**W9-CZH-479**

This coupon entitles you to special discounts when you book your trip through the

## TRAVEL NETWORK®
### RESERVATION SERVICE

### Hotels ♦ Airlines ♦ Car Rentals ♦ Cruises
### All Your Travel Needs

Here's what you get: *

♦ A discount of $50 USD on a booking of $1,000** or more for two or more people!

♦ A discount of $25 USD on a booking of $500** or more for one person!

♦ Free membership for three years, and 1,000 free miles on enrollment in the unique Travel Network Miles-to-Go® frequent-traveler program. Earn one mile for every dollar spent through the program. Redeem miles for free hotel stays starting at 5,000 miles. Earn free roundtrip airline tickets starting at 25,000 miles.

♦ Personal help in planning your own, customized trip.

♦ Fast, confirmed reservations at any property recommended in this guide, subject to availability.***

♦ Special discounts on bookings in the U.S. and around the world.

♦ Low-cost visa and passport service.

♦ Reduced-rate cruise packages and special car rental programs worldwide.

Visit our website at http://www.travelnetwork.com/Frommer or call us globally at 201-567-8500, ext. 55. In the U.S., call toll-free at 1-888-940-5000, or fax 201-567-1838. In Canada, call at 1-905-707-7222, or fax 905-707-8108. In Asia, call 60-3-7191044, or fax 60-3-7185415.

* To qualify for these travel discounts, at least a portion of your trip must include destinations covered in this guide. No more than one coupon discount may be used in any 12-month period, for destinations covered in this guide. Cannot be combined with any other discount or promotion.

**These are U.S. dollars spent on commissionable bookings.

*** A $10 USD fee, plus fax and/or phone charges, will be added to the cost of bookings at each hotel not linked to the reservation service. Customers must approve these fees in advance. If only hotels of this kind are booked, the traveler(s) must also purchase roundtrip air tickets from Travel Network for the trip.

Valid until December 31, 1999. Terms and conditions of the Miles-to-Go® program are available on request by calling 201-567-8500, ext 55.

ENB234

"Amazingly easy to use. Very portable, very complete."

*—Booklist*

♦

"The only mainstream guide to list specific prices. The Walter Cronkite of guidebooks—with all that implies."

*—Travel & Leisure*

♦

"Complete, concise, and filled with useful information."

*—New York Daily News*

♦

"Hotel information is close to encyclopedic."

*—Des Moines Sunday Register*

# Frommer's®
## 22nd Edition

# ENGLAND
## FROM $60 A DAY

The Ultimate Guide to Comfortable
Low-Cost Travel

## by Darwin Porter & Danforth Prince

Macmillan • USA

## ABOUT THE AUTHORS

A native of North Carolina, **Darwin Porter** was a bureau chief for the *Miami Herald* when he was 21 and was assigned to write the very first edition of a Frommer guide devoted solely to one European country. Since then, he has written numerous best-selling Frommer guides, notably to England, France, the Caribbean, Italy, and Germany. In 1982, he was joined in his research efforts across England by **Danforth Prince,** formerly of the Paris bureau of the *New York Times,* who has traveled in and written extensively about England.

## MACMILLAN TRAVEL

A Simon & Schuster Macmillan Company
1633 Broadway
New York, NY 10019

Find us online at **www.frommers.com**
or on America Online at Keyword: **Frommers**.

ISBN 0-02861651-0
ISSN 1042-8399

Editor: Neil E. Schlecht/Robin Michaelson
Production Editor: Lori Cates
Map Editor: Douglas Stallings
Digital Cartography by Peter Bogaty and Ortelius Design
Design by Michele Laseau

## SPECIAL SALES

Bulk purchases (10+ copies) of Frommer's and selected Macmillan travel guides are available to corporations, organizations, mail-order catalogs, institutions, and charities at special discounts, and can be customized to suit individual needs. For more information write to Special Sales, Macmillan General Reference, 1633 Broadway, New York, NY 10019.

Manufactured in the United States of America

# Contents

# List of Maps

## AN INVITATION TO THE READER

In researching this book, we discovered many wonderful places—hotels, restaurants, shops, and more. We're sure you'll find others. Please tell us about them, so we can share the information with your fellow travelers in upcoming editions. If you were disappointed with a recommendation, we'd love to know that, too. Please write to:

*Frommer's England from $60 a Day*
Macmillan Travel
1633 Broadway
New York, NY 10019

## AN ADDITIONAL NOTE

Please be advised that travel information is subject to change at any time—and this is especially true of prices. We therefore suggest that you write or call ahead for confirmation when making your travel plans. The authors, editors, and publisher cannot be held responsible for the experiences of readers while traveling. Your safety is important to us, however, so we encourage you to stay alert and be aware of your surroundings. Keep a close eye on cameras, purses, and wallets, all favorite targets of thieves and pickpockets.

## WHAT THE SYMBOLS MEAN

### ✪ Frommer's Favorites

Our favorite places and experiences—outstanding for quality, value, or both.

The following abbreviations are used for credit and charge cards:

| | | | |
|---|---|---|---|
| AE | American Express | EU | Eurocard |
| CB | Carte Blanche | JCB | Japan Credit Card |
| DC | Diners Club | MC | MasterCard |
| DISC | Discover | V | Visa |
| ER | enRoute | | |

## FIND FROMMER'S ONLINE

Arthur Frommer's Outspoken Encyclopedia of Travel (www.frommers.com) offers more than 6,000 pages of up-to-the-minute travel information—including the latest bargains and candid, personal articles updated daily by Arthur Frommer himself. No other Web site offers such comprehensive and timely coverage of the world of travel.

# The Best of England from $60 a Day

Planning a trip to England presents you with a bewildering array of choices. We've scoured the country in search of the best places and experiences and are happy to report that the best doesn't have to be the most expensive. In this chapter we'll tell you where to go—and where to find the best travel values. We hope our choices will give you some ideas and get you started.

## 1 The Best Destinations for Low-Cost Vacations

- **The Dorset Coast:** In summer, many English vacationers and American visitors flock to high-priced Devon and Cornwall, so hoteliers often double their prices, especially in August. But an equally enchanting—and much less expensive option—is the Dorset coast, the stamping ground of Thomas Hardy and Jane Austen. The coast here is riddled with coves and inlets; the rural and pastoral inland brims with scenic villages. Towns like Dorchester are much more affordable than, say, the artists' colony of St. Ives in Cornwall. See chapter 9.
- **Dartmoor National Park:** Rent a video of *Hound of the Baskervilles* and prepare yourself for a foreboding and haunting—but thrilling—tour of this great national park southwest of London. You could explore the park from Exeter and Plymouth, but it's more fun to stay at a youth hostel or a campground in the area. The best villages for gaining access to these eerie moors are Princeton, Okehampton, or Postbridge. Since public transportation is severely limited, you can rent a bike and head off for adventure. See chapter 10.
- **East Anglia:** There's a lot more to East Anglia than Cambridge. Sure, you'll want to tour the colleges, but we also suggest exploring the backwaters of East Anglia, like the cathedral town of Ely or the little market towns of Thaxted and Saffron Walden. A combined Anglia Plus Pass, which costs £60 ($96) and is only available at train stations in East Anglia, grants you a week's unlimited travel on all rail routes in the region. Or you can just visit Norfolk or Suffolk—which boast the most interesting scenery—for only £26 ($41.60) for a week. You can stay at B&Bs and eat in pubs. See chapter 15.

- **Blackpool:** England's fancier resorts in the south include Brighton and Bournemouth. But droves of working-class Brits, many from the Midlands, flock to Blackpool, a sandy expanse of "fun palaces," neon lights, and even giant "dinosaurs" and palm readers. Sure, it's tacky, but the living is cheap, and a lot of people have been having fun at this monument to unabashed gaudiness ever since the Industrial Revolution. See chapter 17.
- **Central England:** Stratford-upon-Avon is the main draw, but we also suggest exploring some lesser known towns and cities of the Midlands, places such as Hereford, Worcester, and Shrewsbury. Each of these towns is filled with a string of B&Bs and affordable restaurants, and you'll get a lot closer to the literal heart of England than you would hanging out at the more tourist-trodden joints. See chapter 14.
- **Manchester:** London prices are legendary. But England has another sprawling metropolis that's also fascinating and much, much less expensive. It's Manchester, which deserves a stop on your way to the north. It's got everything from museums and galleries to a historic core (Castlefield) that locals have designated an urban heritage park. And there are plenty of places to stay inexpensively. The same goes for dining—this city is full of cash-strapped students, so there are lots of places where you can eat for less than £5 ($8). After dark you can hit the pubs (there's often free music). Perhaps you'll hear the next Oasis. See chapter 17.

## 2  The Best Things to See & Do for Free (or Almost)

- **Seeing the Art Treasures of England:** One of the greatest treasure troves the world has ever known, from Old Masters to the Rosetta stone and the Elgin marbles, can be viewed for free at the British Museum and the Tate Gallery in London. How long the government can continue these subsidies to museums is anybody's guess. But if you go now, you can see great art for free, not only in London but in many regional museums as well, such as the Tate Gallery in Liverpool, a spacious extension of the world-class London branch.
- **Touring England's Cathedrals:** Many people go to England just to tour the cathedral circuit. Nearly all are free, although some request a donation. Such a tour begins, of course, at Westminster Abbey in London. London has another great cathedral, St. Paul's (which does charge admission), but most of its landmark churches are open without charge. From London, you can head in virtually any direction in your cathedral search—we suggest Winchester, Salisbury, Canterbury, Lincoln, Ely, and Liverpool.
- **Pub Crawling:** A pub crawl is one of the most hallowed of British traditions— the pursuit of the pint takes on cultural significance here. Ornate taps fill tankards and mugs in pubs found in every village, hamlet, and town. Such names as the Eagle Arms, the Red Lion, the White Swan, the Bull, and the Royal Oak dot the landscape, their quaint signs beckoning you in. You go not only for the drink but the conviviality, and sometimes even for the entertainment or the food. Log fires roar in winter, and in summer, drinkers like to stand outside in the bracing air. The pub remains the center of English social life. See "The Best Pubs" category for our favorites.
- **Visiting Stonehenge:** One of the world's most celebrated prehistoric monuments, Stonehenge, near Salisbury in Wiltshire, is some 4,000 years old. Its original purpose remains a mystery of the silent Salisbury Plain. There's a small admission fee, or you can see the whole thing from the road for free. Better yet is the perspective from Amesbury Hill, 1 1/2 miles up the road on the A303. See chapter 12.

- **Biking Through the Cotswolds:** There's no better place for cycling than the Cotswolds, less than 100 miles west of London. Its rolling hills and pasturelands are green from nurturing rains, and peppered with ivy-covered inns, stone walls, and honey-colored stone cottages. The names of villages evoke an England of long ago—Bourton-on-the-Water, Upper Slaughter, Chipping Campden, Moreton-in-Marsh, Cirencester, or Wotton-under-Edge (and who can forget Old Sodbury?). See chapter 13.
- **Punting on the Cam:** This expression is "Cantabrigian English" for gliding along in a flat-bottom boat, a long pole (or "punt") pushed into the River Cam's shallow bed, as you bypass the weeping willows along the banks, watch the strolling students along the graveled walkways, and take in the picture-postcard vistas. A summer day is an ideal time to go punting; you can pack a lunch and picnic on the riverbank. It doesn't cost much, and you can share the cost with a few fellow passengers. See chapter 15.
- **Walking the Yorkshire Moors:** A trekker's delight, these purple-heathered moors of *Wuthering Heights* fame sprawl across more than 550 square miles, with some 1,130 miles of public footpaths. In the east, the park opens onto a cliff-studded coastline. But once you go inland, you'll have only the odd sheep, dramatic scenery, and mist to keep you company. We recommend our two favorite walks in "The Best Walks & Rambles" category below. See chapter 19.

## 3 The Best Museums

Terrific news for travelers on a budget: Admission to the London museums and the Fitzwilliam Museum listed below is free (although the Tate sometimes charges for special exhibitions). There's only a modest admission charge for the American Museum and the Walker Art Gallery.

- **The British Museum** (London): When Sir Hans Sloane died in 1753, he bequeathed to England his vast collection of art and antiquities for only £20,000. This formed the nucleus of the collection that would one day embrace everything from the Rosetta stone to the hotly contested Elgin marbles (Greece wants them back). It's all here: two of the four surviving copies of the Magna Carta, a Gutenberg Bible, Shakespeare's First Folio, and much, much more. See chapter 5.
- **The National Gallery** (London): One of the world's greatest collections of Western art—every artist from Leonardo da Vinci to Rembrandt to Picasso—dazzles the eye. The gallery is especially rich in works by Renaissance artists. See chapter 5.
- **The Tate Gallery** (London): Two great national collections encompassing some 10,000 works call this gallery home. Sir Henry Tate, a sugar producer, started the nucleus of the collection, with only 70 or so paintings. But the Tate has grown and grown, and was considerably enlarged when J. M. W. Turner bequeathed some 300 paintings and 19,000 watercolors to England upon his death. Also including avant garde modern art, the Tate's collection is so rich it has to be rotated every year. See chapter 5.
- **The American Museum** (Claverton, 2 miles east of Bath): Housed in a neoclassical country house, this collection presents two centuries of American life and styles—including George Washington's mother's recipe for gingerbread. See chapter 12.
- **The Fitzwilliam Museum** (Cambridge): Although London dominates the museum list, there are some outstanding regional museums, including this gem near

King's College. Exhibits range from paintings by Leonardo da Vinci and Michelangelo to Chinese, Egyptian, and Greek antiquities. See chapter 15.

- **Walker Art Gallery** (Liverpool): One of the finest collections of European and British paintings, this gallery deserves to be better known. A nearly complete study of British paintings is displayed here, from Tudor days to the present. The gallery also owns an outstanding collection of Pre-Raphaelites. Admission is a reasonable £3 ($4.80). See chapter 17.

## 4  The Best Cathedrals

For the most part, entrance to cathedrals is free, although there sometimes are charges to enter the crypts and other areas. Donations are welcomed, however.

- **Westminster Abbey:** One of the world's greatest Anglo-French Gothic buildings, this minster has witnessed a parade of English history—from the crowning of William the Conqueror on Christmas Day 1066 to the World War II blitz. With a few exceptions, the kings and queens of England have all been crowned here, and many are buried here as well. See chapter 5.
- **Canterbury Cathedral:** The object of countless pilgrimages, as described in Chaucer's *Canterbury Tales,* this cathedral replaced one that was destroyed by fire in 1067. A new cathedral, dedicated in 1130, was also destroyed by fire in 1174, when the present structure was built. Its most famous historical event was the murder of Thomas à Becket, whose shrine was an important site for pilgrims until the Reformation. See chapter 7.
- **Winchester Cathedral:** Dominating this ancient city, Winchester Cathedral began to be built in 1079. In time it became England's longest medieval cathedral, noted for its 12-bay nave. Many famous people are buried here, including novelist Jane Austen. See chapter 9.
- **Salisbury Cathedral:** The most stylistically unified of all cathedrals in England, this edifice was built between 1220 and 1265. Its landmark spire—its most striking feature—was constructed from 1285 to 1320. Salisbury Cathedral epitomizes the early-English style of architecture. See chapter 12.
- **Durham Cathedral:** Completed between 1095 and 1133, this cathedral exemplifies Norman architecture on a broad scale. Its nave, a structure of almost majestic power, is its most striking feature. Its outstanding 13th-century Chapel of the Nine Altars was an early-English addition. See chapter 19.
- **York Minster:** The largest Gothic cathedral north of the Alps is also among the grandest, with incredible stained glass—the largest single surviving collection of medieval stained glass in England. Its unusual octagonal Chapter House has a late-15th-century choir screen by William Hyndeley and a wooden vaulted ceiling. See chapter 19.

## 5  The Best Castles, Palaces & Historic Homes

Most of these places charge an entrance fee, which sometimes can be steep, but that's the price you have to pay to see these elegantly appointed mansions, country houses, and palaces. We think it's worth the money! Passes are available from English Heritage and the National Trust that will help you save on the admission fees.

- **Woburn Abbey** (Woburn): A Cistercian abbey for four centuries, Woburn Abbey, the seat of the dukes of Bedford, has been visited by everybody from Queen Victoria to Marilyn Monroe (that's quite a stretch!). You'll see Queen Victoria's

Bedroom and the Canaletto Room, with 21 perspectives of Venice. The grounds, even more popular than the house, house a Wild Animal Kingdom, the best collection in England after the London Zoo. See chapter 6.

- **Hatfield House** (Hertfordshire): Hatfield was the childhood home of Elizabeth I, who was under an oak tree there when she learned she had become queen of England. Hatfield remains one of England's largest and finest country houses, complete with antiques, tapestries, paintings, and even the red silk stockings Elizabeth I wore. See chapter 6.

- **Windsor Castle** (Windsor): The largest inhabited stronghold in the world and England's largest castle, Windsor Castle has been a royal abode since William the Conqueror constructed a motte and bailey on the site four years after conquering England. Severely damaged by fire in 1992, the castle now welcomes visitors to help pay for the restoration. Its major attraction is the great Perpendicular Chapel of St. George's, begun by Edward IV. The chancel is known for its three-tiered stalls, which abound in misericords and ornate carvings. See chapter 6.

- **Blenheim Palace** (Woodstock): England's answer to Versailles, this extravagant baroque palace was the home of the 11th duke of Marlborough as well as the birthplace of Sir Winston Churchill. The structure was designed by Sir John Vanbrugh, of Castle Howard fame. Sarah, the duchess of Marlborough, battled the architects and builders from the beginning, wanting "a clean sweet house and garden be it ever so small." That she didn't get—the structure measures 850 feet from end to end. Capability Brown designed the gardens. See chapter 6.

- **Knole** (Kent): Begun in 1456 by the archbishop of Canterbury, Knole is celebrated for its 365 rooms (one for each day of the year), its 52 staircases (for each week of the year), and its 7 courts (for each day of the week). Knole, one of England's largest private houses and set in a 1,000-acre deer park, is a splendid example of Tudor architecture. See chapter 7.

- **Penshurst Palace** (Kent): One of England's most outstanding country homes, this mansion was the former residence of Elizabethan poet Sir Philip Sidney (1554 to 1586). In its day, the house attracted literati, including Ben Jonson. The original 1346 hall has seen the subsequent addition of Tudor, Jacobean, and neo-Gothic wings. See chapter 7.

- **Hever Castle and Gardens** (Kent): This was the childhood home of Anne Boleyn, second wife of Henry VIII and mother of Queen Elizabeth I. In 1903, William Waldorf Astor, a multimillionaire American and Anglophile, bought the castle, restored it, and landscaped the grounds. From the outside, it still looks like it did in Tudor times, with a moat and drawbridge protecting the castle. See chapter 7.

- **Beaulieu Abbey–Palace House** (Beaulieu, in New Forest): The home of the first Lord Montagu, Palace House blends monastic Gothic architecture from the Middle Ages with Victorian trappings. Yet many visitors consider the National Motor Museum, also on the premises and displaying more than 250 antique automobiles, even more fascinating than the house. See chapter 9.

- **Harewood House** (West Yorkshire): Edwin Lascelles began constructing this house in 1759, and his "pile" has been called an essay in Palladian architecture. The grand design involved some of the major talents of the day, including Robert Adam, Thomas Chippendale, and Capability Brown, who developed the grounds. A $4^1/2$-acre bird garden features exotic species from all over the world. See chapter 19.

- **Castle Howard** (North Yorkshire): This was Sir John Vanbrugh's grand masterpiece, and also the first building he ever designed. Many people will recognize it as the principal location for the popular TV series *Brideshead Revisited.* A gilt-and-painted dome tops the striking entrance, and the park around Castle Howard is one of the most grandiose in Europe. See chapter 19.

## 6 The Best Gardens

- **Kew Gardens** (outside London): This is a delight in any season. Everything from delicate exotics to commonplace flowers and shrubs bloom in profusion here in this 300-acre garden. It's all part of a vast lab that identifies plants from all parts of the globe. Kew Gardens, an easy trip from London, embraces the largest herbarium on earth. Even fabled landscape architect Capability Brown helped lay out some of the grounds. See chapter 5.
- **Wisley Garden:** In Kent, a shire known for being "the garden of England," Wisley Garden sprawls across 250 acres. Maintained by the Royal Horticultural Society, these gardens range from alpinelike meadows to summer "carpets" of flowers. In early summer, the gardens are brilliant in their rhododendron flowering. The landscaped orchid house alone is worth the trip here. See chapter 7.
- **Sissinghurst Castle Garden:** In sunny Kent, these gardens were created by that notorious couple, Vita Sackville West and Harold Nicholson. Although overrun in summer, this garden is the most intriguing on the doorstep of London, some 21 miles northeast of Cranbrook. It was landscaped between the surviving parts of an Elizabethan mansion. We prefer the garden in autumn because of its stunning colors during that time. See chapter 7.
- **Stourhead:** You'll find the most famous garden in England here, at a point 9 miles northwest of Shaftesbury (follow B3081 to B3092) and 30 miles west of Salisbury. This is where English landscape gardening was born. Stourhead is the best-executed example of the "natural landscaping" taste that swept England in the 1700s. The grounds have been compared to the painting of an Old Master like Constable, but in three dimensions, a wealth of flowering shrubs, trees, and beds upon beds of multihued blooms. Grottoes, bridges, and temples add to the allure. See chapter 12.
- **Hidcote Manor Garden:** Four miles northeast of Chipping Campden, one of the most charming Cotswold towns, this stunning garden is laid out around a stone-built Cotswold manor house. It's the largest garden in the Cotswolds and one of the most intriguing in all of Britain. The garden originally bloomed under Major Lawrence Johnstone, an American horticulturist who created it in 1907. He traveled the world and brought back specimens to plant here. See chapter 13.

## 7 The Best B&Bs

- **Vicarage Private Hotel** (London; ☎ **0171/229-4030**): This is the domain of Eileen and Martin Diviney, who share their London home and its traditionally furnished rooms. It's well located, near Kensington High Street, a choice London address. Thoughtful amenities such as sewing kits and hair dryers are provided, all for a cost of £58 ($92.80) in a double room, a bargain in high-priced London. See chapter 4.
- **Adams Guest House** (Oxford; ☎ **01865/556118**): This B&B, in Summertown, 1¹/₄ miles from Oxford, has comfortable and cozy rooms and a host who truly cares about the welfare of his guests. Rates are £38 ($60.80) double. See chapter 6.
- **Alexandra House** (Canterbury; ☎ **01227/767011**): Built around 1901, this is on a quiet road off St. Dunstan's Street, a 10-minute walk from Canterbury

Cathedral. Nothing's fancy here, but the rooms are clean and comfortable, and the price is right: from £36 ($57.60) in a double without bath. See chapter 7.

- **Jeake's House** (Rye; ☎ 01797/222828): This is the premier B&B in Rye, the fabled old seaport (now high and dry) in East Sussex. Once a storehouse for wool, in 1689, then a center for the English literari, the guest house now welcomes the public into its Laura Ashley–style bedrooms, which rent for £39 ($62.40) in a double without bath. See chapter 8.
- **Dudley House** (Brighton; ☎ 01273/676794): This cream-colored Victorian town house features well-decorated bedrooms—some unusually large—in England's premier seaside resort. A double without bath modestly begins at £34 ($54.40). See chapter 8.
- **Ennys** (St. Hilary, near Penzance; ☎ 01736/740262): Begun as a flower farm, Ennys is made of Cornish granite with a slate roof, part of which dates from the 17th century. The rooms are good and comfortable, but another reason to stay here is the home-style cookery, which sometimes shows surprising sophistication. All of that includes a heated swimming pool, with prices beginning at £40 ($64) a night. See chapter 11.
- **The Marlyn Hotel** (Stratford-upon-Avon; ☎ 01789/293752): This place has been welcoming guests who arrive to pay their respects to the Bard since 1890. Near the former home of Shakespeare's daughter, it offers modernized bedrooms and, of course, a complete collection of Shakespeare's works in every bedroom. The cost is £34 ($54.40) for a double (none with bath). See chapter 14.
- **Hambutts Mynd** (Painswick; ☎ 01452/812352): Two blocks from the center of perhaps the prettiest village in the Cotswolds, you'll find this B&B, originally a 17th-century windmill. It has been converted into a Cotswold home of warmth and charm, with windows opening onto views of the nearby fields and hills—all for a price of £40 ($64) for a double without bath. See chapter 13.

## 8  The Best Moderately Priced Hotels

- **Aston's Budget Studios** (London; ☎ 0171/370-0737): This outfit houses you handsomely in a restored row of interconnected Victorian town houses. If you'd like your own comfortably furnished budget studio, this is the place to go; it's just £42 ($67.20) for two. A compact but complete kitchenette helps you cut down on the soaring cost of dining out in London. See chapter 4.
- **Morgan Hotel** (London; ☎ 0171/636-3735): This £80 ($122) per night hotel lies right in the heart of Bloomsbury near the British Museum. In a row of Georgian houses from the 1790s, it offers carpeted bedrooms that have been refurbished. Hospitality is top-notch here. See chapter 4.
- **The Red Lion** (Clovelly; ☎ 01237/431237): In the most charming of all Devonshire villages, this inn lies at the bottom of the steepest cobblestone main street in the country. Once you reach it, at just £80 ($128) for the night, you'll be amply rewarded. Right on the stone seawall of a little harbor, you can bask in time and tradition, having a drink in the pub and a meal in the sea-view dining room before retiring to your cozy lair for the night. See chapter 10.
- **Cott Inn** (Dartington; ☎ 01803/863777): Outside Totnes, in the Devonshire village of Dartington, stands the Cott Inn, built in 1320, although much changed and modified over the years, as you'd expect. It is still a low, rambling two-story building of stone, cob, and plaster, with a thatch roof and walls 3 feet thick. A stay here will introduce you to English life and allow you to feel the pulse of the

village. Yes, your low-ceilinged room will be quaint (watch that you don't bump your head) but a good deal at £55 ($88). See chapter 10.

- **Brompton House** (Bath; ☎ **01225/420972**): In this elegant Georgian city on a bend of the River Avon, you can follow the trail of many leading literary and political figures, including Nelson, Pitt, Dickens, and Thackeray, and enjoy life to the fullest in England's most celebrated spa. Prices tend to run high here, but Brompton House, an elegant Georgian rectory with doubles for £55 to £78 ($88 to $124.80), offers good value. It's set on tranquil grounds within an easy commute from the heart of the city. The rooms are excellent, the management welcoming. See chapter 12.

- **Painswick Hotel** (Painswick; ☎ **01452/812160**): In the heart of the Cotswolds, the sleepy town of Painswick is one of the model villages of England. Count yourself lucky if you get to spend the night here in one of the gems of the Cotswolds. This beautiful, completely refurbished Georgian house was once a vicarage and is encircled by terraces of formal gardens. A double is £87 ($139.20) per night. See chapter 13.

- **Bibury Court Hotel** (Bibury; ☎ **01285/740337**): Bibury is a Cotswold stone-built village that vies with Painswick (see above) as the most idyllic spot in England. You can find affordable lodgings at Bibury Court, which stands beside the gently flowing River Coln, behind St. Mary's Church. Within walled, landscaped gardens, you can wander among the building's fine period furnishings and enjoy the enormous log fires in the drawing room on a cold day—for as little as £78 ($124.80). Bedrooms blend art deco pieces with antiques. See chapter 13.

- **Rothay Garth Hotel** (Ambleside; ☎ **015394/32217**): In one of the most beautiful areas of the Lake District, following in the footsteps of William Wordsworth, you can stay here in an elegant century-old country house set in beautiful gardens—all at a fair price, £106 ($169.90) for a double. Depending on the season, guests enjoy a sunny garden room, or else, when autumn winds blow, retreat to the lounge with its log fires. See chapter 18.

## 9 The Best Dining Bargains

- **Farmer Brown** (London; ☎ **0171/240-0230**): In London's theaterland, you don't expect to find a place called "Farmer Brown." But it offers some of the cheapest eats in town, with a satisfying lunch beginning at only £1.75 ($2.80), plus your drink. At night the action shifts nearby to **Pasta Brown,** 24 Bedford St. (same phone), which feeds you and feeds you well on 29 varieties of pastas and sauces. See chapter 4.

- **Shampers** (London; tel. **0171/437-1692**): Long a favorite of West End wine bar aficionados, Shampers delivers fresh, well-cooked food—everything from pheasant sausage to Irish mussels, with meal platters costing from £8 ($12.80). See chapter 4.

- **The Court Jester** (Windsor; ☎ **01753/864257**): Pub dining has always been the cheap way to go in England. In the historic town of Windsor outside London, site of the fabled castle, The Court Jester proves the rule true. One of the town's most popular pubs, it's housed in a 1790s building and offers traditional pub grub along with a wide range of English ales to wash it down. The Queen doesn't drink here but her security guards at the castle do. Bar snacks—almost a filling meal in themselves—go for £3 ($4.80). See chapter 6.

- **Brown's Restaurant and Bar** (Brighton; ☎ **01273/323501**): Brown's has been almost full every night since it opened in the 1970s. Bistro-style continental food includes Dijon-laced chicken, although we're back in Britain with Scottish sirloin steak or a steak, mushroom, and Guinness pie. Prices begin at £7.50 ($12.50). See chapter 8.

- **Mulberry Room** (Torquay; ☎ **01803/213639**): In one of the premier seacoast resorts of southern England, Lesley Cooper is an inspired cook. Drop in for a fixed-price lunch, for only £5.95 ($9.50), of solid English fare such as baked lamb or honey-roasted chicken. See chapter 10.
- **Harper's Restaurant** (Salisbury; ☎ **01722/333118**): In this fabled cathedral city in the England's "West Countree," the chef-owner takes pride in serving "real food": everything homemade, uncomplicated, and wholesome. A fixed-price lunch of £7.90 ($12.65) is one of the best values in town. See chapter 12.
- **Evans Fish Restaurant** (Bath; ☎ **01225/463981**): This family-run enterprise has served only the freshest of fish ever since it was launched in 1908. Only a 3-minute walk from Bath Abbey and the train station, it offers meals costing from £6 ($9.60). See chapter 12.
- **Arundel House Restaurant** (Cambridge; ☎ **01223/367701**): Overlooking the River Cam is one of the most acclaimed restaurants in Cambridge. Its fixed-price dinner, costing £15.95 ($25.50), is one of the best values in town. This is hearty fare, including fresh salmon, English lamb steak cooked with Calvados, and roast pheasant. See chapter 15.
- **Don Pepe Restaurant and Tapas Bar** (Liverpool; ☎ **0151/231-1909**): This drinking and dining emporium occupies the former headquarters of a local shipping company. Its Spanish cuisine, including delectable tapas, breaks ye olde English monopoly on the dining scene. Meals cost from £10 ($16). See chapter 17.

## 10   The Best Pubs

Pubs come in all styles, but atmosphere is the key to a good pub. Some are extravagant Victorian gin palaces; others occupy parts of long-gone monasteries or abandoned factories. Some are sleek and modern; some are in the country and open onto river banks with weeping willows and white swans floating gracefully by. It is said that Cornwall has the largest concentration of good pubs in England, perhaps 30 for every 100,000 souls living there. Devon, Cumbria (embracing the Lake District), Gloucestershire, Oxfordshire, Somerset, and North Yorkshire also have a roster of good pubs, about 25 per every 100,000 citizens.

- **The Nag's Head** (London; ☎ **0171/235-1135**): It's the smallest pub in London, and it dates from 1780. In the trendy Knightsbridge area, this warm cozy spot is ideal for a pint or a pub grub meal. The cosmopolitan clientele ranges from newspaper people and musicians to auto mechanics. See chapter 4.
- **Spaniards Inn** (London; ☎ **0171/455-3276**): After your ramble across Hampstead Heath in the north of London, there is no better place for a pint than this landmark pub opposite the old tollhouse. Although the original building from 1585 is long gone, the present structure from 1702 has had plenty of time to grow mellow. Quaffing a mug of brew here in days of yore were Dickens, Galsworthy, Byron, and Shelley. See chapter 4.
- **The Ship Inn** (Exeter; ☎ **01392/72040**): Frequented by Sir Francis Drake and Sir Walter Raleigh, this pub on St. Martin's Lane near Exeter Cathedral is the most celebrated in Devon. It still provides tankards of real ale, the same drink swilled down by the likes of Sir John Hawkins. You can also eat here; portions are large, as in Elizabethan times. See chapter 10.

- **Cott Inn** (Dartington, near Totnes, Devon; ☎ **01803/863777**): Built in 1320, this is believed to be the second oldest inn in England. It's a low, rambling two-story building of stone, cob, and plaster under a thatched roof. A gathering place for the people of Dartington, it's a good place for a drink on a windy night, as log fires keep the lounge and bar snug. See chapter 10.
- **The Three Pilchards** (Polperro; ☎ **01503/72233**): What's a visit to England without a pint in a quaint Cornish pub? There's no better choice for it than this time-mellowed boozer near the harbor of this ancient fishing village reached by a steep descent from the main road toward the sea. The interior is all in black oak with a fireplace. You can even order steaks and salads as you eavesdrop and try to decipher the dialect you'll hear from the local Cornish fishers. See chapter 11.
- **Turk's Head** (Penzance, Cornwall; ☎ **01736/363093**): Dating from 1233, and the oldest pub in Penzance, this durable local favorite is filled with artifacts and timeworn beams. Drinkers take their lagers into a summer garden, or else retreat inside to the snug chambers when the wind blows cold. See chapter 11.
- **Lamb Inn** (Burford; ☎ **01993/823155**): This is our favorite place for a lager in all the Cotswolds. In a mellow old house from 1430 with thick stones and mullioned and leaded windows, it's a good place to spend the night, have a traditional English meal, or just a beer. Snacks are served in the timeworn bars and lounges or in a garden in summer. See chapter 13.
- **The Black Swan** (Stratford-upon-Avon; ☎ **01789/297312**): This has been a popular hangout for Stratford players since the 18th century, and over the years we've encountered everybody here from Peter O'Toole to Lord Laurence Olivier having a drink. Locals affectionately call it "The Dirty Duck." In cool weather an open fireplace blazes, and you can stick around if you wish and order the chef's specialty: honey-roasted duck. See chapter 14.

## 11 The Best After-Dark Fun That Won't Cost a Fortune

Many evening entertainment options revolve around music, film, theater, and festivals. Plays and musicals, special festivals, and pub and club shows are posted on many city and town surfaces as well as on student union and tourist office bulletin boards. Film noir and art houses often run classic, cult, foreign, and independent titles at discounted prices. Local listings are generally available in entertainment guides and newspapers; in London, check listings in *Time Out* and *What's On*.

- **The British Music Scene:** In London alone there are five world-class orchestras, two arts centers, two opera houses, and countless concert halls, pubs, and clubs. The city also hosts hundreds of summer jazz festivals, including the **JVC Capital Radio Jazz, Funk, and Soul Festival,** at Royal Albert Hall (☎ **0171/589-8212**), and the **City of London Festival** (☎ **0171/638-8891**). Discounted standing-room-only tickets are often available to musicals and classical and jazz shows in the various theaters and halls, and credit-card reservations can be made for major events by calling **Ticketmaster** at ☎ **0171/344-4444.**

    Throughout Britain, there are hundreds of jazz, folk, and rock clubs. You can also hear live music in pubs, and these gigs can often be enjoyed for just the price of a drink. Clubs often charge a modest cover, but offer a chance to see bands before they become the Next Big Thing. London, Manchester, and Liverpool, in particular, have thriving pop and rock scenes.

- **Bargains on London Theater Tickets:** London theater tickets are priced quite reasonably when compared with those in the United States. Prices vary greatly depending on the seat—anywhere from £12 to £35 ($19.20 to $56). Sometimes gallery seats (the cheapest) are sold only on the day of the performance, so you'll have to head to the box office early in the day and return an hour before the performance to queue up, since they're not reserved seats.

    Many of the major theaters offer discount tickets to students on a standby basis, 30 minutes prior to curtain.

    The **Society of London Theatre** (☎ **0171/836-0971**) operates a discount ticket booth in Leicester Square, where tickets for many shows are available at half price, plus a £2 ($3.20) service charge.

- **Oxford:** A lot of entertainment is offered by, and for, the students—and that means affordable options. College theater productions and concerts are numerous, and along with other options, can be found posted around town, on the bulletin boards of the tourist office, and in the publication *This Month in Oxford.* Summer theater performances are offered at some of the college gardens, while rock, folk, jazz, and comedy can be found at **Freud** and **The Zodiac.** Outstanding national and foreign symphonies and ensembles play classical music at the Sheldonian Theatre, and Oxford Coffee Concerts are held Sunday mornings at the Holywell Music Room, the nation's oldest music venue. See chapter 6.

- **The Bard on Home Turf:** In Stratford, music gives way to theater, with nightly performances at the Royal Shakespeare and Swan theaters, as well as seasonal performances at The Other Place. Offerings range from the mandatory Shakespearean output to more modern, experimental works. Standing-room-only tickets are often available for as little as £4.50 ($7.20), and a few same-day tickets are sold for about £12 ($19.20). Standby tickets, also £12 ($19.20), are offered in theory, but are rarely available. See chapter 14.

- **Cambridge in the Summer:** Summertime in Cambridge is aimed more at tourists than students, and a number of festivals are held. There is the **Midsummer Fair,** dating from the 16th century; the free **Strawberry Fair,** with games and music on the first Saturday in June (☎ **01223/356-0160**); **Summer in the City** and **Camfest,** hosting concerts and special exhibitions throughout the last 2 weeks of August; and the **Cambridge Folk Festival** (contact the Corn Exchange box office at ☎ **01223/335-7851**). The **Cambridge Shakespeare Festival** offers four plays throughout July and August, with tickets available for £8 ($12.80). The **Amateur Dramatic Club (ADC) Theater** (☎ **01223/359547**) offers student-produced plays; **The Arts Cinema** (☎ **01223/504444**) screens comedy classics and undubbed foreign films and hosts a Film Festival during Camfest, with tickets available for £3.30 to £4.30 ($5.30 to $6.90). The **Cambridge Corn Exchange,** besides hosting the folk festival, presents summer band, jazz, and classical concerts. See chapter 15.

# 2

# Getting to Know England

**T**raveling in England is like walking through the pages of an illustrated history book—this is, after all, a country where 2,500 eventful years have left their mark. You can ponder the ancient mystery of Stonehenge, relive the days of Roman Britain as you walk through an excavated villa, and hear in words and place names the linguistic influence of Celtic, Norse, and Norman, as well as Anglo-Saxon. You can stand in the inner courtyard of the Tower of London where Lady Jane Grey was beheaded, walk through Westminster Abbey on the stone grave markers of famous political and literary figures, or visit the homes where Samuel Johnson, Charles Dickens, and Emily Brontë lived and worked.

England is a patchwork quilt of treasures, where you'll find an Elizabethan country estate in Devon, a half-timbered thatched cottage by the sea in Dorset, a regency manor in the Lake District, the great colleges in Cambridge and Oxford. And, of course, there's the exciting, cosmopolitan, colorful city of London, a bastion of tradition, but also the hottest, coolest city in the world at the moment.

## 1 The Regions in Brief

England is a part of the United Kingdom, which is made up of England, Wales, Scotland, and Northern Ireland. Only 50,327 square miles, about the same size as New York State, England has an amazing amount of rural land and natural wilderness and an astonishing regional, physical, and cultural diversity.

The Pennine Chain is the island's backbone, splitting the country in two, with Lancashire on the west of the divide and Yorkshire on the east. Other highland areas include the Cumbrian Mountains (in the Lake District), with the country's highest peak, 3,210-foot Scafell Pike. Several rivers empty into either the North Sea or the Irish Sea—including the Tyne at Newcastle and the Mersey at Liverpool—but the most famous of all is the 209-mile Thames, which empties into the English Channel 20 miles downstream from London Bridge.

**London**     Some seven million city dwellers live in the mammoth metropolis of London, a parcel of land that's more than 609 square miles. The City of London proper is merely 1 square mile, but all the rest of the city is made up of separate villages, boroughs, and corporations. London's neighborhoods are described in chapter 4.

NORTH SEA

SCOTLAND

Glasgow
Edinburgh

Northumberland Nat'l Park
Newcastle upon Tyne

Belfast

Carlisle

NORTHUMBRIA

NORTHERN IRELAND

Solway Firth

THE LAKE DISTRICT

Lake District Nat'l Park

Isle of Man

North York Moors Nat'l Park

IRISH SEA

Yorkshire Dales Nat'l Park

YORKSHIRE

York

Blackpool

Leeds

Liverpool Bay

Liverpool

Manchester

Peak District Nat'l Park

Chester

Lincoln

THE NORTHWEST

EAST MIDLANDS

LINCOLNSHIRE

Nottingham

The Wash

Leicester

Norwich

WALES

Birmingham

EAST ANGLIA

WARWICKSHIRE

Ely

Cambridge

Aldeburgh

Stratford-upon-Avon

THE COTSWOLDS

Bedford

St. George's Channel

Woodstock

Buckingham

Dedham

Swansea

AVON

Oxford

LONDON

Cardiff

Bristol

Bath

OXFORDSHIRE

Windsor

THAMES VALLEY

Canterbury

Bristol Channel

WILTSHIRE

SURREY

KENT

Dover

SOMERSET

HAMPSHIRE

WEST SUSSEX

EAST SUSSEX

Calais

Exmoor Nat'l Park

Salisbury

Southampton

Brighton

Hastings

DEVON

DORSET

Portsmouth

Strait of Dover

Dartmoor Nat'l Park

Lyme Bay

Isle of Wight

CORNWALL

Land's End

Plymouth

Lizard Point

English Channel

Cherbourg

Le Havre

Channel Islands

FRANCE

**The Thames Valley**   England's most famous river runs westward from Kew to its source in the Cotswolds. A land of meadows, woodlands, attractive villages, small market towns, and rolling hillsides, this is one of England's most scenic areas. Many prefer to visit these Thames-side villages by boat. Highlights include **Windsor Castle,** Elizabeth II's favorite residence, and nearby **Eton College,** founded by a young Henry VI in 1440. **Henley,** site of the Royal Regatta, remains our favorite Thames-side town; and at the university city of **Oxford,** you can tour the colleges.

**The Southeast (Kent, Surrey & Sussex)**   This is the land of Charles Lamb, Virginia Woolf, Sir Winston Churchill, and Henry James. Here are all the big-name attractions: **Brighton, Canterbury, Dover,** and dozens of country homes and castles—not only **Hever and Leeds castles** but also **Chartwell,** the more modest abode where Churchill lived. In small villages, such as Rye and Winchelsea in Sussex, and in interesting towns like Haslemere, you discover the charm of the southeast. Almost all of the Sussex shoreline is built up and seaside towns, such as Eastbourne and Hastings, are often tacky. In fact, although the area's major attraction is **Canterbury Cathedral,** the **Royal Pavilion at Brighton** rates as an outstanding, extravagant folly. Teashops, antique shops, pubs, and small inns abound in the area. Surrey is essentially a commuter suburb of London and is easily reached for day trips.

**Hampshire & Wiltshire**   Southwest of London, these two counties possess two of England's greatest **cathedrals (Winchester and Salisbury)** and one of Europe's most significant prehistoric monuments, **Stonehenge.** But there are other reasons for visiting, too. Hampshire is hemmed in by the woodlands and heaths of **New Forest** in its far west. **Portsmouth and Southampton** loom large in naval heritage. You might also want to take a ferry over to the **Isle of Wight,** once Queen Victoria's preferred vacation retreat. In Wiltshire, you encounter the beginning of the **West Country,** with its scenic beauty and monuments—Wilton House, the 17th-century home of the earls of Pembroke, and Old Sarum, the remains of what is believed to have been an Iron Age fortification.

**The Southwest (Dorset, Somerset, Devon & Cornwall)**   These four counties are the great vacation centers and retirement havens of England. Dorset, associated with Thomas Hardy, is a land of rolling downs, rocky headlands, well-kept villages, and rich farmlands. Somerset—the Somerset of King Arthur and Camelot—offers such magical towns as **Glastonbury.** Devon has both **Exmoor and Dartmoor** and northern and southern coastlines with such famous resorts as **Lyme Regis** and such villages as **Clovelly.** In Cornwall you're never more than 20 miles from the rugged coastline, which ends at **Land's End.** Among the cities worth visiting in these counties are **Bath,** with its impressive Roman baths and Georgian architecture; **Plymouth,** departure point of the *Mayflower;* and **Wells,** site of a great cathedral.

**The Cotswolds**   A wonderful region to tour, this is a bucolic land of honey-colored limestone villages where rural England unfolds before you like a storybook. In the Middle Ages, wool made the Cotswolders prosperous, but now they put out the welcome mat for visitors, with famously lovely inns and pubs. Start at **Burford,** the traditional gateway to the region, and continue on to **Bourton-on-the-Water, Lower and Upper Slaughter, Stow-on-the-Wold, Moreton-in-Marsh, Chipping Campden,** and **Broadway. Cirencester** is the uncrowned capital of the south Cotswolds, and **Cheltenham** is the still-elegant Regency spa where Margaret Thatcher's political opponents suggested sending her into retirement. Our two favorite villages are **Painswick,** with its minute cottages, and **Bibury,** with its cluster of former weavers' cottages, Arlington Row.

**Stratford & Warwick**   This is Shakespeare country in the Midlands, also the birth-place of the Industrial Revolution, which made Britain the first industrialized country in the world. Its foremost tourist town is **Stratford-upon-Avon,** but also drawing visitors are **Warwick Castle,** one of England's great castles, and the ruins of **Kenilworth Castle. Coventry,** heavily bombed in World War II, is visited mainly for its outstanding modern cathedral.

**East Anglia (Essex, Cambridgeshire, Norfolk & Suffolk)**   East Anglia, a semicir-cular geographic bulge northeast of London, is the name applied to these four very flat counties. The land of John Constable is still filled with his landscapes. The Fens—that broad expanse of fertile, black soil lying north of Cambridge—remains our favorite district. Go there to see **Ely Cathedral. Cambridge,** with its colleges and river, is the chief attraction. The most important museum is the **Fitzwilliam** in Cam-bridge, but visitors also flock to East Anglia for the scenery and its solitary beauty—fens and salt marshes, villages of thatched cottages.

**The East Midlands (Derbyshire, Leicestershire, Lincolnshire, Northamptonshire & Nottinghamshire)**   This area encompasses some of the worst of industrial En-gland, yet there is great natural beauty to be found, too, as well as stately homes. These include **Chatsworth** in Derbyshire, the seat of the dukes of Devonshire; **Sulgrave Manor** in Northamptonshire, the ancestral home of George Washington; and **Althorp House,** also in Northamptonshire, the childhood home of the princess of Wales. **Lincoln** has one of England's great cathedrals, rebuilt in the 13th and 14th centuries. Bostonians like to visit their namesake, the old seaport town of Boston. **Nottingham** recalls Robin Hood, although the deforested Sherwood Forest is obvi-ously not what it was in the outlaw's heyday. D.H. Lawrence, who lived at Eastwood, fondly recalled this area as "still the old England of the forest and the agricultural past; there were no motor-cars, the mines were, in a sense, an accident in the landscape, and Robin Hood and his merry men were not very far away."

**The West Midlands**   The area known as the West Midlands embraces the so-called "Black Country." **Birmingham,** nicknamed "Brum," is Britain's largest city after London. The sprawling metropolis is still characterized by its overpass jungles and tacky suburbs, as well as great piles of Victorian architecture. Urban renewal is underway. The English marshes cut through the old counties of **Shropshire** and **Herefordshire.** Ironbridge Gorge was at the heart of the Industrial Revolution, and the famous **Potteries** are in Staffordshire.

**The Northwest & the Lake District**   Stretching from Liverpool to the Scottish border, northwest England can be a bucolic delight if you steer clear of its industrial pockets. Most people come here to follow in the footsteps of such romantic poets as Wordsworth, who wrote of the beauty of the Lake District. But **Chester, Manches-ter,** and **Liverpool** merit stopovers along the way. The tawdry resort of **Blackpool** is big, brash, and vulgar, drawing the Midlands factory worker to its Coney Island–like fun by the sea. In contrast, the Roman city of Chester is a well-preserved medi-eval town, known for its encircling wall. And Liverpool is culturally alive and always intriguing, if only to see where the Beatles came from, but it also has a branch of London's Tate Gallery. The literary Lakeland evokes memories of the Wordsworths, Samuel Taylor Coleridge, John Ruskin, and Beatrix Potter, among others. **Windermere** makes the best center, but there are many others as well, including **Grasmere** and **Ambleside.** The Lake District contains some of England's most dra-matic scenery.

**Yorkshire & Northumbria**   Yorkshire will be familiar to fans of the Brontës and James Herriot. **York,** with its immense cathedral and medieval streets, is the city to visit, although more and more visitors are calling on the cities of **Leeds** and **Bradford.** Northumbria comprises **Northumberland, Cleveland, Durham,** and **Tyne and Wear** (the area around **Newcastle**). The whole area echoes the ancient border battles between the Scots and English. **Hadrian's Wall,** built by the Romans, is a highlight. The great cathedral at Durham is one of Britain's finest examples of Norman church architecture, and **Fountains Abbey** is among the country's greatest ecclesiastical ruins. Country homes abound; here you find **Harewood House** and **Castle Howard.**

## 2 History 101

### Dateline

- 54 B.C. Julius Caesar invades England.
- A.D. 43 Romans conquer England.
- 410 Jutes, Angles, and Saxons form small kingdoms in England.
- 500–1066 Anglo-Saxon kingdoms fight off Viking warriors.
- 1066 William, duke of Normandy, invades England and defeats Harold II at the Battle of Hastings.
- 1154 Henry II, first of the Plantagenets, launches their rule (which lasts until 1399).
- 1215 King John signs the Magna Carta at Runnymede.
- 1337 Hundred Years' War between France and England begins.
- 1485 Battle of Bosworth Field ends the War of the Roses between the Houses of York and Lancaster; Henry VII launches the Tudor dynasty.
- 1534 Henry VIII brings the Reformation to England and dissolves the monasteries.
- 1558 The accession of Elizabeth I ushers in an era of exploration and a renaissance in science and learning.
- 1588 Spanish Armada defeated.
- 1603 James VI of Scotland becomes James I of England, thus uniting the crowns of England and Scotland.

*continues*

**FROM MYSTERIOUS BEGINNINGS TO ROMAN OCCUPATION** Britain was probably split off from the continent of Europe some eight millennia ago by continental drift and other natural forces. The early inhabitants, the Iberians, were later to be identified with stories of fairies, brownies, and "little people." These are the people whose ingenuity and enterprise are believed to have created Stonehenge, but despite that great and mysterious monument, little is known about them.

They were replaced by the iron-wielding Celts, whose massive invasions around 500 B.C. drove the Iberians back to the Scottish Highlands and Welsh mountains, where some of their descendants still live today.

In 54 B.C. Julius Caesar invaded England, but the Romans did not become established there until A.D. 43. They went as far as Caledonia (now Scotland), where they gave up, leaving that land to "the painted ones," or the warring Picts. The wall built by the Emperor Hadrian across the north of England marked the northernmost reaches of the Roman Empire. During almost four centuries of occupation, the Romans built roads, villas, towns, walls, and fortresses; they farmed the land and introduced first their pagan religions, then Christianity. Agriculture and trade flourished.

**FROM ANGLO-SAXON RULE TO THE NORMAN CONQUEST** When the Roman legions withdrew, around A.D. 410, they left the country open to waves of invasions by Jutes, Angles, and Saxons, who established themselves in small kingdoms throughout the former Roman colony. From the 8th through the 11th centuries, the Anglo-Saxons contended with Danish raiders for control of the land.

By the time of the Norman conquest, the Saxon kingdoms were united under an elected king, Edward the Confessor. His successor was to rule less than a year before the Norman invasion.

The date 1066 is familiar to every English schoolchild. It marked an epic event, the only successful military invasion of Britain in history, and one of England's great turning points. King Harold, the last Anglo-Saxon king, was defeated at the Battle of Hastings, and William of Normandy was crowned as William I.

One of William's first acts was to order a survey of the land he had conquered, assessing all property in the nation for tax purposes. This survey was called the Domesday Book, or "Book of Doom," as some pegged it. The resulting document was completed around 1086 and has been a fertile sourcebook for British historians ever since.

Norman rule had an enormous impact on English society. All high offices were held by Normans; the Norman barons were given great grants of lands, and they built Norman-style castles and strongholds throughout the country. French was the language of the court for centuries—few people realize that heroes such as Richard Lionheart probably spoke little or no English.

**FROM THE RULE OF HENRY II TO THE MAGNA CARTA**   In 1154 Henry II, the first of the Plantagenets, was crowned (r. 1154–1189). This remarkable character in English history ruled a vast empire—not only most of Britain but Normandy, Anjou, Brittany, and Aquitaine in France.

Henry was a man of powerful physique, both charming and terrifying. He reformed the courts and introduced the system of common law, which not only still operates in moderated form in England today, but also influenced the American legal system. But Henry is probably best remembered for ordering the infamous murder of Thomas à Becket, Archbishop of Canterbury. Henry, at odds with his archbishop, exclaimed, "Who will rid me of this turbulent priest?" His knights, overhearing and taking him at his word, murdered Thomas in front of the high altar in Canterbury Cathedral.

Henry's wife, Eleanor of Aquitaine, the most famous woman of her time, was no less of a colorful character. She accompanied her first husband, Louis VII of France, on the Second Crusade, and it was rumored that there she had a romantic affair with the Saracen leader, Saladin. Domestic and political life did not run smoothly, however, and Henry and Eleanor and their sons were often at odds. The pair have been the subject of many plays and films, including *The Lion in Winter*, *Becket*, and T.S. Eliot's *Murder in the Cathedral*.

- **1620** Pilgrims sail from Plymouth on the *Mayflower* to found a colony in the New World.
- **1629** Charles I dissolves Parliament, ruling alone.
- **1642–49** Civil War between Royalists and Parliamentarians; the Parliamentarians win.
- **1649** Charles I beheaded; England becomes a republic.
- **1653** Oliver Cromwell becomes Lord Protector.
- **1660** Charles II restored to the throne with limited power.
- **1665–66** Great Plague and Great Fire decimate London.
- **1688** James II, a Catholic, is deposed, and William and Mary come to the throne, signing a Bill of Rights.
- **1727** George I, the first of the Hanoverians, assumes the throne.
- **1756–63** In the Seven Years' War, Britain wins Canada from France.
- **1775–83** Britain loses its American colonies.
- **1795–1815** The Napoleonic Wars lead, finally, to the Battle of Waterloo and the defeat of Napoléon.
- **1837** Queen Victoria begins her reign as Britain reaches the zenith of its empire.
- **1901** Victoria dies, and Edward VII becomes king.
- **1914–18** England enters World War I and emerges victorious on the Allied side.
- **1936** Edward VIII abdicates to marry an American divorcée.
- **1939–45** In World War II, Britain stands alone against Hitler from the fall of France in 1940 until America enters the war in 1941. Dunkirk is evacuated in 1940; bombs rattle London during the blitz.

*continues*

- 1945 Germany surrenders. Churchill is defeated; the Labor government introduces the welfare state and begins to dismantle the empire.
- 1952 Queen Elizabeth II ascends the throne.
- 1973 Britain joins the European Union.
- 1979 Margaret Thatcher becomes prime minister.
- 1982 Britain defeats Argentina in the Falklands War.
- 1990 Thatcher is ousted; John Major becomes prime minister.
- 1991 Britain fights with Allies to defeat Iraq.
- 1992 Royals jolted by fire at Windsor Castle and marital troubles of their two sons. Britain joins the European Union. Deep recession signals the end of the booming 1980s.
- 1994 England is linked to the Continent by rail via the Chunnel Tunnel. Tony Blair elected Labor Party leader.
- 1996 The IRA breaks a 17-month cease-fire with a truck bomb at the Docklands that claims two lives. Her Majesty prompts Charles and Di's divorce. The government concedes a possible link between "Mad Cow Disease" and a fatal brain ailment afflicting humans; British beef imports face banishment globally.
- 1997 London swings again. The Labour Party ends 18 months of Conservative rule with a landslide election victory. The tragic death of Diana, Princess of Wales, provokes a worldwide outpouring of grief.

Two of their sons were crowned kings of England. Richard the Lionheart actually spent most of his life outside England, on crusades or in France. John was forced by his nobles to sign the Magna Carta at Runnymede, in 1215—another date well known to English schoolchildren.

The Magna Carta guaranteed that the king was subject to the rule of law and gave certain rights to the king's subjects, beginning a process that eventually led to the development of parliamentary democracy as it is known in Britain today, a process that would have enormous influence on the American colonies many years later. The Magna Carta became known as the cornerstone of English liberties, though it only granted liberties to the barons. It took the rebellion of Simon de Montfort half a century later to introduce the notion that the boroughs and burghers should also have a voice and representation.

**THE BLACK DEATH & THE WARS OF THE ROSES**   In 1348, half the population died as the Black Death ravaged England. By the end of the century, the population of Britain had fallen from four million to two million.

England also suffered in the Hundred Years' War, which went on intermittently for more than a century. By 1371 England had lost much of its land on French soil. Henry V, immortalized by Shakespeare, revived England's claims to France, and his victory at Agincourt was notable for making obsolete the forms of medieval chivalry and warfare.

After Henry's death in 1422, disputes arose among successors to the crown that resulted in a long period of civil strife, the Wars of the Roses, between the Yorkists, who used a white rose as their symbol, and the Lancastrians with their red rose. The last Yorkist king was Richard III, who got bad press from Shakespeare, but who is defended to this day as a hero by the people of the city of York. Richard was defeated at Bosworth Field, and the victory introduced England to the first Tudor, the shrewd and wily Henry VII.

**THE TUDORS TAKE THE THRONE**   The Tudors were unlike the kings who had ruled before them. They introduced into England a strong central monarchy with far-reaching powers. The system worked well under the first three strong and capable Tudor monarchs, but began to break down later when the Stuarts came to the throne.

Henry VIII is surely the most notorious Tudor. Imperious and flamboyant, a colossus among English royalty, he slammed shut the door on the Middle Ages and introduced the Renaissance to England. He is best known, of course, for his treatment of his six wives and the unfortunate fates that befell five of them.

When his first wife, Catherine of Aragon, failed to produce an heir, and his ambitious mistress, Anne Boleyn, became pregnant, he tried to annul his marriage, but the pope refused, and Catherine contested the action. Defying the power of Rome, Henry had his marriage with Catherine declared invalid and secretly married Anne Boleyn in 1533.

The events that followed had profound consequences and introduced the religious controversy that was to dominate English politics for the next 4 centuries. Henry's break with the Roman Catholic Church and the formation of the Church of England, with himself as supreme head, was a turning point in English history. It led eventually to the Dissolution of the Monasteries, civil unrest, and much social dislocation. The confiscation of the church's land and possessions brought untold wealth into the king's coffers, wealth that was distributed to a new aristocracy that supported the monarch. In one sweeping gesture, Henry destroyed the ecclesiastical culture of the Middle Ages. Among those who were executed for refusing to cooperate with Henry's changes was Sir Thomas More, humanist and international man of letters and author of *Utopia.*

Anne Boleyn bore Henry a daughter, the future Elizabeth I, but failed to produce a male heir. She was brought to trial on a trumped-up charge of adultery and beheaded. In 1536, Henry married Jane Seymour, who died giving birth to Edward VI. For his next wife, he looked farther afield and chose Anne of Cleves from a flattering portrait, but she proved disappointing—he called her "The Great Flanders Mare." He divorced her the same year and next picked a pretty young woman from his court, Catherine Howard. She was also beheaded on a charge of adultery, but unlike Anne Boleyn, was probably guilty. Finally, he married an older woman, Catherine Parr, in 1543. She survived him.

Henry's heir, sickly Edward VI (r. 1547–1553), did not live long. He died of consumption—or, as rumor has it, overmedication. He was succeeded by his sister, Mary I (r. 1553–1558), and the trouble Henry had stirred up with the break with Rome came home to roost for the first time. Mary restored the Roman Catholic faith, and her persecution of the adherents of the Church of England earned her the name of "Bloody Mary." Some 300 Protestants were executed, many burned alive at the stake. She made an unpopular and unhappy marriage to Philip of Spain; despite her bloody reputation, her life was a sad one.

Elizabeth I (r. 1558–1603) came next to the throne, ushering in an era of peace and prosperity, exploration, and a renaissance in science and learning. An entire age was named after her—the Elizabethan Age. She was the last great and grand monarch to rule England, and her passion and magnetism were said to match her father's. Through her era marched Drake, Raleigh, Frobisher, Grenville, Shakespeare, Spenser, Byrd, and Hilliard. During her reign, she had to face the appalling precedent of ordering the execution of a fellow sovereign, Mary Queen of Scots. Her diplomatic skills kept war at bay until 1588, when at the apogee of her reign, the Spanish Armada was defeated. She will be forever remembered as "Good Queen Bess."

**CIVIL WAR**   The Stuarts ascended the throne in 1603, but though they held it through a century of civil war and religious dissension, they were not as capable as the Tudors in walking the line between the demands of a strong centralized monarchy and the rights increasingly demanded by the representatives of the people in Parliament.

Charles I, attracted by the French idea of the divine right of the king, considered himself above the law, a mistake the Tudors had never made—Elizabeth, in particular, was clever and careful in her dealings with Parliament. Charles's position was a fatal response to the Puritans and other dissenters who sought for more power. In 1629, Charles dissolved Parliament, determined to rule without it.

Civil War followed, and the victory went to the Roundheads under Oliver Cromwell. Charles I was put on trial and was led to his execution, stepping onto the scaffold through the window of his gloriously decorated Banqueting House. His once-proud head rolled on the ground.

Oliver Cromwell, the melancholy, unambitious, clumsy farmer, became England's first and only virtual dictator. He saw his soldiers as God's faithful servants and promised them rewards in heaven. The English people, however, did not take kindly to this form of government, and after Cromwell's death, Charles II, the dead king's son, returned and was crowned in 1660, but given very limited powers.

**FROM THE RESTORATION TO THE NAPOLEONIC WARS**   The reign of Charles II was the beginning of a dreadful decade that saw London decimated by the Great Plague and destroyed by the Great Fire.

His successor, James II, attempted to return the country to Catholicism, an attempt that so frightened the powers that be that Catholics were for a long time deprived of their civil rights. James was deposed in the "Glorious Revolution" of 1688 and succeeded by his daughter Mary and her husband, William of Orange, thus securing the Protestant succession that has continued to this day. These tolerant and levelheaded monarchs signed a Bill of Rights, establishing the principle that the monarch reigns not by divine right but by the will of Parliament.

Queen Anne, Mary's sister, was the last of the Stuarts: She outlived all her children. Her reign (1702–1714) saw the full union of England and Scotland.

After her death in 1714, England looked for a Protestant prince to succeed her, and they chose George of Hanover. He was invited to take the throne in 1714 as George I and thus began a 174-year dynasty. He spoke only German and spent as little time as possible in England. He left the running of the government to the English politicians and created the office of prime minister. Under the Hanoverians, the powers of Parliament were extended, and the constitutional monarchy developed as we know it today.

The American colonies were lost under the Hanoverian George III, but British possessions were expanded: Canada was won from the French in the Seven Years' War (1756–63), British control over India was affirmed, and Captain Cook claimed Australia and New Zealand for England. The British became embroiled in the Napoleonic Wars (1795–1815), achieving two of their greatest victories and acquiring two of their greatest heroes: Nelson at Trafalgar and Wellington at Waterloo.

**THE INDUSTRIAL REVOLUTION & THE REIGN OF VICTORIA**   The mid- to late 18th century saw the beginnings of the Industrial Revolution. This event changed the lives of the laboring class, created a wealthy middle class, and transformed England from a rural, agricultural society into an urban, industrial economy. England was now a world-class financial and military power. Male suffrage was extended, though women were to continue under a series of civil disabilities for the rest of the century.

Queen Victoria's reign (1837–1901) coincided with the height of the Industrial Revolution. When she ascended the throne, the monarchy as an institution was in considerable doubt, but her 64-year reign, the longest in tenure in English history, was an incomparable success.

The Victorian era was shaped by the growing power of the bourgeoisie, the queen and her consort's personal moral stance, and the perceived moral responsibilities of managing a vast empire. During this time, the first trade unions were formed, a public (state) school system developed, and railroads were built.

Victoria never recovered from the death of her German husband, Albert. He died from typhoid fever in 1861, and the queen never remarried. Although she had many children, she found them tiresome, but was a pillar of family values nonetheless. One historian said her greatest asset was her relative ordinariness.

Middle-class values ruled Victorian England and were embodied by the queen. The racy England of the past went underground. Our present-day view of England is still influenced by the attitudes of the Victorian era, and we tend to forget that English society in earlier centuries was famous for its rowdiness, sexual license, and spicy scandal.

Victoria's son Edward VII (r. 1901–1910) was a playboy who had waited too long in the wings. He is famous for mistresses, especially Lillie Langtry, and his love of elaborate dinners. During his brief reign, he, too, had an era named after him, the Edwardian Age. Under Edward, the country entered the 20th century at the height of its imperial power, whereas at home the advent of the motorcar and the telephone radically changed social life, and the women's suffrage movement began.

World War I marked the end of an era. It had been assumed that peace, progress, prosperity, empire, and even social improvement would continue indefinitely. World War I and the troubled decades of social unrest, political uncertainty, and the rise of Nazism and Fascism put an end to these expectations.

**THE WINDS OF WAR**   World War II began in 1939, and soon thereafter Britain had found a new and inspiring leader, Winston Churchill, whose mother was an American. Churchill led the nation during its "finest hour." For many months, Britain stood alone against Hitler, from the time the Germans took France until they were joined by their U.S. Allies. The evacuation of Dunkirk in 1940, the blitz of London, the Battle of Britain were dark hours for the British people, and Churchill is remembered for urging them to hold onto their courage. Once the British forces were joined by their American allies, the tide finally turned, culminating in the D-day invasion of German-occupied Normandy. These bloody events are still remembered by many with pride, and with nostalgia for the era when Britain was still a great world power.

The years following World War II brought many changes to England. Britain began to lose its grip on an empire (India became independent in 1947), and the Labor government, which came into power in 1945, established the welfare state and brought profound social change to Britain.

**QUEEN ELIZABETH RULES TO THE PRESENT DAY**   Upon the death of the "wartime king" George VI, Elizabeth II ascended the throne in 1952. Her reign has seen the erosion of Britain's once-mighty industrial power and, in recent years, a severe recession.

Political power has seesawed back and forth between the Conservative and Labor parties. Margaret Thatcher, who became prime minister in 1979, seriously eroded the welfare state and was ambivalent toward the European Union. Her popularity soared during the successful Falklands War, when Britain seemed to recover some of its military glory for a brief time.

Although the queen has remained steadfast and punctiliously performed her ceremonial duties, rumors about the royal family abounded, and in 1992, a year which Queen Elizabeth labeled an *annus horribilis,* a devastating fire swept through Windsor Castle, the marriages of several of her children crumbled, and the queen agreed to pay taxes for the first time. Prince Charles and Princess Diana agreed to a separation, and there were ominous rumblings about the future of the House of Windsor. By 1994 and 1995, Britain's economy was improving after several glum years, but Conservative prime minister John Major was coming under increasing criticism.

The IRA, reputedly enraged at the slow pace of peace talks, relaunched its reign of terror across London in February 1996, planting a massive bomb that ripped through a building in London's Docklands, injuring more than 100 people and killing two. Shattered, too, was the 17-month cease-fire by the IRA, which brought hope that peace was at least possible. Another bomb went off in Manchester in June.

Headlines about the IRA bombing gave way to another big bomb—the end of the marriage of Princess Diana and Prince Charles. The Wedding of the Century has become the Divorce of the Century. The lurid tabloids, for a change, had been right all along about this unhappy pair. But details of the $26 million divorce settlement didn't satisfy the curious: Scrutiny of Prince Charles's relationship with Camilla Parker-Bowles, as well as love-related gossip about Princess Diana, continued in the press.

Britain's other bombshell story, Mad Cow Disease, also began to fizzle, although beef sales and prices remain low. The considered destruction of Britain's entire population of 11 million animals was scrapped because of pressure from representatives of the $6.5 billion beef industry. Scientists now claim the epidemic will end naturally by 2001. The handling of the crisis by John Major and the Tories cast a grave shadow of doubt over future reelection prospects.

On May 1, 1997, the Labour Party, led by Tony Blair, ended 18 years of Conservative rule. Blair became Britain's youngest prime minister in 185 years, following in the wake of the largest Labour triumph since Winston Churchill was swept out of office at the end of World War II. Prime Minister John Major, who inherited the Conservative mantle in 1990, handed in his resignation to Queen Elizabeth II at Buckingham Palace. Moments later, Blair arrived to receive instructions from the queen to form a new government. At 44, Blair is Britain's 50th prime minister and the youngest at 10 Downing St. since Lord Liverpool in 1812.

Blair's election had many British entrepreneurs poised and ready to take advantage of what they perceived as enthusiasm for new ideas and ventures. London, certainly, has been acclaimed by the worldwide press for its renaissance in the realms of art, music, fashion, and dining. Parallels to Harold Macmillan and his reign over the Swinging '60s seem inevitable, and insiders agree that something's in the air.

However, events took a shocking and horrific turn on August 31, 1997, when Princess Diana was killed—along with her companion, the Harrods heir, Dodi al-Fayed—in a high-speed car crash in Paris. At press time, it remains to be seen how this tragic event will affect Britain's optimistic mood—and the future of the British Monarchy.

## 3 The Architectural Landscape

**EARLY BEGINNINGS**    The most stirring examples of early English architecture are pre-Celtic religious sites, such as **Stonehenge.** A few well-preserved Roman sites, such as **Bath** and **Verulamium,** and a handful of Saxon churches still exist. The most famous Norman architectural examples are the **White Tower** at the Tower of London and the great **Romanesque cathedrals** of **Durham, Norwich,** and **Ely.**

**THE GOTHIC PERIOD**    England's Gothic period is usually divided into three parts that span the late 12th to mid-16th centuries: early English, decorated, and Perpendicular—each more lavishly ornamented than the previous.

Early English, characterized by narrow pointed arches, ribbed vaults, and lancet windows, lasted from around the mid-12th century until the death of Edward I, in 1307. **Salisbury Cathedral,** in the city of Salisbury, Wiltshire, is one of the most outstanding examples of this style. Actually, it is the only English cathedral built in one style from start to finish. Other examples include **Wells** and **Lichfield cathedrals** and the ruins of **the abbeys** of **Glastonbury** and **Fountains.**

The decorated style, another phase of English Gothic, began around 1280 and lasted approximately until 1377. **Ely Cathedral** (1323–30), with its octagon and lantern, is an outstanding example of this style, as are the facades of **Exeter Cathedral** and **York Minster** and **Lincoln Cathedral's Angel Choir.**

The Perpendicular style of Gothic is peculiarly English. Here attention was paid to vertical lines, and the style's hallmark is paneled decoration all over a structure. Flying buttress and fan-vault roofing were also developed at this time. Exemplary architecture of this period includes the great chapels at **Eton, King's College, Cambridge,** and **St. George's Chapel at Windsor Castle.**

Tudor Gothic began in 1485, when Henry VII came to the throne. **Hampton Court Palace** and **Bath Abbey** are stellar examples of this style; other fine examples include **Penshurst Palace** in Kent and such timber-frame buildings as the **Guildhall** at Lavenham and the **Feathers Inn** in Ludlow, Shropshire.

**THE RENAISSANCE**   The Renaissance came late to England. English architects tended to favor the mannerist approach of Germany and the Low Countries rather than the Italian style, using Flemish gabling and brickwork. Wealthy merchants built lavish mansions, such as **Longleat House** in Wiltshire, and **Hardwick Hall** in Derbyshire. The early 17th-century Jacobean period produced highly decorative domestic architecture; **Hatfield House** in Hertfordshire is a good example.

**THE GREATEST BRITISH ARCHITECTS: INIGO JONES AND CHRISTOPHER WREN**   Inigo Jones (1573–1652), the first great modern British architect, introduced the airily and mathematically precise designs promoted by Italian Renaissance architect Andrea Palladio. This style opted for strict spatial ratios of windows to doors, plus a balanced symmetry that often combined the three classic Greek orders—Doric, Ionic, and Corinthian—in gracefully symmetrical neoclassical grandeur. Two of Jones's most famous buildings are the **Banqueting House** at Whitehall and the **Queen's House** at Greenwich.

This classicism continued to be practiced throughout the 17th century, with baroque and rococo gaining only a foothold.

Sir Christopher Wren, the leading 17th-century English architect, redesigned much of London after the Great Fire of 1666. He constructed a new **St. Paul's Cathedral** and rebuilt 53 churches—two of the most famous are **St. Bride's** in Fleet Street, and **St. Mary-le-Bow.** Other Wren masterpieces include the **Royal Hospital** at Greenwich, the **Sheldonian Theatre,** in Oxford, and the **library** at Trinity College, Cambridge.

At the end of his life, Wren was eclipsed by such famous 18th-century architects as Sir John Vanbrugh (1664–1726), creator of **Castle Howard** and **Blenheim Palace,** and Sir Nicholas Hawksmoor (ca. 1661–1736).

**THE PALLADIAN STYLE**   After 1720, the baroque influence declined and the Palladian style took over, especially in domestic architecture. The architects William Kent and Colin Campbell, among others, built great houses surrounded by parkland and natural landscapes. One example is **Hokham Hall,** where the grounds are dotted with classical sculptures and fountains. Capability Brown was the foremost landscape artist of this period.

**A CLASSICAL REVIVAL**   In the late 18th century a classical revival took place, led by Sir William Chambers and Robert Adam, whose **Syon House,** near London, and **Kedleston Hall,** in Derbyshire, are prime examples.

Robert Adam (1728–92), son of a Scottish architect, is a name you'll frequently encounter when touring the stately homes of Britain. After touring Europe, he and his brothers opened a business in London. At that time the landed gentry of England preferred Palladian designs, but Adam was immediately successful in introducing a lighter and more decorative style. He was the greatest interior designer in England at the time. Whole terraces and crescents—John Wood the Elder's **Royal Crescent,** in Bath, for instance—were laid out in the 18th century. Similar schemes can be seen in Cheltenham and Brighton.

**THE 19TH CENTURY**   In the 19th century, building changed as a result of the Industrial Revolution. Factories, railroad stations, concert halls, and theaters were added to the roster of churches and domestic buildings. All kinds of earlier styles—Romanesque, Byzantine, and Gothic were reinterpreted—as glass and iron were introduced. The very technique of building changed as moldings and other internal decorative elements were mass produced. In the late Georgian and regency periods, the leading architects were John Nash and Sir John Soane.

Beginning in about 1840, there came the craze for Gothic revival that can be seen clearly in the **Houses of Parliament,** the **Law Courts** in London, the **Natural History Museum,** and the controversial **Albert Memorial.** At the end of the century, architects such as Charles Rennie Mackintosh rejected the overdecoration and heaviness of this Victorian style and sought greater simplicity.

The famous architects of the early 20th century include Sir Edwin Lutyens (1869–1944), who built country houses, the **Reuters Building** on Fleet Street, and other commercial buildings, and laid out such grand schemes as the Whitehall cenotaph. He is also associated with the grand designs of British Delhi.

**MODERN ARCHITECTURE**   Modern architecture as we know it really began after World War II. Many early modern buildings were created by immigrants—including **Walter Gropius**—en route to the United States.

Much modern British architecture is blockish and dull (just ask Prince Charles!), with relief provided by such figures as Sir Hugh Casson and Sir Basil Spence. London developers have increased their usage of traditional building materials such as concrete, steel, aluminum, and glass in warmly textured, anthropomorphic forms that manage to combine the rectilinear severity of old-fashioned Bauhaus with the organic shapes of Barcelona's Antonio Gaudí.

The "New Brutalism" manages to combine a powerfully primitive, even primal kind of appeal to buildings erected in the center of some of the most congested neighborhoods of London. Examples include the **Economist Building** in Haymarket and a housing development in London's East End (The **Robin Hood Lane complex**), both designed by award-winning London architects Alison and Peter Simpson.

English architecture today is carefully balanced between a new emphasis on historic preservation and dramatic new statements such as those made by iconoclastic visionary Sir Richard Rodgers in his design of the **Lloyd's Building,** its controlled interior space like Batman looking down into an urban cavern.

The main rival to Rogers is Norman Foster, who is the second most famous London architect. Foster intends to build Europe's tallest building in the midst of the city's financial district, a 76-story **Millennium Tower,** carrying his signature aerodynamic look. As if to counter his rival, Rogers has become the master planner of the world's fairlike **Millennium Festival,** which will be constructed in Greenwich on the meridian. In theory at least, the 21st century will begin at this spot.

# Planning an Affordable Trip to England

# 3

It's completely possible to have a rich and rewarding travel experience without spending a fortune—and that doesn't have to mean that you sacrifice fun or comfort. That goal has been foremost in our minds ever since this guide first appeared in 1964, when it *was* possible to travel England for $5 a day.

Over the years we've made countless trips through the countryside and learned affordable England inside and out. We've often followed that plump and jolly landlady from her first B&B in London, which she eventually sold to open an even better place in Canterbury.

In this chapter, we'll tell you what you need to know in advance, and show you exactly how to set up your trip to find the best bargains.

## 1 How This Guide Can Save You Money

With this guide, you can see the best of England—even the best of pricey London—without spending a fortune. In the pages ahead, we'll show how to save money on lodgings and food, as well as how to cut costs for transportation, sightseeing, after-dark diversions, and the like.

Since we steer clear of tourist traps and expensive diversions, you'll come closer to experiencing the real England and enjoy a truer slice of life. There's great joy is not only discovering a bargain, but meeting people and learning a lot while you travel.

This guide knows what inexpensive travel is all about, but differs from some of its competitors. For example, we believe in paying a little more from time to time in order to secure accommodations that are reasonable in price, but also clean, decent, and welcoming. Likewise, we don't believe in confining ourselves to a diet of "bangers and mash" or cheap fast food. We've picked places to dine that are simple but good, serving well-prepared British, continental, and foreign fare. We also know that you'll feel like splurging sometimes, so we've offered slightly more expensive choices for those occasions—places that are memorable and still offer great value.

Budget travel isn't just about cutting expenses on the road. It's about bringing you into contact with the locals—the folks who run the local B&Bs and pour the pints in the local pubs. We've tried to put you in touch with genuine, warm, and sincere people who, in addition to earning a living in the tourist trade, often take delight in opening their well-kept establishments to others.

Arthur Frommer, the pioneering publisher of this guide, writes that over the years Frommer readers have discovered a major principle of travel: "That the less you spend, the more you enjoy; that the less you spend, the better you encounter the realities of the countries you visit, and thus receive the most lasting rewards of the travel experience."

The best value for money can be found outside London and away from other tourist meccas such as Stratford-upon-Avon, Oxford, Cambridge, or Canterbury. We suggest spending less time in London (perhaps 3 days), then heading out to explore the beautiful English countryside. Spend a few days or more exploring East Anglia, or the Lake District, so beloved by the Romantic poets. Walk the country lanes of Devon, discovering hidden hamlets that look ripe for an Agatha Christie murder mystery. Shopping for bric-a-brac can unearth affordable treasures, and the prices of the B&Bs are affordable. Pub lunches are the way to go, followed by dinner in a small tavern, perhaps one once patronized by Johnson and Boswell.

The daily budget of $60 a day promised in the title of this book is meant to cover your basic living costs while on the road: three meals a day, and half the price of a simple double room. The costs of sightseeing, transportation, shopping, and entertainment are extra, but we'll tell you how to keep those costs trimmed, too. The minimum $60-a-day budget roughly breaks down like this: $30 per person for a double room (which always includes a hearty breakfast in the room price in England), $10 for lunch, and $20 for dinner.

But what about the word "from" in this book's title? We've phrased it that way for a reason. We want to be able to include establishments that are slightly more expensive than the $60-a-day budget, but are still terrific buys. We want to offer you places that have a unique historical, cultural, or architectural features, and let you decide when you're ready to splurge. No place has been included in this book that doesn't offer value, even if it's slightly higher than the figures listed above. (Conversely, we'll tell you about many bargains that could allow you to manage for even less than $60 a day). We've assumed that you demand more comfort than you did in your student days, so we haven't sent you to any marginal properties. We promise to bring you comfortable lodgings, great food, and loads of fun for a reasonable price!

## 2  Visitor Information & Entry Requirements

**VISITOR INFORMATION**   Before you go, you can obtain general information from the **British Tourist Authority,** 551 Fifth Ave., Suite 701, New York, NY 10176-0799 (☎ **800/462-2748** or 212/986-2200).

Canadian travelers will find offices at 111 Avenue Rd., Suite 450, Toronto, ON M5R 3J8 (☎ **800/847-4885** in Canada, or 416/925-6326).

The Australian BTA office is at University Centre, 8th floor, 210 Clarence St., Sydney NSW 2000 (☎ **02/267-4413**). New Zealanders can go to Suite 305, Dilworth Building, at the corner of Queen and Customs streets, Auckland 1 (☎ **09/303-1446**).

The BTA maintains a web page at http://www.bta.org.uk.

For a full information pack on London, write to **London Tourist Board,** P.O. Box 151, London E15 2HF. You can also call the recorded-message service,

**Visitorcall** (☎ **01839/123456**), 24 hours a day. Various topics are listed; calls cost 39p (60¢) per minute cheap rate (Monday to Friday from 6pm to 8am and all day Saturday and Sunday), and 49p (80¢) per minute at all other times.

You can usually pick up a copy of *Time Out,* the most up-to-date source for what's happening in London, at any international newsstand. You can also check it out on the Net at http://www.timeout.co.uk.

**ENTRY REQUIREMENTS**    All U.S. citizens, Canadians, Australians, New Zealanders, and South Africans must have a passport with at least 2 months' remaining validity. No visa is required.

The immigration officer will also want proof of your intention to return to your point of origin (usually a round-trip ticket) and visible means of support while you're in Britain.

If you're planning to fly from the U.S. or Canada to the U.K. and then on to a country that requires a visa (India, for example), you should secure that visa before you arrive in Britain.

If you're planning to drive, you need a valid driver's license and at least one year's driving experience.

**CUSTOMS**    For visitors to England, goods fall into two basic categories—purchases made in a non-European Union (EU) country or bought tax-free within the EU, and purchases on which tax was paid in the EU. In the former category, limits on imports by individuals (aged 17 and older) include 200 cigarettes, 50 cigars, or 250 grams of loose tobacco; 2 liters of still table wine, 1 liter of liquor (over 22% alcohol content), or 2 liters of liquor (under 22%); and 2 fluid ounces of perfume. In the latter category—items on which tax was already paid in the EU—limits are *much* higher: An individual may import 800 cigarettes, 200 cigars, *and* 1 kilogram of loose tobacco; 90 liters of wine, 10 liters of alcohol (over 22%), *and* 110 liters of beer; plus unlimited amounts of perfume.

Returning U.S. citizens who have been away for 48 hours or more are allowed to bring back, once every 30 days, $400 worth of merchandise duty free. You'll be charged a flat rate of 10% duty on the next $1,000 worth of purchases. Be sure to have your receipts handy. On gifts, the duty-free limit is $50. For more specific guidance, write to the **U.S. Customs Service,** P.O. Box 7407, Washington, DC 20044 (☎ **202/927-6724**), requesting the free pamphlet "Know Before You Go."

For a clear summary of Canadian rules, write for the booklet "I Declare," issued by **Revenue Canada,** 2265 St. Laurent Blvd., Ottawa K1G 4KE (☎ **800/461-9999** or 613/993-0534). Canada allows its citizens a $300 exemption, and you are allowed to bring back duty free 200 cigarettes, 2.2 pounds of tobacco, 40 imperial ounces of liquor, and 50 cigars. In addition, you are allowed to mail gifts to Canada from abroad at the rate of CAN$60 a day, provided they are unsolicited and aren't alcohol or tobacco (write on the package: "Unsolicited gift, under $60 value"). All valuables should be declared on the Y-38 Form before departure from Canada, including serial numbers of, for example, expensive foreign cameras that you already own. *Note:* The $300 exemption can be used only once a year and only after an absence of 7 days.

The duty-free allowance in Australia is A$400 or, for those under 18, A$200. Personal property mailed back from England should be marked "Australian goods returned" to avoid payment of duty. Upon returning to Australia, citizens can bring in 250 cigarettes or 250 grams of loose tobacco, and 1 liter of alcohol. If you're returning with valuable goods you already own, such as foreign-made cameras, you should file form B263. A helpful brochure, available from Australian consulates or customs offices, is "Customs Information for All Travellers." For more information, contact **Australian Customs Services,** GPO Box 8, Sydney NSW 2001 (☎ **02/ 213-2000**).

The duty-free allowance for New Zealand is NZ$700. Citizens over 17 years of age can bring in 200 cigarettes, or 50 cigars, or 250 grams of tobacco (or a mixture of all three if their combined weight doesn't exceed 250 grams); plus 4.5 liters of wine and beer, or 1.125 liters of liquor. New Zealand currency does not carry import or export restrictions. Fill out a certificate of export, listing the valuables you are taking out of the country; that way, you can bring them back without paying duty. Most questions are answered in a free pamphlet available at New Zealand consulates and customs offices: "New Zealand Customs Guide for Travellers," Notice no. 4. For more information, contact **New Zealand Customs,** 50 Anzac Ave., P.O. Box 29, Auckland (☎ **09/377-3520**).

Ireland allows its citizens to bring in 200 cigarettes or 100 cigarillos or 50 cigars or 250 grams (approximately 9 ounces) of tobacco, plus 1 liter of liquor exceeding 22% by volume (such as whisky, brandy, gin, rum, or vodka), or 2 liters of distilled beverages and spirits with a wine or alcoholic base of an alcoholic strength not exceeding 22% by volume, plus 2 liters of other wine and 50 grams of perfume. Other allowances include duty-free goods to a value of £34 per person or £17 per person for travelers under 15 years of age. For more information, contact **The Revenue Commissioners,** Dublin Castle, Dublin 1 (☎ **01/679-2777**).

## 3 Money

The British currency is the pound sterling (£), made up of 100 pence (p), which is used throughout the U.K. Notes are issued in £5, £10, £20, and £50 denominations. (A £1 note also circulates in Scotland.) Coins come in 1p, 2p, 5p, 10p, 50p, and £1.

At this writing, the price conversions in this book have been computed at the rates of $1 equals approximately 62p (or £1 = $1.60). Bear in mind, however, that exchange rates fluctuate daily.

**FINDING THE BEST RATES WHEN YOU EXCHANGE YOUR MONEY**   It's always wise to exchange enough money before departure to get you from the airport to your hotel. This way, you avoid delays and the lousy rates at the airport exchange booths.

When exchanging money, you're likely to obtain a better rate for traveler's checks than for cash. London banks generally offer the best rates of exchange; they're usually open Monday to Friday from 9:30am to 3:30pm. Many of the "high street" branches are now open until 5pm; a handful of central London branches are open until noon on Saturday, including **Barclays,** 208 Kensington High St., W8 (☎ **0171/441-3200**).

Money exchange is now also available at competitive rates at major London post offices, with a 1% service charge.

Money can be exchanged during off hours at a variety of bureaux de change throughout the city, found at small shops and in hotels, railway stations (including the international terminal at Waterloo Station), travel agencies, and airports, but their exchange rates are poorer and they charge high service fees. Examine the prices and rates carefully before handing over your dollars, as there's no consumer organization to regulate the activities of privately run bureaux de change.

*Time Out* recently did a survey of various exchange facilities, and American Express came out on top, with the lowest commission charged on dollar transactions.

## The British Pound & the U.S. Dollar

| UK£ | US$ | UK£ | US$ |
|---|---|---|---|
| .16 | .25 | 9.38 | 15.00 |
| .31 | .50 | 12.50 | 20.00 |
| .47 | .75 | 15.63 | 25.00 |
| .625 | 1.00 | 31.25 | 50.00 |
| 1.25 | 2.00 | 46.88 | 75.00 |
| 1.88 | 3.00 | 62.50 | 100.00 |
| 2.50 | 4.00 | 93.75 | 150.00 |
| 3.13 | 5.00 | 125.00 | 200.00 |
| 3.75 | 6.00 | 156.25 | 250.00 |
| 4.38 | 7.00 | 187.50 | 300.00 |
| 5.00 | 8.00 | 218.75 | 350.00 |
| 5.63 | 9.00 | 250.00 | 400.00 |
| 6.25 | 10.00 | 312.50 | 500.00 |

**American Express** is at 6 Haymarket, SW1 (☎ **800/221-7282** or 0171/930-4411) and other locations throughout the city. Other reputable firms are **Thomas Cook,** Oxford St., W1 (☎ **800/223-7373** or 0171/493-4537), branches of which can also be found at Victoria Station, Marble Arch, and other city locations; and, for 24-hour foreign exchange, **Chequepoint,** at 548 Oxford St., W1N 9HJ (☎ **0171/723-1005**) and other locations throughout London (hours will vary).

Try not to change money at your hotel; the rates tend to be horrendous.

**CREDIT CARDS**    The real way to get the best rate of exchange is to buy whatever you can with credit cards. Credit card issuers virtually always offer a rate of exchange better than any you can get by changing your cash, and there's no accompanying service charge. Credit cards are widely accepted in England; American Express, Visa, and Diners Club are the most commonly recognized. A Eurocard or Access sign displayed at an establishment means that it accepts MasterCard.

**ATM NETWORKS**    Plus, Cirrus, and other networks connecting automated-teller machines (ATMs) are accessible throughout London. By using your bank card to withdraw money, you'll debit the amount directly from your account. When using an ATM abroad, the money will be in local currency; the rate of exchange tends to be as good, if not better, than what you would receive at an airport money counter or a hotel. Note that international withdrawal fees will be higher than domestic fees—ask your bank for specifics.

If you're going to be using a credit card at an ATM, always determine the frequency limits for withdrawals and cash advance limits of your credit card.

Check to see if your PIN code must be reprogrammed for usage in London. Most ATMs outside the United States require a four-digit PIN number.

To receive a directory of Cirrus ATMs, call ☎ **800/424-7787;** for Plus locations, call ☎ **800/843-7587.** You can also access the Visa/PLUS International ATM Locator Guide through Internet: http://www.visa.com/visa.

If you have a Citibank Visa or MasterCard, you can call their offices in London at ☎ 0171/500-5500 for information on where to get cash from automatic tellers.

**TRAVELER'S CHECKS**   Traveler's checks are the safest way to carry cash while traveling. Most banks will give you a better exchange rate for traveler's checks than cash. But if you can, go ahead and purchase them in pound denominations.

Major issuers of traveler's checks include American Express (☎ 800/221-7282), Citicorp (☎ 800/645-6556 in the U.S. and Canada, or 813/623-1709 collect from anywhere else in the world), Thomas Cook (☎ 800/223-7373 in the U.S. and Canada, or 609/987-7300 collect from other parts of the world), and Interpayment Services (☎ 800/221-2426 in the U.S. and Canada, or 212/858-8500 collect from other parts of the world).

Issuers sometimes have agreements with groups to sell checks commission-free. For example, the American Automobile Association (AAA) clubs sell American Express checks in several currencies without commission.

**MONEYGRAM**   If you find yourself out of money, a wire service provided by American Express can help you tap willing friends and family for emergency funds. Through MoneyGram, 6200 S. Québec St., P.O. Box 5118, Englewood, CO 80155 (☎ 800/926-9400), money can be sent around the world in less than 10 minutes. Senders should call AMEX to learn the address of the closest outlet that handles MoneyGrams. Cash, credit card (MC or V), or the occasional personal check (with ID) are acceptable forms of payment. AMEX's fee for the service is $10 for the first $300 with a sliding scale for larger sums. The service includes a short telex message. The beneficiary must present a photo ID at the outlet where money is received.

## 4 When to Go

**WHEN YOU'LL FIND BARGAINS**   The cheapest time to travel to England is in the off-season: that means November 1 to December 12 and December 25 to March 14. Weekday flights are cheaper than weekend fares (often by 10% or more).

Rates generally increase between March 14 to June 5 and in October, then hit their peak in the high travel seasons between June 6 and September 30 and December 13 and 24. July and August are also the months when most Britons take their holidays, so besides the higher prices, you'll have to deal with limited availability of accommodations and crowds.

You can avoid crowds by planning trips for November and January through March. Sure, it may be rainy and cold—but England doesn't shut down when the tourists leave! In fact, the winter season includes some of London's best theater, opera, ballet, and classical music offerings, and gives visitors a more honest view of English life. Additionally, many hotel prices drop by 20%, and cheaper accommodations offer weekly rates—unheard of during peak travel times. By arriving after the winter holidays, you can also take advantage of post-Christmas sales to buy your fill of woolens, china, crystal, silver, fashion clothing, handcrafts, and curios.

In short, spring offers the countryside at its greenest, autumn brings the bright colors of the northern moorlands, and summer's warmer weather gives rise to the many outdoor music and theater festivals. But winter offers savings across the board and a chance to see Britons going about their everyday lives largely unhindered by tourist invasions.

**THE CLIMATE**   Yes, it rains, but you'll rarely get a true downpour. Pack an umbrella and prepare yourself for a short daily drizzle. It's heaviest in November (2$\frac{1}{2}$ inches on average).

Temperatures rarely drop below 35°F or go above 78°F. Evenings are cool, even in summer. Note that the British, who consider chilliness wholesome, like to keep the thermostats about 10° below the American comfort level. Hotels have central heating but are usually kept just above the goose-bump (in English, "goose pimple") margin.

**London's Average Daytime Temperature & Monthly Rainfall**

|            | Jan | Feb | Mar | Apr | May | June | July | Aug | Sept | Oct | Nov | Dec |
|------------|-----|-----|-----|-----|-----|------|------|-----|------|-----|-----|-----|
| Temp. °F   | 40  | 40  | 44  | 49  | 55  | 61   | 64   | 64  | 59   | 52  | 46  | 42  |
| Rainfall " | 2.1 | 1.6 | 1.5 | 1.5 | 1.8 | 1.8  | 2.2  | 2.3 | 1.9  | 2.2 | 2.5 | 1.9 |

**HOLIDAYS**   England observes New Year's Day, Good Friday, Easter Monday, May Day (first Monday in May), spring and summer bank holidays (the last Monday in May and August, respectively), Christmas Day, and Boxing Day (December 26).

## ENGLAND CALENDAR OF EVENTS

January

- **London International Boat Show.** Europe's largest boat show, held at the **Earl's Court Exhibition Centre,** Warwick Road. Call ☎ **01784/473377** for details. Early January.
- **Charles I Commemoration,** London. To mark the anniversary of the execution of King Charles I "in the name of freedom and democracy," hundreds of cavaliers march through central London in 17th-century dress, and prayers are said at Whitehall's Banqueting House. Last Sunday in January.
- **Chinese New Year,** London. The famous Lion Dancers in Soho perform free on the nearest Sunday to Chinese New Year. Either in late January or early February (based on the lunar calendar).

February

- **Jorvik Festival,** York. This 2-week festival celebrates this historic cathedral city's role as a Viking outpost. For more information, call ☎ **01904/621756.**

March

- ✪ **Crufts Dog Show,** Birmingham. The English, they say, love their pets more than their offspring. Crufts offers an opportunity to observe the nation's pet lovers dote on 8,000 dogs, representing 150 breeds. It's held at the National Exhibition Centre, Birmingham, West Midlands. Tickets can be purchased at the door. For more information, contact **The Kennel Club,** 1–5 Clarges St., Piccadilly, London W1Y 8AB or call their ticket hotline at ☎ **0171/518-1012.** First week of March.

April

- ✪ **The Shakespeare Season,** Stratford-upon-Avon. The Royal Shakespeare Company begins its annual season, presenting works by the Bard in his hometown, at the **Royal Shakespeare Theater,** Waterside (☎ **01789/295623**). Tickets are available at the box office, or else through such agents as Keith Prowse in London. April to January.
- **London Marathon.** More than 30,000 competitors run from Greenwich Park to Buckingham Palace; call ☎ **0161/703-8161** for information. If you'd like to take the challenge, call from May to June for an application. Mid-April.
- **Devizes to Westminster International Canoe Race.** This 125-mile race runs along the Avon River, the Kennet Canal, and the River Thames. No tickets are needed. Call ☎ **01372/453976** for more information. Three days in mid-April.

- **Easter Parade,** London. A memorable parade of brightly colored floats and marching bands around Battersea Park.

May

- **Chichester Festival Theatre.** Some great classic and modern plays are presented at this West Sussex theater. For tickets and information, contact the **Festival Theatre,** Oaklands Park, West Sussex PO19 4AP (☎ **01243/781312**). The season runs May to October.
- **Brighton Festival.** England's largest multi-arts festival, with some 400 different cultural events. For information, write the **Brighton Festival,** 21–22 Old Steine, Brighton, Sussex BN1 1EL. Most of May.
- ✪ **Bath International Music Festival.** One of Europe's most prestigious international festivals of music and the arts features as many as 1,000 performers at various venues in Bath. For information, contact the **Bath Festivals Trust,** 2 Midland Bridge Rd., Bath, Avon BA2 3EQ (☎ **01225/463362**). Mid-May to early June.
- ✪ **Glyndebourne Festival.** One of England's major cultural events, this festival is centered at the 1,200-seat Glyndebourne Opera House in Sussex, some 54 miles south of London. Tickets, which cost anywhere from £10 to £110 ($16 to $176), are available from **Glyndebourne Festival Opera Box Office,** Lewes, East Sussex BN8 5UU (☎ **01273/813813**). Mid-May to late August.
- **Shakespeare Under the Stars.** The Bard's works are performed at the **Open Air Theatre,** Inner Circle, Regent's Park, NW1, in London. Take the tube to Baker Street. Performances are Monday through Saturday at 8pm; Wednesday, Thursday, and Saturday also at 2:30pm. Call ☎ **0171/486-2431** for more information. Previews begin in late May and last throughout the summer.
- **Chelsea Flower Show,** London. The best of British gardening, with plants and flowers of the season, is displayed at the Chelsea Royal Hospital. Contact your local British Tourist Authority Office to find out which overseas reservations agency is handling ticket sales, or contact the **Chelsea Show Ticket Office,** P.O. Box 1426, London W6 0LQ (☎ **0171/630-7422**). Late May.

June

- **Grosvenor House Art and Antique Fair,** London. This very prestigious antiques fair is held at Grosvenor House, Park Lane. For information, contact **Grosvenor House Art and Antiques Fair,** Grosvenor House, 86–90 Park Lane, London W1A 3AA (☎ **0171/499-8743**). Ten days in mid-June.
- **Kenwood Lakeside Concerts.** These annual concerts on the north side of Hampstead Heath continue a British tradition of outdoor performances for nearly 50 years. Fireworks displays and laser shows enliven the premier musical performances. The audience catches the music as it drifts across the lake from the performance shell. Concerts are held every Saturday from mid-June to early September.
- **Royal Academy's Summer Exhibition,** London. This institution, founded in 1768, has for some 2 centuries held Summer Exhibitions of living painters at **Burlington House,** Piccadilly Circus. Call ☎ **0171/439-7438** for more information. Early June to mid-August.
- ✪ **Trooping the Colour.** This is the queen's official birthday parade, a quintessential British event, with exquisite pageantry and pomp. Seated in a carriage (no longer on horseback), she inspects her regiments and takes their salute as they parade their colors before her. The young men under the bearskins have been known to pass out from the heat. It's held at the Horse Guards Parade, Whitehall.

Tickets for the parade and two reviews, held on preceding Saturdays, are allocated by ballot. Applicants must write between January 1 and the end of February, enclosing a stamped, self-addressed envelope or International Reply Coupon, to the **Ticket Office, HQ Household Division, Horse Guards,** Whitehall, London SW1X 6AA. Exact dates and ticket prices will be supplied later. The ballot is held in mid-March, and only successful applicants are informed in April. Held on a day designated in June (not necessarily the queen's actual birthday).

- **Aldeburgh Festival of Music and the Arts.** The composer Benjamin Britten launched this festival in 1948. For more details on the events, and for the year-round program, write to **Aldeburgh Foundation,** High Street, Aldeburgh, Suffolk IP15 5AX (☎ **01728/452935**). Two weeks from mid- to late June.

✪ **Lawn Tennis Championships,** Wimbledon. Ever since players took to the grass courts at Wimbledon in 1877, this tournament has attracted quite a crowd, and there's still an excited hush at Centre Court and a certain thrill associated with being there. Savor the strawberries and cream that are part of the experience. Tickets for Centre and Number One courts are obtainable through a lottery. Write in from August to December to **A.E.L.T.C.,** P.O. Box 98, Church Rd., Wimbledon, London SW19 5AE (☎ **0181/946-2244**). Outside court tickets are available daily, but be prepared to wait in line. Late June through early July.

- **City of London Festival.** This annual art festival is held in venues throughout the city. Call ☎ **0171/377-0540** for information. June and July.
- **Henley Royal Regatta,** Henley, in Oxfordshire. This international rowing competition is the premier event on the English social calendar. in Oxfordshire. For more information, call ☎ **01491/578034.** Late June to early July.

## July

- **Royal Tournament,** London. In July, Britain's armed forces put on dazzling displays of athletic and military skills at the **Earl's Court Exhibition Centre.** For information about performance times and tickets, call ☎ **0171/244-0244.** Ticket prices range from £5 to £25.
- **The Proms.** A night at "The Proms"—the annual Henry Wood promenade concerts at **Royal Albert Hall**—attracts music aficionados from around the world. Staged almost daily (except for a few Sundays) these traditional concerts were launched in 1895 and are the principal summer engagements for the BBC Symphony Orchestra. Cheering and clapping, Union Jacks on parade, banners and balloons—it's great summer fun. Mid-July through mid-September.

## August

- **Cowes Week,** off the Isle of Wight. This yachting festival takes place in early August. For details, call ☎ **01983/291914.**
- **Notting Hill Carnival,** London. One of the largest annual street festivals in Europe, attracting more than half a million people. There's live reggae and soul music plus great Caribbean food. Two days in late August.

## September

- **Burghley Horse Trials,** Lincolnshire. This annual event is staged on the grounds of the largest Elizabethan house in England, **Burghley House,** Stamford, Lincolnshire (☎ **01780/752451**). Three days in early September.
- **Raising of the Thames Barrier,** Unity Way, SE18. Once a year, usually in September, a full test is done on this miracle of modern engineering; all 10 of the massive steel gates are raised against the low and high tides. Call ☎ **0181/305-4188** for exact date and time.

October

- **Cheltenham Festival of Literature.** This Cotswold event features readings, book exhibitions, and theatrical performances—all in the famed spa town of Gloucestershire. Call ☎ **01242/522878** for more details, or 01242/237377 to receive mailings about the event. Early to mid-October.

- **Opening of Parliament,** London. Ever since the 17th century, when the English beheaded Charles I, British monarchs have been denied the right to enter the House of Commons. Instead, the monarch opens Parliament in the House of Lords, reading an official speech that is in fact written by the government. Queen Elizabeth II rides from Buckingham Palace to Westminster in a royal coach accompanied by the Yeoman of the Guard and the Household Cavalry. The public galleries are open on a first-come, first-served basis. First Monday in October.

- **Quit Rents Ceremony,** London. At the Royal Courts of Justice, the Queen's Remembrancer receives token rents on behalf of the queen. The ceremony includes splitting sticks and counting horseshoes. Call ☎ **0171/936-6131** for more information. Late October.

- **Horse of the Year Show,** Wembley. Riders fly from every continent to join in this festive display of horsemanship (much appreciated by the queen). The British press call it an "equine extravaganza." It's held at **Wembley Arena,** outside London. For more information, call ☎ **0181/902-8833.** Early October.

November

- **London-Brighton Veteran Car Run.** This race begins in London's Hyde Park and ends in the seaside resort of Brighton, in East Sussex. Call ☎ **01580/893413** for more details. First Sunday in November.

- **Guy Fawkes Night,** throughout England. This British celebration commemorates the anniversary of the "Gunpowder Plot," an attempt to blow up King James I and Parliament. Huge organized bonfires are lit throughout London, and Guy Fawkes, the plot's most famous conspirator, is burned in effigy. Check *Time Out* for locations. Early November.

- **Lord Mayor's Procession and Show,** London. The queen has to ask permission to enter the square mile in London called The City—and the right of refusal has been jealously guarded by London merchants since the 17th century. Suffice to say that the lord mayor is a powerful character, and the procession from the Guildhall to the Royal Courts is appropriately impressive. You can watch the procession from the street; the banquet is by invitation only. Second week in November.

## 5 Tips for Travelers with Special Needs

**FOR TRAVELERS WITH DISABILITIES** Before you go, there are many agencies to check with about information for travelers with disabilities.

One is the **Travel Information Service,** Moss Rehab Hospital, 1200 W. Tabor Rd., Philadelphia, PA 19141, which provides information to telephone callers only: Call ☎ **215/456-9603,** or 215/456-9602 (for TTY) for assistance with your travel needs.

You can also obtain a free copy of *Air Transportation of Handicapped Persons,* published by the U.S. Department of Transportation. Request one by writing for Free Advisory Circular No. 12032, Distribution Unit, U.S. Department of Transportation, Publications Division, M-4332, Washington, DC 20590.

You may also want to consider joining a tour specifically for visitors with disabilities. One such tour operator is **FEDCAP Rehabilitation Services** (formerly known as the Federation of the Handicapped), 211 W. 14th St., New York, NY 10011. Call ☎ **212/727-4200** or fax 212/721-4374 for information about membership and summer tours.

For names and addresses of other tour operators and additional relevant information, contact the **Society for the Advancement of Travel for the Handicapped,** 347 Fifth Ave., Suite 610, New York, NY 10016 (☎ **212/447-7284;** fax 212/725-8253). Yearly membership dues are $45, or $30 for senior citizens and students. Send a stamped, self-addressed envelope.

For people who are blind or have visual impairments, the best source is the **American Foundation for the Blind,** 11 Penn Plaza, Suite 300, New York, NY 10001 (☎ **800/232-5463** to order information kits and supplies). It offers information on travel and various requirements for the transport and border formalities for seeing-eye dogs. It also issues identification cards to those who are legally blind.

One of the best organizations serving the needs of people who use wheelchairs or walkers is **Flying Wheels Travel,** 143 West Bridge, P.O. Box 382, Owatonna, MN 55060 (☎ **800/535-6790** or 507/451-5005), offering various escorted tours and cruises internationally, and private tours in a minivan with lift.

For a $25 annual fee, you can join **Mobility International USA,** P.O. Box 10767, Eugene, OR 97440 (☎ **503/343-1284;** fax 503/343-6182), which answers questions on various destinations and also offers discounts on videos, publications, and programs it sponsors.

Many London hotels, museums, restaurants, and sightseeing attractions have wheelchair ramps. Persons with disabilities are often granted special discounts at attractions and, in some cases, nightclubs. These are called "concessions" in Britain. It always pays to ask. Free information and advice is available from **Holiday Care Service,** Imperial Building, 2nd Floor, Victoria Rd., Horley, Surrey RH6 7PZ (☎ **01293/774535;** fax 01293/784647).

The **British Tourist Authority** sells *London Made Easy* (£2.50 [$4]), a booklet offering advice and describing facilities for travelers with disabilities. Bookstores often carry *Access in London* (£4 [$6.40]), an even more helpful publication.

The transport system, cinemas, and theaters are still pretty much off-limits, but **London Transport** does publish a leaflet called *Access to the Underground,* which gives details of elevators and ramps at individual Underground stations; call ☎ **0171/918-3312.** And the London black cab is perfectly suited for those in wheelchairs; the roomy interiors have plenty of room for maneuvering.

In London, the most visible organization for information about access to theaters, cinemas, galleries, museums, and restaurants is **Artsline,** 54 Chalton St., London NW1 1HS (☎ **0171/388-2227;** fax 0171/383-2653). It offers free information about wheelchair access, theaters with hearing aids, tourist attractions, and cinemas. Artsline will mail information to North America, but it's even more helpful to contact Artsline after your arrival in London. Call from 9:30am to 5:30pm on Monday through Friday.

Another organization that cooperates closely with Artsline is **Tripscope,** The Courtyard, 4 Evelyn Rd., London W4 5JL (☎ **0181/994-9294;** fax 0181/994-3618), which offers advice on travel for persons with disabilities in Britain and elsewhere.

**FOR GAY & LESBIAN TRAVELERS**   England has one of the most active gay and lesbian scenes in the world, centered mainly around London. Gay bars, restaurants, and centers are also found in all large English cities, notably Bath, Birmingham, Manchester, and especially Brighton.

For the gay and lesbian traveler to England, the best guides are *Spartacus Britain and Ireland* ($24.95) and *London Scene* ($11.95). For up-to-the-minute activities in Britain, we recommend *Gay Times* (London) for $6.95. If you are traveling elsewhere in Europe, consider *Spartacus,* primarily for gay men, costing $32.95, or *Ferrari's Guides' Women's Travel in Your Pocket* for $14. These books and others are available from **Giovanni's Room,** 1145 Pine St., Philadelphia, PA 19107 (☎ **215/923-2960;** fax 215/923-0813).

*Our World* magazine, 1104 North Nova Rd., Suite 251, Daytona Beach, FL 32117 (☎ **904/441-5367;** fax 904/441-5604), covers options and bargains for gay and lesbian travel worldwide. It costs $35 for 10 issues. *Out and About,* 8 West 19th St., Suite 401, New York, NY 10011 (☎ **800/929-2268** or 212/645-6922; fax 800/929-2215), is another great publication on gay travel that profiles the best gay or gay-friendly hotels, gyms, clubs, and other places worldwide. It costs $49 a year for 10 information-packed issues.

With some 1,200 member agencies, the **International Gay Travel Association** (IGTA), P.O. Box 4974, Key West, FL 33041 (☎ voice mailbox **800/448-8550** or 305/292-0217) specializes in networking travelers with the appropriate gay-friendly service organization or tour specialist. It offers quarterly newsletter, marketing mailings, and a membership directory.

**Our Family Abroad,** 40 West 57th St., Suite 430, New York, NY 10019 (☎ **800/999-5500** or 212/459-1800), operates escorted tours for gay men and women to points throughout the world, including several to Britain. Tour guides serve on a volunteer basis—so you can be sure you won't get a homophobic guide.

In London, the **Lesbian and Gay Switchboard** (☎ **0171/837-7324**) is open 24 hours a day, providing information about gay-related London activities or advice in general. The **Bisexual Helpline** (☎ **0181/569-7500**) offers useful information, but only on Tuesday and Wednesday from 7:30 to 9:30pm. The best bookstore is **Gay's the Word,** 66 Marchmont St., WC1 (☎ **0171/278-7654;** tube: Russell Square), which is the largest such store in Britain. It is open Monday through Wednesday and Friday and Saturday from 10am to 6pm, Thursday 10am to 7pm, and Sunday 2 to 6pm.

**FOR SENIORS** Many discounts are available for seniors. However, in England, you often have to be a member of an association to obtain discounts. Public transportation reductions, for example, are available only to holders of British Pension books. Even if discounts aren't posted, you might ask if they are available.

Senior citizens more than 60 years old receive special 10% discounts on **British Airways** through its Privileged Traveler program. They also qualify for reduced restrictions on APEX cancellations. Discounts are also granted for BA tours and for intra-Britain air tickets if booked in North America.

If you're a member of the **AARP (American Association of Retired Persons),** 601 E St. NW, Washington, DC 20049 (☎ **202/434-AARP**), you may get discounts on car rentals and hotels.

**Elderhostel,** 75 Federal St., Boston, MA 02110-1941 (☎ **617/426-8056**), offers university-based educational programs for seniors in England and other parts of the world. Most courses last about 3 weeks and are remarkable values—the cost includes airfare, accommodations in student dormitories or modest inns, meals, and tuition. Courses emphasize the liberal arts and include field trips and excursions, and best of all, there's no homework or grades. You must be 55 or older to participate.

**SAGA International Holidays,** 222 Berkeley St., Boston, MA 02116 (☎ **800/ 343-0273**), offers inclusive tours and cruises for those 50 and older.

You can write for a helpful publication, *101 Tips for the Mature Traveler,* available from **Grand Circle Travel,** 347 Congress St., Suite 3A, Boston, MA 02210 (☎ **800/ 221-2610** or 617/350-7500; fax 617/350-6206); this travel agency also offers escorted tours and cruises for seniors.

Information on travel for seniors is also available from the **National Council of Senior Citizens,** 8403 Coleville Rd., Suite 1200, Silver Springs, MD 20910 (☎ 301/578-8800). A nonprofit organization, the council charges a membership fee of $13 per couple for which you receive a monthly newsletter and membership benefits, including discounts on hotel and auto rentals, a discount pharmacy program, and accidental death insurance.

**Sears Mature Outlook,** P.O. Box 9390, Des Moines, IA 50306-9519 (☎ **800/ 336-6330;** fax 847/286-5024), is a travel organization for people over 50 years of age. Members are offered discounts at ITC-member hotels and will receive a bimonthly magazine. Annual membership is $14.95 to $19.95, which entitles its members to discounts and in some cases free coupons for discounted merchandise from Sears Roebuck Co.

**FOR FAMILIES**    On airlines, you must request a special menu for children at least 24 hours in advance. If baby food is required, however, bring your own and ask a flight attendant to warm it to the right temperature.

Arrange ahead of time for such necessities as a crib, bottle warmer, and car seat (in England, small children aren't allowed to ride in the front seat).

If you're staying with friends, you can rent baby equipment from **Chelsea Baby Hire,** 83 Burntwood Lane, SW17 OAJ (☎ **0181/540-8830**).

The London black cab is a lifesaver for families; the roomy interior allows a stroller to be lifted right into the cab without unstrapping your baby.

If you want a night out without the kids, you're in luck: London has its own children's hotel, **Pippa Pop-ins,** 430 Fulham Rd., SW6 1DU (☎ **0171/385-2458**), which accommodates children overnight in a wonderful nursery filled with lots of toys and caring minders. Other recommendable baby-sitting services are: **Baby-sitters Unlimited** (☎ **0181/892-8888**) and **Childminders** (☎ **0171/935-2049** or 0171/ 935-3000). Baby-sitters can also be found for you at most hotels.

*Family Travel Times* is published quarterly by TWYCH (Travel With Your Children) and includes a weekly call-in service for subscribers. Subscriptions ($40 a year) can be ordered by mail **TWYCH,** 40 5th Ave., New York, NY 10011 (☎ **212/ 477-5524;** fax 212/477-5173). An information packet, including a sample newsletter, is available for $2.

**Families Welcome!,** 92 N. Main St., Ashland, OR 97520 (☎ **800/326-0724** or 541/482-6121) a travel company specializing in worry-free vacations for families, offers "City Kids" packages to London, featuring accommodations in family-friendly hotels or apartments. Individually designed family packages can include car rentals, train and ferry passes, and special air prices. A welcome kit is available, containing "insider's information" for families traveling in London—such as reliable baby-sitters, where to buy disposable diapers, and a list of family-friendly restaurants.

To find out what's on for children while you're in London, pick up the leaflet *Where to Take Children,* published by the London Tourist Board and Convention Bureau. If you have specific questions, ring **Kidsline** (☎ **0171/222-8070**) Monday to Friday from 4pm to 6pm and summer holidays from 9am to 4pm, or the **London Tourist Board's** special children's information line (☎ **01839/123404**).

**FOR STUDENTS**  **Council Travel** (a subsidiary of the Council on International Educational Exchange) is America's largest student, youth, and budget travel group, with more than 60 offices worldwide. The main office is at 205 E. 42nd St., New York, NY 10017 (☎ **212/661-1450**).

**Council Travel's London Centre** is conveniently located at 28A Poland St., W1V 3DB, just off Oxford Circus (☎ **0171/287-3337** for European destinations, 0171/437-7767 for other destinations). International Student Identity Cards, issuable to all bonafide students for $19, entitle holders to generous travel and other discounts. Discounted international and domestic air tickets are available, and Eurotrain rail passes, Youth Hostel Association (YHA) passes, weekend packages, overland safaris, and hostel/hotel accommodations are bookable. Council Travel sells a number of publications for young people about how to work, study, and travel abroad.

For real budget travelers, it's worth joining **Hostelling International/IYHF** (International Youth Hostel Federation). For information, write Hostelling Information/ American Youth Hostels (HI-AYH), 733 15th St. NW, No. 840, Washington, DC 20005 (☎ **202/783-6161;** fax 202/783-6171). Membership costs $25 annually; those under age 18 pay $10 and those over 54 pay $15.

**STA Travel** is the only worldwide company specializing in student- and youth-discounted airfares. Located at 86 Old Brompton Rd. (tube: South Kensington), it is open Monday to Thursday from 9:30am to 6pm, on Friday from 10am to 6pm, and on Saturday from 10am to 4pm. Call ☎ **0171/361-6161** for more information. Keep in mind that British Airways offers youth fares to anyone 12 to 24.

The **University of London Student Union,** 1 Malet St., WC1E 7HY (☎ **0171/ 580-9551;** tube: Goodge Street or Russell Square), is the best place to go to learn about student activities in the Greater London area. The Union contains a swimming pool, a fitness center, a gymnasium, a general store, a sports shop, a ticket agency, banks, bars, discos, inexpensive restaurants, venues for live events, an office of STA Travel, and many other facilities. It's open Monday through Thursday from 8:30am to 11pm, Friday 8:30am to 1pm, Saturday from 9:30am to 2pm, and Sunday from 9:30am to 10:30pm.

## 6  Getting There

### BY PLANE

The best strategy for securing the lowest fare is to shop around and remain as flexible as you can about dates. Fares are generally lower during the week from Monday through Thursday at noon. There are also seasonal fare differences, with peak season during the summer, basic during winter, and shoulder in between. Travel during Christmas and Easter weeks is usually more expensive.

The following airlines fly the enormously popular routes from North America to Great Britain.

**American Airlines** (☎ **800/624-6262**) offers daily flights to London Heathrow from half a dozen U.S. gateways—New York's JFK (four times daily, six in June), Chicago's O'Hare (twice daily), and Miami International, Los Angeles International, Philadelphia International, and Boston's Logan (each once daily).

**British Airways** (☎ **800/AIRWAYS**) offers flights from 18 U.S. cities to Heathrow and Gatwick airports as well as many others to Manchester, Birmingham, and Glasgow. Nearly every flight is nonstop.

With more add-on options than any other airline, British Airways can make a visit to Britain cheaper than you might have expected. Of particular interest are the "Value

Plus," "London on the Town," and "Europe Escorted" packages that include both airfare and discounted hotel accommodations in Britain.

**Continental Airlines** (☎ 800/525-0280) has daily flights to London from Houston and Newark.

Depending on day and season, **Delta Air Lines** (☎ 800/241-4141) runs either one or two daily nonstop flights between Atlanta and Gatwick. Delta also offers nonstop daily service from Cincinnati and Miami to Gatwick.

**Northwest Airlines** (☎ 800/447-4747) flies nonstop from Minneapolis, Detroit, and Boston to Gatwick, with connections possible from other cities, such as Memphis.

**TWA** (☎ 800/221-2000) flies nonstop to Gatwick every day from its hub in St. Louis. Connections are possible through St. Louis from most of North America.

**United Airlines** (☎ 800/538-2929) flies nonstop from New York's JFK to Heathrow two or three times daily, depending on the season. United also offers nonstop service twice a day from Dulles Airport, near Washington, D.C., plus once-a-day service from Chicago; Newark, N.J.; Los Angeles; and San Francisco to Heathrow.

**Virgin Atlantic Airways** (☎ 800/862-8621) generally offers the best fares from the United States to England. There are daily flights to either Heathrow or Gatwick from Boston; Newark, N.J.; New York's JFK; Los Angeles; and San Francisco. The airline also flies from Miami to Gatwick (four times a week), and five times a week from Orlando. Virgin Atlantic also offers flights to London from Chicago through interconnecting service on Kiwi Airlines. For information, call Virgin Atlantic or Kiwi (☎ 800/JET-KIWI).

For travelers departing from Canada, **Air Canada** (☎ 800/776-3000) flies daily to London Heathrow nonstop from Vancouver, Montreal, and Toronto. There are also frequent direct services from Edmonton, Calgary, Winnipeg, Ottawa, Halifax, and St. John's. All flights are smoke-free.

From Canada, **British Airways** (☎ 800/247-9297) has direct flights from Toronto, Montreal, and Vancouver. You can also fly from Calgary on Canadian Pacific (arranged through British Airways).

For travelers departing from Australia, **British Airways** (☎ 800/247-9297) has flights to London from Sydney, Melbourne, Perth, and Brisbane.

**Quantas** (☎ 800/AIRWAYS) offers flights from Australia to London's Heathrow. Direct flights depart from Sydney and Melbourne. Some flights have free stopovers in Bangkok or Singapore.

Departing from New Zealand, **Air New Zealand** (☎ 800/262-1234) has direct flights to London from Auckland. These flights depart Wednesday, Saturday and Sunday.

Short flights from Dublin to London are available through **British Airways** (☎ 800/AIRWAYS), with four flights daily into London's Gatwick Airport, and **Aer Lingus** (☎ 800/223-6537), which flies into Heathrow. Short flights from Dublin to London are also available through **Ryan Air** (☎ 0541/569-569) and **British Midland** (☎ 0345/554554).

## Discounted Airfares

**BUCKET SHOPS & CONSOLIDATORS**   You might be able to get a great deal on airfare by calling a bucket shop or a consolidator, outfits that act as clearinghouses for blocks of tickets that airlines discount and consign during normally slow periods of air travel. Tickets are usually priced 20% to 35% below the full fare. However, payment terms can vary and you might be assigned a poor seat on the plane at the last minute.

Bucket shops abound from coast to coast. You might try **Travac,** 989 Sixth Ave., New York, NY 10018 (☎ **800/TRAV-800** in the U.S., or 212/563-3303) or 2601 East Jefferson St., Orlando, FL 32803 (☎ **407/896-0014**); **TFI Tours International,** 34 W. 32nd St., 12th Floor, New York, NY 10001 (☎ **800/745-8000,** or 212/736-1140 if calling in New York State); **Unitravel,** 1177 N. Warson Rd., St. Louis, MO 63132 (☎ **800/325-2222;** fax 314/569-2503), **Travel Avenue,** 10 S. Riverside Plaza, Suite 1404, Chicago, IL 60606 (☎ **800/333-3335**), the nation's oldest and largest rebate travel agency; or **TMI** (Travel Management International), 1129–E Wayzata Blvd., Wayzata, MN 55391 (☎ **800/245-3672**).

There's also **1-800-FLY-4-LESS,** RFA Building 5440 Morehouse Dr., San Diego, CA 92121, a nationwide airline reservation and ticketing service that specializes in finding only the lowest fares.

Another option, suitable only for those individuals with extremely flexible schedules, is **Airhitch,** 2641 Broadway, Third Floor, New York, NY 10025 (☎ **212/864-2000**). Prospective travelers inform the company of any 5 consecutive days in which they're available to fly to Europe. Airhitch agrees to fly its passengers within those 5 days from any of three regions of the United States.

**CHARTER FLIGHTS**    Strictly speaking, a charter flight occupies an aircraft reserved months in advance for a one-time-only transit to some predetermined point. Before paying for a charter, check the restrictions on your ticket or contract. You'll pay a stiff penalty (or forfeit the ticket entirely) if you cancel. Charters are sometimes canceled when the plane doesn't fill up.

One reliable charter-flight operator is **Council Charter,** run by the Council on International Educational Exchange, 205 E. 42nd St., New York, NY 10017 (☎ **800/2-COUNCIL** or 212/822-2900), which arranges charter seats on regularly scheduled aircraft. You could also try **Travac,** 989 Sixth Ave., New York, NY 10018 (☎ **800/TRAV-800** or 212/563-3303).

**REBATORS**    Rebators pass part of their commission along to the passenger, although many of them assess a fee for their services. Most rebators offer discounts ranging from 10% to 25% plus a $25 handling charge. They are not the same as travel agents but sometimes offer similar services, including discounted accommodations and car rentals.

Midwest travelers might want to try **Travel Avenue,** 10 South Riverside Plaza, Suite 1404, Chicago, IL 60606 (☎ **800/333-3335** or 312/876-6866). Another major rebator is **The Smart Traveller,** 3111 SW 27th Ave., (P.O. Box 330010) Miami, FL 33133 (☎ **800/448-3338** or 305/448-3338; fax 305/443-3544). They also offer discounts on packaged tours.

**LATE-SAVER FARE    Virgin Atlantic Airways** (☎ **800/862-8621**) offers passage from North America to London that can be reserved within 48 hours of the departure time—if seats are available. This type of fare, known as a Late-Saver fare, is available during off-season when seats are plentiful.

**TRAVELING AS A COURIER**    This cost-cutting technique is not for everyone, but if you choose to do it, you'll get a greatly discounted airfare. As a courier, you're allowed only one piece of carry-on luggage; your baggage allowance is used by the courier firm to transport its cargo. You don't actually handle the merchandise you're "transporting" to Europe; you just carry a manifest to present to customs. Upon arrival, an employee of the courier service will reclaim the company's cargo. You fly alone, so don't plan to travel with anybody. (A friend may be able to arrange to fly as a courier the next day.) Most courier services operate from Los Angeles or

New York, but some operate out of other cities, such as Chicago or Miami. Courier services are often listed in the yellow pages or in advertisements in travel sections of newspapers.

To get started, check with **Halbart Express,** 147-05 176th St., Jamaica, NY 11434 (☎ **718/656-8189;** open daily 10am–3pm), or **Now Voyager,** 74 Varick St., Suite 307, New York, NY 10013 (☎ **212/431-1616;** open daily 10am to 6pm). Now Voyager works with several daily flights to London, one of them  allowing couriers to stay up to 30 days and bring along a modest amount of luggage.

For $45 a year, the **International Association of Air Travel Couriers,** 8 J St., Suite 3, Lake Worth, FL 33460 (☎ **561/582-8320;** fax 561/582-1581), will send six issues of its newsletter, *Shoestring Traveler,* and about six issues of *Air Courier Bulletin,* a directory of worldwide air-courier bargains. The fee also includes access to their 24-hour fax-on-demand system and a computer bulletin board that is updated daily with last-minute flights and bulletin updates.

**TRAVEL CLUBS**   Travel clubs supply an unsold inventory of tickets at discounts of 20% to 60%. You pay an annual fee and are given a hotline number to find out what discounts are available. Many discounts become available several days in advance of the actual departure, sometimes as long as a month in advance. Of course, you're limited to what's available, so you have to be fairly flexible.

**Moment's Notice,** 7301 New Utrecht Ave., Brooklyn, NY 11204 (☎ **718/ 234-6295**), charges $25 per year and offers tours geared for impulse purchases and last-minute getaways. Even nonmembers can call the Moment's Notice hotline (see above) to learn what options are available. Most of the company's best-priced tours depart from the New York metropolitan area.

**Travelers Advantage,** 3033 South Parker Rd., Suite 900, Aurora, CO 80014 (☎ **800/548-1116**), offers a 3-month trial period for $1; the annual membership fee is $49. Benefits include a hotel card, which gets you 50% off the regularly published room rate at more than 3,000 hotels, members-only vacation packages at discounted rates, and a 5% cash bonus on all purchases made through the service (with a copy of your itinerary and any receipts).

## BY FREIGHTER

An offbeat way to get to Britain is getting a cabin aboard a freighter. No freighter can carry more than 12 passengers because a full-time ship's doctor would be required. Your cabin will be adequate, but don't expect organized activities.

Most freighters dock at Le Havre (France), Rotterdam (Holland), or Bremerhaven (Germany), but a few make stops at such unlikely British ports as Felixstowe. Sometimes the final port will change during the crossing, throwing prearranged itineraries into confusion, so you need to be flexible. Passage to Europe from most of North America's Atlantic or Gulf ports takes from 9 to 13 days, depending on the itinerary. Although last-minute berths might suddenly become available, reservations should usually be made at least 6 months in advance. In summer, cabins are often booked as much as a year in advance. Space is more likely to be available in winter.

**Anytime, Anywhere Travel,** 91 N. Bedford Rd., Chappaqua, NY 10514 (☎ **914/ 238-8800**), can book with several different freighter operators for departures from Houston, Savannah, and New Orleans (among others) that dock in several European cities, including Le Havre, Rotterdam, and Bremerhaven. The cost is about $1,500 each way, double occupancy, with meals included.

Other options are described in *Ford's Freighter Travel Guide,* 19448 Londelius St., Northridge, CA 91324 (☎ **818/701-7414;** fax 818/701-7415), which is

# Train Routes in England

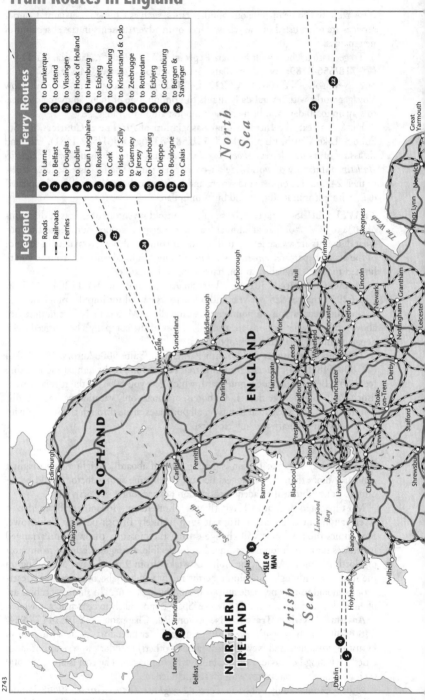

**Legend**

- —— Roads
- ⊣⊢⊣⊢ Railroads
- ‑ ‑ ‑ Ferries

**Ferry Routes**

| | | | |
|---|---|---|---|
| ❶ to Larne | ❽ to Isles of Scilly | ⓮ to Dunkerque | ㉑ to Kristiansand & Oslo |
| ❷ to Belfast | ❾ to Guernsey & Jersey | ⓯ to Ostend | ㉒ to Zeebrugge |
| ❸ to Douglas | ❿ to Cherbourg | ⓰ to Vlissingen | ㉓ to Rotterdam |
| ❹ to Dublin | ⓫ to Dieppe | ⓱ to Hook of Holland | ㉔ to Esbjerg |
| ❺ to Dun Laoghaire | ⓬ to Boulogne | ⓲ to Hamburg | ㉕ to Gothenburg |
| ❻ to Rosslare | ⓭ to Calais | ⓳ to Esbjerg | ㉖ to Bergen & Stavanger |
| ❼ to Cork | | ⓴ to Gothenburg | |

North Sea

ENGLAND

SCOTLAND

NORTHERN IRELAND

Irish Sea

Liverpool Bay

Solway Firth

The Wash

ISLE OF MAN

Edinburgh
Glasgow
Strandraer
Larne
Belfast
Carlisle
Penrith
Newcastle
Sunderland
Middlesbrough
Scarborough
Darlington
Harrogate
York
Hull
Grimsby
Skegness
Kings Lynn
Norwich
Great Yarmouth
Leeds
Bradford
Wakefield
Preston
Huddersfield
Sheffield
Doncaster
Retford
Lincoln
Newark
Nottingham
Grantham
Leicester
Derby
Stoke-on-Trent
Crewe
Stafford
Shrewsbury
Chester
Manchester
Bolton
Blackpool
Barrow
Douglas
Liverpool
Bangor
Pwllheli
Holyhead
Dublin

2743

42

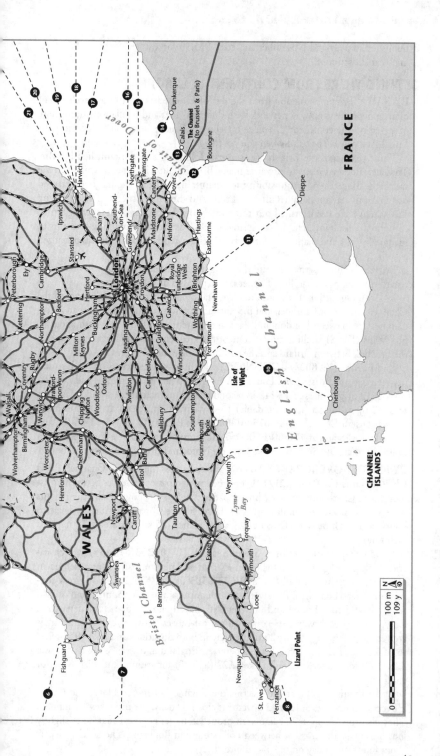

published in May and November and costs $15.95 for a single copy and $24 for a one-year subscription.

## GETTING THERE FROM CONTINENTAL EUROPE

**BY RAIL**   Britain's isolation from the rest of Europe has led to the development of an independent railway network with different rules and regulations from those observed on the continent. If you're traveling to Britain from the continent, your Eurail Pass will *not* be valid when you get there.

Three years ago, the British government, following a lead established by Mrs. Thatcher, initiated plans to privatize major British industries, one of which was the railroads. Since then, responsibility for maintaining the tracks has been farmed out to a private company (Railtrack, Ltd.), and the other aspects of maintaining the system have been farmed out to privately owned caterers, engineering firms, computer consultants, etc. In the spring of 1997, as the last remaining elements of the puzzle (sales and marketing, formerly the responsibility of BritRail) was privatized as well.

BritRail maintains that despite the mergers, absolutely nothing will change as regards pricing or availability of either BritRail Passes or Eurail Passes.

In 1994, Queen Elizabeth and President Françcois Mitterand officially opened the Channel Tunnel, or Chunnel, and the Eurostar Express passenger train began twice-daily service between London and Paris and London and Brussels—both about 3-hour trips. The $15-billion tunnel, one of the great engineering feats of all time, is the first link between Britain and the continent since the Ice Age.

**Rail Europe** (☎ **800/94-CHUNNEL**) sells direct-service tickets on the Eurostar between Paris or Brussels and London. A round-trip fare between Paris and London costs $312 in first class and $248 in second class. You can cut the second-class cost to $152 by making a (nonrefundable) 14-day advance purchase. In London make reservations for Eurostar at ☎ **01345/300003,** in Paris at ☎ **01-44-51-06-02,** and in the United States at ☎ **800/EUROSTAR.** Eurostar trains arrive and depart from London's Waterloo Station, Paris's Gare du Nord, and Brussels's Central Station.

**BY FERRY/HOVERCRAFT**   You can also sail across the English Channel. **P&O Channel Lines** (☎ **01304/212121**) operates car and passenger ferries between Portsmouth and Cherbourg, France (three departures a day; $4^{1}/4$ hours each way, 7 hours at night); between Portsmouth and Le Havre, France (three departures a day; $5^{1}/2$ hours each way); between Dover and Calais, France (25 sailings a day; 75 minutes each way).

P&O's major competitor is **Stena Sealink** (☎ **01233/615455**), which carries both passengers and vehicles on its routes. This company is represented in North America by BritRail (☎ **800/677-8585** or 212/575-2667). It offers conventional ferryboat service between Southampton and Cherbourg (one or two trips a day; 6 to 8 hours) and between Newhaven and Dieppe (four departures daily; 4 hours each way). Its conventional car-ferries between Dover and Calais are very popular; they depart 20 times a day in both directions and take 90 minutes to make the crossing. Typical fares between England and France are as follows: £25 ($40) for a one-way adult ticket, £22 ($35.20) for seniors, and £15 ($24) for children.

By far the most popular route across the Channel is between Dover and Calais. **Hoverspeed** operates at least 12 hovercraft crossings daily; the trip takes 35 minutes. They also run a SeaCat (a catamaran propelled by jet engines) that takes slightly longer to make the crossing between Folkestone and Boulogne. The SeaCats depart about four times a day on the 55-minute voyage.

Traveling by Hovercraft or SeaCat cuts the time of your surface journey from the continent to the U.K. A Hovercraft trip is definitely a fun adventure, since the vessel is technically "flying" over the water. A SeaCat crossing from Folkestone to Boulogne is longer in miles but is covered faster than conventional ferryboats make the Calais-Dover crossing. For reservations and information call Hoverspeed (☎ **01304/240241**). Typical one-way fares are £25 ($40) per person.

**CROSSING THE CHANNEL BY CAR**    If you plan to transport a rented car between England and France, check in advance with the car rental company about license and insurance requirements, and additional drop-off charges, before you begin.

The English Channel is crisscrossed with "drive-on, drive-off" car-ferry services, some of which are covered in other sections of this chapter. In addition, many conventional trains deposit their passengers near embarkation piers for ferryboat crossings, before returning to their point of origin in other parts of England or France.

The most popular ports in France for ferryboat crossings to England include Boulogne and Calais. From either of those ports, Sealink ferries will carry you, your luggage and, if you want, your car. The most popular points of arrival along the English coast include Dover and Folkestone.

There are special Channel Tunnel trains, called Le Shuttle trains that carry freight cars, trucks, lorries, and passenger cars. One-way fares for cars on the Le Shuttle trains vary from £80 to £265 ($128 to $424) according to their size. It's a lot cheaper to transport your car across by conventional ferryboat, but if you insist, here's what you'll need to know: You'll negotiate both English and French customs as part of one combined process, usually on the English side of the channel. You can remain within your vehicle even after you drive it onto a flatbed railway car during the 35-minute crossing. (For 19 minutes of this crossing, you'll actually be under water; if you want, you can leave the confines of your car and ride within a brightly lit, air-conditioned passenger car). When the trip is over, you simply drive off the flatbed car and drive off toward your destination. Total travel time between the French and English highway system is about 1 hour. As a means of speeding the flow of perishable goods across the channel, the car and truck service usually operates 24 hours a day, at intervals that vary from 15 minutes to once an hour, depending on the time of day or night. Neither BritRail nor any of the agencies dealing with reservations for passenger trains through the Chunnel will reserve space for your car in advance, and considering the frequency of the traffic on the Chunnel, they're usually not necessary. For information about Le Shuttle car-rail service after you reach England, call ☎ **01304/288617** or 01990/353535.

Duty-free stores, restaurants, and service stations are available to travelers on both sides of the Channel. A bilingual staff is on hand to assist travelers at both the British and French terminals.

# 7  Getting Around

## BY TRAIN

As it heads for the millennium, British Rail's infrastructure is being altered, although the essential rail network remains intact—and, in some cases, is being expanded. To raise capital and improve service, the government is selling some of its routes to independent operators who agree to maintain the switches, tracks, and rail cars according to standards set by British Rail's supervisory board, Railtrack. None of these behind-the-scenes changes affects the existing procedures for issuing rail passes or for selling individual tickets.

## Train Travel from London to Principal Cities

| To | From London Station | Typical Number of Trains Per Day | Miles | Travel Time |
|---|---|---|---|---|
| Bath | Paddington | 25 | 107 | 1 hr. 11 min. |
| Birmingham | Euston/Paddington | 35 | 113 | 1 hr. 37 min. |
| Bristol | Paddington | 46 | 119 | 1 hr. 26 min. |
| Carlisle | Euston | 10 | 299 | 3 hr. 40 min. |
| Chester | Euston | 16 | 179 | 2 hr. 36 min. |
| Exeter | Paddington | 17 | 174 | 1 hr. 55 min. |
| Leeds | King's Cross | 19 | 185 | 2 hr. 12 min. |
| Liverpool | Euston | 14 | 193 | 2 hr. 34 min. |
| Manchester | Euston | 16 | 180 | 2 hr. 27 min. |
| Newcastle | King's Cross | 26 | 268 | 2 hr. 50 min. |
| Penzance | Paddington | 9 | 305 | 5 hrs. |
| Plymouth | Paddington | 14 | 226 | 2 hr. 35 min. |
| York | King's Cross | 27 | 188 | 1 hr. 57 min. |

## MONEY-SAVING RAIL PASSES

A Eurail Pass is not valid in Great Britain, but there are several special passes for train travel outside London.

For railroad information, go to Rail Travel centers in the main London railway stations—Waterloo, King's Cross, Euston, and Paddington—each of which deals mainly with its own region.

Americans can obtain a BritRail Pass at **BritRail Travel International,** 1500 Broadway, New York, NY 10036 (☎ **800/677-8585** or 212/575-2667 in the U.S., or 800/555-2748 in Canada).

**BRITRAIL CLASSIC PASS**    This pass allows unlimited rail travel during a set time period (8 days, 15 days, 22 days, or 1 month). For 8 days, the pass costs $355 in first class, $249 in "standard" class; for 15 days, $549 in first class, $379 in standard; for 22 days, $700 in first class, $485 in standard; and for 1 month, $815 in first class, $565 in standard.

Senior citizens (60 and over) qualify for discounts, but only in seats within first-class—not standard class—compartments of trains. These cost $305 for 8-day passes; $469 for 15-day passes, $595 for 22-day passes, and $695 for 1 month passes.

If a child age 5 to 15 is traveling with a full-fare adult, the fare is half the adult fare. Children under 5 travel free if not occupying a seat.

**BRITRAIL FLEXIPASS**    This pass lets you travel anywhere on BritRail, and is particularly good for visitors who want to alternate travel days with blocks of uninterrupted sightseeing time in a particular city or region. Flexipasses can be used for 4 days within any 1-month period and cost $305 in first class and $209 in standard. Seniors pay $259 and youths ages 16 to 25 pay $169 to travel standard class. Also available is a Flexipass that allows 8 days of travel within a month and costs $439 in first class, $305 in standard. A senior pass costs $375, the youth standard class $245.

**SOUTHEAST PASS** If you're only planning day trips southeast of London, BritRail's Southeast Pass might make better sense than a more expensive rail pass that's valid in all parts of Britain. This pass allows unlimited travel to accessible destinations throughout BritRail's "Network Southeast," which includes Oxford, Cambridge, Dover, Canterbury, Salisbury, and Portsmouth. Frequent trains—about 41 daily from London to Brighton alone—let you leave early in the morning and return to London in time for the theater or dinner.

A Southeast Pass that's good for 3 days of travel out of any consecutive 8-day period costs $90 in first class, $69 in standard class. A Southeast Pass that's good for 4 days out of any 8-day consecutive period sells for $121 in first class and $90 in standard class. A Southeast Pass that's good for 7 days out of any 15-day consecutive period costs $169 in first class and $121 in standard class. Children under 16 pay $32 and $24 in first and standard class, respectively for any of the three passes. The Southeast Pass must be purchased either from your travel agent or BritRail Travel International in the United States or Canada (see addresses above).

**BRITAINSHRINKERS TOURS** From May to the end of the month of October, Britainshrinkers, Ltd.—an affiliate of BritRail—operates a number of escorted, full-day tours that include, in different combinations, visits to sights of cultural or historic interest outside London. Trips go to such places as Stratford-upon-Avon, the Cotswolds, and many towns and cities in the southeast, including Oxford. They include train transportation and sightseeing by bus. Tours usually include some free time for lunch, shopping, and exploring on your own. Tours return to London in time for dinner or the theater. Rates include entrance fees and value-added tax (VAT), but usually not the price of lunch.

Britainshrinkers offers excellent value for the money. And if you have a BritRail Pass or Flexipass, you'll save up to 60% on the cost of each tour you take. Their tours can be purchased from either your travel agent or BritRail in the United States.

## BY COACH

In Britain, a long-distance touring bus is called a "coach," and "buses" are taken for local transportation. There's an efficient and frequent express motor-coach network—run by National Express and other independent operators—that links most of Britain's towns and cities. Destinations off the main route can be easily reached by stopping and transferring to a local bus.

Tickets are relatively cheap (often half the price of rail fare—worth considering if you've got the extra time) and it's usually cheaper to purchase a round-trip (or "return") ticket than two one-way fares separately.

**Victoria Coach Station,** on Buckingham Palace Road (☎ **0171/730-3466**), is the London departure point for most large coach operators. The coach station is located just 2 blocks from Victoria Station. For credit-card sales (MasterCard and Visa only), call ☎ **0171/730-3499** Monday through Saturday from 9am to 7pm. For cash purchases, get there at least 30 minutes before the coach departs.

**National Express** runs luxurious long-distance coaches that are equipped with hostesses, light refreshments, reclining seats, toilets, and no-smoking areas. Details about all coach services can be obtained by phoning ☎ **01990/808080** daily from 8am to 10pm. The National Express ticket office at Victoria Station is open from 8am to 7pm.

You might want to consider National Express's **Tourist Trail Pass,** which offers unlimited travel on their network. (This company's service is most extensive in England and Wales.) A 3-day pass costs £49 ($78.40), a 5-day pass £79 ($126.40); an 8-day pass, £119 ($190.40); and a 15-day pass, £179 ($286.40).

For journeys within a 35-mile radius of London, try the **Green Line** coach service, Lesbourne Road, Reigate Surrey RH2 7LE (☎ **0181/668-7261**). With a 1-day **Diamond Rover Ticket,** costing £7 ($11.20) for adults and £5 ($8) for children, you can visit many of the attractions of Greater London and the surrounding region, including Windsor Castle and Hampton Court. The pass is valid for 1 day on almost all Green Line coaches and country buses Monday through Friday after 9am and all day on Saturday and Sunday.

Green Line has bus routes called Country Bus Lines that circle through the periphery of London. Although they do not usually go directly into the center of the capital, they do hook up with the routes of the Green Line coaches and red buses that do.

## BY CAR

You can get most places in England by train or coach, but if you want to be on your own and see more of the countryside—and driving on the left appeals to your sense of adventure—here are some guidelines.

The British car-rental market is among the most competitive in Europe. Nevertheless, car rentals are often relatively expensive, unless you avail yourself of one of the promotional deals that are frequently offered by British Airways and others.

Since cars in Britain travel on the left side of the road, their steering wheels are positioned on the "wrong" side of the vehicle. Also keep in mind that most rental cars are manual, so be prepared to shift with your left hand; you'll pay more for an automatic—and you'll need to request one when you reserve.

Most car rental companies will accept your U.S. driver's license, provided you're 23 years old (21 in rare instances) and have had the license for more than a year. Many rental companies will grant discounts to clients who reserve their cars in advance (usually 48 hours) through the toll-free reservations offices in the renter's home country. Rentals of a week or more are almost always less expensive, per day, than day rentals.

When you reserve a car, be sure to ask if the price includes the 17.5% Value-Added Tax (VAT), personal accident insurance (PAI), collision-damage waiver (CDW), and any other insurance options. If not, ask what they will cost, because at the end of your rental, they can make a big difference in your bottom line. As in the United States, the CDW and some added insurance are sometimes offered free by certain credit-card companies if you use the card to pay for the rental. Check directly with your credit-card issuer to see if you are covered by your credit card so you can avoid the sometimes unnecessary coverage.

**British Airways** (☎ **800/AIRWAYS**) offers a relatively inexpensive way to rent a car in Britain through its reservations service. As the U.K.'s largest car renter, BA can offer discounted rates. Depending on size, horsepower, amenities, and season, cars range in price from $20 to $92 per day plus VAT and insurance. Child seats are available free. These arrangements are offered only to passengers flying into Britain on BA.

The major car-rental companies offer services at all major airports. These include **Avis** (☎ **800/331-2112**), which also has a main London office in Mayfair at 8 Balderton St., London W1 (☎ **0171/917-6700;** tube: Bond Street). **Budget Rent-a-Car** (☎ **800/472-3325**), maintains 12 offices in London, including at all the major airports and about 100 other locations throughout the United Kingdom. The busiest London office is near Marble Arch, 89 Wigmore St., W1 (☎ **0171/723-8038;** tube: Marble Arch). **Hertz** (☎ **800/654-3001**) has a London office at 35 Edgeware Rd., Marble Arch, London W1 (☎ **0171/402-4242;** tube: Marble Arch).

**Kemwel Holiday Autos** (☎ 800/678-0678) is among the cheapest and most reliable of the rental agencies. Automobiles are available in two categories: Super Saver, for local rentals in London or Glasgow, and Free Wheeler, which allows pick up and drop off at different stations throughout Great Britain. Call for current prices and information, as advance reservations may be required.

**DRIVING RULES & REQUIREMENTS**    In England, *you drive on the left* and pass on the right. Road signs are clear and the international symbols are unmistakable.

You must present your passport and driver's license when you rent a car in Britain. No special British license is needed. It's a good idea to get a copy of the *British Highway Code,* available from almost any gas station or newsstand (called a "news stall" in Britain).

*Warning:* Pedestrian crossings are marked by striped lines (zebra striping) on the road; flashing lights near the curb indicates that drivers must stop and yield the right of way if a pedestrian has stepped out into the zebra zone to cross the street.

**ROAD MAPS**    The best road map is *The Ordinance Survey Motor Atlas of Great Britain*—whether you're trying to find the fastest route to Manchester or locate some obscure village. Revised annually, it's published by Temple Press and is available at most bookstores, including **W&G Foyle, Ltd.,** 113 and 119 Charing Cross Rd., London, WC2 HOEB (☎ **0171/439-8501**).

**BREAKDOWNS**    You might want to join one of England's two major auto clubs—the Automobile Association (AA) and the Royal Automobile Club (RAC). Membership, which can be obtained through your car-rental agent, entitles you to free legal and technical advice on motoring matters, as well as a whole range of discounts on automobile products and services.

The AA is located at Norfolk House, Priestly Rd., Basingstoke, Hampshire RG24 9NY (☎ **01256/20123**). The RAC can be contacted at P.O. Box 700, Bristol, Avon BS99 1RB (☎ **01454/208000**).

If your car breaks down on the highway, you can call for 24-hour breakdown service from a roadside phone. The 24-hour number to call for AA is ☎ **0800/887766;** for RAC it is ☎ **0800/828282.** All motorways are provided with special emergency phones that are connected to police traffic units, and the police can contact either of the auto clubs on your behalf.

**GASOLINE**    Called "petrol," gasoline is sold by the liter, with 4.2 liters to a gallon. Prices are much higher than Stateside, and you'll probably have to serve yourself. In some remote areas, stations are few and far between, and many are closed on Sunday.

## BY PLANE

**British Airways** (☎ 800/AIRWAYS) flies to more than 20 cities outside London, including Manchester, Glasgow, and Edinburgh. British Airways telephone representatives in North America can give price and schedule information and make reservations for flights within the U.K.

Ask about the British Airways Super Shuttle Saver fares, which can save you up to 50% on travel to certain key British cities. If seats are available on the flight of your choice, no advance reservations are necessary, although to benefit from the lowest prices, passengers must spend a Saturday night away from their point of origin and fly during defined off-peak times. Flights are usually restricted to weekdays between 10am and 3:30pm, whereas most night flights are after 7pm and, in certain cases, on weekends.

For passengers planning on visiting widely scattered destinations within the U.K., perhaps with a side trip to a city on Europe's mainland, British Airways' **Europe Airpass** allows discounted travel in a continuous loop to between 3 and 12 cities anywhere on BA's European and domestic air routes. Passengers must end their journey at the same point they begin it and fly exclusively on BA flights. Such a ticket (for instance, from London to Paris, then to Manchester, and finally to London again) will cut the cost of each segment of the itinerary by about 40% to 50% over individually booked tickets. The pass is available for travel to about a dozen of the most-visited cities and regions of Britain, with discounted add-ons available to most of BA's destinations in Europe as well. (This Airpass is a good bargain for round-trip travel between London and Rome, but not very practical for air travel from, say, Rome to Madrid. You'd be better off traveling between points on the continent by full-fare airline ticket, or by train, bus, or car.)

BA's Europe Airpass must be booked and paid for at least 7 days before your departure from North America. All sectors of the itinerary, including transatlantic passage from North America, must be booked simultaneously. Some changes are permitted in flight dates (but not in destinations) after the ticket is issued. Check with BA for full details and restrictions.

## 8 What You Need to Know About Accommodations Before You Go

**CLASSIFICATIONS**   Unlike some countries, England doesn't have a rigid hotel-classification system.

The local tourist board grades hotels by crowns instead of stars. When you pick up local tourist information, you'll see these rating systems in action. Hotels are judged by their standards for quality and hospitality; budget accommodations are rated "approved" or "commended." There is also a classification of "listed," with no crowns, and these rooms are for the most part very modest.

In a one-crown hotel, buildings are required to have hot and cold running water in all the rooms, but in "listed" hotels, hot and cold running water in the rooms is not mandatory. Crown ratings are posted outside some buildings. However, the system is voluntary, and many hotels do not participate.

Many hotels—especially older ones—still lack private baths for all rooms. However, most have hot and cold running water, and many have modern wings with all the amenities (as well as older sections that are less up-to-date). When making reservations, always ask what section of the hotel you'll be staying in if it has extensions.

All hotels used to include a full English breakfast of bacon and eggs in the room price, but today that is true for only some establishments. A continental breakfast is commonly included, but that usually means just tea or coffee and toast.

**RESERVATIONS**   We recommend making reservations in advance, even in the so-called slow months, from November to April. Tourist travel to London peaks from May to October, when moderate and budget hotels are full.

A hotel or B&B may ask you to send one night's deposit when you reserve. Be forewarned, however, that many readers have reported great difficulty, or even failure, in getting their deposit returned when they were forced to cancel their reservations.

**BED & BREAKFASTS**   Throughout England, you can find the best bargains wherever homeowners take in paying guests. Watch for the familiar bed-and-breakfast (B&B) signs. Generally, these are modest family homes, but sometimes they are like small hotels, with as many as 15 rooms. (If they're that big, they are more properly classified as guest houses.) B&Bs are the cheapest places you can stay in England and still be comfortable.

If you do not have reservations when you arrive in a town or city, go to the local tourist bureau, which can be an invaluable source of information. These offices usually have a free or inexpensive list of vacancies, which is often posted outside their door after business hours. For a fee of about £2 ($3.20), many will help you find a local vacancy and book a room; for an additional £2.50 ($4), you can often "book-a-bed-ahead" by having the office call in reservations to the next town you plan to visit.

**Hometours International,** P.O. Box 11053, Knoxville, TN 37939 (☎ **800/367-4668** or 423/690-8484), will make bed-and-breakfast reservations in England, Scotland, and Wales. This is the only company to guarantee reservations for more than 400 locations in Britain. Accommodations are paid for in the United States in dollars, and prices start as low as $45 per person per night—though they can go as high as $100 per person in London. The company can also arrange for apartments in London or cottages in Great Britain that begin at $550 per week. In addition, it offers walking tours of Great Britain, with prices starting at $560 for 7 days, including meals.

Reservations for bed-and-breakfast accommodations in London can also be made by writing (not calling) the **British Travel Centre,** Rex House, 4–12 Lower Regent St., London SW1 4PQ. Once in London, you can also visit their office (tube: Piccadilly Circus).

In addition, Susan Opperman and Rosemary Lumb run **Bed and Breakfast Nationwide,** P.O. Box 2100, Clacton-on-Sea, Essex CO16 9BW, an agency specializing in B&B accommodations in private homes all over Great Britain. Host homes range from small cottages to large manor houses, as well as working farms, and the prices vary accordingly. One thing you can be sure of is that owners have been specially selected for their wish to entertain visitors from overseas. Remember that these are private homes, so hotel-type services are not available. You will, however, be assured of a warm welcome, a comfortable bed, a hearty breakfast, and a glimpse of British life. Write for a free brochure. For bookings in accommodations outside London, call ☎ **01255/831235** or fax 01255/831437 7 days a week from 9am to 6pm.

**Bed and Breakfast (GB)** covers accommodations in London, England, Scotland, Wales, and Ireland for £15 ($24) a night and up. Contact Bed and Breakfast (GB), Box 66, 94 Bell St., Henley-on-Thames, Oxon, England RG9 1XS (☎ **01491/578803;** fax 01491/410806).

**FARMHOUSES**   In many parts of the country, farmhouses have one, two, even four rooms set aside for paying guests, who usually arrive in the summer months. Farmhouses don't have the facilities of most guest houses, but they have a rustic appeal and charm. This is an option to consider especially if you're driving, as they tend to lie off the beaten path.

Prices are generally lower than bed-and-breakfasts or guest houses, and sometimes you're offered some good country home cooking (at an extra charge) if you make arrangements in advance.

The British Tourist Authority will provide a booklet, *Stay on a Farm,* or you can ask at local tourist offices.

The **Farm Holiday Bureau** (☎ **01203/696909**) publishes an annual directory in early December that includes 1,000 farms and bed-and-breakfasts throughout the United Kingdom. The listings include quality ratings, the number of bedrooms, nearby attractions and activities, and prices as well as line drawings of each property. Also listed are any special details, such as rooms with four-poster beds or activities on the grounds (fishing, for example). Many farms are geared toward children, who can participate in light chores—gathering eggs or just tagging along—for an authentic farm experience. Prices range from £13 to £35 ($20.80 to $56) a night and include an English breakfast and usually private facilities. (The higher prices are for stays at mansions and manor houses.)

Another option is the self-catering accommodations, which are usually cottages or converted barns that cost from £150 to £600 ($240 to $960) per week, including "luxury" items like dishwashers and central heating. Each property is inspected every year not only by the Farm Holiday Bureau, but also by the English Tourist Board. Most properties, except those located in the mountains, are open year-round.

For the directory, contact the **Farm Holiday Bureau,** National Agricultural Centre, Stoneleigh Park, Warwickshire CV8 2LZ (☎ **01203/696909**). It costs £8.50 ($13.60) and may be purchased by credit card.

**RENTING AN APARTMENT OR A HOLIDAY COTTAGE**   Throughout England, there are fully furnished studios, houses, cottages, "flats" (apartments), even trailers suitable for families or groups that can be rented by the month. From October to March, rents are sometimes reduced by 50%.

The British Tourist Authority (see "Visitor Information," above) and most tourist offices have lists available. The BTA's free "Apartments in London and Holiday Homes," lists rental agencies such as **At Home Abroad,** 405 E. 56th St., Apt. 6H, New York, NY 10022 (☎ **212/421-9165;** fax 212/752-1591). Interested parties should write or fax a description of their needs, and At Home Abroad will send listings at no charge.

**British Travel International,** P.O. Box 299, Elkton, VA 22827 (☎ **800/ 327-6097** or 540/298-2232; fax 540/298-2347), represents between 8,000 and 10,000 rental properties in the U.K.—each rented by the week (Saturday to Saturday) and requires a 50% payment at the time of booking. A catalog with pictures of their offerings is available for a $5 fee that is counted toward a deposit. They have everything from honey-colored, thatch-roofed cottages in the Cotswolds to apartments in a British university city. The company represents about 100 hotels in London whose rates are discounted by 5% to 50%, depending on the season and market conditions, and they have listings of some 4,000 B&Bs. They are also the North American representative of the U.K.'s largest bus company, National Express.

The **Barclay International Group (BIG)**, 150 E. 52nd St., New York, NY 10022 (☎ **800/845-6636** or 212/832-3777), specializes in short-term apartment ("flat") rentals in London and cottages in the English countryside. These rentals can be appropriated for families, groups of friends, or businesspeople traveling together, and are sometimes less expensive than equivalent stays in hotels. Apartments, available for stays as short as one night (although the company prefers that guests stay a minimum of three nights and charges a premium if your stay is shorter), are usually more luxurious than you imagine. Furnished with kitchens, they offer a low-cost alternative to restaurant meals. Apartments suitable for one or two occupants begin in winter at around $700 a week (including tax). For extended stays in the English countryside, BIG has country cottages in such areas as the Cotswolds, the Lake District, and Oxford, as well as farther afield in Scotland and Wales. The company can also arrange for tickets for sightseeing attractions, BritRail Passes, and various other "extras." They have recently established an office in England at 6 Hertford St., London W1X 7TB (☎ **0171/495-2986;** fax 0171/499-2312).

**YOUTH HOSTELS**   The **Youth Hostels Association (YHA)** for England and Wales operates a network of 240 youth hostels in major cities, in the countryside, and along the coast. All offer the YHA's Book-a-Bed-Ahead plan, where each hostel will fax ahead, to ensure accommodations are reserved for you when you reach your next stop. Most hostels offer dorm-style living, with large rooms full of bunkbeds, but some have private rooms for couples and families. Many have kitchens, laundry facilities, storage areas, and bike rentals. But check to see if there are restrictions that don't appeal to you, since some hostels feature curfews, daytime "lock-out," a maximum stay period, or chore requirements.

The YHA can be contacted at Customer Services Department, YHA, Travelyan House, 8 St. Stephen's Hill, St. Albans, Hertfordshire, AL1 2DY (☎ **01727/ 855215**). They'll provide a free map showing the locations of each youth hostel and full details, including prices.

For a comprehensive hostel guide to the United Kingdom, check out *Frommer's Complete Hostel Vacation Guide to England, Wales & Scotland*, and the "Internet Guide to Hostelling" (http://www.hostels.com).

**DORMITORIES**   Many colleges and universities will rent tourists rooms in residential halls when schools are not in session—some will even rent unoccupied rooms when the session is in. These facilities are popular with many travelers because they are inexpensive and often offer long-term rentals, so make reservations in advance.

For information, contact the **British Universities Accommodation Consortium,** Box 1432, University Park, Nottingham, England NG7 2RD (☎ **0115/950-4571;** fax 0115/942-2505).

**YWCA & YMCA**   These organizations often offer lodging that is less than a hotel but more than a hostel. Some Young Men's Christian Association locations even accept women, couples, or families. For information and reservations, contact Y's Way International, 224 E. 47th St., New York, NY 10017 (☎ 212/308-2899; fax 212/ 308-3161; Internet: http://www.ymca.org/).

Most **Young Women's Christian Associations** offer accommodations for women, and some even allow couples. Contact **YWCA-USA,** 726 Broadway, New York, NY 10003 (☎ **212/614-2700**).

**CAMPING**   Yes, it may seem strange, but even London has camping options for the budget backpacker. These sites offer the cheapest sleeping accommodations, with many averaging about £5.50 ($8.80) a night per person. However, sooner or later rain will be a factor when camping.

The country has more than 2,500 campsites, and information about the various sites, their accommodations, and prices are available by contacting the **British Tourist Authority** (see "Visitor Information," above) for their free pamphlet, *"Caravan and Camping Parks,"* or the **Automobile Association,** Norfolk House, Basingstoke, Hampshire RG24 9NY (☎ **01256/20123**) for their *Camping and Caravanning,* available for £7.99 ($12.80).

Additional information about camping in England is available from the **Wilderness Press,** 2440 Bancroft Way, Berkeley, CA 94704-1676 (☎ **800/443-7227** or 510/843-8080; fax 510/548-1355), which publishes numerous resources, including *Backpacking Basics* ($11, including postage); and **REI,** P.O. Box 1700, Sumner, WA 98352-0001 (☎ **800/426-4840**), which publishes *Europa Camping and Caravanning* ($20).

**HOME EXCHANGES**   One of the most exciting ways to travel to England is to exchange your home with another family from England. Obviously this is not for everyone, and there are pitfalls. For example, in return for your "mansion" you might inadvertently end up in some hovel in England. But if you're willing to take a chance on swapping your house or apartment for a cottage or flat in England, contact one of the following organizations.

Who knows? With what's going on in the House of Windsor these days, you might end up trading your digs for Buckingham Palace.

**Intervac U.S.,** P.O. Box 590504, San Francisco, CA 94159 (☎ **800/756-HOME** or 415/435-3497), publishes four catalogs a year, listing some 10,000 homes in 36 countries. Members contact each other directly once the details of their homes are published. The cost is $65 plus postage, which includes three company catalogs that will be mailed to you and listing your home in whichever catalog you select. A fourth catalog costs an extra $25.

**The Invented City,** 41 Sutter St., Suite 1090, San Francisco, CA 94104 (☎ **800/ 788-CITY** or 415/252-1141), publishes international home-exchange listings in February, May, and November. A $50 membership fee allows you to list your home and indicate your occupation, hobbies, and when you want to travel.

## 9  Discount Passes to Cut Your Sightseeing Costs

There are several passes available that cut down considerably on entrance costs to the country's stately homes and gardens. If you plan to do extensive touring you'll save a lot of pounds by using one of these passes instead of paying the relatively steep entrance fees on an attraction-by-attraction basis.

Listed below are three organizations that offer passes waiving admission charges to hundreds of historical properties located throughout the U.K. Each is a good deal—the money you'll save visiting just a few of the available sites will pay for the price of the pass.

**The British National Trust** offers members free entry to some 240 National Trust sites in Britain, and more than 100 properties in Scotland. Focusing on gardens, castles, historic parks, abbeys, and ruins, sites include Chartwell, St. Michael's Mount, and Beatrix Potter's House. The membership fee includes a listing of all properties, maps, and essential information for independent tours, and listings and reservations for holiday cottages located on the protected properties.

The Trust's U.S. affiliate, **The Royal Oak Foundation,** offers one or more annual tours, flying from New York and exploring a specific region of Great Britain through a series of day trips.

Both the British and U.S. offices sponsor a series of lectures annually, with 12 to 15 being offered in London, and approximately 30 presented nationwide throughout the U.S.

Individual memberships cost $45 annually, and family memberships, including up to seven people, run $70, so savings on the admission charges, combined with discounts on holiday cottage reservations and British Air or BritRail travel, make this especially appealing. Visa and MasterCard are accepted. Contact The British National Trust, 36 Queen Anne's Gate, London SW1H 9AS (☎ **0171/222-9251**), or The Royal Oak Foundation, 285 W. Broadway #400, New York, NY 10013-2299 (☎ **800/913-6565** or 212/966-6565).

The **English Heritage** sells 14-day passes, 21-day passes, and annual memberships, offering free admission to more than 300 historical sites in England, and half-price admission to more than 100 additional sites in Scotland, Wales, and the Isle of Man. (Admission to these additional sites is free for anyone who renews his or her annual membership after the first year.) Sites include Hadrian's Wall, Stonehenge, and Kenilworth Castle. Also included is free or reduced admission to 450 historic reenactments and open-air summer concerts, a handbook detailing all properties, a map, and, with purchase of an annual membership, events and concerts diaries, and *Heritage Today,* a quarterly magazine.

# How to Get Your VAT Refund

To receive back a portion of the tax paid on purchases made in Britain, first ask the store if they do VAT refunds and what their minimum purchase is. Once you have achieved this minimum, the paperwork must be completed. Fill out the form and present it—along with the goods—at the Customs office in the airport. Allow a half-hour to stand in line. You're required to show the goods at the time of departure, so don't pack them in your luggage and check it!

Once you have the paperwork stamped by the officials, you have two choices: You can mail the papers before you leave and receive your refund in either a British check (no!) or a credit card refund (yes!), or you can go directly to the Cash VAT Refund desk at the airport and get your refund in your hand, in cash. The bad news: If you accept cash other than sterling, you will lose money on the conversion rate.

Also, be advised that many stores charge a flat fee for processing your refund, so that £3 to £5 may be automatically deducted from the total refund you receive. But since the VAT in Britain is 17.5%, you'll still come out way ahead even if you get back 15%.

*Note:* If you're traveling to other countries within the European Union, you don't go through any of this in Britain. At your final destination, prior to departure from the EU, file for all your VAT refunds at one time.

Several readers have reported a scam regarding VAT refunds. The refund forms *must* be obtained from the retailer on the spot (don't leave the store without one). Some merchants allegedly tell customers they can get a refund form at the airport on their way out of the country. *This is not true.* The form must be completed by the retailer on the spot, or there will be no refund later.

A 14-day **Overseas Visitor Pass** runs £12 ($19.20) for an adult, £6 ($9.60) for a child, and £25 ($40) for a family of six or less; and a 21-day pass is £16 ($25.60) for an adult, £8 ($12.80) for a child, and £35 ($56) for a family. Annual memberships are also available with rates of £20 ($32) for an adult, £13.50 ($21.60) for ages 16 to 21, £9.50 ($15.20) for children under 16, and £38.50 ($61.60) for a family. MasterCard and Visa are accepted. For visitor passes, contact Customer Services, English Heritage, 429 Oxford St., London W1R 2HD (☎ **0171/973-3434**), and for membership information, apply to English Heritage Membership Dept., Box 1BB, London W1A 1BB (☎ **0171/973-3403**).

**The Great British Heritage Pass,** available through **BritRail,** allows entry to more than 500 public and privately owned historic properties, including Shakespeare's Birthplace, Stonehenge, Windsor Castle, and Edinburgh Castle. Included in the price of the pass is the *Great British Heritage Gazetteer,* a brochure that lists the properties with maps and essential information. A pass also gains you entrance into private properties not otherwise approachable.

A 7-day pass costs £26.25 ($42), a 15-day pass is available for £40 ($64), and a one-month pass is £56.25 ($90). Passes are nonrefundable and there is no discounted children's rate. A $2 handling fee is charged additionally for each ticket issued. To order passes, contact BritRail Travel International, Inc., 1500 Broadway, New York, NY 10036; visit BritRail's British Travel Shop at 551 Fifth Ave. (at 45th Street), New York, NY 10176; or call ☎ **888/BRITRAIL** or 212/575-2667. Internet access is available at: http://www.britrail.com/us/ushome.htm.

## FAST FACTS: England

For information on London, refer to "Fast Facts: London," in chapter 4.

**Drugstores**   In Britain they're called "chemists." Every police station in the country has a list of emergency chemists. Dial ☎ "0" (zero) and ask the operator for the local police, who will give you the name of the one nearest you.

**Electricity**   British electricity is 240 volts AC, 50 cycles, roughly twice the voltage in North America, which is 115 to 120 volts AC, 60 cycles. American plugs don't fit British wall outlets. Always bring suitable transformers and/or adapters—if you plug an American appliance directly into a European electrical outlet without a transformer, you'll destroy your appliance and possibly start a fire. Tape recorders, VCRs, and other devices with motors intended to revolve at a fixed number of r.p.m. probably won't work properly even with transformers.

**Emergencies**   Dial ☎ **999** for police, fire, or ambulance. Give your name, address, and telephone number and state the nature of the emergency.

**Legal Aid**   The American Services section of "U.S. Embassies & Consulates" (see "Fast Facts: London," in chapter 4) will give advice if you run into trouble abroad. They can advise you of your rights and even provide a list of attorneys (for which you'll have to pay if services are used). But they cannot interfere on your behalf in the legal processes of Great Britain. For questions about American citizens who are arrested abroad, including ways of getting money to them, telephone the Citizens Emergency Center of the Office of Special Consulate Services in Washington, D.C. (☎ **202/647-5225**).

**Liquor Laws**   The legal drinking age is 18. Children under 16 aren't allowed in pubs, except in certain rooms, and then only when accompanied by a parent or guardian. Don't drink and drive. Penalties are stiff.

   In England, pubs can legally be open Monday through Saturday from 11am to 11pm and on Sunday from noon to 10:30pm.

   Restaurants are also allowed to serve liquor during these hours, but only to people who are dining on the premises. The law allows 30 minutes for "drinking-up time." A meal, incidentally, is defined as "substantial refreshment." And you have to eat and drink sitting down.

   In hotels, liquor may be served from 11am to 11pm to both residents and non-residents; after 11pm, only residents, according to the law, may be served.

**Pets**   It is illegal to bring pets to Great Britain—except with veterinary documents, and then most animals are subject to an incredible 6-month quarantine.

**Police**   Dial ☎ **999** if the matter is serious. Losses, thefts, and other criminal matters should be reported to the police immediately.

**Taxes**   To encourage energy conservation, the British government levies a 25% tax on gasoline ("petrol"). There is also a 17.5% national Value-Added Tax (VAT) that is added to all hotel and restaurant bills, and will be included in the price of many items you purchase. This can be refunded if you shop at stores that participate in the Retail Export Scheme (signs are posted in the window). See the "How to Get Your VAT Refund" box earlier in this chapter.

   In October 1994, Britain imposed a departure tax: either £5 ($8) for flights within Britain and the European Union or £10 ($16) for passengers flying elsewhere, including to the United States.

**Telephone**   To call London from home, dial the international code, 44 (Britain's country code), either 0171 or 0181 (London's area codes), and then the seven-digit local telephone number. To call a location outside London, dial the international code, 44, and then the exchange code and the local telephone number.

Once you've arrived, note that British TeleCom is carrying out a massive improvement of its public-phone service.

There are three types of public pay phones: those taking only coins, those accepting only phone cards (called Cardphones), and those taking both phone cards and credit cards. At coin-operated phones, insert your coins before dialing. The minimum charge is 10p (15¢).

Phone cards can be purchased in four denominations—£2 ($3.20), £4 ($6.40), £10 ($16), and £20 ($32)—and are reusable until the total value has expired. You can buy phone cards at newsstands and post offices. Credit-call pay phones operate on credit cards—Access (MasterCard), Visa, American Express, and Diners Club—and are most common at airports and large railway stations.

Outside of major cities, phone numbers consist of an exchange code (like an area code) plus a local telephone number. To reach the number, you will need to dial both the exchange code and the number. The exchange codes are usually posted in the call box. If your code is not there, call the operator by dialing ☎ 100.

In major cities, phone numbers consist of the exchange code and the local number (seven digits or more). These local digits are all you need to dial if you are calling within the same city. If you're calling elsewhere, you'll also need to dial the exchange code for the city you're calling. Again, you can find these codes on the call box information sheets or by dialing the operator (100).

If you need directory assistance or "information," dial ☎ **142** for a number in London. For a number elsewhere in the country, dial 192 and then give the operator the name of the town and then the person's name and address.

To make international calls from England, it's less expensive to dial them yourself from a post office or phone booth than from your hotel room. After you have inserted the coins, dial the international code, then the country code (for the U.S. the code is 1), which is followed by the area code and the local number. If you're calling collect or need the assistance of an international operator, dial 155.

*Caller beware:* Some hotels routinely add surcharges of anywhere from 40% to 300% to local, national, and international phone calls made from your hotel room.

**Time**    England follows Greenwich mean time (5 hours ahead of Eastern Standard Time), with British summer time lasting (roughly) from the end of March to the end of October. Throughout most of the year, including during the summer, Britain is 5 hours ahead of the time observed on the East Coast of the United States. Because of a lead and lag factor associated with the imposition of daylight savings time within the two nations, there's a brief period (about a week) in autumn when Britain is only 4 hours ahead of New York, and a brief period in spring when it's 6 hours ahead of New York.

**Tipping**    For cab drivers, add about 10% to 15% to the fare shown on the meter. However, if the driver personally loads or unloads your luggage, add something extra.

In hotels, porters receive 75p ($1.20) per bag, even if you have only one small suitcase. Hall porters are tipped only for special services. Maids receive £1 ($1.60) per day. In top-ranking hotels the concierge will often submit a separate bill showing charges for newspapers and other items; if he or she has been particularly helpful, tip extra.

Hotels often add a service charge of 10% to 15% to most bills. In smaller bed-and-breakfasts, the tip is not likely to be included. Therefore, tip for special services, such as the waiter who serves you breakfast. If several people have served you in a bed-and-breakfast, you may ask that 10% to 15% be added to the bill and divided among the staff.

In both restaurants and nightclubs, a 15% service charge is added to the bill, which is distributed among all the help. To that, add another 3% to 5%, depending on the service. Tipping in pubs isn't common, but in cocktail bars, the server usually gets about 75p ($1.20) per round of drinks.

Barbers and hairdressers expect 10% to 15%. Tour guides expect £2 ($3.20), although it's not mandatory. Gas station attendants are rarely tipped and theater ushers don't expect tips.

# Settling Into London  4

Europe's largest city is like a great wheel, with Piccadilly Circus at the hub and dozens of communities branching out from it. Since London is such a conglomeration of neighborhoods and districts—each having its own life, hotels, restaurants, and pubs—first-time visitors may be a bit overwhelmed until they get the hang of the city. You'll probably spend most of your time in the West End, where many attractions are located, except for the historic part of London known as "The City," which includes the Tower of London. This chapter will help you get your bearings.

## 1 Essentials

### ARRIVING
### BY PLANE

London is served by four airports. The one you'll arrive at will depend on the airline you're flying and your point of departure.

**HEATHROW AIRPORT** Heathrow, west of London, in Hounslow (☎ **0181/759-4321**), is divided into four terminals. Terminal 4 handles long-haul and transatlantic operations of British Airways. Most transatlantic flights of U.S. airlines arrive at Terminal 3. Terminals 1 and 2 receive the intra-European flights of several European airlines.

**Getting to Central London** The London subway, called the Underground or "tube," connects from Heathrow Central to the center of London; the trip takes 50 minutes and costs £3.80 ($6.10). Airbuses will also take you to central London in about an hour; they cost £6 ($9.60) for adults and £4 ($6.40) for children. For more information about train or bus connections, call ☎ **0171/222-1234.** A taxi will cost no less than £25 to £30 ($40 to $48).

**GATWICK** This smaller and more remote airport (☎ **01293/535353** for flight information) lies 25 miles south of London, in West Sussex. Charter flights as well as many scheduled flights arrive here.

**Getting to Central London** Trains leave for London every 15 minutes during the day and every hour at night; they cost £9 ($14.40) for adults and half price for children ages 5 to 15 (under 5 free). There is also an express Flightline bus (no. 777) from Gatwick to Victoria Station that departs every half hour from

# London at a Glance

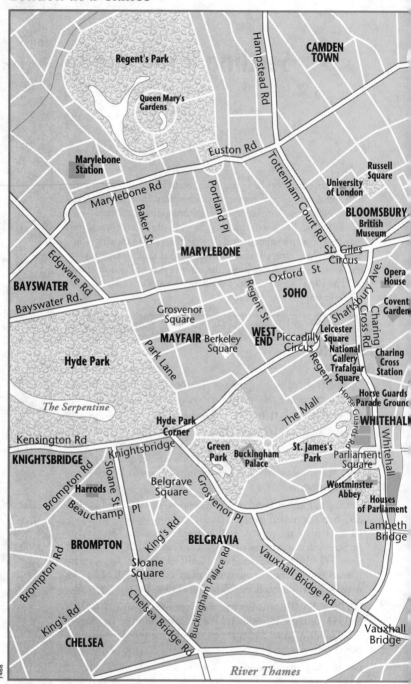

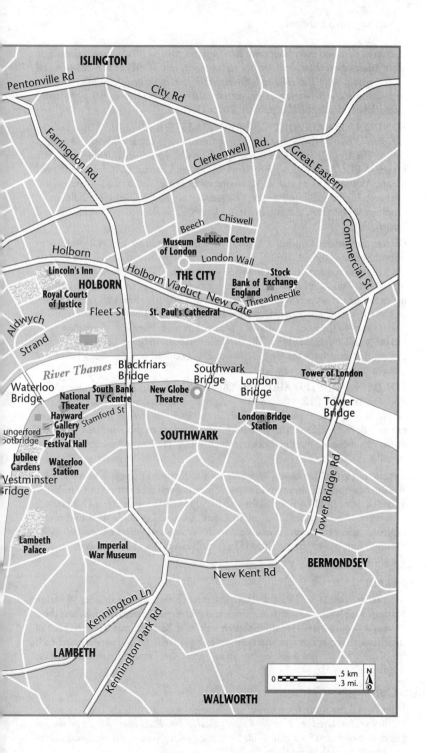

ISLINGTON

Pentonville Rd

City Rd

Farringdon Rd.

Clerkenwell Rd.

Great Eastern

Commercial St

Beech

Chiswell

Museum of London

Barbican Centre

London Wall

Holborn

THE CITY

Lincoln's Inn

HOLBORN

Holborn Viaduct

New Gate

Bank of England

Stock Exchange

Threadneedle

Royal Courts of Justice

Fleet St

St. Paul's Cathedral

Aldwych

Strand

River Thames

Blackfriars Bridge

Southwark Bridge

London Bridge

Tower of London

Waterloo Bridge

National Theater

South Bank TV Centre

New Globe Theatre

Tower Bridge

Hayward Gallery

Stamford St

London Bridge Station

ungerford ootbridge

Royal Festival Hall

SOUTHWARK

Jubilee Gardens

Waterloo Station

Westminster ridge

Tower Bridge Rd

Lambeth Palace

Imperial War Museum

BERMONDSEY

New Kent Rd

Kennington Ln

Kennington Park Rd

LAMBETH

0        .5 km
         .3 mi.

N

WALWORTH

6:30am to 8pm and every hour from 8 to 11pm; it costs £7.50 ($12) per person. For more information about train or bus connections, call ☎ **0171/222-1234.** A taxi usually costs £50 to £60 ($80 to $96); however, you must be careful to negotiate a fare with the driver before you get into the cab—the meter does not apply since Gatwick lies outside the Metropolitan Police District.

**LONDON CITY AIRPORT** (☎ **0171/474-5555;** fax 0171/511-1040) Located just 3 miles East of the bustling business community of Canary Wharf and 6 miles East of The City, London City Airport has a total of 13 airlines (Air Engiadina, Air France, Air Jet, Air UK, Augsburg Airways, CityJet, Crossair, Denimair, Lufthansa, Malmö Aviation, Sabena and VLM) serving 18 European destinations—Amsterdam, Antwerp, Augsburg, Berne, Brussels, Cologne/Bonn, Dublin, Düsseldorf, Edinburgh, Eindhoven, Frankfurt, Geneva, Lugano, Malmö, Paris, Rotterdam, Stockholm, and Zurich.

**Getting to Central London**   A blue-and-white bus charges £3 ($4.80) each way from the airport to the Liverpool Street Station, where you can connect with rail or Underground transportation to almost any destination. The bus runs every 20 minutes Monday through Friday, and every 30 minutes Saturday and Sunday during the hours the airport is open (approximately 7am to 8:30pm). There's also a shuttle bus to Canary Wharf, where trains from the Dockland Line Railway make frequent 10-minute runs to the heart of London's financial district, The City. Here, passengers can catch an Underground from the Bank tube stop. In addition, London Transport bus no. 473 goes from the City Airport to East London, where you can board any Underground at the Plaistow tube stop.

**LONDON STANSTED AIRPORT**   About 50 miles northeast of London's West End, Stansted (☎ **01279/680-500**)—originally conceived as a U.S. airbase during World War II—was expanded massively in the 1980s. It receives most flights from the European continent, although during the lifetime of this edition, the airport expects an increased number of charter flights from the North American mainland as well.

**Getting to Central London**   Your best bet is the Stansted Express, a train that takes you directly from the airport to Liverpool Street rail and tube station in 45 minutes. Tickets cost £11 ($17.60) for adults and £7.90 ($12.65) for children. Daily service runs every 30 minutes from 5:30am to 11pm. A taxi to London's West End is very expensive and takes about 75 minutes; the driver will charge you around £60 ($96) for up to four passengers, and £90 ($144) for between 5 and 6 passengers. Stick to the Express.

## BY TRAIN

Most trains originating in Paris and traveling through the Chunnel arrive at **Waterloo Station.** Visitors from Amsterdam arrive at the **Liverpool Street Station,** and those journeying south by rail from Edinburgh pull in at **King's Cross Station.** Each of these stations is connected to London's vast bus and Underground network, and each has phones, restaurants, pubs, luggage-storage areas, and London Regional Transport Information Centres.

## BY CAR

If you're taking a car ferry across the channel, you can quickly connect with a motorway into London. *First (and most valuable) tip: Remember to drive on the left!* London is encircled by a ring road. Determine which part of the city you wish to enter and follow the signs there.

Once you're in London, we don't recommend driving. Parking is not only scarce, it is expensive. Before you arrive in London, call your hotel and ask advice on where to park your car.

## VISITOR INFORMATION

**The British Travel Centre,** Rex House, 4–12 Lower Regent St., London SW1 4PQ (tube: Piccadilly Circus), caters to walk-in visitors who wait in line for information on all parts of Britain. (Telephone information has been suspended.) On the premises are a British Rail ticket office, a travel agency, a theater-ticket agency, a hotel-booking service, a bookshop, and a souvenir shop. Open Monday through Friday from 9am to 6:30pm, Saturday and Sunday from 10am to 4pm, with extended hours on Saturday from June through September.

Equally useful is the London Tourist Board's **Tourist Information Centre,** forecourt of Victoria Station, SW1 (tube: Victoria). The center deals with accommodations in all size and price categories. It also arranges for travel, tour-ticket sales, and theater reservations; it has a shop that sells books and souvenirs. Open from Easter to October, daily from 8am to 7pm; November to Easter, Monday to Saturday from 8am to 6pm, Sunday from 9am to 4pm.

The tourist board also maintains offices at Heathrow Airport's terminals 1, 2, and 4, Underground Concourse; and at the Liverpool Street Railway Station.

The tourist board has a 24-hour recorded information service, **Visitorcall** (☎ **01839/123456**), which, for fees of 39p or 49p (60¢ or 80¢) per minute, will play a recorded message about current tourist attractions (updated daily). The 39p rate is in effect Monday through Friday from 6pm to 8am and Saturday and Sunday all day; at other times the charge is 49p.

## CITY LAYOUT
### AN OVERVIEW

Although **central London** doesn't have formal geographic boundaries, most Londoners would probably accept the Underground's Circle Line as a fair delimitation. The city center is customarily divided into two areas, **The City** and the **West End.**

The City is where London began; it's the original 1 square mile the Romans called Londinium—and which still exists as a self-governing entity. Rich in historical, architectural, and social interest, The City is today one of the world's great financial centers.

The West End, on the other hand, has no precise borders, but is divided by its main thoroughfares into clearly defined neighborhoods—Mayfair, Soho, Kensington, etc. By merely crossing the street, you can leave behind a neighborhood of very distinct character and enter another that seems to be part of an entirely different world. Most Londoners regard the West End—by virtue of its shops, restaurants, and theaters—as the real city center.

The City and the West End are surrounded by **inner London** (which includes the **East End**) and then by the sprawling hinterland of **outer London.** You'll find the greatest number of hotels in the west, in inner districts such as **Kensington, Chelsea,** and **Victoria,** and in the West End. Even though The City is bejeweled with historic sights, it empties out in the evenings and on weekends.

In much the way that The City is a buffer to the east, so is the river to the south. The Barbican Centre in The City and the South Bank Arts Centre across the river were both conscious attempts to extend the geographical spread of central London's nocturnal life, but central London really fades in The City and only half-heartedly crosses the Thames. Still, the new urban development of Docklands and some up-and-coming residential neighborhoods are infusing energy into the area south of the Thames.

## ORIENTING YOURSELF

Fortunately, the sprawling vastness of Greater London is unlikely to intimidate the traveler, who spends most of his or her time in the pocket north of the River Thames that might be called "Tourist Territory."

Our London begins at **Chelsea,** on the north bank of the river, and stretches for roughly 5 miles north to **Hampstead.** Its western boundary runs through **Kensington,** whereas the eastern boundary lies 5 miles away, at Tower Bridge. Inside this 5-by-5-mile square, you'll find all the major hotels and restaurants and nearly all the sights of interest.

The logical (although not geographical) center of this area is **Trafalgar Square,** which we'll take as our orientation point. Facing the steps of the imposing **National Gallery,** you're looking northwest toward the direction of **Piccadilly Circus**—the real core of tourist London—and the maze of streets that make up **Soho.** Farther north runs **Oxford Street,** and still farther northwest lie **Regent's Park** and the zoo.

At your back—that is, south—runs **Whitehall,** which houses or skirts nearly every British government building, including the prime minister's official residence at **10 Downing Street.** In the same direction, a bit farther south, stand the **Houses of Parliament and Westminster Abbey.**

Flowing southwest from Trafalgar Square is the table-smooth **Mall,** flanked by parks and mansions and leading to **Buckingham Palace.** Farther along in the same direction lie **Belgravia** and **Knightsbridge,** the city's plushest residential areas, and south of them lies chic **Chelsea,** plus the shopping street **King's Road.**

Due west stretches the excellent and pricey shopping area bordered by **Regent Street** and **Piccadilly Street** (as distinct from Piccadilly Circus). Farther west lie the elegant shops and even more elegant homes of **Mayfair.** Then comes **Park Lane.** On the other side of Park Lane is **Hyde Park,** the biggest park in London and one of the largest in the world.

Storied **Charing Cross Road** runs north from Trafalgar Square, past **Leicester Square,** and intersects with **Shaftesbury Avenue.** This is London's theater district. A bit farther along, Charing Cross Road turns into a book browser's paradise, lined with booksellers. At last it funnels into **St. Giles Circus,** where you enter **Bloomsbury,** site of the **University of London,** the **British Museum,** and erstwhile stamping ground of the famed "Bloomsbury group."

Northeast of your position lies **Covent Garden,** today a major shopping, restaurant, and cafe district.

If you follow **The Strand** eastward from Trafalgar Square, you'll come to **Fleet Street. Temple Bar** stands where The Strand becomes Fleet Street; only here do you enter the actual City of London, or The City. Its focal point is the Bank of England on **Threadneedle Street,** with **the Stock Exchange** next door and **the Royal Exchange** across the street. In the midst of all this rises **St. Paul's Cathedral.** At the far eastern fringe of The City looms the **Tower of London.**

## FINDING YOUR WAY AROUND

It's not always easy to locate an address, as London's streets—both their naming and house numbering—follow no pattern whatsoever. London is checkered with innumerable squares, mews, closes, and terraces, which jut into or cross, overlap, or interrupt whatever street you're trying to follow. And house numbers run in odds and evens, clockwise and counterclockwise, when they exist at all. Many establishments do not use house numbers, though a building right next door is numbered.

You're going to get lost, so it's a good idea to buy a detailed street map with an index. The best ones are published by Falk, and they're available at most newsstands and nearly all bookstores. If you can't find one, go **to W. & G. Foyle, Ltd.,** 113–119 Charing Cross Rd., WC2 (☎ **0171/439-8501;** tube: Leicester [pronounced *lester*] Square). The other bible for navigating London's streets is the *A to Z London Guide,* available at newsstands and bookstores.

## LONDON'S NEIGHBORHOODS IN BRIEF

To locate these neighborhoods, see the map on page 60.

### The West End Neighborhoods

**Mayfair**   Bounded by Piccadilly, Hyde Park, Oxford Street, and Regent Street, Mayfair is London's most elegant and fashionable section. Luxury hotels sit side by side with Georgian town houses and swank shops. **Grosvenor Square** (pronounced *Grov*-nor) is nicknamed "Little America" because it is home to the American Embassy and a statue of Franklin D. Roosevelt. Berkeley Square (pronounced *Bark*-ley) is home to the English Speaking Union. One Mayfair curiosity is **Shepherd Market,** a tiny village of pubs, two-story inns, book and food stalls, and restaurants—all sandwiched between Mayfair's greatness.

**Marylebone**   Most first-time visitors head to Marylebone, to explore **Madame Tussaud's** waxworks or walk along **Baker Street** in the make-believe footsteps of Sherlock Holmes. The streets form a near-perfect grid, with the major ones running north-south from Regent's Park toward Oxford Street. Robert Adam laid out Portland Place, one of the most characteristic squares, from 1776 to 1780, and it was at **Cavendish Square** that Mrs. Horatio Nelson waited—often in vain—for the return of the admiral. Marylebone Lane and High Street still retain some of their former village atmosphere, but this is otherwise a now rather anonymous area. Dickens (who was a peripatetic sort) wrote nearly a dozen books when he resided here. At **Regent's Park,** you can visit Queen Mary's Gardens or, in summer, see Shakespeare performed in an open-air theater.

**St. James's**   This area, which begins at Piccadilly Circus and moves southwest, is often called "Royal London." It incorporates **Pall Mall, The Mall, St. James's Park, and Green Park.** Elizabeth II lives at its most fabled address, **Buckingham Palace.** You'll find the American Express office here, on Haymarket, as well as many leading department stores. In this bastion of aristocracy and royalty, a certain pomp still prevails—gentlemen still go to private clubs, where English tradition never dies.

**Piccadilly Circus & Leicester Square**   Piccadilly Circus is the very heart and soul of London, with its statue of Eros being London's gaudy "living room." The circus isn't New York's Times Square yet, but it has the requisite traffic, neon, and jostling crowds. The Piccadilly thoroughfare, the western road out of town, was named for the "piccadill," a ruffled collar created by a tailor in the 1600s. For a bit of grandeur, retreat to the **Burlington Arcade,** a Regency promenade of exclusive shops designed in 1819. Or make your way to **Fortnum and Mason,** 181 Piccadilly, the world's most luxurious grocery store, established in 1788.

Leicester Square is a center of theaters, restaurants, movie palaces, and nightlife. It's a bit tawdry now and not the chic address it was when William Hogarth or Joshua Reynolds lived here.

**Soho**   Every city has its seedier side, of course, but in few are the red lights woven into a texture of such richness and variety as in London's Soho. These densely packed streets in the heart of the West End are famous for their gloriously cosmopolitan mix of people and trades. A decade ago, Soho's decline was much touted when the thriving sex industry threatened to engulf it. But that destruction has now largely been halted: Respectable businesses have returned, and fashionable restaurants and shops prosper; it's also the heart of London's recently expanding cafe society. But Soho wouldn't be Soho without at least a scattering of sex shops and porno theaters.

Soho starts at Piccadilly Circus and spreads out; it's basically bordered by Regent Street, Oxford Street, Charing Cross Road, and the theaters of Shaftesbury Avenue. Carnaby Street, a block from Regent Street, was the center of the universe in the swinging 1960s, but today is just a schlocky sideshow. Across Shaftesbury Avenue, a busy street lined with theaters, is London's **Chinatown,** centered on Gerrard Street: small, authentic, and packed with excellent restaurants. But Soho's heart—full of marvelous French and Italian delicatessens, fine butchers, fish stores, and wine merchants—is farther north, on Brewer, Old Compton, and Berwick streets. Berwick is also a wonderful open-air fresh food market. To the north of Old Compton Street, Dean, Frith, and Greek streets have fine little restaurants, pubs, and clubs—like **Ronnie Scott's** for jazz. The British movie industry is centered in Wardour Street.

**Bloomsbury**   This district, a world within itself, lies northeast of Piccadilly Circus, beyond Soho. It's London's academic heart, site of the **University of London,** several other colleges, and many bookstores. The **British Museum** is also here. Despite its student population, the neighborhood is fairly staid. Its reputation has been fanned by such writers as Virginia Woolf, who lived within its bounds; the novelist and her husband, Leonard, were the unofficial leaders of the celebrated artistic and literary "Bloomsbury group."

The heart of Bloomsbury is **Russell Square,** laid out between 1800 and 1814. The streets jutting off from the square are lined with hotels and bed-and-breakfasts.

Nearby is **Fitzrovia,** bounded by Great Portland, Oxford, and Gower streets, and reached by the Goodge Street tube. Godge Street, with its many shops and pubs, forms the heart of the "village." Once a major haunt of writers and artists, the bottom end of Fitzrovia is a virtual extension of Soho, with a cluster of Greek restaurants.

**Holborn**   The old borough of Holborn, which abuts The City to the west, takes in the heart of legal London—it's home of the city's barristers, solicitors, and law clerks. Still Dickensian in spirit, this area lets you follow in the Victorian author's footsteps, passing the two **Inns of Court** and arriving at Bleeding Heart Yard of *Little Dorritt* fame. If you quench your thirst with a pint of bitter at the **Viaduct Tavern,** 126 Newgate St. (tube: St. Paul's), you'll be sitting at a site built over the notorious Newgate Prison, which specialized in death by pressing and was named after the Holborn Viaduct, the world's first overpass.

**Covent Garden & The Strand**   The flower, fruit, and "veg" market is long gone (since 1970), but memories linger of Professor Higgins and Eliza Doolittle. Covent Garden now contains the city's liveliest groups of restaurants, pubs, and cafes outside Soho, and the restored marketplace is also the home of much trendy shopping. Inigo Jones built St. Paul's Covent Garden between 1631 and 1633; Jones's "handsomest barn in Europe" was rebuilt after a fire in 1795. The restored structure, with its glass and iron roofs, has been called a magnificent example of urban recycling.

Beginning at Trafalgar Square, the Strand runs east into Fleet Street and borders Covent Garden to the south. It's flanked with theaters, shops, hotels, and restaurants. The Strand runs parallel to the River Thames, and to walk it would be to follow in the footsteps of Charles Lamb, Mark Twain, Henry Fielding, James Boswell, William Thackeray, and most definitely Sir Walter Raleigh. The Savoy Theatre helped make Gilbert & Sullivan a household name.

**Westminster & Victoria**   Westminster has been the seat of the British government since the days of Edward the Confessor. Dominated by the **Houses of Parliament** and Westminster Abbey, the area runs along the Thames to the east of St. James Park. **Trafalgar Square,** at the area's northern end and a major landmark, remains a testament to Nelson's naval victory over the French (he died in the moment of his triumph).

**Whitehall** is the principal thoroughfare, linking Trafalgar Square with **Parliament Square.** You can visit **Churchill's Cabinet War Rooms** and walk down **Downing Street** to see no. 10, the world's most famous street address. One of its longest tenants was Margaret Thatcher, Britain's first woman prime minister. No visit would be complete without a call at **Westminster Abbey,** one of the greatest Gothic churches in the world. It has figured into the parade of English history, beginning when William the Conqueror was crowned here on Christmas Day in 1066.

Westminster also encompasses **Victoria,** an area that takes its unofficial name from bustling Victoria Station, known as "the gateway to the Continent."

## The City & Environs

**The City**   When the English speak of "The City," they don't mean all of London; they mean the original square mile that's now the British version of Wall Street. The buildings in this district are known all over the world: the Bank of England (on Threadneedle Street); the London Stock Exchange; and Lloyd's of London. This was Londinium, as it was called by its Roman conquerors. Despite its age, The City doesn't necessarily reveal its past; much was swept away by the Great Fire of 1666, the bombs of 1940, the IRA bombs of the early 1990s, and the zeal of modern developers. Still, elements of its ancient character are very much evident. Some 2,000 years of history unfold at the **Museum of London** and the **Barbican Centre.** At the **Guildhall,** the first lord mayor of London was installed in 1192. Another landmark is **St. Paul's Cathedral,** the masterpiece of Sir Christopher Wren, which stood virtually alone among the rubble after the blitz.

**Fleet Street** has been London's journalistic hub ever since William Caxton printed the first book in English here. *The Daily Consort,* the first daily newspaper printed in England, was launched at Ludgate Circus in 1702. However, most London tabloids have recently abandoned Fleet Street for the new Docklands development across the river.

The City of London still prefers to function independently from the rest of the city; accordingly, it maintains its own **Information Centre** at St. Paul's Churchyard, EC4 (☎ **0171/332-1456**). Tube: St. Paul's.

**Docklands**   In 1981, the London Docklands Development Corporation (LDDC) was formed to redevelop Wapping, the Isle of Dogs, the Royal Docks, and Surrey Docks in the largest, most ambitious scheme of its kind in Europe. Since then, many businesses have moved into the area— bordered roughly by Tower Bridge to the west and London City Airport and the Royal Docks to the east—including most of the Fleet Street newspapers. Thames-side warehouses have been converted to Manhattan-style lofts, and museums, entertainment complexes, shops, and an ever-expanding list of restaurants has popped up at this 21st-century river city in the making.

**Canary Wharf,** on the Isle of Dogs, is the heart of Docklands; this huge 71-acre site is dominated by a 800-foot-high tower, the tallest building in the United Kingdom, designed by Cesar Pelli. The Piazza is lined with shops and restaurants. Across from the country's largest sports complex, **London Arena,** is the **Docklands Visitor Centre** (☎ **0171/512-3000**). On the south side of the river at Surrey Docks, the Victorian warehouses of **Butler's Wharf** have been converted by Sir Terence

Conran into offices, workshops, houses, shops, and restaurants; it's also home to the **Design Museum.**

To get to Docklands, take the London Underground to the Bank or (less conveniently) Tower Hill Station. At either of those stations, transfer to the **Docklands Light Railway** (☎ **0171/538-0311**). Conceived as a silver-colored, computer-controlled monorail, it departs at intervals of between 4 and 10 minutes, daily from 5:30am to 12:15am. Access to its tracks is included as part of the price you'll pay to ride the London Underground.

**The East End**   Traditionally one of London's poorest districts, nearly bombed out of existence by the Nazis. The East End extends from the City Wall east encompassing Stepney, Bow, Poplar, West Ham, Canning Town, and other districts. Many immigrants to London have found a home here, and it's also the home of the cockney, London's most colorful character.

**South Bank**   Although not officially a district, South Bank is the setting today for the **South Bank Arts Centre,** now the largest arts center in Western Europe and still growing. Reached by Waterloo Bridge, it lies across the Thames from the Victoria Embankment. Culture buffs flock to its many galleries and halls, including the **National Theatre, Queen Elizabeth Hall, Royal Festival Hall,** and the **Hayward Gallery.** It's also the setting of the **National Film Theatre** and the **Museum of the Moving Image (MOMI).** Nearby are such neighborhoods as Elephant and Castle and Southwark, home to grand Southwark Cathedral. To get here, take the tube to Waterloo Station.

## Central London Beyond the West End

**Knightsbridge**   One of London's most fashionable neighborhoods, Knightsbridge is a top residential and shopping district, just south of Hyde Park. The classic shopping spot is **Harrods,** on Brompton Road. Founded in 1901, it's been called "the Notre Dame of department stores." Nearby, fashionable Beauchamp Place (pronounced *Beech*-am) is a Regency-era, boutique-lined little street once frequented by Princess Diana.

**Belgravia**   South of Knightsbridge, this area has long rivaled Mayfair as London's aristocratic quarter. Although it reached the pinnacle of its prestige during the reign of Queen Victoria, it's still a chic address; the duke and duchess of Westminster, one of England's richest families, still live at Eaton Square. Its centerpiece is **Belgrave Square** (1825–35). When the town houses were built, the aristocrats followed.

**Chelsea**   This stylish district stretching along the Thames lies south of Belgravia and begins at **Sloane Square.** The area has always been a favorite of writers and artists, including Oscar Wilde (who was arrested here), George Eliot, James Whistler, Henry James, and Thomas Carlyle (whose former home can be visited). Princess Diana and her Sloane Rangers of the 1980s gave it even more fame.

Chelsea's major boulevard is fabled (or hyped) **King's Road,** where Mary Quant launched the miniskirt in the 1960s and the Rolling Stones once lived. Punk fashions and music reigned here in the late 1970s and early 1980s. Running the entire length of Chelsea, King's Road is at its liveliest on Saturdays. Yet the bustle and cutting edge of King's Road is not typical of upscale Chelsea, filled with town houses and little mews dwellings.

On the Chelsea/Fulham border is **Chelsea Harbour,** a luxury development of apartments and restaurants with a private marina. You can spot its tall tower from far away; the golden ball on top moves up and down to indicate tide level.

**Kensington & South Kensington**   This royal borough lies west of Kensington Gardens and Hyde Park and is traversed by two of London's major shopping streets, **Kensington High Street** and **Kensington Church Street.** Since 1689, when asthmatic William III fled Whitehall Palace for Nottingham House (where the air was fresher), the district has enjoyed royal associations. In time Nottingham House became **Kensington Palace,** and the royals grabbed a chunk of Hyde Park to plant their roses. Queen Victoria was born here. "KP," as the royals say, is still home to Princess Margaret (20 rooms with a view), Prince and Princess Michael of Kent, and the duke and duchess of Gloucester. Princess Diana and her two little princes also lived here for a time. The queen permits all these royals to live here free, but insists they pay their own phone, heat, and electricity. Kensington Gardens has been open to the public ever since George II decreed that "respectably dressed" people would be permitted in on Saturday—provided that servants, soldiers, and sailors were excluded. Kensington Square developed in the footsteps of William III, attracting artists and writers such as Thomas Carlyle and Thackeray.

Lying southeast of Kensington Gardens and Earl's Court, primarily residential South Kensington is often called "museumland." Here you'll find **the Natural History Museum, the Victoria & Albert Museum, and the Science Museum;** nearby is **Royal Albert Hall.** One of the district's chief curiosities is the extravagant **Albert Memorial,** completed in 1872 by Sir George Gilbert Scott.

**Earl's Court**   Earl's Court lies below Kensington, bordering the western half of Chelsea. This neighborhood, once a staid residential district, now attracts a new and younger crowd (often gay), particularly at night, to its pubs, wine bars, and coffeehouses. It's long been a popular base for budget travelers, thanks to its wealth of B&Bs and budget hotels and its convenient access to Central London: A 15-minute tube ride will take you into the heart of Piccadilly, via either the District or Piccadilly lines.

Once regarded as "the boondocks," nearby **West Brompton** lies directly south of Earl's Court (take the tube to West Brompton) and directly southeast of West Kensington. Its focal point is the sprawling **Brompton Cemetery,** a flower-filled "green lung" and burial place of such personages as Frederick Leyland, the famous Pre-Raphaelite patron who died in 1892. It also has many good restaurants, pubs, and taverns, as well as some budget hotels.

**Notting Hill & Notting Hill Gate**   Increasingly popular in fashion and frequented by such persons as the Princess of Wales, Notting Hill is bounded on the north by Bayswater Road and on the east by Kensington. It has many turn-of-the-century mansions and small houses on quiet, leafy streets, plus a growing number of trendy restaurants and clubs. On the north end, across Notting Hill Gate, west of Bayswater, is the neighborhood known as Notting Hill Gate, another increasingly hip neighborhood; **Portobello Road** is home to one of London's most famous street (antiques) markets. The adjoining neighborhoods are reachable by taking the tube to Notting Hill Gate, Holland Park, or Ladbroke Grove.

Nearby Holland Park is a chi-chi residential neighborhood visited chiefly by the chic guests of Halycon Hotel, one of the grandest of London's small hotels.

**Paddington & Bayswater**   The Paddington section centers on Paddington Station, north of Kensington Gardens and Hyde Park. It attracts budget travelers who fill up the bed-and-breakfasts at such places as Sussex Gardens and Norfolk Square. Today, this somewhat middle-class and prosperous area is blighted in parts.

Just south of Paddington is Bayswater, also filled with a large number of bed-and-breakfasts. This area's terrace houses and spacious squares became home to a relatively prosperous set of Victorians from the mercantile class.

**North London**

**Greenwich**  Some 4 miles from the city, Greenwich—ground zero for use in the reckoning of terrestrial longitudes—enjoyed its heyday under the Tudors. Henry VIII and both of his daughters, Mary I and Elizabeth I, were born here. Greenwich Palace, Henry's favorite, is long gone, though; today visitors come to this lovely port village for nautical sights along the Thames.

**Hampstead**  This residential suburb of north London, beloved by Keats and Hogarth, is a favorite excursion spot for Londoners on the weekend, and one of the most desirable districts in the Greater London area to call home. Its centerpiece is **Hampstead Heath,** nearly 800 acres of rolling meadows and woodland with panoramic views. Many of the rich and famous live in Hampstead's hilltop village, which is also filled with cafes, tearooms, and dining places. Everybody from Sigmund Freud to D.H. Lawrence, Anna Pavlova to John Le Carré, has lived here. There are pubs galore, some with historic pedigrees. To get here, take the Northern line of the Underground to Hampstead Heath Station.

**Highgate**  Along with Hampstead, Highgate in north London is another choice residential area, particularly those houses on or near Pond Square and along Hampstead High Street. Unless you're living or dining at Highgate, most visitors come here today to see moody Highgate Cemetery, one of the most famous cemeteries in London, at the bottom of a park; it's the final resting place of such illustrious figures as Karl Marx and George Eliot.

## 2  Getting Around

Remember that cars drive on the left, and vehicles have the right-of-way in London over pedestrians. Wherever you walk, always look both ways before stepping off a curb—Americans always have a tough time crossing the street in the first day or two, so take care. In some parts of Kensington and some other districts, the street is actually painted with the instructions "Look Left" or "Look Right" at stop lights.

### BY PUBLIC TRANSPORTATION

Transportation within London can be remarkably easy and inexpensive. Both the Underground (subway, or tube) and bus systems are operated by **London Transport**—with Travel Information Centres in the Underground stations at King's Cross, Hammersmith, Oxford Circus, St. James's Park, Liverpool Street Station, and Piccadilly Circus, as well as in the main line stations at Euston and Victoria and in each of the terminals at Heathrow Airport. They take reservations for London Transport's guided tours and have free Underground and bus maps and other information. A **24-hour telephone information** service is available (☎ **0171/222-1234**).

**Travel Passes**  London Transport offers **Travelcards** for use on the bus, Underground, and main line service inside Greater London. Available in a number of combinations for adjacent zones, Travelcards can be purchased for periods of from 7 days to a year. A Travelcard allowing travel in two zones for 1 week costs £15.70 ($25.10) for adults and £5.30 ($8.50) for children.

To purchase a Travelcard, you must present a Photocard. If you're 16 years old or older, bring along a passport-type picture of yourself when you buy your Travelcard and the Photocard will be issued free. Child-rate Photocards for Travelcards are issued only at Underground ticket offices or Travel Information Centres; in addition to a passport-type photograph, proof of age is required (a passport or birth certificate). Teenagers (14 or 15) are charged adult fares on all services unless they have one of the cards.

For shorter stays in London, you will probably want to purchase the **One-Day Off-Peak Travelcard.** This Travelcard can be used on most bus, Underground, and main line services throughout Greater London Monday through Friday after 9:30am and at any time on weekends and bank holidays. The Travelcard is available at Underground ticket offices, Travel Information Centres, and some newsstands. For two zones, the cost is £3.20 ($5.10) for adults and £1.70 ($2.70) for children aged 5 to 15. Children 4 and under ride free.

The **Visitor Travelcard** is worthwhile if you plan to travel a lot within Greater London. This card allows unlimited transport within all six zones of Greater London's Underground and bus network. You'll most likely travel within the first two zones of the network's boundaries, but you could travel as far as Heathrow during valid times. However, you must buy this pass in North America; it's not available in England. A pass good for 3 consecutive days of travel costs £15.60 ($25) for adults; £6.90 ($11) for children aged 5 to 15; a pass good for 4 consecutive days of travel costs £20.60 ($33) for adults, £8.20 ($13) for children; and a pass good for 7 consecutive days of travel costs £33.10 ($53) for adults, £13.10 ($21) for children. For more information, contact **BritRail Travel International,** 1500 Broadway, New York, NY 10036 (☎ **800/677-8585** or 212/575-2667).

You can now buy **Carnet tickets,** a booklet of 10 single Underground tickets valid for 12 months from the issue date. Carnet tickets are valid for travel only in Zone 1 (central London). They cost £10 ($16) for adults and £4.80 ($7.70) for children (up to 15)—10 for the price of 8 single tickets. Another pass is the one-day **Family Travelcard.** This go-as-you-please card allows as many journeys as you wish on the tube, buses (excluding night buses) displaying the London Transport bus sign, and even the Docklands Light Railway or any rail service within the travel zones designated on your ticket. The family card is valid after 9:30am Monday through Friday, all day on weekends, and public holidays. It costs £3.20 to £4 ($5.10 to $6.40) for adults, or £1.70 ($2.70) for children.

There's also the **Weekend Travelcard** allowing 2 days of weekend transportation on the Underground or buses. The cost ranges from £6.40 to £8 ($10.25 to $12.80) for adults, or £3.40 ($5.45) for children. These passes are available at all Underground stations.

## BUSES

The first thing you learn about London buses is that nobody just boards them. You queue up—that is, form a single-file line at the bus stop.

The comparably priced bus system is almost as good as the Underground, and you'll have a better view—especially from the top of a double decker. You can pick up a free bus map at one of London Regional Transport's Travel Information Centres listed above.

London still has some of the old-style Routemaster buses, staffed by both a driver and conductor. As on a train, a conductor will pass by your seat. You state your destination and pay the fare, receiving a ticket in return. This type of bus is being phased out, however, in favor of newer buses with a single driver. On these, you pay the driver as you enter and exit through one of the rear doors.

Fares vary according to distance traveled. Generally, the cost is 50p to £1.20 (80¢ to $1.90). If you travel for two or three stops, the cost is 60p (95¢); longer runs within zone 1 cost 90p ($1.45). If you want to be warned when to get off, simply

# Central London Bus Routes

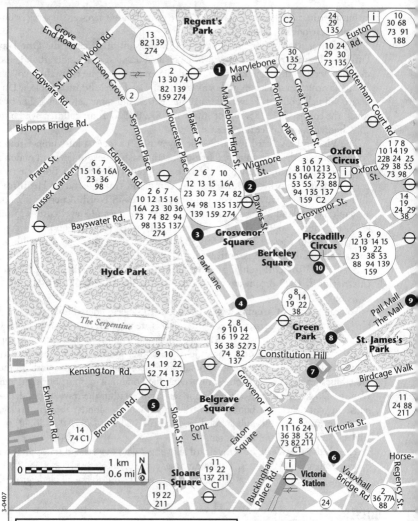

## Using the Map

London bus route numbers are shown in circles at places where routes cross. Locate where you are going and then follow the route circles back toward your starting point. This will show if and where you need to change buses and the bus route number or numbers for your trip.

Tube Station ⊖
British Rail Station ⇌

## MAJOR ATTRACTIONS

Admiralty Arch (9)
Barbican Centre (25)
British Museum (11)
Buckingham Palace (7)
Downing Street (16)
Harrods (5)
Horse Guards (15)
Houses of Parliament (18)
Imperial War Museum (20)

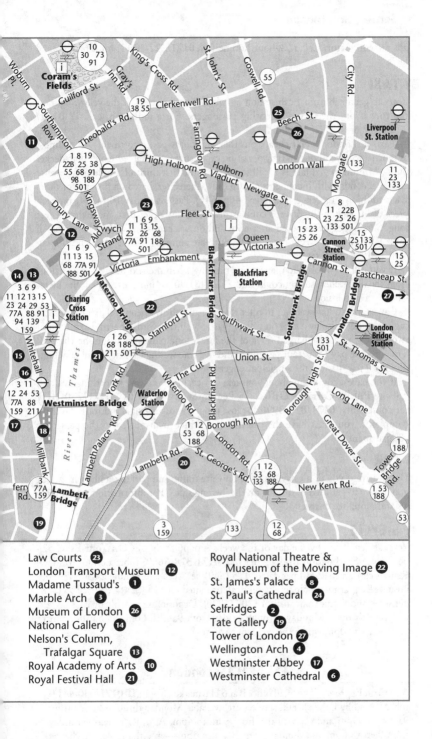

| Law Courts | 23 |
| London Transport Museum | 12 |
| Madame Tussaud's | 1 |
| Marble Arch | 3 |
| Museum of London | 26 |
| National Gallery | 14 |
| Nelson's Column, Trafalgar Square | 13 |
| Royal Academy of Arts | 10 |
| Royal Festival Hall | 21 |

| Royal National Theatre & Museum of the Moving Image | 22 |
| St. James's Palace | 8 |
| St. Paul's Cathedral | 24 |
| Selfridges | 2 |
| Tate Gallery | 19 |
| Tower of London | 27 |
| Wellington Arch | 4 |
| Westminster Abbey | 17 |
| Westminster Cathedral | 6 |

ask the conductor. Call a 24-hour hotline (☎ **0171/222-1234**) for schedules and fares.

## BY TAXI

You can get a cab from a cab station or hail one on the street; if the yellow light on the roof is on, the taxi is accepting passengers. For a radio cab, call ☎ **0171/ 272-0272** or 0171/253-5000.

Taxis in London aren't cheap, but they are roomy and convenient—and almost as much a required London transportation experience as the fabled red double-decker buses. Minimum taxi fare is £1.40 ($2.25) for the first third of a mile or 1 minute and 51 seconds, with increments of 20p (30¢) thereafter, based on distance or time. Each additional passenger is charged 40p (64¢). Passengers pay 10p (16¢) for each piece of luggage in the driver's compartment and any other item more than 2 feet long. Surcharges are imposed after 8pm and on weekends and public holidays. All these tariffs include VAT. Fares usually increase annually. We recommend tipping 10% to 15% of the fare.

If you call for a cab, the meter starts running when the taxi receives instructions from the dispatcher, so you could find £1.20 ($1.90) or more already on the meter when you step inside.

Cab sharing allows cabbies to offer rides for two to five people. The taxis accepting such riders display a sign on yellow plastic with the words Shared Taxi. Each of two sharing riders is charged 65% of the fare a lone passenger would be charged. Three people pay 55%, four pay 45%, and five (the seating capacity of all new London cabs) pay 40% of the single-passenger fare.

If you have a complaint about your taxi service, or if you leave something in a cab, call the **Public Carriage Office,** 15 Penton St., N1 9PU (☎ **0171/230-1631** for complaints; **0171/833-0996** for lost property; tube: Angel Station). To file a complaint, you must have the cab number, which is displayed in the passenger compartment.

## BY CAR

Don't drive if you don't have to. Not only are traffic and parking nightmarish, but you'll have to get used to driving on the "wrong side." For information on car rentals and more, see chapter 3.

## BY BICYCLE

You can rent bikes by the day or the week. A popular shop is **On Your Bike,** 52–54 Tooley St., London Bridge, SE1 (☎ **0171/378-6669;** tube: London Bridge). Rentals cost £8 ($12.80) per day or £25 ($40) per week and require a £50 ($80) deposit. A 21-gear mountain or city bike can be rented for £15 ($24) a day or £55 ($88) per week and require a deposit of £200 ($320). Deposits are payable by MasterCard or Visa. It's open Monday through Friday from 9am to 6pm, on Saturday from 9:30am to 5:30pm, and Sunday 11am to 4pm.

## FAST FACTS: London

**American Express**　The main office is at 6 Haymarket, SW1 (☎ **0171/930-4411;** tube: Piccadilly Circus). Full services are available Monday through Friday from 9am to 5:30pm and on Saturday from 9am to 4pm. At other times—Saturday from 9am to 6pm and Sunday from 10am to 5pm—only the foreign-exchange bureau is open.

**Area Code**    London has two area codes—**0171** and **0181.** The 0171 area code is for central London within a 4-mile radius of Charing Cross (including The City of London, Knightsbridge, and Oxford Street, and as far south as Brixton). The 0181 area code is for outer London (including Heathrow Airport, Wimbledon, and Greenwich). Within London, you'll need to dial the area code when calling from one of these sections of the city to the other, but not within a section. The country code for England is **44.**

**Baby-sitters**    If your hotel won't recommend a sitter, call **Childminders,** 9 Paddington St. (☎ **0171/935-3000;** tube: Baker Street). Rates are £4.65 ($7.45) per hour during the day and £3.35 to £4.40 ($5.35 to $7.05) per hour at night. There is a 4-hour minimum, and hotel guests pay a £5 ($8) booking fee each time they use a sitter.

**Business Hours**    Banks are usually open Monday through Friday from 9:30am to 3:30pm. Business offices are open Monday through Friday from 9am to 5pm. Pubs and bars are legally allowed to stay open Monday through Saturday from 11am to 11pm, and on Sunday from noon to 10:30pm, usually closing for a couple hours in mid-afternoon. London stores are generally open from 9am to 5:30pm, staying open until 7pm on Wednesday or Thursday. Most central shops close on Saturday around 1pm.

**Currency Exchange**    In general, banks provide the best exchange rates, and you're likely to get a better rate for traveler's checks than for cash. Branch offices of the main banks at London's airports charge a small fee. There are also *bureaux de change* at the airports, with offices around London; they charge a fee for cashing traveler's checks and personal U.K. checks and for changing foreign currency into pounds sterling. Some travel agencies, such as American Express and Thomas Cook, also have currency-exchange services.

**Dentists**    For dental emergencies, call **Eastman Dental Hospital** (☎ **0171/ 915-1000;** tube: King's Cross).

**Doctors**    In an emergency, contact **Doctor's Call** (☎ **0181/900-1000**). Some hotels also have doctors on call. **Medical Express,** 117A Harley St. (☎ **0171/ 499-1991;** tube: Regent's Park), is a private British clinic. If you need a prescription filled, stop by, but to fill the British equivalent of a U.S. prescription, there is sometimes a surcharge of £20 ($32) in addition to the cost of the medication. The clinic is open Monday through Friday from 9am to 6pm and on Saturday from 9:30am to 2:30pm.

**Drugstores**    In Britain they're called "chemist shops." A centrally located chemist, keeping long hours, is **Bliss the Chemist,** 5 Marble Arch (☎ **0171/ 723-6116;** tube: Marble Arch), open daily from 9am to midnight. Every London neighborhood has a branch of the ubiquitous **Boots,** the leading pharmacy in Britain.

**Embassies & High Commissions**    The **U.S. Embassy** is at 24 Grosvenor Sq., W1 (☎ **0171/499-9000;** tube: Bond Street). For passport and visa information, go to the U.S. Passport and Citizenship Unit, 55–56 Upper Brook St., London, W1 (☎ **0171/499-9000,** ext. 2563 or 2564; tube: Marble Arch or Bond Street). Hours are Monday through Friday from 8:30am to noon and from 2 to 4pm; on Tuesday, the office closes at noon.

The **Canadian High Commission,** MacDonald House, 38 Grosvenor Sq., W1 (☎ **0171/258-6600;** tube: Bond Street), handles visas for Canada. Hours are Monday through Friday from 8 to 11am only.

The **Australian High Commission** is at Australia House, Strand, WC2 (☎ **0171/379-4334;** tube: Charing Cross or Aldwych). Hours are Monday through Friday from 10am to 4pm.

The **New Zealand High Commission** is at New Zealand House, 80 Haymarket at Pall Mall SW1 (☎ **0171/930-8422;** tube: Charing Cross or Piccadilly Circus). Hours are Monday through Friday from 9am to 5pm.

The **Irish Embassy** is at 17 Grosvenor Place, SW1 (☎ **0171/235-2171;** tube: Hyde Park Corner). Hours are Monday through Friday from 9:30am to 1pm and 2:15 to 5pm.

**Emergencies**    In London, for police, fire, or an ambulance, dial ☎ **999.**

**Eyeglass Repair**    If your glasses are lost or broken, try **Selfridge Opticians** on the street level of Selfridges Department Store, 400 Oxford St. (☎ **0171/629-1234,** ext. 3353; tube: Bond Street or Marble Arch), open Monday through Saturday from 9:30am to 7pm, on Thursday until 8pm. Contact lenses are usually available the same day.

**Fax**    To send a fax, go to the **Chesham Executive Centre** at 150 Regent St. (☎ **0171/439-6288;** tube: Piccadilly Circus). It isn't much cheaper—if at all—than a hotel: A one-page fax to anywhere in the world costs £5.28 ($8.45), plus VAT and the cost of the phone call. Open Monday through Friday from 9am to 5:30pm, Saturday from 9am to noon.

**Hospitals**    The following offer emergency care in London 24 hours a day, with the first treatment free under the National Health Service: **Royal Free Hospital,** Pond Street (☎ **0171/794-0500;** tube: Belsize Park), and **University College Hospital,** Gower Street (☎ **0171/387-9300;** tube: Warren Street). Many other London hospitals also have accident and emergency departments.

**Hotlines**    If you're in some sort of legal emergency, call **Release** at ☎ **0171/ 729-9904,** 24 hours a day. The **Rape Crisis Line** (☎ **0171/837-1600**) accepts calls after 6pm. **Samaritans,** 46 Marshall St. (☎ **0171/734-2800**), maintains a crisis hotline that helps with all kinds of trouble, even threatened suicides, from 9am to 9pm. The 24-hour **AIDS hotline** is toll free at ☎ **0800/567-123. Alcoholic Anonymous** (☎ **0171/352-3001**) answers its hotline daily from 10am to 10pm.

**Information**    See "Visitor Information," earlier in this chapter.

**Luggage Storage & Lockers**    You can rent lockers at Heathrow and Gatwick airports and at all major rail stations, including Victoria Station.

**Newspapers & Magazines**    Of the London papers, the *Times* is tops, then the *Telegraph,* the *Daily Mail,* and the *Manchester Guardian.* The *International Herald Tribune,* published in Paris, and an international edition of *USA Today,* beamed via satellite, are available daily. *Time* and *Newsweek* are also sold at most newsstands. Magazines such as *Time Out* and *City Limits* contain useful information about what's going on, including theatrical and cultural events.

**Photographic Needs**    **The Flash Centre,** 54 Brunswick Centre, WC1 (☎ **0171/ 837-6163;** tube: Russell Square), is the best professional photographic equipment supplier in London.

**Police**    In an emergency, dial ☎ **999** (no coins needed). You can also go to a local police branch, including New Scotland Yard, Broadway (☎ **0171/230-1212;** tube: St. James's Park).

**Post Office**   The main post office is at 24 William IV St. ( ☎ **0171/930-9580;** tube: Charing Cross). It operates as three separate businesses: inland and international postal service and banking (open Monday through Saturday from 8:30am to 8pm), philatelic postage stamp sales (open Monday through Saturday from 8am to 8pm), and the post shop, selling greeting cards and stationery (open Monday through Saturday from 8am to 8pm).

Other post offices and sub–post offices are open Monday through Friday from 9am to 5:30pm and on Saturday from 9am to 12:30pm. Many sub–post offices and some main post offices close for an hour at lunchtime.

**Rest Rooms**   Often called the "loo" by the English, a rest room is usually found where you see signs saying "Public Toilets." Automatic toilets are found on many streets. They are sterilized after each use.

**Safety**   Theft here isn't as big a problem, perhaps, as in U.S. cities like Miami, Los Angeles, and New York. Muggings mainly occur in poor areas. The best advice is to use discretion and a little common sense and keep to well-lit areas.

**Telephone**   For directory assistance for London, dial ☎ **142;** for the rest of Britain, dial ☎ **192.**

**Transit Information**   Call ☎ **0171/222-1234,** daily 24 hours.

**Weather**   Call ☎ **0171/922-8844,** but good luck getting through!

## 3  Where to Stay

London is a challenge for budget travelers; today it is tough to find a place charging less than £35 ($56) a night for a double. You'll often have to pay a lot more than that, and may not like what you get even at a higher price. Rooms can be chilly, and breakfasts meager—perhaps a roll, a tiny glass of juice (from a can), and cornflakes.

Don't be discouraged, though—but we've scoured this expensive city to find a wide assortment of affordable places where you can stay comfortably. Along the way we discovered some real gems, which we'll tell you about below. We were pleased to discover some moderately priced B&Bs, after a terrible slump, bouncing back with a little charm and grace.

But here's the lowdown about London budget accommodations: Most budget hotels aren't hotels at all (in the sense of having elevators, porters, and private baths). Rather, they are family-type guest houses. Hundreds of these four- and five-story hotels dot the city. They may all appear the same, but once inside you'll find varying degrees of cleanliness, service, and friendliness.

Most bed-and-breakfast hotels (B&Bs) serve an English breakfast, or at least a continental one, and rarely serve any other meal. Usually the rooms have sinks, innerspring mattresses, closet and dresser space, a desk, and armchair; rooms on higher floors tend to be smaller. The bathroom may be a half flight down, two flights down, or on the same floor.

Always ask what is included in the room rate; in the case of a B&B, ask to see your room before accepting it. You'll probably have to pay in advance at a B&B.

Incidentally, the designation of a private shower (or tub) on the tariff sheet presented to you doesn't always include a toilet, so ask.

**Reservations by Mail**   Most hotels require at least a day's deposit before reserving a room for you. This can be accomplished either by an international money order or a personal check, if the staff agrees. It can also be done with a credit card.

# Central London Accommodations

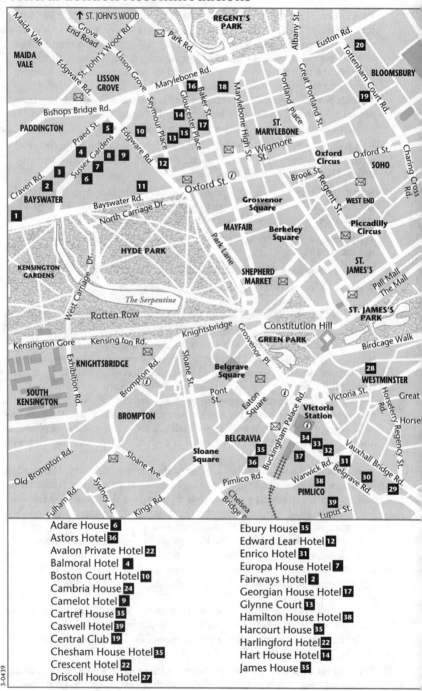

Adare House **6**
Astors Hotel **36**
Avalon Private Hotel **22**
Balmoral Hotel **4**
Boston Court Hotel **10**
Cambria House **24**
Camelot Hotel **9**
Cartref House **35**
Caswell Hotel **39**
Central Club **19**
Chesham House Hotel **35**
Crescent Hotel **22**
Driscoll House Hotel **27**

Ebury House **35**
Edward Lear Hotel **12**
Enrico Hotel **31**
Europa House Hotel **7**
Fairways Hotel **2**
Georgian House Hotel **17**
Glynne Court **13**
Hamilton House Hotel **38**
Harcourt House **35**
Harlingford Hotel **22**
Hart House Hotel **14**
James House **35**

3-0439

78

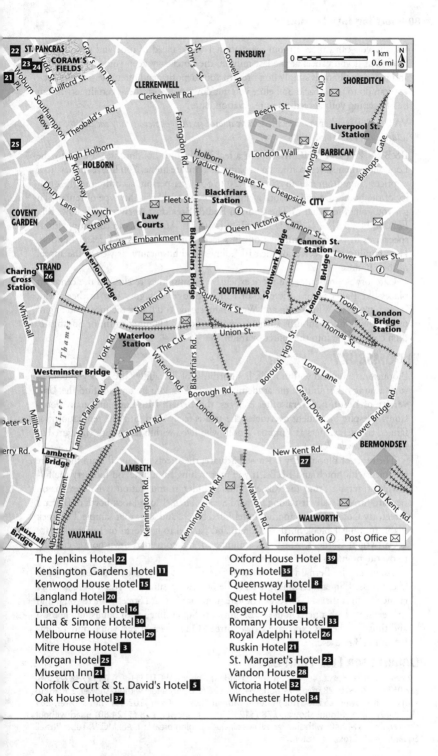

The Jenkins Hotel **22**
Kensington Gardens Hotel **11**
Kenwood House Hotel **15**
Langland Hotel **20**
Lincoln House Hotel **16**
Luna & Simone Hotel **30**
Melbourne House Hotel **29**
Mitre House Hotel **3**
Morgan Hotel **25**
Museum Inn **21**
Norfolk Court & St. David's Hotel **5**
Oak House Hotel **37**

Oxford House Hotel **39**
Pyms Hotel **35**
Queensway Hotel **8**
Quest Hotel **1**
Regency Hotel **18**
Romany House Hotel **33**
Royal Adelphi Hotel **26**
Ruskin Hotel **21**
St. Margaret's Hotel **23**
Vandon House **28**
Victoria Hotel **32**
Winchester Hotel **34**

Usually you can cancel a room reservation 1 week ahead of time and get a full refund. But if you cancel at the last minute, the hotel may keep your deposit. More and more small hotels simply don't return your deposits, and often there is very little you can do to get it back. So before you put down a deposit, be as certain as you can be of keeping your agreed-upon reservation date.

**VAT**    Unless otherwise specified, *rates quoted in this chapter already include the value-added tax (VAT) of* 17¹/2%.

**B&B IN PRIVATE HOMES**    For a real insight into London life, as lived by the Londoners themselves, consider a booking in a private home. You'll save money, too, as prices range from £17 to £35 ($27.20 to $56) per person, according to the quality of the home and its location. Many agencies specialize in this type of rental.  To get you going, see what ✪ **The London Bed & Breakfast Agency,** 71 Fellows Rd., London NW3 3JY (☎ **0171/586-2768;** fax 0171/586-6567), can come up with. It specializes in B&B accommodations in selected private homes in Greater London. Host families are selected for their friendliness and hospitality, as well as the appeal of their homes.

Category A properties are more expensive because they're close to the center in places like Baker Street, Victoria, or Knightsbridge. Category B is further afield, in such places as Wimbledon and West Hampstead. You'll save the most booking in one of the London suburbs such as Camden Town, Hammersmith, or Southgate, then commuting into the center by train.

# BLOOMSBURY

Bloomsbury, a world within itself, lies northeast of Piccadilly Circus, beyond Soho. It is, among other things, the academic heart of London; here you'll find the **University of London,** several other colleges, **the British Museum,** and many bookstores. Despite its student overtones, the area is fairly staid. Still, its reputation was fanned by such writers as Virginia Woolf, who lived within its bounds (it figured in her novel *Jacob's Room*).

The heart of Bloomsbury is **Russell Square;** the streets jutting off from the square are lined with hotels and B&Bs. If you're searching for a hotel on foot, try the following itinerary: From the Russell Square Underground station (whose exit is on Bernard Street), walk first along Bernard Street. Then, 1 long block north of Bernard Street, try Coram Street, another hotel-lined block, and after that sample Tavistock Place, running 1 block north of Coram and parallel to it. North of Tavistock Place is Cartwright Gardens, which has a number of old converted town houses catering to overnight guests.

However, the Bernard Street-Coram Street-Tavistock Place hotels are the most likely Russell Square establishments to be booked in summer. You'll have a better chance on the other side of Russell Square (opposite Bernard Street), where you'll find the relatively high-priced hotels of Bloomsbury Street (lined with publishing houses) and those on the less expensive Gower Street. On Gower Street, you'll find a number of B&B houses.

## DOUBLES FOR LESS THAN £55

**Avalon Private Hotel.** 46–47 Cartwright Gardens, London WC1H 9EL. ☎ **0171/387-2366.** Fax 0171/387-5810. 28 rms, 5 with shower. TV. £36 ($57.60) single without shower, £50 ($80) single with shower; £51 ($81.60) double without shower, £64 ($102.40) with shower; £69 ($110.40) triple without shower, £78 ($124.80) with shower; £78 ($124.80) quad without shower, £89 ($142.40) with shower. All rates include English breakfast. AE, MC, V. Tube: Russell Square, King's Cross, or Euston.

One Victorian-era guidebook claimed Bloomsbury attracted "medical and other students of both sexes and several nationalities, American folk passing through London, literary persons 'up' for a week or two's reading in the British Museum, and Bohemians pure and simple." The same still might be said for the of this hotel, built in 1807 as two Georgian houses, part of the residential Cartwright Gardens. Guests feel privileged to use the semiprivate, horseshoe-shaped garden across the street—that has a tennis court. Top floor rooms, often filled with students, are reached by climbing impossibly steep London stairs; bedrooms on the lower levels have easier access. The decor could only be the work of a wacky decorator, with everything amusingly mismatched in the bedrooms and in the droopy lounge, but the price is right.

**Cambria House.** 37 Hunter St., London WC1N 1BJ. ☎ **0171/837-1654.** Fax 0171/837-1229. 37 rms, 3 with bath. £25.50 ($40.80) single without bath; £40 ($64) double without bath, £50 ($80) double with bath; £60 ($96) triple without bath. Children £5 ($8) (under 3), £12 ($19.20) (3–14). All rates include English breakfast. MC, V. Tube: Russell Square.

The motto says it all: "A Christian church and a registered charity with heart to God and hand to man." Of course, we're talking about The Salvation Army. In the heart of Bloomsbury, this hotel is most assuredly not for smokers, drinkers, or swingers, but if you don't mind a few restrictions, you'll find one of the best bargains in the area. The hotel has been considerably spruced up, though still somewhat institutional. The creaky shared baths in the hallways have plumbing circa WWII, but are free of mold and decently maintained. The cafeteria is very cheap, but bland, only a bit better than a 1940s London canteen.

**The Jenkins Hotel.** 45 Cartwright Gardens, Russell Sq., London WC1H 9EH. ☎ **0171/837-2067.** Fax 0171/383-3139. 15 rms, 6 with bath. TV TEL. £39 ($62.40) single without bath; £52 ($83.20) single or double with bath, £62 ($99.20) double with bath; £76 ($121.60) triple with bath. MC, V. All rates include English breakfast. Tube: Euston Station.

Followers of the Agatha Christie TV series "Poirot," staring David Suchet and Hugh Fraser, might recognize this Cartwright Gardens residence, as it was featured in the series. Back in the 1920s Maggie Jenkins converted the former residence into a hotel and so it remains today. Today a young Virginia Woolf would make her way to the doorstep surrounded by the British Museum, London University, theaters, and antiquarian bookshops. E. M. Forster, a member of the Bloomsbury Set, used to drop in here for tea. The antiques are gone, the rooms are small, but some of the original charm of the Georgian house remains—enough so that the *London Mail on Sunday* recently proclaimed it one of the "ten of best hotel values" in the city. If you've got bulky suitcases, this is probably not the best choice. There are some drawbacks—no lift, no reception or sitting room, but it's a place where you can settle in and feel at home.

**Langland Hotel.** 29–31 Gower St., London WC1E 6HG. ☎ **0171/636-5801.** Fax 0171/580-2227. 30 rms, 6 with bath. £32 ($51.20) single without bath; £42 ($67.20) double without bath, £50 ($80) double with bath. All rates include English breakfast. MC, V. Tube: Goodge Street or Russell Square.

Near the British Museum, this hotel has a 200-year-old facade constructed with the yellow bricks known as "London stock." In a district where many hotels look as if they were furnished with pieces from the curbside, the Langland was recently redecorated and vastly improved. Bedrooms are modestly furnished but comfortable, and many have a TV set. You get a lot of thoughtful extras here—some not normally associated with a small London B&B: room service, in-room massage, twice-daily maid service, and fresh coffee or refreshments in the lobby. This family-run place welcomes other families. The owners have been keeping Langland in good shape for a quarter of a century.

**St. Margaret's Hotel.** 26 Bedford Place, London WC1B 5JH. ☎ **0171/636-4277.** Fax 0171/323-3066. 64 rms, 6 with shower. TV TEL. £40.50 ($64.80) single without shower; £52.50 ($84) double without shower, £62–£68 ($99.20–$108.80) double with shower. All rates include English breakfast. No credit cards. Tube: Holborn or Russell Square.

As you trudge along Bedford Place in the footsteps of William Hogarth, William Butler Yeats, and Charles Dickens, you'll spot this hotel encompassing four interconnected Georgian town houses. The staff here is so loyal they often stay until retirement. Furnishings are a mismatched medley, a bit tattered here and there, but endurable and fine nevertheless. On a spring day you can look out back onto the duke of Bedford's private gardens in full bloom. Rooms are fairly large, except for a cramped single here and there. Many still retain their original fireplaces, which is how the rooms were once heated. Families should ask for room 53, which has a glassed-in garden along the back. A single who doesn't mind sharing a bath will find ample space in room 24. Only a few rooms have private shower, although several bathrooms and showers are variously located throughout the building with unrestricted access. Guests have use of two lounges, one with TV.

## DOUBLES FOR LESS THAN £70

**Central Club.** 16–22 Great Russell St., London WC1B 3LR. ☎ **0171/636-7512.** Fax 0171/636-5278. 100 rms, none with bath. TV TEL. £33.75 ($54) single; £61.25 ($98) double; £21.50 ($34.40) per person triple or quad. All rates include English breakfast. MC, V. Tube: Tottenham Court Road.

After Sir Edwin Lutyens designed this building, Her Majesty, Queen Elizabeth (the Queen Mother) dedicated it in 1932. It's gone through a lot of rough times since, including the blitz, but it's survived. If anything, its accommodations are better than ever, having been modernized. It won't win design awards, but "It's a decent sleep, and quite comfortable at that, old chap," a frequent visitor from Devon told us in the lobby. Even if it doesn't live up to its motto, "a home away from home"—it's too impersonal for that—it offers well-furnished bedrooms, with adequate hallway showers and baths. Bedrooms contain a radio and beverage-making facilities. Although still vaguely affiliated with the YWCA, it now functions as a full-bodied hotel, and accepts men, women, families, and groups traveling together. Facilities include lounges, a coin-operated laundry, a hair salon, a gym, a solarium, and a coffee shop catering to carnivores and vegetarians both.

**Crescent Hotel.** 49–50 Cartwright Gardens, London WC1H 9EL. ☎ **0171/387-1515.** Fax 0171/383-2054. 24 rms, 15 with bath or shower. TV. £37 ($59.20) single without bath, £42 ($67.20) single with shower only, £53 ($84.80) single with bath; £68 ($108.80) double with bath. All rates include English breakfast. MC, V. Tube: Russell Square.

Although Leonard Woolf, Dorothy Sayers, John Ruskin, and Percy Bysshe Shelley no longer pass by, the Crescent continues in the heart of academic London. The private square is owned by the City Guild of Skinners and guarded by the University of London, whose student residential halls are just across the street. You have access to the garden itself, with its private tennis courts. Mrs. Bessolo and Mrs. Cockle, the managers, are the kindest hosts along the street. They view the Crescent as an extension of their private home and welcome you to its comfortably elegant Georgian surroundings, which date from 1810. Some guests have been returning here for four decades, enjoying a range of bedrooms, including small singles with shared baths, although a few have private plumbing. Standard doubles with modest furnishings are available, as are some more spacious twin and double rooms. All rooms have beverage-making facilities. Thoughtful extras include hair dryers. The good ladies will even let you do your ironing so you'll look sharp for your evening out.

**Harlingford Hotel.** 61–63 Cartwright Gardens, London WC1H 9EL. ☎ **0171/387-1551.** Fax 0171/387-4616. 44 rms. TV TEL. £55 ($88) single; £69 ($110.40) double; £78 ($124.80) triple; £90 ($144) quad. All rates include English breakfast. AE, MC, V. Tube: Russell Square.

This hotel is composed of three once-private town houses built in the 1820s that were joined together around 1900 via a bewildering array of staircases and meandering hallways. In the heart of Bloomsbury, the hotel is run by managers who seem genuinely concerned about the welfare of their guests, unlike many of their neighboring rivals. During the Christmas holidays, they distribute little mincemeat pies to their guests—it's a scene straight out of Dickens. Double-glazed windows cut down on the street noise, and all the bedrooms are generally comfortable and inviting, graced with floral prints on the walls. Baths are small, however, since the house wasn't originally designed for them. The most comfortable rooms are on the second and third levels; otherwise, you're climbing these steep English stairs to reach the top (there's no elevator). Resist rooms on ground level, as they are darker and have less security. A key is given for your use of the tennis courts in Cartwright Gardens—a budget privilege.

**✪ Morgan Hotel.** 24 Bloomsbury St., London WC1B 3QJ. ☎ **0171/636-3735.** 17 rms, 4 suites. TV TEL. £48 ($76.80) single; £70 ($112) double; £95 ($152) triple; £90 ($144) suite. All rates include English breakfast. No credit cards. Tube: Russell Square or Tottenham Court Road.

In a row of Georgian houses, each built in the 1790s, this much-restored hotel is distinguished by its gold-tipped iron fence railings. The flower boxes outside preview the warmth and hospitality awaiting you inside. The family managers do all the work themselves, and they have such a devoted following of habitués that it's hard to get a reservation in summer. Much of the paneling and cabinet work was done by one of the owners. Several rooms overlook the British Museum. Even if things are a bit cramped and the stairs rather steep, the rooms are pleasant and the atmosphere congenial. The carpeted bedrooms in this completely refurbished hotel have big beds (by British standards), dressing tables with mirrors, ample wardrobe space, hair dryers, batik bedspreads, and central heating; about 11 of the rooms have air-conditioning. Even though they cost more, the apartments are worth the extra money if you can afford it. They're furnished tastefully with brightly polished dark English pieces, framed English prints, and decorator fabrics, all with spacious bathrooms and daily maid service.

**Ruskin Hotel.** 23–24 Montague St., London WC1B 5BN. ☎ **0171/636-7388.** Fax 0171/323-1662. 32 rms, 6 with bath. TV TEL. £41 ($65.60) single without bath; £58 ($92.80) double without bath, £72 ($115.20) double with bath; £72 ($115.20) triple without bath, £82 ($131.20) triple with bath. All rates include English breakfast. AE, DC, MC, V. Tube: Russell Square or Holborn.

Although the hotel is named for the author John Ruskin, it is the ghost of other literary legends who lived nearby that may haunt you. In this area, Mary Godwin Shelley plotted her novel, *Frankenstein;* James Barrie fantasized about *Peter Pan;* and the provocative Olive Schreiner (1855–1920), an early feminist, advocated women's independence in sexual matters. This hotel has been managed for two decades by a hard-working family who enjoy a repeat clientele. They keep the place spic and span, if without flair; the furnishings, though well polished, are worn. Double-glazing in the front blots out the noise, but we prefer the cozily old-fashioned chambers in the rear as they open onto a park. And a pleasant surprise: There's an elevator. Private baths are usually the way to go, but here they're ridiculously small, whereas the shared baths in the hall are generous and well maintained—so we recommend saving money by opting for one of the bathless rooms. The plants in cellar-level breakfast room are a note of grace, and the breakfast is big enough to fortify you for a full day at the British Museum next door.

## COVENT GARDEN

If you stay in Covent Garden—which lies due east of both the West End and Soho—you'll be right in the thick of things. Once known for its famous flower, fruit, and "veg" market (gone since 1970), Covent Garden is today the site of London's liveliest groups of restaurants, pubs, and cafes outside Soho, and the restored marketplace is home to a wealth of trendy shops. Although there are few budget accommodations choices here, it is a great area in which to hang out. Actors, artists, and generally fashionable people populate this chic area.

**Royal Adelphi Hotel.** 21 Villiers St., London WC2N 6ND. ☎ **0171/930-8764.** Fax 0171/930-8735. 49 rms, 35 with bath. TV TEL. £40 ($64) single without bath; £57 ($91.20) single with bath; £57 ($91.20) double without bath; £75 ($120) double with bath; £96 ($153.60) triple with bath. Extra bed £15 ($24). All rates include continental breakfast. AE, DC, MC, V. Tube: Charing Cross, Embankment.

Close to Covent Garden, theaterland, and Trafalgar Square, this unorthodox choice appeals to some travelers because of its unique location outside the typical B&B stamping grounds. The hotel is upstairs above an Italian restaurant. Though the bedrooms quickly call to mind London's swinging 1960s heyday, accommodations are decently maintained and comfortable. Plumbing, however, is a bit creaky. The higher up you go, the better the view. London has far better B&Bs, but not in this part of town, where you can walk to the Victoria Embankment Garden. If you care most about location, consider this choice. The street was named for George Villiers, duke of Buckingham (1628–87), poet, courtier, wit, and dramatist. Rudyard Kipling also lived on the street (no. 43).

## VICTORIA

Directly south of Buckingham Palace is a section in Pimlico often referred to as Victoria, its namesake being the sprawling Victoria Station. Known as "Gateway to the Continent," Victoria Station is where you get buses or trains to Dover and Folkestone for the trip across the Channel to France. The British Airways Terminal, the Green Line Coach Station, and the Victoria Coach Station are all just 5 minutes from Victoria Station. From the bus stations, you can hop aboard a Green Line Coach to the suburbs. In addition, an inexpensive bus tour of London departs from a point on Buckingham Palace Road just behind the Victoria Railroad Station.

Many of the hotels along Belgrave Road are now occupied by welfare recipients; you'll find the pickings better on the satellite streets jutting off Belgrave Road. Your best bet is to walk about Ebury Street, directly to the east of Victoria Station and Buckingham Palace Road. Here you'll find some of the best moderately priced lodgings in central London.

### DOUBLES FOR LESS THAN £40

✪ **Oak House Hotel.** 29 Hugh St., London SW1V 1QJ. ☎ **0171/834-7151.** 6 rms. TV. £34 ($54.40) double. No credit cards. Tube: Victoria Station.

This little jewel of a hotel, perhaps the smallest in the area, is a real find for London, with lots of homespun charm. The Symingtons from Scotland bring the hospitality from the north of Britain to their home in the Victoria Station area. When Mr. Symington isn't putting on his kilt to do the Scottish war dance, he's out driving a London taxi. Mrs. Symington is here to welcome you to her tidily maintained bedrooms, which are small yet handsomely furnished and appointed. Singles aren't available unless one wants to pay the double rate. Half of the rooms have double beds; the others are twins. Each has beverage-making equipment, color TV, and hair dryer. The closets aren't big enough to stash a Blackbeard. Hang your garments on hooks and store your other items on shelves. Bathrooms are adequate and spotlessly maintained. Rooms are reserved only for 5 or more consecutive days.

**Romany House Hotel.** 35 Longmoore St., London SW1V 1JQ. ☎ **0171/834-5553.** Fax 0171/834-0495. 10 rms, none with bath. TV. £25 ($40) single; £35 ($56) double; £42 ($67.20) family rm for 3. All rates include English breakfast. No credit cards. Tube: Victoria Station.

Established as a hotel in 1937 when a 500-year-old cottage was joined to a 200-year-old white-fronted Georgian town house, the cottage is reputed to have been at one time a hideout for highway robbers. Rumor has it that Guy Fawkes had his last drink here before trying to blow up Parliament. The hotel's name is reportedly taken from a vision by a psychic. The owner, Jaffery Gerard, closed the hotel temporarily in the winter of 1997 to renovate it. It's now up and running again with new wiring, new furniture, new carpeting, and a new decor. All the comfortably furnished rooms have hot and cold running water, beverage-making equipment, and central heating. Shared baths in the hallway are adequate and well maintained. Since the fax number listed above is used by several companies, specify Romany House.

## DOUBLES FOR LESS THAN £55

**Caswell Hotel.** 25 Gloucester St., London SW1V 2DB. ☎ **0171/834-6345.** 18 rms, 7 with bath. TV. £39 ($62.40) single without bath, £55 ($88) single with bath; £50 ($80) double without bath, £70 ($112) double with bath. All rates include English breakfast. MC, V. Tube: Victoria Station.

In the traffic-clogged Victoria area, this hotel, run considerately and thoughtfully by Mr. and Mrs. Hare, lies on a cul-de-sac, a calm oasis in an otherwise busy area. The fancy neighbors are all gone—Mozart lived nearby when he completed his first symphony, and that "notorious couple," Harold Nicolson and Victoria Sackville-West, are long departed. But it's still a choice address. The hotel contains four floors of well-furnished bedrooms, each with such amenities as a hair dryer and beverage-making equipment. Decor is understated, and sometimes you can meet intriguing guests in the chintz-filled lobby, including one chap who told us he'd developed a perpetual motion machine, but would provide no further details. Most guests aren't that eccentric, just people seeking good, inexpensive lodgings. How do they explain the success of the place? One staff member said, "This year's guest is next year's business."

**Chesham House Hotel.** 64–66 Ebury St., London SW1W 9QD. ☎ **0171/730-8513.** Fax 0171/730-1845. 23 rms, 3 with bath. TV. £35 ($56) single without bath; £55 ($88) double without bath, £65 ($104) double with bath; £70 ($112) triple without bath; £75 ($120) quad without bath. All rates include English breakfast. AE, CB, DC, MC, V. Tube: Victoria Station.

Only 5 minutes from Victoria Station, this hotel is often cited in roundups of the best B&Bs in London. Although the street on which it stands is not as grand as it used to be, it's still prime London real estate. The street is wide and uninteresting, with little architectural distinction, yet Thomas Wolfe stayed at no. 75 in 1930 while working on *Of Time and the River*, and Noël Coward lived nearby from 1935 to 1955. The hotel consists of two brick Georgian buildings in a conversation area owned by the duke of Westminster. The buildings are connected on the top floor and in the basement breakfast area. Livinia Sillars, who owns the lease, has decorated the bedrooms in pale peach with patterned quilts and rust-colored curtains, creating a warm, cozy ambience. Rooms without bath have hot and cold running water, with well-maintained and generous shared hallway baths. However, all accommodations have a trouser press. Coffee is available every evening in the reception area. Outside are a pair of old-fashioned carriage lamps and window boxes, a facade that has won various prizes in local competitions.

**Enrico Hotel.** 77–79 Warwick Way, London SW1V 1QP. ☎ **0171/834-9538.** Fax 0171/233-9995. 26 rms, 8 with shower. £26–£30 ($41.60–$48) single without bath; £32–£38 ($51.20–$60.80) double without bath, £40–£46 ($64–$73.60) double with shower. All rates include English breakfast. MC, V. Tube: Victoria Station.

The hotels along Warwick Way have long been able to fill up every night because of their proximity to Victoria Station. Standards, for the most part, however, are low along this street. Even though it's unlikely to appear in *Architectural Digest,* the Enrico has consistently worked to maintain high standards. It charges some of the lowest rates along this well-trodden street. Bedrooms are comfortably furnished, if minimalist in decor. There are no views to speak of, and rooms can be noisy because of heavy traffic. But its a decent, money-saving option. Book a bathless room, since hallway facilities are adequate and spacious; those cramped showers are just not worth the extra pounds. The hotel has a TV room, but no TVs in individual rooms, and a public phone in the hallway.

**۞ James House/Cartref House.** 108 Ebury St. and 129 Ebury St., London SW1W 9QD. ☎ **0171/730-7338** for James House, ☎ **0171/730-6176** for Cartref House. Fax 0171/730-7338. 21 rms, 9 with bath. TV. £42 ($67.20) single without bath; £55 ($88) double without bath, £65 ($104) double with bath; £80 ($128) quad without bath, £90 ($144) quad with bath. Rates include English breakfast. MC, V. Tube: Victoria Station.

Hailed by many publications, including the *Los Angeles Times,* as one of the top 10 B&Bs in London, James House and Cartref House (across the street), deserve the accolades. Derek and Sharon James run both properties, and seem to have real dedication to their work. They are the finest hosts in the Victoria Station area. They are constantly refurbishing, so everything looks state of the art. Each room is individually designed, and some of the large rooms have bunk beds suitable for families. The generous English breakfast might allow you to skip lunch. There's no elevator, but few people complain about any inconveniences at this winning entry. Don't worry about which house you're assigned. Each is as good as the other.

**Luna & Simone Hotel.** 47–49 Belgrave Rd., London SWIV 2BB. ☎ **0171/834-5897.** Fax 0171/828-2474. 36 rms, 15 with bath or shower. TV. £35–£42 ($56–$67.20) single; £40–£57 ($64–$91.20) double; £60–£69 ($96–$110.40) triple. All rates include English breakfast. MC, V. Tube: Victoria Station.

Most of the B&Bs along Belgrave Road, one of the main low-budget hotel streets of London, are too tacky to recommend. On our last inspection, we were about to give up after going through seven of these little horrors. Then we spotted Luna & Simone, which, although impersonally furnished, is one of the better bets along this street. We wish the beds were a little softer and the place had more style, but it is neat and well run. The rooms have hot and cold running water, and you're close to Victoria Station's transportation network. The front rooms are subject to traffic noise, and the view from the rear chambers is hardly of a Devonshire primrose path. This family-run place is a respectable address in spite of its drawbacks. Consider it for its convenient location and its comparatively low price.

**Oxford House Hotel.** 92–94 Cambridge St., London SW1V 4QG. ☎ **0171/834-6467.** Fax 0171/834-0225. 17 rms, none with bath. £32–£35 ($51.20–$56) single; £42–£45 ($67.20–$72) double; £54–£58 ($86.40–$92.80) triple; £72–£76 ($115.20–$121.60) quad. All rates include English breakfast. MC, V. Tube: Victoria Station.

This 1840s Victorian town house is on a quiet one-way street (which taxi drivers have difficulty finding), only a few blocks from Victoria Station. It's owned and operated by an India-born interior designer, Y. A. Kader, and his Irish wife, Terry. They don't like dustballs to collect, and the place is immaculate. It's a real homey place, with Mr. Kader helping with breakfast before leaving for work, and Mrs. Kader staying behind to assist with guest needs throughout the day. They are particularly kind to cost-cutting travelers making their first journey to London. The place overflows with sons and pets, and it has a real homespun quality. Each room is decorated with flowery fabrics and coordinated bedspreads and carpets. Single rooms are rather small and cramped, and up on the fourth floor. The copious breakfast is served in a cozy cellar-level room.

**Vandon House.** 1 Vandon St., off Buckingham Gate, SW1H 0AH. ☎ **0171/799-6780.** Fax 0171/799-1464. 40 rms, 20 with bath or shower. TV TEL. £31 ($49.60) single without bath, £39 ($62.40) single with bath; £48 ($76.80) double without bath, £61.50 ($98.40) double with bath; £89 ($142.40) triple with bath, £112.50 ($180) quad with bath. All rates include an English breakfast. AE, DC, MC, V. Tube: St. James's Park.

Smokers and drinkers will be shown the door here. Otherwise, this is an off-beat budget choice. Owned and run by the Salvation Army, it was for nearly a quarter of a century a charity center dispensing a free bed and a free meal in the tradition of the famous musical, *Guys and Dolls.* Completely overhauled, it was converted into a modest hotel and restaurant. There are drawbacks: The desk is open only from 6:30am until 12:30am, and you're not given a front door key. despite the fact that the clean bedrooms might resemble your college dorm, the attitude here can be slightly stuffy.

Bedrooms have beverage-making facilities ("acceptable" beverages) and hot and cold running water. Some even have a trouser press, and many are equipped with a small bath and shower. Even if you're not staying here, consider their proper English restaurant open Monday through Friday for morning coffee and lunch. A few diners look like Margaret Rutherford in those Miss Marple movies, but where else can you get a good cottage pie, much less a toad-in-the-hole these days?

## DOUBLES FOR LESS THAN £70

**Astors Hotel.** 110–112 Ebury St., London SW1W 9QD. ☎ **0171/730-3811.** Fax 0171/823-6728. 22 rms, 12 with bath. TV. £35–£37 ($56–$59.20) single without bath, £47–£50 ($75.20–$80) single with bath; £52–£55 ($83.20–$88) double without bath, £58–£60 ($92.80–$96) double with bath; £75 ($120) triple without bath, £78 ($124.80) triple with bath. All rates include English breakfast. MC, V. Tube: Victoria Station.

If you'd like a convenient location for your tea with the queen, this might be your best bet. You're not only situated for convenient trips to Buckingham Palace, you're just 5 minutes from the main-line and tube stations of Victoria. The brick-fronted Victorian house was once the home of Margaret Oliphant (1828–97), a popular Victorian novelist. Noël Coward was a neighbor for 20 years, and the great literary men of their time, Wells, Yeats, Bennett, and Shaw came to call when George Moore (1852–1933), the poet, novelist, and racy autobiographer was in residence at no. 153. The guests today don't have such pedigrees, but are travelers looking for a decent, affordable, and respectable address in pricey Londontown. They can find that here, although not a lot of style. Rooms are functional but satisfactory in every way. Space and furnishings vary greatly, so, ask to take a little peek before committing yourself to an overnight stay. Since the hotel is often full, that won't always be possible.

**Ebury House.** 102 Ebury St., London SW1W 9QD. ☎ **0171/730-1350.** Fax 0171/259-0400. 12 rms, none with bath. TV. £45 ($72) single; £60 ($96) double; £75 ($120) triple; £85 ($136) family rm for 4. All rates include English breakfast. MC, V. Tube: Victoria Station.

In days of yore (1920), Ruth Draper wrote: "I was very lucky in finding a sunny top floor room . . . a lovely big double room in front and I am so comfortably fixed . . . for one guinea ($1.05) a week." Only the price has changed. The Baroness Margaret Thatcher lives just around the corner—look for her on the street. This comfortable guest house stands out among its competition here, mainly because of the greeting you get from its owner-manager, Peter Evans. All the bedrooms, fairly plain, are well maintained and have hot and cold running water and hair dryers. There is one full bath per floor and a pay phone on one of the stairwells, in case you need to call home for money. "We get just as many Canadians and Aussies as Yanks," a staff member confided. "They seem to like us." Reserve well in advance in summer as this is not a secret among budget addresses. The pine-paneled breakfast room is the establishment's morning rendezvous point. We were recently delighted to see three copies of this guide at tables.

**Hamilton House Hotel.** 60 Warwick Way, London SW1V 1SA. ☎ **0171/821-7113.** Fax 0171/630-0806. 40 rms, 25 with bath. TV TEL. £44 ($70.40) single without bath, £56 ($89.60) single with bath; £56 ($89.60) double without bath, £60 ($96) double with bath; £82 ($131.20) triple. All rates include English breakfast. MC, V. Tube: Victoria Station.

Admittedly, there is some sterility here, but its renovated bedrooms and comfort—as well as its prices—make it a good choice. The bedrooms have been modernized, and have satellite TV, radio, and a reasonably soothing decor. Most have private plumbing. The hotel lies just off Warwick Square, home for many years of the fabled Oxford University Press, where Charles Williams (1886–1945) was long-time editor. The front rooms can be noisy. The more tranquil rooms are located in the rear, especially those on the third floor. Many shower stalls were added in spaces not really designed for that purpose. A simple restaurant serving English food is on the premises, along with a fully licensed bar.

**Harcourt House.** 50 Ebury St., London SW1W 0LU. ☎ **0171/730-2722.** Fax 0171/730-3998. 10 rms, all with showers. TV. £50 ($80) single; £60 ($96) double. All rates include English breakfast. AE, MC, V. Tube: Victoria Station.

Back in 1890 this was one of the gentleman's clubs in the area, but by the 1940s it had become a spy headquarters for an American sending secret reports to Washington. Since 1980 David and Glesni Wood have turned it into one of the better B&Bs in this popular area. They have seriously upgraded the place, and even if the rooms overdose on flower reproductions—on the walls, on the bedspreads, and on the curtains—it is still a good value for the neighborhood. Recently all the rooms had showers added, even if in some you may as if you were showering in a phone booth. TVs, hair dryers, and full central heating make the place more inviting than ever. If you dream of living in a London garret, take those steep stairs to the top and room 9. The major rail, coach, and tube stations are a 5-minute walk from the Harcourt.

**Melbourne House Hotel.** 79 Belgrave Rd., London SW1V 2BG. ☎ **0171/828-3516.** Fax 0171/828-7120. 16 rms, all with showers. TV TEL. £45 ($72) single; £65 ($104) double; £80 ($128) triple; £100 ($160) quad. All rates include English breakfast. MC, V. Tube: Victoria Station.

If you *must* stay on Belgrave Road—and thousands upon thousands of travelers opt for this budget street annually—consider Melbourne House, which for obvious reasons attracts a slew of Australian visitors. Its bedrooms are better than its nearby competitor, Luna & Simone Hotel, to which you may want to retreat if you can't get in here. It's a family-run hotel with the same management for two decades. Unlike some other grubby choices along this street, the Melbourne is friendly and clean. Totally refurbished but still evocative of a student dorm in Stockholm, the hotel is neat and well polished. Each room is equipped with TV, phone, and beverage-making facilities, and showers have bi-fold doors with very good soft water pressure. King Edward VII would get stuck in the narrow bathtub, but that happened to him at the Ritz in Paris. John and Manuela Desira are congenial hosts and are proud of the repeat travelers who show up on their doorstep every time they're in London.

**Pyms Hotel.** 118 Ebury St., London SW1W 9QC. ☎ **0171/730-4986.** Fax 0171/730-2357. 12 rms, 2 with bath. TV. £40 ($64) single without bath; £60 ($96) double without bath; £75 ($120) double with bath. All rates include English breakfast. AE, CB, MC, V. Tube: Victoria Station.

This "home away from home" in Belgravia lies between Sloane Square and Victoria, just a 3-minute walk from the Victoria Station and its tube stop. The terraced Victorian enjoys a reputation for being "squeaky clean" and rents well-furnished rooms, not the chipped paint and tattered furnishings so often encountered in Victoria Station's B&Bs. Laminated white furniture is a welcome change from the usual flea market stuff. The manager is a Japanese woman who keeps the hallway facilities in mint condition. In general, the place not only charges fair prices but is run efficiently with a welcoming (but not effusive) hospitality. Be warned: There's no elevator but there are other conveniences, including a safe to store your valuables and a public phone in the hall. The full English breakfast—generous in size—is well prepared, fit fortification for a day of London sightseeing.

**Winchester Hotel.** 17 Belgrave Rd., London SW1 1RB. ☎ **0171/828-2972.** Fax 0171/828-5191. 18 rms, all with baths. TV TEL. £65 ($104) double; £85 ($136) triple; £95 ($152) quad. All rates include full English breakfast. No credit cards. Tube: Victoria Station.

One of the best choices along grubby Belgrave Road, this hotel is a privately owned family affair, with an engaging host, Jimmy McGoldrick. The bedrooms have been recently refurbished, and are cozy and comfortable. Many, regrettably, are quite small, so hopefully you won't arrive with too many suitcases. Rooms have private baths, albeit cramped, and there's a sleek modernity throughout, not cozily quaint like many London hostelries. Rooms also have radio and intercom service. McGoldrick sees that his staff maintains a high level of service and cleanliness, a standard that too often doesn't apply to Belgrave Road B&Bs.

## KNIGHTSBRIDGE & BELGRAVIA

Belgravia, south of Hyde Park, is the aristocratic quarter of London, challenging Mayfair for grandness. It's near Buckingham Palace Gardens and Brompton Road; the center is Belgrave Square, one of the more attractive plazas in London. A few town houses once occupied by eminent Edwardians have been discreetly turned into moderately priced hotels—whereas others were built specifically to house guests. Remember, however, that Belgravia is an exclusive address among Londoners, and this pricey district is not overly budget-friendly.

Several major department stores (including Harrods) are in Knightsbridge, a top residential and shopping district adjoining Belgravia just south of Hyde Park. Knightsbridge approximates Belgravia in character, and much of this section to the west of Sloane Street has a distinctive 18th-century architecture and urban layout.

✪ **Diplomat Hotel.** 2 Chesham St., London SW1X 8DT. ☎ **0171/235-1544.** Fax 0171/259-6153. 27 rms. TV TEL. £80 ($128) single; £115 ($184) double. All rates include English breakfast buffet. AE, CB, DC, MC, V. Tube: Sloane Square.

# Accommodations: Kensington to Belgravia

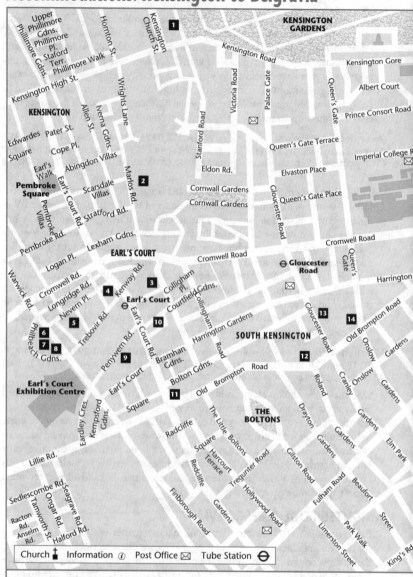

Church ‡   Information ⓘ   Post Office ✉   Tube Station ⊖

## ACCOMMODATIONS

Abbey House **1**
Apollo Hotel/Atlas Hotel **2**
Aston's Budget Studios **12**
Beaver Hotel **7**
Diplomat Hotel **16**
Halifax **7**
Henley House **10**

Hotel 167 **14**
Knightsbridge Hotel **15**
Magnolia Hotel **18**
Nevern Hotel **5**
Oalkey Hotel **19**
Periquito Hotel Kensington **10**
Philbeach Hotel **6**

Plaza Continental **3**
New York Hotel **8**
Rushmore Hotel **4**
Swiss House **11**
Vicarage Private Hotel **1**
Wilbraham Hotel **17**
Windsor House Hotel **9**

3-0580

90

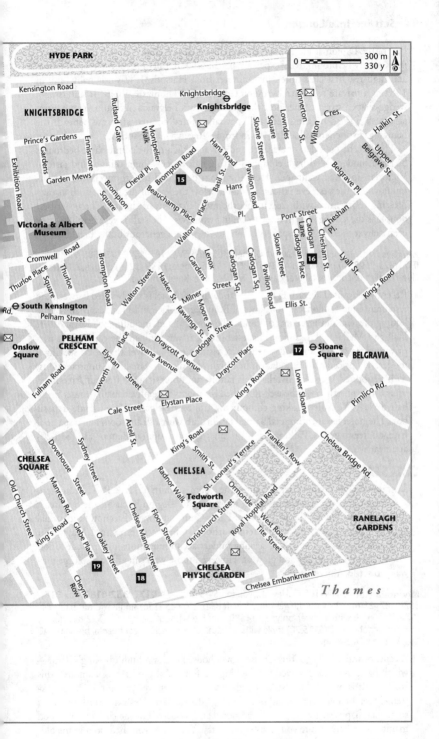

HYDE PARK

KNIGHTSBRIDGE

Kensington Road

Prince's Gardens

Ennismore Gardens

Garden Mews

Exhibition Road

Rutland Gate

Montpelier Walk

Cheval Pl.

Brompton Square

Brompton Road

Beauchamp Place

Knightsbridge

Knightsbridge

Hans Road

Sloane Street

Knightsbridge Square

Lowndes Square

Kinnerton St.

Wilton Cres.

Halkin St.

Upper Belgrave St.

Belgrave Pl.

Basil St.

Hans

Pl.

Pavilion Road

Pont Street

Cadogan Lane

Cadogan Place

Belgrave Pl.

Cheshan Pl.

Lyall St.

15

i

Victoria & Albert Museum

Cromwell Road

Thurloe Place

Thurloe Square

Thurloe

South Kensington

Rd.

Pelham Street

Brompton Road

Walton Street

Hasker St.

Walton

Lenox Gardens

Milner

Rawlings St.

Moore St.

Cadogan Street

Cadogan Sq.

Cadogan Sq.

Street

Sloane Street

Pavilion Road

Ellis St.

Chesham St.

16

King's Road

Onslow Square

PELHAM CRESCENT

Fulham Road

Ixworth Place

Elystan Street

Sloane Avenue

Draycott Avenue

Cadogan Street

Draycott Place

17

Sloane Square

BELGRAVIA

Lower Sloane

Pimlico Rd.

Cale Street

Astell St.

Elystan Place

King's Road

King's Road

Smith St.

Draycott Place

King's Road

Franklin's Row

Chelsea Bridge Rd.

CHELSEA SQUARE

Dovehouse Street

Manresa Rd.

Sydney Street

Glebe Place

Old Church Street

King's Road

Cheyne Row

Oakley Street

Chelsea Manor Street

Flood Street

Radnor Walk

CHELSEA

St. Leonard's Terrace

Christchurch Street

Tedworth Square

Ormonde

Royal Hospital Road

West Road

Tite Street

RANELAGH GARDENS

19

18

CHELSEA PHYSIC GARDEN

Chelsea Embankment

Thames

0    300 m
     330 y
N

91

Part of the Diplomat Hotel's allure lies in its status as a small, reasonably priced hotel in an otherwise prohibitively expensive neighborhood, full of private Victorian homes and high-rise first-class hotels just minutes from Harrods. It was originally built in 1882 as a private residence by the noted architect Thomas Cubbitt. It stands on a wedge-shaped street corner near the site of today's Belgravia Sheraton. You register at a desk framed by the sweep of a partially gilded circular staircase beneath the benign gaze of cherubs looking down from a Regency-era chandelier.

The Regency is a den of elegance and privacy. Each of the comfortable bedrooms boasts a modern tiled bath equipped with a hair dryer, a high ceiling, and tasteful Victorian-inspired wallpaper. Here the room dedicated to Cromwell (for reasons unknown) is the best, even though it's a bit below the level of the street. With its own dressing room lined with closets, it's the most spacious of the lot. The other best double is the Cadogan with floor-to-ceiling windows. The staff is very helpful—they even deliver morning newspapers before serving you a generous buffet breakfast.

**Knightsbridge Hotel.** 12 Beaufort Gardens, London SW3 1PT. ☎ **0171/589-9271.** Fax 0171/823-9692. 40 rms. MINIBAR TV TEL. £85 ($136) single; £135 ($216) double. All rates include English or continental breakfast. AE, MC, V. Tube: Knightsbridge.

Recently renovated according to high standards, this hotel is sandwiched between the restaurants and fashionable boutiques of Beauchamp Place and Harrods. Many of the leading theaters and museums of London lie close at hand, including the Royal Albert Hall and Madame Tussaud's. This establishment was built in the early 1800s as a private town house, and today it attracts visitors from all over the world seeking a moderately priced accommodation in a high-rent district. Small and unpretentious, with a subdued Victorian overlay, this family-run hotel sits on a tranquil, tree-lined square, free of traffic. All the well-furnished bedrooms have private bath, trouser press, hair dryer, TV, coffee-making equipment, minibar/refrigerator, and a safe-deposit box. The hotel has incorporated a small health club with a steam room and a spa pool bath, all free to guests. Parking is free on the street from 6pm to 8am or £12 ($19.20) at a nearby garage.

## CHELSEA

This fashionable district stretches along the Thames, south of Hyde Park, Brompton, and South Kensington, and its main thoroughfare. Beginning at Sloane Square, it runs westward toward the periphery of Earl's Court and West Brompton; its spinal cord is King's Road. As a chic neighborhood, Chelsea doesn't trail Mayfair or Belgravia by much. The visitor seeking budget accommodations might wish to follow Greeley's sage advice and go west. However, those who can afford a splurge may want to settle in here.

**Magnolia Hotel.** 104–105 Oakley St., London SW3 5NT. ☎ **0171/352-0187.** Fax 0171/352-0187. 25 rms, 12 with shower only, 5 with bath. TV. £35 ($56) single without bath, £47 ($75.20) single with shower only; £50 ($80) double without bath, £58 ($92.80) double with shower only; £72 ($115.20) triple without bath. All rates include continental breakfast. AE, MC, V. Tube: Sloane Square.

A century and a half ago, this Chelsea town house hotel was built off King's Road—which back then was reserved for the king. "Lifestyles of the Rich & Famous," this isn't, but it is one of the best-kept little B&Bs in the entire area, and it charges extremely reasonable prices in a "silk stocking" district. Fabrics and furnishings are a somewhat haphazardly medley of traditional and modern, but the comfort and good maintenance here ensure you an affordable stay. You get to your bedroom in the old-fashioned way: you climb the stairs. The little breakfast nook is cozily decorated with shiny copper pots and pans.

**Oakley Hotel.** 73 Oakley St., London SW3 5HF. ☎ **0171/352-5599.** Fax 0171/727-1190. 13 rms, none with bath. £29 ($46.40) single; £38–£49 ($60.80–$78.40) double; £49 ($78.40) triple; £63 ($100.80) quad. All rates include English breakfast. AE, MC, V. Tube: South Kensington; then a £4 ($6.40) taxi ride to hotel or bus 11 or 19 down King's Rd.

A solid and reliable budget choice, this brick-fronted Victorian row house lies north of the Chelsea Embankment and can be reached by a 10-minute taxi from Victoria Station. It's back to basics here. Back in the Victorian era, you would have had an elegant neighbor at no. 87: Lady Jane Wilde ("Speranza"), the poetess, Irish patriot, and pamphleteer best known for giving birth to Oscar Wilde. She lived here from 1886 until her death, and her home became the literary shrine of London. You can have free tea and coffee whenever you want it, and the communal kitchen facilities include a refrigerator and a hot plate. Everything but food is provided for preparing your own meals. Some rooms are large enough for three or four beds; these are rented at low rates. Rooms are comfortable, but you'd hardly call the flea-market furnishings elegant. Some of the shared rooms are really dorm style. There is no hotel sign outside as these are forbidden by local ordinance. The inn has a small garden accessed through the kitchen door. You can take breakfast here if you wish.

**Wilbraham Hotel.** 1–5 Wilbraham Place (off Sloane St.), London SW1X 9AE. ☎ **0171/730-8296.** Fax 0171/730-6815. 53 rms, 6 suites. TV TEL. £57 ($91.20) single; £86–£88 ($137.60–$140.80) double; from £89 ($142.40) suite. No credit cards. Tube: Sloane Square. Parking £12 ($19.20).

This is a dyed-in-the-wool British hotel set on a quiet residential street just a few hundred yards from Sloane Square. If she were alive today, you'd expect Margaret Rutherford to check in. The hotel occupies three Victorian town houses that have been joined together. Sure, it's faded a bit, but the bedrooms are furnished in a traditional style and are well maintained, with fireplaces, leaded glass windows, and wood paneling. The best double—certainly the most spacious—is number 1. Even the towel racks are heated in the bathroom, a lovely, comfort on a cold gray London morning. On the premises is an attractive and old-fashioned lounge, Victorian-styled Bar and Buttery, where you can order drinks, simple lunches, and veddy English dinners.

## KENSINGTON

Kensington, the Royal Borough (W8), not only has great shopping along Kensington High Street; it also contains a number of fine middle-class guest houses, which are located mostly west of Kensington Gardens. This district, close to Kensington Palace, is a convenient place to stay. The rows of houses along Kensington Palace Gardens were once inhabited by millionaires (though Thackeray also lived here). Today the houses are the residences of a good number of foreign ambassadors.

Brompton and South Kensington (SW7), south of Kensington Gardens and Hyde Park, are essentially residential areas, just a notch below the elegance of bordering Belgravia and Knightsbridge. The section is, however, rich in museums—in fact, it's often dubbed "museumland"—and it has a number of colleges and institutes, which draw large numbers of students.

✪ **Abbey House.** 11 Vicarage Gate, London W8 4AG. ☎ **0171/727-2594.** 16 rms, none with bath. TV. £60 ($96) double; £74 ($118.40) triple; £86 ($137.60) quad. All rates include English breakfast. No credit cards. Tube: Kensington High Street.

Some hotel critics have rated this the best B&B in London, and it's recommended by more travel guides than any other B&B in London. It must be doing something right—and it is, offering peace, tranquillity, and affordable rates given its adjacency to Kensington Gardens and the Royal Palace. It's a family-run business, with a keen

---

### ⊕  Family-Friendly Hotels

**Avalon Private Hotel** (*see p. 80*)   In the heart of Bloomsbury, near the British Museum, this 19th-century Georgian town house rents many rooms to families of three or four. Guests also have use of a semiprivate, horseshoe-shaped garden across the street. Children enjoy the park while Mom and Dad play tennis.

**James House/Cartref House** (*see p. 86*)   There is no better address for the value-oriented family in the Victoria Station area than this charmer. Two houses, many with rooms big enough for four, stand on opposite sides of the streets. Some have bunk beds for families.

---

sense of dedication and hospitality. The hotel, built in about 1860 on a typical Victorian square, is renovated and modern, though many of the original features have been retained. Gone are the former bishop and member of parliament who used to live here, giving way to the savvy collector of that small London hotel who wants charm, a touch of class, and a bright, cheery address. The spacious bedrooms have central heating, vanity lights, and hot- and cold-water basins. The hotel's decor may be too frilly for some. The hotel offers shared baths, one to each two-lodging unit. The rooms are refurbished annually. Considering how well run and maintained it is, it gets top marks for value.

✪ **Vicarage Private Hotel.** 10 Vicarage Gate, London W8 4AG. ☎ **0171/229-4030.** Fax 0171/792-5289. 18 rms, none with bath. £36 ($57.60) single; £60 ($96) double; £75 ($120) triple; £84 ($134.40) quad. All rates include English breakfast. No credit cards. Tube: Kensington High Street or Notting Hill Gate.

Eileen and Martin Diviney have a host of admirers on all continents. Their hotel is tops for old-fashioned English charm, affordable prices, and hospitality. A family-run hotel, this Victorian town house retains many original features. It's on a residential garden square close to the shopping bargains of High Street Kensington, Knightsbridge, and Portobello Market. Furnished individually in a homey, English country house style, bedrooms are suitable for singles, couples, or families up to four. Guests meet in a cozy sitting room for conversation or else to watch the telly. As a thoughtful extra, hot drinks are available 24 hours a day. If you want a little nest to hide away in, opt for the top floor eyrie (no. 19), a private little retreat—like Noël Coward used to occupy before he "got rich enough to move downstairs." A hearty English breakfast awaits you.

## BROMPTON & SOUTH KENSINGTON

**Apollo Hotel/Atlas Hotel.** 18–30 Lexham Gardens, London W8 5JU. ☎ **0171/835-1133.** Fax 0171/370-4853. 48 rms in the Apollo Hotel; 54 rms, 45 with bath in the Atlas Hotel. TV TEL. £30 ($48) single without bath, £58–£60 ($92.80–$96) single with bath; £68–£70 ($108.80–$112) double with bath; £78–£80 ($124.80–$128) triple with bath. All rates include continental breakfast. AE, DC, MC, V. Tube: Gloucester Road or Earl's Court.

Both these hotels were originally built as private houses around 1860, and both lie adjacent to one another on a quiet residential street in Kensington, just off Cromwell Road. Despite their proximity and ownership by the same entrepreneur, they maintain separate check-in facilities and entrances, with no connecting doorways. Both have five stories, no-frills bedrooms, and elevators that service all floors. The Atlas is especially recommended for the solo traveler because of its large number of singles. The hotels maintain individual breakfast rooms, but share a bar (it's within the Atlas Hotel). There's a high turnover of clients and an inevitable sense of anonymity, but despite those drawbacks these two hotels have provided clean and uncomplicated (if somewhat cramped) accommodations for thousands of foreign tourists over several decades. The bathless rooms in the hotels are almost always classified as singles.

⭐ **Aston's Budget Studios.** 39 Rosary Gardens, London SW7 4NQ. ☎ **800/525-2810** in the U.S., or 0171/370-0737. Fax 0171/835-1419. 60 studios and apts, 38 with bath. A/C TV TEL. Budget Studios: £41 ($65.60) single; £42 ($67.20) double; £93 ($148.80) triple; £109 ($174.40) quad. Designer Studios: £105 ($168) double. MC, V. Tube: Gloucester Road.

In a restored row of interconnected Victorian town houses, this establishment offers a carefree alternative to the traditional hotel, and many readers find it well suited to their needs. It features comfortably furnished studios and suites, usually (but not always) rented by the week, combining 19th-century nostalgia with the convenience and economy of self-catering. Heavy oak doors and collections of 18th-century hunting scenes give the Aston foyer a traditional atmosphere.

Accommodations are available in Budget Studios or Designer Studios. Regardless of its price, each unit has lots of convenient extras which always include—concealed behind doors—a compact but complete kitchenette. The Budget Studios have fully serviced bathrooms, shared with a handful of other guests. The Designer Studios are decorated with color-coordinated fabrics and furnishings, contain marble-sheathed private bathrooms and have answering machines.

**Hotel 167.** 167 Old Brompton Rd., London SW5 0AN. ☎ **0171/373-0672.** Fax 0171/373-3360. 18 rms. MINIBAR TV TEL. £60–£70 ($96–$112) single; £75–£82 ($120–$131.20) double. Additional bed in rm £14 ($22.40) extra. All rates include continental breakfast. AE, DC, MC, V. Tube: Gloucester Road or South Kensington.

One of the area's more fashionable guest houses, this is sheltered in a Victorian-era, formerly private town house. Including the basement, here there are four floors of living space, all smartly done. Each room is a comfortable medley of contemporary, antique, and Art Deco, with big modern paintings decorating the walls. The basement rooms have big windows. Guests who are at first unsure about being assigned a room in the basement often end up requesting the same room when they return because of its cozy feeling. *Tattler* magazine has compared Hotel 167 with Blakes and Portobello for its amenities, but we wouldn't get that carried away. The hotel attracts many businesspeople and journalists because of its central location. The British rock group Manic Street Preachers wrote a song about the hotel, though it's impossible to judge if the added publicity attracted patrons or scared them away. Owner-manager Frank Cheevers is helpful and friendly, and is a font of information about London.

## EARL'S COURT

Another popular hotel and rooming-house district is the area in and around Earl's Court, below Kensington, bordering the western half of Chelsea. A 15-minute tube ride from the Earl's Court Station will take you into the heart of Piccadilly, via either the District or Piccadilly Line. The area is convenient to both the West End Air Terminal and the exhibition halls. A young crowd is attracted to the district at night, principally to a number of pubs, wine bars, and coffeehouses. In summer, Australians stake out the cheap B&B houses.

### DOUBLES FOR LESS THAN £60

**Beaver Hotel.** 57–59 Philbeach Gardens, London SW5 9ED. ☎ **0171/373-4553.** Fax 0171/373-4555. 38 rms, 24 with bath. TV TEL. £30 ($48) single without bath, £50 ($80) single with bath; £45 ($72) double without bath, £70 ($112) double with bath; £81 ($129.60) triple with bath. All rates include English breakfast. AE, DC, MC, V. Tube: Earl's Court.

On a quiet, tree-lined crescent of Victorian terrace houses dating from the Silver Jubilee of Queen Victoria in 1887, this four-floor hotel offers a choice of rooms. Newly refurbished rooms have private baths; these are the most spacious. Many of the bathless rooms are a bit cramped. Some family rooms contain three beds, and two rooms offer waterbeds. The cheaper basic rooms have hot and cold running water, but there are adequate hallway facilities. Drinks and snacks are available in the self-serve bar. There's also a small pool table and free coffee all day. Breakfast is served in a wood-paneled room that has a touch of the Tyrol about it; the morning specials are written on a blackboard.

**Halifax.** 65 Philbeach Gardens, London SW5 9EE. ☎ **0171/373-4153.** 15 rms, 5 with shower. £30 ($48) single without shower, £38 ($60.80) single with shower; £45 ($72) double without shower, £56 ($89.60) double with shower. All rates include continental breakfast. AE, DC, MC, V. Tube: Earl's Court.

This hotel is often called "Kangaroo Court" because it's the unofficial headquarters of London's large Aussie student community, many of whom seek lodgings at this (relatively) low-budget hotel. Although some hotels around here are among the worst in the city, others, especially some entries along Philbeach Gardens, are quite acceptable. This Victorian town house, a former private residence, has been converted, and up-to-date amenities such as central heating and private, although a bit creaky plumbing, have been added. Bedrooms are modestly but adequately furnished. A few private showers were added in cramped conditions not designed for them. Guests are given their own keys, so they can come and go as they wish. The hotel opens onto a tree-lined crescent near Earl's Court tube stop.

**Nevern Hotel.** 31 Nevern Place, London SW5 9NP. ☎ **0171/370-4827.** Fax 0171/370-1541. 34 rms, 15 with bath or shower. TV TEL. £26–£42 ($41.60–$67.20) single; £36–£62 ($57.60–$99.20) double; £48–£69 ($76.80–$110.40) triple; £60–£80 ($96–$128) quad; £70–£90 ($112–$144) quintet. All rates include continental breakfast. AE, MC, V. Tube: Earl's Court.

Although we've known more welcoming B&Bs, Nevern is still recommendable for its budget prices. The cheapest rates cited above are charged from October to March; otherwise, you pay the higher tariffs. Many of the bedrooms are more spacious than the norm. Each room is furnished in a neutral offensive tone—although the brown curtains would block out a Spanish sun—and most have cramped shower or bathroom facilities along with a toilet. There's a passenger elevator to take you to the rooms. Breakfast is sometimes a communal affair in a bright, pine-paneled room, where, for an extra charge, an English breakfast is available.

**Philbeach Hotel.** 30–31 Philbeach Gardens, London SW5 9EB. ☎ **0171/373-1244.** Fax 0171/244-0149. 40 rms, 20 with bath. TV TEL. £55 ($88) double without bath, £65 ($104) double with bath. All rates include breakfast. AE, DC, MC, V. Tube: Earl's Court.

Catering to a mostly gay (male and female) clientele, this pleasant hotel is composed of two adjacent Victorian row houses. Today painted white, with a facade accented by a green awning, the establishment sports a verdant garden in back. Bedrooms are cozy and comfortable, although simply furnished; they are connected via intercom to telephone calls that arrive for residents at the front desk.

The restaurant on the premises, Wild About Oscar, is adorned with portraits of the restaurant's obvious namesake, Oscar Wilde. The excellent cuisine is mainly French, and both a fixed-price menu and a la carte specialties are offered nightly. Open daily for dinner from 7 to 10:30pm.

**Windsor House Hotel.** 12 Penywern Rd., Earl's Court, London SW5 9ST. ☎ **0171/ 373-9087.** Fax 0171/385-2417. 20 rms, 12 with shower or bath. £22–£32 ($35.20–$51.20) single without bath, £34–£44 ($54.40–$70.40) single with bath; £44 ($70.40) double without bath, £48 ($76.80) double with bath; £68 ($108.80) quad without bath, £78 ($124.80) quad with bath. MC, V. Tube: Earl's Court.

This hotel, the simplest of budget accommodations, will not appeal to everyone. Still, several readers (especially those looking for inexpensive rooms suitable for four occupants) report favorably on its battered but congenial premises.

Originally built in 1842 as a private, stucco-clad town house, this hotel sacrifices a lobby in favor of additional rooms. The polite and amiable owner, Jan Wardle, offers ultrasimple but immaculate bedrooms. There's a camaraderie among clients who associate in the cellar-level breakfast room for afternoon tea (which they prepare for themselves in a small communal kitchen). A pay phone, a shared TV, and—perhaps best of all—a small walled-in garden in back round out the hotel's amenities.

## DOUBLES FOR LESS THAN £85

**Henley House.** 30 Barkston Gardens, London SW5 0EN. ☎ **0171/370-4111.** Fax 0171/370-0026. 20 rms. A/C MINIBAR TV TEL. £59–£70 ($94.40–$112) single; £89–£99 ($142.50–$158.40) double. All rates include continental breakfast. AE, DC, MC, V. Tube: Earl's Court.

This is a standout among the B&Bs around Earl's Court. Barkston Gardens might even become the classic address it used to be when Dame Ellen Terry (1847–1928), the great actress and friend and correspondent of G. B. Shaw, lived nearby at no. 22. This red-brick Victorian row house sits in front of a communal fenced-in garden that guests can enter by borrowing a key from the reception desk. With a bright contemporary decor, Henley House is newly refurbished. The guest rooms have matching curtains and wallpaper, and a ground-floor sitting room overlooks a rear courtyard. A typical room has warmly patterned Anna French wallpaper, chintz-lined curtains, chintz bedspreads, rugs, cushions, and solid brass lighting fixtures. A ground-floor sitting room overlooks a rear courtyard.

**New York Hotel.** 32 Philbeach Gardens, London SW5 9EB. ☎ **0171/244-6884.** Fax 0171/370-4961. 16 rms, 2 with bath. TV TEL. £55 ($88) single with bath; £50 ($80) double with shared bath; £80 ($128) double with bath. All rates include breakfast. AE, MC, V. Tube: Earl's Court.

Another option, though less well-run than others, is this hotel, which caters to a mostly gay male clientele. On a quiet residential street, it offers bland but comfortable bedrooms. On the premises is La Liberté, a dinner restaurant.

**Periquito Hotel Kensington.** 34–44 Barkston Gardens, London SW5 0EW. ☎ **0171/373-7851.** Fax 0171/370-6570. 81 rms. TV TEL. Sun–Thurs £77 ($123.20) single or double; Fri–Sat £85 ($136) single or double. AE, DC, MC, V. Tube: Earl's Court.

When it was first established in 1905, this hotel offered B&B at 5p (10¢) a head, and it rapidly expanded to eventually include six adjoining town houses. By the 1960s it was the first hotel in London acquired by the then-minor Forte Hotel Group, which went on to become one of the world's largest hotel empires. In 1993 the hotel was bought and radically renovated by a British chain, Periquito, noted for its cost-conscious prices. Bedrooms are comfortably contemporary, and filled with the bright primary colors for which the chain is known. Each contains cable-connected TV, a coffeemaker, and a hair dryer. On the premises is a bar and restaurant, called Bistro, decorated in a French country style, serving standard food known more for its affordable prices than its high quality.

**Plaza Continental.** 9 Knaresborough Place, London SW5 0TP. ☎ **0171/370-3246.** Fax 0171/373-9571. 20 rms. TV TEL. £52 ($83.20) single; £76 ($121.60) double; £94 ($150.40) triple. All rates include continental breakfast. AE, DC, MC, V. Tube: Earl's Court.

This newly refurbished B&B is in a white-fronted Victorian row house originally built in the 1870s. Privately owned and managed, it's in a quiet neighborhood about a 2-minute walk from the tube stop, opposite the privately run Cromwell Hospital and a few minutes walk from the Earl's Court and Olympia Exhibition Centres. Each of the compact rooms contains a radio and hot-beverage facilities, and the hotel has full central heating and an elevator. Since rooms may vary in standard, try to get a look at one before agreeing to a firm booking. The bedroom decor is color coordinated, but don't expect miracles here. While you might not want to call this place home, it does provide a good stop over for a night or a few days during your London sojourn.

**Rushmore Hotel.** 11 Trebovir Rd., London SW5 9LS. ☎ **0171/370-3839.** Fax 0171/370-0274. 22 rms. TV TEL. £59 ($94.40) single; £69 ($110.40) double; £79 ($126.40) triple; £89 ($142.40) family rm for 4 or 5. All rates include buffet breakfast. AE, MC, V. Tube: Earl's Court.

Although it had functioned as a run-down hotel since the early 1970s, this Victorian row house received a complete overhaul in 1987, when members of the Saloojee family radically renovated and upgraded it. Today it's one of the most acceptable hotels in a neighborhood filled with sometimes undesirable properties. With a multilingual staff who work hard to make a visit to London rewarding, the hotel offers satellite TV reception and well-maintained, individually decorated rooms. Some singles are woefully small, whereas the rooms in what used to be the attic, beneath sloping eaves, are some of the largest. On the premises are security boxes for valuables and most of the basic services a traveler would need (including dry cleaning, laundry, theater bookings, fax transmissions, and baby-sitting), sometimes at reduced rates. The reception desk also has the authority to rent about 20 apartments in the neighborhood for periods of a week or more. Depending on their size and amenities, apartments range in price from £280–£550 ($448–$880) a week.

**Swiss House Hotel.** 171 Old Brompton Rd., London SW5 0AN. ☎ **0171/373-2769.** Fax 0171/373-4983. 16 rms, 14 with bath. TV TEL. £39 ($62.40) single without bath, £56 ($89.60) single with bath; £72 ($115.20) double with bath. Extra bed £12 ($19.20). All rates include continental breakfast. AE, MC, V. Tube: Gloucester Road.

One of the more desirable B&Bs in the Earl's Court area, this hotel is in a white, Victorian row house festooned with flowers and vines, with a front porch portico. In the heart of South Kensington, the location is close to Harrods, Oxford Street, Hyde Park, and the main exhibition centers of Earl's Court and Olympia. The rear windows overlook a charming communal garden. Its country-inspired bedrooms are individually designed; some have working fireplaces, and there's enough flowering chintz to please the most avid Anglophile. It's best, however, to avoid rooms along the street, as traffic is heavy. One luxury not encountered in most B&Bs is room service from noon to 9pm. Don't expect elaborate food, but the kitchen will prepare sandwiches and soups if you'd like to stay in your room.

This hotel caters to a mostly gay male clientele. A comfortable and pleasant hotel composed of two adjacent Victorian row houses, it offers a verdant garden in back, and one of London's best known gay restaurants, Wild About Oscar. Bedrooms are cozy and simply furnished.

## NOTTING HILL GATE

Notting Hill Gate is bounded on the south by Bayswater Road, on the east by Gloucester Terrace, on the north by West Way, and on the west by the Shepherd's Bush ramp leading to the M40. It has many turn-of-the-century mansions and small houses on quiet, leafy streets.

**The Gate Hotel.** 6 Portobello Rd., London W11 3DG. ☎ **0171/221-2403.** Fax 0171/
221-9128. 6 rms, 3 with bath. MINIBAR TV TEL. £55 ($88) single or double without bath; £65–
£72 ($104–$115.20) single or double with bath. All rates include continental breakfast. DC,
MC, V. Tube: Notting Hill Gate.

Known to antique hunters, this is the only hotel along the entire length of Portobello
Road; because of rigid zoning restrictions, it will probably remain the only hotel here
for many years to come. It was originally built in the 1820s as housing for the farm-
hands working the orchards and vegetable plots at the now-defunct Portobello Farms.
Functioning as a hotel since 1932, it contains two cramped but cozy bedrooms on
each of its three floors, plus a renovated breakfast room in the cellar. Bedrooms are
color coordinated, with a bit of style, and have such amenities as a full length mirror and a built-in wardrobe. Especially intriguing are the wall paintings that show
what the Portobello road market was in its early days, when every character looked
straight out of a Charles Dickens novel. Be prepared for some *very* steep English stairs.
The on-site manager can direct visitors to the nearby antique markets and the attractions of Notting Hill Gate and nearby Kensington Gardens, both of which lie within
a 5-minute walk.

## ST. MARYLEBONE

The principally Georgian district of St. Marylebone (pronounced *Mar*-li-bone) is
below Regent's Park, northwest of Piccadilly Circus, facing Mayfair to the south and
extending north of Marble Arch at Hyde Park. A number of simple but gracious town
houses in this residential section have been converted into private hotels, and little
discreet bed-and-breakfast signs appear in the windows. If you don't have a reservation, start at Edgware Road and walk past Seymour and Great Cumberland Place.
Let the summer crowds fight it out in Bloomsbury.

### DOUBLES FOR LESS THAN £55

**Boston Court Hotel.** 26 Upper Berkeley St., London W1H 7PF. ☎ **0171/723-1445.** Fax
0171/262-8823. 13 rms, 5 with shower only, 8 with bath. TV TEL. £35–£40 ($56–$64) single
with shower only, £40–£49 ($64–$78.40) single with bath; £45–£49 ($72–$78.40) double with
shower only, £60–£69 ($96–$110.40) double with bath; £70–£79 ($112–$126.40) triple with
bath. All rates include continental breakfast. MC, V. Tube: Marble Arch.

Upper Berkeley is a classic B&B street, even though not as well known as Sussex
Gardens. It used to be a prestigious address, home of Elizabeth Montagu (1720–
1800), "queen of the bluestockings," who defended Shakespeare against attacks by
Voltaire. To her house came a host of literary figures, including Dr. Johnson, Boswell
(trailing along), and Horace Walpole. Boston Court is an unfrilly hotel in a building that dates to Victorian times. It's centrally located, within walking distance of
Oxford Street, shops, and Hyde Park. All rooms are refurbished and redecorated,
containing private showers, central heating, hair dryers, coffeemaking equipment, and
small refrigerators.

**Glynne Court.** 41 Great Cumberland Place, London W1H 7LG. ☎ **0171/262-4344.** Fax
0171/724-2071. 12 rms, 11 with bath. TV TEL. £40 ($64) single without bath, £55 ($88) single
with bath; £50 ($80) double without bath, £70 ($112) double with bath; £60 ($96) triple with-
out bath, £90 ($144) triple with bath; £70 ($112) family rm without bath, £100 ($160)
family rm with bath. All rates include continental breakfast. AE, DC, MC, V. Tube: Marble Arch.

In the Marble Arch area of St. Marylebone, this clean and comfortable B&B is in one
of the more desirable places to live. Hyde Park and Oxford Street are close at
hand. White with carriage lamps on each side of the front door, the guest house is
run with a certain flair. There is one shared bath for each pair of rooms; individual
rooms have their own character, as well as color TV, dial-phone, hair dryer, and

beverage-making equipment. Fax service is available upon request. The staff is attentive, carrying a continental breakfast to your room in the morning.

**Kenwood House Hotel.** 114 Gloucester Place, London W1H 3DB. ☎ **0171/935-3473.** Fax
0171/224-0582. 16 rms, 13 with bath. TV. £30 ($48) single without bath, £46 ($73.60) single
with bath; £44 ($70.40) double without bath, £56 ($89.60) double with bath; £64 ($102.40)
triple without bath; £70 ($112) family rm for 4 without bath. All rates include English break-
fast. AE, MC, V. Tube: Baker Street.

This hotel off Baker Street is run by English-born Arline Woutersz and her Dutch
husband, Bryan. The 1812 Adam-style building's front balcony and awning mecha-
nisms are said to be original. The house was a family home until 1942, when the
owner's two sons died in the war. Disheartened, the owner sold it to the British Army,
which used it to billet officers. Now converted into a small hotel, it is a preserved
historical monument. Most of the bedrooms were upgraded and restored in 1993,
and on every floor there are well-maintained, modern bathrooms with shower. Baby-
sitting can be arranged.

## Doubles for Less Than £70

**Edward Lear Hotel.** 28–30 Seymour St., London W1H 5WD. ☎ **0171/402-5401.** Fax
0171/706-3766. 31 rms, 8 with bath; 4 suites. TV TEL. £39.50 ($63.20) single without
bath, £49 ($78.40) single with bath; £60 ($96) double without bath, £79.50 ($127.20)
double with bath; from £85 ($136) suite. All rates include English breakfast. MC, V. Tube: Marble
Arch.

The Edward Lear is a popular hotel, made all the more desirable by the bouquets of
fresh flowers set up around the public rooms. It's 1 block from Marble Arch in a pair
of 1780 brick town houses. The western house was the London home of the 19th-
century artist and poet Edward Lear, whose illustrated limericks adorn the walls of
one of the sitting rooms. He was famous for his nonsense verse. Steep stairs lead up
to the bedrooms. The cozy units are fairly small but have all the usual facilities, such
as coffeemakers and hair dryers. There's only one single room with a private bath in
the hotel, but, oddly, even that requires a trek out into the hallway. Rooms in the
rear are quieter.

**Hart House Hotel.** 51 Gloucester Place, Portman Sq., London W1H 3PE. ☎ **0171/935-2288.**
Fax 0171/935-8516. 16 rms, 10 with bath. TV TEL. £49 ($78.40) single without bath, £60 ($96)
single with bath; £70 ($112) double or twin without bath, £85 ($136) double or twin with bath;
£90 ($144) triple without bath, £100 ($160) triple with bath; £120 ($192) quad with bath. All
rates include English breakfast. AE, MC, V. Tube: Marble Arch or Baker Street.

This is a well-preserved historic building, part of a group of Georgian mansions once
occupied by members of French nobility living in exile during the French Revolution. In the heart of the West End, it lies within easy walking distance of theaters,
as well as some of the most sought-after concentrations of popular shops and public
parks in London. Cozy and convenient, the hotel is run by Andrew Bowden. The
rooms, each with a different character, are very clean. Favorites include no. 7, a triple
with a big bath and shower. On the top floor, ask for no. 11 if you'd like a brightly
lit aerie. The bedrooms combine furnishing styles, ranging from Portobello antique
to modern. This has been a long-enduring favorite with Frommer readers. Glouster
Place itself has many literari associations. The Barrett family, which included the poet,
Elizabeth Barrett, resided at no. 99 for many years.

**Lincoln House Hotel.** 33 Gloucester Place, London W1H 3PD. ☎ **0171/486-7630.** Fax
0171/486-0166. 20 rms. TV TEL. £45–£59 ($72–$94.40) single; £65–£95 ($104–$152) double;
£95 ($152) triple. All rates include English breakfast. AE, DC, MC, V. Tube: Marble Arch or Baker
Street.

Behind a brown-brick facade originally built as part of a private house during the Georgian Age, this much-refurbished guest house offers dependable accommodations in a desirable neighborhood, a 5-minute walk from Marble Arch. Each of the small but cozily furnished bedrooms contains beverage-making facilities, a hair dryer, and a trouser press. A portable ironing center is available upon request. The standard of service is high here—it's not your typical impersonal London B&B. The atmosphere is welcoming and inviting, and the staff genuinely helpful. Many European consumer associations have endorsed the hotel for its good value.

## DOUBLES FOR LESS THAN £85

**Georgian House Hotel.** 87 Gloucester Place, London W1H 3PG. ☎ **0171/935-2211.** Fax 0171/486-7535. 20 rms. TV TEL. £65 ($104) single; £80 ($128) double; £90 ($144) triple; £100 ($160) family rm. AE, MC, V. Tube: Baker Street.

Central London, filled with luxury hotels, has an acute lack of small, personally run hotels. This hotel fills the gap in a famous section of London. The hotel lies near Baker Street (of Sherlock Holmes fame) and is within walking distance of Oxford Street, Regents Park, and the doctors' quarter of Harley Street. Run by the same family since 1973, the Georgian House has a dedicated staff and management intent on improving the hotel. Rooms have many amenities, not just private baths or showers, but shaver points, beverage-making facilities, and individually controlled central heating. There's an elevator to all floors. Bedrooms are neutral in style. The ground-floor accommodations are the least preferred. Don't expect views from some of the back rooms which open onto a wall.

**Regency Hotel.** 19 Nottingham Place, London W1M 3FF. ☎ **0171/486-5347.** Fax 0171/224-6057. 20 rms. MINIBAR TV TEL. £60 ($96) single; £79 ($126.40) double; £95 ($152) family rm. AE, CB, DC, MC, V. Tube: Baker Street or Regent's Park.

The structure that is now the Regency Hotel was originally built in the late 1800s. Although it has functioned as some kind of hotel since the 1940s, in 1991 it was gutted and renovated into its current and tastefully upgraded state. One of the better hotels on the street, it offers simple, conservatively modern bedrooms scattered over four floors, and a breakfast room set in what used to be the cellar. Each room contains a radio, hair dryer, trouser press, and ironing board, and room service is available. The neighborhood is strictly protected as a historic district; Marble Arch, Regent's Park, and Baker Street are all within a 12-minute walk.

# PADDINGTON & BAYSWATER

Another popular hotel area jammed with budget housing (much of it unappealing) is Paddington—the section around Paddington Station, just to the northwest of Kensington Gardens and Hyde Park. Bayswater, slightly to the west of Hyde Park and to the north of Kensington Gardens, is an unofficial district with a number of decently priced lodgings and inexpensive restaurants. Once this area of London had a strong Russian influence, a characteristic that lives on in St. Petersburg Place, the most charming street of Bayswater. Pick and choose carefully among the B&Bs in Bayswater, however; many are quite scruffy. The area abounds in cheap restaurants, mostly Indian and other ethnic cuisines.

Again, you'd be well advised to telephone ahead to see if rooms are available. If you don't have a reservation, begin your trek by taking the Underground to either Paddington or Edgware Road and walking to Sussex Gardens, which is a long avenue flanked by bed-and-breakfast houses, many dreadfully run-down—in fact, many of the budget hotels in this area now deal mostly with homeless people sent from the local authorities. After breakfast hours, when guests have just checked out, is the best time for finding a vacancy. If you're unable to find a room on Sussex Gardens, then try the satellite Norfolk Square, which lies near Sussex Gardens (even closer to Paddington Station).

Tube stops serving the Bayswater and Paddington areas are Paddington, Bayswater, Queensway, Notting Hill Gate, and Ladbroke.

## DOUBLES FOR LESS THAN £60

**Adare House.** 153 Sussex Gardens, London W2 2RY. ☎ **0171/262-0633.** Fax 0171/706-1859. 16 rms, 9 with shower. TV. £32 ($51.20) single without bath, £39 ($62.40) single with shower; £56 ($89.60) double with shower. All rates include full English breakfast. No credit cards. Tube: Paddington.

This place still has a little soul, while so many of its neighbors along Sussex Gardens have lost theirs. You're welcomed by Anne O'Neill, who runs a good ship, and has done so exceedingly well for 25 years. Adare remains one of the best choices for the budget traveler in this neighborhood. The property is well maintained and has been gradually improved over the years with the additions of private baths in admittedly cramped space. The public areas, although relatively modest, still have a touch of class, especially with their smart Regency-era striped wallpaper and red carpeting. Rooms, many quite small, are nevertheless clean and comfortably furnished, although lacking in glamor. They're too down-home for that. Accommodations contain beverage-making facilities, and those with private baths also have a hair dryer.

**Balmoral Hotel.** 156 Sussex Gardens, London W2 1UD. ☎ **0171/723-7445.** Fax 0171/402-0118. 32 rms. TV. £35–£55 ($56–$88) single; £55–£60 ($88–$96) double; £66 ($105.60) triple. All rates include English breakfast. MC, V. Tube: Paddington or Lancaster Gate.

The Balmoral, named after the famous Scottish retreat of Prince Albert and Queen Victoria, stands out on a street with many mediocre B&B choices. The hotel is a converted Victorian row house overlooking Sussex Gardens, and in summer flower boxes decorate the windows. The comfortable rooms are simple but well kept and have hot-beverage equipment facilities. About 15 of this establishment's bedrooms are in a Victorian-era annex across the street, although the reception and breakfast area facilities are located at the above-mentioned address. Bedrooms in both sections were renovated in the early 1990s.

**Europa House Hotel.** 151 Sussex Gardens, London W2 2RY. ☎ **0171/402-1923.** Fax 0171/224-9331. 18 rms. TV TEL. £38–£48 ($60.80–$76.80) single; £48–£60 ($76.80–$96) double; £18–£20 ($28.80–$32) per person family rm. All rates include English breakfast. MC, V. Tube: Paddington.

Another budget find along Sussex Gardens, this family-run hotel attracts those who want their own private plumbing. Like most rooms along Sussex Gardens, bedrooms are a bit cramped, but they are well maintained and often color coordinated. Each contains a direct-dial phone and color TV, plus beverage-making facilities. Some of the rooms are outfitted for sports and university groups, with 3, 4, and 5 beds per unit. In a bright dining room, a hearty English breakfast awaits you every morning.

**Fairways Hotel.** 186 Sussex Gardens, London W2 1TU. ☎ **0171/723-4871.** Fax 0171/723-4871. 17 rms, 10 with bath. TV. £40 ($64) single without bath; £56 ($89.60) double without bath, £62 ($99.20) double with bath. All rates include English breakfast. MC, V. Tube: Paddington.

Near Hyde Park, Jenny and Steve Adams welcome you into one of the finest B&Bs along Sussex Gardens, which, even though it doesn't enjoy the pedigree it used to, is still a favorite address of the value-oriented traveler. This black-and-white town house is easily recognized by its colonnaded front entrance with a wrought-iron balustrade stretching across the front second-floor windows. The Adams family—sorry—prefers the traditional touch, opting for charm and character whenever possible. They call their breakfast room "homely," which Americans might call it homey instead, as it's decorated with photographs of the family and a collection of china. Guests meet fellow guests here and share discoveries of London. The breakfast is hearty and home cooked, fortification for a rainy day in London. Bedrooms are attractively decorated and comfortably furnished, each with hot and cold running water, intercom, color TV, and beverage-making facilities.

**Norfolk Court & St. David's Hotel.** 16–20 Norfolk Sq., London W2 1RS. ☎ **0171/ 723-4963.** Fax 0171/723-3856. 50 rms, 6 with shower. TV. £30 ($48) single without shower, £40 ($64) single with shower; £44 ($70.40) double without bath, £54 ($86.40) double with bath or shower; £54 ($86.40) triple without bath, £64 ($102.40) triple with shower; £65 ($104) quad without bath, £75 ($120) quad with shower. All rates include a full English breakfast. MC, V. Tube: Paddington.

George Neokledos, one of the more welcoming hosts along this stretch of B&Bs, manages to run both these properties with a certain style. These hotels, only a 2-minute walk from Paddington Station, are small and friendly. The properties were built when Norfolk Square knew a grander age during Victoria's reign, attracting luminaries of the time such as John Addington Symonds (1840–93), the eccentric scholar and literary critic and author of the seven-volume *The Renaissance in Italy*. Those blue bloods are long gone, but the area is still safe and recommendable. The decor is mismatched, but each room is well maintained and comfortably—if not elegantly—furnished. There's a homespun quality here. You get good beds, an affordable price, and, in a few rooms, a cubicle shower that's not for long, lingering baths, and certainly not for two.

## DOUBLES FOR LESS THAN £75

**Kensington Gardens Hotel.** 24 Queensway, London W2 4QN. ☎ **0171/221-7790.** Fax 0171/792-8612. 17 rms. TV TEL. £45 ($72) single; £70 ($112) double; £85 ($136) triple. All rates include continental breakfast. AE, DC, MC, V. Tube: Bayswater.

Had Bette Davis checked in a few years ago, she might have proclaimed, "What a dump!" No more! The Kazolides family has seen to that. The place has been vastly renovated and improved, and now stands out as the leader of the pack among the often grubby Bayswater B&Bs. The place now has personality, even though some of the rooms are hopelessly cramped, especially one single recently inspected. Don't arrive loaded down with baggage. Rooms are warm and inviting, made all the more so by a helpful staff. If you don't mind trudging up those narrow English steps, you'll be rewarded with good views from some of the top nests. The staff will direct you to their favorite Greek restaurant, The Halepi, nearby.

**Mitre House Hotel.** 178–184 Sussex Gardens, London W2 ITU. ☎ **0171/723-8040.** Fax 0171/402-0990. 70 rms, 3 suites. TV TEL. £60 ($96) single; £70 ($112) double; £80 ($128) triple; £90 ($144) family rm; £105 ($168) suite. All rates include English breakfast. AE, DC, MC, V. Tube: Paddington or Lancaster Gate.

Sussex Gardens, traditional stamping ground of the value-conscious hotel shopper, is afloat with grubby B&Bs. Mitre House is an exception, one of the best-run properties along the avenue. Managers Michael and Andrew Chris, two brothers, are in charge of the property their parents ran since 1963. Accommodations are divided between the older section, where the rooms are extremely small but well kept, and a newer wing that features a trio of junior suites and such luxuries as Jacuzzis. Suites have minibars. Accommodations on the lower level are the least desirable. This family-run property has a fully licensed bar, a cozy and snug retreat.

○ **Queensway Hotel.** 147–149 Sussex Gardens, London W2 2RY. ☎ **0171/723-7749.** Fax 0171/262-5707. 43 rms. TV TEL. £48 ($76.80) single; £66 ($105.60) double. All rates include continental breakfast. AE, DC, MC, V. Tube: Paddington.

On a tree-lined road close to Hyde Park and Marble Arch, this hotel is ideal for shopping along Oxford Street, Bond Street, and Knightsbridge. Personal service and hospitality have long characterized this place, which received much refurbishment during the mid 1990s. The hotel is one of the most immaculate—if not the most—along the gardens. Bedrooms are moderately spacious and comfortably furnished, with sleek modern bathrooms. Rooms vary in size; some of the more expensive doubles have a Jacuzzi. Lots of extra amenities are found, including a trouser press and beverage-making equipment, along with direct-dial phones and hair dryers. The hotel is actually two Victorian houses joined together. A reception room has the original mantelpiece and deep-cove moldings evoking its former life as a private residence for a "family of character." The dining room is rather elegantly decorated for a London B&B, with pink tablecloths, wall art and—most important of all—a generous breakfast.

## HOLLAND PARK

**Ravina Gora Hotel.** 29 Holland Park Ave., London W11 3RW. ☎ **0171/727-7725.** Fax 0171/221-4282. 21 rms, 3 with bath. TV. £30 ($48) single without bath; £50 ($80) double without bath, £60 ($96) double with bath; £60 ($96) triple without bath; £72 ($115.20) triple with bath; £76 ($121.60) quad without bath, £88 ($140.80) quad with bath. All rates include English breakfast. No credit cards. Tube: Holland Park.

Backpackers, students, and adventure travelers often book here, even though some might find the comfort level the equivalent of the waiting room of a Greyhound bus station. But this place has a devoted following who view Ravina Gora only as a crash pad for the night. James Barrie used to call on the Davies family who lived nearby at no. 23; for the children he composed many of the plots of his fairy stories and plays, including *Peter Pan*. Beginning in 1956, this hotel has been operated by a Yugoslav couple, the Jovanovic family, who don't muck about with frills and bows, but offer basic, no-frills bedrooms. The beds are clean, and the place is quite decent, especially since some of the rooms have been repainted and new hallway showers installed. The location is a bit out of the way, but the tube stop is just across the street.

## AIRPORT HOTELS

Most regularly scheduled planes land at Heathrow, whereas charter flights are likely to go to Gatwick—which more and more is becoming the gateway to London. If you need to be near either airport, consider the following suggestions instead of the well-advertised and more expensive operations.

### NEAR HEATHROW

**The Swan.** The Hythe, Staines, Middlesex TW18 3JB. ☎ **01784/452494.** Fax 01784/461593. 11 rms, 5 with bath; 1 suite. TV TEL. £39–£48.50 ($62.40–$77.60) single without bath; £64 ($102.40) single with bath; £56 ($89.60) double without bath; £71.50 ($114.40) double with bath; £78 ($124.80) suite. All rates include English breakfast. AE, DC, MC, V. Tube: Heathrow; then taxi.

Dating back prior to the days of Samuel Pepys, the Swan is on the south bank of the Thames, beside Staines Bridge, and within easy access of Heathrow (15 minutes). Bedrooms have central heating and tea- or coffee-making facilities. This attractive old inn has a reputation for good food ranging from bar snacks to traditional English "fayre." The food is served in a gazebo-style dining room, featuring wholesome cooking. If you're just arriving in London, this conversation area might be a good introduction to the city's history before you go into the center. The Hythe was established as a port on a curve of the river by the late 7th century. A bridge in time linked it to the town of Staines, an important Roman settlement, across the river. Many surviving buildings in the area date from the 17th century.

**Upton Park Guest House.** 41 Upton Park, Slough, Berkshire SL1 2DA. ☎ **01753/528797.** Fax 01753/550208. 11 rms, 4 with bath. TV. £37 ($59.20) single without bath, £39 ($62.40) single with bath; £49 ($78.40) double without bath, £56 ($89.60) double with bath. All rates include English breakfast. MC, V. Train to Slough Station.

The cab ride from Heathrow to this hotel is about 15 minutes. Kathy and Peter Jones, who run the place, can arrange for a local cab to meet you if you plan in advance (the local cab is cheaper than getting a cab at the airport). All rooms are comfortably furnished and have central heating, hot and cold running water, and complimentary tea and coffee. In the mid 1990s, rooms were redecorated and spruced up a bit. There's also a pleasant bar.

## NEAR GATWICK

**Brooklyn Manor Hotel.** Bonnetts Lane, Ifield, Crawley, West Sussex RH11 0NY. ☎ **01293/546024.** Fax 01293/510366. 11 rms, 4 with bath. TV TEL. £25 ($40) single without bath, £35 ($56) single with bath; £35 ($56) double without bath, £45 ($72) double with bath. AE, MC, V. Bus: C5 to Crawley/Ifield.

The Brooklyn Manor is an old, well-cared-for Victorian house on 5 acres of English countryside, but it's only 5 minutes from Gatwick. The hotel provides free transportation to and from the airport—just call when you arrive and someone will come get you. Martin Davis rents rooms with full central heating and beverage-making facilities. Breakfast costs extra, and you can order a light snack in the evening. In addition, a free courtesy service takes guests to and from a nearby restaurant, and there are two pubs within about a 10-minute walk, both of which serve inexpensive meals. The hotel does not have a bar, but it is licensed, so that you can have drinks served in the lounge if you wish.

**Caprice Guest House.** Bonnetts Lane, Ifield, Crawley, West Sussex RH11 0NY. ☎ **01293/528620.** Fax 01293/531471. 3 rms, 1 with bath. TV. £25 ($40) single without bath, £30 ($48) single with bath; £35 ($56) double without bath, £40 ($64) double with bath. MC, V.

With its own garden and not far from the previously recommended Brooklyn Manor Hotel, this is a small but charming house that has been continuously enlarged since its original construction in the 1950s. Mrs. Jane French maintains a trio of immaculate, cozy, and comfortable bedrooms, each with beverage-making equipment and extensive views over the nearby countryside. Gatwick Airport is about 10 minutes away.

**The Manor House.** Bonnetts Lane, Ifield, Crawley, Sussex RH11 0NY. ☎ **01293/510000.** 6 rms, 4 with private bath. TV. £25–£30 ($40–$48) single; £40 ($64) double; £45 ($72) family rm. All rates include English breakfast. MC, V. Free parking.

The owners, Steve and Joanne Jeffries, include transportation from Gatwick Airport as part of the price of their lodgings. Their home is a sprawling neo-Tudor affair set on two acres of land, amid fields which surround it on all sides. It was originally built in 1894 as a supplemental home for the Lord of Ifield, who occupied an even larger house nearby and never actually moved in. Two of the rooms share a bathroom, whereas the others have private bathrooms. Regardless of its plumbing, each accommodation has flowered wallpaper, and simple, traditional accessories. Breakfast is the only meal served.

# HOSTELS

In London youth hostels, reservations are imperative in summer.

**Astor Hostels** is a group of student hostels for travelers from all over the world that attracts a large American and Australian contingent. They mostly cater to the 18-to-30 age group, but also welcome more mature travelers. Their hostels in London include three of the four listed below—the Museum Inn, Quest Hotel, and the Victoria Hotel.

✪ **Driscoll House Hotel.** 172 New Kent Rd., London SE1 4YT. ☎ **0171/703-4175.** Fax 0171/703-8013. 212 rms, none with bath. £27 ($43.20) single; £50 ($80) double. All rates include breakfast and dinner. No credit cards. Tube: Elephant & Castle.

This imposing neo-Georgian building was inaugurated by Princess Louise in 1913. Since then, it has prided itself on having hosted more than 50,000 guests from around the world. Owned and supervised by Terry Driscoll, an English-born opponent of Franco during the Spanish Civil War, the hotel maintains a personal link with many of its former residents. Bedrooms are cozy and appealingly old-fashioned, each with hot and cold running water. There are abundant private baths on each corridor. The premises contain four TV lounges, sitting rooms, table-tennis rooms, a library, a laundry with coin-operated machines, and no fewer than 10 pianos for the use of guests.

**Museum Inn.** 27 Montague St., London WC1B 5BN. ☎ **0171/580-5360.** Fax 0171/636-7948. 20 rms, none with bath. £10–£16 ($16–$25.60) per person for occupancy of rms with 2 to 10 beds. All rates include continental breakfast. MC, V. Tube: Russell Square, Holborn, or Tottenham Court Road.

Basic and somewhat impersonal, but conveniently located opposite the British Museum, this privately owned hostel provides rock-bottom accommodations for budgeteers looking for an inner-city bargain. Contained in two white-fronted buildings (each located within a 2-minute walk from the other) are 94 beds. These are scattered among one double room, one triple room, and an array of dormitory-style rooms containing between 4 and 10 beds each. On the premises is a communal kitchen available for the preparation of meals or snacks, and a communal pay phone and TV room. Linens and towels are provided in the cost.

**Quest Hotel.** 45 Queensborough Terrace, London W2 3SY. ☎ **0171/229-7782.** Fax 0171/727-8106. 10 rms, 90 beds. £9–£16 ($14.40–$25.60) per person in rms for 2 to 6 occupants. All rates include continental breakfast. MC, V. Tube: Queensway or Bayswater.

Open 24 hours a day, this converted Victorian building has free cable TV, videos, a pool table, and cooking facilities. Rooms are very simple but clean. There are no singles.

**Victoria Hotel.** 71 Belgrave Rd., London SW1 V2BG. ☎ **0171/834-3077.** Fax 0171/932-0693. 12 rms, 70 beds. £12–£14 ($19.20–$22.40) per person in rms containing 4 to 10 beds. All rates include continental breakfast. MC, V. Tube: Pimlico.

The most recent addition to the Astor chain, this exceptionally simple hostel with no-frills rooms is in a white-fronted building near the Pimlico Underground. There's a kitchen on-site if you want to prepare your own meals.

## CAMPING: THE CHEAPEST LIVING IN LONDON

Yes, it may seem strange (can you imagine camping in New York?), but the great city of London has camping options for the budget backpacker. You can't beat these sites for cheap: They average about £6 ($9.60) a night per person, and you can mingle with a lively mix of nomadic sorts from around the world. Keep in mind, however, that England has a very wet climate. Sooner or later rain will be part of your camping experience. In London's **Tent City—Acton,** Old Oak Common Lane, East Acton, London W3 7DP (☎ **0181/743-5708** in winter; 0181/749-9074 in summer; fax 0181/749-9074; tube: East Acton), you can sleep on one of 450 cots in 14 large tents—divided among men's, women's, and mixed—or pitch your own tent. It offers laundry facilities, showers, a snack bar, storage area, and cooking facilities, all for £5.50 ($8.80) a night. After taking the tube, turn left out of the station and again on Wulfstan Road. The campground is a 10-minute walk up Wulfstan Road.

**Tent City—Hackney,** Millsfield Rd., Hackney Marshes, London E5 0AR (☎ **0181/985-7656;** tube: Victoria, Piccadilly Circus), is located 4 miles from London, and offers similar facilities at £6 (9.60) a night. It can be reached by taking Bus 38 from either tube station listed above to Clapton Pond, and walking down Millsfield Road, or by catching Bus 22A from Liverpool St. to Mandeville St. and crossing the bridge to Hackney Marshes.

Neither campground has maximum-stay limitations, but the Acton location is open only from June 1 until September 7, and Hackney from June 1 to August 30.

A third option, located 8 miles from London, is **Crystal Palace Caravan Club Site** (now does that sound like a New Age gathering, or what?), Crystal Palace Parade, London SE19 1UF (☎ **0181/778-7155;** tube: Brixton). You must bring your own tent. There's a 21-day maximum stay, but the facility is open year-round. The daily camping rate is £5 ($8) per night from October 1 through March 25, £6 (9.60) from March 26 through April 5 and in September, and £8 (12.80) from April 6 through August 31. From the tube station take Bus 2A to Crystal Palace.

For more information about these, or any of England's more than 2,500 campsites, contact the **British Tourist Authority,** 551 Fifth Ave., Suite 701, New York, NY 10176-0799 (☎ **212/986-2200**) for their free pamphlet, *Caravan and Camping Parks,* or the **Automobile Association,** Norfolk House, Basingstoke, Hampshire RG24 9NY (☎ **01256/20123**) for their *Camping and Caravaning,* available for £7.99 ($12.80). Additional information is available through the **Wilderness Press,** 2440 Bancroft Way, Berkley, CA 94704-1676 (☎ **800/443-7227** or 510/843-8080; fax 510/548-1355), which publishes numerous resources, including *Backpacking Basics* ($11, including postage); and **REI,** P.O. Box 1700, Summer, WA 98352-0001 (☎ **800/426-4840**), which publishes *Europe Camping and Caravanning* ($20).

# 4 Where to Eat

Once not particularly known as a dining capital, London has, with the pressure of tourism and influx of foreign chefs, seen a dramatic turnaround in culinary offerings. A wave of English-born-and-trained chefs are setting a superb standard of cookery, using high-quality ingredients. *Time Out* has called London a "city of foodies," and food and restaurant columns in local newspapers are read almost as avidly as the latest scandal spinning around the House of Windsor.

Even so, bland, overcooked meat and soggy vegetables abound in many of London's "caffs" (cafes) and other low-cost eateries. But don't despair—across the board, food quality is improving, and even those on the tightest of budgets will find a number of acceptable options. Don't overlook the all-you-can-eat carvery restaurants in central London, which serve up England's famous roasts, especially roast beef and its classic accompaniment, Yorkshire pudding. Roast chicken, roast pork, and roast English lamb are also served at these good-value places.

The once-ubiquitous fish-and-chips shops, known as "chippies," have become harder to find in London, and those that remain are of such varying quality that it's difficult for a visitor to find really good English fish and chips. Proper shops offer a

# Central London Dining

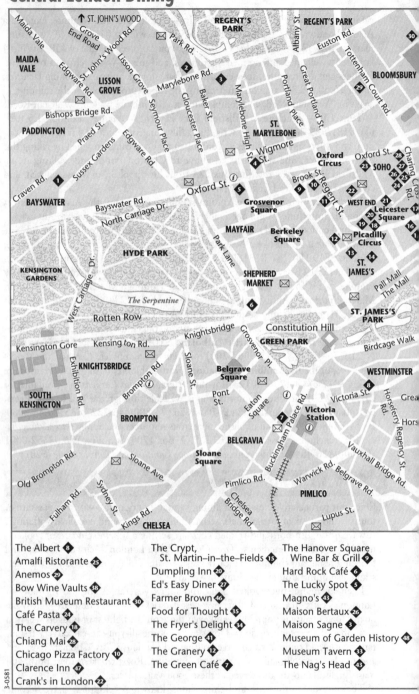

The Albert **8**
Amalfi Ristorante **25**
Anemos **29**
Bow Wine Vaults **38**
British Museum Restaurant **50**
Café Pasta **24**
The Carvery **18**
Chiang Mai **28**
Chicago Pizza Factory **10**
Clarence Inn **47**
Crank's in London **22**

The Crypt,
    St. Martin–in–the–Fields **15**
Dumpling Inn **20**
Ed's Easy Diner **27**
Farmer Brown **46**
Food for Thought **35**
The Fryer's Delight **34**
The George **41**
The Granery **12**
The Green Café **7**

The Hanover Square
    Wine Bar & Grill **9**
Hard Rock Café **6**
The Lucky Spot **5**
Magno's **43**
Maison Bertaux **26**
Maison Sagne **3**
Museum of Garden History **48**
Museum Tavern **33**
The Nag's Head **43**

3-0581

108

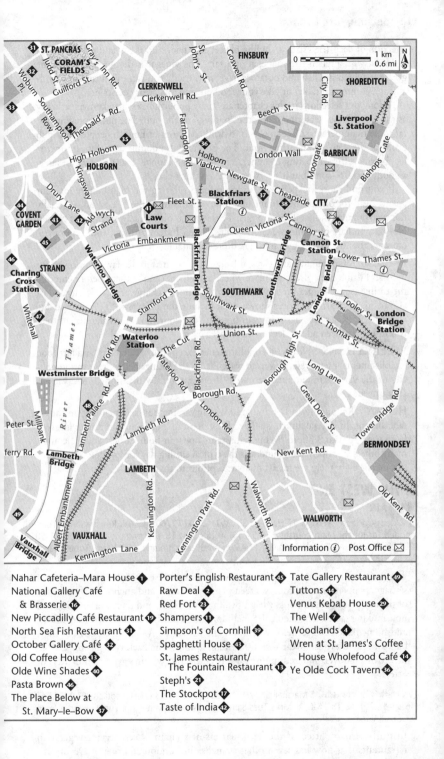

Nahar Cafeteria–Mara House ①
National Gallery Café
  & Brasserie ⑯
New Piccadilly Café Restaurant ⑲
North Sea Fish Restaurant ㉛
October Gallery Café ㉜
Old Coffee House ⑬
Olde Wine Shades ㊵
Pasta Brown ㊻
The Place Below at
  St. Mary–le–Bow ㊲

Porter's English Restaurant ㊺
Raw Deal ②
Red Fort ㉓
Shampers ⑪
Simpson's of Cornhill ㊴
Spaghetti House ㊸
St. James Restaurant/
  The Fountain Restaurant ⑬
Steph's ㉑
The Stockpot ⑰
Taste of India ㊷

Tate Gallery Restaurant ㊾
Tuttons ⑭
Venus Kebab House ㉙
The Well ⑦
Woodlands ④
Wren at St. James's Coffee
  House Wholefood Café ⑭
Ye Olde Cock Tavern ㊱

109

selection of deep-fried fish, including plaice, cod, haddock, skate, and rockfish. This is served with French fries, vinegar and salt. The vinegar is designed to offset the grease in which the fish and potatoes have been fried. You can eat in the shop, usually at a communal table, or take your food outside in a greasy container.

Among our selections in this chapter are many public houses, also known variously as the "local," the "watering hole," the "boozer," or the pub. The pub represents far, far more than merely a place in which to drink. Millions of English people grab "pub grub" at the regular lunchtime hour. The pub can also double as a club, front parlor, betting office, debating chamber, and television lounge. It is not, by and large, a good "pickup" spot, but it's very nearly everything else.

If you find most inexpensive London eateries offering too bland a fare for your palate, head for one of the zillions of ethnic restaurants in the West End, especially the ever-popular Indian dining rooms. These appear on virtually every street corner. Not only Indian, but Chinese, Greek, Italian, West Indian, African, and Cypriot restaurants abound as well, and most are quite reasonable.

**PRICES**    All restaurants and cafes in Britain are required to display the prices of the food and drink they offer in a place where customers can see them before entering the eating area. Charges for service and any minimum charge or cover charge must also be made clear. The prices shown must include the 17$^1/_2$% VAT. Most also add a 10% to 15% service charge to your bill. Look at your check to make sure of that. If nothing has been added, leave a 12% to 15% tip.

**RESERVATIONS**    Nearly all establishments, except pubs, cafeterias, and fast-food establishments, prefer reservations to walk-ins. In the listings below, reservation policies of the various restaurants are noted. If not specifically mentioned, reservations aren't needed.

**HOURS**    Restaurants in London keep widely varying hours, depending on the establishment. In general, lunch is offered from noon to 2 or 3pm, and dinner is served from 6 or 7pm to 9:30pm. Many restaurants open an hour earlier, and, of course, many others stay open later. Sunday is the typical closing day for London restaurants, but increasingly there are many, many exceptions to that rule.

# IN THE WEST END
## MAYFAIR

✪ **Chicago Pizza Factory.** 17 Hanover Sq., W1. ☎ **0171/629-2669.** Reservations recommended for lunch. Main courses £5.95–£11.50 ($9.50–$18.40); pizza for 2 £9.50–£11.50 ($15.20–$18.40). AE, MC, V. Mon–Sat 11:45am–11:30pm; Sun noon–10:30pm. Tube: Oxford Circus. PIZZA.

The specialty here is deep-dish pizza covered with cheese, tomato, and a choice of sausage, pepperoni, mushrooms, green peppers, onions, and anchovies. This is one of the few places where a doggy bag is willingly provided, and there are smoking and nonsmoking tables. The menu also includes stuffed mushrooms, garlic bread, salads, and homemade cheesecake. A video over the bar shows American baseball or football, and the waitresses wear *Chicago Tribune* aprons. The Factory is just off Oxford Street in Hanover Square, opposite John Lewis and within easy reach of Regent Street.

✪ **Crank's in London.** 8 Marshall St., W1. ☎ **0171/437-9431.** Main courses £3.95–£5.45 ($6.30–$8.70). AE, DC, MC, V. Mon–Tues 8am–8pm; Wed–Fri 8am–9pm. Tube: Oxford Circus. VEGETARIAN.

Just off Carnaby Street is the headquarters of a chain of self-service vegetarian restaurants that now has seven other branches in London and one in Devon. It's decorated with natural wood, wicker-basket lamps, bare pinewood tables, and hand-made ceramic bowls and plates. Stone-ground flour is used for making bread and rolls. The uncooked vegetable salad is especially good and there's always a hot stew of savory vegetables (with "secret" seasonings), served in a hand-thrown stoneware pot with salad. Homemade cakes, such as honey cake, gingerbread, and cheesecake, are a specialty. Bakery goods, nuts, and general health-food supplies are sold in an adjoining shop.

**The Hanover Square Wine Bar & Grill.** 25 Hanover Sq., W1. ☎ **0171/408-0935.** Reservations recommended for lunch. Main courses £5.95–£8.95 ($9.50–$14.30); glass of wine £2.50 ($4). AE, CB, DC, MC, V. Mon–Fri 11am–11pm. Tube: Oxford Circus. PROVENÇAL/ CALIFORNIAN.

Established in 1993, this restaurant rapidly gained a repeat clientele among neighborhood office workers and shoppers. Although dinner is served, most business is during lunch hour (when the place can get very crowded). Also popular is after work, when the bar is filled with clients who appreciate the wide choice of wines sold by the glass. The decor is similar to that of a French bistro, though it incorporates certain elements of an English pub. Menu items include several different "grills of the day"; open-face Scottish sirloin sandwiches with mustard, herb butter, and salad; charcoal-grilled prawns with garlic butter; charcoal-grilled Californian sausages with spicy peppers; pork rillettes; and fish grilled "in the California style." Vegetarians will appreciate dishes like sliced eggplant layered with ratatouille, topped with mozzarella, and grilled.

**Hard Rock Cafe.** 150 Old Park Lane, W1. ☎ **0171/629-0382.** Reservations not accepted. Main courses £5.55–£8.75 ($.15–$14). AE, MC, V. Sun–Thurs 11:30am–12:30am; Fri–Sat 11:30am–1am. Closed Dec 25–26. Tube: Green Park or Hyde Park Corner. AMERICAN.

This member of the unstoppable Hard Rock chain offers decent American diner-style food at reasonable prices, with taped music and service with a smile—no different from any of their other locations. The London branch has been here since June 14, 1971; more than 12 million people have been through the doors. Almost every night there's a line waiting to get in, as this continues to be one of the most popular places in town with young people and visitors.

Generous portions are served, and the price of a main dish includes a salad garnish and fries. Specialties include smokehouse steak, filet mignon, and T-bone. The Hard Rock also serves great charcoal-broiled burgers and hot chili. The dessert menu is equally tempting, including homemade hot fudge brownie and thick cold shakes.

**Shampers.** 4 Kingly St., W1. ☎ **0171/437-1692.** Reservations recommended. Main dishes £8–£11.95 ($12.80–$19.10); glass of wine from £2.60 ($4.15). AE, DC, MC, V. Mon–Sat 11am–11pm. Closed Easter and Christmas. Tube: Oxford Circus or Piccadilly Circus. CONTINENTAL.

For a number of years, this has been a favorite of West End wine-bar aficionados who gravitate here, between Carnaby and Regent streets. In addition to the street-level wine bar, where food platters are served, there is a more formal basement-level restaurant. In either section, you can order main dishes like braised leg and breast of guinea fowl, portions of cured and salted ham with new potatoes, and platters of assorted cheese. Salads are especially popular, including chicken with tarragon-cream dressing and tuna and pasta with a spicy tomato sauce. A platter of Irish mussels cooked in a cream-and-tarragon sauce seems to be everybody's favorite. The restaurant is closed in the evening but the bar serves an extended menu, featuring not only the luncheon menu, but such dishes as grilled calves' liver, pheasant sausages, pan-fried tiger prawns, free-range chicken, and a variety of fish dishes.

# PICCADILLY CIRCUS & LEICESTER SQUARE

**The Carvery.** In the Regent Palace Hotel, Glasshouse St., W1. ☎ **0171/734-7000.** Reservations recommended. All-you-can-eat meals £14.95 ($23.90); 2-course buffet £10.95 ($17.50), half price for children 5–16, free for children 4 and under. AE, DC, MC, V. Mon–Fri noon–2:30pm and 5:15–9pm; Sat noon–2:30pm and 5:15–9:30pm; Sun noon–2:30pm and 6–9pm. Tube: Piccadilly Circus. ENGLISH.

Who'd think that just 20 feet from Piccadilly Circus you could have a fabulous all-you-can-eat roast? Incredibly, that's the policy of this renowned all-you-can-eat establishment. There's a wide range of appetizers, and the buffet carving table offers prime rib with Yorkshire pudding, roast leg of Southdown lamb with mint sauce, and a roast leg of English pork with apple sauce. Your choice of roast is carved for you by the chef. Side dishes—buttered peas, roast potatoes, new carrots, and gravy—are self-serve. In another area are cold foods and assorted salads—whatever's in season. Desserts might include chocolate fudge cake, or perhaps a sherry trifle. From 5:15 to 7pm, dinner costs £11.95 ($19.10). Good brewed coffee for "afters" is included in the price.

**The Granery.** 39 Albemarle St., W1. ☎ **0171/493-2978.** Main courses £6.90–£7.90 ($11.05–£12.65). No credit cards. Mon–Fri 11:30am–8pm; Sat–Sun noon–2:30pm. Tube: Green Park. ENGLISH.

Since 1974 this restaurant has served a simple but flavorful array of home-cooked dishes, which are listed every day on a chalkboard. The Granery describes itself as a country-food restaurant, and offers large portions of such dishes as casserole of lamb with mint and lemon, pan-fried cod, and avocado stuffed with prawns, spinach, and cheese. Many dishes are vegetarian-friendly, including mushrooms stuffed with mixed vegetables, stuffed eggplant with curry sauce, and vegetarian lasagna. Desserts are tempting, including bread-and-butter pudding and brown Betty.

**New Piccadilly Café Restaurant.** 8 Denman St., W1. ☎ **0171/437-8530.** Reservations not accepted. Main courses £3.75–£4.75 ($6–$7.60). No credit cards. Daily 11am–9:30pm. Closed Christmas, Boxing Day, Easter Sunday. Tube: Piccadilly Circus. CONTINENTAL.

Just around the corner from the tube station, this eatery is recognizable by the red neon "EATS" sign in the window. Lorenzo Marioni opened it in 1951, and his sister, Rosita, has been cashier ever since. The restaurant is popular with tourists, as demonstrated on the wall covered with postcards sent from around the world. Local color is provided by a regular clientele of show people popping in from the Piccadilly Theatre, located next door.

Omelets, pizza, salads, and dessert are served along with generous portions of sausage or bacon and chips, steak, veal, fresh fish, chicken, pasta, and vegetable dishes. Takeout service is available, and customers are allowed to bring their own beverages.

**Wren at St. James's Coffee House Wholefood Café.** 35 Jermyn St., SW1. ☎ **0171/437-9419.** Main courses £1.95–£4.95 ($3.10–$7.90). No credit cards. Mon–Sat 8am–6pm; Sun 10am–4pm. Tube: Piccadilly Circus or Green Park. VEGETARIAN/WHOLE FOODS.

After visitors see the church, they can eat at the cheerful coffee shop with courtyard service in fair weather. There's always a fresh soup of the day, along with cold appetizers. The restaurant specializes in large potatoes baked in their "jackets," as the British say, and filled with a variety of stuffings, such as chili-bean casserole with sour cream. It's busy at lunchtime, when hot dishes are served. Teatime specialties include homemade cakes and large scones with cream and jam. No smoking is allowed. Every Thursday, Friday, and Saturday from 9am to 7pm a flea market of old clothes and antiques is held in the courtyard.

## (⚇) Family-Friendly Restaurants

**Chicago Pizza Factory** *(see p. 110)*    If your kids are nostalgic for the food back home, they'll find it here at a place whose regular-size pizzas are big enough for two or three diners.

**Deals Restaurant and Diner** *(see p. 124)*    Kids love to take the boat down to Chelsea Harbour where they can enjoy typical North American fare, including "Dealsburgers." Reduced-price children's portions are available.

**Spaghetti House** *(see p. 116)*    Kids beg to go here, where they get their fill of good-tasting pasta dishes—at least 10 different flavors and varieties. For dessert, the cassata siciliana is always a pleaser.

### LEICESTER SQUARE

**Ed's Easy Diner.** 12 Moor St., W1. ☎ **0171/439-1955.** Reservations not accepted. Main courses £3.95–£5.50 ($6.30–$8.80). MC, V. Sun–Thurs 11:30am–midnight; Fri–Sat 11:30am–1am. Closed Christmas. Tube: Leicester Square, Tottenham Court Road. AMERICAN.

This is one of four branches of the popular diner, steeped in retro Americana. It's the kind of place Michael J. Fox might have walked into in *Back to the Future.* Featuring 1950s and 1960s rock and roll on the jukebox, a horseshoe-shaped counter with the kitchen in the middle, and a staff that fit the theme, the restaurant offers not only good diner staples such as burgers, fried onion rings, waffles, hash, and cheesecake, but also good people-watching, with a broad cross-section of fashion trends on parade around the counter.

✪ **Farmer Brown.** 4 New Row, WC2. ☎ **0171/240-0230.** Reservations not accepted. Breakfast and lunch £1.75–£5.40 ($2.80–$8.65). No credit cards. Mon–Sat 7am–5pm. Closed Christmas.

✪ **Pasta Brown.** 24 Bedford St., WC2. Same phone. Reservations not accepted. Breakfast and lunch £1.75–£5.40 ($2.80–$8.65); main courses £4–£6 ($6.40–$9.60). No credit cards. Mon–Thurs 7:30am–11pm; Fri–Sat 7:30am–midnight; Sun noon–7pm. Closed Christmas. Tube: Leicester Square. EGG DISHES/SANDWICHES/PASTA.

These restaurants, owned by the same family and located around the corner from one another, are brimming over with old photos, copper pots, herbs, breads, and hanging sausages; the customers' plates are similarly stuffed. Both locations dish up breakfasts using homemade sausage, high-quality bacon, and the same maize-fed eggs the queen eats. Gears shift at lunch, with a variety of sandwiches (the specialty being corned beef) piled high with layers of meat, cheese, and vegetables.

In the evening, Pasta Brown's menu gives way to 29 varieties of pasta and sauces, from penne to tortellini, Neapolitan to carbonara. Meals include salad and garlic bread, and desserts feature carrot cake and homemade tiramisu.

✪ **The Stockpot.** 40 Panton St., SW1. ☎ **0171/839-5142.** Reservations accepted only for dinner. Main courses £2.20–£5.35 ($3.50–$8.55); fixed-price 2-course lunch £3.20 ($5.10); fixed-price 3-course dinner £6.50 ($10.40). No credit cards. Mon–Sat 7am–11:30pm; Sun 7am–10pm. Tube: Piccadilly Circus or Leicester Square. ENGLISH/CONTINENTAL.

Penny for penny, we believe that this cozy little restaurant offers one of the best dining bargains in London. Meals include minestrone soup, spaghetti bolognese (the eternal favorite), braised lamb, and apple crumble (or other desserts). Offering two levels of dining in a modern atmosphere, the Stockpot has a share-the-table policy during peak dining hours. The little restaurant lies off Haymarket, opposite the Comedy Theatre.

# SOHO

**Amalfi Ristorante.** 29–31 Old Compton St., W1. ☎ **0171/437-7284.** Reservations recommended. Main courses £5–£12 ($8–$19.20). AE, DC, MC, V. Mon–Sat noon–11:15pm; Sun noon–10pm. Tube: Leicester Square. NEAPOLITAN.

Established in the 1950s when many of its patrons were unfamiliar with fare such as pizza, this place has continued to thrive when many competitors have come and gone. Crowded and bargain-priced, its crew of Italian chefs prepare dishes such as spaghetti, pizzas, veal in white wine sauce, minestrone, and lasagna. Fresh salads are served with many of the main courses. If you have room for dessert, an in-house pâtisserie makes excellent Italian pastries.

**Anemos.** 32 Charlotte St., W1. ☎ **0171/636-2289.** Reservations recommended. Main courses £6–£13 ($9.60–$20.80); meze £13 ($20.80) per person. AE, DC, MC, V. Mon–Sat noon–3pm and 6pm–1am. Tube: Tottenham Court Road. GREEK/CYPRIOT.

Anemos, Greek for strong wind or tornado, is the place for breaking plates, dancing, and joining the waiters in a rip-roaring Greek song. There's even a magic show and a floor show with Greek dancing. Specialties include meze, a typical Greek meal encompassing a variety of 12 to 14 different small dishes. A typical meal might be taramasalata, hummus, and kebabs, plus dessert, cheese and coffee, and wine.

**Café Pasta.** 184 Shaftesbury Ave., W1. ☎ **0171/379-0198.** Reservations not accepted. Snacks £1.35–£2.50 ($2.15–$4); main courses £4.95–£6.25 ($7.90–$10). MC, V. Mon–Sat 9:30am–11:30pm; Sun 9:30am–11pm. Closed Christmas. Tube: Tottenham Court Road. ITALIAN.

There are seven Café Pasta restaurants in London, all offering a relaxed dining atmosphere, but this location also has the edge with an exhibition kitchen and outdoor dining in warm weather. This pasta joint chain offers large, filling Italian meals made with fresh ingredients, and it stocks a full bar. The food isn't innovative, but it's good, inexpensive, and served by a helpful staff. Sample menu items include spaghetti with bacon and gorgonzola cheese, rosemary-buttered garlic egg tagliantelle, and penne with cauliflower in a chili, cream, and tomato sauce. In the morning and afternoons, French bread sandwiches and pastries are available.

**Chiang Mai.** 48 Frith St., W1. ☎ **0171/437-7444.** Reservations recommended Sat–Sun. Main courses £5.50–£7.75 ($8.80–$12.40). AE, MC, V. Mon–Sat noon–3pm and 6–11pm; Sun 6–10:30pm. Tube: Leicester Square or Tottenham Court Road. THAI.

In the center of Soho, this restaurant is named after the ancient northern capital of Thailand, a region known for its rich, spicy foods (not to mention its opium growers). Try the hot-and-sour dishes, their chili-laced specials, or one of their special vegetarian meals. It's located next door to Ronnie Scott's, the most famous jazz club in England.

**Dumpling Inn.** 15A Gerrard St., W1. ☎ **0171/437-2567.** Reservations recommended. Main courses £5.65–£11 ($9.05–$17.60); fixed-price lunch or dinner £13–£23 ($20.80–$36.80). AE, MC, V. Daily 11:45am–11:45pm. Tube: Piccadilly Circus. CHINESE.

Despite the incongruous name, this is a cool and rather elegant eatery, serving a delectable Peking Mandarin cuisine that dates back almost 3,000 years and owes some of its special piquancy to various Mongolian ingredients. Their style is best represented by a savory stew called "hot pot." Regulars also come here for shark-fin soup, beef in oyster sauce, seaweed and sesame seed prawns on toast, duck with chili and black bean sauce, and fried sliced fish with sauce. It wouldn't be right if the specialty were not dumplings, and it is; you can make a meal from the dim sum list. Service is leisurely, so don't dine here before a theater date.

**Old Coffee House.** 49 Beak St., W1. ☎ **0171/437-2197.** Main courses £4–£4.50 ($6.40–$7.20). No credit cards. Mon–Sat noon–3pm. Pub, Mon–Sat 11am–11pm; Sun noon–3pm and 7–10:30pm. Tube: Oxford Circus or Piccadilly Circus. BRITISH.

Previously honored as "Soho Pub of the Year," the Old Coffee House takes its name from the coffeehouse heyday of 1700s London—when coffee was "the devil's brew." The pub is heavily decorated with bric-a-brac, including old musical instruments and World War I recruiting posters. It still serves pots of filtered coffee. Have your drink at a long narrow bar, or retreat to the upstairs restaurant where you can enjoy good lunches of such typically English dishes as steak-and-kidney pie, and scampi and chips. Vegetarian dishes and burgers and fries are also popular.

**✪ Red Fort.** 77 Dean St., W1. ☎ **0171/437-2525.** Reservations required. Main courses £9.95–£14.95 ($15.90–$23.90); lunch buffet £12.50 ($20). AE, DC, DISC, MC, V. Daily noon–2:45pm and 5:45–11:45pm. Tube: Leicester Square or Tottenham Court Road. BANGLADESHI/INDIAN.

One of the finest Indian restaurants in London, the Red Fort offers superb meals. The menu, featuring classical north Indian and Bangladeshi dishes, is surprisingly short—which enables the chefs to cook curries fresh to order. Dishes include Murg Jaipuri (a hot dish of chicken cooked with whole spices and red chilies; "Shah Jahan's Last Stew" (boneless pieces of lamb marinated in yogurt with mace, cardamom, and apricot; Sula Salmon (a classical Rajasthani smoked kebab of fresh salmon, and Jhinga Gulnar (jumbo prawns pickled in mustard and fenugreek seeds, ginger, yogurt, and lemon. The restaurant also serves an enormously popular lunchtime buffet with a selection that changes daily. Tandoori dishes sometimes feature quail, and Bangladeshi fish specialties as well as chicken and lamb curries are succulently prepared. The waiters are helpful in explaining the menu.

**Steph's.** 39 Dean St., W1. ☎ **0171/734-5976.** Reservations advisable on weekends but not necessary. Main courses £6.95–£14.95 ($11.25–$23.95). Mon–Thurs noon–3pm and 5:30–11:30pm; Fri noon–3pm and 5:30pm–midnight; Sat 5:30pm–midnight. Tube: Piccadilly Circus. ENGLISH.

Soho's most famous gay restaurant looks like a stage from the John Waters camp classic, *Pink Flamingos*. A theatrical clientele of all sexual persuasions is attracted to this place and its good, wholesome food—likely to include everything from beef-and-oyster pie to selections from the charcoal grill, including swordfish steak.

**Venus Kebab House.** 2 Charlotte St., W1. ☎ **0171/636-4324.** Reservations required in summer. Main courses £4.50–£6 ($7.20–$9.60). MC, V. Daily noon–11:30pm. Tube: Goodge Street or Tottenham Court Road. GREEK/VEGETARIAN.

This corner restaurant is known for Greek specialties, good food, and low prices. Try avgolemono, the Greek national soup, made with chicken stock, rice, egg, lemon, and spices. The standard specialties are dolmades (vine leaves stuffed with lamb, beef, rice, tomatoes, and spices) and moussaka, but the chef also prepares fish and vegetarian meals. The namesake lamb kebabs are especially recommended. In summer, tables are set up outdoors.

## BLOOMSBURY

**British Museum Restaurant.** Great Russell St., WC1. ☎ **0171/580-9212.** Soup £2.75 ($4.40); main courses £5.95–£7.95 ($9.50–$12.70). MC, V. Mon–Sat cold food 10am–4:30pm, hot food noon–3pm; Sun hot and cold food 2:30–5:30pm. Closed holidays. Tube: Holborn or Tottenham Court Road. ENGLISH.

If you've been exploring the wonders of this world-renowned museum, this is obviously the best place for lunch. Located on the lobby level of the East Wing, it is decorated with about a dozen full-size copies of the bas-reliefs from a temple in the town of Nereid in ancient Greece. (You'll find the originals in nearby galleries.) The format is self-service. A few hot specials (there's always something for vegetarians) and crisp salads are made fresh every day, and there's always a good selection of fish and cold meat dishes as well. Desserts include pastries and cakes. On Sunday a hot plate of the day is offered, although most of the emphasis is on soups, salads, and cold platters. There's also a cafe adjacent to the restaurant, serving coffee, sandwiches, and pastries during the same hours as the restaurant.

**Museum Tavern.** 49 Great Russell St., WC1. ☎ **0171/242-8987.** Bar snacks £2–£6 ($3.20–$9.60). AE, DC, MC, V. Mon–Sat 9:30am–11pm; Sun 10:30am–10:30pm. Tube: Holborn or Tottenham Court Road. ENGLISH.

Across the street from the entrance to the British Museum, this circa-1703 pub retains most of its antique trappings: velvet, oak paneling, and cut glass. It is right in the center of the University of London area and is popular with writers, publishers, and researchers from the museum. Supposedly, Karl Marx toiled over a treatise in the pub. Traditional English food is served, with steak-and-kidney pie, sausages cooked in English cider, and chef's specials on the hot-food menu. Cold food includes turkey-and-ham pie, ploughman's lunch, and salads. Beverages include several English ales, Guinness, cold lagers, cider, wines, and spirits. Food and coffee are served all day; the pub gets crowded at lunchtime.

**Spaghetti House.** 15–17 Goodge St., W1P. ☎ **0171/636-6582.** Main courses £5.20–£11.95 ($8.30–$19.10). AE, DC, MC, V. Mon–Thurs noon–11pm; Fri–Sat noon–11:30pm; Sun 5:30–10:30pm. Tube: Goodge Street. ITALIAN.

With healthy eating and today's life-style in mind, Spaghetti House menus feature delicious, freshly made pasta dishes, together with many much-loved regional Italian dishes. There are many Mediterranean foods and ingredients—olive oil, grilled meats and fish, grilled vegetables and salads. The finest Parma ham and the real Parmesan cheese—Simone Lavarini's pride and joy—are stored in special temperature-controlled cellars to keep them in peak conditions until they are needed. Chianti bottles enhance the inviting Italian atmosphere on the four floors of this restaurant. The leader of a chain of spaghetti and pizza houses, it offers at least 10 different varieties of pasta and 10 different meat dishes made from veal, beef, or chicken. Saltimbocca, the classic veal-and-ham dish from Rome, is most popular, but most of the culinary inspiration comes from north-central Italy (Tuscany, Umbria, Emilia Romagna). For dessert, cassata siciliana is a good choice. The restaurant is across Tottenham Court Road in the vicinity of Russell Square.

## COVENT GARDEN & THE STRAND

✪ **Food for Thought.** 31 Neal St., WC2. ☎ **0171/836-0239.** Main courses £2.80–£5 ($4.50–$8). No credit cards. Mon–Sat 9:30am–9pm; Sun noon–4pm. Tube: Covent Garden. VEGETARIAN.

Here you'll find some of the best and least expensive vegetarian food in the neighborhood. During peak dining hours it's usually jam packed, so come after the rush. Food selections change twice a day, but they include excellent soups with whole-meal bread, freshly made salads, quiches, curries, and casseroles, with daily hot specials. All food is prepared from fresh, quality produce. The restaurant is ideally situated for the Covent Garden shopper or the pretheater diner: After leaving the tube at Covent Garden, stroll along Neal Street toward Shaftesbury Avenue; the restaurant is on the left in the second block. Take-out service is also provided; no smoking is allowed.

# In case you want to see the world.

At American Express, we're here to make your journey a smooth one. So we have over 1,700 travel service locations in over 120 countries ready to help. What else would you expect from the world's largest travel agency?

do more®

**Travel**

# In case you want to be welcomed there.

We're here to see that you're always welcomed at establishments everywhere. That's why millions of people carry the American Express® Card – for peace of mind, confidence, and security, around the world or just around the corner.

do more

Cards

# In case you're running low.

**We're here to help with more than 118,000 Express Cash locations around the world. In order to enroll, just call American Express before you start your vacation.**

do more

**Express Cash**

# And just in case.

We're here with American Express® Travelers Cheques and Cheques *for Two*.® They're the safest way to carry money on your vacation and the surest way to get a refund, practically anywhere, anytime.

Another way we help you...

do more

**Travelers
Cheques**

**The George.** 213 The Strand, WC2. ☎ **0171/353-9238.** Bar platters £2.70–£5.95 ($4.30–$9.50). DC, V. Mon–Sat 11:30am–2:30pm. Pub, Mon–Fri 11am–11pm; Sat 11am–3pm. Tube: Temple. PUB GRUB.

Although its half-timbered facade would lead you to believe that it is older than it actually is, this pub was originally built as a coffeehouse in 1723. On the Strand, at the lower end of Fleet Street opposite the Royal Courts of Justice, the place is a favorite of barristers, their clients, and the handful of journalists who haven't yet moved to other parts of London. The establishment's antecedents are illustrious: Samuel Johnson had his mail delivered here, and Samuel Pepys and Oliver Goldsmith enjoyed many tankards of the forerunner of what would become Bass Ale. Today the setting seems only slightly changed from those days, with much of the original architecture still intact. Hot and cold platters are served from a food counter at the back of the pub, including bangers and mash, fish-and-chips, steak-and-kidney pie, lasagna, and the like. Additional seating is available in the basement, where a headless cavalier is said to haunt the same premises where he enjoyed his liquor in an earlier day.

**Magno's.** 65A Long Acre, WC2. ☎ **0171/836-6077.** Reservations required. Main courses £9.95–£15.45 ($15.90–$24.70); fixed-price menus £13.95–£16.95 ($22.30–$27.10); fixed-price pretheater supper (served 5:30–7:15pm) £10.95 ($17.50). AE, DC, MC, V. Mon–Fri noon–2:30pm and 5:30–11:30pm; Sat 5:30–11:30pm. Tube: Covent Garden. FRENCH.

This recommended French restaurant operates in a brasserie-inspired format of green-and-cream-colored walls, closely spaced tables, and efficient service. Menu items are inspired by traditional French bistro cuisine, and might include a feuilleté au Roquefort (bleu cheese in puff pastry), duckling with cabbage and Armagnac, rack of lamb with tarragon sauce, and roast veal or roast pork in the Provençal style served with ratatouille. Although prices here can be a tad high for budget travelers, the pretheater fixed-price menu is a great value. Magno's is especially popular for before- and after-theater meals, so advance reservations at these times are very important.

**The Nag's Head.** 10 James St., WC2. ☎ **0171/836-4678.** Reservations not accepted. Sandwich platters with salad £3–£6 ($4.80–$9.60); full-meal salads £4.75–£5.50 ($7.60–$8.80). AE, DC, MC, V. Mon–Sat 11am–11pm; Sun noon–3pm and 7:30–10:30pm. Tube: Covent Garden. ENGLISH.

The Nag's Head is one of the most famous Edwardian pubs of London. Patrons once had to make their way through lorries of fruit and flowers for a drink here. In the evening, elegantly dressed operagoers used to mix with Cockney cauliflower peddlers at the bar—and 300 years of British tradition happily faded away. With the moving of the market, all that changed long ago, and the pub is now patronized mainly by young people who seem to fill up the tables and bar counter every evening. Lunch is typical pub grub: sandwiches, salads, pork cooked in cider, and garlic prawns. Sandwich platters are served only during the lunch hours (noon to 3:30pm); however, snacks are available in the afternoon.

**✪ Porter's English Restaurant.** 17 Henrietta St., WC2. ☎ **0171/836-6466.** Reservations recommended. Main courses £7.25–£8 ($11.60–$12.80); fixed-price menu £16.50 ($26.40). AE, DC, MC, V. Mon–Sat noon–11:30pm; Sun noon–10:30pm. Tube: Covent Garden or Charing Cross. ENGLISH.

Owned by the seventh earl of Bradford, himself a frequent visitor, Porter's has a friendly, informal, and lively atmosphere in comfortable surroundings on two floors. It specializes in classic English pies, including steak and kidney; lamb and apricot; ham, leek, and cheese; and steak, oyster, and clam. The traditional roast beef with Yorkshire pudding is featured on weekends. With whipped cream or custard, "puddings" come hot or cold, including bread-and-butter pudding and steamed syrup sponge. (The English call all desserts puddings, but at Porter's they really are puddings in the American sense.) The bar does quite a few exotic cocktails, and you can also order cider by the half pint, even English wines or traditional English mead. A traditional English tea is also served, for £3.95 ($6.30).

**Taste of India.** 25 Catherine St., Covent Garden, WC2. ☎ **0171/836-6591.** Reservations required. Main courses £5.75–£10.95 ($9.20–$17.50); fixed-price buffet lunch £7.95 ($12.70); fixed-price 2-course dinner £12.50 ($20); fixed-price pretheater meal (served 5:30–7:30pm only) £8.95 ($14.30). AE, DC, MC, V. Daily noon–2:30pm and 5:30pm–midnight. Tube: Covent Garden. INDIAN.

This is one of the most respected Indian restaurants in London, with a regular clientele of theatergoers, members of Parliament, and businesspeople. In a busy but intimate setting dotted with Indian artwork, you can enjoy the sometimes fiery, sometimes subtle cuisine of northern and southern India. Specialties include a range of Tandoori dishes (prawns, chicken, lamb, or vegetarian dishes slow-cooked in a clay pot), elegant preparations of lamb (including a version cooked with cream and yogurt), and some of the best vegetarian dishes available anywhere.

**Tuttons.** 11–12 Russell St., WC2. ☎ **0171/836-4141.** Main courses £8.50–£11.90 ($13.60–$19.05); pretheater supper or lunch £10.90 ($17.45); fixed-price dinner £14.90 ($23.85). AE, MC, V. Sun–Thurs 9:30am–11:30pm; Fri–Sat 9:30am–midnight. Tube: Covent Garden. BRITISH.

The best place to people-watch in London is this bustling brasserie at the corner of Russell Street and the Piazza, with sun-shaded tables out on the pavement. Even when it's rainy, the giant windows allow you to continue your voyeurism. The color scheme of bullfight red and bright lemon yellow evoke a night in Tijuana. Everybody flocks here: mothers with children, same-sex couples, off-the-record weekenders. The food's not bad, and the fixed-price menus are a good value for pricey Covent Garden. Begin with one of the appetizers such as goat cheese, then follow with the grilled lambsteak or perhaps the poached salmon with spinach and lemon sauce. Spicy fish cakes with tomatoes and coriander is another offering, as is the baked cod or the Thai chicken and mint salad with ginger. For dessert, since you're in Covent Garden, why not take on the Eliza Doolittle favorite, sticky toffee pudding with hot caramel.

## HOLBORN

**The Fryer's Delight.** 19 Theobalds Rd., WC1. ☎ **0171/405-4114.** Reservations not accepted. Fish-and-chips £3.50 ($5.60); pies £1 ($1.60). No credit cards. Mon–Sat noon–10pm; takeout noon–11pm. Tube: Holborn. SEAFOOD/BRITISH.

This restaurant has a reputation for being one of the better fast-food eateries in London, as is illustrated by the line of customers often waiting to place an order. Portions are large, and main courses include fried chicken, fish and chips (including rock cod, plaice, and haddock), steak and kidney or beef and onion pies, sausages, and side dishes of pickled cucumber and onions, peas, or baked beans. Takeout comes wrapped in plain white paper, or else you can eat at five tables on the premises.

**North Sea Fish Restaurant.** 7–8 Leigh St., WC1. ☎ **0171/387-5892.** Reservations recommended. Fish platters £6.30–£12.60 ($10.10–$20.15). AE, DC, MC, V. Mon–Sat noon–2pm and 5:30–10pm. Tube: Russell Square. SEAFOOD.

The fish served in this bright and clean restaurant is purchased fresh every day; the quality is high, and prices are low. Fish is most often deep-fried in batter, but you can also order it grilled. The menu is wisely limited. Students from the Bloomsbury area flock to the place.

**October Gallery Café.** 24 Old Gloucester St., WC1. ☎ **0171/831-1618.** Reservations recommended. Main courses £4.20–£4.80 ($6.70–$7.70). No credit cards. Tues–Sat 12:30–2:30pm (gallery open until 5:30pm). Closed 1st week of Aug to 2nd week of Sept, 2 weeks at Christmas. Tube: Holborn. ENGLISH/CHINESE.

Located in a former Victorian school building near the British Museum, this gallery-eatery was founded in 1979. The dining area is actually within the gallery, and the menu, which changes daily, offers eclectic seasonal dishes as varied as the cross-cultural avant-garde exhibits and performances that take place here. Portions are generous, and half-plates are available for children. Sample menu items include potato and leek soup, spicy eggplant with rice and salad, broccoli and cheese roulade, lemon tarts, and rhubarb crumble. The experience is heightened by surrounding exhibits featuring artists such as William S. Burroughs, Kenji Yoshida, and Aubrey Williams, as well as courtyard performances by the likes of the Bauls of Bengal, Balinese dancers, and Pakistani dervishes, plus readings by authors including Lawrence Durrell and Brion Gysin. Outdoor dining is available in the lush, plant-filled courtyard during warm weather. Bringing your own wine is permissible.

## TRAFALGAR SQUARE

**Clarence Inn.** 53 Whitehall, SW1. ☎ **0171/930-4808.** Reservations not accepted in pub, recommended for upstairs restaurant. Platters and snacks from £3.50 ($5.60); fixed-price menu 3 courses from £8 ($12.80). MC, V. Daily noon–9pm. Pub, Mon–Sat 11am–11pm; Sun noon–3pm. Bus/Tube: Charing Cross or Embankment. ENGLISH.

Just down from Trafalgar Square, this 18th-century inn is a haunt of civil servants from the nearby ministry's office. They enjoy such lunchtime food as braised oxtail, Asian pork chops, and traditional shepherd's pie. There are always at least four hot dishes of the day, plus a range of cold dishes and salads. The pub is at street level, and bar snacks, such as ploughman's lunch and various meat pies, are served during pub hours. The more formal restaurant is upstairs, offering lunch daily. The decor includes blackened beams, a sawdust-strewn floor, church pews, and uncovered tables lit by flickering gaslights.

**National Gallery Café/National Gallery Brasserie.** Trafalgar Sq., WC2. ☎ **0171/839-3321.** Cafe: soups £1.50–£2.25 ($2.40–$3.60); main courses £2.50–£6 ($4–$9.60). Brasserie: main courses £5–£8 ($8–$12.80). AE, DC, MC, V. Mon, Tues, Thurs, Sat 10am–6pm; Wed 10am–8pm; Sun noon–6pm; extended hours during special exhibitions. Tube: Charing Cross. CONTINENTAL.

In addition to its more obvious allure as a repository for art, the National Gallery contains two budget restaurants, either of which might serve as a calming interlude. The less expensive and less formal of the two is the Café, set in the basement of the East Wing, with a self-service format.

More elegant is the Brasserie, which opened in 1992. Set one floor above lobby level in the Sainsbury (West) Wing, the Brasserie provides tableside service, a view over Trafalgar Square, and a stylish continental ambience. In both restaurants, menu items include such dishes as fresh salads, coq au vin (chicken cooked in white wine), beef bourguignonne, quiches, and a tempting array of Austrian-inspired tortes and pastries.

## THE CITY

**Bow Wine Vaults.** 10 Bow Churchyard, EC4. ☎ **0171/248-1121.** Reservations recommended. Main courses £6.50–£8 ($10.40–$12.80). AE, DC, MC, V. The Restaurant and Grill Bar, Mon–Fri 11am–10pm. Pub, Mon–Fri 11am–11pm. Tube: Bank Street or St. Paul's. ENGLISH.

The Bow Wine Vaults existed long before the current wine-bar fad began in the 1970s. One of the most famous wine bars of London, it attracts cost-conscious diners and drinkers who head below ground to its vaulted cellars. Menu choices in the Cellar Grill Bar, as it's called, include such traditional fare as deep-fried Camembert, chicken Kiev, and a mixed grill, along with fish. More elegant meals, served in the street-level dining room, called "The Restaurant," include mussels in cider sauce, English wild mushrooms in puff pastry, beef Wellington, and steak with brown-butter sauce. Adjacent to the restaurant is a cocktail bar, open weekdays from 11:30am to 8pm, which is popular with City employees after work.

**Olde Wine Shades.** 6 Martin Lane, Cannon St., EC4. ☎ **0171/626-6876.** Jacket and tie required. Main courses £6–£14 ($9.60–$22.40). AE, MC, V. Mon–Fri 11:30am–3pm and 5–8pm. Closed bank holidays. Tube: Cannon Street. ENGLISH.

The oldest wine house in The City, dating from 1663, this was the only City tavern to survive the Great Fire in 1666 and Hitler's bombings of 1940. Only 100 yards from the famous monument designed by Sir Christopher Wren to commemorate the Great Fire, it's decorated with oil paintings and 19th-century political cartoons and is one of the many London bars that Dickens used to frequent. There's a restaurant downstairs, and you can also eat light meals upstairs, including Breton pâté and French bread with ham "off the bone." You can order jacket (baked) potatoes filled with cheese, venison pie with a salad garnish, or a large beef salad. Simple fare notwithstanding, men must wear jackets, collars, and ties.

**The Place Below at St. Mary-le-Bow.** St. Mary-le-Bow Crypt, Cheapside, EC2. ☎ **0171/329-0789.** Reservations accepted. Main courses £5.75–£6.25 ($9.20–$10). MC, V. Mon–Fri 7:30am–2:30pm. Tube: St. Paul's. VEGETARIAN.

Curiously located in the 11th-century crypt of Sir Christopher Wren's architectural masterpiece, St. Mary-le-Bow Church, this restaurant has won rave reviews and numerous awards for owner Bill Sewell since opening in the late 1980s. Featuring innovative vegetarian cuisine, the eatery offers self-service breakfast and lunch. Breakfast is composed of cold items such as muffins, fruit salad, and cereal, whereas lunch warms things up with soups like lentils with roast garlic and lime, and main courses including spinach ricotta lasagna, pasta with broccoli pesto and cherry tomatoes, and English vegetables with Stilton. Desserts include fruit crumble, cakes, and tarts. Bringing your own bottle is permissible.

**Simpson's of Cornhill.** 38¹/₂ Ball St., EC3. ☎ **0171/626-9985.** Reservations not accepted. 3-course meal and drink £12–£13 ($19.20–$20.80). AE, DC, MC, V. Mon–Fri noon–3pm. Closed holidays. Tube: Bank. BRITISH.

Established as a pub in 1759, this restaurant (not to be confused with Simpson's on the Strand) was a male eating club from its inception until 1916, when women were finally allowed through the doors. There are two levels; the upstairs houses a traditional bar, whereas the downstairs plays host to a wine bar. The food is traditional English fare, including chops, steaks, rabbit, steak-and-kidney pie, and cold Scotch salmon. The house specialty is stewed cheese, a mixture of melted cheddar with Worcestershire sauce and spices, which is spread on toast. Meals are heavy, but their quality makes this a popular lunch destination.

The restaurant suffered water and smoke damage in a recent fire, but the building is protected by the Heritage Society, so it was refurbished and reopened in 1997. Much of the original decor was salvaged, and the old club look remains intact.

**Ye Olde Cock Tavern.** 22 Fleet St., EC4. ☎ **0171/353-8570.** Reservations recommended. Main courses £9–£14 ($14.40–$22.40); fixed-price 2-course lunch £12 ($19.20). AE, DC,

MC, V. Carvery, Mon–Fri noon–3pm. Pub, Mon–Fri 11am–11pm. Tube: Temple or Chancery Lane. ENGLISH.

Dating from 1549, this is one of the few buildings in London to have survived the Great Fire. It boasts a long line of literary patrons: Charles Dickens used to frequent the pub, Samuel Pepys mentioned the pub in one of his diary entries, and Lord Tennyson referred to it in one of his poems—a copy of which is framed and proudly displayed near the entrance. Downstairs, you can order a pint as well as snack-bar food, steak-and-kidney pie, or a cold chicken-and-beef plate with salad. At the Carvery upstairs, a meal includes a choice of appetizers, followed by all the roasts you can carve—beef, lamb, pork, or turkey.

## WESTMINSTER & VICTORIA

✪ **The Albert.** 52 Victoria St., SW1. ☎ **0171/222-5577.** Reservations recommended. Fixed-price Carvery meals £14.95 ($23.90). AE, DC, MC, V. Carvery, daily noon–9:30pm. Pub, Mon–Sat 11am–11pm; Sun noon–10:30pm. Tube: St. James's Park. ENGLISH.

Once designated "pub of the year," the Albert is a real bit of Victorian England, visited for its sumptuous roasts traditionally prepared and carved for you at its Carvery. The pub, which opened in 1852, was called the Blue Coat Boy until it changed to its present name in 1862 to honor the royal consort of Queen Victoria. It's one of a handful of pubs with bells controlled from the floor of the houses of Parliament, used to notify patrons when an important vote is coming up. At the Carvery you can return as often as you wish, sampling as many helpings of turkey, pork, beef, and other offerings as you want. Fish lovers and vegetarians can also find something to their liking here. Desserts are served from the trolley, and the coffee is unlimited.

**The Green Café.** 16 Eccleston St., SW1. ☎ **0171/730-5304.** Reservations not accepted. Main courses £2.50–£4.50 ($4–$7.20). No credit cards. Mon–Fri 6am–6:30pm; Sat 6:30am–noon. Closed holidays. Tube: Victoria. CONTINENTAL.

This 26-seat cafe has been run by the Fiori family since 1955 and is very popular with neighborhood workers, cabbies, and professionals in suites, counting many of them as regular customers. There is a different special daily, and everything, including bread and pastas, is homemade. Menu items include English breakfast, sandwiches, fresh fish and chips, pastas, and roast beef, lamb, chicken, or pork with vegetables. The restaurant does not offer bar services.

**Tate Gallery Restaurant.** Millbank, SW1. ☎ **0171/887-8877.** Reservations strongly recommended. Main courses £8–£16 ($12.80–$25.60). AE, MC, V. Mon–Sat noon–3pm. Tube: Pimlico. Bus: 77 or 78. BRITISH.

This restaurant offers what may be the best bargains in premium wines to be found anywhere in Britain. It's especially strong on bordeaux and burgundies. The management keeps the markup on wines at 40% to 65%, rather than the 100% to 200% added to the wholesale price in other restaurants. In fact, the prices here are lower even than in most retail wine shops. Wines begin at £10 ($16) per bottle or £2.95 ($4.70) per glass. Wine connoisseurs frequently come for lunch, heedless of the museum's paintings. However, if you're looking for food instead of (or in addition to) wine, the restaurant specializes in an English menu that changes about every month. Menu items include seafood crepe, roast duck with spiced apricots, roast English sirloin of beef with Yorkshire pudding, and a selection of vegetarian dishes. At rare intervals the restaurant also offers dishes inspired by 17th-century English cuisine, including "hindle wakes" (cold stuffed chicken with prunes) and "pye with fruyt ryfshews" (fruit tart topped with meringue). You reach the restaurant through the museum's main entrance on Millbank.

**The Well.** 2 Eccleston Place, SW1. ☎ **0171/730-7303.** Reservations not accepted. Soup £2.65 ($4.25); main course £4.30 ($6.90). No credit cards. Mon–Sat 9:30am–5pm. Tube: Victoria. BRITISH.

Located across the street from Victoria Station, this cafeteria donates profits to benefit St. Michael's Church, and gratuities are donated to a different charity every month. At first you may think you've arrived at a soup kitchen, but the food is surprisingly good, wholesome and hearty. Many pensioners with low incomes eat here every day, finding it cheaper and more convenient than trying to purchase food and cook back in their flats. Roasted coffee, breads, and meals are prepared on the premises, with offerings including an English breakfast, and a variety of hearty three-course lunches with soup and sandwiches. Cakes from the Homemade Cake Company are available by the slice or whole. Only soup is offered on Saturdays, and it is advisable to arrive early on any given day since service stops when the food runs out.

# KNIGHTSBRIDGE & BELGRAVIA

**Arco Bars of Knightsbridge.** 46 Hans Crescent, SW1. ☎ **0171/584-6454.** Reservations not accepted. Breakfast £3.80–£4.80 ($6.10–$7.70); lunch from £4 ($6.40). No credit cards. Mon–Sat 7am–6pm; breakfast 7am–noon and after 3pm. Closed holidays. Tube: Knightsbridge.

Across from Harrods, as well as near Hyde Park and several museums, this restaurant's location makes it an easy stop for tourists. Fresh made sandwiches and Italian cakes are available for dining in or takeout, and yogurt, pastas, desserts, and a full bar are available all day, as is afternoon tea with scones. The food is of the coffee shop/deli variety.

The restaurant has recently remodeled and though it was previously accused of having no atmosphere, it is now a light, airy space done in orange and terra-cotta, with windows that open onto the sidewalk for outdoor dining in warm weather. The walls double as gallery space and feature modern paintings that are also available for purchase.

**Bill Bentley's.** 31 Beauchamp Place, SW3. ☎ **0171/589-5080.** Reservations recommended. Main courses £8.20–£17.25 ($13.10–$27.60). AE, MC, V. Mon–Sat noon–2:30pm and 6–10:30pm. Pub, Mon–Sat 11:30am–11pm; Sun noon–5pm. Tube: Knightsbridge. ENGLISH.

Bill Bentley's stands right on this fashionable restaurant- and boutique-lined block. Its wine list is varied and reasonable, including a good selection of bordeaux. Many visitors come here just to sample the wines, including some "New World" choices along with popular French selections. In summer, a garden patio is open. If you don't wish for a formal dining experience, you can order from the wine-bar menu that begins with half a dozen oysters, or you can enjoy the chef's fish soup with croutons and rouille. Main dishes include Bill Bentley's famous fish cakes, served with tomato sauce, and the day's specialties are written on a chalkboard. In keeping with contemporary trends in London dining, the menu has been simplified and is somewhat less expensive than before. It is changed frequently, but typical dishes might include avocado, crab, and prawn salad as an appetizer, followed by pan-fried calf's liver or a poached stuffed salmon.

**Chicago Rib Shack.** 1 Raphael St., Knightsbridge, SW7. ☎ **0171/581-5595.** Reservations accepted Mon–Fri only. Main courses £6.45–£14.95 ($10.30–$23.90). AE, MC, V. Mon–Sat 11:45am–11:45pm; Sun 11am–11pm. Tube: Knightsbridge. AMERICAN.

Real American barbecued foods cooked in imported smoking ovens and marinated in barbecue sauce made from 15 ingredients are served in this restaurant, just 100 yards from Harrods. The menu also includes their famous onion loaf, which *Harper's*

*& Queen* described as "either a Brobdingnagian French fried onion or the Illinois equivalent of an onion bhaji." Visitors are encouraged to eat with their fingers, and bibs and hot towels are provided. A video is suspended in the bar showing American sports games. The restaurant sports an overwhelming number of Victorian architectural antiques that have been salvaged from demolished buildings all over the country. The 45-foot-long ornate mahogany and mirrored bar was once part of a Glasgow pub, and eight massive stained-glass windows came from a chapel in Lancashire.

✪ **The Nag's Head.** 53 Kinnerton St., SW1. ☎ **0171/235-1135.** Main courses £3.45–£4.95 ($5.50–$7.90). No credit cards. Mon–Sat 11am–11pm; Sun noon–3pm and 7–11pm. Tube: Knightsbridge or Hyde Park. ENGLISH.

This 1780 pub is said to be the smallest in London—although it's not the only one claiming such a distinction. The warm and cozy pub is housed in what was previously a jail; in 1921 it was sold for £12 and 6p. Here, in the midst of a cosmopolitan clientele, you can enjoy real ale sausage (made with pork and ale), shepherd's pie, steak-and-mushroom pie, or even quiche. The pub is patronized by journalists and musicians.

**Pasta Prego.** 1A Beauchamp Place, SW3. ☎ **0171/225-1064.** Reservations recommended. Main courses £6–£9 ($9.60–$14.40). AE, MC, V. Mon–Sat noon–3pm and 6–11pm; Sun noon–3pm and 6–10:30pm. Tube: Knightsbridge. ITALIAN.

Although this hole-in-the-wall Italian eatery is in one of the most expensive districts of London, you get good value and plenty of food. Tables are small; service is helpful. The pasta is fresh and includes some whole-wheat versions. Begin with a selection of antipasto and follow with an order of cannelloni. Main dishes might include ravioli del mar (with seafood) or a delectable risotto. Desserts are excellent, especially the banana pudding. You can also order a moderately priced house wine to go with your meal.

✪ **Stockpot.** 6 Basil St., SW3. ☎ **0171/589-8627.** Main courses £1.95–£5.20 ($3.10–$8.30). No credit cards. Mon–Sat 9:30am–11pm; Sun noon–10:30pm. Tube: Knightsbridge. ENGLISH/ CONTINENTAL.

Serving predominantly English fare with continental dishes scattered throughout the menu, the Stockpot is one of the best dining deals to be found in London. The menu changes twice daily. Starters might include chicken-liver pâté or a mushroom tartlet; main courses Lancashire hot pot, steak-and-kidney pie, filet of chicken with Normandy sauce, or lamb cutlets with red-wine and mushroom sauce. The selection always includes three or four vegetarian meals, with offerings such as vegetable lasagna and moussaka, or pasta with tagliatelle with broccoli. To finish, try the orange sponge pudding with cream, apple crumble, or one of the puddings, such as lemon or rice.

## CHELSEA & CHELSEA HARBOUR

**Boaters Wine Bar.** Harbour Yard, Chelsea Harbour, SW10. ☎ **0171/352-3687.** Main courses £3.75–£4.95 ($6–$7.90). AE, DC, MC, V. Sun–Fri noon–10pm. Take the Chelsea Harbour Hoppa Bus C3 from Earl's Court Mon–Sat; take a taxi on Sun. ENGLISH.

This restaurant occupies the premises of one of London's new "villages," Chelsea Harbour. Well-heeled residents often come here for a glass or bottle of champagne. Visitors from all over the world pour in here as well. Most of the emphasis at the bar is on an impressive array of bottled beers, beers on tap, and wine by either the bottle or the glass; only a minimum array of hard liquor is available. Sandwiches, cheese plates, salads, and such main dishes as chili con carne and mushroom-and-leek Stroganoff are available throughout the day. An impressive list of wines by the glass is offered, beginning at £2 ($3.20) for the house version.

**Chelsea Kitchen.** 98 King's Rd., SW3. ☎ **0171/589-1330.** Reservations recommended. Main courses £2–£5.50 ($3.20–$8.80); fixed-price menu £6 ($9.60). No credit cards. Daily 8am–11:15pm. Tube: Sloane Square. INTERNATIONAL.

This simple restaurant feeds large numbers of artists, musicians, and techno-music fans in a place that has changed very little since its establishment in 1961. The food and the clientele move fast, almost guaranteeing that the entire inventory of ingredients is sold out at the end of each day. There's seating on the street level and additional room in the cellar. Menu items usually include leek-and-potato soup, chicken Kiev, chicken parmigiana, steaks, sandwiches, and burgers. The clientele includes a broad cross section of clients—all having a good and cost-conscious time.

**Deals Restaurant and Diner.** Harbour Yard, Chelsea Harbour, SW10. ☎ **0171/352-5887.** Reservations recommended. Main courses £6–£11 ($9.60–$17.60). MC, V. Mon–Fri noon–3:30pm and 5:30–11pm; Sat noon–11:30pm; Sun noon–10pm. Take the Chelsea Harbour Hoppa Bus from Earl's Court. INTERNATIONAL.

After the Queen Mother arrived here on a barge to order a Dealsburger, the success of this place was assured. Deals is co-owned by Princess Margaret's son, Viscount Linley, and Lord Lichfield. The early 1900s atmosphere includes ceiling fans and bentwood banquettes. The food is a la American diner with a strong Eastern influence: Try teriyaki burgers, prawn curry, spareribs, or even a vegetarian dish, and finish with New England apple pie.

**Henry J. Beans (But His Friends Call Him Hank) Bar & Grill.** 195–197 King's Rd., SW3. ☎ **0171/352-9255.** Main courses £5.50–£6.50 ($8.80–$10.40). AE, MC, V. Mon–Sat 11:45am–11pm; Sun noon–10:30pm. Tube: Sloane Square. AMERICAN.

Popular and uninhibited, this is a likable, no-holds-barred American-style saloon. The clientele tends to be youngish, though on weekends the place fills up with young families. The decor was inspired by the pop-surrealistic 1960s and 1970s, with art and accessories by Andy Warhol wannabees. A commodious bar is the site of lively conversations, as clusters of people gather around stand-up tables or partially secluded booths. Check the chalkboard for daily specials; menu items tend to include chicken-fried chicken, nachos, taco salads, and many kinds of burgers and sandwiches. Also available are an array of health-conscious salads for vegetarians and meat eaters alike, low on fat and high in health value.

**Le Shop.** 329 King's Rd., SW3. ☎ **0171/352-3891.** Reservations required for parties of 6 or more. Crêpes £4–£8 ($6.40–$12.80). MC, V. Daily 10:30am–midnight. Closed Christmas. Tube: Sloane Square, then bus no. 11 or no. 19. CRÊPES.

Offering salads, galettes (buckwheat crêpes) and Breton-style crêpes, this was the first crêpe shop in London, and it remains among the best. Diners can choose from the menu or build their own French snacks from a large selection of meat, vegetable, and sweet fillings. Half portions are available for children, and beverages include a limited array of wines, cider, and beer. Front window tables make for entertaining dining, as this stretch of King's Road offers a pedestrian parade of fashion style setters.

# KENSINGTON

**Benedicts.** 106 Kensington High St., W8. ☎ **0171/937-7580.** Reservations required. Main courses £5–£10 ($8–$16). AE, MC, V. Mon–Fri noon–3pm and 5–10:30pm; Sat noon–10:30pm; Sun 5:30–9:30pm. Tube: Kensington High Street. IRISH/INTERNATIONAL.

After you cross the street from the tube station, climb to the second floor and enter Eire—Ireland. In a district filled with high-priced restaurants, Benedicts keeps its tabs reasonable, with Irish and international meals. Along with a good selection of wines, you can order country pâté, perhaps wild Irish smoked salmon, then follow with steak-and-ale pie or hot Gaelic pepper steak laced with Irish whiskey.

**Britannia.** 1 Allen St., W8. ☎ **0171/937-1864.** Reservations not accepted. Main courses £3–£5 ($4.80–$8). No credit cards. Mon–Sat 11am–11pm; Sun noon–10:30pm. Closed some holidays (call). Tube: High Street Kensington. PUB GRUB.

An old-fashioned pub in the heart of London, this establishment has been run by John and June Eaglestone for more than a decade now. The menu changes daily, but offers the likes of hot casseroles, lasagna, and steak-and-kidney pie for lunch, fish and chips for lunch and dinner, and toasted sandwiches, ploughman's lunch, and salads at all times. For dessert, June Eaglestone's apple pie and apple crumble come highly recommended by the regulars.

The pub features a large bar decorated with Toby mugs and English china plates. Offerings include beer and ale on tap, full liquor service, and several types of wine, including 10 selections available by the glass. Children are allowed, but only in the glassed-in conservatory in the back, which lends a pleasant atmosphere to meals with dining tables set up underneath a variety of hanging plants.

**Stick & Bowl.** 31 Kensington High St., W8. ☎ **0171/937-2778.** Reservations not accepted. Main courses £4–£5.50 ($6.40–$8.80). No credit cards. Daily 11:30am–11pm. Closed Christmas, Boxing Day. Tube: High Street Kensington. CHINESE.

Featuring only 30 seats, this is not a place to linger over dinner, but the fast-paced dining is balanced by more than 50 inexpensive menu selections, including soups, meat and fish dishes, and pork and seafood main courses service with rice and vegetables. Shoppers on Kensington High Street consider this not just a quick meal, but a bargain as well.

**Tumblers Wine Bar and Dining.** 1 Kensington High St., W8. ☎ **0171/937-0393.** Reservations recommended. Main courses £7–£11 ($11.20–$17.60). AE, DC, MC, V. Mon–Fri 11:30am–11pm. Tube: High Street Kensington. ENGLISH.

Shadowy and alluring, this restaurant is set beneath the pavements of London, inside the vaults of a bank originally built in the 1870s. Although a handful of pewter tankards and copper jugs decorate the bar, most of the decoration comes from the many candles that burn in a room almost completely lined with white-glazed ceramic bricks. No one will mind if you stop in just for a drink or a glass of the many French, German, and Australian wines, priced at £2.50 to £4.50 ($4 to $7.20) a glass. But if you want to eat, the menu promises "fine English food prepared and served in the proper manner." Menu items might be Tumbler's homemade pies, including a version made with chicken and chestnuts beneath a flaky pastry top, cod and chips with "mushy peas," bangers and mash, and platters of sliced ham or salmon.

## SOUTH KENSINGTON

✪ **Daquise.** 20 Thurloe St., SW7. ☎ **0171/589-6117.** Reservations recommended. Main courses £5–£10 ($8–$16); fixed-price lunch £5.80 ($9.30). No credit cards. Daily 10am–11pm. Tube: South Kensington. POLISH/EASTERN EUROPEAN.

Established during World War II, this restaurant immediately became a focal point of Polish culture in London, attracting a network of refugees who used it as a center to locate missing persons and organize a tattered but heroic resistance to Hitler. Today, almost all the staff speak Polish and keep alive nationalistic memories amid an old-fashioned decor with framed oil paintings decorating the walls. You might begin with borscht or marinated herring with potato salad, then follow with stuffed cabbage or beef a la Warsaw, perhaps steak a la Daquise. Everything is cooked old country style.

**Luigi Malone's.** 73 Old Brompton Rd., SW7. ☎ **0171/584-4323.** Reservations recommended. Main courses £5.50–£13.95 ($8.80–$22.30); fixed-price lunch £5.65 ($9.05), includes choice of wine, beer, or soft drink. AE, MC, V. Mon–Sat noon–11pm; Sun noon–10:30pm. Closed Christmas. Tube: South Kensington. INTERNATIONAL.

This restaurant's Italina/Irish name and antique American decor only hints at the diversity found in its menu. Offering fajitas, nachos, burgers, pizza, pastas, baby back ribs, steaks, seafood, stir fries, vegetarian dishes, sandwiches, salads, desserts, and a full bar, Luigi Malone's is a popular, ambitious eatery.

The atmosphere is always fun and sometimes hectic, especially on weekends during the 5 to 7:30pm happy hour.

**Noorjahan Restaurant.** 2A Bina Gardens, SW5. ☎ **0171/373-6522.** Main courses £6.50–£10.50 ($10.40–$16.80); fixed-price menu £18.50 ($29.60). AE, DC, MC, V. Daily noon–2:45pm and 6–11:45pm. Tube: Gloucester Road or South Kensington. INDIAN.

Follow in the footsteps of Billy Jean King, Brooke Shields, John Hurt, or Larry Hagman, all of whom beat you here. The chef at this well-established restaurant prepares an interesting selection of Indian food, mostly from the north where they opt for a more delicate mix of fruit and spices and cook with less fat. The temptation in any guidebook is to focus on the new and trendy, but the staff here asked us in all sincerity, "Why not the tried, the tested?" They are so right. Coming back here was like calling on an old friend again. We still prefer the tandoori dishes we enjoyed as students. They are cooked in a clay oven which gives them a unique flavor, especially the chicken Tikka (marinated and barbecued), or the tandoor fish (usually fresh trout in a spicy sauce). The appetizers and soups are exotic, and you can have a wide array of fresh vegetables that follow time-tested recipes. Vegetarians will find items of choice here as well. The lamb dishes are worth the long walk from the tube stop, especially Rogan Josh, cooked with glazed tomatoes, green herbs, and spices—fairly hot but not tear-producing.

**Parsons Restaurant.** 311 Fulham Rd., SW10. ☎ **0171/352-0651.** Reservations not accepted. Main courses £5.70–£7.95 ($9.10–$12.70). AE, DC, MC, V. Mon–Sat noon–12:30am; Sun noon–midnight. Closed Christmas. Tube: South Kensington. BRITISH/INTERNATIONAL.

Just west of the Victoria and Albert Museum and near Hyde Park, the location has made this a popular tourist stopover. The atmosphere is informal, with lots of glass, brass, and wood, and a waitstaff clad in T-shirts and jeans. When Parsons opened in 1971, it was modeled after San Francisco's Old Spaghetti Factory, but the emphasis has turned toward traditional British dishes, such as steak and Guinness pie and sausages and mush, and burgers and steaks using local free-range beef. Other items are available, though, offering soups, nachos, chili, salads, vegetable side dishes, pudding, pies, ice cream, sorbet, and frozen yogurt. Beverages include a limited selection of spirits, beer, and wine.

✪ **Phoenicia.** 11–13 Abingdon Rd., W8. ☎ **0171/937-0120.** Reservations required. Main courses £9–£10.95 ($14.40–$17.50); buffet lunch £11.95 ($19.10); fixed-price dinner £15.30–£28.30 ($24.50–$45.30). AE, DC, MC, V. Daily noon–midnight (buffet lunch, Sun 12:15–3:30pm). Tube: Kensington High Street. LEBANESE.

Phoenicia is highly regarded for both the quality of its Lebanese cuisine and its moderate prices. For the best value, go for lunch when you can enjoy a buffet of more than a dozen *meze* (appetizers), presented in little pottery dishes. The chef prepares two or three home-cooked dishes daily, including chicken in garlic sauce or stuffed lamb with vegetables. Many begin their meal with the apéritif arak, similar to ouzo. Other appetizers include such classic Middle Eastern dishes as hummus or stuffed vine leaves. In a clay oven the kitchen staff bakes its own breads and makes two different types of pizza. Minced lamb, spicy and deliciously flavored, is the eternal favorite. Various charcoal-grilled dishes are also offered.

**Victoria and Albert Museum Restaurant.** Henry Cole Wing, Cromwell Rd., SW7. ☎ **0171/ 938-8500.** Main courses £6–£9 ($9.60–$14.40). AE, DC, MC, V. Mon noon–5:50pm; Tues–Sun 10am–5:50pm. Tube: South Kensington. ENGLISH.

You'll find this to be a grade above your typical museum restaurant, and a remarkably good value as well. On very busy days, the line in the cafeteria moves slowly. The menu changes daily, but is likely to offer a good soup followed by many crisp salads, seafood, and fish and meat dishes. The pastries and cakes make terrific desserts, and an interesting selection of wines is available.

## NOTTING HILL GATE

**Books for Cooks & Ristorante.** 4 Blenheim Crescent, W11. ☎ **0171/221-1992.** Reservations required. Main courses £8–£12 ($12.80–$19.20). AE, DC, MC, V. Mon–Sat 10:30am–5pm. Tube: Notting Hill Gate, Ladbroke Grove. INTERNATIONAL.

Housed in the back room of a shop stocking 8,000 cookbook titles, owner Heidi Lascelles' restaurant not only mimics the diversity of its book selection, but also makes good use of its proximity to Portobello Road Market, as a daily rotation of visiting chefs come here to buy seasonal ingredients, then return to the kitchen to experiment with new recipes. The delectably varied menu changes widely from day to day, but diners can always expect a three-course meal consisting of soup, a vegetable dish, and cake. Seating is limited to just 15, making reservations is imperative, and you may want to get here early to browse through the front shop. Among the selections available is a yearly revision of the recipes tested in the dining room, available for £3.99 ($6.40).

## ST. MARYLEBONE

**The Lucky Spot.** 14 North Audley St., W1. ☎ **0171/493-0277.** Reservations not accepted. Main courses £4.50–£6.50 ($7.20–$10.40). No credit cards. Mon–Sat 7am–7pm. Closed holidays. Tube: Marble Arch, Bond St. ITALIAN.

Located near the American Embassy, this small Italian restaurant is so popular with the office crowd that it is best avoided between noon and 1pm. English breakfast is served in the morning, and 42 varieties of freshly made sandwiches, a number of pasta dishes, pizza, salads, fresh fish, and steaks are available for lunch or dinner. Afternoon tea is served with scones and cakes. There is take-out service, and although the restaurant does not feature a bar, diners are allowed to bring their own wine.

**Raw Deal.** 65 York St., W1. ☎ **0171/262-4841.** Main courses £5.50–£6 ($8.80–$9.60). No credit cards. Mon–Fri 10am–9:30pm (last order); Sat noon–9:30pm (last order). Tube: Baker Street. VEGETARIAN.

In a homelike and unpretentious environment, you can enjoy cafe-style dishes whose ingredients are strictly vegetarian. The good-natured owner, Sandra Barfield, draws inspiration from Italy, central Europe, and England. The format is self-service, and the menu includes at least two freshly made vegetarian specials of the day, perhaps zucchini and eggplant with mozzarella, tomatoes, and hazelnuts, or mushroom tarts, plus an array of salads. Raw Deal is especially popular at lunchtime because of the many office workers who cram in here; in the evening, however, the atmosphere is more relaxed. A full line of beer, wine, and spirits is available.

**Woodlands.** 77 Marylebone Lane, W1. ☎ **0171/486-3862.** Reservations recommended. Main courses £3.50–£4.95 ($5.60–$7.90); fixed-price meal £9.95–£10.95 ($15.90–$17.50). AE, DC, MC, V. Daily noon–3pm and 6–11pm. Tube: Bond Street. INDIAN/VEGETARIAN.

Memories of the British Empire linger at this cost-conscious restaurant where only the vegetarian cuisine of south India is served. In a pastel-colored dining room lined with Indian paintings and filled with Indian music, you'll choose from an unusual selection of *thalis* (variety plates) or *dosas* (spicy vegetarian pancakes). Lentils and rice are among the food group staples here, combinations of which are liberally flavored with herbs. Most of the staff are from south India, and are happy to advise patrons about how and what to order.

Woodlands maintains two other branches, in roughly the same format, near Piccadilly Circus at 37 Panton St., off Haymarket, SW1 (☎ **0171/839-7258;** tube: Piccadilly Circus) and another near Middlesex at 402 High St., HA9 (☎ **0181/ 902-9869;** tube: Wembly Central).

# PADDINGTON & BAYSWATER

✪ **Halepi.** 18 Leinster Terrace, W2. ☎ **0171/262-1070.** Reservations required. Main courses £9–£24 ($14.40–$38.40). AE, DC, MC, V. Daily noon–1am. Closed Christmas. Tube: Queensway. GREEK/CYPRIOT.

Run by the Kazolides family since 1966, this establishment was rated by the AAA Auto Guide of America as the best Greek restaurant in the world. Despite its prestigious reputation, the dining atmosphere is informal, with long rows of brightly clothed tables, *bouzouki* background music, and a large native clientele adding to the authenticity of the place.

Portions are generous, and menu items rely heavily on lamb and include kebabs, *klefticon* (baby lamb prepared with aromatic spices), moussaka (minced lamb and eggplant with bechamel sauce), and dolmades (vine leaves stuffed with lamb and rice). Other main courses include scallops, sea bass, Scotch halibut, huge Indonesian shrimp prepared with lemon juice, olive oil, garlic and spring onion sauce, and *afelia*, filet of pork cooked with wine and spices, served with potatoes and rice. The homemade baklava is recommended for dessert, and the wine list features numerous selections imported from Greece and Cyprus.

**Nahar Cafeteria—Mara House.** 190 Sussex Gardens, W2. ☎ **0171/402-8129.** Reservations not accepted. Main courses £2.90–£10 ($4.65–$16). No credit cards. Daily noon–10pm; Sat– Sun 8–10:30pm. Tube: Paddington. MALAYSIAN.

Off the beaten path, this basement cafeteria is hard to find, the entrance being a non-descript door located next to a steep staircase. Despite its gloomy accommodations, it is popular with local Malays, and offers a wide range of inexpensive, authentically prepared Malayasian dishes with daily menu changes. Sample menu items include eggplant baked in chili sauce, garlic chicken, bean curd in oyster sauce, fish in sweet and sour sauce, and a variety of coconut-based dishes. All main courses are served with rice or noodles and vegetables. Malayasian tea, a mixture of tea, cinnamon and condensed milk, is a popular drink, and rosewater, a sweet, lightly spiced water, is complimentary with all meals.

✪ **Veronica's.** 3 Hereford Rd., W2. ☎ **0171/229-5079.** Reservations required. Main courses £9.50–£15.50 ($15.20–$24.80); fixed-price meals £12.50 ($20). AE, DC, MC, V. Mon–Fri noon– 3pm; Mon–Sat 6:30pm–midnight. Tube: Bayswater or Queensway. ENGLISH.

Called the "market leader in café salons," Veronica's offers some of the finest British cuisine in London—at tabs you don't mind paying. Some dishes are based on recipes used in medieval or Tudor times. For example, your appetizer might be a salad called salmagundy, once enjoyed by Elizabeth I, made with crunchy pickled vegetables. Another concoction might be watersouchy, a medieval stew crammed with mixed seafood. However, each dish is given a current imaginative interpretation by owner Veronica Shaw. One month she'll focus on Scotland; another month, Victorian foods; yet another month, Wales. Many dishes are vegetarian, and everything tastes better when followed with one of the British farmhouse cheeses, or a "pudding." The restaurant is brightly and attractively decorated, and service is warm and ingratiating.

# AWAY FROM THE CENTER
## THE EAST END

**Bloom's.** 130 Golders Green Rd., NW11. ☎ **0181/455-1388.** Reservations optional. Main courses £4.90–£9.90 ($7.85–$15.85). AE, DC, MC, V. Sun–Thurs 11am–1am; Fri 11am–3pm (to 2pm Dec–Feb); Sat 11am–4am. Tube: Golders Green. KOSHER.

This is London's most famous kosher restaurant. Bloom's has a long history in London, beginning in 1920 when Rebecca and Morris Bloom developed an original veal Vienna as well as a new and tastier method of pickling salt beef. They opened their first restaurant in the East End, which was destroyed during the blitz in 1943. After the war they moved to 90 Whitechapel High Street, also in the East End, but eventually left because of the Jewish mass exodus from the area. Today they hope to prosper in their new site. The cooking is strictly kosher at this large, bustling restaurant. Sunday lunchtime is busy, as many visitors come here after browsing through the used-clothing racks and bric-a-brac bins at the Petticoat Lane Sunday market. Bloom's remains the best place in London for things that frighten vegetarians: chopped herring, calves foot jelly, liver Worsht, cold beetroot borsht per glass, hot tongue, boiled fowl leg, and Kishka stuffing, as well as potato Latka, Lockshen pudding, and, of course Ir Israeli wines (red or white). And they still do an egg and onion sandwich.

## HAMPSTEAD HEATH

**Byron's.** 3A Downshire Hill, Hampstead, NW3. ☎ **0171/435-3544.** Reservations recommended. Main courses £9–£13.50 ($14.40–$21.60); fixed-price 3-course lunch £10.95 ($17.50) Mon–Sat, £12.95 ($20.70) Sun. AE, MC, V. Mon–Sat noon–3pm and 7–11pm; Sun 12:30–3:30pm and 7–10pm. Tube: Hampstead. ENGLISH.

Named in honor of Lord Byron, poet and competitor of John Keats (whose home lies within a 3-minute walk), this is a pleasant restaurant with innovative food. In a semidetached, stone-fronted house originally built in the 18th century, it offers a pair of simple and understated dining rooms illuminated with candles. Menu items are updated versions of traditional English recipes, and might include a warm salad of duck livers with lentils on a bed of radicchio and chicory, tempura of winter vegetables with a ginger-flavored dipping sauce, salt-cured salmon stuffed with chicory mousse and served with a mustard-dill sauce, duck breast with pomegranate sauce, a medley of grilled fish with a fennel/chicory/red-wine sauce, and steamed steak-and-kidney pudding with buttered cabbage. The lunch menu might even contain old-fashioned bangers and mash for dyed-in-the-wool traditionalists. Desserts include a black-currant délice with cassis-flavored liqueur.

✪ **Spaniards Inn.** Spaniards Rd., NW3. ☎ **0181/455-3276.** Main courses £4.25–£8 ($6.80–$12.80). MC, V. Daily noon–9:30pm. Pub, Mon–Sat 11am–11pm; Sun noon–10:30pm. Tube: Hampstead or Golders Green. ENGLISH.

A Hampstead Heath landmark, this pub is opposite the old tollhouse, a bottleneck in the road where people had to pay a toll to enter the country park of the bishop of London. The pub was originally built in 1585, and the present building dates from 1702. It still contains some antique benches, open fireplaces, and cozy nooks in rooms with low-beamed ceilings and oak paneling. Old muskets on the walls are survivors of the Gordon Riots of 1780, when a mob stopped in for drinks on their way to burn nearby Kenwood House, property of Lord Mansfield. The innkeeper served so many free drinks that when the Horse Guards arrived they found many of the rioters *hors de combat* from too much libation and relieved the protesters of their weapons. Notables who once patronized the pub include Byron, Shelley, Dickens, and Galsworthy—even Keats may have quaffed a glass here. The pub serves traditional but above-average food, and in summer customers sit at tables on a garden terrace beside an aviary.

## AFTERNOON TEA

In a nation where per-capita consumption of tea has risen to a whopping five cups a day, the tea-taking ritual forms as much a part of the national psyche as football, rugby, Empire-building, and dissing the royal family. Arguments rage regularly (but usually ever-so-politely) about the proper way to prepare a pot of tea, accompanied by lofty debate about how to warm, stir, and flavor it, what blend of leaves is either the most flavorful, most prestigious, or both. Tea is serious business in England.

Taking tea is experiencing a renaissance with the English. Viewed as a civilized pause in the day's activities, it is particularly appealing to people who don't have time for lunch or who plan an early theater engagement. Some hotels feature orchestras and tea dancing in afternoon ceremonies, usually lasting from 3:30 to 6:30pm. This relaxing, drawn-out affair usually consists of three courses: first, dainty finger sandwiches, then scones with jam and clotted cream, and finally an arrangement of bite-sized sweets.

A formal afternoon tea can be a bit pricey for the budget traveler, but if you consider it a late lunch or early dinner you should be able to fit it into your budget. Or you could drop into a local tea shop for a cuppa. If you want to splurge English-style, consider making a reservation at one of the following: **Brown's Hotel** (☎ **0171/493-6020**), **Claridges,** Brook Street (☎ **0171/629-8860**), **Palm Court Lounge,** in the Park Lane Hotel (☎ **0171/499-6321**), or the **Ritz Palm Court,** in the Ritz Hotel (☎ **0171/493-8181**).

**Burgh House.** New End Sq., NW3. ☎ **0171/431-2516.** Reservations required on Sun, accepted at other times. Tea from 50p (80¢); cakes from £1.30 ($2.10). No credit cards. Wed–Sun 11am–5:30pm. Tube: Hampstead. TEA/PASTRIES.

Historic Burgh House, an outstanding example of Queen Anne architecture, hosts concerts, lectures, exhibitions, and a local history museum and buttery. Tea is served throughout business hours, and a variety of fresh baked cakes and pastries are available.

**The Crypt, St. Martin-in-the-Fields.** St. Martin's Place, WC2. ☎ **0171/839-4342.** Tea from 85p ($1.35). No credit cards. Mon–Sat 10am–8pm; Sun noon–8pm. Tube: Charing Cross. TEA/PASTRIES.

This church was built in 1726, and its crypt is the burial place of such notables as Nell Gwynne and Thomas Chippendale. Tea is available throughout the day from the pastry counter, but tea service is from 3:30 to 5pm. Pastries, croissants, cakes, and scones are baked on the premises. The crypt itself makes for interesting browsing, and is in close proximity to several tourist stops, including Trafalgar Square and The National Gallery.

✪ **The Georgian Restaurant.** On the 4th floor of Harrods, 87–135 Brompton Rd., SW1. ☎ **0171/225-5390** or 0171/225-6800. High tea £12.75 ($20.40) per person. AE, DC, MC, V. Teatime Mon–Sat 3:45–5:30pm (last order). Tube: Knightsbridge. TEA

As long as anyone can remember, teatime at Harrods has been one of the most distinctive features of Europe's most famous department store. The Georgian Restaurant, set under elaborate ceilings and belle époque skylights atop London's fabled emporium, is one of the neighborhood's most appealing places for lunch and afternoon tea. Many come here expressly for the tea ritual, where staff haul silver pots and trolleys laden with pastries and sandwiches through the dining hall. One of the rooms, big enough to be a ballroom, features a pianist; music trills among the crystal of the chandeliers. A lunchtime buffet features cold meats and an array of fresh salads. Guests who want a hot meal can head for the carvery, where a uniformed crew of chefs dishes out such offerings as poultry, fish, and pork. The list of teas available (at least 50) is sometimes so esoteric that choosing one might remind you of selecting one of the vintages of a sophisticated wine cellar. Most exotic is Betigala, a rare blend from China, similar to Lapsang Souchong.

**Maison Bertaux.** 28 Greek St., W1. ☎ **0171/437-6007.** Reservations not accepted. Tea from £1.50 ($2.40). No credit cards. Mon–Sat 9am–8pm; Sun 1–3pm. Tube: Piccadilly Circus, Leicester Square. TEA/PASTRIES.

Soho's best loved tea shop, Maison Bertaux was established in 1871 by the Bertaux family, and has had only three owners in its history, including current owner Michelle Wade, who has been there since 1971. There are eight or nine teas to choose from, and fresh baked croissants and pastries are available.

**Maison Sagne.** 105 Marylebone High St., W1. ☎ **0171/935-6240.** Reservations not accepted. Tea from £1.50 ($2.40). AE, MC, V. Mon–Fri 8am–7pm; Sat 8am–6pm; Sun 9am–6pm. Tube: Baker St., Marble Arch. TEA/PASTRIES.

Located near Madame Tussaud's, the Planetarium, Regent's Park, and the Wallace Collection, this tearoom, established in 1926, has remained unchanged in the face of High Street renovations. Croissants, pastries, and scones, baked on the premises, and handmade chocolates are available for takeout as well as tea service.

**Museum of Garden History.** St. Mary-at-Lambeth, Lambeth Palace Rd., SE1. ☎ **0171/261-1891.** Reservations required for parties of 2 or more. Tea from £3 ($4.80). AE, MC, V. Mon–Fri 10:30am–4pm; Sun 10:30am–5pm. Tube: Vauxhall. TEA/SANDWICHES.

Tea is offered throughout the day, and cakes, puddings, and sandwiches are available separately. Visit the churchyard to see the tomb of Admiral Bligh of the HMS *Bounty*. Both the church and the museum are under the patronage of the Tradescant Trust, which was established by the Prince of Wales to maintain them.

✪ **The Orangery.** In the gardens of Kensington Palace, W8. ☎ **0171/376-0239.** Reservations not accepted. Pot of tea £1.60 ($2.55); summer cakes and puddings £1.95–£3.50 ($3.10–$5.60); sandwiches £5.95 ($9.50). MC, V. Mar–Oct 10am–6pm; Nov–Feb 10am–4pm. Tube: High Street Kensington or Queensway. TEA.

In its way, the Orangery is the most amazing place for midafternoon tea in the world. Set about 50 yards north of Kensington Palace, it occupies a long and narrow garden pavilion built in 1704 by Queen Anne as a site for her tea parties. In homage to that monarch's original intentions, rows of potted orange trees bask in sunlight from soaring windows, and tea is still served amid Corinthian columns, ruddy-colored bricks, and a pair of Grinling Gibbons wood carvings. To help accessorize the place, there are even some urns and statuary that the royal family imported to the site from Windsor Castle. The menu includes lunchtime soups and sandwiches, which come with a salad and a portion of upscale potato chips known as "kettle chips." There's also an array of different teas, served with high style, usually accompanied by freshly baked scones with clotted cream and jam, and Belgian chocolate cake.

**The Primrose Patisserie.** 136 Regent's Park Rd., NW1. ☎ **0171/722-7848.** Reservations not accepted. Tea from 60p (95¢). No credit cards. Mon–Fri 7am–7pm; Sat–Sun 8:30am–9pm. Tube: Chalk Farm. TEA/CAKES/SANDWICHES.

Built in Victorian times, this tearoom retains the essence of that era. Tea is served throughout the day, and a variety of cakes, including their most popular, apple crumblet, are available. Salads and sandwiches are served as well. This is a convenient place to rejuvenate oneself before or after a visit to nearby Regent's Park.

**Richoux.** 86 Brompton Rd. (opposite Harrods department store), Knightsbridge, SW3. ☎ **0171/584-8300.** Main courses £6.95–£13.75 ($11.10–$22); full tea (a mini-meal) £11.75 ($18.80); English tea £6.95 ($11.10). AE, DC, MC, V. Mon–Fri 8am–11pm; Sat 8am–11:30pm; Sun 10am–11pm. Tube: Knightsbridge. ENGLISH/TEA.

Try the old-fashioned atmosphere of Richoux, whether for breakfast, lunch, afternoon tea, or supper. You can order four hot scones with strawberry jam and whipped cream, or choose from a selection of pâtisserie behind a display case. Of course, tea is obligatory; always specify lemon or cream, and one lump or two. Also, a full menu is served all day long: At least seven fresh salads are featured, and there are sandwiches, Welsh rarebit, burgers, and an array of other dishes. You can also order main meals, including such dishes as chicken Kiev, Dover sole, and steaks.

Richoux has three other branches: at the bottom of Bond Street, 172 Piccadilly, W1 (☎ **0171/493-2204;** tube: Green Park or Piccadilly Circus); at 41A S. Audley St., W1 (☎ **0171/629-5228;** tube: Hyde Park); and at St. John's Wood, 3 Circus Rd., NW8 (☎ **0171/483-4001;** tube: St. John's Wood). They're open Monday through Saturday from 8:30am to 11pm and on Sunday from 10am to 11:30pm. The restaurants are licensed to serve alcohol only to diners.

✪ **St. James Restaurant/The Fountain Restaurant.** In Fortnum & Mason, 181 Piccadilly, W1. ☎ **0171/734-8040.** St. James: full tea £10.50 ($16.80); high tea £12.25 ($19.60). The Fountain: cream tea £6.95 ($11.10); afternoon tea £9.95 ($15.90). AE, DC, MC, V. Mon–Sat 9:30am–6pm. Closed bank holidays. Tube: Piccadilly Circus. ENGLISH/TEA.

These two tea salons are in London's most prestigious grocery store, Fortnum & Mason, and, as such, carry a great deal of social and culinary style. The more formal of the two tearooms (the St. James Restaurant) is one floor above street level, where a greater choice of teatime options is available. More rapid, less formal, and more tuned to the hectic pace of London shoppers and London commuters is the Fountain Restaurant on the store's street level, where a sense of tradition and urbane manners is very much a part of the teatime experience.

# Exploring London 5

It was Dr. Samuel Johnson who said, "When a man is tired of London, he is tired of life, for there is in London all that life can afford." That statement—which of course applies to women, too—is even truer today than it was when Johnson first made his pronouncement.

Headlines across the globe exclaim the British capital's resurgence: Swinging London! The Hottest, Coolest City in the World! A British Renaissance! London's Got Its Groove Back! It seems like a feeding frenzy, with the press clamoring to champion London as more eclectic and electric than it's been in years. In fact, many don't stop there; some London habitués call it the most pulsating, vibrant city on the planet, rivaling New York for sheer energy, outrageous fashion, trendy restaurants, and an unequaled night scene.

Although London may be on the cutting edge of "the scene," just as in the Swinging '60s, not everyone is obsessed with youth culture. The true spirit of London is still reflected in its diversity of cultures and tastes. That's what makes the city so fascinating today. From Argentina to the Senegal, from Algeria to China, it seems that half the world is flocking to London, giving the city a vital new pulse.

In this chapter, we can only explore a fraction of what is exciting in London. Of course, it's not always the new that attracts visitors; in addition to the buzz in shops and nightlife, we cover the museums, monuments, literary shrines, royal castles, waxworks, palaces, cathedrals, royal parks, and more.

## 1 The Top Attractions

London is not a city to visit in a hurry. It is so vast, so stocked with treasures, that it would take a lifetime to explore everything. But, since your time is no doubt limited, here are the top sights, to help you make your choices of what to see and do.

*Note:* As a rule, and unless otherwise stated, children's prices apply to those aged 16 and under. You must be 60 years of age or older to obtain available senior citizen discounts at some attractions. For students to get available discounted admissions they must have a student ID card.

✪ **The Tower of London.** Tower Hill (on the north bank of the Thames) EC3. ☎ **0171/709-0765.** Admission £8.50 ($13.60) adults, £6.40 ($10.25) students and senior citizens, £5.60 ($8.95) children. Free for children under 5. Family ticket for 5 (but no more than 2 adults) £25.40 ($40.65).

## Impressions

*I love my city, despite its tattered fabric, its antediluvian public transport system (the vast majority of the tube was laid down by the turn of the century; indeed, many stations have been closed since then), and its unutterable cliquishness and snobbery. I love it for the great, ruckled, grimy surface it presents—a surface that has been distressed by the passage of two thousand years of history.*

—Will Self, Author (1996)

Mar Oct Mon–Sat 9am–5pm, Sun 10am–5pm; Nov–Feb Tues–Sat 9am–4pm, Sun–Mon 10am–4pm. Closed Dec 24–26, Jan 1. Tube: Tower Hill. Boats: From Westminster Pier.

This ancient fortress, firmly enshrined in popular culture, continues to pack in visitors. No doubt part of its intrigue is due to its macabre associations with legendary figures imprisoned and/or executed here. James Street once wrote, "There are more spooks to the square foot than in any other building in the whole of haunted Britain. Headless bodies, bodiless heads, phantom soldiers, icy blasts, clanking chains—you name them, the Tower's got them." Plan on spending a lot of time here—although you don't want to stay!

The fortress is actually a compound, in which the oldest and finest structure is the White Tower, begun by William the Conqueror. Here you can view the Armouries, which date from the reign of Henry VIII. A display of instruments of torture and execution recalls some of the most ghastly moments in the tower's history. At the Bloody Tower, the Little Princes (Edward V and the duke of York) were allegedly murdered by their uncle, Richard III. Through Traitors' Gate passed such ill-fated, romantic figures as Robert Devereux, known as the second earl of Essex and a favorite of Elizabeth I. At Tower Green, Anne Boleyn and Catherine Howard, two wives of Henry VIII, lost their lives. Many other notable figures have died at the tower, including Sir Thomas More as well as the four-day queen, Lady Jane Grey, who was executed at Tower Green. Her husband, Lord Guildford Dudley, was put to death at Tower Hill.

To see the **Jewel House,** where the crown jewels are kept, go early in the day during summer; long lines usually form. A major rebuilding of this structure in 1994 eliminated most waiting time except during peak periods, and its ground level allows easy access for wheelchairs. Of the three English crowns, the Imperial State Crown is the most important—in fact, it's the most famous crown on earth. Made for Victoria in 1837, it is worn today by Queen Elizabeth when she opens Parliament. Studded with some 3,000 jewels (principally diamonds), it includes the Black Prince's Ruby, worn by Henry V at Agincourt (the 1415 battle where the English defeated the French). The 530-carat Star of Africa is a cut diamond on the Royal Sceptre with Cross. Ask one of the Yeoman Warders (Beefeaters) in Tudor uniform to tell you how Colonel Blood almost made off with the crown and regalia in the late 17th century.

The Tower of London has an evening ceremony called the **Ceremony of the Keys,** the ceremonial locking of the Tower. The Yeoman Warder will explain the ceremony's significance to guests. For free tickets, write to the Ceremony of the Key, Waterloo Block, Tower of London, London EC3N 4AB, and request a specific date, but also list alternative dates. At least 6 weeks' notice is required. All requests must be accompanied by a stamped, self-addressed envelope (British stamps only) or two International Reply Coupons. With ticket in hand, you'll be admitted by a Yeoman Warder at 9:35pm.

You won't want to miss the ravens. Six of them, as well as two backups, are all registered as official tower residents; each is fed exactly 6 ounces of rations per day.

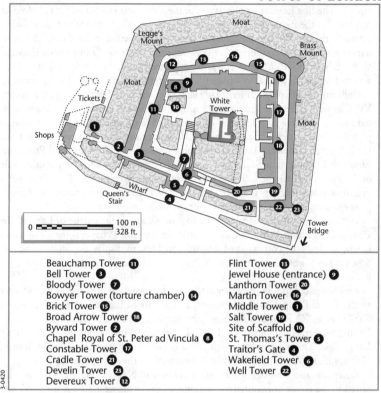

Beauchamp Tower ⑪
Bell Tower ③
Bloody Tower ⑦
Bowyer Tower (torture chamber) ⑭
Brick Tower ⑮
Broad Arrow Tower ⑱
Byward Tower ②
Chapel Royal of St. Peter ad Vincula ⑧
Constable Tower ⑰
Cradle Tower ㉑
Develin Tower ㉓
Devereux Tower ⑫

Flint Tower ⑬
Jewel House (entrance) ⑨
Lanthorn Tower ⑳
Martin Tower ⑯
Middle Tower ①
Salt Tower ⑲
Site of Scaffold ⑩
St. Thomas's Tower ⑤
Traitor's Gate ④
Wakefield Tower ⑥
Well Tower ㉒

According to legend, the Tower of London will stand as long as those black, ominous birds remain in the tower. So, to preserve the tower, one of the wings of each raven is clipped.

A palace once inhabited by King Edward I in the late 1200s was opened to visitors for the first time in 1993. Above Traitor's Gate, it is the only surviving medieval palace in Britain. Guides are dressed in period costumes. Reproductions of furniture and fittings, including Edward's throne, evoke the era, along with burning incense and candles. Admission to the palace is included in the standard ticket price.

One-hour tours are given by the Yeoman Warders at frequent intervals, starting at 9:30am from the Middle Tower near the main entrance. The tour includes the Chapel Royal of St. Peter and Vincula (St. Peter in Chains). The last guided walk starts about 3:30pm in summer, 2:30pm in winter.

The secret to avoid the notoriously long lines here is to come early, as the hordes descend in the afternoon. Your best bet is to be here when the gates open. Crowds are worst on Sunday.

✪ **Westminster Abbey.** Broad Sanctuary, SW1. ☎ **0171/222-7110.** Free admission to abbey; donation suggested. Royal Chapels, Royal Tombs, Coronation Chair, Lady Chapel: £4 ($6.40) adults, £1 ($1.60) children. Mon–Fri 9am–3:45pm; Sat 9:15am–1:45pm and 4–4:45pm. Tube: Westminster or St. James's Park.

Nearly every notable figure in English history has left his or her mark on Westminster Abbey. In 1065 the Saxon king, Edward the Confessor, founded the Benedictine abbey and rebuilt the old Minster church on this spot, overlooking Parliament

Square. The first English king crowned in the abbey was Harold in 1066, before he was killed at the Battle of Hastings later the same year. The man who defeated him, Edward's cousin, William the Conqueror, was also crowned at the abbey. The coronation tradition has continued to the present day, interrupted only twice (Edward V and Edward VIII). Most recently, in September 1997, the abbey held the widely watched funeral of Diana, Princess of Wales, after her death in a tragic car crash.

Built on the site of the ancient lady chapel in the early 16th century, the **Henry VII Chapel** is one of the loveliest in Europe, with its fan vaulting, Knights of Bath banners, and Torrigiani-designed tomb of the king himself over which has been placed a 15th-century Vivarini painting, *Madonna and Child.* Also here are the feuding half-sisters, ironically buried in the same tomb, Catholic Mary I and Protestant Elizabeth I (whose arch-rival, Mary Queen of Scots, is entombed on the other side of the Henry VII Chapel). In one end of the chapel, you can stand on Cromwell's memorial stone and view the RAF chapel and its Battle of Britain memorial stained-glass window, unveiled in 1947 to honor the RAF.

You can also visit the most hallowed spot in the abbey, the **shrine of Edward the Confessor** (canonized in the 12th century). In the saint's chapel is the Coronation Chair, made at the command of Edward I in 1300 to display the Stone of Scone. Scottish kings were once crowned on this stone. The stone has since been returned to Scotland.

Another noted spot in the abbey is the **Poets' Corner,** to the right of the entrance to the Royal Chapel, with monuments to a host of famous writers—Chaucer, Shakespeare, "O Rare Ben Johnson" (his name misspelled), Samuel Johnson, the Brontë sisters, Thackeray, Dickens, Tennyson, Kipling, even the American Longfellow. The most stylized monument is Sir Jacob Epstein's sculptured bust of William Blake. A more recent tablet commemorates the poet Dylan Thomas.

Statesmen and men of science—such as Disraeli, Newton, Darwin—are also interred in the abbey or honored by monuments. Near the west door is the 1965 memorial to Sir Winston Churchill. In the vicinity of this memorial is the tomb of the Unknown Soldier, commemorating the British dead of World War I. Some obscure personages have won the right to be buried in the abbey, including an abbey plumber.

Off the Cloisters, the **College Garden** is the oldest garden in England, under cultivation for more than 900 years. Surrounded by high walls, flowering trees dot the lawns and park benches provide comfort where you can hardly hear the roar of passing traffic. It is open only on Tuesday and Thursday. In the Cloisters, you can make a rubbing at the **Brass Rubbing Center** (☎ **0171/222-2085**).

Far removed from the pomp and glory of this edifice is the **Abbey Treasure Museum,** in the undercroft or crypt, part of the monastic buildings erected between 1066 and 1100. Here are royal effigies used instead of the real corpses for lying-in-state ceremonies—they smelled better. You'll see the almost lifelike effigy of Admiral Nelson (his mistress arranged his hair) and even the effigy of Edward III, his lip warped by the stroke that felled him. Among other assorted oddities are a Middle English lease to Chaucer, the much-used sword of Henry VI, and the Essex Ring Elizabeth I gave to her favorite companion—prior to a change of heart that left her wanting his head.

Photography is only allowed in the abbey Wednesday evenings from 6 to 7:45pm. On Sunday, the Royal Chapels are closed, but the rest of the church is open unless a service is being conducted. For scheduled services, phone the Chapter Office (☎ **0171/222-5152**). Up to six supertours of the abbey are conducted by the vergers Monday through Saturday, beginning at 10am and costing £7 ($11.20) per person.

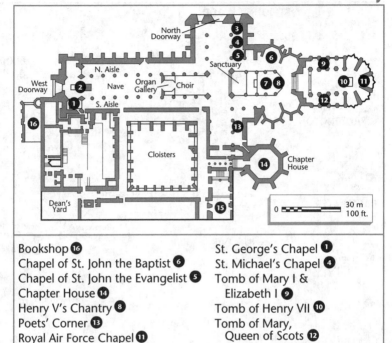

# Westminster Abbey

Bookshop **16**
Chapel of St. John the Baptist **6**
Chapel of St. John the Evangelist **5**
Chapter House **14**
Henry V's Chantry **8**
Poets' Corner **13**
Royal Air Force Chapel **11**
St. Andrew's Chapel **3**
St. Edward's Chapel
  (Coronation Chair) **7**

St. George's Chapel **1**
St. Michael's Chapel **4**
Tomb of Mary I &
  Elizabeth I **9**
Tomb of Henry VII **10**
Tomb of Mary,
  Queen of Scots **12**
Tomb of the Unknown Warrior/
  Memorial to Churchill **2**
Undercroft Museum **15**

3-0422

⭐ **Houses of Parliament.** Westminster Palace, Old Palace Yard, SW1. ☎ **0171/219-4272** for the House of Commons and ☎ **0171/219-3107** for the House of Lords. Free admission. House of Lords: open to public Mon–Thurs 9:30am–3:30pm; also some Fridays (check by phone). House of Commons: open to public Mon, Tues, and Thurs after 2:30pm; Wed and Fri from 9:30am. Join line at St. Stephen's entrance. Tube: Westminster.

The Houses of Parliament are the spiritual and political opposite of the tower; they are the stronghold of Britain's democracy, the assemblies that effectively trimmed the sails of royal power. Both Houses (Commons and Lords) are situated in the former Royal Palace of Westminster, the king's residence until Henry VIII moved to Whitehall.

Debates are often lively and controversial in the House of Commons (seats are at a premium during state crises). Your chance of getting into the House of Lords when it's in session is generally better than for the more popular House of Commons—where even the queen isn't allowed. The old guard of the palace informs us that the members speak their minds more freely and are less likely to adhere to party line than their counterparts in the Commons.

The present Houses of Parliament were built in 1840, but the Commons chamber was bombed and destroyed by the Luftwaffe in 1941. The 320-foot tower that houses Big Ben, however, remained standing and the "symbol of London" continues to strike its chimes. Big Ben, incidentally, was named after Sir Benjamin Hall, a cabinet minister distinguished primarily by his long-windedness (although legend also suggests he was considerable in size).

# Central London Sights

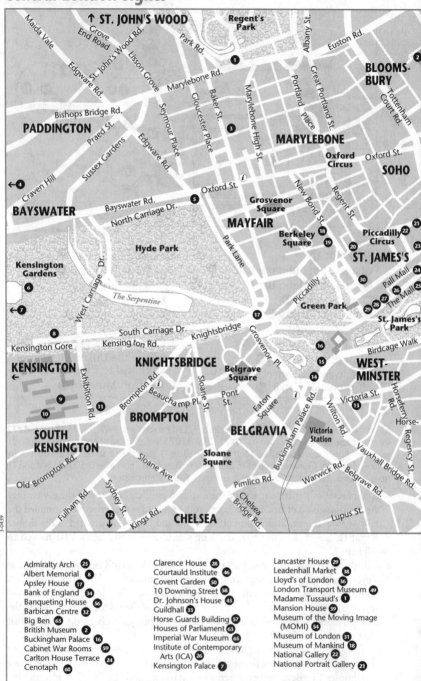

| | | |
|---|---|---|
| Admiralty Arch **25** | Clarence House **28** | Lancaster House **29** |
| Albert Memorial **8** | Courtauld Institute **46** | Leadenhall Market **38** |
| Apsley House **17** | Covent Garden **50** | Lloyd's of London **36** |
| Bank of England **34** | 10 Downing Street **58** | London Transport Museum **49** |
| Banqueting House **56** | Dr. Johnson's House **43** | Madame Tussaud's **1** |
| Barbican Centre **32** | Guildhall **33** | Mansion House **39** |
| Big Ben **63** | Horse Guards Building **57** | Museum of the Moving Image |
| British Museum **2** | Houses of Parliament **63** | (MOMI) **54** |
| Buckingham Palace **16** | Imperial War Museum **65** | Museum of London **31** |
| Cabinet War Rooms **59** | Institute of Contemporary | Museum of Mankind **18** |
| Carlton House Terrace **24** | Arts (ICA) **26** | National Gallery **22** |
| Cenotaph **60** | Kensington Palace **7** | National Portrait Gallery **21** |

3-0439

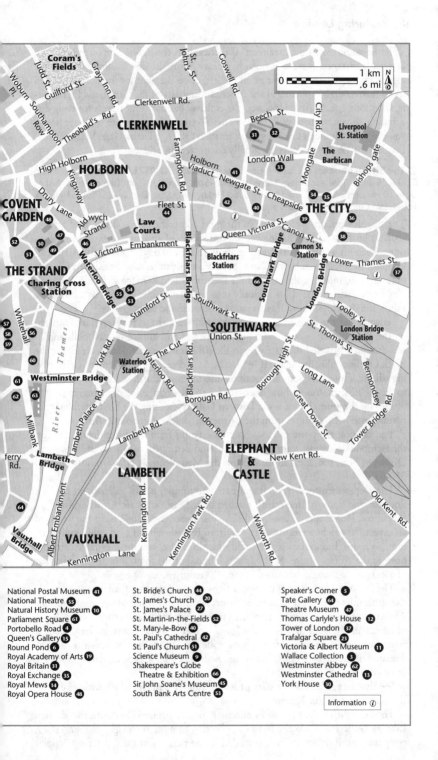

National Postal Museum ④①
National Theatre ⑤⑤
Natural History Museum ⑩
Parliament Square ⑥①
Portobello Road ④
Queen's Gallery ⑮
Round Pond ⑥
Royal Academy of Arts ⑲
Royal Britain ③①
Royal Exchange ③⑤
Royal Mews ⑭
Royal Opera House ④⑧

St. Bride's Church ④④
St. James's Church ⑳
St. James's Palace ㉗
St. Martin-in-the-Fields ⑤②
St. Mary-le-Bow ④⑩
St. Paul's Cathedral ④②
St. Paul's Church ⑤①
Science Museum ⑨
Shakespeare's Globe
   Theatre & Exhibition ⑥⑥
Sir John Soane's Museum ④⑤
South Bank Arts Centre ⑤③

Speaker's Corner ⑤
Tate Gallery ⑭
Theatre Museum ④⑦
Thomas Carlyle's House ⑫
Tower of London ③⑦
Trafalgar Square ㉓
Victoria & Albert Museum ⑪
Wallace Collection ③
Westminster Abbey ⑥②
Westminster Cathedral ⑬
York House ㉚

Information ⓘ

139

To be admitted to the Strangers' Galleries, join the public line outside the St. Stephen's entrance; there is frequently a delay before the line is admitted. The line for the House of Commons forms on the left, or on the right for the Lords. You can speed matters up by applying at the American Embassy or the Canadian High Commission for a special pass. However, the embassy has only four tickets for daily distribution, so you might as well stand in line. To arrange a tour before you leave home, you can write House of Commons Information Office, 1 Derby Gate, Westminister, London SW1A 2DG. Tours are usually conducted on Fridays.

✪ **The British Museum & Library.** Great Russell St., WC1. ☎ **0171/323-8599** or recording 0171/636-1555. Free admission. Mon–Sat 10am–5pm; Sun 2:30–6pm (the galleries start to close 10 minutes earlier). Closed Jan 1, Good Friday, early May, Dec 24–26. Tube: Holborn, Tottenham Court Road, or Russell Square.

The British Museum shelters one of the most comprehensive collections of art and artifacts in the world, including countless treasures of ancient and modern civilizations. Even on a cursory first visit, at a minimum you'll want to see the Asian collections (the finest assembly of Islamic pottery outside the Islamic world), the Chinese porcelain, the Indian sculpture, and the Prehistoric and Romano-British collections. The overall storehouse splits basically into the national collections of antiquities; prints and drawings; coins, medals, and banknotes; and ethnography.

As you enter the front hall, you may want to head first to the **Assyrian Transept** on the ground floor, where you'll find the winged and human-headed bulls and lions that once guarded the gateways to the palaces of Assyrian kings. Nearby is the Black Obelisk of Shalmaneser III (858–824 B.C.) depicting Jehu, king of Israel, paying tribute. From here you can continue into the angular hall of Egyptian sculpture to see the Rosetta stone, whose discovery led to the deciphering of hieroglyphs.

Also on the ground floor is the **Duveen Gallery,** housing the Elgin marbles, consisting chiefly of sculptures from the Parthenon, on the Acropolis in Athens.

The classical sculpture galleries house a caryatid from the Erechtheum, also on the Acropolis, a temple started in 421 B.C. and dedicated to Athena and Poseidon. Displayed here, too, are sculptures from the Mausoleum at Halicarnassus (around 350 B.C.).

The Department of Medieval and Later Antiquities has its galleries on the first floor (second floor to Americans), reached by the main staircase. Of its exhibitions, the Sutton Hoo Anglo-Saxon burial ship, discovered in Suffolk, is, in the words of an expert, "the richest treasure ever dug from English soil." It held gold jewelry, armor, weapons, bronze bowls and cauldrons, silverware, and the inevitable drinking horn of the Norse culture. No body was found, but the tomb is believed to be that of a king of East Anglia who died in the 7th century A.D.

The featured attractions of the upper floor are the **Egyptian Galleries**—especially the mummies. Egyptian Room 63 is extraordinary, resembling the props for *Cleopatra,* with its cosmetics, domestic utensils, toys, tools, and other objects. Items of Sumerian art, unearthed from the Royal Cemetery at Ur (southern Iraq), lie in a room beyond, some dating from about 2500 B.C. In the Iranian room rests "The Treasure of the Oxus," a hoard of riches, perhaps a temple deposit, dating from the 6th to the 3rd century B.C.

See also the galleries of the **City of Rome and its Empire,** which include exhibitions of art before the Romans.

To the right of the museum's entrance, on the ground floor, are the **British Library Galleries.** From the library's collection of more than eight million books, temporary exhibits are erected. Included in the permanent exhibit are two copies

# The British Museum

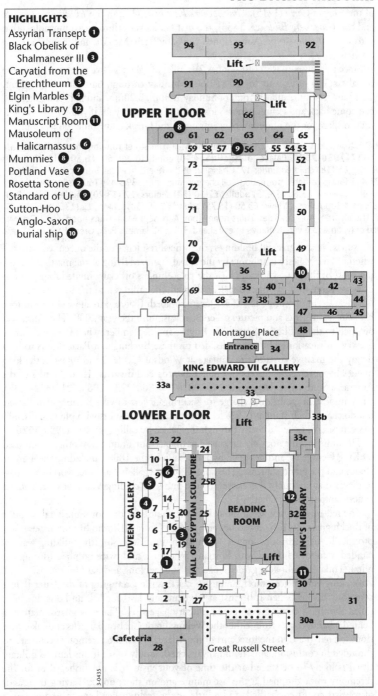

## HIGHLIGHTS

Assyrian Transept ❶
Black Obelisk of
  Shalmaneser III ❸
Caryatid from the
  Erechtheum ❺
Elgin Marbles ❹
King's Library ⑫
Manuscript Room ⑪
Mausoleum of
  Halicarnassus ❻
Mummies ❽
Portland Vase ❼
Rosetta Stone ❷
Standard of Ur ❾
Sutton-Hoo
  Anglo-Saxon
  burial ship ❿

**UPPER FLOOR**

94  93  92
Lift
91  90
Lift
66
60  61  62  63  64  65
59 58 57  56  55 54 53
73  52
72  51
71  50
70  49
Lift
36
35  40  41  42  43
69a  69  68  37 38 39  44
47  46  45
48

Montague Place

Entrance  34

**KING EDWARD VII GALLERY**

33a  33  33b
**LOWER FLOOR**  Lift  33c
23  22  24
10  12  25B  32
9  21  READING  ROOM
5  14  25
4  7  8  15  20
6  16  25  ⑫
5  17  19  2
1  Lift
4  11
DUVEEN GALLERY
HALL OF EGYPTIAN SCULPTURE
KING'S LIBRARY
3  26  29  30
2  1  27  31
Cafeteria  30a
28  Great Russell Street

3-0435

of the *Magna Carta* (1215), *Shakespeare's First Folio* (1623), the *Lindisfarne Gospels,* and the *Gutenberg Bible* (ca. 1453), the first book ever printed with movable—that is to say, reusable—type. Autographed works by Bach, Mozart, and Handel are also on view.

Since the museum is so vast—it has 2½ miles of galleries—we think it makes sense to take a 1½ hour tour for £6 ($9.60) Monday through Saturday at 10:45am, 11:15am, 1:45pm, and 2:15pm, or Sunday at 3pm, 3:20pm, and 3:45pm. Later you can come back and examine more closely what interested you. If you have only minutes to spare for the museum, concentrate on the Greek and Rome rooms (1–15).

✪ **Buckingham Palace.** At the end of The Mall (the street running from Trafalgar Sq.). ☎ **0171/930-9625.** Palace tours: £9 ($14.40) adults to age 60, £6.50 ($10.40) adults over 60, £5 ($8) children under 17. Changing of the guard free (call Visitorcall at ☎ 01839/ 123-411 for up-to-date information; toll charges range from 39p–49p (60¢–80¢) per minute). Queen's Gallery: £3.60 ($5.75) adults, £2.50 ($4) seniors, £2 ($3.20) children 5–17. Daily 9:30am–4:30pm. Royal Mews: £3.50 ($5.75) adults, £2.50 ($4) seniors, £2 ($3.20) children 5– 17. Usually from Apr–July Tues–Thurs noon–4pm; Aug–Sept Mon–Thurs noon–4pm; Oct–Mar Wed only; times are very tentative so call ahead. Tube: St. James's Park, Green Park, or Victoria.

This massive and graceful building is the official residence of the queen; you can tell whether Her Majesty is at home by the Royal Standard flying at the masthead. During most of the year, you can't visit the palace unless officially invited, but you can do what thousands of others do: Peep through the railings into the front yard.

However, in the spring of 1993, Queen Elizabeth II agreed to allow visitors to tour her state apartments and picture galleries, at least until the year 2000. The palace will be open to the public for 8 weeks in August and September, when the royal family is away on vacation. The queen decided on these Buckingham Palace tours to help defray the massive costs of fire damage at Windsor Castle. You can avoid the long queues by purchasing tickets through **Edwards & Edwards,** 1270 Avenue of the Americas, Suite 2414, New York, NY 10020 ( ☎ **800/223-6108** or 212/332-2435). They impose no additional charge for securing tickets to visit Buckingham Palace, but do charge their standard 10% fee, as for all tickets. Visitors with physical disabilities can reserve tickets directly through the palace by calling ☎ **0171/930-5526.**

The tours include not only the state apartments, but a number of other rooms used by King George IV and designed by John Nash in the 1800s, including the Throne Room and the grand staircase. The queen's picture gallery has some world-class masterpieces that are rarely if ever seen by the public, including Van Dyck's celebrated equestrian portrait of Charles I.

The red-brick palace was built as a country house for the notoriously rakish duke of Buckingham. In 1762 it was bought by King George III, who (if nothing else) was prolific; he needed room for his 15 children. From then on, the building was expanded, remodeled, faced with Portland limestone, and twice bombed (during the blitz). Today in a 40-acre garden, it stands 360 feet long and has 600 rooms.

Buckingham Palace's most famous spectacle is the **Changing of the Guard.** This ceremony begins (when it begins) at 11:30am and lasts for half an hour. It's been called the finest existing example of military pageantry. The new guard, marching behind a band, comes from either the Wellington or Chelsea Barracks and takes over from the old guard in the forecourt of the palace. When the ceremony occurs seems shrouded in confusion; you should always check locally to see if this famous military ritual is likely to be staged at the time of your visit. It is not unheard of for the ceremony to be dropped at the last minute and on short notice, leaving thousands of tourists confused, baffled, and a little angry, feeling they have missed out on a London "must see."

Any schedule announced here is not writ in stone. Officials of the ceremony never announce their plans much in advance, posing a dilemma for guidebook writers. In theory at least, the guard is changed daily from about April to mid-July, at which time it goes on "winter" schedule—that is, changing every other day. The cutback is said to derive from budget constraints. The ceremony might also be abruptly canceled during "uncertain" weather conditions. Check tourist information offices or local publications for schedules.

In the **Queen's Gallery,** you can see a sampling of the royal family's art collection. Exhibitions change yearly, but we can tell you that the queen's collection contains an unsurpassed range of royal portraits, including the well-known profile of Henry V; the companion portraits of Elizabeth I as a girl and her brother, Edward VI; four fine Georgian pictures by Zoffany; two portraits of Queen Alexandra from Sandringham; plus paintings of Elizabeth II and other members of the present royal family.

The **Royal Mews,** also on Buckingham Palace Road, is one of the finest working stables in the world today. Housed here are the gilded and polished state carriages—such as the gold State Coach used at every coronation since 1831—along with the horses that draw them.

**Madame Tussaud's.** Marylebone Rd., NW1. ☎ **0171/935-6861.** Admission £8.95 ($14.30) adults, £6.75 ($10.80) seniors, £5.90 ($9.45) children under 16. Combination tickets including the new planetarium cost £11.20 ($35.85) adults, £7.10 ($11.35) children under 16. Mon-Sat 10am–5:30pm. Tube: Baker Street.

In 1770, an exhibition of life-size wax figures was opened in Paris by Dr. Curtius. He was soon joined by his niece, Strasbourg-born Marie Tussaud, who learned the secret of making lifelike replicas of the famous and the infamous. During the French Revolution, the head of almost every distinguished victim of the guillotine was molded by Madame Tussaud or her uncle.

Whereas some of the figures on display today come from molds taken by Madame Tussaud, who continued to make portraits until she was 81, the exhibition also introduces new images of whoever is *au courant.* An enlarged Grand Hall continues to house years of royalty and old favorites, as well as many of today's heads of state and political leaders. In the Chamber of Horrors, you can have the vicarious thrill of walking through a Victorian London street; special effects depict the shadow terror of Jack the Ripper. The instruments and victims of death penalties contrast with present-day criminals portrayed within the confines of prison. You are invited to mingle with the more current stars in the garden party, "meeting" wax dummies of Arnold Schwarzenegger to Elizabeth Taylor.

"Super Stars" offers the latest technologies in sound, light, and special effects combined with new figures from the fields of film and sports.

One of the latest attractions to open here is called "The Spirit of London," a musical show that depicts 400 years of London's history, using special effects that include audio-animatronic figures that move and speak. Visitors take "time-taxis" that allow them to see and hear "Shakespeare" as he writes and speaks lines, to be received by Queen Elizabeth I, and to feel and smell the great fire that started in Pudding Lane in 1666. You'll find a snack bar and gift shops on the premises.

**☼ Tate Gallery.** Beside the Thames on Millbank, SW1. ☎ **0171/887-8725.** Free admission, except special exhibitions varying from £3 ($4.80) to £5 ($8). Daily 10am–5:50pm. Closed Dec 24–26. Tube: Pimlico. Bus: 77A, 36, C10, or 88.

The Tate houses the best groupings of British paintings from the 16th century on, as well as England's finest collection of modern art (the works of British and

# City Sights

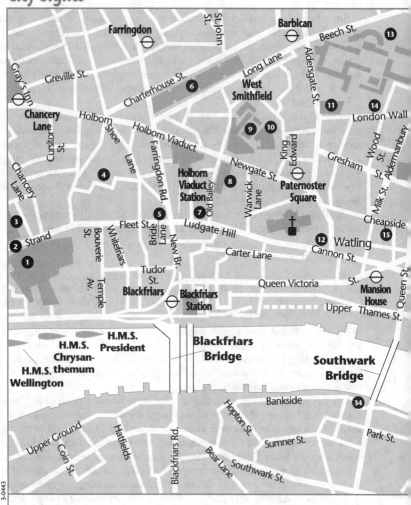

All Hallows Barking by
the Tower of London 28
Bank of England Museum 17
Barbican Centre 13
H.M.S. *Belfast* 31
Cheshire Cheese 7
Docklands 33
Dr. Samuel Johnson's House 4
Fishmonger's Hall 21
Geffrye Museum 16A

Guildhall 16
Inns of Court & Chancery 1
Lloyd's of London 25
London Bridge 22
London Dungeon 24
Mansion House 19
Museum of London 11
National Postal Museum 10
New Globe Theatre 34

144

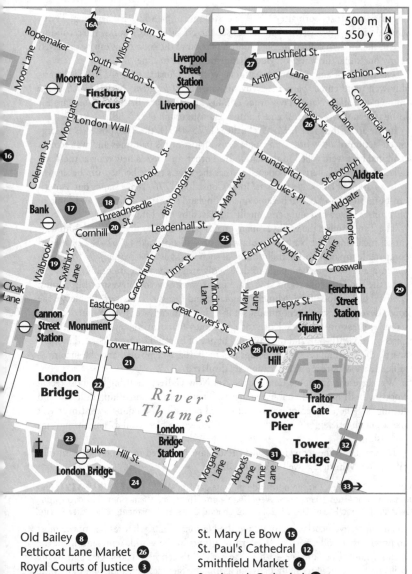

Old Bailey **8**
Petticoat Lane Market **26**
Royal Courts of Justice **3**
Royal Exchange **20**
Royal Mint **29**
St. Bartholomew's Hospital **9**
St. Bride's Church **5**
St. Clement Danes Church **2**
St. Giles Cripplegate **14**

St. Mary Le Bow **15**
St. Paul's Cathedral **12**
Smithfield Market **6**
Southwark Cathedral **23**
Stock Exchange **18**
Tower Bridge **32**
Tower of London **30**
Wesley's Chapel, House & Museum **27**

Church **†**   Tube Station **⊖**   Information **ⓘ**

international artists born after 1860). The volume of paintings is staggering. Try to schedule at least two visits—the first to see the classic English works, the second to take in the modern collection. Since only a portion of the collections can be displayed at any one time, the works on view change from time to time.

The first giant among English painters, William Hogarth (1697–1764), is invariably well represented, particularly by his satirical *O the Roast Beef of Old England* (known as *Calais Gate*). Two other famous 18th-century British painters are Sir Joshua Reynolds (1723–92) and Thomas Gainsborough (1727–88).

In the art of the great J. M. W. Turner (1775–1851), the Tate possesses its largest collection of the works of a single artist. Most of his paintings and watercolors exhibited here were willed to the nation by Turner. In 1987, a new wing at the Tate, called the Clore Gallery, was opened so that the artist's entire bequest can be shown.

In a nation of landscape painters, John Constable (1776–1837) stands out. American-born Sir Jacob Epstein became one of England's greatest sculptors, and some of his bronzes are owned and occasionally displayed by the Tate.

The Tate also has the works of many major painters from the 19th and 20th centuries, including Paul Nash. The drawings of William Blake (1757–1827), the incomparable mystical poet and illustrator of such works as *The Book of Job, The Divine Comedy,* and *Paradise Lost,* perhaps deservedly attract the most attention.

In the modern collections, the Tate owns works by the biggest of big names: Matisse, Dali, Modigliani, Munch, Bonnard, and Picasso. Truly remarkable are the room devoted to several enormous, somber, but rich canvases by the American abstract expressionist Mark Rothko; the group of paintings and sculptures by Giacometti (1901–66); and the paintings of one of England's most celebrated modern artists, the late Francis Bacon. Sculptures by Barbara Hepworth and the incomparable Henry Moore are also occasionally displayed.

We suggest saving some time for the **Art Now Gallery,** housing the most recent works of both new and established artists. There's always something different and cutting edge here. A recent artwork displayed here stirred up quite a controversy: it was a pile of bricks for which the Tate is rumored to have paid a "ghastly and ungodly sum."

Downstairs is the renowned gallery restaurant (reviewed in chapter 4), with murals by Rex Whistler, as well as a coffee shop.

✪ **National Gallery.** On the north side of Trafalgar Sq., WC2. ☎ **0171/839-3321.** Free admission. Mon–Tues 10am–6pm; Wed 10am–8pm; Thurs–Sat 10am–6pm; Sun noon–6pm. Closed Jan 1, Good Friday, Dec 24–26. Tube: Charing Cross, Embankment, or Leicester Square.

In an impressive neoclassical building, the National Gallery houses one of the most comprehensive collections of Western paintings in the world, representing all the major schools from the late 13th to the early 20th century. The largest part of the collection is devoted to the Italians, including the Sienese, Venetian, and Florentine masters, now housed in the Sainsbury Wing.

Of the early Gothic works, the *Wilton Diptych* (French or English school, late 14th century) is the rarest treasure; it depicts Richard II being introduced to the Madonna and Child by John the Baptist and the Saxon king, Edward the Confessor.

A Florentine gem by Masaccio is displayed, as well as notable works by Piero della Francesca, Leonardo da Vinci, Michelangelo, and Raphael.

Among the 16th-century Venetian masters, the most notable works include a rare *Adoration of the Kings* by Giorgione, *Bacchus and Ariadne* by Titian, *The Origin of the Milky Way* by Tintoretto, and *The Family of Darius Before Alexander* by Veronese.

A number of satellite rooms contain works by major Italian masters of the 15th century, such as Andrea Mantegna of Padua, Giovanni Bellini, and Botticelli.

Painters from northern Europe are well represented. For example, there is the Flemish artist Jan van Eyck's portrait of G. Arnolfini and his bride, plus Pieter Brueghel the Elder's Bosch-influenced *Adoration*. With *Young Woman at a Virginal*, the National Gallery has one of just 35 or so examples of the 17th-century master, Johannes Vermeer. Fellow Delftite Pieter de Hooch is represented by the sublime *Courtyard in a House in Delft*.

One of the National's biggest drawing cards is its collection of Rembrandts. His *Self-Portrait at the Age of 34* shows him at the pinnacle of his life; his *Self-Portrait at the Age of 63* is deeply moving and revealing.

Five of the greatest homegrown artists—Constable, Turner, Reynolds, Gainsborough, and Hogarth—have their masterpieces here, as do three giants of Spanish painting. Velázquez's portrait of the sunken-faced Philip IV, El Greco's *Christ Driving the Traders From the Temple*, and Goya's portrait of the duke of Wellington (once stolen) and his mantilla-wearing *Dõna Isabel de Porcel* are on display.

Other rooms are devoted to early 19th-century French painters, such as Delacroix and Ingres; the later 19th-century French impressionists, such as Manet, Monet, Renoir, and Degas; and post-impressionists such as Cézanne, Seurat, and van Gogh.

The National Gallery has a computer information center in the Sainsbury Wing where visitors can design a personal tour map. The computer room, located in the Micro Gallery, includes 12 computer work stations open to the public. The system offers 2,200 paintings to select from, with supporting text for each one. The program includes four indexes that are cross-referenced for your convenience. Using a touch-screen computer, you can design your own personalized tour by selecting a maximum of 10 paintings that you are interested in seeing. Once you have made your choices, you can print a free personal tour map highlighting your selections. There's a small charge, usually about £1 ($1.60), for printouts.

**Kensington Palace.** The Broad Walk, Kensington Gardens, W8. ☎ **0171/937-9561.** Admission £6 ($9.60) adults, £4 ($6.40) children, £4.50 ($7.20) students and seniors. May–Oct 5 daily 10am–6pm by guided tour; last tour leaves at 4:45pm. Closed off-season. Tube: Queensway or Bayswater on the north side of the gardens or High Street Kensington on the south side; a long walk from there.

Home of the state apartments, the palace is located at the far western end of Kensington Gardens; the entrance is from the Broad Walk. The palace was acquired by William III (William of Orange) in 1689 and remodeled by Sir Christopher Wren. George II, who died in 1760, was the last king to use it as a royal residence.

The most interesting chamber to visit is Queen Victoria's bedroom. In this room, on the morning of June 20, 1837, she was aroused from her sleep with the news that she had assumed the throne, following the death of her uncle, William IV. As you wander through the apartments, you'll see many fine paintings from the Royal Collection.

A special attraction is the Royal Ceremonial Dress Collection, which shows restored rooms from the 19th century, i ncluding Queen Victoria's birth room and a series of room settings with the appropriate court dress of the day, from 1760 to 1950.

The palace gardens, originally the private park of royalty, adjoin Hyde Park and are open to the public for daily strolls around Round Pond, near the heart of Kensington Gardens. Also in Kensington Gardens is the ✪ **Albert Memorial,** honoring Queen Victoria's consort. Facing Royal Albert Hall, the statue reflects the ostentation of the Victorian era.

✪ **St. Paul's Cathedral.** St. Paul's Churchyard, EC4. ☎ **0171/248-8348.** Cathedral: £3.50 ($5.60) adults, £2 ($3.20) children (6–16). Galleries: £3 ($4.80) adults, £1.50 ($2.40) children.

Guided tours £3 ($4.80); recorded tours £2.50 ($4). Children 5 and under free. Sightseeing Mon–Sat 8:30am–4pm; galleries Mon–Sat 10am–4:15pm. No sightseeing Sun (services only). Tube: St. Paul's.

St. Paul's has endured its share of hardship and calamity: The cathedral burned down three times and was destroyed once by invading Norsemen. During World War II, newsreel footage reached America showing the dome of St. Paul's Cathedral lit by fires caused by the bombings all around; it was hit badly on another occasion during the early years of the Nazi bombardment of London. During the Great Fire of 1666, the old St. Paul's was razed, making way for a new Renaissance structure designed (after many mishaps and rejections) by Sir Christopher Wren and built between 1675 and 1710.

The classical dome of St. Paul's dominates The City's square mile. Inside, the cathedral is laid out like a Greek cross; it houses few art treasures (Grinling Gibbons's choir stalls are an exception) but many monuments, including one to the "Iron Duke" and a memorial chapel to American service personnel who lost their lives in World War II while stationed in the U.K. Encircling the dome is the Whispering Gallery (so be careful what you say). In the crypt lie not only Wren but also the duke of Wellington and Lord Nelson. A fascinating Diocesan Treasury was opened in 1981. You can climb to the very top of the dome for a spectacular 360° view of London.

Guided tours last 1½ hours and include parts of the cathedral not open to the general public. They take place Monday through Saturday at 11am, 11:30am, 1:30pm, and 2pm. Recorded tours lasting 45 minutes are available throughout the day.

St. Paul's is an Anglican cathedral with daily services at the following times: Matins Monday through Friday at 7:30am, Saturday at 10am, Holy Communion Monday through Saturday at 8am and 12:30pm, and Evensong Monday through Saturday at 5pm. On Sunday, there is Holy Communion at 8am and again at 11am, Matins at 8:45am, and Evensong at 3:15pm. Admission charges do not apply if visitors are attending services.

If you're visiting in spring, be sure to wander through the free gardens of St. Paul's when the roses are in bloom. They are magnificent.

✪ **Victoria and Albert Museum.** Cromwell Rd., SW7. ☎ **0171/938-8500.** Admission £5 ($8) for adults, £3 ($4.80) for students and seniors. Free for children under 18. Mon noon–5:50pm; Tues–Sun 10am–5:50pm. Tube: South Kensington.

Located in South Kensington, this is one of the liveliest and most imaginative museums in London. It's named after the queen and her consort but does not run in their spirit. The general theme here is the fine and decorative arts, adhered to in a pleasantly relaxed fashion.

The medieval holdings include many treasures, such as the Eltenberg Reliquary (Rhenish, second half of the 12th century); the Early English Gloucester Candlestick; the Byzantine Veroli Casket, with its ivory panels based on Greek plays; and the Syon Cope, a highly valued embroidery made in England in the early 14th century. The Gothic tapestries, including the Devonshire ones depicting hunting scenes, are displayed in another gallery. An area devoted to Islamic art houses the Ardabil carpet from 16th-century Persia (320 knots per square inch).

The Victoria and Albert houses the largest collection of **Renaissance sculpture** outside Italy, including a Donatello marble relief, *The Ascension;* a small terra-cotta statue of the Madonna and Child by Antonio Rossellino; a marble group, *Samson and a Philistine,* by Giovanni Bologna; and a wax model of a slave by Michelangelo. The

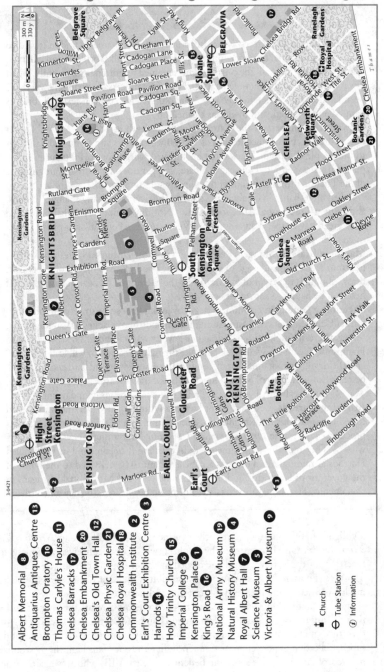

Albert Memorial **8**
Antiquarius Antiques Centre **13**
Brompton Oratory **10**
Thomas Carlyle's House **11**
Chelsea Barracks **17**
Chelsea Embankment **20**
Chelsea's Old Town Hall **12**
Chelsea Physic Garden **21**
Chelsea Royal Hospital **18**
Commonwealth Institute **2**
Earl's Court Exhibition Centre **3**
Harrods **14**
Holy Trinity Church **15**
Imperial College **6**
Kensington Palace **1**
King's Road **16**
National Army Museum **19**
Natural History Museum **4**
Royal Albert Hall **7**
Science Museum **5**
Victoria & Albert Museum **9**

✚■ Church
Ⓣ Tube Station
ⓘ Information

**149**

⭐ **Frommer's Favorite London Experiences**

**Cruising London's Waterways.**  In addition to the Thames, London is riddled with an antique canal system, complete with towpath walks, bridges, and wharves. Replaced by the railroad, the canal system remained forgotten until recently, when it was rediscovered by a new generation. Now, in a process of urban renewal that's been labeled "industrial archaeology," the old system has been restored, bridges painted and repaired, and towpaths cleaned up.

**Viewing the Turners at the Tate.**  Upon his death in 1851, J. M. W. Turner bequeathed his personal collection of 19,000 watercolors and some 300 paintings to the people of Britain. He wanted his finished works, some 100 paintings, displayed under one roof. Today at the Tate, you get not only Turner, but glimpses of the Thames through the museum's windows. How appropriate—the artist lived and died on its banks in Chelsea, and painted the river in its many changing moods.

**Enjoying a Traditional Afternoon Tea.**  Nothing is more typically British, and it's a great way to spend an afternoon. We've suggested our favorite places for tea in chapter 4.

**Making a Brass Rubbing.**  Relive the era of those costumed ladies and knights in armor from England's age of chivalry. One good place to make your very own brass rubbing is the crypt of St. Martin-in-the-Fields in Trafalgar Square; the staff here will be happy to show you how.

**Spending a Sunday in London.**  Begin by looking for some smart or trendy fashions at Camden Market, a Sunday affair in the northern reaches of Camden High Street where stallholders hawk designer jewelry and clothing. Next, walk up to Hampstead Heath off Well Walk and take the right fork, which will lead you to an open field with a panoramic view of London. If you walk long and hard enough, you'll be ready for a traditional Sunday lunch at Jack Straw's Castle at North End Way. Top off your meal with a visit to the Freud Museum, open on Sunday until 5pm.

**Browsing Harrods.**  Regardless of how many times you visit London, it's hard to resist a visit to this vast Knightsbridge emporium. Spread across 15 acres, Harrods proclaims as its motto *Omnia Omnibus Ubique* or "everything for everyone, everywhere." They mean it, too: Someone didn't believe the claim, and in 1975 called Harrods at midnight and ordered a baby elephant to be delivered to the home of the governor of California and his First Lady, Mr. and Mrs. Ronald Reagan, in Sacramento. The animal arrived safely, albeit a bit bewildered. (Nancy sent a "thank

---

highlight of 16th-century art from the continent is the marble group *Neptune With Triton* by Bernini. The cartoons by Raphael, which were conceived as designs for tapestries for the Sistine Chapel, are owned by the queen and can also be seen here.

A most unusual, huge, and impressive exhibit is the Cast Courts, life-size plaster models of ancient and medieval statuary and architecture.

In addition to Chinese and Japanese galleries, the museum has the greatest **collection of Indian art** outside India. Standing in complete contrast are suites of English furniture, metalwork, and ceramics dating earlier than the 16th century, and a superb collection of portrait miniatures, including the one Hans Holbein the Younger painted of Anne of Cleves for the benefit of Henry VIII, who was again casting around for a suitable wife.

The most curious gallery here is devoted to "Fakes and Forgeries." The art impostors in this gallery are amazingly authentic—some seem almost better than the Old Masters themselves.

you" note.) The food hall is our favorite draw, with some 500 different cheeses and 163 brands of whisky among zillions of other goodies. You might have to wait for the famous January sale to find a bargain, but Harrod's is certainly worth a walk around.

**Rowing on the Serpentine.**   When the weather is right, we like to head to this 41-acre artificial lake dating from 1730. A stream was dammed to create the artificial lake, whose name derives from its winding, snakelike shape. At the boat house, you can rent (Brits say "hire") a boat by the hour. With the right companion, it's one of the most idyllic ways to spend a sunny London afternoon. Renoir must have agreed; he immortalized the custom on canvas.

**Strolling Through Covent Garden.**   George Bernard Shaw got his inspiration for *Pygmalion* here, where the character of Eliza Doolittle sold violets to wealthy operagoers and became a household name around the world. The old fruit and vegetable market, with its Cockney cauliflower peddlers and butchers in blood-soaked aprons, is long gone. What's left is just as interesting: Covent Garden today is London's best example of urban renewal. There's an antique market in the square on Monday, and a crafts market Tuesday through Saturday. When you're thirsty, plenty of pubs in the area will quench your thirst.

**Watching the Sunset at Waterloo Bridge.**   Waterloo Bridge is the best place in London to watch the sun set over Westminster. From here, you can also see the last rays of sunlight (if you're lucky enough to get sun) bounce off The City spires in the East End.

**Spending a Night at the West End Theater.**   London is the theater capital of the world. The live stage offers a unique combination of variety, accessibility, and economy—and a preview of next year's Broadway hit. Stop by the half-price ticket booth in Leicester Square for 2-fers.

**Crawling the London Pubs.**   Americans bar hop, Londoners do a pub crawl. With some 5,000 pubs within the city limits, you would be crawling indeed if you tried to have a drink in each of them. Enough traditional pubs remain, especially in central London, to make a crawl worthwhile. While making the rounds, you can partake of that essential British fare known as "pub grub," which might include everything from a ploughman's lunch (a hunk of bread, cheese, and a pickle) to a plate of shepherd's pie.

---

In a major redevelopment plan, about 10% of the entire gallery space of the V&A closed in the summer of 1997. The entirety of the British Galleries won't reopen again until 2001.

A restaurant serves snacks and meals, and two museum shops sell ideal gifts, posters, cards, and books. Note that the museum hosts a jazz brunch on Sunday mornings. You get not only some of the hottest jazz in the city, but a full English breakfast or lunch is included from 11am to 3pm for only £8 ($12.80).

## TRAFALGAR SQUARE

One of the landmark squares of London, Trafalgar Square honors one of England's great military heroes, Horatio, Viscount Nelson (1758–1805), who died at the Battle of Trafalgar. Although he suffered from seasickness all his life, he went off to sea at the age of 12 and became an admiral at the age of 39. Lord Nelson was a hero of the Battle of Calvi in 1794, where he lost an eye, the Battle of Santa Cruz in 1797, where he lost an arm, and the Battle of Trafalgar in 1805, where he lost his life.

The square today is dominated by a 145-foot granite column, the work of E. H. Baily in 1843. The column looks down Whitehall toward the Old Admiralty, where Lord Nelson's body lay in state. The naval hero towers 17 feet high, not bad for a man who only stood 5 feet 4 inches in real life. The capital is of bronze cast from cannons recovered from the wreck of the *Royal George*. Queen Victoria's favorite painter of animals, Sir Edward Landseer, added the four lions at the base of the column in 1868. The pools and fountains were not added until 1939, the last work of Sir Edwin Lutyens.

Political demonstrations still take place at the square and around the column, which has to have the most aggressive pigeons in all London. The pesky birds will land on your head or perform less cute stunts. Actually the birds are part of a long feathery tradition; this site was once used by Edward I (1239–1307) to keep his birds of prey. Called "Longshanks," he came here often before he died of dysentery in 1307. Richard II, who ruled from 1377 to 1399, kept goshawks and falcons here. By the time of Henry VII, who ruled from 1485 to 1509, the square was the site of the royal stables. Sir Charles Barry, who designed the Houses of Parliament, created the present square in the 1830s. The birds remain.

Much of the world trains TV cameras on the square on New Year's Eve. It's a wild and raucous time. Partyers lose all sense of British decorum; revelers jump into the chilly waters of the fountains, and in 1986, five people were crushed to death. The giant Christmas tree installed here every December is an annual gift from Norway to the British people, in eternal appreciation for sheltering their royal family during World War II. Today, street performers, now officially licensed, will entertain you and hope for a token of appreciation for their efforts.

To the southeast of the square, at 36 Craven Street, stands a house once occupied by Benjamin Franklin (1757–74) when he was a general of the Philadelphia Academy. On the north side of the square rises the National Gallery, constructed in the 1830s. In front of the building is a copy of a statue of George Washington by J. A. Houdon.

To the left of St. Martin's Place is the National Portrait Gallery, a collection of British greats (and not-so-greats)—everyone from Chaucer and Shakespeare to Captain Hook and Nell Gwyn. Also on the square is the landmark St. Martin-in-the-Fields by James Gibbs, with its towering steeple, a resting place of such figures as Sir Joshua Reynolds, William Hogarth, and Thomas Chippendale.

# 2 More Attractions

## OFFICIAL LONDON

**Whitehall,** the seat of the British government, grew up on the grounds of Whitehall Palace and was turned into a royal residence by Henry VIII, who snatched it from its former occupant, Cardinal Wolsey. Whitehall extends south from Trafalgar Square to Parliament Square. Along it you'll find the Home Office, the Old Admiralty Building, and the Ministry of Defence.

Visitors today can see the **Cabinet War Rooms,** the bombproof bunker suite of rooms, just as they were when abandoned by Winston Churchill and the British government at the end of World War II. You can see the Map Room with its huge wall maps, the Atlantic map a mass of pinholes (each hole represents at least one convoy). Next door is Churchill's bedroom-cum-office, which has a bed and a desk with two BBC microphones on it for his famous speech broadcasts that stirred the nation.

The Transatlantic Telephone Room, its full title, is little more than a broom closet, even though it housed the Bell Telephone Company's special scrambler phone, called

Sig-Saly, and was where Churchill conferred with Roosevelt. A system of boards with such laconic phrases as "wet," "very wet," "fine and warm," "dry and dull" was used to indicate weather conditions around the world before maneuvers were planned. All visitors are provided with a step-by-step personal sound guide, providing a detailed account of each room's function and history.

The entrance to the War Rooms is by Clive Steps at the end of King Charles Street, SW1 (☎ 0171/930-6961; tube: Westminster or St. James's), off Whitehall near Big Ben. You'll receive a cassette-recorded guided tour, and admission is £4.40 ($7.05) for adults and £2.20 ($3.50) for children. The rooms are open from April to September daily, 9:30am to 6pm (last admission 5:15); and October through March daily, 10am to 5:30pm; they're closed on Christmas holidays.

At the Cenotaph (honoring the dead from two world wars), turn down unpretentious **Downing Street** to the modest little town house at no. 10, flanked by two bobbies. Walpole was the first prime minister to live here, Churchill the most famous. But Iron Maggie, Margaret Thatcher, was around longer than any of them.

Nearby, north of Downing Street, is the **Horse Guards Building,** Whitehall (☎ 0171/414-2396; tube: Westminster), now the headquarters of the horse guards of the Household Division and London District. There has been a guard change here since 1649, when the site was the entrance to the old Palace of Whitehall. You can watch the queen's Life Guards ceremony at 11am Monday through Saturday (10am on Sunday). You can also see the hourly (albeit lesser) change of the guard, when mounted troopers are replaced. At 4pm you can watch the evening inspection, when 10 unmounted troopers and 2 mounted troopers assemble in the courtyard.

Across the street is Inigo Jones's **Banqueting House,** Palace of Whitehall, Horse Guards Avenue (☎ 0171/930-4179; tube: Westminster), site of the execution of Charles I. William and Mary accepted the crown of England here, but they preferred to live at Kensington Palace. The Banqueting House was part of Whitehall Palace, which burned to the ground in 1698, but the ceremonial hall escaped razing. Its most notable feature today is an allegorical ceiling painted by the Flemish master Peter Paul Rubens. Admission to the Banqueting House is £3.25 ($5.20) for adults, £2.15 ($3.45) for children, £2.50 ($4) for seniors and students. It's open Monday through Saturday from 10am to 5pm (last admission 4:30pm).

Finally, stroll to Parliament Square for a view of **Big Ben** (tube: Westminster), the world's most famous timepiece and the symbol of the heart and soul of England. Big Ben is actually the name of the deepest and loudest bell, though it's become the common name for this clock tower on the Houses of Parliament.

## LEGAL LONDON

The smallest borough in London, bustling Holborn (pronounced *HO*-burn) is often referred to as Legal London, home to the city's barristers, solicitors, and law clerks. It also embraces the university district of Bloomsbury. Holburn, which houses the ancient **Inns of Courts**—Gray's Inn, Lincoln's Inn, Middle Temple, and Inner Temple—was severely damaged during World War II bombing raids. The razed buildings were replaced with modern offices, but the borough still retains pockets of its former days.

**Law Courts.** Strand, WC2. Free admission. ☎ 0171-936-6000. During sessions Mon–Fri 10:30am–1pm and 2–4pm. Tube: Holborn/Temple.

At these 60 or more courts presently in use, all civil and some criminal cases are heard. Designed by G. E. Street, the neo-Gothic buildings (1874 to 1882) contain more than 1,000 rooms and 3.5 miles of corridors. Sculptures of Christ, King Solomon, and King Alfred grace the front door; Moses is depicted at the back entrance. On the

## What to See & Do for Free (or Almost)

- **Changing of the Guard.**    This parade in front of Buckingham Palace has more royal pomp and circumstance than any other such royal ceremony on earth—and it's a perennial crowd pleaser.
- **Hampstead Heath.**    For the greatest ramble in London, follow in the footsteps of John Keats and other luminaries and travel north by tube to Hampstead. Here you can take a long ramble on this delightful Heath, where the almost wilderness feel stands in delicious contrast to London's many manicured parks and gardens. Later you can drop in for a pint at one of the local Hampstead pubs.
- **A City With a View.**    Take the tube to Tower Hill or Tower Gateway, and then cross Tower Bridge. If you wander along the south bank of the mighty Thames at night, you can gaze upon the historic landmarks and skyscrapers, floodlit in all their evening spectacle and finery.
- **Regent's Park.**    This area used to be the exclusive hunting grounds of royalty, where both Henry VIII and Elizabeth I chased stags here. Today it's frequented by many Londoners, from footballers to couples strolling barefoot in summer. Regent's Park is home to the London Zoo, the Open Air Theatre's Shakespeare in the Park, Prince Regent's original grand terraces, and Queen Mary's rose gardens. You can take advantage of these attractions or just wander the grounds, enjoying foliage and people watching.
- **The Old Bailey Public Gallery, Warwick Passage of Old Bailey.**    Britain's Central Criminal Court, widely known as "Old Bailey," is an entertaining stop for its tradition as much as its caseload. Robed and bewigged barristers and judges still administer justice with a great deal of formality and theatricality. Built on the foundations of the infamous Newgate Gaol, these

second Saturday in November, the annually elected lord mayor is sworn in by the lord chief justice.

**Old Baziley.** Newgate St., EC4. ☎ **0171/248-3277.** Free admission. Children under 14 not admitted; ages 14–16 must be accompanied by a responsible adult. No cameras or tape recorders allowed. Mon–Fri 10:30am–1pm and 2–4pm. Tube: Temple, Chancery Lane, or St. Paul's.

This courthouse replaced the infamous Newgate Prison, once the scene of public hangings and other forms of "public entertainment." It's affectionately known as the Old Bailey after a nearby street. It's fascinating to watch the barristers, wigs and all, presenting their cases to the high court judges. Entry is strictly on a first-arrival basis, and guests line up outside. Courts 1 to 4, 17, and 18, are entered from Newgate Street, and the balance from Old Bailey (the street). To get here, travel east on Fleet Street, which along the way becomes Ludgate Hill. Cross Ludgate Circus and turn left to the Old Bailey, a domed structure with the figure of "Justice" standing atop it.

## MORE MUSEUMS

**Apsley House.** The Wellington Museum, 149 Piccadilly, Hyde Park Corner, W1. ☎ **0171/499-5676.** Admission £4 ($6.40) adults, £2.50 ($4) seniors and children (12–17, under 12 free), £7 ($11.20) family ticket. Tues–Sun 11am–5pm. Closed Jan 1, May Day, Dec 24–26. Tube: Hyde Park Corner.

This former town house of the Iron Duke, the British general (1769 to 1852) who defeated Napoléon at the Battle of Waterloo and later became prime minister, was courtrooms have seen it all, from Oscar Wilde's conviction on charges of homosexuality to the sentencing of the Yorkshire Ripper (but not Jack!). You can check the court schedule to determine which case you'd like to witness. Wardens, located on each landing, will direct you to the proper gallery.

- **The Voice Box, on Level 5 of the Royal Festival Hall, SE1** (☎ **0171/921-0906**), **and Poetry Library** (☎ **0171/921-0943**).   Part of London's creatively fertile Arts Centre Project, the Voice Box is a stage for poetry and prose readings, usually performed by celebrated writers. The readings are generally held around 7:30pm. There's a small admission charge: £2.50 ($4) for adults and from £2 ($3.20) for students. For a schedule, check a free copy of the "Literature Quarterly" brochure. Next door is the Poetry Library, containing Britain's largest collection of 20th-century poetry. You can also find periodicals of poetry, audio and video recordings, and a bulletin board with information about workshops and contests. Membership is free, but you must bring a current ID. It's open Tuesday through Sunday from 11am to 8pm. Take the tube to Waterloo.
- And don't forget these classic London free attractions:
  **Houses of Parliament, Westminster Palace and Old Palace Yard,** SW1 (☎ **0171/219-4272**). The **British Museum & Library,** Great Russell Street, WC1 (☎ **0171/323-8599**). **Tate Gallery,** beside the Thames on Millbank, SW1 (☎ **0171/887-8725**). The **National Gallery,** on the north side of Trafalgar Square, WC2 (☎ **0171/839-3321**). **National Portrait Gallery,** St. Martin's Place, WC2 (☎ **0171/306-0055**). **Sir John Soane's Museum,** 13 Lincoln Inn Fields, WC2 (☎ **0171/430-0175**).

opened as a public museum in 1952. The building was designed by Robert Adam and was constructed in the late 18th century. Wellington once had to retreat behind the walls of Apsley House, fearing an attack from Englishmen outraged by his autocratic opposition to reform. In the vestibule, you'll find a colossal marble statue of Napoléon by Canova—ironic, to say the least; it was presented to the duke by King George IV.

In addition to the famous *Waterseller of Seville* by Velázquez, the Wellington collection includes works by Correggio, Jan Steen, and Pieter de Hooch. Silver and porcelain collectors should also head here to see some of the finest pieces in Europe. Grateful to Wellington for saving their thrones, European monarchs endowed him with treasures. Head for the Plate and China Room on the ground floor to get the idea. The Sèvres Egyptian service here was intended as a divorce present from Napoléon to Josephine but she refused it, foolish woman. Eventually Louis XVIII of France presented it to Wellington. The Portuguese Silver Service in the dining room was created between 1812 and 1816: it's been hailed as the single greatest artifact of Portuguese neoclassical silver.

**British Library.** British Museum, 96 Euston Rd., NW1. ☎ **0171/412-7000.** Free admission. Mon–Sat 10am–5pm; Sun 2:30–6pm. Tube: Holborn or Tottenham Court Road.

One of the world's greatest libraries is no longer at the British Museum but has moved to St. Pancras, and, although it will be open in parts, the entire library may not be fully functioning until the dawn of the millennium. The move began in

December 1996, and will continue for some 2¹/₂ years. During this period, the library will move some 12 million books, manuscripts, and other items. The first St. Pancras reading room, devoted to humanities, opened in November 1997. You can call for information if you're looking for a specific exhibition or manuscript. The library has special phone lines to provide detailed information about the moves of specific parts of its collection.

Unless you're a scholar working on a paper, most people visit the library to view its rare book collection. The moving of these books began in the summer of 1997, and the rare books room is slated to open in spring 1998. These rare books include items of significant historical and literary interest, featuring two of the four surviving copies of King John's Magna Carta (1215). Almost every major author—Dickens, Jane Austen, Charlotte Brontë, Keats, and hundreds of others—is represented in the section devoted to English literature. Also on display are Nelson's last letter to Lady Hamilton and the journals of Captain Cook.

The history of the book is illustrated by notable specimens of early printing, including the Diamond Sutra of 868, the first dated example of printing, as well as the Gutenberg Bible, the first book ever printed from movable type, 1455. Beneath Roubiliac's 1758 statue of Shakespeare stands a case of documents relating to the Bard, including a mortgage bearing his signature and a copy of the First Folio of 1623. The library's unrivaled collection of philatelic items, including the 1840 Great British Penny Black and the rare 1847 post office issues of Mauritius, are also owned by the library.

✪ **Courtauld Institute Galleries.** Somerset House, The Strand, WC2. ☎ **0171/873-2526.** Admission £4 ($6.40) adults, £2 ($3.20) children. Mon–Sat 10am–6pm; Sun 2–6pm. Tube: Temple, Covent Garden, or Embankment.

These galleries, slated to reopen in July 1998, display a wealth of paintings, including: the great collection of French impressionist and post-impressionist paintings (masterpieces by Monet, Manet, Degas, Renoir, Cézanne, van Gogh, and Gauguin) brought together by the late textile industrialist Samuel Courtauld; the Princes Gate collection of superb old master paintings and drawings, especially those by Rubens, Michelangelo, and Tiepolo; the Gambier-Parry collection of early Italian paintings, ivories, majolica, and other works of art; the Lee collection of old masters; the Roger Fry collection of early 20th-century English and French painting; and the Hunter collection of 20th-century British painting.

Although surprisingly little known, this gallery boasts one of the world's greatest collections of impressionist paintings outside Paris. It's a visual feast, the equivalent of the Frick Collection in New York, a display of superb works of art in a jewel-like setting. We always come here at least once every season to visit one painting: Manet's exquisite *A Bar at the Folies-Bergère.* The galleries are air-conditioned, and most of the paintings are displayed without glass.

**Design Museum.** 28 Shad Thames, London, SE1. ☎ **0171/378-6055.** Admission £5.50 ($8.80) adults, £3.75 ($6) students and children. Mon–Fri 11:30am–6pm; Sat–Sun noon–6pm. Tube: Tower Hill (then walk over the bridge) or London Bridge (then walk along Tooley Street). DLR (Docklands Light Railway): Tower Gateway (then walk over the bridge). Bus: 15, 78, 47, 42, or 188.

Part of the new Docklands development, this museum, located at Butler's Wharf, displays all kinds of manufactured products touted for their design. It's the only museum in Europe that explains why and how mass-produced objects work and look the way they do. You'll see cars, furniture, appliances, graphics, and ceramics, including the Volkswagen Bug and the angle-poise lamp. The museum shop has everything from designer socks to sleek alarm clocks.

**Hayward Gallery.** On the South Bank, SE1. ☎ **0171/928-3144.** Admission £5 ($8) adults; £3.50 ($5.60) children, students, and seniors; under 12 free with adult; family ticket £12 ($19.20). Fees can vary according to exhibitions. Mon, Thurs–Sun 10am–6pm; Tues–Wed 10am–8pm. Tube: Waterloo/Embankment.

Opened by Queen Elizabeth in 1968, this gallery, part of the South Bank Centre, presents a changing program of major contemporary and historic exhibitions. The gallery is closed between exhibitions, so check before crossing the Thames.

**Imperial War Museum.** Lambeth Rd., SE1. ☎ **0171/416-5000.** Admission £4.70 ($7.50) adults, £3.70 ($5.90) seniors and students, £2.35 ($3.75) children; free daily 4:30–6pm. Daily 10am–6pm. Closed Dec 24–26. Tube: Lambeth North or Elephant & Castle.

Built around 1815, this large, domed building, the former Bethlehem Royal Hospital for the Insane (or Bedlam), houses the museum's collections relating to the two world wars and other military operations involving the British and the Commonwealth since 1914. There are four floors of exhibitions, including the Large Exhibits Gallery, a vast area showing historical displays, two floors of art galleries, and a dramatic re-creation of London at war during the blitz. You can see a Battle of Britain Spitfire, the rifle carried by Lawrence of Arabia, and Hitler's political testament, as well as models, decorations, uniforms, photographs, and paintings. It's located just across the Thames.

**London Transport Museum.** The Piazza, Covent Garden, WC2. ☎ **0171/379-6344.** Admission £4.50 ($7.20) adults, £2.50 ($4) seniors and children 5–15. Sat–Thurs 10am–6pm; Fri 11am–6pm. Closed Dec 24–26. Tube: Covent Garden/Charing Cross.

This splendidly restored Victorian building once housed the flower market. Now it's home to horse buses, motor buses, trams, trolleybuses, railway vehicles, models, maps, posters, photographs, and audiovisual displays that trace 200 years of London transport history. The story is enlivened by several interactive video exhibits—you can put yourself in the driver's seat of a bus or tube train. The fabulous gift shops sells a variety of London Transport souvenirs. A cafe overlooks the piazza.

✪ **Museum of London.** 150 London Wall, EC2. ☎ **0171/600-3699.** Admission £4 ($6.40) adults; £2 ($3.20) children, students, and seniors; £9.50 ($15.20) family ticket. Tues–Sat 10am–5:50pm; Sun noon–5:50pm. Tube: St. Paul's, Barbican, Bank, or Moorgate.

In the Barbican district near St. Paul's Cathedral, the Museum of London allows visitors to trace the city's history from prehistoric times to the post-modern era through relics, costumes, household effects, maps, and models. Anglo-Saxons, Vikings, Normans—they're all here, displayed on two floors around a central courtyard. The exhibits are arranged so that visitors can begin and end their chronological stroll through 250,000 years at the museum's main entrance; exhibits have quick labels for museum sprinters, more extensive ones for those who want more background, and still more detail for scholars. It's an enriching experience for everybody—you should allow at least an hour for a full (but still quick) visit.

You'll see the death mask of Oliver Cromwell; the Great Fire of London in living color and sound; reconstructed Roman dining rooms with kitchen and utensils; cell doors from Newgate Prison, which was made famous by Charles Dickens; and an amazing shop counter with pre–World War II prices on the items. But the *pièce de résistance* is the Lord Mayor's coach, built in 1757 and weighing three tons. Still used each November in the Lord Mayor's Procession, this gilt-and-red horse-drawn vehicle is like a fairy-tale coach.

Free lectures on London's history are often given during lunch hours; ask at the entrance hall if one will be given the day you're here. You can reach the museum, which overlooks London's Roman and medieval walls, by going up to the elevated pedestrian precinct at the corner of London Wall and Aldersgate, 5 minutes from St. Paul's. There's a restaurant, opposite the main entrance.

**Museum of Mankind.** In the British Museum, Great Russell St., WC1. ☎ **0171/323-8599.** Free admission. Mon–Sat 10am–5pm; Sun 2:30–5pm. Closed New Year's Day, Good Friday, early May, Dec 24–26. Tube: Holborn or Tottenham Court Road.

It boasts what would seem an impossibly ambitious name, but this is the finest ethnographic collection in the world. It has it all: Eskimo polar-bear pants, an Amazonian's human-head mascot, a painted skull from Mexico honoring the "Day of the Dead," British Columbian stone carvings, Sioux war bonnets. A real curiosity is a Hawaiian god with a mohawk, found by Captain Cook and shipped back to London. The Beninese bronzes from Africa are stunning, as is the Asante West collection of gold jewelry and ornaments from West Africa. The collection is continues to grow.

Following the departure of the British Library from its British Museum site, the Burlington Gardens location of the ethnographic collections will be closed and moved back to its parent, effective December 31, 1997. For the current status of its displays, you can call a special information desk at the museum (☎ **0171/323-8599**).

**National Army Museum.** Royal Hospital Rd., SW3. ☎ **0171/730-0717.** Free admission. Daily 10am–5:30pm. Closed Jan 1, Good Friday, May bank holiday, Dec 24–26. Tube: Sloane Square.

Located in Chelsea, this museum traces the history of the British land forces, the Indian army, and colonial land forces. The collection starts with the year 1485, the date that the Yeomen of the Guard was formed. The saga of the forces of the East India Company is also traced, from its beginning in 1602 to Indian independence in 1947. The gory and the glory are here—everything from Florence Nightingale's lamp to the cloak wrapped around the dying Gen. James Wolfe at Quebec in 1759. There are also "cases of the heroes," mementos of such outstanding men as the duke of Marlborough and the duke of Wellington. But the field soldier isn't neglected either: The Nation in Arms Gallery tells the soldier's story in two world wars, including an exhibit of the British Army in the Far East from 1941 to 1945.

**National Portrait Gallery.** St. Martin's Place, WC2. ☎ **0171/306-0055.** Free admission, except for special exhibitions. Mon–Sat 10am–6pm; Sun noon–6pm. Tube: Charing Cross or Leicester Square.

The National Portrait Gallery was founded in 1856 to collect the likenesses of famous British men and women. Today the collection is the most comprehensive of its kind in the world, constituting a unique record of the men and women who created (and are still creating) the history and culture of the nation. A few paintings tower over the rest, including Sir Joshua Reynold's portrait of Samuel Johnson ("a man of most dreadful appearance"). Among the best are Nicholas Hilliard's miniature of a handsome Sir Walter Raleigh and a full-length Elizabeth I, along with the Holbein cartoon of Henry VIII (sketched for a family portrait that hung, before it was burned, in the Privy Chamber in Whitehall Palace). You'll also see a portrait of William Shakespeare (with gold earring, no less), which is claimed to be the most "authentic contemporary likeness" of its subject of any work yet known. One of the most unusual pictures in the gallery is a group of the three Brontë sisters painted by their brother Branwell. Famous people of today, including the Baroness Thatcher, are celebrated in two floors of the most recent galleries. Diana, Princess of Wales, is on the Royal Landing.

The galleries dedicated to Victorian and early 20th-century portraits were radically redesigned. Occupying the whole of the first floor, they display portraits from 1837 when Victoria ascended to the throne up to the dawn of the Swinging 1960s. Galleries span a remarkable period of British history—from the growth up of the Empire up to the "new Elizabethans." Some of the more flamboyant personalities of the age, from the Pre-Raphaelites to the Bloomsbury group, are on show: T.S. Eliot, Disraeli, Macmillan, Lord Leighton's Sir Richard Burton, and our two favorites—G. F. Watts's famous portrait of his great actress wife, Ellen Terry, and Vanessa Bell's portrait of her sister, Virginia Woolf.

**National Postal Museum.** King Edward Building, King Edward Street, EC1. ☎ **0171/ 600-8914.** Free admission. Mon–Fri 9:30am–4:30pm. Closed all bank holidays. Tube: St. Paul's, the Barbican.

In 1840, Britain introduced the world's first postage stamp, the Penny Black, but for 200 years before that a postal service of sorts was operating. In the main gallery, all the stamps of Britain are on display. Also displayed are valentines and other greeting cards; scales and handstamps; and letter boxes, which were introduced by the post office surveyor and novelist Anthony Trollope in 1852.

✪ **Natural History Museum.** Cromwell Rd., South Kensington, SW7. ☎ **0171/938-9123.** Admission £5.50 ($8.80) adult, £3 ($4.80) seniors, £2.80 ($4.50) children 5–17. Free 4 and under. Mon–Sat 10am–6pm; Sun 11am–6pm. Closed Dec 23–26, Jan 1, and Good Friday. Tube: South Kensington.

With towers, spires, and a huge navelike hall, this terra-cotta building is a wonder in itself. Designed by Alfred Waterhouse and opened in 1881, the museum is one of the finest of its kind. The core of the collection came from Sir Hans Sloane. Today, only a fraction of the museum's natural treasures—fossils, animal and plant life exhibits, and minerals—can be displayed. Among the highlights are the dinosaurs in the main hall; the Human Biology exhibit that features many interactive displays, and an ecology exhibit. There's also an earthquake simulator and an insect display.

**Royal Academy of Arts.** Burlington House, Piccadilly, W1. ☎ **0171/439-7438.** Admission varies, depending on the exhibition. Daily 10am–6pm. Closed Dec 25–26, Good Friday. Tube: Piccadilly Circus/Green Park.

Established in 1768, the academy included Sir Joshua Reynolds, Thomas Gainsborough, and Benjamin West among its founding members. Since its beginning, each academician had to donate a work of art, and so over the years the academy has built up a sizable collection. The annual summer exhibition has been held for more than 200 years.

✪ **Saatchi Gallery.** 98A Boundary Rd., NW8. ☎ **0171/624-8299.** Admission £3.50 ($5.60), free Thurs. Thurs–Sun 12–6 pm. Tube: St. John's Wood or Swiss Cottage.

In the world of contemporary art, the breadth of this collection is unparalleled. The adman Charles Saatchi is one of Britain's greatest private collectors, and his personal museum features rotating displays from vast and continually expanding holdings. Enter through the unmarked metal gateway of a former paint warehouse.

**Science Museum.** Exhibition Rd., SW7. ☎ **0171/938-8000.** Admission £5.50 ($8.80) adult, £2.90 ($4.65) seniors and children 5–17. Four and under free. Daily 10am–6pm. Closed Dec 24–26. Tube: South Kensington.

Among the most notable exhibits here are naval models; the Puffing Billy (1813), one of the oldest locomotives still in existence; Stephenson's Rocket (1829); Arkwright's spinning machine; Wheatstone's electric telegraph; Fox Talbot's first camera; Edison's original phonograph; the Vickers *Vimy* aircraft, which made the first Atlantic crossing in 1919; and Sir Frank Whittle's turbo-jet engine. Three new galleries are designed to appeal to children. The Garden provides water, construction, sound and light shows, and games for 3- to 6-year-olds. The other two galleries appeal to 7- to 12-year-olds allowing them to play on networked terminals and also to investigate the way things work through interactive exhibits.

**Shakespeare's Globe Theatre & Exhibition.** New Globe Walk, Bankside, SE1. ☎ **0171/928-6406.** Exhibition admission £5 ($8) adults, £3 ($4.80) children 15 and under. Guided tours £5 ($8) adults, £4 ($6.40) students and seniors, £3 ($4.80) children. Daily 10am–5pm (guided tours every 30 minutes or so); Closed Dec 24–26. Tube: Mansion House.

This is a re-creation of what was probably the most important public theater ever built—on the exact site where many of Shakespeare's plays were originally staged in the 16th century. The late American filmmaker, Sam Wanamaker, worked for some 20 years to raise funds to re-create the theater as it existed in Elizabethan times, thatched roof and all. A fascinating exhibit tells the story of the Globe's re-creation in modern times, using the materials (including goat's hair in the plaster), techniques, and craftsmanship of 400 years ago. The new Globe isn't actually an exact replica: It seats 1,500 patrons, not the 3,000 that regularly squeezed in during the early 1600s; and this thatched roof has been specially treated with a fire retardant. Guided tours of the facility are offered throughout the day.

In May 1997, the Globe's company staged its first slate of plays. See section 8 in this chapter, "London After Dark," for details on attending a play here. Plans also call for an archival library, shops, an auditorium, and an exhibition gallery, but the full complex may not be fully operational until September 1999.

✪ **Sir John Soane's Museum.** 13 Lincoln's Inn Fields, WC2. ☎ **0171/430-0175.** Free admission. Tues–Sat 10am–5pm; first Tues of each month 6–9pm. Tours given Sat at 2:30pm (free tickets given out at 2pm on a first-come, first-served basis—no groups). Closed bank holidays. Tube: Chancery Lane or Holborn.

This is the former home of Sir John Soane (1753 to 1837), an architect who rebuilt the Bank of England (not the present structure). Employing multilevels, fool-the-eye mirrors, flying arches, and domes, Soane was a master of perspective and a genius of interior space (his picture gallery, for example, is filled with three times the number of paintings a room of similar dimensions would be likely to hold). William Hogarth's satirical series, *The Rake's Progress*, includes his much-reproduced *Orgy* and *The Election*, a satire on mid-18th-century politics. Soane also filled his house with paintings and classical sculpture. On display is the sarcophagus of Pharaoh Seti I, found in a burial chamber in the Valley of the Kings. Also exhibited are architectural drawings from the collection of 30,000 in the Soane Gallery (opened in 1995).

**The Wallace Collection.** Hertford House, Manchester Sq., W1. ☎ **0171/935-0687.** Free admission. Mon–Sat 10am–5pm; Sun 2–5pm. Closed Jan 1, Good Friday, first Mon in May, Dec 24–26. Tube: Bond Street.

This outstanding collection of artworks bequeathed to the nation by Lady Wallace in 1897 is still displayed in the house of its founders, off Wigmore Street. The works of art (mostly French) include important pictures by artists of all European schools. There's also sculpture, furniture, goldsmiths' work, and Sèvres porcelain. Also here are valuable collections of majolica and European and Asian arms and armor. Frans Hals's *Laughing Cavalier* is the most celebrated painting in the collection; Pieter de Hooch's *A Boy Bringing Pomegranates* and Watteau's *The Music Party* are also well known. Other notable artists include Canaletto, Rembrandt, Gainsborough, and Boucher.

# HAMPSTEAD HEATH & VILLAGE

About 4 miles north of the center of London, **Hampstead Heath,** the traditional playground of the Londoner, was dedicated "to the use of the public forever" by a special Act of Parliament in 1872. This 800-acre expanse of high heath entirely surrounded by London is a chain of continuous park, wood, and grassland. On a clear day you can see St. Paul's Cathedral and even the hills of Kent south of the Thames from here. For years, Londoners have come here to fly a kite, sun worship, fish the ponds, swim, picnic, or jog. In good weather, it's also the site of big 1-day fairs. At the shore of Kenwood Lake, in the northern section, is a concert platform devoted to symphony performances on summer evenings. In the northeast corner, in Waterlow Park, ballets, operas, and comedies are staged at the Grass Theatre in June and July.

When the Underground came to **Hampstead Village** (tube: Hampstead) in 1907, its attractiveness as a place to live became widely known, and writers, artists, architects, musicians, and scientists—some from The City—came to join earlier residents. Keats, D. H. Lawrence, Rabindranath Tagore, Shelley, and Robert Louis Stevenson once lived here, and Kingsley Amis and John Le Carré still do.

The Regency and Georgian houses in this village are just 20 minutes by tube from Piccadilly Circus. There's a palatable mix of historic pubs, toy shops, and chic boutiques along Flask Walk, a pedestrian mall. The original village, on the side of a hill, still has old roads, alleys, steps, courts, and inviting groves to stroll through.

✪ **Keats House.** Wentworth Place, Keats Grove, Hampstead, NW3. ☎ **0171/435-2062.** Free admission; donations welcome. Apr–Oct Mon–Fri 10am–1pm and 2–6pm, Sat 10am–1pm and 2–5pm, Sun 2–5pm; Nov–Mar Mon–Fri 1–5pm, Sat 10am–1pm and 2–5pm, Sun 2–5pm. Tube: Belsize Park or Hampstead. Bus: 24 from Trafalgar Square.

The famous poet John Keats lived here for only 2 years, but that was something like two-fifths of his creative life, because he died in Rome of tuberculosis at the tender age of 25 (in 1821). In Hampstead, Keats wrote some of his most celebrated odes, including "Ode on a Grecian Urn" and "Ode to a Nightingale." His Regency house is home to the manuscripts of his last sonnet ("Bright star, would I were steadfast as thou art") and a portrait of him on his deathbed in a house near the Spanish Steps in Rome.

**Kenwood.** Hampstead Lane, NW3. ☎ **0181/348-1286.** Free admission. Apr–Oct daily 10am–6pm; Nov-Mar daily 10am–4pm. Closed Dec 24–25. Tube: Golders Green, then bus no. 210.

Kenwood was built as a gentleman's country home in the early 18th century. In 1754, it became the seat of Lord Mansfield and was enlarged and decorated by the famous Scottish architect Robert Adam in 1764. In 1927 Lord Iveagh gave it to the nation, along with his art collection. The rooms display some fine neoclassical furniture, but the main attractions are the works by old masters and British artists. You can see paintings by Rembrandt (*Self-Portrait in Old Age*), Vermeer, Turner, Frans Hals, Gainsborough, Reynolds, and more. A 19th-century family coach that comfortably carried 15 people stands in the Coach House, where there is also a cafeteria.

**Fenton House.** Windmill Hill, NW3. ☎ **0171/435-3471.** Admission £3.60 ($5.75) adults, £1.80 ($2.90) children, £9 ($14.40) family ticket. Mar Sat–Sun 2–5pm; Apr–Oct Wed–Fri 2–5:30pm, Sat–Sun 11am–5:30pm. Closed Good Friday and Nov–Feb. Tube: Hampstead.

This National Trust property is on the west side of Hampstead Grove, just a short distance north of Hampstead Village. You pass through beautiful wrought-iron gates to reach the red-brick house secluded in a walled garden. Built in 1693, it's one of the earliest, largest, and finest houses in the Hampstead section. The original main staircase, some door frames, and chimneys remain of the early construction. Paneled rooms house furniture, pictures, 18th-century English, German, and French porcelain, and the outstanding Benton-Fletcher Collection of early keyboard musical instruments, dating from 1540 to 1805. Occasional concerts are held.

**Freud Museum.** 20 Maresfield Gardens, NW3. ☎ **0171/435-2002.** Admission £3 ($4.80) adults, £1.50 ($2.40) full-time students, free for children under 12. Wed–Sun noon–5pm. Tube: Finchley Road.

After he and his family left Nazi-occupied Vienna as refugees, Sigmund Freud lived, worked, and died in this spacious three-story red-brick house in northern London. On view are rooms with original furniture, letters, photographs, paintings, and personal effects of Freud and his daughter, Anna. In the study and library, you can see the couch that launched a million psychology theories and metaphors, as well as Freud's large collection of Egyptian, Roman, and Asian antiquities.

## ✪ HIGHGATE VILLAGE

A stone's throw east of Hampstead Heath, Highgate Village has a number of 16th- and 17th-century mansions and small cottages lining three sides of the now-misnamed Pond Square (it no longer has a pond). Its most outstanding feature, however, is **Highgate Cemetery,** entered from Swain's Lane, N6 (☎ **0181/340-1834;** tube: Archway, then walk through Waterlow Park).

Serpentine pathways wind through this beautiful cemetery, laid out around a huge, 300-year-old cedar tree. The cemetery was so popular and fashionable in the Victorian era that it was extended on the other side of Swain's Lane in 1857. The most famous grave belongs to Karl Marx, who died in Hampstead in 1883; his grave, marked by a gargantuan bust, is in the eastern cemetery. In the old western cemetery—only accessible if you take a guided tour, given hourly in summer—are the remains of the scientist Michael Faraday and the poet Christina Rossetti. Admission to the East side is £2 ($3.20); West side, £4 ($6.40), including a guided tour. It's open in April through September daily from 10am to 5pm, October through March daily from 10am to 4pm. Tours are given at 12, 2, and 4pm weekdays, and every hour on weekends, although do call ahead and make an appointment before trekking out to Highgate.

## LANDMARK CHURCHES

Many of the churches listed below offer **free lunchtime concerts**—although it's customary to leave a small donation. A full list of churches offering lunchtime concerts is available from the London Tourist Board.

**St. Martin-in-the-Fields,** overlooking Trafalgar Square, WC2 (☎ **0171/930-0089;** tube: Charing Cross), is the Royal Parish Church. The present, classically inspired church, with its famous steeple, dates from 1726. The first known church on the site dates from the 13th century; among the congregation in years past was George I, who was actually a churchwarden, unique for an English sovereign. From St. Martin's vantage position in the theater district, it has drawn many actors to its door—none more notable than Nell Gwyn, the mistress of Charles II. On her death in 1687, she was buried in the crypt. Throughout the war, many Londoners rode out uneasy nights in the crypt, while blitz bombs rained down overhead. One, in 1940, blasted out all the windows. Today the crypt has a pleasant restaurant, a bookshop, and a gallery. It is home to London's original **Brass Rubbing Centre.**

**St. Bride's Church,** on Fleet Street (☎ **0171/353-1301;** tube: Blackfriars), the eighth one that's stood here, is known as the church of the press. Its spire has four octagonal tiers capped by an obelisk that's topped off with a ball and vane. This soaring confection (234 feet tall) inspired the wedding cakes of a pastry cook who lived in Fleet Street in the late 17th century, it's said. The crypts are now a museum.

Designed in the Italian Renaissance style, **Brompton Oratory,** Brompton Road (☎ 0171/589-4811; tube: South Kensington), is famous for its musical services. Its organ has nearly 4,000 pipes. After Westminster Cathedral and York Minster, this is the widest nave in England.

**St. Etheldreda's,** Britain's oldest Roman Catholic church, lies on Ely Place, Clerkenwell, EC1 (☎ 0171/405-1061; tube: Farringdon or Chancery Lane), leading off Charterhouse Street at Holborn Circus. Built in 1251, it won a mention in both *Richard II* and *Richard III*. One of the survivors of the Great Fire of 1666, the church was built by and was the property of the diocese of Ely in the days when many bishops had their Episcopal houses in London as well as in the actual cathedral cities in which they held their sees. Until this century, the landlord of Ye Olde Mitre public house near Ely Place had to obtain his license from the Justices of Cambridgeshire rather than in London, and even today Ely Place is still a private road, with impressive iron gates and a lodge for the gatekeeper, all administered by six elected commissioners. The church has a distinguished musical tradition, with an 11am Latin mass on Sunday.

The spectacular brick-and-stone **Westminster Cathedral,** Ashley Place (☎ 0171/798-9055; tube: Victoria), is the headquarters of the Roman Catholic church in Britain. Done in high Byzantine style, it's nothing if not massive. One hundred different kinds of marble compose the richly decorated interior. Mosaics emblazon the chapels and the vaulting of the sanctuary. If you climb to the top of the 273-foot-tall campanile, you'll be rewarded with a sweeping view of Victoria and Westminster.

## ALONG THE THAMES

All of London's history and development is linked to this winding ribbon of water—connecting the city with the sea—from which London drew its wealth and its power. For centuries the river was London's highway and main street, and today a row of fascinating attractions lies on, across, and alongside the River Thames.

Some of the bridges that span the Thames have become household words. **London Bridge,** contrary to the nursery rhyme, has never "fallen down," but it was dismantled and shipped to Arizona in 1971, immediately replaced by a new London Bridge; it ran from the Monument (a tall pillar commemorating the Great Fire of 1666) to Southwark Cathedral, parts of which date from 1207.

Its neighbor to the east is the still-standing **Tower Bridge,** SE1 (☎ 0171/378-1928; tube: Tower Hill), one of the city's most celebrated landmarks and probably the most photographed and painted bridge on earth. The Tower Bridge was built from 1886 to 1894 with two towers 200 feet apart, joined by footbridges that provide glass-covered walkways for the public. Exhibitions housed in the bridge's towers utilize advanced technology, including animatronic characters, video, and computers to illustrate the history of the Tower Bridge. The bridge is a photographer's dream, with great views of St. Paul's, the Tower of London, and in the distance, part of the Houses of Parliament.

You can visit the main engine room with Victorian boilers and steam-pumping engines, which used to raise and lower the roadway across the river. One model shows how the 1,000-ton arms of the bridge can be raised in $1\frac{1}{2}$ minutes to allow ship passage. Nowadays, electric power is used to raise the bridge, something that usually happens about once a day, more often in summer. When it's about to open, a bell sounds throughout the bridge and road traffic is stopped. Admission to exhibits is £5.70 ($9.10) for adults and £3.90 ($6.25) for children 5 to 15, students, and seniors. Free 4 and under. From April through October, hours are daily from 10am to 6:30pm; off-season daily 9:30am to 6pm. Last entry is 1¼ hours before closing. It's closed Good Friday, December 24 through 26, and January 1 through 28.

The piece of river between the site of the old London Bridge and the Tower Bridge marks the city end of the immense row of docks stretching 26 miles to the coast. Although most of them are no longer in use, they have long been known as the Port of London.

Particular note should be taken of the striking turn-around in pollution from the Thames during recent decades. The river, so polluted in the 1950s that marine life could not exist in it, can now lay claim to being the cleanest metropolitan estuary in the world, with many fish, even salmon, living in its waters.

## 3 Literary Landmarks

Refer to the discussion of Hampstead Village above for details on Keats's House.

**Carlyle's House.** 24 Cheyne Row, SW3. ☎ **0171/352-7087.** Admission £3 ($4.80) adults, £1.50 ($2.40) children. Easter–Oct Wed–Sun 11am–4:30pm. Tube: Sloane Square. Bus: 11, 19, 22, or 239.

From 1834 to 1881, Thomas Carlyle, author of *The French Revolution,* and Jane Baillie Welsh Carlyle, his noted letter-writing wife, resided in this modest 1708 terraced house. Furnished essentially as it was in Carlyle's day, the house is located about three-quarters of a block from the Thames, near the Chelsea Embankment, along King's Road. It was described by his wife as being "of most antique physiognomy, quite to our humour; all wainscotted, carved and queer-looking, roomy, substantial, commodious, with closets to satisfy any Bluebeard." The second floor contains the drawing room of Mrs. Carlyle, but the most interesting chamber is the less-than-soundproof "soundproof" study in the skylit attic. Filled with Carlyle memorabilia—his books, a letter from Disraeli, personal effects, a writing chair, even his death mask—this is where the author labored over his *Frederick the Great* manuscript.

**Dickens House.** 48 Doughty St., WC1. ☎ **0171/405-2127.** Admission £3.50 ($5.60) adults, £2.50 ($4) students, £1.50 ($2.40) children, £7 ($11.20) families. Mon–Sat 10am–5pm. Closed Christmas and some bank holidays. Tube: Russell Square.

In Bloomsbury stands the simple abode in which Charles Dickens wrote *Oliver Twist* and finished *The Pickwick Papers* (his American readers actually waited at the dock for the ship that brought in each new installment). The place is very nearly a shrine for a Dickens fan; it contains his study, manuscripts, and personal relics, as well as reconstructed interiors.

**✪ Samuel Johnson's House.** 17 Gough Sq., EC4. ☎ **0171/353-3745.** Admission £3 ($4.80) adults, £2 ($3.20) students and seniors, £1 ($1.60) children, 10 and under free. May–Sept Mon–Sat 11am–5:30pm; Oct–Apr Mon–Sat 11am–5pm. Tube: Blackfriars. Walk up New Bridge St. and turn left onto Fleet. Gough Sq. is tiny and hidden, north of Fleet.

Dr. Johnson and his copyists compiled a famous dictionary in this Queen Anne house, where the lexicographer, poet, essayist, and fiction writer lived from 1748 to 1759. Although Johnson also lived at Staple Inn in Holborn and at a number of other places, the Gough Square house is the only one of his residences remaining in London. The 17th-century building has been painstakingly restored, and it's well worth a visit.

**Ye Olde Cheshire Cheese.** Wine Court Office Court, 145 Fleet St., EC4. ☎ **0171/353-6170.** Tube: St. Paul's or Blackfriars.

## A Neighborhood of One's Own: Where Virginia Woolf Lived

Born in London in 1882, the author Virginia Woolf used London as the setting of many of her novels, including *Jacob's Room* (1922). The daughter of Sir Leslie Stephen and his wife, Julia Duckworth, Virginia spent her formative years at 22 Hyde Park Gate, off Kensington High Street, west of Royal Albert Hall. Her mother died in 1895 and her father in 1904.

After the death of their father, the Stephen siblings left Kensington for Bloomsbury and settled in the area around the British Museum. Upper-class Victorians at that time, however, didn't view Bloomsbury as "respectable." From 1905, they lived first at 46 Gordon Sq., east of Gower Street and University College. It was here that the nucleus of the soon-to-be celebrated Bloomsbury Group was created, which would in time embrace Clive Bell (husband of Vanessa) and Leonard Woolf, who was to become Virginia's husband. Later, Virginia went to live at 29 Fitzroy Sq., west of Tottenham Court Road, in a house once occupied by George Bernard Shaw. During the next two decades, Virginia resided at several more addresses in Bloomsbury, including on Brunswick Square, Tavistock Square, and Mecklenburgh Square, these homes have either disappeared or else been altered beyond recognition. During this time, the Bloomsbury Group reached out to include the artists Roger Fry and Duncan Grant, and Virginia became friends with the economist Maynard Keynes and the author E. M. Forster. At Tavistock Square (1924–39) and at Mecklenburg Square (1939–40) she operated Hogarth Press with Leonard. She published her own early work here, as well as T. S. Eliot's *The Waste Land.*

To escape from urban life, Leonard and Virginia purchased Monk's House in the village of Rodmell between Lewes and Newhaven in Sussex. Here, they lived until 1941 when Virginia drowned herself in the nearby Ouse. Her ashes were buried in the garden at Monk's House.

The burly literary figure of G. K. Chesterton, author of *What's Wrong With the World* (1910) and *The Superstition of Divorce* (1920), was a familiar patron at the pub Cheshire Cheese. Flamboyant in manner, he usually swept into the place swathed in a cloak. That, along with his swordstick, became his trademarks. It's said that Oliver Goldsmith, playwright of *She Stoops to Conquer* (1773), earlier patronized the Chesire Cheese. Dr. Johnson, who completed his dictionary at 17 Gough Sq., off Fleet Street, was also a frequent visitor. He must have had some long nights at the pub, because by the time he had compiled his dictionary, he'd already spent his advance of 1,500 guineas.

# 4  London's Parks & Gardens

London's parklands easily rate as the greatest system of "green lungs" of any large city on the globe. Not as rigidly laid out as the parks of Paris, London's are maintained with a loving care and lavish artistry that puts their American equivalents to shame.

Largest of them—and one of the world's biggest—is **Hyde Park,** W2. With the adjoining Kensington Gardens, it covers 636 acres of central London with velvety lawn interspersed with ponds, flowerbeds, and trees. Hyde Park was once a favorite deer-hunting ground of Henry VIII. Running through the width is a 41-acre lake known as the Serpentine. Rotten Row, a 1 1/2-mile sand track, is reserved for horseback riding and on Sunday attracts some skilled equestrians. At the northeastern corner of Hyde Park, near Marble Arch, is **Speaker's Corner,** where anyone can get up and speak. The only rules: You can't blaspheme, be obscene, or incite a riot. The tradition began in 1855—before the legal right to assembly was guaranteed in 1872—when a mob of 150,000 gathered to attack a proposed Sunday Trading Bill. Orators from all over Britain have ascended the soapbox in this spot ever since.

**Kensington Gardens,** W2, blending with Hyde Park, border the grounds of Kensington Palace. These gardens are home to the celebrated statue of Peter Pan, with the bronze rabbits that toddlers are always trying to kidnap. The Albert Memorial is also here.

East of Hyde Park, across Piccadilly, stretch **Green Park** and **St. James's Park,** W1, forming an almost-unbroken chain of landscaped beauty. This is an ideal area for picnics; you'll find it hard to believe it was once a festering piece of swamp near the leper hospital. There is a romantic lake, stocked with a variety of ducks and pelicans, descendants of the pair that the Russian ambassador presented to Charles II in 1662.

**Regent's Park,** NW1, covers most of the district by that name, north of Baker Street and Marylebone Road. Designed by the 18th-century genius John Nash to surround a prince regent palace that never materialized, this is the most classically beautiful of London's parks. The core is a rose garden planted around a small lake alive with waterfowl and spanned by humped Japanese bridges. The **open-air theater** and the **London Zoo** are here, and, as in all the local parks, there are hundreds of deck chairs on the lawns in which to sunbathe. The deck-chair attendants, who collect a small fee, are mostly college students on vacation.

The **London Zoo** is more than 150 years old. Run by the Zoological Society of London, the 36-acre garden is home to some 8,000 animals, including some of the rarest species on earth. Zoo admission is £8 ($12.80) for adults, £6 ($9.60) for children 4 to 14, free for children under 4. The zoo is open daily from 10am to 5:30pm (closes at 4pm from October through February). Take the tube to Camden Town or bus no. 274 or Z2 in summer only.

**Battersea Park,** SW11 (☎ **0181/871-7530**), is a vast patch of woodland, lakes, and lawns on the south bank of the Thames, opposite Chelsea Embankment between Albert Bridge and Chelsea Bridge. Formerly known as Battersea Fields, the present park was laid out in 1852 to 1858 on an old dueling ground. The park, which measures three-quarters of a mile on each of its four sides, has a lake for boating, a fenced-in deer park with wild birds, and fields for tennis and football (soccer). There's even a children's zoo. The park's architectural highlight is a Peace Pagoda, built of stone and wood.

The park, open May through September daily from 7:30am until dusk, is not well serviced by public transportation. The nearest tube is in Chelsea on the right bank (Sloane Square); from here it's a brisk 15-minute walk. If you prefer to ride the bus, take no. 137 from the Sloane Square Station, exiting at the first stop after the bus crosses the Thames.

## 5 Sights on the Outskirts

Several sights just beyond London's city limits are perfect for a morning or afternoon jaunt, and are easily accessible by tube, train, boat, or bus.

## HAMPTON COURT PALACE

On the north side of the Thames, 13 miles west of London in East Molesey, Surrey, the 16th-century ✪ **Hampton Court Palace** of Cardinal Wolsey reminds us of an important lesson: Don't try to outshine your boss—particularly if he happens to be Henry VIII. The rich cardinal did just that, and he eventually lost his fortune, power, and prestige; he ended up giving his lavish palace to the Tudor monarch. Henry took over, eventually even outdoing the Wolsey embellishments. The Tudor additions include the Anne Boleyn gateway, with its 16th-century astronomical clock that tells the high-water mark at London Bridge. From Clock Court, you can see one of Henry's major contributions, the aptly named great hall, with its hammerbeam ceiling. Also added by Henry were the tiltyard, a tennis court, and kitchen.

To judge from the movie *A Man for All Seasons,* Hampton Court had quite a retinue to feed. Cooking was undertaken in the great kitchens. Henry cavorted through the various apartments with his wife of the moment—whether Anne Boleyn or Catherine Parr (the latter, in a variation on a theme, lived to bury her erstwhile spouse). Charles I was imprisoned here at one time and temporarily managed to escape his jailers.

Although the palace enjoyed prestige in Elizabethan days, it owes much of its present look to William and Mary—or rather to Sir Christopher Wren, who designed and had built the Northern or Lion Gates, intended as the main entrance to the new parts of the palace. The fine wrought-iron screen at the south end of the south gardens was made by Jean Tijou around 1694 for William and Mary. You can visit the apartments, which are filled with porcelain, furniture, paintings, and tapestries. The King's Dressing Room is graced with some of the best art here, mainly paintings by old masters on loan from Queen Elizabeth II. Finally, be sure to inspect the royal chapel, which Wolsey wouldn't recognize. To confound yourself totally, you may want to get lost in the serpentine shrubbery maze in the garden, also the work of Sir Christopher Wren.

The gardens—including the Great Vine, King's Privy Garden, Great Fountain Gardens, Tudor and Elizabethan Knot Gardens, Board Walk, Tiltyard, and Wilderness—are open daily year-round from 7am until dusk (but not later than 9pm). They can be visited free except for the Privy Garden, for which admission is £2($3.20), unless you pay for a palace ticket. The cloisters, courtyards, state apartments, great kitchen, cellars, and Hampton Court exhibition are open mid-March to mid-October daily from 9:30am to 6pm, and mid-October to mid-March Monday from 10:15am to 6pm and Tuesday through Sunday 9:30am to 6pm. The Tudor tennis court and banqueting house are open the same hours as above, but only from mid-March to mid-October. Admission to all these attractions is £8.50 ($13.60) for adults, £6.40 ($10.25) for students and seniors, and £5.60 ($8.95) for children 5 to 15 (children under 5, free). For information, call ☎ **0181/781-9500.** A garden cafe and restaurant is in the Tiltyard Gardens.

**GETTING THERE**    You can approach Hampton Court by train, bus, boat, or car. Frequent trains from Waterloo Station (Network Southeast) go to Hampton Court Station. London Transport buses nos. 111, 131, 216, 267, and 461 make the trip, as do Green Line Coaches (ask at the nearest London Country Bus office for routes 715, 716, 718, and 726). Boat service is offered to and from Kingston, Richmond, and Westminster. If you're driving from London, take A308 to the junction with A309 on the north side of Kingston Bridge over the Thames.

## ✪ KEW GARDENS & KEW PALACE

Nine miles southwest of central London at Kew, near Richmond, are the **Royal Botanic Gardens,** better known as **Kew Gardens.** Among the best-known botanical gardens in Europe, Kew has thousands of varieties of plants. But it is no mere pleasure garden—it's essentially a vast (and beautiful) scientific research center. A pagoda, erected in 1761to 1762, represents the "flowering" of chinoiserie. The Visitor Centre at Victoria Gate houses an exhibit telling the story of Kew, as well as a bookshop where guides to the garden are available.

The gardens, on a 300-acre site, encompass lakes, greenhouses, walks, garden pavilions, and museums, together with fine examples of the architecture of Sir William Chambers. No matter what season you visit Kew, there's always something to see, beginning with the first spring flowers and lasting through the winter, when the Heath Garden is at its best. Among the 50,000 plant species are notable collections of arum lilies, ferns, orchids, aquatic plants, cacti, mountain plants, palms, and tropical water lilies.

Admission is £4.50 ($7.20) for adults, £3 ($4.80) for students and seniors, £2.50 ($4) for children, a family ticket is £12 ($19.20). Open Monday to Saturday from 9:30am to 4pm (to 6:30pm April to October), Sunday and public holidays 9:30am to 8pm. Closed New Year's Day and Christmas. For information, call ☎ **0181/940-1171.**

Much interest focuses on the red-brick **Kew Palace** (dubbed the Dutch House), a former residence of King George III and Queen Charlotte. Regrettably, it will be closed for restoration until the spring of 1999.

**GETTING THERE** The least expensive and most convenient way to visit the gardens is to take the District line tube to Kew Gardens on the south bank of the Thames. The most romantic way to come in summer is via a steamer from Westminster Bridge to Kew Pier.

## GREENWICH

Greenwich Mean Time is the basis of standard time throughout most of the world, the zero point used in the reckoning of terrestial longitudes since 1884. But Greenwich is also home to the Royal Naval College, the National Maritime Museum, and the Old Royal Observatory. In dry dock at Greenwich Pier are the clipper ship *Cutty Sark* and Sir Francis Chichester's *Gipsy Moth IV.*

**GETTING THERE** Part of the fun of going to Greenwich, about 4 miles from The City, is getting here. The most appealing mode is to board one of the frequent ferryboats that cruise along the Thames at intervals that vary from every half hour (in summer) to every 45 minutes (in winter). Boats departing from Westminster Pier (tube: Westminster) are maintained by **Westminster Passenger Services, Ltd.** (☎ 0171/930-4097). Boats that depart from the Charing Cross Pier (tube: Embankment) and the Tower Pier (tube: Tower Hill) are run by **Catamaran Cruises, Ltd.** (☎ 0171/987-1185). Depending on the tides and the carrier you select, travel time varies from 50 to 75 minutes each way. Passage for adults costs from £6.30 to £6.80 ($10.10 to $10.90) round-trip for adults; £3.30 to £3.70 ($5.30 to $5.90) children ages 5 to 12. It's free for children under 5.

You can also take the train from Charing Cross Station, which, unsurprisingly, is a lot more prosaic than the ride along the Thames described above. British Rail trains take about 15 minutes to reach Greenwich, charging between £2.10 to £3 ($3.35 to $4.80) round-trip, depending on the time of day you travel. A commuter train that runs independently from British Rail (something of a tourist attraction in its own right) is the Docklands Light Railway, a narrow-gauge railway whose blue and white cars are supported on stilts high above the Docklands. Passengers board the train at Tower Gate (tube: Tower Hill), passing above the Isle of Dogs before arriving at the train's final stop at Island Gardens, in the Docklands. From here, walk through a pedestrian tunnel that extends below a branch of the Thames to a point in Greenwich a few steps from the *Cutty Sark*. One-way fare is £1.60 ($2.55).

A final option, but least desirable of all, involves taking a bus; the trip takes considerably longer. Bus no. 188 goes from Euston Station through Waterloo to Greenwich. One-way fare is £1.70 ($2.70).

**VISITOR INFORMATION**   The **Greenwich Tourist Information Centre** is at 46 Greenwich Church St., London SE10 9BL (☎ 0181/858-6376); April to October, it's open daily from 10am to 5pm. From November to March, hours are Monday to Thursday 11:15am to 4:30pm, Friday to Sunday from 10am to 5pm.

**WALKING TOURS**   The Tourist Information Centre conducts walking tours that visit each of Greenwich's major sights. The tours, which cost £4 ($6.40) each, depart daily at 12:15 and 2:15pm and last $1^{1}/_{2}$ to 2 hours. Advance reservations are not required, but, although the tours are an ongoing service provided by the tourist office, it's nonetheless a good idea to phone in advance to find out if there have been any last-minute changes. Participation in any walking tour, incidentally, includes a 50% reduction in the entrance price to the National Maritime Museum.

## Seeing the Sights

Designed by Inigo Jones, **Queen's House** (1616), on Romney Road (☎ 0181/858-4422), is a fine example of this architect's innovative style. It's most famous for the cantilevered tulip staircase, the first of its kind. Carefully restored, the house contains a collection of royal and marine paintings and other objets d'art.

Adjoining the Queen's House, the **National Maritime Museum** (☎ 0181/858-4422), displays many priceless items associated with Horatio Nelson, including the coat showing the hole made by the bullet that killed him. The 20th-century gallery shows modern naval warfare illustrated with videos, paintings, and ship models both merchant and military.

*Insider's Tip:* Look for some bizarre oddities here—everything from a simulated breakfast at sea long ago (rats, moldy biscuits, stale water), to the dreaded cat-o'-nine tails used to flog sailors until 1879.

Located high on a hill overlooking the Thames, the **Old Royal Observatory,** Flamsteed House, Greenwich Park (☎ 0181/858-4422), is the original home of Greenwich Mean Time. The observatory has the largest refracting telescope in the U.K. and a collection of historic timekeepers and astronomical instruments. You can stand astride the meridian and set your watch precisely by the falling time-ball. Wren designed the Octagon Room. Here the first royal astronomer, Flamsteed, made his 30,000 observations that formed the basis of his *Historia Coelestis Britannica.* Edmond Halley, who discovered Halley's Comet, succeeded him. In 1833, the ball on the tower was hung to enable shipmasters to set their chronometers accurately. Many galleries will be closed intermittently through 1999 to allow for massive renovations.

Admission to all three attractions is £5.50 ($8.80) for adults, £4.50 ($7.20) for seniors, £3 ($4.80) for children.

The **Royal Naval College,** King William Walk, off Romney Road (☎ 0181/858-2154), a complex designed by Sir Christopher Wren in 1696, occupies 4 blocks named after King Charles, Queen Anne, King William, and Queen Mary. Formerly, Greenwich Palace stood here from 1422 to 1640. See the magnificent Painted Hall by Thornhill where the body of Nelson lay in state in 1805 and also the Georgian chapel of St. Peter and St. Paul. Admission is free.

On weekends is the fun **Greenwich Antiques Market,** Greenwich High Road (opposite St. Alfeges Church). This market has everything—books, furniture, crafts, and all kinds of bric-a-brac.

## 6 Especially for Kids

Kids of all ages will enjoy these attractions. For more information about what to do with children in London, call **Kidsline** (☎ **0171/222-8070**), computerized information about current events that might interest kids. The line is open 4pm to 6pm during school term time, 9am to 4pm on holidays. However, it's almost impossible to get through.

**London Dungeon.** 28–34 Tooley St., SE1. ☎ **0171/403-0606.** Admission £7.95 ($12.70) adults, £6.95 ($11.10) students and seniors, £5.50 ($8.80) children under 15. Apr–Sept daily 10am–5:30pm; Oct–Mar daily 10am–4:30pm. Closed Christmas. Tube: London Bridge.

Situated under the arches of London Bridge Station, the dungeon is a series of tableaux, more grizzly than Madame Tussaud's, that faithfully reproduces the ghoulish conditions of the Middle Ages. The rumble of trains overhead adds to the spine-chilling horror of the place. Dripping water and live rats (caged!) make for even more atmosphere. The heads of executed criminals were stuck on spikes for onlookers to observe through glasses hired for the occasion. The murder of Thomas à Becket in Canterbury Cathedral is also depicted. There's a burning at the stake, as well as a torture chamber with racking, branding, and fingernail extraction. The Great Fire of London is brought to crackling life by a computer-controlled spectacular that re-creates Pudding Lane, where the fire started. Of course, this experience may not be to every child's (or adult's) taste.

**Bethnal Green Museum of Childhood.** Cambridge Heath Rd., E2. ☎ **0181/980-2415.** Free admission. Mon–Thurs and Sat 10am–5:50pm; Sun 2:30–5:50pm. Tube: Bethnal Green.

Here you'll find displays of toys past and present. The variety of dolls alone is staggering. The dollhouses range from simple cottages to miniature mansions, complete with fireplaces, grand pianos, carriages, furniture, kitchen utensils, and household pets. In addition, the museum displays optical toys, toy theaters, marionettes, puppets, and soldiers and battle toys of both world wars. There is also a display of children's clothing and furniture.

**London Brass Rubbing Centre.** At All Hallows by the Tower, Byward St., EC3. ☎ **0171/481-2928.** Tube: Tower Hill.

The brass-rubbing center at this fascinating church, next door to the tower, has a crypt museum, Roman remains, and traces of early London, including a Saxon arch predating the tower. Samuel Pepys, the famed diarist, climbed to the spire of this church to watch the raging fire of London in 1666. Materials and instructions are supplied, and the charges range from £1.50 to £11.50 ($2.40 to $18.40) for the largest.

**Blondon Brass Rubbing Centre.** At St. Martin-in-the-Fields Church, Trafalgar Sq., WC2. ☎ **0171/930-9306.** Tube: Charing Cross.

The center is in the big, brick-vaulted, 1730s crypt, alongside the Café-in-the-Crypt, a bookshop, and an art gallery. The center has 88 exact copies of bronze portraits ready for use. Paper, rubbing materials, and instructions on how to begin are furnished, and classical music is played for visitors' enjoyment as they proceed. The charges range from £2 to £15 ($3.20 to $24), the latter price for the largest, a life-size Crusader knight. There's also a gift area where you can buy brass-rubbing kits for children, budget-priced ready-made rubbings, Celtic jewelry, miniature brasses, medieval panels, and model knights. To make brass rubbings in countryside churches, you must obtain permission from the parish of your choice. Once you have received written permission, the center offers instructions and the necessary materials.

# 7  Shopping

London is rather expensive, but there are bargains to be had. The trick is to shop the sales.

American-style shopping has taken Britain by storm, both in concept—warehouse stores and outlet malls—and in actual name: 1 block from Hamley's you'll find The Disney Store, and you'll see The Gap everywhere. (The warning you hear on the London Underground to "mind the gap" has nothing to do with commercial enslavement, however.) Your best bet is to ignore anything American and to concentrate on all things British. You can, surprisingly, find good value in French goods, almost the equivalent of what you find in Paris.

London keeps fairly uniform store hours, mostly shorter than American equivalents. The norm is 10am opening and 5:30pm closing, usually staying open later on Wednesday or Thursday night, until 7pm, maybe 8pm.

The big news in London is that Sunday shopping is now permitted. Stores may stay open 6 hours; usually they choose 11am to 5pm. Stores in designated tourist areas and flea markets are exempt from this law, however, and may be open all day on Sunday. Thus, Covent Garden, Greenwich, and Hampstead are big Sunday venues for shoppers.

**THE SALES**   Traditionally, stores in Britain only held two sale periods: January and July. Now, like their American counterparts, they have sales frequently. July sales begin in June—or earlier. Still, the January sale is the big event of the year. A few stores hold their after-Christmas sale on December 27, the day after Boxing Day, but the really celebrated sales—such as Harrods—usually start after the first week in January. For serious shoppers, January is the time to visit London, and many Europeans jet over from the continent. Round-trip airfares are low, and sale savings pay for your trip, as it were.

Discounts can range from 25% to 50% at leading department stores, such as Harrods and Selfridges. The best buys are on Harrods logo souvenirs, English china (seconds are trucked in from factories in Stoke-on-Trent), and English designer brands like Jaeger. But while the Harrods sale is the most famous in London, it's not the only game in town. Just about every other store—save Boots The Chemist—also has a big sale at that time. Beware, though: There's a huge difference in the quality of the finds bought in genuine sales, where the stores are actually clearing the shelves, and the goods bought at "produced" sales, where special merchandise has been hauled in just for the sale.

**SHIPPING IT HOME**   **Mail + Pack,** 343–453 Latimer Rd., London, W10 (☎ **0181/964-2410;** tube: Latimer Road Station) specializes in packing small to medium-size consignments, although they can also arrange for the shipment of antiques and collectibles. Their rates include all packing charges, customs documentation, and home delivery. The company can arrange to pick up your goods, for a surcharge, at your hotel or at the store where you made the original purchase.

## THE TOP SHOPPING STREETS & NEIGHBORHOODS

Several key streets offer some of London's best retail stores—or simply one of everything—compactly located in a niche or neighborhood so you can just stroll and shop.

**THE WEST END**   The West End includes the tony Mayfair district and is home to the core of London's big-name shopping. Most of the department stores, designer shops, and multiples (chain stores) have their flagships in this area.

The key streets are **Oxford Street** for affordable shopping (start at Marble Arch tube station if you're ambitious, or Bond Street Station if you just want to see just

# London Shopping

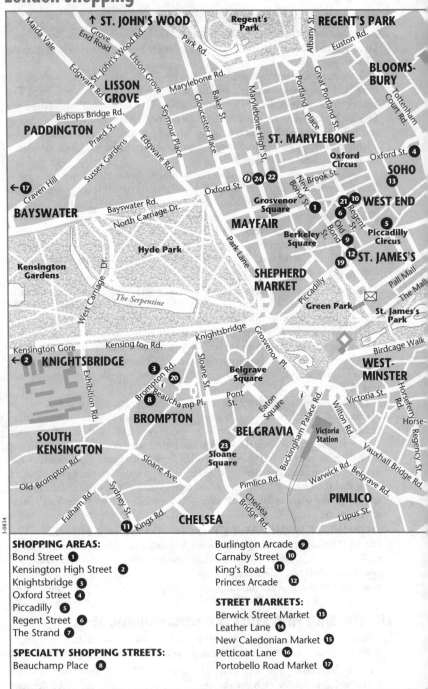

**SHOPPING AREAS:**
Bond Street ❶
Kensington High Street ❷
Knightsbridge ❸
Oxford Street ❹
Piccadilly ❺
Regent Street ❻
The Strand ❼

**SPECIALTY SHOPPING STREETS:**
Beauchamp Place ❽

Burlington Arcade ❾
Carnaby Street ❿
King's Road ⓫
Princes Arcade ⓬

**STREET MARKETS:**
Berwick Street Market ⓭
Leather Lane ⓮
New Caledonian Market ⓯
Petticoat Lane ⓰
Portobello Road Market ⓱

3-0834

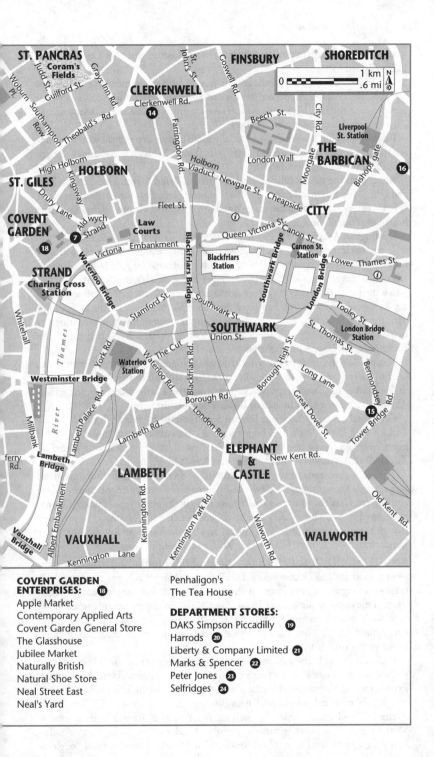

**COVENT GARDEN ENTERPRISES:** 18

Apple Market
Contemporary Applied Arts
Covent Garden General Store
The Glasshouse
Jubilee Market
Naturally British
Natural Shoe Store
Neal Street East
Neal's Yard

Penhaligon's
The Tea House

**DEPARTMENT STORES:**

DAKS Simpson Piccadilly 19
Harrods 20
Liberty & Company Limited 21
Marks & Spencer 22
Peter Jones 23
Selfridges 24

some of it); and **Regent Street,** which intersects Oxford Street at Oxford Circus (tube: Oxford Circus).

While there are several branches of the private label department store **Marks & Spencer,** their Marble Arch store (on Oxford Street) is the flagship store, and worth shopping for their high-quality goods. There's a grocery store in the basement and a home furnishings department upstairs.

Regent Street has fancier shops, especially more upscale department stores (including the famed **Liberty of London**), multiples (**Laura Ashley**), and specialty dealers. It leads all the way to Piccadilly.

In between the two, parallel to Regent Street, is **Bond Street.** Divided into New and Old, Bond Street (tube: Bond Street) connects Piccadilly with Oxford Street and is synonymous with the luxury trade. Bond Street has had a recent revival and is the hot address for all the international designers.

**Burlington Arcade** (tube: Piccadilly Circus), the famous glass-roofed, Regency-style passage leading off Piccadilly, looks like a period exhibition and is lined with intriguing shops and boutiques. The small, smart stores specialize in fashion, jewelry, Irish linen, cashmere, and more. If you linger in the arcade until 5:30pm, you can watch the beadles, those ever-present attendants in their black-and-yellow livery and top hats, ceremoniously put into place the iron grills that block off the arcade until 9am the next morning, at which time they just as ceremoniously remove them to mark the start of a new business day. Also at 5:30pm, a hand bell called the Burlington Bell is sounded, signaling the end of trading.

Just off Regent Street (actually tucked right behind it) is **Carnaby Street** (tube: Oxford Circus), also experiencing a comeback. It's still fun to visit for teens who are in the market for cheap souvenirs, a purple wig, or a little something in leather. There's also a convenient branch of **Boots The Chemist** here.

For a total contrast, check out **Jermyn Street,** on the far side of Piccadilly, a tiny 2-block-long street devoted to high-end men's haberdashery and toiletries shops; many have been doing business for centuries. Several hold royal warrants, including **Turnball & Asser,** where HRH Prince Charles has his pjs made.

The West End leads to the theater district, so there's two more shopping areas: **Soho,** where the sex shops are slowly being turned into cutting-edge designer shops; and **Covent Garden,** which is a masterpiece unto itself. The original marketplace has overflowed its boundaries and eaten up the surrounding neighborhood so that even though the streets run a little higgly-piggly and you can easily get lost, it's fun to just wander and shop. Covent Garden is especially mobbed on Sundays.

**KNIGHTSBRIDGE & CHELSEA** **Knightsbridge** (tube: Knightsbridge) is the second-most famous of London's retail districts because it is home to **Harrods.** A small street nearby, **Sloane Street,** is chock-a-block with designer shops; and another street in the opposite direction, **Cheval Place,** is also lined with designer resale shops.

Walk toward Museum Row and you'll soon find **Beauchamp Place** (tube: Knightsbridge). The street is just 1 block long, but it features the kinds of shops where young British aristocrats buy their duds.

Head out at the **Harvey Nichols** end of Knightsbridge, away from Harrods, and shop your way through the designer stores on Sloane Street (**Hermés, Armani, Prada,** and the like), then walk past Sloane Square and you'll find yourself in an altogether different neighborhood: King's Road.

**King's Road** (tube: Sloane Square), the main street of Chelsea, which starts at Sloane Square, will forever remain a symbol of London in the Swinging 1960s. Today, King's Road is a lineup of markets and "multistores," large or small conglomerations of indoor stands, stalls, and booths within one building or enclosure.

Chelsea doesn't begin and end with King's Road. If you choose to walk the other direction from Harrods, you connect to a part of Chelsea called **Brompton Cross,** another hip and hot area for designer shops made popular when Michelin House was rehabilitated by Sir Terrance Conran for **The Conran Shop.**

Also seek out **Walton Street,** a tiny little snake of a street running from Brompton Cross back toward the museums. About 2 blocks of this 3-block street are devoted to fairy-tale shops for m'lady where you can buy aromatherapy from **Jo Malone,** needlepoint, costume jewelry, or meet with your interior designer, who runs a small shop for objets d'art.

Finally, don't forget all those museums right there in the corner of the shopping streets. They all have great gift shops.

**KENSINGTON & NOTTING HILL   Kensington High Street** (tube: High Street Kensington) is the new hangout of the classier breed of teen, who has graduated from Carnaby Street and is ready for street chic. While there are a few staples of basic British fashion on this strip, most of the stores feature items that stretch, are very, very short or very, very tight.

From Kensington High Street, you can walk up **Kensington Church Street,** which, like Portobello Road, is one of the city's main shopping avenues for antiques. Kensington Church Street dead-ends into the Notting Hill Gate tube station, which is where you would arrive for shopping in **Portobello Road.** The dealers and the weekend market are 2 blocks beyond.

## STREET & FLEA MARKETS

Alternative retail is the secret to making a score in London. You'll have fun, and find bargains at any of the city's street and flea markets.

**APPLE MARKET**   A fun, bustling place, **Apple Market,** Covent Garden Piazza, WC2 (☎ **0171/836-9136;** tube: Covent Garden), almost qualifies as street entertainment and is filled with traders selling . . . well, everything. Many of the items are what the English called collectible nostalgia. Some merchandise is truly unusual, and there's the expected wide array of glassware and ceramics, leather goods, toys, clothes, hats, and jewelry. Many items are truly British and hand made, with some craftspeople selling their own wares.

**BERWICK STREET MARKET**   This market (tube: Oxford Circus or Tottenham Court Road) may be the only street market in the world that's flanked by two rows of strip clubs, porno stores, and adult-movie dens. Don't let that put you off, however. Humming 6 days a week in the scarlet heart of Soho, this array of stalls and booths sells probably the best and cheapest fruit and vegetables in town. It also sells ancient records, tapes, books, and old magazines. It's open Monday to Saturday from 8am to 5pm.

**CAMDEN MARKET (CAMDEN TOWN)**   Don't confuse Camden Passage (upscale) with Camden Market (very, very downtown). Camden Market (tube: Camden Town) is for teens and those into body piercing, blue hair (yes, still), and vintage clothing. Serious collectors of vintage may want to explore during the week, when the teen scene isn't quite so overwhelming. Market hours are daily from 9:30am to 5:30pm, with some parts of the market opening at 10am.

**CAMDEN PASSAGE (ISLINGTON)**   If it's Wednesday, it's time for Islington (tube: Angel), where each Wednesday and Saturday there's a very upscale antique market. It's starts in Camden Passage (☎ **0171/359-9969**) and then sprawls into the streets behind. It's on Wednesdays from 7am to 2pm, and Saturdays from 9am to 3:30pm.

**CHELSEA ANTIQUES MARKET**   245A–253 King's Rd., SW3 (☎ 0171/352-5686; tube: Sloane Square). Sheltered in a rambling old building, this market offers endless browsing possibilities for the curio addict. About one-third of the market is given over to old or rare books. You're likely to run across Staffordshire dogs, shaving mugs, Edwardian buckles and clasps, ivory-handled razors, old velour and lace gowns, wooden tea caddies, antique pocket watches, wormy Tudoresque chests, silver snuff boxes, grandfather clocks, and jewelry of all periods. Of note are the Optical Department, featuring surgeon's tools, microscopes, sextants, and compasses, and Harrington Brothers' selections of antiquarian children's and travel books. Closed Sunday.

**COVENT GARDEN MARKET**   Covent Garden is the most famous market in all of England—possibly all of Europe. There's a crafts market in between the stores—except on Mondays, when the craftspeople are replaced by antique dealers. Meanwhile, out back is **Jubilee Market** (☎ 0171/836-2139), which is also an antique market on Mondays. Every other day of the week, it's sort of a fancy hippie-dippy market with cheap clothes and books. Out front there are a few tents of cheap this and that's, except again on Monday, when antique dealers take over here, too.

Covent Garden Market itself offers one of the best shopping opportunities in London. The specialty shops that fill the building sell fashions and herbs, gifts, toys, books, personalized dollhouses, hand-rolled cigars, automata, and much, much more. There are bookshops and branches of famous stores (**Hamley's, The Body Shop**), and the prices are kept moderate.

**NEW CALEDONIAN MARKET**   It's commonly known as the Bermondsey Market, because of its location on the corner of Long Lane and Bermondsey Street (tube: London Bridge, then bus no. 78 or walk down Bermondsey Street). The market is at the extreme east end, beginning at Tower Bridge Road. It's one of Europe's outstanding street markets in the number and quality of the antiques and other goods offered. The stalls are well known, and many dealers come into London from the country. Prices are generally lower here than at Portobello Road and the other street markets. This market gets under way on Fridays only at 5am and—with the bargains gone by 9am—closes at noon.

**PORTOBELLO MARKET**   A magnet for collectors of virtually anything, Portobello (tube: Notting Hill Gate) is mainly a Saturday happening from 6am to 5pm. Once known mainly for fruit and vegetables (still sold, incidentally, throughout the week), Portobello in the past 4 decades has become synonymous with antiques. The market is divided into three major sections. The most crowded is the antique section, running between Colville Road and Chepstow Villas to the south. *Warning:* There's a great concentration of pickpockets in this area. The second section (and the oldest part) is the "fruit and veg" market, lying between Westway and Colville Road. In the third and final section, Londoners operate a flea market. Looking around makes for interesting fun.

From many of the stores along the route, the serious collector can pick up a helpful official guide, *Saturday Antique Market: Portobello Road & Westbourne Grove,* published by the Portobello Antique Dealers Association. It lists where to find what. *Note:* Some 90 antique and art shops along Portobello Road are open during the week when the street market is closed. This is actually a better time for the serious collector to shop, because you'll get more attention from dealers.

**ST. MARTIN-IN-THE-FIELDS MARKET**   St. Martin's (tube: Charing Cross) is good for teens and tweens who don't want to trek all the way to Camden Town and can make do with imports from India and South America, crafts, and some local football souvenirs. Located near Trafalgar Square and Covent Garden, it runs Monday through Saturday 11am to 5pm, Sundays noon to 5pm.

## THE DEPARTMENT STORES

Contrary to popular belief, Harrod's is not the only department store in London. The British invented the department store, and they have heaps of them—mostly in Mayfair, and each with its own customer profile.

**FENWICK OF BOND STREET**    Dating from 1891, Fenwick (pronounced *Fenick*), 63 New Bond St., W1 (☎ **0171/629-9161**; tube: Bond Street), is a stylish fashion store that offers an excellent collection of designer womenswear, ranging from moderately priced ready-to-wear items to more expensive designer fashions. Lingerie in all price ranges is also sold. They have an excellent selection of hair accessories and creative hair toys.

**✪ FORTNUM & MASON, LTD.**    The world's most elegant grocery store, with its swallow-tailed attendants, is a British tradition dating back to 1707. It's located at 181 Piccadilly, W1 (☎ **0171/734-8040**; tube: Piccadilly Circus). Down the street from the Ritz, it draws the carriage trade, those from Mayfair or Belgravia who come seeking such tinned treasures as pâté de foie gras or a boar's head. Today this store exemplifies the elegance and style one would expect from an establishment with two royal warrants. The grocery department is renowned for its impressive selection of the finest foods from around the world—the best champagne, the most scrumptious Belgian chocolates, and succulent Scottish smoked salmon. You can wander through the four floors and inspect the bone china and crystal cut glass, perhaps find the perfect present in the leather or stationery departments, or browse the antique department. Dining choices include Patio & Buttery, St. James Restaurant, and the Fountain Restaurant.

**✪ HARRODS**    Harrods, 87–135 Brompton Rd., Knightsbridge, SW1 (☎ **0171/730-1234**; tube: Knightsbridge) is an institution. As firmly entrenched in English life as Buckingham Palace and the Ascot Races, it is an elaborate emporium, at times as fascinating as a museum. Some of the goods displayed for sale are works of art, and so are the 300 departments displaying them. The sheer range, variety, and quality of merchandise is dazzling.

The whole fifth floor is devoted to sports and leisure, with a wide range of equipment and attire. Toy Kingdom is on the fourth floor, along with children's wear. The Egyptian Hall, on the ground floor, sells crystal from Lalique and Baccarat, plus porcelain. There's also a men's grooming room, an enormous jewelry department, and the Way In department for younger customers. Along with the beauty of the bounty, check out the tiles and architectural touches. When you're ready for a break, you have a choice of 18 restaurants and bars. Best of all is the Food Halls, stocked with a huge variety of foods and several cafes. Harrods began as a grocer in 1849 and it's still the heart of the business. In the basement you'll find a bank, a theater-booking service, a travel bureau, and Harrods Shop for logo gifts. The motto remains, "If you can eat or drink it, you'll find it at Harrods."

**HARVEY NICHOLS**    Locals call it Harvey Nicks, 109–125 Knightsbridge, SW1 (☎ **0171/235-5000**; tube: Knightsbridge). The late Princess Di's favorite store is large, but doesn't compete with Harrods because it has a much more upmarket, fashionable image. It has its own gourmet foodhall and fancy restaurant, The Fifth Floor, and a huge store crammed with the best designer home furnishings, gifts, and fashions for all, although women's clothing is the largest segment of its business. The store does carry a lot of American designer brands; avoid them, as they're more expensive in London.

**⊙ LIBERTY OF LONDON**    This major British department store, with branches all over the U.K., has its flagship store on 214–220 Regent Street (☎ **0171/ 734-1234;** tube: Oxford Circus). It is celebrated for its Liberty prints. The front part of the store on Regent Street is sort of normal-looking, but don't be fooled: Outside and around back, Liberty is restored to its original Tudor splendor—whitewashed and half-timbered outside, galleries of wooden paneled salons inside. There are six floors of fashion, china, and home furnishings, as well as the famous Liberty Print fashion fabrics, upholstery fabrics, scarves, ties, luggage, and gifts.

**MARKS & SPENCER**    They call it M&S or sometimes Marks & Sparks; it's the most beloved of English institutions, ranking right up there with tea and scones and the Queen Mother. Their fortune has been made in selling high-quality, private la-bel (St. Michael) clothing for all, plus home furnishings and groceries at slightly less-than-regular retail prices.

Despite the fact that the store offers value, it's not considered down market—sim-ply good British common sense. Members of the aristocracy wouldn't shop anywhere else; many businessmen buy their suits here. M&S is also famous for their cotton knit underwear, which 7 out of every 10 women in London are wearing right now as you read this. The main store is at 458 Oxford Street, W1 (☎ **0171/935-7954**).

**PETER JONES**    Founded in 1877 and rebuilt in 1936, Peter Jones, Sloane Square, SW1 (☎ **0171/730-3434;** tube: Sloane Square), is known for household goods, household fabrics and trims, china, glass, soft furnishings, and linens. In fact, they have one of the best linen departments in London.

**SELFRIDGES**    One of Europe's largest department stores, Selfridges, 400 Oxford St., W1 (☎ **0171/629-1234;** tube: Bond Street or Marble Arch), has more than 500 divisions selling everything from artificial flowers to groceries. The store has recently been redone to become more upscale but it features the less expensive, mass-marketed fashion lines as well.

Enter through the cosmetics department; the flagship **Miss Selfridge** boutique is located on one side of the store. There are Miss Selfridge shops all over the U.K. but this one is the best. It features teen fashions, hotshot clothes, accessories, makeup, and the best English and European designers who specialize in moderately priced cutting-edge fashions.

## GOODS A TO Z
### ANTIQUES

**Alfie's Antique Market.** 13–25 Church St., NW8. ☎ **0171/723-6066.** Tube: Marylebone or Edgware Road.

This is the biggest and one of the best-stocked conglomerates of antique dealers in London, all crammed into the premises of what was built before 1880 as a depart-ment store. It contains more than 370 stalls, showrooms, and workshops scattered over 35,000 square feet of floor space. Alfie's has the biggest Susie Cooper collection in Europe. Susie Cooper was a well-known designer of tableware and ceramics for Wedgwood. Closed Sunday and Monday. A whole antique district has grown up around Alfie's along Church Street.

**Antiquarius Antiques Centre.** 131–141 King's Rd., SW3. ☎ **0171/351-5353.** Tube: Sloane Square.

Antiquarius echoes the artistic diversity of King's Road. More than 120 dealers offer specialized merchandise, usually of the small, domestic variety, such as antique and period jewelry, porcelain, silver, first-edition books, boxes, clocks, prints, and paintings, with an occasional piece of antique furniture. You'll find a lot of items from the 1950s. Closed Sunday.

**The Mall at Camden Passage.** Islington, N1. ☎ 0171/351-5353. Tube: Angel.

This mall contains one of Britain's greatest concentrations of antique businesses. Housed in individual shop units are some 35 dealers specializing in fine furniture, porcelain, and silver. This area expands into a street market on Wednesday and Saturday. Closed Sunday and Monday.

## ART

**ACAVA.** 23–29 Faor Rd., W14. ☎ **0171/603-3039.** Tube: Olympia.

Not actually a gallery, this central office represents about 250 artists located in West London. Call for individual open studio schedules, as well as dates for the annual Open Studios weekend, an all-inclusive event. Sales information is also available.

**Delfina Studio Trust.** 50 Bermondsey St., SE1. ☎ **0171/357-6600.** Tube: London Bridge.

This is a registered charity providing studio space for 35 painters, photographers, and sculptors, both British and foreign. Exhibits are hung periodically, at which times the gallery keeps weekend hours. There is also a biannual open house, when the public can enter the studios. All art is for sale, with prices generally around £250 ($400). The Trust takes no commission. This facility features a ground-floor restaurant, and is wheelchair accessible. Call for a list of visiting artists, exhibition schedules, and sales information.

**England & Co.** 216 Westbourne Grove, W11. ☎ **0171/221-0417.** Tube: Notting Hill Gate.

Under the guidance of energetic Jane England, this gallery specializes in Outsider Art (untrained artists), and Art in Boxes, which incorporates a box structure into the composition or frame of a three-dimensional work, while focusing attention on neglected postwar British artists such as Tony Stubbings and Ralph Romney. One-person and group shows are mounted frequently, and many young artists get early exposure here.

**Space Studios.** 8 Hoxton St., N1. ☎ **0171/613-1928.** Tube: Old St.

This is an information center for about 300 artists in the East End, Vauxhall, and Greenwich, who, as working artists, maintain a closed studio policy. The center provides data about an annual exhibition period when studios are open. Call for information.

## AUCTIONS

**Bonhams.** Montpelier St., SW7. ☎ **0171/393-3900.** Tube: Knightsbridge.

Though this auction house has a reputation for being a tad unorganized, it offers some good deals for the bargain shopper. Besides conventional sales of items such as silver, maps and manuscripts, jewelry, musical instruments, and clocks and watches, Bonhams specializes in contemporary ceramics, and it holds a variety of other specialty sales. The Lots Road branch features less expensive items, ranging from architectural fittings to collectibles. Call for information about sales, viewing, and catalogs. There's also a branch called Bonhams Chelsea, at Lots Road, SW10 ( ☎ 0171/393-3900; tube: Fulham Broadway).

**Phillips West.** 10 Salem Rd., W2 ( ☎ **0171/229-9090.** Tube: Bayswater)

Phillips West has weekly sales of lesser quality furniture, glassware, toys, radios, photographic equipment, and collectibles. Its other branch handles the upscale stuff.

## BATH & BODY

Branches of **The Body Shop** seem to be everywhere. Check out the one at 375 Oxford St., W1 (☎ **0171/409-7868;** tube: Bond Street). What you might not know is that prices are drastically lower in the U.K. than they are in the United States.

**Boots The Chemist** has bundles of branches; we like the one across the street from Harrods for convenience and size. It's at 72 Brompton Road, SW3 (☎ **0171/ 589-6557;** tube: Knightsbridge). The house brands of beauty products are usually the best, be they Boots products (try the cucumber facial scrub), Boot's versions of The Body Shop (two lines, Global and Naturalistic), or Boot's versions of Chanel makeup (called No. 7).

**Culpeper the Herbalist** has a store at 8 The Market in Covent Garden, WC2 (☎ **0171/379-6698**) as well as one in Mayfair at 21 Bruton Street, W1 (☎ **0171/ 629-4559**). We stock up on essential oils here; we also like the dream pillows, candles, sachets of letters of the alphabet, and many a shopper's fave: the aromatherapy fan.

**Floris,** 89 Jermyn St., SW1 (☎ **0171/930-2885;** tube: Piccadilly Circus), stocks a variety of toilet articles and fragrances in floor-to-ceiling mahogany cabinets, which are architectural curiosities in their own right, dating from The Great Exhibition of 1851.

**Neal's Yard Remedies,** 15 Neal's Yard, WC2 (☎ **0171/379-7222;** tube: Covent Garden), is noted for their cobalt blue bottles. These homemade-style bath, beauty, and aromatherapy products are chi-chi must-haves for those who deride The Body Shop as too mass market. Prices are much higher in the United States.

Also in Covent Garden, the Victorian perfumery **Penhaligon's,** 41 Wellington St., WC2 (☎ **0171/836-2150;** tube: Covent Garden), holds Royal Warrants. It offers a large selection of perfumes, after-shaves, soaps, and bath oils for women and men. Gifts include antique-silver scent bottles, grooming accessories, and leather traveling necessities. For mail order, call ☎ **800/588-1992** in the U.S.

## BOOKS, MAPS & ENGRAVINGS

**Children's Book Centre.** 237 Kensington High St., W8. ☎ **0171/937-7497.** Tube: High Street Kensington.

This is the best place to go for children's books—it has thousands of titles. Fiction is arranged according to age, up to 16. It also sells videos and toys for children.

**Gay's The Word.** 66 Marchmont St., WC1. ☎ **0171/278-7654.** Tube: Russell Square.

Claiming to be London's only gay and lesbian bookstore, this shop offers fiction, history, gay studies, media studies, and biographies, as well as a selection of magazines, cards, and guides. There is also a used books section.

**Hatchards.** 187 Piccadilly, W1. ☎ **0171/439-9921.** Tube: Piccadilly Circus or Green Park.

On the south side of Piccadilly, Hatchards offers a wide range of books in all subjects and is particularly renowned in the areas of fiction, biography, travel, cookery, gardening, and art, plus history and finance. In addition, Hatchards is second to none in its range of books on royalty.

**Map House.** 54 Beauchamp Place, SW3. ☎ **0171/589-4325.** Tube: Knightsbridge.

This is an ideal place to find an offbeat souvenir. Map House was established in 1907 and sells antique maps and engravings and a vast selection of old prints of London and England, original and reproduction. An original engraving, guaranteed to be more than a century old, can cost as little as £5 ($8), although some rare or historic items sell for as much as £50,000 ($80,000).

# AT&T Direct℠ Service

*How to call internationally from overseas:*

1. Just dial the AT&T Access Number for the country you are calling from.
2. Dial the phone number you're calling.
3. Dial the calling card number listed above your name.

## AT&T Access Numbers

| | | | |
|---|---|---|---|
| Argentina ✱ | 001-800-200-1111 | Costa Rica ●■ | 0-800-0-114-114 |
| Australia | 1800-881-011 | Czech Rep. ▲ | 00-42-000-101 |
| Austria ●○ | 022-903-011 | Ecuador ●▲ | 999-119 |
| Bahamas | 1-800-872-2881 | Egypt ● (Cairo) † | 510-0200 |
| Belgium ● | 0-800-100-10 | France | 0-800-99-0011 |
| Brazil | 000-8010 | Germany | 0130-0010 |
| Canada ■ | 1-800-225-5288 | Greece ● | 00-800-1311 |
| China, PRC ▲ | 10811 | Guam | 018-872 |
| Colombia | 980-11-0010 | Guatemala ○ | 190 |

---

# AT&T Direct℠ Service

*How to call internationally from overseas:*

1. Just dial the AT&T Access Number for the country you are calling from.
2. Dial the phone number you're calling.
3. Dial the calling card number listed above your name.

## AT&T Access Numbers

| | | | |
|---|---|---|---|
| Argentina ✱ | 001-800-200-1111 | Costa Rica ●■ | 0-800-0-114-114 |
| Australia | 1800-881-011 | Czech Rep. ▲ | 00-42-000-101 |
| Austria ●○ | 022-903-011 | Ecuador ●▲ | 999-119 |
| Bahamas | 1-800-872-2881 | Egypt ● (Cairo) † | 510-0200 |
| Belgium ● | 0-800-100-10 | France | 0-800-99-0011 |
| Brazil | 000-8010 | Germany | 0130-0010 |
| Canada ■ | 1-800-225-5288 | Greece ● | 00-800-1311 |
| China, PRC ▲ | 10811 | Guam | 018-872 |
| Colombia | 980-11-0010 | Guatemala ○ | 190 |

## AT&T Access Numbers

| | | | |
|---|---|---|---|
| Honduras ■ | 123 | Panama ■■ | 109 |
| Hong Kong | 800-1111 | Philippines ● | 105-11 |
| Ireland ● | 1-800-550-000 | Saudi Arabia ◇ | 1-800-10 |
| Israel | 177-100-2727 | Singapore | 800-0111-111 |
| Italy ● | 172-1011 | Spain ◇ | 900-99-00-11 |
| Jamaica □ | 872 | Sweden ● | 020-795-611 |
| Japan ● | 0039-111 | Switzerland ● | 0-800-550011 |
| Japan ● ▲ | 0066-55-111 | Taiwan ● | 0080-10288-0 |
| Korea, Republic ● | 00-911 | Thailand ✕ | 0019-991-1111 |
| Mexico ▽ | 95-800-462-4240 | U.K. ▲ | 0800-89-0011 |
| Netherlands ● | 06-022-9111 | U.Arab Emirates ■ | 800-121 |
| New Zealand | 000-911 | Venezuela ● | 800-11-120 |

For a wallet card listing over 140 AT&T Access Numbers, dial the number for the country you're calling from, and ask the operator for customer service. In the U.S., call 1 800 331-1140, ext 704.

● Bold-faced countries permit country-to-country calling outside the U.S.
■ Public phones require coin or card deposit.
◆ Country-to-country calls can only be placed to this country.
◇ Calling available to most countries.
✦ Not available from public phones.
✕ Dial "02" first, outside of Cairo.
▲ May not be available from every phone/pay phone.
▽ Public phones require local coin payment through the call duration.
□ When calling from public phones, use phones marked "Ladatel."
◻ Calling card calls available from select hotels.

© 1996 AT&T

## AT&T Access Numbers

| | | | |
|---|---|---|---|
| Honduras ■ | 123 | Panama ■■ | 109 |
| Hong Kong | 800-1111 | Philippines ● | 105-11 |
| Ireland ● | 1-800-550-000 | Saudi Arabia ◇ | 1-800-10 |
| Israel | 177-100-2727 | Singapore | 800-0111-111 |
| Italy ● | 172-1011 | Spain ◇ | 900-99-00-11 |
| Jamaica □ | 872 | Sweden ● | 020-795-611 |
| Japan ● | 0039-111 | Switzerland ● | 0-800-550011 |
| Japan ● ▲ | 0066-55-111 | Taiwan ● | 0080-10288-0 |
| Korea, Republic ● | 00-911 | Thailand ✕ | 0019-991-1111 |
| Mexico ▽ | 95-800-462-4240 | U.K. ▲ | 0800-89-0011 |
| Netherlands ● | 06-022-9111 | U.Arab Emirates ■ | 800-121 |
| New Zealand | 000-911 | Venezuela ● | 800-11-120 |

For a wallet card listing over 140 AT&T Access Numbers, dial the number for the country you're calling from, and ask the operator for customer service. In the U.S., call 1 800 331-1140, ext 704.

● Bold-faced countries permit country-to-country calling outside the U.S.
■ Public phones require coin or card deposit.
◆ Country-to-country calls can only be placed to this country.
◇ Calling available to most countries.
✦ Not available from public phones.
✕ Dial "02" first, outside of Cairo.
▲ May not be available from every phone/pay phone.
▽ Public phones require local coin payment through the call duration.
□ When calling from public phones, use phones marked "Ladatel."
◻ Calling card calls available from select hotels.

© 1996 AT&T

# I love 0-800-99-0011 in the springtime.

Every country has its own AT&T Access Number which makes calling from France and other countries really easy. Just dial the AT&T Access Number for the country you're calling from and we'll take it from there. And be sure to charge your calls on your AT&T Calling Card. It'll help you avoid outrageous phone charges on your hotel bill and save you up to 60%.* 0-800-99-0011 is a great place to visit any time of year, especially if you've got these two cards. So please take the attached wallet card of worldwide AT&T Access Numbers.

**All you need for the fastest, clearest connections home.**

**Murder One.** 71–73 Charing Cross Rd., WC2. ☎ **0171/734-3485.** Tube: Leicester Square.

Maxim Jakubowski's bookshop is dedicated to the genres of crime, romance, science fiction, and horror. Crime and science fiction magazines, some of them obscure, are also available.

**Silver Moon Women's Bookshop.** 64–68 Charing Cross Rd., WC2. ☎ **0171/836-7906.** Tube: Leicester Square.

Besides stocking literally thousands of titles by and about women, it sells videos, jewelry, T-shirts, and other items. There's also a large selection of lesbian books.

**Stanfords.** 12–14 Long Acre, WC2. ☎ **0171/836-1321.** Tube: Leicester Square or Covent Garden.

The world's largest map shop, Stanfords was established in 1852. Many of its maps, which include worldwide touring and survey maps, are unavailable elsewhere. It's also the best travel bookstore in London (with a complete selection of Frommer's guides).

**W & G Foyle, Ltd.** 113–119 Charing Cross Rd., WC2. ☎ **0171/439-8501.** Tube: Tottenham Court Road.

Claiming to be the world's largest bookstore, W & G Foyle, Ltd., has an impressive array of hardcovers and paperbacks, as well as travel maps. The stock also includes records, videotapes, and sheet music.

## CHINA, GLASS & SILVER

**The Glasshouse.** 21 St. Albans Place, N1. ☎ **0171/359-8162.** Tube: Angel.

Not only can visitors buy beautiful glass here, they can also watch the craftspeople producing glassworks of art in the workshop. Glass can be made to a shopper's own designs.

**Lawleys.** 154 Regent St., W1. ☎ **0171/734-3184.** Tube: Piccadilly Circus or Oxford Circus.

Founded in the 1930s, this store contains one of the largest inventories of china in Britain. The firm specializes in Royal Doulton, Minton, Royal Crown Derby, Wedgwood, Spode, and Aynsley china; Lladró figures; David Winter Cottages, Border Fine Arts, and other famous giftware names. Lawleys also sells cutlery, crystal, and glassware. It has excellent January and July sales.

**London Silver Vaults.** Chancery House, 53063 Chancery Lane, WC2. ☎ **0171/242-3844.** Tube: Chancery Lane.

Don't let the slightly out-of-the-way location, or the facade's lack of charm, slow you down. Downstairs, you go into real vaults—40 in all—that are really filled with tons of silver and silver plate, plus a collection of jewelry. It's a staggering selection of everything from old to new, with excellent prices and friendly dealers.

**Reject China Shop.** 183 Brompton Rd., SW3. ☎ **0171/581-0739.** Tube: Knightsbridge.

Don't expect either too many rejects or too many bargains, despite the name. This shop sells seconds (sometimes) along with first-quality pieces of china from Royal Doulton, Spode, and Wedgwood. You also can find crystal, glassware, and flatware. There are several branches throughout London. If you'd like to have your purchases shipped home for you, the shop can do it for a fee.

## CRAFTS

On Sunday mornings along **Bayswater Road,** pictures, collages, and craft items are hung on railings along the edge of Hyde Park and Kensington Gardens—for more than a mile. If the weather is right, start at Marble Arch and keep walking, shopping or just sightseeing as you go. Along Piccadilly, you'll see much of the same thing by walking along the railings of **Green Park** on a Saturday afternoon.

**Cecilia Colman Gallery.** 67 St. John's Wood High St., NW8. ☎ **0171/722-0686.** Tube: St. John's Wood.

This is one of London's most established crafts galleries, featuring decorative ceramics, studio glass, jewelry, and metalwork. Among the offerings are glass sculptures by Lucien Simon, jewelry by Caroline Taylor, and pottery by Simon Rich. The gallery also has a large selection of mirrors and original design perfume bottles.

**Contemporary Applied Arts.** 2 Percy St., W1. ☎ **0171/436-2344.** Tube: Goodge Street.

This association of craftspeople encourages both traditional and progressive contemporary artwork. The galleries at the center house a diverse retail display that includes glass, ceramics, textiles, wood, furniture, jewelry, and metalwork—all created by outstanding artisans currently producing in the country. There's also a program of special exhibitions that focuses on innovations in the crafts; these are solo or small-group shows from the membership. Many of Britain's best-established makers, as well as promising, lesser-known ones, are represented.

**Crafts Council.** 44A Pentonville Rd., Islington, N1. ☎ **0171/278-7700.** Tube: Angel.

This is the national body for promoting contemporary crafts. Here you can discover some of today's most creative work at the Crafts Council Gallery, Britain's largest crafts gallery. There's also a shop selling craft objects and publications, a picture library, a reference library, and a cafe.

**Neal Street East.** 5 Neal St., WC2. ☎ **0171/240-0135.** Tube: Covent Garden.

This vast shop sells ethnic and tribal crafts from many parts of the world, including the Far East. You'll find an array of dried and silk flowers, toys, calligraphy, modern and antique clothing, along with textiles, baskets, and ethnic jewelry. There is also an extensive cookware department, even a bookshop, selling titles devoted to the mind, spirit, and health, among other topics.

## FABRICS

Also see Liberty of London (refer to "The Department Stores," above).

**Broadwick Silks.** 9–11 Broadwick St., W1. ☎ **0171/734-3320.** Tube: Oxford Circus or Tottenham Court Road.

This cloth shop carries a seemingly endless range of fabrics and is best known for its 200 velvets, bridal silks and brocades, 400 varieties of lace, and fine dress fabrics. Most of London's theater and bridal designers get their supplies here. Just around the corner are two branch stores, the Silk Society, 44 Berwick St. (☎ 0171/287-1881), which concentrates on silks, and Berwick Street Cloth Shop, 14 Berwick St. (☎ 0171/287-2881), which handles a wide range of natural and performance fabrics, ranging from cotton to rubber, PVC, fake fur, sequined, and assorted trims.

## FASHION: THE TRUE BRIT

Whereas every internationally known designer worth his or her weight in shillings has a boutique in London, the best buys are on enduring English styles. Hail Britannia.

**Aquascutum.** 100 Regent St., W1. ☎ **0171/734-6090.** Tube: Piccadilly Circus.

*Time Out* said this about Aquascutum: "It is about as quintessentially British as you'll get this side of Savile Row, and it's a popular stop-off for American tourists wanting to look more British than the Brits." On four floors, this classic shop offers only high-quality British and imported clothing (including leisurewear) for men and women.

**Gieves & Hawkes.** 1 Savile Row, W1. ☎ **0171/434-2001.** Tube: Piccadilly Circus or Green Park.

G & H has a prestigious address and clientele, including the Prince of Wales; yet its prices are not the lethal tariffs of other stores on this street. It's expensive, but you get good quality. Cotton shirts, silk ties, Shetland jumpers (sweaters), and exceptional ready-to-wear and tailor-made (bespoke) suits are sold.

**Next.** 20 Long Acre, WC2. ☎ **0171/836-1516.** Tube: Covent Garden.

This chain of "affordable fashion" stores knew its heyday when it became celebrated in the 1980s for its high street fashion revolution. No longer at its peak (except for its mail-order division), it still merits a stopover. The look is still very contemporary, with a continental flair worn not only by men and women but kids, too.

## FASHION: VINTAGE & SECONDHAND CLOTHING

London is a great place to pick up vintage finds; there's no VAT refund on used clothing, so these shops are doubly attractive. And when you get home, you'll get to put on budget-chic airs and say, "Oh, I got it in a second-hand shop in London."

**Annie's Vintage Costume and Textiles.** 10 Camden Passage, N1. ☎ **0171/359-0796.** Tube: Angel.

The shop concentrates on carefully preserved dresses from the 1920s and 1930s, but has a range of clothing and textiles from the 1880s through the 1960s. A 1920s fully beaded dress will run you about £400 ($640), but there are scarves for £10 ($16), camisoles for £18 ($28.80), and a range of exceptional pieces priced between £50 to £60 ($80 to $96). Clothing is located on the main floor; textiles, including old lace, bed linens, and tapestries, can be found upstairs.

**Old Hat.** 62 & 66 Fulham High St., SW6. ☎ **0171/736-5446.** Tube: Putney Bridge.

A large dealer of secondhand menswear, this is the place to find Savile Row suits, Jermyn Street silk ties, Burberrys raincoats, and Turnbull and Asher shirts for a fraction of their original cost. The shop offers a variety of styles from the last 80 years, and all are in good condition. Prices range from £40 to £90 ($64 to $144), and tailoring is available for about £30 ($48). While here, check out the window displays, which regularly feature such incongruities as a pair of BSA Bantam motorcycles, also available for purchase.

**Pandora.** 16–22 Cheval Place, SW7. ☎ **0171/589-5289.** Tube: Knightsbridge.

A London institution since the 1940s, Pandora stands in fashionable Knightsbridge, a stone's throw from Harrods. Several times a week, chauffeurs will drive up with bundles packed anonymously by the gentry of England. One woman voted best dressed at Ascot several years ago was wearing a secondhand dress acquired here. Prices are generally one-third to one-half the retail value. Chanel and Anne Klein are among the designers you might find. Outfits are usually no more than two seasons old.

**Pop Boutique.** 6 Monmouth St., WC2. ☎ **0171/497-5262.** Tube: Covent Garden.

For the best in original streetwear from the 1950s (those days of Marilyn Monroe and James Dean), the 1960s (the Beatles), and the 1970s (Jane Fonda, John Travolta), this clothing store is tops. Right next to the chic Covent Garden Hotel, it has fabulous vintage wear at affordable prices—leather jackets for £40 ($64), for example, the equivalent of $250 to $300 in New York.

**Steinberg & Tolkein.** 193 King's Road, SW3. ☎ **0171/376-3660.** Tube: Sloane Square.

Steinberg and Tolkein are London's leading dealers in vintage costume jewelry and clothing. There's also some used designer clothing that isn't old enough to be vintage but is prime for collectors; other things are merely secondhand designer thrills.

## FASHION FOR TEENS & TRENDSETTERS

**Dr. Marten's Department Store.** 1–4 King St., WC2. ☎ **0171/497-1460.** Tube: Covent Garden

Dr. Marten makes the shoes (called Doc Martens) that almost every London young person swears by. They're so popular that now there's an entire department store selling accessories, gifts, and even clothes. Teens come to worship here because ugly and clunky is beautiful; prices are far better than they are in the United States, or elsewhere in Europe.

**Hennes.** 261 Regent St., W1. ☎ **0171/493-4004.** Tube: Oxford Circus.

Here are copies of hot-off-the-catwalk fashions at affordable prices. For disposable cutting-edge fashion, you can't beat the prices.

**Hype DF.** 48–52 Kensington High St., W8. ☎ **0171/937-3100.** Tube: High Street Kensington.

This retailer has been showcasing young designers since 1983, but in a different location when it was known as Hyper-Hyper. Designs range from sportswear to evening wear, with plenty of accessories, including shoes. There's a wide range of prices. Hype DF will definitely intrigue. Menswear is also sold.

## FOOD

English food has come a long way lately; it's even worth enjoying and bringing home. Don't pass up the Food Halls in Harrods; consider the Fifth Floor at Harvey Nicks if Harrods is crammed with too many tourists—it isn't the same, but it'll do. Also, Fortnum & Mason is internationally famous as a food emporium. See "The Department Stores," above.

Charbonnel et Walker, One The Royal Arcade, 28 Old Bond St. (☎ 0171/491-0939; tube: Green Park), is famous for its hot chocolate in winter (buy it by the tin) and their strawberries and cream chocolates during the season.

At Neal's Yard Dairy, 17 Shorts Gardens (☎ 0171/379-7646; tube: Covent Garden), you'll enjoy the cheeses as well as foodstuffs, snack items, and picnic supplies.

## FILOFAX

All major department stores sell Filofax supplies, but the full range is carried in their own stores. Go to **The Filofax Centre** in the West End at 21 Conduit Street, W1. (☎ 0171/499-0457; tube: Oxford Circus); it's larger and fancier than the Covent Garden branch at 69 Neal St., with the entire range of inserts and books, and prices that will floor you: They're at least half the U.S. going rate. They also have good sales; calendars for the next year go on sale very early the previous year (about 10 months in advance).

## HOME DESIGN & HOUSEWARES

**The Conran Shop.** Michelin House, 81 Fulham Rd., SW3 ☎ **0171/589-7401.** Tube: South Kensington.

Here you'll find high style at reasonable prices from the man who invented functional chic: Sir Terence Conran. It's great for gifts, home furnishings, and table top—or just for gawking.

**Designers Guild.** 267–271 & 275–277 King's Rd., SW3 ☎ **0171/351-5775.** Tube: Sloane Square.

The Designers Guild is often copied but never outdone. Creative director Tricia Guild and her young designers still lead the pack in all that is bright and whimsical after more than 25 years in business. Selling an exclusive line of handmade furniture and accessories at the 267–271 King's Rd. location, and wallpaper and more than 2,000 fabrics at the neighboring no. 275–277 shop, the colors remain forever vivid and the designs irreverent. Also available are children's accessories, toys, crockery, and cutlery.

## MUSIC

Collectors flock to Covent Garden on the weekends; that's when all the dealers come out with the goods.

The biggies in town are the monster chains, **Tower Records,** 1 Piccadilly Circus, W1 (☎ **0171/439-2500;** tube: Piccadilly Circus), one of the largest tape, record, and CD stores in Europe; and its major rival, the **Virgin Megastore,** 14–16 Oxford St., W1 (☎ **0171/631-1234;** tube: Tottenham Court Road). You'll find whatever you're looking for at either one. Another Megastore is at 527 Oxford St., W1. (☎ **0171/491-8582**). But throughout London, you'll find small, independent record shops with offbeat tastes and discounted prices (new CD prices are considerably higher in Europe compared to the U.S., however, so music purchases probably ought to focus on English bands and the like impossible to find at home.)

A cool London experience is browsing independent and used record stores for that quintessential English toe-gazing band that never quite made it across the Atlantic. Try **Beanos,** 7 Middle St., Croydon, CRO 1RE (☎ **0181/680-1202;** tube: East Croydon or West Croydon). Beanos is the largest secondhand store in England. It has three floors with more than 2$\frac{1}{2}$ million items on display, including 7- and 12-inch vinyl, books, memorabilia, and gold and silver discs. Live bands perform on the second floor, while on the third you can hang out in the 1950s 1960s cafe and watch videos. **Music & Video Exchange,** 38 Notting Hill Gate, W11, (☎ **0171/243-8574;** tube: Notting Hill Gate), carries a full range of soul, jazz, rock, and pop, including rare records and videos. They also buy used items. **Reckless Records,** 30 Berwick St., W1 (☎ **0171/437-4271;** tube: Oxford Circus), is exclusively second hand. They sell all types of music, from soul to dance to rock and pop on vinyl and CDs. Reckless has a branch at 70 Upper St., Islington, N1 (☎ **0171/359-0501**); tube: Angel), where they have a Rarities Shop dealing in collector's items.

## MUSEUM SHOPS

Many museum shops are more than mere afterthoughts, worth visiting in their own right. Particularly wonderful is the **London Transport Museum Shop,** adjacent to Covent Garden Marketplace, WC2 (☎ **0171/379-6344;** tube: Covent Garden), which carries reasonably priced reproduction and antique travel posters as well as tons of fun gifts and souvenirs. The London Underground maps in their original size as seen at every tube station can be purchased here.

The best museum shop in London is the **Victoria & Albert Gift Shop,** Cromwell Road, SW7 (☎ **0171/938-8500;** tube: South Kensington). It sells cards, books, and the usual items, along with reproductions from the museum archives.

## SHOES

**Lilley & Skinners.** 360 Oxford St., W1. ☎ **0171/629-6381.** Tube: Bond Street.

Lilley & Skinners is the largest shoe store in Europe, displaying many different brands of shoes over three floors of showrooms. It specializes in not particularly glamorous names, but offers good value and a wide selection of difficult-to-find sizes.

**Natural Shoe Store.** 21 Neal St., WC2. ☎ **0171/836-5254.** Tube: Covent Garden.

Shoes for both men and women are stocked in this shop, which also does shoe repairs. The selection includes all comfort and quality footwear—from Birkenstock to the best of the British classics.

**Shelly's.** 266 Regent Street, W1. ☎ **0171/287-0939.** Tube: Oxford Circus.

This is the flagship store of the mother of all London shoe shops, where they sell everything from hip shoes for tiny tots to grown-ups' hip shoes and boots. Famous for their Doc Martens, there's more, much more . . . and none of it traditional.

## SHOPPING MALLS

**Whiteleys of Bayswater.** Queensway, W2. ☎ **0171/229-8844.** Tube: Bayswater or Queensway.

Once this was a store that gave Harrods some competition, but it eventually went belly-up. Occupying its former premises is an Edwardian mall whose chief tenant is a branch of Marks & Spencer, but in addition to that, there are around 70 to 80 shops (the number varies from year to year), mostly specialty outlets. On the uppermost floor is an array of some 10 restaurants, cafes, and bars. There's also an eight-screen movie theater.

## TEAS

**The Tea House.** 15A Neal St., WC2. ☎ **0171/240-7539.** Tube: Covent Garden.

This shop is quintessentially British, selling everything associated with tea, tea drinking, and teatime. It boasts more than 70 quality teas and tisanes, including whole-fruit blends, the best tea of China (Gunpowder, jasmine with flowers), India (Assam leaf, choice Darjeeling), Japan (Genmaicha green), and Sri Lanka (pure Ceylon), plus such longtime favorite English blended teas as Earl Grey. The shop also offers novelty teapots and mugs, among other items.

## TRAVEL SERVICES

**British Airways Travel Department Store.** 156 Regent St., W1. ☎ **0171/434-4700.** Tube: Piccadilly Circus or Oxford Circus.

The retail flagship of British Airways, housed on three floors, offers not only worldwide travel and ticketing, but also a wide range of services and shops, including a clinic for immunization, a pharmacy, a bureau de change, a passport and visa service, and a theater-booking desk. The ground floor sells luggage, guidebooks, maps, and other goods. There are various other services, such as a Holiday Centre and a coffee shop. Passengers with hand baggage only can check in here for a BA flight. Travel insurance, hotel reservations, and car rentals can also be arranged.

## WOOLENS & CASHMERES

**British Designer Knitwear Group.** 2–6 Quadrant Arcade, 80 Regent St., W1. ☎ **0171/734-5786.** Tube: Piccadilly Circus.

Here you'll find woolens from all over the British Islands, including the Shetlands in Scotland. Some are handmade; others from well-known designers. You can choose woolens that make you look professorially tweedy or more high fashion.

**Westaway & Westaway.** 62–65 and 92–93 Great Russell St., WC1. ☎ **0171/405-4479.** Tube: Tottenham Court Road.

This shop, opposite the British Museum, is like the Saturday Night Live skit about the store "All Things Scottish." Here you'll find kilts, scarves, waistcoats, capes, dressing gowns, and rugs in authentic clan tartans. The salespeople are knowledgeable about intricate clan symbols. They also sell cashmere, camel-hair, and Shetland knitwear, along with Harris tweed jackets, Burberry raincoats, and cashmere overcoats for men.

## TOYS

**Hamleys.** 188–196 Regent St., W1. ☎ **0171/734-3161.** Tube: Oxford Circus.

This is the finest toy shop in the world—more than 35,000 toys and games on seven floors of fun and magic. A huge selection is offered, including soft, cuddly stuffed animals, as well as dolls, radio-controlled cars, train sets, model kits, board games, outdoor toys, and computer games. There's also a small branch at Covent Garden, and another at Heathrow Airport.

# 8  London After Dark

London's pulsating scene is the most vibrant in Europe. Although pubs still close at 11pm, the city is staying up later. More and more clubs extend partying into the wee hours.

London is on a real high right now, especially in terms of music and dance; much of the current techno and electronica originated in London clubs. London nightlife is notorious for being in a state of constant flux. What is hot today probably just opened; some clubs no doubt will have the lifespan of fruit-flies. **Groucho,** at 44 Dean St., W1 (☎ **0171/439-4685**) remains for the moment the *in* club, though it is still members-only. The Marquee, the legendary live music venue where the Rolling Stones played when they were still bad boys, has regrettably shut its doors. But a few perennials, like Ronnie Scott's, are still around.

London nightlife, however, is not just music and dance clubs. The city abounds with what's probably the world's best live theater scene, pubs oozing historic charm, and many more options for a night out on the town.

Weekly publications such as *Time Out* and *Where* provide the most complete, up-to-the-minute entertainment listings. They contain information on the live music and dance clubs of the moment as well as London's diverse theater scene, which includes everything from big-budget West End shows to fringe productions.

## THE THEATER

In London, you'll have a chance to see the world-renowned English theater on its home ground. Matinees are on Wednesday (Thursday at some theaters) and on Saturday. Theaters are closed on Sunday. It's impossible to describe all of London's theaters in this space, so below are listed just a few from the treasure trove. The biggest theater excitement in London today is being stirred up by the new Globe Theatre. Since this is also a sightseeing attraction, it's previewed above. Refer to Shakespeare's Globe Theatre & Exhibition.

**RESERVATIONS**   If you want to see specific shows—especially hit ones—purchase your tickets in advance. The best way is to buy your ticket from the theater's box office, which you can do over the phone, using a credit card. You'll pay the theater price and pick up the tickets the day of the show. You can also go to a reliable ticket agent (the greatest cluster is in Covent Garden), but you'll pay a fee—which varies depending on the show.

**TICKET AGENTS**   You can also make theater reservations through ticket agents. In the case of hit shows, only brokers may be able to get you a seat, but you'll pay for the privilege.

With offices in London and the United States, **Keith Prowse/First Call** can reserve tickets for hit shows weeks or even months in advance. In the United States, contact them at Suite 1000, 234 W. 44th St. New York, NY 10036 (☎ **800/669-8687** or 212/398-1430). In London, their number is ☎ **0171/836-9001.** The fee for booking a ticket in the United States is 35%; in London, it's 25%.

For tickets and information to just about any show and entertainment in London, **Edwards & Edwards** has a New York office if you'd like to arrange tickets before you go at 1270 Ave. of the Americas, Ste. 2414, New York, NY 10029 (☎ **800/223-6108** or 914/328-2150; fax 914/328-2752). They also have offices in London: **Edwards & Edwards** at the Palace Theatre, Shaftesbury Avenue, W1 8AY (☎ **0171/734-4555**) or at **Harrods'** ticket desk. A personal visit is not necessary; they'll mail tickets to your home, fax confirmation or leave tickets at the box office if you are in a hurry. Instant confirmations are available with special "overseas" rates for most shows. There is a booking and handling fee of 0–20% added to the ticket price.

Another option is **Theatre Direct International (TDI)** (☎ **800/334-8457**), which specializes in providing London theater and Fringe production tickets. Their immediate confirmation lets you arrive in London with your tickets, or else tickets will be held for you at the box office.

**GALLERY & DISCOUNT TICKETS**   London theater tickets are quite reasonably priced compared with those in the United States. Prices vary greatly depending on the seat—from £12 to £35 ($19.20 to $56). Sometimes gallery seats (the cheapest) are sold only on the day of the performance, so you'll have to head to the box office early in the day and return an hour before the performance to queue up, since they're not reserved seats.

Many of the major theaters offer reduced price tickets to students on a standby basis, but not to the general public. When available, these tickets are sold 30 minutes prior to curtain. Line up early for popular shows, as standby tickets go fast and furious. Of course, you must have a valid student ID.

The **Society of London Theatre** (☎ **0171/836-0971**) operates a ✪ **discount ticket booth** in Leicester Square, where tickets for many shows are available at half price, plus a £2 ($3.20) service charge. Tickets are sold only on the day of performance, and there is a limit of four per person. You cannot return tickets, and no credit cards are accepted. Hours are daily from 12:30 to 6:30pm, except on days when there are matinees. Then the booth opens from noon to 6:30pm.

*Warning:* Beware of scalpers who hang out in front of theaters with hit shows. There are many reports of scalpers selling forged tickets, and their prices are outrageous.

**Old Vic.** Waterloo Rd., SE1. ☎ **0171/928-7616** or 0171/928-2651 (box office). £6–£22 ($9.50–$34.75) Plays, £7–£19 ($11.20–$30.40). Tube: Waterloo.

The facade and portions of the interior of this two-century old repertory theater have been restored to their original early 19th-century style. The proscenium arch has also been moved back, the stage tripled in size, and more seats and stage boxes added. Fully air-conditioned and equipped with three bars, the theater presents short seasons of varied plays. Several subscription offerings have been introduced.

**Open-Air Theatre.** Inner Circle, Regent's Park, NW1. ☎ **0171/486-2431.** Tickets £8–£20 ($12.80–$32). Tube: Baker Street.

# Central London Theaters

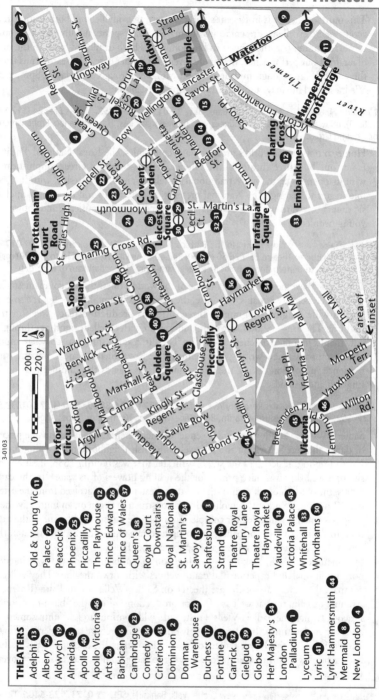

**THEATERS**

| Theater | No. |
|---------|-----|
| Adelphi | 13 |
| Albery | 29 |
| Aldwych | 19 |
| Almeida | 5 |
| Apollo | 40 |
| Apollo Victoria | 46 |
| Arts | 28 |
| Barbican | 6 |
| Cambridge | 23 |
| Comedy | 36 |
| Criterion | 43 |
| Dominion | 2 |
| Donmar Warehouse | 22 |
| Duchess | 17 |
| Fortune | 21 |
| Garrick | 32 |
| Gielgud | 39 |
| Globe | 10 |
| Her Majesty's | 34 |
| London Palladium | 1 |
| Lyceum | 16 |
| Lyric | 41 |
| Lyric Hammersmith | 44 |
| Mermaid | 8 |
| New London | 4 |
| Old & Young Vic | 11 |
| Palace | 27 |
| Peacock | 7 |
| Phoenix | 25 |
| Piccadilly | 42 |
| The Playhouse | 12 |
| Prince Edward | 26 |
| Prince of Wales | 37 |
| Queen's | 38 |
| Royal Court Downstairs | 31 |
| Royal National | 9 |
| St. Martin's | 24 |
| Savoy | 15 |
| Shaftesbury | 3 |
| Strand | 18 |
| Theatre Royal Drury Lane | 20 |
| Theatre Royal Haymarket | 35 |
| Vaudeville | 14 |
| Victoria Palace | 45 |
| Whitehall | 33 |
| Wyndhams | 30 |

3-0103

189

This outdoor theater is in Regent's Park; the setting is idyllic, and both seating and acoustics are excellent. Presentations are mainly Shakespeare, usually in period costume. Its theater bar, the longest in London, serves both drink and food. In the case of a rained-out performance, tickets are given for another date. The season runs from the end of May through mid-September, Monday through Saturday at 8pm, plus Wednesday, Thursday, and Saturday matinees at 2:30pm.

✪ **Royal National Theatre.** South Bank, SE1. ☎ **0171/928-2252.** Tickets £8–£24 ($12.80–$38.40); midweek matinees, Sat matinees, and previews cost less. Tube: Waterloo, Embankment, or Charing Cross.

Home to one of the world's greatest stage companies, the Royal National Theatre is not one but three theaters—the Olivier, reminiscent of a Greek amphitheater with its open stage; the more traditional Lyttelton; and the Cottesloe, with its flexible stage and seating. The National presents the finest in world theater, from classic drama to award-winning new plays, including comedy, musicals, and shows for young people.

**Royal Shakespeare Company.** In the Barbican Centre, Silk St., Barbican, EC2. ☎ **0171/638-8891.** Barbican Theatre £6–£26.50 ($9.60–$42.40); The Pit £10–£17 ($16 to $27.20) matinees and evening performances. Box office daily 9am–8pm. Tube: Barbican or Moorgate.

The Royal Shakespeare Company is one of the world's finest theater companies. The core of its repertoire remains, of course, the plays of William Shakespeare. It also presents a wide-ranging program of three different productions each week in the Barbican Theatre—a 2,000-seat main auditorium with excellent sightlines throughout, thanks to a raked orchestra—and in The Pit, a small studio space where much of the company's new writing is presented. The Royal Shakespeare Company is in residence in London during the winter months; it spends the summer touring in England and abroad.

**Sadler's Wells Theater.** Rosebery Ave., EC1. ☎ **0171/314-8800.** Tickets £7.50–£32.50 ($12–$52). Performances usually 8pm. Box office Mon–Sat 10am–8pm. Tube: Angel.

Sadler's Wells is London's premier venue for the presentation, at reasonable prices, of dance theater. Set within the relatively unstylish neighborhood of Islington, in North London, it occupies the site of a theater that was built in 1683, itself on the site of a well that was once prized for the healing powers of its water. In the early 1990s, the old-fashioned, turn-of-the-century theater that had evolved from the original, 17th-century core was demolished, and construction began on an innovative new design—which is scheduled for completion sometime during the lifetime of this edition. In the interim, performances are being held in a rented, circa 1960, theater, the Peacock on Portugal St., WC2a (same phone; tube: Holborn).

Sometime in 1998, look for something akin to a phoenix rising that will include both traditional and experimental dance venues within two theaters. They will encompass the new, state-of-the-art theater on Sadler Well's original site (Rosebery Avenue, in Islington) as well as offshoot productions within the above-mentioned Peacock (which the Sadlers Wells Trust, Ltd., will continue to rent until sometime after the millennium). Incidentally, this outfit has impressive antecedents: What's known today as the Royal Ballet (originally known as the Sadler's Wells Ballet) had its origins at this theater, before moving to more opulent quarters near Covent Garden.

**Shakespeare's Globe Theatre.** New Globe Walk, Bankside, SE1. ☎ **0171/928-6406.** Tickets £5 ($8) for groundlings, £5–£20 ($8–$32) for gallery seats. Tube: Mansion House.

In May 1997, the new Globe Theatre—a replica of the Elizabethan original, thatched roof and all—staged its first slate of plays (*Henry V* and *A Winter's Tale*) on the exact site of the 16th-century theater where the Bard originally staged his work.

Productions vary in style and setting; not all are performed in Elizabethan costume. In keeping with the historic setting, there's no lighting focused just on the stage, but floodlighting used during evening performances to replicate daylight in theater. Theatergoers sit on wooden benches of yore—in thatch-roofed galleries, no less—but these days you can rent a cushion to make yourself more comfortable. About 500 "groundlings" can stand in the uncovered yard around the stage, just like they did when the Bard himself was here. Mark Rylane, the artistic director of the Globe, told the press he'd be delighted if the audience threw fruit at the actors, as they did in Shakespeare's time. Participatory theater, we think they call it. You're likely to hear an occasional, perhaps witty, comment from the audience (delivered, everyone hopes, in iambic pentameter).

At press time, a performance schedule for 1998 wasn't in place yet. From May through October, the company intends to hold performances Tuesday through Saturday at 2 and 7:30pm, and Sunday at 4pm. There will be a limited winter schedule. In any season, the schedule may be affected by the weather, since this is an outdoor theater. Performances last $2^1/2$ to 4 hours, depending on the play.

Also in the works is a second theater, the Inigo Jones Theatre, based on the architect's designs from the 1600s, where plays will be staged year-round. For details on the exhibition that tells the story of the painstaking re-creation of the Globe, as well as guided tours of the theatre, see "More Museums" earlier in this chapter.

**Young Vic.** 66 The Cut, Waterloo, SE1. ☎ **0171/928-6363.** Tickets £8–£18 ($12.80–$28.80) adults, £5–£6.50 ($8–$10.40) students and children. Performances Mon–Sat 7:30pm, matinee Sat 2pm. Tube: Waterloo.

The Young Vic presents classical and modern plays in the round for theatergoers of all ages and backgrounds, but primarily focuses on young adults. Recent productions have included Shakespeare, Ibsen, Arthur Miller, and specially commissioned plays for children.

## THE PERFORMING ARTS

**English National Opera.** Performing in the London Coliseum, St. Martin's Lane, WC2. ☎ **0171/632-8300.** Tickets £6.50–£8 ($10.40–$12.80) balcony, £12–£55 ($19.20–$88) upper dress circle or stalls; about 100 discount balcony tickets sold on the day of performance from 10am during the season. Tube: Charing Cross or Leicester Square.

The London Coliseum, built in 1904 as a variety theater and converted into an opera house in 1968, is London's largest theater. The English National Opera is one of the two national opera companies and performs a wide range of works, from great classics to Gilbert and Sullivan to new and experimental works, staged with flair and imagination—and every performance is in English. A repertory of 18 to 20 productions is presented five or six nights a week for 11 months of the year (dark in July). Although the balcony seats are cheaper, many visitors prefer the Upper Circle or Dress Circle.

**✪ Royal Opera House—The Royal Ballet & The Royal Opera.** Bow St., Covent Garden, WC2. Box office ☎ **0171/304-4000.** Opera tickets £4–£147.50 ($6.40–$236); ballet tickets £2–£62 ($3.20–$99.20). Tube: Covent Garden.

The nation's most elite opera company and leading ballet company both perform at one of the capital's most glamorous theaters, the Royal Opera House, although they have temporarily been dislodged from their home because of restoration. They will be back on their home stage in fall 1999. In the meantime, the opera and ballet will be appearing at a number of venues within London, such as the Barbican, Royal Albert Hall, and a West End theater, with ballet seasons at the Labatts Apollo in Hammersmith, the Royal Festival Hall, and the London Coliseum. The Royal Opera performs the international repertoire. Performances are usually sung in the original language, but supertitles are projected, translating the libretto for the audience.

Currently under the direction of Sir Anthony Dowell, The Royal Ballet performs a variety of the ballet repertory with a tilt toward the classics and works by its earlier choreographer-directors Sir Frederick Ashton and Sir Kenneth MacMillan.

## Major Concert Halls & All-Purpose Auditoriums

**Barbican Centre.** Silk St., The Barbican, EC2. ☎ **0171/638-8891.** Tickets £6–£30 ($9.60–$48). Tube: Barbican, Moorgate, St. Paul's, Liverpool Street and Bank.

The largest art and exhibition center in Western Europe, the Barbican was created to make a perfect setting to enjoy good music and theater from comfortable, roomy seating. The Barbican Theatre is the London home of the **Royal Shakespeare Company** (see above), and the Barbican Hall is the permanent home address of the **London Symphony Orchestra** and host to visiting orchestras and performers, from classical to jazz, folk and world music.

In addition to the hall and theater, the Barbican Centre has The Pit, a studio theater; the Barbican Art Gallery, a showcase for the visual arts; the Concourse Gallery and foyer exhibition spaces; Cinemas One and Two, which show recently released mainstream films and specialist seasons; the Barbican Library, a general lending library that also places a strong emphasis on the arts; a Conservatory, one of London's largest plant houses; and three restaurants, cafes as well as bars. The box office is open daily from 9am to 8pm.

**Kenwood Lakeside Concerts.** Kenwood, Hampstead Lane, Hampstead Heath, London NW3 7JR. ☎ **0181/348-1286.** Tickets for adults £9–£12 ($14.40 to $19.20) for seats on the grass lawn; £11–£16 ($17.60 to $25.60) for reserved deck chairs. Reductions of 25% for students and persons over 60. Every summer Sat at 7:30pm mid-June to early Sept. Tube: Golders Green or Archway, then bus no. 210.

Presented on the north side of Hampstead Heath, these band and orchestral concerts have been a British tradition for some 50 years. There's more to this than just music: Laser shows and fireworks displays enliven a repertoire that includes everything from rousing versions of the 1812 Overture, complete with fireworks, to jazz, and such operas as *Carmen*. Regardless of the season's individual programs, be assured that the final concert in the season will feature some of the Pomp and Circumstance Marches of Sir Edward Elgar, everyone's favorite imperialistic composer. Music drifts across the lake from the performance amphitheater above a verdant scene that encourages wine and cheese parties on the grass.

**London Palladium.** Argyll St., W1. ☎ **0171/494-5020.** Tickets from £10–£32 ($16–$51.20), depending on show. Closed Sun. Tube: Oxford Circus.

It's hard to encapsulate the prestige of this show-business legend in a paragraph. Performers from Britain, Europe, and America consider that they have "arrived" when they've appeared here. The season's highlight is the Royal Command Performance, held before the queen, which includes an introduction of the artists to Her Majesty.

**Royal Albert Hall.** Kensington Gore, SW7. ☎ **0171/589-8212.** Tickets £8–£120 ($12.80–$192), depending on the event. Tube: South Kensington, Kensington High Street, or Knightsbridge.

Opened in 1871 and dedicated to the memory of Queen Victoria's consort, Prince Albert, this building encircles one of the world's most famous auditoriums with a

seating capacity of 5,200. Since 1941, the hall has been the setting for the BBC
✪ **Henry Wood Promenade Concerts** ("The Proms"), a concert series that lasts for
eight weeks between mid-July and mid-September. (The Proms has been a British
tradition since 1895.) Although most of the audience occupies reserved seats, true
aficionados usually opt for standing room in the orchestra pit for close-up views of
the musicians performing on stage. The programs are outstanding and often present
newly commissioned works for the first time. The last night of The Proms is the most
traditional, as such rousing favorites as "Jerusalem" or "Land of Hope and Glory"
echo through the hall. For tickets call Ticketmaster at ☎ **0171/379-4444** instead
of Royal Albert Hall directly. Sporting events such as boxing also figure strongly here.
For Royal Albert Hall 24-hour events information and ticket availability, call
☎ **01891/500252.**

✪ **Royal Festival Hall.** On the South Bank, SE1. ☎ **0171/960-4242.** Tickets £5–£35 ($8–
$56); credit cards accepted. Box office 10am–9pm. Tube: Waterloo or Embankment.

In the aftermath of World War II, London's musical focus shifted to a uniquely specialized complex of buildings that were erected between 1951 and 1964 on the site
of a bombed-out 18th-century brewery. Out of the industrial wastelands on the south
side of the Thames, across Waterloo Bridge, rose three of the most comfortable and
acoustically perfect concert halls in the world. They include Royal Festival Hall,
Queen Elizabeth Hall, and the Purcell Room. Within their precincts, more than
1,200 performances a year are presented, including classical music, ballet, jazz, popular classics, pop, and contemporary dance. The center also accommodates the internationally famous Hayward Gallery whose exhibitions include both contemporary
and historical art.

  The Royal Festival Hall is open from 10am every day. There are free exhibitions
in the foyers and free lunchtime music from 12:30pm. The Poetry Library is open
from 11am to 8pm, as well as shops selling books, records, and crafts.

  The Festival Buffet offers a wide variety of food at reasonable prices, and there are
numerous bars throughout the foyers. The People's Palace offers lunch and dinner
with a panoramic view of the Thames. Reservations are recommended by calling
☎ **0171/921-0800.**

**Wigmore Hall.** 36 Wigmore St., W1. ☎ **0171/935-2141.** Tickets £5–£35 ($8–$56). Tube:
Bond Street or Oxford Circus.

An intimate auditorium, Wigmore Hall books excellent recitals and concerts. There
are regular series of song recitals, piano, jazz, and chamber music, along with early
music and baroque concerts. A free list of the month's programs is available from the
hall. Performances are given nightly, plus Sunday Morning Coffee Concerts and
additional concerts on Sunday at 4 or 7pm. A cafe-bar and restaurant serves cold
suppers.

## THE CLUB & MUSIC SCENE

Midnight divides the world of bright lights like a curtain. This "midnight curtain"
prevents you from just dropping into a place for a nightcap—you must order something to eat when you have an alcoholic drink after 11pm. You also might have to
pay a cover charge—frequently disguised as a membership fee. This amounts to so-
called temporary membership, which satisfies the letter of the law and allows you to
get in without delay.

### COMEDY

**Comedy Spot.** The Spot, Maiden Lane, WC2. ☎ **0171/379-5900.** Cover £8 ($12.80) Mon,
before 8pm, meal included; £6 ($9.60) after 8pm for comedy show only; £5 ($8) Fri, Sat after

10pm and Sun after 7pm. Open Mon–Thurs, noon–midnight; Fri–Sat noon–1am; Sun noon–10:30pm.

This bar-restaurant has DJs Tuesday through Saturday; singers on Sunday; and "spotlight comedy" on Monday nights, with a host and three comedians, mixing beginners with old pros. If you're into stand-up comedy, English style, this is one of the best places in town.

**The Comedy Store.** 1A Oxendon St., off Piccadilly Circus SW1. ☎ **0142/691-4433.** Cover £9 ($14.40) Mon–Thurs, £10 ($16) Fri–Sun. Daily from 6:30pm. Tube: Leicester Square or Piccadilly Circus.

In the heart of the city's nighttime district, this is London's most visible showcase for established and rising comic talent. Inspired by comedy clubs in the U.S., this London club has given many comics their starts. Today a number of them are established TV personalities. Even if their names are unfamiliar, you'll enjoy the spontaneity of live comedy performed before a British audience. Visitors must be 18 and older; dress is casual. Reservations are accepted through Ticketmaster at ☎ **0171/344-4444,** and the club opens 1 1/2 hours before each show. *Insider's Tip:* Go on Tuesday when the humor is more cutting edge and topical.

## BOUZOUKI

**Elysée.** 13 Percy St., W1. ☎ **0171/636-4804.** Cover £3 ($4.80) Mon–Thurs, £4 ($6.40) Fri–Sat. Meals Mon–Fri noon–3pm; Mon–Sat 7:30pm–4am. Tube: Goodge Street or Tottenham Court Road.

Elsyée is for *Never on Sunday* devotees who like the reverberations of bouzouki and the smashing of plates. The Karegeorgis brothers—Michael, Ulysses, and the incomparable George—offer hearty fun at moderate tabs. You can dance nightly to music by Greek musicians. Two different cabaret shows are presented (the last one at 1am), highlighted by brother George's amusing art of balancing wineglasses. You can book a table on either the ground floor or the second floor, but the Roof Garden is the place to be in summer. The food is good, too, especially the house specialty, the classic moussaka, and kebabs from the charcoal grill.

## ROCK

**The Bull & Gate.** 389 Kentish Town Rd., NW5. ☎ **0171/485-5358.** Cover £4–£6 ($6.40–$9.60). Tube: Kentish Town.

Smaller, cheaper, and often more animated and less touristy than many of its competitors, the Bull & Gate is the unofficial headquarters of London's pub rock scene. Indie and relatively unknown rock bands are often served up back-to-back by the half dozen in this somewhat battered, Victorian pub. If you like spilled beer, this is off-the-beaten-track London at its most authentic. Bands that played here and later ascended to Europe's clubby scene have included Madness, Blur, Pulp, and that 1980s music video oddity, Sigue-Sigue-Sputnik. The place operates pub hours, with music nightly from 8 to 11pm.

**The Rock Garden.** 6–7 The Piazza, Covent Garden, WC2. ☎ **0171/836-4052.** Cover £5 ($8), diners enter free. Open Mon–Thurs 5pm–3am; Fri 5pm–6pm; Sat 4pm–4am; Sun 7:30pm–11pm. Tube: Covent Garden. Bus: Any of the night buses that depart from Trafalgar Square.

A long-established performance site for a wide array of bands, The Rock Garden maintains a bar and a stage in the cellar, and a restaurant on the street level. The cellar, known as The Venue, has hosted such acts as Dire Straits, The Police, and U2 before their rises to stardom. Today bands vary widely, from promising up-and-comers to some who'll never be heard from again. Simple American-style fare is served in the restaurant.

**The VorteX Ltd.** 79 Oxford St. ☎ **0171/439-7250.** Cover £8–£16 ($12.80–$25.60) varies. Open Thurs–Sun 9pm–3am; Fri 9pm–4am; Sat 9pm–6am. Tube: Tottenham Court Road.

Loud, unconventional, and catering to the punk crowd, this brash cellar bar welcomes music lovers and late-night revelers. It's become very touristy, however. The heavily-promoted year-old incarnation of a club opened in the 1970s, The VorteX is set in the basement of an Oxford Street building below, of all things, a Pizza Hut. Entertainment, which includes both recorded and live performers, varies nightly. Thursday's soul and R&B segues into Friday's rock and heavy metal. Saturday is for house and garage jams, while on Sunday, white-suited disco fever returns. Snack items and munchies, and of course beer, are available in quantities.

**Wag Club.** 35 Wardour St., W1. ☎ **071/437-5534.** Cover £5–£10 ($8–$16). Open Tues–Fri 10pm–4am; Sat 10pm–5am; Sun 10pm–3am. No credit cards. Tube: Leicester Square or Piccadilly Circus.

The split-level Wag Club is one of the more stylish live-music places in town. The downstairs stage usually attracts newly signed, cutting-edge rock bands, while a DJ spins dance records upstairs. Door policy can be selective.

## FOLK

**Cecil Sharpe House.** 2 Regent's Pk. Rd., NW1. ☎ **0171/485-2206.** Cover £3.50–£5.50 ($5.60–$8.80). Tube: Camden Town

CSH was the focal point of the folk revival in the 1960s, and it continues to treasure and nurture the style. Here you'll find a whole range of traditional English music and dancing performed. Call to see what's happening and when.

## JAZZ & BLUES

**Ain't Nothing But Blues Bar.** 20 Kingly St., W1. ☎ **0171/287-0514.** Cover £5 ($8) Fri–Sat. Open Mon–Thurs 5:30-1a; Fri–Sat 6pm–3am; Sun 7:30pm–midnight. Tube: Oxford Circus.

The club, which bills itself as the only true blues venue in town, features mostly local acts and occasional touring American bands. On weekends prepare to queue. From the Oxford Circus tube, walk south on Regent Street, turn left on Great Marlborough Street, and then make a quick right on Kingly Street.

**The Blue Note.** 1 Hoxton Sq., N1. ☎ **0171/729-8440.** Cover £5–£12 ($8–$19.20). Open Mon–Sat noon–6pm; Thurs 10pm—3am; Fri–Sat 10pm–5am; Sun 1–6pm and 7pm–midnight. Tube: Old Street.

Owned by the Acid Jazz Record label, this is a cafe bar by day and live music club at night. It became famous on the London night life circuit in its former incarnation as the Bass Clef. Acid Jazz took it over, saved the building from demolition, and it now features bands ranging from jungle, trip hop, and drum and bass to jazz, funk, and soul. Sundays feature soul music upstairs and hot jazz in the basement.

**Bull's Head.** 373 Lonsdale Rd., Barnes, SW13. ☎ **0181/876-5241.** Cover £3–£7 ($4.80–$11.20). Open Mon–Sat 11am–11pm; Sun noon–10:30pm. Tube to Hammersmith, then bus no. 9A to Barnes Bridge, then retrace the path of the bus for some 200 yards on foot; or take Hounslow Look train from Waterloo Station and get off at Barnes Bridge Station, then walk 5 minutes to the club.

This club has showcased live modern jazz every night of the week for more than 30 years. One of the oldest hostelries in the area, it was a mid-19th-century staging post where travelers on their way to Hampton Court and beyond could eat, drink, and rest while coach horses were changed. Today the bar features jazz by musicians from all over the world. Live jazz on Sunday from noon to 10:30pm; Monday through Saturday, from 8 to 11pm. You can order lunch at the Carvery in the Saloon Bar or dinner in the 17th-century Stable Restaurant.

**Jazz Café.** 5 Parkway, NW1. ☎ **0171/344-0044.** Cover £9.50–£14 ($15.20–$22.40); £12 ($19.20) per person to book a table. Tube: Parkway.

Afro-Latin jazz fans are hip to this club hosting combos from around the globe. The weekends, described by one patron as "bumpy jazzy-funk nights," are the best time to decide for yourself what that means. Call ahead for listings, cover, and table reservations (when necessary); opening times can vary.

**100 Club.** 100 Oxford St., W1. ☎ **0171/636-0933.** Cover £8 ($12.80) Fri members and nonmembers; £8 ($12.80) Sat members, £9 ($14.40) nonmembers; £6 ($9.60) Sun. Open Mon–Fri 8:30pm–3am; Sat 7:30pm–1am; Sun 7:30–11:30pm. Tube: Tottenham Court Road or Oxford Circus.

Although less plush and less expensive than some, 100 Club is a serious contender among the city's many dedicated jazz clubs. Its cavalcade of bands includes the best British jazz musicians and some of their Yankee brethren. Rock, R&B, and blues are also on tap.

✪ **Pizza Express.** 10 Dean St., W1. ☎ **0171/439-8722.** Cover £10–£25 ($16–$40). Open Mon–Fri 7:45pm–midnight; Sat–Sun 9pm–12:30am. Tube: Tottenham Court Road.

Don't let the name fool you: this restaurant-bar serves up some of the best jazz in London by mainstream artists. While enjoying a thin-crust Italian pizza, you can check out a local band or a visiting group, often from the U.S. Although the club has been enlarged, it's important to reserve, as it fills up quickly.

✪ **Ronnie Scott's Club.** 47 Frith St., W1. ☎ **0171/439-0747.** Cover £12 ($19.20) Mon–Thurs; £15 ($24) Fri–Sat; with student ID, £8 ($12.80) Mon–Thurs only. Open Mon–Sat 8:30pm–3am. Tube: Leicester Square or Piccadilly Circus.

Inquire about jazz in London and people immediately think of Ronnie Scott's, long the European forerunner of modern jazz. Only the best English and American combos, often fronted by a top-notch vocalist, are booked here. The programs inevitably make for an entire evening of cool jazz. In the heart of Soho, Ronnie Scott's is a 10-minute walk from Piccadilly Circus along Shaftesbury Avenue. You don't have to be a member, although you can join if you wish. In the Main Room you can either stand at the bar to watch the show or sit at a table, from which you can order dinner. The Downstairs Bar is more intimate; among the regulars at your elbow may be some of the world's most talented musicians. On weekends, the separate Upstairs Room has a disco called Club Latino.

**606 Club.** 90 Lots Road, SW10. ☎ **0171/352-5953.** Music charge £4.25 ($6.80) Sun–Thurs, £4.95 ($7.90) Fri–Sat. Open Mon–Sat 8:30pm–2am; Sun 8:30–11:30pm. Tube: Earl's Court. Bus: 11, 19, 22, 31, 39, or C3.

Located in a discreet basement site in Chelsea, the 606 presents live music 7 nights a week. Predominantly a venue for modern jazz, style ranges from traditional to contemporary. Local musicians and some very big names play here, whether planned gigs or informal jam sessions after their shows elsewhere in town. This is actually a jazz supper club in the boondocks of Fulham; because of license requirements, patrons can only order alcohol with food.

## DANCE, DISCO & ECLECTIC

**Bar Rumba.** 26 Shaftesbury Ave., W1. ☎ **0171/287-2715.** Cover £2–£10 ($3.20–$16). Open Mon–Thurs 5pm–3:30am; Fri 5pm–4:30am; Sat 6pm–6am; Sun 8pm–1:30am. Tube: Piccadilly Circus.

Despite its location on Shaftesbury Avenue, this Latin bar and club could be featured in a book of "Underground London." A hush-hush address among Latin types, it leans toward radical jazz fusion on some nights, phat funk on other occasions. Boasting two full bars and a different musical theme every night, Tuesday and Wednesday are the only nights you probably won't have to queue at the door. Monday's "That's How It Is" showcase features jazz, hip hop, and drum and bass; Friday's "KAT Klub" grooves with soul, R&B, and swing; and Saturday's "Garage City" buzzes with house and garage. On weeknights you have to be 18 and up; the age limit is 21 on Saturday and Sunday.

**Camden Palace.** 1A Camden High St., NW1. ☎ **0171/387-0428.** Cover £5 ($8) Tues–Wed, £10–£17 ($16–$27.20) Fri–Sat. Open Tues–Wed 9pm–2:30am; Fri 9pm–4am; Sat 9pm–6am. Tube: Camden Town or Mornington Crescent.

Housed in a former theater built around 1910, Camden Palace draws an over-18 crowd that flocks here in trendy downtown costumes. Energy levels vary according to the night of the week, as does the music, so call in advance to see if that evening's musical program appeals to your taste. A live band performs only on Tuesday. There's a restaurant if you get the munchies.

**The Cross.** The Arches, Kings Cross Goods Yard, York Way, N1. ☎ **0171/837-0828.** Cover £10–£15 ($16–$24). Open Fri 10pm–4:30am; Sat 10:30pm–6am. Tube: Kings Cross.

In the backwaters of Kings Cross, this club has stayed hot since 1993. London hipsters come here for private parties thrown by Rough Trade Records or Red Or Dead, or just to dance in the space's cozy brick-lined vaults. It's always party time here. Call to find out who's performing.

**Equinox.** Leicester Sq., WC2. ☎ **0171/437-1446.** Cover £5–£12 ($8–$19.20), depending on the night of the week. Open Mon–Thurs 9pm–3am; Fri–Sat 9pm–4am. Tube: Leicester Square.

Built in 1992 on the site of the London Empire, a dance emporium that witnessed the changing styles of social dancing since the 1700s, the Equinox has established itself as a perennial favorite among Londoners. It contains nine bars, the largest dance floor in London, and a restaurant modeled after a 1950s American diner. Virtually every kind of dance music is featured here, including dance hall, pop, rock, and Latin. The setting is lavishly illuminated with one of Europe's largest lighting rigs, and the crowd is as varied as London itself.

**Hanover Grand.** 6 Hanover St., W1. ☎ **0171/499-7977.** Cover £8–£16 ($12.80–$25.60). Open Thurs–Sat 10pm–4am. Tube: Oxford Circus.

Thursdays are funky and down and dirty. Fridays and Saturdays the crowd dresses up in their disco-finery, clingy and form-fitting or politicized and punk. Dance floors are always crowded, and masses seem to surge back-and-forth between the two levels. Age and gender is sometimes hard to make out at this cutting-edge club of the minute.

**Hippodrome.** Corner of Cranbourn St. and Charing Cross Rd., WC2. ☎ **0171/437-4311.** Cover £4–£10 ($6.40–$16). Open Mon–Sat 9pm–3am. Tube: Leicester Square.

Located near Leicester Square, the popular Hippodrome is London's grand old daddy of discos, a cavernous place with a great sound system and lights to match. It was once Lady Di's favorite scene, in her youthful bar-hopping days. Tacky and touristy, the 'drome is packed on weekends.

**Iceni.** 11 White Horse St., W1. ☎ **0171/495-5333.** Cover £12 ($19.20) Fri; £10 ($16) Sat. Open Fri 11pm–3am; Sat 10pm–3am. Tube: Queen's Park.

Attracting an older twenty-something crowd on Fridays, and 18-25ers on Saturdays, this funky three-story nightclub features films, board games, tarot readings, dancing to swing, soul, hip hop, and R&B. You can even get a manicure. Leave your name at the door and make a love connection courtesy of Flipside Dating Service.

**Limelight.** 136 Shaftesbury Ave., WC2. ☎ **0171/434-0572.** Cover £2 ($3.20) before 10pm, £12 ($19.20) thereafter. Open Mon–Sat 9pm–3am; Sat 10pm–3am; Sun 6–11pm. Tube: Leicester Square.

Although opened in 1985, this large dance club—located inside a former Welsh chapel that dates to 1754—has only recently come into its own. The dance floors and bars share space with plenty of cool Gothic nooks and crannies. DJs spin the latest house music.

✪ **Ministry of Sound.** 103 Gaunt St., SE1. ☎ **0171/378-6528.** Cover £12–£20 ($19.20–$32). Open Fri and Sat midnight–9am. Tube: Elephant & Castle.

Removed from the city center, this club-of-the-hour is relatively devoid of tourists. With a large bar and an even bigger sound system, it blasts garage and house music to energetic crowds that pack the two dance floors. If the stimulants in the rest of the club have gone to your head, you can chill in the cinema room. Note that the club's cover charge is stiff, and bouncers will definitely decide who is cool enough to enter.

**The Office.** 3–5 Rathbone Place, W1. ☎ **0171/636-1598.** Cover £5 ($8). Open Mon–Sat noon–3am. Tube: Tottenham Court Road.

An eclectic club with a bureaucratic name, one of The Office's most popular nights is Wednesday's "Double Six Club," featuring easy listening and board games from 6pm to 2am. Other nights are more traditional recorded pop, rock, soul, and disco. Ambience wins out over decor.

**Smollensky's on The Strand.** 105 The Strand, WC2. ☎ **0171/497-2101.** No cover except £4 ($6.40) for live music. Open Mon–Sat noon–12:30am; Sun 6:30–10:30pm. Tube: Charing Cross or Embankment.

This American eatery and drinking bar is a cousin to Smollensky's Dover Street. At the Strand location, dance from Thursday through Saturday nights. Sunday night features a special live jazz session. Meals average £20 ($32).

**Stringfellows.** 16–19 Upper St. Martin's Lane, WC2. ☎ **0171/240-5534.** Cover £8–£15 ($12.80–$24). Open Mon–Fri 6pm–3:30am; Sat 8pm–3:30am; Sun 9pm–3:30am. Reservations recommended for restaurant. Tube: Leicester Square.

This would-be glam club has a varied clientele and lots of velvet and gloss. In theory, it's members-only, but—at the discretion of management—nonmembers may be admitted. The disco has a glass dance floor and a dazzling sound-and-light system. A restaurant feeds late-night diners, and there's no charge for admission to the club if you dine in the restaurant. Stringfellows has two drinking areas, one slightly less formal than the other.

**Subterania.** 12 Acklam Rd., W10. ☎ **0181/960-4590.** Cover £8£10 ($12.80–$16). Open Fri–Sat 10:30pm–3am, other nights vary. Tube: Ladbroke Grove.

Affordable, unpretentious, and informal, the feel of this club changes according to the style of the live band that happens to be available at the time. You'll have to phone to discover on what night a favorite local band will appear, or what style of music will be playing on a night you want to go dancing. The place contains a busy street level dance floor and a mezzanine-style bar upstairs, although there is nothing subterranean. The decor is energetic orange, purple, and blue; if those colors work for you, there are also sofas covered in downtown *faux* leopardskin. More or less constant is the Friday music card of soul, funk, hip-hop, and swing, and Saturday's house music. Other nights of the week, it's pot luck.

**Velvet Underground.** 143 Charing Cross Rd., WC2. ☎ **0171/439-4655.** Cover £4–£10 ($6.40–$16). Open Mon–Thurs 10pm–3am; Fri–Sat 10:30pm–4am. Tube: Tottenham Court Road.

All dolled up in red, blue, and yellow velvet, the club's large dance floor pulses to beats provided by DJs Nicky Holloway and Carl Cox. Monday is all-night happy hour with £1 ($1.60) drinks, Thursday is techno, and Friday and Saturday are so hip they've got names: "Ego Trip" and "Tomorrow People." Twenty-somethings can enjoy full bar service, but no food.

✪ **Venom Club/The Zoo Bar.** 13–18 Bear St., WC2. ☎ **0171/839-4188.** Cover £5 ($8) after 10pm for both venues. Zoo Bar daily 4pm–2am, Venom Club daily 9:30pm–3am. Tube: Leicester Square.

Its owners spent millions of pounds outfitting this club with the slickest, flashiest, and most psychedelic decor in London. If you're looking for a true Euro nightlife experience replete with gorgeous *au pairs* and trendy Europeans, this is it. Zoo Bar upstairs is a menagerie of mosaic animals beneath a glassed-in ceiling dome. Downstairs, the music is so intrusive that conversation is futile. Clients are over 18 but younger and hipper than 35. Androgyny is the look of choice. The first Wednesday of every month is devoted to the sugar pop of Boy George, whose groupies cavort here in hopes of glimpsing the campy star.

## LATIN RHYTHMS

**Cuba.** 11 Kensington High St., W8. ☎ **0171/938-4137.** Cover £3–£5 ($4.80–$8) after 10pm. Open Mon–Sat noon–2am; Sun 2–11pm. Tube: High Street Kensington.

This Spanish/Cuban style bar-restaurant, which has a music club downstairs, features live music acts from Cuba, Brazil, Spain, and the rest of Latin America. Odd as it may seem, the crowd is equal parts restaurant diners, after-work drinkers, Latinophiles, and dancers. Salsa dance classes are offered Monday and Wednesday from 8:30 to 9:30pm for £3 ($4.80). Happy hour is Monday to Saturday, noon to 8:30pm.

**Salsa.** 96 Charing Cross Rd., WC2. ☎ **0171/379-3277.** Cover £7 ($11.20) Fri–Sat after 9pm. Open Mon–Sat 5:30pm–2am. Tube: Leicester Square.

This lively bar-restaurant and music club is for Latin music aficionados. It features mostly bands from Central and South America. Dance lessons are available nightly starting at 6:30pm; live music starts at 9pm. Some of the best dancers in London strut their stuff here.

## THE BAR SCENE

**Bracewells Bar.** In the Park Lane Hotel, Piccadilly, W1. ☎ **0171/499-6321.** Tube: Green Park or Hyde Park.

Chic, nostalgic, and elegant, Bracewells is the kind of bar where Edward VII and his stylish companion Mrs. Langtry might have felt at home. With its plush decor of Chinese lacquer, comfortable sofas, and soft lighting, the bar seems like an elegant private club. The bar adjoins the Bracewells restaurant, one of the finest hotel dining experiences in London. Complimentary hors d'oeuvres are offered in the evenings.

**Cocktail Bar.** In the Café Royal, 68 Regent St., W1. ☎ **0171/437-9090.** Tube: Piccadilly Circus.

In business since 1865, this bar was once patronized by Oscar Wilde, James McNeill Whistler, and Aubrey Beardsley. Its 19th-century rococo decor, which includes one of the most beautiful frescoed ceilings in London, exudes glamour. The bartender's specialties are the Café Royal cocktails, which include the Golden Cadillac and the Prince William (Would you drink a Prince William?).

**Lillie Langtry Bar.** In the Cadogan Hotel, Sloane St., SW1. ☎ **0171/235-7141.** Tube: Sloane Square or Knightsbridge.

Next door to Langtry's Restaurant, this 1920s-style bar epitomizes the charm and elegance of the Edwardian era. Lillie Langtry, the turn-of-the-century actress and society beauty (notorious as the mistress of Edward VII), once lived here. Oscar Wilde—arrested in this very hotel bar—is honored on the drinks menu by his favorite libation, the Hock and Seltzer. Sir John Betjeman's poem "The Arrest of Oscar Wilde at the Cadogan Hotel" tells the story. The Cadogan Cooler seems to be the most popular drink here. An international menu is also served in the adjoining restaurant.

**Smollensky's Dover Street.** 1 Dover St., W1. ☎ **0171/491-1199.** Tube: Green Park.

This American eatery and bar is packed during happy hour (Monday to Friday from 5:30 to 7pm) with Mayfair office workers on their way home. You'll find a 1930s piano bar atmosphere, with polished wood and a mirrored ceiling. Standard American-style fare is served, including well-prepared vegetarian dishes.

## THE GAY & LESBIAN SCENE

The most reliable source of information on gay clubs and activities is the **Lesbian and Gay Switchboard** (☎ **0171/837-7324**). The staff runs a 24-hour service for information on places and activities catering to homosexual men and women. *Time Out* also carries listings on such clubs.

**The Box.** 32–34 Monmouth St. (at Seven Dials), WC2. ☎ **0171/240-5828.** Open Mon–Sat 11:30am–11:30pm; Sun noon–6pm. Tube: Covent Garden.

Adjacent to one of Convent Garden's best-known junctions, Seven Dials, this sophisticated Mediterranean-style bar attracts more lesbians than many of its competitors. This is especially the case on women-only Sunday nights, cutely labeled "Girl Bar at the Box." The rest of the week, men slightly outnumber women. From noon to 5:30 pm, this is primarily a restaurant, serving meal-sized salads, club sandwiches, and soups. Food service ends abruptly at 5:30, after which the place reveals its core: a cheerful, popular place of rendezvous for London's gay and countercultural crowds. The Box considers itself a "summer bar," throwing open its doors and windows to a cluster of outdoor tables that attracts a crowd at the slightest hint of sunshine.

**The Edge.** 11 Soho Sq., W1. ☎ **0171/497-3154.** No cover. Open Mon–Sat noon–1am; Sun noon–10:30pm. Tube: Tottenham Court Road.

Few bars in London can rival the tolerance, humor, and sexual sophistication found here. The first two floors are done up with accessories that, like an English garden, change with the seasons. Dance music can be found on the high-energy and crowded lower floors, while the upper floors are best if you're looking for intimate conversation. Three menus are featured: a funky daytime menu, a cafe menu, and a late-night menu. Dancers hit the floors starting around 7:30pm. Clientele ranges from the flamboyantly gay to hetero pub crawlers out for a night of slumming.

**First Out.** 52 St. Giles High St., W1 ☎ **0171/240-8042.** Open Mon–Sat 10am–11pm; Sun noon–10:30pm. Tube: Tottenham Court Road.

First Out prides itself on being London's first (est. 1986) all-gay coffee shop. Set in a 19th-century building whose wood panels have been painted the colors of the gay liberation rainbow, the bar is intimate (that is, not particularly cruisy) and offers an exclusively vegetarian menu, with most items priced at £3.25 ($5.20). Cappuccino and whisky are the preferred libations; curry dishes, potted pies in phyllo pastries, and salads the foods of choice. Don't expect a raucous atmosphere—some clients come here with their grandmothers. Look for the bulletin board with leaflets and business cards of gay and gay-friendly entrepreneurs.

**Heaven.** The Arches, Villiers and Craven sts., WC2. ☎ **0171/930-2020.** Cover £5–£8 ($8–$12.80). Open Tues–Sat 10:30pm–3:30am; Sun 9pm–1am. Tube: Charing Cross or Embankment.

This club in the vaulted cellars of Charing Cross Railway Station is a London landmark. Owned by the same investors who brought the world Virgin Atlantic Airways, Heaven is one of the biggest and best-established gay venues in Britain. Painted black inside, and reminiscent of an air-raid shelter, the club is divided into at least four distinct areas connected by a labyrinth of catwalk stairs and hallways. Each area has a different activity going on. Heaven also has theme nights, which are frequented by predominantly gay men, gay women, or a mostly heterosexual crowd, depending on the night of the week. Thursday in particular seems open to anything. Call before you go.

**Madam Jo Jo's.** 8 Brewer St., W1. ☎ **0171/734-2473.** Cover £12.50–£22.50 ($20–$36). Open Mon–Sat 10pm–3:30am. Tube: Piccadilly Circus.

Tucked alongside Soho's most explicit girlie shows, Madame Jo Jo's also presents "girls"—more accurately described as drag queens. London's most popular transvestite showplace—an eye-popper with decadent Art Nouveau interior—has attracted film directors such as Stanley Kubrick, who filmed scenes from *Eyes Wide Shut*, starring Tom Cruise, here. Other celebrities, including Hugh Grant and Mick Jagger, have dropped in to check out Jo Jo's drag cabaret. Drag shows are Thursday through Saturday nights, with outside promoters organizing entertainment on other nights.

**Mars.** 12 Sutton Row, W1. ☎ **0171/439-4655.** Cover £5–£10 ($8–$16). Open Thurs 10pm–2am; Fri–Sat 11pm–5am. Tube: Tottenham Court Rd.

This large, stark dance club frequently goes gay and lesbian on certain nights of the week. Regardless of sexual preference, Mars is a hot planet for London's dance crowd. Thursday's "Speed" night is heavy on drum and bass; "Kitty Lips" transforms the club into London's hottest lesbian bar on Friday; and Saturday's "Naked" features house music. Occasionally there is a live band.

**Royal Vauxhall Tavern.** 372 Kennington Lane, SE11. ☎ **0171/582-0833.** Cover £2–£3 ($3.20–$4.80) Sat and Sun; no cover other times. Open Mon–Thurs 9pm–1am; Fri 10pm–2am; Sun 2–6pm and 7–10:30pm. Tube: Vauxhall.

Originally a 1880s vaudevillean pub frequented by London's East End working class, this place has long been a bastion of campy humor and wit. It has been a gay pub since the end of World War II. The tavern received a jolt of fame when—as legend has it—Queen Elizabeth's carriage broke down, and the monarch stopped in for a cup of tea. Since then, "Royal" has been gleefully affixed to the name, no doubt suiting the regular queens found here. Charington, one of the largest breweries in England, recently acquired this unabashedly gay pub.

Shaped like an amphitheater, the bar has a large stage area and gay themes on weekends. Friday nights are reserved for women only. Saturday is camp night, when the pub overflows with gay men fawning over their favorite cabaret acts and drag queens.

# 6 Windsor, Oxford & the Home Counties

The historical Thames Valley and Chiltern Hills can easily be reached from London by automobile, train, or Green Line coach. In fact, they are so close that you can explore this area during the day and return to London in time to see a West End show.

The most-visited historic site in England is **Windsor Castle,** 21 miles west of London. It is an especially popular day trip for visitors venturing out of London for the first time. If you base yourself in Windsor, you can spend another day exploring some of the sights on its periphery, including **Eton** (which adjoins Windsor), **Runnymede,** and **Savill Garden.**

If your visit coincides with the spring social sporting season, you can head to Ascot or Henley-on-Thames for the famous—and quintessentially British—social sporting events: **Ascot** and **The Royal Regatta.** Elegant headgear at these events is de rigueur. There are also some great historic homes and gardens in the area, including **Woburn Abbey, Hatfield House, Hughenden Manor, the Mapledurham House,** and the **Wellington Ducal Estate.** If your time is limited, the two most important country mansions to visit are Woburn Abbey, which takes a day to tour, and Hatfield House, which can be visited in a morning or afternoon.

It's not just the historic homes that make the Home Counties intriguing to visit; the land of river valleys and gentle, sweeping hills makes for wonderful drives. The beech-clad Chilterns are at their most beautiful in spring and autumn. The 40-mile chalk ridge extends in an arc from the Thames Valley to the old Roman city of St. Albans in Hertfordshire. The entire region is popular for boating holidays on its 200-mile network of canals.

The principal reason for visiting Oxfordshire is to explore the ancient and still magical university city of Oxford, about an hour's ride from London by car or train. It's not a good day trip, though, because there's so much to see and do. Plan to spend the night, and the following morning you can visit **Blenheim Palace,** England's answer to Versailles. Oxfordshire is also a land of great mansions, old churches of widely varying architectural styles, and rolling farmland.

In a sense, Oxfordshire serves as a kind of buffer zone between the easy living in the southern towns and the industrialized cities of the heartland. Southeast lie the chalky Chilterns, while in the west you'll move toward the wool towns of the Cotswolds. The upper Thames winds its way across the southern parts of the county.

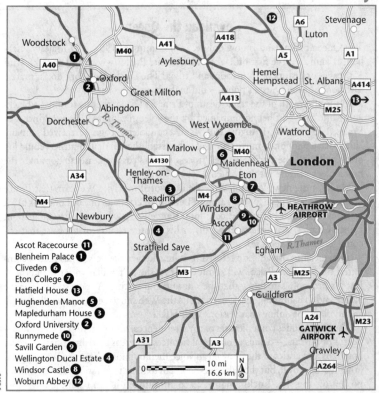

Ascot Racecourse **11**
Blenheim Palace **1**
Cliveden **6**
Eton College **7**
Hatfield House **13**
Hughenden Manor **5**
Mapledurham House **3**
Oxford University **2**
Runnymede **10**
Savill Garden **9**
Wellington Ducal Estate **4**
Windsor Castle **8**
Woburn Abbey **12**

0          10 mi
          16.6 km

## 1 Windsor & Eton

21 miles W of London

Windsor, the site of England's greatest castle and its most famous boys' school at adjoining Eton, was called "Windlesore" by the ancient Britons, who derived the name from winding shore—so noticeable as you walk along the Thames here.

Windsor might still be a charming Thames town to visit, were it not for the castle. But because it is home to the single most famous asset of the royal family, it is virtually overrun in summer by tourists who, unfortunately, obscure much of the town's charm. Windsor Castle remains Britain's second most visited historic building—attracting 1.2 million visitors a year—placing it second to the Tower of London.

The good news is that after the disastrous fire of 1992, things are on the mend—even though some of the new designs for Windsor Castle have been denigrated as a "Gothic shocker" and "ghastly." As work progresses, you'll have to decide for yourself. Actually, the restoration is quite remarkable, as young wood-carvers use ancient draw knives to smooth the 1,200 pound unseasoned oak beams, following the same techniques as did their predecessors in the Middle Ages. Gilders apply gold leaf, and plasterers form little flowers by hand, just as workers did 9 centuries ago when William the Conqueror started the castle.

### ESSENTIALS

**GETTING THERE**   The train from Waterloo or Paddington Station in London makes the trip in 30 minutes. The trip involves a transfer at Slough to the

## Download the Queen

The Queen of England is now online. In the spring of 1997, Her Majesty Elizabeth II launched the first official royal Web site (http://www.royal.gov.uk), with 150 pages of history, information, and trivia. The Duchess of York doesn't rate a mention, but the Queen's pooches did make it onto the net.

In the aftermath of the tragic death of Princess Diana, the site featured a black-and-white image of her accompanied by the solemn caption "Diana, Princess of Wales, 1 July 1961–31 August 1997" and a condolence page. It received so many "hits" that a temporary mirror site had to be established so that mourners could log on. It will surely be a while before Princess Diana's passing ceases to dominate the monarchy's venture into new media.

Much of the new Windsor Web site is devoted to trivia: We learn that Prince Philip uses a Metrocab for trips around London or else takes one of London's black taxis (even though his preference is for a Range Rover). Instead of scandal about Prince Charles, net surfers get details of his favorite charity or his trust that encourages start-up ventures.

The queen has steadfastly refused to state whether she herself has used a computer; Buckingham Palace will admit only that she is "familiar with the Internet." But it's probably safe to say that she's not up and surfing. A spokesperson for the palace said that although the Queen wants the Web site to be "user-friendly," there are no plans for online chat sessions with HRH.

The site includes color pictures of royal residences, historical tidbits, and even—horror of horrors!—details about royal finances. There is a "visitor's page," where both fans and critics of the Crown can voice their opinions about the Web site and other matters royal, but the palace doesn't plan to reply to questions and comments posted on the site. Buckingham Palace announced it can't handle any more communiqués than the 200 to 300 letters a day the Queen already receives.

Though London tabloids heralded the queen's getting wired, her Web site is more educational and PR-oriented than tantalizing. Buckingham Palace claims it's the royal family's way of making the monarchy "more accessible." If the Palace really wants to reach a larger and younger audience—and opinion polls show that British youth care much less about the House of Windsor than their parents do—the Queen might have to do better than a tame Web site, in this day and age. Perhaps an all-night Royal Rave?

Slough-Windsor shuttle train. There are more than a dozen trains per day; the fare is £6.20 ($9.90). Call British Rail at ☎ **0171/262-6767** for more information.

Green Line coaches (☎ **0181/668-7261**) nos. 700 and 702 from Hyde Park Corner in London take about 1¹/₂ hours. A same-day round-trip costs £4.35 to £5.50 ($6.95 to $8.80).

By car from London, take M4 west.

**VISITOR INFORMATION**   A **Tourist Information Centre** is located across from Windsor Castle on High Street (☎ **01753/852010**). There's also an information booth in the tourist center at Windsor Coach Park. Both are open Easter through September daily from 10am to 4pm.

**GETTING AROUND**   The bus will drop you near the Town Guildhall, to which Sir Christopher Wren applied the finishing touches. It's only a short walk up Castle Hill to the top sights.

**Impressions**

*This town, whose name my family bears, is very dear to me. Indeed I regard it as home in a way no other place can be.*

—Princess Elizabeth (1947)

## ✪ WINDSOR CASTLE

When William the Conqueror ordered a castle built on this spot, he began a legend and a link with English sovereignty that has known many vicissitudes: King John cooled his heels at Windsor while waiting to put his signature on the Magna Carta at nearby Runnymede; Charles I was imprisoned here before losing his head; Queen Bess did some noted renovations; Victoria mourned her beloved Albert, who died at the castle in 1861; and the royal family rode out much of World War II behind its sheltering walls. When Queen Elizabeth II is in residence, the royal standard flies. With 1,000 rooms, Windsor is the world's largest inhabited castle.

The apartments display many works of art, porcelain, armor, furniture, three Verrio ceilings, and several 17th-century Gibbons carvings. Several works by Rubens adorn the King's Drawing Room; in the relatively small King's Dressing Room is a Dürer, along with Rembrandt's portrait of his mother, and van Dyck's triple portrait of Charles I. Of the apartments, the grand reception room, with its Gobelin tapestries, is the most spectacular.

In November 1992, a fire swept through part of Windsor Castle, severely damaging it and sending shock waves across Britain. The castle has since reopened, and all the rooms that were once open to the public should be available for viewing in 1998.

**TICKETS & INFORMATION**  Admission is £9.80 ($15.70) for adults, £7.20 ($11.50) for students and seniors, £5.60 ($8.95) for children 16 and under, and £22.50 ($36) for a family of four. The castle is open March through October daily from 10am to 5pm; November through February daily from 10am to 4pm. Ticket sales cease about one hour before closing; last admissions are 1 hour before closing. Closed periods are in April, June, and December when the royal family is in residence. It's always advisable to call ahead and check what's open before visiting. For information, call ☎ **01753/868286.**

### THE CHANGING OF THE GUARD

We find the Windsor changing of the guard a much more exciting and moving experience than the London exercises. In Windsor the guard marches through town when the Queen is in residence, stopping the traffic as it wheels into the castle to the tune of a full regimental band; when the queen is not here, a drum-and-pipe band is mustered up. From May to August, the ceremony takes place Monday through Saturday at 11am. In winter, the guard is changed every 48 hours, Monday through Saturday. It's best to call ☎ **01753/868286** to find out which days the ceremony will take place.

### QUEEN MARY'S DOLL'S HOUSE

A palace in perfect miniature, the Doll's House was given to Queen Mary in 1923 as a symbol of national goodwill. The house, designed by Sir Edwin Lutyens, was created on a scale of 1 to 12. It took 3 years to complete and involved the work of 1,500 tradesmen and artists. Every item is a miniature masterpiece; each room is exquisitely furnished and every item is made exactly to scale. Working elevators stop on every floor, and there is running water in all five bathrooms. There's electric lighting throughout the house.

Castle tickets include admission here. Open same days and hours as Windsor Castle (see above). For information, call ☎ **01753/831118.**

## ✪ ST. GEORGE'S CHAPEL

A gem of the Perpendicular style, this chapel shares the distinction, along with Westminster Abbey, of being a pantheon of English monarchs (Victoria is a notable exception). The present St. George's was founded in the late 15th century by Edward IV on the site of the original Chapel of the Order of the Garter (Edward III, 1348). You first enter the nave, which has fan vaulting (a remarkable achievement in English architecture); it contains the tomb of George V and Queen Mary, designed by Sir William Reid Dick. Off the nave in the Urswick Chapel, the Princess Charlotte memorial provides an ironic touch; if she had survived childbirth in 1817, she—and not her cousin Victoria—would have ruled the British Empire. In the aisle are tombs of George VI and Edward IV. The Edward IV "Quire," with its imaginatively carved 15th-century choir stalls (crowned by lacy canopies and Knights of the Garter banners), evokes the pomp and pageantry of medieval days. In the center is a flat tomb, containing the vault of the beheaded Charles I, along with Henry VIII and his third wife, Jane Seymour. Finally, you may want to inspect the Prince Albert Memorial Chapel, which reflects the opulent tastes of the Victorian era.

Admission is included in admission to Windsor Castle. Open Monday to Saturday from 10am to 4pm, Sunday 2 to 3:45 or 4pm; closed during services, January, and a few days in mid-June.

# ETON

Eton is home to arguably the most famous public school (Americans would call it the opposite, a private school) in the world. For decades the scions of British aristocrats—England's budding business and political leaders—have had their knuckles slapped by their headmasters. From Windsor Castle's ramparts, you can look down on the river and on the famous playing fields of Eton.

You can take a train from Paddington Station, go by car, or take the Green Line coach to Windsor. By car, take the M4 motorway to Exit 5 to go straight to Eton. Since parking is usually a problem, we advise turning off M4 at Exit 6 to Windsor; you can park here and take an easy stroll past Windsor Castle and across the Thames Bridge. Follow Eton High Street to the college.

## EXPLORING ETON COLLEGE

Eton College (☎ **01753/671177**) was founded by 18-year-old Henry VI, in 1440. Some of England's greatest men, notably the duke of Wellington, played on these fields. Twenty prime ministers were educated here, as well as such literary figures as George Orwell, Aldous Huxley, Ian Fleming, and Percy Bysshe Shelley, who, during his years at Eton (from 1804 to 1810), was called "Mad Shelley" or "Shelley the Atheist" by his fellow pupils. If it's open, take a look at the Perpendicular chapel, with its 15th-century paintings and reconstructed fan vaulting.

The history of Eton College since its inception in 1440 is depicted in the **Museum of Eton Life,** Eton College (☎ **01753/671177**), located in vaulted wine cellars under College Hall, which were originally the storehouse for use of the college's masters. The displays, ranging from formal to extremely informal, include a turn-of-the-century boy's room, schoolbooks, sports trophies, canes used by senior boys to apply punishment they felt needful to their juniors, and birch sticks used by masters for the same purpose. Also on view are letters written home by students describing day-to-day life at the school, as well as samples of the numerous magazines produced by students over the centuries, known as ephemera because of the changing writers and ideas. Former Etonians contributed much of the memorabilia.

Admission to the school and museum costs £2.50 ($4) for adults. You can also take guided tours for £3.50 ($5.60). Eton College is open from March 22 to April 16 and June 28 to September 2, daily from 10:30am to 4:30pm; April 17 to June 27 and September 3 to October 5, daily from 2 to 4:30pm. However, it may close for special occasions.

## MORE TO SEE IN & AROUND WINDSOR

The town of Windsor is largely Victorian, with lots of brick buildings and a few remnants of Georgian architecture. In and around the castle are two cobblestone streets, Church and Market, which have antique shops, silversmiths, and pubs. One shop on Church Street was supposedly occupied by Nell Gwynne, who—no doubt for state reasons—needed to be within call of Charles II's chambers. After lunch or tea, you may want to stroll along the 3-mile, aptly named Long Walk.

On Sunday, there are often polo matches in Windsor Great Park and at Ham Common. You may see Prince Charles playing and Prince Philip serving as umpire while the queen watches. The park is the site of the queen's occasional equestrian jaunts. On Sunday she attends church near the Royal Lodge. Traditionally, she prefers to drive herself here, later returning to the castle for Sunday lunch.

**Savill Garden,** Wick Lane, Englefield Green, Egham, Surrey (☎ **01753/860222**), is in Windsor Great Park and is signposted from Windsor, Egham, and Ascot. Started in 1932, the 35-acre garden is one of the finest of its type in the Northern Hemisphere. The display starts in spring with rhododendrons, camellias, and daffodils beneath the trees; then throughout the summer there are spectacular displays of flowers and shrubs presented in a natural and wild state. It's open daily all year (except at Christmas) from 10am to 6pm (to 4pm in winter); admission is £3.50 ($5.60) for adults, free for children 15 and under. It's 5 miles from Windsor along A30; turn off at Wick Road and follow the signs to the gardens. The nearest rail station is at Egham; from here you'll need to take a taxi a distance of 3 miles. There's a licensed, self-service restaurant on the premises.

Adjoining the Savill Garden are the Valley Gardens, full of shrubs and trees in a series of wooded natural valleys running down to the water. It's open daily throughout the year. Entrance to the gardens is free, although parking your car costs £3 ($4.80) per vehicle.

### FROGMORE: THE RESTING PLACE OF QUEEN VICTORIA & PRINCE ALBERT

Queen Victoria died on January 22, 1901, and was buried beside her beloved Prince Albert in a mausoleum at Frogmore (a private estate), a mile from Windsor. The prince consort died in December 1861. The house, gardens, and mausoleum are only open a few days out of the year, usually in May and August, from around 10am to 6pm. The cost for adults is £5 ($8), seniors pay £4 ($6.40). Call ☎ **01753/868286**, ext. 2235 for more details.

### LEGOLAND

On the B3022 Bracknell/Ascot Road, outside Windsor, this 150-acre theme park opened in 1996, based on the one in Denmark. Although a bit corny and not in the class of Denmark's Tivoli, it's a nostalgia trip for parents and fun for the entire family—although for anything but a small family, it could be a budget-buster. Attractions, spread across five main activity centers, include the Duplo Gardens, offering a boat ride, puppet theater, and water works, plus a Miniland, showing European cities or villages re-created in minute detail from millions of Lego bricks. The "Enchanted Forest" has treasure trails, a castle, and animals created from Lego bricks. For reservations and information, call ☎ **01990/040404.** The park is open daily from March through October. Admission costs £15 ($24) for adults, £12 ($19.20) children 3 to 15 (free for 2 and under).

## RUNNYMEDE

Three miles south of Windsor is the 188-acre meadow on the south side of the Thames, in Surrey, where it's believed that King John put his seal on the Great Charter after intense pressure from his feudal barons and lords. Today, Runnymede is also the site of the John F. Kennedy Memorial, an acre of English ground given to the United States by the people of Britain. The memorial, a large block of white stone, is hard to see from the road but is clearly signposted and reached after a short walk. The pagoda that shelters it was placed here by the American Bar Association to acknowledge the fact that American law stems from the English system.

The historic site, to which there is free access all year, lies beside the Thames, half a mile west of the hamlet of Old Windsor on the south side of the A308. If you're driving on the M25, exit at Junction 13. The nearest rail connection is at Egham, half a mile away. Trains depart from London's Waterloo Station, and take about 25 minutes.

## BUS & BOAT TOURS, HORSE RIDES & GUIDED WALKS OF WINDSOR

The tourist office can put you in touch with a Blue Badge (i.e., official) guide to lead you on a walking tour of town. These trained local guides cost £45 ($72) per hour—so if you're interested, get together a group to split the cost. Advance booking is essential.

You can also take a 30-minute carriage ride up the sycamore-lined length of Windsor Castle's Long Walk. Horses with their carriages and drivers line up beside the castle waiting for fares charging about £20 ($32) for up to four passengers.

Boat tours depart from Windsor's main embarkation point along Windsor Promenade, Barry Avenue, for a 35-minute round-trip to Boveney Lock. The cost is £2.90 ($4.65) for adults, half price for children. You can also take a 2-hour tour through the Boveney Lock and up past stately private riverside homes, the Bray Film Studios, Queens Eyot, and Monkey Island, for £4.80 ($7.70) for adults, half price for children. There's also a 35-minute tour from Runnymede on board the *Lucy Fisher,* a replica of a Victorian paddle steamer. You pass Magna Carta Island, among other sights. This tour costs £2.90 ($4.65) for adults, half price for children. In addition, longer tours between Maidenhead and Hampton Court are offered. The boats offer light refreshments and have a well-stocked bar, plus the decks are covered in case of an unexpected shower. Tours in the King's English are given by **French Brothers Ltd.,** Clewer Boathouse, Clewer Court Road, Windsor (☎ **01753/851900**).

## SHOPPING

A colorful, traditional English perfumery, **Woods of Windsor,** Queen Charlotte Street (☎ **01753/868125**), dates from 1770. It stocks a bundle of soaps, shampoos and oils, scented drawer liners, and hand and body lotions, all prettily packaged in pastel flowers and bright old-fashioned wraps. At **The Token House,** High Street (☎ **01753/863263**), you'll find the largest gathering of everyone's favorite china and crystal, but **The Reject China Shop** across the street has items that sell for less.

At **Billings & Edmonds,** 132 High St., Eton (☎ **01753/861348**), you may think you've blundered into a time warp. This distinctive clothing store offers excellent traditional tailoring, suits made to order, and a complete line of cuff links, shirts, ties, and accessories. If you always wanted your kid to look like a prince, English school clothes reflecting the look of early public schools include outfits for boys and girls from age 2 to 18, from school uniforms to shirts, shorts, and gowns for college. The store's other branches carry similar goods.

**Asquith's Teddy Bear Shop,** 33 High St., Eton (☎ **01753/861348**), has every bear imaginable, including Winnie, Paddington, Rupert (a cartoon character in the *Daily Express* 75 years ago), and German Speiss. Bear clothes from dungarees to Eton college uniforms mix with tinware and hatboxes covered in teddy bear prints.

## WHERE TO STAY IN THE WINDSOR AREA

You might opt to make Windsor your base for London sightseeing. Trains leave London as late as 10:30 or 11pm, so it's quite easy to take in an early theater and dinner before returning to Windsor for the night. During the Ascot races and Windsor Horse Show, reservations are necessary far in advance.

### Doubles for Less Than £45.

✪ **Alma House.** 56 Alma Rd., Windsor, Berkshire SL4 3HA. ☎ **01753/862983.** Fax 01753/ 855620. 4 rms, 2 with bath. TV TEL. £28 ($44.80) single without bath; £38 ($60.80) double without bath, £45 ($71.10) double with bath. All rates include English breakfast. No credit cards.

A 5-minute walk south of Windsor Castle, the Alma House is a well-built Victorian guest house that has been managed by the same family since the early 1980s. Many original features of the structure have been retained, including the spacious rooms. Hostess Sally Shipp is known around the world by the many satisfied customers who have stayed here. Many guests spend the night here before making the 20-minute drive to Heathrow for an early-morning departure.

**Mrs. Bronwyn Hughes.** 62 Queen Rd., Windsor, Berkshire SL4 3BH. ☎ **01753/866036.** 4 rms, 2 with bath. TV. £20 ($32) single with or without bath; £36 ($57.60) double without bath, £40 ($64) double with bath. Family rm suitable for up to 3 adults and 3 children, £20 ($32) per adult plus £7.50 ($12) per child. All rates include breakfast. No credit cards.

Your hostess in this sprawling Victorian home is Mrs. Bronwyn Hughes, a former cabin attendant with British Airways, who knows how to make newcomers feel comfortable in her well-furnished bedrooms. Built of brick in 1898, in a position within a 10-minute walk from Windsor Castle, it boasts easy access for guests to cooking facilities, and a well-accessorized layout that's among the most comfortable of any B&B hotel within its price category. No meals are served other than breakfast.

### Doubles for Less Than £65

**Fairlight Lodge.** 41 Frances Rd., Windsor, Berkshire SL4 3AQ. ☎ **01753/861207.** Fax 01753/865963. 10 rms. TV TEL. £47–£53 ($75.20–$84.80) single; £63–£75 ($100.80–$120) double; £90 ($144) family rm for 2 adults and 2 children. All rates include English breakfast. AE, MC, V.

Built in 1885 as the home of the mayor of Windsor, this highly rated B&B in a residential section is only a few minutes' walk south of the heart of Windsor and the castle. Small and privately owned, it has a distinctive warmth and character. The comfortable bedrooms have coffee-making facilities and radio; two rooms have large four-poster beds. The fully licensed Garden Restaurant serves traditional English meals from 7 to 9pm; prices begin at £8.80 ($14.10) for a three-courser. The restaurant also caters to vegetarians and special diets.

**Langton House.** 46 Alma Rd., Windsor, Berkshire SL4 3HA. ☎ **01753/858299.** 3 rms, all with bath. TV. £30 ($48) single; £50 ($80) double. All rates include breakfast. No credit cards.

Set in a quiet residential neighborhood, a 5-minute walk northeast from Windsor Castle, this private home exudes an international flavor acquired by the owners, Mr. and Mrs. Roy Fogg, during his long-term career with British Airways. Built of dark red brick in the 1860s, and adapted for use as a private home from its long-ago role as a nursing home, it offers a trio of well-scrubbed bedrooms on the building's upstairs, interconnected via a hallway-sitting area and a small communal kitchen with tea-making facilities. Bedrooms are larger—in two out of the three cases, much larger—than you might have expected. Each is simply but cozily furnished, with a private bath.

**Suffolk Lodge.** 4 Bolton Ave., Windsor, Berkshire SL4 3JB. ☎ **01753/864186.** Fax 01753/862640. 4 rms. TV TEL. £52 ($83.20) double; £26 ($41.60) extra adult; £13 ($20.80) per child. All rates include English breakfast. MC, V.

Situated on a quiet tree-lined avenue, this B&B is an especially good choice for families. It is a detached Victorian house with private parking. The castle, river, and train station are all within a 10-minute walk, and Legoland is nearby. All rooms have a clock radio, hot beverage facilities, a hair dryer, and a trouser press. In addition, there's a large, heated indoor pool and a full-size snooker table for entertainment.

# WHERE TO EAT

**Clairmont Coffee.** 5 High St. ☎ **01753/621082.** Main courses £1.30–£2.10 ($2.10–$3.35). MC, V. Daily 8:30am–6pm. DELI.

On your way back from seeing Windsor Castle, you might want to stop here for a light lunch or a gourmet coffee. Rest your feet while enjoying a "toastie"—your choice of toppings on white or wheat bread, toasted and served open-faced. The coffeehouse also serves a variety of sandwiches, including vegetarian choices such as avocado and cress on a French baguette. Of course, there are many coffees and teas to choose from, along with croissants, danishes, and cakes to satisfy your sweet tooth.

✪ **The Court Jester.** Church Lane. ☎ **01753/864257.** Bar snacks £3–£6.50 ($4.80–$10.40). MC, V. May–Sept, daily 11:30am–3pm and 6–9:30pm; Oct–Apr, daily 11:30am–2:30pm. Pub: Mon–Sat 11am–11pm; Sun noon–5pm. ENGLISH.

Housed in a 1790s building, this is one of the town's most popular pubs, especially with young people in the evening, when loud music plays. No evening meals are offered, but the traditional pub snacks during the day include hot dishes in winter and an extensive buffet in the summer. A wide range of English ales is served. It's located directly south from the fortification of Windsor Castle and is patronized by many of the household staff and security guards who work there.

**Drury House Restaurant.** 4 Church St. ☎ **01753/863734.** Reservations required. Fixed-price menus £5.95–£7.95 ($9.50–$12.70). No credit cards. Daily 10am–5:30pm. Bus: 704. ENGLISH.

Owner Joan Hearne states with pride that all luncheons served in this wood-paneled 17th-century restaurant are home-cooked "and very English." A visit here could be included in a tour of Windsor Castle, which is only a stone's throw away. A typical meal might include soup, meat, vegetables, and dessert. A refreshing tea is also served, with either homemade scones with jam and freshly whipped cream, or freshly made cream cakes.

**Eton Wine Bar.** 82–83 High St., Eton. ☎ **01753/854921.** Reservations recommended. Main courses £7.50–£12.50 ($12–$20); 2-course dinner £9.95 ($15.90). AE, DC, MC, V. Mon–Sat noon–2:30pm and 6–11pm; Sun noon–2:45pm and 7–10:30pm. FRENCH/ENGLISH/CONTINENTAL.

Just across the bridge from Windsor, this charming place is located on Eton's main street, among the antique shops. It's furnished with pine tables and old church pews and chairs, and there's a small garden out back. Begin with one of the well-prepared soups, or a smoked salmon and artichoke tart. Main dishes include pine nut and spinach risotto topped with pecorino cheese and rack of lamb with a herb crust served with potatoes and vegetables. For dessert, try the pecan pie with cinnamon ice cream or the white and dark chocolate terrine with raspberry coulis. Wine can be ordered by the glass, in half bottles, or in full bottles.

**Jake's.** 10 High St. ☎ **01753/832222.** Reservations recommended. Main courses £7.50–£12.50 ($12–$20). AE, MC, V. Mon–Sat noon–2:30pm and 6–11pm. ENGLISH/INTERNATIONAL.

On the second floor of a building whose ground floor contains the also-recommended Uncle Sam's Steak house, this restaurant is quieter, calmer, and less theme-oriented than its downstairs neighbor. Its sophisticated owner, South Africa–born Jan van Kralingen, maintains a pastel-colored eyrie accented with floral watercolors. Seating is available both at booths and conventional tables (for people-watching). Dishes are both original and fresh, and include such starters as a warm French bean salad with bacon, goat cheese, and oyster mushrooms; and seared Scottish salmon on a chive and potato cake with tomato coulis. Main courses include smoked haddock and herb-flavored fish cakes with a light curry and mussel sauce, or char-grilled shoulder of lamb with black olive cous cous and Mediterranean vegetables.

**Monty's Riverside Restaurant.** Windsor Bridge, Eton. ☎ **01753/860914.** Main courses £8.50–£13 ($13.60–$20.80); fixed-price meal £10.50 ($16.80) at lunch (Mon–Fri only), £16.50 ($26.40) at dinner. AE, DC, MC, V. Daily 11am–3:30pm and 6–11pm. Apr–Oct, cream teas daily 3–6pm. ENGLISH.

This restaurant lies on the Eton side of the river at Windsor Bridge adjacent to the college boat houses and overlooking Windsor Castle. Tables have river views. The chef specializes in fish, including mackerel, lobster, crab, prawns, scallops, and sea bass, brought in fresh daily from the southern and eastern coastal markets. Vegetarian dishes are featured, along with beef courses such as prime Scottish sirloin steak or rack of lamb.

**Slug and Lettuce Pub.** 5 Thames St. ☎ **01753/864405.** Reservations not accepted. Main courses £4.50–£8.75 ($7.20–$14). AE, DC, MC, V. Daily 10am–10:45pm. ENGLISH.

Had this pub existed during the Middle Ages, soldiers from Windsor Castle directly across the street could probably have thrown spears down from their battlements upon the drinkers inside. There's little fear of that today, however, since a member of a nationwide chain (Slug and Lettuce) took over this antique, stone-fronted building. The decor is appropriately dark, antique-looking, and rustic, and includes a busy bar area with an adjacent dining area that serves breakfast from 10am to noon, followed by ongoing lunches or dinners that are offered without interruption from noon until closing. Don't ask for a burger here as an accompaniment to the roster of English and French lagers and ales: Fare is staunchly British, and includes such staples as bangers and mash, steak-and-kidney pie, and steaks, as well as such more esoteric fare as grilled swordfish, steamed mussels in white wine sauce, and supreme of chicken. You'll find a baffling array of English ales on tap, but if in doubt, you can't go wrong with either a Spitfire (to keep that English war theme going) or a Master Brew.

**Thai Castle Restaurant.** 12 Thames St. ☎ **01753/842186.** Reservations recommended. Main courses £5–£7 ($8–$11.20). AE, MC, V. Daily noon–2:30pm and 6:30–11pm. THAI.

Close to the castle, on Windsor's main street near Eton Bridge, this is a welcome change from too constant a diet of British food. Thai cuisine is prepared by Bangkok-born staff who understand both the subtle and fiery nuances of their native dishes. Amid a decor of exposed brick and Thai art, you can enjoy such dishes as satay (marinated chicken or beef grilled on bamboo skewers), minced pork in flaky pastry served with sweet-and-sour sauce, Thai-style fisherman's soup loaded with spices, stir-fried beef with oysters and both red and green peppers, and a wide selection of flavorful prawn, noodle, and seafood dishes. The menu caters to vegetarian palates as well, including a hot-and-sour Thai salad with peanuts and tomatoes, and fresh seasonal vegetables stir-fried in a curry sauce. Dessert might be a banana fritter or coconut ice cream.

**Uncle Sam's American Steak House.** 10 High St. ☎ **01753/866655.** Reservations recommended. Main courses £5–£13 ($8–$20.80). No credit cards. Daily noon–11pm. AMERICAN.

Despite its location near the castle on one of the most English streets in Britain, on the ground floor of a building whose upper level contains the also-recommended Jake's, this restaurant caters wholeheartedly to a resolutely American concept of dining out. The Hollywood/Broadway/Wild West–style bar is adorned with posters of Hollywood's cinematic legends (Marilyn M., Robert de Niro). Menu items in the sometimes boisterous and consciously rustic dining area include juicy versions of 10 kinds of burgers, milk shakes inspired by an American drugstore of long ago, pastas such as spaghetti, and thick, juicy steaks. If you feel guilty afterwards, you could always have fish and chips for breakfast!

**William IV Pub.** 1 Datchet Rd. (at the corner of Thames St., 75 yds. from Eton Bridge). ☎ **01753/851004.** Bar snacks £2–£5 ($3.20–$8). No credit cards. Daily noon–2pm. Pub: Mon–Sat 11am–11pm; Sun noon–10:30pm. ENGLISH.

Although originally built as an inn in 1557, the William IV now functions only as a pub (one of the busiest in town) and a simple lunch-only restaurant. With ceiling beams and a log-burning fireplace, it contains at least three different drinking areas and a busy stand-up countertop where customers place lunchtime food orders. One regular (and legendary) client was Sir Christopher Wren, the great architect of St. Paul's Cathedral, whose house (which he designed and which today functions as an elegant hotel) is located across the street. Other clients of yesteryear included diarists Evelyn and Pepys. The food is simple, home-cooked pub fare, which you can eat at a sidewalk table near the Eton Bridge, while gazing up at the famous castle.

## 2  Henley-on-Thames & The Royal Regatta

35 miles W of London

At the eastern edge of Oxfordshire, Henley-on-Thames, a small town and resort on the river at the foothills of the Chilterns, is the headquarters of the ✪ **Royal Regatta** held annually in late June and early July. Henley, beside a stretch of the Thames that's known for its calm waters, unobstructed bottom, and predictable currents, is like Mecca to rowers. The challenging and entertaining regatta, which dates back to the first years of Victoria's reign, is the major competition among international oarspeople.

The Elizabethan buildings, tearooms, and inns along the town's High Street live up to one's expectations of an English country town. Cardinal Wolsey is said to have ordered the building of the tower of the Perpendicular and Decorated parish church.

Henley-on-Thames is an excellent stopover en route to Oxford. However, lodgings are much less expensive in Oxford; the fashionable inns of Henley-on-Thames (Charles I slept here) are far from cheap.

## ESSENTIALS

**GETTING THERE**   Trains depart from London's Paddington Station but require a change at the junction in Twyford. More than 20 trains make the journey daily; the trip takes about an hour.

About 10 buses depart every day from London's Victoria Coach Station for Henley. Because the bus makes multiple stops, the trip takes about 1 $3/4$ hours. There is no Sunday service in winter.

If you're driving from London, take M4 toward Reading to Junction 819, then drive northwest on A4130.

**VISITOR INFORMATION**   A Tourist Information Centre is at Town Hall, Market Place (☎ **01491/578034**). Open daily from 10am to 7pm; in winter, the center closes at 4pm.

## THE HENLEY ROYAL REGATTA

The Henley Royal Regatta, held during the first week in July, is one of the country's premier racing events. If you want a closeup view from the Stewards' Enclosure, you'll need a guest badge, which is only obtainable through a member. In other words, you have to know someone to obtain special privileges, but admission to the Regatta Enclosure is open to all. Information is available from the Secretary, Henley Royal Regatta, Henley-on-Thames, Oxfordshire RG9 2LY (☎ **01491/572153**).

During the annual 5-day event, up to 100 races are organized each day, with starts scheduled as frequently as every 5 minutes. This event is open only to all-male crews of up to nine at a time. In late June, rowing events for women are held at the 3-day Henley Women's Regatta.

If you want a closer view of the waters of the Thames, even when no regattas are being held, stop by the town's largest and oldest marine outfitter: **Hobbs & Sons, Ltd.,** Station Road Boathouse (☎ **01491/572035**), established in 1870. Their armada of watercraft includes rowboats, which rent for between £6.50 and £9 ($10.40 and $14.40) per hour. On the premises, a chandlery shop sells virtually anything a boat crew could need as well as souvenir items like straw boater's hats and commemorative T-shirts.

## WHERE TO STAY IN THE AREA

✪ **Lenwade Guest House.** 3 Western Rd., Henley-on-Thames, Oxfordshire RG9 IJL. ☎ **01491/573468.** Fax 01491/573468. 3 rms, 2 with bath. TV. £38–£40 ($60.80–$64) double without bath, £42–£45 ($67.20–$72) double with bath. All rates include English breakfast. No credit cards.

As you enter from the small courtyard filled with flowering vines and lush foliage, you'll be greeted by the sight of a 5-foot stained-glass window thought to depict Joan of Arc. Also among the many details that makes this place memorable is the large, winding staircase with its original pine spindles and handrails. The individually decorated rooms are all twins and doubles and contain hot and cold running water and hot-beverage-making facilities. Built in the early 1900s, this Victorian, semidetached guest house is owned and operated by Jacquie and John Williams. Although breakfast is the only meal served, there are plenty of pubs and restaurants close by.

**Shepherds.** Rotherfield Greys, Henley-on-Thames, Oxfordshire RG9 4QL. ☎ **01491/628413.** 3 or 4 rms (depending on circumstances). £23 ($36.80) single; £40–£50 ($64–$80) double. All rates include English breakfast. No credit cards. Closed 1 week at Christmas.

Originally constructed way back in the mid-1600s, this building's recorded history began in 1726 when it was acquired and enlarged by the ancestors of its present owner, Susan Fulford-Dobson. Set amid 8 acres of parklands (six of which are devoted to boarding horses), the building is a creeper-covered country home whose gables face a village green about 3 miles northwest of Henley. A reception area is comfortably furnished with antiques and English country accessories. The bedrooms have chintz curtains, tea- and coffee-making equipment, hair dryers, and, in some cases, TVs. Reductions are offered for stays of 3 nights or more.

# WHERE TO EAT

**Argyll.** 15 Market Place. ☎ **01491/573400.** Buffet lunch £3.10–£4.50 ($4.95–$7.20); Sun lunch £4.95 ($7.90). V. Mon–Sat 11am–midnight; Sun noon–10:30pm. BRITISH.

This very Scottish pub, complete with tartan carpeting and framed prints of Scottish soldiers, is a popular lunch spot with locals. The homemade meals are the main attraction here; Steve and Denise Lothian serve hearty portions of steak-and-kidney pie, shepherd's pie, and other favorites. On Sundays, there's a traditional roast pork or beef lunch, served with vegetables, salads, and desserts.

**The Flower Pot.** Aston, near Henley-on-Thames, Oxfordshire RG9 3DG. ☎ **01491/574721.** Reservations recommended for dinner. Main courses £5.50–£9.50 ($8.80–$15.20). MC, V. Mon–Sat noon–2pm and 6:30–9pm; Sun noon–2pm. Pub: Mon–Sat 11am–11pm; Sun noon–3pm and 7–10:30pm. ENGLISH.

Although it rents a quartet of simple bedrooms on its second floor, this establishment is more famous for its pub and dining facilities than for its accommodations. It's the most important and visible building in Aston, a rural hamlet 2 miles southeast of Henley just off the A423 Henley-Maidenhead road. Built around 1870, the Flower Pot retains much of the Victorian atmosphere of its original construction despite many renovations (the most recent occurred in 1993). The pub grub is far above standard and includes poultry, poached salmon with dill sauce, fish pie, and pan-fried trout.

Two of the four upstairs bedrooms have private bathrooms, and all have TVs. Including an English breakfast, a single without bath costs £33 ($52.80), rising to £39 ($62.40) with bath. A double without bath rents for £41 ($65.60), going up to £49 ($78.40) with bath.

Come here to eat or stay if you appreciate earthy, unpretentious, and straightforward atmosphere that represents honest value.

**The Little Angel.** Remenham Lane, Remenham. ☎ **01491/574165.** Main courses £5.50–£17 ($8.80–$27.20); bar meals from £10 ($16). AE, DC, MC, V. Mon–Sat 11am–2:30pm and 6–10pm; Sun noon–2:30pm. Closed evenings in winter. ENGLISH.

This historic pub was built in the mid-1700s and is today said to be the haunt of the ghost of Mary Blandy, who was hanged on a murder charge. It's a quarter mile east of the center of Henley-on-Thames, beside the London-Henley highway. You can enjoy simple meals in the pub or more elaborate fare in one of two different dining rooms. The establishment features an ale brewed right in Henley (its name is Brakspear's) and is known for its copious quantities of unflinchingly English food. This might include roast beef with Yorkshire pudding, farmer's pie, chicken-and-leek pie, smoked Scottish salmon, and Dover sole in lemon butter. In fair weather, guests enjoy sitting at outdoor tables. In winter the setting is warm and cozy, with softly flickering candles, ceiling beams, and a series of intimate alcoves.

## 3  Oxford: The City of Dreaming Spires

54 miles NW of London; 54 miles SE of Coventry

Oxford, home to one of the greatest universities in the world, is many things: A walk down the long sweep of The High, one of the most striking streets in England; a mug of cider in one of the old student pubs; the sound of May Day dawn, when choristers sing in Latin from Magdalen Tower; the Great Tom bell from Tom Tower, whose 101 peals traditionally signal the closing of the college gates; towers and spires that rise majestically; barges on the upper reaches of the Thames; nude swimming at Parson's Pleasure; the roar of a cannon launching bumping races; a tiny, dusty bookstall where you can pick up a valuable first edition.

Romantic Oxford is still here, but to find it, you'll have to wade through the bustling and crowded city that is also Oxford. You may be surprised by the never-ending stream of polluting buses and the fast-flowing pedestrian traffic—the city core sometimes feels more like London than once-sleepy Oxford. Surrounding the university are suburbs that keep growing, and not in a particularly attractive manner.

At any time of the year, you can enjoy a tour of the colleges, many of which represent an apex of England's architectural kingdom and Victorian contributions. The Oxford Tourist Information Centre (see below) offers guided walking tours daily throughout the year. Comparisons with Cambridge, the *other* university town, are inevitable: Oxford is better known for the arts, Cambridge more for the sciences.

Despite the age of the university, the city predates it—in fact, it was a Saxon town in the early part of the 10th century. By the 12th century, Oxford was growing in reputation as a seat of learning, at the expense of Paris, and the first colleges were founded in the 13th century. The story of Oxford is filled with conflicts too complex and detailed to elaborate here. Suffice to say, the relationship between town and gown wasn't always as peaceful as it is today. Riots often flared, and both sides were guilty of abuses. Nowadays, the young people of Oxford take out their aggressiveness in sporting competitions.

Ultimately, the test of a great university lies in the caliber of the people it turns out. Oxford can name-drop a mouthful: Roger Bacon, Sir Walter Raleigh, John Donne, Sir Christopher Wren, Samuel Johnson, Edward Gibbon, William Penn, John Wesley, William Pitt, Matthew Arnold, Lewis Carroll, Arnold Toynbee, Harold Macmillan, Graham Greene, A. E. Housman, T. E. Lawrence, Emma Thompson, and many others.

## ESSENTIALS

**GETTING THERE**   Trains from Paddington Station reach Oxford in 1¼ hours. Service every hour. A cheap, same-day round-trip ticket costs £12.40 ($19.85). For more information, call **British Rail** at ☎ **0171/262-6767.**

**Oxford CityLink** provides coach service from London's Victoria Station (☎ **0171/824-0056**) to the Oxford Bus Station. Coaches usually depart about every 20 minutes during the day; the trip takes approximately 1¾ hours. A same-day round-trip ticket costs £6.50 ($10.40).

If you're driving, take M40 west from London and just follow the signs. Traffic and parking are a disaster in Oxford, and not just during rush hours. However, there are four large "Park and Ride" parking lots on the north, south, east, and west of the city's ring road, all well marked. Parking is free at all times, but a round-trip bus ride into the city center costs £1.10 ($1.75). In the heart of Oxford, you're taken by bus to St. Aldate's Cornmarket or Queen Street. The buses run every 8 to 10 minutes in each direction. There is no service on Sunday. The parking lots are on the Woodstock road near the Peartree traffic circle, on the Botley road toward Farringdon, on the Abingdon road in the southeast, and on A40 toward London.

**VISITOR INFORMATION**   The **Oxford Tourist Information Centre** is at Gloucester Green, opposite the bus station (☎ **01865/726871**). The center sells maps, brochures, souvenir items, as well as the famous Oxford University T-shirt. It provides hotel booking services for £2.50 ($4). Guided walking tours leave from the center daily (see below). Open Monday through Saturday from 9:30am to 5pm and Sunday and bank holidays in summer from 10am to 3:30pm.

**GETTING AROUND**   Competition thrives in Oxford transportation, and the public benefits with swift, clean service by two companies. The **Oxford Bus Company,** 395 Cowley Rd. (☎ **01865/785400**), has green Park & Ride buses that leave from four car parks in the city using the north-south or east-west routes. Round-trip costs £1 ($1.60). Their Citilink buses are blue and travel to London, Heathrow and Gatwick. The company's red Cityline buses cover 15 routes in all suburbs with a day pass allowing unlimited travel for £1.50 ($2.40). Weekly and monthly passes are available. The competition, **Thames Transit,** Unit 4, Horsepath, Cowley (☎ **01865/ 772250**), uses blue and cream minibuses and red and gray coaches. City buses leave from Cornmarket Street in Oxford center. Day passes cost £1.50 ($2.40). Abington Road buses are marked "Red Bridge" and Iffley Road buses are labeled "Rose Hill."

**STUDENT DEALS**   Many students flock to Oxford in summer for courses and to see what all the excitement is about. For the best travel deals, try **Campus Travel,** 104 St. Aldates St. (☎ **01865/242067**), a student travel agency that offers worldwide flights, coach trips, rail passes, budget accommodations, ferry passes, travel insurance, and car rentals. **Carfax Travel,** 138 High St. (☎ **01865/726172**), handles flights, coach trips, major ferry companies, cruises, holiday bookings worldwide, Continental Coach and Rail, British Rail, National Express Coach Company, and car hire. For long hauls catering to students and young people traveling worldwide, **STA Travel,** 36 George St. (☎ **01865/792800**), is the expert.

## TOURS OF OXFORD

The best way to get a running commentary on the important sights is to take a 2-hour **walking tour** through the city and the major colleges. The tours leave daily from the Oxford Tourist Information Centre at 11am and 2pm. Tours costs £4 ($6.40) for adults and £2.50 ($4) for children; the tours do not include New College or Christ Church.

The Tourist Office also sponsors specialized tours, such as the **William Morris Tour** for arts and crafts enthusiasts, and **Oxford Past & Present,** a good introduction to the university and the city. Both are £4 ($6.40) adults, £2.50 ($4) children. New is the **Inspector Morse Tour,** of TV fame, costing £4.50 ($7.20) adults, £3 ($4.80) children.

The **Oxford Story,** 6 Broad St. (☎ **01865/790055**), is a concise and entertaining audiovisual ride through the campus. It explains the structure of the colleges and highlights architectural and historical features. Visitors are also filled in on the general background of the colleges and the antics of some of the famous people who have passed through the university's portals. The audiovisual presentation is given daily from 10am to 4:30pm. Admission is £4.50 ($7.20) for adults, £3.95 ($6.30) for students, and £3.50 ($5.60) for children. A family ticket for two adults and two children is £14 ($22.40).

For a good orientation, hour-long, open-top bus tours around Oxford are available from **Guide Friday,** office at the railway station (☎ **01865/790522**). Buses leave every half hour winter weekdays, every 20 minutes Saturday and Sunday. In summer, buses leave every 5 minutes. Tickets are good for the day. Tours begin at 9:30am on winter weekends, 10:10am on weekdays. In summer, tours begin at 9:10am. The cost is £7.50 ($12) adults, £5.50 ($8.80) students and seniors, and £2 ($3.20) children. Tickets can be purchased from the driver.

# Oxford

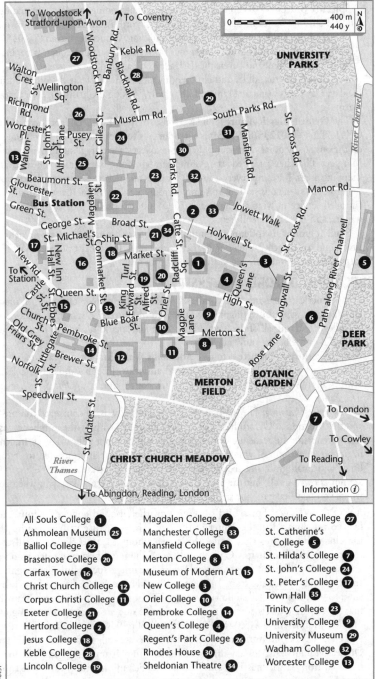

To Woodstock↑
Stratford-upon-Avon    ↑To Coventry

0  400 m
   440 y

**UNIVERSITY PARKS**

River Cherwell

Keble Rd.

Walton Cres.
Wellington Sq.
Richmond Rd.
Worcester Pl.
Walton
Gloucester St.
Green St.
Beaumont St.
George St.
St. Michael's St.
Ship St.
Broad St.
Holywell St.
Market St.
Jowett Walk
High St.
Merton St.
Blue Boar St.
Magpie Lane
Rose Lane
Brewer St.
Littlegate St.
Pembroke St.
Old Grey Friars St.
Church St.
Norfolk St.
Speedwell St.
New Rd.
Castle St.
St. Ebbes St.
Queen St.
King Edward St.
Alfred St.
Oriel St.
Hall St.
New Inn Hall St.
Cornmarket St.
Turl St.
Radcliffe Sq.
Catte St.
Queen's Lane
Longwall St.
St. Cross Rd.
Manor Rd.
Mansfield Rd.
Parks Rd.
Museum Rd.
South Parks Rd.
Woodstock Rd.
Banbury Rd.
Blackhall Rd.
St. Giles St.
Magdalen St.
Pusey St.
Alfred Lane
St. John's St.
Bus Station

To Station

To London
To Cowley
To Reading

St. Aldates St.

Rose Lane

**DEER PARK**

Path along River Cherwell

**MERTON FIELD**

**BOTANIC GARDEN**

*River Thames*

**CHRIST CHURCH MEADOW**

↓To Abingdon, Reading, London

Information ⓘ

| | | |
|---|---|---|
| All Souls College **1** | Magdalen College **6** | Somerville College **27** |
| Ashmolean Museum **25** | Manchester College **33** | St. Catherine's College **5** |
| Balliol College **22** | Mansfield College **31** | St. Hilda's College **7** |
| Brasenose College **20** | Merton College **8** | St. John's College **24** |
| Carfax Tower **16** | Museum of Modern Art **15** | St. Peter's College **17** |
| Christ Church College **12** | New College **3** | Town Hall **35** |
| Corpus Christi College **11** | Oriel College **10** | Trinity College **23** |
| Exeter College **21** | Pembroke College **14** | University College **9** |
| Hertford College **2** | Queen's College **4** | University Museum **29** |
| Jesus College **18** | Regent's Park College **26** | Wadham College **32** |
| Keble College **28** | Rhodes House **30** | Worcester College **13** |
| Lincoln College **19** | Sheldonian Theatre **34** | |

3-0431

**Spires & Shires** (☎ 01865/513998) has tours beginning in March, including a Ghost Tour of 15 sites in the country around Oxford. Another Oxford ghost tour is offered by the **Tourist Office,** Old School Building, Gloucester Green (☎ 01865/726871), on Friday and Saturday evenings from July through October. It begins at 7pm, ends at 8:30pm, and covers the dark alleyways around the ancient schools. The cost is £4 ($6.40) for adults and children; tickets are available at the office during the day. Day tours begin at 11am and 2pm daily, including Christmas, even for one person.

The **Oxford Classic Tour,** Holiday House, Station Road, Didcot, Oxfordshire OX11 7LZ (☎ 01235/819313), is a 1-hour bus tour of the city, but you can get off the bus at any point. The tour passes most colleges, including Summerville, which Margaret Thatcher attended, the Ashmolean Museum, Sheldonian Theatre, and shopping areas. Buses run every 15 to 20 minutes and tickets can be purchased from the driver or at the bus station. In summer, tours are daily from 10am to 5pm, with curtailed service in winter. The cost is £6 ($9.60) adults, £4 ($6.40) students and seniors, and £2 ($3.20) children.

Student groups also offer tours on their own, but prices vary, there are no definite times, and bad weather often derails them altogether. The tourist office provides information on all tours offered at the time of your visit.

## EXPLORING OXFORD UNIVERSITY

Many Americans arriving at Oxford ask: "Where's the college campus?" If a local looks amused when answering, it's because Oxford University is, in fact, made up of 35 colleges. To tour all of these would be a formidable task. It's best to focus on just a handful of the better known colleges.

Our favorite pastime here is to take **Addison's Walk** through the water meadows. The stroll is named after a former Oxford alumnus, Joseph Addison, the 18th-century essayist and playwright noted for his contributions to *The Spectator* and *The Tatler*.

*A Word of Warning:* The main business of a university, is, of course, to educate—and this function at Oxford has been severely interfered with by the number of visitors who disturb the academic work of the university. It is not unheard of for students to politely make fun of visitors oohing and ahhing. Visits are restricted to certain hours and small groups of six or fewer. Furthermore, there are areas where visitors are not allowed at all, but the tourist office will be happy to advise you when and where you may "take in" the sights of this great institution.

**AN OVERVIEW**  For a bird's-eye view of the city and colleges, climb **Carfax Tower,** located in the center of the city. This structure is distinguished by the clock and figures that strike the quarter hours. Carfax Tower is all that remains from St. Martin's Church, where William Shakespeare once stood as godfather for William Davenant, who also became a successful playwright. A church stood on this site from 1032 until 1896. The tower used to be higher, but after 1340 it was lowered, following complaints from the university to Edward III that townspeople threw stones and fired arrows at students during town-and-gown disputes. Admission is £1.20 ($1.90) for adults, 60p (95¢) for children. The tower is open all year. From April through October, hours are daily from 10am to 5:30pm. Off-season hours are Monday through Saturday from 10am to 3:30pm. The tower is closed from Christmas Eve until January 2. For information, call ☎ 01865/792653.

✪ **CHRIST CHURCH**  Begun by Cardinal Wolsey as Cardinal College in 1525, Christ Church (☎ 01865/276492), known as the House, was founded by Henry VIII in 1546. Facing St. Aldate's Street, Christ Church has the largest quadrangle of any college in Oxford.

Tom Tower houses Great Tom, the 18,000-pound bell referred to earlier. It rings at 9:05pm nightly, signaling the closing of the college gates. The 101 times it peals originally signified the number of students in residence at the time when the college was founded. Although the student body has grown exponentially, Oxford traditions seem to live on forever. There are interesting portraits in the 16th-century great hall, including works by Gainsborough and Reynolds. Prime ministers are pictured, since Christ Church was the training ground for 13 prime ministers. There's a separate portrait gallery.

The college chapel was constructed over a period of centuries, beginning in the 12th century. (Incidentally, it's not only the college chapel, but also the cathedral of the diocese of Oxford.) The cathedral's most distinguishing features are its Norman pillars and the vaulting of the choir, dating from the 15th century. In the center of the great quadrangle is a statue of Mercury mounted in the center of a fish pond. The college and cathedral can be visited daily from 9am to 5:30pm. The entrance fee is £3 ($4.80) for adults and £2 ($3.20) for children.

**MAGDALEN COLLEGE**   Pronounced "*Maud*-lin," Magdalen College, High Street (☎ 01865/276000), was founded in 1458 by William of Waynflete, bishop of Winchester and later chancellor of England. Its alumni range from Wolsey to Wilde. Opposite the botanical garden, the oldest in England, is the bell tower, where the choristers sing in Latin at dawn on May Day. The reflection of the 15th-century tower is cast in the waters of the Cherwell below. On a not-so-happy day, Charles I— his days numbered—watched the oncoming Roundheads from this tower. Visit the 15th-century chapel, in spite of many of its latter-day trappings. Ask when the hall and other places of special interest are open. The grounds of Magdalen are the most extensive of any Oxford college; there's even a deer park. You can visit from Easter to September, daily from noon to 6pm; off-season, daily from 2 to 6pm. Admission is £2 ($3.20), but it's charged only from Easter to September.

**MERTON COLLEGE**   Founded in 1264, Merton College, Merton Street (☎ **01865/276310**), is among the three oldest colleges at the university. It stands near Corpus Christi College on Merton Street, the sole survivor of Oxford's medieval cobbled streets. Merton College is noted for its library, built between 1371 and 1379 and said to be the oldest college library in England. There was once a tradition of keeping some of its most valuable books chained up. Now only one book is secured in such a manner, to illustrate the historical custom. One of the library's treasures is an astrolabe (an astronomical instrument used for measuring the altitude of the sun and stars) thought to have belonged to Chaucer. You pay £1 ($1.60) to visit the ancient library, as well as the Max Beerbohm Room (the satirical English caricaturist who died in 1956). The library and college are open Monday through Friday from 2 to 4pm and Saturday and Sunday from 10am to 4pm. It's closed for 1 week at Easter and at Christmas.

**UNIVERSITY COLLEGE**   University College, High Street (☎ **01865/276602**), is the oldest one at Oxford and dates back to 1249, when money was donated by an ecclesiastic, William of Durham (the old claim that the real founder was Alfred the Great is more fanciful). The original structures have all disappeared, and what remains today represents essentially the architecture of the 17th century, with subsequent additions in Victoria's day as well as in more recent times. For example, the Goodhart Quadrangle was added as late as 1962. The college's most famous alumnus, Shelley, was "sent down" for his part in collaborating on a pamphlet on atheism. However, all is forgiven today, as the romantic poet is honored by a memorial erected in 1894. The hall and chapel of University College can be visited daily during vacations from 2 to 4pm for a charge of £1.50 ($2.40) for adults, 60p (95¢) for children. Chapel services are held daily at 4 and 6pm.

**NEW COLLEGE**    New College, New College Lane, off Queen's Lane (☎ **01865/ 279555**), was founded in 1379 by William of Wykeham, bishop of Winchester and later lord chancellor of England. His college at Winchester supplied a constant stream of students. The first quadrangle, dating from before the end of the 14th century, was the initial quadrangle to be built in Oxford and formed the architectural design for the other colleges. In the antechapel is Sir Jacob Epstein's remarkable modern sculpture of Lazarus and a fine El Greco painting of St. James. One of the treasures of the college is a crosier (pastoral staff of a bishop) belonging to the founding father. In the garden, you can stroll among the remains of the old city wall and the mound. The college (entered at New College Lane) can be visited Easter to September, daily from 11am to 5pm; off-season, daily from 2 to 4pm. Admission is £1 ($1.60) from Easter to September, free off-season.

## PUNTING ON THE CHERWELL & OTHER OUTDOOR PURSUITS

Punting (boating) on the River Cherwell remains the favorite outdoor pastime in Oxford. At Punt Station, Cherwell Boathouse, Bardwell Road (☎ **01865/515978**), you can rent a punt (flat-bottom boat maneuvered by a long pole and a small oar) for £8 to £10 ($12.80 to $16) an hour, plus a £30 to £40 ($48 to $64) deposit. Similar charges are made for punt rentals at Magdalen Bridge Boathouse. Punts are rented from March to mid-June and late August to October, daily from 10am until dusk; from mid-June to late August, when a larger inventory of punts is available, daily from 10am to 10pm. However, hours of operation seem to be rather informal; you're not always guaranteed that someone will be here to rent you a boat, even if the punt itself is available.

**Oxford Eights Week** runs from Wednesday to Saturday, mid-afternoon to early evening the last full week in May. Men and women from the university's 36 colleges compete to be "Head of the River." They set off 13 across and try to catch and bump the boat in front. The bumped boat goes down a position and tries again the next day. Spectators watch along the banks.

One of the prettiest club grounds in England, surrounded by great trees, hosts the **Oxford University Cricket Club** from April to June. At the end of the season, the team plays the major foreign team visiting Britain. Games are free and open to the public. The tourist office has details on all these outdoor activities.

## SHOPPING

**Golden Cross,** an arcade of first-class shops and boutiques, lies between Cornmarket Street and the Covered Market (or between High Street and Market Street). Parts of the colorful gallery date from the 12th century. Many buildings remain from the medieval era, along with some 15th- and 17th-century structures. The market also has a reputation as the Covent Garden of Oxford, where live entertainment, from dancing in Radcliffe Square to melodious presentations by the Magdalen College Choir from high atop Magdalen Tower, takes place on Saturday mornings in summer. In the arcade shops you'll find a diverse selection of merchandise, including handmade Belgian chocolates, specialty gifts, and clothing.

About a half hour from Oxford, and a million light years away, you'll find **Bicester Village** (say *Bista*), an American-style outlet mall populated by American and English designers. It's very much a hit-or-miss kind of thing, but local big names include

## Impressions

*Beautiful City! so venerable, so lovely, so unravaged by the fierce intellectual life of our century, so serene!*

*There are our young barbarians, all at play! And yet, steeped in sentiment as she lies, spreading her gardens to the moonlight, and whispering from her towers the last enchantments of the Middle Age, who will deny that Oxford, by her ineffable charm, keeps ever calling us nearer to the true goal of all of us, to the ideal, to perfection,—to beauty, in a word, which is only truth seen from another side?—nearest, perhaps, than all the science of Tübingen. Adorable dreamer, whose heart has been so romantic! who has given thyself so prodigally, given thyself to sides and to heroes not mine, only never to the Philistines! home of lost causes, and forsaken beliefs, and unpopular names, and impossible loyalties!*

—Matthew Arnold (1822–88), Essays in Criticism

Cerruti 1881, Fred Perry, Jigsaw and Monsoon. For information, call ☎ **01869/ 323200.**

**Alice's Shop.** 83 St. Aldate's. ☎ **01865/723793.**

In its way, this establishment might have played a more important role in English literature than any other shop in Britain. Set within a 15th-century building that has housed some kind of shop since 1820, it functioned as a general store (selling brooms, hardware, and the like) during the period that Lewis Carroll, at the time a professor of mathematics at Christ Church College, was creating *Alice in Wonderland.* As such, it is believed to have been the model for important settings within the book. Today, the place is a favorite stop for Lewis Carroll fans from as far away as Japan, who gobble up commemorative pencils, chess sets, party favors, bookmarks, and in rare cases, original editions of some of Carroll's works. An original edition of *Through the Looking Glass* was available for around £400 ($640), but virtually everything else in the store is much, much less expensive.

**Bodleian Library Shop.** Old School's Quadrangle, Radcliffe Sq., Broad St. ☎ **01865/ 277175.**

More than any other shop in Oxford, this one specializes in Oxford-inspired souvenirs that might be appropriate for the desktop or personal collections of anyone with academic pretensions. There are more than 2,000 objects inventoried here, including books describing the history of the university and its various colleges, paperweights made of pewter and crystal, and Oxford banners and coffee mugs.

**Castell & Son (The Varsity Shop).** 13 Broad St. ☎ **01865/244000.**

This is the best outlet in Oxford for clothing (of all degrees of formality) emblazoned with the Oxford logo or heraldic symbol. Objects, which range in price from 35p (55¢) to usually no more than £60 ($96), include both whimsical and dead-on-serious neckties, hats, T-shirts, sweatshirts, pens, bookmarks, beer and coffee mugs, and cuff links. If anyone has commercialized Oxford, albeit with a sense of relative dignity and style, this store has done it.

**Magna Gallery.** 41 High St. ☎ **01865/245805.**

Since 1969, this is one of the best-respected antiquarian galleries in Oxford, with a roster of engravings, maps, and prints made between 1550 and 1896. Sold in both framed and unframed versions, the artworks start from £5 ($8) and are arranged into categories divided by both subject and era, in bins designed for careful rummaging.

Although the botanical prints and maps are among the most intriguing in the store, connoisseurs usually ask for the prints and engravings of 19th-century caricaturist Robert Cruikshank, many of those works are inventoried inside.

**Once a Tree.** 99 Gloucester Green. ☎ **01865/793558.**

Few other shops in England glorify trees and wood products as artfully as this one. A member of a rapidly blossoming chain with at least eight other branches throughout Britain, it stocks wood-carved objects that range from the functional and utilitarian (kitchen spoons and bread boards) to the whimsical and exotic (carved wooden flowers, chunky jewelry, boxes, bowls, mirror frames, furniture, and mantelpieces). Many objects come from England, others from the far corners of the world.

**The Oxford Collection.** 1 Golden Cross Courtyard, off Cornmarket. ☎ **01865/247414.**

Although it stocks a limited number of simple souvenirs selling for less than 50p (80¢), many objects within its inventory bear an aristocratic veneer of discreet good taste. A specialty is souvenirs of Oxford and its university, such as glass beer steins etched with the university's logo and a wool cardigan-like sweater with brass buttons bearing the university crest.

# WHERE TO STAY IN & AROUND OXFORD

Accommodations in Oxford are limited, although the addition of motels on the outskirts has aided the plight of those who require modern amenities. Motorists may want to consider country houses or small B&Bs on the outskirts of town, which offer the best living in Oxford if you don't mind commuting.

The **Oxford Tourist Information Centre** (see "Visitor Information," above), operates a room-booking service or will provide you with the information you'll need to find lodgings on your own.

## CAMPING & A HOSTEL

Oxford camping is a great option for the budget traveler. The **YHA Youth Hostel,** Jack Straw's Lane, Headington (☎ **01865/62997;** national office is **01727/845047**) opens its season in March with tent sites in a garden for £4.55 ($7.30) per person, including hostel facilities. The hostel costs £9.40 ($15.05) with 112 bunk beds in dorms of 6 to 12, with showers, basins, TV in the lounge, and communal kitchens. Breakfast is £2.80 ($4.50), dinner £4.15 ($6.65), and picnic lunches £2.35 ($3.75). The hostel is 2½ miles from Oxford train station, and buses run every 5 minutes until 11pm. Book at least a week ahead in summer. You must be a YHA member (the under-18 rate is £6.30 or $10.10).

Your best chance of getting a site with no reservation is ✪ **Oxford Camping International,** 426 Abington Rd. (☎ **01865/246551**), just off Oxford's Southern Ring Road. Tents and caravans for two adults cost £7.85 ($12.55); motor caravans £7.85 ($12.55); ridge tent £2.60 ($4.15); car £1.80 ($2.90); motorcycle £1.15 ($1.85); extra adult £1.55 ($2.50); child 85p ($1.35); electrical connection £1.95 ($3.10). There are no tents for rent but the shop sells tents and equipment, including outdoor clothing for men and women.

## DOUBLES FOR LESS THAN £45

✪ **Adams Guest House.** 302 Banbury Rd., Summertown, Oxford OX2 7ED. ☎ **01865/ 556118.** 6 rms, all with shower. TV. £25 ($40) single; £38 ($60.80) double. All rates include English breakfast. No credit cards. Bus: 2 or 7 from Cornmarket.

In Summertown, 1¼ miles from Oxford opposite Radio Oxford, is the Adams Guest House, operated by John Strange, and one of the best B&Bs in the northern Oxford area. The comfortable and cozy rooms have private showers and tea- or coffeemakers. Breakfast is served in a dining room decorated in an old-world style. Mr. Strange will provide touring tips, and a bus runs every few minutes to the city center. Adams Guest House is located opposite the Midland Bank, and in its neighborhood are seven restaurants, shops, a post office, a swimming pool, a bicycle-rental shop, and a launderette.

**Bravalia Guest House.** 242 Iffley Rd., Oxford, Oxfordshire OX4 1SE. ☎ **01865/241326.** 5 rms, 4 with bath. TV. £22–£25 ($35.20–$40) single without bath, £25–£30 ($40–$48) single with bath; £36–£38 ($57.60–$60.80) double without bath, £38–£44 ($60.80–$70.40) double with bath. All rates include English breakfast. DC, MC, V. Bus: 3 or 4.

About a mile from the heart of Oxford and about half a mile from Magdalen College, the Bravalia is small and well known, so reserve in advance in summer. Built in the late Victorian era, the semidetached house contains pleasantly furnished bedrooms, two of which are suitable for families. Bedrooms are well maintained and equipped, though showing some wear and tear. The Downes are your hosts, serving breakfast in an airy conservatory at the rear of the B&B.

**Brown's Guest House.** 281 Iffley Rd., Oxford, Oxfordshire OX4 4AQ. ☎ **01865/246822.** 8 rms, 2 with bath. TV. £23–£25 ($36.80–$40) single without bath; £36–£44 ($57.60–$70.40) double without bath, £44–£50 ($70.40–$80) double with bath. All rates include English breakfast. MC, V. Bus: 3, 4, or 4A.

This year-round guest house, run by the Brown family, is a red-brick Victorian structure. The pleasantly furnished guest rooms have hot and cold running water, central heating, and hot-beverage facilities, although some are small. All the bedrooms have recently been refurbished, so this is one of the better bets along Iffley Road. There are adequate showers outside the rooms. Families are catered to, with special breakfasts if requested. Smoking is not allowed in the breakfast room. The house is about a mile from the city center, with such nearby amenities as a post office, launderette, grocery store, drugstore, and bike-rental shop.

**Courtfield Private Hotel.** 367 Iffley Rd., Oxford, Oxfordshire OX4 4DP. ☎ and fax **01865/242991** (but call before faxing). 6 rms, 4 with bath. £26 ($41.60) single without bath, £30 ($48) single with bath; £40 ($64) double without bath, £45 ($72) double with bath. All rates include English breakfast. AE, MC, V. Bus: 4A, 4B, or 4C.

This meticulously maintained B&B is most suitable for motorists who don't want to face the congested city center; it stands on a tree-lined street close to the center of Iffley Village. If you're not driving, you'll find adequate public transportation. The house has been modernized with triple-glazed windows in the bright, spacious bedrooms, most of which contain private baths, one in art-deco marble. Brian Tong, the owner, served with the city police force for 30 years and offers excellent advice to tourists.

**Green Gables.** 326 Abingdon Rd., Oxford, Oxfordshire OX1 4TE. ☎ **01865/725870.** Fax 01865/723115. 9 rms, 6 with bath. TV. £33 ($52.80) single without bath, £40 ($64) single with bath; £39 ($62.40) double without bath, £47 ($75.20) double with bath. All rates include English breakfast. MC, V.

About a mile south of the university city on A4144, this was originally a large Edwardian private residence of a local toy manufacturer. Charles and Connie Ellis are to be applauded for continuing to make improvements to this property. They are some of the best hosts in the Oxford area. Many of their bedrooms are quite large, and each is well maintained in spic-and-span condition. One of the bedrooms on the ground floor is suitable for persons with disabilities. The breakfast room is bright and inviting but doesn't allow smoking. After a stay here, one satisfied guest wrote, "It's like being home." Trees screen the house from the main road, and parking for eight cars is available. If you walk 150 yards to the traffic lights by the Fox & Hounds pub, then turn left, you will come to the River Thames. For a ramble, follow the signposts to the Longbridge Nature Park. Even prettier is the walk to Iffley Lock, past the Isis riverside pub. You can cross the river the lock and climb to Iffley Village, dating from Saxon times and still known for its remarkable Norman church, one of the finest in the country.

**Highfield West.** 188 Cumnor Hill, Oxford, Oxfordshire OX2 9PJ. ☎ **01865/863007.** 5 rms, 3 with bath. TV. £20–£26 ($32–$41.60) single without bath; £39–£50 ($62.40–$80) double with bath. All rates include English breakfast. No credit cards. Bus: 4B.

Three miles from the heart of Oxford, Highfield West is on a good residential road within easy access of the ring road surrounding Oxford. The little village of Cumnor, with its two country inns serving food and drink, is also within walking distance. Blenheim Palace is a few miles away, and a pleasant day can be spent in some of the Cotswold villages. Tina and Robin Barrett offer accommodations in single, double, twin, or family rooms, most with private baths. They have recently completed some major improvements, making the bedrooms more inviting than ever, with new carpets and new bathroom fittings. There is a lounge, and in season visitors can enjoy the heated outdoor pool. A bus into Oxford stops just outside their front garden, and there's also a good local taxi service.

**Lakeside Guest House.** 118 Abingeon Rd., Oxford, Oxfordshire OX1 4PZ. ☎ **01865/244725.** Fax 01865/244725. 6 rms, 3 with bath. TV. £38 ($60.80) single or double without bath; £48 ($76.80) single or double with bath. All rates include English breakfast. No credit cards. Bus: 68.

Proprietors Martin and Daniela Shirley run this Victorian guest house overlooking open fields and parklands that lead to the University Boat Houses. The house, which has been remodeled and updated, is about 5 minutes from Christ Church College, 1 mile south of the center (take A4144). There is hot and cold running water and hot-beverage facilities in all of the centrally heated rooms, each of which is a double.

**Nanford Guest House.** 137 Iffley Rd., Oxford OX4 1EJ. ☎ **01865/244743.** Fax 01865/249596. 65 rms. TV TEL. £20–£23 ($32–$36.80) single; £30–£35 ($48–$56) double. AE, DC, MC, V.

Don't expect the ambience of a private English home if you stay here. With 65 rooms, it's by far the largest B&B in Oxford, and as such has the aura more of a cost-conscious hotel than a home that happens to let out rooms. Built in 1910, it has housed everyone from members of rock and roll bands to academics on sabbatical from universities throughout the world. In the mid-1990s, new carpeting and beds were added to every room. Rooms are simple and unpretentious, each with tea-making facilities and in many cases, a small refrigerator. There's no bar or cocktail lounge on the premises, and other than the English breakfasts that are the norm every morning, no meals of any kind are served.

**Norham Guest House.** 16 Norham Rd., Oxford, Oxfordshire OX2 6SF. ☎ **01865/515352.** Fax 01865/793162. 8 rms, 6 with shower only. TV TEL. £30 ($48) single without bath, £32 ($51.20) single with shower only; £44 ($70.40) double without bath, £51 ($81.60) double with shower only. All rates include English breakfast. No credit cards. Bus: 20, 21, or 22.

Owners Peter and Rosemary Welham provide one of the better B&Bs in the area, with well-kept bedrooms. In North Oxford, this late Victorian building enjoys a tranquil setting near parks. It lies on a quiet leafy road in a conservation area. The Cherwell River is nearby, and it's only a 15-minute stroll to the center of the city.

It boasts many original features of its Victorian days, and all the bedrooms are non-smoking and well equipped with such amenities as color TVs and beverage-making equipment. There is bus service to this district, plus parking for four cars. Breakfast is the only meal served, and vegetarian morning meals can be requested. Breakfast is the full "trad" English one, served in an attractive blue and white dining room. This is a no-smoking establishment.

## DOUBLES FOR LESS THAN £65

**Cotswold House.** 363 Banbury Rd., Oxford, Oxfordshire OX2 7PL. ☎ **01865/310558.** 7 rms, all with bath. TV. £39 ($62.40) single; £57 ($91.20) double. All rates include English breakfast. No credit cards. Bus: 2, 2A, 7, or 7A.

Jim and Anne O'Kane operate this stone house that's one of the better B&Bs in the area. It was featured in the novel *The Way Through the Woods* by Colin Dexter. The bedrooms—all no-smoking—have refrigerators, coffee-making equipment, and hair dryers. Although rooms vary in size, each is comfortable and maintained to a high standard; one ground-floor room is offered. Traditional and vegetarian breakfasts and fresh fruit are always available, all with generous Irish helpings. There is ample off-street parking. The O'Kanes help with maps and give good touring advice. Cotswold House is about 1 1/2 miles from the center, but it's much easier for motorists to use the ring road. Buses pass by about every 5 minutes.

**Dial House.** 25 London Rd., Headington, Oxford, Oxfordshire OX3 7RE. ☎ **01865/69944.** 8 rms. TV. £40–£45 ($64–$72) single; £50–£60 ($80–$96) double. All rates include breakfast. No credit cards. Bus: 7, 7A, 20, 21, or 22.

Two miles east of the heart of Oxford, beside the main highway leading to London, this country-style house was originally built between 1924 and 1927. Graced with mock-Tudor half-timbering and a prominent blue-faced sundial (from which it derives its name), it contains cozy and recently renovated bedrooms, each of which has tea-making facilities and hair dryers. No smoking is permitted in the house. The owners, Julie and Tony Lamb, serve only breakfast in their bright, big-windowed dining room.

**Galaxie Private Hotel.** 180 Banbury Rd., Oxford, Oxfordshire OX2 7BT. ☎ **01865/515688.** Fax 01865/556824. 34 rms, 29 with bath. TV TEL. £32 ($51.20) single without bath, £44 ($70.40) single with bath; £48 ($76.80) double without bath, £60 ($96) double with bath. All rates include English breakfast. MC, V. Bus: 7, 20, 21, or 22.

When it was built about a century ago, this red-brick hotel served as a plush private mansion for a prosperous local family. The hotel was recently refurbished and upgraded, and a conservatory-style lounge was added. Today, although most of its garden has been paved over as a parking lot, it still stands 1 mile north of Oxford's center, in a neighborhood of similar large houses in the suburb of Summertown. Each of the well-maintained bedrooms is equipped with reading lights, electric shaver outlets, hot and cold running water, and central heating. Furnishings are of a high standard. Although no meals other than breakfast are served, the hotel is within a short walk of at least five restaurants and two pubs. A public leisure center, with two indoor pools, is located just behind the hotel. A public bus runs down Banbury Road to the center of Oxford.

**Marlborough House Hotel.** 321 Woodstock Rd., Oxford, Oxfordshire OX2 7NY. ☎ **01865/311321.** Fax 01865/515329. 12 rms, 10 with bath, 2 with shower only. TV TEL. £55–£58 ($88–$92.80) single; £65–£68 ($104–$108.80) double. All rates include continental breakfast. Mid-week and weekend discounts arranged Sept–June. MC, V.

About 1¹/₂ miles north of Oxford, this traditionally designed, three-story structure was built in 1990, unlike most of the Victorian properties in the area. The comfortably furnished rooms contain small refrigerators, microwaves, central heating, and continental breakfast trays. There's a no-smoking policy, and children under 8 years of age are not accepted. Marlborough House offers concessionary membership to Beaumont's Leisure Club at Oxford Moat House. Club facilities include a solarium, indoor pool and spa, fully equipped gymnasium, squash courts, and sauna.

**Pine Castle Hotel.** 290 Iffley Rd., Oxford, Oxfordshire OX4 4AE. ☎ **01865/241497.** Fax 01865/727230. 7 rms. TV TEL. £50–£60 ($80–$96) double. All rates include English breakfast. MC, V. Bus: 3, 4A, 4B, or 4C.

Although it has flourished since the 1960s as one of Oxford's guest houses, the Pine Castle doubled its size in 1994 when its owners, Peter and Marilyn Morris, bought the building's other half as part of an expansion. Today the building retains all the stained-glass windows and old fireplaces of its original construction in 1901. It also housed one of Oxford University's most widely published scholars on the subject of English folklore, Christina Hole. Set about 1¹/₂ miles southeast of the city center, it contains a residents' bar and a small restaurant where fixed-price dinners begin at £8.50 ($13.60). The bedrooms are furnished with simple pine furniture and accessories, and are quiet and comfortable.

**Tilbury Lodge Private Hotel.** 5 Tilbury Lane, Eynsham Rd., Botley, Oxford, Oxfordshire OX2 9OB. ☎ **01865/862138.** Fax 01865/863700. 9 rms. TV TEL. £39–£44 ($62.40–$70.40) single; £52–£64 ($83.20–$102.40) double; £75–£85 ($120–$136) double with 4-poster. All rates include English breakfast. MC, V. Bus: 42, 45, 45A, 45B, or 109.

On a quiet country lane in Botley, about 2 miles west of the center of Oxford, this small hotel is less than a mile from the railway station. Eddie and Eileen Trafford house guests in their well-furnished and comfortable bedrooms, one with a romantic four-poster bed. Some rooms are on the ground floor. The guest house also has a Jacuzzi and welcomes children, who enjoy the play area in the back garden. If you don't arrive by car, Eddie can pick you up at the train station; alternatively, a bus takes visitors to Botley.

**Willow Reaches Hotel.** 1 Whytham St., Oxford, Oxfordshire OX1 4SU. ☎ **01865/721545.** Fax 01865/251139. 9 rms, all with bath. TV TEL. £45 ($72) single; £55 ($88) double; £85 ($136) family rm for 4. All rates include English breakfast. AE, MC, V. Bus: 5, 7, 9, or 11.

This hotel is on a cul-de-sac about a mile south from the center of Oxford and close to the Abingdon Road. All the attractively furnished bedrooms contain private baths and are bright and well-equipped. A three-course table d'hôte dinner of either English or Indian cuisine is served nightly. Guests can relax in the garden or follow a special footpath to a nearby village for a pub meal or an early morning walk. The convivial lounge bar is a favorite rendezvous point for guests who quickly meet and become friends with other guests, comparing Oxford notes.

## WHERE TO EAT

If you just want to have a picnic, or don't mind your food on the run, Oxford abounds in places where you can pick up delicious, low-cost items. A supermarket is an especially good choice if you are using self-catering facilities in a hostel. **Tesco,** 159 Cowley Rd. (☎ **01865/244470**), offers the usual grocery fare, and also has a deli serving sandwiches and salads. **J. Sainsbury,** at the Westgate Shopping Centre (☎ **01865/722179**), doesn't have a deli, but does have a full range of grocery items. Even better, head for the **Covered Market** on Market Street, a half block east of

Cornmarket Street. Here bakers tempt you with their delicious goods and you'll enjoy the greengrocer's bounty from the heart of England. On Wednesday, head for the "Wednesday Market" on Gloucester Green by the bus station. Here you can pick up pies, produce, whatever.

As a college town, Oxford also has plenty of fast-food and ethnic joints, and is known for its "kebab vans" that park around town at night, feeding hungry students with their skewers of spicy meats. They're found at St. Aldate's, High Street, Queen Street, and Broad Street.

✪ **Browns.** 5–11 Woodstock Rd. ☎ **01865/511995.** Main courses £6–£11.50 ($9.60–$18.40); afternoon tea £2–£5 ($3.20–$8). MC, V. Mon–Sat 11am–11:30pm; Sun noon–11:30pm. Bus: 2 or 7. ENGLISH/CONTINENTAL.

Oxford's busiest and most bustling English brasserie suits all groups, from babies to undergraduates to grandmas. A 10-minute walk north of the town center, it occupies the premises of five Victorian shops whose walls were removed to create one large, echoing, and very popular space. Bare wood floors, plaster walls, and a thriving bar trade (where lots of people seem to order Pimms) make the place an evening destination in its own right.

A young and enthusiastic staff serves traditional English cuisine. Your meal might include meat pies, hot salads, burgers, pastas, steaks, and poultry. Afternoon tea here is a justly celebrated Oxford institution. Reservations are not accepted, so if you want to avoid a delay, arrive here during off-peak dining hours.

**Cherwell Boathouse Restaurant.** Bardwell Rd. ☎ **01865/552746.** Reservations recommended. Main courses £9–£14 ($14.40–$22.40); fixed-price dinner £19.50 ($31.20); Sun lunch £17.50 ($28). AE, DC, MC, V. Tues 6–11:30pm; Wed–Sat noon–2pm and 6–11:30pm; Sun noon–2pm. Closed Dec 24–30. Bus: Banbury Road. FRENCH.

This virtual Oxford landmark on the River Cherwell is owned by Anthony Verdin, who has the help of a young crew. A fixed-price menu is offered and the cooks change the menu every 2 weeks to take advantage of the availability of fresh vegetables, fish, and meat. There's a very reasonable, even exciting, wine list. Children are charged half price. In summer, the restaurant also serves on the terrace. Before dinner, you can try "punting" on the Cherwell; punts are rented on the other side of the boat house. The ever-changing menu is always intriguing. On any given night you might face starters such as game terrine with Cumberland sauce or a warm salad of black pudding and bacon with a damson dressing. For a main course, you might opt for breast of guinea fowl with tapenade or, for vegetarians, an eggplant gratin with saffron custard and a mixed bean ragoût. For dessert, who can resist the "fallen" chocolate soufflé with "drunken" prunes and sour cream?

**Chiang Mai Kitchen.** 130A High St. ☎ **01865/202233.** Reservations recommended. Main courses £3.90–£8.50 ($6.25–$13.60). AE, DC, MC, V. Mon–Sat noon–2:30pm and 6–10:30pm. THAI.

Housed in a 17th-century Tudor building with wooden floors and paneling, this restaurant offers a wide array of Thai dishes. Soups may include hot-and-sour chicken or a prawn-and-seafood concoction. The main courses range from various salads to Thai curries, including chicken, beef, and game. An extensive vegetarian menu is also offered featuring several noodles dishes.

**Golden Harvest.** 18 Park End St. ☎ **01865/240686.** Main courses £4.70–£19 ($7.50–$30.40); 3-course fixed-price lunch £7.15 ($11.45); fixed-price dinner for 2 £26.80 ($42.90). AE, DC, MC, V. Mon–Fri noon–2:30pm and 6pm–midnight; Sat–Sun noon–midnight. Bus: 52. CANTONESE.

Located opposite the railway station, Golden Harvest is the first restaurant in Oxford specializing exclusively in the cuisine of Canton and southern China. Set in a 19th-century, brick-fronted corner building with oversize windows, it's maintained by a hardworking China-born family, the Wais. Some of its business derives from a busy take-out service popular with local students, but more frequently diners opt for sit-down lunches and dinners. Menu items change with the seasons, and include king prawns stir-fried in Chinese wine, the Golden Harvest special soup, salmon served with five spicy sauces, fillet of pork in Cantonese sauce, and a wide array of vegetarian dishes.

✪ **Munchy Munchy.** 6 Park End St. ☎ **01865/245710.** Reservations required. Main courses £4.50–£8 ($7.20–$12.80). MC, V. Tues–Sat noon–2pm and 5:30–10pm. Closed 2 weeks in Sept and 3 weeks in Dec. Bus: 52. SOUTHEAST ASIAN/INDONESIAN.

Despite the cute name, some Oxford students claim that this restaurant located near the station offers the best food value in the city. Main dishes depend on what's available in the marketplace, and appetizers are not offered. Ethel Ow is adept at herbs and seasoning, and often uses fresh fruit inventively, as reflected by such dishes as scallops sautéed with ginger and lamb with passion-fruit sauce. Indonesian and Malaysian dishes are popular. Wine is served by the glass or by the bottle. Sometimes, especially on Friday and Saturday, long lines form at the door. Children under 6 are not allowed on Friday and Saturday evenings.

✪ **Nosebag.** 6–8 St. Michael's St. ☎ **01865/721033.** Main courses £3–£7.25 ($4.80–$11.60). No credit cards. Mon 9:30am–5:30pm; Tues–Thurs 9:30am–10pm; Fri–Sat 9:30am–10:30pm; Sun 9:30am–9pm. Bus: 52. ENGLISH.

Another restaurant with a curious name, and one of the most popular places to eat with students, is the self-service upstairs cafeteria on a side street off Cornmarket, opposite St. Michael's Church. At mealtimes there's usually a line on the stairs. At lunch, you can get a homemade soup, followed by the dish of the day, perhaps a moussaka. Baked potato with a variety of fillings is a good accompaniment, as is the hot garlic bread. The menu increasingly leans to vegetarian dishes. Wine is available by the glass.

**Rosie Lee's.** 51 High St. ☎ **08165/244429.** Afternoon tea £6.75 ($10.80); sandwiches £3.20–£4.75 ($5.10–$7.60). No credit cards. Sun–Thurs 9am–6:30pm; Fri–Sat 9am–7pm. ENGLISH.

The casual environment of this restaurant has made it a favorite of the Oxford crowd. Enjoy a variety of cream or lemon teas with a selection of cakes and scones that changes daily. You could also follow the lead of the many students who come here to have a sandwich as they pore over piles of books. *Be warned:* The scholarly patrons tend to crowd the place at afternoon tea; you may want to stop by earlier or later in the day if your plan is to have a more relaxing meal.

**St. Aldate's Church Coffee House.** 94 St. Aldate's. ☎ **01865/245952.** Sandwiches £1.35–£1.60 ($2.15–$2.55); soups £1.85 ($2.95); main courses £1.95–£5.75 ($3.10–$9.20). No credit cards. Mon–Sat 10am–5pm (hot lunches served noon–2pm). Bus: 52. ENGLISH.

Opened by the archbishop of Canterbury in 1963, this is almost opposite the entrance to Christ Church College, adjacent to St. Aldate's Church. Head for the back, where nonsmokers find a large restaurant with counter service run by the church. All the food is homemade, including soups and salads made daily from fresh produce. Portions are generous.

## MORE CHEAP EATS

If you're in the mood for ethnic food, you'll find the best hunting grounds to be the first quartet of blocks along **Cowley Road.** Among the most popular eateries here are **Hi-Lo Jamaican Eating House,** 70 Cowley Rd. (☎ **01865/725984**), which has a goat, chicken, pork, fish, or vegetarian main course served with vegetables, rice, and peas for £4.80 to £5.40 ($7.70 to $8.65) at lunch, or £7 to £7.50 ($11.20 to $12) at dinner. They also have snacks, such as plaintain patties and soups for £2 to £2.20 ($3.20 to $3.50).

Still hungry? Check out **Georgina's Coffee Shop,** Covered Market, above Beaton's Deli (☎ **01865/249527**), and stop to admire the Toulouse-Lautrec posters, as you devour pastries, bagels, and the lunch specials of the day. As you choose from sandwiches and daily specials, priced between £2.60 to £4.50 ($4.15 to $7.20), or snacks such as bagels and pastries.

**Heroes,** 8 Ship St. (☎ **01865/723459**) makes the best Italian-style subs, and their sandwiches range from £1.65 ($2.65) for egg and mayo on sliced bread, to £2.85 ($4.55) for a curried chicken sandwich.

There's always a happening scene at **Café Moma,** 30 Pembroke St. (☎ **01865/722733**), tucked away under the Museum of Modern Art. It attracts the young artsy crowd of Oxford who like its freshly made salads, as well as vegan main courses like the "Nutroast," made from ground nuts, onions, and spices. A vegetarian main course and two salads will run you £4.25 ($6.80), and soup costs £2.15 ($3.45).

**Bret's Burgers** (☎ **01865/245229**) is just a shack on Park End Street, but it sells some of the juiciest burgers in town, along with the inevitable chips. Not so expected is its range of burgers, from traditional to spicy, tandoori and Caribbean burgers, and there's even a veggie burger for the vegan tagging along. A single costs £2 ($3.20), and a double runs £3.20 ($5.10), and you choose from such toppings as garden relish, garlic mayonnaise, Mexican chili, horseradish, and blue cheese.

Where to go for the cheapest but most well-stuffed sandwiches in town? It's **Harvey's of Oxford,** 58 High St. (☎ **01865/791012**). Near Magdalen College, it always seems to have a line at the door—maybe because their sandwiches, each one a meal unto itself, start at just £1.50 ($2.40). If a sandwich really isn't enough, their rich carrot cake will finish you off properly. Oxford students laud their cherry flapjacks, too.

## PUBS WITH PEDIGREE

**Bear Inn.** Alfred St. ☎ **01865/721783.** Snacks and bar meals £2–£6 ($3.20–$9.60). No credit cards. Mon–Sat noon–11pm; Sun noon–3pm and 7–10:30pm. Bus: 2A or 2B. ENGLISH.

A short block from The High, overlooking the north side of Christ Church College, this village pub is an Oxford tradition. Its swinging inn sign depicts the bear and ragged staff, old insignia of the earls of Warwick, who were among the early patrons. Built in the 13th century, the inn has been visited by many famous people who have lived and studied at Oxford. Over the years it has frequently appeared in English literature.

Former owners of the pub developed an astonishing tradition: the clipping of neckties. Around the lounge bar you'll see the remains of thousands of ties labeled with their owners' names. For those of you who want to leave a memento, a thin strip of the bottom of your tie will be cut off (with your permission, of course). After this initiation, you may want to join in some of the informal songfests of the undergraduates.

**The Turf Tavern.** 4 Bath Place, off Holywell St. ☎ **01865/243235.** Main dishes £2.95–£4.95 ($4.70–$7.90). MC, V. Mon–Sat 11am–11pm; Sun noon–10:30pm. Bus: 52. ENGLISH.

This 13th-century tavern, the oldest in Oxford, is tucked away on a very narrow passage in the area of the Bodleian Library, off New College Lane. Thomas Hardy used the place for the setting of *Jude the Obscure*. It was "the local" of Burton and Taylor when they were in Oxford many years ago making a film, and more recent patrons might include Kris Kristofferson and John Hurt. Bill Clinton was a frequent visitor here during his Rhodes scholar days at Oxford. At night, the nearby old tower of New College and part of the old city wall are floodlit, and during warm weather you can select a table in any of the three separate gardens that radiate outward from the pub's central core. For wintertime warmth, braziers are lighted in the courtyard and in the gardens. Inside the low-beamed hospice you can order traditional pub food. The pub prides itself on its old-fashioned earthiness and its wide appeal to beer lovers. Seven kinds of local ales are served here, with brand names that rotate with the seasons. Excellent choices include Broad Cooper and Old Hooky. Every Sunday during winter, mulled wine—a drink guaranteed to bring back a sense of medieval times—is featured throughout the pub's opening hours. The pub is reached via St. Helen's Passage between Holywell Street and New College Lane (you'll probably get lost, but any student worth his beer should be able to direct you).

## OXFORD AFTER DARK

Highly acclaimed orchestras playing in truly lovely settings mark the Music at Oxford series at the ✪ **Oxford Playhouse Theatre,** Beaumont Street (☎ **01865/798600**). The autumn season runs from mid-September to December, the spring-summer season from January to early July. Tickets range from £10 to £27 ($16 to $43.20). Classical music is performed by outstanding groups such as the European Union Chamber Orchestra, the National Symphony of the Ukraine, the Canterbury Musical Society, the Bournemouth Symphony and the Guild Hall String Ensemble of London. All performances are held in the Sheldonian Theatre, a particularly attractive site designed by Sir Christopher Wren with paintings on the ceiling.

**Blackwell's Music Shop,** Holywell Street (☎ **01865/261384**), sells tickets for chamber music in the Oxford Coffee Concerts. Ensembles such as the Praae Piano Trio, Schubert Chamber Players, and the Adderbury Ensemble perform baroque and classical repertoires on Sunday at 11:15am in the Holywell Music Room, a hall dating from 1748, on Holywell Street. Ticket prices are £6 ($9.60) for adults and £5 ($8) for students, seniors, and children under 16. The seasons generally run in 3-month intervals ending just before the Christmas holidays and picking up again in January. Coffee is served at the King's Arms or the Turf Tavern from 10:30am and after the concert upon presentation of your ticket.

**The Apollo,** George Street (☎ **01865/244544**), is Oxford's primary theater. Tickets are £14.50 to £23.50 ($23.20 to $37.60). A continuous run of comedy, ballet, drama, opera, and even rock groups such as Moody Blues play here. Comedies such as *What a Feeling* and musicals such as *Pickwick* are often sold out early. The Welsh National Opera often performs, and The Glyndebourne Touring Opera appears regularly. Advance booking is recommended, although some shows may have tickets the week of performance. It's probably not worth trying to get tickets for popular shows on the same day.

At the **Oxford Stage Company,** Beaumont Street (☎ **01865/798600**), performances at the Oxford Playhouse range from Shakespeare to modern comedy and drama. Tickets are £6 to £14 ($9.60 to $22.40). They are open most nights year-round, but closed Sundays and after Christmas for a week.

For some of the best productions in England, put on by some of the country's most talented actors, ask at the tourist office (see above) about summer performances in some of the college gardens. These used to be student productions, but increasingly are being taken over by professional companies. There are two Shakespeare troupes as well as other groups. Tickets usually cost from £8 to £10 ($12.80 to $16).

## THE CLUBS: BLUES, JAZZ & "CELTIC ROCK"

A sign of the times, ✪ **Freud,** Walton Street. At Great Clarendon Street (☎ **01865/ 311171**), is a converted 19th-century church, stained-glass windows and all, now a jazz and folk club with an array of drink choices. The cover is £3 ($4.80) after 10pm on Saturday and Sunday. The club has art shows that last about a month each, and a restaurant with a regular Mediterranean menu, featuring daily specials. Open Monday and Tuesday from 11am to midnight, Wednesday through Saturday from 11am to 2am, and Sunday 11am to 10:30pm.

The ✪ **Old Fire Station,** 40 George St. (☎ **01865/794494**), covers all the bases, with live entertainment, a bar, theater, art museum, and a new science museum called Curiosity, with a light show and other exhibits. The restaurant, open daily at 8am, serves breakfast until 6pm, with free coffee, tea, and toast. Specials change every few days. The restaurant closes Sunday to Wednesday at 11pm, and Thursday to Saturday at 2 am. School parties are frequent. Music cover charges begin at 9pm and are £4 ($6.40) Thursday and Saturday, and £3.50 ($5.60) Friday. Thursdays are 1970s disco from 9pm to 2am; Fridays see blues and jazz from 11pm to 1am, and Saturdays feature rock and blues. Mondays occasionally have a local band.

The **Zodiac,** 190 Crowley Rd. (☎ **01865/726336**), presents everything from easy listening to "Celtic Rock." Cover varies from £3 to £12 ($4.80 to $19.20) depending on the group featured. It's open Monday through Saturday usually from about 7:30pm to 2am and closed Sunday. Club ownership is shared by the English alt-pop bands Radiohead and Supergrass, and local and big-name bands are featured along with DJs, so call ahead to be sure of what you're getting.

## OTHER PLACES TO TIP A PINT

The **Head of the River,** Abingdon Road at Folly Bridge (☎ **01865/721600**), has been bought by Fuller Smith and Turner, a family brewery. It's a lively place, with barbecues, snooker games, and bucking bronco contests, and they offer true traditional ales and lagers, including award-winning ales such as London Pride, Chiswick, and E.S.B. The pub offers very good sturdy fare such as steak, kidney, beef, and bacon pies, salads, ploughman's, and homemade desserts. In summer, guests sit by the river and can rent a punt or a boat with an engine. Three rooms, all with bath and overlooking the river, are available for £60 ($96) in summer, including breakfast, newspaper, and car park. The location is near the Westgate Center Mall.

**Jolly Farmers,** 20 Paradise St. (☎ **01865/797-3759**), offers real ale, several lagers, and stout year-round, including Stella, Bass, and Murphy's. Lunch is from noon to 2:30pm and carries sandwiches to steak along with the usual pub fare. Entertainment appears infrequently, about every 2 weeks or once a month.

At **The Eagle and Child,** 49 St. Giles St. (☎ **01865/310154**), literary history resonates in the dim, paneled alcoves. For at least a quarter of a century, it was frequented by the likes of C. S. Lewis and J. R. R. Tolkien. In fact, *The Hobbit* and *The Chronicles of Narnia* were first read aloud at this pub. Known as the "Bird and Baby," this literary hallowed ground still welcomes the local dons, and the food is pretty good. Lunch from noon to 2pm offers traditional pub food with Guinness and Carlsberg on tap. It's a settled, quiet place to read the newspapers and listen to classical music on CDs.

**The King's Arms,** 40 Holywell St. (☎ **01865/242369**), hosts a mix of students, gays, and professors. One of the best in-town pubs for conversation, it is owned by Young's Brewery and features six of the company's ales, along with other lagers and bitters that change periodically. Meals are served daily from 11:30am to 3pm and 5:30pm to 9pm. A separate nonsmoking coffee shop offers coffee, tea, sandwiches, and cakes from 10:30am to 5:30pm.

## 4  Woodstock & Blenheim Palace

8 miles NW of Oxford; 62 miles NW of London

The small country town of Woodstock, the 1330 birthplace of the Black Prince, ill-fated son of King Edward III, lies on the edge of the Cotswolds. Some of the stone houses here were constructed when Woodstock was the site of a royal palace. The palace had so suffered the ravages of time that its remains were demolished when Blenheim Palace was built. Woodstock was once the seat of a flourishing glove industry.

### ESSENTIALS

**GETTING THERE**    Take the train to Oxford (see above).

The Gloucester Green bus (no. 20) leaves Oxford about every 30 minutes during the day. The trip takes just over a half hour. Call **Thames Transit** at ☎ **01865/772250** for details.

If you're driving, take A44 from Oxford.

**VISITOR INFORMATION**    The **Tourist Information Centre** is on Hensington Road (☎ **01993/811038**). Open Monday through Saturday in summer, 9:30am to 1pm and 2 to 5:30pm; October through March 10am to 12:00pm and 1 to 3pm.

### ENGLAND'S ANSWER TO VERSAILLES: BLENHEIM PALACE

The extravagant, baroque ✪ **Blenheim Palace** (☎ **01993/811325**) is regarded as England's answer to Versailles. Blenheim is the home of the 11th duke of Marlborough, a descendant of John Churchill, the first duke, who was an on- and off-again favorite of Queen Anne's. In his day (1650 to 1722), the first duke became the supreme military figure in Europe. Fighting on the Danube near a village named Blenheim, Churchill defeated the forces of Louis XIV, and the lavish palace of Blenheim was built for the duke as a gift from the queen. It was designed by Sir John Vanbrugh, also the architect of Castle Howard; the landscaping was created by Capability Brown. The palace is loaded with riches: antiques, porcelain, oil paintings, tapestries, and chinoiserie.

North Americans know Blenheim as the birthplace of Sir Winston Churchill. His birth room is included in the palace tour, as is the Churchill exhibition, four rooms of letters, books, photographs, and other relics. Today the former prime minister lies buried in Bladon Churchyard, near the palace.

The Marlborough Maze, 600 yards from the palace, is the largest symbolic hedge maze on earth. It's like a wonderland with an herb and lavender garden, and a butterfly house, a veritable pleasure garden compound with such attractions as children's inflatable castles. You don't anticipate visiting Blenheim Palace to shop, but you can. The shops are installed in an old palace dairy. Here you can purchase a wide range of souvenirs, handcrafts, and even grandmother's preserves.

Blenheim Palace is open from mid-March to October, daily from 10:30am to 4:45pm. Admission is £7.80 ($12.50) for adults, £5.80 ($9.30) for students and seniors, and £3.80 ($6.10) for children 5 to 15 (free for ages 4 and under). A family ticket is £20 ($32).

# WHERE TO STAY

**Gorselands Farmhouse Auberge.** Boddington Lane, Long Hanborough, Witney AOX8 6PU.
☎ **01993/881895.** Fax 01993/882799. 6 rms. TV TEL. £46 ($73.60) double. AE, MC, V. Take
route A4095 3 miles southwest of Woodstock, following signs to Bladon.

The Gorselands' owner, Barbara Newcombe-Jones, explains with pride some of the
details that went into the restoration of her 200-year-old stone-sided farmhouse.
(Because the bulky roofing slates she needed for an authentic historic renovation
hadn't been mined since the 19th century, she used slates that were culled from other
antique buildings nearby.) Surrounded by many acres of fields, and set within a
1-acre garden of her own, the inn welcomes overnight guests in any of a half-dozen
simple, unpretentiously decorated bedrooms. There's a licensed restaurant on the
premises, serving evening platters of food for £6.75 ($10.80), and three-course full
dinners for £12.95 ($20.70) each. On the premises is a billiard table, a log-burning
fireplace, and many of the agrarian accoutrements found in rural England. Since the
auberge is only 12 miles north of Oxford, some guests prefer to use it as a base for
exploring that city as well.

**The Laurels.** Hensington Rd., Woodstock, Oxfordshire OX20 1JL. ☎ **01993/812583.** 3 rms.
£40 ($64) single; £50 ($80) double. All rates include English breakfast. MC, V. At the Punch Bowl
Public House, turn onto Hensington Rd. and it's 500 yds. ahead on the right.

Built in 1890 for the manager of a then-flourishing glove factory in the area, this guest
house has undergone considerable renovation. The decor is traditional, and Malcolm
and Nikki Lloyd have furnished the house with Victorian and Edwardian pieces in
keeping with the age of the Laurels. The rooms—two doubles and one twin—are
attractively decorated and well maintained. The location is just off the town center,
but within a few minutes' walk of the heart of town and the Blenheim Palace
grounds.

# WHERE TO EAT

**Brotherons Brasserie.** 1 High St. ☎ **01993/811114.** Main courses £7–£10 ($11.20–$16).
AE, DC, MC, V. Daily noon–2:30pm and 6:30–10:30pm. Bus: 206. ENGLISH.

Brotherons, located in the heart of town, is your best bet for a meal. Carefully
chosen fresh ingredients are one of the reasons for the success of this place.
Potted plants, pine chairs and tables, and gas mantels make for a simple but effective decor. Meals are likely to feature a selection of crudités, smoked salmon, or game
pie, and there's always a vegetarian dish of the day. Families with small children are
welcomed.

# WOODSTOCK AFTER DARK

A night out in Woodstock, as you might expect, revolves around the town's
pubs. The **Star Inn** (☎ 01993/811373) has three locally brewed real ales to
choose from—Tetley, Wadworth 6X, and the excellent Marston's Pedigree. The establishment serves the requisite bar munchies as well as full dinners. The management
boasts that its half-shoulder of lamb is the tenderest around because of the flow cooking process. You can also pick and choose from a cold buffet that features salads and
sandwich fixings. The **King's Head** is tucked away at 11 Park Lane (☎ 01993/
812164) in Woodstock. Tourists seem to like the "potato pub," as the locals call it.
The name comes from the wide variety of stuffed potato skins that the pub serves.
Enjoy these with a real ale; the owners are sure to have a different specialty ale every
month. If you come for dinner, a three-course meal—which may include fish, ribs,
or homemade lasagna—costs about £12 ($19.20).

## 5 Aylesbury

46 miles NW of London, 22 miles E of Oxford

The county town of Buckinghamshire since 1725, Aylesbury has retained much of its ancient charm and character. The town has a rich history, and many reminders of times gone by still remain, especially along the narrow Tudor alleyways and in the 17th-century architecture of the houses in the town center. Among the interesting structures is St. Mary's Church, the parish church, which dates from the 13th century and features an unusual spirelet. The 15th-century Kings Head Public House, a National Trust property currently undergoing renovations to restore it to its original splendor, has seen many famous faces in its time. Especially notable are the regular visits to the Inn by King Henry VIII while he was courting Anne Boleyn.

The market, which has been an integral part of the town since the 13th century, is still thriving, with markets held on Wednesdays, Fridays, and Saturdays, and a flea market on Tuesdays. During the 18th and 19th centuries, ducks were the most famous commodity of the Aylesbury market. The pure white ducks were a delicacy and upper-class Londoners desired the ducks for their dinner. The demand for the Aylesbury duck has declined, although not before the breed was threatened with extinction. Today, most ducks found on restaurant menus are raised elsewhere, and the threat to the Aylesbury duck has subsided. The ivory fowl are now enjoyed for their beauty rather than their flavor.

### ESSENTIALS

**GETTING THERE**   Aylesbury is 1 hour by train from London's Marylebone Station, or 25 minutes off the M25 via A41.

**VISITOR INFORMATION**   The **Aylesbury Tourist Information Centre,** 8 Bourbon St. (☎ **01296/330559**), is open April to October, Monday through Saturday from 9:30am to 5pm. From November to March, hours are Monday through Saturday from 10am to 4:30pm.

### SEEING THE SIGHTS

Aylesbury is blessed with an abundance of interesting architecture. We suggest strolling through the town to see the houses and buildings that line the streets. Hickman's Almshouses and the Prebendal Houses are structures that date from the 17th century; you can walk by after enjoying tea at St. Mary's Church, which is just down the road.

Located in two buildings on Church Street, a house and grammar school both dating from the 18th century, is the **Buckinghamshire County Museum.** The newest addition to the recently refurbished museum is the Roald Dahl Children's Gallery. Dahl's famous works, such as *Charlie and the Chocolate Factory,* and *James and the Giant Peach,* come to life as visitors ride in the Great Glass Elevator or crawl inside the Giant Peach. The hands-on exhibits don't stop upon entering the main museum, however. Innovative displays focusing on the cultural heritage of Buckinghamshire are interactive. The museum is open Monday through Saturday from 10am to 5pm and on Sunday from 2 to 5pm. Admission to the main museum is free; the cost for the Children's Gallery is £1.75 ($2.80) for adults, £1.50 ($2.40) for children. Advance arrangements are necessary for the Children's Gallery, because of the large numbers of school groups that visit. Call ☎ **01296/331441** for more information.

While you're here, you'll of course want to see those famous Aylesbury ducks. The best place to catch sight of the once-threatened species is at the **Oak Farms Rare**

**Breeds Park,** off the A41 on the way to Broughton (☎ **01296/415709**). The traditional working farm is home to a variety of animals, from sheep to pigs, many of which are rare breeds. Guests can hand-feed special food to the animals and take a picnic of their own to enjoy. There's also a nature trail that visitors may want to explore. The park is open Easter to the end of August on Wednesday through Friday, 10:30am to 4:30pm; bank holidays and weekends 10:30am to 5:30pm; in September and October, open only on Sundays.

Also in the area is **Waddeson Manor,** Bicester Road (☎ **01296/65182**), which was built by Baron Ferdinand de Rothschild in the 1870s. The manor features French Renaissance architecture and a variety of French furniture, carpets, and porcelain. Eighteenth century artwork by several famous English and Dutch painters is exhibited, and there are, of course, wine cellars representing the family's well-known association with the grape. In the surrounding gardens, an aviary houses exotic birds. On the premises is a restaurant and gift shop, both featuring a vast assortment of Rothschild wines. The grounds and aviary are open March 1 to December 21, Wednesday to Sunday and bank holidays from 10am to 5pm. The house is open March 27 to October 26, Thursday to Sunday and bank holidays from 11am to 4pm. The house is also open in July and August on Wednesdays from 11am to 4pm. Admission to the house and grounds is £9 ($14.40) for adults and £6 ($9.60) for children. Admission to the grounds is £3 ($4.80) for adults and £1.50 ($2.40) for children.

## WHERE TO STAY & EAT

**West Lodge Hotel.** 45 London Rd., Aston Clinton, Aylesbury HP22 5HL. ☎ **0129/663-0331.** Fax 0129/663-0151. 7 rms. TV TEL. £32–£44 ($51.20–$70.40) single; £48–£60 ($76.80–$96) double. All rates include breakfast. AE, DC, MC, V.

Close to Aylesbury, this Victorian hotel on the A41 outdoes all others in the area with its facilities, including a swimming pool and sauna. But it doesn't stop just there. It also offers its own hot air balloon. Rooms are comfortable and furnished with a clock-radio, hair dryer, trouser press, bath items, and tea and coffee fixings.

For dining, there is Montgolfier, a French restaurant named after the brothers who flew the first successful hot air balloon in 1783. It opens for dinner. And a three-star Michelin-trained French chef presides over a guests-only daily table d'hôte two-course dinner for £17.50 ($28). On Thursday, Friday, and Saturday, the dining room is open to the public, serving a three-course table d'hôte for £30 ($48).

**Queen's Head.** 9 High St., Wing. ☎ **0129/668-8268.** Main courses £5.65–£15 ($9.05–$24). MC, V. Mon–Sat noon–11pm; Sun noon–10:30pm. No dinner service on Sun and Mon. ENGLISH.

This old, traditional village pub changed hands recently, and John and Christine Cavanagh, who ran a highly recommended pub in London, have put enough emphasis on food to move this into the restaurant category. Christine, a former caterer, offers up a daily menu that doubles as lunch and dinner. Sunday lunch features a traditional roast, and other recurring menu items, such as chops, fish, lamb hot pot, and a mixed grill. Her pies—pork and apple, steak and kidney, and steak and ale—may help you gain a new appreciation of traditional English fare. Wash your meal down with Carlesburg Export, Calders, Tetley, Marston Pedigree, or Strongbow cider.

## AYLESBURY AFTER DARK

Popular with a younger crowd, the **Hobgoblin,** Kingsbury Square (☎ **0129/641-5100**), has been in operation just 2 years, but it replaced the Red Lion, the original pub built here in 1742. On tap are house ales, Hobgoblin and Wychwood, as well as John Smith's, and there is also a full bar. Snack food is available, as are such distractions as pool tables, televisions, and video games. Sunday nights there's live jazz. There is no cover charge. On weekends, the second floor opens as a nightclub called **Merlin's,** which has a disco. Hours are Friday and Saturday from 10pm to 2:30am, and Sunday from 10pm to 12:30am, with a cover charge of £4 ($6.40).

## 6  St. Albans

27 miles NW of London, 41 miles SW of Cambridge

Reaching back 2,000 years, today's cathedral city of St. Albans was named after a Roman soldier who was the first Christian martyr in England. Medieval pilgrims made the trek to visit the shrine of St. Alban, and visitors today still find inspiration in the ancient cathedral city and the surrounding countryside.

Beatrix Potter created *Peter Rabbit* in this county, and George Bernard Shaw found inspiration in the view from his countryside home near Ayot St. Lawrence. As you explore St. Albans and its nearby attractions, you'll be tracing in the footsteps of the Good Queen Bess and Henry VIII, who passed through before you.

Although industry has crept in, and Greater London continues to expand its circumference, St. Albans is at the center of what was known as "the market basket of England." The 1,000-year-old tradition of the street market continues, as merchants of all kinds set up colorful stalls to display their goods. The market is held on Wednesdays and Sundays, and is one of the largest in the southeast.

Tourism has also become very important to the town, which it is prepared to capture since it is near the M25 and the M1 and on the way to many historic homes and attractions. St. Albans itself is home to several museums, well-preserved Roman ruins, and beautiful gardens.

### ESSENTIALS

**GETTING THERE**   By rail, car, and coach, St. Albans is easily reached from London. North London Railways leaves from London's Euston Station every 40 minutes Monday through Saturday and hourly on Sunday. The rail connection, ThamesLink, takes you from London to St. Albans in just 17 minutes. From London, Green Line coach 724 also runs to St. Albans frequently. Motorists take M25 Junction 21A or 22; M1 Junctions 6, 7, or 9; and A1(M) Junction 3.

**VISITOR INFORMATION**   The **Tourist Information Centre** is at The Town Hall, Market Place (☎ **01727/864511**). From April through October, hours are Monday through Saturday from 9:30am to 5:30pm; off-season hours are Monday through Saturday from 10am to 4pm. From the end of July until mid-September, the office is also open Sunday from 10:30am to 4:30pm.

**WALKING TOURS**   The Association of Honorary Guides, a trained group of local volunteers, provides guided walks. These include a tour of the Roman Verulamium and the Medieval Town, a ghost walk, and a coaching inn walking tour. In addition to prebooked tours, free public guided walks are available on Sunday; the tour begins at 3pm at the clock tower. Guides are also available on Sundays at the Verulamium Museum and Roman Theatre to give short talks on a number of topics concerning the Romans and their time in the area. Full details can be obtained from the Tourist Information Centre (see above) or from the Tours Secretary (☎ **01727/833001**).

# EXPLORING THIS ANCIENT ROMAN TOWN

The **Cathedral of St. Albans,** Holywell Hill and High Street (☎ 01727/860780) is still known as "The Abbey" to the locals, even though Henry VIII dissolved it as such in 1539. Construction of the cathedral was launched in 1077, making it one of the early Norman churches of England. The bricks, especially visible in the tower, came from the old Roman city of Verulamium, located at the foot of the hill. The nave and west front date from 1235.

The new chapter house, the first modern building beside a great medieval cathedral in the country, was opened by the queen in 1982. The structure houses an information desk, a gift shop, and a restaurant. There is also a video detailing the history of the cathedral, which you can view for £1.50 ($2.40).

St. Albans Cathedral and the chapter house are generally open daily from 9am to 6:45pm; closing at 5:45pm in winter. In addition to church services, there are often organ recitals open to the public. The church's choir can sometimes be heard rehearsing, if they're not on tour.

The **Verulamium Museum at St. Michael's** (☎ 01727/819339) stands on the site of the ancient Roman city of the same name. Here you'll see some of the finest Roman mosaics in Britain, as well as re-created Roman rooms. Part of the Roman town hall, a hypocaust, and the outline of houses and shops are still visible in the park that surrounds the museum. The museum is open year-round Monday through Saturday from 10am to 5pm and Sunday from 1 to 5pm. Admission is £2.60 ($4.15) for adults, £1.55 ($2.50) for children, and £7 ($11.20) for a family ticket. By car, Verulamium is a 10-minute drive from Junction 21A on M25; it is also accessible from Junctions 9, 7, or 6 on M1; follow the signs for St. Albans and the Roman Verulamium. Taking a train to St. Albans City Station will put you within 2 miles of the museum.

Just a short distance from Verulamium is the **Roman Theatre** (☎ 01727/835035). The structure is the only theater of the period that is open to visitors in Britain. You can tour the site daily from 10am to 5pm (4pm in winter).

The **Museum of St. Albans,** Hatfield Road (☎ 01727/819340), details the history of St. Albans from the departure of the Romans to the present day. The museum is the home of the Salaman Gallery, which displays trade and craft tools. Special exhibits are often shown and lectures by knowledgeable speakers held. The Museum of St. Albans is open Monday through Saturday from 10am to 5pm and Sundays from 2 to 5pm. Admission is free. It is located in the city center on A1057 Hatfield Road and is a 5-minute walk from St. Albans City Station.

From St. Albans you can visit **Gorhambury,** a classic-style mansion built in 1777. The private home, owned by the Earl and Countess of Verulam, contains 16th-century enameled glass and historic portraits. It's open May to September from 2 to 5pm on Thursday only. Admission for adults is £4 ($6.40), £2.50 ($4) children, and £2 ($3.20) seniors. Gorhambury is located 2¹/₂ miles west of St. Albans near the A5. From the Verulamium Museum, cross Bluehouse Hill Road; the house is about a mile up a private drive.

# OUTDOOR PURSUITS

In St. Albans, visit the swimming pool and aquazooms at **Westminster Lodge,** Holywell Hill (☎ 01727/846031). Also located at the lodge is the 9-hole Abbey View Course. Bathwood's 18-hole golf course is one of the finest public courses in the country. The Batchwood Indoor Tennis Centre, which has four indoor courts, plus outdoor courts, has professional coaches available for all play levels. Both the golf and the tennis center are located on the grounds of the **Batchwood Hall mansion** on Batchwood Drive (☎ **01727/84425**).

## SHOPPING

The twice weekly street market, held every Wednesday and Saturday on St. Peters Street, is defined by a frantic pace. In contrast, modern off-street precincts and small specialty shops in St. Albans combine to create a unique, laid-back atmosphere the rest of the week.

**Jesters,** Christopher Place (☎ **01727/851162**), carries an assortment of wooden toys and games such as trains, cars, and juggling equipment. For souvenirs related to traditional British teatime, visit **Whittard's of Chelsea,** 25 Market Place (☎ **01727/ 867092**). The shop specializes in teas and coffees as well as mugs, tea pots, biscuits, and chocolates.

**The Past Times Shop,** 33 Market St. (☎ **01727/812817**), sells items that cover 12 eras in history. Here you'll find books on historic places, jewelry, clothes such as Victorian-style nightdresses, and compact disks and cassettes. For antiques, visit **By George,** 23 George St. (☎ **01727/853032**), St. Albans' largest antiques center; the building also houses a tearoom and crafts arcade. **Forget-Me-Not Antiques,** 27 High St. (☎ **01727/848907**), specializes in jewelry, especially Victorian name brooches. At **St. Albans Antique Centre,** 9 George St. (☎ **01727/844233**), up to 20 dealers gather to sell their goods. You can browse through the furniture and collectibles, then have a light snack in the tearoom or tour the gardens.

## WHERE TO STAY

**Ardmore House.** 54 Lemsford Rd., St. Albans AL1 3PR. ☎ **01727/859313.** 28 rms. TV TEL. £49.50 ($79.20) single; £59.50 ($95.20) double; £30 ($48) per person family rate with minimum of 3. £10 ($16) for children under 12. All rates include breakfast. AE, V.

This charming Edwardian residence with a Victorian annex is on a residential road close to town and recreational activities, including golf, swimming, and fitness centers. The hotel is privately owned and family run. All rooms are comfortably modern and have coffee and tea facilities. The most desirable room of the house has a four-poster bed for "special occasions." Bedrooms have limed wood fitting and a color-coordinated decor. An elegant lounge bar provides a soothing atmosphere to read or talk to fellow guests. Breakfast is offered in an airy, sunny room overlooking the rear garden.

**Care Inns.** 29 Alma Rd., St. Albans AL1 3AT. ☎ **01727/867310.** 3 rms. TV. £25 ($40) single; £30 ($48) double; £45 ($72) family rm. Children under 12 half price. All rates include breakfast. No credit cards.

The proprietor of this semidetached Victorian house, Karin Arscott, enjoys making her guests feel welcome. She speaks four languages; if you're planning a side trip to France, she'd be happy to help you brush up on your language skills. The Victorian house is located within minutes of the center of town. The hotel only serves breakfast, but several pubs and restaurants are nearby. Also, each room has a small refrigerator; you may want to save money by keeping a few staples in it.

## WHERE TO EAT

The best budget dining in St. Albans is in the pubs.

**Garibaldi.** 62 Albert St., St. Albans. ☎ **01727/855046.** Main dishes £2.55–£4.50 ($4.10–$7.20). MC, V. Daily noon–2:30pm and 6–9pm. Pub: daily 11am–11pm. ENGLISH/ SEAFOOD.

This is one of the most mellow pubs in St. Albans, known for its "hidey-holes" around the small island bar. There is also a cafe-style dining area off the main room where you might want to enjoy your meal. At the front is a patio terrace. The pub serves up ESB, London Pride, and Chiswick beers; you're sure to find one to suit your taste. A variety of dishes, from simple sandwiches to large seafood platters, are served.

**Kingsbury Mill Waffle House.** St. Michael's St., St. Albans. ☎ **01727/853502.** Main courses £5–£8 ($8–$12.80). MC, V. Tues–Sat 11am–5pm; Sun–Mon and bank holidays noon–5pm; open until 6pm in summer. ENGLISH.

As its name implies, the meals here revolve around waffles. Plain or whole wheat Belgian waffles are served with a variety of sweet and savory toppings. As a meal you may enjoy the ham, cheese, and mushroom concoction. Sweet favorites are the pecan and butterscotch and the chocolate ice cream. The restaurant boasts that about half of all ingredients used are organically produced. The restaurant, along with a museum, is housed inside a working mill. Walk upstairs to the museum before your meal to view milling and farming artifacts.

**Rose & Crown.** St. Michael's St., St. Albans. ☎ **01727/851903.** Main courses £1.60–£5 ($2.55–$8). No credit cards. Mon–Sat 11:30am–3pm; Mon–Fri 5:30–11pm, Sat 6–11pm; Sun noon–3pm and 7–10:30pm. ENGLISH.

In a 300-year-old building near Verulamium Park, this pub is often uncrowded and tranquil because of its out-of-the-way location. There are two open fireplaces that are warm and inviting in winter. A variety of beers, including Tetley and Stella Artois are served.

**Ye Olde Fighting Cocks.** Abby Mill Lane, St. Albans. ☎ **01727/865830.** Lunch £3.50–£5.35 ($5.60–$8.55). Dinner £3.75–£7 ($6–$11.20). AE, DC, MC, V. Daily 11am–11pm. ENGLISH.

Listed in the Guinness Book of World Records as the oldest licensed house in England, the original foundation was laid in A.D. 700. William the Conqueror is said to have been a guest here. The inn's name recalls the days when cockfights were a regular event; today you can enjoy a drink in what used to be the pit. Eight real ales are served, along with five guest ales. The place is a real budget eatery. The lunch menu includes ploughman's or steak-and-kidney pie, chili, and other hot meals. Dinners are a tad fancier; favorites are the stuffed prawns and the salmon steak.

## ST. ALBANS AFTER DARK

St. Albans' nightlife is centered around its theaters. The Company of Ten, which has its base at the **Abbey Theatre,** Westminster Lodge, Holywell Hill (☎ **01727/57861**), is one of the leading amateur dramatic companies in Britain. The company presents 10 productions each season in either the well-equipped main auditorium or a smaller studio. Performances begin at 8pm; tickets cost from £4 to £6 ($6.40 to $9.60).

The **Maltings Arts Theatre,** in The Maltings Shopping Center (☎ **01727/844222**), presents performances based on literature—from Shakespeare to modern novels. Plays are presented only once and begin at 8pm on Thursday, Friday, and Saturday. Tickets are £6 to £7.50 ($9.60 to $12).

The **Arena** in the St. Albans Civic Center (☎ **01727/844488**) offers several types of entertainment. Comedies, dramas, and musicals are performed, along with special shows such as The Phantom of the Opera on Ice. Performances are held Monday through Saturday and begin at 8pm. Tickets range from £5 to £22 ($8 to $35.20).

## 7  More Historic Homes & Gardens

### NEAR WINDSOR

If you have time for only one excursion from Windsor, make it Hughenden Manor.

#### HUGHENDEN MANOR

In Buckinghamshire sits **Hughenden Manor,** High Wycombe, a country manor that not only gives us insight into the Victorian age but also acquaints us with a remarkable man. Benjamin Disraeli was one of the most enigmatic figures of 19th-century England. At age 21, "Dizzy" anonymously published his 5-volume novel *Vivian Grey.* In 1839 he married an older widow for her money, although they apparently developed a harmonious relationship. He entered politics in 1837 and continued writing novels; his later ones met with more acclaim.

In 1848, Disraeli acquired Hughenden Manor, a country house that befitted his fast-rising political and social position. He served briefly as prime minister in 1868, but his political fame rests on his stewardship as prime minister from 1874 to 1880. He became Queen Victoria's friend, and in 1877 she paid him a rare honor by visiting him at Hughenden. In 1876, Disraeli became the Earl of Beaconsfield; he died a widower 5 years later. Instead of being buried at Westminster Abbey, he preferred the simple little graveyard of Hughenden Church.

Today, Hughenden houses an odd assortment of memorabilia, including a lock of Disraeli's hair, letters from Victoria, autographed books, and a portrait of Lord Byron, an acquaintance of Disraeli's father. The manor house and garden are open April to October, Wednesday through Sunday from 1 to 5pm, and in March, on Saturday and Sunday only, from 1 to 5pm. It's closed on Good Friday. Admission is £3.70 ($5.90) for adults, £1.85 ($2.95) for children, or £9.50 ($15.20) for a family ticket. A visit to the Garden only costs £1 ($1.60) for adults or 50p (80¢) for children. For more information, call ☎ **01494/532580.**

**GETTING THERE**   From Windsor take the M4 (direction Reading), then A404 to A40. Continue north of High Wycombe on the A4128 for about 1¹/₂ miles. If you're relying on public transportation from London, take coach no. 711 to High Wycombe, then board a Beeline bus (High Wycombe–Aylesbury no. 323 or 324).

### WEST WYCOMBE & THE HELLFIRE CLUB

Snuggled in the Chiltern Hills, 30 miles west of London and 15 miles northwest of Windsor, the village of West Wycombe maintains an early 18th-century atmosphere. The thatched roofs have been replaced by tiles, and some of the buildings have been replaced, but the village is still 2 centuries removed from the present day. From Windsor, take the M4 (direction Reading), then A404 to A40. Signs to follow en route include Maidenhead, Marlow, and Oxford. If you previously visited Hughenden Manor, the village of West Wycombe lies immediately to the west.

In the mid–18th century, Sir Francis Dashwood began an ambitious building program at West Wycombe. His strong interest in architecture and design led him to undertake a series of monuments and parks still considered among the finest in the country. He also sponsored the building of a road, using the chalk quarries on the hill to aid in the support of the poverty-stricken villagers. The resulting caves were used by "The Knights of St. Francis of Wycombe," later known as the notorious **Hellfire Club.** A group drawn from the social circle surrounding the Prince of Wales, its members "gourmandized," swilling claret and enjoying the company of women "of a cheerful, lively disposition . . . who considered themselves lawful wives of the brethren during their stay."

A visit to West Wycombe wouldn't be complete without a tour of **West Wycombe Park,** seat of the Dashwood family, of both historical and architectural interest. Both George III and Ben Franklin stayed here, though not at the same time. The house is one of the best examples of Palladian-style architecture in England. The interior is lavishly decorated with 18th-century paintings and antiques. It is owned by the National Trust.

The house and grounds are open June through August, Sunday through Thursday from 2 to 6pm. Admission is £4 ($6.40) for adults or £10 ($16) for a family ticket. If you wish to visit only the grounds, the cost is £2.50 ($4). The caves are open from March through October, daily from 11am to 5:30pm; off-season hours are only on Saturday and Sunday from 11am to 5:30pm. Admission is £3 ($4.80) for adults and £1.50 ($2.40) for seniors and children. For more information, call the West Wycombe Estate Office at West Wycombe (☎ 01494/524411).

Other sights at West Wycombe include the **Church of St. Lawrence,** perched atop West Wycombe Hill and topped by a huge golden ball. Parts of the church date from the 13th century; its richly decorated interior was copied from a 3rd-century Syrian sun temple. The view from the hill is worth the trek up. Near the church stands the **Dashwood mausoleum,** built in a style derived from Constantine's Arch in Rome.

### Where to Stay & Dine

After your tour of the park, head for **George & Dragon,** High Street, West Wycombe HP14 3AB (☎ 01494/464414) either for a pint or a good, inexpensive lunch. In a building that dates back to 1720, this was a former coaching inn with a cheerful log fire, a comfortable size bar (that gets crowded on weekends), and an impressive oak staircase (complete with its own ghost). The present inn was built on the foundation of a 14th-century hostelry. There is a separate nonsmoking room open to children. The lunch and dinner menu is the same; the daily specials are likely to be game dishes in season. Otherwise, opt for the ploughman's lunch (bread and cheese), homemade meat pies such as lamb, pigeon pudding, or even beef Wellington on occasion. The beer of choice is usually Courage Best and Directors, or else Ushers Fonders on handpump. There's also a garden for outside eating, and a children's play area. If you like West Wycombe and want to stay over, there are eight cozily furnished bedrooms with private bath, phone, and TV, costing £48 ($76.80) for a single and £58 ($92.80) for a double, including breakfast.

### THE COTTAGE WHERE MILTON WROTE *PARADISE LOST*

The modern residential town of **Gerrards Cross** is often called the Beverly Hills of England, as it attracts many wealthy Londoners, among others. To the north of it is **Chalfont St. Giles,** where the poet John Milton lived during the Great Plague in 1665. To reach it, take the A355 north from Windsor bypassing Beaconsfield until you come to the signposted cut off for Chalfont St. Giles to the east.

Chalfont St. Giles is today a typical English village, although its history goes back to Roman times. There is also a Doomsday Book reference to it. The charm of the village is in its center, with shops, pubs, and cafes clustered around the green and the village pond.

At **John Milton's Cottage,** Chalfont St. Giles (☎ 01494/872313), Milton not only completed *Paradise Lost* in this 16th-century structure; he started *Paradise Regained* here. Its four rooms contain many relics and exhibits devoted to Miltoniana. A cottage garden is a further attraction. It is open March through October, Wednesday through Sunday from 10am to 1pm and 2 to 6pm, charging adults £2 ($3.20) and children 60p (95¢). If you're not rushed for time, Beaconsfield, west of Gerrards

Cross, deserves an hour or so. Explore its broad, tree-lined High Street which enjoys many associations with Disraeli.

# NEAR HENLEY-ON-THAMES
## MAPLEDURHAM HOUSE ON THE THAMES

The Elizabethan mansion of the Blount family (☎ 01189/723350) lies beside the Thames in the unspoiled village of Mapledurham. In the house, you'll see the Elizabethan ceilings and the great oak staircase, as well as the portraits of the two beautiful sisters with whom the poet Alexander Pope, a frequent visitor here, fell in love. The family chapel, built in 1789, is a fine example of modern gothic architecture. Cream teas with homemade cakes are available at the house. On the grounds, the last working water mill on the Thames still produces flour.

The house is open Easter to September, on Saturday, Sunday, and public holidays from 2:30 to 5pm; the mill opens at 1pm. Entrance to the house and mill costs £4 ($6.40) for adults and £2 ($3.20) for children 5 to 14. Free 4 and under.

**GETTING THERE**    From Henley-on-Thames, head south along A4155 toward Reading. At the junction with A329 head west. Mapledurham is signposted from this road. But a much more romantic way of reaching the lovely old house is to take the boat that leaves the promenade next to Caversham Bridge at 2pm on Saturday, Sunday, and bank holidays from Easter to September. The journey upstream takes about 45 minutes, and the boat leaves Mapledurham again at 5pm for the return trip to Caversham. This gives you plenty of time to walk through the house.

The round-trip boat ride from Caversham costs £3.50 ($5.60) for adults and £2.40 ($3.85) for children. Further details about the boat can be obtained from **Thames Rivercruises Ltd.,** Pipers Island, Bridge Street, Caversham Bridge, Reading (☎ 01189/481088).

## THE WELLINGTON DUCAL ESTATE

Tangible evidence of the fortune of the duke of Wellington and his descendants is most obvious in this combined house and country park. The complex's center-piece is the **Stratford Saye House,** c/o Wellington Office, Stratford Saye, Reading RG7 2BT (☎ 01256/882882). It lies 1 mile west of Reading, beside the A33 to Basingstoke. To reach Reading from Henry, head south along A1455. It has been the home of the dukes of Wellington since 1817, when the 17th-century house was bought for the Iron Duke to celebrate his victory over Napoléon at the Battle of Waterloo. A grateful Parliament granted a large sum of money for its purchase. Many memories of the first duke remain in the house, including his billiard table, battle spoils, and pictures. The funeral carriage that since 1860 had rested in St. Paul's Cathedral crypt is on display. In the gardens is the grave of Copenhagen, the charger ridden to battle at Waterloo by the first duke. There are also extensive landscaped grounds, together with a tearoom and gift shop. The house can only be visited during the warm-weather months. During May and September, it's open Saturday, Sunday, and bank holidays; from June to August, it's open Saturday to Thursday. On those days, hours are noon to 4pm. Admission costs £5 ($8) for adults, £2.50 ($4) for children 5 to 16, and free for children under 5.

Although extensive parks and gardens surround Stratford Saye, all except those immediately adjacent to the house are closed to the public. If you're looking for greenery, formal landscaping, and a low-tech version of a theme park with historical overtones, you'll find it 3 miles away, on the opposite side of the A33 highway, at the **Wellington Country Park,** Riseley, Reading, Berkshire RG7 1SP (☎ 01189/326444). Under the same administration as Stratford Saye, it's widely used by many local residents as a place for picnics, pedestrian rambles, and exercise. Most of its allure derives from the park's lake, its water fowl, and its miles of well-maintained walking paths. But there's a handful of attractions inside: The park contains the National Dairy Museum (where you can see the relics of 150 years of dairying), a riding school, a miniature steam railway, a deer park, and the Thames Valley Time Trail, a walk-through series of exhibits related to the geology of the region and the dinosaurs that once inhabited it. The park and each of its exhibits are open from March 1 to October 31, daily from 10am to 5:30pm. Admission costs £3.50 ($5.60) for adults, £1.70 ($2.70) for children 5 to 16, and free for children under 5. A combined ticket to the house and the park costs £7 ($11.20) for adults and £3.25 ($5.20) for children.

# NEAR MILTON KEYNES
## ✪ WOBURN ABBEY: ENGLAND'S GREAT GEORGIAN MANOR

Aside from Windsor Castle, the most visited attraction in the home counties is **Woburn Abbey** (☎ **01525/290666**), seat of the dukes of Bedford. It's spectacular, one of the top historic homes destinations near Windsor. The great 18th-century Georgian mansion has been the traditional seat of the dukes of Bedford for more than 3 centuries. The much-publicized estate is signposted half a mile from the village of Woburn, which is 13 miles southwest of the county seat at Bedford and 44 miles north of London.

Its state apartments are rich in furniture, porcelain, tapestries, silver, and art, including paintings by van Dyck, Holbein, Rembrandt, Gainsborough, and Reynolds. A series of paintings by Canaletto, showing his continuing views of Venice, grace the walls of the Venetian Room, an intimate dining room. (Prince Philip said the duke's collection was superior to the Canalettos at Windsor, but Her Royal Highness quickly corrected him.) Of all the paintings, one of the most notable is the *Armada Portrait of Elizabeth I.* Her hand rests on the globe, as Philip's invincible armada perishes in the background.

Queen Victoria and Prince Albert visited Woburn Abbey in 1841; the queen's Dressing Room displays a fine collection of 17th-century paintings from the Netherlands. Among the oddities and treasures at Woburn Abbey are a Grotto of Shells, a Sèvres dinner service (gift of Louis XV), and a chamber devoted to memorabilia of "The Flying Duchess." Wife of the 11th duke of Bedford, she was a remarkable woman who disappeared during a solo flight in 1937 (the same year as Amelia Earhart). The duchess was 72 years old at the time!

In the 1950s, the present duke of Bedford opened Woburn Abbey to the public to pay off his debt of millions of pounds in inheritance taxes. In 1974, he turned the estate over to his son and daughter-in-law, the marquess and marchioness of Tavistock, who reluctantly took on the business of running the 75-room mansion. And what a business it is, drawing hundreds of thousands of visitors a year and employing more than 300 people to staff the shops and grounds.

Today, Woburn Abbey is surrounded by a 3,000-acre deer park that includes the famous Père David deer herd, originally from China and saved from extinction at Woburn. The Woburn Safari Park has lions, tigers, giraffes, camels, monkeys, Przewalski horses, bongos, elephants, and other animals.

The house and park are only open on Saturday and Sunday from January 1 to March 22; visiting times for the house are 11am to 4pm (till 5pm on Sunday and bank holidays). From March 23 to November 2, the house can be visited daily from 11am to 5pm. The park is open Monday through Saturday from 11am to 4pm and Sunday from 11am to 5pm. Admission is £7 ($11.20) for adults, £6 ($9.60) for seniors, and £2.50 ($4) for children. For more information, call ☎ **01525/290666.**

**GETTING THERE** In summer, travel agents can book you on organized coach tours out of London. Otherwise, if you're driving, take the M1 (motorway) north to Junction 12 or 13, where Woburn Abbey directions are signposted.

## SHOPPING

In a wonderful old building, **Town Hall Antiques,** Market Place (☎ 01525/290950), sells a little bit of everything, such as drinking glasses going back to the 1700s, but other items that might read "Dateline 1940." This is a treasure trove of antiquities, including some Early English porcelain. Some unusual commemorative items are also sold, an array of Victorian, Georgian, and Edwardian memorabilia. Goods suit a wide range of pocketbooks, including clocks, Victorian jewelry, brass, copper, and "kitchenalia."

## WHERE TO STAY & EAT

Few visitors stop over here for the night, as they're usually rushing off somewhere else after seeing the abbey. However, if you do wish to stay overnight, Copperfields and Magpie rent simple rooms at affordable prices.

**The Black Horse.** 1 Bedford St. ☎ **01525/290210.** Pub platters £3.95–£6.95 ($6.30–$11.10); main courses £6.95–£17 ($11.10–$27.20). AE, MC, V. Mon–Fri noon–2:30 and 6–10pm; Sat–Sun 11am–11pm. INTERNATIONAL.

This is one of a half-dozen pubs and restaurants in Woburn, but most visitors call it their favorite. Originally opened in 1824 as a coaching inn, and retaining a dark, woodsy interior reminiscent of the era of its construction, it sits behind a stucco-sheathed Georgian facade on the town's main street, doubling as a pub and restaurant. Simple platters, in some cases designed to accompany the ales and lagers served in the pub, include "filled baguettes" (sandwiches on French bread); steaks, lasagna, ploughman's lunches, and spicy soups inspired by Thai cuisine. The restaurant occupies a separate room, and features steaks (including a massive 16-ounce version), and fish such as Dover sole grilled with lemon butter, or salmon with dill and white wine sauce.

**Copperfields.** 15–16 Marketplace, Woburn MK17 9PZ. ☎ **01525/290464.** Cream teas 95p ($1.50); sandwiches and soups £1.50–£2.50 ($2.40–$4). AE, MC, V. Daily 10:30am–6pm. TEA.

Situated on a cobblestone street in the village of Woburn, this tearoom overflows with old-world charm. The low-beamed ceilings and original fireplace are enhanced by lace-covered tables and windows. Homemade cakes are a favorite here—don't count calories; enjoy a piece of chocolate-rum or Victoria's sponge cake. Copperfields is also a B&B, with four rooms that rent for between £16 and £20 ($25.60 and $32) per person. The rather large, simply decorated rooms are in a 1700s Georgian building. Woburn Abbey is nearby, as well as an array of interesting shops.

**Magpie.** Bedford St., Woburn MK17 9QB. ☎ **01525/290219.** Bar lunches, sandwiches £4–£5 ($6.40–$8). AE. Daily noon–2:30pm and 6–11pm. ENGLISH.

After your tour of the abbey, head here for food and drink. This is a very small, family-run pub in a 400-year-old building. The beers of choice are Ruddles Best, Webster's, and Marston's Pedigree. The food is simple but filling fare, including well-stuffed sandwiches or a ploughman's lunch (bread and cheese). Aside from the public bar, there's a separate restaurant in this 16th-century former coaching inn near the Woburn Golf Club. At the side of the pub is a courtyard with tables when the weather's nice. If you'd like to stay over, the pub rents six basic but quite decent bedrooms, costing £35 ($56) for a double without bath or £45 ($72) with bath.

# NEAR ST. ALBANS
## ✪ HATFIELD HOUSE

Six miles east of St. Albans on A414 is **Hatfield House,** one of the great English country houses. Only the banqueting hall of the original Tudor palace remains; the remainder is Jacobean.

Hatfield formed a considerable part of the lives of both Henry VIII and his daughter Elizabeth I. In the old palace, built in the 15th century, Elizabeth romped and played as a child. Although Henry was married to her mother, Anne Boleyn, at the time of Elizabeth's birth, the marriage was later nullified (Anne lost her head and Elizabeth her legitimacy). Henry also used to stash away his oldest daughter, Mary Tudor, at Hatfield. But when Mary became Queen of England and set about earning the dubious distinction of "Bloody Mary," she found Elizabeth a problem. For a while she kept her in the Tower of London, but eventually let her return to Hatfield. In 1558, while at Hatfield, Elizabeth learned of her succession to the throne of England.

The Jacobean house that exists today has much antique furniture, tapestries, and paintings, as well as three oft-reproduced portraits, including the ermine and rainbow portraits of Elizabeth I. The great hall is suitably medieval, complete with a minstrel's gallery. One of the rarest exhibits is a pair of silk stockings, said to have been worn by Elizabeth herself, the first woman in England to don such apparel. The park and the gardens are also worth exploring. Luncheons and teas are available from 11am to 5pm in the converted coach house in the Old Palace yard.

Hatfield is open from March 25 to the second Sunday in October, Tuesday through Saturday from noon to 4pm, on Sunday from 1 to 4:30pm, and on bank holiday Mondays from 11am to 4:30pm; it's closed Good Friday. Admission is ££5.50 ($8.80) for adults and £3.40 ($5.45) for children. For information, call ☎ **01707/262823.**

Elizabethan banquets, staged in the banqueting hall of The Old Palace Tuesday and Thursday through Saturday with much gaiety and music, may be a splurge worth considering. Guests are invited to drink in an anteroom, then join the long tables for a feast of five courses with continuous entertainment from a group of Elizabethan players, minstrels, and jesters. Wine is included in the cost of the meal, but before-dinner drinks are extra. The best way to get here from London for the feast is to book a coach tour for an inclusive fee starting at £44 ($70.40). The Evan Evans agency has tours leaving from Mount Royal Hotel, Cockspur Street, and Herbrand Street in London. The coach returns to London after midnight. If you get here under your own steam, the cost is £28.75 ($46) on Tuesday and Thursday, £30 ($48) on Friday, and £31.50 ($50.40) on Saturday. For private reservations, call ☎ **01707/ 262055.**

**GETTING THERE**    By car from St. Albans, take A414 east and follow the brown signs that lead you directly to the estate. By bus, take the University bus from St. Albans City Station. Hatfield House is directly across from Hatfield Station.

## SHAW'S CORNER

In the village of Ayot St. Lawrence stands **Shaw's Corner** (☎ **01438/820307**), where George Bernard Shaw lived from 1906 to 1950. The utilitarian house, with its harsh brickwork and rather comfortless interior, is practically as he left it at his death—his hats still hang in the hall. Here Shaw wrote 6 to 8 hours a day, even into his 90s—he is said to have muttered, "This damned energy will not let me stop."

Evidence of his love for the written word is obvious throughout the house; one of his old typewriters is even still in position. Shaw was famous for his eccentricities, his vegetarianism, and his longevity. And, of course, for his vast literary output, the most famous of which remains *Pygmalion* (on which the musical, *My Fair Lady,* was based). *Man and Superman, St. Joan,* and *Heartbreak House* are still produced around the world. The house is open April to the end of October, Wednesday through Sunday and bank holidays from 2 to 6pm. Admission is £3.10 ($4.95) for adults and £1.50 ($2.40) for children. Shaw's Corner can be reached from St. Albans by taking B651 to Wheathampstead. Pass through the village, go right at the roundabout and take the first left turn. A mile up on the left is Brides Hall Lane, which leads to the house.

# Kent & Surrey

To the south and southeast of London are the shires (counties) of Kent and Surrey—both fascinating areas within easy commuting distance of the capital.

Of all the tourist centers, Canterbury (in Kent) is of foremost interest and makes the best base for exploring the area. Dover, Britain's historic "gateway" to the continent, is famed for its white cliffs. This port also makes a good base for exploring Kent.

Once an ancient Anglo-Saxon kingdom, Kent lies on the fringes of London but is far removed in spirit and scenery. Since the days of the Tudors, cherry blossoms have enlivened the fertile landscape. Not only orchards, but hop fields abound; conical oat houses with kilns for drying hops dot the rolling countryside. Both the hops and orchards have earned Kent the title of the garden of England—and in England, the competition's steep.

Kent suffered severe destruction during World War II, since it was the alley over which the Luftwaffe flew in its blitz of London. In spite of much devastation, it's still replete with interesting old towns, mansions, and castles. The county is also rich in Dickensian associations—in fact, Kent is sometimes referred to as Dickens Country. The writer's family once lived near the naval dockyard at Chatham.

Long before William the Conqueror marched his bands of pillaging Normans across its chalky North Downs, Surrey held importance for the Saxons. In fact, early Saxon kings were once crowned at what is now Kingston-on-Thames (the Coronation Stone is still preserved near the guildhall). In recent years, this tiny county has been in danger of being gobbled up by the encroaching expansion of London and turned into a sprawling suburb. Although the area bordering the capital is densely populated, Surrey still retains much unspoiled countryside, largely because its many heaths and commons are less than desirable land for postwar suburban houses. Essentially, Surrey is a county of commuters (Alfred Lord Tennyson was among the first; a resident in the remotest corner of Surrey can travel to London in about 45 minutes to an hour.

Kent is filled with some of Europe's grandest mansions. If your time is limited, seek out the big four: **Knole,** one of the largest private houses of England, a great example of Tudor architecture; **Hever Castle,** dating from the end of the 13th century, a gift from Henry VIII to the "great Flanders mare," Anne of Cleves; **Penhurst Place,** a magnificent English Gothic mansion, one of the

# Kent, Surrey & Sussex

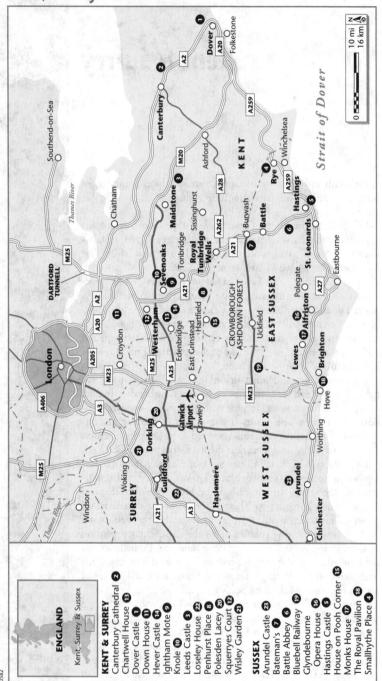

Southend-on-Sea

Thames River

Chatham

DARTFORD TUNNEL

London

Croydon

Woking

Windsor

Dorking

Guildford

Haslemere

SURREY

Gatwick Airport
Crawley

Canterbury

Dover

Folkestone

Strait of Dover

Maidstone

Ashford

K E N T

Sissinghurst

Tonbridge

Royal Tunbridge Wells

Sevenoaks

Westerham

Edenbridge

East Grinstead

Hartfield

CROWBOROUGH ASHDOWN FOREST

Uckfield

Winchelsea

Rye

Hastings

Battle

Burwash

St. Leonards

Eastbourne

EAST SUSSEX

Polegate

Alfriston

Lewes

Brighton

Hove

Worthing

WEST SUSSEX

Arundel

Chichester

**KENT & SURREY**

Canterbury Cathedral ②
Chartwell House ⑬
Dover Castle ①
Down House ⑪
Hever Castle ⑭
Ightham Mote ⑨
Knole ⑩
Leeds Castle ③
Loseley Park ㉒
Penhurst Place ⑧
Polesden Lacey ⑳
Squerryes Court ⑫
Wisley Garden ㉑

**SUSSEX**

Arundel Castle ㉓
Bateman's ⑦
Battle Abbey ⑥
Bluebell Railway ⑲
Glyndebourne
Opera House ⑯
Hastings Castle ⑤
House on Pooh Corner ⑮
Monks House ⑰
The Royal Pavilion ⑱
Smallhythe Place ④

ENGLAND

Kent, Surrey & Sussex

3-0582

outstanding country houses of Britain; and **Leeds Castle,** near Maidstone, dating from A.D. 857, and once called the loveliest castle in the world. Although it doesn't compare with these grand castles, **Chartwell House** also merits a visit because of the man who used to call it home: Sir Winston Churchill. For more advice on how to tour these homes, refer to "Kent's Country Houses, Castles & Gardens," below.

# 1  Canterbury

56 miles SE of London

Chaucer's memorable characters—knight, solicitor, nun, squire, parson, merchant, miller, and others—journeyed under the arch of the ancient West Gate spinning tales. They were bound for the shrine of Thomas à Becket, archbishop of Canterbury, who was slain by four knights of Henry II on December 29, 1170. (The king later walked barefoot from Harbledown to the tomb of his former friend, where he allowed himself to be flogged in an act of penance.) The shrine was finally torn down in 1538 by Henry VIII, as part of a campaign to destroy the monasteries and graven images. Canterbury, by then, had already become a fixed attraction.

The medieval Kentish city on the River Stour stands as the ecclesiastical capital of England. The city was once completely walled, and many traces of its erstwhile fortifications remain. Canterbury was in fact inhabited centuries before the birth of Jesus Christ. Julius Caesar arrived on the Kent coast in 54 B.C., but Roman occupation didn't begin until much later. Although its most famous incident was the murder of Becket, the medieval city witnessed other major events in English history, including Bloody Mary's order to burn nearly 40 victims at the stake. Richard the Lion-Hearted returned this way from crusading, and Charles II passed through on the way to claim his crown.

Canterbury pilgrims still continue to arrive, except today they're called daytrippers, and they overrun the city and its monuments. It's amazing that the central core of the city is as interesting and picture-perfect as it is, considering the enormous damage caused by the Nazi blitz of 1941. The city has an active university life—mainly students from Kent—and an enormous array of pubs. High Street is filled with shoppers in from the country. We suggest exploring Canterbury in the early morning or early evening—before or after the busloads have departed.

## ESSENTIALS

**GETTING THERE**    There is frequent train service from Victoria, Charing Cross, Waterloo, or London Bridge stations. The journey takes 1 1/2 hours.

The bus from Victoria Coach Station takes 2 to 3 hours and leaves twice daily.

If you're driving from London, take A2, then M2. Canterbury is signposted all the way. The city center is closed to cars, but it's only a short walk from several parking areas to the cathedral.

**VISITOR INFORMATION**    The **Visitors Information Centre** is at 34 St. Margaret's St. ( ☎ **01227/766567**), a few doors away from St. Margaret's Church. Open April through October, daily from 9:30am to 5:30pm and November through March, daily 9:30am to 5pm.

**GETTING AROUND BY BIKE**    Modern 10-speeds and mountain bikes make traveling easy and inexpensive. If hills are a problem, pick up an Ordnance Survey map that shows altitude contours from the tourist office. You can also buy the useful *North Downs Way* guide for £2.95 ($4.70), if you'd like to bike around the Kentish countryside.

**Canterbury Cycle Mart,** 19 Lower Bridge St., Canterbury (☎ **01227/761488**), rents 10-speeds for £10 ($16) per day. You'll need a credit card or £50 ($80) cash deposit.

Dutch touring bikes—small, folding bikes—and mountain bikes can be rented at the **House of Agnes Hotel,** 71 St. Dunstan's St., Canterbury (☎ **01227/472185**). A simple map comes with each bike, and an Ordnance Survey map of East Kent is offered for £4.95 ($7.90). A credit card or £50 ($80) deposit is required for city bikes and £100 ($160) for mountain bikes.

## ✪ CANTERBURY CATHEDRAL

The foundation of this splendid cathedral dates back to the arrival of the first archbishop, Augustine, from Rome in A.D. 597, but the earliest part of the present building is the great Romanesque crypt built circa 1100. The monastic "quire" erected on top of this at the same time was destroyed by fire in 1174, only 4 years after the murder of Thomas à Becket on a dark December evening in the northwest transept, still one of the most famous places of pilgrimage in Europe. The destroyed "quire" was immediately replaced by a magnificent early Gothic one, the first major expression of that architectural style in England. Its architects were the Frenchman, William of Sens, and "English" William, who took Sens's place after the Frenchman was crippled in an accident in 1178 that later proved fatal.

The cathedral is noteworthy for its medieval tombs of royal personages, such as King Henry IV and Edward the Black Prince, as well as numerous archbishops. The great 14th-century nave and the famous central "Bell Harry Tower" belong to the later Middle Ages. The cathedral stands on spacious precincts amid the remains of the buildings of the monastery—cloisters, chapter house, and Norman water tower—which have survived intact from Henry VIII's dissolution to the present day.

Becket's shrine was destroyed by the Tudor king, but the site of that tomb is in Trinity Chapel, near the high altar. The saint is said to have worked miracles, and the cathedral has some rare stained glass depicting those feats. Miraculously, the windows escaped both Henry VIII's agents of destruction and Hitler's bombs. The windows were removed as a precaution at the beginning of the war. Even though the war flattened a large area of Canterbury, the main body of the church was unharmed. However, the cathedral library was damaged during a German air raid in 1942. The replacement windows of the cathedral were blown in, proving the wisdom of having the medieval glass safely stored away. East of the Trinity Chapel is "Becket's Crown," where there's a chapel dedicated to the "Martyrs and Saints of Our Own Time." St. Augustine's Chair, one of the symbols of the authority of the archbishop of Canterbury, stands behind the high altar.

The cathedral, located at 11 The Precincts (☎ **01227/762862**), is open Easter to September, Monday through Saturday from 8:45am to 7pm; October to Easter, Monday through Saturday from 8:45am to 5pm; Sunday (all year) from 12:30 to 2:30pm and 4:30 to 5:30pm. Admission is £2.50 ($4) for adults and £1.50 ($2.40) for children. Guided tours, based on demand, are £2.80 ($4.50) for adults and £1.50 ($2.40) for children.

## MORE ATTRACTIONS

**Canterbury Heritage Museum of the City.** Stour St. ☎ **01227/452747.** Admission £1.70 ($2.70) adults, £1.10 ($1.75) students and seniors, 85p ($1.35) children. Year-round Mon–Sat 10:30am to 5pm; Sun 1:30–5pm from June–Oct. Last entry time is 4pm. Closed Christmas week and Good Friday.

In the ancient Poor Priests' Hospital with its medieval interiors and soaring oak roofs, the museum features award-winning displays that showcase the city's treasures.

# Canterbury

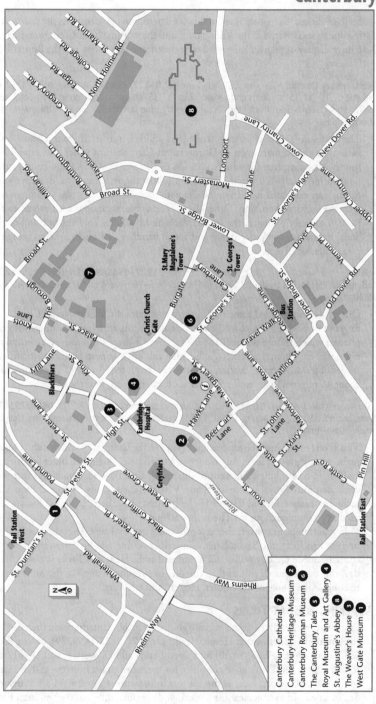

- Canterbury Cathedral **7**
- Canterbury Heritage Museum **2**
- Canterbury Roman Museum **6**
- The Canterbury Tales **5**
- Royal Museum and Art Gallery **4**
- St. Augustine's Abbey **8**
- The Weaver's House **3**
- West Gate Museum **1**

State-of-the-art video, computer, and hologram technology transports the visitor back in time to such events as the Viking raids and the wartime blitz. Collections include a huge display of pilgrim badges from medieval souvenir shops and the Rupert Bear Gallery.

**Canterbury Roman Museum.** Butchery Lane. ☎ **01227/785575.** Admission £1.70 ($2.70) adults, £1.10 ($1.75) students and seniors, 85p ($1.35) children. Year-round Mon–Sat 10am–5pm; Sun 1:30pm–5pm from June–Oct. Last entry time is 4pm. Closed Christmas week and Good Friday.

The museum is located beneath street level and is constructed around actual excavations of the Roman town of Durovernum Cantiacorum which was established shortly after Emperor Claudius's invasion of the area in A.D. 43 and continued to flourish for nearly 400 years. Visitors can follow the archaeologists' detective work through an excavated Roman house site with patterned mosaics that was discovered after the wartime bombing. Other displays and reconstructions are devoted to the Roman military presence, the marketplace, and the household's shrine and family gods. Interactive computer shows and actual handling of Roman artifacts bring the past to life for all ages.

**The Canterbury Tales.** 23 St. Margaret's St. ☎ **01227/454888.** Admission £4.85 ($7.75) adults, £3.95 ($6.30) students, £3.75 ($6) children 5–16. Free 4 and under. Daily 9:30am–5:30pm.

One of the most visited museums in town re-creates the pilgrimages of Chaucerian England through a series of medieval tableaux. Visitors are handed headsets with earphones, which feature oral recitations of five of Chaucer's *Canterbury Tales* and the murder of St. Thomas à Becket. Audiovisual aids bring famous characters to life, and stories of jealousy, pride, avarice, and love are recounted. A tour of all exhibits takes about 45 minutes. The exhibit is located off High Street, near the cathedral.

**St. Augustine's Abbey.** Corner of Lower Chantry Lane and Longport Rd. ☎ **0850/293822.** Admission £1.50 ($2.40) adults, £1.10 ($1.75) students. Apr–Sept daily 10am–6pm; Oct–Mar daily 10am–4pm.

This is one of the most historic religious sites in the country, of which only ruins remain, mostly ground level. Augustine was buried here, along with other archbishops and Anglo-Saxon kings. Adjacent to the remains are the abbey buildings that were converted into a royal palace by Henry VIII and used briefly by several monarchs, including Elizabeth I and Charles I. The buildings have been expanded and are now used as accommodations for The King's School.

In an attempt to convert the Saxons, Pope Gregory I sent Augustine to England in 597. Ethelbert, the Saxon King, allowed Augustine and his followers to build a church outside the city walls; and it endured until Henry VIII tore it down. In its day, the abbey church rivaled the cathedral in size, and enough of the ruins remain to conjure the whole of the cloister, church, and refectory.

## WALKING & BOAT TOURS

From Easter to early November, daily guided tours of Canterbury are organized by the **Guild of Guides,** Arnett House, Hawks Lane (☎ **01227/459779**), costing £3.25 ($5.20) for adults, £2.75 ($4.40) for students and children over 14, and £8 ($12.80) for a family ticket. Don't go to the office for the actual tours; from the end of March to the end of October, meet at the Visitors Information Centre at 34 St. Margaret's St., in a pedestrian zone near the cathedral, daily (including Sunday) at 2pm. From the beginning of July to the end of August there's also a tour Monday through Saturday at 11am.

From just below the Weavers House, boats leave for half-hour **trips on the river;** they feature commentary on the history of the buildings you pass. Umbrellas are provided to protect you against inclement weather.

## OUTDOOR PURSUITS

**GOLF**  For a leisurely stroll on a well-kept public course, try the 18-hole **Canterbury Golf Course** at Littlebourne Road (☎ 01227/453532). The cost per round is £27 ($43.20) for 18 holes, or £36 ($57.60) for the day. There are no golf carts and no clubs for rent. The par 70 club is open to players with established handicaps or proof of membership in another golf club.

**HORSEBACK RIDING**  The **Bourne Park Stables** in Bridge (☎ 01227/ 831927) is open daily from 8am until dark. Riding school horses are available for £15 ($24) for a 1-hour guided hack ride. A Boxing Day hunt (December 26) is open to the public. The stables are closed Christmas and New Year's days. The **Bursted Manor Riding Centre** in Pett Bottom (☎ 01227/830568) is open Tuesday through Sunday from 9am to dusk. On weekdays the last lesson is at 7pm and on Saturday and Sunday at 5pm. Ex-competition and riding school mounts are available at £15 ($24) for a 1-hour group lesson or hack ride and £15 ($24) for a half-hour private lesson. A Boxing Day hunt is open to the public.

**SWIMMING**  The **Kingsmead Leisure Centre** on Kingsmead (☎ 01227/ 769817) has an indoor pool open to the public Monday, Wednesday, and Friday from 9am to 1:30pm. Admission is £1.85 ($2.95), but call ahead because the facility closes at various times for school groups.

## SHOPPING

**Albion Bookstop.** 13 Mercery Lane. ☎ **01227/768631.**

This is the place to find good local folding maps. This small, browser-friendly shop features new books, including children's books and modern fiction. Along with maps, there are many local cookbooks, histories, and biographies.

**Canterbury Pottery.** 38 Burgate (just before Mercury Lane). ☎ **01227/452608.**

Here you'll find practical handmade pottery—vases, mugs, teapots, dinner and tea sets, in earth colors of blues, greens, and browns. This sturdy stuff wears well.

**Chaucer Bookstop.** 6 Beer Cart Lane. ☎ **01227/453912.**

Slap on your tweed jacket and grab your pipe for a trip to a secondhand shop with first editions (both old and modern), out-of-print books, special leather-bound editions, and a large selection of local history books. County maps and prints of local scenery are also available. If you want to amuse (or exasperate) the clerk, ask for a first edition of *The Canterbury Tales*.

**Chaucer Centre.** 22 St. Peter's St. ☎ **01227/470379.**

*The Canterbury Tales* in book and tape formats join all things Chaucerian, including T-shirts, St. Justin jewelry from Cornwall, Ellesmere cards, and balls and plates for juggling.

**Deakins.** 1–2 Sun St. ☎ **01227/462116.**

This classic, well-known men's and boy's outfitter carries clothing from underwear to overcoats. Realbook, Van Heusen, and Double Two shirts join Gurteen, Wellington and Brook Taverner suits and KilSpindie, and Woolsey and Hodgson knitwear. There are regimental ties and walking sticks. They also carry boy's and girl's school uniforms and boy's casual wear, including sport coats.

**English Teddy Bear Company.** 4 St. Peter's St. ☎ **01227/784640.**

English tradition holds firm here in a shop stuffed with hundreds of teddy bears with embroidered noses, humps in their backs, silk feet, and long arms and legs. Famous-name bears don't hang out here—no Rupert, no Winnie, no Paddington. Additional items include bearish T-shirts and sweat shirts, a line of jams and marmalades, and clothes for the bears.

# WHERE TO STAY
## DOUBLES FOR LESS THAN £45

✪ **Alexandra House.** 1 Roper Rd., Canterbury, Kent CT2 7EH. ☎ **01227/767011.** Fax 01227/786617. 7 rms, 3 with bath (tub or shower). TV. £22–£25 ($35.20–$40) single without bath; £36–£38 ($57.60–$60.80) double without bath, £37–£45 ($59.20–$72) double with bath. All rates include English breakfast. No credit cards.

On a quiet road off St. Dunstan's Street, this guest house, built around 1901, is a 10-minute walk from the cathedral. In 1996 it was rated an outstanding B&B. The bedrooms are on any of three different floors and contain hot-beverage facilities, radios, hair dryers, and a simple but clean decor, not the patched carpets and shrunken bedspreads found in many Canterbury B&Bs at this price. Shirley and Terry Barber welcome you to their family-run establishment. In back is a garden with a patio and chairs.

✪ **Ann's Hotel.** 63 London Rd., Canterbury, Kent CT2 8JZ. ☎ **01227/768767.** Fax 01227/768172. 20 rms. TV TEL. £18–£30 ($28.80–$48) single; £34–£44 ($54.40–$70.40) double. All rates include English breakfast. MC, V.

This family-owned B&B stands on an artery leading out of town, a 10-minute walk from the town center (follow the signs to M2 to London). Given the rates, the place is surprisingly luxurious, an imposing Victorian house restored to its original grandeur. Ann Dellaway rents well-furnished and comfortable bedrooms, some with four-poster beds. Each bedroom is individually designed, with all the touches of a fine English country house. Twelve of the rooms have color TVs and coffee-making facilities. A full English breakfast is served in a bright, spacious dining room along with a wide selection of fine teas, marmalades, and jams. Guests convene in an elegant lounge with a Victorian fireplace.

**Chrislyn's Guest House.** 15 Park Ave., Dover, Kent CT16 1ES. ☎ **01304/202302.** TV. 7 rms. £14 ($22.40) single; £24 ($38.40) double. All rates include full English breakfast. No credit cards.

A warm welcome awaits you at this Victorian guest house where Chris and Lyn Heynen provide impeccably clean, comfortable rooms with more amenities than most B&Bs. All rooms have beverage-making equipment and color TV. The Heynens have a special quality that gives their guests that "at home" feeling that you often miss while on vacation. They also have a wealth of knowledge about the Kent area that they are only too happy to share by helping their guests plan bike and walking tours to explore off the beaten path and to picnic.

**Kingsbridge Villa.** 15 Best Lane, Canterbury, Kent CT1 2JB. ☎ **01227/766415.** 13 rms, 8 with bath (tub or shower). TV. £18 ($28.80) single without bath, £30 ($48) single with bath; £32 ($51.20) double without bath, £42 ($67.20) double with bath. All rates include English breakfast. No credit cards.

Located in the historic heart of town, this is a bright, inviting guest house built in the 1750s on Roman foundations. During its lifetime it formerly served as a weaving factory and later as a pub; today it has comfortable furnishings, well-maintained bedrooms, and the remains of an ancient Roman well in its cellar. A small Italian restaurant, Il Pozzo, operates under separate management in the brick-lined basement.

**St. Stephens Guest House.** 100 St. Stephens Rd., Canterbury, Kent CT2 7JL. ☎ **01227/ 767644.** 12 rms, 3 with bath. £21 ($33.60) single without bath; £36 ($57.60) double without bath, £46 ($73.60) double with bath. All rates include English breakfast. MC, V. From Westgate Tower, head down North Lane.

This is in a quiet part of the city, yet is close to the main attractions. Set in well-kept gardens and lawns, St. Stephens is one of the most attractive buildings in Canterbury, and is owned and managed by Jack and Hazel Johnson. While the character of the house has been retained, the accommodations are modern and include central heating, coffee-making facilities, shaver outlets, and hot and cold water. The house can accommodate up to 20 guests.

## DOUBLES FOR LESS THAN £55

✪ **Kingsmead House.** 68 St. Stephens Rd., Canterbury, Kent CT2 7JF. ☎ **01227/760132.** 3 rms. £45–£50 ($72–$80) single or double. All rates include English breakfast. No credit cards. Free parking.

Jan and John Clark, one of the most hospitable couples in the region, welcome you to their 17th-century house. Their timbered house is located about 6 to 8 minutes from the heart of Canterbury off Kingsmead Road. Although you'll pay more here than in a typical peas-in-the-pod B&B, the price is justified because of the taste and comfort level of the place. A stay here is truly like visiting a well-kept and attractive private home. Since there are only three well-furnished rooms, each guest gets personal attention. The rooms are fresh and bright, and the whole atmosphere is state-of-the-art, enough to please the most demanding guest.

**Oriel Lodge.** 3 Queens Ave., Canterbury CT2 8AY. ☎ and fax **01227/462-8452.** 6 rms, 2 with bath. TV. £22–£24 ($35.20–$38.40) single without bath; £37–£41 ($59.20–$65.60) double without bath; £45–£49 ($72–$78.40) double with bath; £63–£69 ($100.80–$110.40) family rm for 3 adults. Children 6–11 half price, no children under 6. All rates include breakfast and afternoon tea. MC, V.

The lodge, built in the style of William Morris in 1907, is an Edwardian house. It is easily accessible to many of the Canterbury sights and to Canterbury Cathedral, which is only a 5-minute walk away. The lodge, run by the Rishworths on a quiet neighborhood off London Road, has an attractive garden and the furnishings are also William Morris style. The rooms have TVs, radio-alarms, and beverage-making equipment. Tea is served from 4 to 5:30pm in the garden in the summer and in front of the log fire in the lounge in the winter. Smoking is permitted in the lounge only, but not during breakfast.

✪ **Pointers.** 1 London Rd., Canterbury, Kent CT2 8LR. ☎ **01227/456846.** Fax 01227/831131. 13 rms, 12 with bath (tub or shower). TV TEL. £32 ($50.55) single without bath, £40 ($64) single with bath; £45 ($71.10) double without bath, £50–£60 ($80–$96) double with bath. All rates include English breakfast. AE, DC, MC, V. Closed from a few days before Christmas to mid-Jan. From the center, follow the signs to the M2/ London Rd.

One of the city's finest guest houses, this Georgian building (ca. 1740) is across from the 10th-century St. Dunstan's Church. Your hosts here are Mary Lanaway, and Christine and Jack O'Brian, proud to be in an area of Canterbury designated as an architectural conservation area. Their inn offers clean, comfortable rooms as well as some family units. Bedroom amenities include radios and beverage-making equipment. It's about a 10-minute walk from the heart of Canterbury, and there's a private parking area. Pointers Restaurant serves English cuisine; a fixed-price dinner costs £13.50 ($21.60). Dinner is prepared by the owner using fresh ingredients, and as such represents extremely good value.

**The White House.** 6 St. Peter's Lane, Canterbury, Kent CT1 2BP. ☎ **01227/761836.** 9 rms. TV. £25–£35 ($40–$56) single; £40–£50 ($64–$80) double; £50–£65 ($80–$104) triple or family rm for 4. All rates include English breakfast. No credit cards.

You'll find this Regency town house on a lane inside the old city walls off St. Peter's Street next to the Marlowe Theatre. The owners, Felicity and Norman Blackman, are welcoming and informed hosts. They add a personal touch to everything, from seeing that bedrooms are well maintained to offering a superb English breakfast. Most of the rooms are good-sized, and each is well-equipped with the comfort and amenities needed for a fine stopover in Canterbury. Breakfast is served at a large communal table in an elegant dining and sitting room.

**Yorke Lodge.** 50 London Rd., Canterbury, Kent CT2 8LF. ☎ **01227/451243.** Fax 01227/462006. 5 rms. TV. £24–£34 ($38.40–$54.40) single; £45–£50 ($72–$80) double; £65–£70 ($104–$112) family rm for 3; £70–£80 ($112–$128) family rm for 4. All rates include English breakfast. MC, V. Follow the signs to the M2/London Rd.

This spacious, elegant Victorian guest house, close to the city center and the cathedral, has been much improved and made even more inviting with new decorations, new beds, fresh linens, and improved plumbing. There's a conservatory opening onto a walled garden, plus a library stocked with information about the area. Breakfasts are large and offer variety. The aim of Robin Hall is to pamper the guests, and this is done exceedingly well. The willingness to please here is admirable. All in all, it's a cozy nook to return to after making your "pilgrim's progress" through Canterbury. Off-street parking is available.

**Zen Stel Lodge.** 140 Dover Rd., Canterbury CT1 3NX. ☎ **01227/453654.** 4 rms, 2 with bath. TV. £38–£44 ($60.80–$70.40) single or double without bath, £42–£48 ($67.20–$76.80) single or double with bath; £50–£60 ($80–$96) triple without bath, £56–£70 ($89.60–$112) triple with bath. All rates include English breakfast. No credit cards.

A very English, very homey Edwardian house with manicured gardens stands next to the Kent County Cricket Grounds. Stained glass abounds, with a beautiful window on the stairs, and original fireplaces in the bedrooms. Ron and Zandra Stedman are welcoming hosts (except they don't allow dogs), and they have furnished the bedrooms comfortably and cozily. Although there are more stylish B&Bs in the Canterbury area, this one is a stand-out for its fair prices and old-fashioned atmosphere. Children are welcome. Guests often meet other guests in the garden, the walls of which exhibit the apprentices' inset fireplace art. Breakfast is the only meal served, but the Stedmans will direct you to some low-cost eateries that are kind to the frugal traveler.

## DOUBLES FOR LESS THAN £70

✪ **Ebury Hotel.** 65–67 New Dover Rd., Canterbury, Kent CT1 3DX. ☎ **01227/768433.** Fax 01227/459187. 15 rms. TV TEL. £45 ($72) single; £65 ($104) double; £73 ($116.80) triple; £85 ($136) quad. All rates include English breakfast. AE, MC, V. Closed Dec 14–Jan 14. Follow the signs to the A2/Dover Rd.

Acclaimed as one of the finest B&B hotels in Canterbury, this gabled Victorian house stands at the edge of the city, set back from the New Dover Road in 2 acres of garden, and within easy walking distance of the town center. Built in 1850, it's composed of two separate houses that were adjoined several years ago. Many of the original and elegant Victorian features have been retained at this family-run hotel. It's important to reserve here, since this owner-operated hotel is quite popular. Rooms are well-furnished, roomy, and pleasantly decorated. The hotel has a heated indoor swimming pool and spa, as well as a spacious lounge and a licensed restaurant serving good English meals prepared with fresh vegetables. Chargrills and dishes based on family recipes are especially good. Lamb chops with watercress are also served: How English do you want to get?

**Ersham Lodge.** 12 New Dover Rd., Canterbury, Kent CT1 3AP. ☎ **01227/463174.** Fax 01227/455482. 13 rms, all with bath. TV TEL. £39 ($62.40) single; £61 ($97.60) double. All rates include English breakfast. AE, MC, V. Closed Dec–Jan.

This long-established lodge is a 5-minute walk from the cathedral, central to major places of interest, entertainment, and shopping. It's an attractive, twin-galleried Victorian period house set back from the road to Dover in the midst of many shade trees. Your hosts, the Pellay family, have been welcoming guests to Canterbury for some 2 decades. The house is distinguished by the personal care of the owners, who seem genuinely concerned about their guests' well-being and comfort. There are a few ground-floor rooms and several especially reserved for nonsmokers. Bedrooms are well appointed, with color TV, radio, phone, hair dryer, and private bath. The public areas include a well-stocked cocktail bar, a bright breakfast room looking out onto a patio and garden, and a ground-floor sitting room. There's also a private parking lot.

✪ **Magnolia House.** 36 St. Dunstan's Terrace, Canterbury, Kent CT2 8AX. ☎ **01227/765121.** Fax 01227/765121. 7 rms. TV. £36–£45 ($57.60–$72) single; £58–£80.50 ($92.80–$128.80) double. All rates include English breakfast. AE, MC, V.

Those who gravitate to the Laura Ashley house of style will flock to the home of Ann and John Davies, who haven't let their honor as a gold winner of the 1995 "Welcome to Kent" hospitality award go to their heads. If anything, they have continued to see that this charming, detached late Georgian House (ca. 1830) is better than ever. Their "Magnolia" lies in a tranquil residential area only a 10-minute walk from the city center, off the London Road. Reservations are important, because of the house's popularity. Each bedroom is individually designed and color-coordinated; one room has a four-poster. Breakfasts are hearty and offered within a bright dining room overlooking a well-kept walled garden with its terraces and a fish pond. An evening meal of three courses at £18 ($28.80) is a very good value. Everything is freshly cooked, using fine, well-chosen ingredients.

## A YOUTH HOSTEL

**Canterbury Youth Hostel.** 54 New Dover Rd., Canterbury, Kent CT1 3DT. ☎ **01227/462911.** Fax 01227/470752. 81 beds. £9.80 ($15.70) per person; £6.30 ($10.10) if under 18. MC, V.

This Victorian lodge is the most bustling hostelry in town, filled with mainly young people from all over the world who flock to the cathedral city. Even families use the place, bunking down in dormitory rooms. Yes, it looks very institutional, but there's a friendliness and welcome here that make it less so. The staff are a bit overworked, but all are welcome; they'll prepare you a bed for the night and feed you well.

There's a self-catering kitchen, but the staff also offers a cafeteria-style or a packaged breakfast for £2.85 ($4.55). A packed lunch costs £2.45 to £3.25 ($3.90 to $5.20), and a surprisingly good dinner goes for £4.25 ($6.80). In spite of its low cost, dinner often has a bit of flair, removing it from the standard boarding school fare. Everything is home cooked, and the staff is "vegetarian sensitive."

Amenities not found in many hostels are found here, including currency conversion, laundry facilities, storage lockers, and a bike storage shed. Parking is available for eight cars and one minibus. This is a nonsmoking facility; it is not equipped for travelers with disabilities, and an 11pm curfew is enforced.

# WHERE TO EAT

✪ **Alberrys Wine and Food Bar.** 38 St. Margaret's St. ☎ **01227/452378.** Main courses £5–£10 ($8–$16). AE, DC, MC, V. Mon–Sat noon–midnight. INTERNATIONAL.

The Victorian cartoons on Alberrys' wine list claim that "Tomorrow morning you'll be able to perform great feats of strength if you drink plenty of wine tonight." Today you eat in the same area where slaves of the Romans once toiled (part of the exposed foundation was a section of a Roman amphitheater). Alberrys offers an inexpensive and frequently changing repertoire of well-prepared food. A meal might include the soup of the day, charcoal-grilled rump steak with pepper sauce, followed by homemade sticky chocolate pudding with vanilla ice cream. Pizzas and quiches are available. Beer and mixed drinks are served, and wine is available by the glass. This fun place is located in the center near the bus station.

**Augustine's Bistro.** 1–2 Longport. ☎ **01227/453063.** Main courses £3.95–£9.50 ($6.30–$15.20). MC, V. Mon–Sat 11:30am–2:30pm and 6:30–10:30pm. Closed the last week in Aug and the 1st week in Sept. ENGLISH.

Located in a Georgian structure 100 yards from St. Augustine's Abbey, this bistro offers English fare in a casual and relaxed atmosphere. Sidney and Branka Agg own the establishment, containing two dining rooms with its uncomplicated decor of wooden floors and tables. To begin, try the mushrooms in cheese and garlic or one of the daily soups, such as leek, mushroom, and tomato; then go on to chicken breast in a cider-and-mustard sauce or roast breast of duckling with cherry sauce. Desserts are traditionally English, including such favorites as the "spotted dick" (no smirking, now) and apple crumb.

**Duck Inn.** Pett Bottom, near Bridge. ☎ **01227/830354.** Reservations recommended. Main courses £5.95–£11.95 ($9.50–$19.10); 2-course fixed-price lunch (Mon–Fri) £7.50 ($12); 3-course fixed-price dinner £10 ($16). AE, DC, MC, V. Lunch noon–3pm; dinner 6:30–11pm. Take the A2/Dover Rd. 5 miles outside Canterbury near the village of Bridge. ENGLISH.

Once called the Woodsmen Arms, this restaurant became known as the Duck Inn because of its low door. (Get it?) Set in the Pett Bottom Valley in a 16th-century structure, the restaurant offers traditional English fare. Although there are bar and restaurant areas, diners can have their meals served to them throughout the establishment, including outside in the English country garden during the summer season. The menu posted on two chalkboards changes weekly, with a few standard English favorites remaining from week to week. You can start with a homemade soup, such as country vegetable or celery and Stilton. For your main course, the menu may include game pies (in season) or mussels marinara, and duck is always served in one form or another. For a finish, try a local favorite—the homemade date pudding with toffee sauce. For James Bond fans this restaurant will be of particular interest: According to the film *You Only Live Twice*, 007 grew up next door to the Duck Inn.

**Fungus Mungus.** 34 St. Peter's St. ☎ **01227/781922.** Main courses £3.50–£5.95 ($5.60–$9.50). No credit cards. Mon–Sat 9am–11pm; Sun 10:30am–11pm. VEGETARIAN.

Perhaps misnamed—the barstools are the biggest mushrooms in this place, and the daily menu features plenty of vegetarian and vegan options. The room is a jungle of greenery, with hanging plants, vines, and tropical bird murals covering the walls. Warm-weather patio dining is available.

**Il Vaticano.** 35 St. Margaret's St. ☎ **01227/765333.** Main courses £5–£8 ($8–$12.80). AE, DC, MC, V. Mon–Sat 11:30am–10:30pm; Sun noon–10pm. ITALIAN.

The best-known pasta parlor in Canterbury is housed in this 14th-century building. All pasta is made on the premises, and you get a choice of sauces. Some of the best include baby clams in a tomato, garlic, and herb sauce, or else black olives and mushrooms in a tomato sauce. Baked lasagna and tortelloni (filled with spinach and ricotta cheese) are also served. The restaurant, decorated in a trattoria style, with bentwood chairs, small marble-top tables, and exposed brick, lies off High Street in the commercial center of the city.

✪ **Queen Elizabeth's Restaurant and Tearoom.** 44–45 High St. ☎ **01227/464080.** Main courses £5–£7.50 ($8–$12); cream teas £3–£4.50 ($4.80–$7.20). No credit cards. Daily 10am–5:50pm. ENGLISH.

The 16th-century interior, with its outstanding relief and wall paneling, recaptures the past admirably. Of special interest is the original room where Elizabeth I entertained the duke of Alençon while she was trying to decide whether to marry him. The food is fresh and home-cooked—from the rich-tasting soups, to the roast beef and vegetables, to the deep-dish apple pie with whipped cream for dessert. If you go early enough, select the seat next to the window so you can look down the High Street. An afternoon cream tea is a specialty. The restaurant is on "The High"; you can spot it easily by its gabled facade with plaster carvings of cherubs.

# CANTERBURY AFTER DARK

**Gulbenkian Theatre,** University of Kent, Giles Lane (☎ 01227/769075), is open during school terms (except Cricket Week, the first week in August) and offers a potpourri of jazz and classical productions, dance, drama, comedy, and a mix of new and student productions. An in-house cinema showcases less popular and student films 3 nights a week. Check newspapers for schedules; tickets cost £5 to £12 ($8–$19.20).

The **Marlowe,** The Friars (☎ 01227/787787), is Canterbury's only commercial playhouse. It's open all year and offers drama, jazz, and classical concerts, and contemporary and classical ballet. Most productions are weekly, but there are also 1-night shows. Rock concerts and "An Evening With . . ." celebrity programs are also featured. Tickets cost from £10 to £12 ($16 to $19.20).

The **Penny Theatre,** 30–31 Northgate (☎ 01227/470512), with a cover charge of £2 to £7 ($3.20–$11.20), is a well-regarded local spot for an eclectic mix of live music, everything from jazz and reggae to indie rock (Canned Heat played here in 1996). The music goes on every day, except Sunday, from noon to midnight, and the bands are well known, both locally and internationally.

## THE BAR SCENE

The already-recommended **Alberrys Wine & Food Bar,** 38A St. Margaret's St. (☎ 01227/452378), features live music, mostly jazz by local and student groups. Shows are once a month in winter and several times a week during summer. Cover charges depend on the group.

The only disco is **The Biz and the Works,** 15 Station Rd. (☎ 01227/462520). The club is open Monday, Tuesday, Thursday, and Friday from 10pm to 2am and Saturday from 9pm to 2am. It is open some Sundays in summer. The club takes bookings for groups, so call ahead. It sports a full bar, and you must be 21 or older. The cover is £2.50 ($4) for early arrivals and £5 ($8) later in the evening.

A laid-back student hangout, **The Cherry Tree,** 10 White Horse Lane (☎ 01227/451266), offers a wide selection of beers, including Bass ale on draft, Cherry Tree ale, three traditional lagers, and four bitters. Popular with students and visitors, the atmosphere is clubby, filled with casual conversations and broadcasts from a TV and a jukebox. If you visit for lunch, you'll find a 35-item menu—the best pub menu in town—plus three types of ploughman's lunch.

Another good choice on your Canterbury pub crawl is **The Flying Horse,** 1 Dover St. (☎ **01227/463803**), which attracts a garrulous mix of young and old. This 16th-century pub bridges generations with "White Cliffs of Dover" oldsters and the hip student crowd. A weekly quiz night stirs conversation.

## 2  The White Cliffs of Dover

76 miles SE of London; 84 miles NE of Brighton

One of the ancient Cinque Ports, Dover is famed for its white cliffs. In Victoria's day, it basked in its popularity as a seaside resort, but today it's known more as a port for cross-channel car and passenger traffic between England and France (notably Calais). Dover was one of England's most vulnerable and easy-to-hit targets during World War II; repeated bombings destroyed much of its harbor. Dover has lately become more important, since the opening of the Channel Tunnel (Chunnel) in 1994.

Unless you're on your way to France or want to use Dover as a base for exploring the English countryside, you can skip a visit here. Except for those white cliffs, Dover has always been rather dull. Even its hotels are second rate; many overnight hotel bookings are made in Folkestone, about 10 miles to the southwest.

## ESSENTIALS

**GETTING THERE**   Frequent trains run between Victoria Station or Charing Cross Station in London and Dover daily from 5am to 10pm. You arrive in Dover at Priory Station, off Folkestone Road. During the day, two trains per hour depart Canterbury East Station heading for Dover. The trip is 1$^1$/$_2$ hours by express train and 2 hours by local train (which makes stops).

Frequent buses leave throughout the day—Monday through Friday 8:30am to 5:30pm and Saturday until 2pm—from London's Victoria Coach Station bound for Dover. The local bus station is on Pencester Road (☎ **01304/240024**). Stagecoach East Kent provides daily bus service between Canterbury and Dover. The buses take about 2$^1$/$_4$ hours, making stops along the way.

If you're driving from London, head first to Canterbury (see above), then continue along A2 southeast until you reach Dover, on the coast. By car it should take about 2 hours.

**VISITOR INFORMATION**   The **Tourist Information Centre** is on Townwall Street (☎ **01304/205108**). Open daily 9am to 6pm.

## EXPLORING DOVER

You'll get the best view of the famous cliffs if you're arriving at Dover by ferry or hovercraft from Calais. Otherwise, you could walk out to the end of the town's Prince of Wales' pier, the largest of the town's western docks. The cliffs loom above you. You could also drive 5 miles east of Dover to the pebble-covered beaches of the fishing hamlet of Deal. Here, a local fisher might take you on an informal boat ride.

**Dover Castle.** Castle Hill. ☎ **01304/211067** or 01304/201628. Admission £6 ($9.60) adults; £3 ($4.80) children under 16; £4.50 ($7.20) seniors and students; £15 ($24) family. Apr–Sept, daily 10am–6pm (last tour at 5pm); Oct–Mar, daily 10am–4pm (last tour at 3pm). Bus: 90 bound for Deal.

Rising nearly 400 feet above the port is one of the oldest and best-known castles in England. Its keep was built at the behest of Becket's fair-weather friend, Henry II, in the 12th century. The ancient castle was called back into active duty as late as World War II. The "Pharos" on the grounds is a lighthouse erected by the Romans in the first half of the 1st century. The Romans first landed at nearby Deal in 54 B.C., but after 6 months they departed and didn't return until nearly 100 years later, in A.D. 43, at which time they stayed and occupied the country for 400 years. The castle houses a military museum and a film center, plus "Live and Let's Spy," an exhibition of WWII spying equipment. The restaurant in the keep room of the castle is open all year. In the summer, there is also a cafeteria open in the tunnels.

**Secret Wartime Tunnels.** Dover Castle, Castle Hill. ☎ **01304/211067** or 01304/201628. Admission free with castle admission. Open same days and hours as the castle. Last tour leaves 1 hour before castle closing time. Bus: 90 bound for Deal.

These secret tunnels, used during the evacuation of Dunkirk in 1940 and the Battle of Britain, can now be explored on a guided tour. Some 200 feet below ground, they were the headquarters of Operation Dynamo, when more than 300,000 troops from Dunkirk were evacuated. Once forbidden ground to all but those with the strongest security clearance, the networks of tunnels can be toured today. You can stand in the very room where Ramsey issued orders; experience the trauma of life in an underground operating theater, and look out over the English Channel from the hidden, cliff-top balcony, just as Churchill did during the Battle of Britain. The tunnels were originally excavated to house cannons to be employed (if necessary) against an invasion by Napoléon. On the Annex level is an Underground Hospital and Field Dressing Station.

**Roman Painted House.** New St. ☎ **01304/203279.** Admission £2 ($3.20) adults; 80p ($1.30) children 15 and under. Apr–Sept, Tue–Sun 10am–5:30pm.

This 1,800-year-old Roman structure—Britain's "buried Pompeii"—has exceptionally well-preserved walls and an under-floor heating system. It's famous for its unique Bacchic murals and has won four national awards for presentation. Brass-rubbing is offered here. You'll find it in the town center near Market Square.

## An Easy Excursion to Deal Castle

**Deal Castle.** On the seafront. ☎ **01304/372762.** Admission £2.80 ($4.50) adults; £2.10 ($3.35) seniors; £1.40 ($2.25) children. Apr–Sept, daily 10am–6pm; Oct–Mar, Wed–Sun 10am–4pm. From Dover, follow A258 north for a distance of 6 1/2 miles. The castle can be clearly seen on the right as you enter the town of Deal. From the center of Deal, it's a 3-minute walk due south along Victoria Rd. The castle is situated on the coast at the edge of town.

Some 5 miles from Dover is Deal Castle, just a mile north of Walmer Castle and a quarter mile south of the Deal town center. A defensive fort built about 1540, it's the most spectacular example of the low, squat forts constructed by Henry VIII. Its 119 gun positions made it the most powerful of his defense forts. Centered around a circular keep surrounded by two rings of semicircle bastions, the castle was protected by an outer moat. The entrance was approached by a drawbridge with a portcullis. The castle, damaged by bombs during World War II, has been restored to its early form. An exhibition on coastal defenses is in the basement.

## WHERE TO STAY

**Ardmore Private Hotel.** 18 Castle Hill Rd., Dover, Kent CT16 1QW. ☎ **01304/205895.** Fax 01304/208229. 4 rms. TV. £40–£47 ($64–$75.20) double; £55–£60 ($88–$96) family rm. All rates include English breakfast. MC,V.

This has long been a winner with the cross-channel crowd, who like its location convenient to the port and hovercraft terminal, and within easy reach of the town center. Carmen and Len Morriss are among the more accommodating hosts in the area. They have done much to modernize this house (ca. 1796), but have retained some of its original architectural style, with many Victorian touches. They keep their non-smoking bedrooms ship-shape, and each unit suitable for a double or twin, or even

## Impressions

*The sea is calm tonight.*
*The tide is full, the moon lies fair*
*Upon the straits;—on the French coast the light*
*Gleams and is gone; the cliffs of England stand*
*Glimmering and vast, out in the tranquil bay.*

—Matthew Arnold, Dover Beach (1867)

a family room. Amenities include private bath or showers, beverage-making facilities, and double glazing on the windows. Some rooms open onto the harbor view. It's located adjacent to Dover Castle, and at the rear is a modern Leisure Center.

✪ **Beulah House.** 94 Crabble Hill, London Rd., Dover, Kent CT17 0SA. ☎ **01304/824615.** 6 rms, 1 with bath. £19 ($30.40) single without bath; £38 ($60.80) double without or with bath. All rates include English breakfast. MC, V. Free parking outside; £2 ($3.20) in the garage.

This elegant late Victorian house, presided over by Ronald and Anita Owens, is convenient to the western docks and the center of Dover. The couple are always making improvements, yet are respectful of their home's original character. What makes this place especially appealing are the gardens in back, with sculptured yews and roses. Bedrooms are nonsmoking, and are handsomely furnished and equipped with such amenities as tea trays. The ideal room is on the ground floor, with a four-poster bed and exclusive use of an adjoining bathroom. Children are welcome here, and some rooms are suitable for families, as they are most spacious. An international crowd of guests is served breakfast and there's also a TV lounge and a small conservatory overlooking the gardens in the rear. Light snacks and cream teas are also available.

**Number One Guest House.** 1 Castle St., Dover, Kent CT16 1QH. ☎ **01304/202007.** 5 rms. TV. £40 ($64) double; £52 ($83.20) triple; £56 ($89.60) family rm for 4. All rates include English breakfast. No credit cards. Free parking outside; £2 ($3.20) in the garage.

The castle overlooks this quaint Georgian town house, which was built in 1800. One of Dover's oldest remaining homes, it was established and run by the same family for more than 22 years. John and Adeline Reidy offer comfortable twin, double, and family rooms, where you'll find courtesy coffee and where you'll be served breakfast. At the rear of this cozy, well-maintained house, which is decorated with Victorian furnishings, is a pretty-in-pink lounge which opens out to a secret walled garden where you can relax on summer evenings. The Reidys provide a smart atmosphere of a bygone age, with old-fashioned hospitality and service. The location is convenient to town, port, or Channel Tunnel and Cruise Terminal.

**St. Martins Guest House.** 17 Castle Hill Rd., Dover, Kent CT16 1QW. ☎ **01304/205938.** Fax 01304/208229. 6 rms, all with showers. TV. £27 ($43.20) single; £32–£42 ($51.20–$67.20) double. All rates include English breakfast. MC,V.

A few blocks from the cross-channel ferries and the hoverport, on the hillside leading to Dover Castle, this hotel is run by Mr. and Mrs. Morriss, who maintain a friendly, relaxed atmosphere. The house is from the 1840s and is maintained and furnished to high standards, with full central heating. The bedrooms, with color-coordinated decor, have double-glazed windows, hot-beverage facilities, and private showers. Guests meet other guests in an attractive pine-furnished breakfast room. The house has a great lounge and a residential license. Ample parking is available.

✪ **Westbank Guest House.** 239 Folkestone Rd., Dover, Kent CT17 9LL. ☎ **01304/201061.** 6 rms, 4 with shower only. TV. £16 ($25.60) single without bath; £32 ($51.20) double without bath, £36 ($57.60) double with shower only. All rates include English breakfast. No credit cards.

One of the best B&Bs in the area, Westbank is an attractive semidetached Victorian house which George and Rosemary Banks have modernized without ruining its character. Convenient to the train station and Dover center, it is a 5-minute ride to the docks and hoverport. Bedrooms are well appointed and very comfortable, ranging from a spacious family to a single. Each contains many amenities such as color TV and shaving points. Shared baths are adequate and maintained in spic-and-span condition, with plenty of towels. It's a family favorite, as cots are made available and high chairs offered in the dining room, where a generous English breakfast is served, beginning at 4:30am for those early channel closings. Mrs. Banks is an excellent cook. If notified in advance, she will prepare a three-course evening dinner for only £8 ($12.80).

## WHERE TO EAT

Finding a good place to eat in Dover isn't easy; France may be just across the channel, but French cuisine often seems light years away. Still, we have some recommendations, all in the town center. For food on the run, your best bet is **Tower Kebab,** 12 Towerhamlets Rd. (☎ **0130/424-2170**), which makes great takeout. They are kings of the kebab, offering several varieties, each accompanied with pita bread and a salad. Prices range from £2.50 to £5 ($4 to $8), and sandwiches, freshly made salads, and tempting desserts round out the menu. The kebab joint is also one of the best places in town to get the ingredients for a picnic.

**Britannia.** 41 Townwall St. ☎ **01304/203248.** Main courses £4.50–£9.95 ($7.20–$15.90). MC, V. Daily noon–2:30pm and 5:30–10pm. Pub: Mon–Sat 11am–11pm; Sun noon–10:30PM. INTERNATIONAL.

If you are a fan of typically English, pub-style meals, try this restaurant whose windows overlook the ferry terminal and the many ships arriving from Calais and Boulogne. Its well-maintained facade has a bow window and lots of gilt and brass nautical accents. A popular pub is on the ground floor, with a restaurant on the upper level. The food is very standard, typical of what you'd get if you stop to eat along a motorway in England. Try a prawn cocktail or a pâté for an appetizer, followed by rump steak or mixed grill. Many different salads are offered, including one made with salmon. Dover sole is a specialty.

**Chaplin's Restaurant and Coffee Bar.** 2 Church St. ☎ **01304/204870.** Main courses £4 ($6.40). MC, V. Oct–Apr Mon–Sat 8:30am–5pm, Sun 11am–5pm; May–Sept Mon–Sat 8:30am–9pm, Sun 11am–9pm. BRITISH.

This restaurant offers the diner a bit of whimsy, with its lace curtains and Charlie Chaplin mementos scattered throughout the dining room. The menu is typically English with such specialties as steak-and-kidney pie, roast lamb, Lancashire hot pot, and cottage pie. Sandwiches, salads, and burgers, including one with cheese, slaw, and pineapple, are also featured. A breakfast special that comprises two sausages, two slices of bacon, beans or tomatoes, an egg, and bread is offered throughout the day, costing £3.35 ($5.35).

**Topo Gigio.** 1–2 King St. ☎ **01304/201048.** Reservations recommended. Pizzas £4–£6 ($6.40–$9.60); main courses £5.50 ($8.80). AE, MC, V. Mon–Thurs noon–2:30pm and 6:30–10:30pm; Fri–Sat noon–2:30pm and 6:30–11pm; Sun noon–2:30pm in the summer. ITALIAN.

Established in 1991 by an Italian entrepreneur from Vicenza, this restaurant was named after the most famous cartoon character in Italy, Topo Gigio, a look-alike for Mickey Mouse. Located a short walk from Dover's market square in a setting accented with brick arches and a wood-burning pizza oven, it serves 15 types of pastas, 16 types of pizzas, and a varied choice of steak, chicken, veal, and fish dishes prepared in the Italian style—or in virtually any way you request. The restaurant's staff and clientele tend to be animated and energetic, which might make an outing here lighthearted and fun. The food's not special, just satisfying and filling.

## 3 Kent's Country Houses, Castles & Gardens

The Westerham area, 20 miles southeast of London, and the Sevenoaks area, 26 miles southeast of London, abound with homes of famous men and a number of the greatest country homes and castles in England, many with splendid gardens.

If you're hoping to see at least two of these attractions in one day, it's good to have a car to save time, because of awkward public transportation. However, trains from Charing Cross run to Sevenoaks, where bus connections take you to Westerham. From the rail or bus stations, you have to rely on taxis to get you to the actual properties. If you're driving southeast from London, as many do, head east along M25, taking the exit to Westerham.

## EXPLORING THE AREA

We've found that guided tours that take in some of these houses are usually too rushed and too expensive to recommend. Each attraction can be toured far more reasonably on your own.

If you have only a day, you might want to visit **Chartwell,** former home of Winston Churchill, and **Knole,** one of England's largest private estates. Everyone seems to want to see where England's wartime prime minister lived, and Knole is like a small town with its vast complex of courtyards and buildings. To reach Knole from Chartwell, drive north to Westerham and pick up A25 and head east for 8 miles.

An entire second day is needed to visit **Leeds Castle** and **Hever Castle.** Leeds has been called "the loveliest castle in the world," and it's even lovelier in that it allows morning visits (most Kentish castles can be visited only in the afternoon). You can then spend your afternoon at Hever Castle. Hever is the stereotypical English castle, with all its battlements and turrets. There's even a moat. Henry VIII courted and won the hand of Anne Boleyn here (poor gal).

If you still have time for castle-hopping, consider yet a third day which will allow you to visit Canterbury Cathedral in the morning (when most castles are closed), then tour **Penshurst Palace** in the afternoon. Penshurst is one of the finest examples of an Elizabethan house in England, and its Baron's Hall is one of the greatest interiors to have survived from the Middle Ages.

The other attractions of great note in the area, regrettably, are also afternoon visits for the most part, except for some early weekend openings. Other major attractions include **Sissinghurst Castle Garden,** which could be visited on a Saturday or Sunday morning (beginning at 10am). Weekdays, it is open only in the afternoon. **Ightham Mote,** a National Trust property dating from 1340, is the other frontranking property in the area. Visits to either of these will occupy an entire afternoon.

What's the bottom line? To see all the stellar historic properties of Kent, most of them taking up an entire afternoon, would occupy a week or more of time, a generous allotment few visitors have. But even those in a rush try to budget time for Knole, Hever, Penshurst, Leeds, and Chartwell, the most deserving of your attention.

## ✪ CHARTWELL: CHURCHILL'S HOME

Chartwell, off B2026, Kent ( ☎ **01732/866368**), was the late prime minister's home from 1922 and is now a museum. Not as grand as Blenheim Palace where Sir

Winston was born in 1874, the rooms of Chartwell remain as the conservative politician left them: They include maps, documents, photographs, pictures, and other personal mementos. Two rooms display gifts that the prime minister received from people all over the world. There is also a selection of many of his well-known uniforms, including his famous "siren-suits" and hats. Terraced gardens descend toward the lake, where you'll find black swans swimming. Many of Churchill's paintings are displayed in a garden studio. You can see the garden walls that the prime minister built with his own hands and the pond where he sat to feed the Golden Orfe. A restaurant on the grounds serves from 10:30am to 5pm on days when the house is open.

The house and garden are open from April to October, Wednesday to Sunday from 11am to 5pm, with the last admission at 4:30pm. The house alone is open from March to November, on Wednesday, Saturday, and Sunday from 11am to 4:30pm, with the last admission at 4pm. Admission for the house only is £3 ($4.80), the gardens only is £2.50 ($4), and a combination ticket to see both is £5 ($8). Children enter for half price. Family tickets cost £11.25 ($18). Drive 2 miles south of Westerham on B2026 and follow the signs.

## DOWN HOUSE (DARWIN'S HOME)

On Luxted Road, in Downe (☎ 01689/859119), the final residence of the famous naturalist/evolutionary theorist Charles Darwin can be found. In 1842, he wrote, "House ugly, looks neither old nor new." He moved into the house with his family in 1842 and lived here "in happy contentment" until his death in 1882. The drawing room, dining room, billiard room, and old study have been restored to the way they were when Darwin was working on his famous—and still controversial—book *On the Origin of Species,* first published in 1859. The museum also includes collections and memorabilia from Darwin's voyage on the HMS *Beagle.* There's also a room dedicated to his famous grandfather, Dr. Erasmus Darwin, and a modest exhibit on evolution is in the new study, the last room to be added into the house. An important feature of the museum is the garden, which retains original landscaping and a glasshouse, beyond which lies the Sand Walk or "Thinking Path," where Darwin took his daily solitary walk.

The house is open April to October, daily from 10am to 6pm, and November to March, daily from 10am to 4pm (closed December 24, 25, 26). Admission is £4 ($6.40) adults, £3 ($4.80) for students and seniors, and £2 ($3.20) for children. Down House is situated a quarter mile southeast of the village of Downe along Luxted Road. From London's Victoria Station, take a daily train to Bromley South, then go by bus no. 146 (Monday to Saturday only) to Downe, or by bus no. R2 to Orpington.

## ✪ HEVER CASTLE & GARDENS

Hever Castle (☎ 01732/865224) dates back to 1270 when the massive gate house, the outer walls, and the moat were first constructed. Some 200 years later, the Bullen (or Boleyn) family added a comfortable Tudor dwelling house inside the walls. Hever Castle was the childhood home of Anne Boleyn, the second wife of Henry VIII and mother of Queen Elizabeth I. The castle holds many memories of her.

In 1903, William Waldorf Astor acquired the estate and invested time, money, and imagination in restoring the castle, building the "Tudor Village," and creating the gardens and lakes. The Astor family's contribution to Hever's rich history can be appreciated through the collections of furniture, paintings, and objets d'art and through the quality of workmanship employed, particularly in the wood carving and plasterwork.

The gardens at Hever Castle were created between 1904 and 1908. They have now reached their maturity and are a blaze of color throughout most of the year. The spectacular Italian Garden contains statuary and sculpture dating from Roman to Renaissance times. William Waldorf Astor acquired these items in Italy and brought them to Hever, where they form a magnificent sight among the displays of shrubs and climbing and herbaceous plants. The formal gardens include a walled Rose Garden, fine topiary work, and a maze. There's a 35-acre lake and throughout the gardens there are streams, cascades, and fountains.

The gardens are open from March 1 to November 30, daily from 11am to 6pm; the castle is open daily from noon to 6pm. Admission to the castle and gardens is £6.50 ($10.40) for adults, £5.70 ($9.10) for seniors and students, and £3.30 ($5.30) for children ages 5 to 16. A family ticket (2 adults, 2 children) is £16.30 ($26.10). Admission to the garden only is £4.90 ($7.85) for adults, £4.30 ($6.90) for seniors and students, and £3 ($4.80) for children ages 5 to 16. A family ticket is £12.80 ($20.50). Children 4 and under enter free.

**GETTING THERE**   Follow the signs northwest of Royal Tonbridge; it's 3 miles southeast of Edenbridge, midway between Sevenoaks and East Grinstead, and 30 minutes from Exit 6 of M25.

## IGHTHAM MOTE

Dating from 1340, Ightham Mote (☎ **01732/810378**) was extensively remodeled in the early 16th century, and remodeling is still going on. The chapel with its painted ceiling, the timbered outer wall, and the ornate chimneys reflect the Tudor period. You'll cross a stone bridge over a moat to its central courtyard. From the Great Hall, known for its magnificent windows, a Jacobean staircase leads to the old chapel on the first floor, where you go through the solarium with an oriel window to the Tudor chapel.

Unlike many other ancient houses in England that have been occupied by the same family for centuries, Ightham Mote passed from owner to owner, with each family leaving its mark on the place. When the last private owner, an American who was responsible for a lot of the restoration, died, he bequeathed the house to the National Trust, who chose to keep the Robinson Library laid out as it was in a 1960 edition of *Homes & Gardens.*

The house is open from April to October on Monday and Wednesday through Friday from noon to 5:30pm, and on Sunday and bank holiday Mondays from 11am to 5:30pm, with the last admission at 5pm. Admission is £4 ($6.40) for adults and £2 ($3.20) for children. Children under 5 are admitted free.

**GETTING THERE**   Drive 6 miles east of Sevenoaks on A25 to the small village of Ivy Hatch; the estate is 2¹/₂ miles south of Ightham; it's also signposted from A227.

## ✪ KNOLE

Begun in the mid–15th century by Thomas Bourchier, archbishop of Canterbury, Knole (☎ **01732/462100**) is one of the largest private houses in England and one of the finest examples of pure English Tudor–style architecture. It's set in a 1,000-acre deer park, 5 miles north of Tonbridge, at the Tonbridge end of the town of Sevenoaks. (Careful not to confuse Tonbridge with Tunbridge Wells.) Virginia Woolf, often a guest of the Sackvilles, used Knole as the setting for her novel *Orlando.*

Henry VIII appropriated the former archbishop's palace from the church in 1537. He spent considerable sums of money on Knole, though there is little record of his spending much time here after emancipating the place from the reluctant Archbishop

Cranmer; history records one visit in 1541. It was then a royal palace until Queen Elizabeth I granted it to Thomas Sackville, first earl of Dorset, whose descendants have lived here ever since. The Great Hall and the Brown Gallery are Bourchier rooms, early 15th century, both much altered by the first earl, who made other additions in about 1603. The earl was also responsible for the Great Painted Staircase.

The house covers 7 acres and has 365 rooms, 52 staircases, and seven courts. The elaborate paneling and plasterwork provide a background for the 17th- and 18th-century tapestries and rugs, Elizabethan and Jacobean furniture, and the collection of family portraits. The building was given to the National Trust in 1946.

If you want to see a bed to die for, check out the state bed of James II in the King's Bedroom. And, unknown to many, you can actually take afternoon tea at Knole. From the early 17th century, the tearooms here were used as a brew house for the regular brewing of beer and ale. Today you can enjoy a pot of tea with scones, jam, and cream, or else devour one of their gateaux such as carrot and walnut sponge topped with a cream cheese and lemon juice icing.

The house is open from April to October on Wednesday, Friday, Sunday, and bank holiday Monday from 11am to 5pm, and on Thursday from 2 to 5pm. The gardens are open on the first Wednesday of the month from May to September, the last admission at 3pm. The park is open daily to pedestrians and open to cars only when the house is. Admission to the house costs £5 ($8) for adults, £2.50 ($4) for children, and a family pass is £12.50 ($20). Admission to the gardens is £1 ($1.60) for adults and 50p (80¢) for children.

**GETTING THERE**    Frequent train service is available from London (about every 30 minutes) to Sevenoaks, and then you can take the connecting hourly bus service, a taxi, or walk the remaining 1¹/₂ miles to Knole.

## ✪ LEEDS CASTLE

Once described by Lord Conway as the loveliest castle in the world, Leeds Castle (☎ 01622/765400) dates from A.D. 857. Originally built of wood, it was rebuilt in 1119 in its present stone structure on two small islands in the middle of the lake; prior to the importation of gunpowder, the castle was an almost impregnable fortress. Henry VIII converted it to a royal palace.

The castle has strong links to America through the sixth Lord Fairfax who, as well as owning the castle, owned 5 million acres in Virginia and was a close friend and mentor of the young George Washington. The last private owner, the Hon. Lady Baillie, who restored the castle with a superb collection of fine art, furniture, and tapestries, bequeathed it to the Leeds Castle Foundation. Since then, royal apartments, known as *Les Chambres de la Reine* (the queen's chambers), in the Gloriette, the oldest part of the castle, have been open to the public. The Gloriette, the last stronghold against attack, dates from Norman and Plantagenet times, with later additions by Henry VIII.

Within the surrounding parklands is a wildwood garden and duckery where rare swans, geese, and ducks abound. The redesigned aviaries contain a superb collection of birds, including parakeets and cockatoos. Even though dogs are not allowed here, dog lovers will enjoy the Dog Collar Museum at the gate house, with a unique collection of collars dating from the Middle Ages. A nine-hole golf course is open to the public. The Culpepper Garden is a delightful English country flower garden. Beyond are the castle greenhouses, with the maze centered on a beautiful underground grotto and the vineyard recorded in the *Domesday Book*. It is once again producing Leeds Castle English white wine.

Don't overlook the aviary. Opened by Princess Alexandra in 1988, it houses a collection of more than 100 rare species of birds. The aviary tries to encourage successful breeding to reintroduce endangered species into their original habitats.

From March to October, the park is open daily from 10am to 5pm; the castle, daily from 11am to 5:30pm. From November to February, the park is open daily from 10am to 3pm; the castle, daily from 10:15am to 3:30pm. The castle and grounds are closed on the last Saturday in June and the first Saturday in July prior to open-air concerts. Admission to the castle and grounds is £8 ($12.80) for adults and £5.50 ($8.80) for children. Students and seniors pay £6.50 ($10.40). For grounds only, £5.50 ($8.80) adults and £3.50 ($5.60) for children. Car parking is free, with a free ride on a fully accessible minibus available for those who cannot manage the half-mile-or-so walk from the parking area to the castle.

Snacks, salads, cream teas, and hot meals are offered daily at a number of places on the estate, including Fairfax Hall, a restored 17th-century tithe barn, and the Terrace Restaurant which provides a full range of hot and cold meals.

If you're really big on the castle, you might consider as a splurge the **Kentish Evenings,** which are presented in Fairfax Hall most Saturdays throughout the year (except in August). They start at 7pm with a cocktail reception, followed by a private guided tour of the castle. Guests feast on smoked salmon mousse, followed by broth and roast beef carved at the table, plus seasonal vegetables. A half bottle of wine is included in the overall price of £41 ($65.60) per person. During the meal, musicians play appropriate music for the surroundings and the occasion. Advance reservations are required, made by calling the castle. Kentish Evenings finish at 12:30am. Participants in Kentish Evenings are advised to arrange nearby overnight accommodations.

**GETTING THERE**   Trains run frequently from London's Victoria Station to Maidstone. Buses run weekdays from London's Victoria Coach Station to Maidstone, 36 miles to the southeast. If you're driving, from London's ring road continue east along M26 and M20. The castle is 4 miles east of Maidstone at the junction of the A20 and the M20 London-Folkestone roads.

## ✪ PENSHURST PALACE

This stately home (☎ **01892/870307**) 6 miles west of Tonbridge is one of the outstanding country houses in Britain. It is also one of England's greatest defended manor houses, standing in a peaceful rural setting that has changed little over the centuries. In 1338, Sir John de Pulteney, four times lord mayor of London, built the manor house, whose Great Hall still forms the heart of Penshurst—after more than 600 years. The boy king, Edward VI, presented the house to Sir William Sidney, and it has remained in that family ever since. It was the birthplace in 1554 of Sir Philip Sidney, the soldier-cum-poet. In the first half of the 17th century, Penshurst was known as a center of literature, attracting such personages as Ben Jonson, who was so inspired by the estate that he wrote one of his greatest poems. Today it's the home of the second viscount de l'Isle.

The Nether Gallery, below the Long Gallery, which has a suite of ebony-and-ivory furniture from Goa, houses the Sidney family collection of armor. You can also see the splendid state dining room. In the Stable Wing is an interesting toy museum, with dolls, toy soldiers, dollhouses, and many other playthings from past generations. On the grounds are nature and farm trails, as well as an adventure playground for children.

On Saturday and Sunday in March and October and daily from April to September, the house is open from noon to 5:30pm; the grounds from 11am to 6pm. Admission to the house and grounds is £5.50 ($8.80) for adults and £3 ($4.80) for children ages 5 to 16. For the grounds only, the cost is £4 ($6.40) for adults and £2.75 ($4.40) for children ages 5 to 16. Children 4 and under enter free.

**GETTING THERE** From M25 Junction follow A21 to Tonbridge, leaving at the Tonbridge (North) exit; then follow the brown tourist signs. The nearest mainline station is Tonbridge.

## QUEBEC HOUSE

This square, red-brick gabled house (☎ **01959/562206**) is the boyhood home of Gen. James Wolfe, who led the English in victory over the French in the battle for Quebec. Wolfe was born in Westerham on January 2, 1727, and lived here until he was 11 years old. A National Trust property, Quebec House contains an exhibition about the capture of Quebec and memorabilia associated with the military hero. See, for example, Wolfe's traveling canteen, which comes complete with a griddle, frying pans, and decanters, evoking the life of an 18th-century officer on a military campaign. Most of the paintings and engravings in the drawing room are linked in some way with Wolfe or Canada. At the rear of the walled garden are the former stables, dating from Tudor times.

The house is open from April to October, on Sunday and Tuesday only from 2 to 6pm. Admission is £2.20 ($3.50) for adults and £1.10 ($1.75) for children. Take B2026 to the junction of Edenbridge and Sevenoaks roads (A25 and B2026).

## ✪ SISSINGHURST CASTLE GARDEN

These gardens (☎ **01580/712850**), situated between surviving parts of an Elizabethan mansion, were created by one of England's most famous and dedicated gardeners, the Bloomsbury writer Vita Sackville-West and her husband, Harold Nicolson. West stated in her *A Joy of Gardening* that "Instead of crawling about on all fours in solitary bad temper and incipient lumbago with trowel or a broken kitchen knife, you may now promenade in a leisurely way, saunter up and down, sprinkling selective death from a watering can as you converse with friends who have to tea on weed killers." It must have been well worth the effort because the spring garden is resplendent with flowering bulbs and daffodils in the orchard. The white garden reaches its peak in June. The large herb garden, a skillful montage that reflects her profound plant knowledge, has something to show all summer long, and the cottage garden, with its flowering bulbs, is at its finest in the fall. Meals are available in the Granary Restaurant. The garden area is flat, so it is wheelchair accessible; however, only two wheelchairs are allowed at a time.

You can see the gardens from April to mid-October on Tuesday through Friday from 1 to 6:30pm, and on Saturday, Sunday, and Good Friday from 10am to 5:30pm. Admission is £6 ($9.60) for adults and £3 ($4.80) for children.

## SQUERRYES COURT

The words of the diarist John Evelyn, written when he visited Squerryes in 1658, still ring true today: "A pretty, finely wooded, well watered seate, the stables good, the house old but convenient." Built in 1681 and owned by the Warde family for 250 years, this still-occupied manor house (☎ **01959/562345**) has—in addition to a fine collection of paintings, tapestries, and furniture—pictures and relics of General Wolfe's family. The de Squerie family lived in a house on this site from 1216 until the mid–15th century. The family crest was a squirrel, and it's thought that they took their name from the place. The family restored the formal gardens, dotting the banks surrounding the lake with spring bulbs, azaleas, herbaceous borders, and old roses to retain its beauty year-round. The reception rooms have been transposed so that the former dining rooms are now the drawing room (as it was when the house was first built). You can enjoy the fine collection of Old Master paintings from the Italian, 17th-century Dutch, and 18th-century English schools, along with antiques, porcelain, and tapestries, all acquired or commissioned by the family in the 18th century. The military hero received his commission on the grounds of the house—the spot is marked by a cenotaph.

From the end of March to September, on Wednesday, Saturday, and Sunday, the grounds are open from noon to 5:30pm; the house is open from 1:30 to 5:30pm. Admission to the house and grounds is £3.70 ($5.90) for adults, £3.40 ($5.45) for seniors and students, and £1.80 ($2.90) for children under 14. To see the grounds only costs £2.20 ($3.50) for adults, £2 ($3.20) for seniors and students, and £1.20 ($1.90) for children under 14. Take A25 just west of Westerham and follow the signs. Squerryes lies half a mile west of the center of Westerham, 10 minutes from Exit 6 or Exit 5 on the M25.

## 4 Royal Tunbridge Wells

36 miles SE of London; 33 miles NE of Brighton

Dudley Lord North, courtier to James I, is credited with the accidental discovery in 1606 of the mineral spring that led to the creation of a fashionable resort. Over the years, the "Chalybeate Spring" became known for its curative properties and was thought to be the answer to everything from too many days of wine and roses to failing sexual prowess. It's still possible to "take the water" today.

The spa resort reached its peak in the mid–18th century under the foppish patronage of "Beau" Nash (1674–1761), a dandy who assumed the role of final arbiter on how to act, what to say, and even what to wear (for example, he got men to remove their boots in favor of stockings).

Tunbridge Wells continued to enjoy a prime spa reputation up through the reign of Queen Victoria, who used to vacation here as a child, and in 1909 Tunbridge Wells received its Royal status. Today the spa is long past its zenith. But the town is a pleasant place to stay—it can be used as a base for exploring the many historic homes in Kent, described above.

## ESSENTIALS

**GETTING THERE**    Two to three trains per hour leave London's Charing Cross Station during the day bound for Hastings, but going via the town center of Royal Tunbridge Wells. The trip takes 50 minutes.

There are no direct bus links with Gatwick Airport or London. However, there is hourly service during the day between Brighton and Royal Tunbridge Wells (call ☎ **01634/832666** for the bus schedule). You can purchase tickets aboard the bus.

If you're driving from London, after reaching the ring road around London, continue east along M25, cutting southeast at the exit for A21 to Hastings.

**VISITOR INFORMATION**    The **Tourist Information Centre,** Old Fish Market, The Pantiles (☎ **01892/515675**), provides a full accommodations list and offers a room reservations service. Open Monday through Friday from 9am to 6pm, on Saturday from 9:30am to 5:30pm, and on Sunday from 10am to 4pm.

## EXPLORING THE TOWN

The most remarkable feature of Royal Tunbridge Wells is **The Pantiles,** a colonnaded walkway for shoppers, tea drinkers, and diners, built near the wells. If you walk around town, you'll see many other interesting and charming spots. Entertainment is presented at the Assembly Hall and Trinity Arts Centre.

Canadians touring in the area may want to seek out the grave of the founder of their country's capital. Lt. Col. John By of the Royal Engineers (1779–1836) died at Shernfold Park in Frant, East Sussex, near Tunbridge Wells, and is buried in the churchyard here. His principal claim to fame is that he established the city of Ottawa and built the Rideau Canal.

Within easy touring distance from Royal Tunbridge Wells are a number of castles, gardens, and stately homes, all with their own history and beauty; for example, Sissinghurst Castle, the home of novelist Vita Sackville-West, and Chartwell, former home of Sir Winston Churchill (see above).

## WHERE TO STAY

**Bankside.** 6 Scotts Way, Royal Tunbridge Wells, Kent TN2 5RG. ☎ **01892/531776.** 3 rms, none with bath. £30 ($48) double. All rates include English breakfast. No credit cards.

For a real taste of English hospitality, try this guest house located in a quiet neighborhood within walking distance of the restaurants, attractions, and train station. Mrs. Anne Kibbey offers pleasant, comfortable rooms, either double or twin (no singles). Her English breakfast will fortify you for the day.

**✪ Clarken Guest House.** 61 Frant Rd., Royal Tunbridge Wells, Kent TN2 5LH. ☎ **01892/533397.** 9 rms, 2 with bath. TV. £18 ($28.80) single without bath; £36 ($57.60) double without bath, £48 ($76.80) double with bath. All rates include English breakfast. No credit cards.

This spacious, comfortable, 19th-century home is on the principal road between Eastbourne and Hastings. It's a 10-minute walk from the main train station, where rail connections are made into London, and it's almost the same distance to the Pantiles. Two bedrooms are suitable for families. The place is kept immaculate, and has a warm, hospitable atmosphere.

**Danehurst House.** 41 Lower Green Rd., Rusthall, near Turnbridge Wells, Kent TN4 8TW. ☎ **01892/527739.** Fax 01892/514-804. 5 rms, 4 with bath. TV TEL. £45 ($72) single with or without bath; £65 ($104) double with or without bath. V.

Set in a residential satellite hamlet (Rusthall) of Tunbridge Wells, about 1 1/2 miles west of the spa's center, this mock-Tudor house was built in 1920 of stone and partially exposed exterior beams, and set within a small garden adjacent to roughly equivalent houses on the left and right. Bedrooms are "antique but newish" according to the owners, with fresh pastel colors, recently upgraded upholstery, and a scattering of old furniture. Public rooms include a conservatory and a library and although someone might whip you up a simple evening meal if you prefer to dine in-house, no meals, other than breakfast, are served on a regular basis for individual travelers.

**Downstairs at Thackeray's.** 85 London Rd. ☎ **01892/537559.** Reservations recommended. Main courses £6.90–£9.90 ($11.05–$15.85); fixed-price menu (Tues–Thurs only) £6.75–£7.95 ($10.80–$12.70). MC, V. Tues–Sat 12:30–2:30pm and 7–10:30pm. FRENCH/ENGLISH.

This restaurant is the less-expensive counterpart to a famous upstairs gastronomical enclave (whose prices are higher than those allowed by the limitations of this guidebook). Downstairs at Thackeray's, however, is fun, likable, reasonably priced, and bustling. Set on the street level of Tunbridge Wells's second-oldest house (built around 1660 and home to novelist William Thackeray), it offers fewer than 30 seats for good but cost-conscious dining. No one will mind if you drop in just for a drink at the stand-up bar, where recorded jazz plays softly. Most visitors, however, opt for full meals, which might include fillet of salmon with asparagus sauce, eggplant with tomatoes and mozzarella, and roast duck with prunes and port sauce.

## 5  Historic Mansions & Gardens in Dorking & Guildford

Dorking: 26 miles S of London
Guildford: 33 miles SW of London

Dorking, birthplace of Lord Laurence Olivier, lies on the Mole River at the foot of the North Downs. Within easy reach are some of the most scenic spots in the shire, including Silent Pool, Box Hill, and Leith Hill.

The guildhall in Guildford, a country town on the Wey River, has an ornamental projecting clock that dates from 1683. Charles Dickens considered High Street, which slopes to the river, one of the most beautiful in England.

## ESSENTIALS

**GETTING THERE**   Frequent daily train service takes 35 minutes from London's Victoria Station to Dorking. The train to Guildford departs from London's Waterloo Station and takes 40 minutes.

Green Line buses (no. 714) leave from London's Victoria Coach Station daily, heading for Kingston with a stop at Dorking. The trip takes 1 hour. National Express operates buses from London's Victoria Coach Station daily, with a stopover at Guildford on its runs from London to Portsmouth. It's usually more convenient to take the train.

If you're driving to Dorking, take A24 south from London. If you're driving to Guildford from London, head south along A3.

**VISITOR INFORMATION**   The **Guildford Tourist Information Centre** is at 14 Tunsgate (☎ **01483/444333**). Open October through April, Monday through Saturday from 9:30am to 5:30pm and May through September, Monday through Saturday from 9am to 6pm and on Sunday from 10am to 5pm.

## A VILLA, MANSION & GARDEN
### POLESDEN LACEY

Three miles to the northwest and 1¹/₂ miles south of Great Bookham, off the A246 Leatherhead-Guildford road, stands Polesden Lacey (☎ **01372/452048**), a former Regency villa built in 1824. It houses the Greville collection of antiques, paintings, and tapestries. In the early part of this century, it was enlarged and made into a comfortable Edwardian country house, thus befitting the owner, Mrs. Ronald Greville—a celebrated hostess and frequent entertainer of royalty from 1906 to 1939. The estate spreads over 1,400 acres. Stroll the 18th-century garden lined with herbaceous borders, and featuring a rose garden.

The grounds are open daily throughout the year from 11am to dusk. The house is open in March only on Saturday and Sunday from 1:30 to 4:30pm; April to October, Wednesday through Sunday from 1:30 to 5:30pm, except on bank holiday Mondays and the Sundays preceding the holiday, when the hours are from 11am to 5:30pm. Admission to the grounds and entrance to the house is £3 ($4.80) each for adults; children under 17 are charged half price and children 5 and under enter free. A family ticket goes for £7.50 ($12). A licensed restaurant on the grounds is open from 11am on the days the house can be visited.

### LOSELEY HOUSE

Lying 2¹/₂ miles southwest of Guildford, Loseley House, Loseley Park (☎ **01483/ 304440**), is a beautiful and historic Elizabethan mansion visited by Queen

Elizabeth I, James I, and Queen Mary. The house has been featured on TV and in numerous films. Its notable features include paneling from Henry VIII's Nonsuch Palace, period furniture, a unique carved chalk chimneypiece, magnificent ceilings, and cushions made by the first Queen Elizabeth.

The mansion is open from June through August, Wednesday through Saturday from 2 to 5pm, charging £4 ($6.40) for adults and £2.50 ($4) for children. Lunches and teas are served in the Courtyard Restaurant from 11am to 5pm, and you can visit the Loseley Park Shop for gifts and souvenirs.

## ○ WISLEY GARDEN

Wisley Garden is one of the great gardens of England. Every season of the year, this 250-acre garden bursts with flowers and shrubs, ranging from the alpine meadow carpeted with wild daffodils in spring, Battleston Hill brilliant with rhododendrons in early summer, the heather garden's colorful foliage in the fall, and a riot of exotic plants in the glasshouses in winter. Recent developments include model gardens and a landscaped orchid house. This garden is the site of a laboratory where botanists, plant pathologists, and entomologists experiment and assist amateur gardeners. A large gift shop stocks a wide range of gardening books. There's also a licensed restaurant and cafe.

The garden (☎ **01483/224234**) is situated in Wisley near Ripley just off M25 (Junction 10) on the A3 London-Portsmouth road. It's open all year, Monday through Saturday from 10am to 7pm (or sunset if earlier). Admission is £4.90 ($7.85) for adults, £1.75 ($2.80) for children 6 to 16, and free for children 5 and under.

# WHERE TO STAY & EAT

## IN DORKING

**Star and Garter Hotel.** Station Approach, Dorking, Surrey RH4 1TF. ☎ **01306/882820.** 10 rms, none with bath. TV. £25 ($40) single; £35 ($56) double; £45 ($72) triple. MC, V.

Most of the income at this establishment is generated at its popular pub, where it seems half the town congregates to drink and munch bar snacks. This tendency became particularly entrenched after its longtime owners sold it to a brewery, Friary Meux (makers of Carlsberg and Tetley beer), in the early 1990s. Today the brewery considers it an important part of their chain. The pub contains pool tables, and offers platters of food ordered at the bar. An American-themed dinner menu includes everything from steaks to sandwiches, with most items ranging in price from £3.50 ($5.60).

Overnight guests appreciate the large size of the self-styled "old-worldy" bedrooms upstairs. Rather spacious, and equipped with hot-beverage facilities and well-used furniture, they're tidy, cozy, and comfortable. The establishment is adjacent to the Dorking railway station, and receives a lot of after-work business from workers commuting from London's Victoria Station, a 35-minute train ride away.

## IN GUILDFORD

**○ Atkinsons Guest House.** 129 Stoke Rd., Guildford, Surrey GU1 1ET. ☎ **01483/38260.** 4 rms, 2 with bath. TV. £20 ($32) single without bath; £36 ($57.60) double without bath; £40 ($64) double with bath. All rates include English breakfast. No credit cards.

This is a most reasonable B&B, considering the warmth of Mrs. Atkinson's welcome and the quality of her rooms, redecorated in 1997. Three rooms have hot-beverage facilities, central heating, and TVs. You can also use ironing facilities. Her breakfasts are plentiful and well prepared. The house is a 10-minute walk to the town center, opposite the scenic park with tennis courts and swimming.

## ON THE OUTSKIRTS: PLACES NEAR GATWICK AIRPORT

**Ashleigh House Hotel.** 39 Redstone Hill, Redhill, Surrey RH1 4BG. ☎ **01737/764763.** Fax 01737/780308. 8 rms, 6 with bath. TV. £25 ($40) single without bath; £38 ($60.80) double without bath, £45 ($72) double with bath. All rates include English breakfast. MC, V.

This former Edwardian residence, long ago converted into a small hotel, stands at the crossroads of the A23 London-Brighton road and A25 to Sevenoaks. It's 15 minutes by car from Gatwick and 30 minutes by train from London. This inviting place is 8 miles east of Dorking, near Reigate, in the town of Redhill. Redhill itself is a town of 30,000 people and a major railway junction linking Gatwick Airport to London. Although Dorking is nearby, it takes about 25 minutes to drive here from there because of the winding, twisty roads. The hosts, Jill and Michael Warren, serve a good English breakfast in their dining room overlooking the garden, which has a heated summer swimming pool. The accommodations, recently updated, are well furnished, and include many amenities, such as hair dryers and radio alarms.

**The King's Arms Inn.** Stanc St., Ockley, near Guildford, Surrey RH5 5TP. ☎ **01306/711224.** Fax 01306/711224. 6 rms, all with bath. TV. £38 ($60.80) single; £50 ($80) double. All rates include continental breakfast. MC, V.

This 14th-century inn standing on an old Roman road is one of the region's most reliable pubs and stopovers. Its comfortable bedrooms upstairs are well kept and cozy, with private baths and beverage-making equipment. Much of the business comes from the on-site restaurant, decorated in a country rustic style. It offers an unusual combination of English, Malay, Burmese, and Thai, unlike anything else around. Its culinary inspiration comes from its resident chef, who traveled widely before returning to put down roots in Ockley. A table d'hôte menu in the dining room costs £15 ($24), although less expensive platters—everything from sandwiches to steaks—are served over the counter in the pub, costing from £1.65 to £10 ($2.65 to $16), depending on the item.

**Lynwood House.** 50 London Rd. Redhill, Surrey RH1 1LN. ☎ **01737/766894.** Fax 01737/778253. 11 rms, all with shower only. TV. £25–£28 ($40–$44.80) single; £40–£45 ($64–$72) double. All rates include English breakfast. MC, V.

This good B&B attracts overnight passengers who plan to catch a plane to Gatwick. Lynwood lies only 15 minutes from the airport either by car or train, 500 yards from Redhill Railway Station, or a 35-minute train ride from London. Accommodations are immaculately maintained and comfortable, all with showers. Breakfast is also generous and well prepared. The guest house is a 6-minute walk from a park with tennis courts, a large shopping center, and a leisure center with swimming.

**The Red Lion Pub.** The Green, Fernhurst. ☎01428/643112. Main courses £5–£10 ($8–$16); pub snacks £2–£5 ($3.20–$8). AE, MC, V. Mon–Sat 11am–3pm and 5:30–11pm; Sun noon–3pm and 7–10:30pm. Pub: Mon–Sat 11am–3pm and 5–11pm; Sun noon–3pm and 7–10:30pm. ENGLISH.

One of the region's most charming pubs lies 3 miles north of Haslemere, on the village green of the hamlet of Fernhurst. Originally built of sandstone and Sussex stone in the 1690s, it offers outdoor seating during warm weather both in front of the pub (where there's a view of the village green) and in back, amid shrubs and flowers specifically chosen for their scent. The staff and regular clients share in a jovial *esprit de corps.* Snacks can be ordered across the bar top, and more elaborate fare, with tableside service, is available in a separate area. Here you can order pepper chicken in a Dijon-flavored cream sauce, steak-and-kidney pie, Armenian lamb with rice pilaf, game pie, and traditional desserts.

✪ **Shrimptons Restaurant.** 2 Grove Cottage, Midhurst Rd., Kingsley Green. ☎ **01428/ 643539.** Reservations recommended. Main courses £10.50–£15 ($16.80–$24); fixed-price meals £12.50 ($20.05) at lunch, £14.95 ($23.90) at dinner. AE, DC, MC, V. Mon–Fri 12:30–1:45pm (last orders) and 6:30–9:45pm (last orders); Sat 6:30–9:45pm (last orders). CLASSICAL ENGLISH/FRENCH.

If you're seeking quality dining, head for this place, housed in a 17th-century build-ing, where Beryl Keeley runs one of the foremost restaurants in the area, and certainly one of the oldest. It's on the A286 Haslemere-Midhurst road, 1 mile outside Haslemere. The vegetables are served separately and in copious quantity, as indeed are all the dishes. Every dish is cooked to order and therefore available without the sauces—which are rich but still light and subtle—if requested. The restaurant is renowned for its fillet of salmon, Dover sole, double pheasant breast, roast grouse, venison steak, roast duck, and roast partridge. Vegetarian dishes are also offered.

# 8 Sussex

If King Harold hadn't so loved Sussex, the course of English history might have been changed forever. Had the brave Saxon waited longer in the north, he could have marshaled more adequate reinforcements before striking south to meet the Normans. But Duke William's soldiers were ravaging the countryside the king knew so well, and Harold rushed down to counter them.

Harold's attachment to Sussex is understandable. The landscape rises and falls like the tides of the Atlantic Ocean. The county is known for its downlands and tree-thickened weald, which produced the timbers to build England's once-mighty fleet. The shires lie south of London and Surrey, bordering Kent in the east, Hampshire in the west, and opening directly onto the English Channel, dotted with (occasionally sunny) seaside towns.

Like the other parts of England's vulnerable south, Sussex witnessed some of the most significant events in the country's lively history. Apart from the Norman landings at Hastings, the most monumental transformation occurred in the 19th century, as middle-class Victorians flocked to the seashore, pumping new spirit into Eastbourne, Worthing, Brighton, even old Hastings. Starved for raw, fresh air, the cult of saltwater worshipers flourished, and their ranks continue to migrate here. Although Eastbourne and Worthing are much frequented by the English, we'd place them several notches below Brighton and Hastings, which are much more suitable for a seaside respite. The Royal Pavilion at Brighton is a John Nash version of an Indian moghul's palace. In Hastings you'll see the Hastings Embroidery, a commemorative needlework tracing 900 years of English history.

Far more intriguing than the seaside resorts, however, are the old towns and villages of Sussex, particularly Rye and Winchelsea. No Sussex village is lovelier than Alfriston (and innkeepers are well aware of this fact), Arundel is noted for its castle, while the cathedral city of Chichester is a mecca for theater buffs. The old market town of Battle was the setting for the Battle of Hastings in 1066.

Traditionally, and for purposes of government, Sussex is divided into East Sussex and West Sussex. If you're exploring the area, the best place to base yourself is Brighton, since it has a wide choice of hotels, restaurants, and nightclubs. There's more excitement here at

"London by the Sea" than there is at tacky Hastings. If you're seeking old English charm and village life, head instead to Alfriston or Rye.

If you like to visit English castles and manors, Sussex does not compare favorably with castle-studded Kent. The only palace here that merits serious exploration is the Royal Pavilion at Brighton, and the only manor castle of worldwide interest is Arundel Castle at Arundel. Each of these memorable sights requires at least half a day.

# 1 The Ancient Seaport of Rye

62 miles SE of London

"Nothing more recent than a Cavalier's Cloak, Hat and Ruffles should be seen in the streets of Rye," said the sniffish Louis Jennings. This ancient town—once an island—flourished in the 13th century. Rye, near the English Channel, and neighboring Winchelsea were once part of the "Antient" Cinque Port Confederation. In its early days Rye was a smuggling center, its residents sneaking in contraband from the marshes to stash away in little nooks.

But the sea receded from Rye, leaving it perched like a giant whale out of water, 2 miles from the channel. Attacked several times by French fleets, Rye was practically razed in 1377. But it rebuilt itself successfully, in full Elizabethan regalia. When Queen Elizabeth I visited in 1573, she was so impressed that she bestowed upon the town the distinction of Royal Rye. The place has long been considered special, over the years attracting a host of the famous and accomplished, such as novelist Henry James.

Its narrow, labyrinthine cobblestone streets twist and turn, and jumbled along them are buildings whose sagging roofs and crooked chimneys reveal the town's medieval origins. The town overflows with architectural interest.

The neighboring Cinque Confederation port to Rye, Winchelsea, has also witnessed the water's ebb. The town traces its history back to Edward I, having experienced many dramatic moments, including its sacking by the French. In the words of one 19th-century writer, Winchelsea is "a sunny dream of centuries ago." The finest sight in this dignified residential town is a badly damaged 14th-century church containing a slew of remarkable tombs.

## ESSENTIALS

**GETTING THERE**   From London, the Southern Region Line offers trains south from Charing Cross or Cannon Street Station, with a change at Ashford, before continuing on to Rye. You can also go via Tunbridge Wells with a change in Hastings. Trains run every hour during the day, arriving at the Rye Train Station off Cinque Ports Street. The trip takes 1½ to 2 hours. Call ☎ **01424/429325** for schedules and information.

You need to take the train to get to Rye, but once you're there you'll find buses departing every hour on the hour for many destinations, including Hastings. Various bus schedules are posted on signs in the parking lot. For bus connections information in the surrounding area, call ☎ **01634/832666.**

If you're driving from London, take M25, M26, and M20 east to Maidstone, going southeast along A20 to Ashford. At Ashford, continue south on A2070.

**VISITOR INFORMATION**   The **Rye Tourist Office** is in the Heritage Centre on the Strand Quay (☎ **01797/226696**). Open mid-March to the end of October, daily from 9am to 5:30pm; November and December, weekdays from 10am to 1pm,

Saturday and Sunday from 10am to 4pm; January to mid-March, weekdays from 10am to 3pm, Saturday and Sunday from 10am to 4pm. The Heritage Centre houses a free exhibition and is also home to Rye Town Model—a sound and light show depicting more than 700 years of Rye's history. Adults pay £2 ($3.20), seniors and students £1.50 ($2.40), and children £1 ($1.60).

## EXPLORING RYE

The old town's entrance is **Land Gate,** where a single lane of traffic passes between massive, 40-foot-high stone towers. The gate parapet has holes through which boiling oil used to be poured on unwelcome and unsuspecting visitors, such as French raiding parties.

A notable historical site is the mid–12th-century **St. Mary's Parish Church,** Church Square (☎ **01797/224935**), with its 16th-century clock flanked by two gilded cherubs (known as Quarter Boys because of their striking of the bells on the quarter hour). The church, expansive and ornately beautiful, is often referred to as "the Cathedral of East Sussex." If you're courageous, you can climb a set of wooden stairs and ladders leading to the bell tower of the church, which affords an impressive view. It's open June through August, daily from 9am to 7pm; off-season, daily from 9am to 4pm. Contributions are appreciated to enter the church. Admission to the tower is £1.60 ($2.55) for adults and 80p ($1.30) for children.

**Lamb House.** West St. (at the top of Mermaid St.). ☎ **01797/224982.** Admission £2.50 ($4) adults and children. Apr–Oct Wed and Sat 2–5:30pm. Closed Nov–Mar.

Henry James lived at Lamb House from 1898 to 1916. James mementos are scattered throughout the house, set in a walled garden. Its previous owner rushed off to join the gold rush in North America but perished in the Klondike, and James was able to buy the freehold for a modest £2,000. Some of his best-known books were written here. In *English Hours,* James wrote: "There is not much room in the pavilion, but there is room for the hard-pressed table and tilted chair—there is room for a novelist and his friends."

**Rye Castle Museum.** Gungarden. ☎ **01797/226728.** Admission £1.50 ($2.40) adults; £1 ($1.60) students and seniors; 50p (80¢) children. Apr–Oct daily 10:30am–5:30pm; Nov–Mar, call for hours open.

This stone fort was constructed in about 1250 by King Henry III, to defend the coast against attack by the French. For 300 years it was the town jail, but it has long since been converted into a museum. In 1996, the Medieval Tower was restored.

### A COUNTRY HOUSE IN WINCHELSEA

On the outskirts of Winchelsea, you can visit **Smallhythe Place,** Smallhythe, near Tenterden (☎ **01580/762334**), for 30 years the country house of Dame Ellen Terry, the English actor acclaimed for her Shakespearean roles. The actor, who had a long theatrical association with Sir Henry Irving, died in the house in 1928. This timber-framed structure, known as a "continuous-jetty house," was built in the first half of the 16th century; it is filled with Terry memorabilia. An Elizabethan barn, converted into a theater in 1929, is open for viewing most days. Insider's tip: The stage memorabilia here—playbills, props, makeup, and a striking display of costumes—are almost worthy of a theater museum by themselves.

The house is on B2082 near Tenterden, about 6 miles north of Rye, and is open April to October, Saturday through Wednesday from 2 to 6pm. Adults pay £2.80 ($4.50) admission; children, £1.40 ($2.25). A family ticket is £7 ($11.20). Take bus no. 312 from Tenterden or Rye.

## SHOPPING IN RYE

Rye has had potteries for centuries and today is no exception. The best pottery outlets include the **Rye Pottery,** Ferry Road (☎ 01797/223038); **Rye Tiles,** Wishward Street (☎ 01797/223038); **David Sharp Ceramics,** The Mint (☎ 0177/222620); **Iden Pottery,** Conduit Hill (☎ 01797/226920); and the **Cinque Ports Pottery,** Conduit Hill (☎ 01797/224019), where you can see the potters at work during the week.

Rye also abounds in antique and collectible shops and bookstores. The best places to shop include **Wish Barn Antiques,** Wish Street (☎ 01797/226797); **Wishward Antiques,** Wishward Street (☎ 01797/226797); **Strand House Antiques,** The Deals (☎ 01797/225008); **Just Books,** The Deals (☎ 01797/321866); **Contraband Centre,** The Deals (☎ 01797/227321); **Martello Bookshop,** High Street (☎ 01797/222242); **Rye Antiques,** High Street (☎ 01797/222259); **Rye Old Books,** Lion Street (☎ 01797/225410); **Landgate Books,** Landgate (☎ 01797/222280); **Landgate Antiques,** Landgate (☎ 01797/224746); and **Ann Lingard Rope Walk Antiques,** Rope Walk (☎ 01797/223486).

## WHERE TO STAY IN THE AREA
### DOUBLES FOR LESS THAN £40

**Cliff Farm.** Military Rd., Iden Lock, Rye, East Sussex TN31 7NY. ☎ and fax **01797/280331.** 3 rms, none with bath. £15 ($24) per person double. All rates include English breakfast. No credit cards. Closed Dec–Feb.

Jeff and Pat Sullivin receive guests on their nearly 4$^{1}/_{2}$ acres of property. Because of the farm's elevated position, you'll have good views of the area, particularly over Romney Marsh. There's a sitting room where a log fire blazes when the weather is cool. Guest rooms in the 200-year-old farmhouse approximate the interior of a comfortable working farm of that era, with antiquated wooden furnishings, hardwood floors, and decorative floral wallpaper. Farm produce means a generous country breakfast and you can see the farm animals as you stroll around. It's located 2 miles east of Rye toward Iden Lock.

✪ **Durrant House Hotel.** East St., Rye, East Sussex TN31 7LA. ☎ **01797/223182.** 9 rms, 7 with bath/showers; 1 suite. TV. £40 ($64) single or double without bath; £56 ($89.60) single or double with bath; £80 ($128) suite. All rates include English breakfast. MC, V.

This beautiful Georgian house is set on a quiet residential street at the end of Market Street off High Street. The charming hotel is full of character and has a cozy lounge with an arched brick fireplace. The decor of the guest rooms helps to create an atmosphere appropriate to the structure and its history, straying only in the wall-to-wall carpet that runs throughout the interior. That aside, the decor features eclectic antique wood furnishings and fabrics combining chintz floral patterns with lace counterpanes. One of the bedrooms features a four-poster bed. The renowned artist Paul Nash lived next door until his death in 1946; in fact, his celebrated view, as seen in his painting *View of the Rother,* can be enjoyed from the hotel's River Room. The house is named for a previous owner, Sir William Durrant, a friend of the duke of Wellington, who bought it in the 18th century. At one time the house was used as a relay station for carrier pigeons; these birds brought news of the victory at Waterloo.

✪ **Jeake's House.** Mermaid St., Rye, East Sussex TN32 7ET. ☎ **01797/222828.** Fax 07197/ 222623. 12 rms, 10 with bath; 1 suite. TV TEL. £22.50 ($36) single without bath; £39 ($62.40) double without bath, £59 ($94.40) double with bath; £82 ($131.20) suite. All rates include English breakfast. MC, V.

The premier B&B in Rye, this hidden treasure is on the same street as the famous Mermaid Inn (see "Where to Eat," below). The five-floor house near the rail station was originally constructed as a wool storehouse in 1689 for a Huguenot, Samuel Jeake II, for whom it's named, and was then joined with a Quaker meeting house next door. The American writer Conrad Aiken, who wrote for *The New Yorker* under the *nom de plume* of Samuel Jeake, Jr., lived here for nearly a quarter of a century and was visited by such guests as T. S. Eliot, Henry James, artist Paul Nash (who had a house nearby), and Radclyffe Hall (author of *The Well of Loneliness*). Today the owners, Jenny and Francis Hadfield, take loving care of this house and are eager to share Aiken's collected letters and poems. The bedrooms, which have central heating and hot-drink trays, have been handsomely styled with Laura Ashley prints, and the bathrooms have hand-painted tiles made at a Sussex factory. Breakfast, traditional or vegetarian, is taken in a former galleried chapel, now elegantly converted.

**Little Saltcote.** 22 Military Rd., Rye, East Sussex TN31 7NY. ☎ **01797/223210.** 5 rms, 2 with bath. TV. £35 ($56) double without bath, £40 ($64) double with bath. All rates include English breakfast. No credit cards.

Owned by Sally and Terry Osborne, this attractive guest house is a 5-minute walk east of the town center, in a peaceful rural setting. The house was built in 1901 on land that, until 1400, lay beneath the surface of the sea. That doesn't seem to impede the fertility of this establishment's rear garden, which in springtime is a riot of color. The well-appointed rooms—all doubles—have central heating, razor outlets, hot-beverage facilities, and hot and cold running water. A vegetarian breakfast can be provided for those who want it, and forecourt parking is available.

## DOUBLES FOR LESS THAN £60

✪ **Little Orchard House.** 3 West St., Rye, East Sussex TN31 7ES. ☎ **01797/223831.** 3 rms, all with bath. TV. £45–£65 ($72–$104) single; £60–£84 ($96–$134.40) double. All rates include English breakfast. MC, V.

You'll find this to be among the most elegant and moderately priced accommodations in the old seaport. The 18th-century Georgian town house was originally the home of Rye's mayor, Thomas Proctor. Other prominent politicians (and/or smugglers) also lived here through the years, including the prime minister, David Lloyd George, who resided near here in the 1920s. The house is tastefully furnished with antiques and Georgian paneling. A large open fireplace in the lounge-study has a blazing fire when needed, a big bouquet of dried flowers otherwise. From this room and the intimate breakfast room, you can see the old-style walled garden with espaliered fruit trees. The bedrooms all have hot-drink trays. The hotel is in the town center at the western end of High Street.

**Playden Oasts Hotel.** Peasmarsh Rd., Playden, Rye, East Sussex TN3 7UL. ☎ **01797/ 223502.** 8 rms. TV TEL. £30–£50 ($48–$80) single; £50–£70 ($80–$112) double. All rates include English breakfast. MC, V.

If you've ever wondered what an oast was, stay at this hotel. The hotel consists of three adjacent towers, each round at the base and capped with a conical roof that tapers to a narrow air vent at the top. The towers were built between 1850 and 1890 as a means of drying the hops (a key ingredient in beer and ale) local farmers once produced in abundance. The three oasts comprising the core of this hotel remained in working use until 1965, when a local entrepreneur interconnected them into a coherent whole.

After a disastrous fire, the oasts were repaired and upgraded again in 1986, and now provide comfortable and unusual accommodations for overnight guests. Only two of the eight accommodations are inside the rounded walls of the original kilns. The other accommodations, rectangular in form, are nonetheless clean and cozy, each with tea-making facilities and comfortably rustic furniture. Bob Press is your host, offering directions to the agrarian hamlet of Playden (a modern corruption of its older name, Pleidenam), about a mile northeast of Rye. It sits on three-quarters of an acre of its own land, surrounded by other residential buildings.

Don't overlook this unusual inn as a place to grab lunch, dinner, or afternoon tea. British cuisine is served at lunch and dinner every day. Advance reservations are required.

✪ **Strand House.** Winchelsea, East Sussex TN36 4JT. ☎ **01797/226276.** Fax 01797/224806. 10 rms. TV. £28–£34 ($44.80–$54.40) single; £40–£58 ($64–$92.80) double. All rates include English breakfast. MC, V.

Sure to catch your eye is this weathered historic house and cottage set in a garden at the foot of a hill; sheep graze in the meadows that separate the hotel from the sea. The owners are conscious of comforts, and their high standard includes wall-to-wall carpeting, hot-beverage facilities, and central heating in all bedrooms. One of the rooms includes a four-poster bed. A private dining room with a huge inglenook fireplace is reserved for the guests, and there's ample parking on the hotel grounds.

The house dates from the 1490s and has irregular oak floors; the low, heavy oak ceiling beams came from ships. It is believed that a tunnel near the house leads up to Winchelsea town, a relic of the days when smuggling was one of the main industries of the area. The house is located just off A259.

## WHERE TO EAT

In addition to the places recommended below, consider **The Olde Bell,** 33 The Mint (☎ **01797/223323**), where you get some of the best pub grub in town. A big plate of lasagna costs £3.50 ($5.60) and makes a filling meal. If you're sightseeing on the run, check out **Anatolian's Kebabs,** 16A Landgate (☎ **01797/226868**), which has Rye's best stuffed pita sandwiches, costing from £2.20 ($3.50). You can also get a filling lunch at **Fletcher's House,** Lion Street (☎ **01797/223101**), where the dramatist, John Fletcher, was born in 1579. Upstairs is an antique-filled, oak-paneled room from the 1400s. Lunches cost from £3.50 ($5.60). Hours are daily from 10am to 5:15pm. It's also a good place for a cream tea at £3.50 ($5.60).

**Casa Conti.** 108 High St. ☎ **01797/222574.** Reservations recommended. Main courses £8.95–£14.95 ($14.30–$23.90). MC, V. Mon–Sat noon–2pm and 7–10pm. ITALIAN/ CONTINENTAL.

Anthony Conti, who graduated from the Lausanne Culinary School, owns this restaurant specializing in flambées. Among the flambées cooked at your table you may find a filet of beef with brandy and green peppers finished off with cream; scampi with butter, onions, white wine, and cream; or escalloped pork and pâté with cognac, lemon, and garlic butter. Other selections include fresh sardines marinated in white wine and onions; breast of chicken with white wine, mushrooms, and cream; and locally caught grilled Dover sole. A vegetarian menu features a number of pasta dishes including cannellini crêpe with spinach and spaghetti al pesto.

✪ **Mermaid Inn.** Mermaid St. ☎ **01797/223065.** Reservations recommended. Fixed-price 2-course lunch £11.50 ($18.40), fixed-price 3-course lunch £14.95 ($23.90); fixed-price 4-course dinner £21 ($33.60). AE, DC, MC, V. Daily 12:30–2:15pm and 7:30–9:15pm. ENGLISH.

This is the most famous of the old smugglers' inns of England—known to the band of cutthroats, the real-life Hawkhurst Gang, as well as to Russell Thorndike's fictional character, Dr. Syn. One of the present bedrooms, in fact, is called Dr. Syn's

Bedchamber, and is connected by a staircase, set in the thickness of a wall, to the bar. The Mermaid had been open for 150 years when Elizabeth I visited Rye in 1573. In addition to serving good food, the most charming tavern in Rye also has 28 comfortable bedrooms to rent, but they are budget bursting.

Even if you don't dine or stay at the Mermaid, drop in to the old Tudor pub, with its 16-foot-wide fireplace (look for a priest's hiding hole). It's located between West Street and the Strand.

**Swan Cottage Tea Rooms.** 41 The Mint, High St. ☎ **01797/222423.** Afternoon tea £4.75 ($7.60); cakes and pastries 75p–£1.75 ($1.20–$2.80). MC. Mon–Wed 10:30am–5pm. ENGLISH TEA.

Dating from 1420, this black and white, half-timbered cottage lies in one of the most historic buildings in town. On the main street, surrounded by antique shops and pottery outlets, it is one of the preferred places for afternoon tea. We prefer the room in the rear, especially on a windy day because it has a big brick-built fireplace. Some rather delectable pastries and cakes await you, along with a selection of Darjeeling, Earl Grey, Pure Assam, and other teas.

## 2  1066 & All That: Hastings & Battle

Hastings: 63 miles SE of London; 45 miles SW of Dover. Battle: 55 miles SE of London; 34 miles NE of Brighton

The world has seen bigger battles, but few are as well remembered as the Battle of Hastings in 1066. When William, duke of Normandy, landed on the Sussex coast and lured King Harold (already fighting Vikings in Yorkshire) southward to defeat, the destiny of the English-speaking people was changed forever. The actual battle occurred at what is now Battle Abbey (8 miles away), but the Norman duke used Hastings as his base of operations. You can visit the abbey, and then have a cup of tea in Battle's main square, and then you can be off, as the rich countryside of Sussex is much more intriguing than this sleepy market town.

Hastings today is a little seedy and rundown. If you're seeking an English seaside resort, head for brighter Brighton instead.

## ESSENTIALS

**GETTING THERE**   Daily trains run from London's Victoria Station or Charing Cross to Hastings hourly. The trip takes $1\frac{1}{2}$ to 2 hours. The train station at Battle is a stop on the London–Hastings rail link. For more information, call the 24-hour line (☎ **01345/484950**).

Hastings is linked by bus to Maidstone, Folkestone, and Eastbourne, which has direct service with scheduled departures. National Express operates regular daily service from London's Victoria Coach Station. If you're in Rye or Hastings in summer, several frequent buses run to Battle. For information and schedules, call ☎ **0990/808080.**

If you're driving from the M25 ring road around London, head southeast to the coast and Hastings on A21. To get to Battle, cut south to Sevenoaks and continue along A21 to Battle via A2100.

**VISITOR INFORMATION**   In Hastings, the **Tourist Information Centre** is at 4 Robertson Terrace (☎ **01424/781111**). Open Monday through Friday from 10am to 5pm and on Saturday from 10am to 1pm and 2 to 5pm.

In Battle, the **Tourist Information Centre** is at 88 High St. (☎ **01424/773721**). Open April through September, daily from 10am to 6pm; off-season Monday through Saturday from 10am to 4pm and on Sunday from 1 to 4pm.

# THE BATTLE SITE LEGACY
## BATTLE ABBEY

King Harold, last of the Saxon kings, fought bravely here encircled by his housecarls not only for his kingdom but for his life. As legend has it, he was killed by an arrow through the eye, and his body was dismembered. To commemorate the victory, William the Conqueror founded Battle Abbey at the south end of Battle High Street (☎ 01424/773792); some of the construction stone was shipped from his own lands at Caen in northern France.

During the dissolution of the monasteries from 1538 to 1539 by King Henry VIII, the church of the abbey was largely destroyed. Some buildings and ruins, however, remain in what Tennyson called "O Garden, blossoming out of English blood." The principal building still standing is the Abbot's House, which is leased to a private school for boys and girls and is open to the general public only during summer holidays. Of architectural interest is the gate house, which has octagonal towers and stands at the top of the Market Square. All of the north Precinct Mall is still standing, and one of the most interesting sights of the ruins is the ancient Dorter Range, where the monks once slept.

The town of Battle flourished around the abbey; even though it has remained a medieval market town, many of the old half-timbered buildings have regrettably lost much of their original character because of stucco plastering carried out by past generations.

This is a great place for the kids. There's a theme play area here, plus, at the gate an activity sheet is distributed, relating the day's events. That's not all. You can relax with a picnic or stroll in the parkland that once formed the monastery grounds.

The abbey is open April to September, daily from 10am to 6pm; October to March, daily from 10am to 4pm. Admission is £3.50 ($5.60) for adults, £1.80 ($2.90) for children, and £2.60 ($4.15) for seniors and students. The abbey is a 5-minute walk from the train station.

**Hastings Castle.** Castle Hill Rd., West Hill. ☎ **01424/781112.** Admission £2.80 ($4.50) adults; £1.90 ($3.05) children. Easter–Sept daily 10am–5pm; Oct–Easter daily 11am–3:30pm. Take the West Hill Cliff Railway from George St. to the castle for 70p ($1.10), 40p (65¢) for children.

In ruins now, the first of the Norman castles built in England sprouted on a western hill overlooking Hastings, around 1067. Precious little is left to remind us of the days when proud knights, imbued with a spirit of pomp and spectacle, wore bonnets and girdles. The fortress was defortified by King John in 1216 and later used as a church. Owned by the Pelham dynasty from the latter 16th century to modern times, the ruins have been turned over to Hastings. There is now an audiovisual presentation of the castle's history, including the famous battle of 1066. From the mount, you'll have a good view of the coast and promenade.

✪ **Hastings Embroidery.** Town Hall, Queen's Rd. ☎ **01424/781111.** Admission £1.50 ($2.40) adults; £1 ($1.60) children and seniors. May–Sept Mon–Fri 10am–4:30pm; Oct–Apr Mon–Fri 11:30am–3pm.

A commemorative work, the Hastings Embroidery is a remarkable achievement that traces 900 years of English history through needlework. First exhibited in 1966, the 27 panels, 243 feet in length, depict 81 historic scenes, including some of the nation's greatest moments and legends: the murder of Thomas à Becket, King John signing the Magna Carta, the Black Plague, Chaucer's pilgrims going to Canterbury, the Battle of Agincourt with the victorious Henry V, the Wars of the Roses, the Little

Princes in the Tower, Bloody Mary's reign, Drake's *Golden Hind,* the arrival of Philip II's ill-fated Armada, Guy Fawkes's gunpowder plot, the sailing of the *Mayflower,* the disastrous plague of 1665, the great London fire of 1666, Nelson at Trafalgar, the Battle of Waterloo, the Battle of Britain, and the D-day landings at Normandy. Also exhibited is a scale model of the battlefield at Battle, with William's inch-high men doing in Harold's model soldiers.

## SEASIDE AMUSEMENTS

Linked by a 3-mile promenade along the sea, Hastings and St. Leonards were given a considerable boost in the 19th century by Queen Victoria, who visited several times. Neither town enjoys such royal patronage today; rather, they do a thriving business with the English on vacation. Hastings and St. Leonards have the usual shops and English sea-resort amusements.

**Smugglers Adventure.** St. Clements Caves, West Hill. ☎ **01424/422964.** Admission £4.20 ($6.70) adults; £2.70 ($4.30) children; £12.50 ($20) family ticket. April–Sept daily 10am–5:30pm; Oct–Mar daily 11am–4:30pm. Take the West Cliff Railway from George St. to West Hill for 70p ($1.10) adults; 40p (65¢) for children.

Here you can descend into the once-secret underground haunts of the smugglers of Hastings. In these chambers, where the smugglers stashed their booty away from customs authorities, you can see an exhibition and museum, a video in a theater, and take a subterranean adventure walk with 50 life-size figures, along with dramatic sound and lighting effects.

## TEATIME

When the wind and rain blow in from the channel, head for **The Willow Tea Room,** 84 All Saint's St., Old Town, in Hastings (☎ **01424/430656**), the favorite spot for afternoon tea. Choose from one of their Indian, Ceylon, China, or fruit teas, each served with an assortment of sandwiches, scones, chunky jam, fresh cream, or a slice of cake. A full tea with all the trimmings costs £4.50 ($7.20).

## WHERE TO STAY IN & AROUND HASTINGS
### DOUBLES FOR LESS THAN £55

**Eagle House Hotel.** 12 Pevensey Rd., St. Leonards, East Sussex TN38 0JZ. ☎ **01424/430535.** Fax 01424/437771. 20 rms. TV TEL. £32 ($51.20) single; £49 ($78.40) double. All rates include English breakfast. AE, DC, MC, V.

One of the best hotels in the area, this three-story mansion, originally built in 1860 as a palatial private home, lies in a residential section about a 10-minute walk from the beaches (it's adjacent to St. Leonards Shopping Centre). The well-furnished bedrooms have central heating and coffee-making facilities, and the hotel has a bar open in the evening. English cuisine is served, a fixed-price dinner costing £18.95 ($30.30).

**Fantail Cottage.** Rosemary Lane, Pett, near Hastings, East Sussex TN35 4EB. ☎ **01424/813637.** 3 rms. TV. £27 ($43.20) single; £39 ($62.40) double. All rates include English breakfast. No credit cards. Closed 2 weeks at Christmas. A public bus marked PETT travels from Hastings every 2 hours Mon–Sat.

One of the most charming bed-and-breakfast hotels in the region lies 4$^1$/$_2$ miles east of Hastings in the hamlet of Pett off A259. Set amid 2$^1$/$_2$ acres of bluebell forest and parkland, the establishment comprises a pair of cottages originally built in 1735 and then connected in the 1950s. Owners Pamela and Bill Waghorn are devoted conservationists who feed flocks of local fantail pigeons (after which the cottage was named), dozens of other birds, and a colony of badgers that emerge every evening at dusk. (All this occurs within a few feet of the living room windows—it's a very pleasant evening ritual.) The bedrooms are decorated in an English country-cottage style, sometimes with family antiques, and are clean, warm, and cozy. A host tray is provided in each room. No evening meals are served, but the Waghorns are familiar with the neighborhood's several recommendable restaurants and pubs.

**Parkside House.** 59 Lower Park Rd., Hastings, East Sussex TN34 2LD. ☎ **01424/433096.** Fax 01424/421431. 5 rms. TV. £25 ($40) single; £52 ($83.20) double. All rates include English breakfast. MC, V.

A 15-minute walk north of Hastings's center, in a neighborhood whose architecture and wildlife are legally protected, this bed-and-breakfast hotel was built in 1880 of red brick and slate. Views from many of the windows overlook a private garden and a duck pond in Alexander Park, a greenbelt that's said to be the largest municipal park in southeast England. Brian Kent, the owner, offers bedrooms that are comfortable and well maintained, each with a color TV and VCR. Guests have access to the hotel's modest inventory of recorded films.

## WHERE TO STAY NEAR BATTLE

**Little Hemingfold Hotel.** Telham, Battle, East Sussex TN33 0TT. ☎ **01424/774338.** Fax 01424/775351. 13 rms, 10 with bath. £40 ($64) single; £69 ($110.40) double. All rates include English breakfast. AE, DC, MC, V. Take A2100 from Battle for 1 1/2 miles and turn at the sign.

Little Hemingfold lies 1 1/2 miles from Battle off A2100 and is reached by going down a steep road. It's a rustic white building that's part 17th century and part early Victorian. Each bedroom is individually decorated in a cozy, homelike way, just like a visit to Grandma's. Guests often enjoy apéritifs on the lawn, and a grass tennis court is available. French and English meals are served.

✪ **Netherfield Hall.** Netherfield, near Battle, East Sussex TN33 9PQ. ☎ **01424/774450.** 4 rms. £30–£35 ($48–$56) single; £40–£50 ($64–$80) double. All rates include English breakfast. No credit cards. Closed Feb. Take A2100—Netherfield is signposted 2 1/2 miles west of Battle.

Opposite the village church in the hamlet of Netherfield, 2 1/2 miles west of Battle, this house was built with architectural remnants salvaged from older buildings throughout Sussex. With the ample use of very old oaken beams and antique stained-glass windows, the house appears older than its 1983 construction. Jean and Tony Hawes offer well-furnished, English country-style bedrooms. Breakfast is served on bone china, and although evening meals are not available, the Hawes can direct overnight guests to the neighborhood's several pubs and restaurants. A tearoom is open daily, except Tuesdays, where coffee is served in the morning and cream teas are served in the afternoon. English-made gifts are available in the tearoom. There is also a beautiful golf course a half mile away. Golf clubs can be rented, if necessary.

## WHERE TO EAT
### IN HASTINGS

Because Hastings is a fishing center, it has a multitude of competitive small seafood restaurants along the street fronting the beach at the east side of the city (on the way to the old part of town). The restaurant listed below is 5 miles outside Hastings.

✪ **Crossways.** Pett Level Rd., at the corner of Waites Lane, in Fairlight, near Hastings. ☎ **01424/812356.** Reservations recommended. Main courses £4.50–£6.50 ($7.20–$10.40) at lunch, £7.50–£12.50 ($12–$20) at dinner; 3-course Sunday lunch £8 ($12.80); 3-course fixed-price dinner £11.75 ($18.80). MC, V. Tues–Sun 12:30–2pm and daily 7–9:30pm. INTERNATIONAL.

This respected restaurant in the hamlet of Fairlight is a 5-mile drive east of Hastings. (The bus that runs between Hastings and Rye stops nearby.) Originally built in 1936 as a butcher shop, the restaurant was established in 1989 by German-born Hartmut Seidler and his wife, Deirdre, who extend a genuine welcome. Known for its honest portions, well-prepared food, and reasonable prices, the restaurant offers such dishes as fresh Dover sole grilled and served with white wine sauce, fresh duck with orange sauce, beef Wellington, several kinds of fresh fish, and a scattering of French and German dishes. Hanging on magnolia-colored walls is a collection of unusual watercolors by local artists.

## IN BATTLE

☼ **The Blacksmith Restaurant.** 43 High St. ☎ **01424/773200.** Reservations recommended. Main courses £7–£15 ($11.20–$24); 2-course fixed-price lunch £9.85–£14.95 ($15.75–$23.90); 2-course fixed-price supper £11 ($17.60). MC, V. Tues–Sun noon–2:30pm and 7–10:30pm. CONTINENTAL/HUNGARIAN.

On the upper (northwestern) edge of Battle, this restaurant is in a 15th-century stone-sided cottage that for many years housed the village blacksmith. Inside, beneath medieval timbers rescued from old galleons, you can appreciate the European cuisine of Martin and Christine Howe. Many dishes are inspired by the cuisine of Hungary, and include grilled avocados stuffed with Hungarian Liptoi cheese, chilled wild-cherry soup, calves' liver prepared Dutch style with smoked ham and onions, and a signature version of roast duck finished with honey and a wild-cherry sauce. The dessert trolley will probably contain an Eszterházy torte or a Shomloi Délice, a concoction of pulverized walnuts, sultanas, sponge cake, rum, and chocolate sauce.

**The Gateway Restaurant.** 78 High St. ☎ **01424/772856.** Reservations required only for Sat dinner. Main courses £4–£5 ($6.40–$8) at lunch; clotted-cream tea £3 ($4.80). MC, V. Sun–Fri 10am–5pm (lunch noon–2:30pm); Sat 10am–5pm and 7–10pm. ENGLISH.

A few paces from the entrance to Battle Abbey, this restaurant is the best place in town for afternoon tea, but it's also a good and reasonably priced restaurant. In a low-beamed building from the 17th century, it was a forge for a blacksmith before its later transformation into a bakery. An avid gardener, the owner, Mrs. Ruth Reeve, along with her husband, Tony, maintains a rose garden with tables set beneath antique arbors. A wide variety of homemade pastries, including chocolate profiteroles, is displayed. In the afternoon, the clotted-cream teas are a delight. Lunches include such classic English dishes as cottage pie, steak-and-kidney pie, chicken-and-leek pie, and beer-and-mushroom casserole.

## 3  Alfriston & Lewes

60 miles S of London

Nestled on the Cuckmere River, Alfriston is one of the most beautiful villages in England. It lies northeast of Seaford on the English Channel, in the vicinity of the resort of Eastbourne and the modern port of Newhaven. During the day, Alfriston is overrun by coach tours (it's that lovely, and that popular). High Street, with its old market cross, is just like what you'd imagine a traditional English village to look like. Some of the old houses still have hidden chambers where smugglers once stored their loot; alas, the loot is long gone. There are also several old inns.

Only about a dozen miles away along A27 toward Brighton, Lewes, an ancient Sussex town centered in the South Downs, is worth exploring. Since the home of the Glyndebourne Opera is only 5 miles to the east, it's difficult to find a place to stay in Lewes during the **Glyndebourne Opera Festival.** The town, although a rather somber appearing market town today, has many historical associations, listing such residents as Thomas Paine, who lived at Bull House, on High Street, now a restaurant.

## ESSENTIALS

**GETTING THERE**   Trains leave from London's Victoria Station and London Bridge Station for Lewes. One train per hour makes the 1¹/₄-hour trip daily. Trains are more frequent during rush hours. Call ☎ **0345/484950** for schedules and information. There is no rail service to Alfriston.

Buses run daily to Lewes from London's Victoria Coach Station, although the 3-hour trip has so many stops that it's better to take the train. A bus runs from Lewes to Alfriston every 30 minutes. It's operated by R. D. H. Services and is called Local Rider no. 125. For bus information and schedules in the area, call ☎ **01273/ 474747.** The bus station at Lewes is on East Gate Street in the center of town.

If you're driving, head east along M25 (the London ring road), cutting south on A26 via East Grinstead to Lewes. Once at Lewes, follow A27 east to the signposted turnoff for the village of Alfriston.

**VISITOR INFORMATION**   The **Tourist Information Centre** is in Lewes at 187 High St. (☎ **01273/483448**). In season, from Easter until the end of October, hours are Monday through Friday from 9am to 5pm, Saturday from 10am to 5pm, and Sunday from 10am to 2pm. Off-season hours are Monday through Friday only, from 10am to 2pm.

## ✪ THE GLYNDEBOURNE OPERA FESTIVAL

In 1934, a group of local opera enthusiasts established an opera company based in the hamlet of Glyndebourne, 1¹/₂ miles east of Lewes and 5 miles northwest of Alfriston. The festival has been running ever since, and now is one of the best regional opera companies in Britain.

In 1994, the original auditorium was demolished, and a dramatic modern glass, brick, and steel structure, designed by noted English architect Michael Hopkins, was built adjacent to some remaining (mostly ornamental) vestiges of the original building. The new auditorium is known for its acoustics.

Operas are presented here only between mid-May and late August, and the productions tend to be unusual works. The 1996 performances include rarely performed pieces such as Handel's *Theodora,* Berg's *Lulu,* Rossini's *Ermionie,* and Tchaikovsky's *Yevgeny Onyegin.*

For information, contact the Glyndebourne Festival, P.O. Box 2624, Glyndebourne (Lewes), East Sussex BN8 5UW (☎ **01273/812321**). You can call the box office at ☎ 01273/813813. Tickets range from £10 to £114 ($16 to $182.40). You usually can get last-minute tickets because of cancellations by season ticket holders. But if you want to see a specific show, it's a good idea to buy a ticket several months in advance. And it's fun to pack your own champagne picnic to enjoy before the performance; you can buy foodstuffs from shops in Lewes.

To get to the theater from Lewes, take the A26 to the B2192, following the signs to Glynde and Glyndebourne. From Alfriston, follow the hamlet's main street north of town in the direction of highway A27, then turn left following signs first to Glynde, then to Glyndebourne.

## EXPLORING THE TWO TOWNS

About 1 mile outside Alfriston off A27 is **Drusilla's Park** (☎ **01323/870656**). The fascinating but not overly large park has a flamingo lake, Japanese garden, and unusual breeds of some domestic animals, among other attractions. Grey Owl Cabin is a replica of a cabin inhabited by a Hastings native living in the Canadian woods in the 1930s; he was a pioneer conservationist who sought to stop the trapping of beaver and the destruction of the Canadian woods. Children particularly like the playland, which now includes a waterplay area. The park is open daily from 10am to 5pm (until 4pm in winter). Admission is £6 ($9.60) for adults, £5 ($8) for children 3 to 12 (free for children 2 and under), and £4 ($6.40) for seniors. It's closed December 24 to 26.

In Lewes, the half-timbered **Anne of Cleves House,** 52 Southover High St. (☎ **01273/474610**), was part of Anne of Cleves's divorce settlement from Henry VIII, but Anne never lived in the house and there's no proof that she ever visited Lewes. Today the house is a Museum of Local History and is cared for by the Sussex Archaeological Society. The museum has a furnished bedroom and kitchen and displays of furniture, local history of the Wealden iron industry, and other local crafts. Admission is £2 ($3.20) for adults, £1 ($1.60) for children, and £1.75 ($2.80) for students. Open April through October, Monday through Saturday from 10am to 5:30pm and Sunday from noon to 5:30pm. From November through March, visits are possible only on Tuesday, Thursday, and Saturday from 10am to 5:30pm. Take bus no. 123.

Lewes, of course, matured in the shadow of its **Norman castle.** Adjacent to the castle is the **Museum of Sussex Archaeology,** 169 High St. (☎ **01273/486290**). A 20-minute audiovisual show is available by advance request. A joint admission ticket to both the castle and the museum costs £3.25 ($5.20) for adults, £1.75 ($2.80) for children, £2.75 ($4.40) for students and seniors, and £8.50 ($13.60) for a family ticket. Both sites can be visited year-round, Monday through Saturday from 10am to 5:30pm, and Sunday and bank holidays from 11am to 5:30pm. Audio tours of the castle are also available. Take bus no. 27, 28, 121, 122, 166, 728, or 729.

## SHOPPING

Lewes, especially along its High Street, thrives as a commercial center. Street musicians regularly entertain shoppers as they browse in the bustling pedestrian precinct, and the town has a particularly impressive range of specialty shops, galleries, and craft centers. Our favorite is the **Old Needlemakers Craft Center,** Market Lane (☎ **01273/475433**).

## TEATIME

Just north of Lewes on the A275 stands **The Old Post House,** Offham (☎ **01273/477358**). We know of no more delightful spot in the area for tea than this romantic setting beside a garden, overlooking two of the village churches, the Norman Hamsey Church from the 1100s and the Offham Church from Victoria's day. The baking is light and delicious, and an afternoon tea costs only £2 ($3.20). However, the room is open only on Saturday and Sunday from 2 to 6pm.

## OUTSIDE LEWES: WHERE THE WOOLFS LIVED & THE BLUEBELL RAILWAY

The small downland village of **Rodmell** lies midway between Lewes and the port of Newhaven on C7. It's known for **Monks House,** a National Trust property that was bought by Virginia and Leonard Woolf in 1919 and was their home until his death in 1969. Virginia wrote of the profusion of fruit and vegetables produced by the garden and of the open-water meadows looking out on the downs. Much of the house was furnished and decorated by Virginia's sister, Vanessa Bell, and the artist Duncan Grant.

Please note that the house has extremely limited visiting hours: from the first Saturday in April until the last Wednesday in October, and then only on Wednesday and Saturday from 2 to 5:30pm. Admission is £2.20 ($3.50) adults, £1.10 ($1.75) children 5 and up, and free for children 4 and under. More information is available by calling the headquarters of the National Trust in East Sussex (☎ **01892/890651**).

Rodmell also has a 12th-century church, a working farm, and a tiny Victorian school still in use. Take Southdown bus no. 123 from the Lewes rail station.

The all-steam **Bluebell Railway** starts at Sheffield Park Station near Uckfield in East Sussex (☎ **01825/722370**) on A275 between East Grinstead and Lewes. The name is taken from the spring flowers that grow alongside the track, running from Sheffield Park to Kingscote. It's a delight for railway buffs, with locomotives dating from the 1870s through the 1950s, when British Railways ended steam operations. You can visit locomotive sheds and a small museum, then later patronize the bookshop or have lunch in a large buffet, bar, and restaurant complex. The round-trip is 1¹/₂ hours as the train wanders through a typical English countryside. It costs £7.20 ($11.50) for adults, £3.60 ($5.75) for children, and £19.50 ($31.20) for a family ticket. Trains run year-round on Saturday and Sunday and daily from May to September.

## WHERE TO STAY
### IN ALFRISTON

**Frog Firle.** Alfriston, near Polegate, East Sussex BN26 5TT. ☎ **01323/870423.** Fax 01323/870615. 68 beds. £8.50 ($13.60) adults; £5.70 ($9.10) under 18 years old. All rates include English breakfast. MC, V.

To beat the high prices of Alfriston, frugal travelers escape to this well-preserved 16th-century farmhouse about a half mile south of Alfriston in the Cuckmere Valley. We love it for its name alone. The stone structure was once a working Sussex farm, and it still retains some of its original character, with its exposed beams, oak timbering, and a room from the early 16th century. On cold nights when the winds blow in from the channel, there's a wood-burning fire glowing. Dinner can be ordered for £4.25 ($6.80), although there's also a self-catering kitchen. Bathroom facilities offer a shower only, and there are no storage lockers or laundry rooms. An 11pm curfew is imposed.

**George Inn.** High St., Alfriston, Polegate, East Sussex BN26 5SY. ☎ **01323/870319.** 8 rms, 6 with bath. TV TEL. £30 ($48) single without bath, £40 ($64) single with bath; £60–£80 ($96–$128) double with bath. All rates include English breakfast. MC, V. Bus: no. 727.

First licensed as an inn in 1397, this long, low, and inviting inn was once a rendez-vous for smugglers. The George, however, is better known for its good food. If you're there for lunch, your meal will cost £8 ($12.80) and up; dinner begins at £15 ($24). Food is served from noon to 2pm and 7 to 9pm. The restaurant specializes in fresh fish, and also serves such dishes as creamy turkey pie, spareribs, and a changing array of daily specials. A garden is in back, but most guests head for the restaurant with its Windsor chairs and beamed ceiling.

✪ **Pleasant Rise Farm.** Off B2108, Alfriston, near Polegate, East Sussex BN26 5TN. ☎ **01323/870545.** 4 rms, 2 with bath. £18.50–£20 ($29.60–$32) single without bath; £35 ($56) double without bath, £37 ($59.20) double with bath. All rates include English breakfast. No credit cards.

This 50-year-old brick-sided farmhouse lies on 100 acres of fertile farmland devoted to vegetable farming, horse grazing, and chickens, in an idyllic position off the Seaford-Alfriston road. Your hosts are Leonard and Diana Savage, who both genuinely welcome their guests and advise visitors about local restaurants, sightseeing, and leisure activities. The bedrooms are cozy and comfortable, and have been much to the liking of many readers of past editions of this guidebook. Indoor and outdoor tennis and badminton courts and country walks add to the bucolic pleasures. The guests like the Savages' Shire horses, and their son often gives the guests rides in his old Sussex wagon. The breakfasts are copious.

## IN LEWES

Accommodations are difficult to find during the Glyndebourne Opera Festival, but are adequate at other times.

**Crown Hotel.** 191 High St., Lewes, East Sussex BN7 2NA. ☎ **01273/480670.** Fax 01273/480679. 12 rms, 4 with bath. TV TEL. £30 ($48) single without bath; £38–£39.50 ($60.80–$63.20) single with bath; £44 ($70.40) double without bath, £49–£55 ($78.40–$88) double with bath. All rates include English breakfast. AE, MC, V.

Built around 1760, this is one of the oldest inns in Lewes, with a Victorian conservatory where lunch is served daily. It is a 30-minute ride from Gatwick and 60 minutes from London. The hotel, run by Brian and Gillian Tolton, is considerably refurbished, though still a bit creaky. All rooms have hot-beverage facilities. Opposite the war memorial, the hotel stands at a traffic circle on the main street. Pub lunches, ranging from £1.50 to £4.25 ($2.40 to $6.80), are available daily from 11:30am to 2:30pm.

✪ **Felix Gallery.** 2 Sun St. (at Lancaster St.), Lewes, East Sussex BN7 2QB. ☎ **01273/472668.** 2 rms, neither with bath. TV. £25–£26 ($40–$41.60) single; £36–£38 ($57.60–$60.80) double. All rates include English breakfast. MC, V.

Completely up-to-date, this inviting cottage, in a tranquil location a short walk from the heart of town and the Lewes Castle, is one of the best buys in town. The comfortably furnished, cozy rooms have hot-beverage facilities, and public parking is available nearby.

# WHERE TO EAT
## IN ALFRISTON

**The George Inn** (see "Where to Stay," above), is known for its good food.

**The Starr Inn.** High St. ☎ **01323/870495.** 2-course meal £16.95 ($27.10); 3-course meal £18.95 ($30.30). AE, DC, MC, V. Mon–Sat 11am–2:30pm and 6–11pm; Sun noon–2:30pm and 7–10:30pm. ENGLISH.

Serving a diverse daily menu, this restaurant inhabits a building dating from the 13th century, and the bar still features wooden posts from that time. Although there's a contemporary British theme, food choices are eclectic and well prepared.

**The Tudor House.** High St. ☎ **01323/870891.** Afternoon tea £4.50 ($7.20); sandwiches £1.50–£2.75 ($2.40–$4.40); cakes and pastries 60p–£1.95 (95¢–$3.10). Daily 10am–5:30pm. No credit cards. TEA/PASTRIES.

This tearoom in a 14th-century building is on the village's main street. The well-lit interior has two tearooms with oak paneling and brass, which provide a calm setting for afternoon tea. Cheese, ham and cheese, and egg salad sandwiches and muffins, danishes, scones, and a variety of cakes are served.

**Ye Olde Smugglers.** Market Cross. ☎ **01323/870241.** Main courses £7.50 ($12). No credit cards. Daily 11am–3pm and 6:30–11pm. ENGLISH.

Housed in a building dating to 1358 that once served as headquarters for the infamous Stanton Collins and his band of smugglers, this restaurant serves sandwiches starting at £2 ($3.20), and main courses including T-bone steak, rump roast, trout, and a vegetable plate. Owing to its checkered past, the place sits atop a series of escape tunnels which have since been filled with concrete. The restaurant itself, however—including the main dining room—is riddled with secret passages, so cleverly concealed that you might never notice. Locals joke that if you aren't careful, you'll get lost and never be found. The chef boasts that once you taste his steaks and roasts, you won't want to leave anyway.

## IN LEWES

**Léonies.** 197 High St., Lewes. ☎ **01273/487766.** Main courses £6–£7 ($9.60–$11.20). AE, MC, V. Mon–Thurs 9am–6pm; Fri–Sat 9am–9:30pm. BRITISH.

Housed in a 17th-century stone structure, this restaurant serves English fare in a congenial atmosphere. For lunch the menu includes pâtés, soups, warm salads, and grilled salmon, while the dinners are more elaborate. The menu changes monthly but may include such dishes as grilled lamb's liver with braised red cabbage, salmon-and-watercress fish cakes, stuffed savory eggplant with Provençal sauce, ginger and mushroom phyllo baskets, herb-crusted cod with aïoli, or roast pigeon with wild mushrooms. To complete the meal, try the rhubarb-and-ginger crumble or one of the fruit meringues.

## 4 Brighton: London by the Sea

52 miles S of London

Brighton was one of the first of the great seaside resorts of Europe. The village on the sea from which the present town grew was named Brighthelmstone, and the English eventually shortened it to Brighton. The original swinger who was to shape so much of its destiny arrived in 1783—it was the prince of Wales, and his presence and patronage that gave immediate status to the seaside town.

Fashionable dandies from London including Beau Brummell turned up. The construction business boomed; Brighton blossomed with charming and attractive town houses and well-planned squares and crescents. From the Prince Regent's title came the voguish word "Regency," which was to characterize an era, but more specifically refers to the period between 1811 and 1820. Under Victoria, and despite the fact that she cut off her presence, Brighton continued to flourish.

Earlier in this century, however, as the English began to discover more glamorous spots on the continent, Brighton lost much of its old *joie de vivre.* It became labeled as "tatty," featuring the usual run of fun-fair–type English seaside amusements. However, that state of affairs long ago changed, owing largely to the huge numbers of Londoners who moved in (some of whom now even commute); the invasion has made Brighton increasingly lighthearted and sophisticated today. For instance, a beach east of town attracts nude bathers—Britain's first such daring.

After London, Brighton is the most extroverted gay city in England. Brighton has developed a reputation for tolerance and humor (and kitsch) that derives from its role as a resort town catering to the whims and eccentricities of outsiders since the Victorian Age. It is perhaps for that reason, according to jaded owners of some of the town's 20-or-so gay bars, that there's a higher percentage of drag queens living within the town's Regency town houses than virtually anywhere else in England. But the gay scene here is a lot less sophisticated than in London.

## ESSENTIALS

**GETTING THERE**  Fast trains—41 a day—leave from Victoria or London Bridge Station and make the trip in 55 minutes.

**Impressions**

*A clean Naples with genteel lazzaroni . . . Brighton that always looks so brisk, gay, and gaudy, like a harlequin's jacket . . .*

—William Makepeace Thackeray, *Vanity Fair* (1847–48)

Buses from Victoria Coach Station take around 2 hours.

If you're driving, M23 (signposted from central London) leads to A23, which takes you into Brighton.

**VISITOR INFORMATION**   At the **Tourist Information Centre,** 10 Bartholomew Sq. (☎ **01273/323755**), opposite the town hall, you can make hotel reservations, reserve tickets for National Express coaches, and pick up a list of current events. Open June to mid-July, Monday through Friday from 9am to 6pm, Saturday from 10am to 5pm, and Sunday from 10am to 4pm; mid-July through August, Monday through Friday from 9am to 6pm and Saturday and Sunday from 10am to 6pm; off-season, Monday through Friday from 9am to 5pm, Saturday from 10am to 5pm, and Sunday from 10am to 4pm.

**GETTING AROUND**   The **Brighton Borough Transport** serves both Brighton and Hove with frequent and efficient service. Local fares are only 60p (95¢), and free maps giving the company's routes are available at Visitor Information (see above). You can also call the company directly at ☎ **01273/606141.**

## ✪ THE ROYAL PAVILION

Among the royal residences of Europe, the Royal Pavilion at Brighton (☎ **01273/603005**), a John Nash version of an Indian moghul's palace, is uniquely ornate and exotic. It has been subjected over the years to the devastating wit of English satirists and pundits, but today we can examine it more objectively as one of the outstanding examples of the English romantic movement's eastern leanings.

Originally a farmhouse, in 1787 a neoclassical villa was created on the site by Henry Holland—but it no more resembled its present appearance than a caterpillar does a butterfly. By the time Nash had transformed it from a simple classical villa into an East Asian fantasy, the Prince Regent had become King George IV, and the king and one of his mistresses, Lady Conyngham, lived in the palace until 1827.

A decade passed before Victoria, then queen, arrived in Brighton. Although she was to bring Albert and the children on a number of occasions, the monarch and Brighton just didn't mesh. The very air of the resort seemed too flippant for her. By 1845, Victoria began packing, and the royal furniture was carted off. Its royal owners gone, the pavilion was in serious peril of being torn down, but by a narrow vote, Brightonians agreed to purchase it. Gradually it was restored to its former splendor, enhanced in no small part by the return of much of its original furniture including many items on loan from Her Majesty The Queen. A new exhibit tours the Royal Pavilion Gardens.

Of exceptional interest is the domed **Banqueting Room,** with a chandelier of bronze dragons supporting lilylike glass globes. In the Great Kitchen, with its old revolving spits, is a collection of Wellington's pots and pans, his *batterie de cuisine,* from his town house at Hyde Park Corner. In the **State Apartments,** particularly the domed salon, dragons wink, serpents entwine, lacquered doors shine. The Music Room, with its scalloped ceiling, is a rollicking fantasy of water lilies, flying dragons, reptilian paintings, bamboo, silk, and satin.

In the first-floor **gallery,** look for Nash's views of the pavilion in its elegant heyday. Other attractions include **Queen Victoria's Apartments,** beautifully re-created, and the impressively restored **South Galleries,** breakfast rooms for George IV's guests. Refreshments are available in the Queen Adelaide Tea Room, which has a balcony overlooking the Royal Pavilion Gardens.

The pavilion is open October to March, daily from 10am to 5pm; April to September, daily from 10am to 6pm; closed December 25 and 26. Admission is £4.10 ($6.55) for adults, £3 ($4.80) for seniors and students, £2.50 ($4) for children 5 to 15, and free for children 4 and under.

## SEASIDE AMUSEMENTS

The Caribbean Brighton is not: Beaches are pebbly and the waters are polluted. So, instead of swimming, most visitors to Brighton sunbathe, promenade along the boardwalk, play video arcade games, hang out in local pubs and "caffs," and generally drink in the sea air. Beachfront areas are more for the promenade crowd, which often consists of sauntering gay men and women.

Brighton is also the site of Britain's first officially designed clothing-optional beach, located a short walk west of the Brighton Marina. Local signs refer to it directly as "Nudist Beach." Telescombe Beach, mostly frequented by gays, lies 4¹/₂ miles to the east of the Palace Pier.

You can't miss the **Palace Pier,** a somewhat battered late Victorian iron structure jutting seaward toward France. Built between 1889 and 1899, and renovated during the early 1990s, it's lined with somewhat tacky concessions and a late-night crowd of somewhat more questionable character than the one that frequents it during the day. The older West Pier is a rusting, abandoned hulk, a solitary reminder of forgotten Steam-Age pleasures and seafront holidays, with a beach in front that's sometimes used as a rendezvous point for gay men.

If you want to rent or charter a boat, stop by the Brighton Marina, at the intersection of A259 and King's Cliff Parade (☎ **01273/693636**).

## OUTDOOR PURSUITS

**CRICKET**  Cricket matches, called "fixtures," are held at **Sussex County Cricket Ground,** Eaton Road, Hove. Admission fees are very reasonable. For a current schedule, call ☎ **01273/732161.**

**FISHING**  **Brighton Marina** (☎ **01273/693636**) offers the best fishing, but the breakwaters near Hove may be better because there aren't as many boats or swimmers in that area. Many different types of fish are caught in these waters, including mackerel and sea whiting and, more rarely, plaice or cod.

**GOLF**  One of the best and most challenging 18-hole golf courses is the **East Brighton Golf Club,** Roedean Road (☎ **01273/603989**). A less challenging 18-hole course is the **Hollingbury Park Golf Club,** Ditching Road (☎ **01273/552010**). Buses from the **Old Steine** are available to both courses.

**GREYHOUND RACING**  Greyhound races are held on Tuesdays, Thursdays, and Saturdays beginning at 7:30pm and on Monday or Wednesday afternoons at the **Coral Stadium,** Nevill Road, Hove (☎ **01273/204601** or 01273/204605). Be sure to call in advance to reserve a table at the restaurant which overlooks the course.

**HORSE RACING**  If you enjoy horse races, the **Brighton Races** are held frequently between April and October at the **Brighton Racecourse,** Race Hill (☎ **01273/603580**). An admission fee is charged.

**SOCCER**  From late August through early May, you can attend the well-supported **Brighton and Hove Albion (Seagulls)** soccer matches at the **Brighton and Hove Albion Ground,** Goldstone Road, Hove (☎ **01273/739535**).

**SWIMMING**  An indoor pool, diving pool, learner's pool, solarium, and water slide are all available daily at the **Prince Regent Swimming Complex,** Church Street (☎ 01273/685692).

**TENNIS**  There are public tennis courses in 12 parks. **Preston Park** has 10 courts in the main park and 10 more courts on the west side of London Road in the **Rockery** section of the park. Since the courts are public courts and cannot be reserved, there is usually a long wait in July and August, and you must provide your own racket. There are three courts open daily in the summer at the **Record Tennis Centre,** Kingsway, Hove (☎ 01273/203795).

# SHOPPING

"Mallers" head for **Churchill Square,** Brighton's spacious shopping center, which has major chain stores including **Habitat,** better known as **Conran's** in the United States. The shopping center runs from Western Road to North Street (about 2 miles long) and offers many inexpensive shops and stalls with great buys on everything from antiques to woolens. On Saturdays there are many more antique exhibits and sidewalk stalls.

The **Regent Arcade,** which is located between East Street, Bartholomew Square, and Market Street, sells artwork, jewelry, and other gift items as well as high-fashion clothing.

Everyone raves about shopping on **The Lanes,** although you may find them too quaint. The Lanes are a closely knit section of alleyways off North Street in Brighton's Old Town; many of the present shops were formerly fishers' cottages. The shopping is mostly for tourists, and, while you may fall for a few photo ops, you'll find that the nearby **North Lanes**—between The Lanes and the train station—is the area for up-and-coming talent and for alternative retail. Just wander along a street called Kensington Gardens to get the whole effect. There are innumerable shops with antique books and jewelry, and many boutiques are found in converted backyards on Duke Lane just off Ship Street. In the center of The Lanes is Brighton Square, an ideal place to relax or people-watch near the fountain on one of the benches or from a cafe-bar. From April through September hour-long guided walking tours are available. Call the Tourist Information Center (☎ 01273/323755) for information on the departure times of these tours.

On Sundays, Brighton has a good flea market in the parking lot of the train station. On the first Tuesday of each month there's the Brighton Racecourse Antiques and Collectors Fair (9am to 3pm) with about 300 stalls.

While browsing around the **Brighton Marina,** bargain hunters can find brand-name goods at discount prices at **Merchants Quay Factory Outlet Shopping** (☎ 01273/818590), with everything from pottery to books and designer clothes to perfumes. Of the many factory outlets to visit, we suggest stopping at **Edinburgh Crystal** (☎ 01273/818702), where you can find cut-glass decanters, vases, glasses, canteens of cutlery, and more, and **Leave It to Jeeves** (☎ 01273/ 818585), where they have old photographs of the local area, illustrations, prints, and a complete framing service. At the **Options Shopping Mall** (☎ 01273/818590), you'll find 30% to 50% discounts on clothes, leatherwear, and furniture from leading designers.

Brighton also abounds in specialty shops. Some of the more special ones follow. **Bears and Friends of Brighton,** 41 Meeting House Lane (☎ 01273/208940), attracts teddy bear buffs, who want to squeeze any number of stuffed animals. **Culpepper,** 12D Meeting House Lane (☎ 01273/327939), is the place for bath salts, fine English soap, herbal medicines, herbs, natural plant oils, potpourri, and spices. **Le Jazz Hot,** 14 Prince Albert St. (☎ 01273/206091), offers a fine selection of art-deco and art-nouveau ceramics, Bakelite jewelry, Deco chrome, and period furniture. **Pecksniff's Bespoke Perfumery,** 45–46 Meeeting House Lane (☎ **01273/328904**), creates a fragrance just for you, keeping your formula on file for when you need a refill. They hand-blend flowers, herbs, and natural oils to make traditional English scents. **The Pavilion Shop,** The Royal Pavilion, East Street, Brighton (☎ **01273/603005**), next door to The Royal Pavilion, is the finest gift shop in Brighton. Here you can purchase many gift and home-furnishing items in the style of the design schools which created the look (from Regency to Victorian) at The Royal Pavilion. Also available are books, jams, needlepoint kits, notebooks, pencils, stencil kits, and other souvenirs. Finally, **Sweet Williams Fudge Shop,** 26A North St., Meeting House Lane (☎ **01273/323234**), is a muse for those with a sweet tooth; choose from homemade fudge, nougat candy, and other goodies.

# WHERE TO STAY
## Doubles for Less Than £45

**Alvia Hotel.** 36 Upper Rock Gardens, Brighton, East Sussex BN2 1QF. ☎ **01273/682939.** 10 rms, 8 with bath (tub or shower). TV TEL. £18 ($28.80) single without bath, £26 ($41.60) single with bath; £32–£38 ($51.20–$60.80) double without bath, £40–£50 ($64–$80) double with bath. All rates include English breakfast. AE, DC, MC, V.

This Victorian structure (renovated in 1994) offers a bit of old-world charm. The rooms are decorated in an English country-house motif, with tea- and coffee-making facilities, and two have four-poster beds. The only meal offered here is breakfast, but there are plenty of dining establishments nearby.

**Brighton Court Craven Hotel.** 2 Atlingworth St., Brighton BN2 1PL. ☎ **01273/607710.** 10 rms, all with shower but without toilet. TV. £33 ($52.80) double Mon–Thurs; £36 ($57.60) Fri–Sun. All rates include breakfast. No credit cards.

Behind an unremarkable stone facade built during the late 1800s, this three-story hotel isn't particularly exciting, and has little to recommend it in terms of facilities or architecture. It's the least enticing of the gay hotels we recommend, but it's also the least expensive. The clientele is mostly male. Breakfasts are served communally, with all the traditional English accompaniments. There's a resident's bar on the premises, and a sense of laissez-faire permissiveness. Owner David Raven is one of Brighton's most active AIDS activists, as well as a well-known star on the drag circuit who performs under the stage name of Maizie Trollette.

**Brighton Marina House Hotel.** 8 Charlotte St., Marine Parade, Brighton, East Sussex BN2 1AG. ☎ **01273/679484** or 01273/605349. 10 rms, 7 with shower. TV TEL. £15–£25 ($24–$40) single without bath; £31–£39 ($49.60–$62.40) single with bath; £35–£49 ($56–$78.40) double with bath. All rates include English breakfast. AE, DC, MC, V. Bus: no. 7 or 27.

One of the best accommodations in its price range at Brighton, this white town house, built in the Regency style, sits about a block from the sea near an interesting collection of antique shops. Many accommodations have high ceilings and elaborate plasterwork. Visitors have free use of the elegant front parlor, and evening meals, at £10 ($16) for four courses, are available upon request.

**✪ Dudley House.** 10 Madeira Place, Brighton, East Sussex BN2 1TN. ☎ **01273/676794.** 6 rms, 3 with bath. TV. £20 ($32) single without bath, £26 ($41.60) single with bath; £34 ($54.40) double without bath, £44 ($70.40) double with bath. All rates include English breakfast. No credit cards. Bus: no. 1, 3, or 7.

A few steps from the sea in a cream-colored Victorian town house, this hotel was upgraded from a run-down boarding house in 1987 when the Lacey family reduced the number of its rooms from 12 to 6. The result is a spic-and-span, well-decorated hotel whose rooms are unusually large, each with enough space for a separate seating area. Some have bay windows. The owners occupy most of the basement level, ensuring the constant presence of the owner-managers.

**Harvey's.** 1 Broad St., Brighton, East Sussex BN2 1TJ. ☎ **01273/699227.** 10 rms, 6 with bath, 3 suites. TV. £15 ($24) single without bath; £17 ($27.20) single with bath; £19 ($30.40) double without bath, £21–£25 ($33.60–$40) double with bath; £25 ($40) suite. All rates include breakfast. MC, V.

Leonard Harvey runs this bed-and-breakfast in the center of Brighton, close to the seafront. The building has been here since the 17th century, but they recently added rooms to the house, and renovated the rest. The rooms are clean and bright, with new furniture, central heating, hair dryers, irons and ironing boards, and color TVs. Most rooms are nonsmoking, and have private and well-maintained baths. Some even have views of the sea and small refrigerators. For breakfast, there is a choice of English, continental, or vegetarian.

## DOUBLES FOR LESS THAN £65

**The Adelaide Hotel.** 51 Regency Sq., Brighton, East Sussex BN1 2FF. ☎ **01273/205286.** Fax 01273/220904. 12 rms. TV TEL. £39–£60 ($62.40–$96) single; £57–£78 ($91.20–$124.80) double. All rates include English breakfast. AE, MC. V.

This small hostelry is in a restored Regency building that has been modernized and decorated without losing its early 19th-century ambience. All units have hair dryers and hot-beverage facilities. The higher prices quoted above are for rooms with a four-poster bed. The Adelaide is in the center of Brighton, just behind the West Pier.

**Ambassador.** 22 New Steine, Marine Parade, Brighton, East Sussex BN2 1PD. ☎ **01273/676869.** Fax 01273/689988. 20 rms. TV TEL. £25–£35 ($40–$56) single; £44–£60 ($70.40–$96) double. Children 11 and under share a room with 2 adults for half price. All rates include English breakfast. AE, DC, MC, V.

A family-run hotel on a waterfront square, the recently expanded Ambassador overlooks the Palace Pier. All the comfortably furnished bedrooms have hot-beverage facilities, and many of the guest rooms were renovated in 1996 and 1997. The front bedrooms have a sea view, and there's also an attractive residents' lounge.

**Ascott House Hotel.** 21 New Steine, Marine Parade, Brighton, East Sussex BN2 1PD. ☎ **01273/688085.** Fax 01273/623733. 12 rms, 10 with bath. TV TEL. £22 ($35.20) single without bath, £35 ($56) single with bath; £50–£70 ($80–$112) double with bath; £23 ($36.80) per person triple with bath; £19 ($30.40) per person quad with bath. All rates include English breakfast. AE, MC, V. Bus: no. 27.

Michael and Avril Strong's establishment enjoys a location within a short walk of the Royal Pavilion. It's also near the pier and the famous Lanes, with their shops and boutiques. This popular licensed hotel has a reputation for comfort, cleanliness, and good breakfasts. The single, double, triple, and family rooms have radio/alarms, hair dryers, and hospitality trays, and most provide full private facilities. The front bedrooms have a sea view.

**Coward's Guest House.** 12 Upper Rock Gardens, Brighton BN2 1QE. ☎ **01237/692677.** 8 rms, all with shower, 6 with toilet. £45–£55 ($72–$88) double. MC, V.

Built in 1807, and extremely well maintained in nearly mint condition, this five-story Regency-era house sits, like many of its neighbors, behind a cream-colored stucco facade that's equivalent to many of the others nearby. Inside, Jerry and his partner Cyril (who's a cousin of the late playwright and *bon vivant* of the same name, Noel Coward), maintain an all-male enclave that appeals to gay men. The bedrooms evoke conservatively standard rooms in modern hotels across Britain, with very few amenities. The owners are charming, and the location is near a wide roster of gay bars.

**Granville Hotel.** 124 Kings Rd., Brighton, BNA 2FA. ☎ **01273/326302.** Fax 01273/728294. 23 rms. TV. £45 ($72) single; £65–£95 ($104–$152) double. All rates include English breakfast. AE, DC, MC, V.

Housed in a black-and-white structure opposite the West Pier, this recommended hotel is owned by Sue and Michael Paskins. The rooms are all individually decorated, some containing added features such as a water bed in the Marina Room, a four-poster bed and double Jacuzzi in the Balcony Room, and the art-deco bath in the Noel Coward Room. At the Café Bar, continental beers and organic wines are served, as well as a light menu including baguettes and omelets. For more substantial fare, Trogs Restaurant features a varied selection of English dishes with continental flair. A fixed-price, four-course dinner is offered for £15.50 ($24.80) and may include such dishes as chicken-and-asparagus crepes, pork steak stuffed with apple, and mushroom-sabayon pie. All the food is prepared using organic ingredients whenever possible.

**Malvern Hotel.** 33 Regency Sq., Brighton, East Sussex BN1 2GG. ☎ **01273/324302.** Fax 01273/324285. 12 rms. TV TEL. £30–£35 ($48–$56) single; £50–£60 ($80–$96) double. All rates include English breakfast. AE, DC, MC, V. Bus: no. 6.

Only a stone's throw from the seafront, this 1820 Regency building is on an attractive square. The rooms are well maintained and brightly furnished and have hot-beverage facilities. There's a small lounge bar with a residential license to serve liquor to hotel guests only. What makes this a winning choice over other similar B&Bs nearby is the personal service by the resident owners and staff.

**New Europe.** 31–32 Marine Parade, Brighton BN2 1TR. ☎ **01273/624462.** Fax 01273/624575. 30 rms. TV. £45–£50 ($72–$80) double. AE, DC, MC, V.

This is Brighton's largest, best-accessorized, busiest, and most fun gay hotel. Unlike many of its competitors, it welcomes women, even though very few tend to be comfortable at this postwar hotel with two mostly male bars on its premises. Bedrooms can sometimes be noisy (from the bars below), but are nonetheless comfortable, clean, and unfrilly. If you want the staff to camp it up for you before your arrival (adding balloons, champagne, flowers, and streamers), someone on the staff will, for a fee, be happy to comply.

## WHERE TO EAT

Of all the towns in the south of England (excluding London, of course), Brighton has the best quality and choice when it comes to restaurants. These are the best of the budget establishments.

✪ **Brown's Restaurant and Bar.** 3–4 Duke St. ☎ **01273/323501.** Main courses £7.50–£12.50 ($12–$20). AE, MC, V. Mon–Sat 11am–11:30pm; Sun noon–11:30pm. Bar: Mon–Fri 9am–11pm; Sat 10am–11pm; Sun noon–3pm and 7–10:30pm. Bus: no. 7 or 52. ENGLISH/CONTINENTAL.

Bustling and popular, Brown's was established in the 1970s in a location off a narrow alleyway that intersects with one of Brighton's main shopping streets, the Lanes. It contains two distinct areas: a bar (whose entrance is technically a few buildings away, at 34 Ship St.) and a large brasserie-style restaurant, where varnished hardwoods contrast pleasantly with white plaster walls. In the bar, "filled baguettes" (sandwiches) start at around £2.15 ($3.45) each, and are served throughout the day. Also in the bar, English breakfasts, priced at £4.65 ($7.45) each, are a morning staple every day until noon. Most customers view the bar, however, as exactly that—a place for drinking and conversation. Diners usually head directly for the restaurant, where a bistro-style menu, with frequent adjustments for seasonal ingredients, is featured. Menu items include spicy chicken wings, Dijon-laced chicken, salads, club sandwiches, Brown's leg of lamb, or a steak, mushroom, and Guinness pie.

**China Garden.** 88 Preston St. ☎ **01273/325124.** Reservations recommended. Main courses £10–£20 ($16–$32); fixed-price menus from £17 ($27.20). AE, DC, MC, V. Daily noon–11:30pm. Closed Dec 25–26. BEIJING/CANTONESE.

The Beijing and Cantonese menu at China Garden, located in the center of Western Road, is large and satisfying. Dim sum (a popular luncheon choice) is offered only until 4pm. Try such dishes as chicken with lemon sauce, crispy sliced pork Szechuan style, or roast duck with pancakes, spring onions, and duck sauce.

**Donatello Pizzeria Ristorante.** 3 Brighton Place, The Lanes. ☎ **01273/775477.** Main courses £5–£10.50 ($8–$16.80); pizza £3.90–£9.50 ($6.25–$15.20); fixed-price menu from £5.20 ($8.30). AE, CB, DC, MC, V. Daily 11:30am–11:30pm. Bus: no. 7. ITALIAN.

A cousin to Pinocchio Pizzeria Ristorante (see below), Donatello brings savory Italian cuisine to a central location in Brighton. It lies in the heart of the Lanes area, a district especially popular with American visitors. Many diners come here to sample the wide variety of pizza, including such delectable offerings as pescatora, with tomato, mussels, peppers, tuna, and garlic. A good selection of fish dishes is offered, along with popular meat and poultry dishes of Italy. The chef also prepares a wide range of antipasti and pasta dishes.

✪ **Food for Friends.** 17A Prince Albert St., The Lanes. ☎ **01273/202310.** Main courses £3.20–£5 ($5.10–$8). No credit cards. Mon–Sat 8am–10pm; Sun 9:15am–10pm. Bus: no. 7 or 52. VEGETARIAN.

A standout on "Restaurant Row" in Brighton, this self-service restaurant offers the freshest food and best value. There may be a wait, but most patrons don't mind. Of course, in a vegetarian restaurant you expect homemade soups, fresh salads, and the like, but here you get many exotic varieties of vegetarian cookery, including dishes from India, Bali, or Mexico, depending on the night. The owners say they never use artificial additives. They make their dishes with organic produce and farmhouse cheeses, homemade yogurts, and unrefined oils. Cakes and breads are baked daily.

**Jesters.** 87 St. James St. ☎ **01273/624233.** Main courses £5.50–£9 ($8.80–$14.40). AE, MC, V. Mon–Fri noon–2:30pm and 5:30–11pm; Sat–Sun noon–11pm. ENGLISH.

Everything about Jesters, including the alert attentions of a kindly matriarch directing the traffic flow near the entrance, evokes a traditional and busy English restaurant, with one rather sizable exception: Its clientele is nearly all gay. Very close to the New Europe Hotel, within a cosmopolitan decor, it serves mostly English food (trout, salmon, pork, beef, and vegetarian items) and to a lesser extent such Italian dishes as lasagna, spaghetti Bolognese, and cannelloni.

**Marmalade & Friends.** 31 Western St. ☎ **01273/772089.** Nightly fixed-price menu £16 ($25.60). AE, MC, V. Tues–Sun 7–9:30pm. ENGLISH/CONTINENTAL.

Run by Franco-Anglo partners, and catering to a clientele usually at least half gay, this is the most upscale and competent gay restaurant in Brighton. A set menu costs £16 ($25.60), and is likely to include a *bouchée* of mushrooms in Chablis sauce; locally smoked salmon; and such main courses as crispy duck in plum and brandy sauce.

**The Mock Turtle.** 4 Pool Valley. ☎ **01273/327380.** Afternoon tea £4.50 ($7.20); sand-wiches £1.55–£2.40 ($2.50–$3.85); cakes and scones 45p–$1.80 (70¢–$2.90). No credit cards. Tues–Sat 10am–6pm. Closed Christmas and 1st 2 weeks in Oct. TEA/PASTRIES.

Although this small but busy tearoom has many locals stopping by to gossip and take their afternoon cuppa, visitors are still most welcome. They offer only a small selec-tion of sandwiches, but the varieties of cakes, flapjacks, tea breads, and light fluffy scones with homemade preserves are dead on. Everything is made fresh daily. The most popular item is the scones with strawberry preserves or Devon cream. They also serve a wide variety of good teas.

**Pinocchio Pizzeria Ristorante.** 22 New Rd. ☎ **01273/677676.** Reservations recom-mended. Main courses £3.90–£9.75 ($6.25–$15.60); fixed-price meal from £5.20 ($8.30). AE, CB, DC, MC, V. Daily 11:30am–11:30pm. ITALIAN.

This popular restaurant is near the Theatre Royal and opposite the Royal Pavilion gardens. It offers a large selection of pastas and pizzas, with specialty Italian desserts. Pinocchio's has a light, airy atmosphere together with a bright, efficient Italian staff. Try breast of chicken with garlic, mushrooms, and a white wine sauce, or fresh monkfish filet in a green-peppercorn, brandy, and cream sauce.

## BRIGHTON AFTER DARK

With its student population and popularity as a seaside resort, Brighton offers lots of entertainment options. You can find out what's happening by picking up the lo-cal entertainment monthly, *The Punter,* and by looking for *What's On,* a single sheet of weekly events posted throughout the town.

If you're here in May, the international **Brighton Festival** (☎ 01273/676926), the largest arts festival in England, features drama, literature, visual art, dance, and concerts ranging from classical to rock. A festival program is available annually in February for those who want to plan ahead. But even if you miss the festival, there's a lot to see and do.

Two theaters offer drama throughout the year: the **Theatre Royal,** New Road (☎ 01273/328488), which has pre-London shows, and the **Gardner Arts Center** (☎ 01273/685861), a modern theater-in-the-round, located on the campus of Sussex University, a few miles northeast of town in Falmer. Bigger concerts in all genres are held at **The Dome,** 29 New Rd. (☎ 01273/674357), and **Brighton Centre,** Russel Road (☎ 01273/202881), a 5,000-seat facility featuring mainly pop music shows.

### NIGHT CLUBS & DANCE SPOTS

Night clubs abound, and dancing is everywhere. Cover charges range from free ad-mission (most often on early- or mid-week nights) to £7 ($11.20), so call the clubs to see about admission fees and updates in their nightly schedules, which often vary from week to week or season to season. It is no secret that many of Brighton's dance clubs and bars cater to gay revelers.

The smartly dressed can find their groove at **Steamers,** King's Road (☎ 01273/775432), located in the Metropole Hotel, which has a dress code. The **Paradox,** West Street (☎ 01273/321628), is a popular 21-plus club that features Gay Night on Monday, and **The Escape Club,** 10 Marine Parade (☎ 01273/606906), home to both gay and straight dancers, has two floors for dancing, downstairs presenting house music on Wednesday, Friday, and Saturday; techno on Thursday; and mixed dance on Monday and Tuesday. The upstairs has disco on Thursday and Friday, and house on Saturday.

You can also head for **Kingswest,** King's Road, a complex that houses two clubs featuring a blend of techno, house, and disco. One of these clubs, **Oriana's** (☎ **01273/325899**), caters to the over-21 crowd, with '80s music on Wednesday, disco on Thursday, mixed dance on Friday and Saturday, and under-18 dance on Sunday. Also at this complex, **Event II** (☎ **01273/732627**), with more than $1 million worth of lighting and dance floor gadgetry, features Eurozone night on Monday, The Zone on Tuesday, Atmosphere on Thursday, '80s on Friday, mixed dance on Saturday, and all-ages disco on Sunday.

**Gloucester,** Gloucester Plaza (☎ **01273/699068**), has a variety of music through the week; Mondays feature '60s to '80s music, Tuesday is alternative night, Wednesday is '70s, Thursday '80s, while Friday showcases Britpop and Saturday groove, pump, and slam. For a change of pace, visit **Casablanca,** Middle Street (☎ **01273/321817**), which features jazz, with an African slant on Wednesday, and Brazilian music on Friday and Saturday.

The largest and usually most frenetic gay disco in the south of England is **Club Revenge,** 32–34 Old Steine (☎ **01273/606064**). Combining architectural elements from the Victorian, art-deco, and post-disco eras, with a sweeping view over the amusement arcades of the Palace Pier, it has two floors and multiple bars. Open Monday to Saturday from 9pm to 2am, it charges £3 ($4.80) entrance.

## PUBS

Pubs are a good place to kick off the evening. Especially good is the **Colonnade Bar,** New Road (☎ **01273/328728**), which has been serving drinks for more than 100 years. The pub gets a lot of theater business because of its proximity to the Theatre Royal. **Cricketers,** Black Lion Street (☎ **01273/329472**), is Brighton's oldest pub, parts of which date from 1549. The **Squid and Starfish,** 77 Middle St. (☎ **01273/727114**), is a good place to meet fellow travelers from the neighboring Backpacker's Hostel; beachside drinking lures them to **Cuba,** 160 King's Rd. (☎ **01273/770505**), and also to **Fortune of War,** 157 King's Rd. (☎ **01273/205065**).

**H J O'Neils,** 27 Ship St. (☎ **01273/748339**), is an authentic Irish pub located at the top of the Lanes. A stop here will fortify you with traditional Irish pub grub, a creamy pint of Guinness, and a sound track of Irish folk music. They make the best Irish stew in town. You can even fill up here on boxty (potato pancakes with a range of filling) or champ (mashed potatoes flavored with chopped spring onions).

There are at least 19 bars or pubs catering to gays in Brighton. For a complete up-to-date roster, check *G-Scene* magazine (☎ **01273/724702**), a gay magazine that's distributed free in gay hotels and bars throughout the south of England. Some of the best include **Doctor Brighton's Bar,** 16 Kings Rd., The Seafront (☎ **01273/328765**), the largest of Brighton's gay bars. Built around 1750, it has more history, and more of the feel of an old-timer Victorian pub, than any of its competitors. It's open Monday to Saturday from 11am to 11pm, Sunday from noon to 10:30pm. Since gay women lack any Brighton venue exclusively for them, Doctor Brighton's tends to be where they congregate most.

Two of the town's busiest and most flamboyant gay bars, **Legends** and **Schwarz,** are located within the previously recommended New Europe Hotel. Legends, a pubby, clubby, woodsy-looking bar with a view of the sea, is open daily from noon to 11pm, and to hotel guests till 5am. Legends features cross-dressing cabarets three times a week (Tuesday and Thursday at 9pm, Sunday afternoons at 2:30pm) when tweedy-looking English matrons and delicate Edwardian vamps are portrayed with tongue-in-cheek satire and humor. The more consciously erotic of the hotel's two bars is Schwarz, a cellar-level "denim and leather" institution that does everything it can to encourage its patrons to wear some kind of uniform. Schwarz is open only Friday and Saturday from 10pm to 2am, and charges a £2 ($3.20) cover.

A final mostly gay staple, which at this writing had just changed ownership, is **The Marlborough,** 4 Princes St. (☎ **01273/570028**). Across from the Royal Pavilion, this is a woodsy-looking Victorian-style pub with a cabaret theater on its second floor. Expect it to remain popular with the gay and, to a lesser degree, straight community, but look out for a changing roster of lesbian performance art and both gay and straight cabaret within the second-floor theater. Open Monday to Saturday from 11am to 11pm, Sunday from noon to 10:30pm.

## 5 Arundel Castle

58 miles SW of London; 21 miles W of Brighton

The small town of Arundel in West Sussex is nestled at the foot of one of England's most spectacular castles. Without the castle it would be just another English market town. The town was once an Arun River port, and its residents enjoyed the prosperity of considerable trade and commerce. However, today the harbor traffic has been replaced with buses filled with tourists.

## ESSENTIALS

**GETTING THERE**    Trains leave hourly during the day from London's Victoria Station. The trip takes 1¼ hours.

Most bus connections are through Littlehampton, opening onto the English Channel west of Brighton. From Littlehampton, you can leave the coastal road by taking bus no. 11, which runs between Littlehampton and Arundel hourly during the day. If you're dependent on public transportation, the tourist office (see below) keeps an update on the possibilities.

If you're driving from London, follow the signs to Gatwick Airport and from there head south toward the coast along A29.

**VISITOR INFORMATION**    The **Tourist Information Centre** (☎ **01903/ 882268**) is at 61 High St. Open from April through October, Monday through Friday from 9am to 5pm and on weekends from 10am to 5pm; off-season, Monday through Friday from 10am to 3:30pm and weekends from 10am to 3pm.

**GETTING AROUND**    A great way to explore the area is by bike, which you can rent from **Arundel Cycle Hire,** 4 School Lane (☎ **01903/883712**), for £10 ($16) per day, plus a deposit. Open March through October, Friday through Wednesday from 9am to 6pm.

## ✪ ARUNDEL CASTLE

The ancestral home of the dukes of Norfolk is a much-restored mansion of considerable importance called the "Song of Feudalism." Its legend is associated with some of the great families of England—the Fitzalans and the powerful Howards of Norfolk. This castle received worldwide exposure when it was chosen as the backdrop for the English movie *The Madness of King George* (it "acted" as Windsor Castle in the film). Nigel Hawthorne came here to play George III, running around the Arundel courtyard in a mad frenzy, chased by actress Helen Mirren.

Arundel Castle has suffered considerable destruction over the years, particularly during the Civil War, when Cromwell's troops stormed its walls, perhaps in retaliation for the 14th earl of Arundel's (Thomas Howard) sizable contribution to Charles I.

In the early 18th century, the castle virtually had to be rebuilt, and in late Victorian times it was remodeled and extensively restored again. Today it's filled with a valuable collection of antiques, along with an assortment of paintings by old masters, such as Van Dyck and Gainsborough.

Surrounding the castle, in the center off High Street, is a 1,100-acre park whose scenic highlight is Swanbourne Lake.

The castle, on Mill Road, is open March to October, Sunday to Friday from noon to 5pm; closed November through March. Admission is £5.50 ($8.80) for adults, £4 ($6.40) for children 5 to 15, and free for children 4 and under. For information, call ☎ 01903/883136.

## MORE SIGHTS

**Arundel Cathedral.** London Rd. ☎ **01903/882297.** Free admission, but donations appreciated. June–Sept daily 9am–6pm; Oct–May daily 9am–dusk. From the town center, continue west from High St.

A Roman Catholic cathedral, the Cathedral of Our Lady and St. Philip Howard stands at the highest point in town. It was constructed for the 15th duke of Norfolk by A. J. Hansom, who invented the Hansom taxi. However, it was not consecrated as a cathedral until 1965. The interior includes the shrine of St. Philip Howard, featuring Sussex wrought ironwork.

**Arundel Toy and Military Museum.** At "Doll's House," 23 High St. ☎ **01903/882908.** Admission £1.25 ($2) adults; £1 ($1.60) children and seniors; £4 ($6.40) family. May–Sept daily 11am–5pm; Oct–Apr Sat–Sun 10:45am–5pm.

In a Georgian cottage in the heart of historic Arundel, this museum displays a vast and intriguing family collection spanning many generations of old toys and games, small militaria, dolls, dollhouses, tin toys, musical toys, famous stuffed bears, Britain's animals and model soldiers, arks, boats, rocking horses, crested military models, an egg cup collection, and other curiosities. The museum is opposite Treasure House Antiques and Collectors Market.

**Brass Rubbing Centre/Heritage of Arundel Museum.** 61 High St. ☎ **01903/882268.** Free admission. May to mid-Oct Mon–Sat 10:30am–4:30 or 5pm. Closed mid-Oct to Apr.

Both these attractions are located in the same stone-sided house as the town's tourist office. The Brass Rubbing Centre is in the cellar, where a collection of movable plaques and gravestones, each of historic and artistic interest, awaits the chalk and heavy paper of those who would like to trace their forms. You're charged according to the stone you choose to copy, usually about £2.50 ($4) per item.

On the street level, adjacent to the rooms housing the tourist information office, is the Heritage of Arundel Museum. It displays postcards, memorabilia, antique costumes, and historic documents relating to the history of Arundel and its famous castle.

## WHERE TO STAY

### DOUBLES FOR LESS THAN £40

**Arden Guest House.** 4 Queens Lane, Arundel, West Sussex BN18 9JN. ☎ **01903/882544.** 8 rms, 3 with shower only. TV. £20 ($32) single without shower, £24–£28 ($38.40–$44.80) single with shower only; £32–£35 ($51.20–$56) double without bath, £36–£40 ($57.60–$64) double with shower only. All rates include English breakfast. No credit cards.

Jeff and Carol Short run this pleasant and uncomplicated bed-and-breakfast hotel consisting of two connected houses a short walk from Arundel Castle. Fronted with dark-colored flint and painted stone, the older of the two houses was originally built in 1804. Each of the comfortable but simple accommodations has hot and cold running water and hot-beverage facilities.

**Arundel House.** 11 High St., Arundel, West Sussex BN18 9AD. ☎ **01903/882136.** 6 rms, 4 with shower only. TV. £17.50 ($28) single without bath, £21.50 ($34.40) single with shower only; £35 ($56) double without bath, £40 ($64) double with shower only. All rates include English breakfast. MC, V. Bus: no. 212.

John and Christine Crowe are the resident owners of this 17th-century guest house and licensed restaurant, which lies a 6-minute walk from the rail station and only seconds away from the castle entrance. It offers snug, comfortable rooms with hot-beverage facilities. The house is open for morning coffee, hot meals, afternoon teas, and Sussex cream teas daily from 9:30am to 6pm.

**Portreeves Acre.** 2 Causeway, Arundel, West Sussex BN18 9JJ. ☎ **01903/883277.** 3 rms. TV. £22–£33 ($35.20–$52.80) single; £36–£42 ($57.60–$67.20) double. All rates include English breakfast. No credit cards. Bus: no. 212.

When this modern, two-story house was built by a local architect within a stone's throw of the ancient castle and rail station, it caused much local comment. Today the glass-and-brick building is the property of Charles and Pat Rogers. Double guest rooms are on the ground floor and have views of the flowering acre in back. The property is bordered on one side by the River Arun.

**St. Mary's Gate Inn.** London Rd., Arundel, West Sussex BN18 7BA. ☎ **01903/883145.** Fax 01903/882256. 7 rms. TV TEL. £30 ($48) single or double. AE, MC, V.

At the foot of Arundel's famous castle, this unpretentious two-story building derives most of its income from the busy pub (see "Where to Eat," below) that fills its street level. In fact, its management refuses to refer to itself as a hotel at all, and stresses its role as a purveyor of simple food and drink, a role it has fulfilled since 1520. The bedrooms upstairs are simple, much renovated, and decent, with modest furnishings and a kind of cozy charm. To check in, you register at the bar—certainly a convenience if you've had a few pints.

## DOUBLES FOR LESS THAN £65

✪ **Dukes.** High St., Arundel, West Sussex BN18 9AD. ☎ **01903/883847.** 5 rms, 1 suite. TV. £30 ($48) single without bath, £40 ($64) single with bath; £60 ($96) double without bath, £65 ($104) double with bath. All rates include English breakfast. MC, V. Bus: no. 212.

The best of the small hotels in town is big on amenities, charm, and character. Mike and Valerie Moore are the guiding light behind this little gem, which has elegantly decorated rooms. The accommodations have coffee-making facilities, hair dryers, and modern baths, whereas a few still retain their Regency detailing and ornate plasterwork. The location is across a busy street from the crenelated fortifications surrounding the castle. The hotel's street-level restaurant is recommended below.

**The Swan Hotel.** High St., Arundel, West Sussex BN18 9AG. ☎ **01903/733381.** Fax 01903/883759. 15 rms. TV TEL. £50 ($80) single; £60 ($96) double. All rates include English breakfast. AE, CB, MC, V. Bus: no. 212.

Although it was already well established as a pub with simple bedrooms, this hotel received a boost in business after it was radically renovated and upgraded in 1994. Owners John Ryan and Steve Lowson are the entrepreneurs who took a Georgian inn, originally built in 1839, and injected it with new life. The rooms are decorated in the style of an English country cottage, and are cozy and comfortable. You'll recognize the building on the town's main street by its white stucco facade and the flowering plants that hang, garden style, from its window boxes.

On the hotel's ground floor, next to the pub, a pink-walled restaurant, illuminated with a pair of skylights and filled with potted plants, serves international food every day at lunch (noon to 3pm) and dinner (6:30 to 10pm).

## A YOUTH HOSTEL

**Arundel Youth Hostel.** Warningcamp, Arundel, West Sussex BN18 9QY. ☎ **01903/ 882204.** Fax 01903/882776. 60 beds. £7.70 ($12.30) adults; £5.15 ($8.25) 18 and under. MC, V.

This Georgian home's oldest section dates to 1720, although several additions have been added over the years; it now functions as a hostel with six dormitories, plus six family rooms. The location is in Warningcamp, about 1¼ mile from the center. Many backpackers, taking in the glory of the South Downs Way, stop off here. There is a self-catering kitchen, and prepared meals are also available. Breakfast runs £2.85 ($4.55), a small packaged lunch is £2.45 ($3.90), a large packaged lunch is £3.25 ($5.20), and a good and filling dinner is £4.25 ($6.80). Packaged meals must be requested the previous night, and a children's menu and vegetarian alternatives are available.

The facility features five showers, laundry facilities, a smoking lounge, and parking for 12 cars. There is no storage available, and an 11pm curfew is enforced. Hours of daily operation are from 7:30 to 10am and from 5 to 11pm.

## WHERE TO EAT
### IN TOWN

**Butler's Wine Bar and Restaurant.** 25 Tarrant St. ☎ **01903/882222.** Reservations recommended. Main courses £7–£15 ($11.20–$24) dinner; lunch £3–£7 ($4.80–$11.20). MC, V. Sept–Dec Mon–Sat 11am–3:30pm and 7–11pm; Jan–Aug Mon–Sat 11am–11pm. ENGLISH.

The building that houses this establishment was originally constructed in the 18th century and converted from a chemist's shop (pharmacy) in the 1960s. Located near the castle, this establishment offers hearty fare at reasonable prices. The menu features fresh meats, fish, pastas, and a few other Italian specialties.

**The Country Life.** 1 Tarrant Sq. ☎ **01903/883456.** Main courses £1.95–£3.80 ($3.10–$6.10). No credit cards. Daily 10:30am–5pm. VEGETARIAN/ENGLISH.

Housed in an 18th-century candle factory, the building itself dates to 1609, although no one seems to know what its function was in its early days. Today, however, it's known as a place to get a good, creative, and reasonably priced meal. There are several vegetarian choices daily, but carnivores can opt for shepherd's pie.

**Dukes.** 65 High St. ☎ **01903/883847.** Reservations required. Main courses £8–£12 ($12.80–$19.20). AE, MC, V. Daily noon–2:30pm and at 7:30pm–10:30pm. FRENCH.

Already recommended as a hotel, Dukes is also one of the town's leading restaurant choices. Owners Valerie and Michael Moore invite guests into their elegant dining room, located on the street level. The restaurant is noted for its 17th-century gilt-carved walnut ceiling, which was originally from a baroque Italian palace; part of this ceiling was once installed in the home of Douglas Fairbanks, Jr. Typical dishes include steak au poivre, trout with almonds, and sole meunière. Though familiar, the fare served up is quite good.

**Partners.** 25A High St. ☎ **01903/882018.** Sandwiches £1.25–£1.75 ($2–$2.80); salads £3–£3.75 ($4.80–$6); burgers and omelets £1.40–£2.40 ($2.25–$3.85). No credit cards. June–Sept daily 9am–5pm; Oct–May daily 9am–4pm. LIGHT MEALS.

The decor is that of a Formica-clad cafe, whose modernity cannot conceal the beamed ceiling and the 1790s building containing it. Service is good natured, and the place is definitely mass market, appealing to those seeking fast food between visits to Arundel Castle. There's take-out service if you'd like to go on a picnic along a country lane in West Sussex. It's located on the main street.

**St. Mary's Gate Inn.** London Rd. ☎ **01903/883145.** Main courses £3.50–£15 ($5.60–$24). AE, MC, V. Mon–Sat 11am–11pm; Sun noon–10:30pm. Pub: Mon–Sat 11am–11pm; Sun noon–10:30pm. ENGLISH.

Recommended for its overnight accommodations (see "Where to Stay," above), this stone-fronted two-story building was originally built in the 1520s as an inn—a function it continues to perform today. Place your food order at the countertop, then someone will carry the plates to a seat in one of four small drinking and dining areas, some of which are paneled. Food items range from simple pub-style snacks (salads, bowls of chili, and sandwiches) to more substantial fare such as pastas, fish dishes, and steaks. There's usually a vegetarian dish of the day offered as well. An outdoor patio in back provides additional seating during clement weather.

## ON THE OUTSKIRTS

**George & Dragon.** Houghton. ☎ **01798/831559.** Main courses £3.95–£10 ($6.30–$16). MC, V. Daily noon–2pm and 7–9pm. Pub: Mon–Sat 11am–2:30pm and 6–11pm; Sun noon–3pm and 7–10:30pm. Hours sometimes extended during midsummer at the whim of the owners. Bus: no. 31. From Arundel, turn off A284 at Bury Hill onto B2139. BRITISH.

Three miles north of Arundel, standing as the most visible building in the agrarian hamlet of Houghton, is one of the neighborhood's most popular pubs, the George & Dragon. Its most prestigious client was Charles II, who stopped for food and drink after his coronation at Scone, in Scotland, with the enemy troops of Cromwell in hot pursuit. (Charles escaped to sanctuary in France, returning in triumph to London in 1660 after the death of Cromwell.) Originally a farmhouse, the George & Dragon is built around a 13th-century core containing two timber-and-flint cottages. Each of the inglenook fireplaces was designed for spit-roasting the huge joints that formed the centerpiece of many an English meal. In winter, fires blaze; in summer, diners and drinkers migrate to a garden and terrace in back. Menu items include fresh fish, homemade soups, pâtés, English cheese, and such traditional dishes as a roast half duckling in a client's choice of orange, apple, port, or gooseberry sauce. Bar snack pies are available for £4.25 to £5.95 ($6.80 to $9.50).

# 6 Chichester

69 miles SW of London; 31 miles W of Brighton

Chichester might have remained a mere market town had the Chichester Festival Theatre not been established in its midst. One of the oldest Roman cities in England, Chichester draws crowds from all over the world for its theater presentations. Other than the theater, however, there's not much else to see. But the town does make a good base for exploring a history-rich part of southern England.

## ESSENTIALS

**GETTING THERE**   Trains depart for Chichester from London's Victoria Station once every hour during the day. The trip takes 1¹/₂ hours. However, if you visit Chichester to attend the theater, plan to stay over—the last train back to London leaves at 9pm.

Buses depart London's Victoria Coach Station four times per day.

If you're driving from London's ring road, head south on A3, turning onto A286 for Chichester.

**VISITOR INFORMATION**   The **Tourist Information Centre** (☎ **01243/ 775888**) is at 29A South St. Open Monday through Saturday from 9:15am to 5:15pm, and in summer, Sunday from 10am to 4pm.

## ✪ THE CHICHESTER FESTIVAL THEATRE

Only a 5-minute walk from the Chichester Cathedral and the old Market Cross, the 1,400-seat theater, with its apron stage, stands on the edge of Oaklands Park. It opened in 1962—its first director was Lord Laurence Olivier. Its reputation has grown steadily, pumping new vigor and life into the former walled city, although many irate locals originally felt the city money could have been better spent on a swimming pool instead of a theater.

The Chichester Festival Theatre, built in the 1960s, offers plays and musicals during the summer season—from May to September—and in the winter and spring months orchestras, jazz, opera, theater, ballet, and a Christmas show for the entire family. Matinee performances begin at 2:30pm and evening performances at 7:30pm, except first nights, which begin at 7pm, and Friday and Saturday when they begin at 8pm.

The **Minerva,** built in the late 1980s, is a multifunctional cultural center that includes a theater plus dining and drinking facilities. The Minerva Studio Theater and the Chichester Festival Theatre are managed by the same board of governors but show different programs and different plays. Performances here begin at 2:45 and 7:45pm. Food service at the Minerva is available daily from 10am to 10pm.

Theater reservations made over the telephone will be held for a maximum of 4 days (call ☎ **01243/781312**). It's better to mail inquiries and checks to the Box Office, Chichester Festival Theatre, Oaklands Park, Chichester, West Sussex PO19 4AP. MasterCard, Visa, and American Express are accepted. Season ticket prices range from £9.50 to £22.50 ($15.20 to $36). Unreserved seats, sold only on the day of performance, cost £6.50 to £7.50 ($10.40 to $12).

## MORE NEARBY SIGHTS

### THE ROMAN PALACE IN FISHBOURNE

A worthwhile sight only 1½ miles from Chichester is the remains of the Roman Palace, Salthill Road, Salthill (☎ **01243/785859**), the largest Roman residence yet discovered in Britain. Built around A.D. 75 in villa style, it has many mosaic-floored rooms and even an underfloor heating system. The gardens have been restored to their original 1st-century plan. The story of the site is told both by an audiovisual program and by text in the museum. There is a cafeteria.

The museum charges £3.80 ($6.10) for adults, £1.80 ($2.90) for children, or £9.50 ($15.20) for a family ticket. From December to February it's open only on Sunday from 10am to 4pm; the rest of the year it's open daily: in March and November from 10am to 4pm, April to October from 10am to 5pm (to 6pm in August). Guided tours are offered twice a day. See what an archaeological dig from July of 1996 unearthed. The museum is situated to the north of A259, off Salthill Road, and signposted from Fishbourne. Parking is free. Buses stop regularly at the bottom of Salthill Road, and the museum is within a 5-minute walk of British Rail's station at Fishbourne.

### OLD BOSHAM VILLAGE

Bosham, 4 miles west of Chichester on A259, is one of the most charming villages in West Sussex. Primarily a sailing resort, linked by good bus service to Chichester, it was the site where Christianity was first established on the Sussex coast. The Danish king Canute made it one of the seats of his North Sea empire, and it was the home of a manor (now gone) of the last of England's Saxon kings, Harold, who sailed from here to France on a journey that finally culminated in the invasion of England by William the Conqueror in 1066.

Bosham's little **church** was depicted in the Bayeux Tapestry. Its graveyard overlooks the boats, and the church is filled with ship models and relics, showing the villagers' link to the sea. A daughter of King Canute is buried inside. Near the harbor, it is reached by a narrow lane.

## WEALD & THE DOWNLAND OPEN AIR MUSEUM

In the beautiful Sussex countryside at Singleton, 6 miles north of Chichester on A286 (the London Road), historic buildings, saved from destruction, are reconstructed on a 40-acre downland site. The structures show the development of traditional building from medieval times to the 19th century in the weald and downland area of southeast England.

Exhibits include a Tudor market hall, a medieval farmstead and other houses dating from the 14th to the 17th century, a working water mill producing stone-ground flour, a blacksmith's forge, plumber and carpenter workshops, a toll cottage, a 17th-century treadwheel, agricultural buildings including thatched barns and an 18th-century granary, a charcoal burner's camp, and a 19th-century village school. A "new" reception area with shops and offices is set in Longport House, a 16th-century building rescued from the site of the Channel Tunnel.

The museum is open March to October, daily from 10:30am to 6pm; November to February, Wednesday, Saturday, and Sunday from 10:30am to 4pm. Admission is £4.50 ($7.20) for adults and £2.20 ($3.50) for children. A family ticket costs £11.50 ($18.40). For further information, call ☎ **01243/811348.** Take bus no. 60 from Chichester.

# WHERE TO STAY

**Bedford Hotel.** Southgate, Chichester, West Sussex PO19 1DP. ☎ **01243/785766.** Fax 01243/533175. 23 rms, 16 with bath. TV. £33 ($52.80) single without bath, £46 ($73.60) single with shower; £70 ($112) double with bath. All rates include English breakfast. AE, DC, MC, V.

This is one of the best all-around moderately priced accommodations in Chichester. The comfortable and quiet rooms contain hot and cold running water, and some also have private baths. In summer, advance reservations are strongly advised. The building, which dates to the 18th century, is located in the town center. Fixed-price meals cost £9 to £14.50 ($14.40 to $23.20).

**Whyke House.** 13 Whyke Lane, Chichester, West Sussex PO19 2JR. ☎ **01243/788767.** 3 rms. TV. £39 ($62.40) double. All rates include continental breakfast. No credit cards.

A short distance from the heart of Chichester, the Whyke makes a good base for seeing a production at the theater and for exploring such attractions in the environs as the Roman Palace and Old Bosham. It has a relaxed atmosphere, and the guest rooms, one of which is suitable for families, are tidily decorated, warm, and comfortable. The house is for the exclusive use of guests (the owners live next door), and a kitchen is available to those who wish to cook their own meals. Reservations are important; smoking is not allowed.

## STAYING IN A PRIVATE HOME

Because Chichester draws a fashionable crowd from London and elsewhere, in town to attend theater, its inns are pricey. So, for cheap digs, we suggest booking into one of the little private B&Bs. These are really family homes where rooms are now rented because the children are gone. The best of them are listed below.

**Chanterelle.** The Lane, Summersvale, Chichester, Sussex PO19 4PY. ☎ **01243/527302.** 1 rm. TV. £44 ($70.40) double. Rate includes English breakfast. No credit cards.

This attractive family home is located in a middle-class residential part of the city, close to the town center. You can relax in the garden, as guests get their own key. The establishment's only bedroom, rented only to nonsmokers, is well furnished and has tea- and coffee-making facilities.

**Hedge Hogs.** 45 Whyte Lane, Chichester, Sussex PO19 2JT. ☎ **01243/780022.** 2 rms, 1 with bath. £22 ($35.20) single without bath; £34 ($54.40) double with bath. All rates include English breakfast. No credit cards.

This family home is located in a tranquil part of the city, near Harvard College, a 10-minute walk from the town center. It sits on a fourth of an acre, and there is a car park in the garden. The bedrooms are nicely furnished and have tea- and coffee-making facilities. A lounge with a TV and a cozy fireplace is available to the guests. This, too, is a nonsmoking facility.

**White Lodge.** Lavant Rd., Chichester, West Sussex PO19 4QY. ☎ **01243/527495.** 3 rms, 1 with bath. £20 ($32) single without bath; £40 ($64) double without bath, £50 ($80) double with bath. All rates include English breakfast. No credit cards.

This family home, a residential section of the city, is not far from the town center. It has a beautiful garden, and the house and bedrooms are furnished with antiques. There is a special welcome waiting for everyone, but especially for those interested in the history and architecture of England, as the owner, Mr. Wingfield-Hayes, is an expert on the subject. His family tree has been called a "who's who" of English history.

## WHERE TO EAT

**The Bedford Hotel Restaurant.** Southgate. ☎ **01243/785766.** Reservations recommended. Main courses £7.50–£10.50 ($12–$16.80); fixed-price Sun menu £14 ($22.40). AE, DC, MC, V. Daily 7–8:30pm. ENGLISH.

One of the best places for a formal dinner is this long-established and previously recommended private hotel dating back to the 1700s. The food is well prepared, the ingredients fresh, and the service relaxed but efficient. Start with mussels in a white wine, onion, and cream sauce, or else Highland smokies (smoked haddock) served with a whisky cream sauce, and proceed through the well-thought-out menu. Sirloin steak appears with a Drambuie sauce, or else you can order trout Véronique with a white wine and grape sauce. Vegetarian dishes are also available. Top your meal off with one of the freshly made desserts of the day.

**Shepherd's Tea Rooms.** 35 Little London. ☎ **01243/774610.** Afternoon tea £4.24 ($6.80), cakes, scones, pastries 40p–£1.55 (65¢–$2.50). No credit cards. Mon–Sat 9:30am–5pm. TEA/PASTRIES

Located in a white building with blue trim in the center of town, the tearoom is casual, with a mix of locals and tourists. The interior is simple but nice, with fine china on lace-covered tables. They have croissants, scones, and a wide variety of cakes, plus chocolate eclairs and meringues. They serve Earl Grey, Darjeeling, English Breakfast, and several other teas.

# Hampshire & Dorset: Austen & Hardy Country

The countryside in this region is reminiscent of scenes from Burke's *Landed Gentry;* logs burn in fireplaces, and wicker baskets swell with apples freshly picked from a nearby orchard. Charming old village houses have been converted into hotels. Beyond the pear trees, on the crest of a hill, you'll find the ruins of a Roman camp. A village pub, with two rows of kegs filled with varieties of cider, is where the hunt gathers. These are Hampshire and Dorset, two shires that protect special rural treasures and are themselves jealously guarded by the English. Everybody knows of Southampton and Bournemouth, but less known is the hilly countryside farther inland. You can travel through endless lanes and discover tiny villages and thatched cottages untouched by the industrial invasion.

The area is rich in legend and in literary and historical associations. Both Jane Austen and Thomas Hardy wrote and set their novels here, and King Arthur held court at the Round Table. Such famous ships as the *Mayflower,* Lord Nelson's *Victory,* the D-day invasion flotilla, and the *QE* all set sail from here.

Hampshire is the country so closely associated with Jane Austen—firmly middle-class, largely agricultural, its inhabitants doggedly convinced that Hampshire is the greatest spot on earth. Austen's six novels, including *Pride and Prejudice* and *Sense and Sensibility,* earned her a permanent place among the pantheon of 19th-century writers and popularity among 1990s film directors and producers. Her books provide insight into the manners and mores of the English in the midst of establishing a powerful empire. Although details of the life she described have now largely faded, the general mood and spirit of the Hampshire she depicted remains intact. You can visit the novelist's grave in Winchester Cathedral and the house where she lived, Chawton Cottage.

Hampshire encompasses the South Downs, the Isle of Wight (Victoria's favorite retreat), and the naval city of Portsmouth. The more than 90,000 acres of the New Forest were preserved by William the Conqueror as a private hunting ground. William lost two of his sons in the New Forest—one was killed by an animal, the other by an arrow. Today this vast woodland and heath is ideal for walking and exploring.

Although Hampshire overflows with many places of interest, for our purposes we've concentrated on two major areas: Southampton for convenience of transportation and accommodations, and

# Hampshire & Dorset

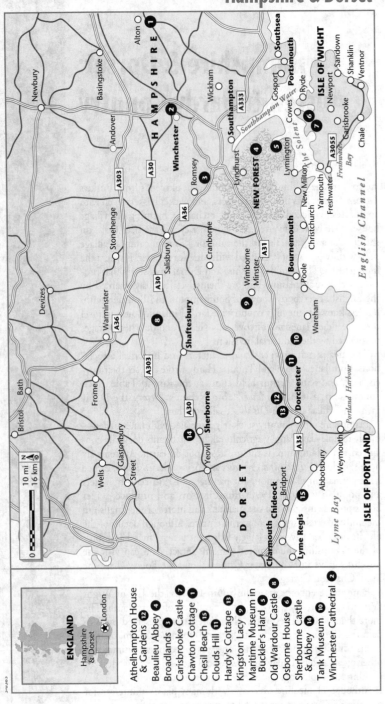

Athelhampton House & Gardens **12**
Beaulieu Abbey **4**
Broadlands **3**
Carisbrooke Castle **7**
Chawton Cottage **1**
Chesil Beach **15**
Clouds Hill **11**
Hardy's Cottage **13**
Kingston Lacy **9**
Maritime Museum in Buckler's Hard **5**
Old Wardour Castle **8**
Osborne House **6**
Sherborne Castle & Abbey **14**
Tank Museum **10**
Winchester Cathedral **2**

Winchester for its history. These counties have many places to stay. You'll find the most hotels—but not the most charm—at the seaside resort of Bournemouth. More intriguing than Bournemouth is much smaller Lyme Regis, with its famed seaside promenade, the Cobb, a favorite of Jane Austen and a setting for *The French Lieutenant's Woman.* If you're interested in the sea, and the ships that sail it, opt for Portsmouth, the premier port of the south and the home of HMS *Victory,* Nelson's flagship. For history buffs and Jane Austen fans, it's Winchester, the ancient capital of England, with a cathedral built by William the Conqueror. Winchester also makes a good base for exploring the countryside.

The best beaches are at Bournemouth, set among pines with sandy beaches and fine coastal views, and Chesil Beach, a 20-mile-long bank of shingle running from Abbottsbury to the Isle of Portland—great for beachcombing. There is no doubt: The most natural spectacle is New Forest, 145 square miles of heath and woodland, once the hunting ground of Norman kings.

Dorset is Thomas Hardy country. Some of the towns and villages in Dorset, although altered considerably, are still recognizable from his descriptions. "The last of the great Victorians," as the writer was called, died in 1928 at age 88. His tomb lies in a position of honor in Westminster Abbey.

One of England's smallest shires, Dorset encompasses the old seaport of Poole in the east and Lyme Regis in the west. Dorset is a southwestern county, bordering the English Channel. It's known for its cows, and Dorset butter is served at many an afternoon tea. This is mainly a land of farms and pastures, with plenty of sandy heaths and chalky downs.

The most prominent tourist center in Dorset is the Victorian seaside resort of Bournemouth, already recommended as an overnight base. If you don't anchor here, you might try a number of Dorset's other seaports, villages, and country towns; we mostly stick to the areas along the impressive coastline. Dorset, as the vacationwise English might tell you, is a frugal traveler's friend.

## 1 Portsmouth & Southsea

75 miles SW of London; 19 miles SE of Southampton

Americans in Virginia, New Hampshire, and even Ohio may have a Portsmouth, but the forerunner of them all is the old port and naval base on the Hampshire coast, seat of the British navy for 500 years. German bombers in World War II leveled the city, hitting about nine-tenths of its buildings. But the seaport was rebuilt admirably and now aggressively promotes its military attractions. It draws visitors interested in the nautical history of England as well as World War II romantics.

Its maritime associations are known around the world. From Sally Port, the most interesting district in the Old Town, countless naval heroes have embarked to fight England's battles. That was certainly true on June 6, 1944, when Allied troops set sail to invade occupied France.

Southsea, adjoining Portsmouth, is a popular seaside resort with fine sands, lush gardens, bright lights, and a host of vacation attractions. Many historic monuments can be seen along the stretches of open space, where you can walk on the Clarence Esplanade and look out on the Solent and view the busy shipping activities of Portsmouth harbor.

## ESSENTIALS

**GETTING THERE**   Trains from London's Waterloo Station stop at Portsmouth and Southsea Station frequently throughout the day. The trip takes 2 hours. Call ☎ **01703/229393** for rail information.

National Express coaches operating out of London's Victoria Coach Station make the run to Portsmouth and Southsea every 2 hours during the day. The trip takes 2 hours and 20 minutes. Call ☎ **0990/808080** for information and schedules.

If you're driving from London's ring road, drive south on A3.

**VISITOR INFORMATION** The **Tourist Information Centre** is at The Hard in Portsmouth (☎ **01705/826722**). Open April through September, daily from 9:30am to 5:45pm, and October through March, daily from 9:30am to 5:15pm.

# EXPLORING PORTSMOUTH & SOUTHSEA

You might want to begin your tour on the Southsea front, where you can see a number of naval monuments. These include the big anchor from Nelson's ship *Victory*, plus a commemoration of the officers and men of HMS *Shannon* for heroism in the Indian Mutiny. An obelisk with a naval crown honors the memory of the crew of HMS *Chesapeake*, and a massive column, the Royal Naval Memorial, honors those lost at sea in the two world wars. A shaft is also dedicated to men killed in the Crimean War. There are also commemorations of those who fell victim to yellow fever in Queen Victoria's service in Sierra Leone and Jamaica.

The Southsea Common, between the coast and houses of the area, known in the 13th century as Froddington Heath and used for army bivouacs, is a picnic and play area today. Walks can be taken along Ladies' Mile if you tend to shy away from the common's tennis courts, skateboard and roller-skating rinks, and other activities.

## MARITIME ATTRACTIONS

You can buy a ticket that admits you to the HMS *Victory*, the *Mary Rose*, the HMS *Warrior 1860*, and the Royal Naval Museum. It costs £10 ($16) for adults, £9 ($14.40) for seniors, and £7 ($11.20) for children.

✪ **The *Mary Rose* Ship Hall and Exhibition.** College Rd., Portsmouth Naval Base. ☎ **01705/750521.** Admission £5.15 ($8.25) adults; £4.55 ($7.30) senior citizens; £3.25 ($5.20) children and students. Daily 10am–5:30pm. Closed Dec 25. Use the entrance to the Portsmouth Naval Base through Victory Gate and follow the signs.

The *Mary Rose*, flagship of the fleet of King Henry VIII's wooden men-of-war, sank in the Solent in 1545 in full view of the king. In 1982, the heir to the throne, Charles, prince of Wales, watched the *Mary Rose* break the water's surface after more than 4 centuries on the ocean floor, not exactly shipshape and Bristol fashion but surprisingly well preserved nonetheless. Now the remains are on view, but the hull must be kept permanently wet.

The hull and the more than 20,000 items brought up by divers constitute one of England's major archaeological discoveries. On display are the almost-complete equipment of the ship's barber-surgeon, with cabin saws, knives, ointments, and plaster all ready for use; long bows and arrows, some still in shooting order; carpenters' tools; leather jackets; and some fine lace and silk. Close to the Ship Hall is the Mary Rose Exhibition, where artifacts recovered from the ship are stored. It features an audiovisual theater and a spectacular two-deck reconstruction of a segment of the ship, including the original guns. A display with sound effects recalls the sinking of the vessel.

For more information, write the Mary Rose Trust, College Road, H.M. Naval Base, Portsmouth, Hampshire PO1 3LX.

**HMS *Victory*.** No. 2 Dry Dock, in Portsmouth Naval Base. ☎ **01705/723549.** Admission £5.15 ($8.25) adults; £4.55 ($7.30) seniors; £3.25 ($5.20) children. Mar–Oct daily 10am–5:30pm; Nov–Feb daily 10am–5pm. Closed Dec 24–25. Use the entrance to the Portsmouth Naval Base through Victory Gate.

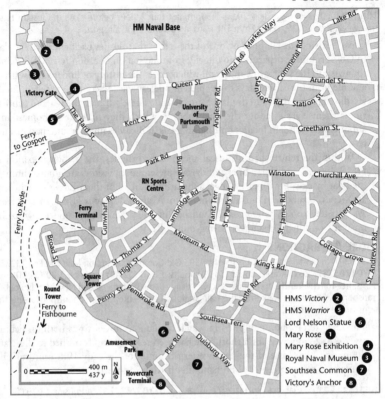

Of major interest is Lord Nelson's flagship, a 104-gun, first-rate ship which is the oldest commissioned warship in the world, launched May 7, 1765. Although it first saw action in 1778, it earned its fame on October 21, 1805, in the Battle of Trafalgar when the English scored a victory over the combined Spanish and French fleets. It was in this battle that Lord Nelson lost his life. The flagship, after being taken to Gibraltar for repairs, returned to Portsmouth with Nelson's body on board (he was later buried at St. Paul's in London).

**Royal Naval Museum.** In the dockyard, Portsmouth Naval Base, (☎ **01705/727562**). Free admission with ticket for HMS *Victory;* otherwise, £3 ($4.80) adults; £2.50 ($4) seniors; £2 ($3.20) children. Summer daily 10am–5:30pm; off-season daily 10am–4:30pm.

The museum is next to Nelson's flagship, HMS *Victory,* and the *Mary Rose* in the heart of Portsmouth's historic naval dockyard. The only museum in Britain devoted exclusively to the general history of the Royal Navy, it houses relics of Nelson and his associates, together with unique collections of ship models, naval ceramics, figureheads, medals, uniforms, weapons, and other naval memorabilia. Special displays feature The Rise of the Royal Navy and HMS *Victory* and the Campaign of Trafalgar. Other exhibits include the Victorian navy, the navy in the 20th century, the modern navy, and representations of the sailor in popular art and culture. The museum complex includes a buffet and souvenir shop.

**Royal Navy Submarine Museum.** Haslar Jetty Rd., Gosport. ☎ **01705/529217.** Admission £3.50 ($5.60) adults; £2.50 ($4) children and seniors; £9.50 ($15.20) family ticket. Apr–Oct daily

10am–4:30pm; Nov–Mar daily 10am–3:30pm, last tour 1 hour before closing. Closed Christmas week. Bus: no. 19. Ferry: From The Hard in Portsmouth to Gosport.

Cross Portsmouth Harbour by one of the ferries that bustles back and forth all day to Gosport. Some departures go directly from the station pontoon to HMS *Alliance* for a visit to the submarine museum, which traces the history of underwater warfare and life from the earliest days to the present nuclear age and contains excellent models, dioramas, medals, and displays from all ages. There's also as much about submariners themselves as about the steel tubes in which they make their homes, and although the museum focuses on English boats, it includes much of international interest.

Within the refurbished historical and nuclear galleries, the principal exhibit is HMS *Alliance*, and after a brief audiovisual presentation, visitors are guided through the boat by ex-submariners. Midget submarines, not all of them English, including an X-craft, can be seen outside the museum. Also on display is HMS *Torpedo Boat No.1*, better known as *Holland I*, launched in 1901, which sank under tow to the breaker's yard in 1913 and was salvaged in 1982.

## MORE ATTRACTIONS

**Charles Dickens's Birthplace Museum.** 393 Old Commercial Rd., off Mile End Rd. (M275). ☎ **01705/827261.** Admission £2 ($3.20) adults; £1.50 ($2.40) seniors; £1.20 ($1.90) students; free for children 12 and under. Apr–Oct daily 10am–5:30pm. Closed Nov–Mar. No public transport. A 10-minute walk from the train station in the center of Portsmouth, following the signs to the museum.

The small terrace house of 1804 in which the famous novelist was born on February 7, 1812, and lived for a short time has been restored and furnished to illustrate the middle-class taste of the southwestern counties of the early 19th century. The museum is near the center of Portsmouth off Kingston Road.

**Southsea Castle.** Clarence Esplanade, Southsea. ☎ **01705/827261.** Admission £1.70 ($2.70) adults; £1.40 ($2.25) seniors; £1 ($1.60) students and children 13–18; free for children 12 and under. Apr–Oct daily 10am–5:30pm; Nov–Mar Sat–Sun 10am–4:30pm. Closed Dec 24–26. From Commercial Rd. S. bus station (between the train station and pedestrian shopping district), bus no.1 or 1A to Southsea Castle, every 20 minutes, Mon–Sat, 7:15am–11pm.

A fortress built of stones from Beaulieu Abbey in 1545 as part of King Henry VIII's coastal defense plan, the castle is now a museum. Exhibits trace the development of Portsmouth as a military stronghold, as well as naval history and the archaeology of the area. The castle is in the center of Southsea near the D-Day Museum.

**D-Day Museum.** Clarence Esplanade, Southsea. ☎ **01705/827261.** Admission £4.50 ($7.20) adults; £3.40 ($5.45) seniors; £2.70 ($4.30) children and students; £11.70 ($18.70) family of 4; children under 5 free. Daily 10am–5pm. Closed Dec 24–26. Next door to Southsea Castle (see directions above).

Right next door to Southsea Castle, this museum—devoted to the Normandy landings—displays the Overlord Embroidery, which shows the complete story of Operation Overlord. The appliquéd embroidery, believed to be the largest of its kind (272 feet long and 3 feet high), was designed by Sandra Lawrence and took 20 women of the Royal School of Needlework 5 years to complete. There's a special audiovisual program with displays, including reconstructions of various stages of the mission with models and maps. You'll see a Sherman tank in working order, Jeeps, field guns, and even a DUKW (popularly called a Duck), an incredibly useful amphibious truck that operates on land and sea. The museum is on the seafront at Southsea.

**Portchester Castle.** Near Farnham. ☎ **01705/378291.** Admission £2.50 ($4) adults; £1.90 ($3.05) seniors; £1.30 ($2.10) children 5–15; free for children 4 and under. Apr–Sept daily

10am–6pm; Oct–Mar daily 10am–4pm. Lies on the south side of Portchester off A27 (between Portsmouth and Southampton, near Farnham).

On a spit of land on the northern side of Portsmouth Harbour are the remains of this castle, plus a Norman church. Built in the late 12th century by King Henry II, the castle is set inside the impressive walls of a 3rd-century Roman fort built as a defense against Saxon pirates when this was the northwestern frontier of the declining Roman Empire. By the end of the 14th century, Richard II had modernized the castle and had made it a secure small palace. Among the ruins are the hall, kitchen, and great chamber of this palace. Portchester was popular with medieval kings, who stayed here when they visited Portsmouth. The last official use of the castle was as a prison for French seamen during the Napoléonic Wars.

## WHERE TO STAY

**The Birchwood Guest House.** 44 Waverly Rd., Southsea, Hants PO5 2PP. ☎ **01705/ 811337.** 6 rms. TV. £30–£42 ($48–$67.20) double. All rates include breakfast. AE, DC, MC, V. With South Parade Pier on left, take 1st right onto roundabout; at 3rd exit turn into Waverly Rd.

This Victorian terraced house is just a few minutes walk from the seafront. The owners create an atmosphere of friendliness and informality with nicely furnished bedrooms and such appointments as hair dryers, electric shaver outlets, color TVs, and beverage-making equipment. There are two nonsmoking bedrooms, and no smoking is allowed in the dining room. Home-cooked evening meals can be prepared upon request. A well-appointed lounge is also available to residents.

**The Elm Guest House.** 48 Victoria Rd. S., Southsea, Hants PO5 2BT. ☎ and fax **01705/ 823924.** 6 rms. TV. £34–£40 ($54.40–$64) double. All rates include breakfast. No credit cards. Turn left at roundabout at end of M275. Go straight ahead at next 3 roundabouts. Guest house 300 yds. on right.

A friendly family-run place, this house dates from Victoria's reign. It has a great location near the seafront, with its shops, cafes, and amusements. The hardworking owners continue to make improvements year after year. For the price, their bedrooms are among the finest of the B&Bs, with such appointments as color TVs, hair dryers, electric shaver outlets, and beverage-making equipment. There is a small bar and lounge, and morning tea is served to early birds.

**Fortitude Cottage.** 51 Broad St., Old Portsmouth, Hampshire PO1 2JD. ☎ and fax **01705/ 823748.** 3 rms. TV. £25–£30 ($40–$48) single; £42 ($67.20) double. All rates include English breakfast. MC, V. Bus: Old Portsmouth.

Carol Harbeck owns this charming waterside cottage overlooking the fishing quay at Portsmouth's harbor. There are three simply but comfortably furnished bedrooms: one double and two twin-bedded rooms. Maintenance is high here. One contains a shower and toilet, although all offer hot and cold running water, TV, and tea- or coffee-making facilities. Breakfast is served in a bow-windowed dining room with a harbor view.

**Mrs. F. E. Fisher.** 9 Bath Sq., Old Portsmouth, Hampshire PO1 2JL. ☎ **01705/823748.** 1 rm. TV. £40 ($64) double. Rate includes English breakfast. No credit cards. Bus: Old Portsmouth.

The mother of Carol Harbeck of Fortitude Cottage (see above) also operates a B&B in this small house in the old part of town on a peninsula overlooking the harbor on both sides. Mrs. Fisher's guest room, a double, overlooks the sea and contains tea- or coffee-making facilities and color TV. The bedroom is delightfully furnished, and the standard of service is high. Breakfast is served in an oak-paneled dining room.

## WHERE TO EAT

The Southsea area in particular has a number of cheap eateries. The best deal is offered at the **Shirin Kebab House,** 58 Kingston Rd. (☎ **01705/699421**). Their pita sandwiches are the best in town, and their spicy kebabs begin at £3.75 ($6). Take-out is done here. Open daily from 5:30pm to 2am.

If you'd like to pick up a pizza or else order a plate of pasta, your best deal is at **Fabio's,** 108 Palmerston Rd. (☎ **01705/811139**), with prices beginning at £5.50 ($8.80). If you order takeout, prices are 25% less. Open daily from noon to 3pm and 5pm to midnight.

Want some English pub grub? Head for that longtime sailor favorite, **The Ship & Castle,** 1 The Hard (☎ **01705/832009**), where prices begin at £5 ($8), and there's a large daily selection made with fresh ingredients. If you'd like to go on a pub crawl later, there are many beer and ale houses nearby that have been quenching the thirst of sailors for years. Although Churchill denounced British naval tradition as "nothing but rum, sodomy, and lash," in these pubs it's more like a bottle of gin or a pint of ale.

**Country Kitchen.** 59 Marmion Rd., Southsea. ☎ **01705/811425.** Soups and salads £1.60–£3.25 ($2.55–$5.20); main courses £2.95–£4.45 ($4.70–$7.10). MC, V. Mon–Sat 9:30am–4:30pm. Bus: no. 3 or 23. VEGETARIAN.

This self-service establishment is a relaxed place to eat. All meals are freshly prepared on the premises daily, and only natural and organic products are used. The place is known locally for its wide range of homemade cakes and varieties of tea. Some dishes are "vegan" (without dairy, eggs, or meat products). Many customers are not vegetarians, though they enjoy the special atmosphere of this well-run establishment. It's housed in a building from the 1840s, and its main dining area is at street level, with an overflow upstairs. Children are welcomed, and there's a policy of no smoking. Take-out service is also available.

A new location has opened 10 miles away at East Street, Havant (☎ **01705/480113**). In the Havant Arts Centre, formerly the town hall, it has the same menu and daytime hours as the Southsea location, but is fully licensed for beer and wine and opens additionally for precinema suppers, with evening hours adjusted monthly according to the neighboring cinema's show times.

**Kumpan Thai Restaurant.** 78 Osborne Rd., Southsea. ☎ **01705/811425.** Main courses £5.50–£8.50 ($8.80–$13.60); fixed-price 2-course lunch £5.95 ($9.50); fixed-price 3-course lunch £10 ($16); fixed-price 3-course dinner £15 ($24). MC, V. Daily noon–2pm and 6–11pm. THAI.

This small, unassuming restaurant serves the zestiest Thai food in the area. This flavorful cuisine, once unknown in the area, has awakened the sleepy tastebuds of Southsea. It's run by immigrants to whom English is, in some cases, not yet a second language. But guests make themselves understood. The service is attentive and you're never rushed. There's little subtlety about the food, though. The dishes are slung together with remarkable abandon, but somehow they emerge full of spice, pepper, and bite. In many dishes, fiery spices are sometimes "tamed" for English tastebuds.

✪ **Rosie's Vineyard.** 87 Elm Grove, Southsea. ☎ **01705/755944.** Reservations recommended. Main courses £6.45–£8.95 ($10.30–$14.30). AE, MC, V. Mon–Sat 7–11pm; Sun noon–3pm and 7–10:30pm. Bus: no. 3 or 23. CONTINENTAL.

Rosie's was named after a since-departed matriarch who patterned her place on a brasserie in France. In summer, guests prefer tables in the pergola garden. The cookery is accomplished and often imaginative, and the menu changes with the season. Look for the daily specials. Dishes include grilled goat's cheese salad, Scottish salmon in puff pastry with white sauce, grilled halibut with ginger and spring onions, and sautéed escalloped pork with a creamy walnut sauce. This wine bar and bistro was originally a Victorian greengrocer, and its understated decor still includes some 19th-century stained-glass accents. Live jazz is heard on Friday at 8pm and at Sunday lunch (the only day lunch is offered), beginning at 12:30pm.

## 2  Southampton

87 miles SW of London; 161 miles E of Plymouth

To many seafaring North Americans, England's number-one passenger port, home base for the *QE2,* is the gateway to Britain. Southampton is a city of sterile wide boulevards, parks, and dreary shopping centers. During World War II, some 31.5 million men set out from here (in World War I, more than twice that number), and Southampton was repeatedly bombed, which destroyed its old character. Today, the rather shoddy downtown section represents what happens when the architectural focus is timeliness, not architectural grace. Sights are meager in the city itself, but rich on the outskirts.

Its supremacy as a port dates from Saxon times when the Danish conqueror Canute was proclaimed king here in 1017. Southampton was especially important to the Normans and helped them keep in touch with their homeland. Its denizens were responsible for bringing in the bubonic plague, which wiped out a quarter of the English population in the mid–14th century. On the Western Esplanade is a memorial tower to the Pilgrims, who set out on their voyage to the New World from Southampton on August 15, 1620. Both the *Mayflower* and the *Speedwell* sailed from here but were forced by storm damages to put in at Plymouth, where the *Speedwell* was abandoned. The memorial is a tall column with an iron basket on top—the type used as a beacon before lighthouses.

If you're spending time in Southampton between ships, you may want to explore some of the major sights of Hampshire near the port—the New Forest, Winchester, the Isle of Wight, and Bournemouth in neighboring Dorset.

## ESSENTIALS

**GETTING THERE**    A small airport outside Southampton is used mainly for flights to the Channel Islands. For information, call ☎ **01703/629600.**

British Rail trains depart from London's Waterloo Station several times daily. The trip takes just over an hour. Call ☎ **01703/229393** for information and schedules.

National Express operates hourly departures from London's Victoria Coach Station. The trip takes 2¹/₂ hours. Call ☎ **0990/808080** for information and schedules.

If you're driving, take M3 southwest from London.

**VISITOR INFORMATION**    The **Tourist Information Centre** is at 9 Civic Centre Rd. (☎ **01703/221106**). Open Monday through Saturday from 9am to 5pm, except on Thursday it is open from 10am to 5pm; closed Good Friday and Easter Monday, Christmas, December 26, and New Year's Day.

**TOURS**    City tourist guides offer a wide range of free guided walks and regular city bus tours. The free walking tours are offered throughout the year on Sunday and Monday at 10:30am and June to September twice daily at 10:30am and 2:30pm. Tours start at Bargate. For details of various boat or bus trips that might be offered at the time of your visit, check with the tourist office.

## EXPLORING SOUTHAMPTON

Ocean Village and the town quay on Southampton's waterfront are bustling with activity and are filled with shops, restaurants, and entertainment possibilities.

**Museum of Archaeology.** God's House Tower, Winkle St. ☎ **01703/635904.** Free admission. Tues–Fri 10am–noon and 1–5pm; Sat 10am–noon and 1–4pm; Sun 2–5pm. Bus: no. 2, 6, 8, or 13.

The museum, housed in part of the town's 15th-century defenses, traces the history and portrays the daily life of the Roman, Saxon, and medieval eras. The lives of the inhabitants are depicted. And you can't beat the address.

**Southampton Maritime Museum.** The Wool House, Town Quay. ☎ **01703/223941.** Free admission. Tues–Fri 10am–1pm and 2–5pm; Sat 10am–1pm and 2–4pm; Sun 2–5pm. Closed bank holiday Mondays, Christmas, and Boxing Day. Bus: no. 2, 6, 8, or 13.

This museum is housed in an impressive 14th-century stone warehouse with a magnificent timber ceiling. Its exhibits trace the history of Southampton, including a model of the docks as they looked at their peak in the 1930s. Also displayed are artifacts from some of the great ocean liners whose home port was Southampton.

## THE HOME OF THE LATE EARL OF MOUNTBATTEN

Eight miles northwest of Southampton in Romsey on A31 stands **Broadlands** (☎ **01794/517888**), the home of the late Earl Mountbatten of Burma, who was assassinated in 1979. Lord Mountbatten, who has been called "the last war hero," lent the house to his nephew, Prince Philip, and Princess Elizabeth as a honeymoon haven in 1947, and in 1981 Prince Charles and Princess Diana spent the first nights of their honeymoon here.

Broadlands is owned by Lord Romsey, Lord Mountbatten's eldest grandson, who has created a fine exhibition and audiovisual show that depicts the highlights of his grandfather's brilliant career as a sailor and statesman. The house, originally linked to Romsey Abbey, was purchased by Lord Palmerston in 1736 and later transformed into an elegant Palladian mansion by Capability Brown and Henry Holland. Brown landscaped the parkland and grounds, and he made the river (the Test) a source of pleasure.

The house and riverside lawns are open from middle of June to September 8 from noon to 5:30pm. Admission is £5 ($8) for adults, £4.25 ($6.80) for students and seniors, £3.50 ($5.60) for children 12 to 16, and free for children 11 and under.

## SHOPPING

West Quay Retail Park, the recently opened first phase of Southampton's £250 million Esplanade development, has become a major venue for shopping. It confirms Southampton's reputation as one of the U.K.'s most successful shopping centers outside of London. The central shopping area has been reserved for pedestrians, and tree- and shrub-filled planters provide a backdrop for summer flowers and hanging baskets. You can sit and listen to the buskers or perhaps watch the world parade by from one of the nearby restaurants or pavement cafes. For a vast array of shops, try the **Town Quay** (☎ **01703/228353**), the **Canutes Pavilion** at Ocean Village (☎ **01703/228353;** same number to call as above for information), or **Kingsland Market** (☎ **01703/221736**).

The most intriguing shopping on the outskirts is at the **Whitchurch Silk Mill,** 28 Winchester St., Whitchurch (☎ **01256/893882**), a working mill in colorful surroundings on the River Test. Historic looms weave silk here as in olden days, and visitors can observe water-wheel powering machinery, warping, and winding. The gift shop sells silk on the roll, ties, scarves, handkerchiefs, jewelry, and souvenirs. Open Tuesday to Sunday from 10:30am to 5pm, although looms don't operate on Sunday.

## WHERE TO STAY

Finding accommodations right in Southampton isn't as important as it used to be. Few ships now arrive, and the places to stay just outside the city are just as good, if not better. For other accommodations in the area, refer to the "New Forest" section, below. However, we'll provide some budget accommodations for those who may want to stay in the city center.

### DOUBLES FOR LESS THAN £35

**Banister House Hotel.** Banister Rd., Southampton, Hampshire SQ1 2JJ. ☎ **01703/221279.** 23 rms, 14 with shower only. TV TEL. £21.50 ($34.40) single without bath, £23.50 ($37.60) single with shower only, £23.50 ($37.60) single with shower and toilet; £29.50 ($47.20) double without bath, £33.50 ($53.60) double with shower and toilet. All rates include English breakfast. AE, DC, MC, V. Bus: no. 5, 11, 15, or 20.

This is one of your best bets if you're seeking affordable rates at a privately run hotel. David and Jackie Parkinson provide a friendly welcome to Southampton and will house you well in one of their well-maintained bedrooms. Rooms have a number of amenities, including hot and cold running water (even in those without full plumbing fixtures), remote-control color TV (and radios), beverage-making equipment, and direct-dial phones. The hotel lies in a residential area close to the city center and convenient to a number of restaurants, pubs, and shops. If you'd like to stay in, a home-cooked meal can be provided for £5 ($8).

**The Linden.** 51–53 The Polygon, Southampton, Hampshire SO15 2BP. ☎ **01703/225653.** 13 rms, none with bath. TV. £15 ($24) single; £29–£31 ($46.40–$49.60) double. All rates include English breakfast. No credit cards. Bus: no. 25 or 29.

This 1905 Edwardian building, which has a green facade and an elaborate twin-gabled roof, is operated by Patricia and David Hutchins, who work continuously to keep the bedrooms upgraded. Each room is equipped with hot and cold running water and coffee-making equipment, and the furnishings are basic but comfortable. Only breakfast is served. The couple are most welcoming with their motto, "Come as strangers, go as friends."

### DOUBLES FOR LESS THAN £55

**Hunters Lodge Hotel.** 25 Landguard Rd., Shirley, Southampton, Hampshire SO15 5DL. ☎ **01703/227919.** Fax 01703/230913. 16 rms. TV TEL. £25 ($40) double. All rates include English breakfast. AE, MC, V. Bus: no. 25 or 29.

This white-fronted villa has front and side gardens, a parking area, and a reputation as one of the best small hotels of Southampton. It lies in the suburb of Shirley, a 5-minute taxi ride from the piers, just south of the town center, a neighborhood of similar buildings and lots of restaurants and shops. The rooms are tastefully decorated and comfortable, each with tea-making facilities. Evening meals are served from 7pm for a fixed-price of £9 ($14.40). In the cozy lounge bar an open fire burns in the winter months, creating a convivial atmosphere. The hotel is easily accessible from the M3 or M27, and is convenient to the city center.

**The Star Hotel.** 26–27 High St., Southampton, Hampshire SO14 2NA. ☎ **01703/339939.** Fax 01703/335291. 45 rms, 39 with bath. TV TEL. £39.50 ($63.20) single without bath, £30–£48 ($48–$76.80) with bath; £54 ($86.40) double without bath, £56 ($89.60) double with bath. All rates include English breakfast. AE, DC, MC, V. Closed Dec 24–27. Bus: no. 2, 6, 8, or 13.

One of the better moderately priced inns in the town center, the Star was a fashionable meeting place in Georgian times. Its origins are uncertain (it may date from 1601). The public Victoria Room commemorates the visit of little Princess Victoria in 1831 at the age of 12. The Star has kept abreast of the times, and today it rents centrally heated bedrooms with radios, tea and coffee trays, and hot and cold running water. There's an informal but popular pub facing the street, plus an inexpensive restaurant on the premises.

## WHERE TO EAT

**La Margherita.** 4–6 Commercial Rd. ☎ **01703/333390.** Main courses £5.50–£12.95 ($8.80–$20.70); pastas and pizzas £5.20–£6.20 ($8.30–$9.90). AE, MC, V. Mon–Sat noon–2pm and 6:30–11pm; Sun 6–11pm. Bus: no. 7, 9, or 10. ITALIAN.

Popular with young people and families, this restaurant offers pizza and pasta, as well as veal, poultry, beef, and fish. It has one of the most extensive menus in town, beginning with appetizers ranging from a medley of antipasti to Parma ham and melon. Look for the catch of the day, which might be shark steak prepared Sicilian style or red mullet. Several vegetarian dishes are offered, including pastas, pizzas, even veggie burgers. The dessert specialty is Claire Francis coup (raspberry sorbet and black currants, with fruits, creams, and liqueur). You can order wine by the glass and end your meal with a strong espresso.

**Pearl Harbour.** 86A Above Bar St. ☎ **01703/225248.** Main courses £5–£9 ($8–$14.40); fixed-price meal £4.50 ($7.20) at lunch, £11.50–£20 ($18.40–$32) at dinner. AE, DC, MC, V. Daily noon–11:30pm. Bus: no. 5. CANTONESE.

Meals here are far superior to those in many other Chinese restaurants on England's southern coast. Set on the second floor of a building in the heart of town, the place serves a tempting array of fish specialties.

**The Red Lion.** 55 High St. ☎ **01703/333595.** Main courses £3.95–£8.75 ($6.30–$14); pub snacks £1.10–£4 ($1.75–$6.40). AE, DC, MC, V. Daily noon–2:30pm and 7–9:30pm. Pub: Mon–Sat 10am–11pm; Sun noon–10:30pm. Bus: no. 1, 2, 6, or 8. ENGLISH.

One of the few architectural jewels to have survived World War II, this pub has its roots in the 13th century (as a Norman cellar), but its high-ceilinged and raftered Henry V Court Room is from Tudor times. The room was the scene of the trial of the earl of Cambridge and his accomplices, Thomas Grey and Lord Scrope, who were condemned to death for plotting against the life of the king in 1415. Today the Court Room is adorned with coats-of-arms of the noblemen who were peers of the condemned trio. The Red Lion is a fascinating place for a drink and a chat. Typical pub snacks are served in the bar, whereas in the somewhat more formal restaurant section the well-seasoned specialties include an array of steaks (including sirloin), roasts, and fish platters.

## 3 The New Forest

95 miles SW of London; 10 miles W of Southampton

Encompassing about 92,000 acres, the New Forest is a large tract created by William the Conqueror, who laid out the limits of this then-private hunting preserve. Rules were strict, to say the least: Successful poachers faced the executioner if caught, and those who hunted but missed had their hands severed. Henry VIII loved to hunt deer in the New Forest, but he also saw an opportunity to build up the British naval fleet by supplying oak and other hard timbers to the boat yards at Buckler's Hard on the Beaulieu River.

Today you can visit the old shipyards and also the museum with its fine models of men-of-war, pictures of the old yard, and dioramas showing the building of these ships, their construction, and their launching. It took 2,000 trees to build one man-of-war. A motorway cuts through the area, and the once-thick forest has groves of oak trees separated by wide tracts of common land that's grazed by ponies and cows, hummocked with heather and gorse, and frequented by rabbits. But away from the main roads, where signs warn of wild ponies and deer, you'll find a private world of peace and quiet.

## ESSENTIALS

**GETTING THERE**   On the train, go to Southampton (see above), where rail connections can be made to a few centers in the New Forest. Where the train leaves off, bus connections are possible to all the towns and many villages.

Southampton and Lymington have the best bus connections to New Forest villages.

If you're driving, head west from Southampton on A35.

**VISITOR INFORMATION**   The information office is at the **New Forest Visitor Centre,** Main Car Park, Lyndhurst (☎ **01703/282269**). Open April through September, daily from 10am to 6pm and October through March, daily from 10am to 5pm.

## SEEING THE SIGHTS

✪ **Beaulieu Abbey—Palace House.** Beaulieu, on B3056 in the New Forest. ☎ **01590/612345.** Admission £8.50 ($13.60) adults; £6.75 ($10.80) seniors and students; £6 ($9.60) children 4–16; free for children 3 and under; £26.50 ($42.40) family ticket (2 adults and up to 4 children). Easter–Sept daily 10am–6pm; Oct–Easter daily 10am–5pm. Closed Dec 25. Buses run from the Lymington bus station Mon–Sat; Sun you'll need a taxi or private car.

The abbey and house, as well as the National Motor Museum, are on the property of Lord Montagu of Beaulieu (pronounced *Bew*-ley), at Beaulieu, 5 miles southeast of Lyndhurst and 14 miles west of Southampton. A Cistercian abbey was founded on this spot in 1204, the ruins of which can be explored today. The Palace House was the great gate house of the abbey before it was converted into a private residence in 1538. It is surrounded by gardens.

The National Motor Museum, one of the best and most comprehensive motor museums in the world with more than 250 vehicles, is on the grounds and is open to the public. It traces the story of motoring from 1895 to the present. Famous autos include four land-speed record holders, among them Donald Campbell's Bluebird. The collection was built around Lord Montagu's family collection of vintage cars. A special feature is called "Wheels." In a darkened environment, visitors can travel in specially designed "pods," each of which carries up to two adults and one child along a silent electric track. They move at a predetermined but variable speed, and each pod is capable of rotating almost 360°. This provides a means by which the visitor is introduced to displays spanning 100 years of motor development without the fatigue of standing in line. Sound-and-visual effects are integrated into individual displays. In one sequence, visitors experience the thrill of being involved in a Grand Prix race. For further information, contact the visitor reception manager, John, at the Montagu Building (☎ **01590/612345**).

**Maritime Museum.** Buckler's Hard. ☎ **01590/616203.** Admission £3 ($4.80) adults; £2.50 ($4) students and seniors; £2 ($3.20) children; £8.30 ($13.30) family ticket. Mar–May daily 10am–6pm; June–Sept daily 10am–9pm; Oct–Feb daily 10am–4:30pm.

Buckler's Hard, a historic 18th-century village 2½ miles from Beaulieu on the banks of the River Beaulieu, is where ships for Nelson's fleet were built, including the admiral's favorite, *Agamemnon,* as well as *Eurylus* and *Swiftsure.* The Maritime Museum highlights the village's shipbuilding history as well as Henry Adams, master shipbuilder; Nelson's favorite ship; Buckler's Hard and Trafalgar; and models of Sir Francis Chichester's yachts and items of his equipment. The cottage exhibits recreate 18th-century life in Buckler's Hard—you can stroll through the New Inn of 1793 and a shipwright's cottage of the same period or look in on the family of a poor laborer at home.

The walk back to Beaulieu, 2½ miles along the riverbank, is well marked through the woodlands. During the summer, you can take a half-hour cruise on the River Beaulieu in the present *Swiftsure,* an all-weather catamaran cruiser.

## WHERE TO STAY

**Bay Tree House.** 1 Clough Lane, Burley, near Ringwood, Hampshire BH24 4AE. ☎ **01425/403215.** 2 rms, none with bath. TV. £18 ($28.80) single; £36 ($57.60) double. All rates include English breakfast. No credit cards. Closed Dec. From the center of the village green at Burley, follow the signs toward Ringwood.

A single and a double room are available for rent in this family home. Guests share the one bathroom, but each room has tea- or coffee-making equipment. For families with children, a cot or a small bed can be added to a room. It's best to write ahead to Annette Allen to reserve your room.

**Caters Cottage.** Latchmoor, Brockenhurst, Hampshire SO42 7UP. ☎ **01590/623225.** 3 rms, none with bath. £19 ($30.40) single; £38 ($60.80) double. All rates include English breakfast. No credit cards.

Caters is among the more reasonably priced hotels in a village filled with thatched cottages and an array of expensive upmarket hotels. In its own patch of the forest, it's a cottage with a lot of character. The bedrooms are comfortably furnished, and each contains hot and cold running water. Early reservations are important, and the owners prefer 2-day bookings. Caters is off Sway Road (B3055); call for travel directions.

**Old Well Restaurant and Guesthouse.** Romsey Rd., Copythorne, Hampshire SO4 2PE. ☎ **01703/812321.** 12 rms, 6 with bath (tub or shower). £22 ($35.20) single without bath, £26 ($41.60) single with bath; £34 ($54.40) double without bath, £42 ($67.20) double with bath. All rates include English breakfast. MC, V.

On A31 in the parish of Copythorne, 10 miles north of Southampton, is Pat and Laurie Martin's guest house. The Martin family used to own the village grocery store, and they are true forest folk, renting simply furnished but comfortable rooms. In 1960 they bought the Old Well, which serves breakfast, morning coffee, and lunch in its restaurant, open Tuesday through Sunday from 11:30am to 2:30pm. A three-course lunch begins at £7 ($11.20). On Sunday they always have a traditional roast joint for lunch. Bar snacks are also available, and dinner is served on Friday and Saturday only, from 7 to 9:30pm.

**The Vicarage.** Church Lane, Burley, near Ringwood, Hampshire BA24 4AP. ☎ **01425/402303.** Fax 01425/403753. 3 rms, none with bath. TV. £17–£22 ($27.20–$35.20) single; £34–£38 ($54.40–$60.80) double. All rates include English breakfast. No credit cards.

This house is set in an informal and secluded garden in a clearing in the New Forest, opposite the church in the village of Burley. The village lies between the A31 and the A35 main roads near Ringwood and is a good center for walking, riding, and enjoying the wildlife of the forest. It's not far from the ancient cathedral cities of

Salisbury and Winchester, the seacoast, and many other places of interest. The house is run by Mrs. Alan Clarkson, the vicar's wife, who can accommodate up to six people. Rooms are pleasant and comfortable, with tea- and coffee-making equipment, and a homelike atmosphere prevails. No smoking is the rule of the house.

✪ **Whitemoor House Hotel.** Southampton Rd., Lyndhurst, Hampshire SO43 7BU. ☎ and fax **01703/282186.** 8 rms, 7 with bath. TV. £25 ($40) per person including breakfast; £35 ($56) per person including half-board double without bath. MC, V.

On A35 going out of Lyndhurst on the road to Southampton is the most desirable of Lyndhurst's inexpensively priced lodgings. It's small, so reservations are strongly recommended. Many of the bedrooms overlook New Forest moors. Each accommodation is immaculately kept and has plenty of room. Breakfast and dinner are now served. A two-course dinner with coffee is £9.50 ($15.20), and a three-course dinner with coffee is £12.50 ($20). All dishes are homemade from local produce. The house was built in the 1930s, and although the public rooms are comfortable, the social center revolves around an outdoor patio within sight of a pleasant garden and an ornamental fish pond.

## WHERE TO EAT

**Alice Lisle.** Rockford Green, near Ringwood. ☎ **01425/474700.** Main courses £4.50–£6.25 ($7.20–$10). MC, V. Daily noon–2:15pm and 6–9:15pm. CONTINENTAL.

This pub is named after a local woman who was accused of housing Royalists during the Civil Uprising of 1685. She was tried for treason and found not guilty, but a certain Judge Jeffries, notorious for his death sentences, overruled the verdict and sentenced her to be burnt at the stake. After a public outcry, the Judge generously agreed to commute the sentence—he ordered her head cut off instead. Obviously displeased with the sentence, a spectral Alice is still spotted with some regularity roaming area forests. These woodlands surround her namesake pub, and a lake lies behind it. The 150-year-old building has existed as a pub since 1960; before that, it was a school, serving as headquarters for the Canadian Air Force during World War II. With beamed ceilings, hardwood floors, paneling, and country bric-a-brac scattered about, it has a playground for children, a patio, and a garden. The menu features 10 daily specials, seafood, vegetarian meals, steaks, a number of pasta dishes, and a children's menu.

**Hunters Wine Bar.** 24 High St., Lyndhurst. ☎ **01703/282217.** Main courses £8.75–£13 ($14–$20.80). MC, V. Daily, noon–2pm; Wed–Sun 7–10pm. ENGLISH.

This small, 250-year-old pub seats 30 in a room featuring original hardwood floors, beamed ceilings, and an inglenook fireplace. The menu is seasonal, based on offerings at the local market. The lunch menu features sandwiches, seafood platters, and pies, whereas dinner includes the likes of salmon cakes, grilled pesto lamb cutlets, and seafood, including fresh crab. Ringwood English bitter is featured on hand pump.

**Mailman's Arms.** 71 High St., Lyndhurst. ☎ **01703/284196.** Main courses £5.50–£11 ($8.80–$17.60). MC, V accepted for bills over £15 ($24). Daily, noon–2:30pm; Thurs–Sat 7–9:30pm. ENGLISH/SEAFOOD.

This 200-year-old pub features the original fireplace and has been updated with wall-to-wall carpeting and a country decor of lacy curtains and wooden furnishings, with plates and old photographs adorning the walls. The daily lunch menu consists of sandwiches, specials, and vegetarian dishes. The dinner menu is primarily seafood, with a sampler platter for two running £25 ($40). There's a beer garden in the back, and Marston's beers are featured on tap.

**The Forester's Arms.** Brookley Rd., Brockenhurst. ☎ **01590/623397.** Main courses £2.50–£5 ($4–$8). No credit cards. Mon–Fri noon–2:30pm and 6–9pm; Sat–Sun noon–9pm. ENGLISH.

This pub dates back hundreds of years—so far, in fact, that locals don't know how old it is. As one pub-goer put it, "It's always been here." The pub features a television and jukebox, but a separate eating area that seats 42 is much quieter. The original beamed ceiling runs throughout, but carpeting and updated wooden furnishings have been added. The menu is the same at lunch and dinner, featuring traditional pub items such as homemade pies, curries, and burgers with chips.

## 4 The Isle of Wight

91 miles SW of London; 4 miles W of Southampton

The Isle of Wight is known for its sandy beaches and ports, favored by the yachting set. The island has long attracted such literary figures as Alfred, Lord Tennyson, and Charles Dickens. Tennyson wrote his beloved poem "Crossing the Bar" en route across the Solent from Lymington to Yarmouth. A holiday on the island sounds a bit dated, although many British families come here just to relax and enjoy the natural beauty of the island. You may want to confine your stay here to a day trip. Some parts are rather tacky, especially Sandown and Shanklin, although other areas out on the island still are tranquil and quite beautiful.

The Isle of Wight is compact in size, measuring 23 miles from east to west, 13 miles from north to south. Ryde is the railhead for the island's transportation system. Yarmouth is something else—a busy little harbor providing a mooring for yachts and also for one of the lifeboats in the Solent area.

Cowes is the premier port for yachting in Britain. Henry VIII ordered the castle built here, but it's now the headquarters of the Royal Yacht Squadron. The seafront, the Prince's Green, and the high cliff road are worth exploring. Hovercraft are built in the town, which is also the home and birthplace of the well-known maritime photographer Beken of Cowes. In winter it's almost *de rigueur* to wear oilskins and wellies, leaving a wet trail behind you.

Newport, a bustling market town in the heart of the island, is the capital and has long been a favorite of British royalty. Along the southeast coast are the twin resorts of Sandown, with its new pier complex and theater, and Shanklin, at the southern end of Sandown Bay, which has held the British annual sunshine record more times than any other resort. Keats once lived in Shanklin's Old Village. Farther along the coast, Ventnor is called the "Madeira of England" because it rises from the sea in a series of steep hills.

On the west coast are the many-colored sand cliffs of Alum Bay. The Needles, three giant chalk rocks, and the Needles Lighthouse, are the farther features of interest at this end of the island. If you want to stay at the western end of Wight, consider Freshwater Bay.

## ESSENTIALS

**GETTING THERE**    A direct train from London's Waterloo Station to Portsmouth deposits travelers directly at the pier for a ferry crossing to the Isle of Wight; ferries are timed to meet train arrivals. Travel time from London to the arrival point of Ryde on the Isle of Wight (including ferry-crossing time) is 2 hours. One train per hour departs during the day from London to Portsmouth.

Drive to Southampton (see above) and take the ferry, or leave Southampton and head west along A35, cutting south on A337 toward Lymington on the coast where the ferry crossing to Yarmouth (Isle of Wight) is shorter than the trip from Southampton.

Red Funnel operates a vehicle ferry service from Terminal 1 in Southampton to East Cowes; the trip takes 55 minutes. An inclusive fare (valid for 5 days) over and back costs from £36 to £55 ($57.60 to $88) for four persons, depending on the season. More popular with train travelers from Waterloo Station in London is a Hi-Speed passenger-only catamaran operating from the Town Quay Terminal 2 in Southampton, going to West Cowes; the trip takes 22 minutes. A day return fare costs £9.30 ($14.90) for adults and £4.66 ($7.45) for children. For ferry departure times, call ☎ **01703/334010.**

The White Line ferry operates between Portsmouth and Ryde, taking 20 minutes and costing £6.20 ($9.90) for adults and £3.10 ($4.95) for children, round-trip. Daytime departures leave every 30 minutes in summer and every hour in winter. A final option involves a Hovercraft that travels from Southsea (Portsmouth's neighbor) to Ryde, charging £7.90 ($12.65) for adults and £3.95 ($6.30) for children. For information on departure times and schedules, call the tourist office in Shanklin (see below) or ☎ **01983/292101** for car-ferries and ☎ **01983/811000** for the Hovercraft or ☎ **01705/827744** for the White Line passenger ferries.

**GETTING AROUND**    Visitors can explore the Isle of Wight just for the day on the Island Explorer bus service. Tickets may be purchased on the bus, and you can board or leave the bus at any stop on the island. The price of a Day Rover is £6.25 ($10) for adults and £3.15 ($5.05) for children. It also entitles you to passage on the island's only railway, which runs from the dock at Ryde to the center of Shanklin, a distance of 8 miles. For further information, call **Southern Vectis** (☎ **01983/ 827005**).

**VISITOR INFORMATION**    The **information office** is at 67 High St., Shanklin (☎ **01983/862942**). Open daily, March through mid-July and September through October from 9am to 6pm, from mid-July through August from 9am to 8:45pm, and from November to March from 9:30am to 5pm. Please call, as these hours are subject to change.

## QUEEN VICTORIA'S FAVORITE RESIDENCE & A MEDIEVAL CASTLE

✪ **Osborne House.** A mile southeast of East Cowes. ☎ **01983/200022.** House and grounds £6 ($9.60) adults; £4.50 ($7.20) seniors; £3 ($4.80) children. Admission to grounds only £3.50 ($5.60). Apr–Sept daily 10am–6pm (house closes at 5pm); Oct daily 10am–5pm. Closed Nov– Mar. Bus: no. 4 or 5.

Queen Victoria's most cherished residence, a mile southeast of East Cowes, was built at her own expense. Prince Albert, with characteristic thoroughness, contributed to many aspects of the design of the Italian-inspired mansion, which stands amid lush gardens, right outside the village of Whippingham. The rooms have remained as Victoria knew them, right down to the French piano she used to play and all the cozy clutter of her sitting room. Grief-stricken at the death of Albert in 1861, she asked that Osborne House be kept as it was, and so it has been. Even the turquoise scent bottles he gave her, decorated with cupids and cherubs, are still in place. It was in her bedroom at Osborne House that the queen died on January 22, 1901.

**Carisbrooke Castle.** Carisbrooke, 1¹⁄₄ miles southwest of Newport. ☎ **01983/522107.** Castle and museum £4 ($6.40) adults; £3 ($4.80) seniors and students; £2 ($3.20) children. Apr–Oct daily 10am–6pm; Nov–Mar daily 10am–4pm. Bus: no. 91A.

This fine medieval castle lies in the center of the Isle of Wight and is one of the island's most recommendable side trips. During one of the most turbulent periods of English history, Charles I was imprisoned here, far from his former seat of power in London, by Cromwell's Roundheads in 1647. On the castle premises is a

16th-century Well House, where during periods of siege, donkeys took turns tread-ing a large wooden wheel connected to a rope that hauled up buckets of water from a well. Accessible from the castle's courtyard is a museum (☎ **01983/523112**) with exhibits pertaining to the social history of the Isle of Wight and the history of Charles I's imprisonment.

# WHERE TO STAY
## IN RYDE

**The Dorset Hotel.** 31 Dover St., Ryde, Isle of Wight PO33 2BW. ☎ **01983/564327.** 21 rms, 11 with bath. TV. £16 ($25.60) single without bath, £19 ($30.40) single with bath; £31 ($49.60) double without bath, £35–£37 ($56–$59.20) double with bath. All rates include English break-fast. No credit cards. Bus: "Around the Island Rover."

Built in the late 19th century to accommodate government officials who accompa-nied Queen Victoria on her summer visits to the Isle of Wight, this hotel is about a 10-minute walk west of the ferryboat terminal in Ryde. Painted cream with beige trim, the stone-sided hotel offers a heated outdoor swimming pool that remains open throughout the year. The rooms are modernized and comfortable. A dining room on the premises charges £6 to £12 ($9.60 to $19.20) for simple fixed-price menus.

**Seaward Guest House.** 14–16 George St., Ryde, Isle of Wight PO33 2EW. ☎ **01983/563168.** 7 rms, 1 with bath. TV. £15–£18 ($24–$28.80) single without bath; £28–£30 ($44.80–$48) double without bath, £36 ($57.60) double with bath. All rates include English breakfast. No credit cards.

A good anchor for the Isle of Wight is the Seaward, as Ryde is an ideal center for ex-ploring the island; many tour buses leave from here, the ferry and hovercraft dock at Ryde, and the train station is here. Dave and Lynn Wood receive guests in their century-old home. Everything is well kept in the comfortably furnished bedrooms, which contain hot and cold running water, color TV, and tea- or coffee-making equipment. Breakfast is four courses. Even if they can't accommodate you in their busy season, they'll have suggestions as to where you can find a room.

## IN SHANKLIN

**The Bondi Hotel.** Clarence Rd., New Shanklin, Isle of Wight PO37 7BH. ☎ **01983/862507.** Fax 01983/862326. 8 rms with shower. TV. £18–£25 ($28.80–$40) single; £36–£50 ($57.60–$80) double. All rates include breakfast. AE, DC, MC, V. From Ryde on A3055, take 3rd turn on right after Texaco garage.

This hotel, run by Brian and Hilary Norton, extends a friendly welcome to its international coterie of guests. The individually decorated and rather personalized bedrooms have amenities as color TVs and beverage-making equipment. For relax-ation, there is a conservatory-style bar and an invitingly furnished lounge. The facility is licensed and serves a five-course dinner made with fresh produce in the nonsmoking dining room opening onto the garden.

**Culham Lodge.** Landguard Manor Rd., Shanklin, Isle of Wight PO37 7HZ. ☎ and fax **01983/862880.** 10 rms with shower. TV. £20–£21 ($32–$33.60) single; £40–£42 ($64–$67.20) double. All rates include breakfast. MC, V. Follow A3055 from Ryde through the traffic signals, go right into Green Lane, then right again into Landguard Manor Rd.

You'll find this small, friendly, family-run hotel located on the border of Shanklin. The bedrooms are attractively decorated with many amenities, including beverage-making equipment. The nonsmoking lounge provides books and games for the guests. There is also a small conservatory that leads to a beautiful garden. Dinner and breakfast—both home cooked—are served in the nonsmoking dining room. There is also a heated outdoor pool and a solarium.

## IN TOTLAND BAY

**Littledene Lodge Hotel.** Granville Rd., Totland Bay, Isle of Wight PO39 0AX. ☎ **01983/ 752411.** 6 rms. £23.50–£24.50 ($37.60–$39.20) single; £39–£41 ($62.40–$65.60) double. All rates include English breakfast. MC, V. Closed Nov–Feb.

Owned and managed by Mrs. Maureen Wright, this hotel is small enough so that you receive plenty of personal attention. The standards in the rooms are high here, and the owner frequently makes changes in the decor and keeps them invitingly spic-and-span for her international array of visitors arriving at the port of Southampton. There's a TV lounge, and the hotel is centrally heated. Maureen is proud of her reputation for serving good food in the spacious bar/dining room. Traditional English meals begin at £9.50 ($15.20). Children are welcome.

**Sentry Mead Hotel.** Madeira Rd., Totland Bay, Isle of Wight PO39 0BJ. ☎ **01983/753212.** 14 rms, all with bath. TV. £20–£30 ($32–$48) single; £40–£60 ($64–$96) double. All rates include English breakfast. AE, MC, V.

This hotel was built in 1891 as the summer home of a Londoner, a Mr. Fox, who disembarked *en famille* complete with a rather large staff and entourage every summer. Today Mike and Julie Hodgson run this year-round establishment in West Wight, 2¹/₂ miles west of the ferry terminal at Yarmouth. The hotel is only a short walk from Alum Bay and Needles. On spacious grounds, it stands at the edge of Totland's Turf Walk and offers a view of the Solent. The bedrooms have private showers and baths, radios, and beverage-making facilities. The breakfast consists of four courses. Mrs. Hodgson, a master chef, prepares international as well as British food that's served in both the dining room and the bar, where lunches are offered.

## WHERE TO EAT

**The Cottage.** 8 Eastcliff Rd., Shanklin. ☎ **01983/862504.** Reservations required. Main courses all £12.95 ($20.70); 3-course fixed-price lunch £9.25 ($14.80). Tues–Sat noon–2pm and 7:30–9:45pm. AE, DC, MC, V. Closed end of Feb to end of Mar, and Oct. ENGLISH/FRENCH.

Established in 1973, this restaurant and adjacent gift shop is in a 1790s stone-sided cottage that's set among the thatch-covered buildings of the center of Shanklin. Inside, two floors of dining rooms contain lace tablecloths and heavy oaken beams. Lunches are fixed-price affairs that feature such dishes as chicken with a mushroom-and-sherry sauce or a roast of the day (pork, lamb, or beef) served with new potatoes and two vegetables as well as a venison dish. Dinners are more elaborate, and include such choices as roast breast of duck with black cherry sauce or fresh salmon in puff pastry with watercress sauce. All desserts including ice creams and sorbets are made fresh daily.

## 5 Winchester

72 miles SW of London; 12 miles N of Southampton

The most historic city in all of Hampshire, Winchester is big on legend—it's associated with King Arthur and the Knights of the Round Table. In the Great Hall, all that remains of Winchester Castle, a round oak table, with space for King Arthur and his 24 knights, is attached to the wall but all that spells is undocumented romance. What is known, however, is that when the Saxons ruled the ancient kingdom of Wessex, Winchester was the capital.

The city is also linked with King Alfred, who is believed to have been crowned here and is honored today by a statue. The Danish conqueror, Canute, came this way too, as did the king he ousted, Ethelred the Unready (Canute got his wife, Emma, in the bargain). The city is the seat of well-known Winchester College, whose

## From Hampshire to Hollywood: The Oh-So-Popular Jane Austen

Jane Austen, one of the most read and reread of English authors, currently enjoys a literary stardom that far exceeds any modern writer. A running (and oft-repeated) joke claims that in the literary Olympics of Britain, Dickens and the Brontë sisters have—thanks to the advent of Austen's made-for-TV movies—been relegated to bronze-medal status, Shakespeare shunted aside to the position of silver medalist, and the authors of the King James version of the Bible have been studiously ignored except by a handful of dusty Anglican vicars. Austen, so the story goes, wins hands-down as ongoing recipient of the gold medal prize given her increasingly recognized role as England's most famous, most cherished, and most frequently emulated classic romantic novelist.

Cinematic versions of Austen's works appeared beginning in the 1940s, and they have graced movie screens everywhere ever since. The most famous of the early cinematic productions included Sir Laurence Olivier and Greer Garson's version of *Pride and Prejudice,* the first of at least four different film versions of that novel alone. Since then, movies have been made (and sometimes remade) of all six of Austen's major novels. Film historians might cite 1995 as the long-deceased writer's cinematic heyday. That year witnessed a BBC production of *Persuasion* (with Amanda Root and Ciaran Hinds); a BBC/A&E remake of *Pride and Prejudice* (with Colin Firth and Jennifer Ehle); and a Columbia Tri-Star production of *Sense and Sensibility* starring the endlessly charming, and endlessly British Emma Thompson and Kate Winslet. Even *Clueless,* a sarcastic teenage comedy, was a modern-day version of *Emma.* In 1996 Hollywood trotted out the traditional *Emma,* this one with Gwyneth Paltrow.

Why the Austenitis of moviegoers and Hollywood producer types? Savvy cinema insiders realized long ago that Ms. Austen's novels provide—in the words of an unemployed and somewhat bitter West End actor—"very pretty, very lovely" platforms for soap operatic made-for-TV dramas. Austen's plots and characters provide the stylish and socially acceptable skeletons for producers whose scenery resembles a painting by John Constable. Interiors focus on salons from the most spectacular country houses in England, and warehouses of historically accurate costumes can be designed with taste and materials that are probably much, much better than their originals. This, coupled with psychologically intriguing characters who seem to stray from the upstanding path, makes Austen's works assets at the box office. Jane Austen's mannered plots have swept through the eastern hemisphere as well, especially Japan.

founding father was the bishop of Winchester, William of Wykeham. Established in 1382, it's reputed to be the oldest public (private) secondary school in England.

And, of course, Winchester is a Mecca for fans of the novelist Jane Austen. You can visit her grave in Winchester Cathedral (Emma Thompson did while writing the screenplay for *Sense and Sensibility*) as well as Chawton Cottage, Jane Austen's house, which is 15 miles east of Winchester.

Traditions are strong in Winchester. You can still go to St. Cross Hospital—which dates from the 12th century and is now an almshouse. Here you'll get ye olde pilgrim's dole of ale and bread (and if there's no bread, you can eat cake). You must arrive, however, on a weekday before 11am.

Its past glory but a memory, Winchester is essentially a market town today, lying on the downs along the Itchen River. Although Winchester hypes its ancient past,

Austen's postmortem catapult to fame has enticed a flood of visitors to her house, Chawton Cottage, in Chawton, 1 mile southwest of Alton off A31 and B3006 (☎ **01420/83262**). The cottage is 15 miles east of Winchester and signposted at Chawton.

Born in 1775, Jane Austen was the daughter of the Oxford-educated rector, the Rev. Mr. George Austen, a typical Hampshire country gentleman, who had lots of charm but little money. In keeping with a custom of the time, the Austens gave their third son, Edward, to a wealthy, childless family connection, Thomas Knight. As Knight's heir, it was Edward who let his mother and sisters live in the house.

You can see where the novelist spent the last 7¹/₂ years of her life, her most productive period. In the unpretentious but pleasant cottage is the table on which she penned new versions of three of her books and wrote three more, including *Emma*. You can also see the rector's George III mahogany bookcase and a silhouette likeness of the Reverend Austen presenting his son to the Knights. It was in this cottage that Jane Austen became ill in 1816 with what would have been diagnosed by the middle of the 19th century as Addison's disease. She died in July 1817.

In 1809, Jane Austen wrote:

> *Our Chawton Home, how much we find*
> *Already in it to our mind;*
> *And how convinced, that when complete*
> *It will all other houses beat*
> *That ever have been made or mended,*
> *With rooms concise or rooms distended.*

Chawton Cottage is open daily March through December, from 11am to 4:30pm, and on Saturday and Sunday only in January and February (same hours). Admission is £2 ($3.20) for adults, 50p (80¢) for children 8 to 18. It's closed Christmas Day and Boxing Day (December 26). There's an attractive garden where you can picnic and an old bake house with Austen's donkey cart. A bookshop stocks new and secondhand books.

Across the road from Jane Austen's house is an idyllic place for tea. **Cassandra's Cup,** Chawton (☎ **01420/831144**), is known for its home baking, especially its delectable scones. Freshly made sandwiches and good-tasting cakes and pastries are also sold. Take your tea such as Darjeeling or Earl Grey in a traditional setting decorated in green and white, with lace curtains and tablecloths. Later you can browse in their shops for souvenirs, perhaps old porcelain.

the modern world has arrived, as evidenced by the fast-food eateries, the reggae music, and the cheap retail clothing stores that mar its otherwise perfect High Street.

## ESSENTIALS

**GETTING THERE**  From London's Waterloo Station there is frequent daily train service to Winchester. The trip takes 1 hour. Arrivals are at Winchester Station, Station Hill; call ☎ **01703/229393** for schedules and information).

National Express buses leaving from London's Victoria Coach Station depart every 2 hours for Winchester during the day. The trip takes 2 hours. Call ☎ **0990/808080** for schedules and information.

If you're driving, from Southampton, drive north on A335; from London, take the M3 motorway southwest.

**VISITOR INFORMATION** The **Tourist Information Centre** is at the Winchester Guildhall, The Broadway (☎ **01962/840500**). Open Monday through Saturday from 10am to 5pm. Beginning in May and lasting through October, guided walking tours are conducted for £2 ($3.20) per person, departing from this tourist center. The tours are Monday through Saturday at 10:30am and 2:30pm, with only one tour offered Sunday at 1:30pm.

## ✪ WINCHESTER CATHEDRAL: JANE AUSTEN'S RESTING PLACE

For centuries, Winchester Cathedral, The Square (☎ **01962/853137**), has been one of the great churches of England. The present building, the longest medieval cathedral in Britain, dates from 1079, and its Norman heritage is still in evidence. When a Saxon church stood on this spot, St. Swithun, bishop of Winchester and tutor to young King Alfred, suggested rather modestly that he be buried outside. Following his subsequent indoor burial, it rained for 40 days. The legend lives on. Just ask a resident of Winchester what will happen if it rains on St. Swithun's Day, July 15, and you'll get a prediction of rain for 40 days.

In the present building, the nave with its two aisles is most impressive, as are the chantries, the reredos (late 15th century), and the elaborately carved choir stalls. Of the chantries, that of William of Wykeham, founder of Winchester College, is the most visited (it's found in the south aisle of the nave). Jane Austen is buried here, and her grave is marked with a commemorative plaque.

There are also chests containing the bones of many Saxon kings and the remains of the Viking conqueror, Canute, and his wife, Emma, in the presbytery. The son of William the Conqueror, William Rufus (who reigned as William II), was also buried at the cathedral.

There are free guided tours April to October, Monday through Saturday at 11am, 12:30pm, 2pm, and 3pm. The crypt is flooded during winter months, but part of it may be seen from a viewing platform. When it's not flooded, there are regular tours, Monday through Saturday at 10:30am and 2:30pm. The cathedral library and the Triforium Gallery are open from Easter to October, on Monday from 2 to 4:30pm and Tuesday through Saturday from 10:30am to 1pm and 2 to 4:30pm; from November to Easter, on Saturday from 10:30am to 4pm. The library houses Bishop Morley's 17th-century book collection and an exhibition room contains the 12th-century Winchester Bible. The Triforium shows sculpture, woodwork, and metalwork from 11 centuries and affords magnificent views over the rest of the cathedral. Admission to the library and Triforium Gallery is £1 ($1.60) for adults and 50p (80¢) for children. No admission fee is charged for the cathedral, although a donation of £2.50 ($4) is requested.

In 1993, Queen Elizabeth II and the Duke of Edinburgh opened a Visitors' Centre, which includes a cathedral refectory and a shop. The refectory offers homemade food ranging from light snacks to three-course lunches, and the shop sells an array of gifts and souvenirs.

## OUTDOOR PURSUITS

You can explore the countryside on one of the lengthy walking trails, such as South Downs Way, a 99-mile trail that goes all the way from Winchester to Eastbourne; Clarendon Way, a 24-mile path from Winchester to Salisbury; and Itchen Way, a beautiful riverside trail from near Cheriton to Southampton.

**FISHING** Winchester and the surrounding area are by far one of the best places to fish in all of England, especially for trout. Try your hand at any of the many nearby rivers including the Rivers Itchen, Test, Meon, Dever and Avon.

**GOLF** When it's tee time, most any of the 12 area golf courses will allow nonmembers on their greens. The tourist office (see above) provides complete details (which change seasonally) on all these outdoor activities.

## SHOPPING

If you have ever dreamed of rummaging through the shelves and stacks of an authentic old English bookstore, stop by **Gilbert's Bookshop,** 19 The Square (☎ **01962/ 852832**). Their wide selection of stock runs the spectrum from rare gems to hot-off-the-press best-sellers. Be sure to strike up a conversation with the staff, too. They've been in business since 1859 and really know the trade. You can spark up your wardrobe at **Cadogan,** 30–31 The Square (☎ **01962/877399**), which sells an upscale and stylish selection of British clothing for both men and women. For a unique piece of jewelry by one of the most acclaimed contemporary designers, stroll into **Carol Darby Jewellery,** 23 Little Minster St. (☎ **01962/867671**). Browse both the shop and workshop for a nice trinket. If by chance nothing suits your fancy, let Carol Darby make one of her special creations tailored to your tastes.

## WHERE TO STAY

**Ann and Tony Farrell.** 5 Ranelagh Rd., St. Cross, Winchester, Hampshire SO23 9TA. ☎ **01962/869555.** 5 rms, 2 with bath. £18 ($28.80) single without bath; £36 ($57.60) double without bath, £40 ($64) double with bath. All rates include English breakfast. No credit cards. Bus: no. 1, 1A, 2, 2A, 29, 47, or 69.

Near the heart of the city, 800 yards south of the town center on St. Cross Road, this Victorian house is furnished in period fashion but has modern comforts. The guest rooms have hot and cold running water and tea-making facilities. Over the years, the rooms and comfort here have drawn some of the most favorable responses from readers, who constantly cite the hospitality extended by the owners.

**Florum House.** 47 St. Cross Rd., Winchester, Hampshire SO23 9PS. ☎ and fax **01962/ 840427.** 10 rms, all with shower only. TV. £36 ($57.60) single; £56 ($89.60) double; £63 ($100.80) family rm for 3. All rates include English breakfast. MC, V. Bus: no. 47.

Half a mile south of Winchester Cathedral, this brick Victorian house from 1887 lies about halfway between the village of St. Cross and Winchester. It's surrounded by about half an acre of private gardens. The comfortably furnished bedrooms contain beverage-making equipment. The house is licensed to serve alcohol to guests, and the management will prepare a dinner, costing £12 ($19.20) and up, if adequate notice is given.

✪ **Harestock Lodge.** Harestock Rd., Winchester, Hampshire SO22 6NX. ☎ **01962/881870.** Fax 01962/886959. 20 rms, all with shower only. TV TEL. £45 ($72) single; £58 ($92.80) double. All rates include English breakfast. AE, MC, V.

One of the best places to stay is this lovely country residence constructed in 1885 on the northern perimeter of the city between the B3420 Andover road and the A272 Stockbridge road. The recently renovated rooms have radios, and the hotel has an outdoor swimming pool. Good British cooking is featured in the restaurant, where meals begin at £6 ($9.60).

✪ **Shawlands.** 46 Kilham Lane, Winchester, Hampshire SO22 5QD. ☎ and fax **01962/ 861166.** 5 rms, 1 with bath. TV. £23–£25 ($36.80–$40) single without bath; £35–£37 ($56–$59.20) double without bath; £40 ($64) double with bath. All rates include English breakfast. No credit cards. From Winchester's center, follow the Romsey road south for a mile.

In an upscale residential neighborhood about a mile south of Winchester's center, Shawlands was built in 1960 across the road from the open fields of a large private estate. Intended for use by the extended family of Kathy Pollock (a retired nutritionist) and her husband, William, the house is comfortable, spacious, and cozy. Made of brick, Shawlands has casement windows with leaded inserts, and larger-than-expected bedrooms. (One of these was converted from a former garage as a "granny flat" for the Pollocks' since-departed parents.) Breakfasts are enhanced by Mrs. Pollock's serving of homemade brown bread and homemade marmalade every morning as part of a time-tested morning ritual.

## A YOUTH HOSTEL

**The City Mill.** 1 Water Lane, Winchester, Hampshire SO23 0ER. ☎ and fax **01962/853723.** 31 beds. £8.50 ($13.60) adults; £5.70 ($9.10) age 18 or under. MC, V.

Straddling the Itchen River, this is an old watermill—now protected by the National Trust—which is split between a hostel and a mill museum. You'll feel as if the clock has turned way back, with the building's barn ceiling, brick walls, and exposed beams. Hostel lovers from all over the world flock here, and some play the piano and sing for the entertainment of guests in the evening. There's not a lot in the way of comfort here—just two large impersonal dormitories—but the setting has so much soul and beauty it compensates somehow. There is no self-catering kitchen, but a rustic common room/dining area offers cafeteria-style service of breakfast for £2.85 ($4.55) and dinner for £4.25 ($6.80). A packaged lunch, ordered the night before, is available for £2.35 ($3.75) to take on your daily excursions. There are no storage lockers or laundry facilities, and an 11pm curfew is enforced.

# WHERE TO EAT

**The Eclipse Inn.** 25 The Square, Winchester. ☎ **01962/865676.** Daily specials, soups, salads, and sandwiches £1.50–£4 ($2.40–$6.40). No credit cards. Mon–Sat noon–3pm and 6–9pm; Sun noon–3pm. PUB GRUB.

Lady Alicia Lisle was hung in The Square, directly in front of this building, after being declared a traitor for harboring Cromwell's army at the inn. Her ghost is said to roam through the building, but regulars don't seem intimidated by her purported presence. In fact, they spent so much time here that they leave their mugs hanging on hooks from the ceiling, readily available for another pint. Stop in for a salad, sandwich or one of their daily specials, including vegetarian and meat pies. Wash it down with one of their cask ales and a lively tale from said regulars.

**Forte Crest Hotel.** Paternoster Row. ☎ **01962/861611.** Reservations recommended. Explorer Restaurant, all-you-can-eat lunch buffet £7 ($11.20). Wessex Restaurant, fixed-price lunch or dinner £20 ($32). AE, DC, MC, V. Explorer Restaurant daily lunch buffet noon–2pm. Wessex Restaurant daily 12:30–2pm and 7–10pm. Bus: no. 25. ENGLISH.

A few steps from the cathedral, this well-known hotel contains the bright Explorer Restaurant, with a separate entrance from the street, where a big spread is laid out for lunch. A typical meal includes soup, breaded plaice with fried potatoes, apple pie and cream, plus coffee. They also offer a traditional afternoon tea. More formal meals are served in the Wessex Restaurant, where a collection of English antiques and a view of the cathedral create one of the most elegant dining spots in town.

**Olde Market Inn.** 34 The Square, at Market St. (opposite the cathedral). ☎ **01962/852585.** Pub snacks £1.65–£3.95 ($2.65–$6.30). MC, V. Mon–Sat noon–6pm. Pub: Mon–Sat 11am–11pm; Sun noon–3pm and 7–10:30pm. ENGLISH.

In the oldest, most historic district of Winchester, this mellow old pub has timbered interiors, cozy nooks, and comfortable chairs. It's ideal for those who enjoy a local pub. A selection of hot and cold bar snacks is available, including home-cooked steak-and-kidney pie, cottage pie, and chicken-and-mushroom pie. Orders are placed over the bar tops. The food is filling, nothing fancy.

**Royal Oak Pub.** Royal Oak Passage. ☎ **01962/842701.** Bar snacks and platters £1.95–£6 ($3.10–$9.60); cask ale from £1.75 ($2.80). MC, V. Daily noon–2pm. Pub: Mon–Sat 11am–11pm; Sun noon–3pm and 7–10:30pm. Bus: no. 25. ENGLISH.

A busy pub with plenty of atmosphere, the Royal Oak reputedly has the oldest bar in England. The cellar of this establishment was originally built in 944 to dispense drink to Winchester's pilgrims, and the present building was constructed in 1630 atop the much older foundation. Various hot dishes and snacks are available, and a traditional Sunday lunch is also served. No culinary awards will be earned here—mainly it's a place for drinking. It is a traditional cask ale house known as a Hogshead. The Royal Oak is found in a passageway next to the God Begot House on the High Street.

## WINCHESTER AFTER DARK

The place to go is **The Porthouse,** Upper Brook Street (☎ **01962/869397**), a pub-cum-nightclub, sprawling across three floors. Different nights are devoted to different themes. Tuesday is student's night, Wednesday is karaoke, and Thursday is ladies night with retro music from the 1960s through the 1980s. On Friday the 25-plus crowd takes over for "Joy on the Weekend." The only cover, ranging from £3 to £5 ($4.80 to $8), is charged on Thursday, Friday, and Saturday nights from 8:30 to 10:30pm. The ground floor pub, where lunch is served, is open from 11am to 3pm; the pub and nightclub are open Monday through Wednesday and on Saturday from 5pm to midnight, Thursday until 1am, and Friday until 2am.

## 6 In & Around Bournemouth

104 miles SW of London; 15 miles W of the Isle of Wight

The south-coast resort at the doorstep of the New Forest didn't just happen: it was carefully planned and executed, a true city in a garden. Flower-filled, park-dotted Bournemouth is filled with an abundance of architecture inherited from those regal arbiters of taste, Victoria and her son, Edward. (The resort was discovered back in Victoria's day, when sea-bathing became an institution.) Other famous names associated with the town include Robert Louis Stevenson, Aubrey Beardsley, and the actor Stewart Granger. Bournemouth's most distinguished feature is its chines (narrow, shrub-filled, steep-sided ravines) along the coastline.

Bournemouth, along with Poole and Christ Church, forms the largest urban area in the south of England. It makes a good base for exploring a historically rich part of England; on its outskirts are the New Forest, Salisbury, Winchester, and the Isle of Wight. It also has some 20,000 students attending the various schools or colleges, who explore, in their off-hours, places made famous by such poets and artists as Shelley, Beardsley, and Turner.

## ESSENTIALS

**GETTING THERE**   An express train from London's Waterloo Station takes 2 hours, with frequent service throughout the day. Contact the Bournemouth Rail Station, Holden Surst Road (☎ **01345/484950**), for complete schedules and information.

Buses leave London's Waterloo Station every 2 hours during the day, heading for Bournemouth. The trip takes 2¹/₂ hours. Call ☎ **0990/808080** for information and schedules.

If you're driving, take M3 southwest from London to Winchester, then A31 and A338 south to Bournemouth.

**VISITOR INFORMATION**   The **information office** is at Westover Road (☎ **01202/451700**). Open May 4 through September 13, Monday through

Saturday from 9:30am to 7pm, Sunday from 10:30am to 5pm; and from September 14 through May 3, Monday through Saturday from 9:30am to 5:30pm.

# EXPLORING BOURNEMOUTH

Of Bournemouth's nearly 12,000 acres, about one-sixth comprise green parks and flower beds such as the Pavilion Rock Garden, which amblers pass through day and night. The total effect, especially in spring, is striking, helping to explain Bournemouth's continuing popularity with the garden-loving English.

The resort's amusements are varied. At the Pavilion Theatre, you can see West End–type productions from London. The Bournemouth Symphony Orchestra is justly famous in Europe. And there's the usual run of golf courses, band concerts, variety shows, and dancing. The real walkers might strike out at Hengistbury Head and make their way past sandy beaches, the Boscombe and Bournemouth piers—all the way to Alum Chine, a distance of 6 miles.

Bournemouth also has an art museum of import, the **Russell-Cotes Art Gallery and Museum,** East Cliff, Bournemouth (☎ **01202/451800** or fax 01202/451851). Based around a remarkable Victorian house (1897) the Russell-Cotes houses an outstanding collection of Victorian fine art and sculpture, ethnography, and modern British art. A new museum extension and newly landscaped gardens are the site for an extension program of contemporary craft and sculpture commissions. Open Tuesday to Sunday from 10am to 5pm. Entrance is free.

True romantics and die-hard fans of Percy Bysshe Shelley should take time to see **The Shelley Rooms,** Beechwood Avenue, Boscombe (☎ **01202/303571**). This small museum and study room are housed in Boscombe Manor, the one-time home of Shelley's son, Sir Percy Florence Shelley. The rooms are devoted to the works of the great poet and his circle. Collections are built primarily around works written during the last few months of Shelley's life when he lived in San Terenzo, Italy. The Shelley Rooms are open Tuesday through Sunday from 2 to 5pm. Admission is free.

## THE BOURNEMOUTH BEACH

This seaside resort has a spectacular beach: 7 miles of uninterrupted sand stretching from Hengistbury Head to Alum Chine. Most of it is known simply as Bournemouth Beach, although its western edge, when it crosses over into the municipality of Poole, is called Sandbanks Beach. Beach access is free and you can swim where a pair of blue flags indicate the water's fine. The flags also signify the highest standards of cleanliness, management, and facilities. A dog-free zone has been established between Fisherman's Walk and Durley Chine. And a health-conscious, nonsmoking zone now exists at Durley Chine, East Beach, and Fisherman's Walk. Fourteen full-time lifeguards patrol on the shore and the water and are helped by three volunteer corps during the busiest summer months. The promenade is traffic-free during the summer. There are two piers, one at Boscombe and the other at Bournemouth.

Amenities at the beach include beach bungalows, freshwater showers, seafront bistros and cafes, boat trips, rowboats, pedaloes, jet-skis, and windsurfers. Cruises run in the summer from Bournemouth Pier to the Isle of Wight.

# WAREHAM

This historic little town on the Frome River 2 miles west of Bournemouth is an excellent center for touring the South Dorset coast and the Purbeck Hills. See the remains of early Anglo-Saxon and Roman town walls, plus the Saxon church of St. Martin, with its effigy of T. E. Lawrence (Lawrence of Arabia), who died in a motorcycle crash in 1935. His former home, **Clouds Hill** (☎ **01929/405616**), lies

7 miles west of Wareham (1 mile north of Bovington Camp) and is extremely small. E. M. Forster wrote about Clouds Hill: "The real framework, the place which his spirit will never cease to haunt." It's open only April to October, on Wednesday, Thursday, Friday, and Sunday from noon to 5pm, and bank holiday Mondays from noon to 5pm. Admission is £2.20 ($3.50), and free for children 4 and under.

Aficionados of Lawrence and/or military history should also head for the **Tank Museum,** in the village and army base of Bovington Camp (☎ **01929/403463**), an installation maintained by the British military. Among the dozens of rare and historic armed vehicles are exhibitions and memorabilia on the life of T. E. Lawrence. Admission is £5 ($8) for adults and £3 ($4.80) for children 5 to 16. It's open daily from 10am to 4:30pm (last admission).

## POOLE & CHRIST CHURCH

True history buffs usually head 5 miles west to Poole, or 5 miles east to Christ Church, both of which predated Bournemouth by thousands of years. Both have large but shallow harbors favored by the ancient Romans.

In Poole, stop by the **Waterfront Museum** on High Street (☎ **01202/683138**). This museum celebrates the nautical influences that made the region great, with exhibits about the effects of seafaring commerce since the days of the ancient Romans. The museum is open April to October from 10am to 5pm; November through March, telephone for details. Admission is £2.50 ($4) for adults, £1.75 ($2.80) for children ages 5 to 16, free for children under 5 in July and August; and £1.95 ($3.10) for adults, £1.25 ($2) for children from April to June and September to October.

In Christ Church, the Priority Church is situated on Quay Road. The present monastic church was begun in 1094 on a site where there has been a church since A.D. 700. It is famous for a number of features, including the "Miraculous Beam," Norman nave and Turret, monks' quire with its Jesse reredos and misericords, Lady Chapel, chantries, 15th-century bell tower, and St. Michael's loft, once a school but now a museum. Open throughout the year Monday through Saturday from 9am to 5pm and on Sundays from 2:15 to 5pm. **The Red House Museum,** also on Quay Road (☎ **01202/482860**) occupies a red-brick building originally constructed in 1764 as a work house. In 1951, a civic-minded resident donated his extensive collection of archaeological and cultural artifacts to form the basis of the town's most visible public monument. An art gallery on the premises has paintings, while exhibits showcase the region's cultural and social history. Open Tuesday to Saturday from 10am to 5pm and Sunday from 2 to 5pm. Admission is £1.60 ($2.55).

## WHERE TO STAY
### DOUBLES FOR LESS THAN £40

**Mayfield Private Hotel.** 46 Frances Rd., Bournemouth, Dorset BH1 3SA. ☎ **01202/551839.** 8 rms, 4 with bath. TV. £15 ($24) single without bath, £18 ($28.80) single with bath; £30 ($48) double without bath, £36 ($57.60) double with bath. All rates include English breakfast. No credit cards. Closed Dec.

In a residential neighborhood about a 15-minute walk east of Bournemouth's center, this hotel was built around 1900 as a private home. A brick house, with a garden, and painted white, it's the domain of the Barling family, whose rooms are well maintained, attractive, and uncomplicated. Residents who opt for evening meals here pay a supplement of around £6 ($9.60) extra per person.

**Sea-Dene Hotel.** 10 Burnaby Rd., Bournemouth, Dorset BH4 8JF. ☎ **01202/761372.** 6 rms. TV. £15–£22 ($24–$35.20) single; £30–£44 ($48–$70.40) double. All rates include English breakfast. No credit cards. Bus: no. 17.

About a mile west of Bournemouth's center, this house was built in 1906, by an Edwardian industrialist for his mistress—part of a turn-of-the-century trend in fashionable Bournemouth for this kind of behavior, encouraged by the then-king, the jovial and occasionally scandalous Edward VII. As you climb the building's stairs, notice the hearts carved into the balustrade, symbols that the genteel owner, Liz Jones, attributes to the building's original motif of love. The euphemistic term used for such a building at the time was a "Grace and Favour" house. The hotel lies a short walk uphill from the sea, and has attractively furnished bedrooms, a lounge, a cozy breakfast area, and a dining room where breakfast is served and evening meals can be prepared, if advance notice is given, for around £6 ($9.60) per person. Two of the building's top-floor bedrooms offer views of the sea.

**Sunnydene.** 11 Spencer Rd., Bournemouth, Dorset BH1 3TE. ☎ **01202/552281** or 01202/ 552269. 11 rms, 2 with bath. £15 ($24) single without bath; £30 ($48) double without bath, £35 ($56) double with bath. All rates include breakfast. No credit cards. Bus: no. 121 or 124.

This Victorian private hotel is in a substantial gabled house on a tree-lined road between the Central Station and Bournemouth Bay. The bedrooms are carpeted and centrally heated, with hot and cold running water; some contain TVs. The hotel is licensed, and drinks and other refreshments are served in the sun lounge.

**Westcliff Hotel.** 27 Chine Crescent, West Cliff, Bournemouth, Dorset BH2 5LB. ☎ **01202/ 551062.** 30 rms. TV. £40–£52 ($64–$83.20) double. All rates include English breakfast. Half board £26–£32 ($41.60–$51.20) per person. MC, V. Bus: no. 25 or 34.

This hotel, a 5-minute walk from the center, near Durley Chine, was once the luxurious south-coast home of the duke of Westminster, who had it built in 1876 in a "chine" (English for dried-out primeval riverbed). Now run by the Blissett family, the hotel enjoys many return customers. All the comfortably furnished and well-maintained rooms have hot-beverage facilities. You can order bar snacks or complete dinners at the hotel's art-deco restaurant. There's a large garden and a parking area, and facilities include a sauna, Jacuzzi, and solarium.

## WHERE TO EAT

**Coriander.** 14 Richmond Hill. ☎ **01202/552202.** Reservations required on weekends. Main courses £6.50–£10.95 ($10.40–$17.50); fixed-price meal £5–£10.95 ($8–$17.50). AE, MC, V. Daily noon–10:30pm. WINE BAR/MEXICAN.

Coriander brings south-of-the-border flair to staid Bournemouth. The restaurant is in a pedestrian zone, and the varied menu includes the usual range of Mexican specialties, plus some interesting vegetarian dishes. All menu items are prepared with fresh ingredients. The coriander soup is a favorite. It's green and spicy and made with fresh coriander, spices, and cream—you are unlikely to find it anywhere else. Main dishes include the standard enchiladas, burritos, and fajitas, although you can also order a crab dinner or a steak Mexicana.

**La Margherita.** 307 Wimborne Rd., Winton, Bournemouth. ☎ **01202/526367.** Reservations recommended. Main courses £3.50–£11.50 ($5.60–$18.40). MC, V. Daily noon–2pm and 6–11:30pm. Closed Mon Sept–June. Bus: no. 2, 3, 4, or 5. ITALIAN/SICILIAN.

Well known as one of the region's best-established Italian restaurants, this place offers red-and-white checked tablecloths, a congenial Italian and Sicilian staff, and dozens of chianti bottles suspended from the ceiling amid verdant plants. Busy and bustling, with a goodly percentage of families with children, it lies in the district of Winton, at the corner of Alma and Wimborne roads. Pizza is a specialty, as well as more elaborate dishes such as tortellini Margherita (with cream, mushrooms, and white wine), scampi amore (with brandy, cream, and rice), and tagliatelle with salmon, cream, and herbs.

## BOURNEMOUTH AFTER DARK

A choice of major art venues offer great performances throughout the year. International Centre's **Windsor Hall** runs personality shows, the **Pavilion** puts on West End musicals as well as dancing with live music, and the **Winter Gardens,** the original home and favorite performance space of the world famous Bournemouth Symphony Orchestra, offers regular concerts. Program and ticket information for all three of these venues is available by calling ☎ **01202/456456.**

## EN ROUTE TO DORCHESTER: KINGSTON LACY

An imposing 17th-century mansion, Kingston Lacy, at Wimborne Minster, on B3082 (Wimborne-Blandford road), 1¹/₂ miles west of Wimborne (☎ **01202/ 883402**), was the home for more than 300 years of the Bankes family, which had as guests such distinguished persons as King Edward VII, Kaiser Wilhelm, Thomas Hardy, George V, and Wellington. The house displays a magnificent collection of artworks by such masters as Rubens, Titian, and Van Dyck. There's also an important collection of Egyptian artifacts.

The present structure was built to replace Corfe Castle, the Bankes' family's home that was destroyed in the Civil War. During her husband's absence while performing duties as chief justice to King Charles I, Lady Bankes led the defense of the castle, withstanding two sieges before being forced to surrender to Cromwell's forces in 1646 because of the actions of a treacherous follower. The keys of Corfe Castle hang in the library at Kingston Lacy.

The house, set on 250 acres of wooded park, is open only from April to October, Saturday through Wednesday from noon to 5:30pm; the park is open from 11:30am to 6pm. Admission to the house, garden, and park is £5.60 ($8.95) for adults and £2.80 ($4.50) for children. Admission to the garden is £2.30 ($3.70) for adults and £1.20 ($1.90) for children.

## 7 Dorchester: Hardy's Home

120 miles SW of London; 27 miles W of Bournemouth

Thomas Hardy bequeathed literary fame to Dorchester in his 1886 novel *The Mayor of Casterbridge.* Actually, Dorchester was notable even in Roman times, when Maumbury Rings, the best Roman amphitheater in Britain, was filled with the sounds of 12,000 spectators screaming for the blood of the gladiators. Dorchester, a county seat, was the setting of another bloodletting, the "Bloody Assize" of 1685, when Judge Jeffreys condemned to death the supporters of the duke of Monmouth's rebellion against James II. Today it's a sleepy market town that seems to go to bed right after dinner. The brewery that makes Thomas Hardy ale is here, however.

## ESSENTIALS

**GETTING THERE**   Trains run from London's Waterloo Station each hour during the day. The trip takes 2¹/₂ hours. Dorchester has two train stations, the South Station at Station Approach and the West Station on Great Western Road. For information about both, call ☎ **01202/292474.**

Several National Express coaches a day depart from London's Waterloo Station heading for Dorchester. The trip takes 3 hours. Call ☎ **0990/808080** for information and schedules.

If you're driving from London, take M3 southwest, but near the end take A30 toward Salisbury where you connect with A354 for the final approach to Dorchester.

**VISITOR INFORMATION** The **Tourist Information Centre** is at Unit 11, Antelope Walk. (☎ **01305/267992**). Open April through October, Monday through Saturday from 9am to 5pm; May through September, Sunday from 10am to 3pm; and November through March, Monday through Saturday from 9am to 4pm.

## SEEING THE SIGHTS

One mile east of Dorchester is **Stinsford Church,** where Hardy's heart is buried. His two wives are buried there as well. To get to the church, officially called the Church of St. Michael, follow the signs from Dorchester for the Kingston Maurward Agricultural College, then just before the entrance gates to the college, turn right, following the signs toward the Stinsford Church.

**Dorset County Museum.** High West St. (next to St. Peter's Church). ☎ **01305/262735.** Admission £2.75 ($4.40) adults; £1.65 ($2.65) children 5–16 and seniors; £8 ($12.80) family ticket; free for children 4 and under. July–Aug daily 10am–5pm; Sept–June Mon–Sat 10am–5pm. Closed New Year's Day. On the main thoroughfare in the heart of town.

This museum has a gallery devoted to memorabilia of Thomas Hardy's life. In addition, you'll find an archaeological gallery with displays and finds from Maiden Castle, Britain's largest Iron Age hill fort, plus galleries on the geology, local history, and natural history of Dorset.

**Hardy's Cottage.** Higher Bockhampton. ☎ **01305/262366.** Admission £2.50 ($4). Apr–Oct Sun–Thurs 11am–1pm and 2–5pm. Closed Nov–Mar. No public transport from Dorchester. Motorists take A35 northeast for 2¹/₂ miles. At Blanford Rd., turn right (south) and drive a half mile to arrive at the cottage, signposted from the road.

Thomas Hardy was born in 1840 at Higher Bockhampton, 3 miles northeast of Dorchester and half a mile south of Blandford Road (A35). His home, now a National Trust property, may be visited by appointment. Approach the cottage on foot—it's a 10-minute walk—after parking your vehicle in the space provided in the wood. Write in advance to Hardy's Cottage, Higher Bockhampton, Dorchester, Dorset DT2 8QJ, England, or call the number above.

**Athelhampton House & Gardens.** On A35, 5 miles east of Dorchester. ☎ **01305/848363.** Admission £4.50 ($7.20) adults; £1.50 ($2.40) children. Mar–Oct Sun–Fri 11am–5pm. Closed Nov–Feb. Take the Dorchester-Bournemouth road (A35) east of Dorchester for 5 miles.

This is one of England's great medieval houses, the most beautiful and historic in the south, lying a mile east of Puddletown. Thomas Hardy mentioned the place in some of his writings but called it Athelhall. It was begun during the reign of Edward IV on the legendary site of King Athelstan's palace. A family home for more than 500 years, it's noted for its 15th-century Great Hall, Tudor great chamber, state bedroom, and King's Room.

In 1992, a dozen of the house's rooms were damaged by an accidental fire caused by faulty wiring in the attic. However, skilled craftspeople restored all the magnificent interiors.

Although many visitors come to see the house, we think the gardens are even more inspiring. Dating from 1891, they have great vistas, and their beauty is enhanced by several fountains and the waters of the River Piddle that flows through. These walled gardens contain the famous topiary pyramids and two pavilions designed by Inigo

Jones. You'll see fine collections of tulips and magnolias, roses, clematis, and lilies, and also a 15th-century Dovecote. Yes, they were visited often by Thomas Hardy.

## TEATIME

The best place for a cuppa in this bustling market town is **Potter Inn,** 19 Durngate St. (☎ **01305/260312**), with its blue-and-white interior and small herb and flower garden out back with several tables. Many guests stop in for some of the delectable ice creams such as butter pecan, but a proper sit-down tea is served for £4.50 ($7.20). You can also order freshly made sandwiches, such as egg and tuna, or else moist cakes, fresh scones, and pastries.

## WHERE TO STAY

**Casterbridge Hotel.** 49 High East St., Dorchester, Dorset DT1 1HU. ☎ **01305/264043.** Fax 01305/260884. 15 rms. TV TEL. £30–£45 ($48–$72) single; £50–£70 ($80–$112) double. All rates include English breakfast. AE, DC, MC, V. Closed Christmas and Dec 26.

In the heart of town, this stone-fronted Georgian house was originally built around 1780 when stones from a demolished prison nearby were recycled and reused. Owned by several generations of the Turner family since the 1930s, this hotel offers clean and well-maintained bedrooms. The cheaper rooms are rather small, but all are "quintessentially English" in their tastes, fabrics, and furniture. Breakfast is the only meal served, although the hotel keeps copies of menus from most of the town's restaurants in its parlor/sitting room.

**Wessex Royale Hotel.** 32 High West St., Dorchester, Dorset DT1 1UP. ☎ **01305/262660.** Fax 01305/251941. 23 rms. TV TEL. £39.95 ($63.90) single; £49.95 ($79.90) double. All rates include English breakfast. AE, DC, MC, V.

Built on medieval foundations, the Wessex is a Georgian structure that was once the home of Lord Ilchester. The public rooms contain much of the original wooden paneling, along with fireplaces and decorative work. The hotel has been modernized and considerably upgraded, each bedroom containing a radio, hair dryer, trouser press, and beverage tray. Located in the town center, it has a busy licensed restaurant, Brooks, and a good wine list. An English cuisine is offered, a complete meal costing £12 to £15 ($19.20 to $24).

**Westwood House Hotel.** 29 High West St., Dorchester, Dorset DT1 1UP. ☎ **01305/ 268018.** Fax 01305/250282. 7 rms, 6 with bath. TV TEL. £27.50–£37.50 ($44–$60) single without bath; £42.50 ($68) double without bath; £49.50–£65 ($79.20–$104) double with bath. All rates include English breakfast. MC, V.

A Georgian town house in the town center, this may have been built as a coaching house for Lord Ilchester. The hotel was recently taken over by Angela and Tom

---

### Impressions

*Casterbridge [Dorchester] was the complement of the rural life around: not its urban opposite. Bees and butterflies in the cornfields at the top of the town, who desired to get to the meads at the bottom, took no circuitous course, but flew straight down High Street without any apparent consciousness that they were traversing strange latitudes. And in autumn airy spheres of thistledown floated into the same street, lodged upon the shop fronts, blew into drains, and innumerable tawny and yellow leaves skimmed along the pavement, and stole through people's doorways into their passages with a hesitating scratch on the floor, like the skirts of timid visitors.*

—Thomas Hardy, *The Mayor of Casterbridge* (1886)

Parsley and restored. The comfortably furnished rooms are equipped with hot-beverage facilities and complimentary drinks. Guests are directed to the Mock Turtle Restaurant 30 yards away (see "Where to Eat," below).

## WHERE TO EAT

**The Horse with the Red Umbrella.** 10 High West St. ☎ **01305/262019.** Soups £1.85 ($2.95); main courses £1.70–£5 ($2.70–$8). No credit cards. In summer Mon–Sat 8am–5:30pm; in winter Mon–Fri 8am–5pm, Sat 8am–5:30pm. ENGLISH/CONTINENTAL.

The window of this shop/coffeehouse on the main street is filled with home-baked goods, and inside you'll find neat tables and chairs where you can watch the passing locals and enjoy quiche and various toasted snacks. They offer such standard fare as stuffed baked potatoes, pizzas, lasagna, omelets, baked macaroni, and other dishes.

✪ **Mock Turtle.** 34 High West St. ☎ **01305/264011.** Reservations recommended. Fixed-price lunch £11.50 ($18.40) for 2 courses, £14.25 ($22.80) for 3 courses; fixed-price dinner £17.25 ($27.60) for 2 courses, £21.75 ($34.80) for 3 courses. MC, V. Mon–Sat 7–9:30pm; Tues–Fri noon–2pm. MODERN BRITISH/CONTINENTAL.

In a Georgian-style building whose stone facade and bow window date to the early 1700s, the Mock Turtle is one of the best restaurants in town. Inside in the dining rooms, exposed stone and brick mingle with strong, dark colors and antiques with an effect like that of a private town house. The menu, conceived by the Hodder family, changes about every 6 weeks, according to the availability of ingredients. Depending on the season of your visit, it might include such dishes as Cajun-blackened chicken steak; medallions of pork with a green-pepper-and-lime sauce; roast duckling with black currants, mango, and crème de casis; and black pudding with onion and apple relish. Fresh fish, prepared in stylish and unusual combinations, is almost always available.

**Webster's Number 6 Wine Bar & Bistro.** 6 North Sq. ☎ **01305/267679.** Main courses £7–£10 ($11.20–$16). MC, V. Mon–Sat noon–2pm and 7–10pm. CONTINENTAL.

Located in a building off High Street, adjacent to the town's prison, this is the second in a chain of wine bars that now stretches across the south of England. Contained in what was originally built as a Victorian forge, it offers an atmospheric interior with racks of wine bottles, plants, and artwork, and a wide selection of wines from virtually everywhere. Menu items include burgers, Caribbean chicken in a sweet-and-sour sauce, steak Napoleon in a pepper sauce, turkey crêpes, ham steak in a parsley sauce, and hot pot of Australian beef.

## 8 Coastal Towns: Chideock, Charmouth & Lyme Regis

Chideock & Charmouth: 157 miles SW of London; 1 mile W of Bridport
Lyme Regis: 160 miles SW of London; 25 miles W of Dorchester

Chideock is a charming hamlet of thatched houses with a dairy farm in the center. About a mile from the coast, it's a gem of a place for overnight stopovers, and even better for longer stays. You may be tempted to explore the countryside and the rolling hills.

On Lyme Bay, Charmouth, like Chideock, is another winner. A village of Georgian houses and thatched cottages, Charmouth provides some of the most dramatic coastal scenery in West Dorset. The village is west of Golden Cap, which, according to adventurers who measure such things, is the highest cliff along the coast of southern England.

Also on Lyme Bay near the Devonshire border, the resort of Lyme Regis is one of the most attractive centers along the south coast. For those who shun big, commercial holiday centers, Lyme Regis is ideal: It's the true English coastal town with a highly praised mild climate. Seagulls fly overhead; the streets are steep and winding; walks along Cobb Beach are brisk and stimulating; the views, particularly of the craft in the harbor, are so photogenic that John Fowles, a longtime resident of the town, selected it as the site for the 1980 filming of his novel *The French Lieutenant's Woman.*

During its heyday, the town was a major seaport. (The duke of Monmouth landed here on return from his exile in Holland in 1685, followed by an unsuccessful attempt to overthrow the regime of his father, Charles II.) Later, Lyme developed into a small spa, including among its visitors Jane Austen. She wrote her final novel, *Persuasion* (published posthumously and based partly on the town's life), after staying here in 1803 and 1804.

## ESSENTIALS

**GETTING THERE**   The nearest train connection to Chideock and Charmouth is Dorchester (see above). Buses run frequently throughout the day west from both Dorchester and Bridport.

To get to Lyme Regis, take the London-Exeter train, getting off at Axminster and continuing the rest of the way by bus. Bus no. 31 runs from Axminster to Lyme Regis at the rate of one coach per hour during the day. There's also National Express bus service (no. 705) that runs daily in summer at 9:50am from Exeter to Lyme Regis, taking $1^3/_4$ hours. Call ☎ **0990/808080** for schedules and information.

If you're driving to Chideock and Charmouth from Bridport, continue west along A35. To get to Lyme Regis from Bridport, continue west along A35, cutting south to the coast at the junction with A3070.

**VISITOR INFORMATION**   In Lyme Regis, the **Tourist Information Centre** is at Guildhall Cottage, Church Street (☎ **01297/442138**). Open November through March, Monday through Friday from 10am to 4pm and Saturday from 10am to 2pm; in April, Monday through Saturday from 10am to 5pm; May through September, Monday through Friday from 10am to 6pm, Saturday and Sunday from 10am to 5pm; and in October, daily from 10am to 5pm.

## WALKING AROUND CHIDEOCK & CHARMOUTH

These are the most beautiful villages in Dorset. It's fun to walk through them to see the lovely cottages, well-manicured gardens, and occasional 18th- or 19th-century churches. Charmouth, more so than Chideock, boasts a small-scale collection of unusual antique shops. Both villages are less than a mile from the western edge of Chesil Beach, one of the Hampshire coast's most famous (and longest) beaches. Although it's covered with shingle (sharp rocks), and hard on your feet if you go bathing, the beach nonetheless provides 5 miles of sweeping views toward France.

## EXPLORING LYME REGIS

Today, one of the town's most visible spokespersons is Richard J. Fox, three-time world champion Town Crier who, although now retired, still does the walks. Famed for his declamatory delivery of official (and sometimes irreverent) proclamations, he followed a 1,000-year-old tradition of newscasting. Dressed as Thomas Payne, a dragoon who died in Lyme Regis in 1644 during the Civil War, Mr. Fox leads visitors on a $1^1/_2$-hour walk around the town every Tuesday at 3pm, beginning at Guildhall, mentioned below. No reservations are necessary; the price is £1.50 ($2.40) for adults and £1.20 ($1.90) for children. He can be reached on the premises of **Country Stocks,** 53 Broad St. (☎ **01297/443568**). This shop sells such wares as sweets, antiques, and gifts and is open daily from 10am to 5pm.

Another famous building is **The Guildhall,** Bridge Street, whose Mary and John Wing (built in 1620) houses the completed sections of an enormous tapestry woven by local women. Depicting Britain's colonization of North America, it's composed of a series of 11- by 4-foot sections, each of which took a team of local women 11 months to weave. Admission is free, but if anyone wants to add a stitch to the final tapestry as a kind of charitable donation, it costs £1 ($1.60). Open Monday through Friday from 10am to 4pm, but only if someone is working on the tapestry.

The surrounding area is a fascinating place for botanists and zoologists because of the predominance of blue lias, a sedimentary rock well suited to the formation of fossils. In 1810, Mary Anning (at the age of 11) discovered one of the first articulated ichthyosaur skeletons. She went on to become one of the first professional fossilists in England. Books outlining walks in the area and the regions where fossils can be studied are available at the local information bureau.

# WHERE TO STAY
## In Chideock

**Betchworth House.** Main St., Chideock, Dorset DT6 6JW. ☎ **01297/489478.** 6 rms, 4 with bath. £17 ($27.20) per person all rms. All rates include English breakfast. No credit cards. Bus: no. 31 from Dorchester.

At the edge of the village is a 17th-century guest house on the main road. The homey (homely, Brits would say) accommodations are always immaculate. There's a large parking area just opposite the house and a walled garden in back of the building.

**Chideock House Hotel.** Main St., Chideock, Dorset DT6 6JN. ☎ **01297/489242.** 9 rms. TV. £35 ($56) single; £50–£70 ($80–$112) double. All rates include English breakfast. AE, MC, V. Bus: no. 31 from Dorchester.

In a village of winners, this 15th-century thatched house is the prettiest. The house quartered the Roundheads in 1645, and the ghosts of the village martyrs still haunt, as their trial was held at the hotel. The resident owners are Anna and George Dunn. Set on the road on the main street with a protective stone wall, the house has a garden in back, and a driveway leads to a large parking area. The beamed lounge has two fireplaces, one an Adams fireplace with a wood-burning blaze on cool days. All the bedrooms have hot-beverage facilities. The restaurant, serving both French and English cuisine, offers a la carte dining daily from 7 to 9pm.

## In Charmouth

**Newlands House.** Stonebarrow Lane, Charmouth, Dorset DT6 6RA. ☎ **01297/560212.** 12 rms, 11 with bath. TV. £21 ($33.60) single without bath; £52 ($83.20) double with bath. Rates include English breakfast. No credit cards. Closed Nov–Feb.

Newlands House stands on the periphery of the village off A35 and within walking distance of the beach. Originally a 16th-century farmhouse, it's set in 1¹/₂ acres of grounds at the foot of Stonebarrow Hill, which is part of the National Trust Golden Cap Estate. The hotel draws favorable reports from readers for its centrally heated bedrooms that are equipped with hot-beverage facilities. Children under 6 are not allowed. Cordon Bleu meals are served, costing £14 ($22.40) and up.

⊗ **Queen's Armes Hotel.** The Street, Charmouth, Dorset DT6 6QF. ☎ **01297/560339.** 11 rms. TV. £28 ($44.80) per person single or double. All rates include English breakfast. MC, V. Closed Nov to mid-Feb.

For those who like a bit of history with their hotel, try this: Catherine of Aragon, the first of Henry VIII's six wives and the daughter of Ferdinand and Isabella of Spain, stayed at this hotel near the sea. The year was 1501 and she'd arrived at nearby Plymouth and was on her way to marry the future king, Henry VIII. A small medieval house, it also figured in the flight of the defeated King Charles with the Roundheads in hot pursuit. The Queen's Armes' hidden virtues include a rear flower garden, oak-beamed interiors, a dining room with dark-oak tables and Windsor chairs, and a living room with Regency armchairs and antiques. There is no smoking in bedrooms. For an additional £12 to £14 ($19.20 to $22.40) per person, you can have dinner here. The hotel specializes in well-prepared English and French fare, and there's also a vegetarian menu.

## IN LYME REGIS

**Coverdale Guesthouse.** Woodmead Rd., Lyme Regis, Dorset DT7 3AB. ☎ **01297/442882.** 8 rms. £16 ($25.60) single without bath, £29–£30 ($46.40–$48) double without bath, £34–£36 ($54.40–$57.60) double with bath. All rates include breakfast. No credit cards. Closed Oct–Feb.

This house, built in the 1920s, is set in a residential neighborhood about 5 minutes from the center of town and the waterfront. Jenny and Ivan Harding run this pretty and inviting home, with its large bay windows with a view of the sea at the front of the house and a small garden out back. The comfortable rooms are all nonsmoking, with central heating. There is a lounge with a television and a dining room where dinners are offered at £9 ($14.40) per person if arranged in advance.

**The White House.** 47 Silver St., Lyme Regis, Dorset DT7 3HR. ☎ **01297/443420.** 7 rms, all with shower only. TV. £34–£42 ($54.40–$67.20) double. All rates include English breakfast. No credit cards. Closed Oct–Mar.

John and Ann Edmondson run this small, centrally heated, well-maintained guest house, which is only a few minutes' walk from the harbor. (It's on the B3175 Axminster–Lyme Regis road.) The attractively furnished house has twin and double rooms, all with hot-beverage facilities. A large lounge is set aside for residents, and there is a private parking area.

# WHERE TO EAT
## IN CHIDEOCK

**George Inn.** On A35, in Chideock. ☎ **01297/489419.** Reservations required. Main courses £2.80–£12.95 ($4.50–$20.70); fixed-price Sun lunch £6.95 ($11.10). MC, V. Daily noon–2pm and 6:30–9:30pm. ENGLISH.

Dating from 1685, this is the oldest hostelry in Chideock, 22 miles west of Dorchester. The owners, Mike and Marilyn Tuck, offer food in the bar, including stuffed omelets, stuffed chicken breast, succulent Dorset steaks, stuffed trout, and chicken chasseur, plus other daily specials and a range of homemade desserts. Many vegetarian meals are offered. The George Inn has two large bars, a comfortable family room, and a 60-seat restaurant.

## IN LYME REGIS

**Pilot Boat Inn.** Bridge St. ☎ **01297/443157.** Reservations recommended. Main courses £3.75–£11.50 ($6–$18.40). V. Daily noon–10pm. Pub: Mon–Sat 10am–11pm; Sun noon–10:30pm. ENGLISH.

Built in 1844, and once a hangout for some of the region's most notorious smugglers, this is the best pub in Lyme Regis. Its lounge bar, accented with a somber local stone known as blue lais, has a nautical decor and views of the River Lyme. Pub fare consists of fresh sandwiches made of locally caught crab, as well as a hot soup of the day. Hot main dishes are likely to include the ubiquitous steak-and-kidney pie and a sea grill. The catch of the day is usually written on a chalk-board menu, and the restaurant also features a special children's menu, as well as a vegetarian menu with at least eight offerings. Desserts are in the old-fashioned English tradition.

## 9 Sherborne

128 miles SW of London; 19 miles NW of Dorchester

A little gem of a town with well-preserved medieval, Tudor, Stuart, and Georgian buildings still standing, Sherborne is in the heart of Dorset, surrounded by wooded hills, valleys, and chalk downs. It was here that Sir Walter Raleigh lived before his fall from fortune.

## ESSENTIALS

**GETTING THERE**   Frequent trains throughout the day depart from London's Waterloo Station. The trip takes 2 hours.

There is one National Express coach departure daily from London's Victoria Coach Station. Call ☎ **0990/808080** for information and schedules.

If you're driving, take M3 west from London, continuing southwest on 303 and B3145.

**VISITOR INFORMATION**   The **Tourist Information Centre** is on Digby Road (☎ **01935/815341**). Open mid-March to mid-October, Monday through Saturday from 9:30am to 5:30pm; mid-October to mid-March, Monday through Saturday from 10am to 3pm.

## EXPLORING SHERBORNE

In addition to the attractions listed below, you can go to **Cerne Abbas,** a village south of Sherborne, to see the Pitchmarket, where Thomas and Maria Washington, uncle and aunt of America's George Washington, once lived.

**Sherborne Old Castle.** Castleton, off A30, half a mile east of Sherborne. ☎ **01935/812730.** Admission £1.50 ($2.40) adults; £1.10 ($1.75) seniors and students; £.80 ($1.30) children 5–16; free for children 4 and under. Apr–Oct daily 10am–6pm; Nov–Mar Wed–Sun 10am–4pm. Follow the signs 1 mile east from the town center.

The castle was built in the early 12th century by the powerful Bishop Roger de Caen, but it was seized by the Crown at about the time of King Henry I's death in 1135 and Stephen's troubled accession to the throne. The castle was given to Sir Walter Raleigh by Queen Elizabeth I. The gallant knight built Sherborne Lodge in the deer park close by (now privately owned). The buildings were mostly destroyed in the Civil War, but you can still see a gate house, some graceful arcades, and decorative windows.

**Sherborne Castle.** Cheap St. (off New Rd. a mile east of the center). ☎ **01935/813182.** Castle and grounds £4.80 ($7.70) adults; £2.40 ($3.85) children; £4 ($6.40) seniors; £12 ($19.20) family ticket (2 adults, 2 children). Grounds only £2.40 ($3.85) adults; £1.20 ($1.90) children. Easter Sat–last Sat in Sept Thurs, Sat–Sun, and bank holidays 12:30–5pm.

Sir Walter Raleigh built this castle in 1594, when he decided that it would not be feasible to restore the old castle to suit his needs. This Elizabethan residence was a square mansion, to which later owners added four Jacobean wings to make it more palatial. After King James I had Raleigh imprisoned in the Tower of London, the monarch gave the castle to a favorite Scot, Robert Carr, and banished the Raleighs from their home. In 1617, it became the property of Sir John Digby, first earl of Bristol, and has been the Digby family home ever since. The mansion was enlarged by Sir John in 1625, and in the 18th century the formal Elizabethan gardens and fountains of the Raleighs were altered by Capability Brown, who created a serpentine lake between the two castles. The 20 acres of lawns and pleasure grounds around the 50-acre lake are open to the public. In the house are fine furniture, china, and paintings by Gainsborough, Lely, Reynolds, Kneller, and Van Dyck, among others.

**Sherborne Abbey.** Abbey Close. ☎ **01935/812452.** Free admission but donations for up-keep welcomed. Apr–Sept daily 9am–6pm; Oct–Mar daily 9am–4pm.

One of the great churches of England, this abbey was founded in 705 as the Cathedral of the Saxon Bishops of Wessex. In the late 10th century it became a Benedictine monastery, and since the Reformation it has been a parish church. It's famous for its fan-vaulted roof, added by Abbot Ramsam at the end of the 15th century; this was the first fan vault of wide span erected in England. Inside are many fine monuments, including Purbeck marble effigies of medieval abbots as well as Elizabethan "four-poster" and canopied tombs. The baroque statue of the earl of Bristol stands between his two wives and dates from 1698. A public school occupies the abbey's surviving medieval monastic buildings and was the setting for a novel by Alec Waugh, *The Loom of Youth,* and for the MGM classic film *Goodbye, Mr. Chips,* starring Robert Donat. The most recent film shot here was Terence Rattigan's *The Browning Version,* starring Albert Finney.

## WHERE TO STAY

**The Alders.** Sanford Orcas, near Sherborne, Dorset DT9 4SB. ☎ **01963/220666.** 3 rms. TV. £18.50–£21 ($29.60–$33.60) double. All rates include breakfast. No credit cards. From town take A3148 toward Marston Magna; after 2¹/₂ miles take signposted turning to Sanford Orcas. At T-junction in village turn left toward Manor House.

The Alders offers the peace and quiet of the picture-postcard village of Sanford Orcas, yet it is only a few minutes from Sherborne. The attractively furnished, non-smoking bedrooms with modern bathrooms also offer color TVs, beverage-making equipment, and electric shaver outlets. A lounge for guests overlooks the garden. A traditional breakfast is served family style at one large table.

**The Antelope Hotel.** Greenhill, Sherborne, Dorset DT9 4EP. ☎ **01935/812077.** Fax 01935/816473. 19 rms. TV TEL. £35–£50 ($56–$80) single; £40–£65 ($64–$104) double. All rates include English breakfast. AE, DC, MC, V.

This personally run, family-type hotel is in the historic district of Sherborne on A30. The inn dates from the 18th century. It's a good base for touring the area and has comfortably furnished bedrooms. The hotel operates an "Olde Worlde" Bar and the Greenhill Restaurant, where English and continental meals cost £5.50 ($8.80) and up.

**Half Moon Toby Hotel.** Half Moon St., Sherborne, Dorset DT9 3LN. ☎ **01935/812017.** 16 rms. TV TEL. £40 ($64) single; £44 ($70.40) double. All rates include English breakfast. AE, DC, MC, V.

Centrally located in Sherborne, across from the abbey, the Half Moon is in a red-brick, 17th-century building with a long history of its own. It was originally built as a coaching inn but has been considerably upgraded and modernized over the years. The guest rooms are well furnished and comfortable. The Toby Carving Room, open Tuesday through Sunday from noon to 2pm and daily from 6 to 10pm, offers one of the best food values in town at a cost of £10 ($16) for a meal. Jazz evenings are presented on alternate Saturdays.

## 10 Shaftesbury

100 miles SW of London; 29 miles NE of Dorchester

The origins of this typical Dorsetshire market town date back to the 9th century when King Alfred founded the abbey and made his daughter the first abbess. King Edward the Martyr was buried here, and King Canute died in the abbey but was buried in Winchester. Little now remains of the abbey, but the ruins are beautifully laid out.

The museum adjoining St. Peter's Church at the top of Gold Hill provides a good idea of what the ancient Saxon hilltop town was like.

Today, ancient cottages with thatched roofs and tiny paned windows line the steep cobbled streets and modern stores compete with the outdoor market on High Street and the cattle market off Christy's Lane. The town is an excellent center from which to visit Hardy Country (it appears as Shaston in *Jude the Obscure*), Stourhead Gardens, and Longleat House. (The gardens and house are covered in chapter 12.)

## ESSENTIALS

**GETTING THERE** There is no direct train access, so you'll have to take the Exeter train leaving from London's Waterloo Station to Gillingham in Dorset, where a 4-mile bus or taxi ride to Shaftesbury awaits you. Trains from London run every 2 hours. Bus connections are possible from London's Victoria Coach Station once a day. There are also two or three daily connections from Bristol, Bath, Bournemouth, and Salisbury. The tourist office (see below) keeps up-to-date transportation hookups in the area. If you're driving, head west from London on M3, continuing along A303 until the final approach by A350.

**VISITOR INFORMATION** The **Tourist Information Centre** is at 8 Bell St. (☎ **01747/853514**). Open April through October, daily from 10am to 5pm; and from November through March, Monday through Friday from 10am to 1pm and on Saturday from 10am to 5pm.

## EXPLORING SHAFTESBURY

Much of Shaftesbury's bucolic allure centers on a (fiercely protected) hearkening back to the agrarian days of Olde England. A promenade on Gold Hill, a steep cobbled hill, is lined on one side with the thatched cottages so evocative of the British countryside. Traffic is prohibited on the road, except for residents of the houses near the top.

Equally charming are the ruins of **Shaftesbury Abbey,** Park Walk, whose boundaries flank one edge of Gold Hill. Founded in 888 by King Alfred—who appointed his daughter, Aethlgeofu, as its first abbess—it was closed during the dissolution of the monasteries in 1539 by Henry VIII, and later fell into ruin. Over the centuries, its stones were used widely for other building projects throughout the town, including those houses on Gold Hill. Excavations of the site continue to this day, but during warm weather, from April 1 to October 30, you can visit the abbey daily from 10am to 5pm. Admission is £1 ($1.60) for adults and 75p ($1.20) for students.

### TEATIME

**King Alfred's Kitchen,** 15 High St. (☎ **01747/852147**), probably should have been named after King Canute who died here or King Edward whose remains were brought here after his murder at Corfe Castle. Nevertheless, it's still the best place in town for tea, lying in an antique house with low ceiling beams. At the top of Gold Hill, this building with its fireplaces and old settle dates back to the 15th century. Afternoon tea costs £4.50 ($7.20), and you can also order a selection of sandwiches, moist cakes, scones, and pastries, along with such teas as Earl Grey or Lapsang Souchong.

Near Shaftesbury in Dorset, on the A350 Blandford road, 20 miles from Warminster, is the **Milestones Tea Room,** Compton Abbas (☎ **01747/811360**). This is really the ideal English tearoom, with a summer garden and a splashing fountain. This 17th-century thatched-cottage tearoom stands right next to the church, and has views over the Dorset hills. The spotless little place is presided over by Ann and

Roy Smith, who serve real farmhouse teas or a ploughman's lunch. Fresh sandwiches are also offered. Open April through October, Friday through Wednesday.

## WHERE TO STAY

**King John Inn.** Tollard Royal, near Shaftesbury, SP5 5PS. ☎ **01725/516207.** 3 rms. TV. £40 ($64) double. All rates include breakfast. MC, V. From Shaftesbury take A3081 to Ringwod Rd., then go up Zigzag Hill and follow the signposts to Tollard Royal. Once in Tollard Royal, take 1st turn left to King John.

Richard Holmes and Diana Campbell own this village house which is located in Tollard Royal, only 7 miles from Shaftesbury. The nonsmoking and comfortably furnished bedrooms are equipped with TVs and beverage-making facilities. The bar and restaurant provide a cozy atmosphere with exposed beams in the ceiling and open fireplaces. Home-cooked meals and locally brewed ales are served in the restaurant.

**The Knoll.** Bleke St., Shaftesbury, Dorset, SP7 8AH. ☎ **01747/855243.** 3 rms, 1 with private bath, 2 with shower. TV. £22 ($35.20) double. All rates include breakfast. No credit cards. Closed Christmas.

This friendly Victorian family house has a large garden with lovely views and a gallery of watercolors painted by owner Bryan Pickard. This nonsmoking facility has been restored by Bryan and his wife Kate who have charmingly decorated the bedrooms and added many special touches designed for your comfort. Breakfast is served in a room overlooking the garden. The house is only a 3-minute walk from the town center and a choice of restaurants.

**Paynes Place Barn.** New Rd., Shaftesbury, Dorset, SP7 8QL. ☎ and fax **01747/855016.** 3 rms. TV. £25–£30 ($40–$48) single; £40–£44 ($64–$70.40) double. All rates include breakfast. No credit cards. Closed Christmas.

This converted stone barn has a magnificent view of the Blackmoor Vale and is in walking distance from the town center. This nonsmoking facility is furnished with all the comforts of home, including TVs and drink-making equipment in the bedrooms. One ground floor room is available. There is a cozy guest lounge, and the traditional English breakfast is served family style around one table.

**Vale Mount.** 17A Salisbury St., Shaftesbury, Dorset SP7 8EL. ☎ **01747/852991.** 5 rms, 1 with shower. £15–£16 ($24–$25.60) single; £30–£32 ($48–$51.20) double. All rates include English breakfast. No credit cards. Parking free nearby.

About 2 minutes from the heart of town, this comfortable, pleasantly furnished house is a good bargain. Several of the rooms were recently redecorated. It's open all year. A free parking area is nearby. Because rooms, especially inexpensive ones, are very limited around Shaftesbury in summer, it's wise to make reservations ahead of time.

## WHERE TO EAT

**Half Moon.** Salisbury Rd. ☎ **02747/852456.** Main courses £5.50–£10 ($8.80–$16). MC, V. Mon–Sat noon–2:30pm and 6:30–9:30pm, Sun 7–9:30pm. BRITISH/INDIAN.

Located about a half mile from the center of town, this local pub has a good restaurant that is popular with townspeople, many of whom come here only to drink during regular pub hours. Your best bet is to opt for one of the daily specials prepared fresh based on whatever looked good at the market. The regular menu features the usual homemade meat pies, some good steaks, a selection of vegetarian dishes, and even some Indian specialties.

**King's Arms.** Bleke St. ☎ **01747/852746.** Main courses £4–£7 ($6.50–$11.20). MC, V. Daily noon–2:30pm and 6–9:30pm. BRITISH.

In the center of town, only 2 blocks from the town hall, this pub serves traditional grub, and does so quite well. Its daily specials are made fresh in the morning, and they attract a lively lunchtime business of locals who call the fare served here "dependable." Although the King's Arms doesn't attract gourmets, its pub dishes are substantial, made with fresh ingredients, and quite tasty. There is also a selection of dishes for the vegetarian, plus what the publicans call "light bites"—meaning sandwiches and the like.

**Two Brewers.** St. James's St. ☎ **01747/82746.** Main courses £3.95–£9.95 ($6.30–$15.90). AE, DC, MC, V. Daily noon–2pm, Mon–Thurs 6–9pm, Fri–Sat 6–10pm, Sun 7–9pm. BRITISH/CONTINENTAL.

Many local B&B owners send their clients here for dinner—and sometimes even join them. Located on one of the main streets of town, this is not only one of Shaftesbury's most venerated pubs; it does a substantial restaurant business as well. For those who are accustomed to dining in England, the food here is familiar fare, including the usual array of pastas, especially a tasty lasagna. You can also order a decent chili, the inevitable scampi that seems to be featured almost everywhere, plus a number of seafood dishes and an assortment of British steaks, some from the Black Angus cattle of Scotland. Service is good, and there's a convivial atmosphere.

The great patchwork-quilt area of southwest England, part of the "West Countree," abounds in cliffside farms, rolling hills, foreboding moors, semitropical plants, and fishing villages—some of the finest scenery in England. It's easy to immerse yourself in West Country life. You can pony trek across moor and woodland, past streams and sheep-dotted fields, or relax at a local pub to soak up the atmosphere and the ales.

The British approach sunny Devon with the same kind of excitement one might reserve for hopping over to the continent. Especially along the coastline—the English Riviera—the names of seaports, villages, and resorts have long been synonymous with holidays in the sun: Torquay, Clovelly, Lynton-Lynmouth. Devon, its red cliffs in the south facing the English Channel, is a land of jagged coasts. The tranquil life prevails in south Devon, the coast from where Drake and Raleigh set sail, and on the bay-studded coastline of north Devon, where pirates and smugglers once found haven.

Much of the district is already known to those who have read *Lorna Doone,* Victorian novelist R. D. Blackmore's romance of the West Country. Aside from the shores, many scenic highlights are in the two national parks: Dartmoor in the south, Exmoor in the north. (Exmoor is covered in chapter 12.)

Almost every hamlet is geared to accommodate visitors. However, many small towns and fishing villages don't allow cars to enter; these towns have parking areas on the outskirts, and then it's a long walk to reach the center of the harbor area. From mid-July to mid-September the most popular villages are quite crowded, so make reservations for a place to stay. Perhaps your oddly shaped bedroom will be in a barton (farm) mentioned in the *Domesday Book* or in a thatched cottage.

Along the south coast, the best bases from which you can explore the region are Exeter, Plymouth, and Torquay. Along the north coast with its more limited facilities, we suggest Lynton/Lynmouth. The area's most charming village (with very limited accommodations) is Clovelly. The greatest natural spectacle is the Dartmoor National Park, northeast of Plymouth, a landscape of gorges and moors filled with gorse and purple heather—home of the Dartmoor pony.

If you're taking the bus around Devon, Stagecoach Devon and Western National bus lines combine to offer a discounted **"Key West Ticket."** Adults can enjoy unlimited use of the lines at these rates: £13.40 ($21.45) for 3 days, £22.65 ($36.25) for 7 days, or 1 month for £83.50 ($133.60). For families (two adults and two children, from 5 to 15 years old), there's only a 3-day ticket at £26.80 ($42.90) or a 7-day ticket at £38.20 ($61.10). You can plan your journeys from the maps and timetables available at any **Western National/ Devon** general office when you purchase your ticket (☎ **01752/222666**). For further information, contact **Stagecoach Devon Ltd.,** Paris Street, Exeter Devon FX1 2JP (☎ **01392/427711**).

## 1  Exeter

201 miles SW of London; 46 miles NE of Plymouth

The county town of Devonshire, Exeter, was a Roman city founded in the 1st century A.D. on the banks of the river Exe. Two centuries later it was encircled by a mighty stone wall, traces of which remain today. Conquerors and would-be conquerors, especially Vikings, stormed the fortress in later centuries; none was more notable than William the Conqueror. Irked at Exeter's refusal to capitulate (perhaps also because it sheltered Gytha, mother of the slain Harold), the Norman duke brought Exeter to its knees on short notice.

Under the Tudors, the city grew and prospered. Sir Walter Raleigh and Sir Francis Drake were two of the striking figures who strolled Exeter's streets. In May 1942, the Germans bombed Exeter, destroying many of the city's architectural treasures. Exeter was rebuilt, but the plastered walls of new, impersonal-looking shops and offices can't replace the Georgian crescents and the black-and-white-timbered buildings. Fortunately, much was spared, and Exeter still has its Gothic cathedral, a renowned university, some museums, and several historic houses.

Exeter is a good base for exploring both Dartmoor and Exmoor National Parks, two of the finest England has to offer. (Exmoor National Park is covered in chapter 12). It's also a good place to spend a day—there's a lot to do in what's left of the city's old core.

## ESSENTIALS

**GETTING THERE**  Exeter Airport (☎ **01392/367433**) serves the southwest, offering both charter and scheduled flights. Lying 5 miles east of the historic center of Exeter, the airport has a modern terminal with excellent facilities, including taxis, car rentals, bars, a food buffet, an exchange bureau, and shops. It has scheduled flights to Belfast, Jersey, Dublin, and the Isles of Scilly among other connections. There are no direct flights to London.

Trains from London's Paddington Station depart every hour during the day. The trip takes 2¹/₂ hours. Trains also run once an hour during the day between Exeter and Plymouth; the trip takes 1¹/₄ hours. Trains often arrive at Exeter Central Station on Queen Street, next to Northernhay Gardens, or else at Exeter St. David's Station at St. David's Hill. Since neither station has a direct line, you have to call Plymouth at ☎ **0345/484950** for information.

A National Express coach departs from London's Victoria Coach Station every 30 minutes during the day; the trip takes 4 hours. You can also take bus no. 38 or 39 between Plymouth and Exeter. During the day, two coaches depart per hour for the 1-hour trip. For information and schedules, call ☎ **0990/808080.**

If you're driving from London, take M4 west, cutting south to Exeter on M5 (junction near Bristol).

# Devon

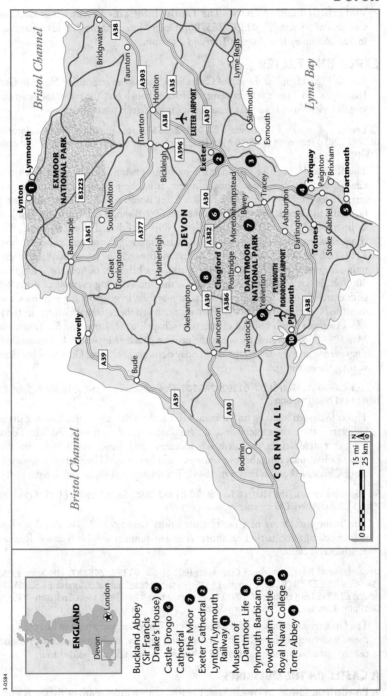

Bristol Channel

EXMOOR NATIONAL PARK

DARTMOOR NATIONAL PARK

CORNWALL

DEVON

Lynmouth
Lynton
Bridgwater
Taunton
Honiton
Lyme Regis
Sidmouth
Exmouth
Tiverton
Bickleigh
South Molton
Barnstaple
Great Torrington
Hatherleigh
Okehampton
Launceston
Tavistock
Yelverton
Postbridge
Moretonhampstead
Bovey Tracey
Ashburton
Dartington
Stoke Gabriel
Totnes
Paignton
Torquay
Brixham
Dartmouth
Exeter
Bodmin
Bude
Clovelly

EXETER AIRPORT

ROBOROUGH AIRPORT

PLYMOUTH
Plymouth

Chagford

A38 A303 A35 A30 A38 A396 A30 A382 A386 A39 A361 A377 B3223 A30

15 mi
25 km
0

ENGLAND
London
Devon

Buckland Abbey (Sir Francis Drake's House) 9
Castle Drogo 6
Cathedral of the Moor 7
Exeter Cathedral 2
Lynton/Lynmouth Railway 1
Museum of Dartmoor Life 8
Plymouth Barbican 10
Powderham Castle 3
Royal Naval College 4
Torre Abbey 5

3-0584

**VISITOR INFORMATION**   The **Tourist Information Centre** is at the Civic Centre, Paris Street (☎ **01392/265700**). Open Monday through Friday from 9am to 5pm, Saturday from 9am to 1pm and 2 to 5pm.

## EXPLORING EXETER

Just off "The High," at the top of Castle Street, stands an impressive **Norman Gate House** from William the Conqueror's Castle. Although only the house and walls survive, the view from here and the surrounding gardens is panoramic.

✪ **Exeter Cathedral.** 1 The Cloisters. ☎ **01392/55573.** Free admission, though a donation of £2 ($3.20) is requested of adults. Mon–Fri 7:30am–6:15pm; Sat 7:30am–6:30pm; Sun 8am–7:30pm.

The Roman II Augusta Legion made its camp on the site where the Cathedral Church of Saint Peter now stands in Exeter. It has been occupied by Britons, Saxons, Danes, and Normans. The English Saint Boniface, who converted northern Germany to Christianity, was trained here in 690. Bishop Leofric was installed here as bishop for Devon and Cornwall in 1050 by Edward the Confessor. The conqueror's nephew, Bishop Warelwast, began building the present cathedral about 1112, and the twin Norman towers still stand. Between the towers runs the longest uninterrupted true gothic vault in the world, at a height of 66 feet and a length of 300 feet. It was completed in 1369 and is the finest existing example of decorated gothic architecture, featuring rare tierceron arches, large matching windows, and decorated corbels and bosses. The Puritans destroyed the cathedral Cloisters in 1655, and a German bomb finished off the twin Chapels of St. James and St. Thomas in May 1942. Now restored, it's one of the prettiest churches anywhere. Its famous choir sings evensong every day except Wednesday during school term. On school holidays, visiting choirs perform.

**Exeter Guildhall.** High St. ☎ **01392/265500.** Free admission. Mon–Sat 10:30am–5pm. It's best to call before visiting.

This colonnaded building on the main street is the oldest municipal building in the kingdom—the earliest reference to the guildhall is in a deed from 1160. The Tudor front that straddles the pavement was added in 1593. Inside you'll find a fine display of silver, plus a number of paintings, including one of Henrietta Anne, daughter of Charles I (born in Exeter in 1644). The ancient hall is paneled in oak.

**St. Nicholas Priory.** The Mint, off Fore St. ☎ **01392/265858.** Admission £1.25 ($2) adults; 75p ($1.20) children. Call for opening arrangements.

This is the guest wing of a Benedictine priory founded in 1070. You'll see fine plaster ceilings and period furniture. A recent summer exhibit featured Russian ceramics and crafts.

**Underground Passages.** Boots Corner, off High St. ☎ **01392/265887.** Admission £2.50 ($4.00) adults; £1.50 ($2.40) children; £6 ($9.60) family ticket. July and August: £3.50 ($5.60) adults; £2.25 ($3.60) children; £9.00 ($14.40) family ticket. July–Sept, Mon–Sat 10am–4:45pm; Oct–June, Tues–Fri 2–5pm, Sat 10am–5pm.

The Underground Passages, accessible from High Street, were built to carry the medieval water supply into the city. By entering the new underground interpretation center, visitors can view a video and exhibition before taking a guided tour.

## A CASTLE ON THE OUTSKIRTS

**Powderham Castle,** in Powderham, Kenton, some 8 miles south of Exeter, is a private house occupied by the Countess and Earl of Devon, who let Ismail Merchant and James Ivory use their home as a setting for the film *Remains of the Day*, starring

Anthony Hopkins and Emma Thompson. It was built in the late 14th century by Sir Philip Courtenay, sixth son of the second earl of Devon, and his wife, Margaret, granddaughter of Edward I. Their magnificent tomb is in the south transept of Exeter Cathedral. The castle suffered damage during the Civil War and was restored and altered in the 18th and 19th centuries.

The castle has many family portraits and fine furniture, including a remarkable clock that plays full tunes at 4pm, 8pm, and midnight, some 17th-century tapestries, and a chair used by William III for his first council of state at Newton Abbot. The staircase hall contains some remarkable plasterwork set in bold relief against a turquoise background, more than 2 centuries old, as well as a detailed pedigree of the Courtenay family, a document more than 12 feet high. The chapel dates from the 15th century, with hand-hewn roof timbers and carved pew ends.

To get to the castle, take the A379 Dawlish road 8 miles south of Exeter; the castle is signposted. It's open Easter through October, Sunday to Friday from 10am to 5:30pm. Admission is £4.95 ($7.90) for adults, £4.45 ($7.10) for seniors, £2.85 ($4.55) for children 5 to 17, free for children 4 and under. For information, call ☎ **01626/890243.**

## SHOPPING

Exeter has long been famous for its silver—in fact, until 1882 it was the silver-assay office for the entire West Country. If you seek, ye shall find old Exeter silver, especially spoons, still sold in local stores. The best merchant for this is **William Burford,** 1 Bedford St. (☎ **01392/54901**), a family business specializing in good antique silver and English made jewelry. You can find spoons dating earlier than the 19th century; look for the three castle mark of Exeter to be sure you're getting the real thing.

**David Trivett Jewelry,** 13A Guildhall Precinct (☎ **01392/276224**), carries antique jewelry as well as secondhand designer jewelry. They also carry original designs by artisans who work in the store or can create a piece that you have designed.

There are a number of antique dealers in Exeter, with at least six on The Quay off Western Way. **The Quay Gallery Antiques Emporium** (☎ **01392/213283**) houses 10 dealers who sell furniture, porcelain, metalware, and other collectibles. **The Antique Centre on the Quay** (☎ **01392/214180**) has 20 dealers. Books and postcards are popular items here.

The **Edinburgh Woolen Mill,** 23 Cathedral Yard (☎ **01392/412318**), carries a large selection of woolen goods, as the name implies. Here you'll find kilts, Aran jumpers, tartan travel rugs, and quality wool suites for women. There is also a daily market on **Sidwell Street,** Exeter's version of an American flea market.

## WHERE TO STAY

Established as a college in the 19th century, and upgraded to university status in the 1950s, **Exeter University,** Birks Hall, New North Road (☎ **0139/221-1500**), offers economical accommodations to the general public in several of its dormitories during Easter break and all summer. A private room will cost you £12.50 ($20), and a private room with a washbasin, laundry facilities, and a cafeteria-style breakfast runs £19 ($30.40) per person. Either choice entitles you to use the sports facilities, which include tennis, squash, badminton, and a heated pool. You can roam the 300 acres of grounds and gardens that make up the school.

Another cheap place to stay is the 90-bed **Exeter YHA Youth Hostel,** 47 Countess Ware Rd., Devon EX2 6LR (☎ **01392/873329**), which offers both dormitory beds and camp sites. It's located on the city outskirts, 2 miles to the south, east off Topsham Road. From the High Street, minibus K or T runs here. On the River Exe, this is a rather inviting hostel with thatch roofs and, beyond, sheep in the meadow. An overnight stay costs £9.40 ($15.05) for adults or £6.30 ($10.10) for those 18 or under, including a hearty English breakfast for £2.85 ($4.55) extra. Ten sites are rented for £6.30 ($10.10) per person. The hostel has 12 showers, laundry facilities, and storage lockers. Check-in time is from 5 to 10:30pm. Once checked in, there is no curfew, as in most hostels, since night doormen are here to let you back in. The hostel closes for 3 weeks in December, and accepts MasterCard and Visa.

## DOUBLES FOR LESS THAN £40

**Claremont.** 36 Wonford Rd., Exeter, Devon EX21 4LD. ☎ **01392/274699.** 2 rms, both with bath; 1 suite. TV. £27 ($43.20) single; £38 ($60.80) double; £64 ($102.40) suite for 4. All rates include English breakfast. No credit cards. Bus: H.

This Regency-style 1840 town house is in a quiet residential part of the city close to the center. The bedrooms are well kept and have beverage-making equipment. Geoff and Jacqueline Self, who run the property, assist visitors in many ways. Nonsmokers only, please.

**Lea-Dene.** 34 Alphington Rd. (A3777), St. Thomas, Exeter, Devon EX2 8HN. ☎ **01392/ 57257.** 11 rms, none with bath. TV. £20–£22 ($32–$35.20) single; £32–£34 ($51.20–$54.40) double. All rates include English breakfast. No credit cards. Blue minibus D from the center.

This Victorian-style guest house was built of red brick before 1930. Set in a southern suburb, a 10- to 15-minute walk from the town center, it contains many original details. The rooms are simply but comfortably furnished. Owners Mr. and Mrs. Colin Foster offer a hearty breakfast.

**Park View Hotel.** 8 Howell Rd., Exeter, Devon EX4 4LG. ☎ **01392/271772.** Fax 01392/ 253047. 15 rms, 10 with bath. TV TEL. £20 ($32) single without bath, £28 ($44.80) single with bath; £35 ($56) double without bath, £43 ($68.80) double with bath. All rates include English breakfast. AE, MC, V.

This landmark Georgian house, near the heart of town and the train station, offers comfortable but plainly furnished bedrooms. Guests take their breakfast in a cozy room opening onto the hotel's garden. Breakfast is the only meal served, but the staff will prepare a packed lunch for touring.

**Trees Mini Hotel.** 2 Queen's Crescent, York Rd., Exeter, Devon EX4 6AY. ☎ **01392/59531.** 12 rms, 1 with bath. TV. £16 ($25.60) single without bath; £28–£30 ($44.80–$48) double without bath, £35 ($56) double with bath. All rates include English breakfast. No credit cards.

This "mini-hotel" lies about a 5-minute walk from the city center, on a quiet street near a small park and the bus station. A red-brick building designed as a private home around the turn of the century, it contains simple but cozy bedrooms, each with tea-making facilities and washbasins. Valerie Daniel, your host, prepares evening meals for around £7 ($11.20) for guests who notify her in advance.

## NEARBY PLACES TO STAY

**Down House.** Whimple, Exeter, Devon EX5 2QR. ☎ **01404/822860.** 9 rms, 2 with bath. TV. £20 ($32) single without bath, £22–£24 ($35.20–$38.40) single with bath; £40 ($64) double without bath, £44–£48 ($70.40–$76.80) double with bath. All rates include English breakfast. No credit cards.

Set in 5 acres of gardens and orchards, this Edwardian farmhouse is secluded and quiet. But it isn't remote—Exeter, the market town of Honiton, and the south Devon coast are all within 9 miles. Down House is an excellent base for touring the area. The well-appointed rooms and hospitable atmosphere are ideal for relaxing after a day of seeing the sights of Devon. Meals here consist of homegrown produce, locally produced eggs and milk, and fresh homemade bread. Guests enjoy wholesome English breakfasts and lively dinners with the other guests of the house.

**The Nobody Inn.** Doddiscombsleigh, near Exeter, Devon EX6 7PS. ☎ **01647/252394.** Fax 01647/252978. 7 rms, 5 with bath. TV TEL. £23 ($36.80) single without bath, £35 ($56) single with bath; £48 ($76.80) double without bath, £59 ($94.40) double with bath. All rates include breakfast. AE, MC, V.

Don't let the name fool you; there is always someone waiting to welcome you to The Nobody Inn. In the tricky-sounding village of Doddiscombsleigh, west of Exeter, this hotel is housed in two buildings. The manor house, where most rooms are located, has a rich history—the ancient structure was given to Ralph de Doddiscomb by King Richard during the holy wars. There are two rooms in the main body of the inn, along with the restaurant and bar. In the bar, which serves lunch and dinner daily, visitors will find an extensive selection of wines and spirits in addition to traditional English dishes such as venison or steak-and-kidney pie. The more formal restaurant is open Tuesday through Saturday for dinner. The inn does not accommodate children under 14.

**Lord Haldon Hotel.** Kings Dr., Dunchideock, near Exeter, Devon EX6 7YF. ☎ **01392/ 832483.** Fax 01392/833765. 21 rms. TV TEL. £39.50 ($63.20) single; £64.50 ($103.20) double. All rates include English breakfast. MC, V.

If you're driving, your best bet might be this hotel 4 miles southwest of Exeter. Constructed in 1735 as a smaller version of what was then Buckingham Palace, this was the seat of the lords of Haldon. A major part of the original structure was destroyed in this century, but the remaining wing has been converted into a country-house hotel that still retains an archway created by 18th-century architect Sir Robert Adam. Most rooms have countryside views, and they all contain hot-beverage facilities. There are four rooms with four-poster beds. Fresh local produce is used for the traditional British dishes that are served in the elegant Chandelier Restaurant, offering a table d'hôte menu for £17.50 ($28).

**Wigham.** Morchard Bishop, Crediton, North Devon EX17 6RJ. ☎ **01363/877350.** 5 rms, all with bath. TV. £39–£46 ($62.40–$73.60) single; £55–£69 ($88–$110.40) double. All rates include English breakfast and 3-course dinner. AE, MC, V.

This thatched Elizabethan longhouse is situated on 30 acres of farmland, 8 miles northwest of Exeter along A377. Stephen and Dawn Chilcott renovated in the late 1980s with hand-hewn furniture and tapestries scattered throughout. While the renovation included the addition of bathrooms to all bedrooms, the structure's cob walls were kept intact. The property includes a heated outdoor swimming pool. Mr. and Mrs. Chilcott offer nonsmoking guests a taste of the country with organically grown produce and livestock—beef and dairy cattle, sheep, pigs, and chickens. Dawn prepares a home-style menu that includes modern English and Mediterranean influences. Communal meals are served at a large elm refectory table and include dishes such as Spanish beef with garlic and onion and a traditional roast lamb braised in wine. Dinners are at 8pm.

# WHERE TO EAT

**Coolings Wine Bar.** 11 Gandy St. ☎ **01392/434184.** Soups £1.95 ($3.10); main courses £3.95–£4.95 ($6.30–$7.90). MC, V. Mon–Sat 11am–11pm. Bus: N. ENGLISH.

Set in a Victorian building on a short cobblestone street that intersects Exeter's High Street near the town center, this is a welcoming place with beams, checkered tablecloths, and tables that spill over into the cellar. The food, prepared on the premises, includes a plentiful selection of meats, pies, and quiches, as well as such changing specialties as chicken Waldorf and sugar-baked ham, each served with freshly prepared salads. There's nothing experimental here—just hearty Devonshire cookery. Wine by the glass includes many dozens of vintages from throughout Europe. Liquor is served Monday through Saturday from 11am to 11pm; however, the full menu is available only at lunch, noon to 2:30pm. After that, a salad bar is served until 4pm and a more limited menu, mainly pub snacks, is offered throughout the afternoon and evening.

**Herbie's Whole Food Restaurant.** 15 North St. ☎ **0139/258473.** Meals £3.75–£4.95 ($6–$7.90). No credit cards. Mon–Fri 11am–2:30pm; Sat 10:30am–4pm; Tues–Sat 6–9:30pm. VEGETARIAN.

This is your best bet not only for the most generous portions of vegetarian fare—and the lowest prices—but as a chance to meet counterculture Exeter, especially those whose lives are attached to the lively Exeter and Devon Arts Centre. Herbie's is known by its trademark sign in front. Homemade meals are the feature here, along with the town's largest variety of vegetarian dishes.

**Port Royal Inn.** The Quay at Larkbeare Rd. ☎ **01392/272360.** Main courses £3.45–£5.95 ($5.50–$9.50). MC, V. Daily 11am–11pm. (Pub: Mon–Sat 11am–11pm; Sun noon–3pm and 7:30–10:30pm.) Blue minibus: R, K, or S. ENGLISH.

With a flowering patio at the edge of the River Exe, this antique pub, a 10-minute walk northeast of the town center, was built in the 1790s as a boat-repair shop. During warm weather, drinkers and diners congregate on the outdoor patio, where a landing stage extends out into the river. The owners pride themselves on stocking 10 types of real ale, some on tap, at all times. Brands rotate. Salads are tempting, and you can order a pâté and toast. Sandwiches made from granary bread are filled with meat or cheese. Two or three hot specials are served on Sundays and may include seafood, roast chicken, or roast lamb. There are also desserts and a good selection of ports and sherries. All food is ordered at the pub but will be delivered to your table.

✪ **The Ship Inn.** St. Martin's Lane. ☎ **01392/272040.** Reservations recommended. Main courses £6–£12 ($9.60–$19.20); pub platters £3–£6 ($4.80–$9.60). MC, V. Restaurant: Wed–Sat noon–3pm and 6–9:30pm. Pub: Mon–Sat 11am–3pm; Sun noon–2pm. Bar: Mon–Sat 11am–11pm; Sun noon–10:30pm. ENGLISH.

The Ship Inn, in the town center, was often visited by Sir Francis Drake, Sir Walter Raleigh, and Sir John Hawkins. Of it Drake wrote: "Next to mine own shippe, I do most love that old 'Shippe' in Exon, a tavern in Fyssh Street, as the people call it, or as the clergie will have it, St. Martin's Lane." The pub still provides tankards of real ales, lager, and stout, and is still loved by locals. A large selection of snacks is offered in the bar every day, whereas the restaurant upstairs provides more substantial but uninspired English fare. At either lunch or dinner, you can order from a wide selection including French onion soup, grilled lemon sole, and five different steaks. Portions are large.

# EXETER AFTER DARK

This lively university town offers an abundance of classical concerts and theater productions, as well as the inevitable nightclub and pub scene. For information concerning cultural events and theaters, contact the **Exeter Arts Booking and Information Centre,** Princesshay (☎ **01392/211080**), open daily from 9:30am to 5pm. They provide a monthly brochure of upcoming events. You can also purchase tickets for any of the listed events at the office.

A classical music lover's dream, the **Exeter Festival,** held for 3 weeks in July, includes more than 150 events, ranging from concerts and opera to lectures. Festival dates and offerings vary from year-to-year, and more information is available by contacting the **Exeter Festival Office,** Civic Center (☎ **01392/265118;** Internet: http//:www.exeter.ac.uk/festival).

An abundance of concerts, opera, dance, and film can be found year-round at the **Exeter & Devon Arts Centre,** Bradninch Place, Gandy Street (☎ **01392/421111**), and Exeter University's **Northcott Theatre,** Stocker Road (☎ **01392/56182**), which is also home to a professional theater company. The Northcott, a fan-shaped theater built in 1967, seats 433 people, and is designed so that there are no view obstructions anywhere in the house. Open daily from 10am until 6pm, and again at 8pm on performance nights. Admission varies, but is usually between £7 to £12 ($11.20–$19.20), with opera performances running a bit more.

For a livelier evening, head to **Volts,** The Quay (☎ **01392/211347**); info line **01392/435820**), a two-story club featuring funk, soul, hard dance, alternative, and indie music on the first floor, and The Hot House, home to disco, pop, classic, and chart music, on the second. The crowd here is young (18+), and there's a full bar and fast food available. The cover charge varies from £1 to £3 ($1.60–$4.80).

Attracting a more diverse crowd, **The Warehouse/Boxes Disco,** Commercial Road (☎ **01392/59292**), is another split club. The Boxes Disco is popular for 1970s and 1980s dance music on Wednesday, soul and jazz on Thursday, and Club 30 on Saturday, which plays motown, 1960s, and contemporary dance music for a 25+ crowd. The neighboring Warehouse gets hopping with indie, classic dance, and hip hop on Thursday. Admission of £3 ($4.80) before 10:30pm, and £5 ($8) afterward gets you into both clubs.

Catering to Exeter's gay scene, **The Lost Club,** Bartholomew Street (☎ **01392/75623**), hosts a Women's Social Group (no men allowed) on the first and third Wednesday of each month, a mixed gay and straight crowd for 1970s and 1980s dance music on Fridays, and a largely gay crowd for house dancing on Saturdays. Cover is £2 ($3.20).

Pubs vary from the ancient and haunted to the haunts of folk music fans, with the **Turks Head,** High Street (☎ **01392/56680**), offering a bit of local color, since it's housed in a 600-year-old dungeon allegedly haunted by the Turks who were tortured and killed here. The first two floors are unchanged from that bygone era, but the top three floors were turned into the existing pub more than 450 years ago. More recently, it was a favorite hangout and scribbling spot of Charles Dickens, whose favorite chair is still on display. Today, it's a lively pub with a computerized juke box and a fast food menu.

The **Well House Tavern,** Cathedral Close (☎ **01392/495365**), is part of the Royal Clarence Hotel—the first establishment in England to be called a hotel, in 1769. It's housed in a building believed to have been constructed in the 14th century, although the Roman well in the basement predates that estimate, lending credence to a debate that the building is actually even older than that. It, too, is said to be haunted—but the ghost here, affectionately called Alice, who purportedly appears in her flowing white dress, is said to be good-spirited. Join Alice and the other regulars for a pint or a light meal.

Featuring a great view of the canal, **Double Locks,** Canal Banks (☎ **01392/56947**), welcomes a varied crowd, largely students. It features live music with no cover charge 2 or 3 evenings a week, and you can get traditional pub grub to go with your pint. Although spaciously spread through a Georgian mansion, the **Imperial Pub,** New North Road (☎ **01392/434050**), is friendly to frugal travelers, with the cheapest brand-name beer in town, ranging from 85p ($1.35), and a fast-food style menu.

Bring your instrument to **The Mill on the Exe,** Bonhay Road (☎ **01392/214464**), for Tuesday evening's Exeter Folk Club, when visitors are encouraged to sit in with the three-piece house band. This place also has a reputation as a good eating pub.

## 2  Dartmoor National Park

213 miles SW of London; 13 miles W of Exeter

This national park lies northeast of Plymouth, stretching from Tavistock and Okehampton on the west to near Exeter in the east, a granite mass that sometimes rises to a height of 2,000 feet above sea level. The landscape offers vistas of gorges with rushing water, gorse, and purple heather ranged over by Dartmoor ponies—a foreboding landscape reserved for the experienced walker.

In Dartmoor, you'll find 500 miles of footpaths and bridleways and more than 90,000 acres of common land with public access. The country is rough, and on the high moor you should always make sure you have good maps, a compass, and suitable clothing and shoes.

## ESSENTIALS

**GETTING THERE**   Take the train down from London to Exeter (see above), then use local buses to connect you with the various villages of Dartmoor.

Transmoor Link, a public transport bus service, usually operates throughout the summer and is an ideal way to get onto the moor. Information on the Transmoor Link and on the bus link between various towns and villages on Dartmoor is available from the Transport Co-ordination Centre (☎ **01392/382800**).

If you're driving, Exeter is the most easily reached "gateway" by highway. From Exeter, continue west on B3212 to such centers of Dartmoor as Easton, Chagford, Moretonhampstead, and North Bovey. From these centers, tiny roads—often not really big enough for two cars—cut deeper into the moor.

**VISITOR INFORMATION**   The main source of information is the **Dartmoor National Park Tourist Information Centre,** Town Hall, Bedford Square, Tavistock (☎ **01822/612938**). It will book accommodations within a 15-mile radius for £3–£3.50 ($4.80–$5.60). Open April through October from 10am to 5pm and in summer on Sunday from 10am to 5pm.

## EXPLORING THE HAUNTING MOORS

About a third of Dartmoor is privately owned by Prince Charles; the remainder belongs mostly to the British government. Regardless of exact ownership, the region is as steeped in myth and legend as anywhere else in Britain. Crisscrossed by about 500 miles of bridle paths and hiking trails and covering about 360 square miles (180 of which comprise the Dartmoor National Park), the moors rest on a granite base with numerous rocky outcroppings.

The Dartmoor National Park Authority (DNPA) runs **guided walks** of varying difficulty, ranging from $1^{1}/_{2}$ to 6 hours for a trek of some 9 to 12 miles. All you have to do is turn up suitably clad at your selected starting point. Details are available from DNP information centers or from the **Dartmoor National Park Authority,** High Moorland Visitor Centre, Tavistock Road, Princetown, near Yelverton PL20 6QF (☎ **01822/890414**). Guided tours cost £2 ($3.20) for a 2-hour walk, £3 ($4.80) for a 3-hour walk, £3.50 ($5.60) for a 4-hour walk, and £4 ($6.40) for a 6-hour walk. These prices are subsidized by the national parks services.

Throughout the area are stables where you can arrange for a day's trek across the moors. For **horseback riding** on Dartmoor, there are too many places to list. All are licensed, and you are accompanied by an experienced rider/guide. The moor can be dangerous since sudden fogs descend without warning on treacherous marshlands. Prices are around £6 ($9.60) per hour, £13 ($20.80) for a half day, and £22 ($35.20) for a full day. Most riding stables are listed in a useful free publication, *The Dartmoor Visitor,* which also provides details on guided walks, places to go, accommodations, local events, and articles about the national park. *The Dartmoor Visitor* is obtainable from DNP information centers and tourist information centers or by mail. Send an International Reply Coupon to the DNPA headquarters (address above).

## ✪ CAMPING IN THE PARK

A few official campsites exist, but many campers prefer the open moor for the night. Since the moor is privately owned land, seek permission before camping. Only 1 night in a single spot is permitted. Campsites include Ashburton Caravan Park, Waterleat, Ashburton (☎ **01364/652552**); River Dart Country Park, Holne Park, Ashburton (☎ **01364/652511**), and Yertiz Caravan and Camping Park, Exeter Road, Okehampton (☎ **01837/52281**). Most sites are open from April through September, and charges begin at £3 ($4.80) per person.

# TOWNS IN & AROUND DARTMOOR

Some 13 miles west of Exeter, the peaceful little town of **Moretonhampstead** is perched on the edge of Dartmoor. Moretonhampstead contains an old market cross and several 17th-century colonnaded almshouses.

The much-visited Dartmoor village of **Widecombe-in-the-Moor** is only 7 miles from Moretonhampstead. The village's fame stems from an old folk song about Tom Pearce and his gray mare, listing the men who were supposed to be on their way to Widecombe Fair when they met with disaster: Bill Brewer, Jan Stewer, Peter Gurney, Peter Davy, Daniel Whiddon, Harry Hawke, and Old Uncle Tom Cobley. Widecombe also has a parish church worth visiting. Called the **Cathedral of the Moor,** with a roster of vicars beginning in 1253, the house of worship in a green valley is surrounded by legends. When the building was restored, a wall plate was found bearing the badge of Richard II (1377 to 1399), the figure of a white hart. However, the town is rather disappointing and unkempt in spite of its fame; you might want to skip it altogether.

The market town of **Okehampton** owes its existence to the Norman castle built by Baldwin de Bryonis, sheriff of Devon, under orders from his uncle, William the Conqueror, in 1068, just 2 years after the Conquest. The Courtenay family lived there for many generations until Henry VIII beheaded one of them and dismantled the castle in 1538. The **Museum of Dartmoor Life,** at the Dartmoor Centre, 3 West St., Okehampton (☎ **01837/52295**), is housed in an old mill with a waterwheel and is part of the Dartmoor Centre, a group of attractions around an old courtyard. Also here are working craft studios, a Victorian Cottage Tea Room, and a Dartmoor National Park information center. Museum displays cover all aspects of Dartmoor's history from prehistoric times, including geology, industries, living conditions, crafts, farm tools, and machinery, and some old vehicles—a Devon box wagon of 1875, a 1922 Bullnose Morris motorcar, a 1937 motorcycle. There's a reconstructed cider press, a blacksmithy, and a tourist information center. The museum is open October to Easter, Monday through Friday from 10am to 5pm and from Easter to October Monday through Saturday from 10am to 5pm. It also opens on Sunday from June through September. Admission is £1.60 ($2.55) for adults, £1.30 ($2.10) for seniors, 80p ($1.30) for children, and £4.50 ($7.20) for a family ticket (two adults, two children).

## SHOPPING

Let yourself drift back in time to the days when craftspeople were the lifeblood of thriving communities. Basket weavers, wood turners, and potters are among the traditional crafters that can still be seen throughout the area, and you can bring home some genuine Devon pieces.

**The Round House Craft Centre,** Town Center, Buckland in the Moor (☎ 01364/653234), contains the output of dozens of local craftspeople accumulated under one roof. Although many objects are derivatives of old-timey Devon, others are modern, slightly New Age expressions with sleek or even abstract lines. Raw materials include wood, ceramics, hand-woven textiles, jewelry, sculptures, and printmaking. Buckland in the Moor lies within the borders of the park, close to its southwestern perimeter.

The richest trove of handcrafts in the region lies just beyond the eastern perimeter of Dartmoor National Park, within the crafts-conscious hamlet of Bovey Tracey. Although there are other contenders in town, three of the best include **The Devon Guild of Craftsmen,** Riverside Mill, Bovey Tracey (☎ 01626/832223), where an upscale roster of wood carvings, wooden furniture and kitchen utensils, weavings, pottery, handmade jewelry (often in intriguing Celtic patterns), stone sculptures, prints, and silk screens are accumulated from crafts studios throughout the region. There's a simple restaurant/cafe on the premises, and an enthusiastic core of salespeople ready, willing, and able to explain the origin of virtually anything in the store. Also in Bovey Tracey, look for **The House of Marbles,** Pottery Road, (☎ 01626/835358), a glass-blowing studio where round glass balls, suitable for small boys playing in the dirt, come in every possible size and shape. Of more enduring appeal for adults are the fanciful paperweights and glass ornaments, wine and water glasses, and examples of how the Victorians might have whiled away a late 19th-century evening. What might this mean? Old-fashioned board games, pitting one contestant in wholesome combat against another via diversions that used to be called "Bagatelle" and "Shove ha'penny." Each of the carved wooden sets comes—fortunately—with an instruction book.

Looking for a novelty teapot so as to pour your tea in a more convincingly British way? Head for the **Cardew Tea Pottery,** High Street (Route A382), on the road leading to Newton Abbott. They only make teacups, tea saucers, teapots, and ceramic teatime accessories, in patterns that are as likely to bewilder as amuse you. If you buy here you won't be alone—buyers for Disney commissioned many of the teapots for its theme parks from this place. Be alert when you remove the lid of one of these teapots-as-camp-art. The face staring back at you from the bottom of the pot evokes a zany character from *Alice in Wonderland.*

In the Dartmoor National Park in West Devon, **The Yelverton Paperweight Centre,** Leg O'Mutton (☎ 01822/854250), has an impressive display of more than 800 glass paperweights for sale along with paintings of Dartmoor scenes. For an interesting outdoor shop, **The Kountry Kit,** 22–23 West St., Tavistock (☎ 01822/613089), carries all the best names in gear and outerwear. It also is a clearinghouse of name-brand seconds. **Green Genie Recycled Crafts,** Mearsdon Manor, Moretonhampstead (☎ 01647/440483), is a treasure trove of wonderful objects and crafts creatively fashioned from "waste" materials.

# WHERE TO STAY & EAT

**Leusdon Lodge.** Leusdon-Lower Town, Poundsgate, Newton Abbot, Dartmoor, South Devon TQ13 7PE. ☎ **01364/631304.** Fax 01364/631599. 7 rms, 6 with bath. TV. £60–£100 ($96–$160) double. All rates include English breakfast. Single supplement £10 ($16). DC, MC, V.

This is an 1840s granite country house set in Dartmoor National Park overlooking the Dart valley; in 1953 it was converted into a hotel. All but one bedroom have a private bath, and there's a family room. Traditional English food and a hearty English breakfast are served in the dining room, with hand-carved walls and an ornate fireplace. A fixed-price dinner costs £24 ($38.40). A log fire burns in the drawing room in winter. There's also a cozy bar. Leisure pursuits include horseback riding, canoeing, fishing, and walking the moors. The kitchen will prepare a picnic lunch for guests who partake of the outdoor activities.

Approaching Exeter or Plymouth on A38, take the Peartree Cross exit to Ashburton (but don't go into Ashburton) and follow the blue signs for Princeton. Continue on this road for 5 miles, crossing two narrow bridges and negotiating a steep hill past the village of Poundsgate. Turn right at the sign halfway up the hill pointing to Leusdon, Ponsworthy, and Widecombe. In less than half a mile, take the right fork at a tall stone called the Jubilee Stone, and at the next small junction turn right, going down a steep hill past Leusdon Church to Leusdon Lodge, about 300 yards on your right.

**✪ Lydford House Hotel.** Lydford, near Okehampton, Devon EX20 4AU. ☎ **01822/820347.** Fax 01822/820442. 13 rms. TV TEL. £35 ($56) single; £70.50 ($112.80) double. All rates include English breakfast. MC, V.

This family-run, country-house hotel stands in some 8 acres of gardens and pastureland on the outskirts of Lydford, just on the edge of Dartmoor. It was built in 1880 for Dartmoor artist William Widgery, and several of his paintings hang in the residents' lounge. All rooms have hot-beverage facilities and hair dryers. Owners Ron and Ann Boulter offer varied and interesting menus, all of which feature home-cooking using local produce. A fixed-price dinner costs £14.50 ($23.20). The property includes a gift shop, tearoom (open for light snacks), and riding stables, run by the owners' daughter, Claire Knight. The hotel is 7 miles south of Okehampton, just off A386, and it's on your right as you approach the hamlet of Lydford.

**✪ Old Walls Farm.** Ponsworthy, near Widecombe-in-the-Moor and Newton Abbot, Devon TQ13 7PN. ☎ **01364/631222.** 3 rms, 1 with bath. £20 ($32) single without bath; £36 ($57.60) double without bath, £40 ($64) double with bath. All rates include English breakfast. No credit cards. Closed Christmas week.

This country home is set on a working farm comfortably in the heart of the moors. The owners will make handmade maps and pinpoint the places of interest within driving distance. Guests relax around a stone fireplace in the drawing room, or on a sunny day enjoy an all-glass sun room (the view of the moorland is exceptional). Breakfast is a special event in the dining room, and you can eat as much as you want.

Old Walls Farm is reached from the A38 divided highway between Exeter and Plymouth. Turn right past Ashburton onto B3357, then right at Poundsgate onto the Ponsworthy-Widecombe road. Go through the hamlet of Ponsworthy, passing the all-purpose post office and store, and look for the B&B sign on the left about 600 yards on.

**Ring of Bells.** North Bovey, near Newton Abbott, Devon TQ13 8RB. ☎ **01647/440375.** 3 rms. £30 ($48) single; £60 ($96) double. All rates include English breakfast. MC, V. To reach Ring of Bells by public transit, take the bus to Moretonhampstead from either Torquay or Exeter, then a taxi the final 1$^1$/2 miles.

Beside the village green of a hamlet consisting almost entirely of thatched cottages, this family-run inn, restaurant, and pub was originally built during the 13th century. Today it retains its thatched roof and cottage garden, though part of the space in back has been transformed into an outdoor pool. The building's walls are as much as 3 feet thick, and some of the bedrooms contain four-poster beds.

Beneath time-blackened beams, you can have meals in the pub, priced from £6 ($9.60). Tony and Brenda Rix, the live-in proprietors, also offer meals in their somewhat more formal restaurant, priced at £6 to £12 ($9.60 to $19.20). Golfers appreciate the proximity of Ring of Bells to the Manor House Hotel, a mile away, which contains an 18-hole golf course.

# 3  Chagford

218 miles SW of London; 13 miles W of Exeter; 20 miles NW of Torquay

Six hundred feet above sea level, Chagford is an ancient Stannary Town; with moors all around, it's a good base from which to explore north Dartmoor. Chagford overlooks the Teign River in its deep valley and is itself overlooked by the high granite tors. There's good fishing in the Teign. From Chagford, the most popular excursion is to Postbridge, a village with a prehistoric clapper bridge.

Surrounded by moors, romantic Chagford is one of the best bases for exploring the often forlorn but romantic north Dartmoor, following in the footsteps of the fictional Lorna Doone. It's also Sir Francis Drake country.

## ESSENTIALS

**GETTING THERE**    Take a train to Exeter, and then take a local bus to Chagford.

By bus from Exeter, take the Transmoor Link National Express bus no. 82.

If you're driving from Exeter, drive west on A30, then south on A382 to Chagford.

## SEEING THE SIGHTS

✪ **Sir Francis Drake's House.** Buckland Abbey, Yelverton. ☎ **01822/853607.** Admission £4.30 ($6.90) adults; £2.10 ($3.35) children. Apr–Oct, Fri–Wed 10:30am–5:30pm; Nov–Mar, Sat–Sun 2–5pm. Last admission 45 minutes before closing. Go 3 miles west of Yelverton off A386.

Constructed in 1278, Sir Francis Drake's House was originally a Cistercian monastery. The monastery was dissolved in 1539 and became the country seat of sailors Sir Richard Grenville and, later, Sir Francis Drake. The house remained in the Drake family until 1946, when the abbey and grounds were given to the National Trust. The abbey is now a museum and houses exhibits including Drake's drum, banners, and other artifacts. Light snacks are available daily.

**Castle Drogo.** 4 miles northeast of Chagford and 6 miles south of the Exeter-Okehampton road (A30). ☎ **01647/433306.** Admission (castle and grounds) £4.90 ($7.85) adults; £2.40 ($3.85) children. Admission (grounds only) £2.30 ($3.70) adults; £1.10 ($1.75) children. Apr–Oct, Sat–Thurs 11am–5pm; grounds daily 10:30am–5pm. Take A30 and follow the signs.

This massive granite castle, in the hamlet of Drewsteignton some 17 miles west of Exeter, was designed and built between 1910 and 1930 by the architect Sir Edwin Lutyens for his client, Julius Drewe. Founder of a nationwide chain of grocery stores, Drewe named his castle after an alleged ancestor, Count Drogo de Teign, who was awarded land in this region by William the Conqueror after the Norman conquest of 1066. The castle occupies a bleak but dramatic position high above the River Teign, with views sweeping out over the moors.

The tour covers an elegant series of formal rooms designed in the best tradition of the Edwardian age, including drawing rooms, dining rooms, salons, a gun room, and a garden. There are two restaurants on the premises, both with waitress service, and a tearoom where tea, pastries, and snacks are served buffet style.

## WHERE TO STAY

**Glendarah House.** Lower St., Chagford, Devon TQ13 8BZ. ☎ **01647/433270.** Fax 01647/433483. 6 rms, all with bath. TV. £25–£30 ($40–$48) single; £50–£54 ($80–$86.40) double. All rates include English breakfast. MC, V. Bus: no. 359.

Located at the edge of town, this comfortable Victorian house, owned by Raymond and Julia Bellenger, makes a good base for exploring Dartmoor National Park. In 1994 the house was refurbished to a high standard, including adding TVs and baths to all rooms, along with all the comforts. Ample breakfasts are provided, and many leisure pursuits are close at hand, including golf, fishing, horseback riding, swimming, walking, and bird-watching.

## WHERE TO EAT

**Ring o' Bells.** 44 The Square. ☎ **01647/432466.** Reservations recommended for dinner; otherwise not necessary. Main courses £4–£10.25 ($6.40–$16.40). MC, V. Daily 8:30–11am; 11:30am–3pm; 3–6pm (tea); and 6–9:30pm. BRITISH.

Food and wine have been dispensed from this site since the 12th century, according to the terse and efficient owners—although the historic building you'll see today dates from sometime around the era of William Shakespeare. The antiquity is enhanced with lots of exposed oak, slate floors, and photographs of old Chagford and the weather-beaten folk who used to work on its surrounding farms. You'll be welcome to hoist a glass of Bass or Butcombe Ale, but if you're hungry, look for various versions of "fish on the bone" (a preparation that locals believe quite accurately adds to the flavor of the dish); venison in red wine sauce; various versions of crab from local water; roast beef with mashed potatoes; and a limited selection of vegetarian dishes.

## 4 Torquay: The English Riviera

223 miles SW of London; 23 miles SE of Exeter

In 1968, the towns of Torquay, Paignton, and Brixham joined to form "The English Riviera"—part of a plan to turn the area into one of the super three-in-one resorts of Europe. The area, the birthplace of mystery writer Agatha Christie, opens onto 22 miles of coastline and 18 beaches. Even palm trees grow here!

Torquay is set against a backdrop of the red cliffs of Devon, with many sheltered pebbly coves. With its parks and gardens, including numerous subtropical plants, it's often compared to the Mediterranean. At night, concerts, productions from the West End (the D'Oyly Carte Opera appears occasionally at the Princess Theatre), vaudeville shows, and ballroom dancing keep the vacationers and many honeymooners entertained.

## ESSENTIALS

**GETTING THERE** The nearest connection is Exeter Airport (see above), 40 minutes away.

Frequent trains run throughout the day from London's Paddington Station to Torquay, whose station is at the town center on the sea front. The trip takes 2¹/₂ hours. Call ☎ **0345/484950** for information and schedules.

National Express coach links from London's Victoria Coach Station leave every 2 hours during the day for Torquay. For information and schedules, call ☎ **0990/ 808080.**

If you're driving, from Exeter, head west on A38, veering south at the junction with A380.

**VISITOR INFORMATION** The **Tourist Information Centre** is at Vaughan Parade (☎ **01803/297428**). Open Monday through Saturday from 9am to 5pm.

## PALM TREES & AGATHA CHRISTIE

The resort is known for one of the balmiest climates in Britain. It's so temperate—because of its exposure to the Gulf Stream—that subtropical plants such as palm trees and succulents thrive. But fans of the British comedy "Fawlty Towers," the television series that made Torquay and the English Riviera known the world over, might be disappointed to learn that it wasn't filmed in Torquay at all, but rather in one of the Home Counties closer to London. (The hotel that served as the comedy's set has since burned down.) Regardless, Torquay continues to be identified with the series, which was inspired by John Cleese's sojourn in Torquay during one of his tours of duty with the Monty Python team.

About a quarter-mile east of Torquay's center is **Torre Abbey,** Kings Drive (☎ **01803/293593**). Originally built as a monastery in 1196, then converted into a private home in the 16th century, it has long been associated with Torquay's leading citizens. Today the Torquay Town Council maintains it as a museum. The museum features a room outfitted in a close approximation of Agatha Christie's private study. After the mystery writer's death, her family donated for display her Remington typewriter, many of her original manuscripts, an oil portrait of Ms. Christie as a young woman, family photographs, and more. Torrey Abbey and its Agatha Christie Room are open daily from Easter or April 1 (whichever is earlier) to October 31; admission is £2.50 ($4) for adults and £1.50 ($2.40) for children.

You'll see the conspicuous consumption of England's Gilded Age at the **Oldway Mansion,** Torbay Road, in Preston, near Paignton (☎ **01803/296244**), a short drive south of the center of Torquay on the main Paignton-Torquay road. The mansion was built in 1874 by Isaac Merritt Singer, founder of the sewing machine empire, and his son Paris then enhanced its decor, massive Ionic portico, and 17 acres of Italianate gardens. The mansion's eclectic decor includes a scaled-down version of the Hall of Mirrors in the Palace of Versailles. During its Jazz Age heyday, Oldway served as a rehearsal space and performance venue for Isadora Duncan, who was having a not-terribly-discreet affair with Paris. The mansion is open year-round Monday to Friday from 9am to 5pm, and from April through October, Saturday and Sunday from 9am to 5pm. Admission is available from May to September to give tours of the mansion. The tours are conducted between 10am and 1pm and cost £1 ($1.60). Admission is free if you do not participate in the guided tour.

## WHERE TO STAY

In addition to the following, the Mulberry Room (see "Where to Eat," below) also rents rooms.

### DOUBLES FOR LESS THAN £40

**Colindale.** 20 Rathmore Rd., Chelston, Torquay, Devon TQ2 6NY. ☎ **01803/293947.** 8 rms, 4 with bath. £17 ($27.20) single without bath, £18.50 ($29.60) single with bath; £34 ($54.40) double without bath, £37 ($59.20) double with bath. All rates include English breakfast. AE, DC, MC, V. Closed Nov–Feb.

This hotel is a good choice, and it's about as central as you'd want: It opens onto King's Garden, a 5-minute walk from Corbyn Beach and a 3-minute walk from the railway station. The hotel has a cocktail bar, a residents' lounge, and a dining room that offers a fixed-price dinner for £8.50 ($13.60). Colindale is one of a row of attached brick Victorian houses, with gables and chimneys. It's set back from the road, with a parking court in front.

**Craig Court Hotel.** 10 Ash Hill Rd., Castle Circus, Torquay, Devon TQ1 3HZ. ☎ **01803/ 294400.** 10 rms, 5 with bath. TV. £16.50–£19.50 ($26.40–$31.20) single without bath, £19.50–£22.50 ($31.20–$36) single with bath; £33–£39 ($52.80–$62.40) double without bath, £39–£45 ($62.40–$72) double with bath. All rates include English breakfast. No credit cards. Take St. Marychurch Rd. (signposted St. Marychurch, Babbacome) from Castle Circus (the town hall), make the first right onto Ash Hill Rd., go 200 yds., and the hotel is on the right.

This hotel is in a large Victorian mansion with a southern exposure and lies a short walk from the heart of town. Owner Ann Box offers excellent value with modernized bedrooms, many with private facilities. In addition to enjoying the good, wholesome food served here, guests can also make use of a well-appointed lounge or an intimate bar opening onto the grounds. A four-course dinner costs £10 ($16).

**Cranborne Hotel.** 58 Belgrave Rd., Torquay, Devon TQ2 5HY. ☎ **01803/298046.** 12 rms, 11 with bath. TV. £17–£24 ($27.20–$38.40) single; £34–£48 ($54.40–$76.80) double. All rates include English breakfast. MC, V. Parking £2 ($3.20).

At this small, family-run enterprise, guests get a personal welcome from Mr. and Mrs. Dawkins, who rent comfortably furnished bedrooms with hot-beverage facilities. Guests mix informally either in a lounge or on the patio. The hotel lies off Torbay Road near English Riviera Centre.

**Cresta Hotel.** St. Agnes Lane, Torquay, Devon TQ2 6QD. ☎ **01803/607241.** 8 rms, all with shower only. £20 ($32) single; £40 ($64) double; £20 ($32) per adult in a family room, free for children 12 and under. All rates include English breakfast. No credit cards. Bus: no. 12 or 14.

This family hotel, full of character, overlooks the sea in a secluded position close to the train station. Hosts John and Lucy Macmillan are helpful and offer comfortably furnished rooms, some with sea views. Five rooms are large enough for families. Free TV and hot-beverage facilities are available in all rooms. Meals include a traditional roast for a four-course evening dinner, costing £7 ($11.20), with tea or coffee in addition to bed and breakfast.

✪ **Glenorleigh.** 26 Cleveland Rd., Torquay, Devon TQ2 5BE. ☎ **01803/292135.** Fax 01803/ 292135. 16 rms, 10 with bath. £14–£18 ($22.40–$28.80) single without bath, £16–£20 ($25.60–$32) single with bath; £28–£36 ($44.80–$57.60) double without bath, £32–£40 ($51.20–$64) double with bath. All rates include English breakfast. MC, V. Closed Nov–Dec. When you reach the traffic lights at Torre Station, bear right into Avenue Rd. (A379); Cleveland Rd. is the first left.

This worthy choice is known in many circles as the best B&B in Torquay. The bedrooms have been tastefully modernized and are well maintained. In summer, many guests are booked for the week, so you'll have to call and see if they have space. The hotel has a solarium and a heated swimming pool. A fixed-price meal ranges from £7.50 to £12 ($12 to $19.20). Every season they seem to try a bit harder around here.

## DOUBLES FOR LESS THAN £60

**Blue Haze Hotel.** Seaway Lane, Torquay, Devon TQ2 6PS. ☎ **01803/607186.** Fax 01803/ 607186. 10 rms. TV. £54–£58 ($86.40–$92.80) double. All rates include English breakfast. Single supplement £8 ($12.80) extra. AE, MC, V. Closed Nov–Apr. Follow the signs to the seafront, turn right along the seafront at the traffic lights by the Grand Hotel, go immediately left between the Grand and the railway station into Hennapyn Rd., and turn right where it meets Seaway Lane; the Blue Haze is about 200 yds. up on the right.

This elegant Victorian house with a large garden is in a residential area 500 yards from the beaches. The spacious bedrooms contain refrigerators, tea and coffeemakers, and hair dryers. The rooms are all doubles. Hosts Doug and Hazel Newton serve home-cooked four-course meals in their licensed hotel, and there's a large private parking area. The English meals cost £14 ($22.40) and up. Try fresh baked rolls, steak-and-kidney pie, a succulent roast beef, and finish off with the apple pie. A full and freshly cooked English breakfast is served daily.

**Fairmount House Hotel.** Herbert Rd., Chelston, Torquay, Devon TQ2 6RW. ☎ **01803/ 605446.** 8 rms. TV. £36.50–£41.50 ($58.40–$66.40) per person. All rates include half board. AE, MC, V. Closed early Nov to early Mar. Follow the signs to Cockington Village and turn right onto Herbert Rd. Bus: no. 24 or 25.

This Victorian building has been well preserved with stained glass, marble fireplaces, and other adornments of that grand age, and lies in a tranquil residential area of the resort about a mile from the harbor. The guest rooms are comfortably furnished, and good, sound British cooking can be ordered. After a meal, guests can relax in the public rooms, which include a conservatory bar lounge where bar lunches are available at noon.

**Norcliff Hotel.** Sea Front, Babbacombe Downs, Torquay, Devon TQ1 3LF. ☎ **01803/ 328456.** Fax 01803/328023. 27 rms. TV TEL. £18–£28 ($28.80–$44.80) single; £36–£56 ($57.60–$89.60) double. All rates include English breakfast. MC, V.

This Italianate Victorian villa is set on a high plateau overlooking Lyme Bay. Painted a shade of lime green with blue trim with a pleasant half-acre garden, it lies in the residential suburb of Babbacombe Downs, about 1 1/2 miles west of the center of Torquay. The bedrooms are conservative and simple, clean and modest, sometimes with sea views. About 10 rooms are in an uninspired modern extension added in 1992, along with an indoor heated swimming pool.

## WHERE TO EAT

**Maggie of Park Lane.** 4–5 Park Lane, The Strand. ☎ **01803/200755.** Reservations recommended. Main courses £7.95–£13.95 ($12.70–$22.30); set menu £17.95 ($28.70). AE, MC, V. Tues–Fri noon–2:30pm; Tues–Sat 7–10pm. BRITISH.

Set within a solid, much-used building that functioned 200 years ago as a warehouse for contraband goods smuggled illegally into Devon from Ireland and France, this restaurant is the creative declaration of Maggie Matthews, who executes much of the cooking from a crowded kitchen in back. The dining room has oak beams, a charming rustic character, and a location 5 minutes from the seafront. Menu items are soothingly old-fashioned, and include many different preparations of fish; surf and turf, where the meat is high-quality rumpsteak; beef casserole; and fried monkfish served with sliced red onions.

✪ **Mulberry Room.** 1 Scarborough Rd., Torquay, Devon TQ2 5UJ. ☎ **01803/213639.** Reservations required for dinner. Main courses £5–£7.50 ($8–$12); fixed-price lunch £5.95 ($9.50) for two courses, £7.95 ($12.70) for three courses. No credit cards. Wed–Sun noon–2pm; Fri–Sat noon–2pm and 7:30–9:30pm. From the seafront, turn up Belgrave Rd., then take the first right onto Scarborough Rd. Bus: no. 35. ENGLISH.

Lesley Cooper is an inspired cook and will feed you well in her little dining room, which seats some two dozen diners at midday. The restaurant is situated in one of Torquay's Victorian villas and faces a patio of plants and flowers, with outside tables for summer lunches and afternoon teas. Dinner is served only on Friday and Saturday. The vegetarian will find selections here and other diners can feast on her baked lamb or honey-roasted chicken, among other dishes. Traditional roasts draw the Sunday crowds. The choice is wisely limited so that everything served will be fresh.

You can even stay here in one of three bedrooms, each comfortably furnished and well kept, with private bath. B&B charges range from £21 to £25 ($33.60–$40) per person daily, making it one of the bargains of the resort.

**No. 7.** The Beacon Terrace, Outer Harbour. ☎ **01803/295055.** Reservations recommended. Main courses £7.95–£12.95 ($12.70–$20.70). AE, MC, V. June–Sept, dinner only, daily 6–10pm; Oct–May Tues–Sat 12:45–1:45pm and 6–10pm. SEAFOOD.

A 2-minute walk of Torquay's center, and within a stone-sided building that's at least a century old, this restaurant recaptures the late-Victorian and Edwardian era, when fish was served to holiday-making factory workers with a minimum of fuss and bother. Dining here means bare pinewood floors, plastic tablecloths, and deliberately simple table settings that include only a napkin, a cup, and a glass. Menu items include carefully prepared versions of fish and chips (cod in winter, plaice in summer); scallops with vermouth and butter sauce; Devon cobbler (a local form of fish pie); and a medley of sole with crabmeat with a cheese sauce.

**Village Brasserie.** 5 Ilsham Rd., Wellswood. ☎ **01803/290855.** Reservations recommended. A la carte menu or three-course dinner £16.95 ($27.10); fixed-price lunch £6.95 ($11.10). AE, MC, V. Tues–Sat noon–2pm and 7–10pm; Sun noon–2pm. CONTINENTAL BRITISH.

In what was originally built around 1900 as a big-windowed storefront, this restaurant lies about half a mile from the center of Torquay in a neighborhood (Wellswood) known for its dozens of shops. Furnished with mahogany tables spaced close together, and staffed with a crew of amiable waitresses, it serves everything from bangers and mash to continental concoctions. Selections include about half a dozen types of fresh seafood, including Mediterranean king prawns pan fried in garlic butter, monkfish wrapped in bacon and served with a hollandaise sauce, and sirloin steak with red wine sauce. Some dishes are prepared with a certain flair; other platters are a little bland.

## TORQUAY AFTER DARK

Torquay bills itself as the "English Riviera," but it's theater, not cinema, that plays to tourists here. Seven theaters in town, all open year-round, offer everything from Gilbert & Sullivan and tributes to Sinatra and Nat King Cole, and Marine Band concerts and comedy shows. Among the most active theaters are the **Palace Avenue Theatre,** Palace Avenue, Paignton (☎ **0180/355-8367**); the **Princess Theatre,** Torbay Road, (☎ **0180/329-9992**); and the **Festival Theatre,** The Esplanade, Paignton (☎ **0180/355-8641**).

Fifteen area nightclubs cater to everyone from teenyboppers to the gay scene, but dancing rules the town, as there's virtually nowhere to catch live club acts. Among the better dance clubs are **Claires,** Torwood Street (☎ **0180/329-2079**), for its Friday and Saturday night house music from 9pm until 2am, with a cover charge from £2 to £5 ($3.20 to $8), depending on the DJ; and **Monroes,** Victoria Road (☎ **0180/329-1149**), which offers "uplifting" dance on Thursday and Saturday, and hard house on Friday, from 9pm until 1am, with a £2 ($3.20) cover on Thursday and Friday, as well as Saturday before 10pm; after which, it's £4 ($6.40). For a later night and a harder groove, try the **Monastery,** Torwood Gardens Road (☎ **0180/329-2929**), on Saturday, the only night this club opens its doors, but you can definitely get your fill of house, hard house, hip hop, and techno here as the dancing starts at midnight and doesn't end until 7am.

The Pleasure Dome/Judy G's, Belgrave Road (☎ 0180/321-1131), has the Juicy Fruit Club, a gay dance night, once a month on Wednesday, and Double Two, Rock Road (☎ 0180/329-2279), is all gay, all the time, open Monday through Saturday, 9:30pm to 1:30am, with a £2 ($3.20) cover at the door.

## 5 Totnes

224 miles SW of London; 12 miles NW of Dartmouth

One of the oldest towns in the West Country, the ancient borough of Totnes rests quietly in the past, seemingly content to let the Torquay area remain in the vanguard of the building boom. On the River Dart, upstream from Dartmouth, Totnes is so totally removed in character from Torquay that the two towns could be in different countries. Totnes has several historic buildings, notably the ruins of a Norman castle, an ancient guildhall, and the 15th-century Church of St. Mary, constructed of red sandstone. In the Middle Ages the town was encircled by walls; the North Gate serves as a reminder of that period.

### ESSENTIALS

**GETTING THERE**    Totnes is on the main London-Plymouth line. Trains leave London's Paddington Station frequently throughout the day.

Totnes is served locally by the Western National and Devon General bus companies (☎ 01752/222555 in Plymouth for information about individual routings).

If you're driving from Torquay, head west on A385.

Many visitors approach Totnes by river steamer from Dartmouth. Contact Dart Pleasure Craft, River Link (☎ 01803/834488), for information.

**VISITOR INFORMATION**    The **Tourist Information Centre** is at the Plains (☎ 01803/863168). Open daily from 9:30am to 12:30pm and 1:30 to 5pm (closes on Sunday off-season).

### EXPLORING TOTNES

The town's most visible monuments include **The Elizabethan Museum,** Fore Street (☎ 01803/863821), the 16th-century home of a wealthy merchant, and repository of furniture, costumes, documents, and farm implements of the Elizabethan Age. One room is devoted to local resident Charles Babbage (1792 to 1871), a mathematician and inventor. He invented a calculating machine that used cards perforated with a coded series of holes and whose memory capacities categorized it as an early version of the computer. His other inventions included the ophthalmoscope, a speedometer, and the cowcatchers that were later used to fend cows off the tracks of railways around the world. The museum is open Easter to October, Monday through Friday from 10:30am to 5pm and Saturday from 2 to 5pm. Admission is £1.50 ($2.40) for adults, 80p ($1.30) for seniors, and 50p (80¢) for children.

Crowing the hilltop at the northern end of High Street is **Totnes Castle,** Castle Street (☎ 01803/864406). Built by the Normans shortly after their conquest of England, it's one of the best examples of mott and bailey construction remaining in the United Kingdom. Although the outer walls survived, the interior is mostly in ruins. It's open April through October daily from 10am to 6pm; in the off-season, the castle closes at 4pm. Admission is £2.20 ($3.50)

The symbol of Totnes is **Totnes Guildhall,** Ramparts Walk (☎ 01803/862147). Originally built as a priory (monastery) in 1553, it contains an old gaol (jail), a collection of civic memorabilia, and the table Oliver Cromwell used to sign documents during his visit to Totnes in 1646. The guildhall is open to the public Monday to Saturday from 10:30am to 1pm and 2 to 4:30pm between Easter and September. Admission is 75p ($1.20) for adults and 25p (40¢) for children.

## SHOPPING

Totnes is known for its colorful markets staged year-round in the center of town at Civic Square on Friday mornings and early afternoons. On Tuesday from May through September, many vendors are in Elizabethan costumes. You may want to wander throughout the town enjoying its old bookstores, antique shops, and retailers hawking handcrafted goods, lace, clothes, knits, and handmade shoes and toys, plus a myriad of other gifts. Although no one particular shop is outstanding, the town as a whole is a shopping destination.

## WHERE TO STAY IN THE AREA

✪ **Broomborough House Farm.** Broomborough Dr., Higher Plymouth Rd., Totnes, Devon TQ9 5LU. ☎ **01803/863134.** 3 rms, 1 with shower only. TV. £18 ($28.80) per person without shower, £20 ($32) per person with shower. All rates include English breakfast. AE.

In a secluded valley with views of Dartmoor National Park, this elegant gabled mansion was designed by Sir George Gilbert Scott, designer of the Albert Memorial and other architecturally important structures in London. The house has central heating and spacious lounges, and the rather basic bedrooms have hot-beverage facilities and electric blankets. Bob and Joan Beale operate the B&B along with their 600-acre farm and will give good advice for touring in the area. The house is a 10-minute walk from the town center; many country inns and restaurants are nearby.

✪ **Cott Inn.** Dartington, near Totnes, Devon TQ9 6HE. ☎ **01803/863777.** Fax 01803/866629. 6 rms. TV TEL. £45 ($72) single; £55 ($88) double. All rates include English breakfast. AE, DC, MC, V. Bus: no. X80 travels from Totnes to Dartington, but most people rent a taxi for the 1$^1$/2 mile journey.

Built in 1320, this hotel on the old Ashburton—Totnes turnpike is the second-oldest inn in England. It's a low, rambling two-story building of stone, cob, and plaster, with a thatch roof and walls 3 feet thick. The owners rent low-ceilinged, double rooms upstairs, with modern conveniences, including hot and cold running water. (If you don't crown yourself, you might have a comfortable night's sleep.) The inn is a gathering place for the people of Dartington, and you'll feel the pulse of English country life.

You'll surely be intrigued with the tavern, where you can also order a meal. A buffet is laid out at lunchtime, priced according to your choice of dish. The a la carte dinners feature local produce: scallops, duck, steak, or fresh salmon may be available. The cookery is more competent than exciting. Even if you're not staying over, at least drop in at the pub (five beers are on draft); it's open Monday through Saturday from 11am to 2:30pm and 5:30 to 11pm, and on Sunday from noon to 3pm and 7 to 10:30pm.

**The Old Forge.** Seymour Place, Totnes, Devon TQ9 5AY. ☎ **01803/862174.** 10 rms. £38–£54 ($60.80–$86.40) single; £48–£64 ($76.80–$102.40) double. All rates include English breakfast. MC, V. From the monument at the foot of Shopping St., cross the bridge over the river and take the second right.

This is a restored former blacksmith's and wheelwright's workshop dating back 6 centuries. The owner of the Old Forge, Peter Allnutt, carried on this ancient tradition until recently. His wife, Jeannie, runs the hotel. Near the River Dart, B&B accommodations are provided in attractively decorated bedrooms, four of which suit families. No smoking is allowed inside. Recent improvements include a Jacuzzi, spa, and a new conservatory.

## WHERE TO EAT IN THE AREA

**Crank's Health Food Restaurant.** Dartington Cider Press Centre, Shinners Bridge. ☎ **01803/862388.** Soups £2.50 ($4); main courses £3.50–£4.95 ($5.60–$7.90); cakes and desserts £1–£2.10 ($1.60–$3.35). DC, MC, V. Daily 9:30am–5:30pm. Closed Sun in winter. Bus: no. X80 travels through Dartington from Plymouth to Torquay. VEGETARIAN.

Affiliated with the Crank's restaurant chain, whose other branches are all in London, this is the region's leading health-food restaurant. Contained in the crafts center of Dartington (actually part of an old Devonshire farmstead), $1\frac{1}{2}$ miles northwest of Totnes, it serves only compost-grown vegetables, live-culture yogurts, and freshly extracted fruit juices. The place is very busy, and strictly self-service, with an ample buffet containing salads. The Devonshire cream teas served include whole-meal scones, whole-fruit jams, and freshly clotted local cream. For our tastes most dishes are underseasoned, although this is what many diners seem to prefer.

**Willow Vegetarian Restaurant.** 87 High St. ☎ **01803/862605.** Reservations required for dinner. Main courses £3.60–£6.50 ($5.75–$10.40). No credit cards. Mon–Sat 10am–5pm; Wed, Fri, and Sat 6:30–9:30pm; additional evenings in July and Aug. VEGETARIAN.

At the top of Totnes' main street, this is a vegetarian whole-food restaurant offering an Indian menu on Wednesday and live music on Friday. Otherwise, it serves both exotic and traditional food, including main dishes, cakes, and salads that are made on the premises from fresh, high-quality, and often organic ingredients. Seasoning is not the kitchen's strong point, but most diners leave satisfied. It's self-service during the day, with table service in the evening. There's also a list of organic wines.

## 6 Dartmouth

236 miles SW of London; 35 miles SE of Exeter

At the mouth of the Dart River, this ancient seaport is the home to the Royal Naval College. Traditionally linked to England's great maritime explorations, Dartmouth sent out the young midshipmen who saw to it that "Britannia ruled the waves." You can take a river steamer up the Dart to Totnes (book at the kiosk at the harbor); the scenery along the way is panoramic, as the Dart is Devon's most beautiful river. Dartmouth's 15th-century castle was built during the reign of Edward IV. The town's most noted architectural feature is the Butterwalk, which lies below Tudor houses. The Flemish influence in some of the houses is pronounced.

## ESSENTIALS

**GETTING THERE**    Dartmouth is not easily reached by public transport. Trains run to Totnes (see above) and Paignton.

There is one bus a day from Totnes to Dartmouth. Call ☎ **01752/222555** for schedules.

If you're driving from Exeter, take A38 southwest, cutting southeast to Totnes on A381; then follow A381 to the junction with B3207.

Riverboats make the 10-mile run from Totnes to Dartmouth, but these trips depend on the tide and operate only from Easter to the end of October. See Totnes, above, for details on obtaining boat schedules.

**VISITOR INFORMATION**    The **Tourist Information Centre** is at the Engine House, Mayors Avenue (☎ **01803/834224**). Open April through October,

Monday through Saturday from 9:30am to 5:30pm and Sunday from 10am to 4pm, off-season Monday through Saturday from 10am to 4pm.

## EXPLORING DARTMOUTH

Many visitors come to Dartmouth to experience the bracing salt air and explore the surrounding marshlands rich with bird life and natural beauty. The historic monuments here are steeped in much of the legend and lore of channel life and historic Devon.

**Dartmouth Castle,** Castle Road (☎ **01803/833588**), originally built during the 15th century and later outfitted with artillery and employed by the Victorians as a coastal defense station, lies about a half-mile south of the town center. A tour of its bulky ramparts and somber interiors provides insight into the changing nature of warfare throughout the centuries, and you'll see sweeping views of the surrounding coast and flatlands. The castle is open daily April through October from 10am to 6pm and from November through March, Wednesday to Sunday from 10am to 4pm. Admission is £2.40 ($3.85) for adults and £1.20 ($1.90) for children.

**Dartmouth Museum,** the Butter Walk (☎ **01803/832923**), contains the region's most interesting maritime exhibit, focusing on the British Empire's military might of the 18th century. Built between 1635 and 1640, it's set amid an interconnected row of 17th-century buildings—**The Butter Walk**—whose overhanging, stilt-supported facade was originally designed to provide shade for the butter, milk, and cream sold there by local milkmaids. Later, it functioned as a warehouse for tobacco from the New World, and then during a low point of its existence, as a parking garage. Today the complex houses the museum as well as shops selling wines, baked goods, and more. The museum is open from March through November, Monday to Saturday from 11am to 5pm. The rest of the year it's open Monday to Saturday from noon to 3pm. Admission is £1 ($1.60) for adults and 40p (65¢) for children.

The town's most historic and interesting church is **St. Petrox,** Castle Road (no phone), a 17th-century Anglican monument with an ivy-draped graveyard whose tombstones evoke the sorrows of Dartmouth's maritime past. The church is open daily from 7am to dusk.

It's also worth walking through the waterfront neighborhood known as **Bayard's Cove,** a cobbled, half-timbered neighborhood that's quite charming. Set near the end of Lower Street, it prospered during the 1600s thanks to its ship repair services. In 1620 its quays were the site for repairs of the Pilgrims' historic ships, the *Speedwell* and the *Mayflower,* just after their departure from Plymouth. Just a 2-minute walk from Bayard's Cove is one of our favorite pubs, **The Cherub,** 13 Higher St. (☎ **01803/832571**). It was originally built in 1380 as the harbormaster's house. Today this charming pub is a great place to drink and dine on simple traditional British platters and bar snacks. It's open Monday through Saturday from 11am to 11pm, with meals served between noon and 2pm and 7 and 10pm. The pub is also open for lunch and dinner on Sunday from noon to 3pm and 6:30 to 10:30pm. In winter, the pub closes from 3 to 6pm daily. There's a more formal dining room upstairs that serves a number of fish dishes, steaks, lamb, and duck.

## WHERE TO STAY
### DOUBLES FOR LESS THAN £50

**Boringdon House.** 1 Church Rd., Dartmouth, Devon TQ6 9HQ. ☎ **01803/832235.** 3 rms. TV. £49 ($78.40) double. All rates include English breakfast. No credit cards. From Dartmouth, head up College Way, take the first left onto Townstal Rd., then take the first right onto Church Road.

---

## Did They Really Say "Clotted"?
## The Best Places for a Devon Cream Tea

No region in England clings as tenaciously to its culinary traditions as Devonshire does to its tea-drinking rituals. Cornish pasties are devoured in pubs scattered between East Anglia and the Lake District, and hearty ales are distributed throughout the vales of England with little regard for their exact origin. But cream teas will always be associated with Devon.

What are the cultural presuppositions of a Devonshire cream tea? Foremost, the ritual includes hints of a Devonshire farmer's wife laboring away on a faraway grange, even if the clotted cream you find alongside your scones derives from a high-tech dairy using ultra-pasteurized processes. These ruddy-cheeked matriarchs perfected the medieval process of simmering at very low temperatures, sometimes for a day or two, a batch of whole cow's milk to create the region's famous Devonshire clotted cream. Don't expect unappetizing globs—or clots—within this national treasure. Silken-textured and rich, with just enough acidity to perk up the tastebuds, it isn't clotted at all, but instead, a very English, urbane, and perishable version of what the French, with subtle variations, call crème fraîche. Thanks to Devon's location at the edge of the English Channel, the debate about the relative excellence of the dairy products of Devon versus those of its French-speaking relative, Normandy, has raged since the days of William the Conqueror.

Devonshire natives rather tartly attribute their clots' taste to the grass consumed by the local herbivores. Warmer than other regions of England, Devonites sometimes hint that valuable nutrients from the rest of Britain trickle their way down to Devonshire soil from the colder, less receptive climes farther north.

What should accompany your clots of cream? Scones, but not just any scone—preferably one just baked, and hopefully, one made without baking soda. The resulting, slightly bitter, slightly sour taste seems to go better with the tangy cream. Preserves? Don't even think of asking for anything except strawberry preserves, and if you should be gauche enough to ask for marmalade, you might be ejected from the tearoom as a uncouth barbarian. The tea itself that figures into the ritual seems less crucial than the accessories accompanying it. Most Devonites opt for strong, unfussy, Indian tea, eschewing the more delicate Chinese blends as something too fancy to muck about with.

As you explore Devon's bylanes and primrose paths, here are Frommer's favorites for your afternoon tea with clotted cream.

Our all-time favorite (and the most convenient, as it lies between Exeter and Plymouth) is Buckfast Abbey at Buckfastleigh (☎ **01364/643301**), also an easy drive from Torquay and Dartmoor. The abbey was built between 1900 and 1930, although it was founded in Saxon days in a valley of the River Dart on the edge of

---

This exceptional up-market B&B wins high marks from the English Tourist Board. Mr. and Mrs. R. Green receive guests in their spacious Georgian house, which stands in a large garden overlooking the town and harbor. The bedrooms are attractively furnished, each one a double- or twin-bedded unit. Parking is in the courtyard, and the house is just a few minutes' walk to the town center by old lanes and steps. No smoking is the rule of the house.

Dartmoor. Today's tearoom is a modern continuation of an old Benedictine tradition of hospitality. The specialty here is a Buckfast wine cake. Prices for a one-scone tea are £2 ($3.20), rising to £2.90 ($4.65) for a two-scone tea. (These prices are typical for all the other tearooms.)

In charming Chagford, Whiddons, High Street (☎ **01647/433406**), is decorated with fresh flowers in summer. They not only have freshly baked scones, but those delectable cucumber sandwiches. After tea, drop in at the Church of St. Michael nearby, where a spurned lover killed Mary Whiddon on her wedding day (later fictionalized in R. D. Blackmore's classic, Lorna Doone).

Or head for The Kettle, 15 Fore St. (☎ **01297/20428**), east of Exeter. You'll know you're at the right place when you see the wooden sign out front of an old lady holding a kettle. The atmosphere inside is mellow in a building 4 centuries old. It's just a short drive from Exeter along the A376 and A3052.

While visiting the coastal towns of Devon, dart inland to Honeybees, High Street (☎ **01404/43392**), in the town of Honiton, long famous for its lace made a century ago. The brick-fronted tearoom with a large bay window is known for its cream teas and "squidgy cakes." From Exeter take A30 straight into Honiton.

Southeast of Exeter, follow the A376 through Exmouth to The Cozy Teapot, Fore Street (☎ **01395/444016**), in Budleigh Salterton. A cozy brick building, this tearoom is tucked away just past a small bridgeway with running water. It serves the best Devon cream tea in the area. You get bone china, lace cloths on the tables, young women in flowery pinafores, and homemade cakes, too.

Our favorite tearoom name has to be Four and Twenty Blackbirds, 43 Gold St., Tiverton (☎ **01884/257055**), reached by following the Old Road (now called A396) from Exeter straight into Tiverton to the north. The black-and-white timbered tearoom stands in a sunken square; R. D. Blackmore attended school nearby. Fresh flowers, mismatched furniture, and an assortment of set teas and tea breads and homemade cakes await you.

In Totnes, whose ruins of a Norman castle are still prominent, Greys Dining Room, 96 High St. (☎ **01803/866369**), sets out its fine silver and china to welcome you in an atmosphere of wood paneling and antiques. About 40 different teas along with homemade cakes and scones will invite you to extend the afternoon.

Finally, unless you have had enough tea (and who could have enough tea?), head for the Georgian Tea Room, High Street (☎ **01392/873465**), in Topsham, reached from Exeter by going along the Polsol Road to A376 (southeast of Exeter). If Aunt Pittipat had been from Devon instead of Atlanta, this is the type of place she'd patronize. Homemade jams accompany the piping-hot scones fresh from the oven.

**Sunny Banks.** 1 Vicarage Hill, Dartmouth, Devon TQ6 9EW. ☎ **01803/832766.** 10 rms, 3 with shower only, 5 with bath. TV. £17.50 ($28) single without bath; £20–£25 ($32–$40) double. All rates include English breakfast. No credit cards. Parking £3 ($4.80). Buses marked Plymouth or Kings Bridge all stop nearby.

This 1880s house in the center of town was originally built as the home and office of a local doctor and now operates as a bed-and-breakfast hotel. Each bedroom contains tea-making facilities, comfortably upholstered furniture, and discreet floral motifs. A patio in the rear garden offers warm-weather seating amid flowering shrubs and trees.

✪ **Victoria Hotel.** 27–29 Victoria Rd., Dartmouth, Devon TQ6 9RT. ☎ **01803/832572.** 10 rms, 9 with bath. TV. £25 ($40) single without bath, £30 ($48) single with bath; £50–£60 ($80–$96) double with bath. All rates include English breakfast. MC, V. Take the "hoppa" bus.

This family-run hotel is in the center of Dartmouth, only 150 yards from the harbor in a row of shops and houses. The characteristic cottage-style bedrooms are tastefully furnished. Bar snacks are available from the spacious bar/lounge area, and an evening meal can be ordered in the restaurant. There's no parking lot, but clients go to the free nearby car parks when space is available.

## WHERE TO EAT

✪ **Billy Budds.** 7 Foss St. ☎ **01803/834842.** Reservations required. Main courses £11.50–£13.95 ($18.40–$22.30); lunch plates £2.50–£5 ($4–$8). MC, V. Bus: no. 93. ENGLISH.

Although the name suggests a Herman Melville connection, the owners insist that the inspiration for its name was the opera by British composer Benjamin Britten. At this simply decorated local favorite, you'll be treated to "cheap and cheerful" lunch dishes that might include omelets, pastas, salads, and such platters of the day as garlic chicken. Dinners are more formal and elaborate, and include locally fattened lamb, salmon from the Dart River, very fresh fish, and desserts made with thick cream from Devonshire cows. Dishes are imaginative, but served with a refreshing lack of pretense.

**Scarlet Geranium.** 10 Fairfax Place. ☎ **01803/832491.** Reservations recommended. Main courses £6.25–£9.75 ($10–$15.60); lunch £1.95–£8.25 ($3.10–$13.20). MC, V. Daily 10am–10pm in summer; 10am–5pm in the off-season. ENGLISH.

Built originally in 1333, this old restaurant in the town center off the Quay was once known as the Albion Inn. Try it for morning coffee, lunch, afternoon tea, or dinner, which features such dishes as roast sirloin of beef and Wiltshire ham. When available, you can order the locally caught and dressed crab or fresh-caught salmon. The food is "tearoomy" in flavor, perhaps no great compliment, but the place has its admirers. A licensed bar is on the premises.

## 7 Plymouth

242 miles SW of London; 161 miles SW of Southampton

The historic seaport of Plymouth is more romantic in legend than reality. But this was not always so. During World War II, the blitzed area of greater Plymouth lost at least 75,000 buildings. The heart of present-day Plymouth, including the municipal civic center on the Royal Parade, has been entirely rebuilt; however, the way it was rebuilt is the subject of much controversy.

For the old part of town, you must go to the Elizabethan section, known as the Barbican, and walk along the quay in the footsteps of Sir Francis Drake (once the mayor of Plymouth) and other Elizabethan seafarers, such as Sir John Hawkins, English naval commander and slave trader. From here in 1577, Drake set sail on his round-the-world voyage.

Of special interest to visitors from the United States is the final departure point of the Pilgrims in 1620, the already-mentioned Barbican. The two ships, *Mayflower* and *Speedwell*, that sailed from Southampton in August of that year put into Plymouth after they suffered storm damage. Here, the *Speedwell* was abandoned as unseaworthy and the *Mayflower* made the trip to the New World alone.

# ESSENTIALS

**GETTING THERE**   Plymouth Airport lies 4 miles from the center of the city. Brymon Airways has direct service from the London airports at Heathrow and Gatwick to Plymouth. For service, call Brymon (☎ **01752/772752**).

Frequent trains run from London's Paddington Station to Plymouth in 3 to 3¹/₂ hours. The Plymouth Train Station (☎ **0345/484950**) lies on North Road, north of the Plymouth Center. Western National Bus 83/84 runs from the station to the heart of Plymouth.

National Express has frequent daily bus service between London's Victoria Coach Station and Plymouth. The trip takes 4¹/₂ hours. Call ☎ **0990/808080** for schedules and information.

If you're driving, from London, take M4 west to the junction with M5 going south to Exeter. From Exeter, head southwest on A38 to Plymouth.

**VISITOR INFORMATION**   The **Tourist Information Centre** is at the Island House, The Barbican (☎ **01752/264849**). A second information center, **Plymouth Discovery Centre,** is at Crabtree Marsh Mills, Plymouth (☎ **01752/266030**). Both open Monday through Saturday from 9am to 5pm and Sunday from 10am to 4pm.

# EXPLORING PLYMOUTH

To commemorate the spot from which the *Mayflower* sailed for the New World, a white archway, erected in 1934 and capped with the flags of Great Britain and the United States, stands at the base of Plymouth's West Pier, on the Barbican. Incorporating a granite monument that was erected in 1891, the site is referred to as both the **Mayflower Steps** or the **Memorial Gateway.**

The **Barbican** is a mass of narrow streets, old houses, and quayside shops selling antiques, brasswork, old prints, and books. Fishing boats still unload their catch at the wharves, and passenger-carrying ferryboats run short **harbor cruises.** A trip includes views of Drake's Island in the sound, the dockyards, naval vessels, and the Hoe from the water. A cruise of Plymouth Harbour costs £3.50 ($5.60) for adults and £1.75 ($2.80) for children. Departures are February through November, with cruises leaving every half hour from 10:30am to 3pm daily. These Plymouth Boat Cruises are booked at 8 Anderto Rise, Millbrook, Torpoint (☎ **01752/ 822797**).

**White Lane Gallery.** 1 White Lane, The Barbican. ☎ **01752/221450.** Free admission. Mon noon–4pm; Tues–Sat 10am–5pm. Bus: no. 39.

This gallery specializes in contemporary art and crafts, with changing exhibitions of paintings and ceramics. It also has three resident craftspeople, including a potter, furniture maker, and silk painter. It's a 5-minute walk from the town center in Plymouth's historic Barbican, near the Mayflower Steps.

**Plymouth Gin Distillery.** Black Friars Distillery, 60 Southside St. ☎ **01752/667062.** Admission £2 ($3.20) adults; £1.25 ($2) children 10–18, free for children 9 and under. Easter–Oct, Mon–Sat 10:30am–4pm. Closed Nov–Easter. Bus: no. 54.

These premises, one of Plymouth's oldest surviving buildings, were where the Pilgrims met prior to sailing for the New World. Plymouth Gin has been produced here for 200 years on a historic site that dates back to a Dominican monastery built in 1425. There are public guided tours. A Plymouth Gin Shop is on the premises. The gin distillery is adjacent to a historic monument, now part of the Distillery Beefeater Restaurant.

**Prysten House.** Finewell St. ☎ **01752/661414.** Admission 75p ($1.20) adults; 30p (50¢) children. Easter–Oct, Mon–Sat 10am–4pm. Closed Nov–Easter.

Built in 1490 as a town house close to St. Andrew's Church, it is now a church house and working museum. Rebuilt in the 1930s with American help, it displays a model of Plymouth in 1620 and tapestries depicting the colonization of America. At the entrance is the gravestone of the captain of the U.S. brig *Argus*, who died on August 15, 1813, after a battle in the English Channel.

## WHERE TO STAY

Present-day pilgrims from the New World looking for affordable lodging are advised to head for the Hoe, where there are a number of inexpensive B&Bs on a peaceful street near the water.

### DOUBLES FOR LESS THAN £40

✪ **Georgian House.** 51 Citadel Rd., The Hoe, Plymouth, Devon PL1 3AU. ☎ **01752/663237.** Fax 01752/253953. 11 rms. TV TEL. £26 ($41.60) single; £39 ($62.40) double. All rates include English breakfast. AE, DC, MC, V. Metered parking 40p (65¢) per hour Mon–Sat 10am–6pm. Closed Dec 23–Jan 10. Bus: no. 54.

This Georgian town house is one of the finest guest houses in Plymouth. Each of the rooms is well maintained and comfortably furnished and contains beverage-making equipment, a hair dryer, and a trouser press. British and international meals are served in the fully licensed candlelit Fourposter Restaurant, costing £7 ($11.20) and up for a meal. The restaurant is open Monday through Saturday from 6:30 to 9pm. The location is on the Hoe, about 5 minutes from the ferry terminal.

**Lamplighter Hotel.** 103 Citadel Rd., The Hoe, Plymouth, Devon PL1 2RN. ☎ **01752/663855.** Fax 01752/263858. 9 rms, all with shower only. TV. £25 ($40) single; £35 ($56) double. All rates include English breakfast. MC, V.

Contained in a Victorian-era house whose stucco-covered 1850 exterior is similar to that of many of its neighbors, this is a comfortable and unpretentious address close to the Hoe and the Barbican. The rooms are clean, simple, and uncluttered, each with tea-making facilities.

**Osmond Guest House.** 42 Pier St., Plymouth, Devon PL1 3BT. ☎ **01752/229705.** Fax 01752/269655. 6 rms, 3 with bath. TV. £16–£18 ($25.60–$28.80) per person single or double. All rates include English breakfast. No credit cards. Bus: no. 25 or 39.

A bay-fronted, three-story house originally built in 1898, this hotel is well known and popular. Inside, the original high plaster ceilings have been carefully preserved. Each basic, simply furnished room has tea- and coffee-making equipment. The owner, Mrs. Carol Richards, will pick guests up at the bus or train station if they arrange it in advance.

**Rosaland Hotel.** 32 Houndiscombe Rd., Mutley, Plymouth, Devon PL4 6HQ. ☎ **01752/664749.** Fax 01752/256984. 9 rms, 5 with bath. TV TEL. £17 ($27.20) single without bath; £30 ($48) double without bath, £35 ($56) double with bath. All rates include English breakfast. MC, V.

Built as a private residence close to the railway station around 1870, this granite-fronted house abuts its neighbors on the left and right, and is fronted with a small but pleasant garden. The bedrooms are simple, cozy, and clean, and the greeting is cheerful. A three-course evening meal can be prepared, if advance notice is given, for around £8 ($12.80) per person.

**St. Rita Hotel.** 76 Alma Rd., Plymouth, Devon PL3 4HD. ☎ **01752/667024.** 16 rms, 6 with bath; 1 suite. TV. £14.50–£16.50 ($23.20–$26.40) single without bath; £29 ($46.40) double without bath, £33 ($52.80) double with bath; £18.50 ($29.60) per person suite. All rates include English breakfast. V. Bus: no. 28B or 43A.

The St. Rita is close to the Plymouth train station in a row of blue Victorian houses on the main bus route to the city center, which is approximately a mile away. The rooms are clean and comfortable, with hot and cold running water and coffee-making facilities. The accommodations at the back are quieter. Evening meals are offered only from October to May, costing £6.50 ($10.40) and up.

**Wiltun.** 39 Grand Parade, West Hoe, Plymouth, Devon PL1 3DQ. ☎ **01752/667072.** 9 rms. TV. £20–£25 ($32–$40) single; £35–£40 ($56–$64) double. All rates include English breakfast. MC, V. Follow the signs to the Hoe, at the western end of the city. Bus: no. 25.

Wiltun is set on Plymouth's historic foreshore overlooking Drake's Island and Plymouth Sound. This Victorian house has many modern facilities, but it retains several of the architectural features of the 1850s. Some rooms are suitable for families. The rooms have recently been refurbished and are fine for an overnight. There's a private lawn to relax on and watch the ships go by.

### DOUBLES FOR LESS THAN £55

**Camelot Hotel.** 5 Elliot St., The Hoe, Plymouth, Devon PL1 2PP. ☎ **01752/221255.** Fax 01752/603660. 17 rms. TV TEL. £39 ($62.40) single; £50 ($80) double; £55–£60 ($88–$96) family room. All rates include English breakfast. AE, DC, MC, V. Bus: no. 54.

This neat, tall hotel stands on a small road just off the grassy expanse of the Hoe. There's a lounge with color TV and video, or you can watch from your own seat in your comfortably furnished bedroom. Guests frequent the pleasant small bar and restaurant, with fixed-price meals and an a la carte menu in the evening. Meals begin at £7 ($11.20). Laundry and dry-cleaning facilities are nearby.

**Imperial Hotel.** 3 Windsor Villas, Lockyer St., The Hoe, Plymouth, Devon PL1 2QD. ☎ **01752/227311.** Fax 01752/674986. 22 rms, 17 with bath. TV TEL. £34 ($54.40) single without bath, £42.50 ($68) single with bath; £47.50 ($76) double without bath, £53.50 ($85.60) double with bath. All rates include English breakfast. AE, CB, DC, MC, V. Bus: no. 54.

Owned by Alan and Prue Jones, this attractive and tastefully decorated Victorian hotel on Plymouth Hoe (off Notte Street) offers a homelike atmosphere. Alan was in the merchant navy for 13 years and is a former chairman of the Personal Service Hotel Group and a director of the Marketing Bureau in Plymouth. With their experience, Alan and Prue are more than able to advise overseas visitors with limited time on where to go and what to see. Ground-floor rooms are available, and there's ample parking space on the premises. Traditional English fare is served in the Imperial Dining Room, where a fixed-price menu costs £12.95 ($20.70).

## WHERE TO EAT

In addition to the selections below, the **Plymouth Arts Centre Restaurant,** 38 Looe St. (☎ **01752/660060**), offers one of the most filling and downhome meals in town. Prices range from £2 to £4 ($3.20 to $6.40), and it's also ideal for a snack. You can even see a movie downstairs if you desire. Service is Monday through Saturday 10am to 8pm.

**The Ganges.** 36 Brettonside. ☎ **01752/220907.** Main courses £5–£11 ($8–$17.60). MC, V. Daily 6pm–midnight. Bus: no. 54. INDIAN.

This Indian tandoori restaurant provides a good change of pace from traditional English cookery. It's part of a chain that has other locations in the West Country. You can dine in air-conditioned, candlelit comfort while enjoying an array of spicy dishes. The chef's specialty of a whole tandoori chicken is superbly spiced and flavored. There's also the usual array of curries and biryanis. Vegetarians will find sustenance here as well.

**Green Lanterns.** 31 New St., The Barbican. ☎ **01752/201313.** Reservations recommended for dinner. Main courses £4.25–£5.50 ($6.80–$8.80) at lunch, £10.45–£14.55 ($16.70–$23.30) at dinner. AE, MC, V. Mon–Sat 11:45am–2:15pm and 6:30–10:45pm. Bus: no. 54. ENGLISH.

A 16th-century eating house on a Tudor street, the Green Lanterns lies 200 yards from the Mayflower Steps. The lunch menu offers a selection of grills, chicken, and fish—all served with vegetables. The kitchen also features chalkboard specials such as Lancashire hot pot. Some unusual dishes are on the dinner menu such as goose breast in breadcrumbs, wild duck (teal), and venison in red wine. Chicken, beef, turkey, plaice, and mackerel are also available—all served with vegetables. Most visitors like the Elizabethan atmosphere, traditional English fare at reasonable prices, and personal service, but chances are you won't be asking for recipes. The restaurant is near the municipally owned Elizabethan House.

**Queen Anne Eating House.** 2 White Lane, The Barbican. ☎ **01752/262101.** Main courses £5.95–£8.95 ($9.50–$14.30); cream teas £2.50 ($4); children's meals £2.75 ($4.40). MC, V. Tues–Sat 6:30–10pm; Sun noon–3:30pm. Bus: no. 54. ENGLISH.

Next to the Barbican Craft Centre, this bow-fronted, white-painted 1790s joint is a nautically inspired place where you can order everything from coffee and tea to full meals. The food is plentiful and wholesome, and includes such English-inspired fare as roast beef and Yorkshire pudding, steak-and-kidney pie, roast fish from the local markets, fish and chips, and other hot meals. Service is fast and polite, and the furniture is solid and oaken. If you're not looking for a full meal, try a Devonshire cream tea (it's served all day) with homemade scones baked with half white and half whole-wheat flour.

**The Ship.** The Barbican. ☎ **01752/667604.** Reservations recommended. Carvery, £8 ($12.80) per adult for 2 courses, £10.49 ($16.80) for 3 courses; £4.95 ($7.90) children's meal. AE, MC, V. Daily 11am–11pm. Bus 54. ENGLISH.

This stone building faces the marina, and its tables are placed to offer a view over the harbor. You pass through a pub and take a flight of stairs one floor above street level, where a well-stocked salad bar and a carvery await you. The carvery presents at least three roast joints, and you're allowed to eat as much as you want; the first course is a help-yourself buffet, and a chef carves your selection of meats for your second course. Desserts cost extra. This is one of the best food values in Plymouth, but it's best to go for lunch, as in the evening the place becomes mainly a drinking establishment. The food is more bountiful than gourmet.

# 8 Clovelly

240 miles SW of London; 11 miles SW of Bideford

This is the most charming Devon village and one of the main attractions of the West Country. From a great height, the village cascades down the mountainside, its narrow, cobblestone High Street making travel by car impossible. You park your car at the top and make the trip on foot; supplies are carried down by donkeys. Every step of the way provides views of tiny cottages, with their terraces of flowers lining the main street. The village fleet is sheltered at the stone quay at the bottom.

To avoid the tourist crowd, stay out of Clovelly from around 11am until teatime. Visit nearby villages such as Bucks Mills (3 miles to the east) and Hartland Quay (4 miles to the west) during the middle of the day when the congestion here is at its height. Also, to avoid the climb back up the slippery incline, go to the rear of the Red Lion Inn and queue up for a Land Rover. In summer the line is often long, but considering the alternative, it's probably worth the wait.

# ESSENTIALS

**GETTING THERE**   From London's Paddington Station, trains depart for Exeter (see above) frequently. At Exeter, passengers transfer to a train headed for the end destination of Barnstable. Travel time from Exeter to Barnstable is 1 1/4 hours. From Barnstable, passengers transfer to Clovelly by bus.

From Barnstable, about one bus per hour, operated by either the Red Bus Company or the Filers Bus Company, goes to Bideford. The trip takes 40 minutes. At Bideford, connecting buses (with no more than a 10-minute wait between the arrival and the departure) continue on for the 30-minute drive to Clovelly. Two Land Rovers make continuous round-trips to the Red Lion Inn from the top of the hill. The visitor center (see below) maintains up-to-the-minute transportation information about how to get to Clovelly, depending on where you are.

If you're driving, from London, head west on M4, cutting south at the junction with M5. At the junction near Bridgwater, continue west along A39 toward Lynton. A39 runs all the way to the signposted turnoff for Clovelly.

**VISITOR INFORMATION**   Go to the **Clovelly Visitor Centre** (☎ **01237/ 431781**), where you'll pay £2.25 ($3.60) for the cost of parking, use of facilities, entrance to the village, and an audiovisual theater admission, offering a multiprojector show tracing the story of Clovelly back to 2,000 B.C. Also included in the price is a tour of a fisherman's cottage and admission to the Kingsley Exhibition (see below). Open April through June, Monday through Saturday from 9:30am to 5:15pm; October through March, Monday through Saturday from 10am to 4:30pm; and July through September, daily from 9am to 6pm.

## SEEING THE STEEP SIGHTS

The major sight of Clovelly is Clovelly itself. Charles Kingsley once wrote "...it is as if the place had stood still while all the world had been rushing and rumbling past it." The price of entry to the village (see above) includes a guided tour of a fisherman's cottage as it would have been at the end of the 1800s. For the same price you can also visit the Kingsley Exhibition. Author of *Westward Ho!* and *Water Babies,* Kingsley lived in Clovelly while his father was curate at the church. This exhibition traces the story of his life.

Right down below the Kingsley Exhibition—and our shopping note for the town—is a Craft Gallery where you have a chance to see and buy works by local artists and craftspeople. Once you've reached the end, you can sit and relax on the quay, taking in the views and absorbing Clovelly's unique atmosphere from this tiny, beautifully restored 14th-century quay. For those who can't make it back up the hill, a trusty Land Rover waits, although the hearty climb all the way back up these impossibly steep cobbled streets to the top and the car park is invigorating.

## WHERE TO STAY & EAT

**New Inn.** High St., Clovelly, Devon EX39 5TQ. ☎ **01237/431303.** Fax 01237/431636. 21 rms, 8 with bath. £17.50–£25 ($28–$40) single without bath; £35–£42.50 ($56–$68) double without bath, £46–£56 ($73.60–$89.60) double with bath. All rates include English breakfast. MC, V.

About halfway down the main street is the village pub, a good meeting place at sundown. It offers the best lodgings in the village, in two buildings on opposite sides of the steep street. Five of the bedrooms contain TV and phone.

This little country inn is also recommended for meals if you're not too demanding. A wide choice of moderately priced meals is offered in the oak-beamed dining room. Some dishes wouldn't be out of place in a pub. Local fare, including

Devonshire cream and fresh-caught lobsters, are featured whenever possible. Motorists can park in the lot at the entrance to the town. It's advisable to pack an overnight bag, as luggage has to be carried down (but is returned to the top by donkey).

✪ **The Red Lion.** The Quay, Clovelly, Devon EX39 5TF. ☎ **01237/431237.** Fax 01237/431044. 11 rms. TV. £80 ($128) double; £10 ($16) supplement single in a double room. All rates include English breakfast. MC, V.

At the bottom of the steep cobblestone street, right on the stone seawall of the little harbor, the Red Lion occupies the jewel position of the village. It rises three stories with gables and a courtyard, and all bedrooms look directly onto the sea or harbor. The rooms have hot and cold running water and adequate furnishings. There's an antique pub here, and dinner is available in the sea-view dining room. Dinners are priced at £14.50 ($23.20) for two courses, with a choice of four main dishes, two of which are always fresh local fish, then a selection from the dessert trolley. The cookery is sensible and wholesome. The manager suggests that the Red Lion is not suitable for children under 7 years of age.

## 9 Lynton-Lynmouth

206 miles W of London; 59 miles NW of Exeter

The north coast of Devon is set off dramatically in Lynton, a village some 500 feet high and a good center for exploring the Doone Valley and that part of Exmoor that overflows into the shire from neighboring Somerset. The Valley of the Rocks, west of Lynton, offers the most panoramic scenery.

## ESSENTIALS

**GETTING THERE**   The resort is rather remote, and the local tourist office recommends that you rent a car. However, local daily trains from Exeter arrive at Barnstable. Call ☎ **0345/484950** for information and schedules. From Barnstable, bus service is provided to Lynton at a frequency of one about every 2 hours. Call ☎ **01598/752225** for schedules. If you're driving, take M4 west from London to the junction with M5, then head south to the junction with A39. Continue west on A39 to Lynton-Lynmouth.

**VISITOR INFORMATION**   The **Tourist Information Centre** is at the Town Hall, Lee Road (☎ **01598/752225**). Open March through October, daily from 8:30am to 6pm and from November through February, Monday through Saturday from 9:30am to 1pm.

## EXPLORING THE TWIN TOWNS

Lynton is linked to its twin, Lynmouth, about 500 feet below, near the edge of the sea, by one of the most celebrated railways in Devon. The century-old train uses no electricity and no power. Instead, the railway covers the differences in distance and altitude by means of a complicated network of cables and pulleys, allowing cars to travel up and down the face of the rocky cliff. The length of the track is 862 feet with a gradient of 1 inch, which gives a vertical height of approximately 500 feet. The two passenger cars are linked together with two steel cables, and the operation of the lift is on the counterbalance system, which is simply explained as a pair of scales where one side, when weighted by water ballast, pulls the other up. The train carries about 40 passengers at a time for 50p (80¢) for adults and 30p (50¢) for children. Trains depart daily from April to October, at 2- to 5-minute intervals, from 8am to 7pm. From November to March, the train is dismantled and repaired.

The East Lyn and West Lyn rivers meet in Lynmouth, a popular resort with the British. For a panoramic view of the rugged coastline, you can walk on a path half-way between the towns that runs along the cliff. From Lynton, or rather from Hollerday Hill, you can look out onto Lynmouth Bay, Countisbury Foreland, and Woody Bays in the west. From Hollerday Hill, the view encompasses the Valley of Rocks, formed during the Ice Age with towering rock formations, and its centerpiece, Castle Rock, which is renowned for its resident herd of wild goats.

From Lynmouth harbor there are regular boat trips along what the English have dubbed, touristlike, "The Heritage Coast" of North Devon. You can cruise past nesting colonies of razorbills, guillemots, dunlin, and kittiwake, with the gulls soaring in the thermals by the highest sea cliffs in England.

Other activities in the locale include fishing, putting, bowls, tennis, pony trekking, and playing golf. Check at the visitor center (see above) for details.

## WHERE TO STAY
### DOUBLES FOR LESS THAN £40

**Bonnicott House Hotel.** 10 Watersmeet Rd., Lynmouth, North Devon EX35 6EP. ☎ **01598/ 753346.** 8 rms. TV. £19–£28 ($30.40–$44.80) per person. Rates include English breakfast. No credit cards. Closed Nov to mid-Mar.

Built as a rectory in 1820 and now listed as a building of historical interest, the Bonnicott is owned by Brenda and Barry Parker Smith. Since acquiring this licensed hotel, Barry and Brenda have embarked on an extensive refurbishing program that has included updating the decor and furnishings and installing central heating. All bedrooms and public rooms have views over Lynmouth Bay or the Lyn Valley. The terraced patio garden overlooks the sea; on a clear day the coast of Wales can be seen. On cooler days, pick up a book from the small library and relax by the log fire. The food is homestyle. Bonnicott House is a no-smoking establishment.

✪ **The Denes Guest House.** Longmead, Lynton, Devon EX35 6DQ. ☎ **01598/753573.** 6 rms, none with bath. £14–£16 ($22.40–$25.60) per person. All rates include English breakfast. No credit cards.

Built during the 1920s in a style popularized by the Victorians, this slate-roofed gabled house sits at the end of a small terrace on a quiet residential street at the western edge of town. The tastefully decorated accommodations are maintained by Nigel and Denise Hill, who accept only nonsmokers. The clean bedrooms are spacious, and each contains hot and cold running water. Dinner is provided for an additional £10 ($16); the tasty and filling meals are served in a cheerful dining room. The guest house sits at the edge of a local geological oddity known as the Valley of the Rocks, whose striations give unusual insights into the glacial activities of the Ice Age.

**Highcliffe House Hotel.** Sinai Hill, Lynton, Devon EX35 6AR. ☎ **01598/752235.** 10 rms. TV. £28–£38 ($44.80–$60.80) double. Single supplement £4 ($6.40). All rates include English breakfast. AE, MC, V.

A small hotel housed in a Victorian house dating from the 1870s, Highcliffe House offers a relaxing getaway. It's located on the side of Sinai Hill above the twin towns of Lynton and Lynmouth, and offers panoramic views of the Lyn River and the coastline. Although the house has been restored and modern amenities have been added to make accommodations more comfortable, none of the Old-World charm has been sacrificed. In the dining room, meals made from fresh ingredients are served. The candlelit dining room adjoins a conservatory where guests can watch as night falls on the cliffs of Devon and Wales.

**Sandrock.** Longmead, Lynton, Devon EX35 6DH. ☎ **01598/753307.** Fax 015989/752665. 9 rms, 7 with bath. TV TEL. £21.50 ($34.40) single without bath, £23 ($36.80) single with bath; £46 ($73.60) double with bath. All rates include English breakfast. AE, MC, V. Closed Dec–Jan.

This substantial three-story house stands on the road that leads from Lynton to the Valley of the Rocks. The house is on the lower part of a hill beside the road, and most of its bedrooms open onto views of the beginning peaks of the Valley of the Rocks. The bedrooms, generally quite large and sunny, are interestingly shaped and have water basins. The third floor has dormer windows, which make the rooms here even cozier. The beds have innerspring mattresses, and there are adequate shared bathrooms. Owners Mr. and Mrs. Harrison take a personal interest in the welfare of their guests. Their baked goods are a delight, especially the lemon lush pie and apple and cherry crumble. In the Anglers' Bar, visitors meet the Lynton locals after a routine dinner, which costs £11.50 ($18.40) and up.

**Victoria Lodge.** Lee Rd., Lynton, Devon EX35 6BS. ☎ **01598/753203.** 9 rms. TV. £22–£32 ($35.20–$51.20) per person. All rates include English breakfast. MC, V.

This elegant hotel, west of Church Hill, has a Victorian theme throughout following a complete refurbishing and redecorating. A nonsmoking hotel, it's known locally for its comfort and cuisine, as well as the hospitality extended by Ben and Jane Bennett. Each of the centrally heated bedrooms is decorated in a Victorian motif, and contains amenities such as color TV, hair dryer, and beverage-making facilities. Some units are deluxe, with four-poster beds. Dinner, at £15 ($24) for three courses, is optional; vegetarians and special diets can be honored. Dinner is served by candlelight in a Victorian dining room. The cuisine is a fairly standard blend of English and continental.

**Woodlands.** Lynbridge Rd., Lynton, North Devon EX35 6AX. ☎ **01598/752324.** 8 rms, 6 with bath. TV. £18.50 ($29.60) single without bath, £20.50 ($32.80) single with bath; £37 ($59.20) double without bath, £41 ($65.60) double with bath. All rates include breakfast. MC, V.

The Woodlands is a small private hotel located in Exmoor National Park but only a few minutes walk from Lynton's city center. Many guests stay at the hotel to enjoy the peaceful, quiet atmosphere; especially nice for relaxing is the large garden that extends down to the river. Most rooms have pleasant views of the wooded valley opposite the hotel and all are equipped with hot-beverage making facilities. All meals are homemade with local ingredients when possible and served in hearty portions. Owners John and Helen Christian also supply guests with a laundry area in which adventurous hikers can leave their muddy boots and wash dirty clothes after trekking through the park. Children under age 12 are discouraged.

## HALF-BOARD BARGAINS

**Hazeldene.** 27 Lee Rd., Lynton, Devon EX35 6BP. ☎ or fax **01598/752364.** 9 rms. TV. £30.50–£33.50 ($48.80–$53.60) per person. All rates include half board. AE, DC, MC, V. Closed mid-Nov to the first week in Jan.

Hazeldene is a Victorian home with a good deal of charm; many consider it among the best of the small B&Bs in the area. The bedrooms, which have beverage-making equipment, are kept sparkling clean and are a pleasure to return to after a day of walking along the coast. You can enjoy a drink in a cozy bar and later a simply prepared meal in the candlelit dining room. It's located west of Church Hill.

**Seawood Hotel.** North Walk, Lynton, Devon EX35 6HJ. ☎ **01598/752272.** 12 rms. TV. £39 ($62.40) single; £78 ($124.80) double. All rates include breakfast and dinner. No credit cards. Closed Nov–Feb.

This pink-walled Victorian house was originally built in 1848 as the vacation home of a local railway magnate. It stands high on a cliff above Lynton, overlooking the bay, and is surrounded by a pleasant garden. Most bedrooms contain traditional furnishings, hair dryers, and tea-making facilities. Four rooms have four-poster beds.

# WHERE TO EAT

**The Greenhouse Restaurant.** 6 Lee Rd., Lynton. ☎ **0159/875-3358.** Reservation required. Main courses £5.95–£13.95 ($9.50–$22.30). AE, MC, V. Mar–May, daily 9am–9pm; June–Sept, daily 9am–10pm. Closed Oct–Feb. INTERNATIONAL.

Established in 1890 as a tearoom, this pink-and-gray Victorian restaurant perched atop a 500-foot cliff offers a panoramic view of the Bristol Channel through its all-glass front. A nautical theme carries through the restaurant, and the bar actually has a waterwheel built into it. Owners Chris and Anjali Peters serve a large menu that's about as varied and multicultural as you're likely to find anywhere—a result, they say, of the fact that he's part Indian and she's part Chinese. Whatever the reason, offerings range from British to American, Chinese, Indian, Italian, and beyond. Locals and tourists alike appreciate the results and flock in to dine on main courses like the popular prawn jalsrezi; succulent shrimp in a spicy, medium-hot curry sauce; fresh local trout with almonds and herbs; a slab of steaming spinach and mushroom lasagna, or a 12-ounce chicken breast in a cheese and ham sauce. Chris Peters said that although orders of their steaks, rack ribs, and other red meat dishes have fallen off since the Mad Cow disease scare, that's not really a problem here, since they have a variety of dishes made with fresh local seafood, as well as more than a dozen vegetarian dishes. If you're in the mood for something lighter, you can choose from several salads, soups, and sandwiches. There's a full bar with a decent wine list.

**The Royal Castle.** Castle Hill, Lynton. ☎ **01598/752348.** Reservations not accepted. Main courses £2.50–£5 ($4–$8) at lunch, £4–£8.50 ($6.40–$13.60) at dinner. No credit cards. Daily noon–2:15pm and 7–9pm. BRITISH.

Because of its position on a hill adjacent to the town's main carpark, on the southern perimeter of Lynton, this 300-year-old pub enjoys sweeping views out over the Bristol Channel's headlands, with panoramas that extend on clear days as far as the coast of Wales. Set behind a tiled, cream-colored facade, it's famous for a period around 1900 when Edward VII, then the Prince of Wales, dropped in several times for drinks with "blokes" that included various royal relatives and the Crown Prince of Siam. The woodsy-looking Victorian decor hasn't changed much since then, although, unlike Edward VII, you'll have to order your food directly from the bar. Give them your table number when you order—the food will eventually be brought to your table. Menu items include steak-and-kidney pie, lasagna, salads, and hearty soups, although at dinner they're likely to be joined by more substantial items such as fried cod, plaice, or scampi, chicken Kiev, pork Somerset, sirloin steak *chasseur,* and beef bourguignonne. There are always about a half-dozen ales and bitters on tap here, many from small-scale nearby breweries, as well as a constant stream of Tetley's.

# 11

# Cornwall

The ancient duchy of Cornwall is in the extreme southwestern part of England, often called "the toe." This peninsula is a virtual island—at least culturally if not geographically. Encircled by coastline, it abounds in rugged cliffs, hidden bays, fishing villages, sandy beaches, and sheltered coves where smuggling was once rampant. Although many of the little seaports with hillside cottages resemble towns along the Mediterranean, Cornwall retains a distinctive flavor.

The Celtic-Iberian origin of the Cornish people is apparent in their superstitions, folklore, and fairy tales. When Cornish people speak of King Arthur and the Knights of the Round Table, they're not just peddling a line to tourists. To them, Arthur and his knights really existed, roaming around Tintagel Castle (now in ruins). In Bolventor, Sir Bediver threw Excalibur into Dozmary Pool at Arthur's request.

The ancient land had its own language until about 250 years ago, and some of the old words (*pol* for pool, *tre* for house) still survive. The Cornish dialect is more easily understood by the Welsh than by those who speak the Queen's English.

We suggest berthing at one of the smaller fishing villages, such as East or West Looe, Polperro, Mousehole, or Portloe—where you'll experience the true charm of the duchy. Many of the villages, such as St. Ives, are artists' colonies. Except for St. Ives and Port Isaac, some of the most interesting places lie on the southern coast, often called the Cornish Riviera. However, the north coast has its own peculiar charm as well. The majestic coastline is studded with fishing villages and hidden coves for swimming, with Penzance and St. Ives serving as the major meccas.

Penzance, a granite resort and fishing port on Mount's Bay, has a Victorian promenade. A little further west is Land's End, where England actually comes to an end. There are also the Isles of Scilly, 27 miles off the Cornish coast, with only five islands inhabited out of more than 100. Here you'll find the Abbey Gardens of Tresco, 735 acres with 5,000 species of plants.

## 1 The Fishing Villages of Looe & Polperro

Looe: 20 miles W of Plymouth; 264 miles SW of London
Polperro: 6 miles SW of Looe; 26 miles W of Plymouth;
271 miles SW of London

# Cornwall

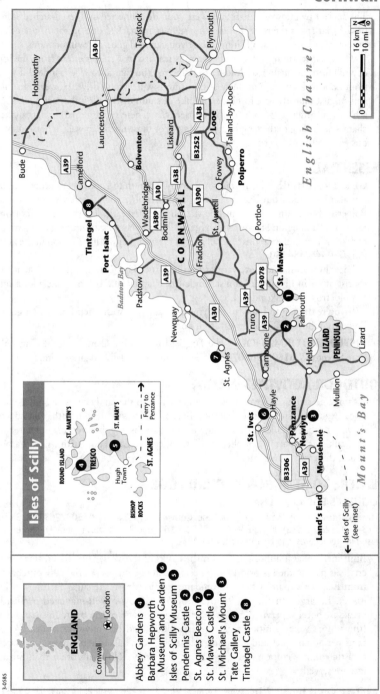

**Isles of Scilly**

ROUND ISLAND
ST. MARTIN'S
TRESCO 4
ST. MARY'S 5
Hugh Town
Ferry to Penzance
ST. AGNES
BISHOP ROCKS

Ferry to Penzance

English Channel

Plymouth
Tavistock
Holsworthy
A30
Bude
A39
Camelford
Launceston
Bolventor
Wadebridge
A389
Bodmin
A30
A38
Liskeard
Looe
A38
B3252
Talland-by-Looe
Polperro
Fowey
A390
St. Austell
Portloe
CORNWALL
Fraddon
A39
Padstow
Bodstow Bay
Tintagel 8
Port Isaac
Newquay
A30
A39
Truro
A39
Camborne
A3078
St. Mawes 1
Falmouth
St. Agnes 7
LIZARD PENINSULA
Helston
Lizard
Hayle
St. Ives 6
Penzance
Newlyn 3
Mousehole
Mullion
B3306
A30
Land's End
Mount's Bay

Isles of Scilly (see inset)

N
16 km
10 mi
0

ENGLAND
London
Cornwall

Abbey Gardens 4
Barbara Hepworth Museum and Garden 6
Isles of Scilly Museum 5
Pendennis Castle 2
St. Agnes Beacon 7
St. Mawes Castle 1
St. Michael's Mount 3
Tate Gallery 6
Tintagel Castle 8

3-0585

385

The ancient twin towns of East and West Looe are connected by a seven-arched stone bridge that spans the river. Houses on the hills are stacked one on top of the other in terrace fashion. In each fishing village you can find good accommodations.

The ancient fishing village of Polperro is reached by a steep descent from the top of a hill from the main road leading to Polperro. You can take the $4^1/_2$-mile cliff walk from Looe to Polperro, but the less adventurous will want to drive. However, in July and August motorists are forbidden to take cars into town unless they are booked at a hotel, in order to prevent traffic bottlenecks. There's a large parking area (that charges according to the length of your stay). For those unable to walk, a horse-drawn bus goes to the town center.

## ESSENTIALS

**GETTING THERE**    Daily trains run from Plymouth to Looe, and rail connections can also be made from Exeter (Devon) and Bristol (Avon). Most visitors drive to Polperro, but the nearest main-line station is at Liskeard, less than 4 hours from London's Paddington Station, with a branch line to Looe. Taxis meet incoming trains to take visitors to the various little villages in the area. For rail information in the area, call ☎ **0345/484950.**

Local bus companies have various routings from Plymouth into Looe. Ask at the tourist office in Plymouth for a schedule (see chapter 10). You can take a local bus to Polperro from Liskeard or Looe.

If you're driving to Looe from Plymouth, take A38 west, then B3253. To get to Polperro, follow A387 southwest from Looe.

**VISITOR INFORMATION**    The **Tourist Information Centre** is at the Guildhall, Fore Street (☎ **01503/262072**). Open summer only daily 10am to 2pm.

## OUTDOOR ACTIVITIES IN LOOE

Fishing and sailing are two of the major sports, and the sandy coves, as well as East Looe Beach, are spots for sea bathing. Beyond the towns are cliff paths and chalky downs worth a ramble. Looe is noted for its shark fishing, but you may prefer simply walking the narrow, crooked medieval streets of East Looe, with its old harbor and 17th-century guildhall.

## WHERE TO STAY IN & AROUND LOOE
### DOUBLES FOR LESS THAN £45

**Harescombe Lodge.** Watergate, near Looe, Cornwall PL13 2NE. ☎ **01503/263158.** 3 rms. £18–£20 ($28.80–$32) single; £36–£40 ($57.60–$64) double. All rates include English breakfast. No credit cards. Closed 1 week at Christmas.

Built in 1760 as a hunting lodge on the banks of the West Looe River, this property was part of the historic Trelawn estate whose lands were originally purchased from Elizabeth I, and whose descendants went on to make sugar fortunes in Jamaica. Enlarged in the 1960s, the property is now a well-managed bed-and-breakfast hotel supervised by Mrs. Jane Wynn. None of the bedrooms has a TV (the house's valley position makes TV reception "terrible" anyway), but each contains period antiques and a comfortable decor, with an aesthetic midway between a rustic country cottage and a stately country home. No meals other than breakfast are served.

**Kantara Guest House.** 7 Trelawney Terrace, West Looe, Cornwall PL13 2AG. ☎ **01503/ 262093.** 6 rms, none with bath. TV. £13–£15.50 ($20.80–$24.80) single; £26–£31 ($41.60–$49.60) double. All rates include English breakfast. AE, MC, V. After crossing the bridge into West Looe, Kantara is on the left-hand side as you bear right up the hill.

This is one of the best bargains in West Looe, a comfortably appointed guest house looking out over the river. It's a leisurely 8-minute stroll from the seafront and the heart of East Looe and 5 minutes from West Looe's town square and quay. The rooms contain color TV, VCR, clock radio, hot and cold water and washbasins, and beverage-making facilities. A video library has about 150 films for guest use. Three rooms are ideal for families. The lounge has a well-stocked bar, and you can also order a three-course meal for £10 ($16) when available. Kantara serves one of the best and most traditional English breakfasts in the area, and you can order it as late as 11am.

⊕ **Klymiarven Hotel.** Barbican Hill, East Looe, Cornwall PL13 1BH. ☎ or fax **01503/262333.** 14 rms. TV TEL. £28–£41 ($44.80–$65.60) per person. All rates include English breakfast. MC, V. Closed Dec–Jan.

Set on 2 acres of woodland and terraced gardens with views of the harbor, this hotel is one of the best accommodations in the area. It has an elegant lounge, a sunny lounge bar, and a terrace overlooking a heated swimming pool. Its tastefully furnished bedrooms include beverage-making equipment, TV, radio, and direct-dial telephones. It's run by Peter and Alison Britchford, who offer a relaxed atmosphere. British and international cuisine is prepared with fresh produce and served in a candlelit restaurant. Meals begin at £15.50 ($24.80) and the dishes are competently cooked. The 1590s cellars have lots of character, with a smugglers' passage, flagstone floors, and old timber beams. The Klymiarven is best approached from Barbican Road from the village of St. Martin.

**Osborne House Licensed Restaurant With Bed & Breakfast Rooms.** Lower Chapel St., East Looe, Cornwall PL13 1AT. ☎ **01503/262970.** 3 rms. TV. £25 ($40) single; £40 ($64) double. All rates include English breakfast. AE, MC, V. Parking £2 ($3.20). Closed Jan.

This 17th-century building stands on one of the tiny streets of this old fishing village, a few minutes' walk to the sea and the main shopping area. All rooms are comfortably but rather plainly furnished, with beverage-making facilities. A few are a little worse for the wear. A small bar is popular with holiday makers. The dining room has Old-World charm, with bright brasses and copper kettles adorning a large hearth. The owners, Wilma and Richard Hatcher, offer a varied menu of fresh fish, Cornish beef, lamb, and game, backed up by a good wine list. The food, although adequate at times, cannot be recommended unreservedly.

## DOUBLES FOR LESS THAN £60

**Coombe Farm.** Widegates, near Looe, Cornwall PL13 1QN. ☎ **01503/240223.** 10 rms. TV TEL. £23–£29 ($36.80–$46.40) single; £46–£58 ($73.60–$92.80) double. All rates include English breakfast. AE, DC, MC, V. Closed Nov–Feb.

About 3¹/₂ miles from Looe is this country house, surrounded by 10¹/₂ acres of lawns, meadows, woods, streams, and ponds, with views down a wooded valley to the sea. Alexander and Sally Low have furnished the centrally heated house with antiques and paintings. Open log fires blaze in the dining room and lounge in cool weather. Dinner, served in the candlelit dining room with views of the sea, includes traditional English and Cornish dishes. The meals—at £15 ($24) and up—offer good value and quality. Food is always prepared with fresh produce and freshly cooked. Nothing is prepared in advance, frozen, and then reheated. Guests may use the heated outdoor swimming pool in the summer.

Coombe Farm lies on the B3253 road just south of Widegates Village between Hessenford (1 mile) and Looe (3¹/₂ miles).

**Panorama Hotel.** Hannafore Rd., West Looe, Cornwall PL13 2DE. ☎ **01503/262123.** Fax 01503/265654. 10 rms. TV. £23.50–£33.50 ($37.60–$53.60) single; £47–£67 ($75.20–$107.20) double. All rates include English breakfast. MC, V.

From this immaculate hotel in the center of this small fishing town, you can enjoy the views of the harbor and rugged coastline. You always get a polite welcome and personal service at this Cornish outpost, and the recently decorated bedrooms are comfortable, and front bedrooms have balconies overlooking the bay. A table d'hôte dinner costs £10.50 ($16.80). Local produce, fresh vegetables, fish from the quay, and vegetarian options are always featured on the menu. Special diets are also catered to.

## WHERE TO EAT IN LOOE

**The Water Rail.** Lower Market St., East Looe. ☎ **01503/262314.** Reservations required in summer only. Fixed-price 3-course menu £12.95 ($20.70). AE, V. Apr–Oct, daily 6:30–10pm; Nov–Mar, Tues–Sat 6:30–10pm. SEAFOOD.

This restaurant, housed in a 14th-century structure near the quay, lies a 2-minute walk from the river and the beach. The kitchen specializes in fresh fish from the area, including, on occasion, sardines. Daily offerings are based on seasonal availability of produce, and the menu is an interesting mix of dishes. The Water Rail has won the praise of many a diner, although some have found the seafood overcooked. Wine is available by the glass.

## EXPLORING POLPERRO

Polperro is one of the handsomest villages in Cornwall; parts of it are still very 17th century in appearance. The village is surrounded by cliffs, and a stream called the Pol runs through it. The heart of the village is its frequently photographed and painted fishing harbor, where the pilchard boats, loaded to the gunwales, used to dock. At one time it was estimated that nearly every man, woman, and child in the village spent time salting down pilchards for the winter, or smuggling. Today the tourist trade has replaced contraband.

## WHERE TO STAY IN POLPERRO

In and around Polperro, you'll find a number of good and colorful cottages, houses, small hotels, and inns that receive paying guests.

### DOUBLES FOR LESS THAN £45

**Lanhael House.** Langreek Rd., Polperro, Cornwall PL13 2PW. ☎ **01503/72428** or 01503/73077. 5 rms, 3 with shower only. TV. £23 ($36.80) single without bath; £38 ($60.80) double without bath, £40 ($64) double with shower only. All rates include English breakfast. No credit cards. Closed mid-Oct to Apr.

One of the best moderately priced accommodations at the resort, Lanhael House, situated off the road to Fowey, dates from the 17th century. Today it has many amenities, including a heated swimming pool and a terrace to capture the sun of the Cornish coast. The bedrooms are comfortable and attractively furnished, each with tea- or coffee-making equipment. An evening meal—nothing special here—can be provided if arrangements are made in advance.

**New House.** Talland Hill, Polperro, Cornwall PL13 2RX. ☎ **01503/272206.** 3 rms, 1 with bath. £18 ($28.80) single without bath; £36 ($57.60) double without bath, £40 ($64) double with bath. All rates include English breakfast. No credit cards. Closed Nov–Mar. From A38, take the first turn to Looe, then turn right over the bridge onto Polperro Rd. and continue for 4 miles; take the left fork at a telephone kiosk and bus shelter, continue 200 yds., and turn right, going down a steep hill; New House is on the left.

This guest house lies on the village outskirts, away from the congestion that sometimes overtakes the town center in summer. It offers a large garden with a view over the harbor and the Eddystone light, and management by owners Ken and Polly Perkins, who welcome their guests warmly. Their house adopted its present form, with several bay windows, in 1911 when a century-old granite cottage was enlarged into the Edwardian style and painted white. The bedrooms are comfortable and well maintained, each with many-paned leaded casement windows that open onto garden or harbor views. Although no meals other than breakfast are served, the Perkinses are adept at directing their visitors to any of the several nearby restaurants.

**Penryn House Hotel.** The Coombs, Main St., Polperro, Cornwall PL13 2RG. ☎ **01503/ 272157.** Fax 01503/273055. 10 rms. TV. £26–£35 ($41.60–$56) single; £40–£56 ($64–$89.60) double. All rates include English breakfast. AE, MC, V.

Bought almost a decade ago by Christine Kay, a most charming hostess, and remodeled over the years, this country-style hotel reflects the peace of its Cornish fishing village heritage. Quaint narrow lanes and whitewashed cottages are home to various potters and artists, and coastal paths offer panoramic sea vistas. All of the bedrooms have televisions, courtesy trays, and beverage-making facilities. The hotel is on the main road, so the car park is an advantage. A fireside lounge bar offers local produce, fresh seafood, and a serviceable wine list. The house often stages murder mystery weekends, with 1920s costumes optional.

## DOUBLES FOR LESS THAN £65

✪ **Landaviddy Manor.** Landaviddy Lane, Polperro, Cornwall PL13 2RT. ☎ **01503/272210.** 7 rms. TV. £29 ($46.40) single; £46–£64 ($73.60–$102.40) double. All rates include English breakfast. MC, V. Closed Nov–Feb. Turn right at the main village parking area (by the Crumplehorn Inn) and follow the lane until you reach a T-junction; then follow the signs to the left to Landaviddy Manor.

This 1790s manor house built of gray Cornish stone sits on a secluded hill above the village and has a view of Polperro Bay. It adjoins National Trust land and is near the cliff paths and coves along the coast; the Cornish moors and Dartmoor are also easily accessible, as are numerous beaches nearby. Landaviddy, run by Eric and Meryl Rowe, may have a period feel to it, but all its bedrooms have hot and cold running water and central heating. All rooms are individually furnished; some have four-poster beds and open onto sea and country views. There's a comfortable lounge with a TV and a log fire. Children 14 and under are not accepted.

# WHERE TO EAT IN POLPERRO

**Crump's Bistro.** Crumplehorn. ☎ **01503/72312.** Reservations recommended for dinner. Main courses £3.70–£5.95 ($5.90–$9.50). MC, V. Daily noon–8pm (tea/coffee daily 10am–11pm). Take the road to Looe, a 10-minute walk north of the town's harbor. ENGLISH.

This unpretentious bistro is in a pair of stone-and-slate farmer's cottages (originally built around 1650) that were architecturally united long ago. Operated by Mr. and Mrs. Westley, it serves lunchtime sandwiches, portions of chili or chicken curry, and ploughman's lunches, and more formal evening fare which might include peppersteak or roast ham with pineapple. When hot meals are not being served, tea and coffee are offered.

✪ **The Three Pilchards.** The Quay. ☎ **01503/72233.** Pub snacks £1.40–£6.95 ($2.25–$11.10). No credit cards. Mon–Sat 11:30am–3pm and 7–11pm; Sun noon–3pm and 7–10:30pm. ENGLISH.

Locals and visitors alike come to this pub near the harbor. It's a large L-shaped room with a black oak interior and a fireplace that burns brightly at night. You can sit in the windowseat and listen to the talk of the villagers, although you may not be able to understand a word of their Cornish dialect. Food items include everything from sandwiches and jacket potatoes to curry, steaks, and salads, instead of the same old fare that's been offered for the last 30 years. Bar snacks and plates of food are served during regular hours.

## 2 The Lizard Peninsula

323 miles SW of London; 21 miles S of Falmouth

The southernmost point in England is the Lizard, a remarkable spot with jagged rocks reaching out into the sea where cormorants and gulls fish. The Lizard is the lesser known of Cornwall's two peninsulas—most people are more familiar with Land's End. The Lizard is characterized by its beaches, small villages, coastal walks, and craft studios. Some of the best beaches are at the coves at Poldhu and Kynance. The seagoing people of the Lizard have long known of the often-furious nature of the coastline, and have given certain places epithets like "the Devil's Frying Pan." Rare flora and fauna can be found at Goonhilly Downs. Many shipwreck victims were buried in the cemetery at the Church of St. Keverne in the village of the same name, and British TeleCom's Goonhilly Satellite Earth Station can be seen from most parts of the peninsula—it beams TV pictures across the Atlantic, and is the country's largest radio-receiving and space-tracking station.

There are those who claim that the Lizard is "the most Cornish place" in Cornwall, and it was the last place where the Cornish language was spoken before the language underwent a modernization.

There are no big resorts here, just scattered small hotels and B&B houses (some of which close in the winter, as this is essentially a summer place). Most of the accommodations and places to eat are at the village of Mullion.

### ESSENTIALS

**GETTING THERE**   The nearest railway station is 23 miles from the Lizard Peninsula in the town of Redruth, which is on the direct London-Penzance line. Trains leave London from Paddington Station. Call ☎ **0345/484950** for schedules and information. No bus service is available. From Falmouth, take A394 west to the junction with A3083, which you can take south to Lizard Point.

**VISITOR INFORMATION**   Go to the **Tourist Information Centre** at 28 Killigrew St. in Falmouth (☎ **01326/312300**). It's open from Easter through September, Monday through Thursday from 9am to 5pm, Friday from 9am to 4:45pm, and Saturday from 9am to 5pm. In July and August, the office is also open on Sunday from 10am to 4pm. In winter, the office is open Monday through Thursday from 9am to 1pm and from 2 to 5pm, and on Friday from 9am to 1pm and from 2 to 4:45pm.

### WHERE TO STAY & EAT

**The Lizard Hotel.** Penmenner Rd., Lizard, Cornwall TR12 7NP. ☎ **01326/290305.** 7 rms, 2 with bath, 5 with shower only. £19–£23 ($30.40–$36.80) single; £38–£46 ($60.80–$73.60) double. All rates include English breakfast. MC, V. From the market town of Helston, take B3083 to Lizard Village; Penmenner Rd. is the first right after the village green.

This informal place, operated by Tess and John Barlow, is in a cul-de-sac at the termination of the point, overlooking Kynance Cove. It is definitely for tranquillity-seekers who enjoy panoramic views. Although the Victorian structure has been renovated several times, many of the original architectural elements are still intact. An evening meal can be arranged at 7:30pm for £12.50 ($20).

**Mrs. Ingrid Sowden's House.** Villa Clare, Lizard Point near Helston, Cornwall TR12 7NU. ☎ **01326/290300.** 2 rms, none with bath. TV. £16–£18 ($25.60–$28.80) single; £30–£33 ($48–$52.80) double. All rates include English breakfast. No credit cards. Closed Dec 24–Jan 2. From Lizard, follow the road signs to "the most southerly point."

This home is definitely the southernmost house in the country, built on solid granite with a terraced garden. It provides fantastic views over the sea and the cliff edge from the garden fence some 170 feet above sea level. Despite the height, the house is frequently showered by spray from the breakers below during storms. The bedrooms have hot and cold running water and beverage-making equipment. Mrs. Sowden will recommend one of her friends in the village if she can't take you in.

## HALF-BOARD BARGAINS

✪ **Penmenner House Hotel.** Penmenner Rd., Lizard, Cornwall TR12 7NR. ☎ **01326/ 290370.** 8 rms, 5 with bath. TV. £20–£23 ($32–$36.80) per person. All rates include half board. MC, V. Take A30 to Redruth, then follow the signs to Helston and Lizard.

Behind a simple facade is one of the most appealing guest houses in the area. Guests receive Cornish hospitality and cozy, comfortable accommodations that have many amenities, such as color TVs, hair dryers, and beverage-making equipment. We strongly recommend that you reserve your room here. Guests of yore have included such writers as Virginia Woolf, Lytton Strachey, and Desmond MacCarthy. The house opens onto views of Lizard lighthouse, as well as coastal scenery.

## 3 Penzance

280 miles SW of London; 77 miles SW of Plymouth

This little harbor town, made famous by Gilbert and Sullivan, is at the end of the Cornish Riviera. It's noted for its moderate climate (it's one of the first towns in England to blossom with spring flowers), and for the summer throngs that descend for fishing, sailing, and swimming. Overlooking Mount's Bay, Penzance is graced in places with subtropical plants including palm trees.

Those characters in *The Pirates of Penzance* were not entirely fictional. The town has been raided by Barbary pirates, destroyed in part by Cromwell's troops, sacked and burned by the Spaniards, and bombed by the Germans. In spite of its turbulent past, it is mostly a tranquil resort today.

The most westerly town in England, Penzance makes a good base for exploring Land's End, the Lizard peninsula, St. Michael's Mount, the old fishing ports and artists' colonies of St. Ives, Newlyn, Mousehole, and even the Isles of Scilly.

## ESSENTIALS

**GETTING THERE**   Ten express trains depart daily from Paddington Station in London for Penzance. The trip takes 5¹/₂ hours. Call ☎ **0345/484950** for information and schedules.

The **Rapide,** run by National Express from Victoria Coach Station in London (☎ **0990/808080**), costs £33.50 ($53.60) for the one-way trip from London, which takes about 8 hours. The buses have toilets and reclining seats, and a hostess dispenses coffee, tea, and sandwiches.

Drive southwest across Cornwall on A30 all the way to Penzance.

**VISITOR INFORMATION**   The **Tourist Information Centre** is on Station Road (☎ **01736/362207**). Open the end of May to the end of August, Monday through Friday from 9am to 5pm, Saturday from 9am to 4pm, and Sunday from 10am to 1pm; and from the end of August through the end of May, Monday through Friday from 9am to 5pm and Saturday from 10am to 1pm.

## SEEING THE SIGHTS AROUND PENZANCE

✪ **Castle on St. Michael's Mount.** On St. Michael's Mount, Mount's Bay. ☎ **01736/ 710507.** Admission £3.90 ($6.25) adults; £1.95 ($3.10) children. Apr–Oct, Mon–Fri

10:30am–4:45pm (open weekends in summer); Nov–Mar, Mon, Wed, and Fri by conducted tour which only leaves at 11am, noon, 2pm, and 3pm, weather and tide permitting. Bus: no. 20, 21, or 22 from Penzance to Marazion, the town opposite St. Michael's Mount.

Rising about 250 feet from the sea, St. Michael's Mount is topped by a part-medieval, part–17th-century castle; it's 3 miles east of Penzance and is reached at low tide by a causeway. At high tide the mount becomes an island, reached only by motor launch from Marazion. In winter, you can go over only when the causeway is dry.

A Benedictine monastery, the gift of Edward the Confessor, stood on this spot in the 11th century. The castle now has a collection of armor and antique furniture. There's a tea garden on the island, as well as a National Trust restaurant, both open in summer. The steps up to the castle are steep and rough, so wear sturdy shoes. To avoid disappointment, it's a good idea to call the number listed above to learn the state of the tides, especially during the winter months.

**Minack Theatre.** Porthcurno. ☎ **01736/810694.** Theater tickets £6 ($9.60). Tour tickets £1.70 ($2.70). Exhibition hall, Easter–Oct 30, daily 10am–5:30pm. Performances, end of May to mid-Sept, matinees Wed and Fri at 2pm, evening shows Mon–Fri at 8pm. Leave Penzance on A30 heading toward Land's End; after 3 miles, bear left onto B3283 and follow the signs to Porthcurno.

One of the most unusual theaters in southern England, this open-air amphitheater was cut from the side of a rocky Cornish hill near the village of Porthcurno, 9 miles southwest of Penzance. Its by-now-legendary creator was Rowena Cade, an arts enthusiast and noted eccentric, who began the theater after World War I by physically carting off much of the granite from her chosen hillside. On the premises an exhibition hall showcases her life and accomplishments. She died a very old woman in the 1980s, confident of the enduring appeal of her theater to visitors from around the world.

Up to 750 visitors at a time can sit directly on grass- or rock-covered ledges, sometimes on cushions if they're available, within sight lines of both the actors and a sweeping view out over the ocean. Experienced theatergoers sometimes bring raincoats for protection against the occasional drizzle. Theatrical events are staged by repertory theater companies that travel throughout Britain, and are likely to include everything from Shakespeare to musical comedy.

# WHERE TO STAY
## DOUBLES FOR LESS THAN £35

**Camilla House Hotel.** 12 Regent Terrace, Penzance, Cornwall. ☎ **01736/363771.** 8 rms, 4 with bath or shower. TV. £16 ($25.60) single without bath, £23 ($36.80) single with bath; £32 ($51.20) double without bath, £46 ($73.60) double with bath. All rates include English breakfast. MC, V.

This comfortable, nicely furnished house is located near the Promenade and is within walking distance of shops and restaurants. The bedrooms have many amenities to give you the feeling of being "at home." Bill and Rosemary Wooldridge are very gracious and most helpful in providing tourist information for attractions in Penzance, St. Michael's, and surrounding areas. If you like, you can drive around the area, but the bus and train are adequate. The Wooldridges provide a delicious English breakfast in their charming dining room. The Wooldridges are also agents for the **Skybus** (airplane), and *Scillonian III* (ferry) and book day trips to the Isles of Scilly.

**Carnson House Hotel.** East Terrace, Penzance, Cornwall TR18 2TD. ☎ **01736/365589.** 8 rms, 2 with bath. TV. £16–£18 ($25.60–$28.80) single without bath; £30–£34 ($48–$54.40) double without bath, £35–£40 ($56–$64) double with bath. All rates include English breakfast. AE, DC, MC, V.

The Carnson House is personally run by the two helpful owners, Trisha and Richard Hilder. Close to the harbor, town center, train station, and beach, their 1740s house is a convenient location for most. The functionally furnished bedrooms have automatic hot-beverage facilities and TVs. There's a comfortable lounge with TV. The Hilders also provide a tourist information service on local things to do and will help to arrange for car rentals and local bus and coach tours, as well as for the steamer service to the Isles of Scilly. The house is licensed to serve alcoholic beverages. A simple four-course dinner is served for £9.75 ($15.60).

**Kimberley House.** 10 Morrab Rd., Penzance, Cornwall TR18 4EZ. ☎ **01736/362727.** 9 rms, none with bath. TV. £14–£16 ($22.40–$25.60) single; £28–£32 ($44.80–$51.20) double. All rates include English breakfast. No credit cards. Closed mid-Dec to mid-Jan.

This B&B is in a Victorian house of character between the Promenade and the town center, opposite Penlee Park and near the Morrab Gardens. Avril and Rex Mudway have run this house since Rex's retirement after a long seagoing career. They are gracious to their guests, providing good food, somewhat basic accommodations, and tips about what to see in the area. A rather large dinner of home-cooked English food goes for £9 ($14.40).

**Lynnwood Guest House.** 41 Morrab Rd., Penzance, Cornwall TR18 4EX. ☎ and fax **01736/365871.** 6 rms, 2 with bath. TV. £12–£15 ($19.20–$24) single; £24–£30 ($38.40–$48) double. All rates include English breakfast. AE, DC, MC, V.

Theresa Stacey owns this bed-and-breakfast located a few hundred yards from the town center. The Victorian house is constructed of granite blocks and is appointed in an English country style. The accommodations are comfortable and include tea- and coffeemaking facilities, TVs, and shaver outlets. Breakfast is the only meal served, but there are many restaurants and pubs nearby. If they're given notice, special diets can be accommodated.

**Mincarlo.** 45 Chapel St., Penzance, Cornwall TR18 4AQ. ☎ **01736/362848.** 3 rms, none with bath. £14 ($22.40) per person double. All rates include English breakfast. No credit cards.

Owner Mrs. Hilda Welsh tends to this large house herself and serves a hearty breakfast in her antiques-filled dining room. The furnishings are basic but adequate with beverage-making equipment in bedrooms; one guest room has a half-tester bed. Mincarlo is near the Admiral Benbow restaurant in the town center connecting with Western Promenade.

**Richmond Lodge.** 61 Morrab Rd., Penzance, Cornwall TR18 4EP. ☎ **01736/365560.** 7 rms, 3 with bath. TV. £15 ($24) single without bath; £30 ($48) double without bath, £34 ($54.40) double with bath. All rates include English breakfast. No credit cards. Closed Nov–Feb.

This comfortable early Victorian house with a nautical flavor is a few steps from Market Jew Street (the main street) and within an easy walk of the Promenade along the seawall; the Morrab Gardens are across the street. The owner, Mrs. Jean Eady, provides helpful service in this homelike place, with full central heating and a fully licensed bar. The best rooms are with bath and a four-poster bed; all rooms have TVs and beverage-making equipment. Dinner can be ordered daily for £8 ($12.80).

**Tremont Hotel.** Alexandra Rd., Penzance, Cornwall TR18 4LZ. ☎ **01736/362614.** 9 rms, 6 with bath (shower). TV. £13 ($20.80) single without bath; £28–£32 ($44.80–$51.20) double with shower only. All rates include English breakfast. No credit cards.

This turn-of-the-century house is on a tree-lined street just up from Mount's Bay off the Promenade and the seafront. Mrs. Maureen Pengelly runs this guest house with its clean, centrally heated bedrooms and comfortable although modest furnishings.

Some rooms are suitable for families, but single rooms have no private baths. A well-prepared dinner will run about £8.50 ($13.60), and you should arrange for it in advance. There's on-street parking.

**The Willows.** Cornwall Terrace, Penzance, Cornwall, TR18 4HL. ☎ **01736/363744.** 6 rms. TV. Apr–Aug £20 ($32) single, £40 ($64) double; Sept–Mar £17.50 ($28) single, £35 ($56) double. All rates include English breakfast. No credit cards.

This 150-year-old Regency house with its wide sweeping staircase, which a seafaring captain had built for himself and his family, is an impressive house and quite different from the usual Victorian bed and breakfast. The Willows is situated in Cornwall Terrace, a stone's throw from the Promenade and the sea. The rooms have TVs and tea- and coffee-making facilities. Lewis and Jenny Mitchell are from Penzance and enjoy chatting to their guests about the area, local politics, and interesting places to visit. Lewis, who is an artist in his spare time, has many of his paintings displayed in the dining room. His wife, Jenny, prepares a delicious breakfast beautifully served in their elegant dining room.

## DOUBLES FOR LESS THAN £60

**Ennys.** St. Hilary, Penzance, Cornwall TR20 9B2. ☎ **01736/740262.** 3 rms, 2 suites. TV. £40 ($64) single; £55–£60 ($88–$96) double; £60–£95 ($96–$152) family suite. All rates include English breakfast. Dinner £17.50. MC, V. Closed Dec 25–26.

Although begun as a flower farm, this property produces mainly vegetables today. Owned by Sue and John White, this farmhouse is made out of Cornish granite and features a slate roof. The exact age of the farm is not known, but the front section dates back to the 17th century and other portions are thought to be much older. The bedrooms are furnished in an old-fashioned farmhouse style with patchwork quilts; all have beverage-making equipment. Mrs. White presents a continental menu featuring fresh vegetables and herbs from the garden. Dinner may include such dishes as tomato-and-basil soup with fresh chives and pan-fried monkfish sautéed with fresh herbs served with Cornish potatoes. Dinner costs £17.50 ($28) and in the summer includes a glass of sherry that can be enjoyed in a large flower garden. The grounds include a heated swimming pool and a grass tennis court.

**Tarbert Hotel.** 11 Clarence St., Penzance, Cornwall TR18 2NU. ☎ **01736/363758.** Fax 01736/331336. 12 rms. TV TEL. £24–£28 ($38.40–$44.80) single; £48–£56 ($76.80–$89.60) double. All rates include English breakfast. AE, MC, V. Closed Dec 23–Jan 26.

The dignified granite-and-stucco walls of this once-private house were built in the 1830s by an earlier incarnation of Harrods department store when it operated a side-line business of home construction. (The present owners state that it was the home of a local merchant sea captain who is believed to have perished at sea between 1893 and 1841.) It's about a 2-minute walk northwest of the town center. Some bedrooms retain their original high ceilings and elaborate cove moldings, and each contains a tea-making facility and comfortable furniture. A restaurant, specializing in fresh seafood brought in by local fishing boats, serves fixed-price evening meals from 7 to 9pm every night, priced from £12.50 ($20) each. During the day, bar lunches are served to residents, and there's also a licensed bar with an extensive wine list and draft beer.

# WHERE TO EAT

In addition to the selections below, consider the **Nelson Bar** in the Union Hotel on Chapel Street in Penzance (☎ **01736/362319**). It's known for its robust pub grub and collection of Nelsoniana. It's also known as the spot where the admiral's death at Trafalgar was first revealed to the English. Food is served daily from noon to 2pm and 6:30 to 9pm.

Other possibilities for very casual eating include **Snatch-a-Bite,** 45 New St. (☎ **01736/366866**), near Lloyds Bank off Market Jew Street. This place is known for its well-stuffed sandwiches costing £2 ($3.20) and freshly made salads, a meal unto themselves, going for £3 ($4.80) and up. Open Monday through Saturday from 9am to 4pm.

**Dolphin Tavern.** 22 Quay St. ☎ **01736/364106.** Summer: Mon–Sat 8am–11pm; Sun 8am–10:30pm. Off-season: Mon–Sat 11am–11pm; Sun 11am–10:30pm. ENGLISH.

Head here for some of the best and most affordable pub grub in town. The staff not only serves a tasty brew, but offers daily specials, and they are particularly known for their tasty Cornish pasties. This is a large, friendly pub that often attracts a young crowd in summer with its variety of menu items. You can get either a hearty breakfast or cream teas at almost any time. The lunch and dinner menus are the same, carrying the usual items such as meat pies, grilled steaks, a roast of the day, and often seafood which usually appears in the half dozen or so daily specials.

**Hungry Horse.** Old Blake House Lane off Chapel St. ☎ **01736/363446.** Main courses £9–£10 ($14.40–$16). MC, V. Oct–May, Tues–Sat 7pm–10pm; June and Sept, Mon–Sat 7pm–10pm; July and August, Mon–Sun 7pm–10pm. INTERNATIONAL.

This comfortable little restaurant is tucked into a quiet lane of shops just off Chapel Street. Patrons can "come as they are," and feel right at home here. The menu offers the normal steak and pizza fare but is perked up with a regular selection of grilled specialties. A typical menu course could be shish kebab–style chicken breast that is marinated in white wine, lemon, and herbs and then grilled on skewers with mushrooms and onions. Dishes are served with a choice of rice, potatoes, or vegetables and include a freshly made salad.

✪ **Turk's Head.** 49 Chapel St. ☎ **01736/363093.** Main courses £4.25–£9.50 ($6.80–$15.20); bar snacks from £1.70 ($2.70). AE, MC, V. Mon–Sat 11am–2:30pm and 6–10pm; Sun noon–2:30pm and 6–10pm. Bar: Mon–Sat 11am–3pm and 5:30–11pm; Sun noon–3pm and 5:30–10:30pm. From the rail station, turn left just past Lloyd's Bank. ENGLISH.

Dating from 1233, this inn is reputed to be the oldest in Penzance—and no doubt, one of the oldest in Britain. It serves passable pub grub, far superior to its chief rival, the nearby Admiral Benbow. In summer, drinkers overflow into the garden. Inside, the inn is decorated in a mellow style, as befits its age, with flatirons and other artifacts hanging from its time-worn beams. Meals include fishermen's pie, local seafood, and chicken curry; and prime-quality steaks include rib eye. See the chalkboards for the daily specials.

# 4  The Isles of Scilly

**27 miles WSW of Land's End**

Several miles off the Cornish coast, the Scilly Isles are warmed by the Gulf Stream—so much so that semitropical plants thrive. Some winters they never see signs of frost. They're the first landfall most oceangoing passengers see on ocean journeys from North America.

There are 5 inhabited and more than 100 uninhabited islands in the group. Some are only a few square miles, whereas others, such as the largest, St. Mary's, encompass some 30 square miles. Three of these islands—Tresco, St. Mary's, and St. Agnes—attract visitors from the mainland. Early flowers are the main export and tourism is the main industry.

The Isles of Scilly figured prominently in the myths and legends of the ancient Greeks and Romans, and in Celtic legend they were inhabited entirely by holy men.

There are more ancient burial mounds on these islands than anywhere else in southern England, and artifacts have clearly established that people lived here more than 4,000 years ago. Today there's little left of this long history for the visitor to see.

St. Mary's is the capital, with about seven-eighths of the total population of all the islands, and it's here that the ship from the mainland docks at Hugh Town. However, if you'd like to make this a day visit, we recommend the helicopter flight from Penzance to Tresco, the neighboring island, where you can enjoy a day's walk through 735 acres mostly occupied by the Abbey Gardens.

## ESSENTIALS

**GETTING THERE** You can fly by plane or helicopter. **Isles of Scilly Skybus Ltd.** (☎ **0345/105555**) operates between two and eight flights per day, depending on the season, between Penzance's Land's End Airport and Hugh Town on St. Mary's Island. Flight time on the eight-passenger fixed-wing planes is 20 minutes each way. The round-trip fare is £53 ($84.80) for same-day return, and £55 ($88) if you plan to stay overnight.

There's also a helicopter service maintained by **British International Helicopters** at the Penzance Heliport Eastern Green (☎ **01736/363871** for recorded information), which operates, weather permitting, up to 12 helicopter flights, Monday through Saturday between Penzance, St. Mary's, and Tresco. Flight time is 20 minutes from Penzance to either island. A same-day round-trip fare is £58 ($92.80), rising to £89 ($142.40) if you spend a night or more on the island. A bus, whose timing coincides with the departure of each helicopter flight, runs to the heliport from the railway station in Penzance for a cost of £1 ($1.60) per person each way.

The rail line ends in Penzance (see above).

Slower but more romantic, you can travel via the **Isles of Scilly Travel Centre,** Quay Street, Penzance (☎ **01736/362009** or fax 01736/351223), which offers daily runs between Penzance and the Scillies from April to October. The trip from Penzance to Hugh Town, St. Mary's, takes approximately 2 hours 40 minutes, with continuing service on to Tresco. The ship departs Monday through Friday at 9:15am, returning from St. Mary's at 4:30pm. Saturday schedules vary according to the time of year, sometimes with two sailings a day. In winter, service is much more limited. A same-day round-trip ticket from Penzance to St. Mary's costs £32 ($51.20) for adults and £16 ($25.60) for children 15 and under. An onward ticket from St. Mary's to Tresco costs an additional £8 ($12.80) for adults and £4 ($6.40) for children under 14.

For information about Tresco's boat schedules, possible changes in hours and prices at the Abbey Gardens, and other matters, call ☎ **01720/422849.**

**VISITOR INFORMATION** **St. Mary's Tourist Information Office** is at Porthcressa Bank, St. Mary's (☎ **01720/422536**). Open April through October, daily from 8:30am to 5pm; November through March, Monday to Thursday from 8:30am to 5pm, Friday from 8:30am to 4:30pm.

## TRESCO & THE ABBEY GARDENS

No cars or motorbikes are allowed on Tresco, but bikes can be rented by the day; the hotels use a special wagon towed by a farm tractor to transport guests and luggage from the harbor.

The ✪ **Abbey Gardens** are the most outstanding feature of Tresco, started by Augustus Smith in the mid-1830s. When he began his work, the area was a barren hillside, a fact visitors are hardpressed to believe today.

The gardens are a nature-lover's dream, with more than 5,000 species of plants from 100 different countries. The old abbey, or priory, now in ruins, is said to have been founded by Benedictine monks in the 11th century, although some historians date it from 964. Of special interest in the gardens is Valhalla, a collection of nearly 60 figureheads from ships wrecked around the islands; the gaily painted figures from the past have a rather eerie quality, each one a ghost with a different story to tell. The gardens are open daily from 10am to 4pm. Admission is £5 ($8) for adults and free for children 13 and under.

After a visit to the gardens, take a walk through the fields, along paths, and across dunes thick with heather. Flowers, birds, shells, and fish are abundant. Birds are so unafraid that they land within a foot or so of you and feed happily. Call ☎ **01720/ 422849** for information about the abbey.

## WHERE TO STAY & EAT

**New Inn.** Tresco, Isles of Scilly, Cornwall TR24 0QQ. ☎ **01720/422844.** Fax 01720/423200. 12 rms. TEL. £52–£75 ($83.20–$120) per person, single or double occupancy, depending on the season. All rates include half board. AE, DC, MC, V.

Composed of an interconnected row of 19th-century fisherman's cottages and shops, the New Inn has been much enlarged by an outdoor area for those who wish to eat and drink. Inside, the bar is a meeting place for locals and visitors alike. Lunch snacks are available, and a bar meal costs £5 ($8) and up for two courses. Fixed-price dinners cost £18.50 ($29.60) and are served nightly between 7 and 9pm. The pictures in the bar show many of the ships that sank or foundered around the islands in the past, as well as some of the gigs used in pilotage, rescue, smuggling, and pillage. The inn has a heated outdoor swimming pool.

## ST. MARY'S

To get around St. Mary's, cars are available but hardly necessary. The **Island Bus Service** charges £2 ($3.20) from one island point to another; children ride for half fare.

Bicycles are one of the most practical means of transport. **Buccabu Bicycle Rentals,** Porthcressa, St. Mary's (☎ or fax **01720/422289**), is the only bike-rental outfit. They stock "shopper's cycles" with three speeds, "hybrid" bikes with 6 to 12 speeds, and 18-speed mountain bikes. All are available at prices that range from £4 to £5 ($6.40 to $8) daily. A sum of £10 ($16) is required for a deposit.

The **Isles of Scilly Museum,** on Church Street in St. Mary's (☎ **01720/422337**), illustrates the history of the Scillies from 2500 B.C. with drawings, artifacts from wrecked ships, and assorted relics discovered on the islands. A locally themed exhibit changes annually. It's open April to October, daily from 10am to noon and 1:30 to 4:30pm, as well as daily from 7:30 to 9pm, May to September; off-season, open only Wednesday from 2 to 4pm. Admission is £1 ($1.60) for adults and 10p (15¢) for children.

There is some shopping here, notably at **The John Hamilton Gallery,** The Parade (☎ **01720/422856**), which sells original paintings, island prints, and melamine mats. For the best selections of island crafts, visit **Phoenix,** Portmellon Ind Est (☎ **01720/422900**), where you can watch original artifacts being made into stained glass. The shops also sell a wide assortment of gifts, including jewelry and leaded weights. **The Isles of Scilly Perfumery,** Porthloo Studios (☎ **01720/423304**), a 10-minute walk from the center of Hugh Town, is packed with an intriguing number of gifts made from plants from the isles—everything from a delicate shell-shaped soap to fine fragrances, cosmetics, potpourri, and other accessories.

## WHERE TO STAY

### Doubles for Less Than £35

**Evergreen Cottage Guest House.** The Parade, Hugh Town, St. Mary's, Isles of Scilly, Cornwall TR21 0LP. ☎ **01720/422711.** 5 rms. £17–£22.50 ($27.20–$36) per person double. All rates include English breakfast. No credit cards.

One of the island's oldest cottages, dating back to the 1790s, the Evergreen was originally the home of sea captains and was at one time a smithy. It has a lot of character, with its maritime artifacts. The guest house has been modernized to provide adequate facilities for guests, and the resident proprietors offer breakfast only. It's located in the town's center and caters only to nonsmokers.

**Mincarlo Guest House.** The Strand, Hugh Town, St. Mary's, Isles of Scilly, Cornwall TR21 0PT. ☎ **01720/422513.** 12 rms, 4 with bath. £17–£21 ($27.20–$33.60) single without bath; £34 ($54.40) double without bath, £52 ($83.20) double with bath. All rates include English breakfast. No credit cards. Closed Nov–Feb.

The Duncan family has owned this lovely house right on the edge of the harbor since the 1950s. Colin and Jill Duncan offer a variety of accommodations, many of them overlooking the harbor, which is only a 5-minute walk away. Colin prepares and cooks the evening meal, featuring a selection of local produce, fish, and shellfish. The cost is £9.50 ($15.20).

### Half-Board Bargains

**Anjeric.** The Strand, Hugh Town, St. Mary's, Isles of Scilly TR2 0PS. ☎ **01720/422700.** 11 rms, 7 with bath. £34.50 ($55.20) per person without bath; £38 ($60.80) per person with bath. All rates include half board. No credit cards. Closed Nov–Mar.

Close to beaches, shops, and the quay, this centrally located B&B is a haven for nonsmokers. A three-story hotel, it is centrally heated, and bedrooms open onto views of the town beach or of off-shore islands. In a friendly relaxed atmosphere, it rents plainly furnished but comfortable and neat bedrooms. The setting is friendly and relaxed, and the food served here is hearty and wholesome, with an emphasis on seafood dishes.

**Crebinick House.** Church St., Hugh Town, St. Mary's, Isles of Scilly, Cornwall TR21 0JT. ☎ **01720/422968.** 6 rms. £64–£75 ($102.40–$120) double. All rates include half board. No credit cards. Closed Nov–Feb.

Named after one of the massive offshore rocks that in the 19th century caused a major shipwreck, this house is owned and operated by two refugees from the urban landscape of London, Lesley and Phillip Jones. Though it was originally built of granite blocks in 1760, modern additions have significantly expanded it in the rear. A landmark building, its facade can't be altered. The house lies in the village center. There are no sea views, but the water is reachable in two directions after a 50-yard walk. The bedrooms are nicely furnished and filled with floral-patterned fabrics. There are no singles. Lesley prepares dinners for residents only.

**Lyonnesse Guest Hotel.** The Strand, Hugh Town, St. Mary's, Isles of Scilly, Cornwall TR21 0PS. ☎ **01720/422458.** 9 rms, none with bath. £30–£31.50 ($48–$50.40) per person. All rates include half board. No credit cards.

This is a large family home in the quieter part of Hugh Town, but close to shops and the harbor. Derek and Melanie Woodcock are both islanders who take pride in telling their guests about the Scillies. There's a large lounge, and the house is well appointed; the front rooms and lounge have views of the harbor and the islands. The simply furnished units have heating, hot- and cold-water basins, and shaver outlets. It's located in the center opening onto Town Beach.

## AN EASY EXCURSION TO ST. AGNES

One of the Isles of Scilly, St. Agnes is a small community that lies as far southwest as any community in Britain and, lucky for travelers, remains relatively undiscovered. Much of the area is preserved by the Nature Conservancy Council. Since the long-established industries for the island are flower farming and fishing, there is little pollution and visitors can enjoy crystal-clear waters ideal for snorkeling and diving. Little traffic moves on the single-track lanes crossing the island, and the curving sandbar between St. Agnes and its neighbor island of Gugh is one of the best beaches in the archipelago. The coastline is diverse and a walker's paradise: A simple trail leads to any number of sandy coves, granite outcroppings, flower-studded heaths and meadows, even a freshwater pool. Sunsets are romantic, usually followed by a brilliant showcase of night stars. This soothing place is truly a natural wonder.

### ESSENTIALS

**GETTING THERE**   There are about three boats in each direction every day between St. Mary's and the much less densely populated island of St. Agnes. Something called a "tripper boat" departs from the quay at St. Mary's every morning at 10:15am and 12:15pm, requiring a 15- to 20-minute transfer to St. Agnes, for a round-trip charge of about £4 ($6.40). Boats return on a schedule determined by the tides, usually at 2:15pm and again at 3pm. The particular boat information is chalked on a chalkboard on the quay at St. Mary's every day. Schedules allow for easy "day-tripping" from St. Mary's. The boats from this island are operated by a couple of different family-run companies: **Briar Boating** (☎ **01720/422886**) and **Hicks Boating** (☎ **01720/422541**).

### WHERE TO STAY

✪ **Coastguards.** St. Agnes, Isles of Scilly, Cornwall TR22 0PL. ☎ **01720/422373.** 3 rms. £26–£29 ($41.60–$46.40) per person. All rates include half board. No credit cards. Closed the last 2 weeks in Dec.

When you visit St. Agnes, it's worth considering a stay at the home of Danny and Wendy Hick, the southwesternmost guest house in the British Isles with excellent sea views. Prince Charles (also the Duke of Cornwall), is the landlord, and he makes regular visits to Scilly, which he regards as a jewel in the Duchy of Cornwall's crown. One of their double rooms has two beds, and there are hot-beverage facilities in the rooms. There's no choice on the daily menu, but special diets are catered to if advance notice is given. The price of half board depends on whether you order a two- or four-course evening meal. Mr. Hick is a model-ship maker who sells his fine works through agents in London and New England, as well as doing work on private commissions. The house is near St. Warna's Cove.

**Covean Cottage.** St. Agnes, Isles of Scilly, Cornwall TR22 0PL. ☎ **01720/422620.** 4 rms, 2 with bath. TV. £60 ($96) double without bath, £64 ($102.40) double with bath. All rates include half board. No credit cards.

Originally built 200 years ago as the home of a local fisher, the home of Heather and Peter Sewell is constructed of solid blocks of local granite, and capped with a slate roof that shuts out the hardiest of gales. Despite the fact that it's a bit drab, and especially so during winter, it's the first bed-and-breakfast you'll see when heading into town after your arrival at the town's pier. There's a garden that wraps itself around the walls of this place, and sweeping views that extend out over the sea. Evening meals are served in a tidy dining room and feature local lamb, plaice, hearty soups, and roast beef.

## WHERE TO EAT

**The Turks Head.** St. Agnes, Isles of Scilly, Cornwall TR22 0PL. ☎ **01720/422434.** Main courses £3–£8.35 ($4.80–$13.35). MC, V. Daily noon–2:30pm and 7–9:30pm. Pub: Mon–Sat 11am–11pm; Sun noon–3pm and 7–10:30pm. Nov–Mar Wed and Sat only 9–11pm. ENGLISH.

In this solid-looking building, originally constructed in the 1890s as a boat house, is the only pub on the island—and the southwesternmost pub in Britain. Prominently located a few steps from the pier, it's run by John and Pauline Dart, who serve pub snacks and also more solid fare, which includes steaks and platters of local fish. The pub is the second building after the arrival point of the ferryboats from St. Mary's. There's also a twin-bedded room with shower for rent here, costing £22 ($35.20) per person.

## 5   Newlyn, Mousehole & Land's End

Newlyn: 1 mile S of Penzance
Mousehole: 3 miles S of Penzance; 2 miles S of Newlyn
Land's End: 9 miles W of Penzance

Reached by traveling through some of Cornwall's most beautiful countryside, Land's End is literally the end of Britain. The natural grandeur of the place has been somewhat marred by theme park–type amusements, but the view of the sea crashing against rocks remains undiminished. If you want to stay in the area, you can find accommodations in either Newlyn or Mousehole. The latter might not sound like a place for a holiday, but it is, in fact, an archetypal Cornish fishing village. If you visit in July and August, you'll need reservations far in advance, as neither Newlyn nor Mousehole has enough bedrooms to accommodate the summer hordes.

## ESSENTIALS

**GETTING THERE**    From London, journey first to Penzance (see above); then take a local bus for the rest of the journey.

From Penzance, take bus A to Mousehole and bus no. 1 to Land's End. There is frequent service throughout the day.

After reaching Penzance, drive south on B3315.

## NEWLYN

From Penzance, a promenade leads to Newlyn, another fishing village of infinite charm on Mount's Bay. In fact, its much-painted harbor seems to have more fishing craft than that of Penzance. The late Stanhope Forbes founded an art school in Newlyn, and in the past few years the village has achieved a growing reputation for its artists' colony, attracting both serious painters and Sunday sketchers. From Penzance, reach the old fishing cottages and crooked lanes of Newlyn by bus.

### WHERE TO STAY & EAT

**Higher Faugan Hotel.** Chywoone Hill, Newlyn, Penzance, Cornwall TR18 5NS. ☎ **01736/62077.** Fax 01736/51658. 11 rms. TV TEL. £41.50–£51.50 ($66.40–$82.40) single; £83–£103 ($132.80–$164.80) double. All rates include English breakfast. Children 11 and under stay free in parents' room. AE, DC, MC, V. Take B3315 ³/₄ of a mile south of Penzance.

The structure was built in 1904 by painter Alexander Stanhope Forbes, whose work is now in demand, as is that of his wife, Elizabeth Adela Forbes, and many other artists from the "Newlyn School." The spacious building's granite walls, big windows, and steep roofs are surrounded by 10 acres of lawn, garden, and woodland, all of which can be covered on foot by adventurous visitors. Amenities include a heated outdoor swimming pool, a putting green, a hard tennis court, a billiards room, and a dining room serving beautifully prepared English and continental specialties. The rooms are traditionally furnished and well maintained.

## MOUSEHOLE

The Cornish fishing village of Mousehole (pronounced *Mou*-sel) attracts hordes of tourists, who, fortunately, haven't changed it too much. The cottages still sit close to the harbor wall; the fishers still bring in the day's catch; the salts sit around smoking tobacco, talking about the good old days; and the lanes are as narrow as ever. About the most exciting thing ever to happen here was the arrival in the late 16th century of the Spanish galleons, whose sailors sacked and burned the village. In a sheltered cove of Mount's Bay, Mousehole today has developed as the nucleus of an artists' colony.

### WHERE TO STAY

**The Lobster Pot.** Mousehole, Cornwall TR19 6QX. ☎ **01736/731251.** Fax 01736/731150. 25 rms, 22 with bath. TV TEL. June–Sept, £26 ($41.60) per person in a single or double without bath; £44–£53.50 ($70.40–$85.60) per person single or double with bath. Oct–May, £22 ($35.20) per person single or double without bath; £36.75–£47.25 ($58.80–$75.60) single or double with bath. All rates include English breakfast. MC, V. Closed Jan. Open weekends only in Feb.

Tasteful, nostalgic, and charming, this little hotel is in four adjacent buildings near the water's edge in Mousehole. In addition to the main hotel, guests are housed in Clipper House, Gull's Cry, or Harbour's Edge. Seven bedrooms open onto sea views across the harbor and Mount's Bay beyond. The bedrooms are comfortably furnished, with such amenities as tea- or coffeemakers, color TVs, direct-dial phones, trouser presses, hair dryers, and razor outlets. Families are especially welcome.

Even if you're not a resident, the Lobster Pot is one of the best dining choices in town. A fixed-price dinner costs £15.50 ($24.80), or you can order a la carte, especially if you want to partake of the chef's specialty, freshly caught lobster (when available). It can be prepared virtually any way you want: steamed, grilled, Newburg, or thermidor. Crab, sole, and salmon are also featured.

**Renovelle.** 6 The Parade, Mousehole, Cornwall TR19 6PN. ☎ **01736/731258.** 3 rms. From £13.50 ($21.60) per person. All rates include English breakfast. No credit cards.

At the edge of the village, just past the large parking area, is a pretty blue-and-white villa on a cliff right beside the sea. Mrs. Stella Bartlett, the owner, has made the inn so inviting that guests keep returning. She's had a B&B since the early 1950s. Each bedroom is comfortable, with good views of the sea. It's a pleasure to have breakfast set before you in the sunny little dining room.

**The Ship Inn.** South Cliff, Mousehole, Penzance, Cornwall TR19 6QX. ☎ **01736/731234.** 3 rms. TV. £30 ($48) double without seaview, £40 ($64) double with seaview. All rates include English breakfast. No credit cards.

This charming pub is located on the harbor in this quaint fishing village. The exterior has a stone facade and the interior has retained much of the original rustic charm with its black beams and paneling, granite floors, built-in wall benches; and, of course, a nautical motif decorates the bar. The bedrooms, offering views of the harbor and the bay, have window seats. Although the rooms are simply furnished with floral chintz fabrics, they all have a TV, hair dryer, and beverage-making equipment. Bar snacks are served during the day. The dinner menu is a la carte with main courses from £4 to £10 ($6.40 to $16).

**White Cottage.** 10 Fore St., Mousehole, Penzance, TR19 6TQ. ☎ **01736/731462.** 2 rms, with shared bath. £15 ($24) single; £22 ($35.20) double. All rates include English breakfast. No credit cards.

This 400-year-old fisherman's cottage, with its 17th-century oak ceilings and antique furniture, is close to the fishing harbor. The nonsmoking cottage is most tastefully decorated, and Mike and Trish Jordan go out of their way to make their guests comfortable. The breakfasts are delicious and made to order. White Cottage is beautifully cared for, with many hanging baskets full of flowers suspended outside. In fact, many tourists stop to take photos of this lovely cottage.

## WHERE TO EAT

**The Lobster Pot** (see above) also serves meals.

**Pam's Pantry.** 3 Mill Lane. ☎ **01736/731532.** Main courses £2.50–£6.80 ($4–$10.90). No credit cards. Daily 9:30am to 5:30pm. SEAFOOD.

Some of the dishes at this small and cheerful cafe on the main road feature fish caught locally. You can order crab salad, a summer favorite, or smoked mackerel. To complete a meal, a homemade apple pie with clotted cream is served. You can also order sandwiches to go and pizzas. Come here more for convenience food than for any subtle flavors or spicing.

# LAND'S END

Craggy Land's End is where England comes to an end. America's coast is 3,291 miles west of the rugged rocks that tumble into the sea beneath Land's End. Some enjoyable cliff walks and panoramic views are available here.

## WHERE TO STAY

**Land's End Youth Hostel.** Letcha Vean, Cot Valley, St. Just, Penzance, Cornwall TR19 7NT. ☎ 01736/788437. Fax 01736/787337. 45 beds. £8.50 ($13.60) adults; £5.70 ($9.10) 18 or under. MC, V. Closed Nov 10–Mar.

One of the most remote but dramatically situated youth hostels in southwest England, this inviting hostel lies outside the town of St. Just, some 5 miles from Land's End. In the old Cornish style, it's reached by going down a rock-strewn road through meadowland with grazing cows. Although a little country-crude, it's welcoming. Rooms open onto the pounding surf or else the bucolic Cot Valley. Young people from all over the world meet in the public areas, often around a fireplace on a windy and rain-swept night. Others retreat to the conservatory with views opening onto the often turbulent Atlantic. Bedrooms are very basic and modest but well kept. There's a self-catering kitchen, although good homemade meals are also served. There's more of the warmth and feeling of a cozy B&B or a small inn here than in your typical impersonal youth hostel.

**The Old Success Inn.** Sennen Cove, Land's End, Cornwall TR19 7DG. ☎ **01736/871232.** Fax 01736/788354. 12 rms, 10 with bath. TV. £21–£36.50 ($33.60–$58.40) per person. All rates include English breakfast. MC, V. Bus: no. 1.

To reach this inn, turn right and follow the road down to Sennen Cove just before you reach Land's End. The Success is at the bottom, facing the sea and wide sandy beaches. Surfing rollers come in from the Atlantic almost to the foot of the seawall beneath this 17th-century fisher's inn. Over the years it has been extended and modernized, and now offers bright, clean rooms with TVs, hot-beverage facilities, electric heaters, and washbasins. The inn has a comfortable lounge with a color TV and panoramic views of the Atlantic. The restaurant features a carvery with meals beginning at £12 ($19.20). Food is also available in Charlie's Bar, which is open for drinks from 11am to 3pm and 6:30 to 11pm.

## WHERE TO EAT

**The King's Arm.** 5 Market Sq., St. Just. ☎ **01736/788545.** Main courses £2–£4 ($3.20–$6.40). No credit cards. Easter–Oct daily 11am–11pm. ENGLISH.

The oldest pub in St. Just is also the best place for affordable meals. Dating back to the 15th century, it stands in the center of town and is your best bet for low-cost food in the Land's End area. Begin with a glass of one of the local cask ales that will be pumped directly "from the wood," as they say here. A pub has stood on this site since 1700 (not when the building was founded), and some of the recipes haven't changed much since then. You can get steaks, roast, and perhaps even fresh crab sandwiches in summer. The kitchen is proud of their Cornish pasties. To go really local at lunch, order the ploughman's lunch with smoked mackerel.

# 6  The Artists' Colony of St. Ives

319 miles SW of London; 21 miles NE of Land's End; 10 miles NE of Penzance

This north-coast fishing village, with its sandy beaches, narrow streets, and well-kept cottages, is England's most famous artists' colony. The artists settled in many years ago and have integrated with the fishers and their families. Today, this large colony of artists live and create their art at various studios or cottages throughout the town.

Artists have been here long enough to have developed several schools or "splits," and they almost never overlap—except in a pub where the artists hang out, or where classes are held. The old battle continues between the followers of representational and abstract art, with each group recruiting young artists all the time. In addition, there are the potters, weavers, and other craftspeople—all working, exhibiting, and selling in this area.

Note that St. Ives becomes virtually impossible to visit in August, when you're likely to be trampled underfoot by busloads of tourists, mostly the English themselves. However, in spring and early fall the pace is much more relaxed, and a visitor can truly experience the art colony.

## ESSENTIALS

**GETTING THERE**   There is frequent service throughout the day between London's Paddington Station and the rail terminal at St. Ives. The trip takes 5$^1/_2$ hours. Call ☎ **0345/484950** for schedules and information.

Several coaches a day run from London's Victoria Coach Station to St. Ives. The trip takes 7 hours. Call ☎ **0990/808080** for schedules and information.

Take A30 across Cornwall, driving northwest at the junction with B3306, leading to St. Ives on the coast.

During the summer months many streets in the center of town are closed to vehicles. You may want to leave your car in the Lelant Saltings Car Park, 3 miles from St. Ives on A3074, and take the regular train service into town, an 11-minute journey. Departures are every half hour. It's free to all car passengers and drivers, and the parking charge is £6 to £8 ($9.60 to $12.80) per day. You can also use the large Trenwith Car Park, close to the town center, for £1.50 ($2.40) and then walk down to the shops and harbor or take a bus that costs 35p (55¢) per person.

**VISITOR INFORMATION**   The **Tourist Information Centre** is at the Guildhall, Street-an-Pol (☎ **01736/796297**). From January to mid-May and from late September through December, hours are Monday through Thursday from 9:30am to 5:30pm and Friday 9:30am to 5pm. From mid-May to June, hours are Monday through Saturday from 9:30am to 5:30pm and Sunday from 10am to 1pm. In July and August, hours are Monday through Saturday from 9:30am to 6pm and Sunday from 10am to 1pm. For the first 3 weeks of September, hours are Monday through Saturday from 9:30am to 5:30pm.

## TWO MUSEUMS DISPLAYING ST. IVES ART

✪ **Tate Gallery St. Ives.** Porthmear Beach. ☎ **01736/796226.** Admission £3 ($4.80) per adult, including 1 child under 16; £1.50 ($2.40) seniors and students 16 or older. Apr–Sept, Tues–Sun 10:30am–6pm; bank holidays 10:30am–5pm. Oct–Mar, Tues–Sun 10:30am–5pm. Closed Dec 24–25.

This branch of London's famous Tate Gallery exhibits changing groups of work from the Tate Gallery's preeminent collection of St. Ives painting and sculpture, dating from about 1925 to 1975. The gallery is administered jointly with the Barbara Hepworth Museum (see below). The collection includes works by artists associated with St. Ives, including Alfred Wallis, Ben Nicholson, Barbara Hepworth, Naum Gabo, Peter Lanyon, Terry Frost, Patrick Heron, and Roger Hilton. All the artists whose works are shown here had a decisive effect on the development of painting and sculpture in the U.K. in the second half of the 20th century. About 100 works are on display at all times.

The museum occupies a spectacular site, overlooking Porthmear Beach, close to the home of Alfred Wallis and to the studios used by many of the St. Ives artists. The museum is a three-story building, backing directly onto the cliff face and exploiting the dramatic sea views afforded by the site.

**Barbara Hepworth Museum & Garden.** Barnoon Hill. ☎ **01736/796226.** Admission £2.50 ($4) adults; £1.25 ($2) children. Apr–Sept, Tues–Sun 10:30am–6pm; bank holidays 10:30am–5pm. Oct–Mar, Tues–Sun 10:30am–5pm. Closed Dec 24–25.

Dame Barbara Hepworth lived at Trewyn from 1949 until her death in 1975 at the age of 72. In her will she asked that her working studio be turned into a museum where future visitors could see where she lived and created her world-famed sculpture. Today the museum and garden are virtually just as she left them. On display are about 47 sculptures and drawings, covering the period from 1928 to 1974, as well as photographs, documents, and other Hepworth memorabilia. You can also visit her workshops, housing a selection of tools and some unfinished carvings. The museum is administered jointly with the Tate Gallery.

## WHERE TO STAY
### DOUBLES FOR LESS THAN £50

**Craigmeor.** Beach Rd., St. Ives, Cornwall TR26 1JY. ☎ **01736/796611.** 3 rms, all with shower. £19–£20 ($30.40–$32) per person. All rates include English or "health-conscious" breakfast. No credit cards. Closed Oct–Mar.

This semidetached building was constructed a few months after World War II, and affords a good view of the coastal footpath that skirts the beaches of Cornwall. Each room has fitted carpets, patterned curtains, and a shower. The owner, Mrs. Ada Taylor, prides herself on her low-cholesterol breakfasts and maintains a rigid ban against smoking on her premises. Each room contains tea- and coffee-making facilities, and the furnishings are very basic. The hotel is a 5-minute walk west of the center, beside Porthmear Beach.

**Hobblers Guest House and Restaurant.** Wharf Rd., St. Ives, Cornwall TR26 1LR. ☎ **01736/ 796439.** 3 rms, none with bath. £20 ($32) single; £40 ($64) double. All rates include English breakfast. AE, DC, MC, V. Closed Nov to 2 weeks before Easter.

This black-and-white building is right on the harborside, next to a surf shop. The house was built in the 17th century as a pilot's house. Renting rooms seems a secondary objective here; most of the staff's attention focuses on operating the more profitable restaurant below. Because it's bull's-eye center, you may have a hard time getting a room here in high season.

**Hollies Hotel.** 4 Talland Rd., St. Ives, Cornwall TR26 2DF. ☎ **01736/796605.** 10 rms. TV. £15–£24 ($24–$38.40) single; £30–£48 ($48–$76.80) double. All rates include English breakfast. No credit cards.

Much of this hotel's charm is because its owners, an Anglo-American couple, John and Beverly Dowland, seem to enjoy what they're doing. Only a 5-minute walk from Porthminster Beach, the house is built of gray granite with a slate roof and lies in a row of about a dozen similar semidetached homes, each constructed a century ago. The bedrooms are well maintained and handsomely equipped. Many open onto views of the water, and several are large enough to shelter families comfortably. In a pine-paneled dining room, guests enjoy a freshly cooked breakfast. Later they return to relax in the spacious lounge or enjoy a pint in the snug bar.

✪ **The Old Vicarage Hotel.** Parc-an-Creet, St. Ives, Cornwall TR26 2ET. ☎ and fax **01736/796124.** 8 rms, 6 with bath. TV. £22–£24 ($35.20–$38.40) single without bath; £38–£42 ($60.80–$67.20) double without bath, £44–£48 ($70.40–$76.80) double with bath. All rates include English breakfast. AE, MC, V. Closed Oct–Easter.

This Victorian house is one of the most desirable of the B&Bs in the area, offering substantial if somewhat unimaginatively furnished bedrooms. It's about half a mile from the heart of the resort and beach area off St. Ives/Land's End Road, away from the bustling tourist activity along the harbor. It also has plenty of parking space, unlike St. Ives center. Guests meet for drinks in the Victorian bar or enjoy one of the books from the hotel library.

**Pondarosa.** 10 Porthminster Terrace, St. Ives, Cornwall TR26 2DQ. ☎ **01736/795875.** 11 rms, 10 with bath. TV. £14–£15 ($22.40–$24) single without bath; £32–£40 ($51.20–$64) double with bath. All rates include English breakfast. MC, V.

This Edwardian house offers good value for the money and is in a prominent location near the harbor and Porthminster Beach. The functionally furnished rooms have hot and cold running water, beverage-making equipment, and central heating, and have recently been upgraded. Patricia Tyldesley, the owner, will prepare an evening meal of good quality if notified in advance. A private parking area adjoins the house.

**Primrose Valley Hotel.** Primrose Valley Hill, St. Ives, Cornwall TR26 2ED. ☎ **01736/794939.** 10 rms. TV. £28–£35 ($44.80–$56) single; £36–£49 ($57.60–$78.40) double. All rates include English breakfast. MC, V. Closed Dec–Jan. Approach the hotel from A3074 and turn right down Primrose Valley Hill.

This was one of the first custom-built hotels in the region, established about a century ago, and reduced in size when about half of it burned down in the 1960s. Today, much repaired, it enjoys a sunny and relatively isolated position in a verdant valley, a 10-minute walk north of the town center, near Porthminster Beach and a putting green. The bedrooms are well furnished and comfortable, children are welcome, and the food is well prepared. Cream teas are served in clement weather on a wide patio, and three-course evening meals cost £10 ($16) each. The place is more solid and reliable than exciting.

# WHERE TO EAT

**Hobblers Restaurant.** The Wharf. ☎ **01736/796439.** Main courses £5.95–£9.95 ($9.50–$15.90). AE, DC, MC, V. Daily 6–10:30pm. Closed Jan–Mar. SEAFOOD.

At this previously recommended guest house, a 5-minute walk from the Tate Gallery, you can order old-style English sea-resort cookery, everything seemingly accompanied by "chips" and frozen peas. Dishes are likely to include scallops, halibut, scampi, and plaice, along with mussels and a cream-of-lobster bisque to start with. If you don't want fish, you might order the chicken Kiev or a fillet steak. The paneled rooms are decorated with pictures of ships and seascapes. Cramped, nautical, and intimate, it's located on the harbor.

**The Sloop Inn.** The Wharf. ☎ **01736/796584.** Bar snacks £2–£9 ($3.20–$14.40); beer £1–£2.10 ($1.60–$3.35). MC, V. Mon–Sat 11am–11pm; Sun noon–3pm and 7–10:30pm. Pub: Mon–Sat 11am–11pm; Sun noon–10:30pm. ENGLISH.

Proud of its long history (it was mentioned in sources as early as 1312), this stone-and-slate building contains one of the busiest and most visible pubs in St. Ives. Most clients come to drink at one of the three different bar areas amid comfortably battered furnishings, but if you're hungry, place your order at one of the bars and carry your platters yourself back to your table. Menu items might include ploughman's lunches, platters of roast chicken or ham, sandwiches, chili, fish-and-chips, "bangers and mash," and lasagna. The aim here seems to be to fill you up more than tantalize the palate. You'll find it located on the harborfront in the town center.

**Woodcote Hotel.** The Saltings, Lelant. ☎ **01736/753147.** Reservations required. Fixed-price 5-course dinner £12.50 ($20). No credit cards. Dinner served around 6:30–7pm for hotel guests; nonguests welcome according to availability. Closed Nov to mid-Mar. The "Hoppa bus" makes frequent trips from St. Ives, or take the local scenic rail line. VEGETARIAN.

Previously recommended as the first vegetarian hotel ever built in Britain, and 3 miles from St. Ives at the edge of a bird sanctuary and saltwater estuary, the Woodcote accepts fill-in bookings from nonresidents if space is available. Typical dishes include lentil-and-cumin soup, eggplant goulash with chickpeas and wild rice, and treacle and ginger tart for dessert. The kitchen uses eggs but no fish.

## 7  Port Isaac

266 miles SW of London; 14 miles SW of Tintagel; 9 miles N of Wadebridge

Port Isaac remains the most unspoiled fishing village on the north Cornish coastline, in spite of large numbers of summer visitors. By all means wander through its winding, narrow lanes and gaze at the whitewashed fishing cottages with their rainbow trims.

## ESSENTIALS

**GETTING THERE**  Bodmin is the nearest railway station. It lies on the main line from London (Paddington Station) to Penzance (about a 4- or 4¹/₂-hour trip). Call ☎ **0345/484950** for schedules. Many hotels will send a car to pick up guests at the Bodmin Station, or you can take a taxi. If you take a bus from Bodmin, you'll have to change buses at Wadebridge, and connections are not good. Driving time from Bodmin to Port Isaac is 40 minutes.

A bus to Wadebridge goes to Port Isaac about six times a day. It's maintained by the Prout Brothers Bus Co. Wadebridge is a local bus junction to many other places in the rest of England.

If you're driving from London, take M4 west, then drive south on M5. Head west again at the junction with A39, continuing to the junction with B3267, which you follow until you reach the signposted cutoff for Port Isaac.

## WHERE TO STAY

**Archer Farm Hotel.** Trewetha, Port Isaac, Cornwall PL29 3RU. ☎ **01208/880522.** 8 rms. TV TEL. £22–£28 ($35.20–$44.80) single; £40–£54 ($64–$86.40) double. All rates include English breakfast. No credit cards. Closed Nov–Apr.

Despite its name, which the long-time owners have deliberately retained out of respect for its 400-year history, this hotel bears no resemblance to a farm. On an acre of its own about three-quarters of a mile southeast of Port Isaac (take B3267), surrounded by the fields of other landowners, it was originally built in the 1600s as dormitory-style housing for laborers. When the Victorian daughter of a 19th-century owner got married, her family added an extension onto the original core for her to raise her family. Since Vickie Welton took over in the 1970s, the place has been gracefully modernized, with many discreet improvements, none of which has detracted from the integrity of the original building. There's a resident ghost whom some guests—perhaps after glasses of wine—claim to have heard or seen (his name is Puck), and a comfortable, unfussy decor that many readers have praised for its understated elegance and dignified good taste.

✪ **Castle Rock Hotel.** 4 New Rd., Port Isaac, Cornwall PL29 3SB. ☎ **01208/880300.** Fax 01208/880219. 14 rms. TV TEL. £32–£37 ($51.20–$59.20) per person. All rates include English breakfast. AE, MC, V.

The most desirable accommodation in Port Isaac, this carefully cared for cream-colored house, originally built in the 1920s, has a panoramic view of the Cornish coast to as far away as Tintagel. Guests meet each other at the well-stocked bar before entering the dining room. The proprietors arrange home-cooked meals priced from £15 ($24) table d'hôte, plus a full a la carte menu, using local produce whenever possible. The good food served here is part of the Castle Rock's attraction. The hotel is adjacent to the town's main parking area, a short walk northwest of the town center.

**The Old School Hotel.** Port Isaac, Cornwall PL29 3RB. ☎ **01208/880721.** 18 rms, 5 suites. TV TEL. £40–£116 ($64–$185.60) double; £116 ($185.60) suite for 2. All rates include English breakfast. MC, V.

Dating from 1875, this guest house on a clifftop overlooks a pier built during the reign of Henry VIII and has views of the harbor and sea. Sports enthusiasts are drawn to the hotel, which offers shark and deep-sea fishing, sailing, wind surfing, and water skiing. Others just enjoy the harbor view and a day or two of rest in the comfortable rooms. All standard rooms are doubles. Breakfast is eaten in the refectory, a long room with tall windows and tables with settle benches. A three- or four-course dinner begins at £12.50 ($20). Owner Mike Warner goes out of his way to make guests comfortable.

## WHERE TO EAT

**Golden Lion.** Fore St. ☎ **01208/880336.** Reservations recommended for the bistro. Main courses £5–£13 ($8–$20.80); pub snacks £2–£5 ($3.20–$8). No credit cards. Bistro: Easter–Oct, daily 7–9:30pm (closed Nov–Easter). Pub: June–Sept, Mon–Sat 11:30am–11pm; Sun noon–3pm and 7–10:30pm. Oct–May, Mon–Sat 11:30am–3pm and 6:30–11pm; Sun 11:30am–3pm and 7–10:30pm. ENGLISH/SEAFOOD.

A few steps from the harbor's edge, this structure has contained some kind of eating house or pub since it was built in the 17th century. Behind stone walls (which in places are 5 feet thick), you'll find a street-level bar with windows that open out over the water and a basement-level bistro. You can always order chili, lasagna, or sandwiches at the bar, or head to the bistro for more formal meals which might include steaks, shellfish, and fresh crab in butter sauce. The mostly standard fare is like that a Cornish family might eat at home at night.

## 8 Tintagel Castle

264 miles SW of London; 49 miles NW of Plymouth

On a wild stretch of the Atlantic coast, Tintagel is forever linked with the legends of King Arthur, Lancelot, and Merlin. If tales of Knights of the Round Table excite you, you can go to Camelford, 5 miles inland from Tintagel. The town claims connections to the legendary Camelot.

## ESSENTIALS

**GETTING THERE**    The nearest railway station is in Bodmin, which lies on the main rail line from London to Penzance. From Bodmin, you'll have to drive or take a taxi for 30 minutes to get to Tintagel (there's no bus service from Bodmin to Tintagel). For railway inquiries, call ☎ **0345/484950.**

If you want to take a bus, you'll travel from London to Plymouth. One bus a day travels from Plymouth to Tintagel, at 4:20pm, but it takes twice the time (2 hours) required for a private car (which only takes about 50 minutes) since the bus stops at dozens of small hamlets along the way. For bus schedule information, call ☎ **01209/719988.**

If you're driving, from Exeter, head across Cornwall on A30, continuing west at the junction with A395. From this highway, various secondary roads lead to Tintagel.

**VISITOR INFORMATION**    **Tourist information** is available at the Municipal Building, Boscawen Street, in Truro (☎ **01872/74555**). Open Easter to November, Monday through Friday from 9am to 6pm and Saturday from 9am to 5pm, and November to Easter, Monday through Friday from 9am to 5pm.

## ✪ TINTAGEL CASTLE

The 13th-century ruins of a castle—built on the foundations of a Celtic monastery from the 6th century—are popularly known as King Arthur's Castle. The ruins stand 300 feet above the sea on a rocky promontory, and to get to them you must take a long, steep, tortuous walk from the parking lot. In summer, many visitors make the ascent to Arthur's Lair, up 100 rock-cut steps. You can also visit Merlin's Cave at low tide.

The castle is half a mile northwest of Tintagel. It's open April to September, daily from 10am to 6pm; October to March, daily from 10am to 4pm. Admission is £2.80 ($4.50) for adults, £2.20 ($3.50) for students and seniors, and £1.60 ($2.55)for children. For information, call ☎ **01840/770328.**

## WHERE TO STAY & EAT IN & AROUND TINTAGEL

**Manor Farm.** Crackington Haven, near Bude, Cornwall EX23 0JW. ☎ **01840/230304.** 5 rms. £32 ($51.20) single; £60 ($96) double. All rates include English breakfast. No credit cards.

This farmhouse, owned by Mr. and Mrs. Knight, is recorded in the *Domesday Book* and is thought to date back to the 12th century with the majority of the structure from the 16th century. On 30 acres, the house is a stone edifice that sports a slate roof with wooden beams scattered throughout the interior. Although centrally heated, fires are lit during the winter on exceptionally cold days. Meals are communal, with breakfast served at 8:30am and dinner between 7 and 7:30pm. Dinners may include such dishes as roast beef with Yorkshire pudding and chicken breast rolled in sea kelp and stuffed with garlic and cheese. Jacket and tie are required for evening meals (not served in August). This is a nonsmoking facility.

**Old Borough House.** Bossiney, Tintagel, Cornwall PL34 0AY. ☎ **01840/770475.** 6 rms, 2 with bath. £18 ($28.80) single without bath, £21 ($33.60) single with bath; £36 ($57.60) double without bath, £42 ($67.20) double with bath. All rates include English breakfast. No credit cards. Walk north from the ruins of Tintagel Castle for 10 minutes.

Run by the Rayner family, this Cornish house has thick stone walls, small windows, low ceiling beams, and a history beginning in 1558. Most of what stands today was completed in the late 1600s, when it served as the residence of the mayor of Bossiney, the hamlet in which it stands. (Bossiney was the seat from which Sir Francis Drake was elected for a brief period to the English Parliament.) Accommodations are cozy, low ceilinged, antique, and very comfortable. There's a sitting room with a TV for use by guests, and if advance notice is given, evening meals can be prepared for £12 ($19.20).

**Trevigue Farm.** Crackington Haven, Bude, Cornwall EX23 0LQ. ☎ **01840/230418.** 6 rms. £20–£28 ($32–$44.80) single; £45–£55 ($72–$88) double. All rates include English breakfast. No credit cards.

The rooms are housed in two stone buildings: four in the 16th-century farmhouse and two in a separate house that offers views of a wooded valley. Although only two of the rooms contain TVs, there is a cozy sitting room with television for guests to enjoy, a log fire, and a wealth of books. Owned by the National Trust, this working dairy farm, whose tenants are Ken and Janet Crocker, is located cliffside, offering access to a beach called The Strangles, where swimming is best experienced during a rising tide. Communal meals feature English fare with international touches. Dinner may include prawn cocktail, chicken à l'orange, and for the finish, a chocolate roulade or apple crumble. Dinner is served at 7:30pm and costs £16 ($25.60).

# 12 Wiltshire & Somerset

For our final look at the "West Countree," we move now into Wiltshire and Somerset, the most antiquity-rich shires of England. When we reach this area of pastoral woodland, London seems far removed.

Most people agree that the West Country, a loose geographical term, begins at Salisbury, with its early English cathedral that has a 404-foot pinnacle. Nearby is Stonehenge, England's oldest prehistoric monument. Both Stonehenge and Salisbury are in Wiltshire. When you cross into Wiltshire, you'll be entering a country of chalky, grassy uplands and rolling plains. Much of the shire is agricultural, and a large part is devoted to pastureland. Wiltshire produces much of England's dairy products and is noted for sheep raising. Here you'll traverse Salisbury Plain, Vale of Pewsey, and Marlborough Downs (the latter making up the greater part of the landmass).

The western shire of Somerset has some of the most beautiful scenery in England. The undulating limestone hills of Mendip and the irresistible Quantocks are especially lovely in spring and fall. Somerset opens onto the Bristol Channel, with Minehead serving as its chief resort. The shire is rich in legend and history, with particularly fanciful associations with King Arthur and Queen Guinevere, Camelot, and Alfred the Great. Its villages are noted for the tall towers of their parish churches.

In Somerset, you may find yourself in a vine-covered inn talking with the regulars; or perhaps you'll discover a large estate in the woods surrounded by bridle paths and sheep walks (Somerset was once a great wool center); or maybe you'll settle down in a 16th-century thatched stone farmhouse set in the midst of orchards in a vale. By the way, Somerset is reputed to have the best cider anywhere. Somerset also encompasses the territory around the old port of Bristol and the old Roman city of Bath, known for its abbey and spa water, beside the river Somerset.

The two best centers for exploring the area are Bath and Salisbury. From Salisbury you can visit Stonehenge and Old Sarum, the two most fabled ancient monuments in the West Country. Yet some say visiting the stones at Avebury is a much more personal experience. And Glastonbury, with its once-great abbey that now is a ruined sanctuary, may be one of Britain's oldest inhabited sites. The greatest natural spectacle in the area is Exmoor National Park, once

# Wiltshire, Somerset & Avon

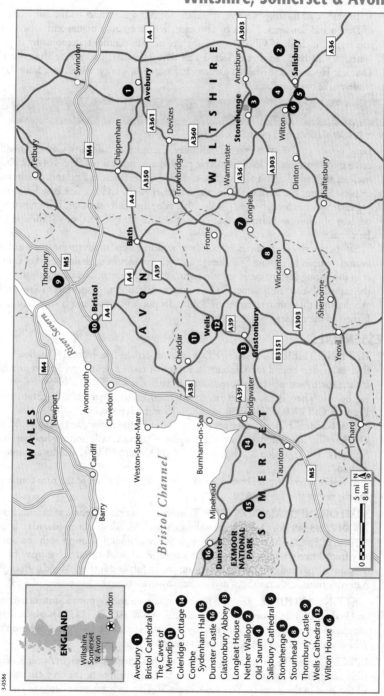

ENGLAND

Wiltshire, Somerset & Avon

London

3-0586

411

an English royal hunting preserve, stretching for 265 square miles on the north coast of Devon and Somerset. There are also many terrific country houses and palaces in this region, including Wilton House, the site of 17th-century staterooms by Inigo Jones. A visit here requires at least a half day. The other two major attractions, Longleat House and the fabled gardens at Stourhead, can be visited in a busy day while you're based at Bath.

## 1   Salisbury

90 miles SW of London; 53 miles SE of Bristol

Long before you've even entered Salisbury, the spire of Salisbury Cathedral will come into view—just as John Constable painted it so many times. The 404-foot pinnacle of the early English and Gothic cathedral is the tallest in England. Salisbury, or New Sarum, lies in the valley of the Somerset River, and is a fine base for touring such sights as Stonehenge. Filled with Tudor inns and tearooms, it is known to readers of Thomas Hardy as Melchester and to fans of Anthony Trollope as Barchester.

Salisbury today is often viewed as only a "refueling stop" or overnight stopover for visitors anxious to explore Stonehenge or Avebury. However, the old market town is an interesting destination in its own right, although most visitors seem only to visit the cathedral, then rush along. There's another reason some visitors like to stop off at Salisbury, the only true city in Wiltshire. Its pub-to-citizen ratio is said to be the highest in the country.

## ESSENTIALS

**GETTING THERE**   A Network Express train departs hourly from Waterloo Station in London bound for Salisbury in a trip that takes 2 hours, and Sprinter trains make a speedy journey from Portsmouth, Bristol, and South Wales, likewise departing hourly. There is also direct rail service from Exeter, Plymouth, Brighton, and Reading. Call ☎ **0345/484950** for schedules and information.

Five National Express buses per day run from London Monday through Friday. On Saturday and Sunday four buses depart Victoria Coach Station heading for Salisbury. The trip takes 2$^1$/$_2$ hours. Call ☎ **0990/808080** for schedules and information.

If you're driving from London, head west on M3 to the end of the run, continuing the rest of the way on A30.

**VISITOR INFORMATION**   The **Tourist Information Centre** is at Fish Row (☎ **01722/334956**). Open October through April Monday through Saturday from 9:30am to 5pm; in May, Monday through Saturday from 9:30am to 5pm and Sunday from 11am to 4pm; in June and September, Monday through Saturday from 9:30am to 6pm and Sunday 11am to 4pm; and in July and August, Monday through Saturday from 9:30am to 7pm and on Sunday from 11am to 5pm.

**GETTING AROUND**   If you'd like to rent a cycle to ride out to Stonehenge, go to **Hayball's Cycle Shop,** 26–30 Winchester St. (☎ **01722/411378**), which rents mountain bikes for £7.50 ($12) per day. For an extra £2.50 ($4) you can keep the bike overnight. A £25 ($40) deposit is required.

**SPECIAL EVENTS**   The **Salisbury St. George's Spring Festival,** in April, is a traditional, medieval celebration of the Patron Saint, thought to be the only celebration of the kind in the country. You can witness St. George slaying the dragon. There's also mummers, damsels, acrobats, fireworks, and much more.

With spring comes the annual **Salisbury Festival,** 75 New St. (☎ **01722/323883;** box office 01722/320333), at the end of May and early June. This festival adds color and activity to the streets of Salisbury. There are symphony orchestra concerts held in Salisbury Cathedral, jazz, folk, children's events, chamber music and much more. And the sidewalks are filled with European street theater, as visual arts, site installations, and outdoor events are staged. At the end of July, you can see **The Salisbury Garden and Flower Show,** Hudson's Field (☎ **01202/870928**). This is positively a treat for gardening enthusiasts—there's a floral marquee packed with Chelsea exhibits, display gardens created especially for the event, specialty food and tastings, antiques, crafts, gifts, vintage and classic cars, and lots for children. In September, you can enjoy "**A Tale of Salisbury:** a celebration of Salisbury, its people, its past, and its present." This action packed weekend includes music, street entertainment and fireworks.

## ✪ SALISBURY CATHEDRAL

You can search all of England, but you'll find no better example of the early English, or pointed, architectural style than Salisbury Cathedral. Construction was begun as early as 1220 and took 38 years to complete; this was rather fast in those days since it was customary for a cathedral building to require at least 3 centuries. The soaring spire was completed at the end of the 13th century. Despite an ill-conceived attempt at renovation in the 18th century, the architectural integrity of the cathedral has been retained.

The cathedral's 13th-century octagonal chapter house (note the fine sculpture), is especially attractive, and it possesses one of the four surviving original texts of the Magna Carta, along with treasures from the diocese of Salisbury and manuscripts and artifacts belonging to the cathedral. The cloisters enhance the beauty of the cathedral, and the exceptionally large close, with at least 75 buildings in its compound (some from the early 18th century and others predating that), sets off the cathedral most effectively.

The cathedral (☎ 01722/328726) is open May to August, daily from 8:30am to 8:30pm; September to April, daily from 8am to 6:30pm. Admission to the cathedral is £2.50 ($4), 30p (50¢) for the chapter house.

In the Cathedral Cloisters is a **Brass Rubbing Centre** (☎ 01722/328726). It's open mid-June through September, Monday to Saturday from 10am to 6pm and Sunday from 11:15am to 4pm. Here you can choose from a variety of exact replicas molded perfectly from the original brasses: local medieval and Tudor knights and ladies, famous historical faces, even Celtic designs. A helpful staff will guide you. The £3 ($4.80) average charge made for each rubbing includes materials and instruction. You can also buy ready-made rubbings and historical gift items.

## MORE SIGHTS IN SALISBURY

There are guided walking tours of Salisbury both during the day and at night. A severed hand, the ghost of the Duke of Buckingham, an arrogant medieval mayor, and a bawdy housekeeper—all (and more!) will be revealed during your tour. Tickets are available from the **Salisbury Tourist Information Centre** (see above) for £2 ($3.20) for adults and £1 ($1.60) for children.

**Mompesson House.** Cathedral Close. ☎ 01722/335659. Admission £3.20 ($5.10) adults; £1.60 ($2.55) children. Apr–Oct Sat–Wed noon–5pm. Next to the cathedral in The Close, in the center of Salisbury, a 5-minute walk from the train station along Fisherton Rd.

This is one of the most distinguished houses in the area. Built by Charles Mompesson in 1701, while he was a member of Parliament for Old Sarum, it is a beautiful example of the Queen Anne style, well known for its fine plasterwork ceilings and paneling. There is also a collection of 18th-century drinking glasses. Visitors can wander through a garden and later order a snack in the garden tearoom.

**The Royal Gloucestershire, Berkshire & Wiltshire Regiment (Salisbury) Museum—Redcoats in the Wardrobe.** The Wardrobe, 58 The Close, Salisbury, Wiltshire. ☎ **01722/414536.** Admission £2 ($3.20) adults; £1.80 ($2.90) seniors; 50p (80¢) children. Feb–Mar and Nov Mon–Fri 10am–4:30pm; Apr–Oct daily 10am–4:30pm. In the center of Salisbury, a 5-minute walk from the train station along Fisherton Rd.

The elegant house housing the museum's collections dates from 1254 and contains exhibits covering 3 centuries of military history. Visitors can relax in the garden leading to the River Somerset (with views made famous by Constable) and enjoy home-made fare from the Redcoats Tea Rooms.

## SHOPPING

Shops in Salisbury are often set in beautiful medieval timber-framed buildings. As you wander through the colorful market or walk the ancient streets, you'll find everything from "medieval" gift shops to modern day retailers. **The Mitre House,** 37 High St. (☎ 01722/333705), reputed to be the oldest house in Salisbury, is a high-quality gift shop owned by the cathedral. It stocks wide ranging, attractive merchandise. For new, secondhand, and antique jewelry and silver, plus watches, clocks, and barometers by leading makers, go to **H. R. Tribbeck & Son,** 12 Bridge St. (☎ 01722/324395). This family jewelers has been in operation since 1905. For those interested in specialty foods, try **David Brown Food Hall & Tea Rooms,** 31 Catherine St. (☎ 01722/329363). They carry the finest fresh foods—meat, delicatessen, bakery, and carvery. This is the best place to gather picnic supplies. **The Old George Mall Shopping Centre,** 23b High St. (☎ 01723/333500), a short walk from the cathedral, has more than 40 individual shops and High-Street stores. Housed in a 14th-century building with hammered beams and some original windows, **Watsons,** 8–9 Queen St. (☎ 01722/320311), carries bone china from Wedgwood and Aynsley; Waterford and Dartington glassware; Royal Doulton china; figurines from Doulton and Coalport; and, for those with light suitcases, a fine line of paperweights.

## ✪ OLD SARUM

Old Sarum is believed to have been an Iron Age fortification. The earthworks were known to the Romans as Sorbiodunum. Much later, Saxons also used the fortification. The Normans built a cathedral and a castle here in what was then a Middle Ages walled town. Parts of the old cathedral were taken down to build the city of New Sarum (Salisbury).

Old Sarum (☎ 01722/335398) is 2 miles north of Salisbury off A345 on Castle Road. Bus nos. 3, 5, 6, 7, 8, and 9 run every 20 minutes during the day from the Salisbury bus station. It's open April to September, daily from 10am to 6pm; other times daily from 10am to 4pm. Admission is £1.90 ($3.05) for adults, £1.40 ($2.25) for seniors, and £1 ($1.60) for children.

## ✪ WILTON HOUSE: A GREAT COUNTRY ESTATE

In the town of Wilton is one of England's great country estates, Wilton House, the home of the earls of Pembroke. Wilton House dates from the 16th century, but has undergone numerous alterations, most recently in Victoria's day. It is noted for its 17th-century staterooms by the celebrated architect Inigo Jones. Many famous personages have either lived at or visited Wilton. It is also believed that Shakespeare's troupe entertained here. Preparations for the D-day landings at Normandy were laid out here by Eisenhower and his advisers, with only the silent Van Dyck paintings in the Double Cube room as witnesses.

The house is filled with beautifully maintained furnishings and displays world-class art, including paintings by Sir Anthony Van Dyck, Rubens, Brueghel, and Reynolds. A dynamic film introduced and narrated by Anna Massey brings to life the history of the family since 1544, the year they were granted the land by Henry VIII. You then visit a reconstructed Tudor kitchen and Victorian laundry plus "The Wareham Bears," a unique collection of some 200 miniature-dressed teddy bears.

Growing on the 21-acre estate are giant Cedars of Lebanon, the oldest of which were planted in 1630. The Palladian Bridge was built in 1737 by the ninth earl of Pembroke and Roger Morris. There are rose and water gardens, riverside and woodland walks, and a huge adventure playground for children. Guides assist in the principal staterooms.

Wilton House (☎ **01722/746729**) is 3 miles west of Salisbury on A30. It's open Easter to October, daily from 11am to 6pm, with the last entrance at 5pm. Admission is £7 ($11.20) for adults, £4.50 ($7.20) for children 5 to 15, free for children under 5. Admission to the grounds only is £4 ($6.40) for adults and £2.75 ($4.40) for children.

# WHERE TO STAY
## DOUBLES FOR LESS THAN £40

**Castlewood Guest House.** 45 Castle Rd., Salisbury, Wiltshire SP1 3RH. ☎ **01722/324809.** 5 rms, 2 with bath. TV. £20 ($32) single without bath; £32 ($51.20) double without bath, £36 ($57.60) double with bath. All rates include English breakfast. No credit cards. Take any of the buses marked STONEHENGE.

This cozy and unpretentious guest house lies a 15-minute walk north of Salisbury's cathedral, on the opposite side of the 6-lane peripheral road (A345) that encircles the city. (The most pleasant way to reach it is by following the riverside walkway that runs parallel to the banks of the Avon.) Built in the early 1900s, with flowerbeds and hanging flower baskets in front, the house is among similar buildings in a neighborhood filled with other B&Bs and a scattering of restaurants. The bedrooms contain tea- and coffee-making facilities and many of their original architectural features.

**Glen Lyn Guest House.** 6 Bellamy Lane, Milford Hill, Salisbury, Wiltshire SP1 2SP. ☎ **01722/327880.** 9 rms, 4 with bath. TV. £19 ($30.40) single without bath; £37 ($59.20) double without bath, £42 ($67.20) double with bath. All rates include English breakfast. No credit cards.

Brian and Sandie Stuart offer a warm welcome to their well-appointed Victorian home on a tree-lined lane just a 5-minute walk from the center of the city. All the comfortably furnished rooms are centrally heated and contain such amenities as beverage-making equipment, shaver outlets, and color TVs. Guests enjoy the garden of the Stuarts. The house is nonsmoking, and children 11 and under aren't accepted.

**Hayburn Wyke Guest House.** 72 Castle Rd., Salisbury, Wiltshire SP1 3RL. ☎ and fax **01722/412627.** 6 rms, 2 with bath. TV. £23–£25 ($36.80–$40) single without bath; £35 ($56) double without bath, £40 ($64) double with bath. All rates include English breakfast. No credit cards. Bus: no. 3.

At this Victorian house, next to Victoria Park and half a mile from the cathedral and Old Sarum, you'll receive a warm welcome from Dawn and Alan Curnow, who do invite families with children. They offer simply furnished bedrooms with hot and cold running water and hot-beverage facilities. Each room is a double, which can be rented as a single for the rate stated above. The full English breakfast is hearty and fortifying for the day. The house is on A345, half a mile from the city center.

**Malvern Guest House.** 31 Hulse Rd., Salisbury, Wiltshire SP1 3LU. ☎ **01722/327995.** 3 rms. TV. £38–£40 ($60.80–$64) double. All rates include English breakfast. No credit cards.

In a solidly comfortable Edwardian house built in 1934, whose rear garden abuts the waters of the River Avon, this family-run inn sits on a quiet cul-de-sac within a 7-minute walk north of the town center. Each room contains tea- and coffee-making facilities, and there's a guest lounge available for the use of residents. Jack and Freda Elkins, former publicans, stock their newly decorated bedrooms with thoughtful extras, and manage to incorporate freshly grown tomatoes (grilled) from their garden and homemade strawberry jam into the breakfasts they serve as part of their overnight arrangements. Nonsmokers only are welcome.

✪ **Richburn Guest House.** 23–25 Estcourt Rd., Salisbury, Wiltshire SP1 3AP. ☎ **01722/325189.** 10 rms, 2 with bath. £18 ($28.80) single without bath; £32 ($51.20) double without bath, £40 ($64) double with bath. All rates include English breakfast. No credit cards.

One of the better bargains in Salisbury, this spacious Victorian home, run by Sandra and David Loader, is located about half a mile north of the town center near several verdant city parks. The bedrooms—functional, but comfortable—have hot and cold running water and beverage-making equipment.

**Rokeby Guest House.** 3 Wain-a-Long Rd., Salisbury, Wiltshire SP1 1LJ. ☎ **01722/329800.** 9 rms, 7 with bath. TV. £28 ($44.80) single without bath, £30 ($48) single with bath; £38 ($60.80) double without bath, £40 ($64) double with bath. All rates include English breakfast. No credit cards.

Beside a busy residential street which eventually becomes the A30 highway, about half a mile east of the town center, this well-managed guest house was originally built in 1901 as a private home. Set on half-acre grounds, and vaguely similar to the red-brick chalets of central Europe, it's owned and managed by Alan and Margo Rogers. Many readers of this guide have lavishly praised these hosts. Breakfasts are served family style in the couple's dining room, and they're quick to offer their discreet assistance to travelers. The bedrooms are high-ceilinged, often large, and filled with the high wainscoting of their original construction. An enclosed gazebo in the rear garden provides a refuge for midsummer glasses of wine.

**White Lodge.** 68 London Rd., Salisbury, Wiltshire SP1 3EX. ☎ **01722/327991.** 6 rms, none with bath. TV. £22 ($35.20) single; £34 ($54.40) double. All rates include English breakfast. No credit cards. Bus: no. 32 or 57.

This is the residence of Mr. and Mrs. Nichols, who receive guests in their attractive, brick-gabled house. The bedrooms are pleasant and the breakfast is personalized. Bedrooms contain beverage-making equipment, hair dryer, and cookies. One room can house four, costing £16 ($25.60) per adult or £8 ($12.80) for a child. The entrance to White Lodge is a glassed-in porch filled with flowers and trailing vines. It's located at the edge of the city on A30 coming in from London, opposite St. Mark's Church.

**Wyndham Park Lodge.** 51 Wyndham Rd., Salisbury, Wiltshire SP1 3AB. ☎ and fax **01722/328851.** 4 rms. TV. £15 ($24) single; £30 ($48) double; £45 ($72) family room for 3. All rates include English breakfast. No credit cards.

From this appealing Victorian 1880 house, it's an easy walk to the heart of Salisbury and its cathedral, and about a 5-minute walk to a swimming pool and the bus station. The bedrooms are comfortably furnished with Victorian and Edwardian antiques and matching floral curtains and wallpaper and have either one double bed or twin beds. Each room contains beverage-making equipment.

## A YOUTH HOSTEL

**Milford Hill House.** Milford Hill, Salisbury, Wiltshire SP1 2QW. ☎ **01722/327572.** Fax 01722/330446. 74 beds. £9.40 ($15.05) adults; £6.30 ($10.10) 18 and under. £1.55 ($2.50) assessment for nonmembers of hostel association. MC, V.

In a landmark 2-century-old building, this hostel is dominated by a Cedar of Lebanon that's almost as old as the building itself. The interior is sterile with few frills. But the reception folks are helpful, and guests from around the world friendly enough. In the dormitory-style rooms you usually share space with nine others. The bathrooms are respectable. Curfew is at 11:30pm, and the hostel closes daily from 10am to 5pm.

The facility has seven toilets and five showers, a laundry room, a large parking lot, and offers free space-available bag storage. There is a self-catering kitchen, and also cafeteria-style meals, including breakfast for £2.85 ($4.55), a packaged lunch for £2.45 ($3.90), and a two-course dinner for £2.60 ($4.15). It is a nonsmoking facility.

## A NEARBY PLACE TO STAY

**The Beadles.** Middleton, Middle Winterslow, near Salisbury, Wiltshire SP5 1QS. ☎ **01980/862922.** 4 rms. TV. £23.50–£25 ($37.60–$40) per person double. All rates include English breakfast. MC, V. Turn off A30 at Pheasant Inn to Middle Winterslow. Enter village, turn first right into the "Flood," right again and first right after "Trevano."

A traditional modern Georgian house with antique furnishings and a view of the cathedral, The Beadles (note: not on Penny Lane) also shows the beautiful Wiltshire countryside with an unobstructed view over the garden. Set on 1 acre, this part of a small, unspoiled English village 8 miles from Salisbury offers excellent access to Stonehenge, Wilton House, the New Forest, and the rambling moors of Thomas Hardy. Even the road to Winchester is an ancient Roman viaduct. Early morning tea and late-night beverages can be ordered through room service, and children are welcome in the 12-seat dining room. Writing materials, hair dryers, and picnic hampers, including vegetarian and special menus, are provided upon request. Warm weather meals are served on the patio or in the conservatory, and a predinner drink is free. Owners David and Anne Yuille-Baddeley delight in providing information on the area. This is a nonsmoking facility.

## WHERE TO EAT

**Charcoal Grill.** 18 Fisherton St. ☎ **01722/322134.** Reservations recommended. Main courses £3–£6 ($4.80–$9.60). No credit cards. Daily noon–midnight. TURKISH.

The cooks here follow recipes that have been handed down for generations in their family, and their Turkish treats have awakened the tastebuds of Salisbury. Kebabs, available for take out, are the most reliable fare, although they also prepare a Turkish moussaka, made with the traditional lamb, potatoes, and eggplant (somehow, though, our latest sampling of this dish tasted suspiciously like English shepherd's pie). Large portions and a staff that seems slightly ill at ease characterize the place, which is still recommendable.

✪ **Harper's Restaurant.** 6–9 Ox Row, Market Sq. ☎ **01722/333118.** Reservations recommended. Main courses £8.50–£11.90 ($13.60–$19.05); 3-course fixed-price meals £7.90 ($12.65) at lunch. AE, DC, MC, V. Mon–Sat noon–2pm and 6:30–10pm; Sun 6:30–9:30pm. Closed Sun Oct–May. ENGLISH/INTERNATIONAL.

The chef-owner of this place prides himself on specializing in "real food"—homemade, uncomplicated, and wholesome—and generally the kitchen succeeds in that goal. The pleasantly decorated restaurant is on the second floor of a red-brick building at the back side of Salisbury's largest parking lot, in the center of town. You can order from two different menus, one featuring cost-conscious bistro-style platters, including beefsteak casserole with "herbey dumplings." A longer menu listing items that take a bit more time to prepare includes all-vegetarian pasta diavolo or spareribs with French fries and rice.

**Michael J. R. Snell.** 8 St. Thomas's Sq. ☎ **01722/336037.** Main courses £5–£8 ($8–$12.80); cream teas £3.50 ($5.60). MC, V. Mon–Fri 6am–6pm; Sat 8:30am–6pm. TEA/PASTRIES/MEALS.

The best all-around tearoom and pâtisserie in Salisbury, this place specializes in tea, coffee, and handmade chocolates. In fact, the present business is an offshoot of a family-run chocolate company that opened here before World War II. In fair weather, umbrella-shaded tables are set out on the square where you can enjoy a Wiltshire clotted-cream tea with scones. You can also ask for a table overlooking the river. Among the dessert specialties, try the Forêt Noire gâteau, a black forest cake. A reasonable luncheon menu, which is likely to include everything from local smoked trout to turkey-and-ham pie, is offered from 11:30am to 2:30pm. Coffee is roasted on the premises, and children's portions are also available.

## SALISBURY AFTER DARK

The **Salisbury Playhouse,** Malthouse Lane (☎ **01722/320117;** box office 01722/320333), produces some of the finest quality theater in the region, from classic drama, musicals, and comedies to new writing and traditional pantomime. Food and drink are available from the bar and restaurant to complete your evening's entertainment.

**The City Hall,** Malthouse Lane (☎ **01722/334432;** box office 01722/327676), has a program of events to suit most tastes. This thriving entertainment center attracts many national touring shows, as well as hosts local amateur events, exhibitions, and sales—an opportunity to enjoy good entertainment at a reasonable price.

**The Salisbury Arts Center,** Bedwin Street (☎ and box office **01722/321744**), housed within the former St. Edmund's Church, offers a wide range of performing and visual arts. A typical program will contain a broad mix of music, contemporary and classic theater, and dance performances plus cabaret, comedy, and family shows. Regular workshops are available for all ages in arts, crafts, theater, and dance. The lively cafe bar is a pleasant meeting place.

Many a Salisbury pub crawl begins at the **Coach & Horses** on Winchester Street (☎ 01722/336254). This is said to be Salisbury's oldest pub, the building dating from 1482. Tank up here on the brew and order pub snacks throughout the day. If you stick around for dinner, a three-course evening meal is served. The fun continues at **The Pheasant,** Salt Lane (☎ **01722/320675**), a quintessential Wiltshire pub attracting both habitués and visitors sharing a pint before descending on Stonehenge. Snacks, ploughman's lunches, and hot meals of pub grub, including meat pies, are served all day. It's all washed down with a goodly assortment of ales. The pub is located near the bus station. To cap the night, head for **Somerset Brewery Inn,** 75 Castle St. (☎ **01722/327280**), decorated like a Victorian saloon from the gay 1890s. It's in an idyllic setting with a garden overlooking the River Somerset. It offers some of the tastiest food in town, and it's affordable, too, as homemade specials run from £4 to £8 ($6.40 to $12.80). You can also order roasts from animals from the Wiltshire plain.

## 2  Prehistoric Britain: Stonehenge & Avebury

### ✪ STONEHENGE

Two miles west of Amesbury and about 9 miles north of Salisbury is the renowned and mysterious Stonehenge, believed to be anywhere from 3,500 to 5,000 years old. This huge circle of lintels and megalithic pillars is the most important prehistoric monument in Britain.

Some visitors are disappointed when they see that Stonehenge is nothing more than concentric circles of (smaller than perhaps expected) stones. Maybe they do not understand that Stonehenge represents an amazing engineering feat—many of the boulders, the bluestones in particular, were moved many miles (perhaps from southern Wales) to this site.

The widely held view of the 18th- and 19th-century romantics that Stonehenge was the work of the Druids is without foundation. The boulders, many weighing several tons, are believed to have predated the arrival in Britain of the Celtic cult. Recent excavations continue to bring new evidence to bear on the origin and purpose of Stonehenge. Controversy surrounds the prehistoric site especially since the publication of *Stonehenge Decoded* by Gerald S. Hawkins and John B. White, which maintains that Stonehenge was an astronomical observatory—that is, a Neolithic "computing machine" capable of predicting eclipses.

Your ticket permits you to go inside the fence surrounding the site that protects the stones from vandals and souvenir hunters. You can go all the way up to a short rope barrier about 50 feet from the stones. In spring 1996 a full circular tour around Stonehenge was started. A modular walkway has been introduced to cross the archaeologically important avenue, the area that runs between the Heel Stone and the main circle of stones. This enables visitors to complete a full circuit of the stones and to see one of the best views of a completed section of Stonehenge as they pass by. This is an excellent addition to the good audio tour.

Stonehenge (☎ **01980/623108**) is at the junction of A303 and A344/A360. It's open March 16 through May and September to October 15, daily from 9:30am to 6pm; June to August, daily from 9am to 7pm; October 16 to March 15, daily from 9:30am to 4pm. Admission is £3.70 ($5.90) for adults, £2.80 ($4.50) for seniors and students, and £1.90 ($3.05) for children.

**GETTING THERE**   It's about a 12-mile trip from Salisbury to Stonehenge. **Wilts & Dorset** (☎ **01722/336855**) runs several buses daily (depending on demand) from Salisbury to Stonehenge, as well as buses from the Salisbury train station to Stonehenge. The bus trip to Stonehenge takes a half hour, and a round-trip ticket costs £4.25 ($6.80) for adults and £2.10 ($3.35) for children under 14. If you're driving, head north on Castle Road from the center of Salisbury. At the first roundabout (traffic circle) take the exit toward Amesbury (A345) and Old Sarum. Continue along this road for 8 miles and then turn left onto the A303 in the direction of Exeter. You'll see signs for Stonehenge, leading you up the A344 to the right.

### ✪ AVEBURY

One of the largest prehistoric sites in Europe, Avebury lies on the Kennet River 7 miles west of Marlborough. Unlike Stonehenge, visitors can walk around the 28-acre site at Avebury, winding in and out of the circle of more than 100 stones, some weighing up to 50 tons. The stones are made of sarsen, a sandstone found in Wiltshire. Inside this large circle are two smaller ones, each with about 30 stones standing upright. Native Neolithic tribes are believed responsible for the circles.

Some visitors claim that a visit to Avebury, in contrast to Stonehenge, is a more "organic" and spiritual experience—you can walk right up and around the stones, as there's no fence keeping you way. The site also isn't mobbed with tour buses.

Avebury is 20 miles north of Stonehenge. **Wilts & Dorset** (☎ **01722/336855**) has two buses (nos. 5 and 6) that it runs between the bus station and Avebury three times a day from Monday through Saturday (twice daily on Sunday). The one-way trip takes 1¹/₂ hours.

**GETTING THERE**    Avebury is on A361 between Swindon and Devizes and a mile from the A4 London-Bath road. The closest rail station is at Swindon, some 12 miles away, which is served by the main rail line from London to Bath. Call ☎ **0345/ 484950** for information and schedules. A limited bus service (no. 49) runs from Swindon to Devizes through Avebury.

## MORE TO DO IN AVEBURY

Also here is the **Avebury Museum** (☎ **01672/539250**), founded by Alexander Keiller, which houses one of Britain's most important archaeological collections. It began with Keiller's material from excavations at Windmill Hill and Avebury, and now includes artifacts from other prehistoric digs at West Kennet, Long Barrow, Silbury Hill, West Kennet Avenue, and the Sanctuary. The Museum is open April to October, daily from 10am to 6pm; November to March, daily from 10am to 4pm. Admission is £1.50 ($2.40) for adults and 80p ($1.30) for children.

You may want to eat at **Stones Restaurant,** High Street (☎ **01672/539514**). This restaurant has been a hit ever since it was opened in 1984 within a converted Victorian stable block by two archaeologists, Dr. Hilary Howard and her husband, Michael Pitts. They specialize in freshly made food grown organically without artificial additives, which is prepared in original ways and sold at reasonable prices. This inexpensive restaurant, which takes MasterCard and Visa, is open April to October, daily 10am to 6pm (serving hot food from noon to 2:30pm); November to March, Saturday and Sunday from 10am to 5pm.

## 3 Dunster & Exmoor National Park

3 miles SE of Minehead; 184 miles W of London

The village of Dunster in Somerset is near the eastern edge of Exmoor National Park. It grew up around the original Dunster Castle, constructed as a fortress for the de Mohun family, whose progenitor came to England with William the Conqueror. The village, about 4 miles from the Cistercian monastery at Cleeve, has an ancient priory church and dovecote, a 17th-century gabled yarn market, and little cobbled streets dotted with whitewashed cottages.

## ESSENTIALS

**GETTING THERE**    The best rail link is to Minehead via Taunton, which is easily reached on the main London-Penzance line from Paddington Station in London. Call ☎ **0345/484950** for information and schedules. From Minehead you have to take a taxi or coach to reach Dunster.

At Taunton, you can take one of the seven Southern National coaches (no. 28), leaving hourly Monday through Saturday; there is only one bus on Sunday. Trip time is 1 hour and 10 minutes. Buses (no. 38 or 39) from Minehead stop in Dunster Village at the rate of one per hour, but only from June to September. Off-season visitors must take a taxi.

If you're driving from London, head west along M4, cutting south at the junction with M5 until you reach the junction with A39 going west to Minehead. Before your final approach to Minehead, cut south to Dunster along A396.

**VISITOR INFORMATION**   Dunster doesn't have an official tourist office, but an **Exmoor National Park Visitor Centre** is found at Dunster Steep (☎ **01643/ 821835**), 2 miles east of Minehead. It's open April to October, daily from 10am to 5pm, plus limited winter opening.

## ✪ DUNSTER CASTLE

The castle is on a tor (high hill), from which you can see Bristol Channel, and it stands on the site of a Norman castle granted to William de Mohun of Normandy by William the Conqueror shortly after the conquest of England. The 13th-century gateway built by the de Mohuns is all that remains of the original fortress. In 1376 the castle and its lands were bought by Lady Elizabeth Luttrell and belonged to her family until given to the National Trust in 1976, together with 30 acres of surrounding parkland. The first castle was largely demolished during the Civil War, and the present Dunster Castle is a Jacobean house built in the lower ward of the original fortifications in 1620, then rebuilt in 1870 to look like a castle. From the terraced walks and gardens you'll have good views of Exmoor and the Quantock Hills.

Some of the outstanding artifacts within are the 17th-century panels of embossed painted and gilded leather depicting the story of Antony and Cleopatra, and a remarkable allegorical 16th-century portrait of Sir John Luttrell shown wading naked through the sea with a female figure of peace and a wrecked ship in the background. The 17th-century plasterwork ceilings of the dining room and the finely carved staircase balustrade of cavorting huntsmen, hounds, and stags are also noteworthy.

The castle (☎ **01643/821314**) is on A396 (just off A39) in Dunster, or you can take bus no. 38 or 39 from Minehead. It is open April through September, Saturday to Wednesday from 11am to 5pm; October, daily 11am to 4pm. The grounds are open February, March, and October through December, daily from 11am to 4pm; April to September, daily 10am to 5pm. Admission to the castle and grounds is £5 ($8) for adults and £2.60 ($4.15) for children. Admission to the grounds only is £2.70 ($4.30) for adults and £1.30 ($2.10) for children.

## EXMOOR NATIONAL PARK

Between Somerset and Devon, along the northern coast of England's southwest peninsula, is Exmoor National Park, an unspoiled plateau whose lonely moors are mostly located 1,000 feet above sea level. One of the most cherished national parks in Britain, it includes the wooded valleys of the rivers Exe and Barle, the Brendon Hills, a sweeping stretch of rocky coastline, and such sleepy but charming villages as **Culbone, Selworthy, Parracombe,** and **Allerford.** Bisected by a network of heavily eroded channels for brooks and streams, the park is distinctive for its lichen-covered trees, gray-green grasses, gorse, and heather. The moors reach their highest point at Dunkery Beacon, at 1,707 feet above sea level.

Although it's one of the smallest national parks in Britain, aficionados praise it for a coastline—which many believe is the most beautiful in England. Softly contoured, without the dramatic peaks and valleys of other national parks, the terrain is composed mostly of primeval layering of sandstone slate. Although noteworthy for its scarcity of trees, the terrain encompasses a limited handful of very old oak groves, which are studied by forestry experts for their growth patterns.

On clear days, the coast of South Wales, 20 miles away, can be spotted across the estuary of the Bristol Channel. The wildlife that thrives on the park's rain-soaked terrain includes a breed of wild ponies (the Exmoor pony) whose bloodlines can be traced back to ancient species.

Despite the region's lack of trees, much of the park's terrain was classified as a Royal Forest and hunting preserve during the Middle Ages. (Part of the explanation for its low population density is the soil's relative infertility.) In 1819, the British government abandoned all attempts to maintain the district as a royal hunting preserve. Although the Royal Forest's boundaries were opened to settlement and investment, it remained sparsely settled until 1954, when it was added to Britain's network of national parks. Today, development programs of all kinds are fostered by the park; there are more than 700 miles of walking trails within the confines of the park, most visitors stay on the coastal trail that winds around the bays and inlets of England's southwestern peninsula or along some of the shorter riverside trails.

The park's administrative headquarters is located within a 19th-century workhouse in the village of Dulverton, in Somerset, near the park's southern edge. A program of walking tours is offered to anyone who's interested, at least five times a week. Themes include Woodland Walks, Moorland Walks, Bird Watching Excursions, and Deer Spottings. Most of the tours last from 4 to 6 hours, and all are free (although you are encouraged to donate). Wear sturdy shoes and raingear.

For the *Exmoor Visitor* brochure, which lists events, guided walks, and visitor information, contact the **Exmoor National Park Visitor Centre,** Dulverton, Somerset TA22 9EX (☎ **01398/323841**). Open Easter to the end of October, daily from 10am to 5pm, and through the winter, daily from 10am to 2pm.

## NEARBY SIGHTS

**Combe Sydenham Hall.** Monksilver. ☎ **01984/656284.** Admission £4 ($6.40) adults; £2 ($3.20) children. Country Park, Easter–Oct Sun–Fri 10am–5pm; courtroom and gardens, May–Sept at 2pm for guided tours only Mon, Thurs, Fri. From Dunster, drive on the A39, following signs pointing to Watchet and/or Bridgwater. On the right, you'll see a minor zoo, Tropiquaria, at which you turn right and follow the signs pointing to Combe Sydenham.

This hall was the home of Elizabeth Sydenham, wife of Sir Francis Drake, and it stands on the ruins of monastic buildings that were associated with nearby Cleeve Abbey. Here you can see a cannonball that legend says halted the wedding of Lady Elizabeth to a rival suitor in 1585. The gardens include Lady Elizabeth's Walk, which circles ponds originally laid out when the knight was courting his bride-to-be. The valley ponds fed by springwater are full of rainbow trout (ask about getting fly-fishing instruction). Woodland walks are possible to Long Meadow with its host of wildflowers. Also to be seen are a deserted hamlet, whose population reputedly was wiped out by the Black Death, and a historic corn mill. In the hall's tearoom, smoked trout and pâté are produced on oak chips, as in days of yore, and there are a shop, working bakery, and car park.

Incidentally, it was from Watchet, a few miles east of Minehead along the coast, that Coleridge's Ancient Mariner sailed.

**Coleridge Cottage.** 35 Lime St., Nether Stowey, near Bridgwater. ☎ **01278/732662.** Admission £1.70 ($2.70) adults; 80p ($1.30) children. Mar 23–Oct 1 Tues–Thurs and Sun 2–5pm. From Minehead, follow the A39 east about 30 miles, following signs to Bridgwater. About 8 miles from Bridgwater, turn right, following signs to Nether Stowey.

The hamlet of Nether Stowey is on A39, north of Taunton across the Quantock Hills to the east of Exmoor. The cottage is at the west end of Nether Stowey on the south side of A39. Here you can visit the home of Samuel Taylor Coleridge—where he wrote his epic "The Rime of the Ancient Mariner." During his 1797 to 1800 sojourn here, he and his friends, William Wordsworth and sister Dorothy, enjoyed exploring the Quantock woods. The parlor and reading room of his National Trust property are open to visitors.

## WHERE TO STAY & EAT IN THE AREA

✪ **Dollons House.** 10 Church St., Dunster TA24 6SH. ☎ **01643/821880.** Fax 01643/822016. 3 rms. TV. £35 ($56) single; £50 ($80) double. All rates include breakfast. MC, V.

Named after nearly forgotten occupants who lived here during the early 1700s, and set very close to the foundation of Dunster Castle, this place provides the most charming and convenient cost-conscious lodging in town. The 350-year-old building that contains it thrived for many generations as a pharmacy and a site where some of the most famous orange marmalade in Britain was mass-produced for consumption by members of Parliament in London. In the early Victorian era, a cream-colored stucco facade accented with egg and dart patterns, was added, causing modern-day newcomers—until they look more closely—to think that the building is actually newer than it is. Today, Hannah Bradshaw and her husband, Humphrey, make marmalade on a small scale—with none of the associations with Parliament of yesterday—that you can taste every morning at breakfast. There's also a gift shop on the premises (it occupies the two front rooms of the building's ground floor) specializing in pottery from local craftspeople. Bedrooms were inspired by the decor of an old-fashioned country cottage, "less frilly than Laura Ashley," and very comfortable.

**Luttrell Arms.** 32–36 High St. ☎ **01643/821-555.** Lunch main courses £6.75–£12.30 ($10.80–$19.70); fixed-price 3-course dinner £19.95 ($31.90); pub meals £3.75–£6.50 ($6–$10.40). AE, DC, MC, V. Restaurant, daily 12:30—2:30pm and 7–9:30pm; pub, daily noon–2:30pm and 6–9pm. ENGLISH.

The latest owners of this inn are continuing a 600-year tradition of providing sustenance to weary travelers. The timbered Tudor pub serves such dishes as scampi, chips, and tea, or a daily pie special. Menu choices can be accompanied by a well-kept Bass Ale, available on handpump. The restaurant serves an a la carte lunch menu that includes dishes like the joint of the day; pan-fried sirloin steak with tomatoes, mushrooms, and onions; a poached salmon fillet; or beef stroganoff served over paprika rice. Main courses are accompanied by a potato and your choice of fresh vegetables or salad. The three-course dinner menu is likely to include such dishes as guinea fowl or baked sugared ham with Somerset cider sauce.

**Tea Shoppe.** 3 High St. ☎ **01643/821-304.** Main courses £4.25–£7.95 ($6.80–$12.70). MC, V. Mar–Oct daily, 10:30am–5:30pm and Fri–Sat, 7pm–10pm (last order 9pm); Nov–Dec, Fri–Sun 10:30am–5:30pm and Fri–Sat 7pm–10pm (last order 9pm). Closed Jan–Feb. ENGLISH.

Parts of this ancient cottage date to 1495, and it's been a popular tea shop and eatery since the 1930s. The well-prepared menu includes such dishes as Exmoor venison trencher prepared in red wine and port, savory rabbit pie, chicken and bacon salad, and a pan-fried chicken fillet in tarragon cream sauce with vegetables. There are also daily vegetarian specials. For starters, we recommend a sampler platter of local cheese. Cream tea is served throughout the day for £3.25 ($5.20). Desserts include a wide variety of freshly made tarts.

## 4 Glastonbury Abbey

136 miles SW of London; 26 miles S of Bristol; 6 miles SW of Wells

Glastonbury may be one of the oldest inhabited sites in Britain. Excavations have revealed Iron Age lakeside villages on its periphery; some of the discoveries dug up may be viewed in a little museum on High Street. After the destruction of its once-great abbey, the town lost prestige. Today it is just a market town with a rich history. The ancient gatehouse entry to the abbey is a museum, and its principal exhibit is a scale model of the abbey and its community buildings as they stood in 1539, at the time of the dissolution.

Instead of Arthurian myth, today you are more likely to see a subculture of mystics, spiritualists, and neo-hippies, all drawn to the kooky legends whirling around the town. Glastonbury has been called England's New Age center and hippie capital. On the streets of Glastonbury, Christian spirituality blends with Druidic beliefs and—well, with just about anything. The average visitor arrives just to see the ruins and the monuments, but is likely to catch an eyeful of unexpected sights. You're as likely to run into people trying to track down Arthur and Guinevere as Jesus.

## ESSENTIALS

**GETTING THERE**   Go to Taunton, which is on the London-Penzance line leaving frequently from London's Paddington Station. Call ☎ **0345/484950** for schedules and information. At Taunton, proceed the rest of the way by bus. Or leave London's Paddington Station for Bristol Temple Meads, and go the rest of the way by Badgerline bus no. 376.

From Taunton, take the Southern National bus (no. 17) to Glastonbury, Monday through Saturday. There are one to three departures per day, and the trip takes 1 hour. A Badgerline bus (no. 376) runs from Bristol via Wells to Glastonbury every hour Monday through Saturday; on Sunday, the schedule is reduced to every 2 hours. The trip takes 1 1/2 hours. For information about bus schedules of Badgerline, call ☎ **01179/553231;** for data about Southern National, call ☎ **01823/272033.** One National Express bus a day (no. 402) leaves London's Victoria Coach Station at 5:30pm and arrives in Glastonbury at 9:40pm. For more information and schedules, call ☎ **0990/808080.**

If you're driving, take M4 west from London, then cut south on A4 via Bath to Glastonbury.

**VISITOR INFORMATION**   The **Tourist Information Centre** is at The Tribunal, 9 High St. (☎ **01458/832954**). Open Easter through September, Sunday to Thursday from 10am to 5pm, Friday and Saturday from 10am to 5:30pm; off-season, daily from 10am to 4pm.

## ✪ GLASTONBURY ABBEY

What was once one of the wealthiest and most prestigious monasteries in England is no more than a ruined sanctuary today, but it provides Glastonbury's claim to historical greatness, an assertion augmented by legendary links to such figures as Joseph of Arimathea, King Arthur, Queen Guinevere, and St. Patrick.

It is said that Joseph of Arimathea journeyed to what was then the Isle of Avalon, with the Holy Grail in his possession. According to tradition, he buried the chalice at the foot of the conical Glastonbury Tor and a stream of blood burst forth. You can scale this more than 500-foot-high hill today, on which stands a 15th-century tower.

Joseph, so the story goes, erected a church of wattle in Glastonbury. (The town, in fact, may have had the oldest church in England, as excavations have shown.) And at one point the saint is said to have leaned against his staff, which was immediately transformed into a fully blossoming tree; a cutting alleged to have survived from the Holy Thorn can be seen on the abbey grounds today—it blooms at Christmastime. Some historians have traced this particular story back to Tudor times.

The most famous link—popularized for Arthurian fans in the Victorian era by Tennyson—concerns the burial of King Arthur and Queen Guinevere on the abbey grounds. In 1191 the monks dug up the skeletons of two bodies on the south side of the lady chapel, said to be those of the king and queen. In 1278, in the presence of Edward I, the bodies were removed and transferred to a black marble tomb in the choir. Both the burial spot and the shrine are marked today.

A large Benedictine Abbey of St. Mary grew out of the early wattle church. St. Dunstan, who was born nearby, was the abbot in the 10th century and later became archbishop of Canterbury. Edmund, Edgar, and Edmund "Ironside," three early English kings, were buried at the abbey.

In 1184 a fire destroyed most of the abbey and its vast treasures. It was eventually rebuilt, after much difficulty, only to be dissolved by Henry VIII. Its last abbot, Richard Whiting, was hanged at Glastonbury Tor. Like the Roman forum, the abbey was used as a stone quarry for years. Today you can visit the ruins of the chapel, linked by an early English "Galilee" to the nave of the abbey. The best-preserved building on the grounds is a 14th-century octagonal Abbot's Kitchen, where oxen were once roasted whole to feed the wealthier pilgrims.

Glastonbury Abbey (☎ 01458/832267) is open daily from 9:30am to 6pm or dusk. Admission is £2.50 ($4) for adults, £2 ($3.20) for students and seniors, £1 ($1.60) for children under 16, and £5.50 ($8.80) for a family ticket.

## A MUSEUM IN THE ABBEY FARM

**Somerset Rural Life Museum.** Abbey Farm, Chilkwell St., Glastonbury. ☎ 01458/831197. Admission £1.80 ($2.90) adults; 50p (80¢) children. Apr–Oct Tues–Fri 10am-5pm, Sat–Sun 2–6pm; Nov–Mar Tues–Fri 10am–5pm, Sat 11am–4pm. A 5-minute walk from the center of Glastonbury. From High St., head toward the A361, through the roundabout to Fisher's Hill, and left onto Bere Lane. Follow Bere Lane to a dead end. The museum is on the left.

The history of the Somerset countryside since the early 19th century is exemplified by this museum based in the abbey farm. The centerpiece of the museum is the abbey barn, built around 1370. The magnificent timbered room, stone tiles, and sculptural details (including the bust of Edward III) make it special. There is also a Victorian farmhouse displaying exhibits that illustrate farming in Somerset during the "horse age" as well as domestic and social life in Victorian times. In summer, there are demonstrations of buttermaking, weaving, basketwork, and many other traditional craft and farming activities, which are rapidly disappearing. There is a museum shop and tearoom.

# WHERE TO STAY

## DOUBLES FOR LESS THAN £45 IN GLASTONBURY

**Little Orchard.** Ashwell Lane, Glastonbury, Somerset BA6 8BG. ☎ 01458/831620. 4 rms, none with bath. £16 ($25.60) single; £30 ($48) double. All rates include English breakfast. No credit cards.

On the A361 Glastonbury-Shepton Mallet road, 1 mile from the center, is a Tyrolean-type brick structure at the foot of Glastonbury Tor, which has striking views of the Vale of Avalon. Rodney and Dinah Gifford rent centrally heated and comfortably furnished bedrooms with hot- and cold-water basins. There is a color TV lounge. In summer, guests can enjoy the sun patio and large garden.

**Market House Inn.** 21 Magdalene St., Glastonbury, Somerset BA6 9EW. ☎ 01458/832220. 7 rms, none with bath. TV. £21.50 ($34.40) single; £35 ($56) double; £46.50 ($74.40) family rm. All rates include English breakfast. No credit cards. Bus: no. 29, 158, or 358.

This 18th-century two-story red-brick building has Georgian detailing, a long history, and a location across from the ruined abbey. Although most of the town's residents appreciate it as a popular pub, it also contains a handful of upstairs bedrooms, which tend to fill up quickly in summertime. The rooms are clean and rather Spartan. Advance reservations are important.

**☼ Woodlands.** 52 Bove Town, Glastonbury, Somerset BA6 8JE. ☎ **01458/832119.** 4 rms, none with bath. £22.50 ($36) single; £42 ($67.20) double. All rates include English breakfast. No credit cards.

Local architects considered this an extremely interesting house. Its oldest section was built in 1720, and interiors range from high-ceilinged Regency to low-beamed and cozy. Two bedrooms have timbered ceilings, and the back of the house—the side opening onto the 1¹/₂-acre garden facing Chalice Hill and the Glastonbury Tor— is early Victorian. Mrs. Yvonne Kerley, a resident of the house for many years, is the owner. The house sits on a road that intersects with Glastonbury's High Street, a 5-minute walk east of the center.

### NEARBY PLACES TO STAY UNDER £40

**Cradlebridge Farm.** Cradlebridge, Glastonbury, Somerset BA16 9SD. ☎ **01458/831827.** 2 rms. TV. £25 ($40) single; £35 ($56) double. All rates include English breakfast. No credit cards. Take A39 from Glastonbury; turn at the second right after passing the Morlands Shoe Factory, then take the first left, and Cradlebridge Farm will be at the end of the road.

This secluded farmhouse is about 2 miles from Glastonbury. Mr. and Mrs. Henry Tinney will go out of their way to make you comfortable and will prepare a traditional farmhouse breakfast. Units have hot-beverage facilities and their own patios, but with rather basic furnishings.

**Havyatt Manor Guest House.** Havyatt, Somerset BA6 8LF. ☎ **01458/832330.** 4 rms, none with bath. TV. £15 ($24) single; £25 ($40) double. All rates include English breakfast. No credit cards.

This 1840s manor house lies in the tiny hamlet of Havyatt, 2 miles west of Glastonbury via the Shepton Mallet road (A361), close to the foot of Glastonbury Tor and the abbey ruins. It grew up over the ruins of a much older manor which burned, and for a time was the center for hundreds of acres of surrounding farmland. Today it has English gardens plus a hothouse where grapes are grown for making wine. All the country-style rooms have beverage-making equipment.

## WHERE TO EAT

**Market House Inn.** 21 Magdalene St. ☎ **01458/832220.** Main courses £3–£12 ($4.80– $19.20); pub platters and snacks £1.40–£5 ($2.25–$8). No credit cards. Daily 9am–3:30pm. (Pub: Mon–Sat 11am–midnight; Sun noon–3pm and 7–10:30pm.) Bus: no. 29, 158, or 358. ENGLISH.

In this previously recommended 18th-century inn (see "Where to Stay," above) you can order restaurant meals on an a la carte menu or bar food. The food is home cooked and prices are reasonable. Roast English meals are featured in the restaurant where recipes seem little changed since the days of Henry VIII. Platters and snacks, including lasagna, chili, and sandwiches, are offered in the pub.

**Rainbow's End Café.** 17A High St. ☎ **01458/833896.** All items 50p–£3.50 (80¢–£5.60). No credit cards. Mon–Sat 10am–4pm; Sun 11:15am–4pm, depending on food inventories. (Café: Mon–Sat 10am–4:30pm.) Bus: no. 158 or 358. VEGETARIAN.

Much appreciated for its all-vegetarian cuisine, this restaurant occupies the street level of a very old white-fronted building on the town's main street. There's a garden terrace in back for outdoor dining during warm weather, and an interior where

## Impressions

*Out of this lake, which filled the center of a beautiful plain, embellished with groupes of beeches and elms, and fed with sheep, issued a river, that, for several miles, was seen to meander through an amazing variety of meadows and woods, till it emptied itself into the sea; with a large arm of which, and an island beyond it, the prospect was closed. On the right of the valley opened another of less extent, adorned with several villages, and terminated by one of the towers of an old ruined abbey, grown over with ivy, and part of the front, which remained still entire.*

—Henry Fielding, *The History of Tom Jones, A Foundling* (1749)

pinewood tables are accented with tablecloths and fresh flowers. Daily specials are posted on a chalkboard, and menu items include quiche, pizza, stuffed baked potatoes, salads, hot vegetarian platters, and cakes. The food, however, is rather bland—the way the locals like it.

## 5 Wells & the Caves of Mendip

21 miles SW of Bath; 123 miles SW of London

The cathedral town of Wells, to the south of the Mendip Hills, is a medieval gem. Wells was a vital link in the Saxon kingdom of Wessex—that is to say, it held a place of importance in England long before the arrival of William the Conqueror. Once the seat of a bishopric, it was eventually toppled from its ecclesiastical hegemony by the rival city of Bath. But the subsequent loss of prestige has paid off handsomely for residents of and visitors to Wells today: The town fell into a slumber, preserving much of its ancient appearance. The town name is derived from the presence of local wells, which were visited by pilgrims to Glastonbury in the hope that their gout could be eased by its supposedly curative waters.

## ESSENTIALS

**GETTING THERE**   Take the train to Bath (see below) and continue the rest of the way by bus.

Wells has good bus connections with its surrounding towns and cities. Badgerline bus no. 175 links Wells with Bath. Departures are every hour Monday through Saturday and every 2 hours on Sunday. Both no. 376 and 378 buses run between Bristol and Glastonbury every hour Monday through Saturday and every 2 hours on Sunday. Call ☎ **01749/673084** for schedules and information.

If you're driving, take M4 west from London, cutting south on A4 toward Bath and continuing along A39 into Wells.

**VISITOR INFORMATION**   The **Tourist Information Centre** is at the Town Hall, Market Place (☎ **01749/672552**). Open Nov to Mar, daily from 10am to 4pm and Apr to Oct from 9:30am to 5:30pm.

## ✪ WELLS CATHEDRAL

Begun in the 12th century, Wells Cathedral (☎ **01749/674483**) in the center of town is a well-preserved example of early English architecture. The medieval sculpture (six tiers of hundreds of statues recently restored) of its west front is without equal. The western facade was completed in the mid–13th century, the landmark central tower erected in the 14th century, and the fan vaulting attached later. The inverted arches were added to strengthen the top-heavy structure.

Much of the stained glass dates from the 14th century. The fan-vaulted lady chapel, also from the 14th century, is in the Decorated style. To the north is the vaulted chapter house, built in the 13th century and recently restored. Look also for a medieval astronomical clock in the north transept. There is no charge to enter the cathedral; however, visitors are asked to make voluntary donations of £3 ($4.80) for adults and £1 ($1.60) for students and children. The Cloister Restaurant and Cathedral Shop are adjacent to the cathedral.

After a visit to the cathedral, walk along its cloisters to the moat-surrounded **Bishop's Palace.** The Great Hall, built in the 13th century, is in ruins. Finally, the street known as the **Vicars' Close** is one of the most beautifully preserved streets in Europe. The cathedral is usually open daily from 7:15am to 6pm or until dusk in summer.

## WEST OF WELLS: THE CAVES OF MENDIP

Easily reached by heading west out of Wells, the **Caves of Mendip** are two exciting natural sightseeing attractions in Somerset—the great caves of Cheddar and Wookey Hole.

**Wookey Hole Caves & Paper Mill.** Wookey Hole, near Wells. ☎ **01749/672243.** 2-hour tour £6.50 ($10.40) adults; £3.50 ($5.60) children 16 and under; £18 ($28.80) family ticket. Apr–Oct daily 9:30am–5:30pm; Nov–Mar daily 10:30am–4:30pm. Closed Dec 17–25. Follow the signs from the center of Wells for 2 miles. Bus no. 172 from Wells.

Just 2 miles from Wells, you'll first come to the source of the Axe River. In the first chamber of the caves, as legend has it, is the Witch of Wookey turned to stone. These caves are believed to have been inhabited by prehistoric people at least 60,000 years ago. A tunnel opened in 1975 leads to the chambers unknown in early times and previously accessible only to divers.

Leaving the caves, you follow a canal path to the mill, where paper has been made by hand since the 17th century. Here the best-quality handmade paper is made by skilled workers according to the tradition of their ancient craft. Also in the mill are "handson vats" where visitors can try their hand at making a sheet of paper, and an Edwardian Penny Pier Arcade where new pennies can be exchanged for old ones with which to play the original machines. Other attractions include the Magical Mirror Maze, an enclosed passage of multiple image mirrors, and Movie Mania, celebrating a century of films. Visitors can use the self-service restaurant and picnic area.

**Cheddar Show Caves & Gorge.** Cheddar, Somerset Gorge. ☎ **01934/742343.** Admission £6.50 ($10.40) adults; £3.95 ($6.30) children 5–15; 4 and under free. Easter–Sept daily 10am–5pm; Oct–Easter daily 10:30am–4:30pm. Closed Dec 24–25. From A38, cut onto A371 to Cheddar village.

A short distance from Bath, Bristol, and Wells is the village of Cheddar, home of Cheddar cheese. It lies at the foot of Cheddar Gorge, within which are the Cheddar Caves, underground caverns with impressive formations. The caves are more than a million years old, including Gough's Cave, with its cathedral-like caverns, and Cox's Cave, with its calcite sculptures and brilliant colors. The Crystal Quest is a dark walk "fantasy adventure" taking you deep underground, and in the Cheddar Gorge Heritage Centre is displayed a 9,000-year-old skeleton. You can also climb Jacob's Ladder for clifftop walks and Pavey's Lookout Tower for views over Somerset—on a clear day you may even see Wales. Adults and children over 12 years of age can book an Adventure Caving expedition for £7.50 ($12), which includes overalls, helmets, and lamps. Other attractions include local craftspeople at work, ranging from the glassblower to the sweet-maker, plus the Cheddar Cheese & Cider Depot and Gough's Shop.

**Chewton Cheese Dairy.** Priory Farm, Chewton Mendip. ☎ **01761/241666.** Admission £2.50 ($4) adults; £2 ($3.20) seniors; £1.50 ($2.40) children 4 to 14; under 4 free. Daily 9am–4:30pm. Head 6 miles north of Wells on the A39 Bristol-Wells rd.

The dairy is owned by Lord Chewton, and visitors are welcome to watch through the viewing window in the restaurant as the traditional cheese-making process is carried out most mornings. A video presentation is featured in a spacious screening room. Guided tours are offered daily April to October at 11:30am, 12:15pm, 1pm, and 1:45pm. Although the dairy is open on Sunday and Thursday, there are no cheese-making demonstrations then. You can purchase a "truckle" (or wheel) of mature Cheddar to send home. The restaurant offers coffee, snacks, farmhouse lunches, and cream teas.

## WHERE TO STAY

You may want to stay in Wells, as its budget places are more reasonably priced than equivalent lodgings at Bath.

### IN WELLS

✪ **Ancient Gate House Hotel.** 12 Sadler St., Wells, Somerset BA5 2RR. ☎ **01749/672029.** 9 rms, 7 with bath. TV. £40 ($64) single with bath; £55 ($88) double without bath, £60 ($96) double with bath. All rates include English breakfast. AE, DC, MC, V.

Run by Francesco Rossi, this hotel faces Sadler Street, and the back has views of the cathedral and the open lawn in front of the cathedral's west door. Each room is comfortable and well furnished (six have four-poster beds). Franco also runs the Rugantino Restaurant attached to the hotel, where pastas and Italian dishes are a specialty. A fixed-price dinner costs £15.70 ($25.10).

**Bekynton House.** 7 Saint Thomas St. (B3139 to Radstock), Wells, Somerset BA5 2UU. ☎ **01749/672222.** 6 rms. TV. £46–£47 ($73.60–$75.20) double; £59 ($94.40) triple. All rates include English breakfast. MC, V.

Built in the 1700s as housing for the clergymen of the nearby cathedral, and named after the region's most famous ecclesiastic (a 12th-century bishop named Bekynton), this stone house is owned and managed by Rosaleen and Desmond Gripper, escapees from the financial district in London. The house contains clean and comfortable bedrooms with a TV and free tea and coffee, and the benefit of a parking lot where guests can leave their cars and walk to the sights in Wells, where parking space is scarce. If you pay with a credit card, expect your total bill to increase by 4%. The house sits a few steps behind the cathedral.

**Sherston Inn.** Priory Rd., Wells, Somerset BA5 1SU. ☎ **01749/673743.** 6 rms, none with bath. TV. £22 ($34.75) single; £42 ($66.35) double. All rates include English breakfast. MC, V.

This is a pub on the edge of town on the road to Glastonbury (A39), with a parking area and beer garden. It's just a 10-minute walk from the cathedral, Bishop's Palace, and Wells Museum. Part of the building is from the 17th century. The owner rents very modest but clean bedrooms. Bar meals are served in the cozy Moat Bar or the more spacious restaurant. Meals are served daily and cost £9 ($14.40) and up in the restaurant; bar platters average £4.75 ($7.60).

**Tor Guest House.** 20 Tor St., Wells, Somerset BA5 2US. ☎ **01749/672322.** 8 rms. £45–£50 ($72–$80) double; £55–£70 ($88–$112) family rate. All rates include English breakfast. MC, V. Bus: no. 173 (Badgerline Bath-Wells line).

One of the more recommendable guest houses, this home dates from 1610, although much altered over the years. From the front rooms there's a view of the Bishop's Palace and the east face of the cathedral, which are reached by a 3-minute walk along the palace moat. Tor House has a Queen Anne shell front porch, and in the front garden is a 1790s magnolia tree said to be the oldest in Europe. The rooms are tastefully furnished but somewhat spare. A sauna, steam room, hydrotherapy, and gym facilities are available to the guests. The house has its own large parking area and is open all year.

## ON THE OUTSKIRTS

**Burcott Mill.** Burcott, Wookey, near Wells, Somerset BA5 1NJ. ☎ **01749/673118.** 6 rms, 3 with bath (tub or shower); 1 suite. £15 ($24) per person single or double without bath; £17 ($27.20) per person single or double with bath; £25 ($40) per person suite. All rates include English breakfast. MC, V.

This hotel was originally built in the 18th century as a stone-sided flour mill. It's set on the outskirts of the village of Wookey (on B3139), beside the River Axe about 2 miles from Wells. The bedrooms are country comfortable and plain. There are three pubs within walking distance of the accommodation, each serving meals. The mill is being restored by its owners, Tony and Alison Grimstad, to become a fully working flour mill. If requested, the Grimstads will show you the electricity-gathering process.

**Crapnell Farm.** Dinder, near Wells, Somerset BA5 3HG. ☎ **01749/342683.** 3 rms, none with bath. £32–£36 ($51.20–$57.60) double. All rates include English breakfast. No credit cards.

Three miles from the Cathedral City of Wells and 1 mile from the local golf club, this 300-year farmhouse offers a bucolic respite from city bustle. The 260-acre working dairy farm is situated on the south side of Mendip Hills. All rooms have tea- and coffee-making facilities. In this warm and friendly atmosphere, you can enjoy watching TV in the guest room or playing snooker in the large snooker room or taking a swim in the outdoor swimming pool. Dinner is available by arrangement.

# WHERE TO EAT

**The City Arms.** 69 High St. ☎ **01749/673916.** Reservations recommended. Main courses £4–£9 ($6.40–$14.40). MC, V. Mon–Sat 10:30am–11pm; Sun noon–3pm and 7–10:30pm. ENGLISH.

The former city jail is now a pub with an open courtyard furnished with tables, chairs, and umbrellas. In summer it's a mass of flowers, and there's an old vine growing in the corner. Full meals are likely to include a homemade soup of the day, fresh salmon, lamb in burgundy sauce, or stuffed quail in Cointreau sauce. From the charcoal grill you can order rump steak or chicken with Stilton cheese, and longtime favorites include beef Wellington or steak, kidney, and ale pie. Vegetarian dishes are also offered. Upstairs is an Elizabethan timbered restaurant. The food is a notch above your typical pub grub. The restaurant is in the center, 2 blocks from the bus station.

**Ritcher's.** 5 Sadler St. ☎ **01749/679085.** Reservations required for the restaurant, not required for the Bistro. Bistro: 2-course fixed-price lunch £6.50 ($10.40), 3-course fixed-price lunch £8.50 ($13.60); 2-course fixed-price dinner £12.95 ($20.70), 3-course fixed-price dinner £14.95 ($23.90). Restaurant: 2-course fixed-price dinner £15 ($24), 3-course fixed-price dinner £18.50 ($29.60). MC, V. Bistro: daily 11:30am–2:15pm and 6:30–9:15pm. Restaurant: lunch by appointment only; dinner Tues–Sat 6:30–9:15pm. FRENCH.

Known as one of the best restaurants in town, it contains a likable bistro on the ground floor and a more formal restaurant one floor above street level. Both are in a 16th-century stone cottage whose entrance lies behind a wrought-iron gate and a tile-covered passageway running beneath another building near the cathedral. Menu items in the bistro include turkey and venison pies, platters of fresh asparagus, and a modernized version of salade niçoise served with a raspberry vinaigrette. The cuisine in the upstairs restaurant is more ambitious, and might include saddle of lamb roasted with garlic-and-herb crust and beaujolais sauce, or slices of Scottish salmon glazed with freshwater prawns in a chablis-flavored cream sauce. The chefs don't always pull off some of these dishes, but there is care and concern with the cuisine.

## 6 Bath: Britain's Most Historic Spa Town

115 miles W of London; 13 miles SE of Bristol

In 1702 Queen Anne made the trek from London to the mineral springs of Bath, thereby launching a fad that was to make the city the most celebrated spa in England.

The most famous personage connected with Bath's popularity was the 18th-century dandy Beau Nash. The master of ceremonies of Bath, Nash cut a striking figure as he made his way across the city, with all the plumage of a bird of paradise. This polished arbiter of taste and manners made dueling déclassé. While dispensing (at a price) trinkets to the courtiers and aspirant gentlemen of his day, Beau was carted around in a sedan chair.

The 18th-century architects John Wood the Elder and his son provided a proper backdrop for Nash's considerable social talents. These architects designed a city of stone from the nearby hills, a feat so substantial and lasting that Bath today is the most harmoniously laid-out city in England. During Georgian times, this city on a bend of the Somerset River was to attract a following among leading political and literary figures, such as Dickens, Thackeray, Nelson, and Pitt. Canadians may already know that General Wolfe lived on Trim Street, and Australians may want to visit the house at 19 Bennett St. where their founding father, Admiral Phillip, lived. Even Henry Fielding came this way, observing in *Tom Jones* that the ladies of Bath "endeavour to appear as ugly as possible in the morning, in order to set off that beauty which they intend to show you in the evening."

Bath has had two lives. Long before its Queen Anne, Georgian, and Victorian popularity, it was known to the Romans as Aquae Sulis. The foreign legions founded their baths here (which may be visited today) to ease their rheumatism in the curative mineral springs. Remarkable restoration and careful planning have ensured that Bath retains its handsome look today. The city suffered devastating destruction from the infamous Baedeker air raids of 1942, when Luftwaffe pilots seemed more intent on bombing historical buildings than in hitting any military target.

After major restoration in the postwar era, Bath today has somewhat of a museum look to it, with the attendant gift shops. Its parks, museums, and architecture continue to draw the hordes to Bath, and prices—because of this massive foreign invasion—remain high. But it's one of the high points of the West Country and a lot more interesting than Bristol. Also from Bath, you can venture out to Avebury.

## ESSENTIALS

**GETTING THERE**    Trains leave London's Paddington Station bound for Bath once every hour during the day. The trip takes about 1 1/2 hours. For schedules and information, call ☎ **0345/484950.**

One National Express coach leaves London's Victoria Coach Station every 2 hours during the day. The trip takes 2 1/2 hours. Coaches also leave Bristol bound for Bath, and make the trip in 50 minutes. For schedules and information, call ☎ **0990/808080.**

Drive west on M4 to the junction with A4, on which you continue west to Bath.

**VISITOR INFORMATION** The **Bath Tourist Information Centre** is at Abbey Chambers, Abbey Church Yard (☎ **01225/477101**), next to Bath Abbey. Open June through September, Monday through Saturday from 9:30am to 7pm, Sunday from 10am to 6pm; off-season Monday through Saturday from 9:30am to 5pm and Sunday from 10am to 4pm.

**GETTING AROUND** One of the best ways to explore Bath is by bike. Rentals are available at **Somerset Valley Bike Hire** (☎ **01225/465-1880**), behind the train station. It's open daily from 9am to 6pm, charging £10.50 to £22.50 ($16.80 to $36) per day, depending on the bike. Deposits range from £20 to £75 ($32 to $120).

## THE BATH INTERNATIONAL MUSIC FESTIVAL

Bath's graceful Georgian architecture provides the setting for one of Europe's most prestigious international festivals of music and the arts. For 17 days in late May and early June each year the city is filled with more than 1,000 performers. The Bath International Music Festival focuses on classical music, jazz, new music, and the contemporary visual arts, with orchestras, soloists, and artists from all over the world. In addition to the main music and art program, there is all the best in walks, tours, and talks, plus free street entertainment and a free Festival Club, and opening night celebrations with fireworks. For detailed information, contact **The Bath Festivals Box Office,** 2 Church St., Abbey Green, Bath BA1 1NL (☎ **01225/463362**).

## BATH ABBEY

Built on the site of a much larger Norman cathedral, the present-day abbey is a fine example of the late perpendicular style. When Queen Elizabeth I came to Bath in 1574, she ordered a national fund to be set up to restore the abbey. The west front is the sculptural embodiment of a Jacob's ladder dream of a 15th-century bishop. When you go inside and see its many windows, you'll understand why the abbey is called the "Lantern of the West." Note the superb fan vaulting, with its scalloped effect. Beau Nash was buried in the nave and is honored by a simple monument totally out of keeping with his flamboyant character. In 1994 the Bath Abbey Heritage Vaults opened on the south side of the abbey. This subterranean exhibition traces the history of Christianity at the abbey site since Saxon times.

The Abbey, Orange Grove (☎ **01225/422462**), is open April to October, Monday to Saturday from 9am to 6pm; November to March, Monday to Saturday from 9am to 4:30pm; year-round Sunday, 1 to 2:30pm and 4:30 to 5:30pm. The Heritage Vaults are open Monday to Saturday from 10am to 4pm. For the abbey, a donation of £1.50 ($2.40) is requested. Admission to the Heritage Vaults is £2 ($3.20) for adults and £1 ($1.60) for students, children, and seniors.

## ✪ THE PUMP ROOM & ROMAN BATHS

Founded in A.D. 75 by the Romans, the baths, in the Abbey churchyard, were dedicated to the goddess Sulis Minerva; in their day they were an engineering feat. Even today they're among the finest Roman remains in the country, and are still fed by Britain's most famous hot-spring water. After centuries of decay, the original baths were rediscovered during Queen Victoria's reign. The site of the Temple of Sulis Minerva has been excavated and is now open to view. The museum displays many interesting objects from Victorian and recent digs (look for the head of Minerva). Coffee, lunch, and tea, usually with music from the Pump Room Trio, can be enjoyed in the 18th-century pump room, overlooking the hot springs. There's also a drinking fountain with hot mineral water that tastes horrible.

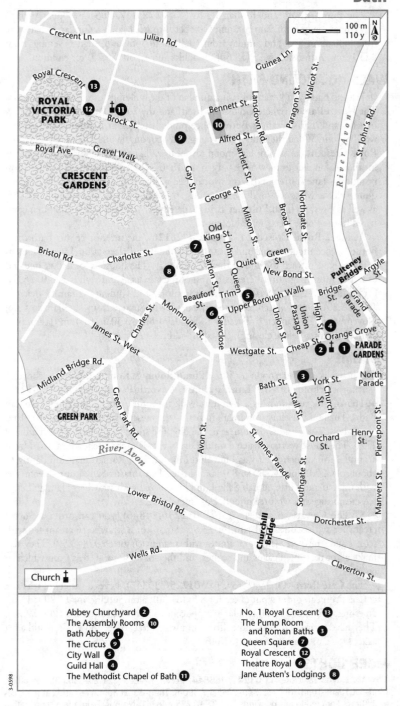

# Bath

0 — 100 m
110 y

N

Crescent Ln.    Julian Rd.

Guinea Ln.

Royal Crescent ❸

ROYAL VICTORIA PARK ❷ ✝❶ Brock St.

Bennett St. ❿

Walcot St.

Paragon St.

Lansdown Rd.

River Avon

St. John's Rd.

Royal Ave.    Gravel Walk

❾

Alfred St.

CRESCENT GARDENS

Gay St.

Bartlett St.

George St.

Milsom St.

Broad St.

Northgate St.

Bristol Rd.    Charlotte St.

Old King St.

❼

John St.

Queen St.

Quiet

Green St.

New Bond St.

Pulteney Bridge

Argyle St.

❽

Barton St.

Beaufort St.

Trim-

❺

Upper Borough Walls

Bridge St.

Grand Parade

Charles St.

Monmouth St.

❻ Sawclose

Union Passage

Union St.

High St.

❹

Orange Grove

James St. West

Westgate St.

Cheap St.

❷ ✝■ ❶

PARADE GARDENS

Midland Bridge Rd.

❸

Bath St.

York St.

Church St.

North Parade

GREEN PARK

Green Park Rd.

River Avon

Avon St.

St. James Parade

Stall St.

Southgate St.

Orchard St.

Henry St.

Pierrepont St.

Manvers St.

Lower Bristol Rd.

Wells Rd.

Churchill Bridge

Dorchester St.

Claverton St.

Church ✝■

3-0598

Abbey Churchyard ❷
The Assembly Rooms ❿
Bath Abbey ❶
The Circus ❾
City Wall ❺
Guild Hall ❹
The Methodist Chapel of Bath ❶

No. 1 Royal Crescent ❸
The Pump Room and Roman Baths ❸
Queen Square ❼
Royal Crescent ❷
Theatre Royal ❻
Jane Austen's Lodgings ❽

433

The Pump Room and Roman Baths (☎ **01225/477785**) are open April to September, daily from 9am to 6pm; October through March, Monday to Saturday from 9:30am to 5pm and Sunday from 10:30am to 5pm, and August evenings from 8 to 10pm. Admission is £6 ($9.60) for adults and £3.60 ($5.75) for children.

## WALKING AROUND BATH

In historic Bath, you'll want to visit a number of the buildings, crescents, and squares. The **North Parade** (where Goldsmith lived) and the **South Parade** (where English novelist and diarist Frances Burney once resided) represent harmony, and are the work of John Wood the Elder. The younger Wood, on the other hand, designed the **Royal Crescent,** an elegant half-moon row of town houses copied by Astor architects for their colonnade in New York City in the 1830s. **Queen Square** is one of the most beautiful—Jane Austen and Wordsworth used to live here (separately)—showing off quite well the work of Wood the Elder. Also of interest is **The Circus,** built in 1754, as well as the shop-lined **Pulteney Bridge,** designed by Robert Adam and often compared to the Ponte Vecchio of Florence.

At **no. 1 Royal Crescent** (☎ **01225/428126**), the interior of this Bath town house has been redecorated and furnished by the Bath Preservation Trust to look as it might have toward the end of the 18th century. The house is located at one end of Bath's most magnificent crescent, west of the Circus. Admission is £3.50 ($5.60) for adults and £2.50 ($4) for children, seniors, and students; a family ticket is £8 ($12.80). Open March to October, Tuesday to Sunday from 10:30am to 5pm; November to December 1, Tuesday to Sunday from 10:30am to 4pm (last admission 30 minutes before closing); closed Good Friday.

## TEATIME

The best place for afternoon tea is the **Pump Room & Roman Baths** (see above).

Another choice is **Sally Lunn's House,** 4 North Parade Passage (☎ **01225/461634**). The restaurant is a 1-minute walk from the Abbey Church and Roman Baths. The house itself is a landmark in Bath—the present wood-frame building dates from about 1482 and is the oldest in the city; the stone facade was erected around 1720. The house was constructed on the site of a monastery kitchen that dated from around 1150, which itself was built upon the site of a Roman mansion dating to about A.D. 200. For £4.28 ($6.85) you can get the Fantastic Sally Lunn Cream Tea with toasted and buttered half Sally Lunn bun served with strawberry jam and clotted cream together with tea or coffee of your choice.

At **The Canary,** 3 Queen St. (☎ **01225/424846**), you can order a clotted cream tea with scones and jam for £3.95 ($6.30) or a strawberry cream tea with scones and strawberry jam or cream tea with a sandwich for £5.95 ($9.50). They also make all of their own cakes and scones, and they have 30 to 40 teas from which to choose.

The **Café Retro,** Orange Grove (☎ **01225/339347**), serves a variety of teas and coffees. You can order a pot of tea for 80p ($1.30), a cappuccino for £1.20 ($1.90), an espresso for £1 ($1.60), or a large cappuccino or large espresso for £1.40 ($2.25). They have a variety of teas and coffees from which to choose, and you can add a tea cake, scone, or crumpet for £1 ($1.60).

## MORE SIGHTS

**Theatre Royal.** Sawclose. ☎ **01225/448844.** Tickets, £7–£23 ($11.20–$36.80). Box office: Mon–Sat 10am–10pm. Shows: Mon–Wed at 7:30pm, Thurs–Sat at 8pm. Wed and Sat matinees at 2:30pm. For credit-card bookings, call ☎ 01225/448861. No bus. From main train station in center of Bath, head northwest on Union St. It's about a 5-minute walk to the theater.

Theatre Royal, located next to the new Seven Dials development, was restored in 1982 and refurbished with plush seats, red carpets, and a painted proscenium arch and ceiling; it is now the most beautiful theater in Britain. It has 940 seats, with a small pit and grand tiers rising to the upper circle. Beneath the theater, reached from the back of the stalls or by a side door, are the theater vaults, where you will find a bar in one with stone walls. The next vault has a restaurant, serving an array of dishes from soup to light a la carte meals.

A studio theater at the rear of the main building opened in 1996. The theater publishes a list of forthcoming events; its repertoire includes, among other offerings, West End shows.

**The American Museum.** Claverton Manor, Bathwick Hill. ☎ **01225/460503.** Admission £5 ($8) adults; £4.50 ($7.20) students and seniors; £2.50 ($4) children 5–16; under 5 free. Late Mar to beginning of Nov Tues–Sun 2–5pm for the museum, and 1–6pm for the garden. Bus: no. 18.

Some $2^1/_2$ miles outside Bath, at the first American museum established outside the United States, you can get an idea of what life was like in America prior to the mid-1800s. In a Greek Revival house (Claverton Manor), the museum sits proudly on extensive grounds high above the Somerset valley. Among the authentic exhibits—shipped over from the States—are a New Mexico room, a Conestoga wagon, an early American beehive oven (try gingerbread baked from the recipe of George Washington's mother), the dining room of a New York town house of the early 19th century, and (on the grounds) a copy of Washington's flower garden at Mount Vernon. A permanent exhibition in the New Gallery displays the Dallas Pratt Collection of Historical Maps, as well as seasonal exhibitions. There is also an American arboretum on the grounds.

Throughout the summer, the museum plays host to various groups who demonstrate a number of events and life-styles from America's attic. These range from displays of Native American dancing and 1700s military drills to very realistic reenactments in the French and Indian War and the Civil War.

## ORGANIZED TOURS

**The Heart of England Tourist Board** (☎ **01905/763436**) and the **West Country Tourist Board** (☎ **01392/276351**) have details of numerous guided tours within their regions, and the staff can book you with registered guides for outings ranging from short walks to luxury tours that include accommodations in stately homes.

Free, $1^3/_4$-hour walking tours are conducted throughout the year by the Mayor's Honorary Society (☎ **01225/477786**). Tours depart from outside the Roman Baths Monday through Friday at 10:30am and 2pm, Sunday at 2:30pm, and Tuesday, Friday, and Saturday at 7pm. A slightly different tour by Bath Parade Tours,

## Impressions

*The Circus is a pretty bauble, contrived for show, and looks like Vespasian's amphitheater turned outside in. If we consider it in point of magnificence, the great number of small doors belonging to the separate houses, the inconsiderable height of the different orders, the affected ornaments of the architrave, which are both childish and misplaced, and the areas projecting into the street, surrounded with iron rails, destroy a good part of its effect upon the eye; and perhaps we shall find it still more defective, if we view it in the light of convenience.*

—Tobias Smollett (1721–71)

costing £3 ($4.80) per person, leaves Saturday at 2:30pm from outside the Roman Baths. Reservations aren't needed for either tour.

**Jane Austen Tours** take you in the footsteps of the author and her characters. Conducted Saturdays, tours begin at Abbey Lace Shop, York Street (☎ **01225/ 436030**). The cost is £3 ($4.80) per person. You'll be told the time to meet for the tour when you make your reservations.

To tour Bath by bus, you can choose among several tour companies—some with open-top buses leaving from the Tourist Information Centre, which can be called for changing schedules and prices. Among the best candidates are **Patrick Driscoll/Beau Nash Guides,** Elmsleigh, Bathampton, BA2 6SW (☎ **01225/46210**). These tours are more personalized than most. Another good outfitter is **Sulis Guides,** 2 Lansdown Terrace, Weston, Bath BA1 4BR (☎ **01225/429681**).

River cruises on the Somerset depart from the river's east bank, adjacent to the Pulteney Bridge, directly across the water from the Parade Gardens. Walk down a slipway/boat ramp to reach the departure point. The 50-minute boat cruises cost between £3 and £3.70 ($4.80 and $5.90) for adults, and between £1.50 and £2 ($2.40 and $3.20) for children. The boats go about 3 miles upstream to Bathampton, then reverse their leisurely, big-windowed junket for their downstream returns to Bath. River tours are offered only from Easter to October via two boats maintained by **The Boating Station** (☎ **01225/466407**); and its competitor, a one-ship out-fit, **The Pulteney Princess** (☎ **01453/836639**).

## OUTDOOR PURSUITS

**GOLF**    Bath has several well-maintained golf clubs. One is the 18-hole **Bath Golf Club** at North Road (☎ **01225/463834**). A round costs £25 ($40) on weekdays and £30 ($48) on Saturday and Sunday. There are no golf carts nor clubs for rent. The club is open to visitors with established handicap certificates or letter with details of their standard of ply from their own club. Before playing, telephone ☎ **01225/466953** for best tee times. To get to Bath Golf Club, take the A36 Warminster Road out of Bath. Turn right into North Road, signed Golf Club, University and American Museum.

Another 18-hole course is the **Lansdown Golf Club,** Lansdown (☎ **01225/ 422138**). The cost per round is £15 ($24) on weekdays and £20 ($32) on Saturday and Sunday. Visitors are accepted only with a handicap certificate from their own club. Tee times are available at any time, but players are advised to telephone ☎ **01225/422138** before playing. To get to Lansdown Golf Club, take Lansdown Road out of Bath toward the racecourse and Lansdown Park and Ride. At the edge of the city, pass the Park and Ride and the Blathwayt Arms and the golf club is on the left-hand side.

A 9-hole public course is the **Entry Hill Golf Course,** Entry Hill (☎ **01225/ 834248**). The cost per round for 9 holes is £5.50 ($8.80) on weekdays and £6.20 ($9.90) on Saturday and Sunday. The cost per round for 18 holes is £8.50 ($13.60) on weekdays and £9.95 ($15.90) on weekends. Golfers need proper golf shoes or trainers, and clubs are available for hire, if needed. Before playing, call ☎ **01225/ 834248** for the best advice on tee times. To get to Entry Hill Golf Course, take the A367 south out of Bath along Wellsway. Turn left into Entry Hill, signed Entry Hill Golf Course.

**HORSEBACK RIDING**    The Wellow Trekking Centre, in Wellow, near Bath (☎ **01225/834376**) is open daily. Rides are available for £11 ($17.60) for a 1-hour, £17 ($27.20) for a 2-hour, and £25 ($40) for a half-day pub ride from 10am–2pm. No public transport. From Bath, follow Warminster Road to Hinton Charter House, then turn right and follow the signposts to Wellow Trekking Centre, a 20-minute drive.

**SWIMMING   The Sports and Leisure Centre on the Recreation Ground** (☎ 01225/462563), has indoor sports, swimming, a sauna, and a solarium. For information on the times, availability, and services, call the sports centre. To get here go across the river via the North Parade Bridge.

**TENNIS**   There are several public courts available with outdoor hard courts at Royal Victoria Park, Sydney Gardens, and Alice Park. For all inquiries regarding public tennis courts in Bath, contact **Excel Tennis** (☎ 01225/425066), from which you can also rent rackets and balls. Courts cost £2.50 ($4) per person, per hour. Pick up a city map from the Tourist Information Centre at Abbey Chambers on your arrival in Bath for details.

## BROWSING BATH

The famous waters of this spa town are for sale by the bottle. The single best day to visit, if you are a serious shopper, is Wednesday, when there are more flea markets in operation than on any other day. The small flea market on Saturday isn't nearly as loaded with merchandise, but it's still fun to browse.

There are antique markets and fairs, antique centers, additional antique shops, and literally hundreds of opportunities to buy (and ship) anything you want. Prices are traditionally less than in London but more than in the British boonies.

The city of Bath is basically one long, slightly uphill shopping opportunity. This is not the kind of British village defined by a single High Street. If you arrive by train, don't be put off by the lack of scenery. Within 2 blocks are several shopping streets. You can go up through the town on one side of the street (which more or less segue into each other) and then go back down on the other side of the street, with only a mere glance at a map. Getting lost is part of the fun.

As you weave through the city, you will find a myriad of items and stores. **Marks & Spencer,** Stall Street (☎ 01225/462591), is a branch of the famous London department store found in most English market towns. There are more fancy stores on nearby Union Street. **The Podium,** at Northgate and Walcot streets (☎ 01225/444678), is a rather modern shopping mall. Here you can find gifts, picnic items, train snacks, and wine and spirits at the **Waitrose** (☎ 01225/442550), a supermarket at The Podium. The ancient **Guild Hall,** High Street, has several open stalls where merchants sell sandwiches, fresh fruits, used paperback books, and more. If you are in need of drugstore items, go to **Boots the Chemist,** 1 Merchant's Passage (☎ 01225/464402).

Bath is second only to London in terms of shopping possibilities. Here is a sampling just to get you started.

**The Bartlett Street Antiques Centre.** Bartlett St. ☎ **01225/466689.**

There are 60 dealers and 160 showcases on three floors displaying furniture, silver, antique jewelry, paintings, clocks, toys, military items, and collectibles.

**Bath Stamp & Coin Shop.** 12–13 Pulteney Bridge. ☎ **01225/463073.**

Established in 1946, this is the largest purveyor of antique coins and stamps in Bath, with hundreds of odd and unusual numismatics from throughout England and its former empire. Part of the inventory is devoted to Roman coins, some of which were imported into England during the 19th century and obtained from estate sales; others of which were unearthed in archaeological excavations at Roman sites near Bath. Also look for antique Venetian glass and a scattering of English antiques.

**Beaux Arts Gallery.** 13 York St. ☎ **01225/464850.**

This is the largest and most important gallery of contemporary art in Bath, specializing in well-known British artists. Closely linked to the art scene as it's unfolding in London, the gallery occupies a pair of interconnected, stone-fronted Georgian houses, in which a half-dozen showrooms exhibit objects ranging from £20 ($32). It's close to Bath Abbey.

**Great Western Antiques Centre.** Bartlett St. ☎ **01225/424243.**

There are 30 dealers on one floor. Here you can find costumes, costume jewelry, trains, and other railway items, lace and linens, porcelain and glass, silver, music boxes, canes, and much more.

**Walcot Reclamation.** 108 Walcot St. ☎ **01225/444404.**

This is Bath's salvage yard. This sprawling and appealingly dusty storeroom of 19th-century architectural remnants is set a quarter-mile northeast of the town center, within what was conceived a century ago as a cabinetmakers' yard. It accumulates into a 20,000-square-foot warehouse the architectural remnants of demolished homes, schools, hospitals, and factories throughout south England. Mantelpieces, panels, columns, fragments of iron fences, and architectural ornaments, each departmentalized and separated into historical eras, entice the memories of other eras. Items range from a complete, dismantled, 1937 version of a Georgian library crafted from Honduran mahogany, to objects costing around £5 ($8) each. Anything can be shipped or altered on site by a battery of artisans who adapt the antique fittings into the context of modern buildings.

**Whittard of Chelsea.** 10 Union Passage. ☎ **01225/447787.**

This is the most charming and unusual emporium in Bath for whatever you'll need to duplicate the tea-drinking ritual after your return to North America, or wherever you happen to like to drink your tea. Inside, you'll find strainers, table and tea services, tea biscuits, tea cozies, tea caddies, and teas that derive from all parts of what used to be known as the British Empire. Looking for a fabulously exotic tea to wow your friends with back home? As for Monkey-Picked Oolong, a Chinese tea from plants so inaccessible that leaves can be gathered only by trained monkeys. Also, you'll find a roster of teapots guaranteed to provoke a response. They include porcelain replicas of London's Big Ben and—more esoteric—the pub featured as a setting for Britain's longest-running soap opera, "Coronation Street."

# WHERE TO STAY
## DOUBLES FOR LESS THAN £60

✪ **Badminton Villa.** 10 Upper Oldfield Park, Bath, Somerset BA2 3JZ. ☎ **01225/426347.** Fax 01225/420393. 5 rms. TV. £38 ($60.80) single; £48–£56 ($76.80–$89.60) double. All rates include English breakfast. MC, V. Bus: no. 14.

Located about half a mile south of the city center, this house was built in 1883 as part of a suburban development that is today an extremely desirable place to live. Constructed of honey-colored blocks of Bath stone, it lies on a hillside with sweeping views down over the world-famous architecture of Bath. When acquired in 1992 by John and Sue Burton, the abandoned villa had fallen into disrepair. The couple gracefully transformed the interior into new configurations suitable to a bed-and-breakfast hotel, added zest and style, and today run one of the most charming small hotels in Bath. Furnishings are an eclectic but unpretentious mix of objects gathered by the Burtons on their travels. The bedrooms have radios, tea-making facilities, and hair dryers. There's a three-tiered garden with patio.

**Cedar Lodge.** 13 Lambridge, London Rd., Bath, Somerset BA1 6BJ. ☎ **01225/423468.** 3 rms. TV. £30–£40 ($48–$64) single; £45–£60 ($72–$96) double. All rates include English breakfast. No credit cards. Bus: no. 3 or 13.

In a residential suburb about a mile east of the town center, this home was originally built in 1778 by a Cotswold wool merchant with ties to the Fairfax family of Virginia. Your hosts are Derek and Maria Beckett, an engaging Anglo-Hungarian couple trained in psychology who spend part of their time conducting research in criminal psychology for the British government. Worldly and charming, they prepare excellent evening meals for clients who give advance notice, from £15 ($24).

**Cheriton House.** Upper Oldfield Park, Bath, Somerset BA2 3JX. ☎ **01225/429862.** Fax 01225/428403. 9 rms. TV. £35–£40 ($56–$64) single; £52–£60 ($83.20–$96) double. All rates include English breakfast. AE, DC, MC, V. Bus: no. 14, 14A, or 14B.

This is an elegant late-Victorian home that still has many of its original architectural adornments, including fireplaces. Mrs. Jo Babbage works hard to make her guests comfortable, and her large house is spotlessly clean. There is ongoing refurbishment in the bedrooms. This is really a house for adults, not young children. Only breakfast is served.

**Grove Lodge Guest House.** 11 Lambridge, London Rd., Bath, Somerset BA1 6BJ. ☎ **01225/ 310860.** Fax 01225/429630. 8 rms, none with bath. TV. £25 ($40) single; £48 ($76.80) double. All rates include English breakfast. No credit cards. Discounts available for 3 or more people. Bus: no. 3, 13, or 23.

This typical Georgian home dates from 1787, and has well-furnished and spacious rooms, most with large windows overlooking a stone terrace, a garden, and the surrounding wooded hills. A warm welcome and personal attention are guaranteed by the owners, Roy and Rosalie Burridge. There are large family rooms available, which can sleep three or four people, and all units are equipped with hot and cold running water. Drinks of all kinds are served until 10:30pm. Near the city center, the lodge is serviced by frequent buses at the front gate.

**Oakleigh Guest House.** 19 Upper Oldfield Park, Bath BA2 3JX. ☎ **01225/315698.** Fax 01225/448223. 4 rms. TV. £35–£45 ($56–$72) single; £50–£60 ($80–$96) double. All rates include English breakfast. AE, MC, V. From the city center take the A367 toward Exeter, then take the first turn on the right.

Situated 10 minutes from the center of Bath, Oakleigh combines Victorian elegance with today's comforts. The rooms are individually decorated and have panoramic views over Georgian Bath. The home is quiet and comfortable, the food excellent, and the service is friendly with special little comforts added by the owner Jenny King. The snug and cozy rooms have color TVs, clock/radios, hair dryers, and coffee- and tea-making facilities. This is a home away from home.

## DOUBLES FOR LESS THAN £75

**Bailbrook Lodge Hotel.** 35–37 London Rd. W., Bath, Somerset BA1 7HZ. ☎ **01225/ 859090.** 12 rms. TV. £50–£70 ($80–$112) double. All rates include English breakfast. AE, DC, MC, V. Bus: no. 3, 13, or 23.

Four of the rooms (the most expensive) in this restored Georgian town house contain four-poster beds, and all rooms offer outstanding views of the Avon Valley. The double rooms have such names as the Jane Austen Suite, the Beau Nash Suite, or the Queen Charlotte Suite. Eight units open onto garden and lawns with views of the Avon Valley, whereas the remaining rooms overlook the grounds of Bailbrook House, a Georgian mansion designed by John Everleigh, a famous architect of his day. The hotel adjoins A4, 2 miles east of Bath.

**✪ Bath Tasburgh Hotel.** Warminster Rd., Bathampton, Bath, Somerset BA2 6SH. ☎ **01225/ 425096.** Fax 01225/463842. 12 rms. TV TEL. £50 ($80) single; £65–£73 ($104–$116.80) double; £85 ($136) triple. All rates include English breakfast. AE, DC, MC, V. Bus: no. 4.

About a mile east of Bath center, amid 7 acres of parks and gardens, this spacious Victorian country house was built in 1890 and was once occupied by one of the royal family's official photographers. The red-brick structure contains a lounge, glassed-in conservatory, original marble fireplaces, stained-glass windows, antiques, and individually decorated bedrooms that usually have sweeping panoramic views. Each contains hot-beverage facilities, and four rooms have four-poster beds. The Avon and Kennet Canal runs along the rear of the property, and guests enjoy summer walks along the adjacent towpath.

**✪ Brompton House.** St. John's Rd., Bathwick, Bath, Somerset BA2 6PT. ☎ **01225/420972.** Fax 01225/420505. 18 rms. TV TEL. £32–£50 ($51.20–$80) single; £55–£78 ($88–$124.80) double. All rates include English breakfast. AE, CB, MC, V. From the M4 motorway, take Exit 18 and proceed along A46 to Bath; at the approach to the city, turn left at the traffic light (signposted to city center) and over the Cleveland Bridge take an immediate left.

This elegant Georgian rectory is set in tranquil grounds within an easy commute of the heart of the city. Formerly the old rectory of St. Mary's Church back in the days when Bathwick was merely a village, it was constructed in 1777 and built on the site of a manor farm from the 16th century. A Victorian wing was added in 1835. Today the hotel is well run, and its owners, David and Susan Selby, are helpful. The rooms are tastefully furnished and decorated and are equipped with color TVs, radio/alarm clocks, direct-dial telephones, hair dryers, and tea- and coffee-making facilities. In the elegant dining room, a traditional English, continental, or whole food breakfast is served.

**Haydon House.** 9 Bloomfield Park, Bath, Somerset BA2 2BY. ☎ and fax **01225/444919.** 5 rms. TV TEL. £45–£55 ($72–$88) single; £60–£75 ($96–$120) double. All rates include English breakfast. AE, MC, V. Bus: no. 14 or 14B.

Originally built of honey-colored stone at the beginning of the Edwardian Age, this house is peacefully situated about a mile from the bustling center of Bath, and since there is so much to do in the area, many guests use Haydon House as a base for an extended visit to see the sights. Gordon Marr, a former commander in the Royal Navy and his wife Magdalene Ashman-Marr can arrange guided tours to the attractions by car at very affordable rates. They also provide a very sustaining Bloomfield Breakfast each morning. Since most guests prefer to sample the many restaurants and pubs in the area, they do not provide an evening meal. They are most helpful with route planning and with recommendations and reservations, including booking seats at the Theatre Royal. The rooms, named and decorated for berries such as gooseberry, strawberry, blueberry, elderberry, or mulberry, include a generous hospitality tray with complimentary sherry and homemade shortbread.

**✪ Leighton House.** 139 Wells Rd., Bath, Somerset BA2 3AL. ☎ **01225/314769.** Fax 01225/ 443079. 8 rms. TV TEL. £47–£53 ($75.20–$84.80) single; £62–£68 ($99.20–$108.80) double; £83–£95 ($132.80–$152) family rm. All rates include English breakfast. MC, V. On approaching Bath, follow A367 Exeter signs but ignore the light vehicles only sign; turn left onto A37/ A367 (the Wells rd.) and follow the black railings uphill (500 yds.); when the railings end, turn left into Hayesfield Park and Leighton House will be on the right.

Marilyn and Colin Humphrey offer one of the best-value accommodations in the area. Their house is a Victorian residence from the 1870s. At the southern side of the city on the A367 road to Exeter (Devon), it's about a 10-minute walk from the center of Bath, and minibuses pass by frequently. A nonsmoking facility, the hotel rents elegant and spacious bedrooms, each individually furnished and decorated, with such extras as a radio alarm, hair dryer, beverage-making equipment, toiletries, and magazines.

**Wentworth House Hotel.** 106 Bloomfield Rd., Bath, Somerset BA2 2AP. ☎ **01225/339193.** Fax 01225/310460. 18 rms. TV TEL. £36–£40 ($57.60–$64) single; £56–£65 ($89.60–$104) double. All rates include English breakfast. AE, MC, V. Bus: no. 14.

In a prosperous residential neighborhood called Bloomfield, about a mile south of the city center, this four-story house was built in 1887 as the home of the region's wealthiest coal merchant. Many original features remain intact, including a staircase that some visitors consider something of a decorative wonder, and many of the ceiling's cove moldings. Set in three-quarters of an acre of gardens, behind a facade of chiseled Bath stone, the house is the property of the Kitching family, who serve snacks and light suppers by advanced arrangement. The bedrooms have been modernized and contain neutrally conservative but comfortable furnishings.

# WHERE TO EAT

**Café Retro.** 18 York St. ☎ **01225/339347.** Cafe dishes £2.50–£5.50 ($4–$8.80); restaurant main courses average £8 ($12.80); 3-course menu £12 ($19.20). AE, MC, V. Cafe: daily 9am–6pm; restaurant: daily 5:30–10:30pm. INTERNATIONAL.

This two-story locale operates as a breakfast and lunchtime cafe on the ground floor and as an evening restaurant on the second floor. A hip, eclectic ambience with wood floors and church pews goes a long way to support a style of food, especially for evening meals, that is affordable, without sacrificing quality. Lunch dishes are simple but filling and include burgers, sandwiches, and salads. Main menu items for dinner such as roast belly of pork stuffed with stilton and walnuts covered with a wild mushroom sauce and twice baked cheese soufflé with celeriac sauce attest to the success and popularity of Café Retro. A three-course dinner menu is offered Monday through Wednesday.

**The Crystal Palace.** Abbey Green. ☎ **01225/423944.** Sandwiches and platters £2.25–£4.95 ($3.60–$7.90). DC, MC, V. Daily noon–2:30pm and 6–8:30pm. Pub: Mon–Sat 11am–11pm; Sun noon–10:30pm. BRITISH.

Set on a small square in the oldest part of Bath, near the abbey, this joint was built as a private house in 1705, during the town's fashionable heyday. Today it's one of Bath's most popular pubs, known for its food service and cozy ambience. Fires flicker in winter; in summer clients move to an outdoor terrace beneath a grape arbor. A Bottle Bar is located in the garden. Food items include sandwiches, steak-and-kidney pie, baked stuffed potatoes, and ploughman's lunches, all the typical pub grub—nothing special.

**Demuth's Vegetarian Restaurant.** 2 North Parade Passage. ☎ **01225/446059.** Main courses £5.25–£7.50 ($8.40–$12). MC, V. Mon–Fri 9am–10pm; Sat 9am–11pm; Sun 10am–10pm. VEGETARIAN.

Here it is! The only vegetarian restaurant in Bath, approved by the Vegetarian Society. This bright, cheery place prepares everything in its kitchen using only fresh produce and organic items. Patrons with special diets or food allergies receive special attention here. Main courses include grilled mozzarella polenta with creamy oyster, mustard, and spinach sauce as well as pan-fried vegetables with rice noodles, seared tofu, and ginger and tamari apple marinade. Fresh salads and puddings for dessert round out the fun menu. As might be expected in a health-conscious establishment, no smoking is allowed.

✪ **Evans Fish Restaurant.** 7–8 Abbeygate St. ☎ **01225/463981.** Main courses £3.50–£4.50 ($5.60–$7.20). MC, V. Mon–Wed 11:30am–6pm; Thurs–Sat 11:30am–8:30pm. SEAFOOD.

Only a 3-minute walk from the abbey and train station, this family restaurant was created by Mrs. Harriet Evans in 1908 and features fish dinners at moderate prices. A meal might include the soup of the day, fried fillet of fish with chips, and a choice of desserts. Only the freshest of fish is served, although some readers find the fish overcooked. The lower floor has a self-service section, and on the second floor is an Abbey Room catering to families. The preferred dining spot is the Georgian Room—so named after its arched windows and fireplace. From the take-out section, you can order a number of crisply fried fish specialties, such as deep-fried scampi with chips.

✪ **Harington's Hotel and Restaurant.** 8–10 Queen St. ☎ **01225/461728.** Reservations recommended. Main courses £9–£11 ($14.40–$17.60); fixed-price dinners £11.50–£13.85 ($18.40–$22.15). AE, CB, DC, MC, V. Daily 8am–9pm. ENGLISH/FRENCH.

This hotel restaurant is an excellent choice for lunch or dinner. Sheltered behind a honey-colored facade of Bath stone originally built in 1752, it's hidden on a narrow cobblestone street in the heart of Bath. The protruding bay window lets in the sun and offers wide-angled views of the passing parade. Fully licensed, the restaurant serves such dishes as suprême of salmon on creamed leeks with butter sauce, poached breast of chicken filled with spiced sausage, and beef with a port sauce.

✪ **Moody Goose Restaurant & Wine Bar.** 7A Kingsmead Sq. ☎ **01225/466688.** Main courses £11–£15 ($17.60–$24). MC, V. Mon–Sat noon–2pm and 6–10pm. ENGLISH/FRENCH.

This is a fine up-market restaurant. Chef's specials feature fresh fish prepared in a variety of ways as well as game in season. A main course might be pan-fried saddle of venison or honey-roasted Devon duck. Desserts feature the traditional bread-and-butter pudding, chocolate desserts, or tart tatin. A large variety of British farmhouse cheeses are available. With advance notice a fixed-price meal may be ordered for pre- or posttheater dining. You may dine al fresco in Kingsmead Square in the summer.

**The New Moon.** 7 Dials Sawclose. ☎ **01225/444407.** Main courses £7.95–£10.95 ($12.70–$17.50). AE, MC, V. Mon–Fri noon–3pm and 5:30–11pm; Sat noon–11pm. ENGLISH/MEDITERRANEAN.

Close to The Theatre Royal, The New Moon is a modern and cosmopolitan restaurant serving English cuisine with a strong Mediterranean influence. Seafood is served every Thursday evening, and the soups are excellent, especially the pumpkin soup with toasted flaked almonds. You might also start with mussels marinière or smoked fish platter with horseradish-spiked sour cream. Delectable main courses run the range from roast herb-crusted rack of lamb with a rosemary jus to breast of duck with a honey and crushed green peppercorn sauce. This is an ideal spot for preshow-goers for lunch or dinner.

**The Pump Room Restaurant.** In the Roman Baths, Stall St. ☎ **01225/444477.** Main courses £6–£12 ($9.60–$19.20). AE, MC, V. Daily 9:30am–4:30pm (5:30pm during summer). ENGLISH.

Run by Milburns Restaurants, this place is a tradition in Bath. The latest incarnation of the Pump Room Restaurant opened in 1988. Guests often enjoy music from the Pump Room Trio or from the resident pianist while they drink or eat. Typical dishes offered during coffee are Bath Bun or plain scones served with clotted cream and strawberry jam. Hot dishes include minute steak and poached salmon fillet. The famous Pump Room tea is a favorite, even among the locals who enjoy their Earl Grey, Darjeeling, or whatever, along with sandwiches, scones, cakes, and pastries for

£6.95 ($11.10). The food sticks to such tried-and-true favorites that it rarely goes wrong.

**Sally Lunn's House.** 4 North Parade Passage. ☎ **01225/461634.** Reservations recommended for dinner. Main courses £5.20–£7.38 ($8.30–$11.80); lunch plates from £3.90 ($6.25). MC, V (for dinner only). Mon 10am–6pm; Tues–Sat 10am–11pm; Sun noon–11pm. ENGLISH.

This is a tiny gabled licensed coffeehouse and restaurant, with a Georgian bow window set in the "new" stone facade put up around 1720. The house is a landmark in Bath—the present wood-frame building, the oldest in the city, dates from about 1482. The restaurant is a 1-minute walk from the Abbey Church and Roman Baths.

Sally Lunn, who may have been a fictional character, is a legend in Bath. She supposedly came from France during the 1680s. Today the cellar bakery where she supposedly worked and recent excavations showing the earlier buildings are a museum open Monday through Saturday from 10am to 6pm and on Sunday from noon to 6pm.

On the ground and first floors, the Sally Lunn buns are served sweet or savory, fresh from the modern bakery on the third floor. Excellent coffee and toasted buns with "lashings" of butter, whole-fruit strawberry jam, and real clotted cream are everybody's favorite. You can have a bun served with various salads, chili, curry, traditional Welsh rarebit, or many other ways. Candlelit dinners, which are served after 6pm, are likely to include a whole poached trout cooked with a soft stuffing, or a quarter of a young roast duck in a rich orange sauce.

**Theatre Vaults Restaurant.** Sawclose at Barton St. ☎ **01225/442265.** Reservations required. Main courses £8–£10.50 ($12.80–$16.80); 2-course fixed-price dinner £9.80 ($15.70). AE, DC, MC, V. Mon–Sat 11am–2:30pm and 6–11pm. INTERNATIONAL.

It took an imaginative entrepreneur to convert the stone vaults beneath the Theatre Royal into an engaging brasserie. Its late closing makes it a favorite of the after-theater crowd. However, daytime people can drop in to enjoy morning coffee, drinks, or lunch. Menu specialties include homemade game terrines and soups, fresh fish of the day, juicy steaks, and regional dishes prepared by the French chef. The chefs don't exert their imaginations too much, but what they concoct is most acceptable.

**The Walrus and the Carpenter.** 28 Barton St. ☎ **01225/314864.** Reservations required Fri–Sun. Main courses £5.50–£11.95 ($8.80–$19.10). AE, MC, V. Mon–Sat noon–2:30pm and 6–11pm; Sun noon–11pm. ANGLO-AMERICAN/VEGETARIAN.

Named after a Lewis Carroll poem, and decorated like a whimsical and hip version of a French bistro, this poster-plastered place defines itself as Bath's "bohemian hangout for everybody." Specialties include steaks and burgers, and such vegetarian dishes as mushroom moussaka with pita bread and salad, spinach lasagna, and an array of salads that are pretty much meals in themselves. The food is filling and competently prepared. The building, incidentally, is a Georgian structure of historical interest. It's in the town center, near the Theatre Royal.

## BATH AFTER DARK

To gain a very different perspective of Bath, you might want to take the **Bizzare Bath Walking Tour** (☎ 01225/335124), an 1¼-hour improvisational tour of the streets during which the tour guides pull pranks, tell jokes, and in general are amusingly annoying to tourgoers and unsuspecting residents alike. This seasonal affair runs nightly at 8pm from March 24 through the end of summer. No reservations are necessary; just show up, ready for anything, at the Huntsman Inn at North Parade Passage. The tour costs £3 ($4.80) for adults and £2.50 ($4) for students.

After your walk, you might need a drink, or maybe you just want to check out the local club and music scene. At **The Bell,** 103 Walcot St. (☎ **01125/460426**), music ranges from jazz to country, reggae, or blues on Monday and Wednesday nights and Sunday at lunch. It's a long, narrow 400-year-old room covered in post-cards from around the world. On music nights, the band anchors in the center of the room, so sit near the middle to watch the music or on the outskirts to socialize a bit. Be warned—if you're hungry, the only food they have is a selection of rolls. The two-story **Hat and Feather,** 14 London St. (☎ **01225/425672**), has live musicians or DJs playing funk, reggae, or dance music nightly and all day Sunday. Cold snacks are available at the bar. For dancing, **The Hub,** The Paragon (☎ **01125/446288**), plays cutting edge–English scene music. Go find out why the locals dig this place. Open Thursday through Saturday from 9:30pm to 2am. The cover charge varies from £4 to £6 ($6.40 to $9.60).

# EASY EXCURSIONS FROM BATH
## LACOCK

From Bath, take A4 about 12 miles to A350, then head south to Lacock, a National Trust village showcasing English architecture from the 13th- through the 18th-century. It is so well preserved in fact, that you'll be hard-pressed to find signs of change since the 18th century, when the village's cottage wool industry was overcome by the Industrial Revolution.

Unlike many villages that disappeared or were absorbed into bigger communities, Lacock was largely owned by the Talbot family who liked their traditional village and maintained it. Turned over to the National Trust in 1944, it's now one of the best preserved bits of the old England with many 16th-century homes, gardens, and churches. Notable is **St. Cyriac Church,** Church Street, a perpendicular-style church built by wealthy wool merchants between the 14th and 17th centuries. **Lacock Abbey,** High Street (☎ **01249/730227**) founded in 1232 for Augustinian canonesses, was updated and turned into a private home in the 16th century. It fell victim to Henry VIII's Dissolution, when, upon establishing the Church of England, he seized existing church properties to bolster his own wealth. Admission for house, cloister, and grounds is £4.20 ($6.70) for adults and £2.20 ($3.50) for children. Admission for cloister and grounds only is £3 ($4.80) for adults and £1.50 ($2.40) for children. Open April through October, Wednesday through Monday 11am to 5pm. Tuesday, only the cloister and grounds are open.

While on the grounds, stop by the medieval barn, home to the **Fox Talbot Museum** (☎ **01249/730459**). Here William Henry Fox Talbot carried out early experiments with photography, making the first known photographic prints in 1833. In his honor, the barn is now a photography museum featuring some of those early prints. Open March through October, daily from 11am to 5pm. Admission is £2.40 ($3.85) for everyone.

**Where to Stay**
**The George Inn,** see below, also offers rooms at a nearby farmhouse.

✪ **The Old Rectory.** Lacock, Wiltshire SN15 2JZ. ☎ **01249/730335.** 3 rms. £45 ($72) double. All rates include English breakfast. No credit cards.

The Addisons have taken their Victorian home and have turned it into a great little B&B. They offer three rooms, two of which have four-poster beds. Guests have free roam of 7 acres where they can even play croquet if they so choose.

## Where to Eat

**The Carpenter's Arms.** 22 Church St. ☎ **01249/730203.** Reservations recommended on weekends. Lunch and dinner £5–£8 ($8–$12.80). AE, MC, V. Daily 11am–2:30pm and 6–11pm. ENGLISH.

With its origins as a 16th-century pub, this real public house's charm is due in part to its many small rooms and nooks and crannies. The locals know that the food is good here. Lunch is typical bar food—steak-and-kidney pie, salads, jacket potatoes, and the like. An a la carte menu gives patrons a range of more substantial choices during dinner, including homemade soups and a collection of fresh meat, fish, and vegetarian dishes.

**The George Inn.** 4 West St., Lacock, Wiltshire SN15 2LH. ☎ **01249/730263.** Main courses £4.50–£10.25 ($7.20–$16.40). AE, MC, V. Easter–Oct daily 11am–11pm; Nov–Easter daily 10am–3pm and 5:15pm–11pm. ENGLISH.

In a building that has housed a pub since 1361, the George Inn has been equipped with some modern conveniences since then, like running water, and is today run by John Glass. It still maintains many of its vestiges from the past—uneven floors, a large, open fireplace with its very own dog-wheel once used for spit roasting—and has an extensive garden used as a dining area in the summer. There's even a children's playground. About 30 daily specials are chalked on a blackboard in addition to a regular menu containing fish, meat, and vegetarian dishes. You can even order kangaroo and ostrich steak or a beef steak with a Stilton sauce. Two popular desserts are bread-and-butter pudding and sticky toffee pudding.

John Glass's wife, Judy, runs a B&B out of the family farmhouse. **The Lower Home Farm** (☎ **01225/790045**) has three double rooms, each with a private bath, that go for £35 ($56) per night, including an English breakfast. The grounds are made up of 100 acres of gardens, walks, and a lake that all blend together to create a peaceful and serene setting. No credit cards are accepted at the farm, but rates include taxi service to the George Inn which puts guests in walking distance to all the attractions in this National Trust village.

## 7 Longleat House & Stourhead Gardens

### ✪ LONGLEAT HOUSE

Between Bath and Salisbury, Longleat House, Warminster, in Wiltshire (☎ **01985/844400**), owned by the seventh marquess of Bath, is one of the great country homes of England. This magnificent Elizabethan house, built in the early Renaissance style, is stunning and unquestionably romantic; the wealth of paintings and furnishings in its lofty rooms is dazzling.

**GETTING THERE**    Longleat House lies 35 miles southeast of Bristol, 20 miles southeast of Bath, 24 miles northwest of Salisbury, and 120 miles west of London. Daily trains run from Bath and Salisbury to Longleat. The trip takes about 30 minutes. From both Bath and Salisbury, take the train to Warminster; then take a taxi or Davron Coach no. 53 (the local bus) to Longleat which takes about 10 minutes. You'll have to walk the last 2 miles from the bus stop up the road to Longleat House.

By bus from Bath take bus no. 265 or 267, which run only Monday through Saturday, to Frome Market Place; then change buses in Frome and take the bus to Warminster. In Warminster, take Davron Coach no. 53 to Corsley Avenue and walk the last 2 miles to Longleat House.

From Salisbury, take bus no. X4 to Warminster. In Warminster, take Davron Coach no. 53 to Corsley Avenue and walk the last 2 miles to Longleat House.

If you're driving from Bath, take A36 south to Warminster; then follow the signposts to Longleat House. From Salisbury take A36 north to Warminster, then follow the signposts to Longleat House.

## SEEING THE HOUSE

From the Elizabethan Great Hall to the library, the staterooms and the grand staircase, the house is incredibly varied. The state dining room is full of silver and plate, and fine tapestries and paintings adorn the walls in profusion. The sumptuous library represents the finest private collection in the country. The Victorian kitchens are open, offering a glimpse of life "below the stairs" in a well-ordered country home. Various exhibitions are mounted in the stable yard.

The house itself is open Easter through September, daily from 10am to 6pm and October to Easter, daily from 10am to 4pm.

## WANDERING THE GROUNDS

The **Longleat Safari Park**—unique in Europe—offers you a chance to walk among giraffes, zebras, camels, and llamas. From your car you can see lions and tigers, including England's only white tiger. You'll also experience the rather dubious thrill of having wolves prowl around your car. Longleat is home to many of the world's majestic and endangered wild animals, including rhinoceroses and elephants, free to roam these bucolic surroundings in all their splendiferous bulk.

You can take the safari boat around the lake to see the gorillas or feed the sea lions. You can also enjoy the park by train for a railway adventure. Moreover, the park provides the thrills of the Simulator, where you can lose yourself in the Adventure Castle and maze, marvel at the butterflies in the tropical Butterfly Garden, and explore the science-fiction world in the Doctor Who Exhibition. Longleat justifiably has been Britain's no. 1 Safari Park for more than 30 years.

The world's longest (and one might say over the top) maze is Safari Park's **The Maze of Love,** commissioned by the Marquess of Bath and designed by Graham Burgess. It was inspired by the Garden of Love in Villandry in France and Botticelli's painting—*Primavera*. It lies between Longleat House and the Orangery. It appears as a traditional parterre with gravel paths and small leafed box hedging (*Buxus sufruticosa sempervirens* of which 5,000 were planted), forming symbolic patterns. The most obvious are the four giant hearts and the female lips, but there are many more. The flower that has embodied love for the generations, the rose, has been planted in the beds and climbing roses trained over the heart-shaped arches. More than 1,300 rose bushes have been planted; their names—First Kiss, Eve, Seduction, Sleeping Beauty, Irresistible, and Romance—leaving no doubt what the story's about. The journey through the maze tells the whole erotic tale: Enticement, Falling in Love, Romantic Associations, the Impassioned Embrace, Satisfaction, and Fulfillment in Love. At the center is the original Scallop Fountain (a symbol of fertility) retained from the previous garden, as were the surrounding yew hedges and the four urns. As you walk through the maze, you are expected to kiss your partner when you pass under each heart-shaped arch, and at the exit path you leave hand-in-hand straddling the final length of hedge. This is probably not the best place for an awkward blind or first date. The Maze of Love will not open to the public until St. Valentines Day A.D. 2000, but visitors can view it before then from either end to enjoy the designs and the scent of the roses in summer.

In 1997, the **Airborne I,** a giant passenger balloon began operation from Longleat, adding to its entertainment possibilities. This new ride for visitors of all ages takes you in a balloon gondola up to a height of some 400 feet, providing amazing panoramic views. The balloon ride is suitable for all ages and has facilities for wheelchair access. Passengers take off from a launch site and rise smoothly and silently some 120 meters. The balloon, 5,000 cubic meters in size, supports a gondola carrying an average of 25 adult passengers with a pilot. The pilot operates the balloon from the gondola by radio-linked controls to a powerful winch on the ground. Lord Bath, who commissioned the balloon's construction, hopes that this new attraction will provide visitors with yet another new angle from which to enjoy Longleat. You may be able to memorize the correct route in and out of the Maze—although he hopes that you will have forgotten it by the time you come back to earth.

Admission to Longleat House is £4.80 ($7.70) for adults and £3.50 ($5.60) for children; admission to Safari Park is £5.50 ($8.80) for adults and £4 ($6.40) for children. Special exhibitions and rides require separate admission tickets. Passport tickets for all Longleat's attractions cost £12 ($19.20) for adults and £10 ($16) for children, including admission to the Butterfly Garden, Simulator Doctor Who Exhibition, Postman Pat's Village, Adventure Castle, and more. It's open from mid-March to September, daily from 10am to 6pm; October to Easter, daily from 10am to 4pm. The park is open mid-March to November 3, daily from 10am to 6pm (last cars are admitted at 5:30pm or sunset).

## ✪ STOURHEAD

In a country replete with gardens and gardeners, Stourhead (☎ **01747/841152**), is the most fabled. The gardens are the most celebrated example of the English 18th-century taste for natural landscaping. As you wander the grounds, they take on the aura of a three-dimensional Old Master painting, with their bridges, grottoes, and temples, everything hidden among trees, flowers, and colorful shrubs. Although Stourhead is truly a garden for all seasons, it is at its most idyllic in summer when the rhododendrons are in full bloom.

**GETTING THERE**   Trains run from Bath Monday through Saturday; however, you can't get to Stourhead by train from Salisbury. From Bath, take the train to Gillingham; in Gillingham, take Southern National bus no. 58 or 58A to Stourhead, about a 20-minute trip.

From Bath you can take the direct bus to Stourton, but it runs only on the first Saturday of each month. The return journey is via Frome. From Salisbury, bus service is very limited; however, you can take bus no. 26 to Hindon or Tewesbury where you'll have to change buses to Stourton.

If you're driving from Bath take A36 south to Warminster about 28 miles; then get on A350 toward Mere. When you come to the crossroads, turn right onto A303 toward Mere and follow the signposts about 2 miles to Stourhead. From Salisbury, take A36 north to Warminster for 10 miles; then follow A303 toward Exeter. About 15 miles along on A303 look for signposts to Stourhead. Many visitors in one very busy day try to visit Longleat (see above) and Stourhead. If you're among them, after Longleat you can drive 6 miles down B3092 to Stourton, a village just off the highway, 3 miles northwest of Mere (A303).

### EXPLORING THE GARDENS

The Palladian house of Stourhead was built in the 18th century by the banking family of Hoare. You can enjoy 100 acres of 18th-century landscaped gardens, with classical temples, lakes, and grottoes. Henry Hoare II (1705–85), known as "Henry the

Magnificent," contributed greatly to the development of the landscape of this magnificent estate. The Temple of Flora was the first building in the garden, designed by the architect Henry Flitcroft in 1744. The wooden seats are copies of those placed near the altar where images of pagan gods were laid. Marble busts of Marcus Aurelius and Alexander the Great can be seen in the niches on the wall.

The Grotto, constructed in 1748, is lined with tufa, a waterworn limestone deposit. The springs of the Stour flow through the cold bath, where lies a lead copy of the sleeping Ariadne. In a cave beyond her, the white lead statue of the River God is seen dispensing justice to the waves and to the nymphs who inhabit his stream. The origin of the Gothic Cottage is uncertain: It was not part of the garden plan until 1806 when the trees around it were cleared and Colt Hoare added the Gothic seat and porch.

The Pantheon was built in 1753 to house Rysbrack's statues of Hercules and Flora and other classical figures. Brass grilles originally heated the temple. The Iron Bridge close by replaced a wooden one in 1860. In 1765 Flitcroft built the Temple of Apollo, the route to which takes the visitor over the public road via a rockwork bridge constructed in the 1760s. The Apollo Temple is copied from a round temple excavated at Baalbec: The statues which used to be in the niches are now on the roof of Stourhead House. The Turf Bridge was copied from Palladio's bridge in Vicenza.

The Bristol High Cross dates from the early 15th century and commemorates the monarchs who benefited the City of Bristol. It was removed from Bristol and set up by Henry Hoare at Stourhead in 1765. Colen Campbell, a leader in the Palladian revival, designed and built the house at Stourhead for Henry Hoare I between 1721 and 1725; it reflects 16th-century Venetian villas created by the architect Palladio. The magnificent interior hosts an outstanding library and picture gallery and a wealth of paintings, art treasures, and Chippendale furniture.

The three fine red-brick walled terraces were built in the early 19th century to supply cut flowers, fresh fruit, salads, and vegetables to the mansion house. They were in use up to the deaths of Sir Henry and Lady Alda Hoare in 1947. The lower was an herbaceous garden together with peach and vine house. The pool was part of an irrigation system fed by rainwater from the greenhouses and stable yard.

You can take the recommended walks to appreciate fully the panoramic sights in more than 90 acres of landscape garden and lake, an ever-changing scene of color and fragrance throughout the seasons. The landscape garden is of historic importance—it shows the influence of William Kent in design and use of buildings.

Henry Hoare II's 18th-century red-brick folly, **Alfred's Tower,** on the borders of Wiltshire, Somerset, and Dorset, is 160 feet high and has 221 steps. **The Obelisk** was built in 1839–40 of Bath stone and replaced the original of Chilmark stone constructed by William Privet for Henry Hoare in 1746.

The plant center is situated near the entrance to the main car park in part of the Old Glebe Farm—a small estate dairy farm. This was a working farm until the early 1970s. This new feature provides visitors with the opportunity of buying plants often seen in the gardens.

Lunches and suppers are served at the **Spread Eagle Inn** near the entrance to the garden. Boxes are available to order for picnics, which are allowed in the grounds and garden. The Spread Eagle is noted for dinner in the evening and for its Sunday lunches in the autumn, winter, and spring. A self-service buffet is available in the Village Hall tearoom.

The gardens are open March through October, daily from 9am to 7pm (or until dusk), costing £4.30 ($6.90) for adults and £2.30 ($3.70) for children. Off-season tickets cost £3.30 ($5.30) for adults and £1.80 ($2.90) for children. The house is open from March 30 through October 30, Saturday through Wednesday from noon to 5:30pm, costing £4.30 ($6.90) for adults and £2.30 ($3.70) for children.

# 8  Bristol

13 miles NW of Bath; 120 miles W of London

Bristol, the largest city in the West Country, is just across the Bristol Channel from Wales and a good center for touring western Britain. This historic inland port is linked to the sea by 7 miles of the Somerset River. Bristol has long been rich in seafaring traditions and has many links to the early colonization of America. In fact, some claim that the new continent was named after a Bristol town clerk, Richard Ameryke. In 1497, John Cabot sailed from Bristol, and pioneered the discovery of the northern half of the New World.

Whereas Bath is more elegant and pretentious, Bristol has a working-class feel. Although it's been called "the Seattle of England," Seattle has a lot more going for it. Even so, Bristol has some limited attractions like a colorful harbor life that make it a good overnight stop in your exploration of the West Country.

## ESSENTIALS

**GETTING THERE**   Bristol Airport (☎ **01275/474444**) is conveniently situated beside the main A38 road, just over 7 miles from the city center.

Rail services to and from the area are among the fastest and most efficient in Britain. British Rail runs frequent services from London's Paddington Station to each of Bristol's two main stations: Temple Meads in the center of Bristol, and Parkway on the city's northern outskirts. The trip takes $1\frac{1}{2}$ hours. For more information and schedules, call ☎ **0345/484950.**

National Express buses depart every hour during the day from London's Victoria Coach Station, making the trip in $2\frac{1}{2}$ hours. For more information and schedules, call ☎ **0990/808080.**

If you're driving, head west from London on the M4. The trip should take between 2 and $2\frac{1}{2}$ hours.

**VISITOR INFORMATION**   The **Tourist Information Centre** is at St. Nicholas Church, St. Nicholas Street (☎ **0117/926-0767**). Open Monday through Saturday from 9:30am to 5:30pm and Sunday from 11am to 4pm in winter and from 9:30am to 5:30pm in summer.

## EXPLORING BRISTOL

Guided walking tours are conducted in summer and last about $1\frac{1}{2}$ hours. The tours depart from Neptune's Statue on Saturday at 2:30pm and on Thursday at 7pm. Guided tours are also conducted through Clifton, a suburb of Bristol, which has more Georgian houses than Bath. Consult the tourist office (see above) for more information.

**SS *Great Britain*.** City Docks, Great Western Dock. ☎ **0117/926-0680.** Admission £3.90 ($6.25) adults; £3 ($4.80) seniors; £2.70 ($4.30) children. Apr–Oct daily 10am–5:30pm; Nov–Mar daily 10am–4:30pm. Bus: no. 511 from city center, a rather long haul.

In Bristol, the world's first iron steamship and luxury liner has been partially restored to its 1843 appearance, although it's still a long way from earning its old title of a "floating palace." This vessel, which weighs 3,443 tons, was designed by Isambard Brunel, a Victorian engineer.

Incidentally, in 1831 (at the age of 25), Brunel began a Bristol landmark, the Suspension Bridge, over the 250-foot-deep Somerset Gorge at Clifton.

**Bristol Cathedral.** College Green. ☎ **0117/926-4879.** Free admission; donation requested £2 ($3.20). Daily 8am–6pm. Bus: no. 8 or 9.

Construction of the the cathedral—formerly an Augustinian abbey—began in the 12th century; the central tower was not added until 1466. The chapter house and gatehouse are good examples of late Norman architecture. Sir John Betjeman, the late poet laureate singled out the cathedral's interior for praise.

In 1539 the abbey was closed and the incomplete nave demolished. The building was converted into the Cathedral Church of the Holy and Undivided Trinity 3 years later. In 1868 plans were drawn up to complete the nave to its medieval design. The architect, G. E. Street, found the original pillar bases, so that the cathedral is much as it would have been when it was still the abbey church. J. L. Pearson added the two towers at the west end and further reordered the interior.

The eastern end of the cathedral, especially the choir, is unique among British and European architecture. The nave, choir, and aisles are all of the same height, composing a large hall. Bristol Cathedral is the major example of a "hall church" in Great Britain and one of the finest in the world.

**St. Mary Redcliffe Church.** 10 Redcliffe Way. ☎ **0117/929-1487.** Free admission. June–Aug daily 8am–8pm; Sept–May daily 8am–5pm. No public transport. Just a 100-yd. walk downhill from the main train station.

Meanwhile, the parish church of St. Mary Redcliffe is one of the finest examples of Gothic architecture in England. Queen Elizabeth I, on her visit in 157, is reported to have described it as "the fairest, goodliest and most famous parish church in England," and Thomas Chatterton, the boy poet, called it "the pride of Bristol and the western land." The American Chapel houses the tomb and armor of Adm. Sir William Penn, father of Pennsylvania's founder.

**Theatre Royal.** King St. ☎ **0117/949-3993.** Box office 0117/987-7877. Tickets £4.50–£18 ($7.20–$28.80). Any City Centre bus. Show times Mon–Wed, 7:30pm; Thurs–Sat 8pm.

Built in 1766, this—the home of the Bristol Old Vic—is now the oldest working playhouse in the U.K. Backstage tours leave from the foyer. Tours are run Friday and Saturday at 12:30pm and cost £2 ($3.20) for adults and £1.50 ($2.40) for children and students under 19. Call the box office for the current schedule.

## SHOPPING

Many major Bristol shopping spots are now open on Sunday. The biggest shopping complex is **Broadmead,** mainly pedestrian and housing branches of all main street stores, plus cafes and restaurants. Many specialty shops are found at **Clifton Village,** in a Georgian setting where houses are interspaced with parks and gardens. Here you'll find a wide array of shops selling antiques, arts, and crafts, along with designer clothing. The **Galleries** is a totally enclosed mall, providing three levels of shopping and eateries. **St. Nicholas Markets** opened in 1745, and are still going strong, selling antiques, memorabilia, handcrafted gifts, jewelry, and haberdashery. The **West End** is another major shopping area, taking in Park Street, Queen's Road, and Whiteladies Road. These streets are known for their clothing outlets, book stores, and unusual gift items from around the world, as well as wine bars and restaurants.

The best antique markets are **The Bristol Antique Centre,** Brunel Rooms, Broad Plain, and **Clifton Antiques Market** and **New Antiques Centre,** the Mall in Clifton, and **Clifton Arcade,** Boyces Avenue, also in Clifton. Both Clifton outlets are closed on Monday but the Bristol Antique Centre is open daily, including Sunday.

## WHERE TO STAY
### DOUBLES FOR LESS THAN £50

**Alandale Hotel.** 4 Tyndall's Park Rd., Clifton, Bristol, Somerset BS8 1PG. ☎ **0117/973-5407.** Fax 0117/923-7965. 11 rms. TV TEL. £40 ($64) single; £48 ($76.80) double. All rates include English breakfast. MC, V. Bus: no. 8 or 9.

This elegant early Victorian house retains many of its original features, including a marble fireplace and ornate plasterwork. Note the fine staircase in the imposing entrance hall. The hotel is under the supervision of Mr. Burgess, who still observes the old traditions of personal service; for example, afternoon tea is available, as are sandwiches, drinks, and snacks in the lounge (up to 11:15pm). A continental breakfast is served in your bedroom until 10am, unless you'd prefer the full English breakfast in the dining room. All the plainly furnished bedrooms have hot-beverage facilities and hair dryers.

**Downlands Guest House.** 33 Henleaze Gardens, Henleaze, Bristol, Somerset BS9 4HH. ☎ **0117/962-1639.** 8 rms, 3 with bath. TV. £25 ($40) single without bath, £36 ($57.60) single with bath; £42 ($67.20) double without bath, £46 ($73.60) double with bath; £53 ($84.80) family room for 3 without bath. All rates include English breakfast. MC, V. Bus: no. 1, 2, 3, or 501.

This well-appointed Victorian home is on a tree-lined road on the periphery of the Durdham Downs. About 2 miles from the center of Bristol, it lies on a bus route in a residential suburb. The Newman family receives guests all year, and will provide a 6pm meal if it's arranged in advance. The bedrooms are well kept and many have recently been redecorated; all contain TV and hospitality trays. It's fairly basic, but inviting.

**Oakfield Hotel.** 52–54 Oakfield Rd., Clifton, Bristol, Somerset BS8 2BG. ☎ **0117/973-3643.** Fax 0117/974-4141. 27 rms, none with bath. TV. £26 ($41.60) single; £37 ($59.20) double. All rates include English breakfast. No credit cards. Bus: no. 8 or 9.

Instead of finding lodgings in the center of Bristol, many visitors prefer to seek out accommodations in the leafy Georgian suburb of Clifton, 1 mile north of the center, near the famous Suspension Bridge. This impressive guest house from the 1840s, with an Italian facade, would be called a town house in New York. It's on a quiet street, and everything is kept spic-and-span under the watchful eye of Mrs. P. Hurley. Each bedroom has hot and cold running water and central heating, although the furnishings are modest. For another £6.50 ($10.40), you can enjoy a simple dinner.

## WHERE TO EAT

**Cherries Bistro.** 122 St. Michael's Hill, Clifton. ☎ **0117/929-3675.** Reservations recommended. Main courses £8.45 ($13.50); 3-course fixed-price dinner (Mon–Fri) £13.95 ($22.30). MC, V. Mon–Sat noon–2:30pm and 7–11:30pm. Bus: no. 8 or 9. INTERNATIONAL.

This popular and informal bistro does a thriving business from a position in Clifton, about 1½ miles northeast of Bristol's center, near the university. Its walls are adorned with intricate collages crafted from magazine clipouts from the 1950s, as well as scattered accessories from the Jazz Age. Although in previous years Cherries gained a steady clientele because of its focus on all-vegetarian cuisine, it relented recently and added several meat dishes to its repertoire. These include crabmeat and lobster roulades, brochettes of beef and lamb flambéed in cognac, and Malay chicken in peanut sauce. The vegetarian dishes change frequently, but include phyllo pastry pie with vegetables in a tomato-garlic-mustard coulis. The cuisine rises above the ordinary.

**51 Park Street.** 51 Park St. ☎ **0117/921-4616.** Main courses £6.50–£10.75 ($10.40–$17.20). AE, DC, MC, V. Mon–Sat noon–11pm; Sun noon–10pm. INTERNATIONAL.

An established favorite with Bristolians, "51" is stylish and relaxed despite the hurly-burly of Bristol's main shopping street. The restaurant is in a Georgian building where diners watch the passing world through an enormous window. The menu is varied, meaning that you can order anything from a snack to a three-course meal during opening times. That might mean a brunch of traditional favorites such as kedgeree. A la carte tea often attracts shoppers in the afternoon. More substantial fare includes such house specialties as rack of lamb with pearl barley risotto and onion marmalade served with vegetables and rosemary sauce, spicy stir-fried beef, and lamb in red-currant sauce. Pastas, steaks, and burgers are also available. There is a good selection of desserts. Many dishes are quite flavorful; others just standard fare. A full bar service is also available for those not wishing to eat.

**The Flipper.** 6 St. James Barton. ☎ **0117/929-0260.** Main courses £2.50–£3.95 ($4–$6.30). No credit cards. Mon–Sat 7:30am–6pm. Bus: no. 20, 22, or 75. FISH-AND-CHIPS.

A short distance from the bus station, in the center of the city's biggest cluster of stores, the Flipper serves the best fish and chips in Bristol. Good-tasting codfish (and slightly more expensive plaice and halibut) is dished out from a fast-food countertop on the street level. Breakfast is served all day, and an upstairs wood-paneled dining room offers waitress service.

**Rocinantes Café and Tapas Bar.** 85 Whiteladies Rd. ☎ **0117/973-4482.** Reservations recommended. Tapas £2–£5 ($3.20–$8); main courses £7.50–£14 ($12–$22.40). AE, MC, V. Mon–Sat 9am–11pm; Sun 10am–10:30pm. MEDITERRANEAN.

Here's a great place for a drink, tapas, or a full meal. It's particularly popular with locals. Patrons can choose from a varied and hearty selection of tapas or, if they prefer, a great Mediterranean meal with such dishes as grilled tuna steak, vegetable lasagna, and, everyone's favorite, shellfish risotto. In the summer, eating on the patio is très chic.

# BRISTOL AFTER DARK

Unlike the stiff formality of Bath, Bristol clubs and pubs are more laid-back and in-formal, drawing more working-class Brits than the yuppies of Bath. Hot spots include **Lakota,** 6 Upper York St. (☎ 0117/942-6193), off Stokes Croft. It's known for its all-night "groove parties," with a funk/jungle sound track. However, the cover is a bit steep, from £7 to £12 ($11.20 to $19.20), depending on what's featured that night.

In a converted freight steamer moored on The Grove, **Thelka** (☎ 0117/929-3301), is the place for acid jazz. The cover is usually £5 ($8). The other leading venues for jazz are **The Old Duke,** King Street (☎ 0117/929-7137), and the **Bebop Club** at The Bear, Hatwell Road (☎ 0117/987-7796). The premier gay club is **Just,** 1 Fiennes St. (☎ 0117/930-4675), charging only a £1 ($1.60) cover.

The leading comedy club is **Comedy at The Shed,** Watershed, Canons Road (☎ 0117/925-3845).

Some of the best pubs are along King Street, especially **Llandoger Trow,** 5 King St. (☎ 0117/926-0783), with its mellow West Country ambience. If you'd like to meet up with some students, their favorite watering hole is **The Hobgoblin,** 2 Bryon Place (☎ 0117/929-9322).

# The Cotswolds 13

Between Oxford and the River Severn, about a 2-hour drive west of London, the pastoral Cotswolds occupy a stretch of sometimes grassy limestone hills, deep ravines, and barren plateaus known as *wolds*—Old English for "God's high open land." Ancient villages with names like Stow-on-the-Wold, Wotton-under-Edge, and Moreton-in-Marsh dot this bucolic area, most of which is in Gloucestershire, with portions in Oxfordshire, Wiltshire, and Worcestershire.

Enriched by the sale of sheep wool, landowners here invested in some of the finest domestic architecture in Europe, distinctively built with honey-brown Cotswold stone. The wool-rich gentry didn't neglect their spiritual obligations, for some of the simplest Cotswold hamlets today boast churches that, in architectural style and ornamentation, seem to exceed their modest means. Cotswold stone varies in tone and shade, but as a general rule, stone quarried in the southern Cotswolds, around Painswick, is more gray than the honey-colored sandstone quarried in the north.

You'll also see thatched cottages in the Cotswolds, fiercely protected by local bylaws yet endlessly impractical because of their need for repair, maintenance, and replacement. Natives will tell you that they cost "a bloody fortune" to insure against fire. More common are the Cotswolds roof shingles fashioned from split slabs of stone, which required massive buttressing from medieval carpenters as a means of supporting the weight of the roof. Buildings erected as of the 1700s, however, mostly have slate roofs.

Tourist-trodden Broadway, with its 16th-century stone houses and cottages, is justifiably the most popular locus of touring in this area, but savvy travelers also will head for Bibury, Painswick, or other small villages to capture the true charm of the Cotswolds. You'll find the widest range of hotels and facilities in Cheltenham, once one of England's most fashionable spas with a wealth of Regency architecture. In Cirencester, check out the Corinium Museum's collection of Roman antiquities. Families might head to Birdland, in Bourton-on-the-Water, where you can see some 1,200 birds of 361 different species.

# 1 Tetbury

113 miles W of London; 27 miles NE of Bristol

Tucked in the rolling Cotswolds, Tetbury remained outside the tourist mainstream until the heir to the British throne and his beautiful bride took up residence at the Macmillan Place, a Georgian building on nearly 350 nearby acres. The presence of royalty prompted crowds from all over the world to come here in the hopes of catching a glimpse of Prince Charles straddling a horse and Princess Di shopping in the village. Today, of course, villagers and visitors content themselves watching for Charles and his ladyfriend, Camilla Parker-Bowles. Hounded (and wounded) by the media, they no longer frequent any of the local establishments; the best locals can do is spot them whizzing by en route to their homes.

The nine-bedroom Windsor mansion, Highgrove, lies $1\frac{1}{2}$ miles southwest of Tetbury on the way to Westonbirt Arboretum, but it cannot be seen from the road. The town of Tetbury has a 17th-century market hall and a number of antique shops and boutiques. Tetbury's inns weren't cheap before royalty moved in, so you can imagine where they stand today.

Charles isn't the only royal who lives around Tetbury. The home of the Princess Royal is 4 miles to the north; slightly further north, at Nether Lypiatt Manor, is the country home of Prince and Princess Michael of Kent.

## ESSENTIALS

**GETTING THERE**  Frequent daily trains run from London's Paddington Station to Kemble, 7 miles east of Tetbury. For more information and schedules, call ☎ **0345/484950.** Buses run from there to Tetbury.

National Express buses leave from London's Victoria Coach Station with direct service to Cirencester, 10 miles northeast of Tetbury. For more information and schedules, call ☎ **0990/808080.** Several buses a day connect Cirencester to Tetbury.

If you're driving from London, take the M40 northwest to Oxford, continuing along A40 to the junction with A429. Drive south to Cirencester, where you connect with A433 southwest into Tetbury.

**VISITOR INFORMATION**  The **Tourist Information Centre** is in The Old Court House, 63 Long St. (☎ **01666/503552**). Open March through October, Monday to Saturday from 9:30am to 4:30pm.

## EXPLORING THE TOWN

The town, with its antique shops and old houses, deserves at least a morning. The **Parish Church of St. Mary the Virgin,** which boasts a spire that's the fourth highest in England, was built between 1777 and 1781. It's been hailed as the best Georgian Gothic church in the country. Extensive restoration work has returned the interior to its original 18th-century appearance and feel. For more information, call ☎ **01666/502333;** it's more than likely the vicar himself will answer.

One of the finest examples of a Cotswold pillared market house is the 1655 **Market House of Tetbury.** It is still in regular use as a meeting place and market. If you visit on a Wednesday, you'll encounter one of the most interesting markets in the Cotswolds. There are antique stalls in the oak-beamed meeting hall and general stalls at street level. Who knows? Some of that bric-a-brac might be cast-offs from Camilla's house.

After the market, head for **Chipping Steps.** The Chipping (meaning market) was for centuries the site of "Mop Fairs" where farm hands and domestic staff offered themselves for employment. Many of the surrounding buildings have medieval origins. In the northeast corner, the steep cobbled steps and weavers' cottages retain

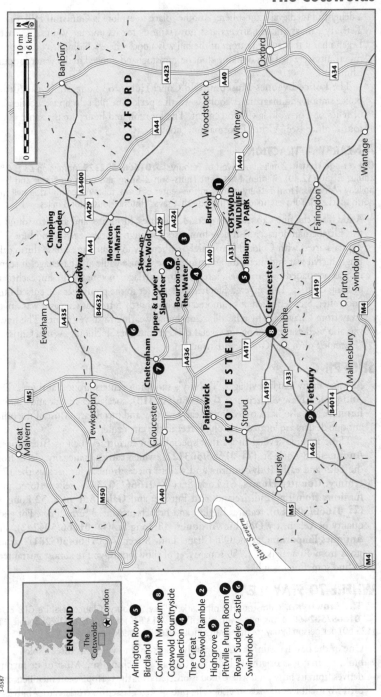

# The Cotswolds

N

10 mi
16 km
0

OXFORD

Banbury

A423

A40

Woodstock

Witney

A34

Wantage

Faringdon

A3400

Chipping
Campden

A429

A44

Moreton-
in-Marsh

A424

A429

Stow-on-
the-Wold

**1** Burford

COTSWOLD
WILDLIFE PARK

**3**

A40

A33

Bilbury

**2**

Bourton-on-
the-Water

**4**

**5**

Cirencester

**8**

A419

Purton

Swindon

M4

Evesham

A435

Broadway

B4632

Upper & Lower
Slaughter

**6**

Cheltenham

**7**

A436

A417

Kemble

A419

Painswick

GLOUCESTER

Stroud

**9** Tetbury

A33

B4014

Malmesbury

A46

Dursley

M5

River Severn

M4

Great
Malvern

M5

Tewkesbury

Gloucester

M50

A40

A44

Kemble

3-0587

ENGLAND

The
Cotswolds

★ London

Arlington Row **5**
Birdland **3**
Corinium Museum **8**
Cotswold Countryside
Collection **4**
The Great
Cotswold Ramble **2**
Highgrove **9**
Pittville Pump Room **7**
Royal Sudeley Castle **6**
Swinbrook **1**

455

a delightful medieval atmosphere. Another place to explore is **Gumstoll Hill,** one of Tetbury's most ancient streets and now famous for its annual Woolsack Races. Legend has it that at the bottom of the hill was a pool where scolding wives and other miscreants were tied to a dunking stool or gumstool and dunked under water for punishment.

The **Police Bygones Museum,** Old Court House, 63 Long St., in the former police station and magistrates court, is worth a peek. The old cells house a collection of relics of Cotswold law enforcement. The location and hours are the same as the tourist office (see "Visitor Information," above).

## A NEARBY ATTRACTION

**Chavenage House.** 2 miles northwest of Tetbury. ☎ **01666/502329.** Admission £3 ($4.80) adults; £1.50 ($2.40) children. May–Sept Thurs–Sun 2–5pm; also open on Easter and bank holiday Mondays. From Tetbury market in the center of town, follow Avening Rd. a half mile north to its end. Turn left, following the sign that says "Historic House" for 3 miles.

Aside from the fine Cromwellian-period tapestries, furniture, and artifacts found in this Elizabethan house, a visit here immerses you in its drama, legend, and lore. The drama started with Colonel Nathaniel Stephens, who owned the house during the English civil war and met with an unfortunate demise while at Chavenage. It seems he was persuaded by Cromwell, a relative by marriage, to vote for the impeachment of King Charles. This angered Stephens's daughter to the point that she cursed him. Soon after, Stephens died; it's rumored that his ghostly form was seen as it was driven away from Chavenage by a headless coachman wearing royal vestments. The house was also used as the location for several BBC productions, including Agatha Christie's "Hercule Poirot and Grace and Favour."

## SHOPPING

As in so many English villages, Tetbury's shopping centers around antiques. **Day Antiques,** 5 New Church St. (☎ 01666/502413), specializes in oak and country furniture and also has a collection of early pottery and metalware. Most of the other antique dealers are located on Long Street in the city center.

These include several shops that specialize in furniture, such as **Breakspeare Antiques,** 18 Long St. (☎ **01666/503122**), which carries mahogany pieces from the 18th and early 19th centuries and walnut pieces from as far back as the 17th century. **Country Homes,** 61 Long St. (☎ **01666/502342**), sells restored pine furniture from England, Ireland, and Europe; and **Gales Antiques,** 52 Long St. (☎ **01666/502686**), features English and French provincial furnishings. For good quality porcelain, try **Dolphin Antiques,** 48 Long St. (☎ **01666/504242**). The **Antiques Emporium,** at the Old Chape, Long Street (☎ **01666/505281**), gathers stock from 40 dealers in 1,750 square feet of showrooms; you're almost guaranteed to find something you like.

## WHERE TO STAY & EAT

✪ **The Crown Inn.** Gumstool Hill off Market Place, Tetbury, Gloucestershire GL8 8DG. ☎ **01666/502469.** 4 rms, none with bath. TV. £19 ($30.40) single; £32 ($51.20) double; £16 ($25.60) per person family room. All rates include English breakfast. AE, MC, V.

One of the best bargains in this expensive Cotswold town is this three-gabled stone building that was originally built in 1693 as a coaching inn. Most of its income derives from its busy pub, where food is ordered over the bartop. (Staff members then carry your choices to seats in either the pub or in a glassed-in conservatory in back.) Platters cost £3.25 to £12 ($5.20 to $19.20) each. The inn's quartet of pub-type accommodations are on the building's third floor, under the sloping eaves. To reach them, overnight guests climb a 17th-century Jacobean staircase. The rooms are small and cozy, usually with exposed beams and tea makers.

**The Hare & Hounds Hotel.** Westonbirt, Tetbury, Gloucestershire GL8 8QL. ☎ **01666/880233.** Fax 01666/880241. 30 rms. TV TEL. £58–£68 ($92.80–$108.80) single; £80–£88 ($128–$140.80) double. All rates include English breakfast. AE, MC, V. Take A433 2¹/₂ miles southwest of Tetbury.

One of the more substantial buildings in the area, this hotel has stone-mullioned windows and gables and is set on 10 acres of private grounds with two hard-surface tennis courts. Originally a 19th-century farmhouse, The Hare & Hounds was turned into a Victorian inn, and the lounge and country bars remain from those days. The main hotel building was added in 1928, but it was constructed so faithfully in the original stone that it looks much older. This traditional country hotel, often favored as a conference place, is run by the Price brothers. They do a good job of entertaining their guests, and make the place a worthy splurge choice. Under a hammerbeam ceiling, the restaurant serves a combination of British and continental dishes, with seasonal specialties. A four-course fixed-price dinner goes for £16.75 to £18.75 ($26.80 to $30), with lunches costing £11.75 to £12.25 ($18.80 to $19.60).

# 2 Cirencester & Painswick

Cirencester: 89 miles W of London; 16 miles S of Cheltenham; 17 miles SE of Gloucester; 36 miles W of Oxford
Painswick: 4 miles N of Stroud; 107 miles W of London; 10 miles SW of Cheltenham; 15 miles NW of Cirencester

Cirencester is the unofficial capital of the Cotswolds, a throwback to the Middle Ages, when it flourished as the center of the great Cotswold wool industry. Then known as Corinium, five roads converged here during the Roman occupation. In size, it ranked second only to London. Today it is chiefly a market town and a good base for touring. And don't worry about how to pronounce Cirencester. There's disagreement even among the English. Say *Siren-cess-ter* and you won't be too far off.

Some 15 miles northwest of Cirencester, the sleepy, enchanting little town of Painswick is so well preserved today it affords an escape from often dull English market towns. Although erected over different periods, its houses blend harmoniously—builders used only Cotswold stone. The one distinctive feature on the Painswick skyline is the spire of its 15th-century parish church. It's also known for its annual Clipping Feast, when the congregation joins hands and circles around the church as if it were a maypole, singing hymns as they do. Ancient tombstones dot the churchyard.

## ESSENTIALS

**GETTING THERE**   Cirencester has no railway station, but trains depart several times a day from London's Paddington Station for the 80-minute trip to Kemble, 4 miles southwest of Cirencester. You may have to transfer trains at Swindon. For schedules and information, call ☎ **0345/484950.** From Kemble, a bus travels to Cirencester four to five times a day. If traveling to Painswick, trains depart from London's Paddington Station several times a day for Stroud, the nearest railway station, 3 miles away. The trip takes from 1¹/₂ to 2 hours, and you may have to change trains at Swindon. From Stroud, buses run to Painswick, some as frequently as once every hour. Many taxis also wait at the Stroud railway station.

National Express buses leave from London's Victoria Coach Station with direct service to Cirencester. For schedules and information, call ☎ **0990/808080.** For Painswick, buses depart from Bath in the direction of Cheltenham on Wednesday and Saturday, stopping in Painswick (and many other small towns) along the way.

If you're driving to Cirencester from London, take the M40 northwest to Oxford, continuing along A40 to the junction with the A429. Drive south on the A429 to Cirencester. From Cirencester, continue west along A419 to Stroud, then head north on A46 to Cheltenham and Painswick.

**VISITOR INFORMATION**    In Cirencester, The **Tourist Information Centre** is at Corn Hall, Market Place (☎ **01285/654180**). Open April through October, Monday 9:45am to 5:30pm and Tuesday to Saturday from 9:30am to 5:30pm. From November through March it closes at 5pm.

The Painswick **Tourist Information Centre** is at the Painswick Library, Stroud Road (☎ **01452/813552**). Open April through September, Monday to Saturday from 10am to 6pm, October through March, Monday to Saturday from 10am to 5pm.

# CIRENCESTER
## SEEING THE SIGHTS

Cirencester has some of the best walks and scenic views of any town in the Cotswolds. And you don't have to go miles out of town to enjoy these strolls; they are easily reached from the center at Market Place. On the grounds of the parish church, attractive trees and shrubs evoke a well-manicured landscape. You can see swans and wild fowl on the River Churn and the lake, even remnants of the town's Roman walls. For a great stroll, take the riverside walk alongside the Churn from Barton Lane to the Abbey Grounds. If you want more, head west from Market Place until you reach **Cirencester Park,** 3,000 acres of parkland with woodland walks. The park is open daily for horse riding and walking. Pedestrian access is from Cecily Hill (no vehicles).

**Brewery Arts Centre.** Brewery Court. ☎ **01285/657181.** Free admission. Year-round Mon–Sat 10am–5pm. No bus or public transport, but Cirencester attractions lie within walking distance (a quarter mile) of the town's main marketplace at the center of town. All sights are pinpointed on a free map provided by the visitor information center.

The living heart of this arts complex is the workshop area of 15 resident craftworkers who produce everything from baskets to chandeliers. Other components of the center include three galleries with exhibitions in both crafts and fine art, a theater, education classes, a shop selling the best in British craftwork, a cafe, and a coffeehouse.

✪ **Corinium Museum.** Park St. ☎ **01285/655611.** Admission £1.75 ($2.80) adults; £1.20 ($1.90) students; 80p ($1.30) children. Mon–Sat 10am–5pm; Sun 2–5pm. Closed Mon in winter.

The museum houses one of the finest collections of archaeological remains from the Roman occupation, found locally in and around Cirencester. Mosaic pavements excavated on Dyer Street in 1849 and other mosaics are the most important exhibits. Provincial Roman sculpture, including such figures as Minerva and Mercury, pottery, and artifacts salvaged from long-decayed buildings, provide a link with the remote civilization that once flourished here. The museum has been completely modernized to include full-scale reconstructions and special exhibitions on local history and conservation.

**Cirencester Parish Church.** Market Place. ☎ **01285/653142.** Free admission; donations invited. Mon–Fri 9:30am–4:30pm; Sun 12:30–5:30pm in summer; 2:15–5:30pm in winter.

A church may have stood on this spot in Saxon times, but the present building overlooking the Market Place in the town center dates to Norman times and Henry I. In size, it appears more like a cathedral than a mere parish church, with a variety of styles, largely perpendicular, as in the early-15th-century tower. Among the treasures inside are a 15th-century "wineglass" pulpit and a silver-gilt cup given to Queen Anne

Boleyn 2 years before her execution. In the Trinity Chapel you can rub some great 15th-century brasses.

## OUTDOOR PURSUITS

Want to take a cool dip? Check out the **Cirencester Open Air Swimming Pool,** Thomas Street (☎ **01285/653947**). Opened in 1869, this is one of England's oldest outdoor pools, fed by cold, refreshing well water. Both a paddling pool and a main pool make up the swimming complex here. Admission is free. If the weather is too cold for outdoor swimming, visit the **Cotswold Leisure Centre,** Tetbury Road (☎ **01285/654057**), for a range of healthy activities including badminton, squash, swimming, and the "Relax Zone" sauna/solarium steam and spa. Admission is 50p (80¢) for adults and 25p (40¢) for seniors and children.

## SHOPPING

For antiques in Cirencester, try **William H. Stokes,** The Cloisters, 6–8 Dollar St. (☎ **01285/653907**), which specializes in furniture, tapestries, and other items from the 16th and 17th centuries. **Rankine Taylor Antiques,** 34 Dollar St. (☎ **01285/ 652529**), sells items from the 17th, 18th, and early 19th centuries, including silver, glass, and furniture. The arts complex known as the **Brewery Arts,** Brewery Court (☎ **01285/657181**), has 15 independent workshops of area craftspeople ranging from jewelers to weavers and basket makers. There are three galleries and a craft shop recognized by the Crafts Council with wares on display and for sale.

## WHERE TO STAY

**Raydon House Hotel.** 3 The Avenue, Cirencester, Gloucestershire GL7 1EH. ☎ and fax **01285/653485.** 10 rms. TV. £25–£35 ($40–$56) single; £45–£55 ($72–$88) double; £66 ($105.60) family rm. All rates include English breakfast. MC, V. From Market Place, drive along Cricklade St. and Watermoor Rd., and turn left on The Avenue.

This Victorian mansion is only 5 minutes from the town center in a peaceful residential area. All the comfortable units have hot-beverage facilities and furnishings that have been chosen to complement the style of the building. The hotel has a suitable restaurant and bar where a fixed-price dinner costs £12 ($19.20). Parking is available.

**Warwick Cottage Guest House.** 75 Victoria Rd., Cirencester, Gloucestershire GL7 1ES. ☎ **01285/656279.** 4 rms, all with shower only. TV. £32–£36 ($51.20–$57.60) double. All rates include English breakfast. No credit cards.

This attractive Victorian town house with full central heating is owned and run by Pat and Dave Gutsell, and is within easy walking distance of the town center and the Cirencester parish church. The bedrooms have color TVs, hot and cold running water, radios, and hot-beverage facilities. Evening meals are served at 6:30pm and range from £7.50 ($12). Packed lunches are also available. Children sharing a room with their parents are granted a reduced rate.

✪ **Wimborne House.** 91 Victoria Rd., Cirencester, Gloucestershire GL7 1ES. ☎ **01285/ 653890.** 5 rms. TV. £20–£28 ($32–$44.80) single; £28–£35 ($44.80–$56) double. All rates include English breakfast. No credit cards.

This Cotswold stone house built in the Victorian era (1886) is a 5-minute walk from the town center and Market Place, which is dominated by the parish church. Cirencester Park, with 3,000 acres of beautifully wooded parkland, the abbey grounds, and the Corinium Museum are nearby. A welcoming atmosphere is provided by the owners, Dianne and Marshall Clarke. All the centrally heated and functionally furnished bedrooms have hot-beverage facilities and clock radio alarms. This is a nonsmoking house.

## WHERE TO EAT

**Cottage of Content.** 117 Cricklade St. ☎ **01285/652071.** Reservations recommended. Main courses £5.65–£13.25 ($9.05–$21.20). No credit cards. Tues–Fri 7:30–9:30pm; Sat 7:30–10:30pm. Closed bank holidays. ENGLISH/INTERNATIONAL.

This delightful little restaurant in the center near the Cirencester parish church is owned and run by Mr. and Mrs. Pugh, who cook, serve, and even do the washing up. Open only in the evening, they have a variety of succulent T-bone steaks, all served with fresh vegetables, salads in season, and a dessert. They've also added some international dishes to the menu, which liven it up a bit.

✪ **Harry Hare's Restaurant and Brasserie.** 3 Gosditch St. ☎ **01285/652375.** Reservations recommended. Main courses £8.95–£12.50 ($14.30–$20); lunches from £5.95 ($9.50). AE, MC, V. Mon–Sat 11am–11pm; Sun noon–11pm. ENGLISH.

Near the town center, in what was originally a 15th-century barn, is this lighthearted brasserie that's popular on weekends. The place remains open throughout the day for full meals, afternoon teas, or snacks virtually anytime. The polite but hurried staff offers a changing array of such specialties as rack of lamb red-currant and port wine sauce, fish cakes and hollandaise sauce, lamb's liver with shallots and smoked bacon, and a cassoulet pie filled with duck confit, pork sausage, and haricot beans. The food is above the ordinary, and many dishes have real flavor.

**Slug and Lettuce.** 17 W. Market Place. ☎ **01285/653206.** Main courses £5–£6 ($8–$9.60). MC, V. Mon–Sat noon–9pm; Sun noon–7pm. Pub: Mon–Sat 11:30am–11pm; Sun noon–10:30pm. ENGLISH.

This is the best-loved and most popular pub in town, with a flower- and vine-ringed beer garden in back adding to the ambience. A coaching inn since the 14th century, it stands opposite the parish church. Many of its original architectural features have been preserved. The setting is one of log fires, country chairs, cushioned pews, and plain stonework. The Slug and Lettuce serves pub food that's far better than the usual. Daily specials are written on a chalkboard and might include homemade eggplant casserole, grilled sausages, and black pudding with scrambled eggs.

### CIRENCESTER AFTER DARK

Head for the town favorite, **Slug and Lettuce,** 17 W. Market Place (☎ **01285/653206**), a friendly pub enjoyed by locals and students alike, without out-of-towners predominating in summer. The pub is known not only for its good brew, but for its fish cakes. You can eat here inexpensively as well as drink: The menu includes the usual steak, chicken, fish dishes, and meat pies. It has the most convivial after-dark atmosphere in town.

## PAINSWICK

### THE CLIPPING FEAST

The Clipping Feast of Painswick—also referred to as the Clipping Ceremony—is an unusual, early medieval ceremony anthropologists suspect might have been inspired by the dim Celtic prehistory of Britain. Every September, a month that coincides with the harvest ceremonies of the pagans, adults and as many children as can be mustered hold hands in a circle around **St. Mary's Anglican Church.** The circle moves first one way, then the other, and the participants sing hymns and pray out loud in a celebration of thanksgiving. Participants and observers come from all over the region to take part in this important rite.

St. Mary's Church, the centerpiece of the village, was originally built between 1377 and 1399, and rebuilt into its present form in 1480. Its churchyard contains 99 massive yew trees, each of which is at least 200 years old. Local legend states that no matter how hard well-meaning gardeners have tried, they've never been able to grow more than 99 of them.

## EXPLORING PAINSWICK

Most of Painswick's charm derives from its historic Cotswold architecture. For example, the post office, on New Street, was built in 1420, whereas most of New Street itself dates from 1450. A specific attraction, regrettably open only by appointment, is **Painswick House,** Gloucester Street, Highway B4073, Painswick Stroud (☎ **01452/813204**); it's about a half-mile west of the town center. This 18th-century Georgian and Palladian mansion, built by Charles Hyett in 1734 and enlarged in 1830, has been home to eight generations of the same family. Today it's the home of Lord and Lady Dickinson. The building's rococo gardens are open between February 1 and mid-December every Wednesday to Sunday from 11am to 5pm. Admission is £1.90 ($3.05) for adults and children; no appointment is necessary for the gardens.

For woodcrafts influenced by William Morris, stop by **Dennis French,** New Street (☎ **01453/883054**).

## WHERE TO STAY & EAT

✪ **Hambutts Mynd.** Edge Rd., Painswick, Gloucestershire GL6 6UP. ☎ **01452/812352.** 3 rms, 1 with bath. TV. £22 ($35.20) single without bath; £40 ($64) double without bath, £42 ($67.20) double with bath. All rates include English breakfast. No credit cards. Closed Jan 15–Feb 15.

Set in half an acre of gardens about 2 blocks southwest from the center of Painswick, this hotel occupies a structure originally built in the 17th century as a windmill for the grinding of corn. Since the 1970s it has functioned as the home and bed-and-breakfast hotel of sprightly Elizabeth Warland. Behind a somber and severely dignified facade of Cotswold stone, the hotel is warm, the subject of many letters of praise from satisfied clients, and filled with an idiosyncratic (and highly pleasing) collection of furniture that includes everything from William and Mary chests to 1930s kitsch. Windows in each of the bedrooms encompass sweeping views over the nearby hills and fields.

✪ **Painswick Hotel.** Kemps Lane, Painswick, Gloucestershire GL6 6YB. ☎ **01452/812160.** Reservations recommended. Main courses £14.75–£28.75 ($23.60–$46); fixed-price dinner £20.50–£28.50 ($32.80–$45.60); fixed-price 2-course lunch £7.50 ($12); fixed-price Sun lunch £14.75 ($23.60). AE, MC, V. Daily 12:30–2:30pm and 7:30–9:30pm. ENGLISH/FRENCH.

The hotel that contains this restaurant is the most prestigious place to stay in this most delightful of English villages. Nevertheless it offers one of the finest and most reasonably priced lunches (and some of the more elegant, if pricier, dinners) in the area. Lunches are served one flight above street level. The more formal evening meals are served in the street-level oak-paneled dining room. Typical menu items might include terrine of chicken and lobster served with a French bean-and-tomato salad, poached filets of lemon sole with a spinach mousse glazed under a white-wine sabayon, and a pastry tartlet of veal kidneys served on a bed of spinach with a grain-mustard sauce. The hotel sits immediately behind the village church.

Staying here might tug at your budget, but if you do, you'll find an elegantly decorated series of rooms, with stunning fabrics, antiques, and period engravings. The more standard rooms, rather than the lavishly adorned units with four-poster beds, begin at £87 ($139.20) per night in a double.

# 3 Cheltenham

99 miles NW of London; 9 miles NE of Gloucester; 43 miles W of Oxford

Legend has it that the Cheltenham villagers discovered a mineral spring by chance when they noticed pigeons drinking from a spring and observed how healthy they were (the pigeon has been incorporated into the town's crest). King George III arrived in 1788 and launched the town's career as a spa. The duke of Wellington came to ease his liver disorder, and Lord Byron came this way, proposing marriage to Miss Millbanke.

Cheltenham today remains one of England's most fashionable spas. A winner of the "Beautiful Britain in Bloom" contest, Cheltenham attracts many visitors to see its gardens from spring to autumn. The architecture is mainly Regency, with lots of ironwork, balconies, and verandas. Attractive parks and open spaces of greenery make the town especially inviting. The main street, the Promenade, has been called the most beautiful thoroughfare in Britain. Rather similar are such thoroughfares as Lansdowne Place and Montpelier Parade. The design for the dome of the Rotunda was based on the Pantheon in Rome. With caryatids separating its stores, Montpelier Walk is one of England's most interesting shopping centers.

The **International Festival of Music** and the **Festival of Literature** take place each year in July and October, respectively, and attract internationally acclaimed performers and orchestras.

## ESSENTIALS

**GETTING THERE**   Twenty-one trains depart daily from London's Paddington Station for the 2¹/₄-hour trip. You may have to change trains at Bristol or Swindon. For schedules and information, call ☎ **0345/484950.** Trains between Cheltenham and Bristol take only an hour, with continuing service to Bath.

National Express offers nine buses daily from London's Victoria Coach Station to Cheltenham. The ride takes about 2¹/₂ hours. For schedules and information, call ☎ **0990/808080.**

If you're driving from London, head northwest on the M40 to Oxford, continuing along A40 to Cheltenham.

**VISITOR INFORMATION**   The **Tourist Information Centre** is at 77 Promenade (☎ **01242/522878**). Open September through June, Monday to Saturday from 9:30am to 5:15pm; July and August, Monday to Friday from 9:30am to 6pm, Saturday from 9:30am to 5:15pm, and Sunday from 9:30am to 1:30pm.

**COACH TOURS OF THE COTSWOLDS**   Escorted coach tours of the Cotswolds depart Cheltenham every Tuesday, Wednesday, Thursday, and Sunday from June 18 through September 29; for details, call the information center.

## TAKING THE WATERS

**Pittville Pump Room/Gallery of Fashion.** East Approach Dr., Pittville Park. ☎ **01242/523852.** Pump Room free. Gallery £1.50 ($2.40) adults; 50p (80¢) children, students, and seniors. May–Sept Wed–Mon 10am–4:30pm; Oct–Apr Wed–Mon 11am–4pm. From the center take Portland St. and Evesham Rd.

Cheltenham Waters are the only natural, consumable alkaline waters in Great Britain, and are still taken at one of the spa's finest Regency buildings. The Pittville Pump Room is open Sundays from the end of May until the end of September for a host of activities, including lunch, afternoon cream teas, live classical music, landau carriage rides around the city, and brass bands playing in Pittville Park—it's real traditional England.

The Gallery of Fashion, also located in the pump room, depicts the social history of Cheltenham Spa. Memorabilia include photographs and prints of the U.S. Army when it was stationed at Pittville in the 1940s. A prized collection in the gallery is the Hull Grundy Gift, a dazzling display of jewelry from the Regency period through Art Nouveau. You can see tiaras made from glittery paste stones, fine examples of jewelry made from human hair, a brooch made of tiny mosaics, and much more.

## MORE SIGHTS

**Cheltenham Art Gallery & Museum.** Clarence St. ☎ **01242/237431.** Free admission. Mon–Sat 10am–5:20pm. Closed bank holiday Mondays.

This gallery houses one of the foremost collections of the arts-and-crafts movement, notably the fine furniture of William Morris and his followers. One section is devoted to Edward Wilson, Cheltenham's native son who died with Captain Scott in the Antarctic in 1912. The gallery is located near Royal Crescent and the Coach Station.

**Everyman Theatre.** Regent St. ☎ **01242/572573.** Admission £4.50–£21.50 ($7.20–$34.40), depending on the event. Box office: Mon–Sat 9:30am–8:30pm on performance days, 9:30am–6pm otherwise.

Cheltenham is the cultural center of the Cotswolds, a role Everyman Theatre maintains at least in part. Designed in the 1890s as an opera house by Frank Matcham, Victorian England's leading theater architect, it retains its ornate cornices, sculpted ceilings, and plush velvets despite extensive renovations to its stage and lighting facilities.

The theater has recently become a touring venue, attracting some of England's top dramatic companies. Shakespeare, musicals, comedies, and a variety of other genres are performed in the small (658 seats) and charming hall. Some examples of last season's works include *The Adventures of Robin Hood, Don Giovanni, Antony and Cleopatra,* and several performances by musical groups. Also in the theater are a restaurant and bars, all serving both food and drink.

**Holst Birthplace Museum.** 4 Clarence Rd. ☎ **01242/524846.** Admission £1.50 ($2.40) adults; 50p (80¢) children and seniors. Year-round Tue–Sat 10am–4:20pm.

In 1874 this Regency terrace house saw the birth of Gustav Theodore Holst, who went on to become a great composer and teacher and whose works were heavily influenced by English folk music and Hindu literature. He is most famous for "The Planets," which he wrote in 1918. During the first 8 years of his life, he lived here, and visitors can see rooms restored to illustrate the "upstairs-downstairs" life-style he and his family enjoyed. The house also includes Holst's original piano, a Regency drawing room, a children's nursery, and a kitchen in working condition.

## SHOPPING

The different quarters that make up Cheltenham's shopping district turn shopping into an unusually organized event. Start in the Montpelier quarter for a host of individual boutiques and an abundance of craft and specialty shops. Then continue to the nearby Suffolk quarter to find most of the town's antique stores. And an enjoyable short stroll to the Promenade will take you to Cheltenham's heart of high fashion, shoes, and books. From the Promenade, take Regent Street to High Street, which is mostly pedestrian-only, and you'll find brand-name department stores. The weekly market is in the Henrietta Street car park on Thursday and in Coronation Square on Friday. Weather permitting, markets open around 9am and close toward 4pm.

## WHERE TO STAY

If you don't mind roughing it a bit, here are some cheap sleep options. The **YMCA,** 6 Vittoria Walk, Cheltenham ( ☎ **01242/524024;** fax 01242/232635), has 47 single rooms and three doubles, none of which has a bath. Rates of £13 ($20.80) per person go down to £11.70 ($18.70) on the third night, and breakfast is included. Laundry facilities are also available on the premises. Call first, though, because students rent most of the rooms and, outside of July and August, they can be hard to come by.

If a night under the open sky is more what you had in mind, try **Longwillow's Camping Site,** Woodmancote, outside Cheltenham ( ☎ **01242/674113**), which offers sites for tents, caravans, or RVs at rates of £6 ($9.60) per night for up to two adults with two children or three adults, during the high season; £5.50 ($8.80) in the low season. For larger parties, the extra person rate is £1.25 ($2). You don't really have to rough it here though, because electricity is available for £1.60 ($2.55) a night, and there are also laundry facilities, hot water, and showers. In addition, a popular Indian restaurant and bar are located at the entrance to the camp, and there are other restaurants and a supermarket, open 7 days a week, about a half-mile up the road.

### DOUBLES FOR LESS THAN £50

**Beaumont House Hotel.** Shurdington Rd., Cheltenham, Gloucestershire GL53 0JE. ☎ **01242/245986.** Fax 01242/520044. 17 rms. TV TEL. £37 ($59.20) single; £48 ($76.80) standard double; £58 ($92.80) 4-poster rm; £60 ($96) family rm. All rates include English breakfast. AE, MC, V. Bus: "Metro."

This Victorian-era building with gardens offers a tranquil environment, only minutes from the town center. The licensed house has been tastefully converted to receive paying guests. Most of the bright, airy, color-coordinated bedrooms have private baths or showers; all have hot drinks tray, direct-dial phone, radio alarm clock, satellite TV, and some have video players. Good British fare is also served in the dining room, where you may want to reserve for dinner. Served Monday through Saturday, the cost for a multicourse meal is £17.75 ($28.40).

**Central Hotel.** 7–9 Portland St., Cheltenham, Gloucestershire GL52 2NZ. ☎ **01242/582172.** 15 rms, 6 with bath. TV TEL. £24 ($38.40) single without bath, £34 ($54.40) single with shower only; £40 ($64) double without bath, £48 ($76.80) double with shower only. AE, DC, MC, V.

Within easy reach of Cheltenham's range of attractions, this white-fronted hotel consists of a pair of stone houses that were originally built in the 1700s and then combined. Today, strictly protected from exterior changes by local building codes, it's a family-run hotel, with a street-level public house. Meals are served in the bar for under £10 ($16) each. The bedrooms are conservatively modern, with tea-making facilities inside.

✪ **Lawn Hotel.** 5 Pittville Lawn, Cheltenham, Gloucestershire GL52 2BE. ☎ **01242/526638.** 9 rms, 4 with bath. TV. £17.50–£19.50 ($28–$31.20) single; £35–£37 ($56–$59.20) double. All rates include English breakfast. No credit cards. Bus: no. 1A, 2A, or 3A.

Built in 1830 with a stucco exterior, this elegant landmark Regency house lies just inside the iron gates leading to Pittville Park and the Pump Room. It's one of 300 town houses built in an area landscaped in the early 19th century by Joseph Pitt. Owned by the Armitage family, it offers pleasantly decorated rooms with tea-making equipment, hot and cold running water, and TV. Evening meals can be arranged, beginning at £7.50 ($12) per person, as well as afternoon teas. The hotel is convenient to the town center and its Promenade, about a 10-minute walk away.

# WHERE TO EAT

✪ **Below Stairs Restaurant**. 103 Promenade. ☎ **01242/234599.** Reservations recommended. Main courses £7.75–£16.75 ($12.40–$26.80). AE, DC, MC, V. Mon–Sat noon–2:30pm and 6–10:30pm. CONTINENTAL.

In the heart of the spa, this restaurant is indeed below street level; you enter from the Promenade through a basement doorway. But this is no dank, Dickensian cellar: It's one of the best and most rewarding places for food and drink in Cheltenham. The menu caters to local and foreign tastes alike. You may choose, for example, a bowl of mussels marinara or a fresh crab crêpe with a mixed salad. Fish comes up from Devon three times a week, and oysters and mussels arrive from Cherbourg (France) every Wednesday. Meat is obtained from a beef specialist in Scotland, and fresh vegetables are delivered daily. Vegetarian specialties are a feature.

**Caffè Uno.** 15–17 Clarence St. ☎ **01242/221186.** Main courses £5–£6 ($8–$9.60) lunch; £4.50–£8 ($7.20–$12.80) dinner. AE, MC, V. Mon–Thurs 10am–11pm; Fri–Sat 10am–midnight; Sun 11am–10:30pm. ITALIAN.

Part of the Garfunkel chain of Italian restaurants, this large dining room is pleasantly light and airy with its flagstone floors, modern art prints, and abundant greenery. Lunch tends to feature pastas, pizza, sandwiches, and salads, whereas dinner offers traditional steak, chicken, and fish dishes. The food is only standard fare, but ingredients are fresh, and locals often cite this as one of their more "affordable" choices.

**Montpelier Wine Bar.** Montpelier St. ☎ **01242/527774.** Reservations recommended. Main courses £4.95–£6.50 ($7.90–$10.40) lunch; £7.50–£12 ($12–$19.20) dinner. MC, V. Mon–Fri noon–2:30pm and 6–10pm; Sat–Sun noon–10pm. Bar: Mon–Sat 11am–11pm; Sun noon–10:30pm. BRITISH.

Housed in a distinctive bow-fronted Regency building, this four-story restaurant is so bowed that its front is actually a semicircle with sweeping windows favored by diners on nice days. The upstairs dining room is light and airy and, along with the outdoor patio, a favorite place to eat in warm weather. The downstairs dining room is cozy but up to date, with a large stone fireplace balanced by original contemporary paintings and polished wooden floors and tables. There is a daily menu of seasonal dishes with fish, steak, pork, chicken, British game, and vegetarian items all rotating into a list of creative, well-prepared choices. The bottom two floors house a wine bar and a full bar, with a generous listing of vintages.

**Moran's Eating House and Wine Bar.** 123–129 Bath Rd. ☎ **01242/581411.** Reservations recommended on Fri–Sat. Main courses £4–£10 ($6.40–$16). No credit cards. Mon–Sat 10am–2:30pm and 6–11pm. CONTINENTAL.

A lively and popular place, especially on Friday and Saturday nights, this restaurant/bar inhabits two connected mid–19th century homes, one a comfortable wine bar with wicker and padded leopard-skin furniture, and the other an unassuming dining room with polished wood floors and pine furniture. The two halves are unified by a lush garden, popular in warm weather. Main courses include such items as fresh seafood pie with crunchy cheese topping, beef bourguignon, and large mushrooms stuffed with pasta and ratatouille, with a wine list offering selections to go with everything.

**The Orange Tree.** 317 High St. ☎ **01242/234232.** Main courses £4.95–£5.95 ($7.90–$9.50). No credit cards. Tues–Sat 9am–9pm. VEGETARIAN.

This small vegetarian restaurant is simply laid out, with an orange tree motif around the walls and polished wooden floors and tables. The menu changes daily, and standard dishes such as lasagna, quiche, cottage pie, stroganoff, and vegetable curry are given new life with innovative vegetable and seasoning combinations.

**Pepper's Café Bar.** Regent St. near the Playhouse. ☎ **01242/573488.** Main courses £6–£7 ($9.60–$11.20) cafe-pub; £8–£9 ($12.80–$14.40) restaurant. AE, MC, V. Daily 11am–3pm and 6–10:30pm. Cafe-pub: Mon–Sat 8am–11pm; Sun 8am–10:30pm; food service 8am–8pm. BRITISH.

This European-style cafe is a great place to relax and have a snack or a meal. Split into a cafe-pub and a 300-seat dining room, a comfortable atmosphere is established through the use of low-level lighting and music in combination with polished wooden floors, raised carpeted sitting areas, and comfortable chairs and settees. There's also an outdoor terrace for warm weather drinking and dining. The cafe has snacks, pies, fish and chips, and pasta dishes, along with a wide variety of draft and bottled beer. The restaurant serves an array of specialty breads to accompany a more extensive selection of steaks, traditional English dishes like steak and ale pie, and Italian fare.

**The Retreat.** 10–11 Suffolk Parade. ☎ **01242/235436.** Reservations recommended. Main courses £4.50–£7.25 ($7.20–$11.60); glass of wine from £1.30 ($2.05). AE, DC, MC, V. Mon–Sat noon–2:15pm. Pub: Mon–Sat noon–11pm. INTERNATIONAL/VEGETARIAN.

In a red-brick building at least a century old, this is the most popular pub/wine bar in town. Its most distinctive feature is a plant-filled courtyard that's packed with diners during fine weather. Only lunch is served—the rest of the day the place is devoted to imbibing. Meals (you place your order at a food counter) are likely to include an array of fresh salads, with health-conscious ingredients blended into imaginative combinations. The Retreat is a 5-minute walk south of the village center.

## CHELTENHAM AFTER DARK

The major nighttime venue is the **Everyman Theatre** (see above), a premier sightseeing attraction of Cheltenham. But there's lots more theater at the **Playhouse,** Bath Road (☎ 01242/522852), with new local, amateur productions of drama, comedy, dance, and opera being staged at the dizzying pace of every 2 weeks, with 1 week of rehearsal and 1 week of performance. Tickets are £3 to £6 ($4.80 to $9.60).

For theater and beyond, **Axiom Centre for the Arts,** 57–59 Winchcombe St. (☎ 01242/253183), is a stage for working artists, musical performance, and traveling exhibitions. The complex houses studio spaces, two galleries featuring works by local artists as well as those further afield, a theater specializing in fringe productions, a cafe-bar, and **The Back Bar,** the only local venue for live music, with entertainment every night but Wednesday and Sunday. Bands range from indie to jazz and Saturdays they break out the turntables as DJs play an eclectic dance mix. Mainly free, there can be a cover charge, dependent upon the performance.

Dancers flock to **Mondo,** Bath Road (☎ 01242/263456), for mixed crowds and dance styles, with students only on Monday, an over-25 crowd on Wednesdays, and come one, come all on Thursday through Saturday. The cover charge varies from £1 to £5 ($1.60 to $8).

You can choose your groove at **Gas,** St. James Square (☎ 01242/52770), where it's soul and R&B upstairs, or house and techno downstairs on Monday and Wednesday through Saturday nights from 9pm to 2am. The cover charge varies from £3 to £5 ($4.80 to $8), depending on the night. **Enigma,** Regent Street (☎ 01242/224085), seems like a quiet two-story club until Tuesday, when it heats up with salsa lessons on one level and karaoke on the other, and Friday and Saturday, when upstairs house dancing and downstairs eclectic dance raise the temperature again.

## A SIDE TRIP TO ROYAL SUDELEY CASTLE

In the Cotswolds village of Winchcombe, just 6 miles northeast of Cheltenham, stands one of England's finer stately homes, the 15th-century Royal Sudeley Castle (☎ 01242/602949 or 01242/603715). From Cheltenham, take the regular bus to

## The Great Outdoors in the Cotswolds

One of the principal reasons to visit the Cotswolds is to take advantage of its natural beauty, whether from the banks of a river or from the fairway of a scenic golf course. But for many, the main reason to visit is to take a ramble across a meadow where sheep graze or hike along hidden paths and trails next to a fast-flowing stream.

✪ **BIKING**    Bicycling down the country roads of the Cotswolds is one of the best ways to experience the quiet beauty of the area. **Country Lanes,** 9 Shaftesbury Street, Fordingbridge, Hampshire SP6 1JF (☎ **01425/655022**), rents 21-speed bicycles fully equipped with mud guards, a water bottle, lock and key, a rear carrier rack, and, of course, safety helmets. The day trips with easy-to-follow route sheets are self-guided, and therefore at your own pace. En route you'll pass manor farms and pretty cottages of honey-colored stone. Several villages are also along the path, and the Hidcote Manor Garden is a perfect spot to relax if your legs tire of pedaling. The 10-, 20-, or 28-mile trips all end at the Manor House Hotel, a former 16th-century coaching inn at Moreton-in-Marsh. Here, you'll be served afternoon tea in the garden. The £25 ($40) price includes everything mentioned above and a souvenir T-shirt. Advanced booking is essential; call ☎ **01608/650065** to book by credit card.

**GOLF    Cotswold Hills Golf Club,** Ullenwood, Cheltenham (☎ **01242/515263**). Open year-round, the only requirements at this par 71 golf course are a reasonable standard of play, your own clubs, and no jeans or sneakers. Rates on weekdays are £24 ($38.40) for 18 holes and £30 ($48) for unlimited play; on Saturday and Sunday £30 ($48) for 18 holes and £35 ($56) for unlimited play.

At the **Tewkesbury Park Golf and Country Club,** Lincoln Green Lane, Tewkesbury, 12 miles north of Cheltenham (☎ **01684/295405**), the requirements at this year-round 73-par course are a reasonable standard of play, a golf bag, and no jeans, sneakers, or club sharing. Clubs are available for rent at £10 ($16). Eighteen holes costs £20 ($32) on weekdays and £30 ($48) on Saturday and Sunday.

The 70-par **Gloucestershire Golf and Country Club** course, Matson Lane, Gloucester (☎ **01452/411331** or 01452/425653), requires a reasonable standard of play and disallows jeans and sneakers, though tailored shorts are okay. Club rentals are available for £5 to £6 ($8–$9.60). Eighteen holes costs £19 ($30.40) on weekdays and £25 ($40) on Saturday and Sunday.

**FISHING**    The Cotswolds feature trout fishing unparalleled in all of England, with the River Test, running through Stockbridge, offering the best, and streams near Bibury and Fairford also providing a challenge. Unfortunately, all are privately owned, so the best way to take advantage of the region's fishing is to stay in a hotel aimed at anglers. Among these, try the **Bibury Court Hotel,** Bibury GL7 5NT (☎ **01285/740337**); the **Swan Hotel,** Bibury GL7 5NW (☎ **01285/740695**); or **Wroxton House Hotel,** Wroxton St. Mary, Wroxton OX15 6PZ (☎ **01295/730777**).

**WALKING**    With such a large area in which to ramble, it's a good idea to know where you are, and where you aren't, welcome. The **Cotswold Wardens,** c/o County Planning Department, Shire Hall, Gloucester (☎ **01452/425000,** ext. 7542), offers free brochures highlighting trails and paths for your hiking pleasure. Other sources of information include the *Cotswold Way Handbook* by the **Rambler's Association,** c/o R. A. Long, 27 Lambert Ave., Shurdington, Cheltenham (☎ **01242/862594**); *The Cotswold Way: a Walker's Guide* by Mark Richards (Thornhill Press), and *A Guide to the Cotswold Way* by Richard Sale (Constable).

Winchcombe and get off at Abbey Terrace. Then walk the short distance along the road to the castle. If you're driving, take the B4632 north out of Cheltenham, through Prestbury, and up Cleve Hill to Abbey Terrace where you can drive right up to the castle.

Royal Sudeley Castle has a rich history that begins in Saxon times, when the village was the capital of the Mercian kings. Later, Katherine Parr, the sixth wife of Henry VIII, lived and died here. Her tomb is in a chapel on the grounds along with a host of formal gardens like the Queen's Garden, now planted with Old World roses. While exploring the gardens, you're sure to see the waterfowl and flamboyant peacocks who call Sudeley home.

For the past 30 years, Lady Ashcombe, an American by birth, has owned the castle and welcomes visitors from the world over. The castle houses many works of art by Constable, Turner, Rubens, Van Dyck, among others, and has several permanent exhibitions, magnificent furniture and glass, and many artifacts from the castle's past. In the area to the right of the keep, as you enter the castle, workshops are devoted to talented local artisans who continue to use traditional techniques to produce stained glass, textiles, wood and leather articles, and marbled paper. There is also a design exhibition illustrating how these articles have been incorporated in country houses through the ages.

Royal Sudeley Castle is open Easter through October, daily from 11am to 5pm. The grounds open 30 minutes earlier at 10:30am. Admission is £5.50 ($8.80) for adults, £4.80 ($7.70) for seniors, £3 ($4.80) for children, and £15 ($24) for a family ticket.

## 4 Bibury

86 miles W of London; 30 miles W of Oxford; 26 miles E of Gloucester

On the road from Burford to Cirencester, Bibury is one of the loveliest spots in the Cotswolds. In fact, the utopian romancer of Victoria's day, the poet William Morris, called it England's most beautiful village. In the Cotswolds, it is matched only by Painswick for its scenic village beauty and purity. Both villages are still unspoiled by modern invasions.

## ESSENTIALS

**GETTING THERE**   About five trains per day depart from London's Paddington Station for the 1-hour, 10-minute trip to Kemble, the nearest station 13 miles south of Bibury. Some will require a rapid change of train in Swindon (the connecting train waits just across the tracks). For schedules and information, call ☎ **0345/484950.** There are no buses from Kemble to Bibury, but most hoteliers will arrange transport if you make arrangements in advance.

Five buses leave London's Victoria Coach Station daily for Cirencester, 7 miles from Bibury. For schedules and information, call ☎ **0990/808080.** There are no connecting buses into Bibury, but local hotels will send a car, and taxis are available.

If you're driving from London, take the M4 to Exit 15, head toward Cirencester, then follow A33 (on some maps this is still designated as B4425) to Bibury.

## SEEING THE SIGHTS

On the banks of the tiny Coln River, Bibury is noted for **Arlington Row,** a group of 17th-century gabled cottages protected by the National Trust. These houses were originally built for weavers. They are its biggest and most-photographed attraction, but it's not polite to peer into the windows, as many do, because people still live here.

To get a view of something a bit out of the ordinary for the Cotswolds, check out **St. Mary's Parish Church.** As the story goes, the wool merchants who possessed power and money in the area were rebuilding the churches. However, they did not finish the restoration of St. Mary's, and as such, much of the original Roman-style architecture has been left intact. The 14th-century decorated-styled windows have even survived the years. This is an often-overlooked treasure.

The once-prosperous mill has been silenced and converted into the **Cotswold Country Museum** (☎ **01451/860715**) where visitors are treated to a host of anti-quated wagons and machines once used in the area and a variety of display rooms that illustrate the way people used to handle day-to-day existence. Open mid-March through mid-November, Monday to Saturday from 10:30am to 5pm, and Sunday from 2pm to 5pm; mid-November through mid-March, Saturday and Sunday from 10:30am to dusk. Admission is £1.50 ($2.40) for adults, £1.25 ($2) for seniors, and 75p ($1.20) for children.

Just next to the museum is the **Bilbury Trout Farm** (☎ **01285/740212**), a target for tourists. However, if you have children, go. Fish can be fed by visitors, and in an ironic twist, fish can be bought to feed visitors. The farm is open Monday through Saturday from 9am to 6pm and Sunday from 10am to 5pm. Admission is £1.90 ($3.05) for adults, £1.50 ($2.40) for seniors, and 90p ($1.45) for children.

One of the most delightful walks in all the Cotswolds begins at the grounds of Bibury Court and winds to the next village of Coln St. Aldwyn, following the riverbank. Tennyson described it well: "Grey twilight poured on dewy pastures, dewy trees, softer than sleep—all things in order stored a haunt of ancient peace."

## WHERE TO STAY & EAT

**The Catherine Wheel Guest House.** Arlington, near Bibury, Gloucestershire GL7 5ND. ☎ **01285/740250.** 4 rms. TV. £40 ($64) single, double, or triple. AE, DC, MC, V.

These rooms are equivalent to those within most of the three-star hotels of Britain, but carry the added advantage of being in the annex of a rustically timbered house built during the 1400s. The main building, set in the heart of town, contains Bibury's only pub, and as such, serves hearty platters of food Monday to Saturday from noon to 10pm, and Sunday from noon to 2:30pm and 7 to 10pm, from any of four bar areas within its historically evocative, richly beamed and paneled, premises. As many as three fireplaces blaze away almost constantly between October and March, illuminating platters that include the predictable roster of bangers and mash and steak-and-kidney pie, as well as more esoteric choices like swordfish, calamari, ham pie, and lobster casserole. Platters range from £3.50 to £10.50 ($5.60 to $16.80).

Bedrooms contain touches of half-timbering and functional but comfortable furnishings, and lie a short walk from the noise and activities of the pub, within an annex that functioned throughout the early 20th century as a storage building. Why is it called The Catherine Wheel? The publican hasn't a clue but will offer a pint or two to anyone who can accurately research the origin of the name. Regular patrons suspect it has something to do with a Catholic virgin martyred by the Romans for her virtuous behavior.

## 5 Burford

76 miles NW of London; 20 miles W of Oxford

Built of Cotswold stone and serving as a gateway to the area, the unspoiled medieval town of Burford is largely famous for its Norman church (ca. 1116) and its High Street lined with coaching inns. Oliver Cromwell passed this way, as did Charles II and his mistress, Nell Gwynne. Burford was one of the last of the great wool centers, the industry bleating out its last breath as late as Queen Victoria's day. Be sure to photograph the bridge across the Windrush River where Queen Elizabeth I once stood. As the antique shops along High Street will testify, Burford today is definitely equipped for tourists.

The River Windrush, flanked by willows through meadows toward Burford, passes beneath the packhorse bridge and goes around the church and away through more meadows. Its banks make for one of the most delightful walks in the Cotswolds, ranking with Bibury and Lower Slaughter.

## ESSENTIALS

**GETTING THERE**   Many trains depart daily from London's Paddington Station to Oxford, a 45-minute trip. For schedules and information, call ☎ **0345/484950.** From Oxford, passengers walk a very short distance to the entrance of the Taylor Institute, from which about three or four buses per day make the 30-minute run to Burford.

A National Express bus runs from London's Victoria Coach Station to Burford several times a day, with many stops along the way. It's a 2-hour ride. For schedules and information, call ☎ **0990/808080.**

If driving from Oxford, head west on A40 to Burford.

**VISITOR INFORMATION**   The **Tourist Information Centre** is at the Old Brewery, Sheep Street (☎ **01993/823558**). Open November through March, Monday to Saturday from 10am to 4:30pm; April through October, Monday to Saturday from 9:30am to 5:30pm.

## EXPLORING BURFORD

To approach Burford from the south is to confront one of the finest views of any ancient market town in the country. The main street sweeps down to the River Windrush, past an extraordinary collection of houses of various styles and ages. The hills opposite provide a frame of fields and trees and, with luck, panoramic skies.

*Burh-ford* (meaning a defended settlement by a ford) was mentioned in the *Domesday Book* in 1086, with a population of 200. The crossing of the river later progressed from a mere ford to a bridge. Burford's ancient packhorse bridge is still doing duty at the bottom of the hill.

Although the wool trade has long since vanished, most of Burford remains unchanged in appearance, with its old houses, both great and small, to be seen in the High Street and side streets. Nearly all are built of the local stone, lending harmony to the scene. Many Cotswold towns have their Sheep Street, as does Burford, with many fine stone-built houses covered with roofs of Stonesfield slate. Burford Church is almost cathedral-like in proportion, begun about 1175. It was enlarged throughout succeeding centuries until the decline of the wool trade. Little has changed here since about 1500. Traders and vendors still set up their stalls under the Tolsey on Friday, where the guild since 1107 used to collect tolls from anyone wishing to trade in the town. It still stands at the corner of Sheep Street. On the upper floor is the minor Tolsey Museum, where you can see a medieval seal bearing Burford's insignia, the "rampant cat."

Two miles south of Burford on A361 lies the **Cotswold Wildlife Park** (☎ **01993/823006**). The 120 acres of gardens and forests around this Victorian manor house have been transformed into a jungle, of sorts, with a Noah's Ark consortium of animals ranging from voracious ants to rare Asiatic lions. Children can romp around the farmyard and the adventure playground. A narrow-gauge railway runs from April to October, and there are extensive picnic areas plus a cafeteria. Hours are Easter through October, daily from 10am to 6:30pm; off-season, daily from 10am to 5:30pm. Admission is £5.10 ($8.15) for adults, £3.40 ($5.45) for seniors and children 3 to 16, free for ages 2 and under.

As a final *adieu* to Burford, we suggest a visit immediately east to **Swinbrook,** a pretty village by the Windrush River, best known for its link to the fabled Mitford sisters who lived here. Visit the local parish church to see the grave of writer Nancy Mitford and the impressive tiered monuments to the Fettiplace family.

## SHOPPING

On High Street in Burford, you'll find several antique shops, including **Manfred Schotten Antiques,** The Crypt, 109 High St. (☎ **01993/822302**). Sporting antiques and collectibles, they also carry library and club furniture. **Jonathan Fyson Antiques,** 50–52 High St. (☎ **01993/823204**), carries English and continental furniture and porcelain, glass, and brass items. On Cheltenham Road, **Gateway Antiques** (☎ **01993/823678**) has a variety of items displayed in large showrooms. English pottery, metalware, and furniture dominate the inventory. Unique arts and craft items and interesting decorative objects are fun to browse through, even if you're not looking to buy.

## TEATIME

After you've browsed through the antique shops, head for your cuppa to **Burford House,** High Street (☎ **01993/823151**), an old Cotswold house long known as the Andrews Hotel. Retaining a mellow charm, it serves tea daily from 11am to 6pm. Freshly baked goods, including flans, scones, cakes, and muffins are here to tempt. The English tea comes not only with a pot of tea, but clotted cream, scones, jam, flan, and fruit, whereas the queen's tea is more modest: a cup of tea with some scones and jams. Pehaps they've put the queen on a diet.

## WHERE TO STAY & EAT

**The Boltons.** 9 Windrush Close, Burford, Oxfordshire OX18 4SL. ☎ **01993/822051.** 3 rms. TV. £17 ($27.20) single; £24 ($38.40) double. All rates include English breakfast. No credit cards. From High St., head east on Swan Lane.

Mrs. E. Barrett's guest house was built in 1955 about an eighth of a mile from Burford's center. Cotswold stone and Cotswold slate were used to build the house, which has small but pleasant gardens in front and in back. From many of the windows, you can look out over green fields and hills, although a housing development has been built to the south. Mrs. Barrett is a warm hostess; there's a home-away-from-home ambience here, although the bedrooms are back-to-basics.

✪ **The Bull.** 105 High St., Burford, Oxfordshire OX18 4RG. ☎ **01993/822220.** 16 rms, 15 with shower only. TV TEL. £45 ($72) single without bath; £65 ($104) double with shower only. All rates include English breakfast. AE, MC, V.

This three-star hotel on the main street is the oldest in Burford, dating from at least 1475. The priory was given by Henry VIII to his barber-surgeon in 1544 after the monasteries were dissolved, and from 1603, when John Silvester became inn holder, the history of the Bull can be traced. The storied inn has had such visitors as the king's troops in the battle with Cromwell's Parliament Dragoons, Cromwell himself, and later Charles II and Nell Gwynne. The hotel is distinguished by its brick-and-stone front dating from 1658, when additions increased the size of the hostelry. Today Old-World charm blends with modern comfort. All bedrooms have central heating. Even if you don't stay here, drop in for a drink at the pub or a good meal.

Pub snacks, priced from £4 to £9 ($6.40 to $14.40) each, are served daily from noon to 10pm. The dining room begins serving dinner at 7pm.

## BURFORD AFTER DARK

Although an elegant and expensive inn, dating from the 15th century, the drinking facilities at ✪ **Lamb Inn,** Sheep Street (☎ **01993/823155**), attract many from all walks of life who appreciate its mellow atmosphere and charm. Guinness, cider, and a carefully chosen collection of ales, including a local brew, Wadworth, are on tap. Bar meals are served Monday through Saturday from 11am to 2pm, and an English/ French menu is available Monday through Friday from 7 to 9pm. On Sunday a traditional English roast is served from noon to 2pm.

## 6 Bourton-on-the-Water

85 miles NW of London; 36 miles NW of Oxford

You may feel like Gulliver voyaging to Lilliput when you arrive in this scenic Cotswold village. Bourton-on-the-Water lies on the banks of the tiny Windrush River. Its mellow stone houses, its village greens on the banks of the water, and its bridges have earned it the title of the Venice of the Cotswolds. But that label tends to obscure its true charm.

Its fans consider Bourton-on-the-Water the quintessential Cotswold village, with a history going back to the Celts. Actually, a loyal cadre of historians would risk everything to protect the village's 15th- and 16th-century architecture. Populated in Anglo-Saxon times, it developed into a strategic outpost along the ancient Roman road, Fosse Way, that traversed Britain from the North Sea to the St. George's Channel, facing Ireland and Wales. During the Middle Ages, prosperous land-owners produced wool in abundance. And during the Industrial Revolution, its central core was never modernized because of the town's backwater status as a producer of wool but not finished textiles. (That honor went to nearby Northleach, a town that is consequently less well-preserved than Bourton).

Despite its small size, Bourton remains quite popular. It's also the site of a legend-ary river, the Windrush, an upper tributary of the Thames, which, at this point, runs swift, clear, cold, and not particularly deep.

## ESSENTIALS

**GETTING THERE**   Trains leave from London's Paddington Station to nearby Moreton-in-Marsh, a trip of 2 hours. For schedules and information, call ☎ **0345/ 484950.** From here, take a Pulhams Bus Company coach 6 miles to Bourton-on-the-Water. Trains also run from London to Cheltenham and Kingham; while somewhat more distant than Moreton-in-Marsh, both have bus connections to Bourton-on-the-Water.

National Express buses run from Victoria Coach Station in London to both Cheltenham and Stow-on-the-Wold. For schedules and information, call ☎ **0990/ 808080.** Pulhams Bus Company operates about four buses per day from both towns to Bourton-on-the-Water.

If driving from Oxford, head west on A40 to the junction with A429 (Fosse Way). Take it northeast to Bourton-on-the-Water.

## LILLIPUT, BIRDS, VINTAGE CARS & MORE

Within the town are a handful of minor museums, each of which were established from idiosyncratic collections amassed over the years by local residents. They include the **Bourton Model Railway Exhibition and Toy Shop** (☎ **01451/820686**), and **Birdland,** described below.

**Birdland.** Rissington Rd. ☎ **01451/820480.** Admission £3.75 ($6) adults; £2.75 ($4.40) seniors; £2 ($3.20) children 4–14; under 3 free. Apr–Oct daily 10am–6pm; Nov–Mar daily 10am–4pm.

This handsomely designed homage to the ornithological splendors of the world was established in 1958 on $8^{1}/_{2}$ acres of field and forests on the banks of Windrush River about a mile east of Bourton-on-the-Water. It houses about 1,200 birds representing 361 species, many of them on exhibition for the first time. Included is the largest and most varied collection of penguins in any zoo, with glass-walled tanks that allow observers to appreciate their agile underwater movements. There's also an enviable collection of hummingbirds. Birdland has a picnic area and a children's playground in a wooded copse.

**Cotswold Motor Museum.** The Old Mill. ☎ **01451/821255.** Admission £1.40 ($2.25) adults; 70p ($1.10) children. Feb–Nov daily 10am–6pm.

This museum has fun displays of cars, bikes, caravans from the 1920s, toys, and the largest collection of advertising signs in Europe. Visitors can also see village shops from the past. The museum is actually in a historic watermill from the 1700s and is the site where the British TV program, "Brum," was filmed. "Brum" revolves around the adventures of a little car, somewhat like the Disney favorite *Herbie the Lovebug.*

**Cotswold Perfumery.** Victoria Street. ☎ **01451/820698.** Admission £1.75 ($2.80) adults; £1.50 ($2.40) children and seniors. Apr–Sep Mon–Sat 9:30am–6pm and Sun 10:30am–6pm; Oct–Mar Mon–Sat 9:30am–5pm and Sun 10:30am–5pm. Closed Dec 25–26.

This permanent perfume exhibition details the history of perfume and the perfume industry and also focuses on its production. The museum, believed to be unique in Europe, incorporates an audiovisual show housed in a "smelly vision" theater, a perfume quiz, a perfume garden full of plants grown exclusively for their fragrance, and a genealogy chart that can be used by visitors to select their personal perfume. Perfumes are made on the premises and sold in the shop.

**The Model Village at the Old New Inn.** High St. ☎ **01451/820467.** Admission £1.50 ($2.40) adults; £1.20 ($1.90) seniors; £1 ($1.60) children. Daily 9am–6pm or dusk in summer; 10am–4pm in winter.

Beginning in the 1930s, a local hotelier, Mr. Morris, whiled away some of the doldrums of the Great Depression by constructing a scale model (1:9) of Bourton-on-the-Water as a testimony to its architectural charms. This isn't a tiny and cramped display set behind glass—the model is big enough so you can walk through this near-perfect and most realistic model village.

**Cotswold Countryside Collection.** Fosse Way, Northleach (Cotswold District Council). ☎ **01451/860715.** Admission £1.50 ($2.40) adults; £1.25 ($2) seniors; 75p ($1.20) children; £3.75 ($6) family ticket. Apr–Oct Mon–Sat 10am–5pm; Sun 2–5pm.

This museum of rural life is located off A40 between Burford and Cheltenham. You can see the Lloyd-Baker collection of agricultural history, including wagons, horse-drawn implements, and tools, as well as a seasons-of-the-year display. A Cotswold gallery records the social history of the area. Below Stairs is an exhibition of laundry, dairy, and kitchen implements. The museum was once a house of correction, and its history is displayed in the reconstructed cell block and courtroom.

## TEATIME

A quaint little tearoom, **Small Talk,** High Street (☎ **01451/821596**), is full of dainty lace and fine china and appetizing scones and pastries. Sit at a table overlooking the water and enjoy a pot of tea and the good conversation of a friend. Weather permitting, tea can be served in the open air.

## WHERE TO STAY

**Broadlands Guest House.** Clapton Row, Bourton-on-the-Water, Cheltenham, Gloucestershire GL54 2DN. ☎ **01451/822002.** 11 rms. £40–£58 ($64–$92.80) double. All rates include English breakfast. No credit cards.

One of the more distinctive B&Bs in the area is in a renovated Victorian building that retains many of its original features, including a glassed-in conservatory. If arrangements are made in advance, dinner can be ordered. One of the bedrooms contains a four-poster bed, and each unit is a double. The hotel sits in a pleasantly isolated spot, somewhat removed from the congestion of the village itself but only 5 minutes away. Overflow guests are housed at Landsdowne Villa, at Landsdowne, Bourton-on-the-Water.

**Duke of Wellington.** Sherbourne St., Bourton-on-the-Water, Cheltenham, Gloucestershire GL54 2BY. ☎ **01451/820539.** 4 rms. TV. £30 ($48) single; £45 ($72) double. All rates include English breakfast. No credit cards.

Most of the town's residents define this place as a pub rather than a hotel, but it does offer a handful of cozy if rather plain accommodations. It was constructed as an inn in 1588, and has remained one throughout most of its long life. Each room has tea-making facilities. Even if you don't stay in one of the upper bedrooms, you might consider dropping in for a drink or informal meal in its antique premises. Its pub is divided into three different bar areas, each of which is among the most consistently popular drinking places in the village; it's open daily from 11am to 11pm. Order your drinks and food at the bar, and waitresses will carry it to your table. Platters, priced at £3.95 to £8 ($6.30 to $12.80), include steaks, jacket potatoes stuffed with various fillings, trout, fish, ham, and shepherd's pie. There's also a bistro-style restaurant that is open for dinner Monday through Saturday and for lunch on Sunday. It offers a variety of meals, including some vegetarian dishes. Main courses cost between £7 and £11 ($11.20 and $17.60).

**Farncombe.** Clapton, Bourton-on-the-Water, Cheltenham, Gloucestershire GL54 2LG. ☎ and fax **01451/820120.** 3 rms, 2 with shower only, 1 with bath. £42 ($67.20) double. All rates include English breakfast. No credit cards. Take A429 toward Cirencester, then the first left after Bourton.

On the outskirts, Farncombe lies 2 1/2 miles from Bourton-on-the-Water. The little hamlet of some 20 houses is an address known only to the discerning English who stay here when the more popular and more famous place is overrun with tourists. Mrs. Julia M. Wright receives guests all year. Her nonsmoking house makes a good base for touring the Cotswolds. The three simply furnished rooms are all doubles and have hair dryers. Coffee and tea is available in the dining room. The property opens onto views of the Windrush Valley. Julia has many menus of the surrounding restaurants and pubs available, as well as maps and tourist-attraction brochures for her guests' convenience.

## WHERE TO EAT

**Old New Inn.** High St. ☎ **01451/820467.** Fixed-price meals £12 ($19.20) at lunch, from £18 ($28.80) at dinner; bar snacks £2.50–£6.50 ($4–$10.40). MC, V. Daily 12:30–1:45pm and 7:30–8:45pm. ENGLISH.

With its popular wine garden, this is one of the best places for food in Bourton-on-the-Water, even though nothing fancy. At lunchtime, guests not only enjoy the snacks but can also play darts or chat with the villagers. The local residents know of its good, fresh, and reasonably priced bar snacks (which can easily be turned into a full meal), and you can also have a more formal dinner in the evening, enjoying good but plain English cookery.

**The Old Well Restaurant.** In the Chester House Hotel and Motel, Victoria St. ☎ **01451/ 820286.** Reservations required. Main courses £6–£8 ($9.60–$12.80) at lunch, £6.95–£12.50 ($11.10–$20) at dinner. AE, DC, MC, V. Daily noon–2pm and 7–9:30pm. Closed Dec–Jan. ENGLISH/CONTINENTAL.

Part of this popular motel in the village center was constructed around what was once a stable for horses. This restaurant is in one of the busiest hotels in the village, catering to a kindly share of business travelers. The chef relies on quality ingredients, producing a good menu. Try the rack of lamb with a port and red-currant sauce, pepper steak, or a casserole of wood pigeon. Traditional English soups are served as appetizers. The simpler the dish and the less challenging to the kitchen, the better it is.

## 7 Stow-on-the-Wold

9 miles SE of Broadway; 10 miles S of Chipping Campden; 4 miles S of Moreton-in-Marsh; 21 miles S of Stratford-upon-Avon

Stow-on-the-Wold is an unspoiled Cotswold market town, in spite of the busloads of tourists who stop off en route to Broadway and Chipping Campden. The town is the loftiest in the Cotswolds, built on a wold about 800 feet above sea level. In its open market square you can still see the stocks where the townspeople threw rotten eggs at past offenders. The final battle between the Roundheads and the Royalists took place here. The town, which is really more of a market village today, is used by many as a base for exploring the Cotswold wool towns, as well as Stratford-upon-Avon.

## ESSENTIALS

**GETTING THERE**   Several trains run daily from London's Paddington Station to Moreton-in-Marsh (see below). For schedules and information, call ☎ **0345/ 484950.** From Moreton-in-Marsh, Pulhams Bus Company makes the 10-minute ride to Stow-on-the-Wold.

National Express buses also run daily from London's Victoria Coach Station to Moreton-in-Marsh, where you can catch a Pulhams Bus Company coach to Stow-on-the-Wold. For schedules and information, call ☎ **0990/808080.** Several Pulhams coaches also run daily to Stow-on-the-Wold from Cheltenham.

If driving from Oxford, take A40 west to the junction with A424, near Burford. Head northwest along A424 to Stow-on-the-Wold.

**VISITOR INFORMATION**   The **Tourist Information Centre** is at Hollis House, The Square (☎ **01451/831082**). Open April through October, Monday to Saturday from 9:30am to 5:30pm, Sunday from 10:30am to 4pm; November through March, Monday to Saturday from 9:30am to 4:30pm.

## ANTIQUES & MORE

Don't be fooled by the hamlet's sleepy, bucolic setting: Stow-on-the-Wold has developed over the last 20 years into the antique-buyer's centerpiece of Britain, and as such has at least 60 merchandisers scattered throughout the village and its environs. Some visitors thrill to rummaging at random through the town's various venues, dusty and otherwise. Barring that, and if your time is a bit more limited, here's a selection of the town's most interesting and unusual emporiums.

**Anthony Preston Antiques, Ltd.** The Square. ☎ **01451/831586.**

Four showrooms inside an 18th-century building on the town's main square compose this emporium of good taste. It specializes in English and French furniture, including some very large pieces such as bookcases, and decorative objects.

**Baggot Church Street, Ltd.** Church St. ☎ **01451/830370.**

This is the smaller, and perhaps more intricately decorated, of two shops founded and maintained by a well-regarded local antique merchant, Duncan "Jack" Baggott. A dealer since 1965, and a frequent denizen at estate sales of country houses throughout Britain, the shop contains four showrooms loaded with furniture and paintings from the 17th to the 19th century. Prices range from £50 ($80) per object.

**Huntington's Antiques Ltd.** Church St. ☎ **01451/830842.**

Covering about half a block in the heart of town, this emporium contains one of the largest stocks of quality antiques dating from the Middle Ages to the end of the 17th century. The informal (i.e., country "vernacular" pieces) span the Middle Ages to the end of the 18th century. Wander at will through 10 ground-floor rooms, then climb to the second floor where a long gallery and a quartet of additional showrooms bulge with refectory tables, unusual cupboards, and the salable heritage of centuries of objects that, until relatively recently, adorned the private homes of thousands of since-deceased owners. Mike Golding is the knowledgeable owner.

**Woolcomber House.** Sheep St. ☎ **01451/830662.**

More eclectic and wide-ranging in its inventory than Baggott Church Street, Ltd. (see above), this is the second of the two shops maintained by local authority Duncan Baggott. Among the largest retail outlets in the Cotswolds, it contains about 17 rooms that during the 16th century functioned as a coaching inn, and which today are each lavishly decorated according to a particular era of English decorative history.

## TEATIME

The best place for tea is a lovely cottage home by the name of **Tea at the Peggums,** Church Street (☎ **01451/830102**). The place usually sells out well before closing, so you may want to arrive early. Menu items include a choice of teas and tasty tea breads, scones, and other pastries.

## WHERE TO STAY
### DOUBLES FOR LESS THAN £50

✪ **Cross Keys Cottage.** Park St., Stow-on-the-Wold, Gloucestershire GL54 1AQ. ☎ **01451/ 831128.** 3 rms, 1 with bath. TV. £42–£45 ($67.20–$72) double without bath; £48–£52 ($76.80–$83.20) double with bath. All rates include breakfast. No credit cards.

Within a minute's drive east of Stow's center, this is one of the district's most charming B&Bs, partly because of its owners, Margaret and Roger Welton, who themselves are charming, and partly because of its origins in 1640 as a brewery. The narrow cottage you'll see from the road is only part of the picture; the site includes three interconnected stone cottages, with nos. 2 and 3 built in 1660 and 1950, respectively, and a walled-in cottage garden. All the rooms are doubles. The managerial expertise derives from time the Weltons spent directing a sports program at a resort hotel in Cyprus, and complements the comfortable interior that includes a log-burning fireplace. Open year-round, the place prides itelf on the care and attention it devotes to its guests, the warmth of their welcome, and the quality of their breakfasts.

# The Great Cotswold Ramble

A walking tour between the villages of Upper and Lower Slaughter, with an optional extension to Bourton-on-the-Water, is one of the most memorable in England. It's 1 mile each way between the Slaughters, or 2¹/₂ miles from Upper Slaughter to Bourton-on-the-Water. The walk, depending upon your dalliances and appreciation of the scenery, could take between 2 and 4 hours.

The architecture of Upper and Lower Slaughter is so unusual that you're likely to remember this trek for many years. By striking out on foot, you avoid at least some of the roadway traffic which taxes the nerves and goodwill of local residents during peak season. En route, you're likely to glimpse the waterfowl that inhabit the rivers, streams, and millponds that crisscross this much-praised region.

A well-worn footpath known as **Warden's Way** meanders beside the edge of the swift-moving River Eye. From its well-marked beginning in Upper Slaughter's central car park, the path passes sheep grazing in meadows, antique houses crafted from honey-colored local stone, stately trees arching over ancient millponds, and footbridges that have endured centuries of foot traffic and rain.

The rushing river powers a historic mill on the northwestern edge of Lower Slaughter. In quiet eddies, you'll see ample numbers of waterfowl and birds, including wild ducks, gray wagtails, mute swans, coots, and Canadian geese.

Most visitors turn around at Lower Slaughter, but for the more adventurous, Warden's Way continues another 1¹/₂ miles to Bourton-on-the-Water by following the Fosse Way, route of an ancient Roman footpath. The path leaves the river's edge and strikes out across cattle pastures in a southerly direction. Most of the path from Lower Slaughter to Bourton-on-the-Water is covered by tarmac; it's closed to motor traffic, but ideal for trekkers or cyclists. You're legally required to close each of the several gates that stretch across the footpath.

Warden's Way will introduce you to Bourton-on-the-Water through the hamlet's northern edges. The first landmark you'll see will be the tower of St. Lawrence's Anglican Church. From the base of the church, walk south along The Avenue (one of the hamlet's main streets) and end your Cotswold ramble on the Village Green, directly in front of the War Memorial.

You can follow this route in reverse, but parking is more plentiful in Upper Slaughter than in Lower Slaughter.

**The Limes.** Evesham Rd., Stow-on-the-Wold, Gloucestershire GL54 1EJ. ☎ **01451/830-034.** 4 rms, 3 with bath (shower). TV. £34 ($54.40) double without bath, £39 ($62.40) double with bath. All rates include English breakfast. No credit cards.

This Victorian building of character is along A424 (Evesham Road), about a 4-minute walk from the heart of this famed Cotswold village. It has a lovely garden, and in chilly weather log fires make it warm and inviting. The bedrooms—all doubles—have washbasins and hot and cold running water, TV, and beverage-making equipment; one has a four-poster bed. The amenities are there, but it's still rather plain. The owners, Mr. and Mrs. Keyte, personally supervise the operation of The Limes, and cater to vegetarians.

**The Royalist Hotel.** Digbeth St., Stow-on-the-Wold, Gloucestershire GL54 1BN. ☎ **01451/830670.** 12 rms, all with bath. TV TEL. £40 ($64) single Sun–Thurs, £45 ($72) single Fri–Sat; £50–£75 ($80–$120) double Sun–Thurs, £60–£85 ($96–$136) double Fri–Sat. All rates include English breakfast. AE, MC, V.

Dating from A.D. 947, (you might want to read that again!) The Royalist Hotel is listed in the *Guinness Book of World Records* as the oldest inn in England. Over the centuries, the building has naturally passed through many hands; a number of clues to its long history still remain. Ask the proprietors to tell you about the ancient tunnels leading to the church and Maugersbury Manor or about the young John Shellard, who died in 1638 but, amazingly, is still a frequent visitor to the hotel's bar. The charm and character of the inn were not sacrificed when 20th-century comforts were added. Each room now has a private bathroom, independently controlled heating, and hot beverage-making facilities; rooms in a more modern annex lack the intrigue of the accommodations in the original building, of course.

**South Hill Farm House.** Fosseway, Stow-on-the-Wold, Gloucestershire GL54 1JU. ☎ **01451/ 831219.** Fax 01451/831554. 4 rms. TV. £38–£40 ($60.80–$64) double; £50–£60 ($80–$96) family rm. All rates include English breakfast. No credit cards.

This honey-colored stone Victorian farmhouse lies a quarter of a mile south of Stow along A429, on large grounds with plenty of parking. Shaun and Gaye Kenneally offer a high standard of traditional B&B accommodation and service. All the farmhouse-style rooms are centrally heated.

**West View.** Fosseway, Stow-on-the-Wold, Gloucestershire GL54 1DW. ☎ **01451/830492.** 3 rms, none with bath. TV. £13 ($20.80) single; £27 ($43.20) double; £32 ($51.20) family rm. All rates include English breakfast. No credit cards.

Nancy White, a gracious hostess, has furnished the place attractively, in part with antiques. The bedrooms all have hot and cold running water, tea and coffee facilities, and TVs. The shared bathroom has a shower with plenty of hot and cold running water. The location is about a 3-minute walk from the center of Stow.

**The White Hart.** The Square, Stow-on-the-Wold, Gloucestershire GL54 1AF. ☎ **01451/ 830674.** 8 rms, 5 with bath. TV. £17–£24 ($27.20–$38.40) single without bath, £22–£28 ($35.20–$44.80) single with bath; £34–£38 ($54.40–$60.80) double without bath, £44–£46 ($70.40–$73.60) double with bath. All rates include English breakfast. AE, DC, MC, V.

This limestone-fronted building is on the main square of town. You register at the bar of the street-level pub, which is laden with brass accents and open fireplaces. Since 1698 this has been a thriving coaching inn, welcoming wayfarers from all over the world. There is a healthy respect for the traditional around here, and the place has a mellow period atmosphere, with its uneven floors and low doorways. All the rather basic guest rooms have coffee-making equipment. The food, such as steak-and-kidney pie and grilled local trout, and especially the steak, is good but simple. Meals cost £3 to £13 ($4.80 to $20.80).

## WHERE TO EAT

**The Old Stocks Hotel.** The Square, Stow-on-the-Wold. ☎ **01451/830666.** Lunch platters in bar £3–£6.25 ($4.80–$10); fixed-price dinners £9.99–£16.25 ($16–$26). MC, V. Daily noon–2pm. BRITISH.

The food served in this restaurant is as straightforward, old-fashioned, and British as the simple hotel it is housed in. The woodsy, dark-stained setting fills most of the ground floor of Stow's most visible and cost-conscious hotel, a previously recommended stone-fronted building facing the stocks (site of public punishments and humiliations) of the village green. At lunchtime, you'll place your food order at the battered bar, and someone will carry the finished product to your table. At night, the venue is more formal, and somewhat more expensive, with staff members duplicating some of the ambience (and certainly the cuisine) of an unpretentious cuisine reminiscent of the Edwardian Age. Don't expect fancy sauces or garnishes here. Menu items include steak-and-kidney pie; grilled or pan-fried trout served simply—just with lemon juice; plain grilled Dover sole with seasonal vegetables; chicken supreme; and grilled steaks with potatoes and vegetables.

**Prince of India.** 5 Park St., Stow-on-the-Wold. ☎ **01451/831198.** Reservations recommended. Main courses £3.75–£12.50 ($6–$20). AE, MC, V. Daily noon–2:30pm and 6–11:30pm. INDIAN.

The cuisine here features spices skillfully used in a wide range of dishes. If you have a brave palate, try the meat vindaloo, but you can also order less tongue-wilting fare, including tandoori chicken or hot-and-sour prawns Madras. Leavened bread is served, and there are many vegetarian dishes. A savory beginning is the lentil soup. The restaurant is a short walk from the town center, near the bus stop.

**The Queen's Head.** The Square, Stow-on-the-Wold. ☎ **01451/830563.** Reservations not accepted. Main courses £3–£7 ($4.80–$11.20). MC, V. Mon–Sat noon–2pm and Tues–Sat 6:30–9pm. BRITISH.

Set on the town's main square, this is the oldest and one of the most centrally located pubs in town. Amid the rich patina of generations of spilled beer and tobacco smoke, you'll find a pair of bars, many exuberant local residents, at least three kinds of beer on tap, including Carlsberg lager and an ale brewed within a few miles of Stow called Donnington's, and platters of traditional, well-seasoned food. Place your food order at the bar, and someone will carry it to your table. Platters are likely to include steak-and-kidney pie, duck in orange sauce, platters of pâté with lettuce and pickles, lasagna, and chicken-and-leek pie. The pub stays open till 11pm Monday to Saturday, till 10:30pm on Sunday, and it's closed every day between 2:30 and 6pm.

## 8  Moreton-in-Marsh

83 miles NW of London; 4 miles N of Stow-on-the-Wold; 7 miles S of Chipping Campden; 17 miles S of Stratford-upon-Avon

Near many other villages of interest, Moreton-in-Marsh is an important center for rail passengers headed for the Cotswolds. Don't take the name "Moreton-in-Marsh" too literally, since "Marsh" derives from an old word meaning "border." Look for the 17th-century market hall and the old curfew tower, then walk down the shop-flanked High (the main street), where Roman legions trudged centuries ago along the Fosse Way.

## ESSENTIALS

**GETTING THERE**   British Rail provides daily service from London's Paddington Station to Moreton-in-Marsh, a nearly 2-hour trip. For schedules and information, call ☎ **0345/484950.**

National Express buses run from London's Victoria Coach Station to Moreton-in-Marsh daily. For schedules and information, call ☎ **0990/808080.**

If driving from Stow-on-the-Wold (see above), take A429 north.

**VISITOR INFORMATION**   The nearest tourist office is at Stow-on-the-Wold (see above).

## SEEING THE SIGHTS

For a fascinating lesson on birds of prey, stop by the **Cotswold Falconry Centre,** Batsford Park (☎ **01386/701043**). These great birds are flown daily by experienced falconers for visitors to see first hand the remarkable speed and agility of eagles, hawks, owls, and falcons. The center also has a falconry museum and breeding pairs of birds.

Open daily from 10:30am to 5:30pm. Flying displays are daily at 11:30am, 1:30pm, 3pm, and 4:30pm. Admission is £3 ($4.80) for adults and £1.50 ($2.40) for children 4 to 16. Free for children 3 and under.

Touted as a Cotswold farm with a difference, **Sleepy Hollow Farm Park,** 32 Sleepy Hollow Farm Park (☎ **01386/701264**), is a great place for children and adults to explore. This plot of land is the home of many rare and unusual farm animals that coexist with an array of interesting wild animals, including a family of otters and ever-curious raccoons. The animals, with noticeably distinct personalities, will win your heart. Admission is £2.70 ($4.30) for adults, £1.95 ($3.10) for seniors, and £1.40 ($2.25) for children (free 2 and under). It is open March through October, daily from 9am to 5pm.

# WHERE TO STAY
## DOUBLES FOR LESS THAN £45

✪ **Blue Cedar House.** Stow Rd., Moreton-in-Marsh, Gloucestershire GL56 0DW. ☎ **01608/ 650299.** 5 rms, 2 with bath. TV. £36 ($57.60) double without bath, £40 ($64) double with bath only. All rates include English breakfast. No credit cards. Closed Dec–Jan.

Named after an enormous tree in the front yard, this brown brick house was erected in 1952 on the edge of the village center along A429. It's owned and operated by Sandra and Graham Billinger, who offer comfortable bedrooms—all doubles or twins—plus a TV lounge. The house stands on half an acre of land with a fish pond, and is within a 10-minute walk of the rail station. Dinner costs £8.50 ($13.60). Tea and coffee facilities are provided in the guest rooms as well as in the lounge. Hair dryers, TVs, and radios are also in the bedrooms.

**The Cottage.** Oxford St., Moreton-in-Marsh, Gloucestershire GL56 0LA. ☎ **01608/651740.** 1 cottage with bath, 2 rms without bath. TV. £42 ($67.20) single or double occupancy of the cottage; £30 ($48) single without bath; £36 ($57.60) double without bath. All rates include English breakfast. No credit cards. Closed Jan 15–Feb 15.

This house, along with the cottage that lies behind it, was originally built of Cotswold stone more than 400 years ago, and as such, is the oldest surviving residence in Moreton-in-Marsh. Originally the home and workshop of the settlement's wheelwright (i.e., maker of wheels), it's the sedate and ever-so-polite domain of Lorraine and Richard Carter, who outfit their premises with many accoutrements common to a long-ago elegant country life. The most charming of the three accommodations is the cramped but cozy independent cottage ("The Peter Rabbit Cottage"). The other pair of rooms shares a communal bathroom. This place has been praised by many readers of this guide for its calm, comfort, and careful maintenance.

**Moreton House Guest House.** High St., Moreton-in-Marsh, Gloucestershire GL56 0LQ. ☎ **01608/650747.** Fax 01608/652747. 11 rms, 7 with bath. TV. £22 ($35.20) single without bath; £42 ($67.20) double without bath; £46 ($73.60) double with bath. All rates include English breakfast. MC, V.

On the main street, this is the most desirable budget accommodation in the center of this popular Cotswold village. A mellow old house with a Tudor facade of honey-colored sandstone, it has an attractive tearoom on street level, where you register at a small reception desk. Evening meals are served nightly from 6:30 to 8:30pm, costing £9.50 ($15.20). The house is at the junction of A429 and A44. Coffee- and tea-making facilities are in each room, and hair dryers and irons are available upon request.

**New Farm.** Dorn, Moreton-in-Marsh, Gloucestershire GL56 9NS. ☎ **01608/650782.** 3 rms, all with bath. TV. £16–£17 ($25.60–$27.20) per person. All rates include English breakfast. No credit cards.

Catherine Righton accepts guests at this B&B, which is a mile north of Moreton-in-Marsh, just off A429. The farmhouse was built in the 1790s of Cotswold stone. The house has a large and impressive fireplace in the dining room where guests enjoy breakfast served with hot crispy bread. All rooms are spacious and have private bath, color TV, and beverage-making equipment. Hair dryers and irons are available upon request. Many rooms contain antiques.

**Treetops.** London Rd., Moreton-in-Marsh, Gloucestershire GL56 0HE. ☎ **01608/651036.** 6 rms. TV. £30 ($48) single; £42 ($67.20) double. All rates include English breakfast. MC, V.

Treetops dates from 1983, when Brian and Elizabeth Dean realized their dream of designing and building their own house. Though not a tree fort, their home stands amid fir and beech trees in almost an acre of garden, about a 5-minute stroll from the heart of Moreton-in-Marsh. Its driveway is identified with a sign visible from the main A44 highway. Each room contains coffee- and tea-making facilities. A simple three-course dinner is served at 7pm sharp for £10 ($16).

# WHERE TO EAT

**The Black Bear.** High St., Moreton-in-Marsh. ☎ **01608/650705.** Main courses £4–£6 ($6.40–$9.60). AE, DC, MC, V. Daily noon–2:15pm and 6:30–9:30pm. BRITISH.

It isn't the oldest pub in town (that honor goes to the White Hart, a few steps away), but its regular clients claim that it serves the best food and is, at its best, the most fun. The 17th-century setting includes exposed stone, heavy beams, and paneling that reveals the patina of many generations of cigarette smoke and spilled beer. At lunch, you'll place your food order at the bar; at dinner, someone will come to your table to note what it is you'd like. Menu items include the usual roster of lasagna, steak-and-kidney pie, and ploughman's lunches, although there's usually a limited number of dishes (duck breast in orange and brandy sauce, or peppercorn-encrusted steaks) that raise the cuisine beyond the usual pub grub. There's a wide roster of lagers and stouts on tap, including a local bitter (Donnington) brewed within a few miles of the place. As regards coffee and drinks, the place is open daily from 10am to midnight.

**Inn on the Marsh.** Stow Rd. (Hwy. A492), Moreton-in-Marsh. ☎ **01608/650709.** Main courses £4.25–£7.50 ($6.80–$12). MC, V. Daily noon–2pm and Tues–Sun 7–9pm. BRITISH.

This is the most substantial and well-rounded of the cost-conscious restaurants in town. It has made significant improvements recently thanks to its recent acquisition by Irish-born Richard Patrick Prince and his wife Catherine. It's the last pub on the road headed south of town, about a half-mile from the center. The setting is a chronological hodgepodge that includes an Elizabethan "boozer," (site of today's bar area, lined with turn-of-the-century photos of the nearby marshes before they were drained), and a *faux* Edwardian conservatory, added in 1991, where most sit-down meals are served. Menu items are very good value and include chicken-and-mushroom pie, deep-fried scampi or plaice, char-broiled chicken, lamb with mint sauce, pork with apple sauce, and an 8-ounce rumpsteak. Everything is served with chips or roasted potatoes and vegetables. Naturally, no one will mind if you preface or follow your meal with a round of drinks in the pub.

**Market House.** 4 High St., Moreton-in-Marsh, ☎ **01608/650767.** Reservations recommended for large parties. Main courses £3–£9.50 ($4.80–$15.20). No credit cards. June–Sept Mon–Sat 9am–5pm; Sun 11am–5pm. Oct–May Mon–Sat 9am–4:30pm; Sun 11am–4:30pm. ENGLISH.

Set behind a prominent bow window and a facade of Cotswold stone, this 1590s building provides a tearoom-style setting that's ideal for morning coffee, a flavorful lunch, or a reasonably priced early supper. You can enjoy relatively simple dishes that include prawn cocktails or soups, steaks, or chicken Kiev, fried plaice, haddock, or cod, followed by a piece of moist cake or some other dessert. Sandwiches and fresh salads are also served. In fair weather, a patio is opened. Market House is on the town's main street, a few paces from the Town Hall.

## 9  Broadway

15 miles SW of Stratford-upon-Avon; 93 miles NW of London; 15 miles NE of Cheltenham

Although the most overrun and tourist-trodden town of the Cotswolds, Broadway is also one of the most beautiful—hence its enduring popularity. Many of the prime attractions of the Cotswolds, as well as Shakespeare country, lie within easy reach of Broadway, which is near Evesham at the southern tip of Hereford and Worcester. Overlooking the Vale of Evesham, it's a major stopover for bus tours and is positively mobbed in summer; however, it manages to retain its charm in spite of the annual invasion. Broadway has a wide and beautiful High Street flanked with honey-colored stone buildings, remarkable for their harmony of style and design.

## ESSENTIALS

**GETTING THERE**   Rail connections are possible from London's Paddington Station via Oxford. The nearest railway stations are at Moreton-in-Marsh (7 miles away) or at Evesham (5 miles away). For schedules and information, call ☎ **0345/484950.** Frequent buses arrive from Evesham, but one has to take a taxi from Moreton.

One bus departs daily from London's Victoria Coach Station to Broadway, a 2¹/₂-hour ride. For schedules and information, call ☎ **0990/808080.**

If driving from Oxford, head west on A40, then A434 to Woodstock, Chipping Norton, and Moreton-in-Marsh.

**VISITOR INFORMATION**   The **Tourist Information Centre** is at 1 Cotswold Court (☎ **01386/852937**). Open March through December, Monday to Saturday from 10am to 1pm and 2 to 5pm.

## EXPLORING BROADWAY

Henry James once wrote, "The place has so much character that it rubs off on the visitor . . . it is delicious to be at Broadway." Too many visitors may have heeded the words of this author, as Broadway today is overrun with summer tourists and tour buses. It's the most visited town in the Cotswolds, and with good reason.

Its **High Street** or main street is one of the most beautiful in England—perhaps the most beautiful, as William Morris or J. M. Barrie might testify if they were still around. Many of its most striking facades date from 1620 to the early 1800s. The most famous is that of the **Lyon Arms,** High Street (☎ **01386/852255**), a venerated old inn. On its own 3 acres of formal gardens, it's been serving way farers since 1532. Even if you're not staying here, you might want to visit for a meal or a drink.

Also along the street you can visit the **Broadway Teddy Bear Museum,** 76 High St. (☎ **01386/858323**), a showcase shop for teddy bear and doll artisans. The site is also the setting for a unique museum displaying hundreds of antique and collectors' teddy bears, toys, and dolls. This 18th-century stone shop is an ideal setting for a historical look at the world of teddy bears, ranging from Steiff through Hermann and all the way up to such long-time favorites as Pooh, Paddington, and Rupert. Bears from all leading manufacturers are also for sale. Hours are from mid-March to mid-November, daily from 9am to 6pm; off-season, daily from 10am to 5pm. Admission is £1.50 ($2.40) for adults and £1 ($1.60) for children under 14 and seniors.

On the outskirts of Broadway stands **The Broadway Tower Country Park** on Broadway Hill (☎ **01386/852390**), a "folly" created by the fanciful mind of the sixth earl of Coventry. Today, you can climb this tower for a panoramic vista of 12 shires, at least on a clear day. It's the most sweeping view in the Cotswolds, having earned the praise of William Morris and his Pre-Raphaelite friend, Dante Gabriel Rossetti. At the time of its construction, the tower was denounced as a "superfluous attempt to gild the lily," meaning the Cotswold scenery was beautiful enough without further adornment. The tower is open from early April to late October, daily from 10am to 6pm. Admission is £2.95 ($4.70) for adults and £1.95 ($3.10) for children. There's also a family ticket costing £7.95 ($12.70). Also on site is a 150-year-old barn with exhibits relating to the area's geology. You can also bring the makings for a picnic here and spread out your lunch in designated areas.

You might also seek out **St. Eadurgha's Church,** a place of Christian worship for more that 1,000 years. It's located just outside Broadway on Snowshill Road and is open most days, though with no set visiting hours. If it's closed at the time of your visit, a note on the porch door will tell you what house to go to for the key. There are only occasional Sunday services here.

South of Broadway, a final attraction is **Snowshill Manor,** at Snowshill (☎ **01386/852410**), a house which dates mainly from the 17th century. The house was once owned by the eccentric Charles Paget Wade, who collected virtually everything he could between 1900 and 1951. Queen Mary once remarked that Wade himself was the most remarkable artifact among his entire flea market. There's a little bit of everything here: Flemish tapestries, toys, lacquer cabinets, narwhal tusks, mousetraps, and cuckoo clocks—in other words, a glorious mess, almost a giant attic of the 20th century. Wade used to live in an adjoining building without electricity. The property, now owned by the National Trust, is open October through April, Wednesday to Monday from 1 to 5pm; May through September, Wednesday to Monday from 1 to 6pm. Admission is £5.20 ($8.30) or £13 ($20.80) for a family ticket. On the grounds is a restaurant and shop.

## TEATIME

The best place in Broadway for a cup of tea is **Tisanes,** The Green (☎ **01386/ 852112**). The shop offers perfectly blended teas with a variety of light food choices, such as sandwiches and salads. Sweet offerings include fruit tarts, baked cheesecake, and several types of cake. Basic teas are priced from £3 ($4.80). Tisanes also sells tea accessories, including teapots, china, and of course, a wide variety of specialty teas.

## WHERE TO STAY
### DOUBLES FOR LESS THAN £45

**East Bank.** Station Dr., Broadway, Hereford and Worcester WR12 7DF. ☎ **01386/852659.** 6 rms. TV. £38–£50 ($60.80–$80) double; £60–£80 ($96–$128) family room. All rates include English breakfast. No credit cards.

The stone house where Anne and Ken Evans receive B&B guests is a bargain for Broadway, in a tranquil location off A44, about a 12-minute walk from the village center. There's unlimited parking on the grounds of the house and on the approach drive. The house is centrally heated, but in addition a log fire blazes in the guest lounge during cooler weather.

**Pennylands.** Evesham Rd., Broadway, Hereford and Worcester WR12 7DG. ☎ **01386/ 858437.** 3 rms. TV. £37 ($59.20) double. All rates include English breakfast. No credit cards.

This is a former private home, built in Edwardian times, but now receiving B&B guests in its comfortably furnished rooms, all doubles. It lies on the outskirts of Broadway, a mile from the center, and can be a base for touring the historic village and also the Cotswolds. Josephine and John Brazier, the owners, will help you plan day outings. Tea and coffee facilities and chocolate and fresh milk are available in each room, and hair dryers and irons are available upon request.

**Southwold House.** Station Rd., Broadway, Hereford and Worcester WR12 7DE. ☎ **01386/853681.** Fax 01386/858653. 7 rms, 5 with shower only. TV. £17 ($27.20) single without bath, £34 ($54.40) single with shower only; £34 ($54.40) double without bath, £44 ($70.40) double with shower only. All rates include English breakfast. MC, V. Free parking (limited).

Built as a private home in Edwardian times (1910), now Southwold House welcomes B&B guests all year. It's about 5 minutes from the heart of the village along A44. Your hosts, Daphne and Glyn Price, offer a warm welcome, comfortable bedrooms, friendly service, and advice about where to locate a range of pub and restaurant food. Coffee- and tea-making equipment is available in each room. Hair dryers and irons are available upon request.

✪ **Whiteacres.** Station Rd., Broadway, Hereford and Worcester WR12 7DE. ☎ **01386/852320.** 6 rms. TV. £38–£42 ($60.80–$67.20) double. All rates include English breakfast. No credit cards. Closed Nov–Feb.

One of the best and most charming B&Bs in this high-priced town, Whiteacres occupies an unpretentious Victorian house on the southern extension of High Street, a 5-minute walk from the center. Owned and operated by Helen and Alan Richardson, its bedrooms, all doubles, are pretty and very comfortable. Its public rooms are cozy, with white walls adorned with porcelain that was either collected or inherited by the congenial owners. Three rooms contain four-poster beds. Tea- or coffee-making equipment and hair dryers are found in each room.

## DOUBLES FOR LESS THAN £55

**The Crown and Trumpet.** Church St., Broadway, Hereford and Worcester WR12 7AE. ☎ **01386/853202.** Fax 01386/853874. 5 rms, all with shower only. TV. £47–£50 ($75.20–$80) double. All rates include English breakfast. No credit cards.

Better known in Broadway as a public house than as a hotel, this 16th-century inn nonetheless offers a handful of simple upstairs double bedrooms to visitors passing through. Coffee- or tea-making facilities are in all rooms, and hair dryers and irons are available upon request. Set behind a facade of honey-colored Cotswold stone, the pub serves snacks throughout the day priced at £3.50 to £7 ($5.60 to $11.20) each. The pub is open Sunday to Friday from 11am to 3pm and 6 to 11pm, and on Saturday from 11am to 11pm. Dinners begin at £3.50 to £10 ($5.60 to $16). It's located just behind the town's village green.

**Olive Branch Guest House.** 78–80 High St., Broadway, Hereford and Worcester WR12 7AJ. ☎ and fax **01386/853440.** 8 rms, 6 with bath (tub or shower). TV. £19.50 ($31.20) single without bath; £45–£48 ($72–$76.80) double with bath. All rates include English breakfast. AE, MC.

In the heart of an expensive village, this budget oasis is managed by Mark Riley. The house, dating back to the 16th century, retains its old Cotswold architectural features. Behind the house is a large walled English garden and parking area. Guests are given a discount for purchases at the owners' attached antique shop. Tea and coffee facilities are in each room. Hair dryers and irons are available upon request. Furnishings are basics, but comfortable.

**Pathlow House.** 82 High St., Broadway, Hereford and Worcester WR12 7AJ. ☎ **01386/ 853444.** 5 rms, all with bath; 1 family cottage. TV. £42–£46 ($67.20–$73.60) double; £80 ($128) cottage. All rates include English breakfast. No credit cards.

The rates are quite reasonable considering the location, right in the heart of the village. From spring to autumn, guests from around the world are received here. Rooms are available in the house as well as in a small cottage in the courtyard. Each unit is a double and is plainly furnished. The house, run by Des and Iris Porter, is centrally heated and all bedrooms have hot-beverage facilities.

## WHERE TO EAT

**Broadway Hotel.** The Green. ☎ **01386/852401.** Fixed-price lunch £9.95 ($15.90) for 2 courses, £10.95 ($17.50) for 3 courses; fixed-price dinner £17.95 ($28.70). AE, MC, V. Daily noon–2pm and 7–9pm. ENGLISH.

Even the locals agree that this hotel bar is the best low-cost lunch stop in Broadway. Lunches are always served at the bar, where you can place your order for one of the platters of the day. Dinner, however, is served in the more formal dining room in this centrally located place, right on the village green. Formerly used by the abbots of Pershore, the building combines the half-timbered look of the Vale of Evesham with the stone of the Cotswolds. Traditional English food is featured, including fresh fish, duckling, and (in season) venison. The ingredients are generally good, and most dishes seem to satisfy.

✪ **Goblets Wine Bar.** High St. ☎ **01386/853568.** Main courses £6.50–£8.50 ($10.40–$13.60). AE, DC, MC, V. Mon–Sat noon–2pm and 6–9:30pm; Sun noon–2pm and 7–9:30pm. ENGLISH.

With black-and-white timbered walls, this 17th-century inn built of Cotswold stone and filled with antiques is frequented by Broadway locals and tourists. Additions to the menu, changed every season, are marked on the chalkboard, and orders should be placed at the bar. The limited but tasty menu begins with such appetizers as duck pâté with toasted onion bread and goes on to such daily specials as Cotswold lamb and apricot casserole. About four desserts appear daily, including, for example, a hot gingerbread pudding. The coffee is good, and the atmosphere is warm. The inn is next to the Lygon Arms, a historic inn which owns the wine bar.

## 10  Chipping Campden

36 miles NW of Oxford; 12 miles S of Stratford-upon-Avon; 93 miles NW of London

Regardless of how often they visit the Cotswolds, the English are attracted in droves to this town, once an important wool center. Off the main road, it's easily accessible to major points of interest, and double-decker buses frequently run through here on their way to Oxford or Stratford-upon-Avon.

A Saxon settlement on the northern edge of the Cotswolds above the Vale of Evesham, Campden was recorded in the *Domesday Book*. In medieval times, rich merchants built homes of Cotswold stone along its model High Street, described by historian G. M. Trevelyan as "the most beautiful village street now left in the island." Today the houses have been so well preserved that Chipping Campden remains a gem of the Middle Ages. Its church dates from the 15th century, and its old market hall is the loveliest in the Cotswolds. Look also for its alms-houses, which, along with the market hall, were built by a great wool merchant, Sir Baptist Hicks, whose tomb is in the church.

# ESSENTIALS

**GETTING THERE**    Trains depart from London's Paddington Station for Moreton-in-Marsh, a 1¹/₂ to 2 hour trip. For schedules and information, call ☎ **0345/484950.** A bus operated by Castleway's travels the 7 miles from Moreton-in-Marsh to Chipping Campden five times a day. Many visitors opt for a taxi from Moreton-in-Marsh to Chipping Campden.

The largest and most important nearby bus depot is Cheltenham, which receives service several times a day from London's Victoria Coach Station. For schedules and information, call ☎ **0990/808080.** From Cheltenham, Barry's Coaches are infrequent and uncertain, departing at the most three times per week.

If you're driving from Oxford, take A40 west to the junction with A424. Follow it northwest, passing by Stow-on-the-Wold. The route becomes A44 until you reach the junction with B4081, which you take northeast to Chipping Campden.

**VISITOR INFORMATION**    The summer-only **Tourist Information Centre** is at Noel Court, High Street (☎ **01386/841206**). Open daily from 10am to 5pm.

# ✪ HIDCOTE MANOR GARDEN

The year 1907 was a momentous time in the life of the American horticulturalist Major Lawrence Johnstone; he created the treasure of Hidcote Manor Garden, 4 miles northeast of Chipping Campden and 9 miles south of Stratford-upon-Avon (☎ **01386/438333**). Set on 10 acres, this masterpiece is composed of small gardens, or rooms, separated by a variety of hedges, old roses, rare shrubs, trees, and herbaceous borders. The garden opens April through September, Monday, Wednesday, Thursday, and Saturday and Sunday from 11am to 7pm. October weekend hours are 11am to 6pm. In June and July, it is also opened on Tuesday from 11am to 7pm. Last admission is either at 6pm or 1 hour before sunset. Admission is £5.20 ($8.30).

In summer, Shakespeare's plays are performed on the Theatre Lawn; there is truly no more memorable experience in the Cotswolds than watching *A Midsummer's Night Dream* performed here on a balmy evening in July.

# SHOPPING

For most of his life, the poet, artist, and craftsman William Morris (1834 to 1896) called the Cotswold countryside home. The talent and dedication of this "dreamer of dreams" had an enormous impact on the artisans of his day. And, as destiny would have it, Morris became a leader of the arts and crafts movement that flourished from 1850 to 1920. The movement quickly spread to Europe and North America. Today, his legacy continues to inspire artists and craftspeople in this area.

At the studio of **D. T. Hart,** The Guild, The Silk Mill, Sheep Street (☎ **01386/841100**), silver is expertly smithed by descendants of George Hart, an original member of the Guild of Handicraft, in the original Ashbee workshop. **Robert Welch Studio Shop,** Lower High Street (☎ **01386/840522**), is where Robert Welch has been crafting silverware, stainless steel, and cutlery for more than 40 years. **Ann Smith,** Peacock House (☎ **01386/840879**), creates high-quality, handcrafted 18-carat gold jewelry along with enamel and gem work. **Martin Gotrel,** The Square (☎ **01386/841360**), designs and makes fine contemporary and traditional jewelry.

**Campden Needlecraft Centre,** High St. (☎ **01386/840583**), is widely known as one of the leading specialist embroidery shops in England with an interesting selection of embroidery and canvaswork as well as fabrics and threads.

If antiques and antique hunting are your passion, visit **School House Antiques,** High Street (☎ **01386/841474**), or **The Barn Antiques Centre,** Long Marston on the Stratford-upon-Avon Road (☎ **01789/721399**). For new, secondhand, and antiquarian books, look up **Campden Bookshop,** High Street (☎ **01386/840944**), or **Draycott Books,** 1 Sheep St. (☎ **01386/841392**).

# WHERE TO STAY

**Marnic House.** Broad Campden, Chipping Campden, Gloucestershire GL55 6UR. ☎ **01386/ 840014.** 3 rms. TV. £30 ($48) single; £42 ($67.20) double. All rates include English breakfast. No credit cards.

This house, in the agrarian hamlet of Broad Campden, about a mile north of Chipping Campden's center, was built of Cotswold stone around 1913. It's set on a country lane with similar houses on either side, and views over fields and grazing sheep in front and back. The house is surrounded by a rock garden and outdoor terrace, which provide places to sit during warm weather. Owners Janet and Roy Rawlings named their place after an anagram taken from the names of their two children, Mark and Nicola. No meals other than breakfast are served, although the village pub, a short walk away, serves well-prepared food. The bedrooms are comfortable, and each has tea-making facilities.

**Orchard Hill House.** Broad Campden, near Chipping Campden, Gloucestershire GL55 6UU. ☎ **01386/841473.** Fax 01386/841030. 4 rms, 3 with bath. TV. £44 ($70.40) single without bath; £47–£56 ($75.20–$89.60) double with bath. All rates include English breakfast. No credit cards. Closed Christmas.

Located in a village on the outskirts of Chipping Campden, this hotel is a beautifully restored 17th-century farmhouse, with two bedrooms in the main house, and two private-entrance bedrooms in a converted barn, which also houses a lounge and dining room. There is no smoking. A pub within walking distance serves evening meals. The English breakfast is the highlight of the stay here. It's served at an old-fashioned wooden farmhouse table in a dining hall paved with flagstones and including an inglenook fireplace.

**Sandalwood House.** Back-Ends, Chipping Campden, Gloucestershire GL55 6AU. ☎ **01386/ 840091.** 2 rms. £23–£25 ($36.80–$40) single; £44 ($70.40) double. All rates include English breakfast. No credit cards. Turn right off High St. at the Roman Catholic church, and walk for about 3 minutes.

Peacefully situated in a garden just south of the town center, this house was built in traditional tile-roofed Cotswold style in the early 1970s. The two rentable bedrooms are spotless, large, and airy, with comfortable beds, washbasins, and hot-beverage facilities. Diana Bendall, the hostess, has two dining rooms where you have a choice of dishes, which you'll select from a breakfast menu. Every evening Mrs. Bendall serves hot drinks at 9:30pm in the cozy lounge. Sandalwood House accepts non-smokers only. In writing for information, return postage is appreciated.

# WHERE TO EAT

**The Bantam Tea Room.** High St. ☎ **01386/840386.** Main courses £2.90–£4.90 ($4.65–$7.85); cream tea £2.90 ($4.65). No credit cards. Tea Mon–Sat 9:30am–5:15pm, Sun 3–5pm; lunch daily noon–2pm. Closed Mon late Oct to early July. ENGLISH.

Opposite the historic market hall is a bow-windowed, 17th-century stone house where old-fashioned English afternoon teas are served. Tea can be just a pot of the brew and a tea cake, or you can indulge in homemade scones, crumpets, sandwiches, and homemade pastries and cakes. Lunches are served, with a selection of local ham and salad, chicken pie, pâtés, omelets, and salads.

**Forbes Brasserie.** In the Cotswold House Hotel, The Square. ☎ **01386/840330.** Main courses £4.75–£11.50 ($7.60–$18.40). MC, V. Daily 9:30am–11pm. ENGLISH.

You eat a whole day's meals here. Mr. and Mrs. Forbes, who own and run Chipping Campden's most elegant hostelry, oversee a staff serving dishes that change with the seasons. Starters include a salad of roasted peppers in olive oil with green beans, herbs, and parmesan cheese and the "Forbes Cotswold Cup"—button mushrooms and cubes of blue cheese and bacon pieces under a puff pastry top. These can be followed by a selection of pasta, fish, and meat dishes—perhaps the mixed game and vegetable casserole or freshly made basil and garlic tagliatelle with smoked chicken, mushrooms, and a creamy herb sauce. A popular dessert is the homemade ice cream; there's always vanilla plus a selected flavor-of-the-day.

**Kings Arms.** The Square. ☎ **01386/840256.** Reservations recommended. Main courses £5.50–£7.50 ($8.80–$12); fixed-price lunch platter £5 ($8); fixed-price dinner £18 ($28.80). MC, V. Daily 6–9:30pm; Pub: noon–3pm and 6–9:30pm. ENGLISH/CONTINENTAL.

A full restaurant and pub are in the Kings Arms, one of the town's leading inns (rooms are beyond our budget). Even if you don't stay here, try to visit for the best bar snacks in Chipping Campden. You're likely to be tempted with artichokes and Stilton dressing, baked eggs, crab with Gruyère cheese and cream, fresh fillet of mackerel with a mustard-cream sauce, plus more prosaic soups and pâtés. Main dishes include such continental fare as roast duck in a piquant orange sauce, beef stroganoff, and fillet of pork Calvados. The kitchen at least tries to add zest and flavor to the food.

**The Vinery Restaurant.** In the Seymour House Hotel & Restaurant, High St. ☎ **01386/840429.** Reservations recommended. Fixed-price meal £14.50 ($23.20) at lunch, £19.75–£29.50 ($31.60–$47.20) at dinner. AE, MC, V. Mon–Sat 7–10pm; Sun noon–2:30pm and 7–10pm. ENGLISH/CONTINENTAL.

The Vinery, part of this previously recommended hotel, serves homemade pasta dishes and other delectable items. The chef's specialty is filetto al piatto, thin layers of Scottish beef cooked on an extremely hot plate with olive oil, rosemary, and garlic. A selection of fresh seasonal vegetables accompanies main courses. For dessert you might sample the crème brûlée. At the Malt House Bar, the other dining spot at the hotel, you can order simple lunches costing £2.50 to £10.50 ($4 to $16.80) and served daily from 11am to 3pm.

# Shakespeare Country & the Heart of England

Second only to London, Shakespeare Country—in the heart of England—is the district most visited by North Americans. Many don't recognize the county name, Warwickshire, but do know its foremost tourist town, Stratford-upon-Avon, birthplace of England's (and many would say the English language's) greatest writer, William Shakespeare.

The county and its neighboring shires are a land of industrial cities, green fields, and market towns dotted with buildings. Most of these structures obviously weren't here in Shakespeare's time, but a few were standing back when the Bard was born in Stratford-upon-Avon in 1564. They help make this one of the great meccas for writers, readers, and theatergoers from around the world.

Shakespeare's hometown is the best center for touring this part of England. You'll want to take in some theater while in Stratford-upon-Avon and branch out for day excursions—notably to Warwick Castle in nearby Warwick, to Kenilworth Castle, and to Coventry Cathedral.

But once you've seen the Shakespeare Country, you have the heart of England at your doorstep. You might start by visiting nearby Birmingham, England's second city. It is said that all roads in England lead here to this city now undergoing gentrification, although countless abandoned warehouses and bleak factories remain.

The heart of England is no longer filled with the "dark satanic mills" that William Blake saw when mines were, in the words of D. H. Lawrence "like black studs on the countryside linked by a loop of fine chain, the railway." Today you'll find many lovely old market towns and bucolic spots. Monuments, museums, scenery, and a good time await the visitor who'd like to seek out the more esoteric England found in such cities as Worcester (of Royal Worcester Porcelain fame), the scenic Malverns, or even the historic town of Shrewsbury. Pottery lovers flock to Stoke-on-Trent for a day or so visiting the fabled potteries.

## 1 Stratford-upon-Avon

91 miles NW of London; 40 miles NW of Oxford; 8 miles S of Warwick

Reams of tourists overrun this market town on the Avon River during the summer months. Stratford today aggressively hustles its

Shakespearean connection, a bit suffocatingly so, as everybody seems in business to make a buck off the Bard. If he could return today, Shakespeare could buy a Bard T-shirt, purchase a china model of Anne Hathaway's cottage, sample a Big Mac, and then look for a less trampled town to live out his final days. The throngs dwindle in winter, however, when you can at least walk on the streets and seek out the places of genuine historic interest.

Actor David Garrick really launched the shrine in 1769 when he organized the first of the playwright's commemorative birthday celebrations. Little is known about Shakespeare's early life, and many of the stories connected with his days in Stratford are largely fanciful, invented to amuse and entertain the vast number of literary fans who make the pilgrimage.

Another magnet for tourists today is the Royal Shakespeare Theatre, where Britain's foremost actors perform during a long season that lasts from early April until late January. Other than the theater, Stratford is pretty much devoid of any rich cultural life; you may want to rush back to London after you've seen the literary pilgrimage sights and a production of Hamlet. But Stratford-upon-Avon is also a good center for trips to Warwick Castle, Kenilworth Castle, and Coventry Cathedral (see below).

## ESSENTIALS

**GETTING THERE**   Amazingly, considering the demand, there are no direct trains from London. However, from London's Paddington Station you can take the train to Leamington Spa, where you can change trains for Stratford-upon-Avon. The journey takes about 3 hours, a round-trip ticket costing £20 ($32). For schedules and information, call ☎ **0345/484950.** The train station at Stratford is on Alcester Road (☎ **01203/555211**). On Sundays from October through May, it is closed, so you'll have to rely on the bus.

Eight National Express buses (☎ **0990/808080**) a day leave from London's Victoria Station, with a trip time of 3¼ hours. A single-day round-trip ticket costs £13.50 ($21.60) except Friday when the price is £16 ($25.60). For schedules and information, call ☎ **0990/808080.**

If you're driving from London, take the M40 toward Oxford and continue to Stratford-upon-Avon on A34.

**VISITOR INFORMATION**   The **Tourist Information Centre,** Bridgefoot, Stratford-upon-Avon, Warwickshire, CV37 6GW (☎ **01789/293127**), provides any details you might wish about the Shakespeare properties and will assist in booking rooms (see "Where to Stay," below). Open March to October, Monday to Saturday from 9am to 6pm, Sunday from 11am to 5pm; November to February, Monday to Saturday from 9am to 5pm.

To contact **Shakespeare Birthplace Trust,** which administers many of the attractions, send a self-addressed envelope and International Reply Coupon to the Director, the Shakespeare Centre, Henley Street, Stratford-upon-Avon, Warwickshire CV37 6QW (☎ **01789/204016**).

## ✪ THE ROYAL SHAKESPEARE THEATRE

On the banks of the Avon, the **Royal Shakespeare Theatre,** Waterside, Stratford-upon-Avon CV37 6BB (☎ **01789/295623**), is a major showcase for the Royal Shakespeare Company. Seating 1,500 patrons, the theater's season runs from November until September. The company has some of the finest actors on the British stage. In an average season, five Shakespearean plays are staged.

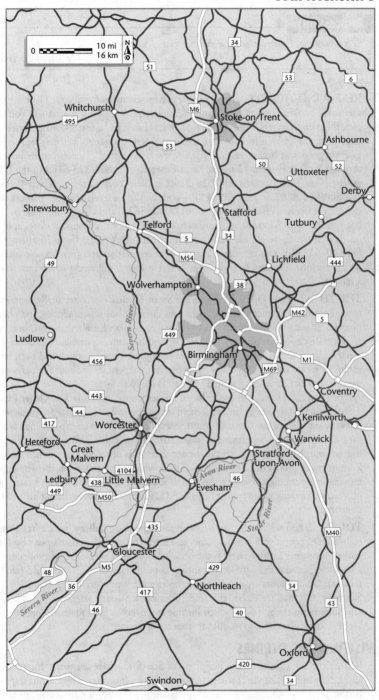

## Impressions

*It is something, I thought, to have seen the dust of Shakespeare.*

—Washington Irving

**RESERVING TICKETS**  You'll usually need reservations for tickets. There are two successive booking periods, each one opening about 2 months in advance. You can pick these up from a North American or an English travel agent. A small number of tickets are always held for sale on the day of a performance, but it may be too late to get a good seat if you wait until you arrive in Stratford. Tickets can be booked through New York agents **Edwards and Edwards** (☎ **800/223-6108** in the U.S., except New York City, or 914/328-2150 in New York City) or **Keith Prowse** (☎ **800/669-8687** or 212/398-1430)—both will add a service charge. You can also call the theater box office directly (☎ **01789/295623**) and charge your tickets. The box office is open Monday to Saturday from 9am to 8pm, although it closes at 6pm on days when there are no performances. Seat prices range from £6.50 to £46 ($10.40–$73.60). You can make a credit-card reservation and pick up your tickets on the performance day, but you must cancel at least 2 full weeks in advance to get a refund.

**THE THEATRES**  Opened in 1986, the **Swan Theatre** is architecturally connected to the back of its older counterpart and shares the same box office, address, and phone number. It seats 430 on three sides of the stage, as in an Elizabethan playhouse, an appropriate design for plays by Shakespeare and his contemporaries. The Swan was erected after a fire in 1926 destroyed The Memorial Theatre, which had been built in the Victorian style in 1879. The Swan presents a repertoire of about five plays each season, with tickets ranging from £9 to £30 ($14.40 to $48).

The most recent addition to the Royal Shakespeare complex is **The Other Place,** a small, starkly minimalist theater located on Southern Lane, about 300 yards from its better-established counterparts. It was redesigned in 1996 as an experimental work-shop theater without a permanent stage; seats can be radically repositioned (or re-moved completely) throughout the theater. Examples of recent productions include a "promenade production" of *Julius Caesar,* in which the actors spent the whole play moving freely among a stand-up audience. Tickets are sold at the complex's main box office and generally range from £12 to £18 ($19.20 to $28.80) each, but are subject to change.

**TOURS**  Based within the Swan Theatre is a **painting gallery,** which has a basic collection of portraits of famous actors and scenes from Shakespeare's plays by 18th and 19th century artists. There is the occasional small exhibition. It also operates as a base for guided tours with lively running commentary through the world-famous theaters. Guided tours are conducted at 1:30 and 5:30pm (excluding Thursday and Saturday, the matinee days), and four times every Sunday afternoon, production schedules permitting. Tours, which include stopovers at the souvenir shop, cost £4 ($6.40) for adults and £3 ($4.80) for students or seniors.

## VISITING THE SHRINES

Besides the attractions on the periphery of Stratford, there are many Elizabethan and Jacobean buildings in town; many of them are administered by the Shakespeare Birthplace Trust. One ticket—which costs £8.50 ($13.60) for adults, £7.50 ($12) for seniors and students, and £4 ($6.40) for children—lets you visit the five most

# Stratford–upon–Avon

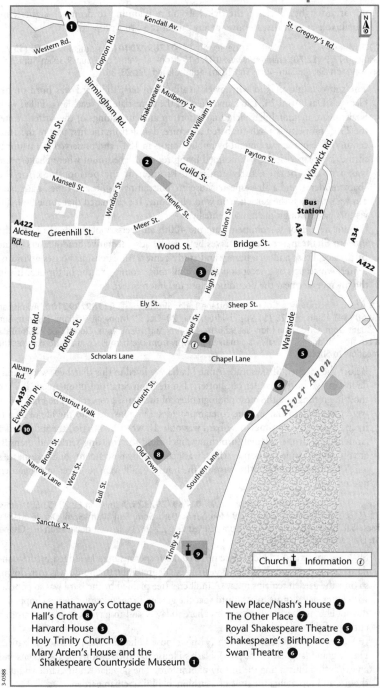

Church ✝  Information ⓘ

Anne Hathaway's Cottage ⑩
Hall's Croft ⑧
Harvard House ③
Holy Trinity Church ⑨
Mary Arden's House and the
    Shakespeare Countryside Museum ①

New Place/Nash's House ④
The Other Place ⑦
Royal Shakespeare Theatre ⑤
Shakespeare's Birthplace ②
Swan Theatre ⑥

3-0588

important sights. Pick up the ticket if you're planning to do much sightseeing (obtainable at your first stopover at any one of the Trust properties).

✪ **Shakespeare's Birthplace.** Henley St. ☎ **01789/204016.** Admission £3.60 ($5.75) adults; £1.70 ($2.70) children. Mar 20–Oct 19 Mon–Sat 9am–5pm; Sun 9:30am–5pm. Off-season Mon–Sat 9:30am–4pm; Sun 10am–4pm. Closed Dec 23–26.

The son of a glover and whittawer (leather worker), the Bard was born on St. George's Day, April 23, 1564, and died on the same date 52 years later. Filled with Shakespeare memorabilia, including a portrait and furnishings of the writer's time, the Trust property is a half-timbered structure, dating from the first part of the 16th century. The house was bought by public donors in 1847 and preserved as a national shrine. You can visit the oak-beamed living room, the bedroom where Shakespeare was probably born, a fully equipped kitchen of the period (look for the "babyminder"), and a Shakespeare Museum, illustrating his life and times. Later, you can walk through the garden. You won't be alone: It's estimated that some 660,000 visitors pass through the house annually.

Built next door to commemorate the 400th anniversary of the Bard's birth, the modern **Shakespeare Centre** serves both as the administrative headquarters of the Birthplace Trust and as a library and study center. An extension houses a visitors' center, which acts as a reception area for all those coming to the birthplace. It's in the town center near the post office close to Union Street.

✪ **Anne Hathaway's Cottage.** Cottage Lane, Shottery. ☎ **01789/292100.** Admission £2.50 ($4) adults; £1.20 ($1.90) children. Mar 20–Oct 19 Mon–Sat 9:30am–5:30pm; Sun 9:30am–5pm. Off-season Mon–Sat 9:30am–4:30pm; Sun 10am–4pm. Closed Dec 23–26. Take a bus from Bridge St. or walk via a marked pathway from Evesham Place in Stratford across the meadow to Shottery.

Before she married Shakespeare, Anne Hathaway lived in this thatched, wattle-and-daub cottage in the hamlet of Shottery 1 mile from Stratford-upon-Avon. It's the most interesting and the most photographed of the Trust properties. The Hathaways were yeoman farmers, and the cottage provides a rare insight into the life of a family in Shakespearean times. The Bard was only 18 when he married the much older Anne. Many of the original furnishings, including the courting settle and utensils, are preserved inside the house, which was occupied by descendants of Shakespeare's wife's family until 1892. After visiting the house, you'll want to linger in the garden and orchard.

**New Place/Nash's House.** Chapel St. ☎ **01789/292325.** Admission £2.20 ($3.50) adults; £1 ($1.60) children. Mar 20–Oct 19 Mon–Sat 9:30am–5pm; Sun 10am–5pm. Oct 20–Mar 19 Mon–Sat 10am–4pm; Sun 10:30–4pm. Closed Dec 23–26. Walk west down High St.; Chapel St. is a continuation of High St.

Shakespeare retired to New Place in 1610, a prosperous man as judged by the standards of his day, and died here 6 years later. Regrettably, the house was torn down, so only the garden remains today. A mulberry tree planted by the Bard was so popular with latter-day visitors to Stratford that the garden's cantankerous owner chopped it down. The mulberry tree that grows here today is said to have been planted from a cutting of the original tree.

You enter the gardens through Nash's House (Thomas Nash married Elizabeth Hall, a granddaughter of the poet). Nash's House has 16th-century period rooms and an exhibition illustrating the history of Stratford. The popular Knott Garden adjoins the site and represents the style of a fashionable Elizabethan garden.

## Impressions

*We love him [Shakespeare]. It's not even Oedipal anymore, or, let me say as a woman, Electral, for he's ceased being a father figure and has become the very source of our literary culture and language, at least if we are English-speaking. Love means we want him to be with us, and so we have to renew him, out of joy, pleasure and desire, every time we feel him slipping away.*

—Author Jane Smiley (1996)

**Mary Arden's House and the Shakespeare Countryside Museum.** Wilmcote. ☎ **01789/ 293455.** Admission £3.50 ($5.60) adults; £1.60 ($2.55) children. Mar 20–Oct 19 Mon–Sat 9:30am–5pm; Sun 10am–5pm. Off-season Mon–Sat 10am–4pm; Sun 10:30–4pm. Closed Dec 23–26. Take the A3400 (Birmingham) road for $3^1/_2$ miles.

Reputedly this Tudor farmstead, with its old stone dovecote and various outbuildings, was the girlhood home of Shakespeare's mother—or so claimed an 18th-century entrepreneur. There is no evidence to prove that she lived here, but the house contains country furniture and domestic utensils. In the barns, stable, cowshed, and farmyard, you'll find an extensive collection of farming implements illustrating life and work in the local countryside from Shakespeare's time to the present.

Visitors can also see the neighboring Glebe Farm, whose interior evokes farm life in late Victorian and Edwardian times. Light refreshments are available, and there is a picnic area.

**Hall's Croft.** Old Town. ☎ **01789/292107.** Admission £2.20 ($3.50) adults; £1 ($1.60) children; £20.50 ($32.80) family ticket (2 adults, 3 children) for all 5 Shakespeare related houses and £13.50 ($21.60) for the 3 houses in town. Mar 20–Oct 19 Mon–Sat 9:30am–5pm; Sun 10am–5pm. Off-season Mon–Sat 10am–4pm; Sun 10:30–4pm. Closed Dec 23–26. To reach Hall's Croft, walk west from High St., which becomes Chapel St. and Church St. At the intersection with Old Town, go left.

This house is on Old Town street, not far from the parish church, Holy Trinity. It was here that Shakespeare's daughter Susanna probably lived with her husband, Dr. John Hall. Hall's Croft is an outstanding Tudor house with a beautiful walled garden, furnished in the style of a middle-class home of the time. Dr. Hall was widely respected and he built up a large medical practice in the area. Exhibits illustrating the theory and practice of medicine in Dr. Hall's time are on view. Visitors to the house are welcome to use the adjoining Hall's Croft Club, which serves morning coffee, lunch, and afternoon tea.

**Holy Trinity Church (Shakespeare's Tomb).** Old Town. ☎ **01789/266316.** Church: free; Shakespeare's tomb: donation 60p (95¢) adults; 40p (65¢) students. Mar–Oct Mon–Sat 8:30am–6pm; Sun 2–5pm. Nov–Feb Mon–Sat 8:30am–4pm; Sun 2–5pm. Walk 4 minutes past the Royal Shakespeare Theatre with the river on your left.

In an attractive setting near the Avon River is the parish church where Shakespeare is buried ("curst be he who moves my bones"). The Parish Register records his baptism in 1564 and burial in 1616 (copies of the original documents). The church ranks as one of the most beautiful parish churches in England.

You'll find Shakespeare's tomb in the chancel, a privilege bestowed upon him as a "lay rector," which he became in 1605. Alongside his grave are those of his widow, Anne, and other members of his family. Nearby on the north wall is the bust of Shakespeare, which was fashioned within 7 years of his death and during the lifetime of his widow and many of his friends.

## Impressions

*After we had seen Shakespeare's tomb and birthplace, we went back to the inn there, where we slept that night, and I recollect that all night long I dreamt of nothing but a black gentleman, at full length, in plaster-of-Paris, with a lay-down collar tied with two tassels, leaning against a post and thinking; and when I woke in the morning and described him to Mr. Nickleby, he said it was Shakespeare just as he had been when he was alive, which was very curious indeed.*

—Charles Dickens, Nicholas Nickleby

**Harvard House.** High St. ☎ **01789/204507.** Admission £2 ($3.20) adults; £1 ($1.60) students and children. Mar 20–Oct 19 daily 10am–4pm.

The most ornate home in Stratford, Harvard House is a fine example of an Elizabethan town house. Rebuilt in 1596, it was once the home of Katherine Rogers, mother of John Harvard, founder of Harvard College. In 1909, the house was purchased by a Chicago millionaire, Edward Morris, who presented it as a gift to the famous American university. The rooms are filled with period furniture, and the floors are made of local flagstone. Look for the Bible Chair, used for hiding the Bible during the days of Tudor persecution. Their newest acquisition is a Neish pewter collection.

**The Royal Shakespeare Theatre Summer House.** Avonbank Gardens. ☎ **01789/297671.** Free admission. Apr–Oct daily 10am–6pm; Nov–Mar daily 11am–4pm.

This is a brass-rubbing center, where medieval and Tudor brasses illustrate the knights and ladies, scholars, merchants, and priests of a bygone era. The Stratford collection includes a large assortment of exact replicas of brasses. Entrance is free, but visitors are charged depending on which brass they choose to rub. According to size, the cost ranges from 95p ($1.50) to make a rubbing of a small brass, to a maximum of £19.95 ($31.90) for a rubbing of the largest, a 7-foot behemoth that takes an enthusiast a full day to complete. The price includes all the necessary paper and waxes, and a demonstration of the methodology of rubbing.

## GUIDED TOURS

Guided tours of Stratford-upon-Avon leave from near the Guide Friday Tourism Center, Civic Hall, Rother Street (☎ **01789/294466**). In summer, open-top double-decker buses depart every 15 minutes daily from 9:30am to 5:30pm. You can take a 1-hour ride without stops, or you can get off at any or all of the town's five Shakespeare's Properties. Anne Hathaway's Cottage and Mary Arden's House are the two likely stops to make outside the town center. Although the bus stops are clearly marked along the historic route, the most logical starting point is on the sidewalk in front of the Pen & Parchment Pub, at Bridgefoot, at the bottom of Bridge Street. Tour tickets are valid all day so you can hop on and off the buses wherever you want. The tours cost £8 ($12.80) for adults, £2.50 ($4) for children under 12, and £6 ($9.60) for seniors or students.

## AN EXCURSION TO RAGLEY HALL

A magnificent 115-room Palladian country house built in 1680, **Ragley Hall,** in Alcester, is the home of the earl and countess of Yarmouth. The house has been restored and appears much as it did during the early 1700s. Great pains have been taken to duplicate colors and, in some cases, the original wallpaper patterns. The pictures, furniture, and works of art that fill the vast and spacious rooms represent 10 generations of collecting by the Seymour family. Ragley Hall may be a private home, but it has a museumlike quality; many of its artifacts have great historical importance. The most spectacular attraction is the lavishly painted south staircase hall. Muralist Graham Rust painted a modern trompe l'oeil work depicting the Temptation. A new mural in the tearoom depicts a Victorian kitchen and the characters who inhabit it.

Ragley Hall is near Alcester, 9 miles from Stratford-upon-Avon. You must drive or go by taxi, since there is no suitable bus service. Ragley Hall is located off A435 or A46 to Evesham, about 1¹/₂ miles west of the town of Alcester. There is easy access from the main motorway network, including the M40 from London.

The house is open Easter through September, Thursday to Sunday from 11am to 5pm; the gardens are open 10am to 6pm. Admission to the house, garden, and park is £4.50 ($7.20) for adults, £4 ($6.40) for seniors, and £3 ($4.80) for children. For information, call ☎ **01789/762090.**

## SHOPPING

The largest shop of its kind in the Midlands, **Arbour Antiques, Ltd.,** Poets Arbour, off Sheep Street (☎ **01789/293493**), sells antique weapons, used for both warfare and sport, from Britain, Europe, and in some cases, India and Turkey. If you've always hankered after a full suit of armor, you'll find one here, perhaps a 15th-century suit from England, Germany, or Italy. More modest purchases might include an Indian bullet mold, circa 1850, selling for around £10 ($16), or any of several Indian swords, priced at £40 ($64).

More than any other pottery studio in Stratford, **Dianthus,** 1 Centre Craft Yard, off Henley Street (☎ **01789/292252**), emphasizes unique creative statements cast in stoneware. Set within spacious quarters where a trio of potters display their technique on their potter's wheels, the place is owned and managed by English-born Mike Steveni, his California-trained wife, Dinah, and their associate, James Pavitt. Prices begin at £3 ($4.80), come in a pleasing assortment of sky and earth tones, and include their oft-duplicated version of a creamware mug.

Everything in **Pickwick Gallery,** 32 Henley St. (☎ **01789/294861**), is a well-crafted work of art produced by copper or steel engraving plates, or printed by means of a carved wooden block. As such, hundreds of botanical prints, landscapes, and renderings of artfully arranged ruins, each suitable for framing, can be purchased at prices beginning at £5.50 ($8.80). Look for the engravings by William Hogarth showing satirical scenes that lampooned Parliamentary corruption during the late 18th century. Topographical maps of regions of the U.K. are also available if you're planning on doing any hill climbing or trekking.

**The National Trust Shop,** 45 Wood St. (☎ **01789/262197**), is imbued with a sense of national pride at the English heritage that the National Trust was designed to protect. Here you'll find textbooks and guidebooks describing esoteric places in the environs of Stratford, descriptions of National Trust properties throughout England, stationery, books, china, pewterware, and toiletries, each inscribed, embossed, or painted with logos that evoke some aspect of English tastes and traditions.

Few other shops in England glorify trees and wood products as artfully as **Once a Tree,** Bard's Walk (☎ **01789/287790**). A member of a rapidly blossoming chain with at least eight other branches throughout Britain, it stocks wood-carved objects that range from the functional and utilitarian (kitchen spoons and bread boards) to the whimsical and exotic (carved wooden flowers, chunky jewelry, boxes, bowls, mirror frames, furniture, and mantelpieces).

Within an antique house across from the Shakespeare Birthplace Centre, **The Shakespeare Bookshop,** 39 Henley St. (☎ **01789/292176**), is the region's premier source for textbooks and academic treatises on the Bard and his works. Books cover all levels of Shakespearean expertise, from picture books to weighty tomes geared to anyone pursuing a Ph.D. in literature.

Scattered over three floors of an Elizabethan house said to have been occupied by one of Shakespeare's daughters as an adult, **Trading Post,** 1 High St. (☎ **01789/ 267228**), offers a jammed and slightly claustrophobic assortment of gift items that might appeal to your taste for the kitschy and nostalgic. Included are doll's houses and the furnishings to go inside, a scattering of small, easy-to-transport antiques, and memorabilia, some desirable, sometimes not, of your visit to the Midlands.

## TEATIME

After visiting the birthplace of Shakespeare, pop across the street for tea at **Mistress Quickly,** Henley Street (☎ **01789/295261**). This airy tearoom is quite the place in town for tea, but the very attentive staff more than compensates for the vast number of patrons that graces its doors. Choose from an array of tea blends, cream tea, and various gateaux, pastries, and tea cakes—all freshly baked in their own kitchen.

Housed in a mellowed building from the 1590s, **Hathaway Tea Rooms,** 19 High St. (☎ **01789/292404**), is as timbered and rickety as its across-the-street neighbor, Harvard House. It's also near the landmark Holy Trinity Church. You pass through a bakery shop and climb to the second floor, into a forest of oaken beams. You can order wholesome food that might include a vegetarian dish of the day, Welsh rarebit, quiches and salads, and the traditional favorite of steak-and-kidney pie. A classic steaming fruit pie might round off your meal. You can also visit for high tea or cream tea.

**The Cottage Tea Garden,** Cottage Lane, Shottery (☎ **01789/293122**), is set in its own rose garden a few paces from Anne Hathaway's Cottage, on a country lane 1¹/₂ miles from Stratford-upon-Avon. The tearoom offers a verdant and refreshing place for respite from the whirlwind of sightseeing. Though most visitors prefer a chair on the outdoor patio, a glassed-in conservatory offers indoor seating for 25. Available throughout the day are at least five kinds of countryman platters, which include salads, raw vegetables, and cheese (a ploughman's lunch); ham (a huntsman's lunch); tuna (a fisher's lunch); cold roast beef (a cowman's lunch); and Cornish pasties (a Cornishman's lunch). Stratford's "blue minibus" passes nearby every 10 minutes throughout the day.

## WHERE TO STAY

During the long theater season, it's best to arrive with a reservation. However, the **Tourist Information Centre** (part of the national "Book-a-Bed-Ahead" service that enables visitors to make reservations in advance through the nationwide Tourist Information Centre Network) will help find a room for you in the price range you're seeking. The fee for room reservations made is 10% of the first night's stay (bed-and-breakfast rate only), deductible from the visitor's final bill.

### DOUBLES FOR LESS THAN £40

**Aidan Guest House.** 11 Evesham Place, Stratford-upon-Avon, Warwickshire CV37 6HT. ☎ **01789/292824.** 6 rms. £32–£40 ($51.20–$64) double. All rates include English breakfast. AE, MC, V. From the center at the police station on Rother St., walk west. Bus: no. 16 or 18.

This large Victorian family house belongs to Lilly and John Thompson. Close to the town center, the house is a 5-minute walk from the theater and railway station. All the rather spartan but impeccably clean rooms have central heating, hot and cold running water, and hot-beverage facilities. Each room is a double. The place is particularly recommended for those with small children, as baby-sitting can be arranged, and children's cots are also available.

**Church Farm.** Long Marston, Stratford-upon-Avon, Warwickshire CV37 8RH. ☎ **01789/ 720275.** 2 rms. TV. £35–£38 ($56–$60.80) double. All rates include English breakfast. No credit cards. From Stratford, take A3400 south, forking right onto B4632; go for about 4 miles and, after passing an airfield on your right, turn right (signposted Long Marston); at the T-junction, turn right again into the village and Church Farm is on your left. Bus: no. 215 from Stratford.

This 17th-century farmstead in a secluded garden is about 6 miles from Stratford. The owner, Mrs. Wiggy Taylor, enjoys meeting people from other countries and welcomes children (she can provide baby-sitting services). You can rent a large room, with private shower and beverage-making equipment. She is continually updating the decor in the bedrooms.

**Kawartha House.** 39 Grove Rd., Stratford-upon-Avon, Warwickshire CV37 6PB. ☎ **01789/ 204469.** Fax 01789/292387. 7 rms, 6 with bath. TV. £15 ($24) single without bath; £30 ($48) double without bath, £32–£36 ($51.20–$57.60) double with bath. All rates include English breakfast. MC, V.

This solid house was built in the late 1800s in the mock-Tudor style by a family who had greatly enjoyed one of their trips to North America. Its unusual name derives from a spot they had found particularly beautiful, the Kawartha Lakes of Canada. Set on a street lined with other B&B hotels, it lies a 5-minute walk from Stratford's theater complex. Although it has provided overnight accommodations since the early 1970s, it was tastefully renovated in the late 1980s. It offers a well-maintained garden in front, and very pretty, pastel-colored bedrooms upstairs. Some overlook a park, and each contains tea- and coffee-making facilities.

**Lemarquand.** 186 Evesham Rd., Stratford-upon-Avon, Warwickshire CV37 9BS. ☎ **01789/ 204164.** 3 rms, 2 with shower only. £17 ($27.20) single without bath; £34–£38 ($54.40–$60.80) double with shower only; £40 ($64) family rm with shower only. All rates include English breakfast. No credit cards. From the center at the police station on Rother St., walk west. Bus: no. 218.

The functionally furnished bedrooms here are comfortably equipped and contain hot and cold running water and tea- and coffee-making facilities. Each unit is a double, although often rented to solo travelers. There are other more glamorous properties along Evesham Road, but you're likely to pay more to stay at them. Anne Cross gives good service, and the location is close to the theater and town center.

**✪ The Marlyn Hotel.** 3 Chestnut Walk, Stratford-upon-Avon, Warwickshire CV37 6HG. ☎ **01789/293752.** 8 rms, 3 with shower only. £18–£22 ($28.80–$35.20) single without bath, £26 ($41.60) single with shower only; £34 ($54.40) double without bath, £44 ($70.40) double with shower only; £43.50 ($69.60) family rm (triple) with shower only. All rates include English breakfast. AE, MC, V.

This Victorian house has been welcoming guests since 1890. It's conveniently situated near Hall's Croft, the former home of Shakespeare's daughter, and is within a 5-minute walk of the town center and the Royal Shakespeare Theatre. The hotel is centrally heated, and each bedroom contains tea- and coffee-making facilities. There's also a small lounge with a TV. If you don't want to pack your Shakespeare, don't worry—a copy of the complete works of the Bard is in every bedroom. Evening meals are available. The Marlyn has been owned and managed since 1994 by the Evans family, and Rosemary Ann Evans endeavors to make guests comfortable throughout their stay.

**Parkfield Guest House.** 3 Broad Walk, Stratford-upon-Avon, Warwickshire CV37 6HS. ☎ and fax **01789/293313.** 7 rms, 5 with shower only. TV. £18 ($28.80) single without bath;

£35 ($56) double without bath, £41 ($65.60) double with shower only. All rates include English breakfast. MC, V.

Jo Pettitt has received many reader recommendations. She runs this "smoke-free" place with her husband, Roger. The rooms at this conveniently located guest house have hot-beverage facilities. Breakfast is superb. Mrs. Pettitt, if possible, will help guests obtain theater tickets. The house is just off B439 (Evesham Road), a 5-minute walk from the Royal Shakespeare Theatre.

**Salamander Guest House.** 40 Grove Rd., Stratford-upon-Avon, Warwickshire CV37 6PB. ☎ **01789/205728.** Fax 01789/205728. 7 rms, all with shower only. TV. £18 ($28.80) single; £34–£44 ($54.40–$70.40) double. All rates include English breakfast. No credit cards. Bus: no. X16.

One of the better guest houses of Stratford-upon-Avon, the Salamander is well maintained and homelike, fronting a woodsy park. Maurice and Ninon Croft rent comfortably furnished rooms, including one for families. Evening meals, prepared by Maurice, who is a chef, can be ordered; the cost is £7.50 ($12) and up for three courses. Serving is timed at 6pm sharp so patrons can get to the theater for the evening performance. The house is about a 5-minute walk from the town center just off B439 (Evesham Road).

## DOUBLES FOR LESS THAN £55

### In Town

**Craig Cleeve House Hotel.** 67–69 Shipston Rd., Stratford-upon-Avon, Warwickshire CV37 7LW. ☎ **01789/296573.** Fax 01789/299452. 15 rms, 9 with shower only. TV. £20.50 ($32.80) single without bath; £39 ($62.40) double without bath, £50 ($80) double with shower only. All rates include English breakfast. AE, DC, MC, V.

This hotel was originally built of red brick in 1906 as two separate residences. Later, they both functioned as independently operated guest houses, the Craig and the Cleeve, and in the late 1980s they were combined into the single hotel you'll see today. It sits within a 10-minute walk of Stratford's center, on the far side of the Clopton Bridge, off A3400 road leading to Oxford. The Palmer family, Terry and Margarita, the congenial owners, paved over most of their garden to create their much-needed parking lot, although there's still a pretty landscaped garden in the rear.

**The Croft.** 49 Shipston Rd., Stratford-upon-Avon, Warwickshire CV37 7LN. ☎ and fax **01789/ 293419.** 9 rms, 7 with bath. TV. £20 ($32) single without bath, £28–£38 ($44.80–$60.80) single with bath; £35 ($56) double without bath, £42–£50 ($67.20–$80) double with bath. All rates include English breakfast. Family rates available for 3 to 5 people. DC, MC, V.

Kevin Hallworth runs this traditional guest house, which has been in business many years and is kept up-to-date. Fully modernized, the house has central heating and hot-beverage facilities in all rooms. A pretheater evening meal can be arranged at £10.50 ($16.80). Gardens lead to the River Avon, and there's a swimming pool on the grounds. The Croft stands on A3400 only 5 minutes from the town center and the Royal Shakespeare Theatre.

**Courtland Hotel.** 12 Guild St., Stratford-upon-Avon, Warwickshire CV37 6RE. ☎ **01789/ 292401.** 7 rms, 3 with bath. TV. £18–£25 ($28.80–$40) single without bath, £30–£35 ($48–$56) single with bath; £40–£46 ($64–$73.60) double with bath; £48 ($76.80) family rm without bath. All rates include English and continental breakfast. AE, CB, MC, V.

The hotel is in a large Georgian house with antique furniture. The rooms have hot and cold running water, and the owner, Mrs. Bridget Johnson, gives them her personal attention. She will also pick up guests from the station upon request. The

Courtland, in the town center, is a minute from the bus station, a 5-minute walk from the rail station, and 3 minutes from the theater. The preserves served with breakfast are homemade, and special diets will be catered to upon request.

**The Hollies Guest House.** 16 Evesham Place, Stratford-upon-Avon, Warwickshire CV37 6HQ. ☎ **01789/266857.** 6 rms, 3 with bath. TV. £28 ($44.80) single without bath; £35 ($56) double without bath, £45 ($72) double with bath. All rates include English breakfast. No credit cards. From the center at the police station on Rother St., walk west for about 3 minutes. Bus: no. 16 or 18.

This inn is run by a mother and daughter, Mrs. Mavis Morgan and Mrs. L. Burton, and named after a beloved pet (a mongrel named Holly) that died long ago. Their guest house is a renovated three-story building that was originally built in 1875 as a school, although it looks like a stately old home. The bedrooms are large with plenty of wardrobe space, and the beds have good, firm mattresses. The rooms are technically defined as doubles, although some can be rented as singles if not otherwise engaged. The place serves a good, plentiful breakfast in a sunny dining room. Babysitting can be arranged.

**Hunters Moon.** 150 Alcester Rd., Stratford-upon-Avon, Warwickshire CV37 9DR. ☎ **01789/292888.** Fax 01789/204101. 8 rms. TV. £17–£25 ($27.20–$40) per person single or double. All rates include English breakfast. V. From town center, take the bus marked West Green Drive.

Amid a half-acre garden near Anne Hathaway's Cottage is this guest house owned and operated by Stratfordians Rosemary and David Austin. Built of brick in the early 1900s, and enlarged many times since, the house was completely refurbished in 1994. All rooms have dual-voltage shaver outlets, hair dryers, radio, and beverage-making facilities. It lies 1¹/₂ miles north of Stratford on the A422 Stratford-Worcester road.

✪ **Moonraker House.** 40 Alcester Rd., Stratford-upon-Avon, Warwickshire CV37 9DB. ☎ **01789/267115.** Fax 01789/295504. 15 rms, all with shower only; 3 suites. TV. £35–£50 ($56–$80) single; £45–£55 ($72–$88) double; £65–£75 ($104–$120) suite. All rates include English breakfast. MC, V.

The hardworking owners, Mike and Mauveen Spencer, rent pretty rooms with hair dryers and hot-beverage facilities. A luxury suite is available with a bedroom, lounge, and kitchenette, plus two more suites, each with two rooms. Among the amenities are four-poster beds, a nonsmoking lounge area, and garden patios. Start the morning with a hearty and full English breakfast, followed by toast and homemade marmalade and jams, all personally served and prepared by Mauveen and Michael. The house is 2 minutes by car from the heart of town on A422.

**Newlands.** 7 Broad Walk, Stratford-upon-Avon, Warwickshire CV37 6HS. ☎ and fax **01789/298449.** 4 rms, 3 with shower only. TV. £19 ($30.40) single without bath; £42 ($67.20) double with shower only; £55 ($88) triple. All rates include English breakfast. MC, V.

Sue Boston welcomes guests, especially fellow theatergoers, to her home and enjoys helping them plan their sightseeing. Each room is comfortably furnished and well maintained and contains hot-beverage facilities, hair dryers, and an iron. Most of the bedrooms have recently been redecorated. The house is just off B439 (Evesham Road), a 10-minute walk from the Royal Shakespeare Theatre.

**Ravenhurst Hotel.** 2 Broad Walk, Stratford-upon-Avon, Warwickshire CV37 6HS. ☎ **01789/292515.** 5 rms. TV. £21–£22 ($33.60–$35.20) double. All rates include English breakfast. AE, MC, V.

On a quiet street near the town center is this Victorian town house within easy reach of the historic district. Richard Workman invites guests to enjoy the comfortable rooms, all of which have beverage-making facilities. Each unit is a double, and one has a four-poster. Mr. Workman's extensive knowledge of the area can be a big help. The house is directly west of the center, just off B439 (Evesham Road).

✪ **Twelfth Night.** Evesham Place, Stratford-upon-Avon, Warwickshire CV37 6HT. ☎ **01789/ 414595.** 6 rms, all with shower only. TV TEL. £48–£57 ($76.80–$91.20) double. Rates include English breakfast. MC, V. From the center at the police station on Rother St., head west for 200 yds.

This inn is aptly named—for a quarter of a century it accommodated actors from the Royal Shakespeare Theatre Company, many of whom appeared in productions of *Twelfth Night.* Today this privately owned Victorian house is rated one of the finest guest accommodations in Stratford. The bedrooms, each a double, are cozily and comfortably furnished and include clock radios, hair dryers, and beverage-making facilities. Only nonsmokers are accepted.

### Nearby

**Graveside Barn.** Binton, Stratford-upon-Avon, Warwickshire CV37 9TY. ☎ **01789/750502.** Fax 01789/298056. 4 rms. TV TEL. £20–£30 ($32–$48) per person. All rates include English breakfast. MC, V.

Denise and Guy Belchambers welcome you not into a hotel or a guest house, but an extension of their own home. An old thatched barn, carefully converted, it today has modern comforts. In the open countryside, its bedrooms open onto views of the Cotswolds and the Malvern Hills. The bedrooms contain such amenities as central heating, tea- or coffee-making equipment, phones, and a small refrigerator. Breakfasts are cooked to order, catering to both the health-conscious and those who prefer the traditional English cooked breakfast. With prior notice, evening meals can also be provided. Graveside Barn lies 4 miles west of Stratford along B439, only 15 minutes from the M40 and M42 motorways.

**Loxley Farm.** Loxley, Warwickshire CV35 9JV. ☎ and fax **01789/840265.** 2 rms, both with bath. TV. £44 ($70.40) double. All rates include English breakfast. No credit cards.

The nearby village of Loxley, just 4 miles from Stratford-upon-Avon and 7 miles from Warwick, is an ancient community, boasting one of the oldest Saxon churches in England, the parish church of St. Nicholas. This country village, claimed by some to be the original home of Robin Hood (Sir Robin of Loxley), is a quiet little place with a delightful old pub. At historic Loxley Arm, Roderick and Anne Horton live in a real dream of a thatched cottage with windows peeping from the thatch and creeper climbing up the old walls. The garden is full of apple blossoms, roses, and sweet-scented flowers. A stone path leads across the grass and into the flagstone hall, with nice old rugs and a roaring fire. Accommodations are in the Shieling, a recently converted 17th-century single story building also thatched and half-timbered. It stands in the garden of Loxley Farmhouse. It has two double bedrooms each with private bathroom, a sitting room, and small kitchen. In the house there is a twin suite sometimes available. Breakfast is served in the house on a table made from a panel from the wall of the Royal Mint in London.

**Moss Cottage.** 61 Evesham Rd., Stratford-upon-Avon, Warwickshire CV37 9BA. ☎ and fax **01789/294770.** 2 rms. TV. £17–£19 ($27.20–$30.40) per person. All rates include English breakfast. No credit cards.

Pauline and Jim Rush provide thoughtful care and service at this charming cottage built in 1922. They go to great lengths to assure your comfort. Rooms are spacious and include tea- and coffee-making facilities. Guests can relax in the pretty English cottage garden. Baby-sitters and room service are available upon request. It is within walking distance to town, theaters, and places of interest, and it is an ideal base for touring the Cotswolds. This is a nonsmoking facility.

**Pear Tree Cottage.** Church Rd., Wilmcote, Stratford-upon-Avon, Warwickshire CV37 9UX.
☎ **01789/205889.** Fax 01789/262862. 7 rms. TV. £30 ($48) single; £45 ($72) double.
All rates include English breakfast. No credit cards.

In the home village of Shakespeare's mother, Mary Arden, is this late 16th-century
farmhouse (with later additions). Exposed beams and antique furniture give the house
a period charm, whereas such things as modern plumbing and central heating add
20th-century comfort. No longer a farmhouse, the cottage stands in nearly an acre
of lawn and gardens. Mr. and Mrs. Mander can accommodate up to 15 guests. Three
of the bedrooms are in the original buildings and the remainder are in a modern wing
"with an old feel" added on in 1987. Mary Arden's birthplace is visible across the field
from the house. The cottage is 3¹/₂ miles northwest of Stratford-upon-Avon toward
Wilmcote (1 mile off A3400 to Birmingham).

**Winton House.** The Green, Upper Quinton, Stratford-upon-Avon, Warwickshire CV37 8SX.
☎ **01789/720500.** 3 rms, 2 with bath. £46 ($73.60) double. All rates include English
breakfast. No credit cards.

This enchanting house is located on the border of the Cotswolds near Warwick
Castle. Mrs. Lyon, the owner, goes out of her way to make her guests comfortable,
and her breakfasts are a delight. The rooms are comfortably decorated with high ceilings and homey touches. The house is surrounded by many footpaths, and bicycles
are for hire for £6 ($9.60) per day.

## A YOUTH HOSTEL

✪ **Stratford-upon-Avon International YHA Centre.** Hemmingford House, Alveston,
Warwickshire CV37 7RG. ☎ **01789/297093.** Fax 01789/205513. 28 rms, 120 beds. £12.95
($20.70) adults; £9.65 ($15.45) youths. All rates include breakfast. AE, MC, V.

This remodeled 200-year old Georgian mansion is popular with students, backpackers, and families wanting cheap accommodations, so call in advance for
reservations as they are often booked up. Besides the dormitory bunk beds, there are
standard doubles, double suites, and family rooms. Six rooms feature private baths.

There is a common game room, television room, and smokers lounge. Amenities
include a laundry drop-off where, for £1.50 ($2.40) per load, you can get clothes
washed, then dry them yourself in the drying room, free bag storage and parking, and
currency exchange. Curfew is midnight.

Breakfast can be eaten in or packed, and lunch, costing £3.25 ($5.20), is a packed
affair, but all requests for packaged meals must be made by 10pm the previous night.
Dinner is a three-course meal for £4.25 ($6.80). Package deals are available, where
you can purchase bed, breakfast, lunch, and dinner for £20.45 ($32.70) adult or
£17.50 ($28) youth. Do-it-yourselfers can use the self-catering kitchen.

## WHERE TO EAT

**The Box Tree/The River Terrace Restaurant.** In the Royal Shakespeare Theatre, Waterside.
☎ **01789/293226.** Reservations required. Box Tree: fixed-price lunch or dinner £24 ($38.40).
River Terrace: main courses £6.50–£7 ($10.40–$11.20). AE, MC, V accepted in Box Tree; no
credit cards in the River Terrace. Box Tree: lunch Thurs and Sat noon–2pm; dinner daily 5:45–
11:30pm. River Terrace: Mon–Sat 10:30am–9:30pm; Sun 10:30am–5pm. ENGLISH.

This pair of restaurants satisfies the hunger pangs of actors, directors, stage hands, and
members of the audience. The more formal of the two places is the Box Tree, where
English meals are served with style by a polite and hardworking staff. Less formal,
and more affordable, is the River Terrace, whose view extends over the back of
the theater as far as the River Avon. Menu items include typical English and pasta
dishes, baked ham, salads, and vegetarian dishes, as well as morning coffee and
afternoon tea.

**Lambs.** 12 Sheep St. ☎ **01789/292554.** Reservations required Sat night. Main courses £5.95–£12 ($9.50–$19.20); fixed-price menu £5.95 ($9.50). AE, DC, MC, V. Mon–Sat noon–2:30pm and 5:30–11pm; Sun 6:30–10:30pm. ENGLISH/CONTINENTAL.

Only a stone's throw from the Royal Shakespeare Theatre, this cafe and bistro is housed in a building dating back to 1547 that has connections with author Lewis Carroll. For a quick light meal or a pretheater dinner, it's ideal. The menu changes seasonally. You might begin with a tomato-and-mozzarella salad, perhaps Scottish smoked salmon or a pasta, then follow with such dishes as pan-fried filet of beef with roasted shallots or grilled fillet of halibut with an avocado-and-tomato salsa. The chef takes chances with some dishes (no doubt inspired by trips to the continent), and it's a nice departure from the bland tearoom food that has been served for decades in Stratford.

**Marlowe's Restaurant.** Marlowe's Alley, 17–18 High St. ☎ **01789/204999.** Main courses £5.50–£8.50 ($8.80–$13.60); 3-course fixed-price dinner £18.50 ($29.60). AE, DC, MC, V. Mon–Fri noon–2:30pm and 5:45–10:30pm; Sat noon–2:30pm and 5:45–11pm; Sun noon–2:30 and 7–9:30pm. ENGLISH.

Marlowe's is made up of the Elizabethan Room, a 16th-century oak-paneled dining room, and Georgies, once the hayloft to this ancient house. A la carte meals in the Elizabethan Room start at around £12 ($19.20), although you can also order a fixed-price meal. There is a garden patio, and the owners invite you to have a drink or even an alfresco meal here. Hours are timed so that you can make the opening curtain at the theater. A traditional Sunday lunch is also featured, with prime ribs of beef and Yorkshire pudding. Marlowe's serves such dishes as chateaubriand with Yorkshire pudding and béarnaise sauce, or drunken duck marinated in red wine, gin, crushed peppercorns, lemon juice, and juniperberries. Georgies is across the patio from Marlowe's, serving lunches and dinners that begin at a modest £6 ($9.60). Georgies keeps the same dinner hours as Marlowe's (see above). Try such dishes as rib of beef, rack of lamb with mint and rosemary sauce, and fresh fillet of bream with a white wine sauce. Theatergoers are welcome for dessert and coffee after the theater during regular business hours.

**No. 6.** 6 Union St. ☎ **01789/269106.** Reservations recommended, especially Fri–Sat nights and for pretheater. Main courses £6–£12 ($9.60–$19.20). AE, MC, V. Mon–Sat noon–2:15pm and 5:30–10:30pm. ENGLISH.

This bistro is near Slug & Lettuce, north of Bridge Street in the town center. Its mood is informal and its bright, breezy atmosphere has the feel of a French bistro. The chef specializes in typically British food, such as "bangers and mash" (sausages and mashed potatoes). About 12 fresh fish dishes are also offered daily—brought in from Birmingham's fish markets. The staff informs us that the most popular dinner is camembert fried in phyllo pastry and served with a black currant sauce followed by salmon and haddock fish cakes with tarragon and dill hollandaise. To finish, the bread-and-butter "pud" is a special delight—made with brioche, croissants, and apricots served with a vanilla custard.

**Russons.** 8 Church St. ☎ **01789/268822.** Reservations required. Main courses £7.95–£11.95 ($12.70–$19.10). AE, MC, V. Tues–Sat 11:30am–2pm and 5:30–10pm. INTERNATIONAL.

Mr. and Mrs. D. G. Russon have been proprietors of this two-room eatery for just 2 years now, and have gained a loyal local following. Since the theater is a short stroll away, this is a great place for a preshow meal. The restaurant is housed in a 400-year-old building and the two simply furnished dining rooms, one with a hardwood floor, the other with flagstones, both feature inglenook fireplaces. The menu changes regularly to reflect availability of seasonal ingredients, with fresh seafood being the specialty. Daily specials are posted on a blackboard, and include such items as rack of lamb, chicken, guinea fowl, and numerous vegetarian dishes. Finish with a home-made dessert, which ranges from fresh fruit sorbet to a warm pudding.

**Vintner Wine Bar.** 5 Sheep St. ☎ **01789/297359.** Reservations recommended. Main courses £3.75–£10 ($6–$16). AE, MC, V. Mon–Sat 10:30am–11pm; Sun 10:30am–10:30pm. Bus: no. X16 or X18. CONTINENTAL.

The Vintner demonstrates why dining at wine bars is all the rage in England. The Elizabethan decor is fitting in the town of Shakespeare, and its name derives from one of Stratford's most famous vintners and wine merchants, John Smith, who operated from these premises in 1600. Around the corner from the Shakespeare Hotel, a short walk from the Royal Shakespeare Theatre, this popular drinking and dining spot has daily specials posted on the chalkboard. Many guests prefer one of the tempting cold plates at lunch. You can also order a vegetable dish of the day, a vegetarian soup, an oven baked tuna steak or spicy meatballs in rich tomato sauce with spaghetti. The cookery is not always with verve and elan, but is straightforward and filling, the way locals like it. Food is available more or less continuously while the joint is open.

## PUBS

✪ **The Black Swan (aka Dirty Duck).** Waterside. ☎ **01789/297312.** Reservations required. Main courses £7–£15 ($11.20–$24); bar snacks £1.50–£4 ($2.40–$6.40). MC, V (restaurant only). Pub: Mon–Sat 11am–11pm; Sun noon–3pm and 6–10:30pm. Restaurant: Dinner Mon–Sat 6–11:30pm; lunch Tues–Sun noon–2pm. ENGLISH.

Affectionately known as the Dirty Duck, this has been a popular hangout for Stratford players since the 18th century. The wall is lined with autographed photos of its former patrons, such as Lord Olivier. In the spring and fall an open fire blazes. In the Dirty Duck Grill Room, typical English grills, among other dishes, are featured. You'll be faced with a choice of a dozen appetizers, most of which are a meal in themselves. Main dishes include braised kidneys or oxtails, and honey-roasted duck. In fair weather, you can have drinks in the front garden and watch the swans on the Avon glide by. The service is perfunctory and the quality of the food can be erratic, but this has always been a place where the food was secondary to talk about "the play." The pub overlooks the Avon between the Royal Shakespeare Theatre and Holy Trinity Church.

**The Garrick Inn.** 25 High St. ☎ **01789/292186.** Main courses £5–£9 ($8–$14.40). MC, V. Daily noon–8:30pm. Pub: Mon–Sat 11am–11pm; Sun noon–10:30pm. ENGLISH.

This black-and-white timbered Elizabethan pub has an unpretentious charm. It's named after David Garrick, one of England's greatest actors. The front bar has tapestry-covered settles and an open fireplace where the locals gravitate. The black bar has a circular fireplace and mementos on the triumphs of the English stage. The pub is open on Sunday from 3 to 7pm only to those dining here. The specialty is homemade pies such as steak and ale, steak and kidney, and chicken and mushroom.

**Slug and Lettuce.** 38 Guild St. ☎ **01789/299700.** Reservations recommended. Main courses £9.95–£10.95 ($15.90–$17.50). MC, V. Pub: Mon–Wed 11am–3pm and 5:30–11pm; Thurs–Sun noon–11pm. Restaurant: Mon–Wed noon–2pm and 5:30–9pm; Thurs noon–3pm and 5:30–9pm; Fri–Sat noon–9pm; Sun noon–3pm and 7–9pm. ENGLISH.

This brick-fronted pub was created in the early 1980s when two much older ones were connected to form a larger whole. Popular with both locals and visitors, the pub is rustic and cozy, with hearty food and ale. In fair weather, tables are set up on the sidewalk outside. The menu is prepared with fresh ingredients, and might include pork chops cooked with apples and flavored with Calvados, fresh mussels in garlic butter, and Cumberland sausage served in a mushroom-and-mustard sauce. The restaurant is a 5-minute walk north of the center, on a busy street eventually designated A38 leading to Birmingham.

**White Swan.** Rother St. ☎ **01789/297022.** Reservations recommended. Bar snacks £2–£6 ($3.20–$9.60); 3-course fixed-price dinner £17.95 ($28.70). AE, DC, MC. V. Morning coffee daily 10am–noon; self-service bar snacks daily 12:30–2pm; afternoon tea daily 2–5pm; dinner Mon–Thurs 6–9pm, Fri–Sat 6–9:30pm, Sun 7–9pm. ENGLISH.

This is one of the most atmospheric pubs in Stratford-upon-Avon. Once you step inside, you're drawn into a world of cushioned leather armchairs, old oak settles, oak paneling, and fireplaces. It's believed that Shakespeare may have come here to drink back when it was called the Kings Head. At lunch you can partake of the hot dishes of the day along with fresh salads and sandwiches. The pub is in the center near the police station.

# 2 Warwick: England's Finest Medieval Castle

92 miles NW of London; 8 miles NE of Stratford-upon-Avon

Most visitors come to this town just to see Warwick Castle, the finest medieval castle in England. Some combine it with a visit to the ruins of Kenilworth Castle (see below), but the historic center of ancient Warwick has a lot more to offer.

A devasting fire swept through the heart of Warwick in 1694, but a number of Elizabethan and medieval buildings still survive, along with some fine Georgian structures from a later date. Except for the East and West Gates, very few traces of the town walls remain. Warwick cites Ethelfleda, daughter of Alfred the Great, as its founder. But most of its history is associated with the earls of Warwick, a title created by the son of William the Conqueror in 1088. The story of those earls—the Beaumonts, the Beauchamps (such figures as "Kingmaker" Richard Neville)—makes for an exciting episode in English history.

## ESSENTIALS

**GETTING THERE**    Trains run frequently between Stratford-upon-Avon and Warwick. Call ☎ **0345/484950** for schedules and information.

One Midland Red bus per hour (no. 18 or no. X16) departs Stratford-upon-Avon during the day. The trip takes 15 to 20 minutes. Call the tourist office (☎ **01789/293127**) for schedules.

Take A46 if you're driving from Stratford-upon-Avon.

**VISITOR INFORMATION**    The **Tourist Information Centre** is at The Court House, Jury Street (☎ **01926/492212**). Open daily from 9:30am to 4:30pm; closed December 24 to 26 and Jan 1.

## ✪ WARWICK CASTLE

Perched on a rocky cliff above the Avon in the town center, this stately, late-17th-century-style mansion is surrounded by a magnificent 14th-century fortress. It is the finest medieval castle in England. The first significant fortifications were built here in 915 by Ethelfleda, daughter of Alfred the Great. William the Conqueror ordered the construction of a motte and bailey castle in 1068, 2 years after the Norman Conquest. The mound is all that remains today of the Norman castle, which was sacked by Simon de Montfort in the Barons' War of 1264. Surrounded by gardens, lawns, and woodland, where peacocks roam freely, and skirted by the Avon, Warwick

Castle was described by Sir Walter Scott in 1828 as "that fairest monument of ancient and chivalrous splendor which yet remains uninjured by time."

The Beauchamp family, the most illustrious medieval earls of Warwick, are responsible for the appearance of the castle today, and much of the external structure remains unchanged from the mid-1300s. When the castle was granted to Sir Fulke Greville by James I in 1604, he spent £20,000 (an enormous sum in those days) converting the existing castle buildings into a luxurious mansion. The Grevilles have held the earl of Warwick title since 1759, when it passed from the Rich family.

The staterooms and Great Hall house fine collections of paintings, furniture, arms, and armor. The armory, dungeon, torture chamber, ghost tower, clock tower, and Guy's tower create a vivid picture of the castle's turbulent past and its important role in the history of England.

The private apartments of Lord Brooke and his family, who in recent years sold the castle to Tussaud's Group, are open to visitors. They house a display of a carefully reconstructed Royal Weekend House Party of 1898. The major rooms contain wax portraits of important figures of the time: young Winston Churchill; the duchess of Devonshire; Winston's widowed mother, Jennie; and Clara Butt, the celebrated singer, along with the earl and countess of Warwick and their family. In the Kenilworth bedroom, the likeness of Prince of Wales, who later became King Edward VII reads a letter. The duchess of Marlborough prepares for her bath in the red bedroom. Among the most lifelike of the figures is a little uniformed maid bending over to test the temperature of water running into a bathtub.

You can also see the Victorian rose garden, a re-creation of an original design from 1868 by Robert Marnock. The original garden had fallen into disrepair, and a tennis court was built on the site. In 1980, however, it was decided to restore the garden and, as luck would have it, Marnock's original plans were discovered in the county records office. Near the rose garden is a Victorian alpine rockery and water garden. The romantic castle is host to various colorful pageants. Even 3 hours may not give you enough time to see everything.

The castle is open daily from 10am to 5pm (except Christmas Day). Admission is £8.95 ($14.30) for adults, £5.40 ($8.65) for children 4 to 16, £6.40 ($10.25) for seniors and students, and free for children 4 and under. There's free parking. For information, call ☎ **01926/408000.**

## EXPLORING WARWICK

**St. Mary's Church.** Church St. ☎ **01926/400771.** Free admission; donations accepted. Apr–Sept daily 10am–5pm; Oct–Mar 10am–4pm. All buses to Warwick stop at Old Square.

Destroyed in part by the fire of 1694, this church, with its rebuilt battlemented tower and nave, is among the finest examples of late 17th- and early 18th-century architecture. The Beauchamp Chapel, spared from the flames, encases the Purbeck marble tomb of Richard Beauchamp, a well-known earl of Warwick who died in 1439 and is commemorated by a gilded bronze effigy. Even more powerful than King Henry V, Beauchamp has a tomb that's one of the finest remaining examples of perpendicular-Gothic style from the mid-15th century. The tomb of Robert Dudley, earl of Leicester, a favorite of Elizabeth I, is against the north wall. The perpendicular-Gothic choir dates from the 14th century, and the Norman crypt and the chapter house are from the 11th century.

**Lord Leycester Hospital.** High St. ☎ **01926/491422.** Admission £2.50 ($4) adults; £1.75 ($2.80) students and seniors; £1.25 ($2) children. Easter–Oct Tues–Sun 10am–5pm; Nov–Easter Tues–Sun 10am–4pm.

The great fire also spared this group of half-timbered almshouses at the West Gate. The buildings were erected about 1400, and the hospital was founded in 1571 by Robert Dudley, earl of Leicester, as a home for old soldiers. It's still used by ex-service personnel and their spouses. On top of the West Gate is the attractive little chapel of St. James, dating from the 12th century but renovated many times since.

**Warwick Doll Museum.** Oken's House, Castle St. ☎ **01926/495546.** Admission £1 ($1.60) adults; 70p ($1.10) children. Easter–Sept Mon–Sat 10am–5pm; Sun 1–5pm. Oct–Easter Sat 10am–5pm.

One of the most charming Elizabethan buildings in Warwick houses this doll museum near St. Mary's Church. Founded in 1955, its seven rooms display an extensive collection of dolls in wood, wax, and porcelain. Fabric dolls are housed in a new display case. Off Jury Street in the center, the house once belonged to Thomas Oken, a great benefactor of Warwick.

**Warwickshire Museum.** Market Hall, The Market Place. ☎ **01926/412500.** Free admission. Mon–Sat 10am–5:30pm; Sun (May–Sept) 2–5pm. From Jury St. in the center, take a right onto Swan St., which leads to the museum.

This museum was established in 1836 to house a collection of geological remains, fossils, and an exhibit of amphibians from the Triassic period. There are also displays illustrating the history, archaeology, and natural history of the county, including the famous Sheldon tapestry map.

**St. John's House Museum.** St. John's. ☎ **01926/412021.** Free admission. Oct–Apr Tues–Sat (and bank holidays) 10am–12:30pm and 1:30–5:30pm. May–Sept Tues–Sat 10am–12:30pm and 1:30–5:30pm; Sun 2:30–5pm.

At Coten End, not far from the castle gates, this early 17th-century house has exhibits on Victorian domestic life. A schoolroom is furnished with original 19th-century furniture and equipment. During the school term, Warwickshire children dress in period costumes and learn Victorian-style lessons. Groups of children also use the Victorian parlor and the kitchen. Since it's impossible to display more than a small number of items at a time, a study room is available where you can see objects from the reserve collections. The costume collection is a particularly fine one, and visitors can study the drawings and photos that make up the costume catalog. These facilities are available by appointment only. Upstairs is a military museum, tracing the history of the Royal Warwickshire Regiment from 1674 to the present. For more information or for an appointment to use the study room, telephone the Keeper of Social History at the number above. St. John's House is at the crossroads of the main Warwick-Leamington road (A425/A429) and the Coventry road (A429).

## TEATIME

For ancient ambience, experience a tea at **Brethren's Kitchen,** Lord Leycester Hospital (☎ **01926/491580**). This tearoom is part of the 16th-century hospital that the earl established in 1571. It's built with cool stone floors and exposed oak beams. Indian, Chinese, and herbal teas are all available. Enjoy the house specialty of scones with fresh cream, sponge cake, or fruit cake.

## WHERE TO STAY

Many people prefer to stay in Warwick and commute to Stratford-upon-Avon, although the accommodations here are much inferior to those at Stratford.

### DOUBLES FOR LESS THAN £35

**Cambridge Villa.** 20A Emscote Rd., Warwick, Warwickshire CV34 4PL. ☎ and fax **01926/ 491169.** 15 rms, 10 with bath. TV. £18.50 ($29.60) single without bath, £26 ($41.60) single with bath; £35 ($56) double without bath, £45 ($72) double with bath. All rates include English breakfast. AE, DC, MC, V. From St. John's, continue along Coten End leading to Emscote Rd. toward Leamington Spa.

This place is a 4-minute walk west of Warwick Castle, but you can also take an even more pleasant walk through St. Nicholas Park to reach it. The bedrooms are decorated in a comfortable modern style, although a bit plain. The hotel has a good Italian restaurant on the premises.

**Warwick Lodge Guest House.** 82 Emscote Rd., Warwick, Warwickshire CV34 5QJ. ☎ **01926/492927.** 7 rms, none with bath. TV. £16–£18 ($25.60–$28.80) single; £32–£34 ($51.20–$54.40) double. All rates include English breakfast. MC, V. From St. John's, continue along Coten End leading to Emscote Rd. toward Leamington Spa. Bus: no. X16 or X18.

Run by Grace and Bernard Smith, this informal place is close enough to Stratford-upon-Avon to be a base for touring Shakespeare Country. All the rather basic rooms have hot-beverage facilities, central heating, hot and cold running water, and comfortable beds. The location is half a mile from Warwick.

**Westham Guest House.** 76 Emscote Rd., Warwick, Warwickshire CV34 5QG. ☎ **01926/ 491756.** 7 rms, 2 with bath. TV. £15–£16 ($24–$25.60) single without bath; £30 ($48) double without bath, £34 ($54.40) double with bath. All rates include English breakfast. No credit cards. From St. John's, continue along Coten End leading to Emscote Rd. toward Leamington Spa. Bus: no. X16 or X18.

In a residential section of town along a busy road, this canopied building with a garden is managed by the Donald family. It's about a 5-minute walk from Warwick center. The bedrooms are utterly plain but reasonably comfortable and clean—and hard to match for the price. The guest house is licensed to serve drinks to guests and has an extensive bar menu served nightly from 7 to 9pm. A three-course meal costs £10 to £12 ($16 to $19.20). The guest house lies on A445, the main road leading to Leamington Spa. Approaching from London, come in from M1, then follow the signs for Coventry onto A46, leading into Warwick.

## DOUBLES FOR LESS THAN £55

**Agincourt Lodge.** 36 Coten End, Warwick, Warwickshire CV34 4NP. ☎ and fax **01926/ 499399.** 7 rms, all with bath. TV TEL. £28.50–£31.50 ($45.60–$50.40) single; £40–£52 ($64–$83.20) double. All rates include English breakfast. AE, MC, V.

This place was built in 1838, positioned by the architect so that it wouldn't harm the enormous copper beech in the front yard. Today the Blackband family receives guests, and the beech tree is bigger than ever. The bedrooms are comfortable and contain such amenities as private baths, beverage-making equipment, TVs, and phones; one features a four-poster bed. There's also a bar and lounge for residents. There's a long and narrow garden in back (the hotel actually occupies only half the original house), and visitors can walk in St. Nicholas Park, whose entrance is just 50 yards from Agincourt Lodge. The house is a 5-minute walk from the castle toward Leamington Spa Road.

✪ **The Old Rectory.** Vicarage Lane, Stratford Rd., Sherbourne, near Warwick, Warwickshire CV35 8AB. ☎ **01926/624562.** 14 rms. £33 ($52.80) single; £40–£52 ($64–$83.20) double; £50–£80 ($80–$128) family rm. All rates include English breakfast. MC, V.

This 1790s farmhouse has been restored and decorated with antiques by the owners, Sheila and Martin Greenwood. It's a delightful old place, with a wealth of beams, inglenook fireplaces, and flagstone and elmwood floors. The rectory stands in a half an acre of lovely walled gardens, and enjoys government protected land mark status. In its early days it was known as the White Horse Inn, later becoming the home of the Canon of St. Mary's Church in Warwick. There are rooms in the main house, as well as a converted carriage house suitable for a family. Several bedrooms have antique brass beds, but each has individual styling, all with such amenities as satellite TV, radio alarms, trouser press, hair dryer, and beverage-making equipment. The Elm Restaurant offers a variety of fine foods and wines, each dish freshly prepared. It's just off A46 between Warwick and Stratford-upon-Avon, less than 3 miles southwest of Warwick and half a mile from M40 (Junction 15).

✪ **Tudor House Inn & Restaurant.** 90–92 West St., Warwick, Warwickshire CV34 6AW. ☎ **01926/495447.** Fax 01926/492948. 11 rms, 8 with bath. TV TEL. £25 ($40) single without bath, £39.95 ($63.90) single with bath; £55.90 ($89.45) double with bath. All rates include English breakfast. AE, MC, V. Opposite the main Warwick Castle car park, $^1/_2$ mile south of town on A429.

At the edge of town is a black-and-white timbered inn built in 1472. It's one of the few buildings to escape the fire that destroyed High Street in 1694. Off the central hall are two large rooms, each of which could be the setting for an Elizabethan play. All the simply furnished bedrooms have washbasins, and two contain doors only 4 feet high. In the corner of the lounge is an open turning staircase. Bar snacks are available, and the restaurant offers a standard English and continental menu. Tudor House is on the main road from Stratford-upon-Avon leading to Warwick Castle.

# WHERE TO EAT

**Fanshaw's Restaurant.** 22 Market Place, Warwick. ☎ **01926/410590.** Reservations recommended. Lunch main courses £2.50–£8.50 ($4–$13.60); dinner main courses £14–£16 ($22.40–$25.60). Set menus (not available Sat night) £13–£16 ($20.80–$25.60). AE, MC, V. Tues–Sat noon–3pm and Mon–Sat 6–10pm. BRITISH/FRENCH.

In the heart of Warwick, at the edge of the city's commercial focal point, this restaurant occupies a late-Victorian building whose somber-looking brick facade is enlivened by flowered window boxes. Inside, there are only 32 seats within a well-maintained, feminine-looking dining room accented in pink and white, filled with fresh flowers, and lined with mirrors to give the illusion that it's actually bigger than it is. A well-trained staff serves food from a menu that changes every 2 months, and which usually includes sirloin steak, grilled plaice, steak-and-kidney pie, lamb's liver with smoked bacon, Wellington-style saddle of lamb, and prime filet of beef with sundried tomatoes, black olives. Especially elegant, usually offered during game season, is a brace of quail with a hazelnut and apricot stuffing.

**Findon's Restaurant.** 7 Old Sq., Warwick. ☎ **01926/411755.** Reservations recommended. Set lunches £6.95–£19.95 ($11.10–$31.90); set dinners Mon–Fri £10.95–£19.95 ($17.50–$31.90); set Sat night dinner £19.95 ($31.90). AE, DC, MC, V. Sun–Fri noon–2pm and Mon–Sat 7–10pm. BRITISH.

The building is authentically Georgian, built in 1700 after a disastrous fire had wiped out part of the neighborhood that contains it. You'll dine surrounded by original stone floors and original pinewood cupboards, within a setting for only 43 diners to dine in snug comfort. Michael Findon, owner and sometime chef, works hard at orchestrating a blend of traditional and modernized British cuisine. The set menus include such dishes as chicken livers with Calvados and sliced apples, and baked goat's cheese with a mushroom crust, red onion relish, and an herb salad. A la carte meals might include medallions of venison with a mousse of peas and a port sauce; "chump" of lamb with green lentils and garlic with a mint and basil fumet; breast of chicken with tarragon cream sauce; flaked smoked haddock with savoy cabbage and an English mustard sauce; and a filet of beef with a green tapénade and truffle jus. If you're cutting costs, consider a lunchtime visit to this place, when a two-course "plat du jour" includes a soup of the day followed by such platters as venison sausages with a mustard sauce and fresh vegetables (or a suitable vegetarian substitute), all for only £6.95 ($11.10), about what you might have paid for a platter in a local pub.

**Nicolini's Bistro.** 18 Jury St. ☎ **01926/495817.** Reservations recommended. Main courses £8.75–£15.50 ($14–$24.80). AE, CB, DC, MC, V. Mon–Sat noon–2pm and 6–10:30pm. ITALIAN.

This restaurant features an appealing blend of the cuisines from northern and central Italy. Lynne and Nicky, as they are known locally, welcome you into their pleasant restaurant decorated with greenery. Check out the crisp salads and luscious desserts. You're faced with an array of appetizers, including king prawns cooked in garlic butter or Nicky's polenta served with a napoletana sauce and baked in the oven. Pastas such as lasagna can be served as either an appetizer or a main course. Main courses include daily specialties, as well as such standard Italian fare as pork marsala or veal milanese. The restaurant stands in the center of town near the castle.

**Piccolino's.** 31 Smith St., between Jury St. and Coten End. ☎ **01926/491020.** Main courses £4.50–£10.50 ($7.20–$16.80). MC, V. Mon–Thurs noon–2:30pm and 5:30–11pm; Fri noon–2:30pm and 5:30–11:30pm; Sat noon–11:30pm; Sun noon–2:30pm and 5:30–10:30pm. ITALIAN.

This Italian restaurant is informal and fun, serving a wide selection of pizzas, including a "red hot Mamma" with a zesty chili flavor. You can also order such filling pasta dishes as tortellini alla crema and tagliatelle carbonara. Many dishes taste as if they had been prepared from recipes handed down by one's *mamma mia.* Italian wine may be ordered by the glass.

## 3 Kenilworth Castle

5 miles N of Warwick; 13 miles N of Stratford-upon-Avon; 102 miles NW of London

The main attraction in the village of Kenilworth, an otherwise dull English market town, are the ruins of Kenilworth Castle—reason enough to go here.

## ESSENTIALS

**GETTING THERE**   InterCity train lines make frequent and fast connections from London's Paddington and Euston stations to either Coventry or Stratford-upon-Avon. For schedules and information, call ☎ **0345/484950.** Midland Red Line buses make regular connections from both towns to Kenilworth.

If you're driving from Warwick, take A46 toward Coventry.

**VISITOR INFORMATION**   The **Tourist Information Centre** is in the village at the Kenilworth Library, 11 Smalley Place (☎ **01926/852595**). Open Monday, Tuesday, Thursday, and Friday from 9:30am to 7pm, and Saturday from 9:30am to 4pm.

## THE MAGNIFICENT RUINS OF KENILWORTH CASTLE

Kenilworth Castle was built by Geoffrey de Clinton, a lieutenant of Henry I. Its walls at one time enclosed an area of 7 acres, but it is now in magnificent ruins. Caesar's Tower, with its 16-foot-thick walls, is all that remains of the original structure.

Edward II was forced to abdicate at Kenilworth in 1327 before being carried off to Berkeley Castle in Gloucestershire, where he was undoubtedly murdered. In 1563, Elizabeth I gave the castle to her favorite, Robert Dudley, earl of Leicester. He built the gate house, which the queen visited on several occasions. After the Civil War, the Roundheads were responsible for breaching the outer walls and towers and blowing up the north wall of the keep. This was the only damage inflicted following the earl of Monmouth's plea that it be "Slighted with as little spoil to the dwellinghouse as might be."

The castle is the subject of Sir Walter Scott's romance *Kenilworth*. In 1957, Lord Kenilworth presented the decaying castle to England, and limited restoration has since been carried out.

From Good Friday through September, the castle is open daily from 10am to 6pm; in other months, daily from 10am to 4pm. The castle is closed January 1 and December 24 to 26. Admission is £2.50 ($4) for adults, £1.30 ($2.10) for children 5 to 16 (under 5, free), £1.90 ($3.05) for seniors. For information, call ☎ **01926/ 852078.**

## WHERE TO STAY

**Abbey.** 41 Station Rd., Kenilworth, Warwickshire CV8 1JD. ☎ **01926/512707.** Fax 01926/ 859148. 7 rms, 3 with shower. TV. £21 ($33.60) single without bath, £25 ($40) single with shower; £36 ($57.60) double without bath, £42 ($67.20) double with shower. All rates include English breakfast. No credit cards. Bus: no. X16 or X17.

One of the preferred guest houses in the area near the train station, Trevor and Angela Jefferies' home has a certain old-fashioned Victorian quality. Built in 1900, it has charm and an inviting atmosphere, although all the modern amenities have been installed. Many guests here are frequent visitors. Bedrooms are well furnished, with such amenities as color TV, beverage-making equipment, and electric shaver points. Breakfast offers a good choice, and in the residents' lounge guests gather and enjoy the house's license to serve drinks. Limited parking is available.

**Castle Laurels.** 22 Castle Rd., Kenilworth CV8 1NG. ☎ **01926/8561795.** Fax 01926/ 854954. 11 rms. £32 ($51.20) single; £51 ($81.60) double; £21.25 ($34) per person family rm, reduced slightly for children depending on age. All rates include English breakfast. MC, V. Closed week of Christmas.

Winter is a popular time to stay here because of the unhindered view of Kenilworth Castle ruins, opposite this Victorian house owned by Nick and Pam Moore. The surroundings are so pleasant, though, that it makes for a good stop year-round. The owners create a homey atmosphere by spending evenings socializing with lodgers, chatting and answering questions about the surrounding area. Public areas are made bright with flowers, and bedrooms with tasteful fabrics. Further comforts are provided by a lounge bar and restaurant, which has an a la carte dinner menu of homemade dishes like Pam's pâté and vegetarian offerings, made with seasonal produce. There is a strict nonsmoking policy in effect.

**Enderly Guest House.** 20 Queens Rd., Kenilworth, Warwickshire CV8 1JQ. ☎ **01926/55388.** 4 rms. TV. £25 ($40) single; £38 ($60.80) double; £43 ($68.80) family rm. All rates include English breakfast. No credit cards.

This family-operated place off Warwick Road offers newly decorated, well kept, and inviting bedrooms. The guest house is within easy reach of the town center, the castle, and the "heart" of England. In fact, you might choose to stay here and let the summer crowds fight it out in Stratford-upon-Avon.

**The Priory Guest House.** 58 Priory Rd., Kenilworth, Warwickshire CV8 1LQ. ☎ **01926/ 856173.** 5 rms, 3 with shower. TV. £19 ($30.40) single without bath, £24 ($38.40) single with shower only; £34 ($54.40) double without bath, £38 ($60.80) double with shower. All rates include English breakfast. No credit cards.

This small Victorian guest house in Kenilworth center is the home of Nina and Richard Haynes, who take deserved pride in running a hotel with charm and character. They offer tastefully furnished, comfortable rooms with coffee-making equipment and hot and cold running water. Many guests use the house as a base for exploring the countryside.

## WHERE TO EAT

**Ana's Bistro.** 121–123 Warwick Rd. ☎ **01926/853763.** Reservations recommended Tues–Thurs, required Fri–Sat. Main courses £6.95–£9.95 ($11.10–$15.90). AE, DC, MC, V. Tues–Sat 7–10:30pm; Sun noon–2:30pm. Closed Aug 1–21 and 1 week at Easter. ENGLISH/FRENCH.

Ana's is located downstairs under the Restaurant Diment (which some consider the finest in Kenilworth for those willing to spend the extra money). At Ana's you get food that's well prepared and based on the availability of fresh produce. Try grilled whole plaice, homemade lasagna, or sirloin steak in red-wine sauce. It's located south of town toward Warwick.

**Harrington's.** 42 Castle Hill. ☎ **01926/52074.** Reservations recommended. Main courses £4.75–£10.50 ($7.60–$16.80). AE, MC, V. Daily noon–2pm and 7–10pm. ENGLISH/CONTINENTAL.

With room for 60 diners, this is a suitable choice for lunch or dinner. Only a few steps from the castle in a room filled with English knickknacks, it prepares simple, familiar fare. You can order sole or pan-fried filets of beef, along with a selection of appetizers and vegetables, based on the seasons. Vegetarian dishes are also available. There are friendlier service staffs in England, and the food could use more seasoning, but the place has its habitués.

## 4 Coventry

20 miles NE of Stratford-upon-Avon; 18 miles SE of Birmingham; 52 miles SW of Nottingham; 100 miles NW of London

Coventry has long been noted in legend as the ancient market town through which Lady Godiva took her famous ride in the buff—giving rise to the expression, "Peeping Tom." The veracity of the Lady Godiva story is hard to ascertain. It's been suggested that she never appeared nude in town, but was the victim of scandalmongers. Coventry today is a Midlands industrial city. The city was partially destroyed by German bombers during World War II, but the restoration is miraculous.

### ESSENTIALS

**GETTING THERE**   From London's Victoria Coach Station, buses depart every hour throughout the day, for the 2-hour trip. From Stratford, bus no. X16 runs from the town's bus station every hour for Coventry's bus station at Pool Meadow, Fairfax Street. This bus takes 60 to 90 minutes, and stops at Kenilworth and Warwick en route. For schedules and information, call ☎ **0990/808080.**

**VISITOR INFORMATION**   The **Coventry Tourist Office,** Bayley Lane (☎ **01203/832303**), is open Easter to mid-October, Monday to Friday from 9:30am to 5pm, Saturday from 10am to 4:30pm; and mid-October to Easter, Monday to Friday from 9:30am to 4:30pm, Saturday and Sunday from 10am to 4:30pm.

### ✪ COVENTRY CATHEDRAL

Consecrated in 1962, Sir Basil Spence's controversial cathedral is the city's foremost attraction. The cathedral is on the same site as the 14th-century perpendicular building, and you can visit the original tower. Many locals maintain that the structure is more likely to be appreciated by the foreign visitor, since Brits are more attached to traditional cathedral design. Some visitors consider the restored sight one of the most poignant and religiously evocative modern churches in the world.

Outside is Sir Jacob Epstein's bronze masterpiece, *St. Michael Slaying the Devil.* Inside, the outstanding feature is the 70-foot-high altar tapestry by Graham

Sutherland, said to be the largest in the world. The floor-to-ceiling abstract stained-glass windows are the work of the Royal College of Art. The West Screen (an entire wall of stained glass installed during the 1950s) depicts rows of stylized saints and prophets with angels flying around among them.

In the undercroft of the cathedral is a visitor center, where a 20-minute documentary film, *The Spirit of Coventry*, is shown more or less continually. Also within the visitor center is the Walkway of Holograms, whose otherwise plain walls are accented with three-dimensional images of the stations of the cross created with reflective light. One of the most evocative objects within the collection of artifacts is a charred cross wired together by local workmen from burning timbers which crashed to the cathedral's floor during the bombing. An audiovisual exhibit on the city and church includes the fact that 450 aircraft dropped 40,000 firebombs on the city in 1 day.

The Cathedral, on Priory Row (☎ **01203/227597**), is open October through Easter, daily from 9:30am to 4:30pm, and Easter through September, daily from 9:30am to 6pm. The Visitor Center is open from Easter to October, daily except Sunday from 10am to 4:30pm. Admission to the cathedral is free, but there's a suggested donation of £2 ($3.20). Admission to the tower is £1 ($1.60) for adults, 50p (80¢) for children, and to get into the visitor center you'll have to pay £1.25 ($2) for adults and 75p ($1.20) for children ages 6 to 16. After visiting the cathedral, you may want to have tea in Benedict's Coffee Shop.

## 5 Birmingham

120 miles NW of London; 25 miles N of Stratford-upon-Avon

England's second largest city may fairly lay claim as the birthplace of the Industrial Revolution. James Watt first hatched in Birmingham the profitable application of the steam engine to mine the area's Black Country. Watt and other famous 18th-century members of the Lunar Society regularly met under a full moon in the nearby Soho mansion of manufacturer Matthew Boulton. Together—Watt, Boulton, and other "lunatics" such as Joseph Priestly, Charles Darwin, and Josiah Wedgwood cheerfully called themselves—launched the revolution that thrust not only England but the world into our modern technological era.

Today, this brawny and unpretentious metropolis still bears some of the scars of Birmingham's industrial excess and the devastation of the Nazi *Luftwaffe*'s bombing during World War II. Fueled by an energetic building boom in recent years, *Brummies* have nurtured the city's modern rebirth as a "meeting place for Europe" that hosts 80% of all U.K. trade exhibitions.

Birmingham lies at the heart of Central England in the West Midlands. As a trading hub where roads, rail, and canals converge, the city's center has more miles of canals than Venice. At the nexus of canal waterways that traverse the British Isles, and with its abundance of coal, iron, and wood, Birmingham readily attracted manufacturers, craftworkers, and traders to set up shop. The city's reputation as a trading center began as early as 1166 when Henry II granted Peter de Birmingham a charter to operate a market known as the Bull Ring. Profit-seekers later paid dearly for equipping Parliamentary forces with swords, pikes, armor, and other weapons during the English Civil War in the 17th Century. King Charles' unforgiving soldiers sacked and burned the city for its disloyalty to the Crown.

Undeterred by the fortunes of war, Birmingham's entrepreneurial merchants and artisans later established gun making as a primary trade. With the expansion of the nation's industrial might in the 19th century, Birmingham rapidly became known as the "city of 1,001 trades" and, later, the "workshop to the world." Many of today's industrial practices began in Birmingham, including the first mass-production Austin car factory built at Longbridge in 1906.

Birmingham has worked diligently in recent decades to overcome the blight produced by overindustrialization, poor urban planning, and post–World War II, concrete-slab modernization. The expansion of green space, cultivation of a first-rate symphony, ballet company, art galleries, museums, and shopping areas, along with the restoration of the few surviving Victorian and Elizabethan buildings, all contribute to Birmingham's newfound allure for the traveler.

Although not an obvious tourist attraction, Birmingham today serves as a gateway to England's north and a magnet for business travelers who do business in Birmingham's extensive trade centers and exhibition halls. With more than one million inhabitants, Birmingham serves up a vibrant nightlife and restaurant experience. Its three universities, 6,000 acres of parks and nearby pastoral sanctuaries, and restored canal walkways also offer welcome quiet places for the busy traveler who visits "England's Workshop."

# ESSENTIALS

**GETTING THERE   By Plane**   Three major international carriers fly transatlantic flights directly to Birmingham International Airport (BHX) from four North American Gateways. **British Airways** ( ☎ **800/AIRWAYS** in the U.S. and Canada, or 0345/222111) flies daily direct flights from Toronto (Monday and Wednesday through Sunday) and New York's JFK airport (Monday and Tuesday and Thursday through Sunday). BA and other international carriers also fly regularly between Birmingham and major U.K. and European airports.

**American Airlines** ( ☎ **800/882-8880**) flies nonstop 7 days a week from Chicago's O'Hare Airport and Birmingham. With the proposed alliance of British Airways and American Airlines, some coordination of flight schedules throughout the combined current network is likely. **Continental Airlines'** ( ☎ **800/525-0280**) new North American daily service between Newark Airport (New York) and Birmingham began in July 1997.

Direct air service between Birmingham and London is almost nonexistent. Many air carriers, however, maintain a virtual air-shuttle service between London airports and nearby Manchester, which is a 1$^1/_2$-hour trip to Birmingham via ground transport. For example, British Airways operates 28 daily flights from London's Heathrow to Manchester, 17 daily flights from London's Gatwick, and 6 daily flights from Stansted to Manchester. BA runs even more return flights each day from Manchester to London. Ground transportation links between Manchester and Birmingham, as well as between London and Birmingham, are plentiful.

Details on Birmingham flights and schedules are available through the airport ( ☎ **0121/767-5511,** or brochure hotline 0121/767-7000, or via Internet Web site http://www.bhx.co.uk).

## GETTING FROM THE AIRPORT TO TOWN

Birmingham's airport is about 8 miles southeast of the Birmingham City Centre and is easily accessible by a variety of public transport. **AirRail Link** offers a shuttle bus service every 10 minutes at no charge from the airport to the Birmingham International Rail Station and National Exhibition Centre (NEC). **InterCity** train services operate a shuttle from the airport to New Street Station in the City Centre, just a 10-minute trip. InterCity also offers half-hourly train service (Monday through Friday) between London's Euston Station and Birmingham, a 90-minute rail trip. Frequent train service between Birmingham and Manchester airports, and surrounding areas is also available.

## BY TRAIN, BUS & CAR

Regular train service connects Birmingham with London, southwest England, central Wales, and England's North Country. Trains depart London's Euston Station every 2 hours for Birmingham. Birmingham's New Street Station in City Centre and the airport's International Station link the city to the national rail network. The London-Birmingham train trip takes about 2 hours. Trains to Birmingham leave Manchester's Piccadilly Station nearly every hour for the 90-minute train trip. Contact **British Rail Train** (☎ **0345/484950**) for train schedules and fares.

**National Express** (☎ **0990/808080**) and **Flightlink** (☎ **0990/757747**) provide regular bus service between Birmingham and London, Manchester, and regional towns.

If you are traveling by car, Birmingham's City Centre is easily reached from national motorways via M5 and M6 linking to the M1, M42, M40, and M69. Birmingham's City Centre is easily accessible from London by driving north on the M5 and connecting to the A38 which directly leads to the Bristol Street/Suffolk Street Queensway to the heart of the city. Because Birmingham sits at the junction of central England's road network, it is easily reached by car. The drive to Birmingham from London takes about 2 to 2 1/2 hours. Parking is available at various city locations and at the Birmingham Airport for short- and long-term stays. Contact **National Car Parks** (☎ **0121/767-7861**).

**VISITOR INFORMATION**   The **Birmingham Convention & Visitor Bureau (BCVB),** 2 City Arcade near New Street in the City Centre (☎ **0121/643-2514**) is open Monday through Saturday from 9:30am to 5:30pm and Sunday from 10am to 4pm. The BCVB assists travelers in arranging accommodations, obtaining theater or concert tickets, and planning tourist trips and conference programs. The BCVB also operates offices at the National Exhibition Centre, International Exhibition Centre, and at 130 Colmore Rd., Victoria Square.

**GETTING AROUND**   Birmingham's City Centre hosts a number of attractions within easy walking distance. **Centro** (☎ **0121/200-2787,** or hotline 0121/200-2700) provides information on all local bus and rail service within Birmingham and the West Midlands area. A **Day Saver Pass** costs £2.20 ($3.50) and is an economical way to use the Centro bus and local train system. A weekly **Centro Card** costs £13.50 ($21.60). Exact change is required on one-way local bus and train trips.

**Travel West Midlands** (☎ **0121/200-2700**) links Birmingham and surrounding Midland towns with regular bus service. Taxis queue at various spots in City Centre, rail stations, and the National Exhibition Centre. Travelers can also ring up radio cab operators such as **BB's** (☎ **0121/233-3030**) and **Beaufort Cars** (☎ **0121/784-3166**).

## EXPLORING BIRMINGHAM

Unbeknownst to many, Birmingham features an intriguing variety of museums, galleries, concert and exhibition halls, shops, canal walking paths, and public spaces. This city has different urban edges, some rough-hewn, others smooth and refined—as different as a steam engine exhibit from J. M. W. Turner's painting *The Great Western Railway*—yet all with a special character in which the sum is greater than any part, and well worth exploring.

**Birmingham Museum and Art Gallery.** Chamberlain Sq. ☎ **0121/235-2834.** Free admission. Special exhibition charge. Mon–Sat 10am–5pm; Sun 12:30pm–5pm. Train to New St. station; 10-minute walk to Victoria Square and Museum.

Known chiefly for its collection of Pre-Raphaelite paintings, the city gallery also houses exceptional samples of English watercolor masters from the 18th century. The

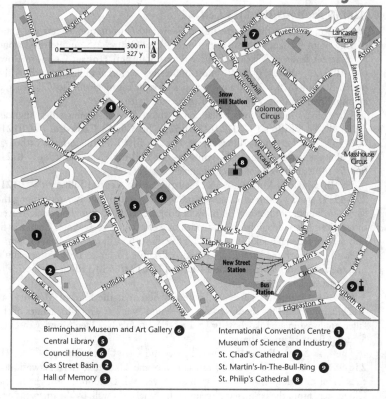

Birmingham Museum and Art Gallery 6
Central Library 5
Council House 6
Gas Street Basin 2
Hall of Memory 3

International Convention Centre 1
Museum of Science and Industry 4
St. Chad's Cathedral 7
St. Martin's-In-The-Bull-Ring 9
St. Philip's Cathedral 8

museum is instantly recognized by its "Big Brum" clock tower. Represented here are works such as Bellini's *Mother and Child* and a *Roman Beggar Woman* by Degas, but the focus is Pre-Raphaelite art by Brotherhood members such as Ford Maddox Brown, Dante Gabriel Rossetti, Edward Burne-Jones, and Holman Hunt, among others.

**Barber Institute of Fine Arts.** University of Birmingham, off Edgbaston Rd., near the University's East Gate, 2¹/₂ miles south of City Centre. ☎ **0121/472-0962.** Free admission. Mon–Sat 10am–5pm; Sun 2–5pm. Bus: no. 61, 62, or 63 from central city.

Don't be put off by the stark, stone-and-brick building that houses the Barber Institute collection. Some critics consider it the finest small art museum in England and the equal of any museum outside London. The choice selection of paintings includes works by Bellini, Botticelli, Brueghel, Canaletto, Delacroix, Gainsborough, Gauguin, Guardi, Murillo, Renoir, Rubens, Turner, Van Gogh, and Whistler.

**Museum of Science and Industry.** Newhall St. ☎ **0121/235-1661.** Free admission. Mon–Sat 10am–5pm; Sun 12:30–5pm. From New St. train station, take bus no. 101.

Birmingham's industrial history is captured in this homage to the engineering marvels of James Watt, Matthew Boulton, and other innovators of the 17th through 20th centuries that irrevocably changed modern life. While some may ignore the exhibits of steam engines, machine tools, vehicles, early aircraft, firearms, and other historical gadgets, to do so would be to neglect what makes Birmingham unique.

## WALKING AROUND THE CITY CENTRE

Stephenson Place at the intersection of New and Corporation Streets is a good starting point for sampling the attractions of City Centre. A 5-minute stroll along New Street leads to Victoria Square where **Council House,** Colmore Row, (☎ 0121/235-2040), the city's most impressive Victorian building, anchors the piazza. Built in 1879, it is still a meeting place for the Birmingham City Council and an impressive example of the Italian Renaissance style.

A few blocks from Victoria Square on Colmore Row is Birmingham's Anglican cathedral, **St. Philip's** (☎ 0121/236-6323). **St. Chad's Cathedral** (☎ 0121/236-5535) on St. Chad's Queensway, was the first Roman Catholic cathedral built after the Reformation. **St. Martin's-In-The-Bull-Ring** parish church (☎ 0121/643-5428) is at the edge of the city's ancient market area.

The Birmingham Museum & Art Gallery and the **Central Library** (☎ 0121/235-4511) stand nearby on Chamberlain Square. Central Library ranks among the largest in Europe, with nearly 34 miles of bookshelves and 1.5 million books—even though its modern design has been derided by architecture expert Prince Charles as fit only for incinerating books. It's open Monday through Saturday from 9am to 5pm.

Passing through the covered courtyard at Paradise Forum to Broad Street, you'll find the **International Convention Centre** (☎ 0121/665-6116) at the far side of Centenary Square.

Across Convention Centre on Centenary Square is the **Hall of Memory,** an octagonal memorial for those who died in World War I at which the names of the fallen are listed in a book whose pages are turned regularly. Open Monday through Saturday from 10am to 4pm.

The **Gas Street Basin** (operated by Second City Canal Cruises, ☎ 0121/236-9811) along Broad Street forms the hub of the 2,000-mile canal network that runs in all directions from Birmingham to Liverpool, London, Nottingham, and Gloucester. From the basin, a cruise along the canals or a walk by the towpaths or a short trip beyond the city's center yields other sights and experiences, such as **Aston Hall.** This 17th-century Jacobean mansion (☎ 0121/327-0062) is located on Trinity Road, Aston Park, about 2¹/₂ miles north of City Center. Open March through October, daily from 2 to 5pm.

## EXCURSIONS TO THE BLACK COUNTRY

Drawing its name from the black smoke that billowed and covered the iron-working era, "The Black Country" merits exploration as an insight into the Industrial Revolution. That era is best remembered at the **Black Country Museum** (☎ 0121/557-9643), Tipton Road, Dusley, about 10 miles northwest of Birmingham and 3 miles from Junction 2 on the M5. The museum occupies a sprawling landscape in the South Staffordshire coal field that was one of the early forges of the Industrial Revolution. The museum re-creates what it was like to work and live in the Black Country of the 1850s. An electric tramway draws visitors to view a thick underground coal seam, and trolleys move through a reconstructed industrial village comprising a schoolhouse, trade shops, rolling mill, working replica of a 1712 steam engine, an anchor forge, and other examples of early industrial life. From March through October, open daily from 10am to 5pm; November through February, Wednesday through Sunday from 10am to 4pm. Admission is £5.95 ($9.50).

## SHOPPING

From industrial grime to shopping: With more than 100 jewelry shops, **Jewelry Quarter** at 77–70 Vyse St. (☎ 0121/554-3598), is a 200-year-old jewelry-making quarter, just a 10-minute walk from City Centre. The skill of the jeweler's craft can be viewed at the Discovery Centre's restored Smith and Pepper factory displays or by visiting shop workbenches that still produce most of the jewelry made in Britain. A unique time capsule of the ancient craft of jewelry-making and working with precious metals, the quarter offers bargain hunters the opportunity to arrange repairs, design a custom piece, or just browse. Admission to the Discovery Centre is £2 ($3.20). Open Monday through Friday from 10am to 4pm and Saturday from 11am to 5pm.

## WHERE TO STAY

The cheapest living in Birmingham is provided by one of the "Ys," all of which accommodate long-term guests. Call ahead to make sure a room is available. There are several choices, including the **YMCA,** at 300 Reservoir Rd., Birmingham B23 6DB. Both men and women over 20 are accommodated at the rate of £15.50 ($24.80) per night, including breakfast. Take bus no. 102, 103, or 104 to Six Ways in Erdington. Another **YMCA,** 200 Bunbury Rd., Birmingham B31 2DL (☎ **0121/ 475-6218**), caters to women and men over 18, charging them £15 ($24) per night for bed and breakfast. You can also get dinner here for only £2.50 ($4). Take bus no. 61, 62, or 63 to Church Road, Northfield, or else a train heading to Northfield from New Street Station.

There's a **YWCA,** at the Alexandra Residential Centre, 27 Norfolk Rd., Birmingham B15 EPY (☎ **0121/454-8134**), which accepts men and women over 18 at the cheapest rate of all the Ys, only £7 ($11.20) per night. No meals are available here, and a key deposit of £10 ($16) is imposed. Take bus no. 9 or 19 from Colmore Row.

The **YWCA** at Stone Road, Birmingham B15 2HH (☎ **0121/440-2924**), admits men and women 16 years and older. The charge is £9.50 ($15.20) per night; no meals are served although there is a communal kitchen. This is not the safest area of Birmingham and guests should be particularly leary getting here at night. The Y also charges a £10 ($16) key deposit. Take bus no. 61, 62, or 63 to the McDonalds on Bristol Road. The Y is next door.

✪ **Ashdale House Hotel.** 39 Broad Rd., Acock's Green B27 7UX. ☎ and fax **0121/706-3598** or 0121/707-2324. 9 rms, 6 with bath. TV. £20 ($32) single without bath, £25 ($40) single with bath; £32 ($51.20) double without bath, £38 ($60.80) double with bath. All rates include English breakfast. AE, DC, MC, V.

A spacious Victorian terrace house, this is one of Birmingham's best B&Bs. Your hosts, Evelyn and Richard, invite you to use their library with its generous number of titles. Their bedrooms are cozy and comfortable, each well maintained and inviting. Organic produce is offered at breakfast, along with some vegetarian choices. Naturally in such an eco-friendly environment, smoking isn't allowed. It's a very inviting and homelike place for an affordable stay in Birmingham.

**Awentsbury Hotel.** 21 Spencer Rd., Selly Park B29 7HU. ☎ and fax **0121/472-1258.** 16 rms, 11 with bath. TV TEL. £26 ($41.60) single without bath, £30–£36 ($48–$57.60) single with bath; £40 ($64) double without bath, £44–£48 ($70.40–$76.80) double with bath. All rates include English breakfast. AE, DC, MC, V.

University and Pebble Mill Studio visitors will find this lodging convenient and comfortable. The place is kept spic and span, and the bedrooms, while not stylish, are decent and acceptable in every way, with beverage-making equipment and direct-dial phones from the bedrooms. One room is large enough for (normal-sized) families. No smoking is allowed in the dining room, where you can get a large English breakfast that will fortify you for the day. Take the A38 from City Centre for about 2 miles, then turn left at Bournebrook Road, and the first right onto Serpentine Road.

**Copperfield House Hotel.** 60 Upland Rd., Selly Park, Birmingham B29 7JS. ☎ **0121/472-8344.** 18 rms. TV. Mon–Fri £52.50 ($84) single; £62.50 ($100) double; Sat–Sun £42.50 ($68) single, £52.50 ($84) double. All rates include English breakfast. AE, V.

This red-brick, Victorian Gothic house is sited on a steep slope along a residential street; some rooms are difficult to reach. Rooms vary remarkably in spaciousness and quality. The basement level no. 2 is especially desirable, with its smart modern aura and prints, and most recommended is no. 4 on the ground floor with its smartly tiled bath and handsome furnishing. A small restaurant and sitting room provide comfortable food and surroundings. It is reached via the M5, Junction 4 to the A38 to City Centre. Turn left at Priory Road, then right at first light (A441) and right again at Upland Road.

**Lyndhurst Hotel.** 135 Kingsbury Rd., Erdington B24 8QT. ☎ and fax **0121/373-5695.** 14 rms. TV. £30–£39.50 ($48–$63.20) single; £39.50–£52.50 ($63.20–$84) double. All rates include English breakfast. AE, DC, MC, V.

Nine miles from the airport, this stone-exterior Victorian hotel in the northern suburbs is convenient to Convention and City Centre and Aston University. The bedrooms are well maintained and equipped, with everything from a remote control TV to a hostess tray, along with a clock radio alarm and hair dryer. Although the house is Victorian, furnishings are contemporary. For those who have a problem with steps, some bedrooms are on the ground floor. A bar and a homelike dining room serve guests, as does a separate TV lounge. The garden view restaurant serves standard but very affordable dishes in a relaxed environment. From Junction 6 of the M6 motorway, follow A5127; take a right signposted Minworth into Kingsbury Road. The hotel is on the right.

## WHERE TO EAT

A growing phenomenon called the **Birmingham Balti Experience** may interest the more adventurous seekers of spicy food. *Balti* literally means bucket, but it refers to a Kashmiri style of cooking over a fast, hot flame. Birmingham boasts a large Kashmiri population, and many *baltihouses* have sprung up in the Sparkbrook, Balsall Heath, Moseley, and south Birmingham neighborhoods. Most are bare-bones, unlicensed-for-spirits affairs where one often brings along wine or beer. Best to check first with the city visitors' bureau which provides details on Balti establishments.

**Chung Ying.** 16 Wrottesley St., City Centre. ☎ **0121/622-5669.** Main courses £5.50–£9.50 ($8.80–$15.20). AE, DC, V. Mon–Sat noon–11:30pm; Sun noon–10:30pm. CHINESE.

With a substantial Chinese community in town, this Birmingham restaurant offers more than 300 flavorful items on its provincial-styled Cantonese menu. There are 40 dim sum items alone. Samples include pan-cooked Shanghai dumplings, stuffed crispy duck packed with crabmeat, steamed eel in bean sauce, and a variety of tasty casseroles. If you want to go really authentic and sample some of the dishes the locals in this revitalized Chinese *quartier* eat, try the fried frogs' legs with bitter melon, steamed pork pie with dried or fresh squid, and fish cakes with mangetout (snow peas). The Chung Ying Garden, another restaurant owned by the same proprietor, is at 17 Thorpe St. (☎ **0121/666-6622**).

✪ **Left Bank.** 79 Broad St., City Centre. ☎ **0121/643-4464.** Main courses £11–£15 ($17.60–$24). AE, DC, MC, V. Mon–Fri noon–2:30pm; Mon–Sat 7–11pm. BRITISH.

This winning restaurant in a former bank premises in the vicinity of the International Convention Centre occupies the ground floor of a grand Victorian building. It's one of the few places in Birmingham where you can almost be guaranteed a good meal. The bistro has a high coffered, gilted ceiling, oil paintings, and seating in wicker chairs. The menu from the talented chef, William Marmion, is eclectic. Some of the more delectable items include rump of lamb cooked with beans, a confit of duck with chili salsa and wild rice, a millefeuille of salmon and spinach in a herb-flavored sauce, and char-grilled chicken with couscous risotto and a tomato salsa.

**Maharaja.** 23 Hurst St., near the Hippodrome. ☎ **0121/622-2641.** Main courses £6–£7.50 ($9.60–$12). Mon–Sat noon–2:15pm and 6–11:15pm. AE, DC, MC, V. INDIAN.

A few doors down from the Birmingham Hippodrome, this winning Indian restaurant is decorated in framed fragments of Indian cloth, prints, and paintings, a fit backdrop for a culinary journey to the subcontinent. You can make a savory selection from some of the best dishes from the Mughlai and northern Indian cuisines. Dining is on two floors, with light oak paneling. The menu features such popular dishes as lamb dhansak (cubes of lamb in thick lentil sauce), chicken patalia (cooked in spices, herbs, and fruit) and prawn madras. The balanced use of spices, herbs, and other flavorings gives this cuisine an aromatic but delicate taste.

# BIRMINGHAM AFTER DARK
## THE PERFORMING ARTS

For further information, the Birmingham tourist office distributes a free guide, *What's on Birmingham,* as well as *Pocket Guide to Birmingham,* which contains after-dark listings. For alternative hangouts, you can pick up a copy of *Wow,* an underground paper with additional listings.

**CONCERTS**   Connected to the Convention Centre, **Symphony Hall** at Broad Street (☎ **0121/212-3333**), hailed since completion in 1990 as an acoustical gem, is home to the **City of Birmingham Symphony Orchestra.** The venue also features visiting artists and performing companies. Ticket prices vary from £5.50 to £31 ($8.80 to $49.60) depending on the event

**National Indoor Arena,** King Edward's Road, (☎ **0121/200-2202**), seats 13,000 and is another favorite site for concerts, sporting events, and conventions.

The **Birmingham Repertory Theatre** (☎ **0121/236-4455**), on Broad Street at Centenary Square, houses one of England's most established acting companies. A roster of the world's greatest actors have performed with the repertory company, beginning in 1913 when it opened, and including the stars Lord Olivier, Albert Finney, Paul Scoffield, Dame Edith Evans, Kenneth Branaugh, and many others. The widely known "Rep" comprises the **Main House,** which seats 900 theatergoers, and the **Studio Theatre,** a more intimate, 140-seat venue that often stages new and innovative works. The box office is open Monday through Saturday from 9:30am to 8pm. Tickets cost £6.50 to £15 ($10.40 to $24).

The **Midlands Arts Centre** (☎ **0121/440-3838**) in Cannon Hill Park is close to the Edgbaston Cricket Ground and reached by car or bus (routes 1, 35, 45, 47, 61, 62, and 63). The MAC houses three performance areas and stages a lively range of drama, dance, music, comedy, and film. Box office is open Monday through Saturday from 9am to 11pm. The **Crescent Theatre,** Cumberland Street (☎ **0121/643-5858**), is Birmingham's leading amateur theater.

The **Alexandra Theatre,** Station Street (☎ **0121/633-3325**), hosts national touring companies, including productions from London's West End. Tickets for all theaters are available through Birmingham visitors' offices. The Alexandra Theatre is home to the **D'Oyly Carte** Opera Company (☎ **0121/643-3168**), widely acclaimed for its renditions of Gilbert & Sullivan light opera.

The **Birmingham Hippodrome,** Hurst Street (☎ **0121/622-7486**), is home to the **Birmingham Royal Ballet** and visiting companies from around the world. Built as a music hall in 1899, the Hippodrome was renovated in the 1970s and now seats 1,950 persons who attend a variety of events, from the Welsh National Opera to musicals, and dance. The box office is open Monday through Saturday from 10am to 10pm. Ticket prices range from £5 to £20 ($8 to $32) by event.

## THE CLUB & MUSIC SCENE

Birmingham's nightlife scene is richly diverse. **Bobby Brown's The Club,** 48 Gas St. along the City Centre canal (☎ **0121/643-2573**), is a converted warehouse with several small bars and a disco. **Ronnie Scott's,** 258 Broad St. (☎ **0121/643-4525**), lets guests unwind with live jazz in a casual setting. **Liberty's** 184 Hagley Rd. (☎ **0121/454-4444**), is a large, fashionable club featuring French cuisine in the Piano Bar restaurant, champagne, cocktail, and other smaller bars.

Five casinos serve the betting Birmingham visitor. British law requires you to be 18 years or older and to obtain membership at the casino at least 48 hours in advance of your intended gambling. The better known betting parlors are **Stakis Regency International** 84 Hill St. (☎ **0121/643-1777**), and **Sergeant Yorke** on Gas Street (☎ **0121/631-2414**). Both casinos are open each day from 2pm to 4am.

## PUBS

Dozens of pubs liven up Birmingham after hours. "Brummies" have their their individual allegiances to particular spots. **The Old Varsity Tavern Public House** 56 Bristol Rd. (☎ **0121/472-3186**), ranks as the third largest pub in England and is popular with university students. One local fan and reviewer claims that it's "good for pulling and for dodgy music," but another laments that while it is "generally a good pub, there are vast numbers of wasted students." That may or may not be your speed. The **City Tavern Public House,** Bishopsgate Street (☎ **0121/622-2898**), dates to 1901 and is a popular, three-story pub with live music.

## THE GAY & LESBIAN SCENE

The gay scene is so thriving here that there is actually a Gay Village overlapping Chinatown. It's bordered by Bristol, Wrentham, Sherlock, and Hurst streets, with Hurst being the center of most activities. You'll know you're there when you see the Hippodrome Theatre, a neighborhood landmark.

There are sometimes special events, but most of the nightlife centers around the pubs and clubs, of which there is an ample supply, regardless of your taste. Among the better gay pubs are the **Angel Café Bar,** 127–131 Hurst Street (☎ **0121/ 622-2525**), continental cafe by day, bar by night. A predominantly male bar, **The Jester,** Holloway Circle (☎ **0121/643-0155**), is very cruisy, in its spacious basement setting with lively talk and a good sound system. Another all-male enclave is the **Australian Bar,** Hurst Street (☎ **0121/622-4256**), a quieter, more traditional pub than The Jester. **The Fox,** 17 Lower Essex St. (☎ **0121/622-1210**) is an aptly named lesbian hangout; and **The Green Room,** Hurst Street (☎ **0121/622-4343**), is a comfortable mixed gay-friendly pub.

Dance fiends head out to **Nightingales,** Essex House, Kent Street (☎ **0121/ 622-1718**), a huge complex housing two dance floors, five bars, a restaurant, cafe, and game room. There's dancing Monday through Saturday until 2am, and Sunday until midnight. Wednesday night is Women's Night. This is actually a members-only club, but with a friendly clientele, and someone will generally sign you in as a guest at the door. After that, an admission fee of £5 ($8) will give you run of the place.

## 6  Hereford & Worcester

Hereford: 133 miles NW of London; 51 miles SW of Birmingham
Worcester: 124 miles NW of London; 26 miles SW of Birmingham; 61 miles N of Bristol

With some of the most magnificent and lushest river scenery in all of Europe, the Wye Valley (and its namesake river) meanders through open farmland that is home to some of the most charming small villages in the west-central region of England. Whereas wool used to be the main industry in this area, most locals today make their living by fruit growing, dairy farming, and to an increasing degree, tourism.

The former county of Herefordshire combined with Worcestershire to make "Hereford and Worcester"–shire. Worcestershire has become a household name around the world thanks to the famous sauce used to accent a myriad of dishes and perk up any respectable Bloody Mary. One of the quaintest of the Midland counties, it covers portions of the rich valleys of the Severn and Avon. Herefordshire's Black Mountains give way to the Welsh Brecon Beacons National Park, and between the two cathedral cities of Hereford and Worcester the ridge of the Malverns rises from the Severn Plain.

Using your BritRail Pass to travel to the heart of England, you can take the train from Paddington Station in London. The train takes you through many of the previously mentioned towns and villages, and you can stop and visit Windsor, Henley-on-Thames, and Oxford, plus numerous Cotswold villages such as Chipping Campden. It's one of the loveliest train rides in the country, and you can also take a side trip by bus from Evesham to Stratford-upon-Avon. Or catch the bus back from Stratford to Oxford via Woodstock, then the train back into London.

## HEREFORD

Situated on the Wye River, Hereford's city charters date back to 1189, when Richard I conferred it such status, freeing all of its citizens from direct crown control. This cathedral city easily lays claim to being one of the most colorful towns in England—as well as the birthplace of both David Garrick, the actor, producer, and dramatist who breathed life back into London theater in the mid-18th century, and Nell Gwynne, the actress-cum-mistress of Charles II. Dating from 1080, the red-sandstone Hereford Cathedral contains an eclectic roster of differing architectural styles, from Norman to perpendicular.

Surrounded by pristine countryside, including orchards and lush pasturelands, Hereford is home to the world-famous, white-faced Hereford cattle and some of the finest cider around, best sampled in one of the city's many traditionally atmospheric pubs.

### ESSENTIALS

**GETTING THERE**  By train from London's Paddington Station, Hereford is a 3-hour trip. For schedules and information, call ☎ **0345/484950.**

To make the 4-plus hour trip by bus from London, you'll need to catch a National Express from Victoria Station. For schedules and information, call ☎ **0990/808080.**

The trip to Hereford is a scenic 3-hour drive from London. Take the M5 to either Ledbury or Romp-on-Wye, then turn onto the A49 toward Hereford.

**VISITOR INFORMATION  Hereford's Tourist Information Centre** (☎ **01432/268430**) is located at 1 King St. Open Monday through Saturday from 9am to 5pm. During the summer months, it opens on Sunday, as well, from 9am to 5pm.

## EXPLORING HEREFORD

**The Old House,** High Town (☎ **01432/364598**), is a completely restored Jacobean period museum with 17th-century furnishings on three floors. The painstakingly restored half-timbered building, constructed in 1621—originally part of Butcher's Row—includes a kitchen, hall, and rooms with four-poster beds. The house is open all year. Summer hours are Tuesday through Sunday from 10am to 5:30pm. In winter, it is open Tuesday through Saturday from 10am to 1pm and then from 2pm to 5:30pm. Admission is £1 ($1.60) for adults and 40p (65¢) for children.

**The Churchill Gardens Museum and Hatton Gallery,** Venns Lane, Aylestone Hill (☎ **01432/267409**), can be visited on a joint ticket combined with The Old House (see above). The museum and gallery stand on the outskirts of town, located in a large park. The museum boasts collections of fine furniture, costumes, and paintings from the 18th and 19th centuries, while the Hatton Gallery is devoted to the work of a local artist, Brian Hatton, killed in World War I. They are open Tuesday through Sunday from 2 to 5pm in summer. In winter, hours for both are Tuesday through Saturday from 2 to 5pm. Admission is £1 ($1.60) for adults and 60p (95¢) for children and seniors over 60. The museum is at the top of Aylestone Hill, off the main Worcester Road (A465), a 10-minute walk from the city center.

**The Cider Museum and King Offa Citer Brandy Distillery,** Pomona Place, Whitecross Road (the A438 to Brecon; ☎ **01432/354207**), tells the story of traditional cider making from its heydey during the 17th century right through to the modern factory methods. Detailed displays include orcharding, a 17th-century French beam press, a cooper's shop, an old farm cider house, traveling cider makers' "tack" what used to be trundled from farm to farm, and the original champagne cider cellars with tiers of bottles. You can also see a 1920s press house and factory bottling line and the great oak vats of the Napoleonic period. The King Offa Distillery has been granted the first new license to distill cider in the United Kingdom in more than 250 years, and visitors can see it being produced from the beautiful copper stills brought from Normandy. The museum is open from April to the end of October, daily from 10am to 5:30pm; from November to March, Monday to Saturday from 1 to 5pm. Admission is £1.50 ($2.40) for adults and £1 ($1.60) for children. The museum is a 5-minute walk from the city center and a quarter of a mile from the city Ring Road on the A438 to Brecon.

✪ **The Hereford Cathedral** (☎ **01432/59880**) is one of the oldest cathedrals in England, with its cornerstone laid in 1080. The cathedral is primarily Norman and includes a 13th-century Lady Chapel erected in 1220, and houses a majestic "Father" Willis organ—one of the finest in the world. Exhibited together in the new library building at the west end of the Hereford Cathedral are two of Hereford's unique and priceless historical treasures: the Mappa Mundi of 1290, which portrays the world oriented around Jerusalem, and the 1,600-volume library of chained books, with some volumes dating back to the 8th century. The cathedral also contains the Diocesan Treasury and the St. Thomas Becket Reliquary. You'll find the cathedral open year-round; entrance is free. The Mappa Mundi and Chained Library exhibition is also open Monday to Saturday, from 10am to 4:15pm and on Sunday from noon to 3:15pm. Admission is £4 ($6.40) for adults and £3 ($4.80) for children and seniors. A special family ticket (two adults and three children) is available for £10 ($16). Children under 5 are admitted free. The cathedral can be found easily in the Hereford city center.

## SHOPPING

The city's richest inventory of shops lies within a labyrinth of historic and character buildings, known collectively as **High Town.** Limited to pedestrian traffic, it's enhanced by street performers and visiting entertainers. The town's interpretation of a U.S.–style shopping mall, with 40 shops of various sizes, is **Maylord Orchards,** combining state-of-the-art goods with a sense of the historic, close to the town center. Principal shopping streets include Widemarsh Street, Commercial Road, St. Owen's Street, and most charming and artfully old-fashioned of them all, Church Street.

**The Hereford Market,** city center, evokes the old West Country street fairs with a cornucopia of both treasures and junk displayed in an open-air setting of regional charm. It's conducted throughout the year every Wednesday and Saturday morning from 8am to 1pm. The area pulsates with life as vendors sell items ranging from sweatshirts and saucepans to paintings and pet food.

**Andrew Lamputt, The Silver Shop,** 28 St. Owen St. (☎ **01432/274961**), is *the* place in the city for that perfect silver gift. It boasts a large array of quality old silverware and fine gold jewelry and even maintains a stable of skilled craftspeople who work in the shop's own workshop restoring old silverware and jewelry.

**The Country Furniture Store,** Cross Keys at Withington (on the A465 Hereford Bromyard Road; ☎ **01432/820612**), offers Herefordshire's finest selection of traditional country furniture in oak, elm, ash, beech, and pine. These talented craftspeople can also make furniture to suit your individual tastes and needs.

## WHERE TO STAY

✪ **Charades.** 34 Southbank Rd., Hereford, Hereford & Worcester HR1 2TJ. ☎ **01432/ 269444.** 7 rms, 6 with bath. TV. £17.50 ($28) per person single or double without bath; £20 ($32) per person single or double with bath. All rates include breakfast. No credit cards.

The inn's name derives from a frustrating moment in the life of its Scottish-born owner, Mrs. Betty Mullen, who referred to the slow pace of her hotel's renovation (five men working for a full year) as "a charade." Since the work was completed, however, this charming bed-and-breakfast has emerged as one of the most likable and appealing in Hereford. On 1¹/₂ acres of private grounds, within an 8-minute walk south of the town center, it's composed of mirror-image brick-sided houses, each built in the 1830s, that Mrs. Mullen joined together in the 1980s. Bedrooms are high-ceilinged, carefully outfitted with built-in furnishings, personalized knickknacks, and views that stretch out over the Black Mountains. Breakfast, the only meal served, is elaborate, formal, and generous.

**Felton House.** Felton, Hereford HR1 3PH. ☎ **01432/820366.** 5 rms. £21 ($33.60) single; £42 ($67.20) double. All rates include breakfast. No credit cards. From Hereford, follow the A465 or the A49, then turn on the A417 to Felton.

About 8 miles north of Hereford, this B&B lies within what was originally built in 1851 as the rectory for the Anglican church next door. Other than an immersion in the English countryside, don't expect a lot in Felton. Except for church services held briefly every other week, Felton's only other attraction is a pub serving meals, about 400 yards away. The hotel is outfitted much like a late Victorian/Edwardian private home, a role it fulfilled for 20 years as the residence of its live-in managers, Brian and Marjorie Roby. There's a conservatory, a library, a breakfast room overlooking the garden, and cozy, well-insulated bedrooms with a smattering of what look like family heirlooms and antiques. Breakfast is the only meal served. Interested in medieval history? The site the inn occupies was mentioned in the *Domesday Book* (ca. 1087) as the residence of a Frenchman, and site of a much older church that preceded the rarely used one you'll see today.

**The Merton Hotel.** 28 Commercial Rd., Hereford, Hereford & Worcester HR1 2BD. ☎ **01432/265925.** Fax 0432/354983. 17 rms. TV TEL. £40 ($64) single; £50–£65 ($80–$104) double. All rates include breakfast. AE, MC, V.

Closer to Hereford's railway station than any of its competitors, this hotel was built in the 1790s as the home for the overseer of the local prison—which at the time stood across the street. All vestiges of the original punitive function of this place long ago disappeared in favor of a not particularly exotic hotel, with clean but slightly cramped bedrooms and conservatively modern furnishings. Rooms contain tea-making facilities and a comfortable but otherwise undistinguished decor. There's an exercise area on the premises, as well as a restaurant that's open Monday to Saturday only, from noon to 2pm and 6:30 to 9:30pm. Main courses include such well-prepared dishes as grilled local salmon with hollandaise sauce.

**The Somerville.** Bodenham Rd., Hereford, Hereford & Worcester HR1 2TS. ☎ **01432/ 273991.** 10 rms, 6 with bath. TV TEL. £20 ($32) single without bath, £25 ($40) single with bath; £32 ($51.20) double without bath, £40 ($64) double with bath. All rates include breakfast. AE, MC, V.

A 15-minute walk northeast of Hereford's cathedral, this imposing Victorian-style house was built of red brick around 1900, and functioned briefly as a retirement home before being converted into this efficiently decorated hotel in the early 1980s. The front garden was long ago converted into a parking lot, but the back garden retains some of its original plantings, and can be overlooked during the breakfast rituals in the large, much-renovated dining room. Bedrooms are spacious with high ceilings, tea-making facilities, and functional, old-fashioned furnishings. The staff have a sense of humor, but don't indulge in the personalized fussing you're likely to find in more intimate B&Bs.

## WHERE TO EAT

The best bet for a pub grub lunch is The Orange Tree (see "Hereford After Dark," below).

**Shires Restaurant.** In The Green Dragon Hotel, Broad St. ☎ **01432/272506.** Main lunch courses £6.50 ($10.40); main dinner courses £12.95–£16.95 ($20.70–$27.10); set-price dinner £18.95 ($30.30). AE, DC, MC, V. Daily 12:30–2pm and 6:45–9:15pm. ENGLISH/FRENCH.

Set within the street level of the town's most historic and prestigious hotel, this restaurant is sheathed with very old paneling, some of it 17th century, carved from Herefordshire oak. Virtually everyone in town considers it the stateliest restaurant around, suitable for formal venues and important family celebrations, of which you may see several during your meal. Main courses at lunchtime are selected from an all-English carvery table, where a uniformed attendant carves from roasted joints of beef, turkey, or ham, garnished with all the traditional fixings. Dinners are more French in flavor, and are conducted with as much fanfare as anything else around. Menu items include a pâté of duck meat and wild mushrooms served with a juniper chutney; filet of beef with red wine and mushroom sauce; navarin (lamb stew) with garden vegetables; and fillet of salmon with white wine sauce and sole.

**The Restaurant at the Castle Pool Hotel.** Castle St. ☎ **01432/356321.** Reservations recommended. Set lunch £7.90 ($12.65); set dinner £14.50 ($23.20); main courses £7.95–£12.50 ($12.70–$20). MC, V. Daily noon–2pm and 7:30–9:30pm (till 10:30pm on Fri–Sat). ENGLISH/ INTERNATIONAL.

Inside the building that served as the 19th-century residence of the bishop who administered the nearby cathedral, this restaurant overlooks a well-planned garden through the windows of a modern extension that enlarged the floor plan of the hotel's original design. Lunches are straightforward, mostly British affairs presented in a no-nonsense (and relatively inexpensive) manner that includes steak-and-kidney pie and fisherman's platters. Dinners, however, are much more experimental by local standards. The menu reads something like a travelogue (chicken San Remo, spinach

Verona, or Polynesian pork satay). Despite that, food is well prepared and more imaginative than anywhere else around. Chicken San Remo is prepared with peaches, raspberries, apricot brandy, and cream. Spinach Verona is garnished with cottage cheese and herbs, while the more predictable Steak Diana, served with wild mushrooms and cream, is one of the most consistently reliable choices on the menu.

## HEREFORD AFTER DARK

Nightlife in this provincial headquarters is small-scale but sometimes cozy, focusing on drink in any of the town's many pubs, and sometimes attendance at one of the erratically scheduled concerts, operattas, and musical comedies. Contact the Hereford Tourist Information Centre (see above) or the **Hereford Arts in Action,** 89 East St. (☎ **01432/278118**) for complete information. If you want to enjoy a simple and relaxed evening, consider the Green Dragon Hotel (see above) for jazz or a walk through the town's historically evocative central district.

At **The Orange Tree,** 16 King St. (☎ **01432/267698**) there's nothing particularly unusual about this woodsy pub, and never any live music to perk up the usual diet of locals kibbutzing with one another about local events and daily gossip. But it is one of the most consistently popular "locals" in town, attracting all generations of beer lovers and tipplers from across the county. Beers on tap include Buddington's and a changing roster of ales and lagers sent on spec from local breweries, sometimes as part of local sales promotions. If you're hungry, don't get your hopes up: Other than lunches, served Monday to Saturday from 11am to 3pm, when pub grub costs from £1.40 to £4.95 ($2.25 to $7.90) per snack, food generally isn't available.

# WORCESTER

The River Severn flows through the heart of this world-famous porcelain center and has attracted visitors throughout the ages to Worcester. In medieval times, the river served as the hub of commercial life (now found a short distance away in the bustling scene of High Street). Today the river plays host to more leisurely activities like boat trips, fishing, rowing, and steeplechases at the riverside Worcester Racecourse. The magnificent Worcester Cathedral has dominated the skyline for more than 900 years; the best view of it is from the river bridge.

The town was loyally supported by the Stuarts during England's civil war and was dubbed "the city faithful in war and peace." Birthplace of England's premier composer, Sir Edward Elgar, Worcester also has an impressive history of musical and cultural events.

## ESSENTIALS

**GETTING THERE**   Regular trains from London's Paddington Station take about 2¼ hours. For schedules and information, call ☎ **0345/484950.**

The National Express bus leaves throughout the day from London's Victoria Coach Station. For schedules and information, call ☎ **0990/808080.**

If you're driving, take the M5 to Junction 7 toward Worcester. Give yourself about 3 hours for the road trip.

**VISITOR INFORMATION**   **Worcester Tourist Information Centre,** High Street (in the Queen Anne's Guildhall) (☎ **01905/726311**), is open from mid-March through October, Monday to Saturday from 10:30am to 5:30pm; and from November to mid-March, Monday to Saturday from 10:30am to 4pm.

## EXPLORING WORCESTER

**Worcester Cathedral** (☎ **01905/611002**) with its 200-foot tower stands majestically beside the river. The original crypt, dating from 1084, is a classic example of Norman architecture and is still in daily use. The tombs of King John (died 1216), whose claim to fame is the Magna Carta, and Prince Arthur (died 1502), the elder brother of Henry VII, can both be found near the High Altar. The 12th-century Chapter House is one of the finest in England and, along with the Cloisters, evokes a rich monastic past. The cathedral has a long tradition of the finest choral music and hosts the oldest choral festival in Europe, the Three Choirs Festival. The cathedral is open daily from 7:30am to 6pm. There is no admission charge, but each adult visitor is asked to donate £2 ($3.20).

The premier attraction is the **Royal Worcester Porcelain Factory,** Severn Street (☎ **01905/23221.** With the sole objective of creating "ware of a form so precise as to be easily distinguished from other English porcelain," the factory has continued to achieve its goal ever since its founding in 1751. It produces a unique range of fine china and porcelain that remains unsurpassed throughout the world. Behind-the-scenes tours are given Monday through Friday beginning at 10:25am and costing £4.95 ($7.90) for adults and £4.50 ($7.20) for seniors and £3.25 ($5.20) for children over 11. Tours last about 45 minutes. Children under 11, very senior citizens, and travelers with disabilities can't take the tour because of safety regulations. Call ahead to reserve your place on a tour (for that day, phone before 10am). The **Retail and Seconds Shops** at the factory are open to all and offer a chance to buy the beauty of Royal Worcester at bargain prices. Many pieces are marked as seconds, though most of the time the flaws are unnoticeable. The **Dyson Perrins Museum** is also located at the factory and houses the world's largest collection of Worcester Porcelain. The museum is open Monday to Saturday from 9am to 5:30pm. Admission is £1.75 ($2.80) for adults and £1 ($1.60) for seniors and children.

The **Commandery,** Sidbury (☎ **01905/355071**), originally the 11th-century Hospital of St. Wulstan, was transformed over the years into a sprawling 15th-century, medieval timber-framed building that served as the country home of the Wylde family. This was the headquarters of King Charles II during the Battle of Worcester, which finally ended the English Civil War in 1651. The great hall has a hammerbeam roof and a minstrels' gallery. England's premier **Civil War Centre** is now situated here. This exciting, interactive, and hands-on museum marvelously incorporates life-size figures, sound systems, and videos to take you through the bloody and turbulent years of England's Civil War. You can even try on helmets, handle weapons, and dare to pick up cannon balls. The Commandery also has canalside tearooms, a picnic area, and a Garden of Fragrance. The house is open Monday to Saturday from 10am to 5pm and on Sunday from 1:30 to 5:30pm. Admission is £3.40 ($5.45) for adults, £2.30 ($3.70) for children and seniors, or £9 ($14.40) for a family ticket. The Commandery is a 3-minute walk from Worcester Cathedral.

Another site in Worcester to check out is the **Museum of Local Life,** Friar Street (☎ **01905/722349**), with its displays portraying life in the city during the past 200 years. Opening times are Monday to Saturday (closed on Thursday) from 10:30am to 5pm. Admission prices are £1.50 ($2.40) for adults and 75p ($1.20) for children, students, and seniors.

**Queen Anne's Guildhall,** High Street (☎ **01905/723471**), was built between 1721 and 1723. Here you'll find statues dutifully erected by the Royalists honoring Charles I and Charles II as well as one of the most beautifully decorated Queen Anne rooms in England. Open Monday to Saturday from 9am to 5pm. Admission is free. Be sure to check with the Tourist Information Centre (☎ **01905/726311**), conveniently located in the guildhall, for details on summer walking tours and Pump Room teas.

**Sir Edward Elgar's Birthplace,** Crown East Lane, Lower Broadheath (☎ **01905/ 333224**), about 3 miles west of Worcester off A44, is a charming, inviting red-brick country cottage, stable, and coach house—all set on well-tended grounds. Elgar, England's greatest composer, was born in this early 19th-century house on June 2, 1857. Today, the cottage houses a unique collection of manuscripts and musical scores, photographs, and other personal memorabilia depicting Elgar's achievements and wide range of interests. Musicians and conductors come from afar to pay homage to Elgar. To reach the house, drive out of Worcester on the A44 toward Leominster. After 2 miles, turn off to the right at the sign. The house is in the village, half a mile down a side road. It's open in summer from 10:30am to 6pm, and in winter from 1:30 to 4:30pm; closed Wednesday and from mid-January to mid-February. Admission is £3 ($4.80) for adults, £2 ($3.20) for seniors, 50p (80¢) for children.

## OUTDOOR PURSUITS

**Bickerline River Trips,** south quay near the Cathedral (☎ **01531/670679**), lets you leisurely see Worcester from the river aboard the 88-passenger *Marianne*. These 45-minute trips set sail every day on the hour from 11am to 5pm and until 6pm on Saturday and Sunday. Light refreshments are served and party bookings are available.

**Worcester Racecourse,** Pitchcroft (☎ **01905/25364**), gives you an ideal spot to enjoy the spectacle of the "sport of kings." This riverside course is an oval of about 1 mile and 5 furlongs with a finishing straight of 4 furlongs and run-in of 220 yards. Open on a variety of days from mid-April to the beginning of December (call for race days and admission).

## SHOPPING

For elegant Royal Worcester porcelain, stop by the Retail Best and Seconds Shops at the **Royal Worcester Porcelain Factory** (see above). Stroll down the architecturally important **Friar Street** to experience the most interesting collection of individual timber-framed and brick shops in Worcester.

**G. R. Pratley & Sons,** Shambles (☎ **01905/22678** or 01905/28642), offer a smorgasbord of glass, china, and earthenware. **Bygones of Worcester,** 55 Sidbury & Cathedral Sq. (☎ **01905/23132** or 01905/25388), is actually two shops packed with an intriguing and eclectic collection of antiques and odds and ends. Wander through this store to find furnishings for your home that range from the bizarre to the decorative and fanciful—all from cottages and castles in England.

## WHERE TO STAY

**Burgage House.** 4 College Precincts, Worcester, Hereford & Worcester WR1 2LG. ☎ and fax **01905/25396.** 9 rms, 2 with bath. TV. £28–£30 ($44.80–$48) single without bath, £40 ($64) single with bath; £40–£42 ($64–$67.20) double without bath, £48 ($76.80) double with bath. No credit cards.

Within a stone's throw of the cathedral, this brick-sided Georgian-style house, whose components were built as two separate houses in 1750, were combined into a single unit in 1858. Soon after, the British government acquired it as the headquarters of a branch of its local bureaucracy, a fact that caused untold headaches for its eventual renovator (and savior), Janette Ratcliffe. Assisted by her son, Martin, she ripped out the worst vestiges of drab officialdom after her takeover in 1987, installing in its place a country-cottage look of soft chintzes. Scattered throughout, you'll find clusters of old, sometimes antique (occasionally Jacobean) furnishings in the public rooms. Carefully choreographed breakfasts are part of your experience here.

**40 Britannia Square.** 40 Britannia Sq., Worcester, Hereford & Worcester WR1 3DN. ☎ **01905/611920.** Fax 01905/27152. 3 rms, 2 cottage suites. TV. £45 ($72) single; £55 ($88) double; £70 ($112) cottage suite for 1 or 2. All rates include breakfast. MC, V.

It's only subtly different from the 50-or-so equivalent stucco-fronted buildings that surround what civic boosters refer to as one of the largest fully intact Regency squares in England. Operated by John and Val Lloyd, and outfitted with a carefully matched collection of early 19th-century furnishings, it incorporates dozens of laboriously stenciled or *faux* marbelized walls and ceilings, and frequent reminders of the era of the house's original construction in 1820. Rooms have touches of vaguely feminine frills, and lots of modern convenience and comforts. Largest of all are the pair of cottage suites within what were originally constructed as outbuildings, stables, and/or servant's quarters.

## WHERE TO EAT

**Farriers Arms.** 9 Fish St. ☎ **01905/27569.** Platters £3.45–£12 ($5.50–$19.20). No credit cards. Mon–Sat 11am–11pm; Sun noon–10:30pm. BRITISH.

This is the most historic and evocative drinking and dining haven in Worcester. Housed within the second-oldest building in town—a 15th-century half-timbered affair that's exceeded in age only by the Cardinal's House. Don't expect grand cuisine, as the viands are ham-fisted, very British, without a shred of continental artistry. Food, rather, is crafted as an appropriate foil for any of the quintet of ales and lagers (including Courage Directors Bitter) that management keeps flowing from taps. Rib-sticking platters usually include steak and ale pie; fisherman's pie; steaks, fried plaice with tartar sauce, and an old-fashioned version of pork and cider cobbler that doesn't frequently appear in many other pubs.

**Pasha Indian Cuisine.** 56 St. Johns. ☎ **01905/426327.** Main courses £4.50–£9.25 ($7.20–$14.80). AE, MC, V. Mon–Sat noon–2pm and 5:30pm–midnight; Sun 1–3pm and 5:30pm–midnight. INDIAN.

This is the best and most authentic Indian restaurant in town, purveying a spicy, slow-cooked cuisine from a position across the River Severn from the city's cathedral. Within an ambience dotted with the handcrafts and lore of India, you can enjoy such dishes as chicken with yogurt, lamb with coriander and cumin, and a particularly succulent version of Tandoori shahi masala (king prawns slow-cooked in a tandoori oven).

## WORCESTER AFTER DARK

Set aside some time and energy to experience the river charm and friendliness of this town at night. If you have a penchant for down-home English pubs and neighborhood bars, a host of local haunts awaits your discovery. Or if you're more in the mood for a cultural experience from the other end of the spectrum, give the **Worcester Swan Theatre** (☎ 01905/27322) a go. It is the county's only professional repertory venue and provides year-round entertainment of the highest quality—plays, concerts, and dance.

One of Worcester's most whimsical and gently irreverent pubs is the **Little Sauce Factory,** London Road (☎ 01905/350159), where the layer of sawdust scattered across the floor is designed to mop up the beer you might happen to spill whilst laughing at an off-color joke. The entire place is a takeoff on Worcester's famous sauce, and contains posters advertising food flavorings, all the accessories of an old-fashioned kitchen, and an enormous ceiling map of Britain set out in ceramic tiles as a kind of quirky art object. Bar platters (grilled chicken, steak pies) cost from £5 to £7 ($8 to $11.20) each, and go swimmingly well when accompanied with such sauces as Carlsberg lager.

For a more authentic, somewhat less contrived atmosphere, you might drop into a pub favored by local residents—known for welcoming the seamstresses and laborers at Worcester's famous (now mostly defunct) glove factories. **The Pub at Ye Old Talbot Hotel,** Friar Street (☎ **01905/23573**), across from the cathedral, contains lots of Victorian nostalgia and old-fashioned wood paneling darkened by generations of billowing cigarette smoke and beer. It offers the kind of pub grub that nobody expects to be any good but that's darn well acceptable, especially when accompanied with a pint of the house's half-dozen ales on tap. If you get too potted to find your way home after an evening here, there are 29 simple, no-frills rooms upstairs, each with bathroom, for between £35 to £49.50 ($56 to $79.20) for a single, and for £49.50 to £59.50 ($79.20 to $95.20) for a double.

# LEDBURY

119 miles NW of London; 14 miles W of Hereford; 16 miles SW of Worcester

A thriving market town since 1120, Ledbury's wealth of historic black-and-white half-timbered buildings set against a rustic backdrop creates a magical fairy tale town, especially in springtime when bluebells and wild daffodils abound and the scent of apple blossoms fills the air. Famous 19th-century poet Elizabeth Barrett Browning spent here childhood in nearby Wellington at Hope End (now a hotel), and the renowned poet laureate John Mansfield was born and raised in Ledbury.

## ESSENTIALS

**GETTING THERE**    From London by train, board at the Paddington Station for the $2^{1}/_{2}$ hour trip. For schedules and information, call ☎ **0345/484950.**

Two National Express buses leave daily from London's Victoria Coach Station for the 3-plus–hour trip to Ledbury. For schedules and information, call **0990/808080.**

By car take the M50 south toward Wales and exit northwest on the A417 toward Ledbury.

**VISITOR INFORMATION**    The **Ledbury Tourist Information Centre** is located at 3 The Homend (☎ **01531/636147**). It is open daily from 10am to 5pm all year.

## EXPLORING LEDBURY

Within easy walking distance of the Tourist Information Centre, you will find the delightfully cobbled **Church Lane,** which is so well preserved that it is often used as a movie set. *Little Lord Fauntleroy* and *By the Sword Divided* are two films in which you'll be able to spy Church Lane. **The Painted Room** (☎ **01531/635457**), located in the Old Council Offices in Church Lane, features a series of 16th-century frescoes found during 1991 renovations to the building. Open daily from 11am to 2pm if a staff member is available or a tour can be arranged by phoning ahead. The tour costs £1 ($1.60) per person.

**Eastnor Castle,** $2^{1}/_{2}$ miles east of Ledbury on the A438 (☎ **01531/633160**), transports you back to a more romantic time. Built in 1812 by a local aristocrat, Eastnor has undergone a virtual renaissance thanks to the hard work, dedication, and youthful vitality of the Hervey-Bathursts, descendants of the castle's original owner. The many rooms are spectacularly appointed and overflow with early Italian fine art, 17th-century Venetian furniture, and Flemish tapestries, plus medieval armor and paintings by Van Dyck, Reynolds, Romney, and Watts. Lunches and teas are also available. Open from Easter to the end of September on Sunday and bank holiday Mondays from 11am to 5pm. During July and August, the castle is open Sunday to Friday. Admission is £4 ($6.40) for adults and £2 ($3.20) for children.

**Hellen's Much Marcle,** 4 miles southwest of Ledbury in Much Marcle (☎ 01531/660668), begun in 1292, is the boyhood home of the original Knight of the Garter. This ancient manor, brimming with a haunting atmosphere, still houses the great fireplace by which Queen Isabella of England waited for the Great Seal and abdication of King Edward II in 1326 as well as the bedroom prepared for Bloody Mary Queen of England in 1554. Guided tours are available on the hour from 2 to 5pm Good Friday to the beginning of October. Admission is £3 ($4.80) for adults and £1 ($1.60) for children.

**Westons Cider Mill,** The Bounds, Much Marcle (☎ 01531/660233), in the middle of cider apple and perry pear orchards, was established in 1880 by the tenant farmer Henry Weston. Although a somewhat long affair lasting $2^{1}/_{2}$ hours, the tour of the mill is a real treat and includes a tasting of ciders and perries in the Visitors Centre and shop. The mill is open all year, Monday to Friday from 9:30am to 4:30pm and on Saturday from 10am to 1pm. Tours need to be booked ahead of time and admission is £3 ($4.80) for adults and £2 ($3.20) for children. Cider tasting without the tour is free in the mill's shop.

## SHOPPING

Ledbury has always been a crossroads for commerce and trade and was recognized in King Stephen's charter more than 850 years ago for its commercial importance. Today, Ledbury is still a busy center of shopping and quality craftwork. Every street is worth exploring for the many unique craft galleries and antique shops.

**Homend Pottery,** 205 The Homend (☎ 01531/634571), is a gallery and showroom of practical pots ranging from kitchen to conservatory design. All wares are hand thrown and decorated in the Homend workshops.

## WHERE TO STAY

**The Barn House.** New St., Ledbury, Hereford & Worcester HR8 2DX. ☎ 01531/632825. 3 rms, 1 with bath. TV. £35 ($56) single without bath, £40 ($64) single with bath; £42 ($67.20) double without bath, £48 ($76.80) double with bath. All rates include breakfast. MC, V.

In the heart of Ledbury, this charming B&B occupies what was built around 1600 as a farmhouse and barn. During the late Victorian age, it functioned as the corporate headquarters of a local bottling plant for mineral water. Most of the improvements that made the place livable were added in the 1920s, guaranteeing oaken panels and fine woodwork that add an Edwardian flavor to an otherwise purely 17th-century design. Bedrooms are homey and uncomplicated—very much like what you'd find in the private homes of tasteful but unflashy homes throughout England. Your hosts are Richard and Judy Holland, whose family has lived in the house for at least 30 years prior to the day they began accepting overnight guests. Under rare circumstances, you might arrange an evening meal on the premises, but since many of the town's restaurants lie within walking distance, many patrons prefer to try their luck in town.

✪ **Wall Hills Country Guesthouse.** Hereford Rd., Ledbury, Hereford & Worcester HR8 2PR. ☎ 01531/632833. 3 rms. TV. £30–£38 ($48–$60.80) single; £52 ($83.20) double. Discounts offered for stays of 2 nights or more. MC, V.

Its builders, during its original construction in 1750, positioned the brick walls of this manor in ways that profited most artfully from the sweeping views that still lead downhill through cider apple orchards and fields of hops. This place lies $1^{1}/_{2}$ miles west of Ledbury, beside the A438 highway. In the late 1980s, it was bought and refurbished by David and Jennifer Slaughter, devoted hosts and chefs, who accurately maintain that the highlight of a visit to their home is one of their set-price evening meals (available only with a few hour's advance notification) that's reasonably priced at £15.75 ($25.20) per person. Menu items are carefully crafted by David, a master chef who grows at least some of the produce that goes into his craft. Especially succulent are seasonal versions of Blue Nile perch prepared with vermouth and fresh fennel, salmon with a saffron cream sauce, or a broiled breast of pheasant stuffed with herbs and wrapped in bacon. If for any reason you've opted to be a teetotaler during your trip to England, be warned that the cuisine at this place derives at least some of its allure from the copious amounts of vermouth, sherry, whisky, or wine the chef laces into his stew and saucepots. All but a few of the patrons here approve of that wholeheartedly, but if you object, you'll have to make your wishes understood in advance. Accommodations are large, high-ceilinged, comfortable, with a refreshing lack of trendiness. The 6 acres associated with this place contain architectural oddities from the 15th century (an A-framed cruck barn and an oast house). Even more impressive, the somber-looking ruin of an Iron Age fort lies within a farmer's field atop a nearby hill.

**Ye Olde Talbot Hotel.** New St., Ledbury, Hereford & Worcester HR8 2DX. ☎ **01531/ 632963.** 6 rms, 2 with bath. TV. £31.50 ($50.40) single or double without bath; £36.50 ($58.40) single or double with bath. AE, MC, V.

Among centrally located Ledbury restaurants and pubs, the Elizabethan authenticity of this place is rivaled (but not exceeded) only by the half-timbering of The Feathers hotel and restaurant, which in some ways this place closely resembles. The main allure of the place derives from its restaurant and pub (see "Where to Eat," below). It describes itself as a "restaurant and pub with rooms"; those rooms are evocative, but a bit more battered, with floors a bit more squeaky, than you might have hoped. The barkeep here stayed in a room during a business trip and returned to the place as its full-time employee. Rooms in back allow you to sleep through the morning road traffic in front, and of them all, room 7 is the most appealing.

## WHERE TO EAT

**Ye Olde Talbot Hotel.** New St. ☎ **01531/632963.** Main courses £4.95–£10 ($7.90–$16). AE, MC, V. Daily noon–2:30pm and 6:30–9:30pm. BRITISH.

This place is one of the most evocative pubs in town, having seen thousands of pints of beer quaffed or spilled by clients who at one time or another have included virtually everyone in town. If your tipples last longer than you thought, a half-dozen rooms upstairs can shelter you for the night (see "Where to Stay"), and you can even dine on simple but rib-sticking dishes that are usually marked on the morning of your arrival on the chalkboard. Examples include bangers and mash (sausage and mashed potatoes), steak and ale pies, turkey scalloppine, halibut steak with tartar sauce, and pork tenderloin. Place your food order at the bar, and wait until a staff member transports the finished product to your table.

# 7 Shropshire

Immortalized by A. E. Housman's *A Shropshire Lad,* this hilly county borders Wales, which accounts for its turbulent history. The bloody battles are over today, and the towns of Shropshire, with their black-and-white timbered houses, are peaceful and quiet. The county makes a good base for touring in the Welsh mountains.

When Parliament redistricted and even renamed some of the shires of England in 1973, the name of Shropshire was changed back to a much older name—Salop. However, in this case, the name just didn't catch on, and you'll find the county still called Shropshire on recent maps and by most of its inhabitants.

# SHREWSBURY

164 miles NW of London; 39 miles SW of Stoke-on-Trent; 48 miles NW of Birmingham

Before the Norman conquest, Shrewsbury was the Saxon town of Scrobbesbyrig and occupied two hills within the horseshoe bend of the Severn River. The river almost enclosed the town serving as a natural fortification, and its well-preserved castle (built after the Norman conquest by a powerful kinsman of William the Conqueror) still commands the land approach. Shrewsbury, with its skyline of towers and spires, is the capital of Shropshire. Known for its cakes and ale, Shrewsbury contains one of the best-known schools in England. It was also the birthplace of Charles Darwin. And Ellis Peters' chronicles of the 12th-century detective monk, Brother Cadfael, are set in and inspired by this medieval market town.

The finest Tudor town in England, Shrewsbury is noted for its black-and-white buildings of timber and plaster, including Abbot's House from 1450 and the tall gabled Ireland's Mansion from 1575 standing on High Street. These houses were built by the powerful and prosperous wool traders or Drapers. Charles Dickens wrote of his stay in Shrewsbury's Lion Hotel, "I am lodged in the strangest little rooms, the ceilings of which I can touch with my hands. From the windows I can look all downhill and slantwise at the crookedest black and white houses, all of many shapes except straight shapes." The town also has a number of Georgian and Regency mansions, some old bridges, and handsome churches, including the Abbey Church of St. Peter and St. Mary's Church.

## ESSENTIALS

**GETTING THERE**   Taking the train from London's Euston Station, you'll have to change in Birmingham. Allow 3 hours for this trip. For schedules and information, call ☎ **0345/484950.**

Three National Express buses leave daily from London's Victoria Coach Station for the 5-hour trip. For schedules and information, call ☎ **0990/808080.**

If you make the 2¹/₂-hour car trip, you'll take the M1 to the M6 to the M54 and exit onto the A5 which will take you directly to Shrewsbury.

**VISITOR INFORMATION**   The Shrewsbury **Tourist Information Centre,** The Square (**01743/350761**), is open May 26 to September 30, Monday to Saturday from 10am to 6pm and on Sunday from 10am to 4pm; and October to late May, Monday to Saturday from 10am to 5pm plus in April and May on Sunday before bank holidays from 10am to 4pm.

## SEEING SHREWSBURY

Many tales and stories are locked within Shrewsbury's winding narrow streets and black-and-white structures. And the best way to get the scoop on all the local lore and characters from the past is to take one of the many walking or coach tours hosted by an official Shrewsbury guide. Special themed walking tours such as Ghosts, Brother Cadfael, and the Civil War are also available. A typical town tour starts in the town center and lasts on average 1¹/₂ hours. Tickets can be purchased from the Tourist Information Centre (see above).

**Shrewsbury Castle,** Castle Street (☎ **01743/358516**), built by a Norman earl, Roger de Montgomery, in 1083 as a powerful fortress of central strategic importance to secure the border with Wales, stands in a dominating position where the River Severn almost surrounds the town. The Great Hall and walls were constructed during the reign of Edward I. Then Thomas Telford extensively remodeled the castle inside and out 200 years ago. It houses the Shropshire Regimental Museum, including the collections of the King's Shropshire Light Infantry, the Shropshire

Yeomanry, and the Shropshire Royal Horse Artillery. The collections represent more than 300 years of regimental service and include a lock of Napoléon's hair and an American flag captured in 1814 when the White House was seized and burned in the War of 1812. The castle is open Easter through September, Tuesday to Saturday from 10am to 4:30pm and Sunday from 10am to 4:30pm.

**Rowley's House Museum,** Barker Street (☎ **01743/361196**), is housed in a fine 16th-century timber-frame warehouse and an adjoining 17th-century brick and stone mansion dating from 1618. This museum includes displays on art, local history, Roman and prehistoric archaeology, geology, costumes, and natural history. The great treasures include the Hadrianic forum inscription and silver mirror, both from the nearby Roman city of Viroconium (Wroxeter). There is also a new display of Shropshire ceramics and tiles. The museum is open year-round Tuesday to Saturday from 10am to 5pm; and also from June to September and April/May bank holidays on Sunday from 10am to 4pm. Admission is £2 ($3.20) for adults, £1 ($1.60) for students and seniors, and 50p (80¢) for children.

**Clive House Museum,** College Hill (☎ **01743/354811**), a Georgian town house of Clive of India when he served as mayor and M.P. for Shrewsbury in the 1760s, contains period rooms and local pottery and porcelain, early watercolors, and textiles, plus displays on the natural historians of 19th-century Shrewsbury such as Charles Darwin. There is also a secluded walled garden. Open Tuesday to Saturday from 10am to 4pm. Admission is £2 ($3.20) for adults, £1 ($1.60) for students and seniors, and 50p (80¢) for children.

**Attingham Park,** Shrewsbury (☎ **01743/709203**), an elegant classical house set on 250 acres of woodlands and landscaped deer park, is graced with superbly decorated staterooms, including a red dining room and blue drawing room. Treasures of the house include Regency silver used at 19th-century ambassadorial receptions and elegant Italian furniture. The house is open March 22 to November 2, Saturday to Wednesday from 1:30 to 5pm; on bank holiday Mondays from 11am to 5pm; and in October, Saturday and Sunday from 1:30 to 5pm. The park and grounds are open daily during daylight hours. House admission is £3.80 ($6.10) for adults, £1.90 ($3.05) for children, and £10 ($16) for a family ticket. Park and grounds admission is £1.50 ($2.40) for adults and 75p ($1.20) for children.

**Shrewsbury Abbey,** Abbey Foregate (☎ **01743/232723**), founded in 1083, became one of the most powerful Benedictine monasteries and is the center of the Brother Cadfael tales made so famous by Ellis Peters's mystery books and more recently adapted for television. The church remains in use to this day, and visitors can see displays devoted to the abbey's history as well as the remains of the 14th-century shrine of St. Winefride. Open Easter to October, daily from 9:30am to 5:30pm, and November to Easter, daily from 10:30am to 3pm. Admission is free, but donations are requested for the Abbey Fund.

**The Shrewsbury Quest,** Abbey Foregate (☎ **01743/243324** or 01743/355990), on the site of the 5-century-old Benedictine Abbey of St. Peter and St. Paul, brings the world of the medieval monastary to life with busy tradespeople, a great store, sweet sounds of dulcimer, harp, and lute, Vesper bells, plus monastic gardens planted with a collection of herbs dating from the 12th century. Visitors can participate in different activities, including the making of a decorated manuscript in the Scriptorium, solve mysteries like Ellis Peters's Brother Cadfael, and play ancient games of skill in the Cloisters. Open April to October, daily from 10am to 5pm and November to March, daily from 10am to 4pm. Closed December 25 and January 1. Admission is £3.95 ($6.30) for adults, £3.20 ($5.10) for seniors and students, and £2.50 ($4) for children under 12.

## SHOPPING

Walk down any of the narrow, cobbled streets of Shrewsbury for a shopping experience filled with the character of small, independent shops and the charm of Tudor-fronted stores vending an array of secondhand books, Art-Deco bric-a-brac, geological specimens, musical instruments, and antiques.

**St. Julian's Craft Centre,** Wyle Cop (☎ **01743/353516**), housed in a 12th-century tower, has been the symbol of high-quality locally made crafts for 16 years. Shoppers can also see craftspeople at work in the center of the tower. Examples of wares include prints, frames, jewelry, boots and shoes, cards, handmade clothes, pottery, woodwork, slatework, pine furniture. Saturday craft fairs and art exhibitions every fortnight provide constantly changing attractions.

**Mansers Antiques,** 53–54 Wyle Cop (☎ **01743/351120**) always ready to give free advice, offers one of the largest comprehensive stocks of antiques in the U.K. Items for sale include furniture of all periods, silver and plate, china and glass, clocks and metal goods, jewelry, linen, pictures, and items from Asia. The establishment has a restoration department and will ship purchases. **Carnival Crafts,** 26–27 The Parade Shops, St. Mary's Place (☎ **01743/366713**), boasts a fun and beautiful assortment of unusual handcrafted gifts from Britain and around the world. Crafts available include African and Balinese carvings, Italian music boxes and ceramics, unique glass from Britain, Gozo, and Gibraltar.

Some shopping destinations for books, maps, and prints include the **Victorian Gallery** (prints) at 40 St. John's Hill (☎ **01743/356351**) and **Quarry Books** (secondhand and antiquarian) at 24 Clarmemont Hill (☎ **01743/361404**).

## WHERE TO STAY

**The Manse.** 1 Swan Hill, Shrewsbury, Shropshire SY1 1NL. ☎ **01743/242659.** 2 rms, 1 with bath. TV. £25 ($40) single without bath, £30 ($48) single with bath; £36 ($57.60) double without bath, £38 ($60.80) double with bath. All rates include breakfast. No credit cards. Closed 1 week at Christmas.

Until around 1975, this Georgian house (ca. 1770) functioned as the residence of a local minister, who conducted services, partly in Welsh, within the adjacent Congregationalist Church. Today, it's the home of Maureen Cox, a genteel host who opens two of the bedrooms within her red-brick house to paying guests who appreciate a position within a 2-minute walk of both the river and the town center. Accommodations are outfitted with tea makers and a medley of antique and old furniture, and permeated with a lot of personalized charm. Breakfast is the only meal served.

**Sydney House Hotel.** Coton Crescent, Coton Hill, Shrewsbury, Shropshire SY1 2LJ. ☎ and fax **01743/354681.** 7 rms, 4 with bath. TV. £35 ($56) single without bath, £45 ($72) single with bath; £46 ($73.60) double without bath, £60 ($96) double with bath. AE, MC, V.

Your hosts, Terence and Pauline Hyde, are transplants to Shrewsbury from the English Midlands, and as such, probably work harder than dyed-in-the-wool locals at promoting the attractions of their adopted town. Their headquarters lies within a whimsical-looking Edwardian house, which combines red brick walls with vague aspects of a Teutonic chalet. Built around 1900, it lies only 700 yards from the railway station, and a 10-minute walk north of the town center. Inside, you'll find a comfortably upholstered but not at all lavish set of public areas and bedrooms, each sunny and bright and very clean, but without any particularly antique references. The street level is devoted to a restaurant, where the Hydes prepare dinners (but not lunches) every day of the week from 7:30 to 8:30pm. Two- and three-course meals are reasonably priced at £9 ($14.40) and £11.50 ($18.40), respectively, and include simple and unpretentious versions of deep-fried brie with cranberry sauce; baked whole rainbow trout; and braised pork steak in a creamy paprika sauce. Liquor is served, but only to residents of the hotel or clients consuming a meal.

## WHERE TO EAT

**The Peach Tree.** 21 Abbey Foregate. ☎ **01743/355055.** Reservations recommended. Main courses £7.95–£11.95 ($12.70–$19.10). AE, MC, V. Tues–Sun 12:30–2pm; Tues–Sat 7–9:30pm. BRITISH/EUROPEAN.

Its name derives from the hundreds of ripe peaches, fruiting peach trees, and peach boughs that someone laboriously stenciled onto the walls. The setting dates from the 15th century, when the big-windowed site functioned as a weaver's cottage set adjacent to the abbey. Cuisine is based on solid, time-tested recipes concocted from fresh ingredients with dollops of European savoir-faire, and as such are among the most interesting of any offered by any competitor in town. They include roast breast of duck with traditional blackberry and red wine sauce; filet steak with mushrooms, garlic, white wine, and cream; and such vegetarian main courses as a cashew and hazelnut loaf served with an apricot and ginger sauce. The dessert that keeps everyone coming back for more is homemade meringue with ice cream, traditional butterscotch sauce, and shreddings of roasted coconut. Although the culinary pomp and circumstance of this place is most visible within the upstairs restaurant, any of the platters can be served informally in the street-level bar if you're alone or in a hurry.

**Porter's Food Pub.** 62–63 Mardol. ☎ **01743/352214.** Reservations not accepted. Snacks and platters £1.95–£6.95 ($3.10–$11.10). No credit cards. Food service Mon–Sat 9am–5pm; Wed–Sat 7–9pm, bar service till 11pm. BRITISH.

It isn't the only antique pub in Shrewsbury, but according to its fans, it's the most evocative for dialogue and chitchat among strangers. Until 1995, its antique premises, somberly rustic premises had housed just about anything anyone could ever think of, including a chemist shop and a wine bar. Since then, members of the Richards family have promoted local trade, especially among office workers during their lunch hour, thanks to Bass Ale and Carling lager on tap, and a simple but flavorful roster of platters (baguette sandwiches, stuffed "jacket," or baked, potatoes, deep-fried breaded brie, and ham or tuna salads, and heartier fare such as breaded plaice or cod; sirloin steaks, and main-course pies made with beef and stout. Fish fingers and chicken nuggets are whipped up as part of children's platters.

## SHREWSBURY AFTER DARK

Nightlife in this capital city provides a healthy mix of pubs, clubs, and theaters—all of which offer you ample opportunity to rub elbows with the locals. Whet your thirst, if it appeals to you at the **Lion & Pheasant Hotel** bar, 49–50 Wyle Cop (☎ **01743/236288**), which has an inviting ambience of firelight in the colder months and a restaurant with an ample selection of food.

You may also want to check out the **Boat House Pub,** New Street (☎ **01743/362965**), located beside a beautiful old park on the River Severn. It is a favorite with the young crowd and has a fun terrace for the summer months and a lounge overlooking the river and fully bedecked with rowing regalia. Patrons here enjoy a healthy selection of beers and ales with grub ranging from soup to sandwiches to pies.

For clubs, the **Buttermarket Nightclub** (☎ **01743/241455**), set in the old buttermarket on Howard Street, caters to the over-25 crowd. It has 2 "theme" nights: a huge disco complete with DJs on Saturday and a world music night on Thursday featuring any number of styles of music ranging from reggae to jazz. Other clubs include the **Jazz and Roots Club** at the old buttermarket on Howard Street (☎ **01743/365913**) and the **Park Lane Nightclub,** Ravens Meadows

(☎ **01743/243283**), which attracts a younger scene. **The Music Hall,** The Square (☎ **01743/350763**), a virtual revolving door of performances, has musicals, plays, and concerts year-round. Tickets range from £10 to £20 ($16 to $32).

# IRONBRIDGE: BIRTHPLACE OF THE INDUSTRIAL REVOLUTION

135 miles NW of London; 36 miles NW of Birmingham; 18 miles SE of Shrewsbury

Ironbridge, located in the Ironbridge Gorge, is famous for being the place where the Industrial Revolution started. Indeed, this stretch of the Severn River valley has been an important industrial area since the Middle Ages when coal and limestone were exploited. And iron has been made here since the time of Henry VIII. But the real event that clinched this area's importance came in 1709, when the Quaker iron-master, Abraham Darby I discovered the method of smelting iron using coke as a fuel instead of charcoal. This paved the way for the first iron rails, boats, wheels, iron aq-ueducts, iron-framed buildings, and of course the first iron bridge which was cast in Coalbrookdale in 1779. So momentous was this accomplishment that the area was renamed from Coalbrookdale to Iron Bridge. The area literally buzzed with the new transportation and engineering innovations that soon followed.

This area is the location of an intriguing complex of museums that documents and brings to life the rich history of Ironbridge Gorge. The Ironbridge Gorge Museums spread over some 6 square miles of the Severn Gorge, encompassing a unique series of industrial monuments and displays. A passport ticket can be purchased at any of the museums for a special price. This passport ticket admits the visitor to all of the museums and remains valid until each site has been visited once.

## ESSENTIALS

**GETTING THERE**   Trains leave from London's Euston Station and run to Telford Central Station in Telford after which you'll need to take a bus or taxi onto Ironbridge. Expect a 3-hour trip. For schedules and information, call ☎ **0345/484950.**

Buses leave daily from London's Victoria Coach Station and arrive in Telford about 5 hours later. For schedules and information, call ☎ **0990/808080.** Local buses that leave Telford for the 20 minute ride to Ironbridge include nos. 6, 8, 9, and 99.

If you're driving a car from London, take the M1 to the M6 to the M54 which takes you right to Ironbridge.

**VISITOR INFORMATION**   The Ironbridge **Gorge Tourist Information Centre,** 4 The Wharfage (☎ **01952/432166**) is open Monday through Friday from 9am to 5pm and Saturday and Sunday from 10am to 5pm.

## THE IRONBRIDGE GORGE MUSEUMS

The Ironbridge Valley plays host to seven main museums and several smaller ones, collectively called the Ironbridge Gorge Museums, Ironbridge, Telford (☎ **01952/43352** on weekdays and 01952/432166 on Saturday and Sunday). Some of the museums include the **Coalbrookdale Museum** with its Darby Furnace of Iron and sound-and-light display along with Rosehill and Dale House (restored 19th-century homes of the Quaker ironmasters); the **Iron Bridge** with its original tollhouse; the **Jackfield Tile Museum** and Craven Dunnill where the visitor can see historic tiles as well as tile-pressing, decorating, and firing—all while having basic techniques explained; the **Blists Hill Open Air Museum** with a re-creation of a 19th-century town with costumed demonstrators; and **Coalport China Museum** devoted to the collection of Coalport china and the people who created it.

The sites are open September to June, daily from 10am to 5pm, and July and August daily from 10am to 6pm. The Iron Bridge Tollhouse and Rosehill House are closed November to March. A ticket to all the museums of the Ironbridge Gorge (passport ticket) is £9 ($14.40) for adults, £8 ($12.80) for seniors, £5.30 ($8.50) for students and children, and £28 ($44.80) for a family of two adults and up to five children.

## SHOPPING

The Ironbridge Valley, with its many museums, presents great shopping for Coalport china at the **Coalport China Museum** and decorative tile from the **Jackfield Tile Museum.** Another shopping locale worth visiting, located just beyond the Jackfield Museum, is **Maws Craft Workshops** (☎ **01952/883967** or 01952/883843), where 25 craft workshops are in an old Victorian tile works beside the River Severn. You'll find porcelain dolls, glass sculptures, dollhouses, original and Celtic art, pictures with frames made while you wait, pottery, jewelry, woodcraft, furniture, stained glass, art castings, hobby ceramics, hats, and children's clothes. There's also a tearoom open for lunch and afternoon tea.

## WHERE TO STAY

**Bridge House.** Buildwas, Telford, Shropshire TF8 7BN. ☎ **01952/432105.** 6 rms, 4 with bath. £48 ($76.80) double with bath. All rates include breakfast. AE, MC, V. Closed 2 weeks at Christmas.

Set 1¹/₂ miles west of Ironbridge, on the outskirts of the hamlet of Buildwas, this ivy-draped, half-timbered building originated in 1620 as a coaching inn ("The Abbey Inn") at the junction of routes heading to Much Wenlock and Shrewsbury. From 1911 to just after World War II, it functioned as a privately owned farmhouse until it was subdivided into two private houses. In 1985, the buildings were reunited into the inn you'll see today by resident proprietor Janet Hedges. She'll tell you unusual stories if you listen, including legends about there being 365 nails (one for every day of the year) holding together the planks of the front door; and the fact that the building's front porch was removed from the nearby abbey. Bedrooms are cozy, genteel, and comfortable in ways you'd expect in a private home, sometimes with touches of Edwardian drama (lavishly draped beds, in some cases). Some are even cluttered with exposed beams and testimonials (creaking floors, uneven walls) to the age of the building. No meals are served other than breakfast. The name of the hotel (Bridge House), incidentally, doesn't refer to the town's famous Iron Bridge, but to an older version nearby that, because it was decrepit and unsafe, was replaced several decades ago with a more modern version.

**Severn Lodge.** New Rd., Ironbridge, Telford, Shropshire TF8 7AS. ☎ and fax **01952/432148.** 3 rms. £24 ($38.40) single; £38 ($60.80) double. No credit cards.

It was built in l832 by a prosperous local landowner, Sir Buckworth Soames as a wedding gift for his daughter, at the time of her marriage to the local doctor. Brick built in the Georgian style, on impressive sandstone foundations, it remained a medical office until 1975, when it was taken over as a bed-and-breakfast hotel by your hosts, Nita and Alan Reed. Bedrooms are outfitted, Laura Ashley style, in a l9th-century style that's appropriate to the age of the house, with the personal touch of Mrs. Reed, a skilled decorator and former educator. With her husband, Alan, they're well-intentioned guides to the charms (both geological and sociological) of their region. No meals are served other than breakfast.

## WHERE TO EAT

**Restaurant Chez Maw.** In The Valley House Hotel. ☎ **01952/432247.** Reservations recommended. Main courses £15.50–£18.50 ($24.80–$29.60); set menus £15.50–£18.50 ($24.80–$29.60). AE, DC, MC, V. Daily noon–2pm and 7–9:30pm. BRITISH.

Its name has nothing to do with somebody's idea of an affectionate name for their mother: It refers to Arthur Maw, long-ago owner of the house, and founder and director of a nearby factory that produced decorative tiles during the 19th century. Prized examples of his ceramic creations line the reception area and the monumental staircase leading upstairs. Outfitted with crisp napery, Windsor-style chairs, formal draperies, and a high ceiling, the restaurant serves such food as tortellini laced with cream, herbs, and slices of Parma ham; platters of smoked tuna and marinated salmon; oriental-style salmon, sliced breast of duck with avocados and orange sauce; and filets of pork and beef drizzled with sauce made from Shropshire blue cheese. Anyone can precede a meal here with a round of drinks in the hotel's cocktail lounge.

## IRONBRIDGE AFTER DARK

If your after-dark desires include a rebuilt Victorian pub complete with a chicken coop in the backyard, the **New Inn** located within the Blists Hill Museum complex (☎ **01952/583003**) is just for you. It has atmosphere—dare we say ambience—with its gas lamps, sawdust floors, and its knowledgeable and friendly staff who all sport vintage Victorian garb. You'll find a goodly selection of ales, hearty, rib-sticking home-cooked meals, and a choice of favorite pub games.

# 8  Staffordshire & the Potteries

Virtually in the heart of England, halfway between the Irish and the North Seas, Staffordshire is a county of peaceful countryside, rugged Staffordshire Moorlands, and Cheshire Plains. Pottery is really Staffordshire's claim to fame. It's been in use in the area since 2000 B.C. Then when the Romans rolled through in A.D. 46, they set up a pottery kiln at Trent Vale. Later, a medieval kiln was established at Sneyd Green. But the town of Stoke-on-Trent is where people today go for pottery. Actually, Stoke-on-Trent is a loose confederation of six neighboring towns. Thanks to one of its famous native sons, the author Arnold Bennett (1867 to 1931), confusion surrounds the number of towns that actually makes up Stoke-on-Trent (also called The Potteries). In his novel, Anna of the Five Towns, which is set in the Stoke-on-Trent of his youth, Bennett writes of there being only five towns. However, since 1832, when the Parliamentary Borough of Stoke-on-Trent was established, six towns have made up Stoke-on-Trent: Tunstall, Burslem, Hanley, Stoke, Fenton, and Longton.

Other famous Staffordshire residents include the "Father of English Potters," Josiah Wedgwood (born in Burslem in 1730), and the famous pottery designer Susie Cooper (born in Tunstall in 1902), who struck out on her own and opened several successful pottery studios. In 1940, she was the first woman to be honored with the Royal Designer for Industry award.

## STOKE-ON-TRENT

162 miles NW of London; 46 miles N of Birmingham; 59 miles NW of Leicester; 58 miles SE of Liverpool; 41 miles S of Manchester

During and thanks mainly to the Industrial Revolution, the area known collectively as Stoke-on-Trent became the world's leading producer of pottery. Today, because of the worldwide interest in the making of pottery, this town has found itself a tourist attraction. It's the home of the pottery made famous by Josiah Wedgwood, along with other well-known names such as Coalport, Minton, and Spode. Stoke-on-Trent is actually an amalgamation of six towns that covers an area of 7 miles. The town of Hanley is the actual City Centre of Stoke-on-Trent.

## ESSENTIALS

**GETTING THERE**   It's a direct train ride of 2 hours to Stoke-on-Trent from London's Euston Station. For schedules and information, call ☎ **0345/484950.**

The National Express bus leaves London's Victoria Coach Station for the 4- to 5-hour trip to Stoke. For schedules and information, call ☎ **0990/808080.**

By car from London, drive along the M1 to the M6 to the A500 at Junction 15. It will take you 2 to 3 hours by car.

**VISITOR INFORMATION**   The Stoke-on-Trent **Tourist Information Centre,** Quadrant Road, Hanley, Stoke-on-Trent (☎ **01782/234600**), is open Monday through Saturday from 9:15am to 5:15pm.

## SEEING THE SIGHTS

While in Stoke-on-Trent, a retreat into the past is in order to get a good grounding in the town's history. Start at the **Stoke-on-Trent City Museum and Art Gallery,** Bethesda Street, Hanley (☎ **01782/232323**), for an overview on Stoke-on-Trent history. It houses departments of fine arts, decorative arts, natural history, archaeology, and social history. It also has one of the world's largest and finest collections of ceramics. Admission is free. Open Monday through Saturday from 10am to 5pm and Sunday from 2 to 5pm.

**The Gladstone Pottery Museum,** Uttoxeter Road at Longton (☎ **01782/319232**), is the only Victorian pottery factory from the era of coal-fired bottle ovens that has been restored as a museum, with craftspeople providing daily demonstrations in original workshops. Various galleries depict the rise of the Staffordshire pottery industry; tile history; sanitary ware with washstand bowls and jugs plus toilets of all shapes, sizes, colors, and decoration. There are replicas of a potter's house and a factory manager's office. Great hands-on opportunities for visitors to the museum include plate painting, pot throwing, and ornamental flower making. Gladstone is open daily from 10am to 5pm with the last admission at 4pm. Admission is £3.75 ($6) for adults, £2.75 ($4.40) for seniors and students, and £2.25 ($3.60) for children.

## SHOPPING

Stoke-on-Trent is a mecca for pottery and bone china. Get in shape for this adventure—there are over 40 factory shops in "The Potteries," as this area of England is so affectionately called. All of the factories have gift shops and seconds shops on site—in fact, some have several shops on site, that sell anything from fine china dinner services to hand-painted tiles. Seconds are always a great bargain—they are still high-quality pieces that have imperfections that only the professional can detect. Shops do reduce the price of their best ware at times but do not always offer shipping. Prices of first wares are the same in Stoke-on-Trent as they are in London or anywhere else in England. Therefore, you don't come here expecting to purchase first wares at discounts.

## WHERE TO STAY

**Corrie Guest House.** 13 Newton St., Basford, Stoke-on-Trent, Staffordshire ST4 6JN. ☎ **01782/614838.** 8 rms, 3 with bath. TV. £19 ($30.40) single without bath, £26 ($41.60) single with bath; £33 ($52.80) double without bath, £38 ($60.80) double with bath. No credit cards.

## Visiting the Potteries

**The Wedgwood Visitor Centre,** at Barlaston (☎ **01782/204218**), includes a demonstration hall where you can watch clay pots being formed on the potter's wheel, see how the raised motifs so well known on Wedgwood Jasper are made and added to the pieces, as well as witness how plates are turned and fired, then painted. Highly skilled potters and decorators are happy to answer your questions about their special occupation. An on-site cinema continually shows a video covering the 230 years of Wedgwood history and craftsmanship.

An art gallery and a gift shop showcase samples of factory-made items that also can be purchased. Wedgwood "seconds," which are available at reduced prices, are not sold at the center but are available at the **Wedgwood Group Factory Shop,** King Street Fenton (☎ **01782/316161**).

Also located at the Wedgwood Centre, the **Wedgwood Museum** covers 3 centuries of design and features "living" displays including Josiah Wedgwood's Etruria factory and his Victorian showroom. Other room settings can also be seen at the museum. The Josiah Wedgwood Restaurant is perfect in which to relax with a coffee or a full meal. You can even have your postcards franked with a special Portland vase stamp to say that they were mailed at the Wedgwood Centre; however, you must ask to have this done at the reception area.

Factory tours last 2 hours and are given Monday through Thursday at 10am and 2pm. Tours must be booked in advance. The center is open Monday through Friday from 9am to 5pm, Saturday from 10am to 5pm, and Sunday from 10am to 4pm. Tour admission is £7.25 ($11.60) for adults, seniors, students, and children 15 and older. Admission to everything else is £3.25 ($5.20) for adults; £1.60 ($2.55) for seniors, students, and children; and £7.95 ($12.70) for a family ticket (up to two adults and three children).

For the tour of the **Royal Doulton Pottery Factory,** Nile Street Burslem, near Stoke-on-Trent (☎ **01782/292434**), wear comfortable shoes. During the tour, you'll walk nearly a mile and tackle 250 steps, but you will see how plates, cups, and figures are made from start to finish. If this seems physically demanding, you can always see a factory tour in Royal Doulton's Video Theater. Live demonstrations of how figures are assembled from a mold and decorated are given at the Visitor Centre, which also has the world's largest collection of Royal Doulton figures.

Next door to the Visitor Centre is the **Minton Fine Art Studio** where plates and pillboxes are hand painted and richly decorated with gold before your eyes. As a note of interest, the training period for Royal Doulton figure painters is 2 years, and the raised paste gilders train for 7 years. Sir Henry Doulton Gallery contains a host of stoneware pieces, Lambeth wares, and other exhibits from the past 180 years. The Gallery Restaurant serves cakes and coffee, light lunches, and afternoon tea. Of course, everything is served on the finest bone china.

The gift shop is stocked with a full range of Royal Doulton figures and tableware. Tours are conducted Monday through Thursday from 10:30am to 2pm and Friday from 10:30am to 1:30pm. Tours must be booked in advance. The Visitor Centre is open Monday through Saturday from 9:30am to 5pm and Sunday from 10am to 4pm, and the shop is open Monday to Saturday from 9am to 5:30pm and Sunday from 10am to 4pm. Admission to just the Visitor Centre is £2.50 ($4) for adults; £1 ($1.60) for children aged 5 to 9; £2 ($3.20) for children aged 10 to 16, students, and seniors; and £7 ($11.20) for family tickets. Admission for both the tour and the Visitor Centre is £5 ($8) for adults; £4.50 ($7.20) for children aged 10 to 16, students, and seniors; and £17 ($27.20) for family tickets.

Since 1896, the **John Beswick Studios of Royal Doulton,** Gold Street, Longton, near Stoke-on-Trent (☎ **01782/291237**), have built a reputation for fine ceramic sculpture. Most renowned for its authentic studies of horses, birds, and animals, the studio also creates the famed Character and Toby Jugs of Royal Doulton. You may be lucky enough to see Peter Rabbit and other Beatrix Potter figures in the making during a visit. The 1¹/₂-hour tour ends in the factory shop so you can indulge your purchasing whims. Factory tours are Monday through Thursday at 10:15am and 2pm, and Friday at 10:15am and 1:30pm. Tours need to be booked in advance by calling ☎ **01782/291213.** The shop is open Monday through Friday from 9am to 4:30pm, and tour admission is £2.50 ($4) for adults and £2.25 ($3.60) for seniors and children 10 and older.

The oldest English pottery company still operating on the same site since 1770 and the birthplace of fine bone china, **Spode,** Church Street, Stoke-on-Trent (☎ **01782/744011**), offers regular factory tours lasting approximately 1¹/₂ hours and connoisseur tours lasting 2¹/₂ hours. In the Craft Centre, visitors can also see craftsmanship demonstrations of engraving, lithography, hand painting, printing, and clay casting. An unrivaled collection of Spode's ceramic masterpieces are on display in the Spode Museum. The Blue Italian Restaurant cooks up refreshments and lunch—all served on Spode's classic blue tableware, Blue Italian. The Factory Shop sells "seconds" at reduced prices.

Tours are conducted Monday through Thursday at 10am and 1:30pm and Friday at 10am. Tours need to be booked in advance. Spode Visitor Centre and accompanying sights are open Monday through Saturday from 9am to 5pm and Sunday from 10am to 4pm. Admission for the Visitor Centre and Museum is £2 ($3.20) for adults and £1 ($1.60) for children 5 years and older, students, and seniors. Children younger than 5 are free. For the regular factory tour, admission is £3.50 ($5.60) for adults and £1.75 ($2.80) for children 12 years and older, students, and seniors. For the connoisseur factory tour, admission is £6 ($9.60) for adults and £4 ($6.40) for children 12 years and older, students, and seniors.

**Moorcroft Pottery,** W. Moorcroft, Sandbach Road, Burslem, Stoke-on-Trent (☎ **01782/207943**), is a welcome change to the world-famous names. Founded in 1898 by William Moorcroft, who produced his own special brand of pottery and was his own exclusive designer until his death in 1945, the pottery is unique in that the decoration is part of the first firing, giving it a higher quality of color and brilliance than, say, Spode. Today, design is in the hands of William's son, John, who carries on the personal traditions of the family firm, creating floral designs in bright, clear colors. There is much to admire and buy in the factory seconds shop. There is always someone around to explain the various processes and to show you around the museum. Tours must be booked in advance and are given Monday, Wednesday, and Thursday at 11am and 2pm, and Friday at 11am. The museum and shop are open Monday through Friday from 10am to 5pm and Saturday from 9:30am to 4:30pm. Admission is £2.50 ($4) for adults and £1.50 ($2.40) for seniors and children under 16.

To help navigate The Potteries, purchase a **China Day Rider ticket** for £3.50 ($5.60). This special ticket is offered by the local bus company PMT and lets you travel by bus to the different factories and shops for the entire day that you buy the ticket. It can be bought on the bus. A special attraction to this ticket is the discount voucher sheet that China Day Rider passengers can use to get discounts off purchases and entrance fees at various potteries. Ask for the voucher sheet at the first attraction or shop you visit. You may also want to pick up a China Experience visitor map from the Stoke-on-Trent Tourist Information Centre.

This house is brick-fronted and substantial thanks to the fact that it's composed of a pair of late Victorian terraced houses that were interconnected by a previous owner. The owners live at this straightforward and competent inn. Bedrooms are conservatively outfitted in traditional, not particularly experimental ways, but are nonetheless comfortable and neat, always with tea-making facilities. The location is on a quiet cul-de-sac.

**Haydon House Hotel.** 1–9 Haydon St., Basford, Stoke-on-Trent, Staffordshire ST4 6JD. ☎ 01782/711311. Fax 01782/717470. 22 rms, 8 suites. TV TEL. Mon–Thurs £52.50 ($84) single, £62.50 ($100) double, £120 ($192) suite. Fri–Sun £35 ($56) single, £50 ($80) double, £100 ($160) suite. AE, DC, MC, V.

Between 1952 and 1980, this imposing dark-brick late Victorian house served as the family home of the Machin family, who reared two children within its premises. Since 1980, they've acquired a pair of smaller but roughly equivalent houses across the road, added a collection of built-in mahogany furniture to the bedrooms, and reconfigured their home and their lives to welcome paying overnight guests. Today, you'll find many of the original Victorian fittings (paneling, elaborate cove moldings, bay windows, a dignified staircase), an unusual collection of clocks, and many of the modern amenities to make your overnight stay comfortable. A restaurant on the premises serves meals every day at lunch and dinner, and every day except Sunday night to nonresidents. Suites each have efficiently arranged kitchenettes.

**Westfield House.** 312 Princes Rd., Penkhull, Stoke-on-Trent, Staffordshire ST4 7JP. ☎ 01782/844582. 2 rms, none with bath. £20 ($32) single; £32 ($51.20) double. All rates include breakfast. No credit cards.

Originally built in 1892, in a position within a 10-minute uphill walk from the center of Stoke-on-Trent, the main allure of this place derives from a location that's convenient to the region's many potteries. Set within a neighborhood that's adjacent to many equivalent houses, it's run by members of the White family. Westfield is very much like a private home that accepts paying guests, and as such, can be either an intimate experience or a limiting one.

## WHERE TO EAT

**George Hotel.** Swan Sq., Burslem. ☎ 01782/577544. Reservations recommended. Set-price lunches £10.95 ($17.50); set-price dinners £12.95–£15.95 ($20.70–$25.50). AE, DC, MC, V. Daily noon–2pm and 7–9pm. BRITISH/INTERNATIONAL.

Although no one will enforce this, the restaurant at the George Hotel is the kind of place where it might be preferable for men to wear a jacket and necktie. It's in the town's most visible hotel, a red-brick pile from 1929. The restaurant is one of the best in town, a long narrow room with a tactful, well-trained staff that serves dishes that have a touch of flair but appeal nonetheless to conventional palates. Examples include sirloin steak garni, Devon-style pork (in this case, inspired by Normandy, in France, because of its use of apples, Calvados, and cream), and grilled halibut with a tomato and onion enhanced white wine sauce.

**Reagan's.** 325 Hartshill Rd., Hartshill. ☎ 01782/634925. Main courses £4.60–£9.25 ($7.35–$14.80). AE, DC, MC, V. Daily noon–midnight. INTERNATIONAL.

It's the restaurant that virtually every hotel owner in The Potteries cites as the most whimsical and fun in the district. You'll find it 2 miles outside of Stoke, beside the road leading to Newcastle, within what was built 200 years ago as a stone-sided cottage, and which has served as a home, a cafe, and a flower shop before its most recent incarnation. Peter Harber is the creative force, and his vision derives from his many trips to such citadels of sophisticated marketing as New York and Las Vegas.

There's a bar (either the Hollywood Bar or the Ivy League Bar, depending on who you happen to talk to) on the ground floor, that's supplemented with a restaurant upstairs. Both are outfitted with U.S–derived memorabilia that includes framed letters of recognition from the restaurant's namesake former actor and former president Ronald Reagan) in which he acknowledges the use of his name. Why Ronald? The owner's acquisition of the restaurant and Reagan's election victory occurred almost simultaneously, and as such, was adopted as a lucky talisman. The menu? Stiff drinks, plus eight kinds of burgers, filet and/or sirloin steaks, a half-dozen pastas and pizzas, salads, and daily specials of fish, vegetarian dishes, pork, or lamb.

## STOKE-ON-TRENT AFTER DARK

One word of caution is in order here—don't spend all your money or energy shopping. Save some of both for an evening on the town in and around Stoke-on-Trent.

The **New Victoria Theatre,** Etruria Road, Newcastle-under-Lyme (☎ **01782/717962**), is Britain's first theater in the round. It still has a lively program to suit every taste from traditional plays to modern blockbusters. Tickets are £7 to £10 ($11.20 to $16) and can be bought at the box office and the Tourist Information Centre.

If nightclubs are more your speed after a full day of shopping, hot spots with the younger crowd include **Valentino's,** Etruria Road, Hanley, Stoke-on-Trent (☎ **01782/214494**); and **The Place,** Bryan Street, Hanley, Stoke-on-Trent (☎ **01782/284433**). For a slightly older crowd, check out **Maxims,** Stanier Street, Newcastle-under-Lyme (☎ **01782/717325**), but only on Monday, Friday, and Saturday nights.

# STAFFORD

142 miles NW of London; 17 miles S of Stoke-on-Trent

The county town of Staffordshire was the birthplace of Izaak Walton, the British writer and celebrated fisherman. Long famous as a boot-making center, it contains many historic buildings, notably St. Chad's, the town's oldest church; St. Mary's, with its unusual octagonal tower; and the Ancient High House, the largest timber-frame town house in England.

## ESSENTIALS

**GETTING THERE**   From London, take a train from Euston Station for the approximately 2-hour trip. For schedules and information, call ☎ **0345/484950.**

By bus, catch a National Express from London's Victoria Coach Station. The trip will take about 5 hours. For schedules and information, call ☎ **0990/808080.**

For the 3-hour car trip, take the M40 to the M6 which will carry you right to Stafford.

**VISITOR INFORMATION**   The Stafford **Tourist Information Centre,** located in the Ancient High House, Greengate Street (☎ **01785/240204**), is open Monday to Friday from 9am to 5pm and Saturday from 10am to 3pm (November to March) and Saturday from 10am to 4pm (April to October).

## SEEING THE SIGHTS

On Greengate Street, the **Ancient High House** (☎ **01785/240204**) was built in 1595 and served as living quarters for King Charles I and his nephew Prince Rupert at the start of England's civil war in 1642. The next year, the house was turned into a prison for Royalist officers by the Parliamentarians. Many of the rooms throughout the house have been restored in a variety of styles, each of which corresponds with an important period in the house's history. The **Staffordshire Yeomanry Museum** is also located in the Ancient High House and documents the history of the Queen's Own Royal Regiment over the past 200 years. Other rooms include the Wallpaper Room displaying samples of 18th- and 19th-century wallpapers, the Civil War Room commemorating the visit of King Charles I and Prince Rupert, and the Victorian Room with its period furnishings. There is also a garden planted with herbs that were actually used by the house inhabitants during the Elizabethan period. The house is open year-round Monday to Friday from 9am to 5pm. Saturday hours from April to October are 10am to 4pm and from November to March are 10am to 3pm. Admission is £1.60 ($2.55) for adults; £1 ($1.60) for students, children, and seniors; £4 ($6.40) for family (two adults, two children).

Built on an easily defendable promontory, **Stafford Castle,** Newport Road (☎ **01785/257698**), began as a timber fortress in A.D. 1100, a scant 40 years after the Norman invasion. Its long history peaked in 1444 when its owner, Humphrey Stafford, became the duke of Buckinghamshire. In the 17th century, during the English civil war, the castle was defended by Lady Isabel but was eventually abandoned and almost entirely destroyed. In 1813, the ruins of the castle were reconstructed in the Gothic Revival style but nonetheless fell into disarray by the middle of this century. The Visitor Centre has the floorplan of a Norman guard house from the 12th century and, along with its collection of artifacts from on-site excavations, is designed to bring to life the tumultuous history of Stafford Castle. Many programs, events, and re-enactments are scheduled throughout the year that allow visitors to step back in time. During winter, torchlight tours of the castle can be arranged for organized groups. The castle also has a 16-bed herb garden and a host of arms and armour that visitors can try on. Stafford Castle and Visitor Centre is open April to October, Tuesday to Sunday from 10am to 5pm and November to March from 10am to 4pm. Admission is £1.60 ($2.55) for adults; £1 ($1.60) for students, children, and seniors; £4 ($6.40) for family (two adults, two children).

In 1654, **Izaak Walton** bought this 16th-century, typical mid-Staffordshire cottage, located on Worston Lane (☎ **01785/760278** from April to October and 01785/240204 from November to March), as part of the Halfhead Estate. Walton wrote *The Compleat Angler* in 1653, the year before buying the cottage. To this day, the book is the greatest classic of angling literature that celebrates the English countryside. After a rough history which includes two 20th-century fires, the cottage has been rethatched and restored to its original condition. A cottage garden and an angling museum can be found on the cottage grounds, too. The cottage is open April to October, Tuesday to Saturday from 11am to 4:30pm. Admission is £1.60 ($2.55) for adults; £1 ($1.60) for children, students, and seniors; and £4 ($6.40) for a family (two adults, two children).

## SHOPPING

Stafford's shopping area runs the gamut from dust-encrusted antiquarians to upscale, one-of-a-kind galleries. The **Schott Zwiesel Factory Shop,** Drummond Road, Astonfields Industrial Estate (☎ **01785/223166**), is Europe's largest manufacturer of blown crystal glassware and is hailed as extravagantly inexpensive. Established more than 100 years ago, Schott Zwiesel combines tradition with advanced glass technology while maintaining the finest quality and design. You can find plain and fine cut crystal stemware, giftware, and blown decorative crystal.

**The Shire Hall Gallery,** Market Square (☎ **01785/278345**), housed in the richly restored historic courthouse built in 1798, is an important visual arts complex that offers a lively program of exhibitions and a craft shop that stocks a wide range of contemporary craft including ceramics, textiles, jewelry, and glass objects.

## WHERE TO STAY

**Abbey Hotel.** 65–68 Lichfield Rd. Stafford, Staffordshire ST17 4LW. ☎ **01785/258351.** Fax 01785/246875. 31 rms, 19 with bath. TV. £19 ($30.40) single without bath, £28.50–£35 ($45.60–$56) single with bath; £33 ($52.80) double without bath, £46–£50 ($73.60–$80) double with bath. AE, MC, V.

About 1¹/₂ miles south of Stafford's historic core, this hotel is composed of a quintet of early 20th-century houses that were interconnected either by breaking down interior walls, or by means of a glass canopy extending over what had originally been the alleyways that separated them. Brick built, but painted in contrasting shades of black and white, they provide comfortable and unpretentious, but blandly contemporary accommodations, each in a monochromatic color scheme of green, peach, yellow, or blue. All of those in the main building have private baths and, except for one under the eaves, lie one flight above street level. There's no elevator. Those without baths lie in the annex. There's a restaurant and cocktail lounge, both of which are open only to residents. Set dinners are a bargain at £7.50 ($12) each.

**The Vine Hotel.** Salter St., Stafford, Staffordshire ST16 2JU. ☎ **01785/244112.** Fax 01785/246612. 27 rms. TV TEL. £40 ($64) single; £50–£52 ($80–$83.20) double. All rates include breakfast. AE, MC, V.

Built around the half-timbered core of a greatly expanded Elizabethan inn from the 15th century, this is a reliable, slightly dowdy hotel which retains its Old-World allure despite modernizations that have combined it with what were originally conceived as the mew houses and stables in back. Although about three of them retain vestiges of half-timbering, most bedrooms are modern and uncomplicated, and despite the layer of wall-to-wall carpeting that sheathes their floors, still retain such eccentricities as squeaking floors and slightly uneven walls. There's a pub and restaurant on the premises.

## WHERE TO EAT

**Da Vinci's.** 13 Bailey St., Woodings Yard. ☎ **01785/246265.** Reservations recommended. Pasta platters £5.25–£6.95 ($8.40–$11.10); main courses £8.75–£11.95 ($14–$19.10). MC, V. Mon–Sat noon–2pm and 7–10:30pm. ITALIAN.

This is the best restaurant in town, providing Mediterranean flair from a white-sided Victorian cottage adjacent to central Stafford's only cinema. The twin dining rooms are outfitted mostly in green and gold, reflecting the colors of an Italian harvest as interpreted by the Tuscan-born owners. Menu items are a welcome relief after too constant a diet of all-British staples, and include such pastas as pappardelle alla cacciatore (wide noodles with diced chicken, mushrooms, and basil); spaghetti all posillipo (with baby prawns and clams); prawns with a paprika and brandy sauce, and a succulent version of stuffed mushrooms (funghi ripiene) that's one of the most popular dishes on the menu. Steaks, prepared with gorgonzola, pizzaiola, or red wine with pesto, are grilled in the Tuscan style, and usually tender and flavorful.

## STAFFORD AFTER DARK

Try a go at the local pubs to relax after dark in Stafford. **The Stafford Arms,** 43 Railway St. (☎ **01785/253313**), tends to be a very happening place. Though never trendy, it always has a fun, friendly aura about it. The staff is outgoing and ready to strike up a conversation in an instant. This true ale pub offers a fine array of ales, ever-changing micro-brewery specials, and good inexpensive grub.

**The Malt & Hops,** 135 Lichfield Rd. (☎ **01785/258555**), is a pub with an easy-going atmosphere that is less chaotic than the Stafford Arms. It, too, has a wise choice of ales and good food. Thursday through Saturday evenings often see an energetic, young crowd.

## LICHFIELD: BIRTHPLACE OF SAMUEL JOHNSON

128 miles NW of London; 16 miles NE of Birmingham; 23 miles SW of Derby; 30 miles SE of Stoke-on-Trent

Set in proximity to the industrial heartland of the English Midlands, Lichfield, which dates back to the 8th century, has escaped many of the industrial trappings from the past 200 years. Visitors can reflect on earlier times while strolling down the medieval streets of Lichfield complete with a mix of Georgian, Tudor, and Victorian architectural styles. Fans of Samuel Johnson take pilgrimages to this historic city to see where the author of the first important English dictionary was born in 1709. The city is noted for its cathedral, whose three spires are known as "Ladies of the Vale." Buildings in the Close such as the Vicar's Close with its half-timbered houses and the 17th-century Bishops Palace have survived the sieges down through the years.

During the summer months, Lichfield District is home to many different small festivals. June festivals include a jazz and blues festival, a real ale festival with more than 50 different ales to sample, and a folk festival. The Lichfield Festival plus Fringe occurs in July and is a music, arts and drama extravaganza. Contact the Tourist Information Centre for exact dates.

### ESSENTIALS

**GETTING THERE**    A few direct trains leave daily out of London's Euston Station in the early morning and evening. The trip takes about $2^1/_2$ hours. For schedules and information, call ☎ **0345/484950.**

By bus, you'll have to take the National Express from London's Victoria Coach Station to Birmingham, at which point you'll have to change to local bus no. 912 through to Lichfield. For schedules and information, call ☎ **0990/808080.** Plan on about 4 hours for the bus trip, depending on your connection in Birmingham. The Birmingham to Lichfield leg of the trip takes about 1 hour.

If making the 3-hour trip by car from London, take the M1 to the M42 and then the A38.

**VISITOR INFORMATION**    The Lichfield **Tourist Information Centre,** Donegal House, Bore Street, Lichfield (☎ **01543/252109**), is open September to May, Monday through Saturday from 9am to 5pm and June to August, Monday through Saturday from 9am to 6pm and Sunday 1pm to 5pm.

### SEEING THE SIGHTS

**The Samuel Johnson Birthplace Museum,** Breadmarket Street (☎ **01543/ 264972**), is in the restored house where Dr. Johnson was born in 1709 and is dedicated to the life, work, and personality of one of England's most gifted writers. Johnson wrote poetry, essays, biographies, and, of course, the first important English dictionary. He is also famous for his provocative sayings—such as "When two Englishmen meet their first talk is of the weather" or "A tavern chair is the throne of human felicity." The museum contains tableaux rooms revealing how the house looked in the early 18th century, four floors of exhibits illustrating Johnson's life and work, a bookshop, a reading room, and displays of Johnson's manuscripts and other personal effects. It is open February to October, Monday through Sunday from 10:30am to 4:30pm and November to January, Monday through Saturday from 10:30am to 4:30pm. The last admission is at 4:15pm. Admission is £1.20 ($1.90) for adults, 70p ($1.10) for children and seniors, and £3.20 ($5.10) for a family ticket (up to two adults and four children).

Across the street from Dr. Johnson's Birthplace Museum stands the **Heritage Centre & Treasury,** located in St. Mary's Centre, Breadmarket Street in Market

Square (☎ **01543/256611**). The former parish church, which still maintains the Dyott Chapel for worship, has been transformed into a treasury and exhibition room with a coffee shop and a gift shop. The exhibition tells the story of Lichfield through its people and events, including audiovisual presentations of the history of Lichfield and the English civil war as it unfolded in and around Lichfield. The treasury houses a display on the art of silversmithing where visitors can see chalices, goblets, and other examples of civic, regimental, and church plate. Ancient charters and documents are displayed in the Muniment Room. The Heritage Collection Gallery contains costumes, old photographs, and newspapers that trace recent Lichfield history. And the best panoramic views of the town can be seen from the 40-meter viewing platform in the spire of St. Mary's Centre. The centre is open Monday through Sunday from 10am to 5pm with the last admission at 4:15pm. Admission is £1.30 ($2.10) for adults; 80p ($1.30) for children, seniors, and students; and £3.30 ($5.30) for a family ticket. The viewing platform admission is £1 ($1.60) for adults and 80p ($1.30) for children over the age of 10, students, and seniors.

Just behind the Heritage Centre is the Victorian Gothic **Guildhall,** Bore Street (☎ **01543/250011**). Rebuilt in 1846, this former meeting place of the city council is actually built over the medieval city dungeons where it is reported that a man was imprisoned for 12 years for counterfeiting a sixpence. Many of its prisoners were burned at the stake in Market Square. The dungeons are open June through mid September on Saturday from 10am to 4pm. Admission is 30p (50¢) for adults and 20p (30¢) for seniors and children.

The west front end of the **Lichfield Cathedral,** The Old Registry, The Close (☎ **01543/250300**), was built around 1280. The entire cathedral received heavy damage during the civil war but was restored in the 1660s and later in the 1800s. Thanks to the careful restoration, its three spires, known as the "Ladies of the Vale," can still be seen from miles around, with its tallest spire rising more than 250 feet. The cathedral's many treasures include the illuminated manuscript known as "the Lichfield Gospels," Sir Francis Chantrey's famous sculpture "the Sleeping Children," 16th-century Flemish glass in the Lady Chapel, and a High Victorian pulpit and chancel screen by Gilbert Scott and Francis Skidmore. The cathedral is open daily from 7:45am to 5:30pm, and the Visitors Study Centre is open June to September, daily from 7:45am to 5:30pm.

## WHERE TO STAY

**Oakleigh House.** 25 Chad's Rd., Lichfield, Staffordshire WS13 7LZ. ☎ **01543/262688.** Fax 01543/418556. 10 rms. TV TEL. £35–£42.50 ($56–$68) single; £55 ($88) double. MC, V.

The most sophisticated and whimsical inn in Lichfield lies within a dignified villa that was built in 1909 as the private home of the building contractor (J. R. Deacon) who erected many of the upscale homes throughout the district. Consequently, you'll find a wealth of Edwardian-style decorative touches here that reflect his professional taste and sense of craftsmanship. They include decorative tiles in the hall, a trio of log-burning fireplaces (including our favorite, the one in the cozy bar), and views over a 6-acre lake (Stowe Pool) where ducks, geese, and local fishers enjoy the waters. Half the bedrooms are in the main house; the rest are in what was originally built as the servants quarters and stables or garage. Rooms are dignified but cozy, ripe with a sense of English aesthetic and comfort. Despite the allure of the hotel that contains it, and the house-party ambience that prevails thanks to the humor of its owners, the place is better known for its restaurant.

## WHERE TO EAT

**Little Barrow Restaurant.** Beacon St. ☎ **01543/414500.** Reservations recommended. Bar: platters £2.20–£7.95 ($3.50–$12.70). Restaurant: fixed-price lunch £10 ($16); main lunch and dinner courses £9.50–£13.50 ($15.20–$21.60). AE, MC, V. Bar meals daily noon–2pm and 6:30–9pm; restaurant daily noon–2pm and 7–9:30pm. BRITISH.

This respectable, highly competent restaurant has the same kind of genteel decor you might have expected in the dining room of a country club, and tactful service from a well-trained staff. Most business at lunchtime is conducted over the reasonably priced £10 ($16) set menu; evening meals are a la carte, more leisurely, and more elaborate. Menu items include prime filet of scotch sirloin with a cream, brandy, and black pepper sauce; whole breast of chicken with shallots, almond slivers, cream, and diced ham; and rack of lamb coated with honey and herbs and served atop a port and red currant jus. Less formal, and less expensive, meals are served in the bar, where platters range from sandwiches to steaks.

**Pig & Truffle Bar & Bistro.** Tamworth St. ☎ **01543/262312.** Main courses £3–£7.95 ($4.80–$12.70). AE, MC, V. Daily noon–2:30pm; Mon–Thurs 6–9pm. FARM-STYLE BRITISH.

No other inexpensive joint in Lichfield can match the level of service and the whimsical charm of this very popular pub and bistro. The setting (a stone, stucco, and *faux* timbered facade that rests on 17th-century foundations) lies in the heart of town. Diners and drinkers alike congregate at the same tables, as a staff maneuvers around what can sometimes, especially on Friday and Saturday nights, be mobbed with locals who use the place as both rendezvous and gossip exchange. (Be warned that because of the crush, no dinners are served on weekends.) No one will mind if you drop in just for a drink, but if your intention involves sustenance, know in advance that every menu item in the place derives its inspiration from some sort of barnyard nomenclature. Your barbequed sandwich is a pigsty baguette, your burger (any of about a half-dozen variations) is a bullyburger; and your stuffed baked potato is a "Percy (the pig's) boot." Expect wit and dialogue—you'll probably get it.

**The Swan Hotel.** Bird St. ☎ **01543/414777.** Reservations not accepted. Bar snacks and platters £1.25–£4.75 ($2–$7.60). AE, DC, MC, V. Mon–Thurs 11am–3pm and 6:30–11pm; Fri–Sat 11am–3pm and 7–11pm; Sun noon–3pm and 7–10:30pm. BRITISH.

In an 18th-century coaching inn, this pub has a black-and-white facade, and an interior that hasn't changed much since the days of Charles Dickens. A roster of ales on tap ("real ales" that management specifies as "cask ales") and lagers are served along with pub-style lunches where simple platters of pub-inspired staples include strips of fajita-style beef, stuffed potatoes, baguette sandwiches, and lasagna. The menu is a lot more appealing at lunch than at dinner, when, frankly, you might want to drop in only for a drink. Dance alert: Disco isn't dead, at least not in Lichfield. Every Friday and Saturday nights, from 8pm till the 11pm closing, the site is transformed into a dance club.

## LICHFIELD AFTER DARK

Why not put a pub featuring a bit of live local music on the agenda for an evening out in Lichfield? **The King's Head,** Bird Street (☎ **01543/256822**), saw quite a bit of action during the English Civil War and has no problem still attracting a noisy, animated, and frenetic crowd. Housed in a 15th-century coaching inn decorated with military memorabilia, the town's under 25-ers enjoy live music, reasonable ales, good food, and a disco on Friday, Saturday, and Sunday.

    **The Shoulder of Mouton,** London Road (**01543/263279**), has been recently renovated and has a more relaxed atmosphere and a more mature clientele than the

King's Head. This is a friendly place filled with lots of big comfy chairs just perfect for listening to its Monday evening live jazz sessions. Traditional pub-style food and drink are available.

One of the most cheerful and comfortably old-fashioned watering holes is within the previously recommended **Swan Hotel,** Bird Street (☎ **01543/414777**). Its interior hasn't changed much since the days of Charles Dickens. A host of cask ales on tap and lagers are served along with pub-style lunches, really simple platters of British staples. Dancin' fools take note: Disco ain't dead, at least not in Lichfield. Every Friday and Saturday night, from 8pm till the 11pm closing, the site is transformed into a disco. The only cover charge you'll pay is the purchase of a pint.

# 15 Cambridge & East Anglia

The four essentially bucolic counties of East Anglia—Essex, Suffolk, Norfolk, and Cambridgeshire—were an ancient Anglo-Saxon kingdom dominated by the Danes. Beginning in the 12th century, the area's cloth industry brought it prosperity, witnessed today in the impressive spires of some of its churches. In part, it's a land of heaths, fens, marshes, and inland lagoons known as "broads." Cambridge is home of the university of the same name, one of the world's most famous, and nearby stands Ely Cathedral, dating from 1081. Suffolk and Essex—Constable Country—boast some of England's finest landscapes. Seat of the dukes of Norfolk, Norwich is less popular, but those who do venture toward the North Sea will be rewarded with an area whose scenery rivals any in the country.

Cambridge is the most visited city in East Anglia. The little village of Thaxted makes a good base for exploring Essex. Either Long Melford or Lavenham are the most idyllic centers for exploring the Constable country of Suffolk. In Norfolk the best base is Norwich, the county seat, from which you can branch out and visit "the Broads."

Cambridgeshire is in large part an agricultural region, with some distinct geographic features, including the black peat soil of the Fens, a district crisscrossed by dikes and drainage ditches. Many old villages and market towns abound, including Peterborough, which sits on the divide between the flat Fens and the wolds of the East Midlands. Bird watchers, fishing enthusiasts, walkers, and cyclists are all drawn to the area. Of course, most people visit Cambridge, which is in the center of Cambridgeshire. Many famous figures in English history came from this land, including Oliver Cromwell (1699–1758), the Lord Protector during the English Civil War.

Most motorists drive through Essex on the way to Cambridge. Even though close to London and itself industrialized in places, this land of rolling fields has a number of rural areas and villages, many on the seaside. Essex stretches east to the English Channel, where its major city, Colchester, is known for oysters and roses. Fifty miles from London, Colchester was the first Roman city in Britain and is the oldest-recorded town in the kingdom. Parts of its Roman fortifications remain. A Norman castle has been turned into a museum, housing a fine collection of Roman-British artifacts. Among the

# East Anglia

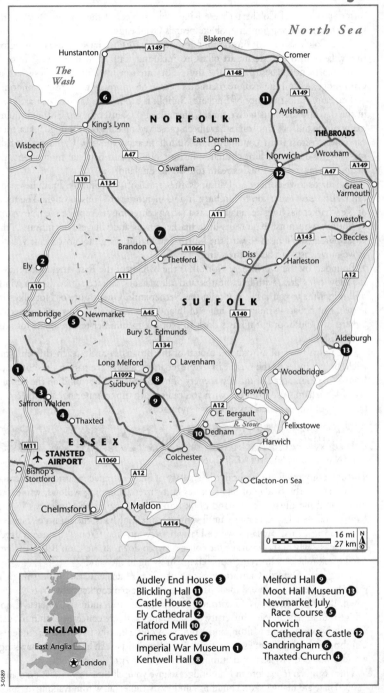

North Sea

The Wash

Hunstanton
Blakeney
Cromer
A149
A148

NORFOLK

**6** King's Lynn
**11** Aylsham
THE BROADS
Wisbech
East Dereham
Norwich **12** Wroxham
A149
A47
Swaffam
Great Yarmouth

A10
A134
A47

Ely **2**
A11
Brandon **7**
Thetford
Diss
Harleston
Lowestoft
Beccles
A143
A12

A10
A11
A1066

SUFFOLK

Cambridge
Newmarket **5**
A45
Bury St. Edmunds
A140
Aldeburgh **13**

**1**
A134
Long Melford
Lavenham
Woodbridge
Saffron Walden **3**
A1092
Kentwell Hall **8**
Sudbury
Melford Hall **9**
Ipswich
Thaxted **4**
E. Bergault
Felixstowe
R. Stour
Dedham **10**
Harwich

M11
ESSEX
STANSTED AIRPORT
A1060
Colchester
A12
Bishop's Stortford
Clacton-on Sea

Chelmsford
Maldon
A414

0    16 mi / 27 km    N

ENGLAND
East Anglia
★ London

| | |
|---|---|
| Audley End House **3** | Melford Hall **9** |
| Blickling Hall **11** | Moot Hall Museum **13** |
| Castle House **10** | Newmarket July |
| Ely Cathedral **2** | Race Course **5** |
| Flatford Mill **10** | Norwich |
| Grimes Graves **7** | Cathedral & Castle **12** |
| Imperial War Museum **1** | Sandringham **6** |
| Kentwell Hall **8** | Thaxted Church **4** |

3-0589

553

former residents of Colchester were King Cole, subject of the nursery rhyme, and Cunobelinus, the warrior king, Shakespeare's Cymbeline.

Since Colchester is not on the route of most visitors, we have focused instead on tiny villages in the western part of Essex, including Saffron Walden and Thaxted, which represent the best part of the shire. They are roughly 25 to 30 miles south of Cambridge, so you can explore them quite easily on your way there from London.

The easternmost county of England, Suffolk is a refuge for artists, just as it was in the day of its famous native sons, Constable and Gainsborough. Through them, many of the Suffolk landscapes have been preserved on canvas. Although a fast train can whisk visitors from London to East Suffolk in approximately 1 1/2 hours, its fishing villages, dozens of flint churches, historic homes, and national monuments remain far removed from mainstream tourism in England.

The major town is Bury St. Edmunds, the capital of West Suffolk. From here, you can take an easy excursion to Sudbury and its memories of Gainsborough. The town of Newmarket has long been famous as a racing center. But to capture the true charm of Suffolk, you must explore its little market towns and villages. Beginning at the Essex border, we'll head toward the North Sea, highlighting the most scenic villages as we move eastward across the shire.

Bounded by the North Sea, Norfolk is the biggest of the East Anglian counties. It's a low-lying area, with fens, heaths, and salt marshes. An occasional dike or windmill might make you think you're in the Netherlands. One feature of Norfolk is its network of Broads—miles and miles of inland lagoons, shallow in part, connected by streams. Outdoor enthusiasts flock to Norfolk in summer to hire boats for sailing or fishing.

The resort town of Wroxham, capital of the Broads, is easily reached from Norwich, only 8 miles to the northeast. Motorboats regularly take parties on short trips from Wroxham. Some of the best scenery of the Broads is to be found on the periphery of Wroxham. Also from Norwich you can make a trip to Sandringham, the country home of four generations of British monarchs.

# 1 Cambridge: Town & Gown

55 miles N of London; 80 miles NE of Oxford

The university town of Cambridge is a collage of images steeped in history, academia, and romance: the Bridge of Sighs; spires and turrets; drooping willows, witness to much punting; dusty secondhand bookshops; carol singing on Christmas Eve in King's College Chapel; dancing until sunrise at the May balls; the sound of Elizabethan madrigals; narrow lanes where Darwin, Newton, and Cromwell once walked; the "Backs," where the lawns of the colleges sweep down to the Cam River; the tattered black robe of a hurrying upperclassman flying in the wind.

Along with Oxford, Cambridge is one of Britain's ancient seats of learning. In many ways their stories are similar, particularly the age-old conflict between town and gown. Beyond the campus, Oxford has a thriving high-tech industry, whereas Cambridge is dominated by its university. As far as the locals are concerned, alumni such as Isaac Newton, John Milton, and Virginia Woolf aren't just yesterday's students. Cambridge today continues to graduate famed scientists such as Stephen Hawking, world-renowned physicist and author of *A Brief History of Time*.

There is much to explore in Cambridge, so give yourself time to wander, even aimlessly. There are many historic buildings in the city center, all within walking distance, including Great St. Mary's Church (from which the original Westminster chimes come), St. Benet's Church, the Round Church, the Fitzwilliam Museum (one of the

# Cambridge

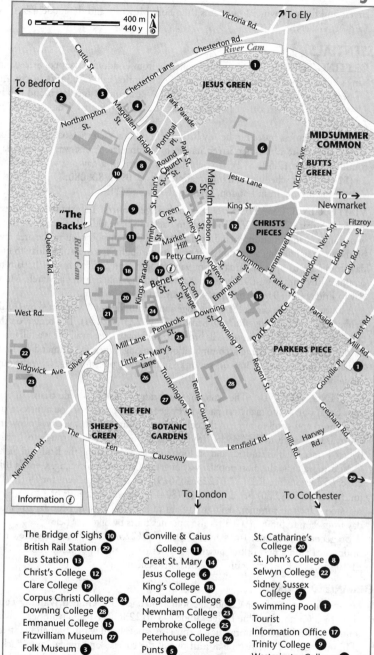

0 ——— 400 m
——— 440 y

To Ely
Victoria Rd.
Chesterton Rd.
River Cam
Castle St.
To Bedford
Northampton St.
Chesterton Lane
Magdalen Bridge
Portugal Pl.
Park Parade
JESUS GREEN
Round Church St.
Park St.
St. John's St.
Green St.
Trinity St.
Malcolm St.
Jesus Lane
King St.
Sidney St.
Hobson St.
St. Andrews St.
MIDSUMMER COMMON
BUTTS GREEN
Victoria Ave.
To Newmarket
Fitzroy St.
New Sq.
Clarendon St.
Eden St.
City Rd.
CHRISTS PIECES
Emmanuel Rd.
Parker St.
"The Backs"
Queen's Rd.
River Cam
Market Hill
Petty Curry
Kings Parade
Benet St.
Corn Exchange St.
Emmanuel St.
Drummer St.
Downing St.
Downing Pl.
Park Terrace
Parkside
Parkside
PARKERS PIECE
East Rd.
Mill Rd.
West Rd.
Pembroke St.
Mill Lane
Little St. Mary's Lane
Silver St.
Sidgwick Ave.
Trumpington St.
Tennis Court Rd.
Regent St.
Gonville Pl.
Cresham Rd.
Harvey Rd.
Hills Rd.
Lensfield Rd.
THE FEN
SHEEPS GREEN
BOTANIC GARDENS
The Fen
Newnham Rd.
Causeway
To London
To Colchester

Information ⓘ

## Legend

| | | |
|---|---|---|
| The Bridge of Sighs ⑩ | Gonville & Caius College ⑪ | St. Catharine's College ⑳ |
| British Rail Station ㉙ | Great St. Mary ⑭ | St. John's College ⑧ |
| Bus Station ⑬ | Jesus College ⑥ | Selwyn College ㉒ |
| Christ's College ⑫ | King's College ⑱ | Sidney Sussex College ⑦ |
| Clare College ⑲ | Magdalene College ④ | Swimming Pool ① |
| Corpus Christi College ㉔ | Newnham College ㉓ | Tourist Information Office ⑰ |
| Downing College ㉘ | Pembroke College ㉕ | Trinity College ⑨ |
| Emmanuel College ⑮ | Peterhouse College ㉖ | Westminster College ② |
| Fitzwilliam Museum ㉗ | Punts ⑤ | |
| Folk Museum ③ | Queen's College ㉑ | |
| General Post Office ⑯ | | |

3-0430

555

largest and finest provincial museums), the Folk Museum, and the modern Kettles Yard Art Gallery.

# ESSENTIALS

**GETTING THERE**   Trains depart frequently from London's Liverpool Street and King's Cross stations, arriving an hour later. For inquiries, call ☎ **0345/484950.** An off-peak same-day round-trip is £12.50 ($20). A peak-time same-day round-trip is £14.90 ($23.85). An off-peak longer stay round-trip (up to 5-day period) is £17 ($27.20).

National Express buses run hourly between London's Victoria Coach Station for the 2-hour trip to Drummer Street Station in Cambridge. A one-way or same-day round-trip costs £7.50 ($12). If you'd like to return in a day or two the cost is £9 ($14.40). For schedules and information, call ☎ **0990/808080.**

If you're driving from London, head north on the M11.

**VISITOR INFORMATION**   The **Cambridge Tourist Information Centre,** Wheeler Street (☎ **01223/322640**), is in back of the Guildhall. The center has a wide range of information, including data on public transportation in the area and on different sightseeing attractions. Open April through September, Monday to Friday from 9am to 6pm, Saturday from 9am to 5pm, and Sunday from 10:30am to 3:30pm; July and August, daily from 9am to 7pm; October through March, Monday to Friday from 9am to 5:30pm, Saturday from 9am to 5pm.

A tourist reception center for Cambridge and Cambridgeshire is operated by **Guide Friday Ltd.** at Cambridge Railway Station (☎ **01223/362444**). The center, on the concourse of the railway station, sells brochures and maps. Also available is a full range of tourist services, including accommodations booking. Open in summer daily from 9:30am to 6pm (closes at 3pm off-season). Guided tours of Cambridge leave the center daily.

**GETTING AROUND**   The center of Cambridge is made for pedestrians, so park your car at one of the many car parks (they get more expensive as you approach the city center) and stroll to some of the colleges spread throughout the city. Follow the courtyards through to the "Backs" (the college lawns) and walk through to Trinity (where Prince Charles studied) and St. John's Colleges, including the Bridge of Sighs.

Next to walking, the most popular way of getting around is bicycling. **Geoff's Bike Hire,** 65 Devonshire Rd. (☎ **01223/365629**), has bicycles for rent for £4 ($6.40) for 3 hours, £6 ($9.60) per day, or £15 ($24) per week. A deposit of £25 ($40) is required. Open in summer, daily from 9am to 6pm; off-season, Monday to Saturday from 9am to 5:30pm. Geoff's also operates tours by bike (see below).

**Stagecoach Cambus,** 100 Cowley Rd. (☎ **01223/423554**) services the Cambridge area with a network of buses, with fares ranging in price from 50p (80¢) to £1.10 ($1.75). The local tourist office has bus schedules.

## ORGANIZED TOURS

For an informative spin on Cambridge, join in on one of the **Guided Walking Tours** given by a Cambridge Blue Badge Guide (☎ **01223/322640**). Two-hour walking tours leave the Tourist Information Centre (see above) and wind through the streets of historic Cambridge, visiting at least one of the colleges and the famous "Backs." From mid-June through August, drama tours are conducted during which participants may see various costumed characters walk in and out of the tour. Henry VIII, Queen Elizabeth I, Isaac Newton, and others help to breathe life into the history of Cambridge during the drama tours. Regular tours are given April through mid-June, daily at 11:30am and 1:30pm; mid-June through September, daily at 10:30am,

11:30am, 1:30pm, and 2:30pm; October through March, daily at 1:30pm and Saturday at 11:30am. Drama tours are offered mid-June through August, daily at 6:30pm. Admission for regular tours is £5.75 ($9.20) per person and for drama tours £3.90 ($6.25) per person.

In addition to its visitor information services (see "Essentials," above), **Guide Friday Ltd.,** on the concourse of Cambridge Railway Station (☎ **01223/362444**), has daily guided tours of Cambridge via open-top, double-decker buses. In summer, they depart every 15 minutes from 9:45am to 6pm; in winter, there are hourly departures. The tour can be a 1-hour ride, or you can get off at any of the many stops and rejoin the tour whenever you wish. Tickets are valid all day. The fare is £7 ($11.20) for adults, £5.50 ($8.80) for seniors and students, and £2 ($3.20) for children 5 to 12, free for kids 4 or under.

**Geoff's Bike Hire,** 65 Devonshire Rd. (☎ **01223/365629**), has guided bicycle tours on Tuesday, Wednesday, Thursday, and Saturday at 2:30pm. A 10:30am tour on Saturday is also offered. These cost £7.50 ($12) including bike rental. Or you can just rent a bike.

## VISITING CAMBRIDGE UNIVERSITY

Oxford University slightly predates Cambridge, but by the early 13th century scholars also made their presence known here. Eventually, Cambridge won partial recognition from Henry III, rising or falling with the approval of subsequent English monarchs. The university consists of 31 colleges for both men and women. Colleges are closed for exams from mid-April until the end of June.

*A Word of Warning:* Because of the disturbances caused by the influx of tourists to the university, Cambridge has had to limit visitors, or even exclude them altogether, from various parts of the university. In some cases, a small entry fee will be charged. Small groups of up to six people are generally admitted with no problem, and you can inquire from the local tourist office about visiting hours (see above).

The following listing is only a sample of some of the more interesting colleges. If you're planning to stop in Cambridge for a long time, you might also want to visit **Magdalene College,** on Magdalene Street, founded in 1542; **Pembroke College,** on Trumpington Street, founded in 1347; **Christ's College,** on St. Andrew's Street, founded in 1505; and **Corpus Christi College,** on Trumpington Street, which dates from 1352.

*Note:* All the colleges are closed Easter, bank holidays, during exams, graduation, and at other times without notice.

✪ **KING'S COLLEGE**   The adolescent Henry VI founded King's College on King's Parade (☎ **01223/331212**) in 1441. Most of its buildings today are from the 19th century, but its crowning glory, the perpendicular **King's College Chapel,** dates from the Middle Ages and is one of England's architectural gems. Owing to the chaotic vicissitudes of the English kings, the chapel wasn't completed until the early 16th century.

Henry James called King's College Chapel "the most beautiful in England." Its characteristic features are the magnificent fan vaulting—all of stone—and the great windows, most of which were fashioned by Flemish artisans between 1517 and 1531 (the west window, however, dates from the late Victorian period). The stained glass portrays biblical scenes, in hues of red, blue, and amber. The long range of the windows all the way around the back of the chapel, from the first on the north side at the west end to the first on the south side, depicts the Birth of the Virgin; the Annunciation; the Birth of Christ; the Life, Ministry, and Death of Christ; the Resurrection; the Ascension; the Acts of the Apostles; and the Assumption. The upper

## Punting on the Cam

Punting on the Cam, in wood-built, flat-bottomed boats somewhat like Venetian gondolas, is a traditional pursuit of students and visitors to Cambridge. The punt is called, in fact, the gondola of England. Downstream, you pass along the ivy-covered "backs" of the colleges, their lush gardens sweeping down to the Cam. About 2 miles upriver lies Grantchester, immortalized by Rupert Brooke (author of the sonnet, "The Soldier"), perhaps best known for the verse cited on the following page.

Literary types flock to Grantchester, which can be reached both by punting and by taking the path following the River Granta for less than an hour to Grantchester Meadows. The town lies about a mile from the meadows. When the town clock stopped for repairs in 1985, its hands were left frozen "for all time" at 10 to 3 in honor of Brooke's famed verse.

After so much activity, you're bound to get hungry or thirsty, so head to **The Green Man,** 59 High St. (☎ **01223/841178**), a 400-year-old inn named in honor of Robin Hood, where a crackling fire warms you in cold weather and summer features a back beer garden, leading off toward the river where your punt is waiting to take you back to Cambridge.

People sprawled along the banks of the Cam on a summer day wait to judge and ridicule you as you maneuver your punt with a pole about 15 feet long. The river's floor is muddy, and many a student has lost his pole in the riverbed shaded by the willows. If your pole gets stuck, it's better to leave it sticking in the mud instead of risking a plunge into the river.

**Scudamore's Boatyards,** Granta Place (☎ **01223/575431**), by the Anchor Pub, has been in business since 1910. Punts and rowboats rent for £10 ($16) per hour. A £40 ($64) cash or credit-card deposit is required. There is a maximum of six persons per punt. They are open from March to late September or October daily from 9am until dusk, depending on the weather and number of clients. You may prefer a chauffeur, in which case there is a minimum cost of £20 ($32) for two people and £5 ($8) per person after that.

The **Cambridge Punt Company,** working out of The Anchor Pub, Silver Street (☎ **01223/327280**), is recommended for its 45-minute punt tours. A guide (usually a Cambridge student) appropriately dressed in a straw boater hat will both punt and give running commentary to groups of between one and six persons. Tours cost a minimum of £20 ($32) for two and £5 ($8) per each adult after two, £2.50 ($4) for children 5 to 12. Kids 4 and under ride free. The Anchor Pub's service staff can call a guide over to your table. If you want to row yourself along the Cam, "unchauffeured" boats rent for £10 ($16) per hour. The company is open daily from 9am to dusk, although everyone packs up and goes home if it rains or if the winds get too high.

range contains Old Testament parallels to these New Testament stories. The chapel also houses Rubens' *The Adoration of the Magi.* The rood screen is from the early 16th century.

The chapel is open during vacation time Monday to Saturday from 9:30am to 4:30pm, and on Sunday from 10am to 4:30pm. During the term, the public is welcome to attend choral services Tuesday to Saturday at 5:30pm and on Sunday at 10:30am and 3:30pm. During the term, the chapel is open to visitors Monday to

Saturday from 9:30am to 3:15pm and on Sunday from 1:15 to 2:15pm and 5 to 5:30pm; it is closed December 23 to January 1. It may be closed at other times for recording sessions, broadcasts, concerts, etc.

There is an exhibition in the seven northern side chapels showing why and how the chapel was built. Admission to the college and chapel, including the exhibition, is £3 ($4.80) for adults, £2 ($3.20) for students and children 12 to 17, free for children under 12.

**PETERHOUSE**   This college, on Trumpington Street (☎ **01223/338200**), is the oldest Cambridge college, founded in 1284 by Hugh de Balsham, the bishop of Ely. Of the original buildings, only the hall remains, but this was restored in the 19th century and now boasts stained-glass windows by William Morris. Old Court, constructed in the 15th century, was renovated in 1754; the chapel dates from 1632. Ask permission to enter at the porter's lodge.

**TRINITY COLLEGE**   On Trinity Street, Trinity College (not to be confused with Trinity Hall) is the largest college in Cambridge. It was founded in 1546 by Henry VIII, who consolidated a number of smaller colleges that had existed on the site. The courtyard is the most spacious in Cambridge, built when Thomas Nevile was master. Sir Christopher Wren designed the library. For admission to the college, apply at the porter's lodge, or call ☎ **01223/338400** for information. There is a charge of £1.50 ($2.40) March to May 4 and June 21 to November 2.

**EMMANUEL COLLEGE**   On St. Andrew's Street, Emmanuel (☎ **01223/ 334274**) was founded in 1584 by Sir Walter Mildmay, a chancellor of the exchequer to Elizabeth I. Harvard grads take note: John Harvard, founder of Harvard University, studied here. You can take a nice stroll around its attractive gardens and visit the chapel designed by Sir Christopher Wren and consecrated in 1677. Both the chapel and college are open daily from 9am to 6pm.

**QUEENS' COLLEGE**   On Queens' Lane, Queens' College (☎ **01223/335511**) is the loveliest of Cambridge's colleges. Dating back to 1448, it was founded by two English queens, one the wife of Henry VI, the other the wife of Edward IV. Its second cloister is the most interesting, flanked by the early–16th-century half-timbered President's Lodge. Admission is £1 ($1.60), free for children under 12 accompanied by parents. A short printed guide is issued. Individual visitors are normally admitted daily from 1:45 to 4:30pm, but during March through October the college is also open to visitors daily from 10:15am to 12:45pm. Entry and exit is by the old porter's lodge in Queens' Lane only. The old hall and chapel are usually open to the public when not in use.

The Grove occupies the ground fronting the west bank of the River Cam on the north side of the bridge. It's a riot of blossoms in spring. The walk along the riverbank reveals the best view of the college and of King's College, but ends at a small branch channel in the river. Beyond the lawn on the other side of the river, the high stone wall dividing the two colleges is the last remaining fragment of a Carmelite monastery dissolved in 1538.

**ST. JOHN'S COLLEGE**   On St. John's Street, this college (☎ **01223/338600**) was founded in 1511 by Lady Margaret Beaufort, mother of Henry VII. A few years earlier she had founded Christ's College. Before her intervention, an old hospital had stood on the site of St. John's. The impressive gateway bears the Tudor coat of arms, and Second Court is a fine example of late Tudor brickwork. But its best-known feature is the Bridge of Sighs crossing the Cam, built in the 19th century and patterned after the bridge in Venice. It connects the older part of the college with New

Court, a Gothic revival on the opposite bank from which there is an outstanding view of the famous "Backs." The Bridge of Sighs is closed to visitors but can be seen from the neighboring Kitchen Bridge. Wordsworth was an alumnus of St. John's College. The college is open from March to October, daily from 9:30am to 5pm. Admission is £1.50 ($2.40) for adults and 75p ($1.20) for children. Visitors are welcome to attend choral services in the chapel.

## CAMBRIDGE'S OTHER ATTRACTIONS

✪ **The Fitzwilliam Museum.** Trumpington St., near Peterhouse. ☎ **01223/332900.** Free admission. Tues–Sat 10am–5pm; Sun 2:15–5pm. Guided tours, Sun 2:30pm. Closed Jan 1, Good Friday, May Day, and Dec 24–31. From the train station, walk down Station Rd., turn right on Trumpington Rd., walk $^1/_4$ mile and turn left on Lensfield Rd., following it to its end. Turn right on Trumpington St.; the museum is on the left.

One of the finest museums in Britain, founded by the bequest of the 7th Viscount Fitzwilliam of Merrion to the University of Cambridge in 1816, this museum is worth the trip here. Although it features temporary exhibitions, its permanent collections are noted for their antiquities from ancient Egypt, Greece, and Rome. Roman and Romano-Egyptian art are displayed in newly created galleries and in the refurbished Western Asiatic displays. The Applied Arts section features English and European pottery and glass, along with furniture, clocks, fans, and armor, Chinese jades and ceramics from Japan and Korea, plus rugs and samplers. The museum is also noted for its rare coin collection, including ancient and medieval coins, along with medals created from the Renaissance on down. Many rare printed books and illuminated manuscripts, both literary and music, are also on display. The best is saved for last: the paintings, including masterpieces by Simone Martini, Domenico Veneziano, Titian, Veronese, Rubens, Van Dyck, Canaletto, Hogarth, Gainsborough, Constable, Monet, Degas, Renoir, Cézanne, and Picasso. There is also a fine collection of other 20th century art, miniature, drawings, watercolors, and prints.

Occasional musical events, including evening concerts, are held in Gallery III. For more details, call ☎ 01223/332900. There are also great lectures staged here; call the same number above for more details.

**Great St. Mary's.** King's Parade. ☎ **01223/350914.** Admission to tower £1.50 ($2.40) adults; 50p (80¢) children. Mon–Sat 10am–4:30pm and Sun 12:30–4:30pm; church open daily 9am–6pm.

Cambridge's central church was built on the site of an 11th century church, but the present building dates largely from 1478. It was closely associated with events of the Reformation. The cloth that covered the hearse of King Henry VII is on display in the church. There is a fine view of Cambridge from the top of the tower. Great St. Mary's is the university church.

## SHOPPING

There are several main shopping districts in Cambridge, each with its own atmosphere and type of shops.

For an ambience of 400-year-old buildings intermingled with a young, collegiate feel, forage around the shops lining St. John's Street, Trinity Street, King's Parade, and Trumpington Street. Check out **English Teddy Bear Company,** 1 King's Parade (☎ 01223/300908), which sells teddy bears handmade in cottages all over the U.K.—a real British souvenir. **Primavera,** 10 King's Parade (☎ 01223/357708), is a showplace of British crafts, featuring pottery, glass, ceramics, jewelry, ironwork, and fabric crafts ranging from ties to wall hangings. While at Primavera, be sure to explore the basement exhibition of paintings and craft items. String music buffs will want to visit **Cambridge Music Shop,** 1-A All Saints' Passage (☎ **01223/351786**), which carries non-electric stringed instruments, musical scores, music books, and accessories. For a bit of energy to fuel your shopping frenzy, stop by **Fitzbillies,** 52 Trumptin St. (☎ **01223/352500**), a bakery since 1922, and try the house specialty, a devilishly delectable sticky Chelsea bun. They also make cakes, pastries, bread, and pack picnic baskets with a hearty assortment of goodies. Their upstairs restaurant is open for breakfast, lunch, and dinner Wednesday through Saturday.

Another well-defined shopping district comprises Bridge Street, Sidney Street, St. Andrew's Street, and Regent Street. Particularly of note in this area is **James Pringle Weavers of Inverness,** 11 Bridge St. (☎ **01223/361534**), a Scottish haven. You'll find a mind-boggling array of Scottish tartans, kilts, tweeds, fine knitwear, Scottish food, and of course postcards. For unique British-designed jewelry, stop in **Workshop,** 3 Bridge St. (☎ **01223/354326**). You can also get pieces made to order and shop for studio glass as well as handmade leather goods.

Cambridge's pedestrian shopping district runs between Market Square and St. Andrew's Street and is known as the Lion Yard. **Culpepper The Herbalists,** 25 Lion Yard (☎ **01223/367370**), carries a complete herbal line that includes everything from extracts of plants to jellies, honeys, teas, cosmetics, bath products, pillows, and potpourri. **Mothercare,** 12–15 Lion Yard (☎ **01223/362001**), sells items that every mother and mother-to-be needs, including maternity and baby clothes, furniture, and toys.

If you're a bookworm, Cambridge shopping is going to be a paradisiacal experience for you. **Heffers of Cambridge** is a huge book, stationery, and music store with six branches, each specializing in a certain product area. All stores can be contacted through their central telephone number: ☎ **01223/568568.** The main store, 20 Trinity St., carries academic books; the children's book shop is at 30 Trinity St.; the stationery store can be found at 19 Sydney St.; Heffers' paperback and video shop is at 31 St. Andrews St.; their art and graphics shop has an address of 15–21 King St.; the music store, 19 Trinity St., features classical and popular cassettes, CDs, and choral college music. Heffers also has a shop in the mall at Grafton Centre that carries new fiction and nonfiction titles.

Also owned by Heffers, **Deighton, Bell & Co.,** 13 Trinity St. (☎ **01223/568568**), sells art and architecture books downstairs and antiquarian as well as secondhand books upstairs. **G. David,** 16 St. Edward's Passage (☎ **01223/354619**), hawks secondhand books, publishers' overruns at reduced prices, and antiquarian books. **Dillons,** 27 Sydney St. (☎ **01223/351688**), deals exclusively in varied new books. **Haunted Bookshop,** 9 St. Edward's Passage (☎ **01223/312913**), specializes in out-of-print children's books and first editions. **W. H. Smith,** 14–15 Market St. (☎ **01223/311313**), peddles magazines, newspapers, stationery, books, and videos.

And when you want tea and some more shopping, a huge selection of bed and table linens is what you'll find when you stop in **Perfect Setting,** All Saints Passage (☎ **01223/354188**), on the way to the little tearoom that shares the premises. A specialty that patrons should experience with their tea is one of the many sandwiches made with the tearoom's freshly baked bread.

## WHERE TO STAY
### DOUBLES FOR LESS THAN £40

**Avimore Guest House.** 310 Cherryhinton Rd., Cambridge, Cambridgeshire CB1 4AU. ☎ **01223/410956.** Fax 01223/576957. 6 rms, 3 with bath. TV TEL. £18 ($28.80) single without bath, £27 ($43.20) single with bath; £32 ($51.20) double without bath, £38 ($60.80) double with bath. All rates include English breakfast. MC, V. Bus: no. 4 or 5.

This guest house is 1.7 miles from the heart of Cambridge, near Addenbrookes Hospital. Now well established, it offers a good standard of B&B accommodation, but reservations are important. The accommodations are somewhat bland but contain beverage-making equipment and hot and cold running water. Parking is available, or you can depend on reliable public transportation to go back and forth (many visitors prefer to walk to the center in about 20 minutes).

**The Bridge Guest House.** 151–153 Hills Rd., Cambridge, Cambridgeshire CB2 2RJ. ☎ **01223/247942.** Fax 01223/416585. 12 rms. TV TEL. £25 ($40) single; £40 ($64) double. All rates include English breakfast. MC, V. Bus: no. 5 or 6.

A mile south of the city center, this hotel is a pair of interconnected houses that were built shortly after World War II. An extension, constructed around 1987, juts into the rear garden and contains some of the simple but clean and well-maintained accommodations. Your hosts are Venice-born Archimedes and Maria della Libere, who emigrated from Italy in the late 1960s. A fixed-price dinner is offered, if advance notification is given, for around £9 ($14.40) per person.

**Hamilton Hotel.** 156 Chesterton Rd., Cambridge, Cambridgeshire CB4 1DA. ☎ **01223/365664.** Fax 01223/314866. 26 rms, 17 with bath. TV. £20 ($32) single without bath, £30–£35 ($48–$56) single with bath; £35 ($56) double without bath, £45–£50 ($72–$80) double with bath. All rates include English breakfast. AE, DC, MC, V. Bus: no. 3 or 3A.

One of the better and more reasonably priced of the small hotels of Cambridge, this red-brick establishment lies about a mile northeast of the city center, close to the River Cam. A well-run, modestly accessorized hotel, it stands on a busy highway, but there's a parking area out back. The well-furnished bedrooms contain beverage-making equipment and phones. The hotel has a small, traditionally styled licensed bar, offering standard pub food and snacks.

## DOUBLES FOR LESS THAN £60

**Ashley Hotel.** 74 Chesterton Rd., Cambridge, Cambridgeshire CB4 1ER. ☎ **01223/350059.** Fax 01223/367721. 10 rms, 8 with bath; 6 studios, 4 with bath. TV TEL. £27.50 ($44) single without bath, £39.50 ($63.20) single with bath; £49.50 ($79.20) double with bath; £35 ($56) per person studio for 1 or 2 (3-day minimum). All rates include English breakfast. MC, V. Bus: no. 3 or 3A.

One of the most popular B&Bs in Cambridge, Ashley Hotel is a gray stone Edwardian building originally constructed as a private home. About half a mile north of the center, near the River Cam and Jesus Green, it offers standard bedrooms as well as functional but comfortable studio apartments (without kitchens) to clients interested in rentals of 3 days or more. Each room contains a radio and tea-making facilities, and there's a rose garden in back. Although only breakfast is served, guests are welcome to use the dining and drinking facilities of this establishment's companion hotel, the Arundel House Hotel, at 53 Chesterton Rd.

**Dresden Villa Guest House.** 34 Cherryhinton Rd., Cambridge, Cambridgeshire CB1 4AA. ☎ **01223/247539.** Fax 01223/410640. 13 rms. TV. £24–£26 ($38.40–$41.60) single; £42–£44 ($67.20–$70.40) double; £60 ($96) family rm for 3. All rates include English breakfast. No credit cards. Bus: no. 1, 2, 4, or 5.

This guest house has an Edwardian-era painted facade with four sunny bay windows. Within a 10-minute walk of the Cambridge Railway Station, it's owned by the Ruggiero family, who came here many years ago from a village near Sorrento, Italy. The place is neat and tidy, and most of the rooms have recently been redecorated. English or Italian fixed-price meals can be arranged in the evening for £9 ($14.40) per person. The location is about 1 1/4 miles south of the Market Place in Cambridge.

**Helen Hotel.** 167–169 Hills Rd., Cambridge, Cambridgeshire CB2 2RJ. ☎ **01223/246465.** Fax 01223/214406. 28 rms. TV TEL. £35–£45 ($56–$72) single; £55–£60 ($88–$96) double; £75–£80 ($120–$128) family room. All rates include English breakfast. AE, MC, V. Bus: no. 5 or 6.

This yellow-fronted Victorian hotel, about a mile south of the town center, is a Mediterranean-inspired refuge maintained by Gino and Helen Agodino. Born in San Remo and Naples, respectively, they prepare some of the best Italian dinners in Cambridge (featuring homemade ravioli and pastas) for guests who reserve in advance. A four-course dinner costs £13.50 ($21.60). This hostelry is much bigger than many other hotels in this section, and benefits from gardens laid out with boxwood in a symmetrical and formal Italian style. The hotel contains a lounge and cocktail bar, and each bedroom has tea-making facilities, a hair dryer, and a radio, and rather bland furnishings that obviously have serviced a number of guests before you.

✪ **Number 136.** 136 Huntington Rd., Cambridge, Cambridgeshire CB3 0HL. ☎ or fax **01223/461142.** 3 rms. TV. £35 ($56) single; £56 ($89.60) double. All rates include English breakfast. V. Bus: no. 2.

Small but choice, this charming Edwardian guest house lies only a 10-minute walk from Magdalene College, in a leafy residential neighborhood about half a mile north of the center of Cambridge. Built of red brick in 1911, the house is known for the venerable cedar that graces its front yard, its large and verdant rear garden, and the gracious dialogue of its owner, Alice Percival. Born of English colonial parents in Kenya, she offers comfortable accommodations on the street level of her house, along with advice on touring possibilities in the Cambridge region.

**Parkside Guest House.** 25 Parkside, Cambridge, Cambridgeshire CB1 1JE. ☎ **01223/311212.** Fax 01223/356926. 11 rms, 5 with shower only. TV TEL. £29 ($46.40) single without bath, £33 ($52.80) single with shower only; £50 ($80) double without bath; £53 ($84.80) double with shower only. All rates include English breakfast. No credit cards. Bus: no. 78 or 79.

Originally built in the 1850s as a residence for lecturers at Peterhouse College, this house was transformed during World War II into the headquarters for the Peterhouse Jewish Association, and sheltered Jewish academics from other parts of Europe. Later, the organist from St. John's College lived here and, after a brief period when it was owned by another college (Robinson College) within Cambridge University, it was sold to Mr. John Sutcliffe and Mrs. Shirley Heaton, who operate it today as a hotel. Located very close to the town center, it's one of the city's better B&Bs. The rooms are a good safe haven but devoid of a lot of charm. The establishment contains a tiny laundry, a bar and lounge, a small walled garden, a collection of reference books about the city and university, and a variety of breakfast cereals for those who wish to supplement the bacon and eggs. With advance notice, an evening meal can be arranged.

**Regency Guest House.** 7 Regent Terrace, Cambridge, Cambridgeshire CB2 1AA. ☎ **01223/329626.** Fax 01223/871816. 8 rms, 3 with bath. TV. £27–£29 ($43.20–$46.40) single without bath; £45–£48 ($72–$76.80) double without bath; £55–£58 ($88–$92.80) double with bath. All rates include continental breakfast. No credit cards. Bus: no. 5.

In a desirable location near the town center, overlooking the verdant expanse of a city park known as Parker's Piece, this hotel was built as a private house around 1850. Set behind a stone facade, and similar in design to many of its neighbors, it offers tea-making facilities in each of the bedrooms, and 1950s-style furniture which in recent years has acquired a nostalgic kind of glamour. The rooms are painted about every 6 months and have a bright, fresh look. Breakfast includes ample portions of continental-inspired fast-breakers, although cooked English breakfasts can be arranged for a supplement of £3 ($4.80).

**The Suffolk House.** 69 Milton Rd., Cambridge, Cambridgeshire CB4 1XA. ☎ **01223/ 352016.** Fax 01223/566816. 8 rms. TV. £35–£45 ($56–$72) single; £50–£65 ($80–$104) double. All rates include English breakfast. MC, V. Guests using the M11 motorway or the A14 Cambridge bypass should exit at Junction A10 (Ely), entering Cambridge on A1309, which is Milton Rd. Bus: no. 4 or 5.

Once the home of a well-known local doctor, it has long since been turned into one of the more winning B&Bs in Cambridge. Mary and Michael Cuthbert run this hotel, which is only a 15-minute stroll to the colleges. All rooms, furnished rather functionally and blandly, have tea- and coffee-making facilities, and hair dryers and irons are available upon request. In the back of this detached house is a garden, and the location is peaceful.

## A Youth Hostel

**Cambridge Youth Hostel.** 97 Tension Rd., Cambridge, Cambridgeshire CB1 2DN. ☎ **01223/354601.** Fax 01223/312780. 24 rms, 100 beds. £10.30 ($16.50) adults; £7 ($11.20) 18 and under. MC, V.

This converted Victorian town house with newer wings is popular for its location only 10 minutes from the center of Cambridge—as well as for its convenience—no curfew, free storage lockers, and bicycle and baggage storage, as well as currency exchange, laundry facilities, and a hostel shop selling postcards, stamps, laundry soap, and other necessities. There is a self-catering kitchen, but meals are also provided in the cafeteria-style dining room, with breakfast costing £2.85 ($4.55); a small packed lunch running £2.45 ($3.90), and a large one available for £3.25 ($5.20); and dinner for £4.25 ($6.80). Another bonus is the hostel's table license, allowing service of beer and wine with meals. The staff, professional and friendly, can answer your questions, suggest things to do, and point you to a bicycle rental shop up the block. Call ahead to reserve a room, because the hostel has such good amenities that many backpackers end up staying over for an extra day or two. If you're driving, the one big drawback is the complete lack of parking, meaning you'll have to scramble around for 2-hour metered spaces.

# WHERE TO EAT

In addition to the selections below, consider the **Rainbow Vegetarian Bistro,** King's Parade, across from Kings College (☎ **01223/321551**), a cellar whole-food and vegetarian establishment with less than a dozen tables. The a la carte menu of freshly prepared dishes is served all day, and includes breakfast with eggs or vegetarian sausage for £3.75 ($6) and main courses for £5.25 ($8.40). There are daily specials, plus an array of gluten-free and vegan dishes. Open daily from 9am to 9pm.

A popular student hangout, **Clown's Café,** 54 King St. (☎ **01223/355711**), is named for the clown art on its walls, remnants of its annual clown art competition. Serving daily from 9am until midnight, the cafe offers sandwiches, salads, quiches, lasagna, and daily specials, priced between £2 to £5.95 ($3.20 to $9.50). The satellite **Clown's II,** 8 Market Passage (☎ **01223/322312**), has a similar decor, but offers salads, pasta dishes, and cakes from £3 to £4.50 ($4.80 to $7.20). It also serves wine, and a pasta dish with a glass of wine runs £7 ($11.20). Service is daily from 10am to 11pm.

If you need a little spice in your life, try **Cambridge Curry Centre,** 45–47 Castle St. (☎ **01223/302687**), a two-story eatery offering traditional curry and tandoori dishes, as well as the flavorful chicken jalfrazi. Open daily from noon to 2:30pm and 6pm to midnight, it sells main courses for £4 to £7 ($6.40 to $11.20). For healthy self-catering or takeout, try **Cambridge Health Food,** 5 Bridges St. (☎ **01223/ 350433**), which offers a wide variety of whole-food supplies and supplements as well as a carry-out section of items such as pastas, quiche, and pizza.

**The Anchor.** 15 Silver St. ☎ **01223/353554.** Bar snacks and platters £2.95–£5.95 ($4.70–$9.50). MC, V. Daily noon–6pm. (Pub: Mon–Sat 10am–11pm; Sun noon–10:30pm.) ENGLISH.

Set a few steps from the Cam, beside the Silver Street Bridge, this verdant and time-tested establishment was opened in the 1970s in what was originally built as a ware-house for the storage of grain and flour. It has a bar and an outdoor terrace where punters will agree to row up to four visitors up and down the river, giving a running commentary en route. In 1994 it was refurbished, most modern accessories were ripped out, and the place was restored to an Old-World decor with lots of exposed wood and an assortment of real ales on tap. There's dining and drinking on two lev-els, with a choice of food items including lasagna with salad, roast beef platters, scampi, chicken nuggets, hot pots, and steak-and-ale pies. It's the same fare served almost anywhere in England.

✪ **Arundel House Restaurant.** In the Arundel Hotel, 53 Chesterton Rd. ☎ **01223/367701.** Reservations recommended. Main courses £8–£13 ($12.80–$20.80); fixed-price lunch £9.75 ($15.60) for 2 courses, £10.95 ($17.50) for 3 courses; Sun lunch £11.25 ($18); 2-course fixed-price dinner £13.50 ($21.60); 3-course fixed-price dinner £15.95 ($25.50). AE, DC, MC, V. Daily 12:15–1:45pm and 6:30–9:30pm. Bus: no. 3 or 5. FRENCH/BRITISH/VEGETARIAN.

One of the best and most acclaimed restaurants in Cambridge is in this 105-bedroom hotel on Chesterton Road overlooking the River Cam and Jesus Green. The location is a short walk from the city center. Winner of many awards, the cuisine is noted not only for its excellence and use of fresh produce, but also for its good value. The de-cor is warmly inviting, with Sanderson curtains, Louis XV–style upholstered chairs, and spacious tables. The menu changes frequently, and you dine both a la carte or from the fixed-price menu. There's also a children's menu, where the maximum price is £2.25 ($3.60). Perhaps you'll begin with a country game soup (venison, pheasant, hare, and rabbit) or a creamy fish soup. Fish choices are likely to include trout or salmon, or try English lamb steak cooked with Calvados, roast pheasant, or filet steak.

✪ **Browns.** 23 Trumpington St. ☎ **01223/461655.** Main courses £7.55–£11.45 ($12.10–$18.30). AE, MC, V. Mon–Sat 11am–11:30pm; Sun noon–11:30pm. Bus: no. 2. ENGLISH/CONTINENTAL.

Long a favorite at Oxford, Browns became a sensation at Cambridge some time ago. With a neoclassical colonnade in front, it has all the grandeur of the Edwardian era. It was actually built in 1914 as the outpatient department of a hospital dedicated to Edward VII. Today it's the most lighthearted place for dining in the city, with wicker chairs, high ceilings, pre–World War I woodwork, and a long bar covered with bottles of wine. The extensive bill of fare includes various spaghetti, fresh salads, several se-lections of meat and fish (from charcoal-grilled leg of lamb with rosemary to fresh fish in season), hot sandwiches, and the chef's daily specials. Service is often frantic, the waiters too busy to explain anything, but it's still a good choice—even if we did get served someone else's supper on our last visit. If you drop by in the afternoon, you can also order thick milkshakes or natural fruit juices. In fair weather, outdoor seating is provided. The location is opposite the Fitzwilliam Museum, 5 minutes from King's College.

**Cambridge Arms.** 4 King St. ☎ **01223/359650.** Bar snacks from £3–£6.50 ($4.80–$10.40). AE, V. Mon–Sat noon–5:30pm; Sun noon–2:30pm. (Pub: Mon–Sat 11am–11pm; Sun noon–3pm and 7–10:30pm.) ENGLISH.

This bustling, no-nonsense pub in the center of the town's busiest commercial dis-trict was originally built in 1866 as a brewery. Decorated with the original brickwork, photographs of the building's earlier incarnations, and assorted paraphernalia of the brewery trade, it dispenses endless platters of food to clients who order them over the bar's countertop. Menu possibilities include chef's daily specials, grilled steaks, lasagna, and an array of both hot and cold dishes. Some dishes are overcooked for our tastes, but few people go away hungry. Also on site is a Victorian-style coffee shop open daily from 10am to 10pm with access to six computers equipped with business software, Internet access, and E-mail.

**Free Press.** 7–9 Prospect Row. ☎ **01223/368337.** Bar snacks £1.75–£5 ($2.80–$8). No credit cards. Mon–Sat noon–2pm and 6–8:30pm; Sun noon–2pm and 7–9pm. (Pub: Mon–Sat noon–2:30pm and 6–11pm; Sun noon–3pm and 7–10:30pm.) ENGLISH.

The place was named after a radical local newspaper, the *Free Press,* which was bankrupted in the 1830s partly as a result of its fervent editorials against the dangers of alcohol. In 1840 the matriarch who founded this pub gleefully attached its name to her new watering hole, thereby ensuring an endless round of local jokes that have continued to the present day. The place is crowded and convivial; owners Chris Lloyd and his American-born wife, Debbie, praise their establishment as the only pub in Britain never visited by royalty. Its decorative theme includes lots of rowing and punting memorabilia. Food items include freshly made soups, meat pies, moussaka, vegetarian platters, and hot chef's specials of the day. Curiously enough, the more lager you have, the better the food tastes. There are a limited number of outdoor tables, which are much in demand during warm weather. Smoking isn't allowed.

**✪ Hobbs Pavilion.** Park Terrace, off Regent St. ☎ **01223/367480.** Crepes £4.10–£7.95 ($6.55–$12.70); 2-course fixed-price lunch £7.25 ($11.60); 3-course fixed-price dinner £8.75–£12.75 ($14–$20.40). No credit cards. Tues–Sat noon–2:15pm and 7–9:45pm. Closed mid-Aug to mid-Sept. CREPES.

In the vicinity of the University Arms Hotel is this deservedly popular place. Labeled "a creperie with a difference," it's located in the historic brick Cricket Pavilion. You get a choice of nearly 4 dozen crepes, both as a main course and as a dessert. Stuffings range from spicy mushrooms to black pudding. (We make a point of skipping the latter selection.) This savory list is backed up by a selection of freshly prepared soups and salads. The owner makes his own ice cream, which is usually served with chocolate sauce made from Belgian chocolate.

**Martin's Coffee House.** 4 Trumpington St. ☎ **01223/361757.** Sandwiches £1–£1.50 ($1.60–$2.40); pastries 90p–£1.20 ($1.45–$1.90); English breakfast £3.50 ($5.60). No credit cards. Mon–Sat 8:15am–5pm; Sun 9:15am–5pm. Bus: no. 4 or 5. TEA/SANDWICHES/PASTRIES.

Near the Fitzwilliam Museum is a small, simple, and modern coffeehouse with high standards. It offers a pleasing array of sandwiches and pastries, along with English breakfasts. Whole-meal rolls are filled with turkey, ham, beef, salad, cheese, and eggs. Homemade cakes, scones, and doughnuts are also sold, usually to accompany the endless pots of tea that emerge, steaming, from a modern samovar. Basically it's the kind of food you'd get at a church supper in England.

**Shao Tao.** 72 Regent St. ☎ **01223/353942.** Reservations recommended Fri–Sat. Main courses £4.50–£6 ($7.20–$9.60); 4-course fixed-price meal £15.50 ($24.80). AE, DC, MC, V. Daily noon–2:30pm and 6–11pm. Bus: no. 1, 4, or 5. CHINESE.

On a busy commercial street in the town center, this pastel-colored restaurant specializes in Hunan, Szechuan, and Peking cuisine. The menu offers such dishes as aromatic crispy duck, crispy shredded beef with chili and carrots, "three kinds of meat" soup, and a host of other dishes. The restaurant also caters to vegetarians. If you're confused, order the "leave it to us" feast, and you're likely to be happily surprised. The cookery is delicate and light, unlike some of the horrors dispensed by so-called Chinese restaurants in Cambridge.

**Varsity Restaurant.** 35 St. Andrew's St., between Sidney and Regent sts. ☎ **01223/356060.** Main courses £4.50–£8.90 ($7.20–$14.25). AE, CB, DC, DISC, MC, V. Daily 11:30am–3pm and 5:30–11pm. GREEK/CONTINENTAL.

This is one of the oldest and best-established restaurants in Cambridge, having opened in the 1950s in a building dating from 1650. In a bare, whitewashed room with black beams and pictures of boats and islands on the walls, you can dine on such Greek specialties as stuffed vine leaves. Kebabs are served with rice and salad, and there are some continental dishes for less adventurous palates. The recipes from the old country have lost a little in translation from the Greek, but students come here for a "good tuck in," nevertheless.

## CAMBRIDGE AFTER DARK

Cambridge's artistic bent comes to a head from the middle of June to the middle of July when **Camfest** (☎ 01223/359547) hosts a visual and performing arts festival all over town. Event tickets are generally between £3.50 to £7 ($5.60 to $11.20).

In fact, during the summer months Cambridge holds a number of festivals, aimed primarily at tourists. You might want to visit the **Midsummer Fair,** which has been around since the 16th century; the free **Strawberry Fair,** with games and music on the first Saturday in June (☎ 01223/356-0160); **Summer in the City;** and the **Cambridge Folk Festival** (contact the Corn Exchange box office at ☎ 01223/ 335-7851). The **Cambridge Shakespeare Festival** offers four plays throughout July and August, with tickets available for £8 ($12.80). The **Cambridge Corn Exchange,** besides hosting the folk festival, presents summer band, jazz, and classical concerts.

Most of the year you can find dramatic entertainment where Emma Thompson and other well-known thespians got their start, at **The Amateur Dramatic Club,** Park Street near Jesus Lane (☎ 01223/359547; box office 01223/504444). The stage presents two student productions nightly, Tuesday through Saturday, with the main show tending toward classic and modern drama and opera and the late show usually of comic or experimental nature. The theater is open 40 weeks a year, closing in August and September. Tickets to the main show run from £4.50 ($7.20) early in the week to £5.50 ($8.80) late in the week; late show tickets start at £2.50 ($4) and edge up to £3 ($4.80) late in the week.

You may see ADC alumni on screen when you go to the **Arts Cinema,** Market Passage (☎ 01223/504444), which runs five shows a day ranging from subtitled European films to cult films to blockbusters. Science fiction is often the genre of choice late night, and summertime offers afternoon children's features. Tickets are £3.20 ($5.10) for general seating in the afternoon and late night, £4.20 ($6.70) for reserved seating in the evening.

There's also musical entertainment, which you can find out about by checking out flyers posted around town, or reading the *Varsity.* **The Corn Exchange,** Wheeler Street and Corn Exchange (☎ 01223/357851), is a venue for everything from classical concerts to bigger-name rock shows. Call for specific listings and ticket prices, which generally vary from £5 to £25 ($8 to $40). The **Fresher & Firkin,** 16 Chesterton Rd. (☎ 01223/324325), a pub located in a former movie theater, has live music or DJs on Friday and Saturday, providing mainly rock and dance music free of charge. Entertainment in some form can be found 7 nights a week at **The Junction,** Clifton Road, near the train station (☎ 01223/511511), where an eclectic mix of acts take to the stage weeknights to perform all genres of music, comedy, and theater, and DJs take over on the weekend, playing dance styles ranging from soul to jungle. Cover charges vary from £7.50 to £10 ($12 to $16), depending on the event.

For dancing only, **5th Avenue,** Lion Yard (☎ **01223/364222**), a second-story club, has a huge dance floor and plays everything from house to the latest pop hits, Monday through Saturday from 9pm until 2am. Sometimes they even DJ the old-fashioned way—by taking requests. The cover charge ranges from £2.50 to £6 ($4 to $9.60), depending on the night.

## A PUB CRAWL

For further nightlife, do as the locals do and pub crawl. The list of pubs is far too extensive to review here, but regardless of whether your goal is to wind down or get wound up, rub shoulders with lifelong residents or students, there's a pint waiting for you. When crawling, why not start at the place from which all local pub life evolved, the **Pickerel,** Bridge Street (☎ **01223/355068**), Cambridge's oldest pub, dating back to 1432. Pubs don't get more traditional than this. If the ceiling beams or floorboards groan occasionally, well, they've certainly earned the right over the years. Real ales on tap include Bulmer's Traditional Cider, Old Speckled Hen, or Theakston's 6X, Old Peculiar, and Best Bitter.

The **Maypole,** Portugal Place at Park Street (☎ **01223/352999**), is the local hangout for actors when they're not in the nearby ADC Theatre. It's known for cocktails rather than ales, but you can get a Tetley's 6X or Castle Eden anyway. Flowing just as freely is conversation of a very dramatic nature.

The **Eagle,** Benet Street off King's Parade (☎ **01223/505020**), will be forever famous as the place where Nobel Laureates Watson and Crick first announced their discovery of the DNA double helix. Be prepared to pay up front though, as the barkeeper wouldn't even serve them a toast until they'd settled an outstanding tab of 4 shillings. Real ales include local brewery Greene King's Abbott, so make your order and raise a pint to the wonders of modern science.

For an encounter with less revered academics, join local students at the **Anchor,** Silver Street (☎ **01223/353554**), or **Tap and Spile (The Mill),** Mill Lane, off Silver Street Bridge (☎ **01223/357026**) for a pint of Greene King's IPA or Abbott. Anchor-goers claim the bridge itself as drinking grounds in fair weather, whereas the Tap and Spiel's clientele lays claim to the entire riverside park.

If none of these pubs meets your needs, ask locals, but expect varied responses: The **Baron of Beef,** 19 Bridge St. (☎ **01223/505022**); **Henry's,** Quayside (☎ **01223/324649**); **Champion of the Thames,** 68 King St. (☎ **01223/352043**); or **The Rat & Parrot,** Thompsons Lane (☎ **01223/311701**); are but a few of the other pubs that enjoy popularity with students.

## 2 Ely

70 miles NE of London; 16 miles NE of Cambridge

Ely Cathedral is the top attraction in the fen country, outside of Cambridge. The town of Ely used to be known as the Isle of Ely, until the surrounding marshes and meres were drained. The last stronghold of Saxon England, it was defended by Hereward the Wake, until his capitulation to the Normans in 1071. After you've seen the cathedral, you can safely be on your way, as Ely is a sleepy market town, its glory belonging to another day, and it can hardly compete against the life and bustle found at Cambridge. Nearby attractions include a Neolithic Flint Mine and a war museum.

## ESSENTIALS

**GETTING THERE**    Ely is a major railway junction served by express trains to Cambridge. Service is frequent from London's Liverpool Street Station. For schedules and information, call ☎ **0345/484950.**

## Impressions

*Next morning went with H. M.[his mentor, Horace Moule, son of the Vicar of Fordington] to King's Chapel early. M. opened the great West doors to show the interior vista: we got upon the roof where we could see Ely Cathedral gleaming in the distant sunlight. A never-to-be-forgotten morning. H. M. saw me off for London. His last smile.*

—Thomas Hardy

Frequent buses run between Cambridge and Ely. Call ☎ **01223/423554** for schedules and information.

If you're driving from Cambridge, take A10 north.

**VISITOR INFORMATION**    The **Tourist Information Centre** is at Oliver Cromwell's House, 29 St. Mary's St. (☎ **01353/662062**). Open April through October, daily from 10am to 6pm; November through March, Monday to Saturday from 10am to 5:15pm.

## ✪ ELY CATHEDRAL

The near-legendary founder of the cathedral was Etheldreda, the wife of a North Umbrian king who established a monastery on the spot in 673. The present structure dates from 1081. Visible for miles around, the landmark octagonal lantern is the crowning glory of the cathedral. Erected in 1322 following the collapse of the old tower, it represents a remarkable engineering achievement. Four hundred tons of lead and wood hang in space, held there by timbers reaching to the eight pillars.

You enter the cathedral through the Galilee West Door, a good example of the early English style of architecture. The lantern tower and the octagon are the most notable features inside, but visit the lady chapel, too. Although its decor has deteriorated over the centuries, it's still a handsome example of the perpendicular style, having been completed in the mid–14th century. The entry fee goes to help preserve the cathedral. Monday to Saturday, guided tours gather at 11:15am and 2:15pm; in the summer, tours occur throughout the day.

Admission is £3 ($4.80) for adults, £2.20 ($3.50) for seniors, students, children ages 12 to 16; it's free for children under 12. Open April to October, daily from 7am to 7pm; November through March, Monday to Saturday from 7:30am to 6pm and Sunday from 7:30am to 5pm. For information, call ☎ **01353/667735.**

You might want to visit the Brass Rubbing Centre, which has a large selection of replica brass. Rubbings can produce remarkable results for wall-hangings or special gifts. All materials are provided to make your own rubbings. The center is open all year in the North Aisle, outside the Cathedral Shop.

And the **Cathedral Shop** within Ely Cathedral is one of the best of all cathedral shops in England, with an exceptional range of unusual gifts, souvenirs, and cards. It is especially recommended for its well-stocked bookshelves and its selection of choral, organ, and other classical music on CD and cassette.

## MORE ATTRACTIONS IN & AROUND ELY

**Ely Museum.** The Old Goaf, Market St. ☎ **01353/666655.** Admission £1.80 ($2.90) adults; £1.25 ($2) children, students, and seniors; free for children 6 and under. Tues–Sun and bank holiday Mondays 10:30am–4:30pm.

In the Ely Museum, a gallery presents a chronological history of Ely and The Isle from the Ice Age to the present day. Displays include archaeology, social history, rural life, local industry, and military as well as a tableaux of the debtor's cell and condemned cell which are also on view.

**Oliver Cromwell's House.** 29 St. Mary's St. ☎ **01353/662062.** Admission £2.30 ($3.70) adults; £1.80 ($2.90) children, seniors, and students; £5 ($8) family ticket. Apr–Sept daily 10am–6pm; off-season Mon–Sat 10am–5:15pm.

This recently restored house was owned by Oliver Cromwell, a name hardly beloved by the royals even today. He rose to fame as a military and political leader during the English civil wars of 1642 to 1649. These wars led to the execution of Charles I and the replacement of the monarchy by the Commonwealth. In 1653 Cromwell was declared Lord Protector, and this local farmer became the most powerful man in the land until his death in 1658. His house stands next to St. Mary's Church in the heart of Ely. Exhibitions, displays, and period rooms offer an insight both into Cromwell's character and into 17th-century domestic life. Rooms include a Portrait Room, a Civil War Exhibition, Cromwell's Study, and a Haunted Bedroom, and videos depict Cromwell's life and times. The tourist center is also located here.

**Grimes Graves.** On B1107, 2³/4 miles northeast of Brandon, Norfolkshire. ☎ **01842/810656.** Admission £1.60 ($2.55) adults; £1.20 ($1.90) students and seniors; 80p ($1.30) children 5–15; free for children 4 and under. Apr–Oct daily 10am–1pm and 2–6pm; Nov–Mar Wed–Sun 10am–1pm and 2–4pm.

This is the largest and best-preserved group of Neolithic flint mines in Britain, and produced the cutting edges of spears, arrows, and knives for prehistoric tribes throughout the region. Because of its isolated location within sparsely populated, fir-wooded countryside, it's easy to imagine yourself transported back through the millennia.

Most visitors get here by taking A134 for 7 miles northwest of Thetford, then transferring to B1107. A guardian will meet you near the well-signposted parking lot. After determining that you are physically able to take the tour, he or she will open one or several of the mine shafts, each of which requires a descent down an almost-vertical 30-foot ladder (a visit here is not recommended for very young children, seniors, or travelers with disabilities). Since the tunnel and shaft have been restored and reinforced, it's now possible to see where work took place during Neolithic times. Although not essential, many archaeologists, professional and amateur, bring their own flashlights with them. The mines, incidentally, are situated close to the military bases that housed thousands of American air force personnel during World War II.

**Imperial War Museum.** Duxford Airfield, on A505, at Junction 10 of M11. ☎ **01223/835000.** Admission £6.40 ($10.25) adults; £4.20 ($6.70) seniors; £3.20 ($5.10) children and students; £18 ($28.80) families. Mid-Mar to Oct daily 10am–6pm; Nov to mid-Mar daily 10am–4pm. Closed Dec 24–26. Bus: Cambus no. 103 from Drummer St. Station in Cambridge. Take M11 to Junction 10, 8 miles south of Cambridge.

In this former Battle of Britain station and U.S. Eighth Air Force base in World War II, you'll find a huge collection of historic civil and military aircraft from both world wars, including the only B-29 Superfortress in Europe. Other exhibits include midget submarines, tanks, and a variety of field artillery pieces, as well as a historical display on the U.S. Eighth Air Force.

In 1997, Elizabeth II opened the American Air Museum here as part of the larger complex. It houses Europe's finest collection of historic American combat aircraft and is the largest precast concrete structure in Europe. Aircraft on show ranges from a World War I biplane to the giant B-52 jet bomber. A number are dramatically suspended from the ceiling as in flight. The museum uses aircraft and other exhibits to explain the significance of U.S. air power and its part in 20th-century history.

## TEATIME

Around the corner from St. Mary's Church is **Steeplegate,** 16–18 High St. (☎ **01353/664731**), a tearoom and craft shop. The tearoom with its wood tables and ancient windows, serves its tea with selections from a menu that includes light lunch items like sandwiches as well as scones and creamy gateaux. After tea, venture downstairs to the craft shop and have a look at the variety of handmade pottery, glass, and baskets.

## WHERE TO STAY

**Cathedral House.** 17 St. Mary's St., Ely, Cambridgeshire CB7 4ER. ☎ **01353/662124.** 3 rms, 2 suites, all with bath. TV. £35 ($56) single; £50 ($80) double and suites. No credit cards. Closed Christmas and New Year's.

This Georgian house from the mid-1800s has been lovingly restored by Jenny and Robin Farndale. The house, with its walled garden, sits in the shadow of the cathedral and is close to Cromwell's House. They retained the original features and added new decor and furnishings to both the public and the private rooms. All the bedrooms are with private bath and well appointed, with garden views. All rooms have coffee- and tea-making facilities, and children are welcome.

**The Nyton.** 7 Barton Rd., Ely, Cambridgeshire CB7 4HZ. ☎ **01353/662459.** 10 rms. TV. £38 ($60.80) single; £60 ($96) double. All rates include English breakfast. AE, DC, MC, V.

In a quiet residential section of Ely is this licensed family-run hotel surrounded by a 2-acre flower garden with lawns and trees. It's also right next to an 18-hole golf course. You'll have views of a wide area of fenland and of the cathedral. Each time-worn bedroom has beverage-making equipment. Bar snacks are available from noon to 2pm, and dinner is offered nightly from 7 to 8:30pm, costing £15 ($24). Barton Road is accessible from the cathedral and railway station, lying on the A142 Ely-Newmarket road off the A10 Ely-Cambridge road.

## WHERE TO EAT

An unusual choice is **The Almonry Restaurant & Tea Rooms** in The College, Ely Cathedral (☎ **01353/666360**). Housed in the medieval college buildings on the north side of the cathedral, this is a comfortable tearoom with table service and a restaurant in a beautiful 12th-century Undercroft licensed to sell drinks. You can take your food or drink out in warm weather to a garden seat. It is open for morning coffee, lunches, and afternoon teas. Meals cost from £5 ($8). Hours are Monday through Saturday from 10am to 5pm and on Sunday from 11am to 5pm.

✪ **The Old Fire Engine House.** 25 St. Mary's St. ☎ **01353/662582.** Reservations recommended. Main courses £11.50–£13.80 ($18.40–$22.10). MC, V. Mon–Sat 12:30–2pm and 7:30–9pm; Sun 12:30–2pm. Bus: no. 109. ENGLISH.

Opposite St. Mary's Church is one of the finer restaurants in East Anglia. It's worth making a detour to this converted fire station in a walled garden, in a complex of buildings that includes an art gallery. Soups are served in huge bowls, accompanied by course-grained crusty bread. Main dishes include beef braised in beer, jugged hare, steak-and-kidney pie, pike baked in white wine, rabbit with sherry sauce, and pigeon with bacon and black olives. Desserts include fruit pie and cream, although we'd recommend the syllabub, made with cream and liquor. In summer you can dine outside in the garden, even order a cream tea. It's owned and in large part run by Ann Ford, who still finds time to talk to customers.

## 3 Saffron Walden & Thaxted

43 miles NE of London; 15 miles SE of Cambridge

In the northern corner of Essex, a short drive from Thaxted, is the ancient market town of **Saffron Walden,** named for the crop of crocus sativus grown here between the 15th and 18th centuries for use as a spice, as well as an additive in medicine and dye. Despite its proximity to London, it isn't disturbed by heavy tourist traffic, although residents of Cambridge use it as a quiet weekend escape.

Saffron Walden has a settlement history going back to the Bronze Age, and the architecture of its perpendicular-style Church of Saffron Walden, castle ruins, and 15th- through 17th-century homes reflects the town's medieval roots as a trade center for wools and malts, as well as saffron. A prevailing characteristic of its timber-framed structures is the ornamental facades of parget, whitewashed plasterwork sometimes made with cow dung. It is also one of the few market towns in England that still has its original medieval street pattern.

**Thaxted,** a couple of miles southeast of Saffron Walden on the B184, is home to the beautiful 14th-century Church of St. John the Baptist, Our Lady and St. Lawrence, and the rare 15th-century Guildhall. The town is famous for having a number of well-preserved Elizabethan houses. Thaxted is also known as the venue for the famous Morris Ring, the first weekend after spring bank holiday, a processional street dance that attracts more than 300 dancers and culminates with a haunting horn dance as dusk falls.

## ESSENTIALS

**GETTING THERE**   Trains leave London's Liverpool Street Station in the direction of Cambridge several times a day. Two or three stations before Cambridge, passengers should get off in the hamlet of Audley End, 8 miles north of Thaxted and 1 mile from Saffron Walden. There is a bus from Audley End, but it meanders around so much that most visitors prefer to take a taxi instead. For schedules and information, call ☎ **0345/484950.**

Cambus no. 122 leaves Cambridge Monday to Saturday at 12:15pm, 2:40pm, and 5:35pm for Saffron Walden. Cambus no. 9 departs only Sunday every 1¹/₂ hours between 10am to 6pm. The last bus back on Sunday departs Saffron Walden at 7:10pm. Call ☎ **01223/423554** for information and schedules. National Express buses leave London's Victoria Coach Station several times a day and stop at Saffron Walden, 6 miles north of Thaxted. For schedules and information, call ☎ **0990/808080.** From here, about three (at most) buses head on to Thaxted. However, most visitors find it easier to take a taxi.

If you're driving from Cambridge, take A1301 southeast, connecting with B184 (also southeast) into Saffron Walden and the adjoining village of Thaxted.

Thaxted is 5 miles south of Saffron Walden. To reach Thaxted from Saffron Walden, drive along the B184 (the Thaxted Road), following signs to Thaxted and Great Dunmow. A bus follows this route Monday to Saturday five to six times a day.

**VISITOR INFORMATION**   The **Tourist Information Centre** is at 1 Market Sq. (☎ **01799/510444**) in Saffron Walden. Open November through March, Monday to Saturday from 10am to 5pm and April through October, Monday to Saturday from 9:30am to 5:30pm. This office also handles inquiries for Thaxted.

## SEEING THE SIGHTS
### IN SAFFRON WALDEN

One mile west of Saffron Walden (on B1383) is **Audley End House** (☎ **01799/522842**), one of the finest mansions in East Anglia. Begun by Thomas Howard, treasurer to the king, in 1605, this Jacobean house was built on the foundation of a monastery. James I is reported to have said, "Audley End is too large for a king, though it might do for a lord treasurer." Among the house's outstanding features is an impressive Great Hall with an early–17th-century screen at the north end, one of the most beautiful ornamental screens in England. The rooms decorated by Robert Adam feature fine furniture and works of art. Among the attractions are a "Gothick" chapel and a charming Victorian ladies' sitting room. Landscaped by Capability Brown, the park surrounding the house has a lovely rose garden, a river and cascade, and a picnic area.

From April 3 until the end of September, the house and grounds are open Wednesday to Sunday and on bank holidays from noon to 6pm. Admission to the house and grounds is £5.50 ($8.80) for adults, £4.10 ($6.55) for students and seniors, and £2.80 ($4.50) for children 5 to 16. The grounds only are open daily from 10am to 6pm and cost £3.30 ($5.30) for adults, £2.50 ($4) for students and seniors, and £1.70 ($2.70) for children. It's located 1¼ miles (a 20-minute walk) from Audley End Station—on B1383, a country road 1 mile west of Saffron Walden—where trains arrive from Cambridge.

In a maze of narrow medieval streets, on the grounds of the **Saffron Walden Museum,** stand the ruins of the 11th-century Norman **Castle Keep.** Next door is the museum (☎ **01799/510333**) with its rotating exhibits, natural history and archaeological exhibits, and decorative arts. Admission to the grounds and ruins is free; museum admission is £1 ($1.60) adults, children free. Open March through October, Monday through Saturday, from 10am to 5pm, Sunday and bank holidays 2:30pm to 5pm; November through February, Monday through Saturday from 11am to 4pm, Sunday and bank holidays 2:30pm to 4pm; closed Christmas Eve and Christmas Day.

## IN THAXTED

Sitting on the crest of a hill 43 miles north of London, the Saxon town of Thaxted has the most beautiful small church (☎ **01371/830221**) in England. The graceful spire of **The Church of St. John the Baptist, Our Lady and St. Lawrence** can be seen for miles around. Its belfry has special chimes that call parishioners to church services. Dating back to 1340, the church is a nearly perfect example of sacred architecture.

Other sights include the **Thaxted Guildhall** (no telephone), located next to the church and the site of medieval market place. It is a fine example of a medieval Guildhall, few of which now remain. It was built between 1393 and 1420, possibly the Cutlers Guild. Open April through September, Sundays and bank holiday Mondays only from 2 to 6pm.

**Thaxted Windmill** (☎ **01371/830285**), stands on the site of the earlier Church Mill and was constructed of local bricks. It was built in 1804 by John Webb, a local farmer, at a time when the demand for milled wheat and malt was increasing. It ceased working between 1900 and 1907, and fell into increasing disrepair until 1973 when the Thaxted Society commenced work to restore it. Open May through September, Saturdays, Sundays, and bank holiday Mondays from 2 to 6pm.

## OUTDOOR PURSUITS

Uttlesford is the northwest corner of Essex, 10 miles south of Cambridge and a half an hour's drive from London up the M11. This rich agricultural area is full of ancient woods and villages with names ending in "don" and "den," signifying the rolling hills and valleys, respectively, that make up the area.

It is home to the National Trust's **Hatfield Forest,** more than 1,000 acres of woodland, lying south of the A120 between Takeley and Great Hallingbury, once part of the royal forests that covered large parts of West Essex. Open to the public, it offers wide valleys, woodland walks, lake fishing, nature reserves, and a 1½-mile nature trail. Refreshments are available at the Lakeside Café. For further information, contact The Head Warden (☎ **01279/870678**).

# WHERE TO STAY
## IN SAFFRON WALDEN

**The Cross Keys Hotel.** 32 High St., Saffron Walden, Essex CB10 1AX. ☎ **01799/522207.** Fax 01799/526550. 5 rms, 3 with bath. TV. £30 ($48) single without bath; £39 ($62.40) double without bath, £50 ($80) double with bath; £55 ($88) triple with bath; £65 ($104) honeymoon suite. All rates include English breakfast. AE, MC, V.

As famous for its pub as it is for its rooms, this fine example of Elizabethan architecture was built in 1449 and retains its black-and-white half-timbered facade. The bedrooms are cozily arranged beside crooked upstairs hallways, and each has comfortable furnishings and vaguely modernized charm. Even if you don't stay here, consider dropping into the pub for a pint of ale beside the huge inglenook fireplace where fleeing priests used to hide in what was known as a priest's hole. Meals, chosen from a large menu that's supplemented by daily specials, are served daily from noon to 10pm. Fairly routine meals begin at £10 ($16) and include soups, prawn cocktails, mixed grills, ham steak, and the chef's daily specials. The hotel sits opposite the post office, at the northern end of the town's main street.

**Queen's Head Inn.** High St., Littlebury, near Saffron Walden, Essex CB11 4TD. ☎ **01799/522251.** Fax 01799/513522. 6 rms. TV TEL. £29.95 ($47.90) single; £49.95 ($79.90) double. All rates include continental breakfast. AE, DC, MC, V.

In the environs, the Queen's Head is on B1383, 5 minutes from Junction 9 (M11) if you're coming from the south, or Junction 10 if you're coming from the north. The hotel and licensed restaurant rents comfortably furnished although somewhat dowdy bedrooms, all with beverage-making equipment. The inn dates from the 16th century, and is only minutes from the heart of Saffron Walden by car. The Queen's Head provides a large parking area, and it also has a good restaurant, serving English and classic French food and doing so competently instead of grandly.

## NEAR THAXTED

**Four Seasons Hotel.** Walden Rd., Thaxted, Essex CM6 2RE. ☎ **01371/830129.** Fax 01371/830835. 9 rms, all with bath. TV TEL. £50–£60 ($80–$96) single; £65–£75 ($104–$120) double. All rates include English breakfast. AE, MC, V.

This country hotel stands on 2 acres of well-maintained lawns and gardens with a natural pond. On the outskirts of Thaxted, the hotel has been modernized to a high standard, although the original features remain. It lies half a mile northwest of the village center, beside the B184 highway. The rooms are comfortable and centrally heated, not only with private baths, but color TVs, hospitality trays, and direct-dial phones. The hotel lounge bar is warm and inviting, popular with locals and visitors alike. In the intimate restaurant, an a la carte menu is presented for both lunch and dinner Monday through Saturday. Sunday is family day, when a traditional lunch is served to those who have made a reservation. The cuisine is made even better by the fresh produce from local suppliers. A little more flavor in the dishes would help. This is a strictly nonsmoking facility, and there is a dress code in the restaurant and bar.

# WHERE TO EAT
## IN SAFFRON WALDEN

**Eight Bells.** 18 Bridge St. ☎ **01799/522790.** Reservations recommended on weekends only. Main courses £6.25–£14.95 ($10–$23.90); fixed-price 3-course Sun lunch £10.75 ($17.20); bar menu £2.10–£13.75 ($3.35–$22). AE, V. Daily noon–2:30pm and 6–9:30pm. INTERNATIONAL.

Behind an Elizabethan-era black-and-white half-timbered facade, this is the most popular pub in town, a favorite of students visiting from Cambridge. Depending on business, a formal dining room, the Tudor Barn, may or may not be open at the time of your arrival. This timbered hall, with oaken beams and furniture, serves menus with a wide choice of meat, vegetables, and fish. The cookery doesn't aspire to grandeur; the aim is merely to feed you. When business is less brisk, meals are served in a warmly traditional dining room located a few steps from the busy pub, in something the staff refers to as "The Top Bar." The Eight Bells lies beside the main road leading to Cambridge, a 5-minute walk from the center.

## IN THAXTED

**Recorder's House Restaurant.** 17 Town St. ☎ **01371/830438.** Reservations recommended. Main courses £8.50–£14 ($13.60–$22.40); fixed-price lunch £13.75 ($22). AE, MC, V. Wed–Sun noon–10pm. ENGLISH/CATALAN.

Near the guildhall in the village center, the Recorder's House was built in 1450 and is believed to have once incorporated part of the medieval Thaxted Manor House. It's named after the recorder who used to live here, collecting taxes for the Crown. Apparently there were objections to these taxes, as the winding staircase was built with steps that pitch outward, so that an attacking swordsman would be thrown off balance. In front of an inglenook fireplace, you'll dine in a room with the same linenfold paneling, wide oak floors, and candlelit atmosphere as Edward VII enjoyed when he honeymooned here with his queen. The cuisine—which combines English and Catalan cooking—is the best in the area, although that's not saying a lot. Featured are such dishes as noisettes of lamb in a red wine and rosemary sauce, sautéed calf's liver in a rosemary-walnut sauce, and butter-glazed rainbow trout with mussels and spring onions, served with a lime sabayon. Weather permitting, guests can dine outside in the medieval walled gardens.

# 4  Dedham

63 miles NE of London; 8 miles NE of Colchester

Remember Constable's *Vale of Dedham?* The Vale of Dedham lies between the towns of Colchester and Ipswich in a wide valley through which runs the River Stour, the boundary between Essex and Suffolk. It's not only the link with Constable that has made this vale so popular. It is one of the most beautiful unspoiled areas left in southeast England. In this little Essex village on the Stour River you're in the heart of Constable Country. Flatford Mill is only a mile farther down the river. The village, with its Tudor, Georgian, and Regency houses, is set in the midst of the water meadows of the Stour. Constable painted its church and tower. Dedham is right on the Essex-Suffolk border and makes a good center for exploring both North Essex and the Suffolk border country.

## ESSENTIALS

**GETTING THERE**   Trains depart every 20 minutes from London's Liverpool Street Station for the 50-minute ride to Colchester. For schedules and information, call ☎ **0345/484950.** From Colchester, it's possible to take a taxi from the railway station to the bus station, then board a bus run by the Eastern National Bus Company for the 5-mile trip to Dedham. (Buses leave about once an hour.) Most people take a taxi from Colchester directly to Dedham.

National Express buses depart from London's Victoria Coach Station for Colchester, where you have the choice of taking either another bus or a taxi to Dedham. For schedules and information, call ☎ **0990/808080.**

If you're driving from the London ring road, branch northeast on A12 to Colchester, turning off at East Bergholt onto a small secondary road leading east to Dedham.

## VISITING THE PAINTERS' HOMES

Less than a mile from the village center is **The Sir Alfred Munnings Art Museum,** East Lane (☎ **01206/322127**), home of Sir Alfred Munnings, president of the Royal Academy from 1944 to 1949 and painter extraordinaire of racehorses and other animals. The house and studio, which have sketches and other works, are open from early May to early October, on Sunday, Wednesday, and bank holidays (plus Thursday and Saturday during August) from 2 to 5pm. Admission is £3 ($4.80) for adults and 50p (80¢) for children.

The English landscape painter John Constable (1776–1837) was born at East Bergholt, directly north of Dedham. Near the village is **Flatford Mill,** East Bergholt (☎ **01206/298283**), subject of one of his most renowned works. The mill, in a scenic setting, was given to the National Trust in 1943, and has since been leased to the Field Studies Council for use as a residential center. The center offers more than 170 short courses each year in all aspects of art and the environment. Fees are £102 ($163.20) for a weekend (Saturday and Sunday) and £272 ($435.20) for a full week. The fee includes accommodation, meals, and tuition. Write to Director of Studies, Field Studies Council, Flatford Mill Field Centre, East Bergholt, Colchester, Essex CO7 6UL.

## WHERE TO STAY & EAT

**Dedham Hall.** Brook St., Dedham, Essex C07 6AD. ☎ **01206/323027.** 16 rms. £40 ($64) single; £60 ($96) double. All rates include English breakfast. MC, V.

Built in 1380, today this is a rambling Elizabethan farmhouse, with a pink stucco exterior and a partially half-timbered interior. Set on 5 acres of park, garden, and field, it's the domain of Jim and Wendy Sarton, who raise sheep and geese, and run a small evening restaurant on the premises. From the front windows of much of the house, you can see a privately owned pond and the steeple of the village church. There's a resident's bar near the dining room, and a trio of sitting rooms for extended conversations. Fresh-cooked, three-course meals with a wide choice of dishes are served at dinnertime Tuesday through Saturday for a set price of £19.50 ($31.20). Lunch is served only on Sunday, three courses for £17.50 ($28). Meals might include scrambled eggs with smoked salmon, or grilled Dover sole with butter sauce, and at least one vegetarian dish of the day. Advance reservations for nonresidents are recommended. Dedham Hall is a 3-minute walk east of the town center.

**The Marlborough Head Hotel.** Mill Lane, Dedham, Essex CO7 6DH. ☎ **01206/323250.** Main courses £4.60–£11.95 ($7.35–$19.10); sandwiches £1.95–£3.25 ($3.10–$5.20). AE, DC, MC, V. Daily 10am–10pm. (Pub: Mon–Sat 10am–11pm; Sun 10am–10:30pm.) ENGLISH.

This is the most historic and popular pub in the area, and it also rents four bedrooms upstairs to passersby. Set opposite Constable's old school, and known for its stone and frame construction, it contains sections that date from the 1400s. During warm weather the crowd moves onto an outdoor patio near a small garden. Children are welcome and you're likely to see more than one family dining together. Place your food order at the bar counter and an employee will bring it to your table. Food items include an array of pâtés, quiches, beef, fish, poultry, and offal (such as kidney-and-liver) dishes, each prepared in solidly conservative English ways.

The inn's four simple but adequate bedrooms each contain plaster walls and wooden floors engagingly skewed and sloped because of their age. Each contains a shower, toilet, sink, and TV. For B&B, rates are £32.50 ($52) for a single and £50 ($80) for a double.

## 5  Stately Homes in Long Melford

61 miles NE of London; 34 miles SE of Cambridge

Long Melford has been famous since the days of the early cloth makers. Like Lavenham, it attained prestige and importance during the Middle Ages. Of the old buildings remaining, the village church is often called "one of the glories of the shire." Along its 3-mile-long High Street—said to boast the highest concentration of antique shops in Europe—are many private homes erected by wealthy wool merchants of yore. Of special interest are Long Melford's two stately homes, Melford Hall and Kentwell Hall.

## ESSENTIALS

**GETTING THERE**   Trains run from London's Liverpool Street Station toward Ipswich and on to Marks Tey. Call ☎ **01223/423554** for information and schedules. Here you can take a shuttle train going back and forth between that junction and Sudbury. From the town of Sudbury, it's a 3-mile taxi ride to Long Melford.

From Cambridge, take a Cambus Bus Company coach to Bury St. Edmunds, then change for the final ride into Long Melford. These buses run about once an hour throughout the day and early evening.

If driving from Newmarket, continue east on A45 to Bury St. Edmunds, but cut south on A134 (toward Sudbury) to Long Melford.

**VISITOR INFORMATION**   There is a **Tourist Information** office in the Town Hall, Sudbury (☎ **01787/881320**), open daily Monday through Saturday from 10am to 4:45pm.

## BEATRIX POTTER'S ANCESTRAL HOME & A TUDOR MANSION

Standing in Long Melford on the east side of A134 is **Melford Hall,** the ancestral home of Beatrix Potter, who often visited. Jemima Puddleduck still occupies a chair in one of the bedrooms upstairs, and some of her other figures are on display. The house, built between 1554 and 1578, has paintings, fine furniture, and Chinese porcelain. The gardens alone make a visit here worthwhile.

Melford Hall (☎ **01787/880286**) is open May to September, Wednesday through Sunday and bank holiday Mondays from 2 to 5:30pm; April and October, Saturday, Sunday, and bank holiday Mondays from 2 to 5:30pm. Admission is £4.20 ($6.70) for adults and £2.10 ($3.35) for children.

At the end of an avenue of linden trees, the red-brick Tudor mansion, **Kentwell Hall,** surrounded by a broad moat has been restored by its owners, Mr. And Mrs. Patrick Phillips. A 15th-century moat house, interconnecting gardens, a brick-paved maze, and a costume display are of interest. There are also rare-breed farm animals here. Two gate houses are constructed in 16th-century style. The hall hosts regular re-creations of Tudor domestic life, including the well-known annual events for the weeks June 16 to July 7 when admission prices tend to escalate slightly.

Kentwell Hall (☎ **01787/310207**) is on A134 between Sudbury and Bury St. Edmunds; the entrance is north of the green in Long Melford on the west side of A134, about half a mile north of Melford Hall. It's open only March 15 to June 14 and October, Sunday only from noon to 5pm; July 10 to September 18, daily from noon to 5pm. Admission is £4.90 ($7.85) for adults, £4.20 ($6.70) for seniors, and £2.90 ($4.65) for children.

## WHERE TO STAY

**The Black Lion Hotel.** The Green, Long Melford, Suffolk CO10 9DN. ☎ **01787/312356.** Fax 01787/374557. 9 rms; 1 suite. TV TEL. £50–£60 ($80–$96) single; £70–£80 ($112–$128) double; £95 ($152) suite. All rates include continental or English breakfast. AE, MC, V.

Since the 1100s some kind of inn has stood on this spot. Fourteenth-century documents mention it as the spot where drinks were dispensed to revolutionaries during one of the Peasants' Revolts. The present building dates from the early 1800s, and it has been richly restored by its present owners. It overlooks one of the loveliest village greens in Suffolk. Each of the individually decorated bedrooms contains tea- and coffee-making facilities. An added bonus is the hotel's well-patronized Countrymen Restaurant (see "Where to Eat," below).

## WHERE TO EAT

✪ **Bull Hotel.** Hall St. ☎ **01787/378494.** Reservations recommended. Fixed-price 3-course meal £15 ($24) at lunch; £19.95 ($31.90) at dinner. AE, DC, MC, V. Daily noon–2:30pm and 7–9:30pm. ENGLISH/CONTINENTAL.

If you're passing through, try to visit one of the oldest (1540) inns of East Anglia. Built by a wool merchant, it's Long Melford's finest and best-preserved building. Incorporated into the general inn is a medieval weavers' gallery and an open hearth with Elizabethan brickwork. The dining room is the Bull's outstanding feature, with its high-beamed ceilings, trestle tables, settles, and handmade chairs, as well as a 10-foot fireplace. Menu items are likely to include sweet pickled herring with dill sauce, grilled rump steak with a whole-grain-mustard sauce, and such vegetarian dishes as baked avocado with a tomato-and-basil sauce. Some dishes fall short of the mark, but others have continental flair and flavoring.

✪ **The Countrymen Restaurant.** In the Black Lion Hotel, The Green. ☎ **01787/312356.** Reservations required. Fixed-price meals £14–£35 ($22.40–$56). AE, MC, V. Tues–Sun noon–2pm and 7–9:30pm. ENGLISH/CONTINENTAL.

The restaurant operates out of a fully restored 17th-century coaching inn overlooking one of Suffolk's loveliest village greens near Holy Trinity Church. At night the dining room is warmed by candlelight, and during the day there are views of a Victorian walled garden. Fixed-price meals are available at both lunch and dinner, with menus changing every 6 to 8 weeks. Dinner is expensive, but well worth the splurge. Prices include unlimited coffee. The kitchen is likely to turn out such dishes as a delicate poached fillet of sole, sirloin steak with piquant sauce, freshwater crayfish Newburg style, or deep-fried whitebait. Roast prime English beef is a Sunday feature. Flavor, taste, and imagination emerge from the kitchen here.

## 7 Lavenham

66 miles NE of London; 35 miles SE of Cambridge

Once a great wool center, Lavenham is the classic Suffolk village, beautifully preserved today. It features a number of half-timbered Tudor houses washed in the characteristic Suffolk pink. The town's wool-trading profits are apparent in its guildhall, on the triangular main "square." Inside are exhibits on Lavenham's textile industry, showing how yarn was spun, then "dyed in the wool" with woad (the plant used by the ancient Picts to dye themselves blue), and following on to the weaving process. There is also a display showing how half-timbered houses were constructed.

The Church of St. Peter and St. Paul, at the edge of Lavenham, has interesting carvings on the misericords and the chancel screen, as well as ornate tombs. This is one of the "wool churches" of the area, built by pious merchants in the perpendicular style with a landmark tower.

# ESSENTIALS

**GETTING THERE**   Trains depart London's North Street Station at least once an hour, sometimes more often, for Colchester, where they connect quickly to the town of Sudbury. For schedules and information, call ☎ **0345/484950.** From Sudbury, Beeston's Coaches, Ltd., has about nine daily buses making the short run to Lavenham. The trip from London takes between 2 and $2^1/2$ hours.

National Express buses depart from London's Victoria Coach Station, carrying passengers to the town of Bury St. Edmunds, some 9 miles from Lavenham. For schedules and information, call ☎ **0990/808080.** From Bury St. Edmunds, you can take another bus onto Lavenham. The trip takes about $2^1/2$ hours.

If you're driving from Bury St. Edmunds, continue south on A134 toward Long Melford, but cut southeast to Lavenham at the junction with A1141.

**VISITOR INFORMATION**   The **Tourist Information Centre** is on Lady Street (☎ **01787/248207**). Open April through October, daily from 10am to 4:45pm.

## SHOPPING & TEATIME

Shoppers from all over East Anglia flock to **Timbers,** 13 High St. (☎ **01787/ 247218**), which is a center housing 24 dealers—everything from antiques to various collectibles, including books, toys, military artifacts, glass, porcelain, and much more. It's open every day except Wednesday.

After strolling the medieval streets of Lavenham, stop by **Tickle Manor Tea Rooms,** High Street (☎ **01787/248438**). This two-story timber-frame home was built by the son of a priest in 1530 and provides an ample dose of history for patrons to absorb while sipping any one of a selection of teas that are served with English breakfast, sandwiches, or a piece of cake.

## WHERE TO STAY

✪ **The Angel.** Market Place, Lavenham, Suffolk, CO10 9QZ. ☎ **01787/247388.** Fax 01787/ 248344. 8 rms. TV TEL. Sun–Thurs £37.50 ($60) single; £50 ($80) double; £60 ($96) family rm. Fri–Sat £47.50 ($76) single; £60 ($96) double; £70 ($112) family rm. All rates include English breakfast. AE, MC, V. Bus: no. 17 or 27.

The best B&B in town is this inn, first licensed in 1420, standing right in the center of Lavenham overlooking the marketplace and the guildhall. Family-run, it's a good restaurant, a popular pub for the locals, and a comfortable place to spend the night. All bedrooms are well maintained, with direct-dial phone, color TV, and beverage-making equipment. A cot is available on request, and extra amenities include hair dryers, shoe-cleaning, ironing, and laundry facilities. The bar contains a double inglenook Tudor fireplace and a rare Tudor shuttered shop-window front. Home-cookery is a feature of the restaurant, with a daily-changing menu. You might begin with a chicken-liver pâté, perhaps king prawns in garlic butter, then follow with steak-and-ale pie, pheasant with walnuts and cranberries, or lamb chops marinated in rosemary and garlic. Dinners cost £12 ($19.20) and up.

A few other places offer bed-and-breakfast in and around Lavenham, usually renting a room or two in the summer months. The Angel is the best and most substantial B&B.

## WHERE TO EAT

**The Bell Inn.** The Street, Kersey, near Ipswich, Suffolk IP7 6DY. ☎ and fax **01473/823229.** Reservations recommended. Restaurant/bar menu main courses £4.95–£10.95 ($7.90–$17.50). AE, DC, MC, V. Daily 11am–2pm and 6:30–11pm. ENGLISH.

Off the A1141/B1115 road from Lavenham to Hadleigh, and 15 minutes from the main A12 trunk road, the Bell Inn lies in what has been called "the most photographed village in the world," with a "watersplash" right in the middle of the main street (that means a river running across a road). The inn, dating from the 13th century, has a blazing fireplace and ceiling beams. The Bell offers good snacks in a timbered bar with glinting horse brasses. In the Pink Room, the main restaurant, lunches and dinners include the finest lamb, duck, sole, and fish dishes, even some vegetarian specialties, typically standard English "soul food."

## 7  Woodbridge & Aldeburgh

Woodbridge: 81 miles NE of London; 47 miles S of Norwich
Aldeburgh: 97 miles NE of London; 41 miles SE of Norwich

On the Deben River, the market town of Woodbridge is a yachting center. Its best-known, most famous resident was Edward FitzGerald, Victorian poet and translator of the "Rubaiyat of Omar Khayyam." FitzGerald died in 1883 and was buried some 4 miles away at Boulge. Woodbridge is a good base for exploring the East Suffolk coastline, particularly the small resort of Aldeburgh, noted for its moot hall.

On the North Sea 15 miles from Woodbridge, Aldeburgh is a favorite resort of discriminating travelers, and it attracts many Dutch, who make the sea crossing via Harwich and Felixstowe, both major entry ports for traffic from the continent. Aldeburgh dates from Roman times, and has long been known as a small port for North Sea fisheries. The Aldeburgh Festival, held every June, is the most important arts festival in East Anglia, and one of the best attended in England.

## ESSENTIALS

**GETTING THERE**   Woodbridge is on the rail line to Lowestoft from either Victoria Station or Liverpool Street Station in London. Get off two stops after Ipswich. For schedules and information, call ☎ **0345/484950.** The nearest rail station to Aldeburgh is on the same line, at Saxmundham, six stops after Ipswich. From Saxmundham, you can take a taxi or one of six buses that run the 6 miles to Aldeburgh during the day.

One National Express bus a day passes through Aldeburgh and Woodbridge on the way from London's Victoria Coach Station to Great Yarmouth. It stops at every country town and narrow lane along the way, so the trip to Aldeburgh takes a lamentable 4¼ hours. For schedules and information, call ☎ **0990/808080.** Many visitors reach both towns by Eastern County Bus Company's service from Ipswich. That company's no. 80/81 buses run frequently between Woodbridge and Aldeburgh.

If driving from London's ring road, take A12 northeast to Ipswich, then continue northeast on A12 to Woodbridge. To get to Aldeburgh, stay on A12 until you reach the junction with A1094, then head east to the North Sea.

**VISITOR INFORMATION**   The **Tourist Information Centre** is at the Cinema, 51 High St., Aldeburgh (☎ **01728/453637**). Open Easter through October, Monday to Friday from 9am to 4:30pm and on Saturday and Sunday from 10am to 4:30pm.

## ✪ THE ALDEBURGH FESTIVAL

Aldeburgh was the home of Benjamin Britten (1913–76), renowned composer of the operas *Peter Grimes* and *Billy Budd*, as well as many orchestral works. Many of his compositions were first performed at the Aldeburgh Festival, which he founded in 1946. The festival takes place in June, featuring internationally known performers. There are other concerts and events throughout the year. Write or call the tourist office for details. The Snape Maltings Concert Hall nearby is one of the more successful among the smaller British concert halls; it also houses the Britten-Pears School of Advanced Musical Studies, established in 1973.

## OUTDOOR ACTIVITIES & SIGHTS IN ALDEBURGH

There are two golf courses, one at Aldeburgh and another at Thorpeness, 2 miles away. A yacht club is situated on the River Alde 9 miles from the river's mouth. There are also two bird sanctuaries nearby, Minsmere and Havergate Island. Managed by the Royal Society for the Protection of Birds, they are famous for their waterfowl.

Seek out **Crag Path,** running along Aldeburgh's wild shore. It is unusually attractive, with its houses of different dates and architectural styles. The two lookout towers were built early in the 19th century so that watch could be kept for vessels putting down or needing pilots.

Constructed on a shelf of land at the sea level, High (or main) Street runs parallel to the often-turbulent waterfront. A cliff face rises some 55 feet above the main street. A major attraction is the 16th-century **Moot Hall Museum,** Market Cross Place, Aldeburgh (☎ **01728/453295**). The hall dates from the time of Henry VIII, but its tall twin chimneys are later additions. The timber-frame structure displays old maps, prints, and Anglo-Saxon burial urns, as well as other items of historical interest. It is open July and August, daily from 10:30am to 12:30pm and 2:30 to 5pm. It also is open Easter to June, Saturday and Sunday from 2:30 to 5pm, and June to September, daily from 2:30 to 5pm. Admission is 50p (80¢) for adults and free for children.

Aldeburgh is also the site of the nation's northernmost martello tower, erected to protect the coast from a feared invasion by Napoléon.

## WHERE TO STAY
### NEAR WOODBRIDGE

**The King's Head Inn.** Front St., Orford, near Woodbridge, Suffolk IP12 2LW. ☎ **01394/ 450271.** 3 rms. TV. £45 ($72) single or double. All rates include English breakfast. MC, V. Take B1084 for about 10 miles east of Woodbridge, following the signs to Orford.

At this ancient town, known for the ruins of its 12th-century castle, you can stay at the King's Head, a 13th-century inn reported to have a smuggling history, lying in the shadow of St. Bartholomew's Church. The bedrooms, all doubles, are comfortably furnished and well maintained. A wealth of old beams and a candlelit dining room add to the ambience of the inn, which is owned and run by Tracey and Will Hughes. Tasty meals are served, using fresh fish from the sea and locally caught game. Lunchtime bar snacks are available. If you'd like to visit just to eat, hours are noon to 2pm and 6 to 9pm daily, and main courses cost £6 to £12 ($9.60 to $19.20), the latter for locally caught lobster. A boat trip on the River Ore on *The Lady Florence,* suitable for up to 12 passengers, costs £9 ($14.40) per person for 4 hours.

### IN ALDEBURGH

**Uplands Hotel.** Victoria Rd., Aldeburgh, Suffolk IP15 5DX. ☎ **01728/452420.** Fax 01728/ 454872. 20 rms, 17 with bath; 7 chalets. TV TEL. £35 ($56) single without bath, £45 ($72) single with bath; £65 ($104) double with bath. All rates include English breakfast. AE, DC, MC, V.

Opposite the parish church on the main road into Aldeburgh, this privately owned and family-run hotel was once the residence of Elizabeth Garrett Anderson, the first woman doctor in England. Set in award-winning gardens lovingly cultivated by the owners, Uplands offers a welcoming atmosphere and comfortable accommodations. All rooms are for two people, equipped with tea- or coffee-making equipment. The restaurant with its sculpted Italian ceiling overlooks the garden. The menu features standard English cooking, using fresh local produce complemented by a fine wine selection with dinner costing £14.50 ($23.20).

# WHERE TO EAT
## IN WOODBRIDGE

**Captain's Table.** 3 Quay St. ☎ **01394/383145.** Reservations recommended. Main courses £7–£12 ($11.20–$19.20); fixed-price lunch or dinner £12.95 ($20.70); bar snacks £2.50–£7 ($4–$11.20). AE, DC, MC, V. Tues–Sat noon–2pm and 6:30–9:30pm. SEAFOOD.

This is a good choice for intimate dining near the railway station. No one knows the exact age of the building, but it's estimated to be some 600 years old. Its outside is sheathed in a layer of plaster or stucco, and the interior is filled with old timbers and nautical accessories. The food is well prepared and the atmosphere near the wharf is colorful. The licensed restaurant serves a number of specialties, including Dover sole, and scallops cooked in butter with bacon and garlic. Vegetables are extra, and the desserts are rich and good tasting. The day's specials are written on a chalkboard, and might include oysters, sea salmon, and turbot in lobster sauce.

**The Spice Bar.** 17 Thoro'fare. ☎ **01394/382557.** Reservations recommended. Main courses £4.50–£7.50 ($7.20–$12). AE, MC, V. Mon–Sat noon–2pm and 7–10pm. Closed 1 week in Jan. CONTINENTAL/MALAYSIAN/MEDITERRANEAN.

Built as an alehouse in the 1640s, this popular dining spot in the village center offers reasonably priced food and drink. The home-cooked meals are based on seasonal produce. Many guests come just for a glass of wine (25 labels plus 3 house wines available by the glass) or a draft beer or spirits, and many dishes have flair and flavor. Main courses include strips of beef with chiles and Chinese greens or King Prawn Sanbal. The desserts are sumptuous, including the favorite crème brûlée.

## IN ALDEBURGH

**Aldeburgh Fish and Chip Shop.** 226 High St. ☎ **01728/452250.** Reservations accepted only for parties of 11 or more. Main courses £2.20–£3 ($3.50–$4.80). No credit cards. Daily 11:45am–1:45pm and 5–9pm. Closed Sun–Mon early Oct to May. FISH-AND-CHIPS.

Despite its humble appearance and lack of indoor seating, this is one of the region's most famous fish-and-chips emporiums. Set on the town's main street, it sells only one version of either plaice or cod. The product is wrapped in paper, doused (according to Victorian tradition) in malt vinegar, and usually consumed by enthusiasts on the open-air seawall outside. The greasy-but-flaky products have been enjoyed here since around 1900 by clients who have included composer Benjamin Britten and his longtime companion, Peter Pears, who used to bring visitors from London or America for walks along the oceanfront followed by fish with chips.

**Ye Old Cross Keys.** Crabbe St. ☎ **01728/452637.** Main courses £4–£12 ($6.40–$19.20). No credit cards. Daily noon–2pm and 7–9pm. (Pub: Mon–Sat 11am–3pm and 6–11pm; Sun noon–3pm and 7–10:30pm.) ENGLISH/SEAFOOD.

A few paces from the sea in the town center, this genuine 16th-century pub has the atmosphere of a Suffolk local. In the summer, drinkers take their mugs of real English ale or lager out and sit on the seawall and watch the pounding waves, always within the sight lines of the many flowering baskets that hang from the building's eaves. The pub is favored by local artists, who during the cooler months sit beside an old brick fireplace and eat smoked salmon, seafood platters, seafood pie, and lasagna. Place your food order at the special counter and someone will call your number when it's ready. Don't expect too much in the way of cuisine here.

## 8 Norwich

109 miles NE of London; 20 miles W of the North Sea

The county town of Norfolk, Norwich still clings to its claim as the capital of East Anglia. Despite its partial industrialization, it's a charming and historic city. In addition to the cathedral, it has more than 30 medieval parish churches built of flint. It's also the most important shopping center in East Anglia and has a lot to offer in the way of entertainment and interesting hotels, many of them in its narrow streets and alleyways. There also is a big open-air market, busy every weekday, where fruit, flowers, vegetables, and other goods are sold from stalls with colored canvas roofs.

## ESSENTIALS

**GETTING THERE**    There is hourly train service from London's Liverpool Street Station. The trip takes nearly 2 hours. For schedules and information, call ☎ **0345/484950.**

National Express buses depart London's Victoria Coach Station once each hour for the 3-hour ride. For schedules and information, call ☎ **0990/808080.**

If you're driving from London's ring road, head north toward Cambridge on the M11. Turn northeast at the junction with A11, which will take you all the way to Norwich.

**GETTING AROUND**    To see Norwich and the surrounding countryside, try a bicycle. **East Anglia Cycles,** 72–A Gloucester St. (☎ **01603/632467**), has the best selection. Bicycles are rented by the day or the week. Hours are Monday to Saturday from 9am to 6pm, and rates are £5 ($8) per day. There is a 20% discount for rentals over 7 days as well as a discount for card-carrying students.

## VISITING THE CATHEDRAL & CASTLE

**Norwich Cathedral.** 62 The Close. ☎ **01603/764385.** Admission to cathedral free; suggested donation £2 ($3.20) per person. Oct–May daily 7:30am–6pm; June–Sept daily 7:30am–7pm.

Dating from 1096 and principally of Norman design, the cathedral is noted primarily for its long nave with lofty columns. Built in the late perpendicular style, the spire rises 315 feet; together with the keep of the castle, it forms a significant landmark on the Norwich skyline. More than 300 bosses (knoblike ornamental projections) on the ceiling depict biblical scenes. The impressive choir stalls with handsome misericords date from the 15th century. Edith "Patriotism is not enough" Cavell, an English nurse executed by the Germans during World War I, is buried on the cathedral's Life's Green. The quadrangular cloisters, which date back to the 13th century, are the largest monastic cloisters in England. A short walk from the cathedral will take you to Tombland, one of the most interesting old squares in Norwich.

**Norwich Castle (Norfolk Museums Service).** Castle Meadow. ☎ **01603/223624.** Admission Oct–June £2.30 ($3.70) adults, £1 ($1.60) children; July–Sept £3.10 ($4.95) adults, £1.40 ($2.25) children. Museum: Apr–Sept daily 10am–5pm; Oct–Mar Sun 2–5pm.

Formerly the county jail, the castle sits in the center of Norwich on a partly artificial mound. Its huge 12th-century Norman keep and the later prison buildings are used as a civic museum and headquarters of the countywide Norfolk Museums Service. There are guided tours of the battlements and dungeons throughout the day.

The museum's art exhibits include an impressive collection of paintings by artists of the Norwich School, the most distinguished of whom were John Crome (b. 1768) and John Sell Cotman (b. 1782). The castle museum also has the best collection of

## Impressions

*Yes, there it spreads from north to south, with its venerable houses, its numerous gardens, its thrice twelve churches, its mighty mound, which, if tradition speaks true, was raised by human hands to serve as the grave heap of an old heathen king, who sits deep within it, with his sword in his hand and his gold and silver treasures about him. There is an old grey castle on top of that mighty mound; and yonder, rising three hundred feet above the soil, from among those noble forest trees, behold that old norman master-work, that cloud-encircled cathedral spire around which a garrulous army of rooks and choughs continually wheel their flight. Now, who can wonder that the children of that fine old city are proud of her, and offer up prayers for her prosperity.*
—George Borrow (1816)

British ceramic teapots in the world and unrivaled collections of Lowestoft porcelain and Norwich silver. Rare prehistoric gold jewelry and other archaeological finds help to illustrate Norfolk's wealth and importance and the life of its people. A set of dioramas shows Norfolk wildlife in its natural setting. You can also visit a geology gallery. The cafeteria is open Monday to Saturday from 10am to 4:30pm, Sunday from 2 to 4:30pm.

## NORWICH'S OTHER SIGHTS

**Sainsbury Centre for Visual Arts.** University of East Anglia, Earlham Rd. ☎ **01603/ 456060.** Admission £2 ($3.20) adults; £1 ($1.60) children and students. Tues–Sun 11am–5pm. Bus: no. 3, 4, 12, 27, or 76 from Castle Meadow.

The center was the gift in 1973 of Sir Robert and Lady Sainsbury, who contributed their private collection to the University of East Anglia, 3 miles west of Norwich on Earlham Road. Together with their son David, they gave an endowment to provide a building to house the collection. Designed by Foster Associates, the center was opened in 1978 and has since won many national and international awards. Features of the structure are its flexibility, allowing solid and glass areas to be interchanged, and the superb quality of light, which permits optimum viewing of works of art. Special exhibitions are often presented in the 1991 Crescent Wing extension. The Sainsbury Collection is one of the foremost in the country, including modern, ancient, classical, and ethnographic art. Its most prominent works are those by Francis Bacon, Alberto Giacometti, and Henry Moore. There's a regular program of special exhibitions.

**The Mustard Shop Museum.** 3 Bridewell Alley. ☎ **01603/627889.** Free admission. Mon– Sat 9:30am–5pm. Closed bank holidays.

The Victorian-style Mustard Shop is, yes, a museum dedicated to that storied condiment. It displays a wealth of mahogany and shining brass. The standard of service and pace of life reflect the personality and courtesy of a bygone age. The Mustard Museum features exhibits on the history of the Colman Company and the making of mustard, its properties and origins. There are old advertisements, as well as packages and "tins." You can browse in the shop, selecting whichever mustards you prefer, including the really hot, English-type. The shop also sells aprons, tea towels, pottery mustard pots, and mugs.

**Second Air Division Memorial Library.** 71 Ber St. ☎ **01603/215206.** Free admission. Mon–Fri 10am–5pm; Sat 9am–5pm.

A memorial room honoring the Second Air Division of the Eighth United States Army Air Force is part of the central library. The library staff will assist veterans who wish to visit their old air bases in East Anglia. At the library, one can find pertinent books, audiovisual materials, and records of the various bomber groups.

## A NEARBY JACOBEAN HOUSE

**Blickling Hall.** Blickling, near Aylsham. ☎ **01263/733084.** House and gardens: Tue–Sat £5.60 ($8.95) adults, £2.80 ($4.50) children; Sun and bank holiday Mon £6.60 ($10.55) adults, £3.30 ($5.30) children. Gardens only: Tue–Sat £3.20 ($5.10) adults, £1.60 ($2.55) children; Sun and bank holiday Mon £3.50 ($5.60) adults, £1.75 ($2.80) children. Apr–Oct Thurs–Sun and bank holiday Mon, plus additional days July–Sept 1pm–4:30pm. (Garden, Shop, Restaurant and Plant Centre, open as Hall plus additional days, 10:30am–5:30pm). Blickling Hall lies 14 miles north of the city of Norwich, 1½ miles west of Aylsham on B1354; take A140 toward Cromer and follow the signs. Telephone before visiting to confirm opening arrangements.

Massive yew hedges bordering a long drive frame your first view of Blickling Hall, a great Jacobean house built in the early 17th century, one of the finest examples of such architecture in the country. The long gallery has an elaborate 17th-century ceiling, and the Peter the Great Room, decorated later, has a fine tapestry on the wall. The house is set in ornamental parkland with a formal garden and an orangery. Meals and snacks are available.

# WROXHAM: A BASE FOR EXPLORING THE BROADS

Wroxham, 7 miles northeast of Norwich, is the best center for exploring the Broads—mostly shallow lagoons connected by streams. These are fun to explore by boat, of course, but some folks perfer to ride their bikes along the Broads.

To get to Wroxham from Norwich, take bus no. 51. The 30-minute ride costs £1.80 ($2.90) for a return ticket. Information about touring the Broads is provided by the **Hoveton Tourist Office,** Station Road (☎ 01603/782281), open Easter through October, daily from 9am to 1pm and 2 to 5pm. At this office you can get a list of boat rentals.

If you don't want to handle your own boat, you can take an organized tour. The best ones are offered by **Broads Tours,** near the Wroxham bridge (☎ 01603/782207). Their cruises last 1¼ to 3½ hours. In summer, most departures are either at 11:30am or 2:30pm. The cost ranges from £4.40 to £6.75 ($7.05 to $10.80) for adults and £3.40 to £5 ($5.45 to $8) for children.

# SHOPPING

For the best in antiques, books, crafts, and pleasant scenery, shoppers can search out the historic lanes and alleys in the center of Norwich. **Norwich Antiques Centre,** 14 Tombland (☎ **01603/619129**), is a three-floor house opposite the cathedral where 60 plus dealers set up shop. The selection is wide and varied and includes everything from small collectibles to antique furniture. There's also a small coffee shop in the house. Right next to the Antiques Centre, **James and Ann Tillett,** 12–13 Tombland (☎ **01603/624914**), have a marvelous shop specializing in antique silver, barometers, and new as well as antique jewelry.

**St. Michael-at-Plea,** Bank Plain (☎ **01603/618989**), calls a 13th-century church home. The church's stained-glass windows were stolen by Henry VIII. Here, 30 dealers sell toys, books, linens, ceramics, furniture, among other things. Browsers can get snacks, sandwiches, and coffee at the small on-site restaurant.

For book fanciers, **Peter Crowe,** 75 Upper St. Giles St. (☎ **01603/624800**), specializes in 17th- and 18th-century scholarly books, well-bound and illustrated 19th-century books, general secondhand books, and modern first editions.

If you count yourself among the growing number of doll enthusiasts around the world, don't miss **Elm Hill Craft Shop,** 2 Elm Hill (☎ **01603/621076**), with their

## The Royal Residence of Sandringham

Some 110 miles northeast of London, 7,000-acre Sandringham has been the country home of four generations of British monarchs, ever since Queen Victoria's son, the Prince of Wales (later King Edward VII), purchased it in 1861. He and his Danish wife, Princess Alexandra, rebuilt the house, which in time became a popular meeting place for British society. The red-brick and stone Victorian-Tudor mansion consists of more than 200 rooms, some of which are open to the public, including two drawing rooms, the ballroom, and a dining room. The atmosphere of a well-loved family home is a contrast to the formal splendor of Buckingham Palace. Guests can also view a loft salon with a minstrel's gallery used as a sitting room by the royal family and full of photographs and mementos.

A **Land Train** designed and built on the estate makes it easy for visitors to reach Sandringham House, which sits at the heart of 60 acres of beautiful grounds. The train's covered carriages have room for wheelchairs.

**Sandringham Museum** holds a wealth of rare items relating to the history of the royal family's time here, and displays tell the story of the monarchs who have owned the estate since 1862. Visitors can see the big game trophies in settings that include a safari trail.

Sandringham is some 50 miles west of Norwich and 8 miles northeast of King's Lynn (off A149). King's Lynn is the end of the main train route from London's Liverpool Street Station that goes via Cambridge and Ely. Trains from London arrive at King's Lynn every 2 hours, a trip of 2¹/₂ hours. From Cambridge, the train ride takes only 1 hour. Buses from both Cambridge and Norwich run to King's Lynn, where you can catch bus no. 411 to take you the rest of the way to Sandringham.

The grounds and museum of Sandringham (☎ **01553/772675**) are open Easter to October 2, daily from 11am to 4:45pm (closed July 21 to August 16). Admission to the house, grounds, and museum is £4.50 ($7.20) for adults, £3.50 ($5.60) for seniors, and £2.50 ($4) for children. Admission to the grounds and museum is £3 ($4.80) for adults, £2.50 ($4) for seniors, and £2 ($3.20) for children.

custom-made dollhouses and furnishings. They also carry traditional children's toys, books, and children's jewelry.

## WHERE TO STAY

Norwich is better equipped than most East Anglian cities to handle guests who arrive without reservations. The **Norwich City Tourist Information Centre** maintains an office at the Guildhall, Gaol Hill, opposite the market (☎ **01603/666071**). Each year a new listing of accommodations is drawn up, including both licensed and unlicensed hotels, B&B houses, and even living arrangements on the outskirts.

### CAMPING, YOUTH HOSTELS & MORE

From camping to youth hostels to student housing, Norwich has the cheapest accommodations in all of East Anglia.

Right in the center of town, the **YMCA,** 48 St. Giles St., Norwich, Norfolk NR2 1LT (☎ **01603/620269**), has 90 beds in a number of standard rooms that are clean and separated by gender. The YMCA is open all year, and there is no curfew or self-catering. This Y has laundry facilities, a TV lounge, and a games room. Rates are £12.50 ($20) B&B single and £8.50 ($13.60) for a bed in a dorm room. Key deposits are £5 ($8) for a room and £1 ($1.60) for the dorm.

Although primarily a special needs homeless hostel, rooms are available occasionally at the **YWCA,** 61 Bethel St., Norwich, Norfolk NR1 2NR (☎ **01603/625982**). This Y is open only to women, the rooms are sparse and clean, and a communal kitchen is available. Call ahead for availability. Rates are £11.43 ($18.30) per person. Key deposit is £10 ($16).

A 20-minute walk from the town center, **YHA Youth Hostel,** 112 Turner Rd., Norwich, Norfolk NR2 4HB (☎ **01603/627647**), has 66 different-size bunk rooms with 2 to 6 beds in each. YHA accepts both men and women, and there is an 11pm curfew. They are open daily from February to October; closed Sunday November and January, and in the month of December. July and August are their busiest months, so call ahead for availability. Kitchen facilities are available or meals can be bought: £2.85 ($4.55) breakfast, £2.45 ($3.90) packed lunch, £4.25 ($6.80) dinner. Rates are £8.50 ($13.60) for adults and £5.70 ($9.10) for children under 18.

One of the most economical ways to spend some time in Norwich is to pitch a tent at **Lakenham Camp Site,** Martineau Lane, located 1 mile from the center of town (☎ **01603/620060**). Facilities include clean toilets and showers. Gates close at 11pm so if you're in a car, get here before then. But if you're traveling by foot, you can still get in after 11pm. Call ahead for availability of sites, which are open April through September. Rates July through August are £3.85 ($6.15) for adults and £1.40 ($2.25) for children; September through June, £3.50 ($5.60) for adults and £1.40 ($2.25) for children. Nonmembers pay a £3.50 ($5.60) pitch fee.

Reduced-rate campus housing rooms for bona fide, card-carrying university students are available through **Student Housing,** University of East Anglia, Accommodations & Conference Office, Norwich, Norfolk NR4 7TJ (☎ **01603/593277**). Nonstudents are still welcome, but they pay more. The small rooms are fairly typical of student housing—bed, wardrobe, desk, and chair. There is a laundry service available. Book rooms ahead through the Conference Office. Student rates during summer vacation (end of June through mid-September) are £7.25 ($11.60) single without bath and £9.25 ($14.80) single with bath. Student rates mid-September to end of June are £14.60 ($23.35) single without bath but with breakfast and £22.60 ($36.15) single with bath and breakfast. Nonstudent rates year-round are £21.50 ($34.40) single without bath but with breakfast and £29.50 ($47.20) single with bath and breakfast.

## DOUBLES FOR LESS THAN £55

**Crofters Hotel.** 2 Earlham Rd., Norwich, Norfolk NR2 3DA. ☎ **01603/613287.** 12 rms. TV. £39–£54.50 ($62.40–$87.20) single with bath; £54.50–£64.50 ($87.20–$103.20) double. All rates include English breakfast. MC, V.

Built in 1840 of yellow brick that long ago turned gray, this structure was originally intended as a gentleman's private residence. Located next door to St. John's Cathedral, it is today the personal domain of Jonathan and Dawn Cumby, who maintain a separate TV lounge for their guests, and serve (if notified in advance) three-course evening meals for £9.50 ($15.20) per person. The bedrooms are a little dowdy and worn, but adequate. Families are welcome, and on weekends an evening salad buffet is provided free. During the summer cream teas are served on the terrace.

**Marlborough House Hotel.** 22 Stracey Rd., Norwich, Norfolk NR1 1EZ. ☎ and fax **01603/ 628005.** 11 rms, 6 with bath. TV. £16–£18 ($25.60–$28.80) single without bath, £26 ($41.60) single with bath; £36 ($57.60) double with bath; £50 ($80) family rm with bath. All rates include English breakfast. No credit cards.

This centrally heated hotel offers pristine and simple bedrooms with hot-beverage facilities. Evening meals with home-style cooking, costing £6.50 ($10.40) and up, are served daily from 5:30 to 7pm. There's a comfortable TV lounge and a licensed bar. The hotel has a small parking area on its grounds, and there is adequate off-street parking as well. It's centrally situated close to the railway station, Riverside Walk, the cathedral, and the central library.

**Wedgewood Guest House.** 42–44 St. Stephens Rd., Norwich, Norfolk NR1 3RE. ☎ **01603/ 625730.** Fax 01603/615035. 13 rms, 10 with bath. TV. £22 ($35.20) single without bath; £36 ($57.60) double without bath, £42 ($67.20) double with bath. All rates include English breakfast. AE, MC, V.

A large, rambling, Edwardian-era house originally built in 1902, this pleasant guest house is painted white with Wedgwood-blue trim. Popular with repeat visitors because of its convenient parking and its location near the city's hospital, and located within a 5-minute walk south of the city center, the house is clean, cozy, and run with a lighthearted sense of irreverent fun. The much-traveled owners, Charles and Terry Pugh (who lived, among other places, in Zambia, Saudi Arabia, and aboard the Cunard Line's *QE2*), provide keys to the front door so guests can come and go as they wish.

## WHERE TO EAT

**Brasted's.** 8–10 St. Andrews Hill. ☎ **01603/625949.** Reservations required. Main courses £12–£19.50 ($19.20–$31.20). MC, V. Mon–Fri noon–2pm and 7–10pm; Sat 7–10pm. ENGLISH/ FRENCH.

Within an easy stroll of both the cathedral and the castle, Brasted's is set in a lovely home in the oldest part of Norwich. After exploring the two major sights of Norwich, you can come here to sample the savory cooking of John Brasted, for whom the restaurant is named. The owner and chef de cuisine, Mr. Brasted knows how to combine the best of yesterday with modern cooking techniques and innovations. As you enjoy the rather flamboyant interior, you can peruse the a la carte menu. You'll probably settle for one of the fresh fish dishes of East Anglia. Other dishes, including roast Norfolk pheasant, vegetarian plates, and desserts are equally well prepared.

✪ **Briton Arms Coffee House.** Elm Hill. ☎ **01603/623367.** Main courses £3.30–£4.15 ($5.30–$6.65). No credit cards. Mon–Sat 9:30am–5pm (lunch 12:15–2:30pm). CONTINENTAL.

In the heart of the old city near the train station, the Briton Arms overlooks the most beautiful cobblestone street in Norwich. Tracing its history back to the days of Edward III, it's now one of the least expensive eating places in town. It's certainly one of the most intimate and informal, with old beamed ceilings and Tudor benches. The coffeehouse has several rooms, including one in back with an inglenook. The procedure here is to go to the little counter, where you purchase your lunch and bring it to the table of your choice. Everything we've tried was homemade and well prepared. Try lamb casserole and white wine and juniper berries or seafood gratin. Every day a different kind of soup is offered. It's a good place to stop after you tour the cathedral, only a block away.

**Pinocchio's.** 11 St. Benedict St. ☎ **01603/613318.** Reservations recommended. Main courses £6–£10 ($9.60–$16). MC, V. Mon–Wed 6:30–11pm; Sun 6:30–11pm. ITALIAN/ MEDITERRANEAN.

This restaurant brings a touch of the Mediterranean to the Norwich dining landscape. The cookery is competent and often filled with flavor, though an occasional dish could stand more Italian flavor and flair. The menu changes every 4 to 6 weeks and always features at least six pasta and six vegetarian dishes. The menu may include smoked goose salad, tagliatelle carbonara, eggplant stuffed with chestnut-and-spinach risotto, or haunch of venison with a red wine sauce. Italian wines are featured here, with wine tastings held every 6 weeks. If you're looking to splurge a little, the wine tasting costs £25 ($40) and includes a five-course dinner, a glass of wine with each course, and a talk conducted by a member of the company that produces the featured wines. On Monday and Thursday evenings you can enjoy live jazz that's showcased here around 8pm.

## NORWICH AFTER DARK

From fine arts to pop arts, there's quite a bit of entertainment happening in Norwich at night. Information on almost all of it can be found at **The Ticket Shop,** Guildhall (☎ **01603/764764**), a clearinghouse of local entertainment calendars and costs, where you can also pick up tickets to just about any event.

**Theatre Royal,** Theatre Street (box office ☎ **01603/630000**), hosts touring companies performing drama, opera, ballet, and modern dance. The Royal Shakespeare Company and London's Royal National troupe are among the regular visitors. Ticket prices run £10 to £25 ($16 to $40), with senior and student discounts usually available for Wednesday, Thursday, and Saturday matinees. The box office is open Monday through Saturday from 9:30am until 8pm on performance days, and closes at 6pm on nonperformance days.

Hosting productions of classic drama on most evenings, the **Norwich Playhouse,** Gun Wharf, 42–58 St. George's St. (☎ **01603/766466**), offers tickets ranging from £3.50 to £12.50 ($5.60 to $20). The box office is open daily from 10am until 8pm.

An Elizabethan-style theater, the **Maddermarket Theatre,** 1 St. John's Alley (☎ **01603/620917**), is home to the amateur Norwich Players' productions of classical and contemporary drama. Tickets, ranging from £3.50 to £7.50 ($5.60 to $12), and schedules are available at the box office, Monday through Saturday from 10am to 5pm. On nonperforming Saturdays, it closes at 1pm.

The city's **Theatre in the Parks** (☎ **01603/212137**) includes about 40 outdoor performances each summer in various venues. Located in a converted medieval church, **Norwich Puppet Theatre,** St. James, Whitefriars (☎ **01603/629921**), offers original puppet shows most afternoons and some mornings in an octagonal studio that holds about 50 people. Tickets are £5 ($8) for adults, and £3.75 ($6) for children, available at the box office, Monday through Saturday from 9:30am to 5pm.

Before or after your cultural event, check out the local culture at **Adam and Eve,** 17 Bishopgate (☎ **01603/667423**), the oldest pub in Norwich, founded in 1249, which serves a well-kept John Smith's or Old Peculiar. A traditional bare-wood pub, the **Finnesko & Firkin,** 10 Dereham Rd. (☎ **01603/666821**), serves five real ales brewed on the premises, and **The Gardener's Arms,** 2–4 Timberhill (☎ **01603/621447**), pours Boddington's and London Pride to a lively crowd of locals and students. A good place to wait for the next film, **Take 5,** St. Andrew's St. (☎ **01603/763099**), a cafe-bar located next door to Cinema City, is hangout to the local arts crowd.

After the pubs close, you can wander down to the river and check out the **Waterfront,** 138–141 King St. (☎ **01603/632717**), which hosts live bands during the week and DJs playing the latest dance mixes on weekends. The cover charge varies from £2 to £4 ($3.20 to $6.40). Switching from a daytime pub to a nightclub, **Boswell's,** 24 Tombland (☎ **01603/626099**), offers live music earlier in the evening and disco after midnight. The cover charge after 9pm varies from £1 to £3 ($1.60 to $4.80).

# 16 The East Midlands

The East Midlands is a mix of dreary industrial sections and incredible natural scenery, particularly in the Peak District National Park, centered in Derbyshire. Byron asserted that the landscapes in the Peak District rivaled those of Switzerland and Greece. In the East Midlands you'll also find the tulip land of Lincolnshire, the 18th-century spa of Buxton in Derbyshire, and the remains of Robin Hood's Sherwood Forest in Nottinghamshire. George Washington looked to Sulgrave Manor in Northamptonshire as his ancestral home. If you have Pilgrims in your past, you can trace your roots to the East Midlands.

Except for Sulgrave Manor and Althorp House, where Princess Di spent her girlhood and is now buried, Northamptonshire is not on the tourist circuit. If you do decide to stop here, the best center for food and lodging is Northampton, the capital.

In Leicestershire, you can use the industrialized county town of Leicester as a base to explore many notable sights in the countryside, including Belvoir Castle, setting for Spielberg's *Young Sherlock Holmes,* and Bosworth Battlefield, site of England's most important battle after the 1066 Battle at Hastings and the 1940 Battle of Britain.

Derbyshire is noted primarily for the Peak District National Park, but it also has a number of historic homes—notably Chatsworth, the home of the 11th duke of Devonshire. The best centers here are Buxton, Bakewell, and Ashbourne.

In Nottinghamshire, the city of Nottingham is a good center for exploring what's left of Sherwood Forest, the legendary stamping grounds of Robin Hood.

The goal of the pilgrim to Lincolnshire is the cathedral city of Lincoln itself, with stopovers at the old seaport of Boston, which lent its name to the famous American city.

## 1 Northamptonshire

In the heart of the Midlands, Northamptonshire has been inhabited since Paleolithic times. Traces have been found here of Beaker and other Bronze Age people, and remains of a number of Iron Age hill-forts can still be seen. Two Roman roads—now Watling and Ermine streets—ran through the county, and relics of Roman settlements have been discovered at Towcester, Whilton, Irchester, and Castor.

West Saxons and Anglicans invaded in the 7th century. In 655, the first abbey was established at Medehamstede, now Peterborough.

# NORTHAMPTON

69 miles NW of London; 41 miles NE of Oxford

Fortified after 1066 by Simon de Senlis (St. Liz), the administrative and political center of Northamptonshire was a favorite meeting place of Norman and Plantagenet kings. The barons trying to force policy changes that finally resulted in the Magna Carta besieged King John here. During the War of the Roses, Henry VI (before he achieved that title) was defeated and taken prisoner, and during the Civil War, Northampton stuck with Parliament and Cromwell.

From reports of the time, Northampton before 1675 was a fascinating town architecturally, but a fire destroyed the medieval city. Defoe once called it "the handsomest and best town in this part of England." That is no longer true. Nothing of the castle (ca. 1100) where Thomas à Becket stood trial in 1164 is left standing. The town you see today was created essentially after the railway came in the mid-19th century. If ancient architecture is your interest, Lincoln is more interesting.

## ESSENTIALS

**GETTING THERE**   Trains depart from London's Euston Station every hour and 5 minutes throughout the day for the 1-hour trip to Northampton. For information in Northampton and the rest of the Midlands, call the BritRail Travel Information Line (☎ **0345/484950**).

Between three and five motorcoaches depart every day from London's Victoria Coach Station, requiring about 2 hours for the ride to Northampton, with many sometimes annoying stops in between. For schedules and information, call ☎ **0990/ 808080.**

If you're driving from London, follow the M1 due north to junction 15, then follow the signs into Northampton. Depending on traffic, the trek takes about an hour.

**VISITOR INFORMATION**   The **Northampton Visitor Centre** is at Mr. Grant's House, 10 St. Giles Sq. (☎ **01604/22677**). Open Monday to Friday from 9:30am to 5pm, Saturday from 9:30am to 4pm, Sunday from early June to late August from noon to 3pm.

## SEEING THE SIGHTS

The **Church of the Holy Sepulchre,** on Sheep Street, is one of five Norman round churches in England. It was founded by Simon de Senlis, famous veteran of the First Crusade. You can see its circular ambulatory and round nave. Victorian Gothic architecture swept Northampton after the coming of the railway, and the style is best exemplified by the **Guildhall,** on St. Giles Square. It was built by Edward Godwin in the 1860s, an architect then only in his 20s.

**Central Museum & Art Gallery.** Guildhall Rd. ☎ **01604/39415.** Free admission. Mon–Sat 10am–5pm.

One of Britain's most unusual provincial museums and Northampton's key attraction, this establishment was enlarged in the early 1990s with four new galleries. It celebrates Northampton's rich cultural and industrial traditions. Proud of the city's status as the boot- and shoe-making capital of Britain, it devotes much of its gallery space to exhibitions of the largest collection of antique shoes in the world, spanning centuries of footwear, with emphasis on the Victorian era. Also on display are artworks from Italy spanning the 15th to the 18th centuries, a wide spectrum from the history of British art, and objects uncovered from nearby archaeological sites dating back to the Stone Age. Some gallery space is devoted to temporary exhibitions, showcasing, for the most part, displays that are of interest to Northampton and its region.

## WHERE TO STAY

**Hollington.** 22 Abington Grove, Northampton, Northhamptonshire NN1 4QW. ☎ **01604/ 32584.** 7 rooms, none with bath. TV. £16–£18 ($25.60–$28.80) single; £30–£35 ($48–$56) double; £39–£50 ($62.40–$80) family of 3 or 4. All rates include English breakfast. MC, V. Closed for 2 weeks during Christmas.

Sometimes you can walk into a house and feel and smell and sense a rich history that leads you back in time. That is the feeling guests stumble upon when first entering Hollington. This "very English," red-brick Victorian guest house sits across the street from a landscaped park. The rooms are all rather small, fitted simply with wardrobes, tea- and coffee-making facilities, as well as art that includes landscapes and tapestries. Dark mahogany woodwork abounds throughout and melds into a nicely carved fireplace in the dining room, where guests are served a filling breakfast around individual tables.

**The Poplars Hotel.** Cross St., Moulton, Northampton, Northhamptonshire NN3 1RZ. ☎ **01604/643983.** Fax 01604/790233. 18 rooms. TV TEL. £30–£39.50 ($48–$63.20) single; £42–£47.50 ($67.20–$76) double. £6 ($9.60) older children. All rates include English breakfast. AE, MC, V. Closed Christmas week.

This renovated 17th-century farmhouse has been transformed into a charming hotel in this small country village just 4 miles from the center of Northampton. Plenty of personal attention is lavished upon guests from the moment they check in. The farmhouse feels 17th century, with its oak beams and dark wood panels. The average-size guest rooms have been outfitted in period country-style furnishings and fit the ambience established for the house in the public areas. Two lounges and a dining room complete the public rooms. Guests can have a set-price dinner Monday through Thursday for £12 ($19.20). No smoking areas include 10 bedrooms, the dining room, and one lounge.

**Quinton Green.** Quinton, Northamptonshire NN7 2EG. ☎ **01604/863685.** Fax 01604/ 862230. 3 rooms. TV. £22 ($35.20) per person, single or double. All rates include English breakfast. No credit cards. Closed Dec 25.

On a gentle slope overlooking 1,200 acres of beautiful green pastures and wheat fields, this 17th-century farmhouse, constructed of heavy slabs of local stone, welcomes guests with a certain warmth and charm that can be attributed in large part to the house's owners, the Turneys, whose family has lived here since 1919. The upstairs bedrooms are large with oak and pine furnishings that include wardrobes and comfy armchairs. All the rooms have views of rolling countryside—the kind that make you want to fling the windows open, lean out, and drink in the fresh air and brilliant sunshine. The country-style ground floor, with its wood and brick fireplaces, has a sitting room, billiards room, and dining room, where guests sit around a huge oak table for breakfast. Just beyond the front door, the Turneys have created a romantic walled garden.

## WHERE TO EAT

**Buddies.** The Old Mission School, Dye Church Lane. ☎ **01604/20300.** Lunch fixed-price £3.99 ($6.40); main courses £8–£12 ($12.80–$19.20). AE, MC, V. Mon–Thurs noon–10:30pm; Fri–Sat noon–11pm; Sun noon–9pm. AMERICAN.

If you're craving good American food and atmosphere, Buddies is for you. Americans will feel right at home here where walls are plastered with Stateside memorabilia

# The East Midlands

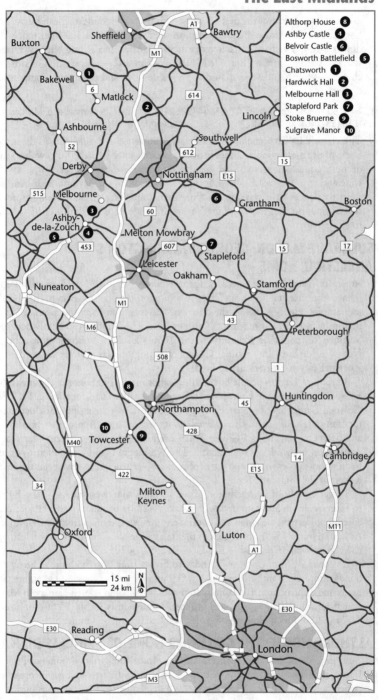

Althorp House 8
Ashby Castle 4
Belvoir Castle 6
Bosworth Battlefield 5
Chatsworth 1
Hardwick Hall 2
Melbourne Hall 3
Stapleford Park 7
Stoke Bruerne 9
Sulgrave Manor 10

donated by clients over the past 15 years. This lively and loud American bistro/cafe, housed in a 200-year-old church mission school, has a huge 400-item lunch and dinner menu. The fixed-price lunches include nachos, salads, and burgers. Dinner selections range from a dish called "New York meats"—a hearty duo of ribs and chicken—to fish and vegetarian dishes. A side salad and potatoes accompany all dinners.

**Luigi's.** 50 Wellingborough Rd. ☎ **01604/28621.** Reservations recommended. Main courses £5–£10 ($8–$16). AE, DC, MC, V. Mon–Sat 7–midnight. ITALIAN.

This classical Italian restaurant overflows with ambience, as candlelight sets the mood. Some of the more popular dishes include a cooked-to-order steak Luigi with a sauce of mushrooms, onions, red wine, cilantro, and cream; or baked chicken with a white wine and cream sauce. All dishes include a vegetable of the day or a salad. And the must-try dessert has always been a more-than-ample slice of the heavenly espresso-soaked tiramisu. Bottles from Luigi's wine list range from £7.95 to £13.95 ($12.70 to $22.30)

# SULGRAVE MANOR: GEORGE WASHINGTON'S ANCESTRAL HOME

American visitors will be especially interested in this small mid–16th-century Tudor manor, the ancestral home of George Washington. As part of a plan to dissolve the monasteries, Henry VIII sold the priory-owned manor in 1539 to Lawrence Washington, who had been mayor of Northampton. The Washington family occupied Sulgrave for more than a century, but in 1656, Col. John Washington left for the New World. Born in Virginia, George Washington was a direct descendant of Lawrence (seven generations removed).

A group of English people bought the manor in 1914 in honor of the friendship between Britain and the United States. Beginning with a large donation in 1927, the Colonial Dames have been largely responsible for raising the money for a major restoration to return it as much as possible to its original state. Appropriate furnishings and portraits—including a Gilbert Stuart original of the first president—have been donated on both sides of the Atlantic. The Washington family coat of arms on the main doorway—two bars and a trio of mullets—is believed to have been the inspiration for the "Stars and Stripes."

To get here from Northampton, drive 18 miles southwest on A43, then B4525 to Sulgrave. From Stratford-upon-Avon, take A422 via Banbury (whose famous cross entered nursery rhyme fame) and continue to Brackley; 6 miles from Brackley, leave A422 and join B4525, which goes to the tiny village of Sulgrave. Signs will lead you to Sulgrave Manor, on Manor Road (☎ **01295/760205**).

It is open April to October, Monday to Friday from 2 to 5:30pm, Saturday and Sunday from 10:30am to 1pm and 2 to 5:30pm; November through December, Saturday and Sunday from 10:30am to 1pm and 2 to 4:30pm (closed January to March except for schools and prebooked groups). Admission is £3.50 ($5.60) for adults, £1.75 ($2.80) for children ages 5 to 16, and free for children under 5.

## ALTHORP HOUSE: THE GIRLHOOD HOME OF PRINCESS DIANA

Built in 1508 by Sir John Spencer, Althorp House, the girlhood home of Princess Diana, receives a sometimes unwelcome dose of fame. Interest in it has increased exponentially since Diana's tragic demise. On September 6, 1997, she was buried on a small island in the middle of a lake on the grand estate. At press time, Diana's family was considering the possibility of opening the estate twice a year for visitors to pay their respects to the Princess. Her family decided not to bury Diana in the small church cemetery nearby—the final resting place of several generations of Spencers—to preclude pilgrimages that would overwhelm the tiny hamlet of Harlestone.

Althorp house was brought back to life and a degree of glamour by Raine Spencer, Diana's sometimes undeservedly maligned stepmother. Since the death of Lord Spencer, Diana's father, the estate has been under the jurisdiction of Charles Spencer, Diana's younger brother, who emigrated to South Africa partly because of the glare from the British monarchy's fall from grace. Charles Spencer's recent efforts to sell some of Althorp House's art and antiques have been hindered by the legal actions of Raine Spencer. The collection includes paintings by Van Dyck, Reynolds, Gainsborough, and Rubens, as well as an assortment of rare French and English furniture, and porcelain by Sèvres, Bow, and Chelsea.

Althorp House (☎ **01604/770107**) is 6 miles northwest of Northampton on A428, in Althorp, near Harlestone. It's only open in July and August daily, except July 12 and 13, from 2 to 5pm, but it's best to call before you visit. Admission is £6 ($9.60) for adults, £3 ($4.80) for children under 14.

## 2 Leicester

107 miles NW of London; 43 miles NE of Birmingham; 24 miles NE of Coventry; 26 miles S of Nottingham

Hang onto your hats, because this county town is definitely no Sleepy Hollow. Leicester, one of the 10 largest cities in England, overflows with hustle and bustle and is by far the most cosmopolitan city in the East Midlands. Britain's first environmental city is a busy industrial center—a city of firsts that has thrived on its spirit of discovery and adventure. Beethoven's music was first performed here; the BBC's first local radio station was BBC Radio Leicester; and the first and only footwear and contour design degree program in Britain is offered through De Montfort University. Leicester is also the birthplace of genetic fingerprinting and home to the Sir Norman Chester Centre for Football Research—charged with discovering the causes of football hooliganism. Although it has some historic attractions, Leicester makes a better base for exploring the surrounding history-rich countryside. Its real attraction to locals and tourists alike is its shopping, art scene, and night life.

Historically speaking, Leicester was called *Ratae Coritanorum* during Roman times, and it was the capital of Lear's kingdom. The town was also the seat of the East Mercian bishops in the 8th century. William I once constructed a castle here, which was inhabited by Simon de Montfort, the earl of Leicester, and by John of Gaunt. In 1360, Chaucer became a husband in St. Mary de Castro Church, and merchants amassed huge sums of wealth from hosiery production during the Middle Ages.

## ESSENTIALS

**GETTING THERE**   Trains depart from London's St. Pancras Station every 30 minutes throughout the day for Leicester, a trip of about 90 minutes. The fare costs £26 ($41.60) each way Saturday to Thursday and £32 ($51.20) on Friday. For schedules and information, call ☎ **0345/484950.**

About 10 buses a day leave London's Victoria Coach Station for Leicester. They call at several secondary stops en route, thus taking 2³/₄ hours each way. The round-trip fare is £15.75 ($25.20) Saturday to Thursday and £19 ($30.40) on Friday. For schedules and information, call ☎ **0990/808080.**

If driving from London, follow the M1 north to junction 21 toward Leicester. The drive takes 2 hours.

**VISITOR INFORMATION**   The main **tourist information office** is at 7–9 Every St., Town Hall Square (☎ **0116/265-0555**). Open Monday to Wednesday and Friday from 9am to 5:30pm, Thursday from 10am to 5:30pm, and Saturday from 9am to 5pm.

## SEEING THE SIGHTS

Although it's primarily a base for exploring one of the most history-rich parts of the Midlands, Leicester is worth a look if you have an afternoon to spare. In addition to the sights mentioned below, the town has a boating lake, riverside walks, and ornamental gardens. The tourist office will give you a map pinpointing the sightseeing highlights that can be covered on foot.

**Jewry Wall and Archaeology Museum.** St. Nicholas Circle. ☎ **0116/247-3021.** Free admission. Mon–Sat 10am–5:30pm; Sun 2–5:30pm.

Set near the excavation of an ancient Roman bath, this museum has nothing at all to do with Jewish history. Its name derives from a corruption of the Norman French "Jurad," which referred to the governing magistrates of an early medieval town, who used to gather in the shadow of this wall for their municipal decisions. More than 40 feet high, the wall is higher than Hadrian's Wall, the Baths at Cirencester, or any other piece of ancient Roman architecture in Britain. Exhibits within the museum include a pair of ancient Roman mosaics, the Peacock Pavement and the Blackfriars Mosaic, which are the finest of their kind in the British Midlands. Each was laboriously sliced from the masonry of ancient villas within the district and set into new masonry beds here. The site is about a quarter-mile from the town center, adjacent to the Holiday Inn.

**Leicester Abbey.** Abbey Park, S. Margaret's Way. ☎ **0116/251-0641.** Free admission. Daily dawn to dusk.

Set within a verdant public park that's favored by joggers and picnickers about three-quarters of a mile north of Leicester's historic core, these evocative, poetically shattered remains were built in 1132 to house what became the richest Augustinian monastery in England. In 1530, Cardinal Wolsey came here to die, demoralized and broken after his political and religious conflicts with Henry VIII. The abbey was torn down during the Reformation and stones were used in the construction of Cavendish House next door. Charles I and his officers based here before the 1645 Battle of Naseby.

**Leicester Guildhall.** Guildhall Lane. ☎ **0116/253-2569.** Free admission. Mon–Sat 10am–5:30pm; Sun 2–5:30pm.

Built in stages between the 14th and 16th centuries, Leicester's most prominent public building was Leicester's first town hall and contains one of the oldest libraries in Britain. Plaques commemorate its role as a die-hard last bastion of the Parliamentarians during the Civil War. On its ground floor, you'll see a 19th-century police station with a pair of original prison cells, whose mournful effigies afford a powerful testimony to the horrors of the Victorian penal system. Shakespeare's troupe is said to have appeared here.

**Leicestershire Museum and Art Gallery.** 96 New Walk. ☎ **0116/255-4100.** Free admission but donations accepted. Mon–Sat 10am–5:30pm; Sun 2–5:30pm.

This multipurpose museum has two distinctly separate features. The street level contains exhibits of archaeology and natural history. Star exhibits include a dinosaur bone found in a field near Leicester, a collection of Egyptian mummies and artifacts brought back to the Midlands by Thomas Cook, the 19th-century travel mogul, and exhibits relating to geology. One floor above street level is a collection of paintings by British and European artists (including some by Gainsborough) between the 18th and 20th centuries. The collection of early–20th-century canvasses by German expressionists is one of the largest in Europe.

**St. Martin's Cathedral.** 1 St. Martin's East. ☎ **0116/262-2594.** Free admission. Daily 7:30am–5pm.

Despite the fact that it lacks the soaring grandeur of the cathedrals of York or Lincoln, this is the most venerated and historic church in Leicester. In 1086, it was one of the region's parish churches, and enlarged during the 1300s and the 1500s. In 1927, it was designated as the cathedral of Leicester, a nomenclature that adds considerably to its pomp and circumstance. The oak vaulting beneath the building's north porch is one of the most unusual treatments of its kind in England.

## SHOPPING

This university town dazzles with freshly constructed shopping venues like the Victorian-style **Shires Shopping Centre** with its designer and collectible stores, wide walkways, fountains, and sunny skylights. And **St. Martins Square,** in the city center, has taken on a new life with restored buildings that are home to retailers, cafes, and tea shops. The lively pedestrian-only avenues of **Church Gate, Gallowtree Gate,** and **Market Street** with their beautifully landscaped green areas play host to an energetic atmosphere of shopping and street entertainment.

Venture out from the center of town to Belgrave Road and you'll discover the **"Golden Mile."** This neighborhood is home to the largest sari shop outside of India, and the store windows along Belgrave Road overflow with fine Indian silks, organzas, and cottons. Sari shops also generally carry a variety of accessories including bags, jewelry, shoes, and shawls. **Alankar,** 95–101 Belgrave Rd. (☎ **0116/261-2594**), creates a traditional Indian atmosphere for shoppers with Moghul-style decor and provides free refreshments. **Benzer,** 153 Belgrave Rd. (☎ **0116/261-1411**), carries Tussar silk saris, salwar kameez (trouser suits) in cotton and silks, and men's traditional wedding outfits.

## WHERE TO STAY

**Alexandra House.** 342 London Rd., Stoneygate, Leicestershire LE2 2PJ. ☎ **0116/270-3056.** Fax 0116/270-5464. 5 rooms. TV. £30 ($48) single; £40 ($64) double. All rates include English breakfast. MC, V.

Built in 1876, this brilliantly preserved Victorian house stands in a quiet suburb about 2 miles from Leicester's center. Walking in from the street, guests are greeted with a large lounge with paneled walls, a decorated fireplace, and an assortment of bric-a-brac. The bedrooms range in size from average to large and have period wardrobes, desks, and beds, plus coffee- and tea-making facilities. A full English breakfast is served to guests in the smoke-free dining room.

**Red Cow Hotel.** Hinckley Rd., Leicester Forest East, Leicester, Leicestershire LE3 3PG. ☎ **0116/238-7878.** Fax 0116/238-6539. 31 rms. TV TEL. Mon–Thurs £39.50 ($63.20) single or double; Fri–Sun £28.50 ($45.60) single or double. AE, DC, MC, V.

Accommodations at this inn are in a two-story, red-brick annex, built in the early 1990s as an enlargement of one of the region's most famous pubs (See "Where to Eat," below). The decor is functional and simple. Opt at least for a drink or a barside platter at the Red Cow—it's as authentic and cozy as a corner you're likely to find within the neighborhood. And it's got a great name to boot.

**Scotia Hotel.** 10 Westcotes Dr., Leicester, Leicestershire LE3 0QR. ☎ **0116/254-9200.** 16 rooms, 4 with bath. TV. £21 ($33.60) single without bath, £27 ($43.20) single with bath; £38 ($60.80) double without bath, £44 ($70.40) double with bath. All rates include English breakfast. No credit cards.

This Victorian building has ecclesiastic roots. In its former life, it belonged to the Church of England and was used to house clerics and others who were in town on church business. Today, the hotel retains much of the building's original character and architectural features including cupboards and fireplaces. The rooms are of average size and have been redecorated, complete with free-standing wardrobes, so as to maintain the Victorian flavor of the house. The restaurant, with its dark paneling and chandeliers, serves a three-course, fixed-price menu on Monday through Thursday. Smoking is not allowed in the restaurant in the morning.

**The Stanfre House Hotel.** 265 London Rd., Leicester, Leicestershire LE2 3BE. ☎ **0116/270-4294.** 11 rooms. TV. £20 ($32) single; £32 ($51.20) double. All rates include English breakfast. Closed Dec 24–Jan 3. No credit cards.

This formerly private home, built in 1892, has been turned into a rather nondescript little hotel with a scattering of modern reproduction furnishings throughout—a grandfather clock here, a coffee table there. Rooms are small to average in size and have been decorated in a charmingly run-of-the-mill style. Guests sit around eight tables in the dining room for breakfast; a choice of restaurants are nearby for lunch and dinner. There is no smoking allowed in the dining room.

**Stoneycroft Hotel.** 5–7 Elmfield Ave., Leicester, Leicestershire LE2 1RB. ☎ **0116/270-7605.** Fax 0116/2706067. 47 rooms, 27 with private bath. TV TEL. £27 ($43.20) single without bath, £29–£36 ($46.40–$57.60) single with bath; £39–£42 ($62.40–$67.20) double with bath. All rates include English breakfast. AE, MC, V.

This commercial-style, three-story hotel started off as two separate rooming establishments around the turn of the century and was later joined into the present-day structure. It's about a 15-minute walk from the center of town on a quiet residential street. The average-sized rooms are similarly decorated with built-in furnishings and include coffee- and tea-making facilities. Guests have access to a hotel lounge, a bar, and a games room. The restaurant, which does not allow smoking in its dining room, opens for dinner if there are enough guests.

## WHERE TO EAT

**Friends Tandoori Restaurant.** 41–43 Belgrave Rd. ☎ **0116/266-8809.** Main courses £5–£9 ($8–$14.40). AE, MC, V. Mon–Sat noon–2pm and 6–11:30pm; Sun 6:30pm–10:30pm. INDIAN.

This spacious, two-story restaurant specializes in the cuisine of northern India—Punjabi—and lies along the famous Belgrave Road where you can also shop for a sari. The upstairs is a bar and lounge where smoking is allowed. You can relax, have a drink, and place your order here. Downstairs is the nonsmoking dining room and another bar. An assortment of plants and Indian artwork sets the mood for your meal. Menu items can be seasoned to suit individual tastes and may include offerings of chicken and lamb tikka, vegetable dishes, and a selection of prestigious curries. A popular buffet featuring a wide range of vegetarian and meat starters along with main courses takes place Sunday evenings.

**Pierre Victoire.** 34 Belvoir St. ☎ **0116/291-9922.** Lunch £4.90 ($7.85); main courses £6–£9 ($9.60–$14.40); fixed-price meal £7.95 ($12.70) from 6–8pm. MC, V. Mon–Sat noon–3pm and 6–11pm. FRENCH.

This franchise restaurant, one of 105 around the country, is wildly popular and serves French-style dishes from a menu that changes daily. Emphasis is placed on fresh ingredients, and everything is homemade—not your average chain restaurant. Lunch is a table d'hôte, 3-course meal along the lines of coq au vin (chicken in white wine) or broccoli and blue cheese quiche with a salad, dessert, and cheese. Dinner selections are a la carte and include such dishes as rib-eye steak with lemon and watercress, salmon with ginger and spring onions, and a vegetarian combination of Provençale vegetables with basmati rice. A choice from the extensive list of wines, beers, and liquors complements meals perfectly.

**The Red Cow Pub and Restaurant.** Hinckley Rd., Leicester Forest East. ☎ **0116/238-7878.** Reservations recommended for restaurant. Bar platters £4.75–£6.95 ($7.60–$11.10). Main courses in restaurant £7.25–£11.95 ($11.60–$19.10). AE, DC, MC, V. Mon–Fri 11am–11pm; Sat 11am–3pm and 6–11pm; Sun noon–2:30pm and 6–11pm. ENGLISH/GAME.

Some 5 miles north of the center of Leicester, this historic inn prides itself on a 200-year-old tradition of providing food and drink to travelers, and for its status as the only pub in Leicestershire with a genuine thatched roof. Amid low ceilings, dark paneling, and antique accessories of brass and leather, you can order simple but wholesome platters in the bar (ploughman's lunches, fish and chips, shepherd's pie); or more substantial fare in the cozy restaurant. Here, menu items include different preparations of chicken, fish, beef, and vegetarian fare, as well as such exotica as kangaroo, wild boar, pheasant, and guinea fowl. Beers on tap include Carling, LaBatt's, and the Belgian staple lager Stella Artois.

**Rise of the Raj.** 6 Evington Rd. ☎ **0116/255-3885.** Main courses £4.75–£11 ($7.60–$17.60). AE, MC, V. Sat–Thurs noon–2pm and daily 6–11:30pm. INDIAN.

This restaurant occupies the first two floors of a three-story terrace house and serves northern Indian dishes. The menu is the same for lunch and dinner, with main courses of chicken, prawns, and lamb all prepared in traditional Punjabi style served with sauces that range in intensity from mild to hot. The most popular menu item is a thali. This is essentially a taste of just about everything served accompanied by basmati rice and nan (a thin, warm, unleavened bread, very similar to pita bread).

## LEICESTER AFTER DARK

The **Haymarket Theatre,** Belgrave Gate (☎ **0116/253-9797**), one of the nation's leading provincial theaters, has been the launching point for many successful West End productions, including *Me and My Girl,* and well-known faces from television and film often turn up in leading roles. Popular musicals like *West Side Story* are the house specialty, but don't be surprised to see anything from contemporary drama to visiting dance companies gracing the stage.

**Phoenix Arts Centre,** Newarke St. (☎ **0116/255-4854**), hosts dance, music, and theatrical productions from around the world, but local dancers, musicians, and actors also entertain from its stage, and there's even an occasional cinema screening.

In May and June, the **Leicester Early Music Festival** (☎ **0116/270-7820**), brings a series of concerts emphasizing harp, keyboard, brass, wind, and dance. Tickets for the whole series cost £20 to £25 ($32 to $40). In June, the **Leicester International Music Festival** (☎ **0116/251-7759**), attracts some of the biggest names in classical music. Each year there is a theme and an emphasis on string chamber music. Ticket prices vary, but average about £6 ($9.60).

On weekends, the area around the **Clock Tower** in the center of town is alive with bustling crowds headed out to the clubs and bars on Church Gate, Silver Street, and High Street. **Mosquito Coast,** 37 St. Nicholas Place (☎ **0116/251-7471**), and **Krystals,** 97 Church Gate (☎ **0116/262-5720**), offer varied entertainment acts from around the world to crowds that flock in from all over the Midlands. Call for information since on any given night the cover charge depends on the act.

## HISTORIC HOMES AROUND LEICESTER

If you've read Sir Walter Scott's *Ivanhoe,* you will remember Ashby-de-la-Zouch, 18 miles northwest of Leicester, a town that retains a pleasant country atmosphere. The main attraction here is the ruined Norman manor house, **Ashby Castle** (☎ **01530/ 413343**), where Mary Queen of Scots was imprisoned. The building was already an antique in 1464 when its thick walls were converted into a fortress. Open April through October, daily from 10am to 6pm. Off-season hours are Wednesday to Sunday from 10am to 4pm. Admission is £1.60 ($2.55) for adults, £1.20 ($1.90) for seniors, and 80p ($1.30) for children under 16.

On the northern border of Leicestershire overlooking the Vale of Belvoir (pronounced "Beaver"), **Belvoir Castle** has been the seat of the dukes of Rutland since the time of Henry VII. Rebuilt by Wyatt in 1816, the castle contains paintings by Holbein, Reynolds, and Gainsborough, as well as tapestries in its magnificent staterooms. Seven miles west-southwest of Grantham, between the A607 to Melton Mowbray and the A52 to Nottingham, the castle was the location of the movies *Little Lord Fauntleroy* and Steven Spielberg's *Young Sherlock Holmes.* In summer it's the site of medieval jousting tournaments. It's open from April through September Tuesday to Thursday and Saturday and Sunday from 11am to 5pm. Admission is £4.50 ($7.20) for adults, £3.50 ($5.60) for senior citizens and £3 ($4.80) for children under 16, and £13 ($20.80) for a family ticket (2 adults, 2 children). For more information, call the estate office at ☎ **01476/870262.**

## 3 Derbyshire & Peak District National Park

The most magnificent scenery in the Midlands is found in Derbyshire, between Nottinghamshire and Staffordshire. Some travelers avoid this part of the country because it's ringed by the industrial sprawl of Manchester, Leeds, Sheffield, and Derby. But missing this area is a pity, for Derbyshire has been less defaced by industry than its neighbors. The north of the county, containing the **Peak District National Park,** contains waterfalls, hills, moors, green valleys, and dales. In the south the land is more level, and the look becomes, in places, one of pastoral meadows. Dovedale, Chee Dale, and Millers Dale are worth a detour.

## ✪ EXPLORING PEAK DISTRICT NATIONAL PARK

Peak District National Park covers some 542 square miles, most of it in Derbyshire, with some spilling over into South Yorkshire and Staffordshire. It stretches from Holmfirth in the north to Ashbourne in the south, and from Sheffield in the east to Macclesfield in the west. The best central place to stay overnight is Buxton (see below).

The peak in the name is a bit misleading, since there is no actual "peak"—the highest point being 2,100 feet. What the park has instead is some 4,000 walking trails that riddle some of the most beautiful hill country in England. The southern portion of the park, called **White Peak,** is filled with limestone hills, tiny villages, old stone walls, and hidden valleys. August and September are the best and most beautiful time to hike these rolling hills. In the north, called **Dark Peak,** the scenery changes to rugged moors and deep groughs or gullies. This area is best visited in the spring when the purple heather, so beloved by Emily Brontë, comes into bloom.

Many come to the park not for its natural beauty but for the **"well dressings."** A unique park tradition, this festival with pagan origins is best viewed in the villages of Eyam, Youlgrave, Monyash, and Worksworth. Local tourist offices will supply details. The dressings began as pagan offerings to local "water spirits," but later became part of Christian ceremonies. Dressings of the wells take place from early May to August of every year. Designs are pricked on large boards covered in clay. The board is then decorated with grasses, lichens, bark, seeds, and flowers and placed by the spring or well and blessed.

If you're planning an extensive visit to the park, write for details to the **Peak Park Joint Planning Board,** National Park Office, Aldern House, Bakewell, Derbyshire DE45 1AE. A list of publications will be sent to you, and you can order according to your wishes.

## GETTING TO THE PARK

You can reach Buxton (see below) by rail from Manchester. It's also possible to travel by bus, the Transpeak, taking 3$^1$/$_2$ hours to go from Manchester to Nottingham, with stops at such major centers as Buxton, Bakewell, Matlock, and Matlock Bath. If you're planning to use public transportation, consider purchasing a Derbyshire Warfarer, sold at various rail and bus stations. For £6.95 ($11.10) for adults or £3.50 ($5.60) for children, you can ride all the bus and rail lines within the peak district for 1 day. If you're driving, the main route is A515 north from Birmingham with Buxton as the gateway. From Manchester, Route 6 heads southeast to Buxton.

## GETTING AROUND THE PARK

Many visitors prefer to walk from one village to another. If you're not so hearty, you can take local buses that connect various villages. Instead of the usual Sunday slow down in bus service, more buses run on that day than during weekdays because of the increased demand, especially in summer. Call ☎ **01298/23098** daily between the hours of 7am to 8pm for bus information.

Another popular way to explore the park is by bicycle. Park authorities operate six **Cycle Hire Centres,** renting bikes for £7.70 ($12.30) a day for adults, and £5.80 ($9.30) for children 15 and under, with a £20 ($32) deposit, helmet included. Centers are at Mapleton Lane in Ashbourne (☎ **01335/343156**); near the Fairholmes Information Centre at Derwent (☎ **01433/651261**); near New Mills on Station Rd. in the Sett Valley at Hayfield (☎ **01663/746222**); near Matlock on the High Peak Trail at Middleton Top (☎ **01629/823204**); at the junction of Tissington and High Peak Trails at Parsley Hay (☎ **01298/84493**); and between Ashbourne and Leek on the A523 near the southern tip of the Manifold Truck at Waterhouses (☎ **01538/308609**).

## AN INEXPENSIVE PLACE TO STAY: CAMPING BARNS

Hikers and bikers can't find cheaper accommodations than the region's 11 National Park–operated camping barns, which provide a rudimentary raised sleeping platform, water faucet, and toilet for £3 ($4.80) a night per person. Advance booking and payment is mandatory. Contact **Peak National Park Office,** Aldern House, Baslow Road, Bakewell, Derbyshire DE45 1AE (☎ **01629/816316**), to make reservations or obtain further information.

## BUXTON: A LOVELY BASE FOR THE PARK

172 miles NW of London; 38 miles NW of Derby; 25 miles SE of Manchester

One of the loveliest towns in Britain, Buxton in the 18th century rivaled the spa at Bath. Its waters were known to the Romans, whose settlement here was called *Aquae Arnemetiae.* The thermal waters were pretty much forgotten from Roman times until the reign of Queen Elizabeth I, when the baths were reactivated. Mary Queen of Scots was brought here to take the waters by her caretaker, the earl of Shrewsbury.

Buxton today is mostly the result of the 18th-century development carried out under the direction of the duke of Devonshire. Its 19th-century spa days have come and gone, but it's still the best center for exploring the peak district. The climate is amazingly mild, considering that at 1,000 feet altitude, Buxton is the second highest town in England.

The town hosts a well-known **opera festival** during a 2$^1$/$_2$ week period in July, followed by a 2$^1$/$_2$ week **Gilbert & Sullivan festival** that draws people from around the world. The tourist office will supply details.

## ESSENTIALS

**GETTING THERE**    Trains depart from Manchester at least every hour during the day. It's a 30-minute trip.

About a half-dozen buses also run between Manchester and Sheffield, stopping in Buxton en route, after a 40-minute ride.

**VISITOR INFORMATION**    The **Tourist Office** is at The Crescent (☎ 01298/25106). Open between March and October, daily from 9:30am to 5pm; off-season, daily from 10am to 4pm. It arranges a limited roster of 2-hour guided walking tours of the town between June and September on Monday at 10:30am. Although they're free, a gratuity to the guide is appreciated. More practical are the self-guided tours that meander through the historic streets of the town, beginning and ending at the tourist office. Most visitors require between 75 and 90 minutes for the circuit. The tourist office also sells pamphlets outlining the town's most remarkable sites for 30p (50¢) a copy.

## SEEING THE SIGHTS

Water from nine thermal wells is no longer available for spa treatment except in the hydrotherapy pool at the Devonshire Royal Hospital, behind The Crescent. It is also used in the swimming pool at the 23-acre **Pavilion Gardens.** You can purchase a drink of spa waters at the tourist information center or help yourself at the public fountain across the street. An exhibition hall in the gardens, which are open at all times and are free, is the venue for weekend-only events likely to include everything from craft fairs to antique dealers sales.

Another sight, **Poole's Cavern,** Buxton Country Park, Green Lane (☎ 01298/26978), is a cave that was inhabited by Stone Age people, who may have been the first to marvel at the natural vaulted roof bedecked with stalactites. Explorers can walk through the spacious galleries, viewing the incredible horizontal cave, which is electrically lighted. It is open April through October, daily from 10am to 5pm. Admission is £3.80 ($6.10) for adults, £2 ($3.20) for children 5 to 15, and free for kids 4 and under.

About 1$^1$/$_4$ miles south of Buxton's town center is one of the oddest pieces of public architecture in the Midlands, **Solomon's Temple,** whose circular design might remind you of a straight castellated Tower of Pisa as interpreted by the neo-Gothic designers of Victorian England. It was conceived as a folly in 1895, and donated to the city by a prominent building contractor, Solomon Mycock. It sits atop a tumulus (burial mound) from the Neolithic Age. Climb a small spiral staircase inside the temple for impressive views over Buxton and the surrounding countryside. It's open all the time, day and night, and admission is free.

## WHERE TO STAY

**Buxton Wheel House Hotel.** 19 College Rd., Buxton, Derbyshire SK17 9DZ. ☎ **01298/24869.** 9 rooms. TV. £26 ($41.60) single; £42–£45 ($67.20–$72) double. All rates include English breakfast. MC, V.

A Victorian house doesn't have to be drab and tattered around the edges. At least that's the case with this turn-of-the-century B&B, which recently underwent floor-to-ceiling renovations. This family-run establishment is in a quiet area and is a short 8-minute walk from the center of town. Upon entering the house, guests can't help but notice the big, bright sun lounge with its soft couches. Large, airy guest rooms have been outfitted with modern, comfortable furnishings that even include sofas and tables. And guests breakfast in the dining room that also has a small bar area. All but one of the guest rooms are for nonsmoking guests.

**Coningsby.** 6 Macclesfield Rd., Buxton, Derbyshire SK17 9AH. ☎ **01298/26735.** 3 rooms. TV. £37.50 ($60) single; £50–£70 ($80–$112) double. All rates include English breakfast. No credit cards. Closed Nov–Jan.

This charming stone Victorian B&B has been rated as one of the country's top 20 guest houses by Britain's *Which* magazine. It sits back from the road on about one-third of an acre with a storybook garden and tiny pond. The Harry's own and run Coningsby, and in their witty and humorous manner, invite guests "to have a go at weeding the garden whenever the mood strikes them." Not surprisingly, Linda Harry muses that most never take her up on the offer—rather they more often choose simply to sit in the garden and sip wine while watching the ornamental fish in the pond. All the guest rooms are very large, have marble fireplaces, double-pane windows, and are decorated in a B&B/Laura Ashley style. Guests have access to a cheerful sitting room and dining room, where breakfast is served and a set-price dinner is available with a little advance notice. Smoking is not allowed in the house. It's a 5-minute walk to town.

**The Grosvenor House Hotel.** 1 Broad Walk, Buxton, Derbyshire SK17 6JB. ☎ **01298/72439.** 8 rooms. TV. £45–£47.50 ($72–$76) single; £50–£70 ($80–$112) double. All rates include breakfast. No credit cards.

This rather grandiose Victorian house sits on a quiet street in town and is a stone's throw from the Pavilion Gardens and the Opera House. Built in the 1850s of stone with a gray slate roof, it has an elegant interior and atmosphere that is often described by guests as being "home away from home"—a place that is lovely but not too formal. The rooms range in size from small to very large and have period antique furniture. The largest rooms have more antiques and the best views of the gardens and the River Wye. Smoking is not allowed in the guest rooms. Public areas include an inviting lounge with a small bar, a dining room where guests can have breakfast and an optional 3-course dinner, as well as an adjacent coffee shop which is open from Easter to September. The coffee shop serves hotel guests and locals, and pre-opera dinners served at the hotel have become a tradition.

**Lakenham Guest House.** 11 Burlington Rd., Buxton, Derbyshire SK17 9AL. ☎ **01298/70069.** 7 rooms, 6 with bath. MINIBAR TV. £35 ($56) single without bath; £44 ($70.40) double without bath; £50 ($80) double with bath. All rates include English breakfast. No credit cards.

A 5-minute walk from the center of town will lead you to a quiet, residential area of large stately houses where you'll find this B&B situated. This fine Edwardian house lies in nearly an acre of lavish lawns and gardens that the guest rooms overlook. The rooms vary in size from small to large and are all appointed with Victorian antiques, as is the entire house. The public areas of the house include a large lounge and dining room with private tables where guests can take breakfast.

## WHERE TO EAT

**The George.** The Square. ☎ **01298/24711.** £2.50–£4.75 ($4–$7.60). No credit cards. Mon–Sat noon–3pm and 7–11pm; Sun noon–10:30pm. BRITISH.

In a town not known for its cuisine, this pub is a good bet. Lying in a building even older (no one knows just how old) than the Royal Crescent, it serves the least expensive food at Buxton. Bar snacks, well-filled sandwiches, and even a ploughman's lunch of cheese, bread, and pickle are available throughout the day, all at reasonable prices. The clients are a mixture of visitors to Buxton and locals.

**Hydro Café Tea Rooms.** 75 Spring Gardens. ☎ **01298/25106.** Main courses £4–£5 ($6.40–$8). No credit cards. Mon–Sat 9:30am–5pm; Sun 10:30am–4:30pm. BRITISH.

These tearooms have been serving visitors for years in an atmosphere typical of an English tearoom. Walls are decorated with pictures depicting the development of the town tied to the harnessing of water power. All the food is homemade and prepared fresh daily. Portions are generous and prices among the most reasonable in town. You can get a wide selection of well-stuffed sandwiches. Locals often come in and make an entire meal out of potatoes cooked in the skins, which are then covered with various toppings. You can also order a number of meat and poultry pies. They do a good chicken pot pie and also offer steak-and-kidney pie daily. In addition, a selection of freshly made salads, various pastas, and vegetarian dishes are featured daily.

# THE HISTORIC MARKET TOWN OF ASHBOURNE

146 miles NW of London; 48 miles SE of Manchester; 33 miles NW of Nottingham

Another center for exploring the Peak District, this historic market town has a 13th-century church, a 16th-century grammar school, ancient almshouses, a population that doesn't exceed 5,000, and no fewer than 13 pubs, more than virtually any town its size in the district.

## ESSENTIALS

**GETTING THERE**    There's no train service to Ashbourne, as the rail lines that used to run into the village have been reconfigured into a walking trail.

The bus connecting Manchester with Derby stops in Ashbourne en route. It runs five times a day, and takes about 1 1/4 hours.

From Nottingham, you can take the train to Derby, then transfer to the Trent bus no. 107. The bus takes about an hour and runs hourly from Monday to Saturday.

**VISITOR INFORMATION**    The town's **Information Centre** is at 13 Market Place (☎ **01335/343666**). Open early March to early October, Monday to Saturday from 9:30am to 5pm; in August also on Sundays from 9:30am to 5pm; off-season. Monday to Saturday from 10am to noon and from 1 to 4pm.

## WHERE TO STAY

✪ **Biggin Mill House.** Biggin-by-Hulland, Derbyshire DE6 3FN. ☎ **01335/370414.** 2 rooms with private bath. TV. £75 ($120) double. Rate includes English breakfast. AE, MC, V.

Built in 1757 as a farmhouse by a wealthy landowner, this stone country home is called a Derbyshire long house. Located 10 minutes by car from Ashbourne, the house lies in the middle of 3 acres complete with gardens and a babbling brook. The Bazeley's, who own and run this little B&B, are warm and friendly and make sure that everyone feels at ease in this very inviting place. One of their special touches is to fill all the rooms with fresh flowers. The guest rooms are lovingly described by the Bazeley's as "cottage size" and are furnished with solid wood antiques and, of course, fresh flowers every day. And the dining room turns into a relaxing social area each morning as guests wake up to a hearty breakfast.

**Greenman Royal Hotel.** St. John's St., Ashbourne, Derbyshire DE6 1GH. ☎ **01335/345783.** Fax 01335/346613. 18 rooms. TV TEL. £38 ($60.80) single; £50 ($80) double. All rates include English breakfast. AE, DC, MC, V.

Originally a 17th-century coaching inn, this establishment has new owners who have completely renovated the place and added nine new guest rooms. Given the building's age, guest rooms do vary in size from small to average, but are smartly decorated, and include free-standing furniture plus coffee- and tea-making facilities. Guests can enjoy two bars and a lounge. The larger oak-paneled bar with two fireplaces, the Boswell, serves breakfast. The hotel is ideally located in the very center of town, close to shops, cafes, and restaurants. And its unusual sign actually crosses over the road and has become somewhat of a local landmark—you can't miss it.

**Lichfield Bridge View.** Mayfield, Derbyshire DE6 2HN. ☎ **01335/344422.** 4 rooms, 2 with private bath. TV. £20 ($32) single without bath; £42 ($67.20) double with bath. £8.50 ($13.60) per child. All rates include English breakfast. No credit cards. Closed Dec 25–26.

Located about 1¹/₂ miles from Ashbourne, this gracious Georgian house with its sentinel-like chimneys sits on 3 acres of landscaped lawn and well-tended gardens overlooking the River Dove. Guest rooms have beautiful country views and are all very spacious with high ceilings and old pine furnishings. The theme of pinewood furnishings is carried from the bedrooms through to the timbered breakfast room with warm-toned pine tables and chairs. Smoking is not allowed in the house.

**✪ Llam Hall Youth Hostel.** Ashbourne, Derbyshire DE6 2AZ. ☎ **01335/350212.** Fax 01335/350350. 148 beds. £12.25–£14.05 ($19.60–$22.50) adults; £9.15–£10.50 ($14.65–$16.80) 18 and under. All rates include breakfast. MC, V.

A fine and stately old English mansion set in the middle of an estate of green lawns, gardens, and thick forest has been transformed into one of the country's most extraordinary hostels. Paths behind the house lead down to the river, and an old church and stables share the property. The interior with its dark wood, massive pieces of art, and wallpaper still has the look and feel of a private home, despite its conversion. The rooms range in size from two to nine beds, with most of the larger rooms located in the part of the house known as the Brewhouse Wing. Public areas include a classroom and a games room. A packed lunch costs £2.45 to £3.25 ($3.90 to $5.20), and evening meals are £4.25 ($6.80).

## WHERE TO EAT

**TEATIME**   For the best pot of tea around, try **The Old Post Office Tea Room,** Alstonefield, near Ashbourne (☎ **01335/310201**). Ernie and Jean Allen, owners and tea aficionados, offer a set tea menu which includes tea and all the proper food accoutrements like scones, sandwiches, and fruitcake. They also prepare an assortment of homemade goodies such as baked quiche, soup, and cold roasted meats—all perfect for a light lunch. A unique curiosity is their boiled egg tea.

**Ashbourne Gingerbread Shop.** St. John St. ☎ **01335/346753.** Snack meals £1.50–£5 ($2.40–$8). No credit cards. Winter Mon–Sat 8:30am–5pm; summer daily 8am–5:30pm. ENGLISH.

Before you walk into this delightful bakery, prepare yourself to be wafted by the sweet, spicy aroma of warm, freshly baked gingerbread. As Billy Crystal might say, it's marvelous! This nearly 200-year-old bakery can be found in a 400-year-old building that began as the Roebuck Inn. The Spencer-Pearson family took over the business in 1979, and maintain an active role. You can buy a snack meal or light lunch here—something like a burger or sandwich—but this place is famous around these parts for its gingerbread. They make all shapes and sizes of gingerbread, including gingerbread men, gingerbread boys, gingerbread animals, and gingerbread slab cakes.

**The Caverns Bistro.** St. Johns St. ☎ **01335/300305.** Lunch £2–£5 ($3.20–$8); main courses £6.50–£13.50 ($10.40–$21.60). AE, MC, V. Mon–Sat 11am-2:30pm and 7–9:30pm (10pm in summer). INTERNATIONAL.

You'll find this fun eatery in three basement rooms beneath the city's marketplace. If it sounds dreary to you (basement rooms), rest assured, it's not. Stone walls have been painted white and lots of red carpet sparks up the wee space. For lunch, you can choose from an array of different sandwiches and various light meals like lasagna or grilled trout. The dinner menu features regularly changing bistro specials including steak, fish, pastas, and vegetarian dishes.

**The Horns Inn.** Victoria Sq. ☎ **01335/300737.** Lunch £4–£6 ($6.40–$9.60); main courses £5.50–£8.50 ($8.80–$13.60). No credit cards. Mon–Sat 11am–11pm; Sun noon–10:30pm. Food served daily noon–2:30pm. Dinner available some days in summer. ENGLISH.

This bustling, cozy restaurant opens its doors in the warm summer weather and fills the sidewalk with tables and chairs to meet the demand from its constant flow of patrons. The food is simple but good at this mainly lunchtime gathering place. The menu offers a standard fare of soup, homemade pies like steak and kidney or chicken and mushroom, along with burgers, and a special or two that changes every couple of days.

**Smiths Tavern.** 36 St. John's St. ☎ **01335/342264.** Main courses £4.75–£12 ($7.60–$19.20). AE, MC, V. Mon–Sat 11am–11pm; Sun noon–10:30pm. Meals and snacks daily noon–2:30pm and 6–9:30pm. ENGLISH.

A series of three rooms in a tall, narrow stone building make up this "proper old-fashioned pub," as it is so proudly described by owners John and Elaine Bishop. Supported by its fair share of antique wood beams adorned with an assortment of pots and horse brasses, the pub's middle room, which gives way to the dining room, dates back to 1300. Guests sit on well-aged settles and time-worn chairs at plain, sturdy tables. Snacks and homemade hot dishes, yes, and desserts, make up the menu here. Main courses include such favorites as steak-and-kidney pie, fresh fish, steak, and sides of fresh vegetables. Children are welcomed in the dining room as long as they are with their parents.

# BAKEWELL
160 miles NW of London; 26 miles N of Derby; 37 miles SE of Manchester; 33 miles NW of Nottingham

Lying 12 miles southeast of Buxton, Bakewell is yet another center for exploring the southern Peak District, especially the beautiful valleys of Ashwood Dale, Monsal Dale, and Wyedale. On the River Wey, Bakewell is but a market town, but its old houses constructed from the gray-brown stone and its narrow streets give it a picture-postcard look. Its most spectacular feature is a medieval bridge across the river with five graceful arches.

Still served in local tearooms is the famous Bakewell Tart, which was supposedly created by accident. A local chef spilled a rich cake mixture over some jam tarts, and tearoom history was made. The best time to be here is market day—Mondays—when local farmers come in to sell their produce. Entrepreneurs from throughout the Midlands also set up flea market–style stands in the town's main square, The Market Place. Sales are conducted from 8:30am until 5:30pm in winter, and until 7:30pm in summer.

If you're here on a Tuesday, you can watch a livestock auction from the public car parks adjacent to the Market Place. The livestock are housed in aluminum-sided sheds and barns and hauled in and out on trucks and trailers, but the event is somewhat evocative of agrarian life in the Middle Ages, as large numbers of cattle and sheep are bartered and sold. This is not a particularly happy event, since most of the livestock are hauled off for slaughter.

Well dressing festivals (rituals with pagan roots, described in the above section on Peak District National Park) are held in June.

## ESSENTIALS

**GETTING THERE**   The best way to get to Bakewell by car is from either Derby or Manchester by taking the A6 and following the signs. To Bakewell from both Derby and Manchester, buses run daily about every 2 hours. Bakewell is about an hour from Derby and 1$^1$/$_2$ hours from Manchester.

**VISITOR INFORMATION   Bakewell Information Centre** is available at the Old Market Hall, Bridge Street, in Bakewell (☎ **01629/813227**). Open Easter through August, Monday through Friday from 9:30am to 5:30pm and on weekends and bank holidays 9:30am to 6pm; and November to Easter, Friday through Wednesday from 9:30am to 5pm and on Thursday 9am to 1pm.

## WHERE TO STAY

The **Castle Inn,** see below, also rents rooms.

**The Ashford Hotel & Restaurant.** Church St., Ashford-in-the-Water, Derbyshire DE45 1QI. ☎ **01629/812725.** Fax 01629/814749. 7 rooms. TV. £50 ($80) single; £85–£95 ($136–$152) double. All rates include English breakfast. AE, MC, V.

This stone-and-timber building dates from the 1780s and originally served as a coaching inn where coach horses, hot and exhausted from a full-day's ride, were changed out for fresh steeds. It is a very public place today with a pub and restaurant on the ground floor that is open to the general masses. The hotel's interior is graced with old beams and two huge stone fireplaces. Guest rooms, located upstairs, range in size from small to large and are furnished with modern to more distinctively aged pieces including several four-poster beds. The restaurant serves bar meals and snacks during the day and in the evening hosts candlelight British dinners ranging from £7.50 to £12 ($12 to $19.20).

**Barleycorn Croft.** Sheldon, Derbyshire DE45 1QS. ☎ **01629/813636.** 2 rooms, none with bath. £35 ($56) double. Rate includes English breakfast. No credit cards.

Housed in a converted stone barn that is attached to the main living residence, this is essentially an apartment with two bedrooms and a bath upstairs. The downstairs is a TV room and a dining room. Bedrooms are rather small but are furnished with loving care in old oak pieces, as is the rest of the apartment. If one couple books a bedroom, the other bedroom will stay empty, so, in essence, the shared bath could become a private bath. Guests receive a key and can come and go as they please. Breakfast is served in the dining room, and the village has a pub that serves evening meals. Guests tend to become regulars here. Bakewell is 3$^1$/$_2$ miles from this little B&B apartment.

**Holly House.** The Avenue, Bakewell, Derbyshire DE45 1EQ. ☎ **01629/813207.** 2 rooms, none with bath. TV. £36 ($57.60) double. Rate includes English breakfast. No credit cards.

This Victorian house, located in a quiet cul-de-sac about 5 minutes from the town center, offers two medium-size rooms outfitted in a comfortable yet nonetheless smart style. The up-to-date bath that serves these two no-smoking guest rooms is only across the hall, a few steps away. Public areas include a separate lounge/sitting room and a bright, cheerful dining room where guests take their hearty, home-cooked breakfast. A bounty of pubs and restaurants can be found a short walk from the house.

✪ **Milford House.** Mill St., Bakewell, Derbyshire DE45 1DA. ☎ **01629/812130.** 12 rooms. TV. £40 ($64) per person, single or double. Rate includes English breakfast. MC, V. Closed Nov 1–Easter.

Less than 300 yards north of Bakewell's main square, behind a facade that's defined by its friendly owners as Derbyshire gritstone, this Georgian-style house was built in 1872. It served for many years as the home of Robert Cross—the chief water engineer for the entrepreneur who invented the Spinning Jenny—who lived here with his wife and seven daughters. You'll get the sense that this is very much a working family home, thanks to the homey touches, carefully maintained patinas, and high-ceilinged bedrooms with personal knickknacks, tea-making facilities, and chintz curtains. Usually, no meals are served other than breakfast, but if you advise the owners in advance, they'll prepare you an evening meal for £17.50 ($28) per person, served within their family dining room. There's a garden in back.

## WHERE TO EAT

**TEATIME** For a look at a working 19th-century flour mill and a taste of baked goods made from its stone-ground flour, stop in at **Caudwell's Mill,** Bakewell Road (☎ **01629/733185**). Here you can take an afternoon tea, along with its many freshly baked cakes, breads, and pastries, and then stroll through a variety of shops at the mill, including a handcrafted-furniture store, a glass-blowing studio, a jewelry shop, and an art gallery.

**Carriage House Restaurant.** Chatsworth, near Bakewell. ☎ **01246/582204.** Lunch £3.75–£6 ($6–$9.60). No credit cards. Mid-Mar–Oct daily 11am–2:15pm. ENGLISH.

If you visit the Chatsworth House, you should eat at this restaurant. And if you eat at this restaurant, you should visit the Chatsworth House. Located at the top of a hill about 100 yards from the House, the restaurant is actually a converted 17th-century carriage house. This place is quite grand. So when you read that lunch is a self-service buffet, remember that it's not just any lunch buffet, but an elegant one that is being served on the Chatsworth Estate. The 16-item buffet changes daily depending on what is available at the market. Typical main courses include poached salmon, meat and potato pie, and char-grilled chicken. Fresh vegetables and salads along with a nice selection of fluffy desserts and rich cakes round out the buffet.

**Castle Inn.** Bridge St., Bakewell DE45 1DU. ☎ **01629/812103.** Main courses £2–£6 ($3.20–$9.60). MC, V. Mon–Sat 11am–11pm and Sun noon–10:30pm. ENGLISH.

This stone and ivy-covered building has been a pub for 400 years and is ideally located in the center of town right on the banks of the River Wye. The lunch and dinner menus are the same and range from bar snacks to hot and hearty meals, including chicken curry, prawn and cod bake, Yorkshire pudding, and meat and potato pie. Daily specials are also posted. The inside of this pub is dark with lots of wood and beams along with two huge open fireplaces. Ales on draft are Boddingtons, Castle Eden, Murphy's, and Stella.

A newer feature of the Castle Inn is its four clean, bright double rooms. They are only about 5 years old, are of modest size and furnishings, and include bath, TV, and coffee- and tea-making facilities. Doubles are £36.50 ($58.40).

**Val Verde.** Water St. ☎ **01629/814404.** Reservations recommended. Lunch £3.50–£5 ($5.60–$8); main courses £6.50–£9 ($10.40–$14.40). AE, MC, V. Summer daily 10:30am–2:30pm, tea 3–5pm, 7–9:30pm; winter daily 11:30am–2:30pm and 7–9:30pm. ITALIAN.

Don't pass this restaurant by just because it is small. Rather, think of it as intimate and then prepare to be swept off your feet by the simple, often times understated, elegance of the food. This recently renovated restaurant is pleasantly light, full of flowers and hanging plants, and is graced by the occasional exhibition of a local artist's works. In the summer, the garden becomes an extravaganza of dining alfresco. Lunch items include the typical Italian mainstays like pasta and pizza as well as soups and salads. But dinner is the real event here, with a menu that entices with the likes of truffles with wild mushrooms in sauce, turkey breast with Madeira wine sauce, and trout filled with ginger and spring onions. Of course, pizza and pasta dishes are also available.

## HISTORIC HOMES NEAR BAKEWELL

The tourist office in Bakewell (see above) will provide you with a map outlining the best routes to take to reach each of the attractions below.

### ✪ Chatsworth

Four miles east of Bakewell beside the A623 and 10 miles north of Matlock stands one of the great country houses of England, Chatsworth, the home of the 11th duke of Devonshire and his duchess, the former Deborah Mitford (sister of Nancy and Jessica). With its lavishly decorated interior and a wealth of art treasures, it has 175 rooms, the most spectacular of which are open to the public.

Dating from 1686, the present building stands on a spot where the eccentric Bess of Harwick built the house in which Mary Queen of Scots was held prisoner upon orders of Queen Elizabeth I. Capability Brown (who seems to have been everywhere) worked on the landscaping of the present house. But it was Joseph Paxton, the gardener to the sixth duke, who turned the garden into one of the most celebrated in Europe. Queen Victoria and Prince Albert were lavishly entertained here in 1843. The house contains a great library and such paintings as the *Adoration of the Magi* by Veronese and *King Uzziah* by Rembrandt. On the grounds you can see spectacular fountains, and there is a playground for children in the farmyard.

Chatsworth is open March 19 to November 2, daily from 11am to 4:30pm. Admission is £5.90 ($9.45) for adults, £3 ($4.80) children 5 to 15, and free for children 4 and under. Call ☎ **01246/582204** for more information.

### Hardwick Hall

Another great house in the district, Hardwick Hall, Doe Lea, Chesterfield (☎ **01246/850430**), lies 9¹/₂ miles southeast of Chesterfield. The approach from M1 is at junction 29. The house was built in 1597 for Bess of Hardwick, a woman who acquired an estate from each of her four husbands. It is particularly noted for its "more glass than wall" architecture. The high great chamber and long gallery crown an unparalleled series of late–16th-century interiors, including an important collection of tapestries, needlework, and furniture. The house is surrounded by a 300-acre country park, which is open daily all year. Walled gardens, orchards, and an herb garden are just part of its attractions.

The house itself is open April 1 through the end of October, Wednesday, Thursday, Saturday, Sunday, and bank holiday Mondays from 12:30 to 5pm. Admission is £5.80 ($9.30) for adults and £2.90 ($4.65) for children.

### Melbourne Hall

At Melbourne, 8 miles south of Derby on A447 stands **Melbourne Hall Church Square** (☎ **01332/862502**). Built by the bishops of Carlisle in 1133, it stands in one of the most famous formal gardens in Britain. The ecclesiastical structure was restored in the 1600s by one of the cabinet ministers of Charles I and enlarged by Queen Anne's vice chamberlain. It was the home of Lord Melbourne, who was prime minister when Victoria ascended to the throne. He was born William Lamb, and Melbourne Hall was also the home of Lord Byron's friend, Lady Caroline Lamb.

Lady Palmerston later inherited the house, which contains an important collection of pictures, antique furniture, and works of art. A special feature is the beautifully restored wrought-iron pergola by Robert Bakewell, noted 18th-century ironsmith.

The house is open daily (except for August, on the first three Mondays) from 2 to 5pm, but the gardens are open from April through September, Wednesday, Saturday, Sunday, and bank holidays from 2 to 6pm. Admission to the house is £2.50 ($4) for adults, £2 ($3.20) for students and seniors, £1 ($1.60) for children ages 5 to 15, and free for kids 4 and under. Visits to the garden cost £4.50 ($7.20) for adults, £3.50 ($5.60) for students and seniors, £2.50 ($4) for children 5 to 15, and free for kids 4 and under.

## THE ROYAL CROWN DERBY FACTORY

Royal Crown Derby, at 194 Osmaston Rd. in Derby (☎ 01332/712-8000), is the only pottery factory allowed to use both the words "royal" and "crown" in its name, a double honor granted by George III and Queen Victoria. At the end of a 90-minute tour, you can treat yourself to a bargain in the gift shop and visit the Royal Crown Derby Museum. Tours begin at 10:30am and 1:45pm, Monday to Friday, and cost £3 ($4.80) per person. Admission is free to the museum, which is open Monday to Friday from 10am to 12:30pm and from 2 to 4pm. The gift shop is open Monday to Friday from 9am to 5pm, Saturday from 9am to 4pm, and Sunday from 10am to 4pm.

To get to the National Tram Museum, take the A6 south through Matlock Bath to Cromford. Turn left at the traffic light and look for a sign to the museum. To go to the Peak District Mining Museum, take the A6 south through Matlock to Matlock Bath. It's in The Great Pavilion on the left. To get to the Royal Crown Derby Factory, take the A6 to Derby. The factory is in the center of town next to the Derby Tourist Office.

## 4 Nottinghamshire: Robin Hood Country

"Notts," as Nottinghamshire is known, lies in the heart of the East Midlands. Its towns are either rich in folklore or have bustling markets. Many famous people have come from Nottingham, notably those 13th-century outlaws from Sherwood Forest, Robin Hood and his merry men. It also was home to the romantic poet Lord Byron; you can visit his ancestral home at Newstead Abbey. D. H. Lawrence, author of *Sons and Lovers* and *Lady Chatterley's Lover,* was born in a tiny miner's cottage in Eastwood, which he later immortalized in his writings.

## SHERWOOD FOREST

Ranking alongside Germany's *Schwarzwald* in Europe's litany of lore and legend, Sherwood Forest is 450 acres of oak and silver birch trees owned and strictly protected by a local entity, the Thoresby Estate, and maintained by the county of Nottinghamshire. Actually very little of this area was forest even when it provided cover for Robin Hood, Friar Tuck, and Little John.

### THE LEGEND OF ROBIN HOOD

Robin Hood, the folk hero of tale and ballad, fired the imagination of a hardworking, sometimes impoverished English people, who particularly took to his adopted slogan: "Take from the rich and give to the poor."

Celebrating their freedom in verdant Sherwood Forest, Robin Hood's eternally youthful band rejoiced in "hearing the twang of the bow of yew and in watching the gray goose shaft as it cleaves the glistening willow wand or brings down the king's proud buck." Life was one long picnic beneath the splendid oaks of a primeval forest, with plenty of ale and flavorful venison poached from the forests of an oppressive king. The clever guerrilla rebellion Robin Hood waged against authority (represented by the haughty, despotic, and overfed sheriff of Nottingham) was punctuated by heroic exploits and a yearning to win justice for the victims of oppression. Later, such historical figures as the Scottish bandit and soldier of fortune Robert MacGregor, known as Rob Roy (1671–1734), were imbued with the heroism and bravado of Robin Hood, and many English reformers drew upon his heroism as they battled the forces of oppression.

## EXPLORING SHERWOOD FOREST

Then as now, the forest consists of woodland glades, agricultural fields, villages, and hamlets. The surroundings are considerably built up, relegating Robin Hood to a place far removed in time and space.

The **Sherwood Forest Visitor Centre** (☎ 0623/823202) is in Sherwood Forest Country Park at Edwinstowe, some 18 miles north of Nottingham city off the A614, or 8 miles east of Mansfield on B6034. It stands near the Major Oak, popularly known as Robin Hood's tree, although analysis of its bark reveals that it wasn't around in the 13th century. Many marked walks and footpaths lead from the visitor center through the woodland. There's an exhibition of life-size models of Robin and the other well-known outlaws, as well as a shop with books, gifts, and souvenirs. The center will provide as much information as is known about the merry men and Maid Marian, whom Robin Hood is believed to have married at Edwinstowe Church near the visitor center. Little John's grave can be seen at Hathersage (36 miles away), Will Scarlet's at Blidworth (9$^1$/$_2$ miles away).

The center also contains a visitor information facility and the **Forest Table,** which offers cafeteria service and meals with an emphasis on traditional English country recipes.

Opening times for the country park are dawn to dusk and for the visitor center April to October, daily from 10:30am to 5pm and November to March from 10:30am to 4:30pm. Entrance to the center is free, but for "Robin Hood's Sherwood" exhibition, there is a charge of 50p (80¢) for adults, 25p (40¢) for children and seniors. There is a year-round program of events mainly on weekends and national and school holiday periods. Car parking costs £1 ($1.60) per car per day, April to October.

An odd and somewhat archaic holdover from medieval times are **The Dukeries,** large country estates that contain privately owned remnants of whatever trees and vales remain of Sherwood Forest. Most lie on the edge of heavily industrialized towns, and may or may not have privately owned houses of historic merit. Very few can actually be visited without special invitations from their owners. On the other hand, **Clumber Park,** a 3,800-acre tract of park and woodland maintained by National Trust authorities, is favored by local families for picnics and strolls. It contains an 80-acre lake at its center, a monumental promenade flanked with venerable lime (linden) trees, and the Gothic Revival **Clumber Chapel.** Built between 1886 and 1889 as a site of worship for the private use of the seventh Duke of Newcastle, it's open from early March until mid-January, daily from 10am to 4pm. The park itself is open year-round during daylight hours, although its allure and the services it provides are at their lowest ebb during November and December. The gift shop and tearoom are open January through March, daily from 10am to 5pm, and from April to late October, daily from 10:30am to 6pm. Admission to the park, including the chapel, ranges from £3 ($4.80) and £4.30 ($6.90), depending on the size of your vehicle.

If you're specifically interested in the botany and plant life, head for the park's **Conservation Centre,** a walled garden with extensive greenhouses. It's open from April 1 to September 24 on Saturday, Sunday, and bank holiday Mondays from 1 to 5pm. For information about the park and its features, contact the **Clumber Park Estate Office,** Worksop, Nottingham SKO 3AZ (☎ **01909/476592**).

# NOTTINGHAM

121 miles N of London; 72 miles SE of Manchester

Although an industrial center, Nottingham nevertheless makes a good base for exploring Sherwood Forest and the rest of the shire. Long famous for its lace, Nottingham is known to literary buffs for its association with author D. H. Lawrence and its medieval sheriff who played an important role in the Robin Hood story.

Once known as Snotingeham, it was an important pre-Norman settlement guarding the River Trent, the gateway to the north of England. Followers of William the Conqueror arrived in 1068 to erect a fort here. In a later reincarnation, the fort saw supporters of Prince John surrender to Richard the Lionheart in 1194. Many other exploits occurred here—notably Edward III's capture of Roger Mortimer and Queen Isabella, the assassins of Edward II. From Nottingham, Richard III marched out with his men to face defeat and his own death at Bosworth Field in 1485.

With arrival of the Spinning Jenny in 1768, Nottingham launched into the forefront of the Industrial Revolution. It's still a center of industry and home base to many well-known British firms, turning out such products as John Player cigarettes, Boots pharmaceuticals, and Raleigh cycles.

Nottingham has meager attractions, but it's a city of youth and vitality, a very student-oriented place. Its Hockley neighborhood has been called as hip as anything this side of Manchester or London. Culturally, Nottingham finds a place on the maps with its Nottingham Festival, a premier musical and artistic festival lasting throughout the summer.

## ESSENTIALS

**GETTING THERE**   The best rail connection is via Lincoln, from which 28 trains arrive Monday through Saturday, and about eight trains on Sunday. The trip takes about 45 minutes. Trains also leave from London's St. Pancras Station; the trip takes about $2^1/_2$ hours. For schedules and information, call ☎ **0345/484950.**

Buses from London arrive at the rate of about seven per day. For schedules and information, call ☎ **0990/808080.**

If you're driving from London, the M1 motorway runs to a few miles west of Nottingham. Feeder roads, including the A453, are well-marked the short distance into town. The drive takes about 3 to $3^1/_2$ hours.

**VISITOR INFORMATION**   Information is available at the **City Information Centre,** 1–4 Smithy Row (☎ **0115/915-5330**). Open Easter to the first week in October, Monday through Friday from 8:30am to 5pm, Saturday from 9am to 5pm, and Sunday from 10am to 4pm; the rest of the year open Monday to Friday from 8:30am to 5pm, Saturday from 9am to 5pm.

## SEEING THE SIGHTS: MUSEUMS & MORE

**Nottingham Castle Museum.** Castle Rd. ☎ **0115/915-3700.** Admission Sat–Sun £1.50 ($2.40) adults; 75p ($1.20) children (free Mon–Fri). Open Mar–Oct daily 10am–5pm; Nov–Feb daily 1–5pm.

Overlooking the city, Nottingham Castle was built in 1679 by the duke of Newcastle on the site of an old Norman fortress. After restoration in 1878, it was opened as a provincial museum surrounded by a charmingly laid-out garden. Of particular interest are the History of Nottingham Gallery re-creating the legends associated with the city, a rare collection of ceramics, and a unique exhibition of medieval alabaster carvings, which were executed between 1350 and 1530. These delicately detailed scenes illustrate the life of Christ, the Virgin Mother, and various saints. Paintings cover several periods but are strong on 16th-century Italian, 17th-century French and Dutch, and the richest English paintings of the past 2 centuries.

The only element from the original Norman castle to survive is a subterranean passage, Mortimer's Hole. The passage leads to Ye Olde Trip to Jerusalem (see "Where to Eat," below).

**Brewhouse Yard Museum.** Brewhouse Yard, Castle Rock. ☎ **0115/948-3504.** Admission Sat–Sun £1.50 ($2.40) adults; 75p ($1.20) children (free Mon–Fri). Daily 10am–5pm. Closed Christmas Day and Boxing Day.

This museum consists of five 17th-century cottages at the foot of Castle Rock, presenting a panorama of Nottingham life in a series of furnished rooms and shops. Some of them, open from cellar to attic, display much local history, and visitors are encouraged to handle the exhibits. The most interesting features are in a series of cellars cut into the rock of the castle instead of below the houses, plus an exhibition of a Nottingham shopping street circa 1919 to 1939. This is not a typical folk museum, but attempts to be as lively as possible, involving both visitors and the Nottingham community in expanding displays and altering exhibitions on a bimonthly basis.

**The Galleries of Justice.** Shire Hall, High Pavement, Lace Market. ☎ **0115/952-0555.** Admission £4.25 ($6.80) adults; £2.95 ($4.70) seniors, students, and children; £11.95 ($19.10) family ticket for two adults and two children. Apr–Aug Tue–Sun and bank holidays 10am–6pm; Sep–Mar Tue–Sun and bank holidays 10am–5pm. Closed Dec 24–26.

This is an interactive attraction that centers around two Victorian courtrooms and a 19th-century prison/dungeon with sandstone cave cells located beneath the courtrooms. Over the many years, prisoners entered this complex with well-founded fear—it was a veritable chamber of horrors with rats, leg irons, putrid gruel for food, and torture. Today visitors can experience the dark reality of 19th-century life here through an interpretative drama called "Condemned!". Everyone is given a criminal identity number, tried in court, found guilty, and promptly escorted downstairs to the prison to serve sentence. Upon returning to the free world and sunlight, visitors can enjoy a drink in the Judge's Pantry and browse in "Shopped," the galleries-themed retail store.

**Museum of Costume & Textiles.** 51 Castle Gate. ☎ **0115/948-3504.** Free admission. Daily 10am–5pm.

This is one of the half-dozen or so best collections of period costumes in Britain, with exhibitions ranging from the 17th century to the Carnaby Street era of the 1960s. It's not as comprehensive as the collection at London's Victoria & Albert Museum, but then, what is? Many garments date from the 1700s, and include exhibitions of "fallals and fripperies" (gewgaws and accessories as designated by the disapproving Puritans), as well as lace, weavings, and embroideries, each of them a celebration of the textile industry that dominated part of Nottingham's economy for many generations. Look for the Eyre Map Tapestries, woven in 1632 and depicting the geography of the region. Two of the map's three sections are on display; the third is part of a private collection elsewhere in England.

**The Canal Museum.** Canal St. ☎ **0115/959-8835.** Free admission. Wed–Sun 10am–noon and 1–5pm.

One of the smallest museums in town lies adjacent to the castle. Set within a compound of 19th- and early–20th-century buildings that once serviced and maintained the many barges that meandered through town, it's a nostalgia-laden tribute to a long-ago commerce that added incalculably to the commercial prosperity of the Midlands.

## HISTORIC HOMES NEAR NOTTINGHAM

### Newstead Abbey

Lord Byron once made his home at Newstead Abbey, one of eight museums administered by the city of Nottingham. Some of the original Augustinian priory, purchased by Sir John Byron in 1540, still survives. In the 19th century, the mansion was given a neo-Gothic restoration. Mementos, including first editions and manuscripts, are displayed inside. You can explore the parkland of some 300 acres, with waterfalls, rose gardens, a Monk's Stew Pond, and a Japanese water garden.

Newstead Abbey (☎ 01623/793557) is on A60 (Mansfield Road) 12 miles north of Nottingham center in Linby. It's open April to October, daily from noon to 6pm. The gardens are open year-round from 9:30am to dusk. Admission to the gardens only is £1.70 ($2.70) for adults and £1 ($1.60) for children. Admission to the house and grounds is £3.50 ($5.60) for adults, £2 ($3.20) for students and seniors, and £1 ($1.60) for children.

### Wollaton Hall

This well-preserved Elizabethan mansion, finished in 1588, is the most ornate in England. Today it houses a natural history museum with lots of insects, invertebrates, British mammals, birds, reptiles, amphibians, and fish. The hall is surrounded by a deer park and garden. See the camellia house with the world's earliest cast-iron front dating from 1823. The bird dioramas here are among the best in Britain.

Wollaton Hall (☎ 0115/915-3900) is in Wollaton Park, 3 miles from Nottingham center. Drive southwest along the A609 (Ilkeston Road), which will become Wollaton Road. Open April to September, Monday to Saturday from 10am to 5pm, Sunday 1 to 5pm; off-season, Monday to Saturday from 10am to 4:30pm, Sunday 1:30 to 4:30pm. Admission on Saturday, Sunday, and bank holiday Mondays is £1.50 ($2.40) for adults and 75p ($1.20) or children.

## SHOPPING

You better put on some of your most comfortable shopping shoes to tackle the more than 800 shops in and around the streets of this town, which boasts some of England's best shopping. Start in the city center with its maze of pedestrian streets and work your way out toward the two grand indoor shopping malls, the Victoria and the Broad Marsh, located to the north and to the south of the center of town. Then head over to Derby Road for your fill of antiques.

Fine Nottingham lace can be found in the **Lace Centre,** Castle Road, across the street from Nottingham Castle (☎ 0115/941-3539), or in the shops around the area known as the **Lace Market** along High Pavement.

Of course in a shopping mecca like Nottingham, unique art items abound. **International Fine Arts,** no. 5, The Poultry (☎ 0115/941-2580), bills itself as Nottingham's most prestigious art gallery, selling original oil paintings; watercolors; limited editions; and collections by David Shepherd, Sir William Russell Flint, Gordon King, and LS Lowry. **Patchings Farm Art Centre,** Oxton Road, near Calverton (☎ 0115/965-3479), is a 60-acre art haven. Restored farm buildings house three galleries, working art and pottery studios, a gift shop, and art and framing shops. And long known as Britain's first real craft center, **Longdale Craft Centre,** Longdale Lane, Ravenshead (☎ 01623/794858), is a labyrinth of re-created Victorian streets where professional craftspeople work on a whole range of craft items, including jewelry, pottery, and prints.

## TEATIME

For your cuppa, head for the **Lace Hall,** High Pavement (☎ 01159/484221), where you can sit in an ancient chapel and admire the softly colored sunlight filter through the stained-glass windows.

## WHERE TO STAY

**Balmoral Hotel.** 55–57 Loughborough Rd., West Bridgford, Nottingham, Nottinghamshire NG2 7LA. ☎ **0115/945-5020.** Fax 0115/955-2991. 31 rooms. TV TEL. £25.50–£35 ($40.80–$56) single; £39.50–£45 ($63.20–$72) double. All rates include breakfast. AE, MC, V.

If you're into football (read soccer) and cricket, you may want to stay here. This hotel, formerly two brick Victorian houses from the 1880s that have been combined and extended into one large establishment, is situated within a stone's throw of the cricket field where the International Test Matches are played as well as the football grounds for two of the Nottingham teams. Rooms are on the small side here and have built-in modern furnishings. Public areas include a dining room, where breakfast is served; a lounge; and a billiard room. It is about 1¹/₄ miles from the center of town and is also near the River Trent and the National Water Sports Center. The hotel serves a three-course dinner from £7.50 to £11 ($12 to $17.60) during the week, and bar snacks on weekends.

**Castle Rock Guest House.** 79 Castle Blvd., Nottingham, Nottinghamshire NG7 1FE. ☎ **0115/948-2116.** 4 rooms, none with bath. TV. £16.50 ($26.40) per person (single or double). Rate includes English breakfast. No credit cards.

A bit of amusing history surrounds this terrace guest house, located just across the street from the castle. It starts with the duke of Newcastle building a group of large houses for the Nottingham lace barons. But it seems that the good duke, always a man with the best of intentions, had a weakness: an obsession for gambling. When it came time to pay the piper and resolve one of his many gambling debts, he ended up forfeiting all the buildings on the Castle Rock side of the street, including this guest house. This three-floor, brick B&B has high ceilings and a rather simple interior with spotless guest rooms outfitted in a basic array of modern furniture and spring colors. Breakfast is served at individual tables in the dining room. And Castle Rock is a short 5-minute walk to the center of town as well as the bus and train stations.

**Claremont Hotel.** 2 Hamilton Rd., Sherwood Rise, Nottingham, Nottinghamshire NG5 1AU. ☎ **0115/960-8587.** 14 rooms, 10 with bath. TV. £20 ($32) per person without bath; £25 ($40) per person with bath. All rates include English breakfast. MC, V. Closed Dec 23–Jan 2.

This red-brick Victorian was built as a private house between 1872 and 1875, and sits in a quiet residential street lined with other Victorian homes about a mile from the center of town. The ground floor has some typically extravagant Victorian architectural features, including marbled pillars, stone carvings, and goldleaf cornices. The average-size bedrooms are more simple and basic in design, style, and furnishings. But all do have tea- and coffee-making facilities. The dining room has big windows through which guests can admire the small garden while eating breakfast.

**Lucieville St. James.** 349 Derby Rd., Nottingham, Nottinghamshire NG7 2DZ. ☎ **0115/978-7389.** Fax 0115/979-0346. 5 rms, 1 suite. TV TEL. £45 ($72) single; £55 ($88) double; £75 ($120) suite. AE, DC, MC, V.

This two-story, brick-and-timber B&B sits on a rather busy residential road that leads right into the center of town. But the grounds in back are landscaped with an illuminated garden complete with a small fish pool and its own waterfall. The hypnotic effect of the water trickling into the pool can be enjoyed from one of the four balconied guest rooms. The size of the guest rooms teeters between medium and large, all pleasantly decorated with antiques. The large bridal suite runs from the front to the back of the hotel, has a romantic balcony, and of course a four-poster bed. Breakfast and dinner are served in the spot-lighted dining room with breakfast costing £4.50 to £9.50 ($7.20 to $15.20) and dinner ranging from £6 to £22.50 ($9.60 to $36).

## WHERE TO EAT

**Higoi.** 57 Lenton Blvd. ☎ **0115/942-3379.** Main courses £15–£25 ($24–$40). AE, DC, MC, V. Mon–Sat 6:30–10pm and Sat noon–2pm. JAPANESE.

This is the best place in town for Japanese food. This small restaurant has been decorated in a simple, traditional style. Mr. Kato, the owner, has assembled a varied menu that provides customers with meals ranging from sushi and sashimi to tempura. Favorites include teriyaki chicken and salmon.

**Hiziki Wholefood Collective and Out to Lunch Café.** 15 Goose Gate. ☎ **0115/950-5523** and 0115/948-1115. Lunch £2.50–£4 ($4–$6.40). No credit cards. Daily 9am–6pm and 9am–4pm for the cafe. VEGETARIAN.

These two establishments are found in the same building, which is located in a rather alternative area of town. Hiziki Wholefood Collective sells vegetarian and vegan foodstuff like dried beans and organic fruit and vegetables. They do have a small take-away food section where you can buy vegetarian snacks like quiche and pizza and a few sweet items like pastries. The cafe upstairs is a great little place to have breakfast or lunch. It has lots of lush green plants scattered about here and there, on the hardwood floors and counters. Tables are placed so patrons can look out the big windows and watch the street life below. Breakfast items include vegetarian sausage, toast, and beans. Lunch is just as simple and good with choices like vegetarian burgers and chips, salads, vegetable pie with roasted potatoes, and soups.

**Loch Fyne Oyster Bar.** 17 King St. ☎ **0115/950-8481.** Main courses £6.95–£8.95 ($11.10–$14.30). MC, V. Mon–Thurs 9am–8pm; Fri–Sat 9am–9pm. Closed bank holidays, Christmas, and Good Friday. SEAFOOD.

Good, fresh seafood is the hallmark of this boisterous restaurant. Walk in and you'll immediately notice the commanding mural of a woman carrying an oyster basket surrounded by fish and crustaceans. Favorite menu items include poached salmon with cucumber sauce, whole brown crabs, Loch Fyne kippers, pan-fried marinated salmon with ginger and lime, and platters of fish, lobster, or both. Homemade hearty soups like mulligatawny round out the menu, and pies and puddings are perennial dessert favorites.

**Pinchinello's.** 35 Forman St. ☎ **0115/941-1965.** Lunch £3–£5 ($4.80–$8); main courses £6.95–£12.50 ($11.10–$20). AE, MC, V. Mon–Sat 9:30am–10:30pm (food available from noon to close). INTERNATIONAL.

Across the street from the Theatre Royal, this fun establishment has become a tradition with theatergoers, who regularly stop by for a post-theater special that features a starter and a dessert for £5.95 ($9.50). Pinchinello's is housed in a row of three 13th-century brick cottages. The old oak-beam ceilings, terra-cotta tile floor, and sturdy tables combine with two large open fireplaces to create a vibrant atmosphere. Pasta and vegetable dishes are the most popular lunch items, and the dinner menu features homemade soups like carrot and French onion served with crusty bread, pasta with roasted vegetables, Spanish chicken with baked rice, and supreme of chicken in oriental sauce. An all-you-can-eat salad bar is a lunch and dinner favorite.

**Saagar.** 473 Mansfield Rd., Sherwood. ☎ **0115/962-2014.** Main course £9–£13.40 ($14.40–$21.45); set-price dinner for two £32 ($51.20). AE, MC, V. Mon–Sat noon–2pm and 5:30pm–midnight. Closed Dec 25. INDIAN.

Owner Mohammed Khizer and chef Amjaid Parvaiz have created one of the best restaurants around. The same a la carte menu is used for both lunch and dinner and includes selections of chicken, lamb, and prawns prepared in traditional recipes from the Madras area of India. Don't worry about the sizzle of your food here. Most sauces are mild, including the cream and coconut sauce used in the Kurma chicken. Main courses are quite large and also include rice. The set-price dinner for two includes starters, main course, rice, vegetables, bread, and dessert.

**Ye Olde Trip to Jerusalem.** 1 Castle Rd. ☎ **0115/947-3171.** Bar snacks £2–£5 ($3.20–$8). AE, MC, V. Mon–Sat 11am–11pm; Sun noon–10:30pm. ENGLISH.

Constructed in 1189, this is reputedly the oldest inn in England. It was, however, a regular resting spot for righteous knights and fools on the long road to the holy land during the Crusades. The establishment was built into the rock base of Nottingham Castle. A natural fault in the stone next to the fireplace served as a secret passage to the castle. In fact, a whole maze of passages and tunnels are hidden behind the inn, leading in one way or another to the castle. It is said that in these passages, many a secret assassination took place. The intrigue doesn't stop there. In the inn's gallery, the model of a galleon is said to have a curse on it—death within a year to anyone who touches it. During a recent renovation, the galleon needed to be moved. So a psychic was actually called to the inn to check everything out. There have been no reports of curse-related deaths to date as a result of temporarily moving the galleon during the renovations. However, just to be on the safe side, the galleon is back on display under the protection of a glass case. Typical pub food along the line of meat pies and sandwiches can be had here every day. On Sunday, patrons are treated to roast beef and Yorkshire pudding. Ales on draft include Kimberley Classic, Best Mild, and Marston's Pedigree. This inn now sports a new paint job, reupholstered settles, and new wood tables and chairs. In warmer weather, there's outdoor eating on both front and back patios.

## NOTTINGHAM AFTER DARK

Whether you're looking for theater, film, music, or dancing, there's always something going on. *Now* and *City Lights* are two publications that will steer you toward mainstream offerings. *Overall There's a Smell of Fried Onions* covers more underground happenings. *Out Right,* a regional gay magazine, covers not just Nottingham, but Leicester and Derby as well.

If you need a little drama in your life, **Nottingham Playhouse,** Wellington Circus (☎ **0115/941-9419**), presents theater most of the year, closing for 8 to 10 weeks every summer. Performances are held every Monday through Saturday nights, and range from the works of Shakespeare to Tennessee Williams, presented by both Nottingham Playhouse Productions as well as visiting theater companies. Ticket prices are £6.75 ($10.80), £9.75 ($15.60), and £13 ($20.80).

For truly varied musical entertainment from around the world, call the **Theatre Royal,** Upper Parliament St. (☎ **0115/948-2626**), to find out their upcoming schedule of musicals, opera, or concerts. Tickets generally cost between £17 to £38 ($27.20 to $60.80). Pop music fans have several good local options, starting with

**Rock City,** 8 Talbot St. (☎ **0115/941-2544**), a large club staging shows by local and touring rock bands. When bigger shows aren't scheduled, Friday night is Rock Night and Saturday night is Alternative Night, each with a cover of £4 ($6.40). When there are shows, tickets range from £5 to £12 ($8 to $19.20). On Thursday through Saturday, **Old Vic,** 22 Fletcher Gate (☎ **0115/950-9833**), has local and regional bands playing everything from jazz to rock, with a cover charge of £1 ($1.60) after 10pm, and £2 ($3.20) after 11pm. Sunday night it's all comedy, and the laughs will cost you £5 ($8). Located in a former brewery next to the BBC, the **Filly & Firkin,** 36 Mansfield Rd. (☎ **0115/947-2739**), has live bands, mostly of the indie and Britpop ilk, every Thursday through Saturday night, with the band(s) setting their own cover charge.

The building housing **The Salutation Inn,** Houndsgate, Castle Road (☎ **0115/958-9432**), has hosted a pub continuously since the 13th century, and was built over a series of caves that sheltered 8th-century farmers. Add to that atmosphere the largest range of cask ales in the country, and this just may be as good as a pub gets. The regulars are friendly, and if you're lucky you'll show up during one of their regular storytelling sessions. Sure you can get Flowers or Castle Eden, but be adventurous and try a pint of Bread of Heaven or Molly Malone.

For a pub with a different flavor, stop by **Gatsby's,** Huntingdon Street (☎ **0115/950-5323**), Nottingham's premier gay pub, which offers conversation over a pint during the week, then picks up the pace with a free disco on Friday and Saturday nights. Traditional pub lovers may leave Nottingham with a new conception of what they've been missing.

## 5  Lincolnshire

This large East Midlands county is bordered on one side by the North Sea. Its most interesting section is Holland, in the southeast, a land known for its fields of tulips, its marshes and fens, and windmills reminiscent (logically) of the Netherlands. Although much of the shire is interesting to explore, most visitors don't linger long here. North American tourists generally tip-toe across the tulip fields, stopping in the busy port of Boston before making the swing north to the inland cathedral city of Lincoln.

### BOSTON

122 miles N of London; 35 miles SE of Lincoln; 55 miles E of Nottingham

New Englanders like to visit this old seaport in the riding of Holland that gave its name to the more famous Massachusetts city. It's ironic that the Pilgrims named their seaport after the English town of Boston, as they suffered more here than in virtually any other town in England. In 1607, about a dozen years before their eventual transit to the New World on the *Mayflower,* some Pilgrims arranged for a ship to carry them to new lives in Holland via *The Wash* and the sea lanes of the North Sea. The captain of the ship betrayed them and absconded with their money; as a result, the group was imprisoned in Boston's guildhall for a month for attempting to emigrate from England without the king's permission. The cells they occupied can still be visited within Boston's guildhall. Also at Scotia Creek, on a riverbank near town, is a memorial to those early Pilgrims.

### ESSENTIALS

**GETTING THERE**    From Lincoln, there are about a half-dozen trains a day, each of which require a transfer in the town of Sleaford. The trip takes about an hour. From London, about 10 trains a day depart from King's Cross Station, for the 2½-hour trip. For schedules and information, call ☎ **0345/484950.**

There's no bus service from Lincoln, and perhaps one or two buses a day depart from London's Victoria Coach Station to Boston. For schedules and information, call ☎ **0990/808080.**

If you're driving from Lincoln, take A17 southeast for 35 miles; the trip takes about 45 minutes. From London, take the A1 motorway north to Peterborough, then follow the signs to Boston. It's about a 3$^1$/$_2$-hour drive.

**VISITOR INFORMATION**   The **Boston Tourist Office,** Market Place (☎ **01205/356656**), is open Monday through Saturday from 9am to 5pm.

## WALKING AROUND BOSTON

The center of Boston is closed to cars, so you will have to walk to visit attractions such as the **Boston Stump,** the lantern tower of the Church of St. Botolph with a view for miles around of the all-encircling fens. As it stands, the tower was finished in 1460. In the 1930s the people of Boston, Massachusetts, paid for the restoration of the tower, known officially as St. Botolph's Tower. The stairs aren't in good shape, so we don't recommended that you climb the tower. The city officials were going to add a spire, making it the tallest in England, but because of the wind and the weight, they feared the tower would collapse. Therefore, it became known as "the Boston Stump." An elderly gentleman at the tower assured us it was the tallest in England— that is, 272$^1$/$_2$ feet tall.

The **Boston Borough Museum,** St. Mary's Guildhall, South St. (☎ **01205/ 365954**), is a 15th-century guildhall that contains the courtrooms where the pilgrims were tried and the cells where they were imprisoned. It is open April to September, Monday to Saturday from 10am to 5pm and Sunday from 1:30 to 5pm. The admission of £1 ($1.60) for adults or 75p ($1.20) for seniors includes a 45-minute audio guided tour. Children accompanied by adults are admitted free.

Next door to the guildhall, the 1700s **Fydell House,** South St. (☎ **01205/ 351520**), is an adult education center but has a room set aside to welcome visitors not only from Boston, Massachusetts, but also from the rest of the U.S. It is open Monday to Friday from 9:30am to 12:30pm and 1:30 to 4:30pm. Admission is free.

## PUBS WHERE YOU CAN EAT, DRINK & STAY

**Admiral Nelson Pub.** Main Rd., Bennington, near Boston, Lincolnshire. ☎ **01205/760460.** 2 rms, none with bath. TV. £15–£25 ($24–$40) per person, single or double. All rates include English breakfast. No credit cards.

Five miles north of Boston, it isn't plush or luxurious, and you might get the feeling that the accommodations are intended for those too drunk to drive home after an alcoholic binge. But if you're not too fussy, and want an insight into the goings on at the main pub of an English village, this establishment maintains a pair of battered but clean accommodations upstairs from its antique premises. Don't overlook the charms of the pub, where log-burning fireplaces add a glow to the old-fashioned panels and much-used bar area. Platters of pub grub cost from £3 to £5.50 ($4.80 to $8.80) each, and tend to go well with the roster of Bateman's Ales that, along with a changing roster of "guest ales," provide much of the drinking staple here.

**Castle Inn.** Haltoft End, Freiston, Boston, Lincolnshire PE22 0MY. ☎ **01205/760393.** 4 rms, none with bath. TV. £12 ($19.20) single; £21 ($33.60) double. No credit cards.

These are about as basic as any units we're willing to recommend, but for cost-conscious travelers who want easy access to the sociability and warmth of a busy pub, they're a worthwhile choice. They are upstairs from a traditional pub, the Castle Inn, whose brick facade and old-timey aura lies about 1$^1$/$_2$ miles from the center of Boston, beside the A52 highway. (To reach it from Boston's center, follow the signs to

Skegness.) Bedrooms have tea-making facilities, two twin beds, and congenially battered, strictly utilitarian furniture. None contain sinks or any plumbing fixtures.

**Kings Arms Inn.** Horncastle Rd., Boston, Lincolnshire PE21 9BU. ☎ and fax **01205/364296.** Platters £1.30–£9.50 ($2.10–$15.20). No credit cards. Mon–Sat 11am–11pm; Sun 11am–3pm and 7–10:30pm. ENGLISH.

The neighborhood's most charming pub, built of softly weathered red bricks, lies a half-mile west of Boston's center, across the road from the Mard Foster Canal, near what used to function as a windmill. It was built in the 1830s to assuage the hunger pangs and thirst of men who operated the longboats carrying grain up and down the canal. (The fifth-generation publicans who own the place, the Cooper family, remember when downing 8 pints of beer in one sitting was considered normal for most of the clients of this place.) Today, the site retains its antique aura, but with a somewhat more temperate attitude toward food and drink. Bateman's Ale, a brand that's brewed fewer than 18 miles away, is the beverage of choice, along with Bass Ale and whatever promotional brew is being marketed at the time. Menu items are flavorful and come in very generous portions—especially the English-style mixed grill that wins again and again as the most popular platter. (If it doesn't appeal to you, consider any of the curries, the ham steak, any of the chicken dishes, or perhaps something as simple as a sandwich.)

Looking for lodging? Consider one of the quartet of cozy bedrooms on the inn's second floor. Each has a TV, tea-making facilities, a shower, and a sink, but shares a communal toilet off the second floor hallway. A "proper English breakfast" is included in the price of £25 ($40) per night for a single, and £35 ($56) for a double.

# LINCOLN

140 miles N of London; 94 miles NW of Cambridge; 82 miles SE of York

One of the ancient cities of England, Lincoln was the site of a Bronze Age settlement. Originally known as Lindon, the city's name was latinized by the Romans into Lindum. In the 3rd century, Lincoln was one of the four provincial capitals of Roman Britain. In the Middle Ages it was the center of Lindsey, a famous Anglo-Saxon kingdom. After the Norman conquest, it grew increasingly important and was known throughout the land for its cathedral and castle. Its merchants grew rich by shipping wool directly to Flanders.

Much of the past lives on in Lincoln today to delight visitors who wander past half-timbered Tudor houses, the Norman castle, and the towering Lincoln Cathedral. Medieval streets climbing the hillsides and cobblestones re-create the past. Lincoln, unlike other leading East Midlands centers such as Nottingham and Leicester, maintains somewhat of a country town atmosphere. But it also extends welcoming arms to tourists, the mainstay of its economy.

## ESSENTIALS

**GETTING THERE**    Trains arrive every hour during the day from London's King's Cross Station, a 2-hour trip usually requiring a change of trains at Newark. Trains also arrive from Cambridge, again necessitating a change at Newark. For schedules and information, call ☎ **0345/484950.**

National Express buses from London's Victoria Coach Station service Lincoln, a 3-hour ride. For schedules and information, call ☎ **0990/808080.** Once in Lincoln, local and regional buses service the county from the City Bus Station, off St. Mary's Street opposite the train station.

If you're driving from London, take the M1 north to the junction with A57, then head east to Lincoln.

**VISITOR INFORMATION**    The **Tourist Information Centre** is at 9 Castle Hill (☎ **01522/529828**). Open Monday to Thursday from 9:30am to 5:30pm, Friday from 9am to 5pm, Saturday and Sunday from 10am to 5pm.

## ✪ LINCOLN CATHEDRAL

No other English cathedral dominates its surroundings as does Lincoln's. Visible from up to 30 miles away, the central tower is 271 feet high, which makes it the second tallest in England. The central tower once carried a huge spire, which, prior to heavy gale damage in 1549, made it the tallest in the world at 525 feet. Construction on the original Norman cathedral was begun in 1072, and it was consecrated 20 years later. It sustained a major fire and, in 1185, an earthquake. Only the central portion of the West Front and lower halves of the western towers survive from this period. The present cathedral is Gothic style, particularly the early English and decorated periods. The nave is 13th century, but the black font of Tournai marble originates from the 12th century. In the Great North Transept is a rose medallion window known as the Dean's Eye. Opposite it, in the Great South Transept, is its cousin, the Bishop's Eye. East of the high altar is the Angel Choir, consecrated in 1280, and so called after the sculpted angels high on the walls. The exquisite wood carving in St. Hugh's Choir dates from the 14th century. Lincoln's roof bosses, dating from the 13th and 14th centuries, are handsome, and a mirror trolley assists visitors in their appreciation of these features, which are some 70 feet above the floor. Oak bosses are in the cloister.

In the Seamen's Chapel (Great North Transept) is a window commemorating Lincolnshire-born Capt. John Smith, one of the pioneers of early settlement in America and the first governor of Virginia. The library and north walk of the cloister were built in 1674 to designs by Sir Christopher Wren. In the Treasury is fine silver plate from the churches of the diocese.

Lincoln Cathedral (☎ **01522/544544**) is open June through August, Monday to Saturday from 7:15am to 8pm, Sunday from 7:15am to 6pm; September through May, Monday to Saturday from 7:15am to 6pm, Sunday from 7:15am to 5pm. The coffee shop is open Monday to Saturday from 10am to 4:30pm. Admission by suggested donation is £2.50 ($4) for adults and £1 ($1.60) for seniors, students, and children.

## WALKING AROUND LINCOLN

The best lanes to walk are those tumbling down the appropriately named Steep Hill to the Witham River. It's also fun to pop in and out of the stores along High Street.

One of the most visited attractions in Lincoln, **Greyfriars City and County Museum,** is currently closed for repairs. Check with the Tourist Office for reopening dates.

The **Museum of Lincolnshire Life,** on Burton Road (☎ **01522/528448**), is the largest museum of social history in the Midlands. Housed in what was built as an army barracks in 1857, it's a short walk north of the city center. Displays here range from a Victorian schoolroom to a collection of locally built steam engines. Admission is £1.20 ($1.90) for adults and 60p (95¢) for children. Open May through September, daily from 10am to 5:30pm; October through April, Monday to Saturday from 10am to 5:30pm, Sunday from 2 to 5:30pm. Closed Good Friday, Dec 24 to 27, and New Year's Day.

## SHOPPING

The cathedral is a good starting point for your shopping tour of Lincoln, as the streets leading down the hill are lined with a melange of interesting stores. Wander in and out of these historical lanes, down Steep Hill, along Bailgate, around the Stonebow gateway and Guildhall, and then down High Street. Following this route, you'll find all sorts of clothing, books, antiques, arts and crafts, and gift items.

While walking down Steep Hill, stop in **Harding House Gallery,** 53 Steep Hill (☎ 01522/523537), to see one of the best local venues for local craftspeople. They carry ceramics, teddy bears, textiles, wood, metal sculptures, and jewelry. Another Steep Hill address to visit is **David Hansord,** 32 Steep Hill (☎ 01522/530044), where you'll find a great collection of Georgian English furniture from 1730 to 1820, plus clocks, barometers, and various sundry works of art. You can peek down St. Paul's Lane, just off Bailgate, to investigate **Cobb Hall Centre,** 28 St. Paul's Lane (☎ 01522/527317), a small cluster of specialty shops selling outdoor gear, candies and gift items, German figures, and antiques.

## WHERE TO STAY

The cheapest lodgings are those at the **YHA Lincoln Youth Hostel,** 77 S. Park, Lincoln, Lincolnshire LN5 8ES (☎ 01522/522076), which stands at the end of Canwick Road across from South Common. This is back to basics, but it's clean and cheap, offering 52 dormitory beds for the night, with shared baths. Rates are £8.50 ($13.60) for adults or £5.70 ($9.10) for those under 18. The reception is closed from 10am to 5pm daily, with a strict 11pm curfew imposed. You can also get decent meals here, with a cafeteria breakfast costing £2.85 ($4.55), and a decent dinner going for only £4.25 ($6.80). The hostel is open daily July and August; Monday through Saturday, April through June; Tuesday through Saturday from mid-February to March, and September and October; and only on Friday and Saturday in winter. You can take bus no. 51 from the station, getting off at Canwick Road Old Cemetery.

### Doubles for Less Than £50

✪ **Carline Guest House.** 1–3 Carline Rd., Lincoln, Lincolnshire LN1 1HN. ☎ 01522/ 530422. 12 rms all with bath. TV. £30 ($48) single; £40 ($64) double; from £50 ($80) family rm. All rates include English breakfast. No credit cards. Bus: no. 15, 17, or 18. From the Cathedral, take Drury Lane to Carline Rd.

Among the finest B&Bs in this city, the Carline, is a charming double fronted Edwardian house. Since 1977, when the house was first opened, Gill and John Pritchard have established a reputation for excellence and competitive pricing and provide a warm, welcoming atmosphere. It is only a 6-minute stroll to the center of Lincoln, where you'll find the cathedral, castle, and museums as well as shops and attractions. The bedrooms, which have been individually and traditionally furnished, each have private bath, hospitality tray, and hair dryer. For your safety and comfort, this is a nonsmoking facility. There is also a sitting room in which you can relax and browse through the stocks of tourist literature and information to be sure you get the most from your visit to Lincoln. Gill and John are only too happy to recommend some of the better eating establishments to you for your lunch or dinner.

**Duke William Hotel.** 44 Bailgate, Lincoln, Lincolnshire LN1 3AP. ☎ 01522/533351. 11 rms. TV TEL. £25 ($40) single; £35 ($56) double; £45 ($72) family rm. All rates include English breakfast. AE, DC, MC, V.

The Duke William is in the heart of historic Lincoln near the Roman arch, within walking distance of the cathedral. Although the structure, built in 1791, has undergone many architectural changes, care has been taken to preserve the atmosphere of an 18th-century inn; many bedrooms still have their original heavy timbers.

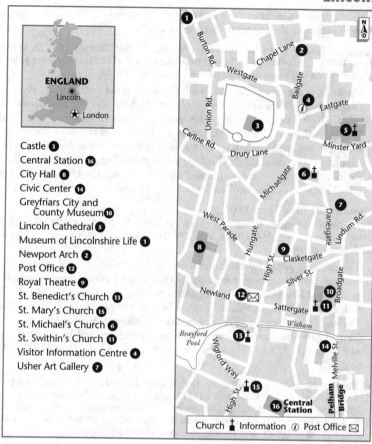

Castle **3**
Central Station **16**
City Hall **8**
Civic Center **14**
Greyfriars City and
    County Museum **10**
Lincoln Cathedral **5**
Museum of Lincolnshire Life **1**
Newport Arch **2**
Post Office **12**
Royal Theatre **9**
St. Benedict's Church **13**
St. Mary's Church **15**
St. Michael's Church **6**
St. Swithin's Church **11**
Visitor Information Centre **4**
Usher Art Gallery **7**

Church ✝ Information ⓘ Post Office ✉

    The hotel features a good restaurant and a cozy bar. Bar snacks are served every day from noon to 2pm, priced at £1.50 to £9 ($2.40 to $14.40). Dinners, costing £8 to £10 ($12.80 to $16), are offered Monday through Wednesday from 5:30 to 9:30pm and Thursday through Sunday from 7 to 9pm. Since the hotel's owner also owns a brewery, featuring Simon Bitter, you'll naturally find that brew on tap in the bar.

**Hollies Hotel.** 65 Carholme Rd., Lincoln, Lincolnshire LN1 1RT. ☎ and fax **01522/522419.** 11rms, 6 with bath (tub or shower). TV TEL. £28 ($44.80) single without bath, £45 ($72) single with bath; £50 ($80) double without bath, £65 ($104) double with bath. All rates include English breakfast. AE, MC, V.

Built around 1850, and today owned by the Colston family, this cream-fronted hotel sits in a busy commercial neighborhood half a mile west of Lincoln's cathedral. This hotel is an elegant former Victorian residence with many of the original features remaining, including the terra-cotta floor and pitch pine staircase of the entrance hall. The resident proprietors, Richard and Dena Colston, personally ensure that you have a pleasant and comfortable stay. The individually designed bedrooms (most of which are en-suite and all have hot and cold running water) have remote control TV with satellite channel, radio, direct-dial telephone, and welcome refreshment tray. Some ground-floor rooms are also available. The dining room has a licensed bar where your evening meal can be chosen from a varied menu which includes a variety of vegetarian meals, with specialty and vegan diets catered for.

**Tennyson Hotel.** 7 S. Park Ave., Lincoln, Lincolnshire LN5 8EM. ☎ and fax **01522/521624.** 8 rms. TV TEL. £26 ($41.60) single; £38 ($60.80) double; £46 ($73.60) family (three persons). All rates include English breakfast. AE, DC, MC, V. Bus: no. 24 or 27.

The hotel, at the edge of the wide South Common, is run warmly by Maybelle and Lino Saggiorato. The small and comfortable hotel has bedrooms with a radio, color television, self-set alarm, and tea- and coffee-making facilities. A fortifying English breakfast is served in the dining room which also offers a full choice of breakfasts. A well-appointed lounge contains original features including a fine old fireplace. You can relax here at the end of the day and have a quiet drink. Lying $1^1/_2$ miles from the cathedral precincts in the vicinity of South Park Common, near the A15 and A1434 junction, Tennyson makes a good base for exploring the area, especially if you have a car.

### Doubles for Less Than £70

**Castle Hotel.** Westgate, Lincoln, Lincolnshire LN1 3AS. ☎ **01522/538801.** Fax 01522/575457. 19 rms. TV TEL. £54 ($86.40) single; £70 ($112) double. All rates include English breakfast and newspaper. MC, V.

This privately owned red-brick three-story traditional English hotel in old Lincoln has been carefully converted from the North District National School dating back to 1858 and boasts views of the castle and cathedral—just a 3-minute walk away. The bedrooms have been individually decorated and are named after British castles. Good English-style cooking can be enjoyed by candlelight amid tapestry screens in the oak-paneled Knights Restaurant, open daily from 7 to 9:30pm and Sunday from noon to 2pm; lunch is £8.95 ($14.30) and a la carte dinner is from £12 to £22 ($19.20 to $35.20).

✪ **Hillcrest Hotel.** 15 Lindum Terrace, Lincoln, Lincolnshire LN2 5RT. ☎ and fax **01522/510182.** 17 rms. TV TEL. Mon–Thurs £47 ($75.20) single; £65 ($104) double. Fri–Sun £37 ($59.20) single; £62 ($99.20) double. All rates include English breakfast. AE, MC, V. To get here, from Wragby Rd., connect with Upper Lindum St.; continue to the bottom of this street, make a left onto Lindum Terrace, and the hotel is 200 yards along on the right.

This fine red-brick house was built in 1871 as the private home of a local vicar, and although it has been converted into a comfortable, small licensed hotel, it retains many of its original features. The Hillcrest suits travelers who appreciate a cozy atmosphere where personal tastes can be accommodated. It's on a quiet, tree-lined road overlooking 26 acres of parkland, in the old high town and within easy walking distance of Lincoln Cathedral and the Roman remains. All bedrooms are well furnished and kept in shape. The Terrace Restaurant offers a wide variety of English dishes with a European flavor cooked to order, with special menus for vegetarians and children.

### WHERE TO EAT

**Brown's Pie Shop.** 33 Steep Hill. ☎ **01522/527330.** Reservations recommended. Main courses £8.75–£13.50 ($14–$21.60). MC, V. Daily 11:30am–11pm. ENGLISH.

This restaurant, housed in a building dating from 1527, was previously a hotel and sheltered Lawrence of Arabia several times. Near the cathedral, it is today a beamed and rustic English dining room. As the name suggests, it specializes in pies, including fish pies, vegetarian pies, steak-and-kidney pies, chicken-and-chestnut pies, and more. Don't like pies? Try Cumberland sausage or honey-glazed spareribs. Some of the dishes are based on 15th-century recipes. It's good, wholesome cooking, aimed at filling you up.

**Crust.** 252 Upper High St. ☎ **01522/540322.** Reservations recommended. Main courses £5.95–£11.70 ($9.50–$18.70); three-course fixed-price meals £6.35 ($10.15) at lunch, £10–£13 ($16–$20.80) at dinner, £9.65 ($15.45) vegetarian meal. AE, DC, MC, V. Sun–Mon 11:30am– 2:30pm; Tues–Sat 11:30am–2:30pm and 7–10:15pm. INTERNATIONAL/VEGETARIAN.

This bistro-style steak house restaurant in a 1790s building is in a pedestrian zone in the town's center; there are ample parking facilities. Lincoln's cathedral is a 10-minute walk away up one of the town's most historic streets. The chef and patron, Malta-born Victor Vella, has won a number of awards. His talent is reflected in dishes such as veal maréchale, coq au vin (chicken in white wine), and traditional versions of roast beef with Yorkshire pudding. More imagination in the kitchen is shown here than at most Lincoln eateries. Vegetarian menus are also served. Since the restaurant is located on the second floor, it is not wheelchair accessible.

**Lion and Snake.** 79 Bailgate. ☎ **01522/523770.** Main courses £4.10–£7.95 ($6.55–$12.70); pub snacks from £1.25 ($2); three-course Sun lunch £6.75 ($10.80). AE, MC, V. Pub: Mon–Sat 11am–11pm; Sun noon–3pm and 7:30–10:30pm. Restaurant: Mon–Fri 11:30am–2:30pm; Sat noon–2pm; Sun noon–3pm. TRADITIONAL BRITISH.

The oldest pub in Lincoln, still with its original windows, was once the old stables. The place is reputedly haunted; ghosts have been spotted in the basement and also upstairs. It also has great views of the sites of Lincoln including the cathedral which can be seen from the pub. You'll enjoy a traditional steak-and-kidney pie, fish and chips, roast beef, or a three-course meal, and a restorative pint in this unique, old pub. A particularly good bet is the fisherman's selection, including filet of cod, breaded haddock, and salmon steak.

**Lord Tennyson.** 72 Rasen Lane. ☎ **01522/530690.** Main courses £4–£9 ($6.40–$14.40). No credit cards. Mon–Sat noon–2:30pm and 5:30–9pm; Sun noon–2:30pm. BRITISH.

This busy, old pub is located just off Yarborough Road at the top of the hill near the cathedral. You can enjoy excellent traditional British food at reasonable prices. A two-course lunch special costs only £2.99 to £3.99 ($4.80 to $6.40) Monday through Saturday from noon to 2pm, or you can get a huge steak dinner and a bottle of wine for two for £10.99 ($17.60).

**Stokes High Bridge Café.** 207 High St. ☎ **01522/513825.** Morning and afternoon teas £2–£4.60 ($3.20–$7.35); lunches from £4 ($6.40). MC, V. Mon–Sat 9am–5pm. BRITISH.

This busy tearoom is located in a 16th-century half-timbered style house built on a medieval high bridge, circa 1160, over the Witham River. Morning tea is served from 9am to 11:20am when you can get anything with your tea from scones and jam and tea cakes from 85p ($1.35) to a fried egg over toast for £2 ($3.20). Lunch is served from 11:20am to 2pm when you can get a steak pie or quiche for a little over £4 ($6.40). From 2 to 4:40pm afternoon tea, which is similar to the morning tea, is served. This is truly a relaxing experience; sip your tea while you watch the calming water and the swans go by.

## LINCOLN AFTER DARK

To add a little variety to your nightlife, check in with the **Theatre Royal,** Clasketgate (☎ **01522/525555**), a small Victorian theater near the city center, featuring drama, comedy, opera, ballet, and touring musical groups year-round. The box office is open Monday through Saturday from 10am until 6pm, and tickets for most shows range from £7 to £16 ($11.20 to $25.60).

If you're looking for a drink and maybe a band in a unique atmosphere, visit **Cornhill Vaults,** Cornhill Exchange, opposite the Central Market (☎ **01522/535113**), a Roman wine cellar converted into a subterranean pub and club full of nooks and crannies scattered with brewery relics. Weekends often feature free hard rock bands, and the place gets packed and smoky.

Pubs remain one of the best ways to gauge the temperament of a town or village, and Lincoln's pubs are largely friendly places. Drop by the **Adam & Eve Tavern,** Lundum Hill (☎ **01522/537108**), the oldest pub in Lincoln, dating to 1701, where you can knock back a Magnet, Old Speckled Hen, or Theakston's Best Bitter in a homey, cottage atmosphere complete with gas fires and a large front garden for warm weather drinking and browsing. The **Jolly Brewer,** 27 Broadgate (☎ **01522/ 528583**), dates to 1850; it's a basic wooden floorboards place where you'll be welcomed into a mixed straight and gay drinking crowd. If you're hungry, there's pub grub at lunchtime only, and draft ales include Spitfire no. 3 and Bass, as well as rotating guests.

# 17

# The Northwest Cities: Manchester, Liverpool & Chester

Great industrial developments of the 19th century cast an extended shadow of darkness over England's northwest, so much so that the area has been relatively neglected by visitors. Most Americans who make it here tend to rush through it en route to the glories of the Lake District and Scotland. In spite of its industry and bleak commercial area, however, England's northwest has considerable beauty. Manchester, Lancaster, Morecambe, and Southport—to name just a few—are all cities of interest, and much of the beautiful countryside has inns, restaurants, and pubs worth visiting, along with many other sightseeing attractions.

We will concentrate on three of the region's more popular cities: Manchester, Liverpool, and Chester. We'll take a side trip to Blackpool, which is Coney-Island tacky, but also the largest vacation resort in Europe. You may want to visit it not so much for its beaches but for its kitschy, Old-World appeal.

Once-dull Manchester, which only began as a city in 1853 but became a major center of the Industrial Revolution, is taking on new vitality. Many North Americans whose plane lands here instead of London sometimes wish they'd budgeted more time for this city; today it's one of the hippest in England, with good restaurants, attractions, and hotels. It is increasingly gentrified and no longer the "devil's darkness," as Ruskin memorably described it.

Many travelers make a pop culture pilgrimage to Liverpool, birthplace of the Beatles, to retrace the steps of the group that redefined pop and rock music the world over. But the city has done much in recent years to revitalize its tourist industry beyond its Beatle connection, especially since the restoration of its waterfront, which today houses many museums and exhibitions. An extension of London's Tate Gallery also opened here in 1988, with a collection of modern art.

Chester, world renowned for its cheese, is in Cheshire. This low-lying, largely agricultural northwestern county borders Wales and has had a turbulent history. The towns and villages of Cheshire offer a good base for touring north Wales, the most beautiful part of that little country.

## 1 Manchester: Gateway to the North

202 miles NW of London; 86 miles N of Birmingham; 35 miles E of Liverpool

The second largest metropolitan region in England, Manchester is gaining increased importance for foreign travelers because major airlines now fly here from North America, making the city a gateway to northern England; once the only option was to fly into London. In recent years, Manchester has made great strides to abandon its image as an industrial wasteland. Although chimneys still spike the skyline, they no longer make the metropolitan sky an ash-filled canopy. As in New York, abandoned warehouses are being renovated to provide posh quarters for upscale urbanites. Rustic factory equipment turns up in museums rather than piling up in salvage yards. Even the Victorian architecture that gave a beautiful facade to the town in its "heyday" has been given a face-lift. The overall effect is a rough-around-the-edges charm—like a favorite uncle who just happens to be a chimney sweep.

The stars of Manchester today are the hit band Oasis, known for their rowdy rock star antics. If the band, which pays overt homage to the Beatles, haven't done for Manchester what their idols did to put Liverpool on the charts, many of their fans would say they're on their way. *Definitely Maybe* was the fastest selling debut album in British history.

Manchester's roots go all the way back to A.D. 79, when the Romans settled here. It remained under Roman occupation until A.D. 410, when the empire began its storied decline. The west gate has since been reconstructed upon the original site. Little is known of Manchester's Middle Ages.

The historical images most popularly associated with the city derive from the mid-17th century, when this harbinger of the Industrial Revolution first began to capitalize on the wealth of opportunity that the burgeoning textile industry offered. The ubiquitous sheep population of England had afforded the town a prosperous lot in woolens, but with the mass production of cotton and silks in the 18th century, Manchester became the Dickensian paradigm of the industrial complex and urban plight. The railways were equally responsible for catapulting the city to the forefront of the industrial movement. Still the grand empire, England found a town in Manchester that was at once both a convenient terminus and refinement center through which raw goods became viable exports. Appropriately, the Museum of Science and Technology resides here.

Many of the factory laborers were immigrants who flocked to the city for the promise of work. The atrocity of their conditions is well documented. What remains lesser known is the profound effect these migrations ultimately had on the city's culture. Today, nearly 20,000 descendants of Chinese immigrants give Manchester England's highest Chinese population outside London. The Chinese residents have adapted their surroundings to fit their heritage. Faulkner Street, particularly the monumental Imperial Chinese Archway, is brought to life by the murals, gardens, and vibrant decor that pay homage to the once-displaced working force.

## ESSENTIALS

**GETTING THERE    By Plane**    More and more North Americans are flying directly to Manchester to begin their explorations of the United Kingdom. **British Airways** (☎ **0345/222111,** only accessible in the U.K., or 800/247-9297 in the U.S. and Canada) is able to issue tickets that start your tour of England in Manchester and bring it to its conclusion in London, thus avoiding the traffic jams of London during one leg of a visit. British Airways has daily flights departing New York's JFK airport for Manchester at 6:15pm, arriving after 7 hours in the air at 6:10am local

ENGLAND

The Northwest

★ London

Keswick

*Ullswater*

**LAKE DISTRICT NATIONAL PARK**

A591

Grasmere ○ ○ Rydal

A6 M6

○ Ambleside

Hawkshead ○

Coniston ○ ○ Windermere

A595

A5084 A592 A5074

Bowness ○

A6068

○ Kirby Lonsdale

**YORKSHIRE DALES NATIONAL PARK**

Barrow-in-Furness ○

*Morecambe Bay*

A6

M6

Morecambe ○ ○ Lancaster A65

Heysham ○

Fleetwood ○

A6 M6

**LANCASHIRE**

○ Keighley

*Irish Sea*

**Blackpool** ○

M55

M65 ○ Burnley

Preston ○

Blackburn ○

Huddersfield ○

Halifax ○

Southport ○

M6

Rochdale ○

A59

Bolton ○

A565

A6

Bury ○

Oldham ○

*Liverpool Bay*

○ Wigan

Birkenhead ○

A580

M62

A628

**Liverpool** ○

M62

**Manchester**

M53

Warrington ○

○ Stockport

*R. Hersey*

A34

A55

A54 ○ Northwich

Macclesfield ○

**Chester** ○

M6

A34

A53

0    85 km
     50 mi

N

↓ Stoke-on-Trent

3-0590

**THE PENNINES**

time the next day. All flights are nonstop and nonsmoking. You can also fly from BA's many North American gateways nonstop to London, and from here, take the almost shuttlelike service from either Gatwick or Heathrow airports to Manchester, a 50-minute flight.

**American Airlines** (☎ 800/433-7300 in the U.S. and Canada) offers a daily nonstop flight to Manchester from Chicago's O'Hare Airport that departs at 6:10pm, arriving the following morning. American also flies from London's Heathrow back to Chicago.

Manchester is also the target for dozens of flights coming in from the European continent. **Lufthansa** (☎ 800/645-3880) has frequent nonstop flights each week between Frankfurt and Manchester, depending on the season. Flight time is 1 hour and 45 minutes.

To get the details of international arrivals, call the airport flight line at ☎ 0839/888747. For more information on domestic arrivals, call ☎ 0839/888757.

**By Train, Bus & Car**   From London's Euston Station take **British Rail** (☎ 0345/484950,** only accessible in the U.K.) directly to Manchester. The trip takes 2¹/₂ hours.

**National Express** (☎ 0990/808080,** only accessible in the U.K.) buses serve the Manchester region from London's Victoria Coach Station.

If you're driving from London to Manchester, go north on the M1 and the M6. At junction 21A, go east on the M62, which becomes the M602 as you enter Manchester. London-to-Manchester usually takes from 3 hours to 3¹/₂ hours, but it could be longer because of traffic and construction.

## GETTING FROM THE AIRPORT TO TOWN

Manchester's airport, 15 miles south of the town center, is convenient for those staying overnight. Visitors are linked to the center by both public transportation and a motorway network. The Airport Link, a modern above-ground train, connects the airport terminal to the Piccadilly Railway Station downtown in Manchester. Trains leave every 15 minutes from 5:15pm to 10:10pm, sometimes through the night. The ride takes 25 minutes. Direct rail lines link the airport to surrounding northern destinations such as Edinburgh, Liverpool, and Windermere.

Buses numbered 44 and 105 run between the airport and Piccadilly Gardens Bus Station every 15 minutes (hourly during the evenings and on Sunday). The bus ride takes 55 minutes.

**VISITOR INFORMATION**   The **Manchester Visitor Centre,** Town Hall Extension, Lloyd Street (☎ 0161/234-3157) is open Monday to Saturday from 10am to 5:30pm and Sunday from 11am to 4pm. To reach it, take the Metrolink tram to St. Peter's Square. Especially useful are a series of four free pamphlets with information on accommodations, dining, city attractions, and cultural/entertainment options.

**GETTING AROUND**   It's not a good idea to try to "hoof it" in Manchester. It's better to take the bus and Metrolink. Timetables, bus routes, fare information, and

## Impressions

*With a population of 2.6 million, Manchester today is second only to London in terms of employment, in the importance of its financial and business sectors, and in the diversity of its cultural, sporting, and leisure facilities. And as Mancunians say: "What Manchester thinks today, London thinks tomorrow—so, London the game is on!"*
                                                          —Samantha Hannam, Writer, 1997

# Manchester

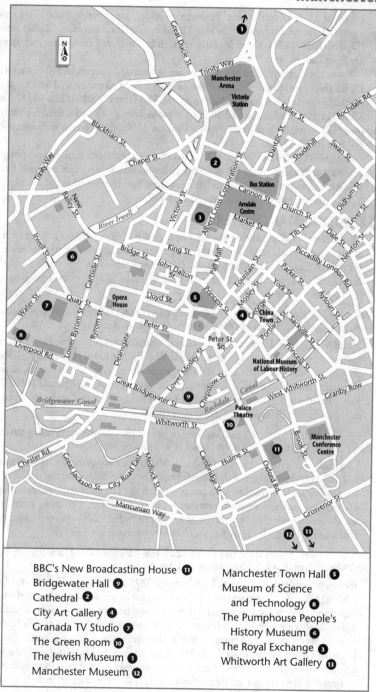

BBC's New Broadcasting House ⑪
Bridgewater Hall ⑨
Cathedral ②
City Art Gallery ④
Granada TV Studio ⑦
The Green Room ⑩
The Jewish Museum ①
Manchester Museum ⑫

Manchester Town Hall ⑤
Museum of Science
  and Technology ⑧
The Pumphouse People's
  History Museum ⑥
The Royal Exchange ③
Whitworth Art Gallery ⑬

a copy of a helpful leaflet, the "Passenger's Guide," are available from The Kiosk, a general information booth within the Piccadilly Gardens bus station, Market Street (☎ **0161/627-2828**). Open Monday through Friday from 7am to 8pm and Saturday from 8am to 8pm.

Buses begin running within Manchester at 6am and operate in full force until 11pm, then continue with limited routes until 3am. Tickets are sold at a kiosk at Piccadilly Gardens bus station. A day pass, the **Wayfarer** (☎ **0161/228-7811**) costs £5.50 ($8.80) for adults and £2.80 ($4.50) for children 5–15 and is valid for a complete day of public bus travel. Another source of bus information is **Stagecoach** (☎ **0161/273-3377**).

**Metrolink** (☎ **0161/205-2000**) streetcars connect the bus stations and provide a useful north-south conduit. Self-service ticket machines dispense zone-based fares. The streetcars operate Monday to Saturday from 6am to midnight, and on Sunday from 7am to 11pm. They are wheelchair accessible.

## EXPLORING MANCHESTER

Manchester has all the attractions most equate with a big city. There's the town hall at St. Peter's Square, and the usual fare of museums and galleries, plus canals and waterways, Castlefield, Chinatown, the Gay Village behind the bus station, and the Northern Quarter. There's enough here to make Manchester a single-stop destination.

**Manchester Town Hall.** St. Peter's Court. ☎ **0161/234-3157.** Free admission. Mon–Fri 9am–5pm. Guided tours 2nd and 4th Wed 2pm. Piccadilly train station.

Alfred Waterhouse designed this neo-Gothic structure that first opened in 1877, and extensions were added just prior to World War II. The tower rises nearly 300 feet above the town. The Great Hall and its signature hammerbeam roof houses 12 pre-Raphaelite murals by Ford Max Brown, commissioned between 1852 and 1856. The paintings chronicle the town's storied past from the 1st-century Roman Occupation to the Industrial Revolution of the 19th century.

**Cathedral.** Victoria St., beside the river. Free admission. Daily 8am–6pm. Piccadilly train station; "Central Line" bus or walk down Market St. and turn right on Victoria St.

Originally just a medieval parish in 1421, Manchester was granted cathedral status in 1847 with the creation of the new diocese. The cathedral's nave, the widest of its kind in Britain, is formed by six bays, as is the choir. The choir stall features unique 16th-century misericord seats—caricatures of medieval life. The choir screen is a wood carving from the same era. Carel Weight provided a 20th-century canvas rendition of the beatitudes as well as a sculpture by typographer Eric Gill.

**City Art Gallery.** Mosley St. ☎ **0161/236-5244.** Free Admission. Mon 11am–5:30pm; Tues–Sat 10am–5:30pm; Sun 2–5:30pm. Metrolink Tram to Albert Sq.

Its stately neoclassical premises, built between 1827 and 1834, contain many of the paintings that were accumulated by the city's wealthy industrialists during the heyday of their prosperity. Consequently, the museum boasts one of the best collections of Pre-Raphaelite paintings in Britain, with at least 30 by one of the genre's leaders, Ford Madox Brown. The entrance hall is lined with plaster castings made directly from the Elgin marbles, exact duplicates of the originals in London that used a process that would never be allowed today. Other artworks include an eclectic collection of British and European art dating from the 1300s to the present, including some works by Gainsborough, Turner, and a collection of paintings by such postwar artists as Derek Jarman.

If you're here between May and September, consider a visit to **Heaton Hall,** the museum's annex 4 miles to the east. It's the centerpiece of 650 acres of rolling parkland, accessible via the Metrolink tram (get off at Heaton Park). Built of York stone in 1772, and filled with furniture and decorative art of the 18th and 19th centuries, it is open only between May and September. Contact the City Art Gallery for opening hours. Admission is free. Address all inquiries about Heaton Hall to the City Art Gallery.

**The Jewish Museum.** Cheetham Hill Rd. ☎ **0161/834-9879.** Admission £2.50 ($4) adults; £1.75 ($2.80) children, students, and seniors; £6.50 ($10.40) family ticket. Mon–Thurs 10:30am–4pm; Sun 10:30am–5pm. Bus: no. 21, 59, or 60.

The premises here were built in the Moorish revival style in 1874 as a Sephardic synagogue. It's one of only two such museums in Britain (the other is in London). It traces the culture and history of Manchester's Jewish community, estimated today at around 40,000. Part of the emphasis is on the experiences of immigrants, many from Eastern Europe, whose recorded voices describe the experience of life in Manchester's Jewish quarter in the years before World War II.

**The Pumphouse People's History Museum.** Left Bank, Bridge St. ☎ **0161/839-6061.** Admission £1 ($1.60) adults Sat–Thurs, free Fri; free for students, seniors, and children. Tues–Sun 11am–4:30pm. Tram: Metrolink to Albert Sq.

Few other museums in Europe catalog and commemorate the social history of the working class as carefully and with as much academic neutrality as this one. The origins of this museum began in 1990 when it was designated as the resting place of most of the archives of Britain's communist party. Despite the fact that every exhibit is carefully couched in apolitical terms, it remains the most controversial museum in the Midlands, the focus of the hopes and dreams of hundreds of supporters and detractors both within and outside the local Labourite government. The building was constructed as a pumping station during the Victorian age. Today it contains the largest collection of trade union flags in the country. Of special note are exhibitions that relate the 1819 Peterloo Massacre of trade union activists by government forces, and the ongoing struggles of the coal miners of Yorkshire in their fight for higher wages and better working conditions.

**Manchester Museum.** University of Manchester, Oxford Rd., near Booth St. ☎ **0161/839-6061.** Free admission. Mon–Sat 10am–5pm. Tram: Metrolink to St. Peter's Sq., then bus no. 41, 42, or 45.

Maintained under the auspices of the local university, this venerable museum showcases an eclectic and sometimes eccentric collection of the spoils brought back by local industrialists from their adventurous forays outside of England. Among archaeological ornaments excavated from all over the world, it contains England's largest collection of ancient Egyptian mummies outside the British Museum in London.

## CASTLEFIELD: THE CITY'S HISTORIC CORE

Manchester's origins began in Castlefield, the city's historic core that local authorities have recently designated an "urban heritage park." It comprises the densely populated neighborhood that housed as many as 2,000 civilians beginning in A.D. 79, when Manchester was *Mancestra,* a fortified Roman camp strategically positioned between other Roman outposts Chester and Carlisle. The roots of modern-day Manchester began here, providing the basic goods and services that supplied the soldiers in the nearby fort. After the Romans abandoned their fortress in A.D. 411, the settlement stood alone throughout the Dark Ages, a bastion of once and future prosperity.

Castlefield's name derives from the early Middle Ages, when the remains of the Roman fort and its surrounding parklands were known as the Castle in the Field.

Castlefield's next major development was the Bridgewater Canal, which transferred coal from Worsley. Many other goods passed through this center because of the ease of transportation. Warehouses arose around the wharfs, their names suggesting their wares (i.e. Potato Wharf). Later, Liverpool Road housed the world's first passenger railway station, today home to the Museum of Science and Technology. Although the city atrophied for decades after its reign as industrial capital of the world, an interest in historical renewal emerged in the 1970s. Many of the grand canals and warehouses have been restored, and Castlefield is once again a thriving vibrant area full of attractions.

The **Granada TV Studio,** Water Street, Castlefield (☎ **0161/832-9090**), produces many of the most popular and most widely distributed TV series in Britain. A private corporation, Granada is Britain's second largest producer of television programs, behind only the BBC. Many of its made-for-TV movies and series ("A Tale of Two Cities"; "Adventures of Sherlock Holmes"; and "Children's Ward") have been staples on public television in the United States.

With a style and flair that evokes Atlanta's CNN, Granada opens the backstage area of its studios to public scrutiny every day except Monday (when the areas are used for filming). As such, the studio is one of the most popular attractions in the Midlands. Although tours last for only 45 minutes, there are so many exhibitions and displays on view that many participants extend their visits to fill several hours touring through the memorabilia of TV shows that are household words throughout the U.K. Between May and September, tours are conducted Tuesday to Sunday from 9:45am to 4:30pm. Between October and April, they're conducted Tuesday to Sunday from 9:45am to 7pm. Participation in the tour and access to the exhibits costs £12.99 ($20.80) for adults, £9.99 ($16) for children 5 to 14, and free for kids 4 and under. Reservations in advance are a good idea, if only to learn about last-minute changes to the activities and opening hours. The tour entrance is across the street from the Victoria & Albert Hotel.

The **Museum of Science and Industry,** Liverpool Road, Castlefield (☎ **0161/832-1830**), is located 1 mile north of Manchester's center. Set within five separate and antique buildings, the premises were built in 1830 as the first railway station in the world. Its many exhibits celebrate the Industrial Revolution and its myriad inventions and developments, such as printing, the railway industry, the role of electricity in the factory and home, textile manufacturing, the use and manufacture of machine tools and industrial machinery, plus the history of flight and aerospace exploration. Admission is £5 ($8) for adults and £3 ($4.80) for children. Parking costs £1.50 ($2.40). The museum is open daily from 10am to 5pm, except Dec 24 to 26. Take bus route 33.

For the more aesthetically minded, the **Whitworth Art Gallery,** located at the University of Manchester on Oxford Road near the corner of Denmark Road (☎ **0161/275-7450**), was originally established in 1889 with a bequest to the city from a wealthy industrialist. The gallery was opened to the public in 1908 with a magnificent red-brick facade. Today, behind that same facade lies a light and spacious interior. The gallery is one of the richest research sources in England for antique patterns of wallpaper and textiles and the weaving techniques that produced them. There's a superb collection of 18th- and 19th-century watercolors on display, including many by Turner and by the offspring of wealthy businesspeople who produced sketches and drawings during their grand tour of the continent of Europe. There's no charge for admission, and the gallery stays open Monday to Saturday from 10am to 5pm and on Sunday from 2 to 5pm. Take the Metrolink to St. Peter's Square then hop on bus no. 41, 42, or 45.

## SHOPPING MANCHESTER: MILL SHOPS, MALLS & MORE

This gateway city of the north is a shopping megalopolis. Not only does it offer a vast number and variety of boutiques, shops, galleries, and craft centers, but Manchester is also one of the last remaining strongholds for shopping bargains in all of England.

Although not located in one centralized location, most of the larger shopping precincts in the city are reserved for pedestrians and include the main shopping street of **King Street** and **St. Ann's Square,** full of exclusive boutiques and designer stores; **Market Street** with its many major chain and department stores along with Arndale Centre which is Manchester's largest covered shopping center; and the recently revitalized **Piccadilly and Oldham Street** for fashion, music, and plenty of bargains. Deansgate Street is not pedestrian-only, but it does have a lot of adventure sports and outdoor shops.

You should also know that some of the best shopping around is found in the outlying suburbs of Manchester. So don't overlook Bolton, Oldham, Bury, Wigan, and Trafford.

### SPECIALTY SHOPS

**ANTIQUES & FINE ART**   Those of you who like to search through stacks of stuff complete with dust, soot, and grime will find Manchester and the greater Manchester area prime hunting grounds. For "recent antiques," which seem to be all the rage, go to **Design Goes Pop,** Basement Cafe Pop, 34–36 Oldham St. (☎ **0161/ 237-9688**), which stocks original decorations and "artifacts" from the 1950s, 1960s, and 1970s. **The Ginnel Antique Centre,** 18–22 Lloyd St. (☎ **0161/833-9037**), has a massive selection of books, collectibles, Art Deco and Art Nouveau pottery, glass, and furniture. Check out **The Antiques Gallery,** Royal Exchange Shopping Centre, St. Ann's Square (☎ **0161/834-3731**), for a stash of all kinds of wares down through the ages. More refined and stylish antiques can be found along Bury New Road in Prestwich village, just outside of Manchester.

**ART GALLERIES**   If you're into contemporary art, stop by the artist-run **Castlefield Gallery,** Liverpool Road (☎ **0161/832-8034**). **The Gallery Manchester's Art House,** 131 Portland St. (☎ **0161/237-3551**) focuses on artists whose work can be classified as being from the Northern School.

**ARTS & CRAFTS**   You can really rack up a lot of one-of-a-kind items while exploring the many venues devoted to craftspeople and their art. For ceramics, glass, textiles, jewelry, toys, dollhouses, and the like, visit the exquisite Victorian building that houses **Manchester Craft Centre,** 17 Oak St. (☎ **0161/832-4274**); **The Alexandra Craft Centre,** Upper Mill, Oldham (☎ **01457/876675**); and **St. George's Craft Centre,** St. George's Road, Bolton (☎ **01204/398071**).

**FASHION**   Most of the fashion stores are centered around St. Ann's Square and King Street. Men's and women's avant-garde clothing can be found at **Flannels,** Police Street (☎ **0161/834-9442**). Classic clothes for both sexes are sold at **Racing Green,** 33 King St. (☎ **0161/835-2022**). British designers reign supreme at **De La Mode,** 24 Deansgate (☎ **0161/839-3637**).

**MARKETS**   Here in the north, markets are a tradition and offer you a great chance to jump in and barter with the locals. Locals are who you'll mainly find while wandering amongst the vendors' stalls in these old Victorian market halls. Although markets tend to sell everyday items and foodstuff, some stalls are devoted to flea-market type goods and "antiques." Market days vary throughout the city, but you're bound to find at least one in full swing each day of the work week.

Markets and their locations include Arndale Market, Market Hall, Manchester Arndale Centre; Grey Mare Lane Market, Beswick District Shopping Centre, Beswick; Moss Side Market, Moss Lane East, Moss Side. For information on Manchester's markets, call ☎ **0161/234-1282.**

**MILL SHOPS**   Manchester is an industrial stronghold with lots of textile mills. Most mills used to have a store on site, or mill shop, where customers could come to buy mill goods. Today, more and more of the mills are setting up shop in towns across the country. **Bury New Road** in Cheetham Hill near Boddingtons Brewery has a great selection of factory shops, discount stores, warehouses, cash and carry outlets, and street stalls on Sunday mornings. Some stores along this road do not sell to the general public and others require a minimum purchase.

**Jaeger Factory Shop,** Thomas Burnley, Gomersal, Cleakheaton (☎ **01274/ 852303**), has an extensive chain of outlet stores all over England (you can get a list of stores and addresses). Stock includes overruns, damages, and unhappy colors in both men's and women's clothing. This is the place to find the best price in the world on cashmere sweaters and factory knits seconds. A good line of Van Heusen shirts are available.

**A. Sanderson & Sons,** 2 Pollard St., Ancoats (☎ **0161/272-8501**), is one of England's most famous brands. The shop is right outside the heart of downtown and easy to get to. It's clean, modern, and fun to shop for fabrics by the yard, gift items made of Sanderson fabrics, as well as bed linen, carpet, and draperies.

**MUSIC**   Audiophiles take note: There's more than live Britpop to be found in Manchester. The largest secondhand album and CD shop in all of England is the city's **Vinyl Exchange Used Record & CD Shop,** 18 Oldham St. (☎ **0161/ 228-1122**), with recordings from all musical genres split between vinyl, on the first floor, and CDs, upstairs. With more than 25,000 selections in stock, it's worth setting aside some browsing time. Who knows, you may just walk out with that U.K.– only single you've been trying to track down for the past few years. Also check out the secondhand music stalls found near Piccadilly Station along Church Street. For newer music, go to **Virgin Megastore,** 52–56 Market St. (☎ **0161/8331111**). Or if you have more classical tastes, **Forsyth Brothers,** 126 Deansgate (☎ **0161/ 8343281**), vends classical music and instruments.

# WHERE TO STAY

**Blooms Hotel.** 11 Bloom St., Manchester M1 3HS. ☎ **0161/236-7198.** Fax 0161/236-1876. 31 rms, all with bath. TV TEL. Sun–Thurs £39.50 ($63.20) single; £79 ($126.40) double; Fri– Sat £34.50 ($55.20) single, £69 ($110.40) double. All rates include continental breakfast. AE, MC, V.

Located in the city center, this hotel is within walking distance of many attractions and activities. Rooms are basic but comfortable, featuring a private bath, hair dryer, and coffee- and tea-making facilities. An on-premises restaurant serves a la carte British, French, and Italian fare, and there is also a full bar located in the lobby. The hotel is gay friendly, and there's a gay nightclub, The Carousel, located on the lower level.

**The Cornerhouse Hotel.** Gravel Lane, Greengate, Manchester M3 7WQ. ☎ and fax **0161/ 833-0272.** 13 rms, 9 with shower. £15 ($24) single without shower, £25 ($40) single with shower; £25 ($40) double without shower, £35 ($56) double with shower. No credit cards.

This small hotel, located about 3 minutes by foot from the city center, offers basic accommodations at truly budget prices in the heart of Manchester. Nine rooms have a wash basin and shower, and these also feature television and tea- and coffee-making facilities. The other rooms are very simple with no amenities. At a communal kitchen you can prepare your own meals.

**Kempton House Hotel.** 400 Wilbraham Rd., Chorlton-Cum-Hardy M21 0UH. ☎ and fax **0161/881-8766.** 13 rms, 6 with bath. TV. £23 ($36.80) single without bath, £28 ($44.80) single with bath; £37 ($59.20) double with bath. All rates include English breakfast. MC, V.

A large Victorian house located 2¹/₂ miles south of the city center, this hotel provides basic, centrally located accommodations at a reasonable rate. Rooms also include tea- and coffee-making facilities, and the hotel features a small bar and lounge. Several buses run by the hotel on a regular basis. Since deregulation, there are so many independent bus companies active that it's difficult to keep track of numbers and schedules. These are best checked at the Victoria Station bus depot in city center.

**New Central House.** 144–146 Heywood St., Cheetham M8 0PD. ☎ and fax **0161/205-2169.** 10 rms, 7 with shower. TV. £20 ($32) single without shower, £21.50 ($34.40) single with shower; £33 ($52.80) double without shower, £35 ($56) double with shower. All rates include English breakfast. MC, V.

Located just off the A665 Cheetham Hill Road, 1¹/₂ miles from Victoria Station, this house offers simple but comfortable accommodations. Each room features tea- and coffee-making facilities, and there is a lounge and a bright, pleasant dining room where you can arrange dinner service upon request. Be sure and specify your needs when booking a room, since three rooms share all facilities, and none has private toilet facilities.

**Thistlewood Hotel.** 203 Urmston Lane, Stretford M32 9EF. ☎ **0161/865-3611.** Fax 0161/866-8133. 9 rms. TV. £29 ($46.40) single; £44 ($70.40) double. All rates include English breakfast. DC, MC, V.

This large Victorian house is located 4 miles from city center, close to junction 7 of the M63. Besides bathing facilities, rooms feature tea- and coffee-making facilities, trouser press, and a hair dryer. There's a comfortable lounge, and a dining room looking out over a stepped garden. In the evening, a good variety of hot and cold snacks and light meals can be arranged. Several buses stop outside the hotel.

## A YOUTH HOSTEL

✪ **YHA Manchester.** Potato Wharf, Liverpool Rd., Castlefield, Manchester M3 4NB. ☎ **0161/839-9960.** Fax 0161/835-2054. 160 beds in 40 rms. £10.60–£14 ($16.95–$22.40) adult; £7.40–£10.15 ($11.85–$16.25) youth under 18 years of age, for occupancy of rooms with 4 beds. MC, V.

Situated in a newly constructed £2 million ($3.2 million) waterfront building in the middle of the city center's Castlefield urban renewal project, this is billed as England's premiere YHA hostel, and guests have told staff that it's the nicest hostel in the world.

Each 4-bed suite has its own shower, toilet, and wash basin. Premium suites have their own television and coffee- and tea-making facilities, and private or family rooms are available as well. Besides a self-catering kitchen, the facility offers full catering and meals can either be purchased separately, or you can pay for bed-and-breakfast, half-board, or full-board accommodations, ranging from economy to premium in all categories. Purchased individually, breakfast costs £2.85 ($4.55), a standard packed lunch is £2.45 ($3.90), and a large one is £3.25 ($5.20), and dinners runs £4.25 ($6.80) for three courses. Laundry facilities include washing machines and dryers, and there is a television lounge and a game room with pool tables and video games. Free amenities include storage lockers (provide your own lock) bicycle storage, and parking (40 cars). The facility is open year-round, and allows 24-hour access to rooms, meaning no curfews or daytime lockout.

# WHERE TO EAT

**Al-Faisal Tandoori.** 58 Thomas St. ☎ **0161/834-3266.** Main courses £1.70–£3 ($2.70–$4.80). No credit cards. Mon–Fri 11am–6pm. INDIAN.

One of several nondescript Indian eateries in the immediate area, this is primarily a carryout kitchen, although a few tables are available. What is remarkable about this place is its inexpensive menu, with a chicken or lamb tikka running £2.80 ($4.50), and a large spicy vegetable curry costing £1.70 ($2.70). Prices like these keep students and budget travelers coming back.

**Atlas Bar.** 376 Deansgate. ☎ **0161/834-2124.** Lunch specials £4.95 ($7.90); main courses £5.95 ($9.50). MC, V. Food service: daily noon–2:30pm and 6–8pm. Bar hours: Mon–Sat 11am–11pm; Sun 11am–10:30pm. ITALIAN/VEGETARIAN.

This cafe and bar, located in the renovated Knott Mill complex, runs through a two-story shopfront and the undercroft of a railway arch, then spills out in back over a landscaped terrace. The front is composed entirely of glazed glass screens, creating an open atmosphere in which street traffic and cafe patrons are mutually exposed. Birch, pitch pine, York stone, and Kirkstone slate are combined to create a warm, modern interior. The menu includes a variety of salads and pasta dishes such as brown mushroom lasagna or parpadelle with roast peppers, goat cheese, and pine nuts, and specials such as a smoked salmon tart or roast vegetables with couscous and harissa dressing. Breakfast is served on Sunday from 11am until 1pm.

**Duke 92.** Castle St., below the bottom end of Deansgate. ☎ **0161/839-8646.** Ploughman's lunch £3.20 ($5.10). No credit cards. Mon–Sat 11am–11pm; Sun noon–10:30pm. BRITISH.

This pub sits in the middle of what still appears to be an old industrial area, but there's more than meets the eye going on around here, as the neighborhood is in the midst of urban renewal and is actually becoming quite trendy and full of hidden away places like this one. Built out of converted old canal horse stables, the spacious interior is a mixture of black wrought iron and whitewashed plaster walls with a handsome marble bar and Edwardian furniture placed about. A beautiful spiral staircase leads up to an upper room and balcony. It's a rather elegant interior in which to find a bargain meal but, nonetheless, this sibling to the Mark Addy "cheese" pub, offers a similar ploughman's lunch featuring a huge portion of two cheeses, two pâtés, or one of each with fresh granary bread for only £3.20 ($5.10), with cheese choices running into obscure offerings like a black currant Lancashire. The bar sells not only Boddingtons on tap but also the Belgian white wheat beer Hoegaarden. When the weather's pleasant, you can go out and sit alongside the canal.

**Lass O'Gowrie Brewhouse.** 36 Charles St. ☎ **0161/273-6932.** Lunch £1–£4 ($1.60–$6.40). Daily 11am–11pm. BRITISH.

This Victorian pub is popular with office workers at lunch, and students in the evening. It features a long bar illuminated by gas lights and a central glass cage through which you can watch beer being made in the cellar microbrewery. Its malty ales, LOG35 and LOG 42 named for their specific gravity (strength), are quite popular, as are their inexpensive lunch items, such as baps (large bread rolls filled with a variety of meats and vegetables), ploughman's lunches, sausages, and pies.

**Mark Addy.** Stanley St., Salford. ☎ **0161/832-4080.** Ploughman's lunch £3.20 ($5.10). No credit cards. Mon–Sat 11:30am–11pm; Sun noon–10pm. BRITISH.

This pub, named after a 19th-century hero who rescued more than 50 drowning people from the River Irwell outside, is one of Manchester's two great cheese pubs. A ploughman's lunch here comes with a choice of two cheeses, two pâtés, or one of each to go with fresh-baked granary bread, and they throw in a pickle as well. There are more than 50 English and European cheeses to choose from, and servings are so large that a doggy bag automatically comes with your order. Order a pint of Boddingtons or Timothy Taylors Landlord to wash it down. You may find yourself lingering here if you settle into one of the private and comfortable barrel-vaulted red sandstone bays. Outside, in warm weather, there's a courtyard bursting with color from the blossom of many flowers.

**Royal Oak.** 729 Wilmslow Rd., Didsbury. ☎ **0161/434-4788.** Ploughman's lunch £3.30 ($5.30). No credit cards. Pub daily 11am–11pm; food daily noon–2pm. BRITISH.

This old worn room is known, of all things, as a "cheese pub." Order a ploughman's lunch with your pint of Batemans Mild or Marstons Bitter or Pedigree, and you can choose either two cheeses, a cheese and a pâté, or two pâtés to go with a substantial hunk of bread. It's the 50-plus cheeses that keep lunch patrons coming back, though. Even rare cheeses are plopped down in front of you by the pound, so expect to ask for a doggy bag—it's a request the friendly staff hears all the time.

**Royal Orchid Thai Restaurant.** 36 Charlotte St. ☎ **0161/236-5183.** Main courses £3.20–£9.50 ($5.10–$15.20). AE, MC, V. Tues–Fri 11:30am–2:30pm; Mon–Sat 6:30–11:30pm. THAI.

Located close to city center, this popular restaurant offers an extensive menu of authentic Thai cuisine. Seafood, pork, chicken, and beef are available with a variety of sauces, vegetables, and noodles, and menu items include dim sum, crab claws fixed six different ways, mild Thai chicken or beef Muslim curry, garlic fried beef, pork, or chicken, or steamed fish with preserved plums. There's a respectable wine list, and house wines are available by the glass. Dine on the last Friday of the month, and you may be entertained by traditional Thai dancing.

## MANCHESTER AFTER DARK

Everyone knows about the teeming rock scene in Manchester, but the fine arts are thriving as well. There are far too many cultural events in Manchester to cover them completely, so contact **Arts About Manchester,** 23 New Mount St. (☎ **0161/953-4035**), for more detailed listings.

For drama with an unobstructed view, go to the nation's largest theater-in-the-round, **The Royal Exchange,** St. Ann's Square (☎ **0161/833-9833**), housed in a futuristic glass-and-steel structure built within the Great Hall of Manchester's former Cotton Exchange, and offering 48 weeks of in-house dramaturgy every year. Tickets for Monday through Thursday night, and Wednesday and Saturday matinee run £5 ($8), £11 ($17.60), and £14 ($22.40); tickets for Friday and Saturday night cost £6 ($9.60), £13 ($20.80), and £16 ($25.60).

Home of the renowned **Halle Orchestra, The Bridgewater Hall,** Lower Mosley Street (☎ **0161/834-3697**), a state-of-the-art, 2,400-seat concert hall, hosts a series of concerts by the orchestra through the year; while other performances booked in the hall are mainly of a classical nature, there's a little pop and comedy thrown in as well. Tickets for classical events tend to range between £5 to £26 ($8 to $41.60) with poppier events averaging about £13 ($20.80).

**The University of Manchester's Department of Music,** Dunmark Road (☎ **0161/275-4982**), is home to one of the nation's most distinctive classical string quartets, the **Lindsay String Quartet,** which performs a series of eight evening concerts in the department's auditorium during the year, with tickets £8.50 ($13.60), or £3 ($4.80) for students. For a real bargain, check on their luncheon recital series, which is free.

The BBC's **New Broadcasting House,** Oxford Road (☎ **0161/244-4001**), has free tickets to musical performances that are taped in its Studio Seven for broadcast on BBC Radio 3. Renowned ensembles perform chamber music on Tuesday and/or Friday evenings, and there's a brass festival held annually in February. The internationally acclaimed **BBC Philharmonic** performs Saturday evening concerts 12 times a year at Bridgewater Hall (box office ☎ **0161/907-9000**), with tickets ranging from £4.50 to £26 ($7.20 to $41.60).

Presenting new theater, dance, and live art at the local, national, and international levels, **The Green Room,** Whitworth West Street (☎ **0161/950-5777;** box office 0161/950-5900), a theater-cafe bar, mainly hosts performances during its two main seasons, spring (February through May) and autumn (September through December). Tickets are £5.50 ($8.80) and £6.50 ($10.40).

Check out the happenings at the **Nia Centre,** Chichester Road, Hulme (☎ **0161/226-6461;** box office 0161/227-9254), where African and Caribbean culture are explored through performances of dance, theater, and music. Tickets average between £5 to £8 ($8 to $12.80).

## THE CLUB & MUSIC SCENE

Above all else, Manchester is known for its recent contributions to pop music. From 1980s stalwarts New Order and The Smiths to the Stone Roses and Oasis, the "Manchester sound" is known throughout the world. Surprisingly enough, however, live music venues went by the wayside in the early 1990s and have been in short supply until the last couple of years, in which time they've made a steady comeback. The city's most famous music club, **The Hacienda,** 11–13 Whitworth St. W. (☎ **0161/236-5051**), never disappeared, but ironically it was always a dance club featuring only 1 night of live music. The former yacht showroom, once co-owned by New Order and Factory Records, struck boldly, launching The Smiths, New Order, and the Stone Roses out of its Tuesday night "Stone Love" showcase, when three bands took to the stage every week. As popular as it is legendary, "Stone Love" still happens on Tuesday, when a chance to see the next big thing will cost you £1.50 ($2.40) before 10pm, and £3.50 ($5.60) thereafter.

Hooking up with the same booking agents, the **Boardwalk,** Little Peter Street (☎ **0161/228-3555**), has gained popularity by hosting "Stone Love II," an extension of the Hacienda's showcase. The club features live bands on Friday, when the cover charge is £5 ($8) before 11pm, and £7 ($11.20) after, and Saturday, when the cover charge is £3.50 ($5.60) before 11pm, and £4.50 ($7.20) thereafter.

Other nights of the week, head to **The Roadhouse,** Newton Street (☎ **0161/228-1789**), the hottest small venue in Manchester, which hosts bands up to 7 nights a week, with a cover charge varying from £1 to £5 ($1.60 to $8). Monday through Saturday check out **Band on the Wall,** 25 Swan St. at Oak Street (☎ **0161/832-6625**), where live rock, blues, jazz, and reggae can be heard for a cover charge varying between £5 to £7 ($8 to $11.20). For edgier music, check the stage at **Star & Garter,** Barefield Street (☎ **0161/273-6726**), on Wednesday through Friday, when harder rock and hardcore acts will get in your face for a mere £2 ($3.20).

Live venues are on their way back, but dance clubs have taken over the town in the past 5 years. Just stroll through the Castlefield district on a weekend night, and check out all the bars featuring a DJ. Clubs are everywhere, and among the best are the aforementioned **Hacienda,** which plays everything from old soul to drum-and-bass, and **The Roadhouse,** where Friday night's "One Tree Island," featuring dub-ambient music, is a hot stop for £5 ($8).

On York Street near Oxford Road, **The Holy City Zoo** (☎ **0161/273-7467**), offers up everything from garage to house on Thursday through Saturday nights, with a cover charge of £4 ($6.40) on Thursday, £6 ($9.60) on Friday, and £7 ($11.20) on Saturday. Located in the old three-story headquarters of Factory Records, **Paradise Factory,** 112–116 Princess St. (☎ 0161/273-5422), offers up techno and disco to a mainly gay crowd. Admission is free Tuesday through Thursday, and the cover charge on Monday is £1 ($1.60) before 11pm and £2 ($3.20) thereafter; Friday it's £2 ($3.20), and Saturday, when you can dance until 4am, the cover is £5 ($8) before 11:30pm, and £7 ($11.20) thereafter. Also catering to a mainly gay crowd, **Dickens,** Oldham St. (☎ 0161/236-4886), pumps out disco and other dance styles on weekends, when the cover charge is £3.50 ($5.60) before 11:30pm, and £4 ($6.40) thereafter.

## A PUB CRAWL

The rock and dance scenes start late, so prepare for your evening with an early pint or two in one of the pubs. The city's oldest, **Old Wellington Inn,** Shambles Square (☎ 0161/832-7619), dates back to 1378 and feels like it. Ask about the pub's long history over a pint of Bass or Worthington's.

The **Peveril of the Peak,** Great Bridgewater Street (☎ 0161/236-6364), is easy enough to find: Just look for a 380-year-old triangular building covered in tile from top to bottom. No one seems to know why it was designed or built that way, but you can step inside and enjoy a pint of Wilson's Original, Theakston's Best Bitter, Yorkshire Terrier, or Webster's Best Bitter while you puzzle over it.

**Manto,** 46 Canal St., behind Chorlton Street Coach Station (☎ 0161/236-2667), is more than a gay pub, it's a major scene unto itself, and serves as a sort of clearinghouse of information on the hottest happenings in the gay scene weekly. Read the flyers posted around the interior and strike up a conversation with an employee or regular to find out what's what if you're out and about.

An 18th-century pub nestled in the midst of Manchester's urban renewal, **Sinclairs,** Shambles Square (☎ 0161/834-0430), in Arndale Centre between Deansgate and Corporation Street, looks lost among the surrounding modern architecture, but offers the weary laborer or traveler a friendly, charming place to grab a pint or a quick bite to eat. There's a series of small rooms with low-beam ceilings and oak paneling in which you can settle while enjoying a Sam Smiths, or maybe some lamb and apricot casserole or chicken, leek, and cider bake.

A late Victorian drinking house renowned for its environment as well as its ales, the **Marble Arch,** 73 Rochdale Rd., Ancoats, corner of Gould Street (☎ 0161/832-5914), just east of Victoria Station, has high barrel-vaulted ceilings, extensive marble and tile surfaces, mosaic barroom floor, carved wooden mantlepiece, and glazed brick walls. It's a great place to linger over a pint of Hopwood Bitter, Oak Wobbly Bob, or Titanic Captain Smith. If you get hungry, they offer all day breakfast or chili. If you like slapstick, the Laurel and Hardy Preservation Society shows old movies on the third Wednesday of the month.

# 2  Liverpool

219 miles NW of London; 103 miles NW of Birmingham; 35 miles W of Manchester

Liverpool, with its famous waterfront on the River Mersey, is a great shipping port and industrial center that gave the world such famous figures as the fictional Fannie Hill and the Beatles. King John launched it on its road to glory when he granted it a charter in 1207. Before that, it had been a tiny 12th-century fishing village, but it quickly became a port for shipping men and materials to Ireland. In the 18th century it grew to prominence as a result of the sugar, spice, and tobacco trade with the Americans. By the time Victoria came to the throne, Liverpool had become Britain's biggest commercial seaport.

Recent refurbishing of the Albert Dock, establishment of a Maritime Museum, and the converting of warehouses into little stores similar to those in Ghirardelli Square in San Francisco have made this an up-and-coming area once again, with many attractions for visitors. Liverpudlians are proud of their city, with its new hotels, two cathedrals, shopping and entertainment complexes, and parks with 2,400 acres of open spaces in and around the city. Liverpool's main shopping street, Church, is traffic free. And of course, whether Beatles fans or not, most visitors to Liverpool want to see where Beatlemania began.

## ESSENTIALS

**GETTING THERE**   Liverpool has its own airport, **Speke** (☎ **0151/486-8877**), which has frequent daily flights from many parts of the United Kingdom, including London, the Isle of Man, and Ireland.

Frequent express trains depart London's Euston Station for Liverpool, a 2¼-hour trip. For schedules and information, call ☎ **0345/484950.** There is also frequent service from Manchester, a 1-hour ride away.

National Express buses depart London's Victoria Coach Station depart every 2-hours for the 4¼-hour trip to Liverpool. Buses also arrive every hour from Manchester, a 1-hour ride away. For schedules and information, call ☎ **0990/808080.**

If you're driving from London, head north on the M1, then northwest on the M6 to the junction with M62, which heads west to Liverpool.

**VISITOR INFORMATION**   The **Tourist Information Centre,** at the Atlantic Pavilion, Albert Dock (☎ **0151/708-8838**), is open daily from 10am to 5:30pm. There is also a Tourist Information Centre in the City Centre: Merseyside Welcome Centre, Clayton Square (☎ **0151/708-8838**) that's open Monday and Wednesday to Saturday from 9:30am to 5:30pm and on Tuesday from 10am to 5:30pm.

## BEATLEMANIA: BUS TOURS & MORE

**Cavern City Tours** (☎ **0151/236-9091**) presents a daily 2-hour Magical Mystery Tour, departing from Albert Dock at 2:20pm and from Clayton Square at 2:30pm. The bus tour covers the most famous attractions associated with the Beatles, including Strawberry Field, Penny Lane, the registry office where Lennon married his first wife, and the site of the Cavern Club. Tickets cost £6.50 ($10.40) and are sold at the Tourist Information Centre at the Atlantic Pavilion on Albert Dock or at the Merseyside Welcome Center on Clayton Square. For more information about tickets, call either ☎ **0151/708-8838** or 0151/236-9091.

The annual Beatles Festival, which attracts about 100,000 people, is held at the end of August featuring music, performances, and much more.

In the Britannia Pavilion at Albert Dock, you can visit **"The Beatles Story"** (☎ **0151/709-1963**), a museum housing memorabilia of the famous group, including a yellow submarine with live fish swimming past the portholes. It's open daily from 10am to 6pm. Admission is £5.45 ($8.70) for adults and £3.95 ($6.30) for children and students.

### Impressions

*A sunny optimism permeated everything and possibilities seemed limitless . . . The Beatles were at their peak and were looked up to in awe as arbiters of a positive new age in which the dead customs of the older generation would be refreshed and remade through the creative energy of the classless young.*

—Ian MacDonald, *Revolution in the Head* (1996)

# Liverpool

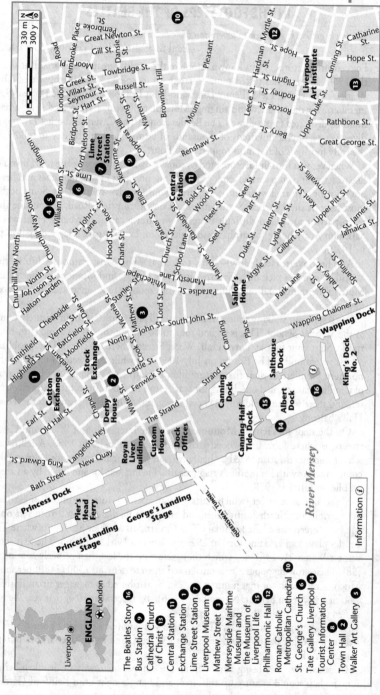

330 m
300 y

N

Great Newton St.
Pembroke St.
Gill St.
Dansie St.
Moor pl.
Pembroke Place
London Road
Greek St.
Villars St.
Seymour St.
Hart St.
Birdport St.
Lord Nelson St.
Lime St.
William Brown St.
Churchill Way South
Churchill Way North
Islington
North St.
Johnson St.
Halton Garden
Cheapside
Vernon St.
Batchelor
Dale St.
Moorfields
Smithfield St.
Highfield St.
Tithebarn St.
Earl St.
Old Hall St.
Chapel St.
Derby House
Vernon St.
Victoria St.
Stanley St.
North John St.
Mathew St.
Lord St.
South John St.
Castle St.
Fenwick St.
Cook St.
Water St.
Langelots Hey
New Quay
King Edward St.
Bath Street

Towbridge St.
Russell St.
Tong St.
Warren St.
Brownlow Hill
Mount Pleasant
Renshaw St.
Mount
Leece St.
Roscoe St.
Rodney St.
Pilgrim St.
Hardman St.
Myrtle St.
Hope St.
Catharine St.
Canning St.
Hope St.
Rathbone St.
Great George St.
Berry St.
Upper Duke St.
Cornwallis St.
Kent St.
Upper Pitt St.
St. James St.
Jamaica St.
Sparling St.
Tabley St.
Park Lane
Com. St.
Henry St.
Lydia Ann St.
Gilbert St.
Argyle St.
Duke St.
Seel St.
Parr St.
Fleet St.
Wood St.
Bold St.
Elliot St.
Church St.
Parker St.
Ranelagh St.
Hanover St.
School Lane
Manesty Lane
Paradise St.
Whitechapel
Canning
Canning
Strand St.
place
Wapping
Chaloner St.
The Strand

Liverpool Art Institute

Lime Street Station

Central Station

Sailor's Home

Stock Exchange

Cotton Exchange

Royal Liver Building

Custom House

Dock Offices

Pier's Head Ferry

Princess Dock

Princess Landing Stage

George's Landing Stage

QUEENSWAY TUNNEL

River Mersey

Canning Dock

Salthouse Dock

Canning Half Tide Dock

Albert Dock

Wapping Dock

King's Dock No. 2

Information ℹ

1  4  5  6  7  8  9  10  11  12  13  14  15  16  2  3

## Legend

The Beatles Story **16**
Bus Station **9**
Cathedral Church of Christ **13**
Central Station **11**
Exchange Station **1**
Lime Street Station **7**
Liverpool Museum **4**
Mathew Street **3**
Merseyside Maritime Museum and the Museum of Liverpool Life **15**
Philharmonic Hall **12**
Roman Catholic Metropolitan Cathedral **10**
St. George's Church **6**
Tate Gallery Liverpool **14**
Tourist Information Center **8**
Town Hall **2**
Walker Art Gallery **5**

ENGLAND
London
Liverpool

3-0591

643

## IN THE FOOTSTEPS OF THE BEATLES

*Get back, get back, get back to where you once belonged.*
—Paul McCartney/John Lennon, "Get Back"

For centuries Liverpool was known as one of the world's greatest seaports. But since the 1960s its fame has rested more squarely on its role as "The Birthplace of The Beatles." Strawberry Field, Penny Lane, and John Lennon's "There are Places I Remember," set the whole world singing. More than 30 years have passed since a few hundred dedicated fans followed The Beatles around The Cavern and other Liverpool dives, yet every year hundreds of thousands of visitors flock to the city to follow in the early footsteps of the mop-topped "Fab Four."

Wherever you turn in Liverpool today, somebody is hawking a Beatle tour. If you'd like to set your own pace and explore at will, put on a pair of walking shoes and head out on your own trail with a little help from your friends—meaning us. Some of the most famous sites, such as Strawberry Field on Beaconsfield Road, are outside the main part of town and difficult to reach without a car. (Strawberry Field was a Salvation Army home for orphans, to which John Lennon gave a large donation to in 1970.)

At The Cavern (see below)—now touted as "The Most Famous Club in the World"—you can pick up a Cavern City Tour map to find locations in the center. More in-depth explorations will require a "Liverpool A to Z" map available at most newsstands.

We'll start our walking tour at the Town Hall and finish 2 1/2 hour leisurely hours at the St. Silas School. This is a good tour to do during the day to avoid rush-hour traffic. Start your tour at **Town Hall,** Water Street, where the city of Liverpool held a civic reception for The Beatles on July 10, 1964, while they were in town for the northern premiere of their first feature film, A Hard Day's Night. Nearly a quarter of a million fans turned out, lining the way from Liverpool Airport into the city center, and there was an explosion of cheering when they finally appeared on the Town Hall's balcony.

On the steps of **Victoria Monument,** near the intersection of Water and Castle streets, is where John first wooed girlfriend Thelma Pickles in 1958. A fellow art school student also abandoned by her father, she is best remembered for helping John come to terms with his mother's tragic death. Thelma was hit and killed by an automobile on July 15, 1958.

Walk up Castle Street (which starts at Water Street), turn left onto Cook Street, take a right on North John Street and almost immediately you'll turn left onto Mathew Street, site of the legendary **The Cavern,** 10 Mathew St. This is where The Beatles played an amazing total of 292 gigs between 1961 and 1963. The first show was on March 21, 1961, for which they were paid the less than princely sum of £5 ($8). Their growing popularity soon allowed them to demand £300 ($480) per show. Much of the credit for that jump in pay can be attributed to manager Brian Epstein, who first saw them here on November 9, 1961. By December 10 of that year, he had signed a contract with the band.

Through much of its heyday, The Cavern was without a drinking license, so The Beatles and other bands would cross Mathew Street and enter **The Grapes** pub for a quick drink.

Occasionally, after being barred from The Grapes for rowdy or drunken behavior, the lads would venture up the street and hang a right onto Rainford Gardens where **The White Star** stood ready to haul out the pints.

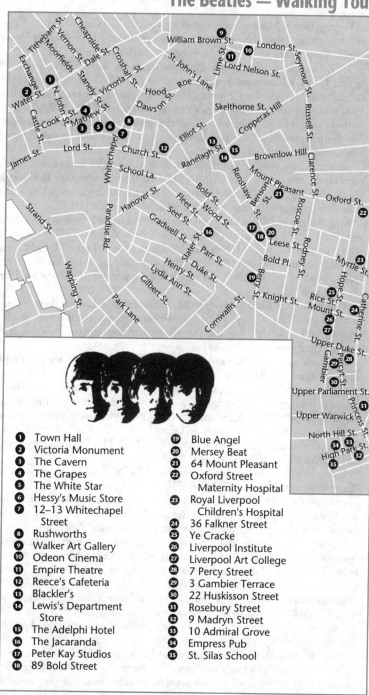

1. Town Hall
2. Victoria Monument
3. The Cavern
4. The Grapes
5. The White Star
6. Hessy's Music Store
7. 12–13 Whitechapel Street
8. Rushworths
9. Walker Art Gallery
10. Odeon Cinema
11. Empire Theatre
12. Reece's Cafeteria
13. Blackler's
14. Lewis's Department Store
15. The Adelphi Hotel
16. The Jacaranda
17. Peter Kay Studios
18. 89 Bold Street
19. Blue Angel
20. Mersey Beat
21. 64 Mount Pleasant
22. Oxford Street Maternity Hospital
23. Royal Liverpool Children's Hospital
24. 36 Falkner Street
25. Ye Cracke
26. Liverpool Institute
27. Liverpool Art College
28. 7 Percy Street
29. 3 Gambier Terrace
30. 22 Huskisson Street
31. Rosebury Street
32. 9 Madryn Street
33. 10 Admiral Grove
34. Empress Pub
35. St. Silas School

Heading back to Mathew Street, continue away from The Cavern, and you'll dead-end on Stanley Street. Hang a right and just around the corner stands **Hessy's Music Shop,** where John's Aunt Mimi bought him his first guitar for £17 ($27.20) in 1957. Continue up Stanley Street and you'll come to Whitechapel. Take a right to find **12–13 Whitechapel Street,** situated on your left. Now an appliance store called Rumbelows, this was the home of **NEMS** (Northern End Music Stores), Brian Epstein's family-owned record shop, where repeated requests for The Beatles record (actually a single by fellow Hamburg nightclub performer Tony Sheridan, on which The Beatles appeared as "The Beat Brothers") made him curious enough to head to The Cavern and catch a show.

Backtrack now, walking past the intersection with Stanley Street again. Also located on the east side of Whitechapel, you'll find Hessy's competitor **Rushworths,** the shop that upgraded John and George to Gibson acoustic guitars in 1962—their prize for being named Liverpool's best band in a Mersey Beat poll.

Keep walking up Whitechapel until you come to a five-way intersection and veer right (east) onto William Brown Street, home of the **Walker Art Gallery,** on the left, which housed the John Moores Exhibit where Moores himself bought Stuart Sutcliffe's painting, providing the £65 ($104) with which he bought his Hofner bass. (John's good friend, Sutcliffe, "The fifth Beatle," was recruited into the band for a short stint on bass.)

Walk further up William Brown Street, and it turns into London Road. A couple of blocks up on the right, you'll find the **Odeon Cinema,** venue for the northern premiere of A Hard Days Night, in July 1964, coinciding with the city's civic reception for The Beatles at the Town Hall.

Backtrack to Lime Street and take a left. On the left you'll see the **Empire Theatre,** where The Beatles, still undecided about their moniker, had a 1959 audition, as Johnny & the Moondogs, for the Caroll Lewis "Discoveries" show. They returned to the stage as The Beatles in October 1962, and again several times in their English tours of 1963–1965, including the 1963 Beatles Christmas shows. It was also the site of their last Liverpool show on December 5, 1965. Way before any of that, it is the place where a 12-year-old Paul may have decided his fate while attending his first concert, a show by Eric Delaney's Band.

Continue straight (south) where Lime Street and St. John's Lane converge into Renshaw Street, then veer right on Elliot Street. To your left you'll find the intersection of Parker and Leigh streets, home of **Reece's Cafeteria,** site of John and Cynthia's wedding reception on August 23, 1962, when Brian escorted them to lunch here after their ceremony, with witnesses George and Paul in tow. Brian not only picked up the bill, he also announced that he was giving them his comfortable apartment at 36 Falkner Street as a wedding present—although his real motive was probably to protect John's marketable single image by hiding away the pregnant Cynthia.

Backtrack along Elliot Street, and turn right on Great Charlotte Street. To your left you'll see **Blackler's,** the site of George's apprenticeship as an electrician in 1960. Though short-lived, he learned enough to do amplifier maintenance and repairs in The Beatles' early years.

Keep moving up Great Charlotte Street and turn left on Ranelagh Street. To your right will be **Lewis's Department Store.** Upon returning to home life after the excitement of Hamburg, Paul was instructed by his father to quit moping around the house, so he found short-lived employment here as a delivery van assistant during the 1960 Christmas season. The doorway of this store is also where John and Cynthia met to start many an evening on the town when they were dating.

Just across Renshaw Street, between Copperas Hill and Brownlow Hill, sits **The Adelphi Hotel,** Ranelagh Place, employer of John's father, Freddie Lennon, in his youth. This is also where John the art student, dressed as a vicar, persuaded the staff to lend him a mop and bucket with which he mopped the pedestrian crosswalk out front while singing at the top of his lungs. Later, in the mid-1960s, it hosted not only The Beatles, but other pop luminaries, including Bob Dylan, when they passed through town.

Backtrack down Ranelagh Street, and turn left on Bold Street; take a right on Slater. Just before the intersection of Seel Street, on the left, you'll find **The Jacaranda,** 23 Slater St., Allan Williams' wine cellar converted into a music club with a dance floor. Although he claimed to have never liked their music, Williams acted as the quartet's first manager and occasionally booked them here in 1960. It is from this location that Williams drove them to the ferry on their way to Hamburg in August 1960. Murals still visible on the walls were supposedly painted by John and Stuart when the club was preparing to open. Backtrack to Bold Street and turn right. On the left you'll see **Peter Kay Studios,** 83 Bold St., the professional studio responsible for many of the early Beatles promo shots. Just past it stands **89 Bold St.,** the former site of the Odd Spot Club, where the four performed several times in 1962. John Dykins, boyfriend of Julia Lennon (John's mother), was the doorman here. John often called to see if it was slow enough for him and the boys to come in for a little anonymous relaxation.

Keep walking up Bold Street and veer right onto Berry Street. Near the intersection of Berry and Seel streets, you'll find Allan Williams' other club, the **Blue Angel,** 108 Seel St., the site in May 1960 (when it was called "Wyvern Social Club") of an audition (as the Silver Beatles) for British promoter Larry Parnes (the U.K.'s answer to Colonel Tom Parker). The band was chosen to accompany Parnes' crooner, Johnny Gentle, on a nine-stop tour of Scotland—their first professional gig as The Beatles. In August of that year, desperately needing a drummer to accept their infamous Hamburg gig, they auditioned Pete Best on this stage. It actually opened as the Blue Angel on March 22, 1961, and was later the site of the first meeting between Ringo and Brian.

Follow Berry Street back onto Renshaw, and past Leese Street, on the right. Here you'll find the former offices of **Mersey Beat,** 81A Renshaw St. Opened on a £50 ($80) loan, the first issue of this newspaper hit the streets on July 6, 1961. It wasn't long before publisher Bill Harry (an art school friend of John), photographer Dick Matthews, and writer Bob Wooler (also the DJ/impresario of The Cavern) were touting The Beatles to all of Liverpool. In a readers' poll published in the January 4, 1962, issue, The Beatles were named the best group in Merseyside, thus winning their Gibson guitars from Rushworths. Continuing back along Renshaw, take a right onto Benson Street, then turn right again on Mount Pleasant. To your right sits **64 Mount Pleasant,** the site of the former Register Office where John and Cynthia were married on August 23, 1962, with Brian, George, and Paul in attendance.

Continue up Mount Pleasant (east) until it becomes Oxford Street. A couple of blocks up, on the right, you'll see the **Oxford Street Maternity Hospital,** Cambridge Street, where John was born during a 7am air raid on October 9, 1940. Backtrack just a bit to Hope Street and turn left, following it south to Myrtle Street, on the left. Turn onto Myrtle, and on the left you'll see the **Royal Liverpool Children's Hospital,** where Ringo convalesced for 11 months when he was 6, after a burst appendix and peritonitis left him in a coma for weeks.

Continue up Myrtle to Catherine Street and take a right. Several blocks down, on the right, you'll find Falkner Street, site of Brian's apartment at **36 Falkner St.** His wedding present to John and Cynthia, this apartment is where the pregnant Cynthia was sequestered, starting in August, 1962.

Follow Falkner to Hope Street, turn left, and then take a right on Rice Street, where you can take a much deserved break and have a pint at **Ye Cracke.** Located close to the Liverpool Art College, this was a hangout to John Lennon and Stuart Sutcliffe in their art school days. It was here that John brought future Cynthia, plying her with alcohol until she agreed to return with him to Stuart's flat at 3 Gambier Terrace, Hope Street, where he seduced her for the first time. (Note: Regulars here are seemingly sick of talking to tourists about John's drinking days in the pub. Your best bet is just to absorb the little changed atmosphere and move on.)

Backtrack to Hope Street, where you'll turn right. The next intersection on your right is with Mount Street. Sitting at the corner, on Mount Street, is the **Liverpool Institute,** the high school of both George and Paul. Adjacent to it on Hope Street is the old **Liverpool Art College,** now John Moores University, where John Lennon enrolled in 1958, majoring in lettering. It was here that John met Cynthia, Stuart, and Bill Harry, his art school friend. Owing to the proximity of their schools, Paul and George often took their guitars to school and met John at the art college, holding impromptu jam sessions in the canteen or in Room 21.

Continue south on Hope Street and turn left on Duke Street. Take a right on Percy Street, and you can view **7 Percy St.,** the basement flat which was Stuart Sutcliffe's private studio. He often came here, skipping classes, to spend time alone and paint. Backtrack yet again to Hope Street and turn left. The street changes names here and becomes Gambier Terrace. Stuart's former apartment is at **3 Gambier Terrace,** on the left. This is the Liverpool flat shared by John and Stuart in early 1960. An unknown John appears sprawled on the floor of this apartment in a photo accompanying a derogatory article about beatniks in a July 1960 article from The People. This is where John used to sleep in a satin-lined coffin because he claimed it was comfortable.

Continue south on Gambier Terrace, and turn left on Huskisson Street, where on your right, you'll find a large, four-story Victorian house at **22 Huskisson St.,** the childhood home of John's mother, Julia, Aunt Mimi, and his other three aunts. Backtrack to Gambier Terrace, turn left, take a left on Upper Parliament Street, then go right on Princess Road. To your left you'll find **Rosebury Street.** A block party held here, to celebrate the 750th anniversary of Liverpool receiving its first Royal Charter from King John, is touted as "The Quarry Men's" first professional gig, on June 22, 1957. Performing on the back of a coal lorry, a picture from this gig of John Lennon playing and singing in a checkered shirt is famous today as the first photo of the future superstar at work. The gig was so successful that The Quarry Men had to wait inside a friend's home for a police escort, as some local toughs, noticing the amount of female attention they were receiving, threatened them with bodily harm.

Go back to Princess Road, turn left and walk down to High Park Street, on your left. You are now in the Dingle district, domain of young Ringo. To the right off High Park is **9 Madryn St.,** where Ringo was born on July 7, 1940. He lived here until his parents divorced in 1943.

He and his mother then moved just across High Park to the small, modest house at **10 Admiral Grove.** Directly on High Park is the **Empress Pub.** Returning to his roots after The Beatles' breakup, Ringo featured a photo of the pub on his first solo recording, "Sentimental Journey."

Just across the street stands **St. Silas School,** Ringo's primary school, though he rarely attended classes because of his sickly nature.

# MORE LIVERPOOL SIGHTS

In addition to the Beatles sights, Liverpool has a wealth of things for the visitor to see and enjoy, including major cathedrals, restored waterfront glories, and cultural centers.

## THE CATHEDRALS

✪ **Cathedral Church of Christ.** Saint James Mount. ☎ **0151/709-6271.** Free admission to cathedral; tower and embroidery gallery £2 ($3.20) adults, £1 ($1.60) children. Daily 8am–6pm. From train station, best to walk (10 minutes) or take a taxi (about £2, or $3.20). From Line St. station, head down Renshaw St. to its end, then cross the street to Berry St. Follow this to the end and turn left.

The great new Anglican edifice was begun in 1904 and was largely completed 74 years later. On a rocky eminence overlooking the River Mersey, this is the last gothic-style cathedral to be built worldwide. Dedicated in the presence of Queen Elizabeth II in 1978, it is the largest church in England and the fifth largest in the world. Its vaulting under the tower is 175 feet high, the highest in the world, and its length—619 feet—makes it one of the longest cathedrals in the world. The organ has nearly 10,000 pipes, the most found in any church. The tower houses the highest (219 feet) and the heaviest (31 tons) bells in the world, and the gothic arches are the highest ever built. From the tower, you can see to North Wales.

After winning a competition in 1903 for this building's design, architect Giles Scott went on to rebuild the House of Commons after it was gutted by bombs during World War II. He personally laid the last stone on the highest tower pinnacle here.

In 1984, a Visitor Centre and Refectory was opened, and its dominant feature is an aerial sculpture of 12 huge sails, with a ship's bell, clock, and light that changes color on an hourly basis. You can enjoy full meals in the charming refectory.

**Roman Catholic Metropolitan Cathedral of Christ the King.** Mount Pleasant. ☎ **0151/709-9222.** Free admission. Daily 8am–6pm (closes 5pm Sun in winter). From Line St. station, no. 79 or no. 14 bus.

Half a mile away from the Anglican cathedral stands the Roman Catholic cathedral; the two are joined by a road called Hope Street. The sectarian strife of earlier generations has ended, and a change in attitude, called by some the "Mersey Miracle," was illustrated clearly in 1982 when Pope John Paul II drove along Hope Street to pray in both cathedrals.

The construction of the cathedral, designed by Sir Edwin Lutyens, was started in 1930, but when World War II interrupted in 1939, not even the granite and brick vaulting of the crypt was complete. At the end of the war it was estimated that the cost of completing the structure as Lutyens had designed it would be some £27 million. Architects throughout the world were invited to compete to design a more realistic project to cost about £1 million and to be completed in 5 years. Sir Frederick Gibberd won the competition and was commissioned to oversee the construction of the circular cathedral in concrete and glass, pitched like a tent at one end of the piazza that covered all the original site, crypt included.

Construction was completed between 1962 and 1967, and today the cathedral provides seating for more than 2,000, all within 50 feet of the central altar. Above the altar rises a multicolored glass lantern weighing 2,000 tons and rising to a height of 290 feet. Called a "space age" cathedral, it has a bookshop, a tearoom, and tour guides.

## THE WATERFRONT

A fun thing to do is to take the famous **Mersey Ferry** that travels from the Pier Head to both Woodside and Seacombe. Service operates daily from early morning to early evening throughout the year. Special cruises run throughout the summer including trips along the Manchester Ship Canal. For more information, contact **Mersey Ferries,** Victoria Place, Seacombe, Wallasey (☎ 0151/630-1030).

**Albert Dock.** Albert Dock Co. Ltd. ☎ **0151/708-8838.** Free admission. Shops: daily 10am–6pm. Bars and restaurants: daily 10am–11pm. Smart Bus from city center.

Built of brick, stone, and cast iron, this showpiece development on Liverpool's waterfront opened in 1846, saw a long period of decline, and has been renovated and refurbished so that it's now England's largest Grade 1 Listed Building, a designation for landmark buildings. The dockland warehouses now house quality shops, restaurants, cafes, an English pub, and a cellar wine bar. One pavilion encompasses the main building of the Merseyside Maritime Museum (see below) and another is the home of the Tate Gallery Liverpool, the National Collection of modern art in the north of England (see below). Parking is available.

**The Conservation Centre.** Whitechapel, Liverpool. ☎ **0151/478-4999.** Admission £1.50 ($2.40) adults; £1 ($1.60) children, students, and seniors. Mon–Sat 10am–5pm; Sun noon–5pm. Closed Dec 23–26 and Jan 1. Take a no. 61, 78, or 79 bus.

The Conservation Centre in the heart of Liverpool is the first of its kind in Europe to open its doors to the public. The "Caught in Time" exhibition uncovers the secret world of museum conservation and reveals how the 1.2 million artifacts in national museums and galleries on Merseyside collections are kept from the ravages of time. Using state-of-the-art hand-held audio guides, video link-ups, demonstrations, behind-the-scenes tours, and interactive displays, visitors can see how everything from fine art, a Beatles gold disc, to a mummified crocodile are saved from decay by the expert conservators using the most up-to-date techniques.

✪ **Merseyside Maritime Museum and the Museum of Liverpool Life.** Albert Dock. ☎ **0151/478-4499.** Admission £3 ($4.80) adults; £1.50 ($2.40) children, seniors, and students. Daily 10am–5pm. Bus: "Albert Dock Shuttle" from city center.

Set in the historic heart of Liverpool's waterfront, this museum provides a unique blend of floating exhibits, craft demonstrations, working displays, and special events. In addition to restored waterfront buildings, exhibitions present the story of mass emigration through Liverpool in the last century, shipbuilding on Merseyside, the Battle of the Atlantic Gallery, and Transatlantic Slavery. The Museum of Liverpool Life explores the history of Liverpool, its people and their contribution to national life. "Anything to Declare," the National Museum of H. M. Customs & Excise, tells the story of customs. You can also see a restored pier master's house and a working cooperage. A fine restaurant, a coffee shop, a waterfront cafe, gift shops, and ample parking space are among the facilities. There is wheelchair access and toilet facilities for persons with disabilities.

✪ **Tate Gallery Liverpool.** Albert Dock. ☎ **0151/709-3223.** Free admission except special exhibitions; £2.50 ($4) adults, £1 ($1.60) children. Tues–Sun 10am–6pm. Bus: "Albert Dock Shuttle" from city center.

Opened in 1988, this museum displays much of the national collection of 20th-century art, complemented by changing art exhibitions of international standing. Three- and four-month special exhibitions are frequently mounted here, perhaps the prints of the Spanish artist Joan Miró or the sculptures of the iconoclastic British sculptress Rachel Whiteread. The tourist office has full details of all special exhibitions, or else you can call the museum directly. Closing in 1997, the Tate Gallery will reopen in May 1998 with a big art celebration of its 10th anniversary.

✪ **Walker Art Gallery.** William Brown St. ☎ **0151/478-4199.** Admission £3 ($4.80). Mon–Sat 10am–5pm; Sun noon–5pm. Closed Dec 23–26 and Jan 1. Lime St. station. Go out back entrance; the gallery is across the street from the Empire Theatre.

One of Europe's finest art galleries offers an outstanding collection of European art from 1300 to the present day. The gallery is especially rich in European Old Masters, Victorian and pre-Raphaelite works, and contemporary British art. It also has an award-winning sculpture gallery, featuring works from the 18th and 19th centuries. Seek out, in particular, Simone Martini's *Jesus Discovered in the Temple* and Salvator Rosa's *Landscape With Hermit.* Rembrandt is on show, as is an enticing *Nymph of the Fountain* by Cranach. The work of British artists is strongest here, ranging from *Horse Frightened by a Lion* by Stubbs to *Snowdon from Llan Nantlle* by Richard Wilson. Among the Pre-Raphaelites is Ford Madox Brown's *Coat of Many Colours* and narrative paintings such as *When Did You Last See Your Father?* by W. R. Yeames. French impressionists include the works of Monet, Seurat, and Degas, among others. Modern British paintings include works by Lucien Freud and Stanley Spencer. The admission charged is good for 1 year's admission into any and all of the eight museums and galleries on Merseyside.

✪ **Liverpool Museum.** William Brown St. ☎ **0151/207-0001.** Free admission. Mon–Sat 10am–5pm; Sun noon–5pm.

One of Britain's finest museums features collections from all over the world—from the earliest beginnings with giant dinosaurs through centuries of great art and inventions. At the Natural History Centre, you can use microscopes and video cameras to learn about the natural world. Living displays from the vivarium and aquarium form a large part of the collections, and a planetarium features daily programs covering modern space exploration—an armchair tour toward the beginning of the universe and the far-flung reaches of the cosmos. There is a small charge for the planetarium and temporary exhibitions.

## SHOPPING

Pedestrian-only shopping precincts with an array of boutiques, specialty shops, and department stores include Church Street, Lord Street, Bold Street, Whitechapel, and Paradise Street. Right on the river, Albert Dock also houses a collection of small shops.

For shopping centers, go to **Cavern Walks** on Mathew Street, the heart of Beatleland (☎ **0151/236-9091**), or **Quiggins Centre,** 12–16 School Lane (☎ **0151/709-2462**).

If you want to buy that special something related to the Beatles or John Lennon, then you need to wander through the **Beatles Shop,** 31 Mathew St. (☎ **0151/236-8066**). Another choice for Beatle items is the **Heritage Shop,** 1 The Colonnades, Albert Dock (☎ **0151/709-7474**), which also carries other English and Liverpool memorabilia.

For a huge selection of British crafts, visit **Bluecoat Chambers,** School Lane (☎ **0151/709-4014**), with its gallery of metal, ceramics, glass, jewelry, and wood pieces by some 350 British craftspeople. **Frank Gzeen's,** 10 Britannia Pavilion, Albert Dock (☎ **0151/709-3330**), is where you'll find prints by this famous local artist who has been capturing the Liverpool scene on canvas since the 1960s. His work includes city secular buildings, churches, and street life.

Two of Liverpool's best bookshops include **Waterstone's,** 52 Bold St. (☎ **0151/709-0866**), and **Gallery Shop,** Tate Gallery, Albert Dock (☎ **0151/709-0507**).

A few other specialty shops that warrant a visit include **Sewill Marine,** Cornhill House, 24 Cornhill St. (☎ **0151/708-7744**), who have been making nautical instruments longer than anyone in the known world and where you can buy a barometer, a watch, or a clock. At **Thornton's,** 6 Whitechapel (☎ **0151/708-6849**), you can choose from a dizzying selection of continental and traditional English chocolates, toffees, and mints.

# WHERE TO STAY
## DOUBLES FOR LESS THAN £45

**Aachen Motel.** 89–91 Mount Pleasant, Liverpool, Merseyside L3 5TB. ☎ **0151/709-3477.** Fax 0151/709-1126. 18 rms, 12 with bath. TV TEL. £24 ($38.40) single without bath, £30–£32 ($48–$51.20) single with bath; £38 ($60.80) double without bath, £42–£46 ($67.20–$73.60) double with bath. All rates include English breakfast. AE, DC, MC, V. Parking £2 ($3.20).

Five minutes from the city center, this well-run establishment is a Grade III Listed Building (an English designation for landmark status) in a conservation area. Each of the modernized bedrooms here has a hair dryer, in-house movies, beverage-making facilities, and a trouser press. It's short on charm, but good on value. The hotel has a bar, and the location is near the Roman Catholic Metropolitan Cathedral.

**Aplin House Hotel.** 35 Clarendon Rd., Garston, Liverpool, Merseyside L19 6PJ. ☎ **0151/427-5047.** 5 rms, 2 with shower only. TV. £22.50–£25.50 ($36–$40.80) single without shower; £38 ($60.80) double without shower, £40 ($64) double with shower only. All rates include English breakfast. No credit cards. Northern Line train to Garston. Bus: no. 80 or 86.

This well-kept residence facing the park is run by Mr. and Mrs. Atherton, and was built in 1901, the year of Queen Victoria's death. The rooms are comfortable and all contain color TVs and tea- and coffee-making equipment. Mrs. Atherton makes breakfast "as you like it." Because this establishment is located within a mile of where the Beatles lived and went to school, Mrs. Atherton will be happy to arrange a private tour through "Beatles Country." The hotel is about 10 minutes by train from the city center, 2 miles from the Liverpool airport, and 20 minutes by car from the Irish ferries. It's off A561, close to the Garston Railway Station.

**Feathers Hotel.** 119–125 Mount Pleasant, Liverpool, Merseyside L3 5TF. ☎ **0151/709-9655.** Fax 0151/709-3838. 84 rms, 60 with bath. TV TEL. £29.95 ($47.90) single without bath, £44.95 ($71.90) single with bath; £44.95 ($71.90) double without bath, £59.95 ($95.90) double with bath. All rates include English breakfast. AE, DC, MC, V. Bus: no. 80 (the airport bus).

The largest privately owned hotel in Liverpool, this brick-fronted establishment is composed of four separate Georgian-style town houses. It sits in the heart of town, adjacent to the city's modern Metropolitan Cathedral. The hotel contains a cocktail lounge (Zach's) serving bar snacks, as well as the Peacock restaurant, which is recommended separately (see "Where to Eat," below). The bedrooms are comfortable, with uncomplicated traditional furniture, but don't expect much charm.

# WHERE TO EAT

✪ **Don Pepe Restaurant and Tapas Bar.** 19–21 Victoria St. (Union House). ☎ **0151/231-1909.** Reservations recommended. Main courses £3.75–£12 ($6–$19.20). In tapas bar: beer and wine from £1.70 ($2.70); tapas £1.20–£4.50 ($1.90–$7.20). AE, CB, DC, MC, V. Mon–Sat 11am–3pm and 5:30–11pm. SPANISH.

This drinking and dining emporium is inside the imposing stone walls of one of the city's most architecturally distinguished buildings. (Built a century ago as the headquarters of a local shipping company, it had degenerated into a derelict fruit warehouse until its restoration.) Inside, a group of local investors have created one of the most vividly evocative Spanish decors in England, complete with hand-painted tile murals and Iberian fountains. No meal here would be complete without a before-dinner visit to the marble-topped tapas bar. Choices include portions of fried calamare (squid), spicy sausage (chorizo), salty but savory slices of Serrano ham, and well-seasoned croquetas of potatoes. Many visitors extend their time here by moving on to a meal in the adjacent dining room, where merluza a la romana (hake in a light batter), zarzuela de pescado (seasoned fish stew), escalopes of pork fried in bread crumbs, and an array of lamb dishes (especially the cordero de la casa) are highly recommended. The service is performed by a well-trained battalion of Spanish waiters.

**Everyman Bistro.** 9 Hope St. ☎ **0151/708-9545.** Main courses £2.80–£5.20 ($4.50–$8.30). No credit cards. Mon–Sat noon–midnight. INTERNATIONAL.

The Everyman Bistro, part of the Everyman Theatre complex, is informal, crowded on weekends, fun, and reasonably priced. Because the bistro has been at this location for 23 years, many locals consider it a city institution. A buffet is offered with a wide range of pâtés, quiches, pizzas, soups, meat and vegetarian main courses, seasonal salads, cheeses, desserts, and pastries. The menu, changed twice daily, is influenced by the season, with only fresh produce used. A typical three-course meal might consist of carrot soup with French bread, chicken pie with new potatoes and green salad, strawberries in white wine with cream, and coffee. These are simple heart-warming dishes that won't wow, but are varied and plentiful. It's on the street connecting the Catholic and Anglican cathedrals.

**La Bouffe.** 48A Castle St. ☎ **0151/236-3375.** Reservations recommended. Main courses £9–£13 ($14.40–$20.80); 3-course fixed-price lunch £10.95 ($17.50); fixed-price dinner (Tues–Fri) £12.75 ($20.40). AE, MC, V. Mon–Fri noon–3pm and 6–10:30pm. Bus: no. 20, 21, or 80. INTERNATIONAL.

A French-inspired cellar bistro in the center of the city's commercial heartland, La Bouffe offers satisfying food at reasonable prices: The fixed-price lunch is one of the best values in Liverpool. The menu changes often, but the chefs use fresh ingredients and handle them deftly. Dinners tend to be more relaxed than meals served to the lunchtime crowds. Menu choices might include a terrine of duck meat with pistachios, smoked fillet of halibut served with aromatic Chinese pickles and cabbage, supreme of chicken in a fresh tarragon sauce, and fillet of pork with raisins, pine nuts, and balsamic vinegar. Not all these dishes may be successful, but the cuisine is often inventive if not always enlightened.

**The Peacock.** In the Feathers Hotel, 119–125 Mount Pleasant. ☎ **0151/709-9655.** Main courses £6–£11 ($9.60–$17.60). AE, DC, MC, V. Daily 6:30–9pm. ENGLISH.

In the Edwardian-era premises of a well-known Liverpudlian hotel, this restaurant was renovated and upgraded in 1994. Painted a cerulean blue, and ringed with blow-ups of mountaineers scaling impossible peaks, the restaurant serves well-flavored versions of Lancashire hot pot, steaks, grills, and salads to local residents and tourists alike. The management sometimes features special theme nights, where the cuisine might stress the recipes of, among others, China or Mexico, but it's better to stick to the country cooking of the northwest that the chefs know.

✪ **Philharmonic Dining Rooms.** 36 Hope St. ☎ **0151/709-1163.** Main courses £3.95–£7.65 ($6.30–$12.25). No credit cards. Mon–Sat 11:30am–3pm and 6–9pm. Pub: Mon–Fri 11:30am–11pm; Sat 11:30am–11pm. Bus: no. 86, 87, or H25. ENGLISH.

This favorite pub has splendid turn-of-the-century architectural features, such as stained glass, carving, and plasterwork. You pass through wrought-iron gates into a selection of different rooms, named after the composers Brahms and Liszt. The heart of the pub is the Horseshoe Bar, which has a mosaic floor and stained glass—fine Edwardian flamboyance. Attracting art, drama, and music students as well as actors, it serves pub snacks which include scouse (a specialty of Liverpool composed of stewed beef with rich gravy and potatoes), fried haddock with chips, lasagna, and curried chili. Some dishes may be a little heavy, particularly with all that rich gravy, but that's what the locals like. Waitresses take your food and drink orders, and carry your dishes to your table. Pay the cashier for your meal as you leave.

✪ **St. George's Carvery.** In St. George's Hotel, St. John's Precinct, Lime St. ☎ **0151/ 709-7090.** Reservations recommended. 3-course carvery lunch or dinner £13.50 ($21.60) adults, half price for children 5–14, free for children 4 and under. AE, DC, MC, V. Daily 7–10am and 6–9:30pm; Sun noon–2:30pm. Bus: no. 12 or 13. ENGLISH.

In the very modern premises of one of Liverpool's busiest commercial hotels, this is one of the best food values in Liverpool. A uniformed assistant will help you carve portions of honey-baked ham, turkey, beef, leg of lamb, and pork, and you'll serve yourself from steaming dishes of vegetables and seasonal specialties. These dishes might qualify as soul food to the English—or "heady realism," as one diner put it.

## LIVERPOOL AFTER DARK

From high-profile fine arts performances to word-of-mouth underground events, Liverpool's nightlife is nothing if not diverse. Several publications and places will help you get a handle on the vast array of entertainment options around Liverpool. The evening *Liverpool Echo* is a good source of daily information about larger and fine arts events, while the youth-oriented *L: Scene* magazine will provide you with a thorough calendar of club dates and gigs for £1 ($1.60), and the free *City X Blag*, available in most clubs and pubs, will do the same. Available free in gay clubs and pubs, *Pulse* lists gay activities and events throughout the region. The **Student Entertainment Office** (☎ **0151/794-4143**) at the University of Liverpool can tell you about the range of activities sponsored by the school, or you can stop by the student union on Mt. Pleasant and check out the bulletin board. Chic shopping centers that offer everything from club clothes to body piercing, **The Palace,** Slater Street (☎ **0151/ 708-8515**), is a little more upscale, while **Quiggins Centre,** School Lane (☎ **0151/709-2462**), is funkier and cheaper, but both are prime locations to find out the latest happenings around the alternative scene, as each is overflowing with flyers advertising local events.

Open year-round, the **Liverpool Empire,** Lime Street (☎ **0151/709-1555**), hosts visiting stage productions ranging from dramas and comedies to ballets and tributes. The box office is open Monday through Saturday from 10am until 8pm on show days, and closes at 6pm when there's no show. Tickets generally range from £7 to £22 ($11.20 to $35.20), but students should check on discounts available the week of performance.

A small-scale theater, **Unity Theatre,** Hope Place off Hope Street (☎ **0151/ 709-4988**), presents new work, theater, and some dance and themed work. Each year a new piece of gay theater is commissioned, and there is a traditional Christmas show. Tickets are £4 to £8 ($6.40 to $12.80).

Located in a historical red brick building dating to 1717, the **Bluecoat Arts Centre,** School Lane (☎ **0151/708-8877**), is home to music and contemporary dance performances and workshops, as well as housing a gallery for art exhibits. Performance tickets range from £4 to £7 ($6.40 to $11.20), and most workshops are free.

The **Philharmonic Hall,** Hope Street (☎ **0151/709-2895**), is home to **The Royal Philharmonic Orchestra,** one of the best orchestras outside of London, which performs twice weekly. When the orchestra is not on, there are often concerts by touring musicians, and films are sometimes shown as well. Concert tickets range from £7 to £20 ($11.20 to $32, and film tickets run £3.50 ($5.60).

The **Robins 051 Cinema,** 1 Mt. Pleasant (☎ 0151/707-0257), screens new, foreign, and classic films every evening. Tickets run about £3.50 ($5.60).

## THE CLUB & MUSIC SCENE

Obviously the immeasurable popularity and influence of The Beatles gained this northern port a lot of positive pop attention, but even before that, the Liverpool sound, dubbed the "Mersey beat," brought national stardom to Gerry and the Pacemakers, and Cliff Richards and the Shadows. Acts that have come up since The Beatles era include late 1970s and early 1980s college radio mainstays The Teardrop Explodes and Echo and the Bunnymen. More recently, those bands' frontmen, Julian Cope and Ian McCulloch, respectively, have enjoyed some solo success, and Orchestral Maneuvers in the Dark (OMD) is still going strong, often recording at the local studio Pink Museum. There's even an Oasis connection, as they recorded their first single at that studio. Music scene insiders aren't touting one band over another, but several newer bands have signed record deals in the past few months and any one of them may be the next Liverpool sensation. Among the up-and-coming groups: The Real People, Cast, The Sunlight Experience and Bullyrag, The La's, Blue Seed, and Space.

Open Wednesday through Saturday nights, **Lomax,** 34 Cumberland St. (☎ 0151/236-6458), is a good place to catch local and touring indie bands, both new and established. The cover charge is usually £3 to £5 ($4.80 to $8). Home to two venues, **Krazy House,** Wood Street (☎ 0151/708-5016), hosts live music 7 nights a week in both its 300-capacity and 1,000-capacity rooms. Within its split layout, you can catch everything from unknown locals to popular touring bands, with the cover charge generally ranging from £3 to £10 ($4.80 to $16).

The best of both worlds, **The Buzz,** Skelhorne Street (☎ 0151/707-2122), hosts a live music showcase on Friday, when admission will cost you £7 to £8 ($11.20 to $12.80), but its reputation as a dance club is unparalleled when it hosts Saturday appearances by the **Porn Kings,** million-selling DJs as revered in the U.S. and Canada as they are at home. If you're a dancer, the £5 ($8) cover charge is a bargain.

House music keeps the dancers rocking all week at **Mello Mello,** 40–42 Slater St. (☎ 0151/707-0898), where there's no cover charge to join in. Formerly Bourbon Street Jazz Club, the **Zanzibar Club,** 43 Seel St. (☎ 0151/707-0633), has changed its name to more accurately reflect its dance orientation. DJs spin acid jazz, salsa, and other Latin styles Monday through Saturday nights, and if you like your dancing exotic, the first Friday of each month has a Brazilian Carnival theme, with samba music, costumed dancers, stilt walkers, and a rowdy, party atmosphere. Cover is generally £2 to £3 ($3.20 to $4.80).

**Cream/Nation,** Parr Street, north of Slater Street (☎ 0151/709-1693), is where the Nation, a huge warehouse club consists of three rooms, hosts one of England's top rated dance clubs, Cream, every Saturday night and the last Friday of the month, when Cream pulls an all-nighter and attracts clubgoers from all over England. Admission to Cream is £10 ($16).

A mixed gay nightclub, **Garlands,** 8–10 Eberle St., off Dale Street (☎ 0151/236-3307), sometimes hosts bizarre special events, but you can always count on dancing Thursday through Saturday, when the cover charge will range from £4 to £9 ($6.40 to $14.40).

A cafe by day, **Baa Bar,** 43–45 Fleet Street (☎ 0151/707-0610), still serves tapas at night, but free dancing to a DJ brings in a lot of the evening's business. A pub with a Fab Four spin, **Ye Cracke,** Rice Street (☎ 0151/709-4171), was a favorite watering hole of John Lennon in pre- and early-Beatles days, but expect regulars to suggest you quit living in the past if you ask about those days. Better just soak up the little changed atmosphere over a pint of Oak Wobbly Bob, Cains, or Pedigree.

A hangout for gay groups and clubs, **Time Out,** 30 Highland Rd. (☎ 0151/236-6768), is a continental pub that offers all the latest information on happenings in the local gay scene. A friendly place, it's mainly male in its clientele.

## 3 The Walled City of Chester

207 miles NW of London; 19 miles S of Liverpool; 91 miles NW of Birmingham

A Roman legion founded Chester on the Dee River in the 1st century. The town reached its pinnacle as a bustling port in the 13th and 14th centuries but declined following the gradual silting up of the river. While other walls of medieval cities of England were either torn down or badly fragmented, Chester still has 2 miles of fortified city walls intact. The main entrance into Chester is Eastgate, which dates only from the 18th century. Within the walls are half-timbered houses and shops, although not all of them date from Tudor days. Chester is unusual in that some of its builders used black-and-white timbered facades even during the Georgian and Victorian eras.

Chester today has aged gracefully and is a lovely old English city to visit, if you don't mind the summer crowds who virtually overrun the place. It has far more charm and intimacy than either Liverpool or Manchester, and is one of the four most interesting medieval cities to visit in England, the others being the even more intriguing York and, to a lesser degree, Lancaster and Shrewsbury.

## ESSENTIALS

**GETTING THERE**    About 21 trains depart London's Euston Station every hour daily for the 3-hour trip to Chester. Trains also run every 30 minutes between Liverpool and Chester, a 45-minute ride. For schedules and information, call ☎ 0345/484950.

One National Express bus every hour runs between Birmingham and Chester; the trip takes 2 hours. The same bus line also offers service between Liverpool and Chester. It's also possible to catch a National Express coach from London's Victoria Coach Station to Chester. For schedules and information, call ☎ 0990/808080.

If you're driving from London, head north on the M1, then the M6 at the junction near Coventry. Continue northwest to the junction with A54, which leads west to Chester.

**VISITOR INFORMATION**    The **Tourist Information Centre** is at the Town Hall, Northgate Street (☎ 01244/318356). It offers a hotel-reservation service as well as information. Arrangements can also be made for coach tours or walking tours of Chester (including a ghost-hunter tour). Open May through October, Monday to Saturday from 9am to 7:30pm and Sunday from 10am to 4pm; off-season Monday to Saturday from 9am to 5:30pm (except on Wednesday when they close at 4:45pm) and Sunday from 10am to 4pm.

## EXPLORING CHESTER

In a big Victorian building opposite the Roman amphitheater, the largest uncovered amphitheater in Britain, the **Chester Visitor Centre,** Vicars Lane (☎ 01244/319019), offers a number of services to visitors. A visit to a life-size Victorian street complete with sounds and smells helps your appreciation of and orientation to Chester. The center has a gift shop and a licensed restaurant serving meals and snacks.

# Chester

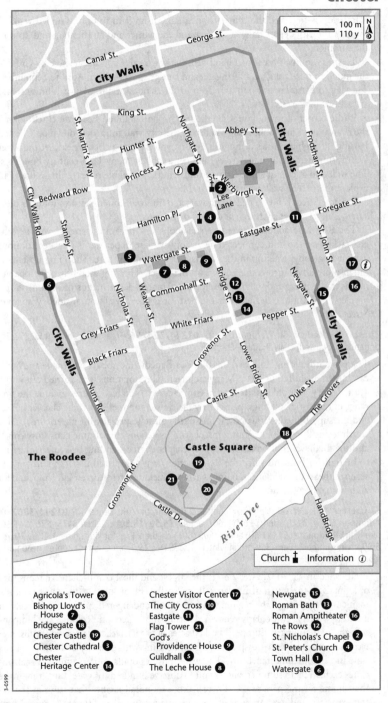

0 ___ 100 m
___ 110 y

George St.

Canal St.

**City Walls**

King St.

Abbey St.

St. Martin's Way

Hunter St.

Princess St.

Northgate St.

St. Werburgh St.

**3**

**City Walls**

Frodsham St.

ⓘ **1**

Bedward Row

**2**

Lee Lane

City Walls Rd.

Hamilton Pl.

**4**

**11**

Foregate St.

Stanley St.

Eastgate St.

St. John St.

**10**

**5**

Watergate St.

**9**

**17** ⓘ

**6**

**7** **8**

Commonhall St.

Bridge St.

**12**

Newgate St.

**16**

Nicholas St.

Weaver St.

**13**

**15**

White Friars

**14**

Pepper St.

**City Walls**

Grey Friars

Grosvenor St.

Lower Bridge St.

Black Friars

Nuns Rd.

Castle St.

Duke St.

The Groves

**The Roodee**

**Castle Square**

**18**

Grosvenor Rd.

**19**

**21**

**20**

HandBridge

Castle Dr.

*River Dee*

Church ✝ Information ⓘ

3-0599

Agricola's Tower **20**
Bishop Lloyd's
   House **7**
Bridgegate **18**
Chester Castle **19**
Chester Cathedral **3**
Chester
   Heritage Center **14**

Chester Visitor Center **17**
The City Cross **10**
Eastgate **11**
Flag Tower **21**
God's
   Providence House **9**
Guildhall **5**
The Leche House **8**

Newgate **15**
Roman Bath **13**
Roman Ampitheater **16**
The Rows **12**
St. Nicholas's Chapel **2**
St. Peter's Church **4**
Town Hall **1**
Watergate **6**

Admission is free, and the center is open daily from 9am to 6pm. Guided walking tours of the city depart daily at 10:30am in the winter and at 10:30am and 2pm in the summer.

To the accompaniment of a hand bell, the **town crier** appears at the City Cross—the junction of Watergate, Northgate, and Bridge streets—from April to September, Tuesday to Saturday at noon and 3pm to shout news about sales, exhibitions, and attractions in the city.

In the center of town, you'll see the much-photographed **Eastgate clock.** Climb the nearby stairs and walk along the top of the **city wall** for a view down on Chester. Passing through centuries of English history, you'll go by a cricket field, see the River Dee, formerly a major trade artery, and get a look at many 18th-century buildings. The wall also goes past some Roman ruins, and it's possible to leave the walkway to explore them. The walk is charming and free.

Eastgate Street is now a pedestrian way, and musicians often perform for your pleasure beside St. Peter's Church and the Town Cross.

**The Rows** are double-decker layers of shops, one tier on the street level, the others stacked on top and connected by a footway. The upper tier is like a continuous galleried balcony; walking in the rain is never a problem here. Shopping upstairs is much more adventurous than down on the street. Thriving establishments operate in this traffic-free paradise: tobacco shops, restaurants, department stores, china shops, jewelers, and antique dealers. For the best look, take a walk on arcaded Watergate Street.

**Chester Cathedral.** St. Werburgh St. ☎ **01244/324756.** Free admission but £2 ($3.20) donation suggested. Daily 7:30am–6:30pm.

The present building, founded in 1092 as a Benedictine abbey, was made an Anglican cathedral church in 1541. Many architectural restorations were carried out in the 19th century, but older parts have been preserved. Notable features include the fine range of monastic buildings, particularly the cloisters and refectory, the chapter house, and the superb medieval wood carving in the quire (especially for misericords). Also worth seeing are the long south transept with its various chapels, the consistory court, and the medieval roof bosses in the lady chapel. A free-standing bell tower, the first to be built in England since the Reformation, was completed in 1975 and may be seen southeast of the main building. Facilities include a refectory, a gift shop, and an audiovisual presentation.

✪ **Chester Zoo.** Off A41, Upton-by-Chester, 2 miles north of the center. ☎ **01244/380280.** Admission £8 ($12.80) adults; £6 ($9.60) seniors; £5.50 ($8.80) children 3–15; £26 ($41.60) family ticket. Monorail £1 ($1.60) adults; 50p (80¢) children. Free for kids under 3. Daily 10am–5:30pm in summer; 10am–3:30pm in winter. Closed Dec 25. From Chester's center, head north along Liverpool Rd.

Established in 1934, Chester Zoo is the largest and most comprehensive repository of animals in the north of England. It is also the site of some of the most carefully manicured gardens in the region. Many rare and endangered species breed freely in a setting which is particularly renowned for the most successful colonies of chimpanzees and orangutans in Europe. The 110 acres of gardens feature unusual shrubs, rare trees, and warm-weather displays of carpet bedding with as many as 160,000 plants timed to bloom simultaneously. The water bus, a popular observation aid that operates exclusively in summer, allows you to observe hundreds of water birds that make their home on the park's lake. There's also a monorail facility that stops at the extreme eastern and western ends of the zoo, making visits less tiring. Youngsters love the Monkey's Island exhibit. Year-round restaurants include the fully licensed Oakfield Restaurant and the Jubilee self-service cafeteria.

## SHOPPING

You will want to focus on three main areas for the bulk of your shopping in and around Chester. The **Grosvenor Precinct** is filled with classy, expensive shops and boutiques that sell a lot of trendy fashion and art items. This area is bordered on three sides by Eastgate Street, Bridge Street, and Pepper Street.

For stores with more character and lower prices, explore **the Rows**—a network of double-layered streets and sidewalks with an assortment of shops including jewelers, art galleries, craft centers, and carpet dealers. The Rows runs along Bridge Street, Watergate Street, Eastgate Street, and Northgate Street.

Another town worth exploring in the environs is **Boughton,** which is hardly a shopping secret any more, as every transatlantic dealer seems to go here. Along A41, a mile from the heart of town, Boughton is filled with antique shops along Christledon Road. It doesn't have the charm of Chester, but shopping values are often better here than in the more historic city. Some outlets have as many as a dozen showrooms, even though they often are hidden behind rather dreary facades.

Chester has a large concentration of antique and craft shops. Some of the better ones include **Lowe & Sons,** 11 Bridge St. Row (☎ 01244/325850), with their antique silver and estate jewelry; **The Antique Shop,** 40 Watergate St. (☎ 01244/316286), specializing in brass, copper, and pewter items; **Adam's Antiques,** 65 Watergate Row (☎ 01244/319421), focusing on 18th- and 19th-century antiques; and **Melodies Galleries,** 32 City Rd. (☎ 01244/328968), a cluster of eight antique dealers in a three-story 18th-century grain storage building. **Three Kings Studios,** 90–92 Lower Bridge St. (☎ 01244/317717), is a gallery for local artisans and craftspeople that sells pottery, prints, embroidery, and wood items.

For a good selection of cheeses, chutneys, olives, pastas, and English fruit wines, seek out **The Cheese Shop,** 116 Northgate St. (☎ 01244/346240). Another specialty food store is **Owen Owen,** Bridge Street (☎ 01244/321555), where you can get spices and preserves, a variety of coffee and teas, chocolates, and even prepared picnic baskets.

**Chester Candle Shop,** 75 Bridge St. Row (☎ 01244/346011), has every shape, size, and color candle imaginable, as well as snuffers, flower rings, and holders. Shoppers can also watch candles being carved, and children can try their hand at dipping candles.

Finally, for a general, but big, bookshop, go to **Bookland,** 12 Bridge St. (☎ **01244/347323**).

## WHERE TO STAY

### DOUBLES FOR LESS THAN £55

✪ **Cavendish Hotel.** 42–44 Hough Green, Chester, Cheshire CH4 8JQ. ☎ **01244/675100.** Fax 01244/681309. 19 rms. TV TEL. £45 ($72) single; £55 ($88) double. All rates include English breakfast. AE, MC, V. Bus: no. 28.

In one of Chester's most prestigious neighborhoods, this hotel lies beside A5104, on a tree-lined street about a mile west of the city center. It was built around 1840 as two semidetached houses that were connected and transformed into a hotel in the 1980s. Completely renovated in 1991–92, it's owned by Scotland-born Jennifer Jones and her partner, Jan Sumner. The restaurant has been expanded under the new ownership. Each of the comfortable bedrooms contains an array of toiletries and lots of cozy charm. A residents' lounge and bar contains a scattering of early 20th-century furniture.

**Derry Raghan Guest Hotel.** 54 Hoole Rd., Chester, Cheshire CH2 3NL. ☎ **01244/318740.** 8 rms. £17–£19 ($27.20–$30.40) per person. All rates include English breakfast. No credit cards. Take A56 north from the city center. Bus: no. 53.

This Victorian guest house lies about a mile from the heart of Chester and some 3 miles from the zoo. Meryl and Peter Bold welcome guests to their pleasantly furnished rooms, complete with hot-beverage facilities. The furnishings are comfortable, the place is a cozy stopover for the night. The ground floor and second floor bedrooms (first floor to the English) are spacious and tastefully decorated, all with private baths. In the morning a wide variety of choices is served in the breakfast room, including a full and fortifying English breakfast.

**Eversley Hotel.** 9 Eversley Park, Chester, Cheshire CH2, 2AJ. ☎ **01244/373744.** 11 rms, 9 with bath. TV TEL. £23 ($36.80) single without bath; £43 ($68.80) double with bath. All rates include English breakfast. MC, V. Head north from the center toward the zoo. Bus: no. C40.

The Eversley lies off Liverpool Road, three-quarters of a mile from the heart of old Chester in a residential section. The owners have fully modernized the Victorian residence with hot-beverage facilities, hot- and cold-water basins, razor outlets, radios, and telephones in the simply furnished bedrooms. Evening meals, costing £7 ($11.20) and up, are available in the candlelit dining room, and you can order snacks in the Deva Bar.

✪ **Redland Hotel.** 64 Hough Green, Chester, Cheshire CH4 8JY. ☎ **01244/671024.** Fax 01244/681309. 13 rms, 2 suites. TV TEL. £45 ($72) single; £55–£60 ($88–$96) double; £75 ($120) honeymoon suite. All rates include English breakfast. MC, V. Bus: no. 28.

Many judges have rated this the finest small hotel in Chester. It's a Victorian town house of character and charm, with oak paneling and stained-glass windows. Open year-round, it lies but a mile from the center of Chester opposite the Chester Golf Course in the direction of the Welsh border, and many guests use it as a base for exploring North Wales. Mrs. T. M. White has added such amenities to the hotel as a sauna and solarium, and she has a residential license for serving alcohol. Guests have the use of a laundry room.

**Ye Olde King's Head Hotel.** 48–50 Lower Bridge St., Chester, Cheshire CH1 1RS. ☎ **01244/ 324855.** Fax 01244/315693. 8 rms. TV TEL. £46 ($73.60) single or double.

A 5-minute walk from the bus station, this hotel is a 16th-century museum piece of black-and-white architecture. From 1598 to 1707, it was occupied by the well-known Randle Holme family of Chester, noted heraldic painters and genealogists (some of their manuscripts have made it to the British Museum). Since 1717, the King's Head has been a licensed inn. The host rents bedrooms with hot-beverage facilities and central heating, although they're nowhere near the equal of the public rooms as regards charm and character. Many of the walls and ceilings are sloped and highly pitched, with exposed beams.

## WHERE TO EAT

✪ **Francs Restaurant.** 14 Cuppin St. ☎ **01244/317952.** Reservations required. Main courses £7.15–£10.90 ($11.45–$17.45); fixed-price 3-course meal £9.85 ($15.75); Sun lunch £8.45 ($13.50). Separate children's menu. AE, MC, V. Daily 11am–11pm. Take any bus heading into the city center. FRENCH.

This restaurant serves what many consider the finest food for the price in Chester. Within the city walls, it's housed in a building constructed with oak beams in the 1600s. Inside, the cuisine is French—the way they cook in the countryside—and you can order an array of dishes including homemade sausages, a good-tasting cassoulet, and *plats du jour,* which might be your best bet. The wine list is reasonably priced, and the atmosphere is formal and convivial. The location is adjacent to the police station just off the main North Wales circular road.

**Gallery Restaurant.** 24 Paddock Row, Grosvenor Precinct. ☎ **01244/347202.** Lunch plates £2.95–£6.50 ($4.70–$10.40); full lunch menu £5.50 ($8.80); afternoon teas £1 ($1.60). MC, V. Mon–Sat 9:30am–5pm. ENGLISH.

Walking into this old English tearoom is a little like going into an indoor garden—it's festooned with masses of green plants. A varied English and continental menu is offered, including prawns, steak-and-kidney pie, smoked salmon, and crêpes. These are simple dishes, and you shouldn't expect more than a good "tuck-in." It's located in the town center.

✪ **Garden House Restaurant.** 1 Rufus Court, Northgate St. ☎ **01244/320004.** Reservations recommended. Main courses £10.25–£16 ($16.40–$25.60); fixed-price menus £12–£15 ($19.20–$24). MC, V. Mon–Sat noon–2pm and 6:30–10pm. Take any bus heading to the city center. INTERNATIONAL/VEGETARIAN.

The renovation of this restaurant's building (as well as the food served inside) has won several civic awards. It's housed in a complex of Georgian buildings, originally designed as an archbishop's palace, and later occupied by the city's hangman. The lower floor is a comfortable lounge, which is connected to the dining room by a sweeping Georgian staircase. During clement weather, additional tables are on the patio, set in the large outdoor garden directly beneath the city walls. Menu items include a choice of vegetarian specialties, fish, meat, and game (in season).

**Ye Olde Boot Inn.** 9 Eastgate Row. ☎ **01244/314540.** Bar snacks £1.45–£5.80 ($2.30–$9.30). MC, V. Daily noon–2pm. Pub: Mon–Sat 11am–11pm; Sun noon–10:30pm. Bus: no. 10 or 18. ENGLISH.

One of Chester's most atmospheric pubs was established in 1643 on a street immediately adjacent to the back of the cathedral. In 1986, its original premises expanded into what had been a covered alleyway and a row of shops, although it still retains low ceilings, stone or wood floors, most of the original ceiling beams, and a very old oak bar in back. In front, in what's known as the Eastgate Room, is the only view from any pub in Chester of the legendary Eastgate clock. Most visitors come here just to drink, although at lunchtime the place is crowded because of its food values. These include such fare as ploughman's lunches, a "giant's Yorkshire pudding" made by treating a leaf of "pud" like a crêpe and filling it with steak-and-kidney stew, Boozy Boot (lean chunks of steak marinated in old brewery cask bitter, mixed with fresh vegetables), lasagna, or scampi. The most enduring food item has remained basically unchanged since the inn was founded: Known as a hot boot sandwich, it contains oversize slices of beef with gravy nestled between two sides of a thick granary roll—it sells for £2.95 ($4.70).

# CHESTER AFTER DARK

The last 2 weeks of July are an active time in Chester, as the **Chester Summer Music Festival** (box office ☎ **01244/320700** or 01244/341200, Monday through Saturday, from 9:30am to 5:30pm) hosts orchestras and other classical performers from around Britain in lunch concerts, with tickets averaging £5 ($8), small indoor evening concerts, where tickets cost between £6 to £10 ($9.60 to $16), and large outdoor shows, with tickets ranging between £14 to £18 ($22.40 to $28.80). For additional information about the music festival, you can also write to the Chester Summer Music Festival Office, Gateway Theatre, Hamilton Place, Chester CH1 2BH. Occurring simultaneously, the **Chester Fringe Festival** (box office ☎ **01244/340392**), focuses on other musical genres, offering Latin, rock, cajun, folk, and jazz concerts, with ticket prices varying widely, depending on the performer.

If you want to relax in a pub, grab a pint of Marston's at the **Olde Custom House,** Watergate Street (☎ **01244/324435**), a 17th-century custom house with many original features still intact. The **Pied Bull,** Northgate Street (☎ **01244/325829**), is an 18th-century coaching inn where you can still eat, drink, or rent a room. Real ales on tap include Flowers, and Greenall's Bitter and Traditional. At **Ye Olde King's Head,** Lower Bridge Street (☎ **01244/324855**), ales are not the only spirits you might encounter. This bed-and-breakfast pub, built in 1622, is said to be haunted by three ghosts, a crying woman and baby in room no. 6, while the ghostly initials "ST" appear in steam on the bathroom mirror of room no. 4. If you prefer you're spirits in a glass, stick to the pub, where you can sip on a Boddington's Bitter, or Greenall's original or local.

Live Irish music and atmosphere can be sampled at **Scruffy Murphy's,** 59 Northgate St. (☎ **01244/321750**), where you can hear traditional music on Wednesday and Friday nights for the price of a pint of Guinness.

**Alexandre's,** Rufus Court off Northgate Street (☎ **01244/340005**), offers more varied musical entertainment every night except on Wednesday and Saturday, which are comedy nights. Sunday and Monday vary from week to week, but Tuesday there's acoustic blues and folk, Thursday brings big band and electric blues, and on Friday, DJs spin soul, funk, and acid house for your dancing pleasure. The cover charge varies between £2 to £6 ($3.20 to $9.60).

For strictly dancing, head to **Raphael's,** Love Street off Foregate (☎ **01244/340754**), or **Connections,** 39 Watergate St. (☎ **01244/320619**), Chester's only gay club, on weekends, when the dance styles are mixed and admission will cost you about £4 ($6.40).

## 4  Blackpool

246 miles NW of London; 88 miles W of Leeds; 56 miles N of Liverpool; 51 miles NW of Manchester

Even its detractors admit that the least appealing thing about Blackpool is its name. No, don't expect a British version of the La Brea tar pits. Rather, you'll find a once-antiquated Midlands resort struggling to make a comeback by marketing its Victorian and modern charms to new generations of holiday makers. The result is a revitalization attempt that may remind you of the newest version of Las Vegas. The city has a midwinter population of 125,000, which swells to three or four times that much in midsummer.

The country's largest resort boasts 7 miles of beaches, the most extensive illumination of any city in England (6 miles of colored lights), lots of Disney-wannabe attractions and rides, and a free-for-all venue similar to that of Las Vegas make Blackpool one of the most entertaining (and least apologetic) pieces of razzle-dazzle in England.

Disadvantages include dicey or unpredictable weather that brews over the nearby Irish Channel; a sandy, flat-as-a-pancake landscape that's less than inspiring; and a sometimes undeserved reputation for dowdiness that might raise an eyebrow or two in swinging (but faraway) London. On the other hand, you've got a brisk sea air, frequent architectural remnants of Britain's greatest Imperial Age successes, an utter lack of pretentiousness that's a welcome relief when compared to more stylish—but snobbier—venues, and a sense of nostalgia over a departed age.

## ESSENTIALS

**GETTING THERE**   Trains from Manchester pull in at the rate of 2 per hour (a 1¹/₂-hour trip) and one every 2 hours from Liverpool (a 2-hour trip). For schedules and information, call ☎ **0345/484950.**

National Express buses arrive from Chester at the rate of 3 per day (a 4-hour trip), Liverpool at the rate of 6 per day (a 3$^1$/$_2$-hour trip), Manchester 5 per day (a 2-hour trip), and London, 6 per day (a 6$^1$/$_2$-hour trip). For schedules and information, call ☎ **0990/808080.**

If you're driving from Manchester, take the M61 north to the M6 and then to the M55 toward Blackpool. The trip takes about 1 hour. From London, take the M25 west around London until you reach the turnoff for M40. Get on M40 and go all the way to Birmingham, where you take the M42 link east to the M6. Continue north along the M6 toward Preston, at which point you cut west along M55 to Blackpool.

**VISITOR INFORMATION**   The helpful **Tourist Office** staff is at 1 Clifton St. (☎ **01253/21623**), open Monday through Thursday and Saturday from 9am to 5pm, Friday from 9:30am to 5pm, and Sunday from 10am to 3:45pm.

## SEEING THE SIGHTS

Blackpool is famous for the **Illuminations**—an extravaganza of electric lights affixed to just about any stationary object along the Promenade. It features hundreds of illuminated figures, including Diamonds Are Forever, Santa's Workshop, Lamp Lighters, and Kitchen Lites. The tradition began in 1879 with just eight electric lights and has grown with time and technology to include 6 miles of fiber optics, low-voltage neon tubes, and traditional lamps. The illuminations burn bright into the night from the end of August to the end of November. Take a tram ride down the Promenade for a great view of these tackily festive lights.

The undisputed, most famous landmark in this town is its **Tower,** along the Central Promenade (☎ **01253/22242**). In 1891, during the reign of Queen Victoria, a mad-cap idea started floating around to construct a 518-foot tower that resembled Paris's Eiffel Tower (but half its size). The idea was first formerly presented to the town leaders of Brighton, who laughed at the idea, thinking it was a joke. But the forward-thinking leaders of Blackpool, when presented the plan, immediately saw the advantages of having such an attraction, and quickly approved the tower's construction. You be the judge of its value. Lighted by more than 10,000 bulbs, this landmark has become a tower of fun. It is truly an indoor entertainment complex both day and night and features the Tower Ballroom (one of the great Victorian ballrooms of Britain), the Tower Circus, the Hornpipe Galley, Jungle Jims Indoor Adventure Park and Dawn of Time dinosaur ride for kids, as well as the Tower Aquarium. An elevator takes visitors to the top of the Tower for a 60-mile view. The Tower is open from Good Friday through October, daily from 10am to 11pm. The circus has two shows daily (with the exception of Friday evening) at 2:30pm and 7:30pm. Tower admission is £5 ($8).

## BLACKPOOL BEACH ATTRACTIONS

Blackpool is, first and foremost, a beach resort of the Coney Island or Myrtle Beach variety. The promenade is littered with campy tourist attractions such as water slides, miniature golf, and roller coasters. The best of these are a couple of complexes that encompass a variety of attractions within their gates. The **Blackpool Sandcastle Centre,** South Promenade (☎ **01253/343602**), offers water slides, a wave pool, game room, bars, cafes, and gift shops during its summer opening. The admission fee in June is £4.50 ($7.20) all day, or £3.50 ($5.60) after 2pm for adults and children over 5 years of age. In July and August, the price goes up to £4.80 ($7.70) all day, and £3.70 ($5.90) after 2pm. This ticket includes unlimited admission to all water attractions, and children under 5 years of age are admitted free with guardian. Featuring more than 140 rides and amusements, **Blackpool Pleasure Beach,**

(☎ **01253/341033**), opts to charge per attraction, with no admission fee to enter the park. It claims to have the biggest roller coaster in the world, a 235-foot-high track featuring cars that achieve speeds of up to 85 miles per hour. Besides a plethora of other common amusement park rides, they also offer an ice show and a musical review. Attractions fall into three categories: A, with an admission of £2 ($3.20); B, at £1.50 ($2.40); and C, which costs £1 ($1.60).

## SHOPPING

Your best bets for smaller specialty shops and boutiques in this souvenir-laden town are found along Waterloo Road and Ocean Boulevard in the southern part of town and then along Red Bank Road in the northern section called Bispham. Hounds Hill Shopping Centre in the town center has all the major retail stores under one roof.

## WHERE TO STAY

**The Berwyn Hotel.** 12 Finchley Rd., Gynn Sq., Blackpool FY1 2LP. ☎ **01253/352896.** Fax 01253/594391. 20 rms. TV TEL. £34 ($54.40) single; £56 ($89.60) double. All rates include breakfast. DC, MC, V.

Although the plot of land it sits on isn't any bigger than those of most of the equivalent guest houses in town, you'll get the feeling that you're occupying a large estate thanks to its location overlooking the city's municipal park, Gynn Gardens. Because of this, there are large numbers of windows set into the ground-floor facade of this (ca. 1910) house that flood the interior with sunlight and views of greenery. Originally built as two houses designed to look like one, it was interconnected in 1942 into the spacious and much-modernized establishment you'll see today. Bedrooms are simple and somewhat banal, but comfortable and restful. Evening meals, some of the best served within any comparable establishment in Blackpool, sell for a supplement of £9 ($14.40) per person. Your hardworking hosts are Phil and Jeanette Prescott.

**Burlees Hotel.** 40 Knowle Ave., North Shore, Blackpool FY2 9TQ. ☎ **01253/354535.** 9 rms. TV. £21 ($33.60) single; £42 ($67.20) double. Discounts available for stays of 3 nights or more. MC, V. Closed Nov–Feb.

This is one of many dozens of equivalent guest houses dotting the urban landscape of Blackpool, although it's probably a bit better maintained than the norm. Presenting a bow-windowed, stucco-sheathed facade to the neighborhood of equivalent houses nearby, it's run by members of the Lawrence family. Don't expect grandeur— what you see is what you get. There's a resident's bar on the premises, as well as a small restaurant (nonsmokers only) serving simple and uncomplicated food. The garden faces south, a fact prized by the folk who maintain it.

**Grosvenor View Guesthouse.** 7–9 King Edward Ave., North Shore, Blackpool FY2 9TD. ☎ **01253/352851.** 17 rms, 10 with bath. £16–£19 ($25.60–$30.40) per person, single or double, without bath; £19–£22 ($30.40–$35.20) per person, single or double, with bath. All rates include breakfast. AE, MC, V.

Built as two halves of a brick-fronted house in the 1930s, these premises were united by a previous owner into the free-standing guest house you'll see today. Public areas are bright thanks to the large bay windows whose leaded glass breaks sunlight into geometric shapes. Bedrooms are clean, well-maintained, and comfortably traditional, and a pair of TV lounges (designated respectively for smokers and non-smokers) provide places to socialize. Part of the appeal of this place derives from owners Dave and Sheila Jackson, whose set-price evening meal, served only to residents, is a genuine bargain at £6 ($9.60) per person. Its only drawback is the hour it's served (5pm), a scheduling that transforms the venue into something like a high tea instead of a bona fide dinner. Why so early? Virtually everyone who opts to attend is committed to heading off to one of Blackpool's many pubs, nightlife venues, shows, or concerts. As such, it's a convenient way to sustain life and enjoy the nocturnal pleasures of the town as well.

**Sunray Hotel.** 42 Knowle Ave., Blackpool FY2 9TQ. ☎ **01253/51937.** 9 rms. TV TEL. £25–£28 ($40–$44.80) single; £50–£56 ($80–$89.60) double. All rates include breakfast. Discounts offered for stays of 2 nights or more. AE, MC, V.

The real charm of this place derives from the conscientious management of its owner, Mrs. Jean Dodgson, who makes sometimes heroic efforts to make her guests feel comfortable. Custom-built as a hotel in 1935, and set on a street corner within 300 yards of the oceanfront, it's the mirror image of a competing guest house next door, Burlees, which is also recommended. Public areas are flooded with sunlight thanks to large bay windows, and upstairs bedrooms are clean, cozy, and outfitted in pale colors suitable for a summertime resort hotel. Evening meals are served at 5:30pm to any resident who's interested, for a price of £12 ($19.20) per person.

# WHERE TO EAT

**Autumn Leaves.** 82 Topping St. ☎ **01253/20730.** Reservations recommended. Main courses £9–£12 ($14.40–$19.20). DC, MC, V. Daily 6pm–midnight. ENGLISH.

This wood-beamed restaurant has Old-World decor and ambience with dining tables set around a central stage that offers sporadic musical and theatrical entertainment during the summer months. Even during the mad cow scare, it has been known as a place to get a good steak, traditional chicken and seafood dishes are also available. The restaurant is fully licensed.

**Brewer's Fayre.** Yeadon Way. ☎ **01253/341415.** Main courses £4.75–£8.25 ($7.60–$13.20). AE, DC, MC, V. Daily 10am–11pm. CONTINENTAL.

This restaurant is in a contemporary building attached to the Whitbread brewery. It's decorated to re-create the ambience of a traditional brewer's pub with red floral carpets, brick walls and a fireplace, wooden beams and furnishings, and a row of decorative plates, mugs, and bottles running around the walls just below the ceiling. They serve mixed grills, salads, and pasta dishes, accompanied, of course, by Whitbread's selection of beers. The menu is designed to appeal to the widest possible tastes, with the usual range of English roasts, pasta dishes, and the standard fish and scampi. Steaks are one of the most popular items to order, although the chef occasionally goes exotic with a chicken tandoori.

**Harry Ramsden's.** 60–63 The Promenade. El. ☎ **01253/294386.** Reservations recommended. Set menus £5.35–£9.95 ($8.55–$15.90). Apr–Oct daily 11:30am–11pm; Nov–Mar daily 11:30am–7pm. MC, V.

This is one of the most appealing of a chain of 21 restaurants whose personalized mission involves exporting British fish-and-chips to the world at large. Since it was established from a storefront in Guisley, West Yorkshire, in the early 1920s, it's award-winning formula for the seafood staple has been duplicated as far away as Jeddah, Singapore, and Heathrow airport. The restaurant's allure has rooted itself especially deeply in Blackpool, where one of the chain's most opulent restaurants combines a takeout counter—where a portion of haddock and chips, suitable for munching during a Promenade on the nearby pier, sells for £2.25 to £4 ($3.60–$6.40). More appealing is the salmon-colored and wood-paneled restaurant, where the nostalgia of yesteryear is preserved with a uniformed staff, big chandeliers, and frequent reminders of the Art Deco age. In addition to fish and chips, there's a steak-and-kidney pudding "filled with savory goodness," plain salmon with tartar sauce or lemon, and such meat dishes as sausages, and several vegetarian selections.

**Peppermill.** 15 Barley St. ☎ **01253/22253.** Main courses £3–£8 ($4.80–$12.80). No credit cards. Daily 8am–5:30pm. ENGLISH/CONTINENTAL.

"Come on, Ducky, let's go over to the Peppermill," may sound like a curious phrase, but it is often heard in Blackpool. This newly refurbished restaurant has what the headwaiter terms a "French continental decor." No one in the kitchen dares to get too imaginative, but the cooks will turn out the usual array of soups, salads, sandwiches, and pastas, the preferred fare during the day. At night, they get a little fancier, preparing their best seafood and steak dishes. This is where blue-collar Manchester dines a bit upmarket, but at an affordable price.

## BLACKPOOL AFTER DARK

Blackpool musical venues attempt to be all things to all people, and the entertainment is a mixed bag, ranging from theatrical offerings to classical and pop concerts. The **Opera House,** Church Street (☎ 01253/27786), is a largely unadorned hall that seats 3,000, and the nearby **Grand Theater,** Church Street (☎ 01253/28372) has the appeal of an intimate and ornate theater. Both book entertainment throughout the year. On the beach, The **North Pier** (☎ 01253/20980), **South Pier** (01253/343096), and **Central Pier** (☎ 01253/23422) add their eclectic bookings in summer months only.

With a 3,000-person capacity, you can almost definitely find somebody to dance with at **The Palace,** Central Promenade (☎ 01253/26281), where DJs play largely commercial dance music for two dance floors surrounded by mirrors and lit by flashing lights and pulsing laser beams. The cover charge ranges from £1 to £6 ($1.60 to $9.60) through the week. Dedicated dancers often end up downstairs in the basement club **Main Entrance** (☎ 01253/292335), which features the heavier rhythms of house and garage, and the heftier cover charge of £6 to £10 ($9.60 to $16).

If you just want to unwind with a drink, head to **Yates Wine Lodges,** Talbot Square (☎ 01253/752443), and relax in smart Victorian surroundings complete with a marble bar. For a more Dickensian ambience, head to **The Counting House,** Talbot Square (☎ 01253/290979).

Locals seem fond of two Irish theme pubs. **Scruffy Murphy's,** Corporation Street (☎ 01253/24538), is part of a chain that offers Irish atmosphere and, occasionally, music, all for the price of a pint of Guinness. If it's too crowded there, you may want to spill over to **O'Neil's,** Talbot Road (☎ 01253/28617), where a similar offering is found.

# The Lake District 18

The Lake District, often referred to as a "miniature Switzerland," is actually quite small, measuring about 35 miles wide. Most of the district is in Cumbria, although it begins in the northern part of Lancashire.

Driving in the wilds of this picturesque shire is fine for a start, but the best way to take in its beauty is by walking—an art best practiced here with a crooked stick. There is a great deal of rain and heavy mist, and sunny days are few. When the mist starts to fall, try to be near an inn or pub, where you can drop in and warm yourself beside an open fireplace. You'll be instantly transported back to the good old days, since many places in Cumbria have valiantly resisted change.

Bordering Scotland, the far northwestern part of the shire used to be called Cumberland. Now part of Cumbria, it is generally divided geographically into a trio of segments: the Pennines, dominating the eastern sector (loftiest point at Cross Fell, nearly 3,000 feet high); the Valley of Eden; and the lakes and secluded valleys of the west, by far the most interesting.

So beautifully described by the romantic lake poets, the area enjoys many literary associations. In its time it lured such writers as Samuel Taylor Coleridge, Charlotte Brontë, Charles Lamb, Percy Bysshe Shelley, John Keats, Alfred, Lord Tennyson, and Matthew Arnold. In Queen Victoria's day, the Lake District was one of England's most popular summer retreats.

Windermere is the best center for exploring the Lake District. Not only will you be located beside one of Britain's most beautiful lakes, you can use it as a base for excursions, including to Rydal Mount, former home of William Wordsworth, and Brantwood, home of John Ruskin, that towering figure of the Victorian Age. You can also explore natural wonders from here, including **Scafell Pike,** which rises to a height of 3,210 feet. The largest town is Carlisle up by the Scotland border, a possible base for exploring Hadrian's Wall (see chapter 19), but we will concentrate on the district's lovely lakeside villages.

## 1 Exploring the Great Outdoors

Created in 1951, the **Lake District National Park** covers 885 square miles and is one of England's most beautiful spots, visited by some 14 million people annually. Attracted by the descriptions from the romantic lake poets, these visitors arrive to take in the wealth of mountains, wildlife, flora, fauna, and secluded waterfalls. Much of the area is privately owned, but landowners work with national park officers to preserve the landscape and its 1,800 miles of footpaths.

Before setting out to explore the lake, stop in at the **National Park Visitor Centre** (☎ 015934/46601), at Brockhole, on the A591 between Windermere and Ambleside. You can reach it by bus or one of the lake launches from Windermere. Here you can pick up useful data as well as explore 30 acres of gardens and parklands.

When setting out anywhere in the Lake District, it's wise to take adequate clothing and equipment, including food and drink. Weather conditions can change rapidly in this area, and in the high fells it can be substantially different from that found at lower levels. A weatherline service provides the latest conditions: call ☎ 017687/75757. In an emergency, dial the police at ☎ 999.

For more information on all the outdoor pursuits possible from Windermere, see below.

## BOATING IN CONISTON

**Coniston Water** and the Coniston Boating Centre are a part of the Lake District National Park. Coniston Water lies in a tranquil wooded valley between Grisedale Forest and the high fells of Coniston Old Man and Wetherlam. **Coniston Boating Centre,** Lake Road, Coniston LA21 (☎ 015394/41366), occupies a sheltered bay at the lake's northern end. The center provides launching facilities, boat storage, and parking. You can rent rowing boats that carry from two to six people, sailing dinghies that carry up to six passengers per boat, or Canadian canoes that transport two. There is a picnic area and access to the lakeshore. From the gravel beach you may be able to spot the varied water birds and plants that make the margins of Coniston Water a valuable but fragile habitat for wildlife.

You can also cruise the lake in an original Victorian steam-powered yacht, the *Gondola.* Launched in 1859 and in regular service until 1937, this unique boat was rescued and completely restored by the National Trust. Since 1980 it has become a familiar sight on Coniston, and sailings to Park-a-Moor and Brantwood run throughout the summer. Service is subject to weather conditions, of course. For more information, call ☎ 015394/41288.

**Coniston Launch** is a traditional timber boat which calls at Coniston, Monk Coniston, Torver, and Brantwood with a running commentary. Reductions are offered to individuals buying a Brantwood house ticket. What makes this boating outfitter exceptional is that special cruises are conducted in summer. The "Swallows and Amazons" tour was inspired by Arthur Ransome's classic story. For more information, call or fax ☎ 015394/36216.

**Summitreks** is a company that operates from the lakeside at Coniston Boating Centre, offering qualified instruction in canoeing and windsurfing. A wide range of equipment can be hired from the nearby office at Lake Road (☎ 015394/41212) or purchased from the shop at Yewdale Road, Coniston (☎ 01539/41487).

## CRUISING ULLSWATER

The two 19th-century **Ullswater Steamers** provide the best way to see Ullswater and the panoramic mountain scenery around the lake. In season three scheduled services run daily between Glenridding, Howtown, and Pooley Bridge as well as five shorter 1-hour cruises. Passengers may choose to walk back along the lakeside path or break for lunch at either end of the lake. The steamers run from the end of March to the beginning of November and cost £1.95 to £5.30 ($3.10 to $8.50). For more information, call ☎ 01539/721626. Glenridding is on the A592 at the southern end of Ullswater. Pooley Bridge is 5 miles from the M6 junction 40 Penrith.

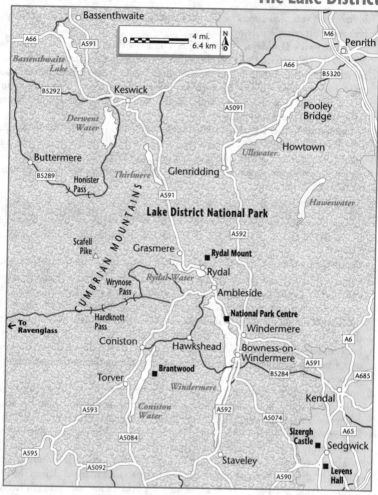

## SAFARI TOURS FROM AMBLESIDE

**Lakeland Safari Tours,** 23 Fisherbeck Park, Ambleside (☎ **015394/33904**), help you discover Lakeland's hidden beauty, heritage, and traditions. The local owner/driver, a qualified Blue Badge Guide, provides an exciting selection of full-day and half-day safaris in his luxury six-seater vehicle with collection and return to your accommodation. Admission is from £15 ($24) half day to £25 ($40) full day.

## RAILWAY TOURS IN RAVENGLASS

From the Irish Sea at Ravenglass, the little trains of the **Ravenglass & Eskdale Railway** carry you 7 scenic miles into Lakeland's mountains. You can visit the railway's own pub, "The Ratty Arms," cafes, shops, the Railway Museum, and a working water mill. For more information call ☎ **01229/717171.**

## WALKING TOURS

On one point, almost all Lake District devotees agree: The best way to see this part of England is on two legs, preferably with a staff if you do your best Wordsworth imitation. If you need directions to your trekking, the two outfitters below offer the best and most reliable walking tours.

**Countrywide Holidays,** Grove House, Wilmslow Road, Didsbury, Manchester M20 2HU (☎ **0161/448-7112**), has offered walking and special interest holidays for more than 100 years. Safe and sociable guided walks are led by experienced leaders, for all ages and abilities. It's ideal for independent walkers, with boot-drying rooms provided. They have four comfortable, informal and welcoming guest houses set in beautiful Lakeland locations.

**Lakeland Natural Walking Holidays,** Low Slack, Queens Road, Kendal LA9 4PH (☎ **01539/733011**), explores the Lakeland Fells on one of its 2-, 5-, and 7-day holidays in safety with qualified, informative leaders. Then you can relax and delight in one of the vegetarian guest houses in Kendal where you'll find comfort, plentiful food, and wine.

## 2 Kendal

270 miles NW of London; 64 miles NW of Bradford; 72 miles NW of Leeds; 9 miles SE of Windermere

The River Kent winds its way through a rich valley of limestone hills and cliffs, known as "fells," and down through the "Auld Grey Town" of Kendal, whose name refers to the large number of gray-stone houses found in and about the town. Many visitors to the Lake District simply pass through Kendal, much like the River Kent, on their way to more attractive vacation destinations—thus making the town a gateway rather than a true stopping place. As such, the town has never been entirely dependent on the tourist dollar. This fact should not deter you, however, from taking a bit of time to discover some of this market town's more intriguing areas.

In Kendal are the ruins of a castle where Catherine Parr, the last wife of Henry VIII, was allegedly born, although there's been recent speculation about her actual birthplace. Even if she wasn't in fact born here, it is still said that she most likely lived at the castle during some time in her life. Among other historic sites, Kendal has a 13th-century parish church that merits a visit.

The town was also associated with George Romney, the 18th-century portrait painter (Lady Hamilton was his favorite subject) who used to travel all over the Lake District trying to get someone to sit for him. He held his first exhibition in Kendal, married, and had children here. He deserted them in 1762, not returning until the end of his life, dying in Kendal in 1802.

Today, Kendal is famous for its mint cake and surrounding limestone fells, which offer excellent vistas of the area and make for great hiking excursions.

## ESSENTIALS

**GETTING THERE**  Trains from London's Euston Station do not go directly to Kendal, per se—rather the seven daily trains arrive in Oxenholme, which is about 1¹/₂ miles from Kendal. From here, you'll be able to take one of the local trains that leave approximately every hour to Kendal proper (a 3¹/₂-hour trip). For train schedules and information, call ☎ **0345/484950.**

To Kendal from London by bus, take one of the three daily National Express buses (a 7-hour trip). For schedules and information, call National Express at ☎ **0990/808080.**

If you drive, follow the M1 out of London, then the M6 to Kendal (a 5-hour trip).

**VISITOR INFORMATION**  **The Tourist Information Centre,** Town Hall, Highgate (☎ **01539/725758**), is open November to Easter, Monday to Saturday from 9am to 5pm; Easter through October, Monday to Saturday from 9am to 5pm and Sunday from 10am to 4pm.

## SEEING THE SIGHTS

For a good survey of the area's history, visit the local museums. **Kendal Museum,** Station Road (☎ 01539/721374), one of England's oldest museums, takes visitors on a journey of discovery from Roman times to the present. A natural history section includes a nature trail from mountaintop to lakeside on which visitors are brought face to face with many of the inhabitants of the area. The World Wildlife Gallery displays a vast collection of exotic animals. One exhibition introduces visitors to the fell-tops' best-known visitors—Alfred Wainwright, who walked, talked, and wrote with passion and flair about the region. Wainwright worked diligently until his death in 1991. Open mid-February through March, daily from 10:30am to 4pm and from April through late December, daily from 10:30am to 5pm. Admission is £2.50 ($4) for adults, £1.90 ($3.05) for seniors, and £1 ($1.60) for children.

Another museum devoted to the old ways of life in Kendal is the **Museum of Lakeland Life and Industry,** Kirkland (☎ 01539/722464). From the re-creation of a Victorian Kendal street, complete with pharmacy and market, the visitor can discover the lost craft and trades of the region and the ways of life that have accompanied them. Open mid-February through March, daily from 10:30am to 4pm and from April through late December, daily from 10:30am to 5pm. Admission is £2.50 ($4) for adults, £1.90 ($3.05) for seniors, and £1 ($1.60) for children.

The Georgian elegance of Kendal's **Abbot Hall Art Gallery,** Kirkland (☎ 01539/722464), has created an ideal setting for its display of fine art. Paintings by the town's famous son, 18th-century portrait painter George Romney, fill the walls of rooms furnished by Gillows of Lancaster. A major display of work by 20th-century British artists such as Graham Sutherland, John Piper, and Ben Nicholson are on permanent display. Visitors to the Lake District can see the region through the eyes of the many painters who have been inspired by the area in another of the gallery's permanent exhibitions housed in The Peter Scott Gallery. Open mid-February through March, daily from 10:30am to 4pm and from April through late December, daily from 10:30am to 5pm. Admission is £2.50 ($4) for adults, £1.90 ($3.05) for seniors, and £1 ($1.60) for children.

Just a few miles outside of town sit two historic residences. **Sizergh Castle,** $3^{1}/_{2}$ miles south of Kendal, northwest of interchange A590/591 (☎ 015395/60070), has a pele tower that dates from the 14th century. Inside, visitors can see a collection of Elizabethan carvings and paneling, fine furniture, and portraits. The complete garden, largely from the 18th century, incorporates a rock garden and a famous planting of hardy ferns and dwarf conifers. The castle is surrounded by a show of fiery colors during the autumn. Open April through October, Sunday through Thursday from 1:30pm to 5:30pm. The last admission is at 5pm. Admission is £3.80 ($6.10) for adults, £1.90 ($3.05) for children, and £10 ($16) for a family ticket (two adults and two children).

**Levens Hall,** Levens Park, Levens, 4 miles south of Kendal (☎ 015395/60321), is an Elizabethan mansion constructed in the 1500s by James Bellingham. Today the house is filled with Jacobean furniture and a working model of steam collection. The estate also has a topiary garden dating from 1692 in which grow a host of yews and box hedges clipped into a variety of intriguing shapes. Open April through September, Sunday to Thursday from 11am to 5pm. Admission is £4.20 ($6.70) for the house and gardens, and £2.50 ($4) for the gardens only.

From tiny tree frogs to 15-foot pythons, **Kendal Reptiles,** Stircklandgate (☎ 01539/721240), is a haven for those who like creepy, crawly things. Creatures like snakes, lizards, frogs, and spiders are all housed in a carefully controlled, heated micro-climate which makes up this modern and attractive nature exhibit. Open November though March, Monday to Saturday from 9am to 5pm; and April through October, Monday to Saturday from 9am to 5pm and Sunday from 10:30am to 4:30pm. Admission is free.

## SHOPPING

A variety of shops can be found throughout the town, but the three areas with the densest concentration of stores are Finkle Street, Blackhall Yard on Blackhall Road, and Westmorland Shopping Centre on Stricklandgate.

In the heart of Kendal is **Westmorland Shopping Centre,** Stricklandgate (☎ **01539/740060**), with major stores like Argos and Principles, smaller specialty shops, traditional restaurants, and events and entertainment all year-round. On the upper level of Westmorland is **The Market Hall** (☎ **01539/733333**), where 18 permanent traders set up their stalls, plus different daily traders operate at about 20 additional tables. Monday is secondhand goods day. And outdoor markets are held in the marketplace off Stricklandgate on Wednesday and Saturday, with more stalls along Stramongate.

**Kentmere Pottery,** Kentmere, Staveley, north of Kendal (☎ **01539/821621**), produces and sells fine handpainted English enamels and lustres such as lamps, jardinières, individual pieces, tableware, and commissions that are specially designed to meet your requirements. Nearby, **Peter Hall & Sons Woodcraft Workshop,** Kentmere, Staveley (☎ **01539/821633**), is the site of a genuine cabinetmakers workshop. Craftspeople work on new and antique furniture, including tables, chairs, dressers, traditionally upholstered suites, bowls, lazy Susans, lamps, and wine coasters.

You can also wander the many acres that make up **Webb's Garden Centre,** Burnside Road (☎ **01539/720068**), an undercover complex containing thousands of plants and gifts, which also has a cafe on site.

## WHERE TO STAY

**Holmfield.** 41 Kendal Green, Kendal, Cumbria LA9 5PP. ☎ **01539/720790.** 3 rms, none with bath. TV. £20–£22 ($32–$35.20) per person single and double. All rates include English breakfast. No credit cards.

This rather whimsical, stone Edwardian house, with its pink-tiled, Dutch barn roof, sits at the end of a very private 100-yard drive. Built in 1904 for a Kendal snuff baron, the house was ironically one of the first B&Bs in England to go completely nonsmoking. The bedrooms are all very large, with high ceilings, antique furnishings, and warm colors. An added plus is that all rooms look out over landscaped gardens and the distant hills of the Lake District. Guests can enjoy a sitting room and, in the morning, a sunlit-filled dining room that offers panoramic views of the countryside and an Inglenook fireplace. This is the room where the owners cheerfully say that they "throw breakfast parties instead of dinner parties." Indeed, breakfast here is quite the social event. The grounds include a heated swimming pool and a croquet lawn, and Holmfield is a 10-minute walk from the center of town. No pets or children are allowed.

**Lane Head House.** Helsington, Kendal, Cumbria LA9 5RJ. ☎ **01539/731283.** Fax 01539/721023. 6 rms, 2 suites. TV TEL. £40 ($64) single; £60 ($96) double; £70 ($112) suite. All rates include English breakfast. V.

Guests can soar across the countryside with the views from this B&B of the River Kent Valley and the Lake District. This 17th-century manor house was actually constructed on an elevated plot of land that had ruins of a Pele Tower—a fortress location used during the battles between the English and Scots so many years ago. Guest rooms here are average size with original oak beams from the 1600s and are appointed with period-style reproductions. All rooms have romantic arch windows with views of the landscaped gardens, the Elizabethan knot garden and maze, and the fruit orchard of apples, pears, and plums. Beyond that is pasturelands and the River Kent. Breakfast is served in the dining room, and all public rooms have dark wood paneling and similar wood accents. There is no smoking in the dining room, and a three-course dinner can be had upon prior arrangement.

## A YOUTH HOSTEL

**Kendal Youth Hostel.** 118 Highgate, Kendal, Cumbria LA9 4HE. ☎ **01539/724066.** Fax 01539/724906. 54 beds. £8.50 ($13.60) adults; £5.70 ($9.10) children under 18. MC, V.

This hostel is right in the center of town, next door to the Brewery Arts Centre and plenty of restaurants and nightlife. The hostel is located in a Georgian town house built in 1740 by the owner of the town's brewery, as his personal residence. When the brewery closed it was converted into the neighboring Brewery Arts Centre. The house was turned into a hostel 10 years ago and successfully maintains its old character and original features, like an ornate and winding staircase, alongside many modern conveniences. The 12 guest rooms, all clean and bright, are located upstairs and have anywhere from two to six beds in them. They are all decorated with old show posters from the Brewery Arts Centre. Breakfast costs £2.85 ($4.55), a packed lunch is £2.45 ($3.90), and dinner is £4.25 ($6.80). If the wholesome food here is not to your liking, or if you want to check out the local nightlife, there are plenty of restaurants, pubs, and shows to see in the town center. The hostel opens from mid-February through December. The 11pm curfew is enforced, and the reception is open from 7:30 to 10am and from 5 to 11pm.

## WHERE TO EAT

**Don Gaeta.** 24 Finkle St. ☎ **01539/720547.** Reservations recommended. Lunch £2.50–£12 ($4–$19.20); main courses £3–£12 ($4.80–$19.20). MC, V. Mon–Sat noon–2pm and 6–10:30pm; Sun 6–10:30pm. ITALIAN.

You've got to look a little for this one, but it's well worth the effort. It's down a little alley off Finkle Street, then up a flight of stairs to the first floor. Inside, you'll find a happy, if not unusual, marriage of a large sitting area with a cozy feel—in all, a romantic candlelit ambience. Lunch dishes can be ordered from a menu or a daily specials board with such items as pizza or bow tie pasta with lobster sauce. The dinner menu includes tagliatelle with leeks and scampi in a rich cream sauce; a house lasagna consisting of layers of egg, ham, and pepperoni all in a bolognese sauce; and baked chicken stuffed with salami and cheese with a mushroom and Napoli sauce. The wine list constantly changes and favors robust red wines.

**Moon.** 129 Highgate. ☎ **01539/729254.** Main courses £7.45–£9.75 ($11.90–$15.60). MC, V. Tues–Fri and Sun 6:30–10pm; Sat 6–10pm. INTERNATIONAL.

This bistro-style restaurant cooks up what has been called "the best food in Kendal." In a building that's more than 250 years old and was once a grocery store, the dining room offers patrons a close, friendly, and informal environment filled with lively conversations. Main courses include filet steak in Roquefort cheese sauce wrapped in phylo pastry and served with mushroom coulis; monkfish prepared in Thai tomato, lime, and coriander sauce; and, for vegetarians, creamed parsnip, lentil, and tomato tortillas with parmesan sauce.

## KENDAL AFTER DARK

For performing arts along the lines of theater, jazz, and other live musical events, try the **Brewery Arts Centre,** Highgate (☎ 01539/725133), which is also the headquarters for the **Kendal Jazz and Blues Festival,** held every year in and around the arts center.

For a more earthy adventure to start or end your evening, try one of the many character-filled (both in ambience and patrons) pubs including **Gateway,** Crook Road (☎ **01539/724187**); **Globe,** Market Place (☎ **01539/724042**); and **Ring o' Bells,** Kirkland (☎ **01539/720326**), which shares the parish church grounds.

## 3  Windermere & Bowness

274 miles NW of London; 10 miles NW of Kendal; 55 miles N of Liverpool

The largest lake in England is Windermere, whose eastern shore washes up on the town of Bowness (or Bowness-on-Windermere), with Windermere the town 1¹/₂ miles away. From either town, you can climb **Orrest Head** in less than an hour for a panoramic view of England's Lakeland. From that vantage point, you can even see **Scafell Pike,** rising to a height of 3,210 feet—the peak pinnacle in all of England.

## ESSENTIALS

**GETTING THERE**    Trains to Windermere meet the main line at Oxenholme for connections to both Scotland and London. Information about rail services in the area can be obtained by calling the Oxenholme Railway Station (☎ **0345/484950**, only available for use in the U.K.). Frequent connections are possible throughout the day. To get to Bowness and its ferry pier from Windermere, turn left from the rail terminal and cross the center of Windermere until you reach New Road, which eventually changes its name to Lake Road before it approaches the outskirts of Bowness. It's about a 20-minute walk downhill. The CMS Lakeland Experience bus also runs from the Windermere Station to Bowness every 20 minutes.

The National Express bus link, originating at London's Victoria Coach Station, serves Windermere, with good connections also to Preston, Manchester, and Birmingham. For schedules and information, call ☎ **0990/808080.** Local buses operated mainly by Cumberland Motor Services (CMS) (☎ **01946/63222**) go to Kendal, Ambleside, Grasmere, and Keswick. Call for information on various routings within the Lake District.

If you're driving from London, head north on the M1 and M6 past Liverpool until you reach the A685 junction heading west to Kendal. From Kendal, A591 continues west to Windermere.

There are launch and steamer cruises from Bowness daily throughout the year operated by **Windermere Lake Cruises Ltd. (☎ 015394/43360**). Service is available from Bowness to Ambleside and to Lakeside at rates ranging from £5.30 to £8.75 ($8.50 to $14) for adults and £2.65 to £4.40 ($4.25 to $7.05) for children. There is a 45-minute Island Cruise for £4.20 ($6.70) for adults and £2.10 ($3.35) for children. At Lakeside you can ride a steam train to Haverthwaite. A combination boat/train ticket is £8.15 ($13.05) for adults and £4.15 ($6.65) for children. A new attraction at Lakeside, near Newby Bridge, is the Aquatarium (☎ **015395/30153**) with an exhibit of fish and wildlife. Combination boat/admission tickets from Ambleside are £11.95 ($19.10) for adults, £7 ($11.20) for children, and £36.75 ($58.80) for a family; and from Bowness £9.30 ($14.90) for adults, £5.40 ($8.65) for children, and £28.70 ($45.90) for a family.

## Impressions

*The two views we have had of it are of the most noble tenderness—they can never fade away—they make one forget the divisions of life; age, youth, poverty and riches; and refine one's sensual vision into a sort of north star which can never cease to be open lidded and stedfast over the wonders of the great power.*

—John Keats on Lake Windermere (1818)

**VISITOR INFORMATION**  The **Tourist Information Centre** at Windermere is on Victoria Street (☎ **015394/46499**). Open November through February, daily from 9am to 5pm; March through June, daily from 9am to 6pm, and in July and August, daily from 9am to 7:30pm. The **Tourist Information Centre** at The Glebe in Bowness (☎ **015394/42895**) is open April through October, daily from 9:30am to 5:30pm.

# WINDERMERE

There is regular **steamer service** around Windermere, the largest of the lakes, about $10^{1}/_{2}$ miles long. It's also possible to take a steamer on Coniston Water, a small lake that Wordsworth called "a broken spoke sticking in the rim." Coniston Water is a smaller and less heavily traveled lake than Windermere. Ullswater, a lake measuring $7^{1}/_{2}$ miles long, used to be called "Ulfr's Water." It is second in size to Lake Windermere and can also be crossed by lake steamer. For details about how to explore these bodies of water, see "Enjoying the Great Outdoors," above.

## WINDERMERE STEAMBOAT MUSEUM

The Windermere Steamboat Museum, on Rayrigg Road (☎ **015394/45565**), houses the finest collection of steamboats in the world. Important examples of these elegant Victorian and Edwardian vessels have been preserved in working order. The steamboats are exhibited in a unique wet dock where they are moored in their natural lakeside setting. The fine display of touring and racing motorboats in the dry dock links the heyday of steam with some of the most famous names of powerboat racing and record-breaking attempts on Windermere, including Sir Henry Segrave's world water speed record set in 1930.

All the boats have intriguing stories, including the veteran S.L. *Dolly,* built around 1850 and probably the oldest mechanically driven boat in the world. The vessel was raised from the lake bed of Ullswater in 1962 and, following restoration, ran for 10 years with its original boiler. *Dolly* is still steamed on special occasions.

The wet dock also houses the Chris-Craft speedboat *Jane* dating from 1938. In the dry dock is the first glider to take off from the water (1943), and the record-breaking hydroplane *Miss Windermere IV.* There is also Beatrix Potter's rowing boat and the sailing dinghy *Amazon* from Arthur Ransome's classic story "Swallows and Amazons."

Also displayed is the *Esperance,* an iron-hulled steam yacht built for a local industrialist, Henry William Schneider, in 1869, and the S.S. *Raven* constructed in 1871 to carry everything from coal and timber to farm produce and beer to the scattered communities around the lake when the only alternative would have been to transport these goods by horse and cart over very poor roads.

The museum is open daily from Easter to the end of October, 10am to 5pm. Admission is £2.90 ($4.65) for adults and £1.50 ($2.40) for children. The S.L. *Osprey* (1902) is steamed most days and visitors can make a 50-minute trip on the lake, at a cost of £4.75 ($7.60) for adults and £3.50 ($5.60) for children, with the crew serving tea or coffee made using the Windermere steam kettle.

## MORE ATTRACTIONS

**The World of Beatrix Potter** (The Old Laundry, Bowness-on-Windermere (☎ **015394/88444**), uses the latest technology to tell the story of Beatrix Potter's fascinating life. A video wall and special film describe how her tales came to be written and how Beatrix Potter became a pioneering Lakeland farmer and conservationist. There is also a shop where you will discover a wealth of top quality Beatrix Potter merchandise from Wedgwood ceramics to soft toys. Admission is £2.99 ($4.80) for adults and £1.99 ($3.20) for children. To get here, take the A591 to Lake Road and follow the signs.

Outside of Windermere, you can visit the **National Park Visitor Centre** at Brockhole (☎ **015394/46601**), on the road to Ambleside. Brockhole has extensive landscaped gardens, offers lake cruises, exhibitions, and film shows. Some of the special events for all the family include "Environmentally Yours," "Animal Extravaganza," and "A Victorian Affair." Lunches and teas are served in Gaddums tearooms which have terrace seating, and 30 acres of gardens and parkland can be explored. Normally there is free admission, except for special events staged here. Parking costs £2.50 ($4) for 2 hours or £3.50 ($5.60) for the day. To get here take the A591 midway between Windermere and Ambleside on the shores of Windermere.

## SHOPPING

In the center of Windermere, visitors drop in to **John Kershaw's Workshop and Showroom** (☎ **015394/44844**). At this pottery workshop and showroom you'll find a wide range of work that is produced in a very distinctive style using strong shapes and textures, heavily influenced by ancient and ethnic pottery.

Another intriguing shopping possibility is **Made in Cumbria Craft Shop** on Victoria Street (☎ **015394/46499**). This craft shop is located downstairs at Windermere Tourist Information Centre. Here you'll find a wide selection of craftwork made by Cumbria's top craftspeople on display at affordable prices.

## WHERE TO STAY

The **Queens Head** and the **Punch Bowl** (see "Where to Eat," below) also rent rooms.

### Doubles for Less Than £35

**Brendan Chase.** 1–3 College Rd., Windermere, Cumbria LA23 1BU. ☎ and fax **015394/ 45638.** 8 rms, 4 with bath. TV. £14 ($22.40) single without bath, £20 ($32) single with shower only; £28 ($44.80) double without bath, £30 ($48) double with shower only. All rates include English breakfast. No credit cards. Take High St.

Mr. and Mrs. Graham are pleased to welcome guests to their long-established Edwardian home 150 yards off A591 leading into town. In the center of the Lakeland resort, the guest house is nevertheless in a tranquil location yet convenient to the attractions. Each comfortably furnished room has a TV and beverage-making equipment, and there's also a TV lounge. Families are welcomed and quoted special rates. There is adequate parking adjacent to the guest house.

**Kenilworth Guest House.** Holly Rd., Windermere, Cumbria LA23 2AF. ☎ **015394/44004.** 6 rms, 3 with bath. TV. £14.50–£16.50 ($23.20–$26.40) single without bath; £29–£33 ($46.40– $52.80) double without bath; £34–£38 ($54.40–$60.80) double with bath; £45–£55 ($72–$88) family rm with bath. All rates include English breakfast. No credit cards.

This house is known for its cleanliness, comfort, and good value. Tony and Cynthia Roberts offer centrally heated, pleasant bedrooms, each with hot and cold running water. Guests are received year-round. An informal atmosphere prevails. It's located near Broad Street in the town center.

✪ **Rockside Guest House.** Ambleside Rd., Windermere, Cumbria LA23 1AQ. ☎ **015394/ 45343.** Fax 015394/45533. 15 rms, 10 with bath (shower). TV TEL. £16.50 ($26.40) single without bath, £22.50 ($36) single with bath; £34 ($54.40) double without bath, £37–£45 ($59.20–$72) double with bath. All rates include English breakfast. MC, V.

This guest house near the train station is run by Neville and Mavis Fowles, who came to this area to achieve their ambition of living in "the most beautiful corner of England." They have since made Rockside one of the best B&B establishments in the area. Standard rooms have hot and cold running water basins, whereas those listed as "top choice" contain private showers and toilets, beverage-making facilities, and hair dryers. The breakfast menu gives you a wide choice. At the rear of the house is a parking area for 12 vehicles, but Rockside is only a 2-minute walk from the bus, train, or village of Windermere. The Fowles, who like to make sure their guests see what the area has to offer, can also organize a half- or full-day minibus tour of the Lake District.

### Doubles for Less Than £50

✪ **Fir Trees.** Lake Rd., Windermere, Cumbria LA23 2EQ. ☎ and fax **015394/42272.** 7 rms. TV. £25–£31 ($40–$49.60) single; £40–£52 ($64–$83.20) double. All rates include English breakfast. AE, MC, V.

This is by most accounts the finest guest house in Windermere. It's very well run, and you get hotel-like standards at B&B tariffs. Opposite St. John's Church halfway between the villages of Bowness and Windermere, Fir Trees is a Victorian house furnished with antiques. Proprietors Allene and Ira Fishman offer a warm welcome and rent well-furnished and beautifully maintained bedrooms, each with beverage-making equipment and other thoughtful amenities. Some units are large enough for families. The Fishmans know the Lake District extremely well and provide their guests with detailed information on restaurants, country pubs, or on where to go and what to see. This is a nonsmoking facility.

✪ **Hawksmoor.** Lake Rd. (between Windermere and Bowness), Windermere, Cumbria LA23 2EQ. ☎ **015394/42110.** 10 rms. TV. £24–£31 ($38.40–$49.60) single; £48–£62 ($76.80–$99.20) double. All rates include English breakfast. MC, V.

Bob and Barbara Tyson have restored this old Lake District home, which must be at least a century old. A modern extension was added in the 1980s. Some family-style rooms are available. Mrs. Tyson reveals her decorating flair in her warm, inviting dining room, which is of a standard far superior to your typical B&B. Here you can order a four-course evening meal, costing £11.50 ($18.40) and up per head. Always call or write in advance.

## WHERE TO EAT

✪ **Miller Howe Café.** Lakeland Plastics, Station Precinct. ☎ **015394/46732.** Main courses £5–£7.50 ($8–$12). MC, V. Mon–Fri 9am–5pm; Sat 10am–5pm; Sun 10am–4pm. INTERNATIONAL.

This restaurant was opened by former actor John Tovey, the celebrated owner of the Miller Howe Hotel, a prestigious (and expensive) lakeside inn known for fine dining. Now owned by his former head chef, Ian Dutton, this charming little cafe lies at the back of a shop that is known as one of the largest retailers of "creative kitchenware" in Britain. Amid a very modern decor, clients place their food orders at a countertop, then wait until the dishes are brought to their tables by waitresses. The cuisine draws upon culinary traditions from around the world, and includes such dishes as diced and curried beef in a spicy sauce, fillet of salmon with a fresh garden herb sauce, macaroni baked with heavy cream and red Cheddar cheese, and breast of chicken served in a red wine gravy. The restaurant is adjacent to the town's railway station.

**Porthole Eating House.** 3 Ash St. ☎ **015394/42793.** Reservations recommended. Main courses £7–£13 ($11.20–$20.80). AE, DC, MC, V. Sun–Fri noon–3pm; Wed–Mon 6:30–11pm. FRENCH/ITALIAN/ENGLISH.

In a white-painted Lakeland house near the center of town, this restaurant, owned and operated by Gianni and Judy Barten for the last quarter of a century, serves French, English, and Italian cuisine inspired by Italian-born Gianni. Amid a decor enhanced by rows of wine and liqueur bottles and nautical accessories, you can enjoy well-flavored specialties that change with the seasons. Examples include lobster-and-crab bisque; goat cheese and leek timbale; tomato tart; noisette of pan-fried lamb; vegetarian lasagna made with mixed vegetables, fresh herbs, and a fresh tomato coulis and basil sauce; and fillet of beef lightly grilled and served with a reduction of butter, fresh herbs, and a touch of white wine.

**Punch Bowl.** Crosthwaite, Windermere, Cumbria LA8 8HR. ☎ **015395/68237.** Reservations recommended. Main courses £6.75–£9 ($10.80–$14.40). MC, V. Daily noon–2pm and 6–9pm. CONTINENTAL.

Since chef Stephen Doherty has taken over this 16th-century inn, it's known for more than beds and a pint in the pub. Doherty, who studied under the brothers Roux, has brought a flare to the dining room that has locals and visitors alike coming in to sample his fare. In fact, the place has become so popular that there's no guarantee you'll get a table if you don't call first. Menu items include Cumbrian air-dried ham with Italian-style marinated and grilled vegetables and fillet of sea bass with a ginger, spring onion, and soy sauce. Starters include a deliciously simple tomato and basil soup and pork terrine with homemade chutney. Besides the a la carte menu, there are daily blackboard specials, and the menu changes every 6 months to reflect spring/summer dishes and autumn/winter dishes. The restaurant/pub service area is very spacious, including a large main room with a high-beamed ceiling and upper minstrel galleries, as well as four additional rooms off a hallway just a few steps down from the main area. There are also three comfortable sleeping rooms available, each equipped with two twin beds. The rate for a single room is £35 ($56); a double is £50 ($80).

**Queens Head.** A592 north of Windermere, Cumbria LA23 1TW. ☎ **015394/32174.** Reservations recommended. Main courses £6.60–£13.50 ($10.55–$21.60). DC, MC, V. Daily 6:30–9pm. CONTINENTAL.

Voted the Cumbria Dining Pub of the Year in 1996, this unusual 17th-century coaching inn uses a huge Elizabethan four-poster bed as its serving counter and has other eclectic antiques scattered in among its traditional wooden bar furniture. The menu, which changes every 3 to 4 weeks, feels much the same way, combining common items in unusual ways, taking traditional dishes and making them more exotic. A recent sampling included main courses such as chicken rolled in garlic and herbs served on a bed of creamed leeks with beetroot sauce and roasted breast of duck served on creamed cabbage bordered with plum sauce. You can finish with one of their lovely puddings, perhaps an orange and chocolate tart with a Grand Marnier sabayon. There's also a full bar and reasonable wine selections. If you're looking for a place to stay in the area, they also have eight well-furnished rooms with rates of £40 ($64) single or £60 ($96) double.

**Swainsons.** Cross St., Windermere, Cumbria LA23 1AE. ☎ **015394/43120.** Main courses £5.50–£11 ($8.80–$17.60). AE, MC, V. Restaurant: daily noon–2:30pm and 6–9:30pm. Public bar: Mon–Sat 11am–11pm; Sun noon–3pm and 7–10:30pm. BRITISH/CONTINENTAL.

This restaurant, located at the Elleray Hotel, is the top choice of the local guest houses for where to eat in Windermere. They offer a relaxed atmosphere, gracious service, and beautifully presented and reasonable priced good food. The menu is available in both the cozy Lounge Bar with a glowing fire in the winter, or in the nonsmoking restaurant. All dishes are prepared only with fresh produce. The menu might include grilled ham steak served with pineapple or fried egg, garden peas, and french fries, or prime roast of beef with Yorkshire pudding, fresh vegetables, and potatoes. Fresh fish, seafood specialties, and desserts are displayed on the blackboard. They also serve a "special of the day" from 6 to 7pm. The Elleray Hotel, a local B&B, offers bedrooms with central heating, washbasins, TVs, and tea- and coffee-making facilities from £15 ($24).

## WINDERMERE AFTER DARK

Drive a short distance south of Windermere to Cartmel Fell, situated between A592 and A5074, and you'll find a pub lover's dream. The ✪ **Mason Arms,** Strawberry Bank (☎ **01539/568486**), is a Jacobean pub offering a stunning view of the Winster Valley. Retaining its original oak paneling and flagstone floors, there's sturdy, comfortable wooden furniture spread through a series of five rooms in which you can wander or settle. The outside garden, attractive in its own right, offers the most dramatic view of the valley beyond. The pub offers so many beers that they have a 24-page catalog to help you order. You can find some rare selections or stick to their house brews—Amazon, Big Six, or Great Northern. If you're in the mood for something a little more exotic, try their damson (plum) beer or Knickerbockerbreaker, a hard cider from local apples. A creative, reasonable menu includes several tasty vegetarian options.

There's an eclectic mix of seating, ales, and whiskies at the **Watermill** (☎ **01539/ 821309**), just east of Windermere off A591 in Ings. Choose a padded or wooden chair, pew, or stool; then look over the selection of six regular ales, including Lees Moonraker and Blacksheep Bitter, eight rotating guest ales, and more than 50 whiskies. If any of the numerous outdoor activities nearby whet your appetite, there's good tradition pub grub here as well.

# BOWNESS

Directly south of Windermere, Bowness is an attractive old lakeside town with lots of interesting architecture, much of it dating back to Queen Victoria's day. This has been an important center for boating and fishing for a long time, and you can rent boats of all descriptions to explore the lake.

## WHERE TO STAY

**Belsfield Guest House.** 4 Belsfield Terrace, Kendal Rd., Bowness-on-Windermere, Cumbria LA23 3EQ. ☎ **015394/45823.** 9 rms. TV. £21–£27 ($33.60–$43.20) single; £36–£44 ($57.60–$70.40) double. All rates include English breakfast. No credit cards.

Built in the 1830s by a wealthy industrialist from the Midlands, this house has walls made from Lakeland slate, a facade covered with white stucco and layers of white paint, and from the back a view out over Lake Windermere. In the heart of town, the building is owned by the Grantham family, who have performed many renovations. The bedrooms are modernized and cozy. Breakfast is the only meal served.

**Thornleigh Guest House.** Thornbarrow Rd., Bowness-on-Windermere, Cumbria LA23 2EW. ☎ **015394/44203.** 5 rms, 4 with shower only. TV. £17–£23 ($27.20–$36.80) single; £34–£46 ($54.40–$73.60) double. All rates include English breakfast. No credit cards.

Set amid a cluster of other houses, overlooking fields and forests (but not the lake), this guest house is a late Victorian stone-sided Lakeland house that has been maintained as a B&B since the 1970s. You'll find it midway between the settlements of Bowness and Windermere. The bedrooms are simply furnished and outfitted with fresh and light-pastel colors, and contain tea makers and accessories. No meals are served other than breakfast.

## BOWNESS AFTER DARK

Established in 1612, the **Hole in t' Wall**, Lowside (☎ **01539/443488**), is Bowness' oldest pub and is viewed as a treasure by regulars and visitors alike because of its character and friendliness. The barroom is decorated with a hodgepodge of antiquated farming tools, and there's a large slate fireplace lending warmth on winter days. Real ales on tap include Robinsons Frederics, Old Tom, and Old Stockport. The menu is determined daily and there's real ingenuity illustrated in an eclectic mix of vegetarian, seafood, and local game dishes. There's a small flagstoned terrace in the front for lingering on warmer days and evenings.

# 4 Ambleside & Rydal

278 miles NW of London; 14 miles NW of Kendal; 4 miles N of Windermere

An idyllic retreat, Ambleside is one of the major centers of the Lake District, attracting pony trekkers, fell hikers, and rock scalers. The charms are here all year, even in late autumn, when it's fashionable to sport a mackintosh. Ambleside is perched at the north end of Lake Windermere. Just a small village with few attractions, it's used primarily as a refueling stop or overnight stopover for those exploring the Lake District.

Between Ambleside and Wordsworth's former retreat at Grasmere is Rydal, a small village on one of the smallest lakes, Rydal Water. The village is noted for its sheep-dog trials at the end of summer. It's 1¹/₂ miles north of Ambleside on A591.

## ESSENTIALS

**GETTING THERE**   Take a train to Windermere (see above), then continue the rest of the way by bus.

Cumberland Motor Services (CMS) (☎ **01946/63222**) has hourly bus service from Grasmere and Keswick (see below) and from Windermere. All these buses into Ambleside are labeled either no. 555 or no. 557.

If you're driving from Windermere, continue northwest on A591.

**VISITOR INFORMATION**   The **Tourist Information Centre** is at Old Courthouse, Church Street, in Ambleside (☎ **015394/32582**). Open April through October, daily from 9am to 5pm and from November through March on Tuesday to Saturday with reduced hours.

## ✪ RYDAL MOUNT: WORDSWORTH'S HOME

Off A591, 1¹/₂ miles north of Ambleside, Rydal Mount (% 015394/33002) was the home of William Wordsworth from 1813 until his death in 1850. Part of the house was built as a farmer's lake cottage around 1575. A descendant of Wordsworth's now owns the property, which displays numerous portraits, furniture, and family possessions as well as mementos and the poet's books. The 4¹/₂-acre garden, landscaped by Wordsworth, is filled with rare trees, shrubs, and other features of interest.

The house is open March to October, daily from 9:30am to 5pm; November to February, daily from 10am to 4pm (closed Tuesday in winter). Admission is £3 ($4.80) for adults, £2.50 ($4) for seniors and students, £1 ($1.60) for children 5 to 16, and free for kids 4 and under. Entrance to the garden is £1.50 ($2.40).

# SHOPPING

**Adrian Sankey,** Rydal Road (☎ 015394/33039), is an open workshop with a distinctive collection of both traditional and contemporary lead crystal studio glass. Here you can watch craftspeople manipulate the molten material into countless different forms. There are delightful perfume bottles, bowls, vases, paperweights, drinking vessels, period lamps, and contemporary atmospheric lighting. The Glass House Café Restaurant is open for your refreshment. To get here go to Rydal Road in Ambleside behind Bridge House.

**The Kirkstone Galleries,** Ambleside (☎ 015394/34002), originated by crafting Lakeland stone, and now it displays one of the largest and most unusual collections of crafts and home furnishings in Cumbria. It has everything from kitchen worktops to Kirkstone jewelry, elegant colored glass, handcrafted picture frames, lamps, and so much more. If you need a respite from shopping and sightseeing, try some of their home-baked cakes, which are served in Chesters, their coffee shop. To get here take the A593 from Ambleside to Coniston. It's on the banks of the River Brathay at Skelwith Bridge.

# WHERE TO STAY

## IN AMBLESIDE

**Crow How Hotel.** Rydal Rd., Ambleside, Cumbria LA22 9PN. ☎ **015394/32193.** 9 rms, 8 with bath. TV. Mon–Thurs £18 ($28.80) single without bath, £28.50 ($45.60) single with bath; £36 ($57.60) double without bath, £58 ($92.80) double with bath. Fri–Sun £24 ($38.40) single without bath, £32.50 ($52) single with bath; £48 ($76.80) double without bath, £65 ($104) double with bath. All rates include English breakfast. AE, MC, V. Closed Dec–Jan.

Along a private drive off A591 north of Ambleside, the Crow How is only a few minutes' walk from Rydal Water. This was originally a large Victorian farmhouse of Lakeland stone. The proprietors are Pattie and Edward Scott. The bedrooms are plainly furnished and have beverage-making facilities and controllable heaters, whereas the public rooms are centrally heated. The hotel has a large guest lounge, a small but well-stocked bar, and 2 acres of gardens. Dinner is optional at £13.50 ($21.60) per person.

**Queens Hotel.** Market Place, Ambleside, Cumbria LA22 9BU. ☎ **015394/32206.** Fax 015394/32721. 26 rms. TV TEL. Mon–Thurs £25–£33 ($40–$52.80) single; £50 ($80) double. Fri–Sun £28–£33 ($44.80–$52.80) single; £56 ($89.60) double. AE, DC, MC, V.

In the heart of the resort area is the Queens, an old-fashioned and long-established family-run hotel where guests are housed and fed well. Victorians erected the building as a private house, and it was later transformed into a hotel, with some restoration completed in 1992. Since the hotel has two fully licensed bars and restaurants, you may want to dine here. The food is good and hearty. Locals and tourists alike gravitate to the hotel bar. Bar meals are served throughout the day. Residents pay only £15 ($24) for a fixed-price four-course dinner, whereas non-residents are charged £17.50 ($28). The Queens is centrally heated in winter.

**✪ Rothay Garth Hotel.** Rothay Rd., Ambleside, Cumbria LA22 0EE. ☎ **015394/32217.** Fax 015394/34400. 16 rms, 14 with bath; 1 suite. TV TEL. £47 ($75.20) single without bath, £53 ($84.80) single with bath; £106 ($169.60) double with bath; £122 ($195.20) suite. All rates include English breakfast and a 5-course gourmet dinner with a minimum 2-night stay. AE, DC, MC, V. Free parking.

On the southern edge of Ambleside, along A591 from Kendal, is an elegant, century-old country house set in beautiful gardens. The bedrooms are tastefully decorated, warm, and comfortable, with hair dryers and tea- and coffeemakers. A varied cuisine is served in the restaurant where a table d'hôte menu costs £18.50 ($29.60). Fresh flowers are arranged throughout the hotel daily, and guests can enjoy a sunny garden room or the cozy lounge with its seasonal log fires. A wide choice of bar lunches is served all year in the Loughrigg Bar. The special ploughman's lunch has received much praise. Yachts, canoes, and sailboards can be rented. Tennis courts, a pitch-and-putt golf area, and a croquet lawn are adjacent to the hotel, and laundry and ironing facilities are available.

## IN RYDAL

**✪ Foxghyll.** Under Loughrigg, Rydal, near Ambleside, Cumbria LA22 9LL. ☎ **015394/ 33292.** 3 rms. TV. £25 ($40) single; £50 ($80) double. All rates include English breakfast. No credit cards.

You may need good directions to find Foxghyll, but if you succeed you'll have arrived at one of the best-value small B&Bs in the Rydal and Ambleside district. You're welcomed by Timothy and Marjorie Mann, who are happy to share this handsomely restored house that was once occupied by the writer Thomas De Quincey (*Confessions of an English Opium Eater*). Each room contains a radio, a hair dryer, and a comfortable chair or settee for reading. One room has a Jacuzzi-style tub and another has a four-poster bed. The Manns can only accept about six guests a night, so reservations are important. Solo travelers are accepted only off-season at the rates quoted above. Much of the house has a decorative overlay familiar to Queen Victoria, but parts of the building are said to date from the 1600s. The house stands on extensive grounds, which you can explore at leisure. It's about a 1-mile walk north of town.

## IN ELTERWATER

**Britannia Inn.** Elterwater, Ambleside, Cumbria LA22 9HP. ☎ and fax **015394/37210.** 9 rms, 8 with shower only. TV TEL. £24 ($38.40) single without bath; £56 ($89.60) double without bath; £62 ($99.20) double with shower only. All rates include English breakfast. AE, MC, V. Closed Christmas. Take A593 from Ambleside to Coniston for 2¹/₂ miles, then turn right onto B5343 to Elterwater. Bus: no. 516 from Ambleside.

Just off B5343 4 miles west of Ambleside is a 1690s traditional village inn adjoining the green in the unspoiled village of Elterwater. Views from the inn are over the meadows to the three tarns making up Elterwater ("lake of the swan") and the fells beyond. Bar meals are served in the cozy bar where a log fire blazes in cool weather. David Fry, the innkeeper, rents well-appointed double bedrooms, all with tea- and coffeemakers and hair dryers. Evening meals start at £5.50 ($8.80).

# WHERE TO EAT

## IN AMBLESIDE

**Apple Pie Eating House.** Rydal Rd. ☎ **015394/33679.** Soups £1.85 ($2.95); sandwiches £2.20–£2.80 ($3.50–$4.50); main courses £3.50–£4.50 ($5.60–$7.20). No credit cards. Mon–Sat 9am–5:30pm; Sun 10am–5:30pm. Closed Dec 20–26. Bus: no. 555. ENGLISH.

The most visible aspect of this bustling restaurant is its animated take-out counter. Lines form for the pastries, sandwiches, salads, and soups, which are dispensed by a hardworking group of waitresses. You'll also find a self-service cafeteria where quiches, pastries, meat pies, sandwiches, and snacks are served to dozens of hungry daytime diners. Whether you decide to buy "take-away food" or to eat at one of the simple tables, you might opt for a slice of the joint's trademark pastry, a cinnamon-laced chunk of apple pie. Weather permitting, you can dine outside on the patio. The restaurant is beside Ambleside's main parking area, in the town center.

**Sheila's Cottage Country Restaurant and Tea Room.** The Slack. ☎ **015394/33079.**
Reservations recommended for dinner. Lunch main courses £5–£8 ($8–$12.80); dinner main
courses £10–£12 ($16–$19.20); fixed-price afternoon cream tea £3.50 ($5.60); fixed-price
dinner £16–£19 ($25.60–$30.40). AE, MC, V. Morning coffee Mon–Sat 11am–noon; lunch
daily noon–2:30pm; afternoon tea Mon–Sat 2:45–5pm; dinner Mon–Sat 7–9:30pm.
MODERN ENGLISH.

Established many years ago by a since-departed woman named Sheila, this restaurant
is in a 1740s stone-sided Lake District cottage in the town center. Lunches are
relatively informal, featuring side dishes which might include a salad made with tiny
shrimp from nearby brackish estuaries, and Swiss-inspired Rösti made from shredded potatoes laced with cream and leeks. Dinners are more ambitious, with such
dishes as a tartare of Argyll salmon, smoked filet of Lakeland trout with fresh asparagus and chive vinaigrette, roast loin of lamb with a herb crust covered with a fricassée
of sweetbreads. As one satisfied diner told us—and we agree—"the food here tastes
like it used to."

**Zeffirellis.** Compston Rd. ☎ **015394/33845.** Main courses £4.95–£6.50 ($7.90–$10.40).
MC, V. Garden Room Café: daily 10am–5:30pm. Pizzeria and restaurant: Mon–Fri 6–9:45pm;
Sat–Sun noon–2pm and 5–9:45pm. Bus: no. 555. WHOLE-FOOD VEGETARIAN.

In the town's only movie theater, these restaurants are tucked away into simply decorated corners. At least some of the diners come as part of an evening on the town,
incorporating a movie into their dinner schedule. The theater itself is an old-fashioned
small-scale piece of architecture with a Japanese-inspired art-deco theme. The food
is completely vegetarian and includes pastas, pizzas, salads, and platters of fresh
vegetables covered, perhaps, in a sauce of Stilton cheese. Don't come here expecting
exciting taste sensations; all the dishes taste . . . well, wholesome. Wine and beer are
sold, too. Films are shown twice daily now that a second screen has been added.

## AMBLESIDE AFTER DARK

The friendliest pub in Ambleside is the **Golden Rule,** Smithy Brow (☎ **01539/
433363**), named for the brass yardstick mounted over the bar. There's a country hunt
theme, provided by hanging pictures and fox masks, in the barroom which features
comfortable leather furniture and cast-iron tables. You can step into one side room
and throw darts, or go into the other for quiet contemplation in a sitting room.
Behind the bar, a small but colorful garden provides a serene setting for a warm
weather pint; choose from Hartleys XB, Hatters Mild, Old Stockport, and Robinsons
Best. There's inexpensive pub grub if you get hungry.

Located 3 miles west of town, off the A593 in Little Langdale, **Three Shires**
(**015394/37215**), a stone-built pub with a stripped timber and flagstone interior,
offers stunning views of the valley and wooded hills. You can get good pub grub here,
as well as a pint of Black Sheep Bitter, Ruddles County, or Websters Yorkshire. Malt
whiskies are well represented as well.

## 5  Grasmere

282 miles NW of London; 18 miles NW of Kendal; 43 miles S of Carlisle

On a lake of the same name, Grasmere was the home of Wordsworth from 1799 to
1808. He called this area "the loveliest spot that man hath ever known."

## ESSENTIALS

**GETTING THERE**   Take a train to Windermere (see above) and continue the rest
of the way by bus.

Cumberland Motor Services (CMS) (☎ **01946/63222**) runs hourly bus service to Grasmere from Keswick (see below) and Windermere (see above). Buses running in either direction are marked no. 555 or 557.

If you're driving from Windermere (see above), continue northwest along A591.

**VISITOR INFORMATION** The summer-only **Tourist Information Centre** is on Red Bank Road (☎ **015394/35245**). Open April through October, daily from 9:30am to 5:30pm.

## ✪ DOVE COTTAGE & THE WORDSWORTH MUSEUM

The nature-loving poet lived with his writer-and-diarist sister, Dorothy, at Dove Cottage, which is now part of the Wordsworth Museum administered by the Wordsworth Trust. Wordsworth, who followed Southey as poet laureate, died in the spring of 1850 and was buried in the graveyard of the village church at Grasmere. Another tenant of Dove Cottage was Thomas De Quincey (*Confessions of an English Opium Eater*).

The Wordsworth Museum houses manuscripts, paintings, and memorabilia. There are also various special exhibitions throughout the year, exploring the art and literature of English romanticism. The property is open daily from 9:30am to 5:30pm; closed from December 24 to 26 and January 6 to February 2. Admission to both Dove Cottage and the adjoining museum is £4.10 ($6.55) for adults and £2.05 ($3.30) for children. Call ☎ **015394/35544** for museum information. In the Dove Cottage Tearoom and Restaurant (☎ **015394/35268**) afternoon tea is served. A good selection of open sandwiches, scones, cake, and tea breads is offered along with Darjeeling, Assam, Earl Grey, and herbal teas. The tearoom is open daily from 10am to 5pm. Both Dove Cottage and the restaurant are located on A591 directly south of the village of Grasmere on the road to Kendal.

## WHERE TO STAY
### DOUBLES FOR LESS THAN £50

**The Traveller's Rest** (see "Where to Eat," below) also rents rooms.

**Riversdale.** Grasmere, Cumbria LA22 9RQ. ☎ **015394/35619.** 3 rms. TV. £22–£24 ($35.20–$38.40) single; £36–£40 ($57.60–$64) double. All rates include English breakfast. No credit cards.

This lovely old house, built in 1830 of traditional Lakeland stone, is situated on the outskirts of the village of Grasmere on the banks of the River Rothay. The bedrooms are tastefully decorated and offer much comfort, including views of the surrounding fells, hair dryers, toiletries, tea- and coffee-making facilities, and hospitality trays. Mrs. Joyce Edwards and her sister Jean Newnes are gracious, witty, and full of fun. They are a wealth of information on day trips whether by car or hiking. Their breakfasts, which are a delight, are served in the dining room which overlooks Silver How and the fells beyond Easdale Tarn. There is a comfortable lounge in which to relax, watch TV, or read. This is a nonsmoking facility.

**Rothay Lodge Guest House.** White Bridge, Grasmere, Cumbria LA22 9RH. ☎ **015394/ 35341.** 5 rms. TV. £23–£25.75 ($36.80–$41.20) single; £46–£51.50 ($73.60–$82.40) double. All rates include English breakfast. No credit cards. Closed Nov–Feb. Bus: no. 555.

This is a traditional 19th-century Lakeland house built of stone and standing in landscaped grounds by the Rothay River at White Bridge. It's about a 5-minute walk from Grasmere center. The house is known for its commanding views of the countryside. The guest rooms are tastefully decorated and furnished with antiques. An evening meal can be arranged for £12 ($19.20).

## DOUBLES FOR LESS THAN £65

✪ **Craigside House.** Grasmere, Cumbria LA22 9SG. ☎ **015394/35292.** Fax 015394/35691. 3 rms. TV. £54–£62 ($86.40–$99.20) double. All rates include English breakfast. No credit cards.

This house is set in 1¹/₂ acres of garden, with views over the lake to the hills beyond. It's just above Wordsworth's Dove Cottage, and it was Wordsworth, back in 1839, who originally pointed out that this site was an ideal location for a house. Ken and Shirley Wood, who operate the Moss Grove Hotel (see below), run this guest house as well. One of the rooms has a Hepplewhite four-poster bed.

✪ **How Foot Lodge.** Town End, Grasmere, Cumbria LA22 9SQ. ☎ **015394/35366.** Fax 015394/35748. 6 rms. TV. £40–£46.50 ($64–$74.40) single; £50–£58 ($80–$92.80) double. All rates include English breakfast. MC, V.

This 1840s Victorian house that once belonged to Wordsworth's friends lies directly south along A591, the road from Dove Cottage and Rydal Mount. The bedrooms, which are elegant, all have radios and tea- and coffeemakers. No meals other than breakfast are served. The hotel is owned by the Wordsworth Trust, and will direct you to Dove Cottage Museum to see the series of paintings from the Wordsworth Collection. Several paintings are by Percy Horton, who was director of the Royal Academy of Fine Arts in World War II and was responsible for evacuating many British masterpieces out of London during the blitz bombings. The managers will also direct you to the Dove Cottage Restaurant for meals. Dove Cottage Museum and Dove Cottage Restaurant are also owned by the Wordsworth Trust.

**Moss Grove Hotel.** Grasmere, Cumbria LA22 9SW. ☎ **015394/35251.** Fax 015394/35691. 14 rms, 13 with bath. TV TEL. £29.50 ($47.20) single without bath, £35.50 ($56.80) single with bath; £65 ($104) double with bath. All rates include English breakfast. MC, V. Closed Dec–Jan. Bus: no. 555.

This old Lakeland house in the town center, just past the Grasmere church, is owned and run by Ken and Shirley Wood. The hotel is warm and well furnished (some of the accommodations contain four-poster beds). There are two lounges: one with TV, the other with a small bar. Dinner is a well-cooked meal, usually with a roast joint or poultry along with fresh vegetables. Meals cost £10 to £15 ($16 to $24). Facilities include free use of a nearby swimming pool.

## A YOUTH HOSTEL

**Grasmere Youth Hostel (Butterlip How).** Easedale Rd., Grasmere, Cumbria LA22 9XG. ☎ **015394/35316.** Fax 015394/35798. 90 beds. £8.50 ($13.60) adults; £5.70 ($9.10) children under 18. MC, V.

This was built as a stone-and-slate Victorian farmhouse. The immediate area in front of the hostel, known as Butterlip How, has a great deal of history. It was a stronghold for the Vikings, and archaeologists believe that it later served as a repository for the final remains of King Bothar's soldiers who fell in battle. Four rooms sleep two each, and 10 family rooms can handle up to 4 people per room. Public rooms include a lounge, dining room, drying room, and games room. Breakfast is £2.85

### Impressions

*. . . Had never seen so humble a ménage: and, contrasting the dignity of the man with this honourable poverty, and his courageous avowal of it, his utter absence of all effort to disguise the simple truth of the case, I felt my admiration increase to the uttermost by all I saw.*

—Thomas De Quincey on Dove Cottage (1807)

($4.55), a packed lunch, which must be ordered the previous night, is available for £2.45 ($3.90) or £3.25 ($5.20), and a dinner is £4.25 ($6.80). The majority of the hostel is a nonsmoking environment. It is open from January through October. The 11pm curfew is enforced, and the reception is open from 7 to 9:30am and 1 to 11:30pm.

## WHERE TO EAT

**Baldry's.** Red Lion Sq. ☎ **015394/35301.** Main courses £3.50–£5.50 ($5.60–$8.80). No credit cards. July–Aug Thurs–Tues 9:30am–6pm; Sept–June Thurs–Tues 9:30am–5pm. ENGLISH.

This family-run place serves wholesome homemade food at prices that most diners find appetizing. In a stone-sided Lake District house whose walls are adorned with framed newspaper clippings and mementos of the district's history, Elaine and Paul Nelson have created a cozy refuge in this lovely old tearoom. Many dishes are vegetarian, such as whole-meal pasta in a mushroom-and-cream sauce, as well as such light fare as soups, salads, quiche, welch rarebit, roast ham, pastries, tea, and scones. The food is stronger on portions than subtlety. A good tea with scones and pie can be enjoyed for £1 to £2 ($1.60 to $3.20).

**The Traveller's Rest.** Dunmail Raise, Hwy. A591, Grasmere, Cumbria LA 22 9RR. ☎ **015394/ 35604.** Main courses £4.75–£13 ($7.60–$20.80). No credit cards. Easter–Oct noon–10pm; Nov–Easter Mon–Sat noon–3pm and 6–10pm, Sun noon–3pm and 7–10pm. (Pub: Mon–Sat 11am–11pm; Sun noon–3pm and 7–10:30pm.) ENGLISH.

In a carefully connected trio of late 16th-century stone cottages, this much-patronized pub attracts locals as well as summer visitors and Lakeland hikers. Place your order for one of the platters at the bar and enjoy it either in the pub itself or at a seat in the adjacent dining room. Typical dishes include steak-and-kidney pie, hamburgers, ploughman's lunches, and lasagna. Most visitors wash everything down with lager or ale, sometimes from a seat on the panoramic patio.

The pub also contains eight unpretentious guest rooms on the upper floors, four of which have private showers. With an English breakfast included, singles rent for £22.95 ($36.70) and doubles go for £45 ($72). The pub is half a mile north of Grasmere beside the highway.

## 6 Hawkshead & Coniston

263 miles NW of London; 52 miles S of Carlisle; 19 miles NW of Kendal

Discover for yourself the village of Hawkshead, with its 15th-century grammar school where Wordsworth studied for 8 years (he carved his name on a desk that is still there). Near Hawkshead, in the vicinity of Esthwaite Water, is the 17th-century Hill Top Farm, former home of author Beatrix Potter.

At Coniston, 4 miles west of Hawkshead, you can visit the village famously associated with John Ruskin. Coniston is a good base for rock climbing. The Coniston "Old Man" towers in the background at 2,633 feet, giving mountain climbers one of the finest views of the Lake District.

## ESSENTIALS

**GETTING THERE**    Take a train to Windermere (see above) and proceed the rest of the way by bus.

Cumberland Motor Services (CMS) (☎ **01946/63222**) runs three buses from Windermere to Hawkshead and Coniston Monday to Saturday, two on Sunday. Take either bus no. 505 or 515 from Windermere.

By car from Windermere, proceed north on A591 to Ambleside, cutting southwest on B5285 to Hawkshead.

The **Windermere Lake Cruises** (☎ 015394/43360) operates a ferry service in summer from Bowness, directly south of Windermere, to Hawkshead. It reduces driving time considerably (see "Windermere & Bowness," above).

**VISITOR INFORMATION**   The **Tourist Information Centre** (☎ 015394/ 36525) is at Hawkshead in the Main Car Park. Open March 23 through October, daily from 9:30am to 5:30pm.

## SEEING THE RUSKIN SIGHTS

**Brantwood.** Coniston. ☎ **015394/41396.** Admission £3.70 ($5.90) adults; £1 ($1.60) children 5–15. Nature walk £1.50 ($2.40) adults; £1 ($1.60) children. Mid-Mar to mid-Nov daily 11am–5:30pm; mid-Nov to mid-Mar Wed–Sun 11am–4pm. Closed Christmas Day and Boxing Day. From Coniston, follow the B5285 and "Brantwood" signs for 2 miles. The museum is across the lake from Coniston.

John Ruskin, the poet, artist, and critic, was one of the great figures of the Victorian Age and a prophet of social reform, inspiring such diverse men as Proust, Frank Lloyd Wright, and Gandhi. He moved to his home, Brantwood, on the east side of Coniston Water, in 1872 and lived here until his death in 1900. The house today is open for visitors to view much Ruskiniana, including some 200 pictures by him. Also displayed are his coach and boat, the *Jumping Jenny.* A video program tells the story of Ruskin's life and work.

The house is owned and managed by the Education Trust, a self-supporting registered charity. Part of the 250-acre estate is open as a nature trail. The Brantwood stables, designed by Ruskin, have been converted into a tearoom and restaurant, the Jumping Jenny. Also in the stable building is the Coach House Craft Gallery, which follows the Ruskin tradition of encouraging contemporary craft work of the finest quality.

Literary fans may want to pay a pilgrimage to the graveyard of the village church, where Ruskin was buried; his family turned down the invitation to have him interred at Westminster Abbey.

**John Ruskin Museum.** Yewdale Rd., Coniston. ☎ **015394/41164.** Admission £2 ($3.20) adults; £1 ($1.60) children. Easter–Oct daily 10am–1pm and 2–4pm. Closed Nov–Easter. From Coniston bus station, to Yewdale Rd.; the museum is opposite the fire station.

At this institute, in the center of the village, you can see Ruskin's personal possessions and mementos, pictures by him and his friends, letters, and his collection of mineral rocks. The museum closed in 1997 for refurbishment but should be up and running at the time of your visit. Hours may change as a result; phone ahead to be certain that the museum is open.

## SHOPPING

In Hawkshead, the **Beatrix Potter Gallery** (☎ 015394/36355), has an annually changing exhibition of Beatrix Potter's original illustrations from her children's story books. The building was once the office of her husband, the solicitor, William Heelis and the interior remains largely unaltered since his day. To get here take bus no. 505 from Ambleside-Coniston to the square in Hawkshead.

## WHERE TO STAY

In addition to the following listings, the **Queen's Head** (see "Where to Eat," below), also has sleeping accommodations.

### IN HAWKSHEAD

**The Kings Arms Hotel.** The Square, Hawkshead, near Ambleside, Cumbria LA22 0NZ. ☎ **015394/36372.** 9 rms, 6 with bath. TV. £29 ($46.40) single without bath, £34 ($54.40) single with bath; £47 ($75.20) double without bath, £57 ($91.20) double with bath. All rates include English breakfast. MC, V.

This is an old coaching inn in the middle of the village near the police station, with leaded windows and sloping roofs. Inside, low beams and whitewashed walls complete the picture, along with a friendly bar patronized by locals. There's also a neat buttery, and in the rear, a room for bar games. The inn offers grills and steaks at mealtimes. Dinners start at £12 ($19.20). The bedrooms are routine pub style, clean and decent, perhaps a little noisy on occasion.

### A Youth Hostel

**Hawkshead Youth Hostel.** Esthwaite Lodge, Hawkshead, Ambleside, Cumbria LA22 0QD. ☎ **015394/36293.** Fax 015394/36720. 117 beds. In the house £9.40 ($15.05) adults, £6.30 ($10.10) children under 18; in the courtyard £28.50 ($45.60) per rm for up to 3 people and £38 ($60.80) per rm for up to 4 people. AE, MC, V.

A room with a view is surely guaranteed in this stately brick and stone Regency mansion. Thomas Beck, an English noble and builder of the house, made sure of it. He loved the views of Esthwaite Water from this plot of land, and designed his residence here so that he could always gaze out from the house and be assured of a panorama. The hostel still has a residential feel with carpeted halls and Beatrix Potter prints all about. Bedrooms are found in two areas: the main house and the courtyard. The dorm rooms for 4 to 18 people are in the house, and three- and four-bed family rooms are in the courtyard. Breakfast is available for £2.85 ($4.55); a packed lunch, if ordered prior to 10:30pm the night before, is £2.35 ($3.75); and dinner costs £4.25 ($6.80). The hostel accepts visitors from February to December 24, but is closed Sunday to Monday from November to mid-March. There is an 11pm curfew, but people staying in the family rooms in the courtyard receive keys and can come and go as they please. The reception is open from 7:15 to 10:30am and 1 to 10:30pm.

## IN CONISTON

**Coniston Sun Hotel.** Coniston, Cumbria LA21 8HQ. ☎ **015394/41248.** 11 rms. TV TEL. Mon–Thurs £30 ($48) single; £60 ($96) double. Fri–Sat £35 ($56) single; £70 ($112) double. All rates include English breakfast. MC, V.

This is the most popular, traditional, and attractive pub, restaurant, and hotel in this Lakeland village. In reality, it's a country-house hotel of much character, dating from 1902, although the inn attached to it is from the 16th century. Standing on its own grounds above the village, it lies at the foot of the Coniston "Old Man." Donald Campbell made this place his headquarters during his attempt on the world water-speed record. Each bedroom is decorated with style and flair, and two contain four-poster beds. Fresh local produce is used whenever possible in the candlelit restaurant. Log fires take the chill off a winter evening, and guests relax informally in the lounge, which is like a library. Many sports can be arranged. The hotel is near the village center off A593.

## IN FAR SAWREY

✪ **Sawrey Hotel.** Hawkshead Rd., Far Sawrey, near Ambleside, Cumbria LA22 0LQ. ☎ **015394/43425.** 20 rms, 18 with bath (tub or shower). TV TEL. £31 ($49.60) single without bath, £36 ($57.60) single with bath; £62 ($99.20) double without bath, £72 ($115.20) double with bath. All rates include half board. MC, V.

This hotel is in the village where Beatrix Potter lived the happiest years of her life. The inn was built of stone and "pebble-dash" (a form of stucco) as a coaching inn in the early 1700s. Most residents opt for the half-board plan where five-course dinners are served in a stone-sided pub whose premises were converted from a very old

*The first thing which I remember, as an event in life, was being taken by my nurse to the brow of friar's crag on Derwentwater; the intense joy, mingled with awe, that I had in looking through the hollows in the mossy roots, over the crag, into the dark lake, has associated itself more or less with all twining roots of trees ever since.*

—John Ruskin

stable. (Popular with local townspeople, the pub still retains its antique hayracks and stall dividers.) Nonresidents are welcome to dine on a fixed-price evening meal priced at £15.50 ($24.80) and served every evening from 7 to 8:45pm. David Brayshaw and his family are the hosts, offering comfortable accommodations in either the older part of the hotel, in rooms with thick plaster walls, or in somewhat more modern and plainer rooms added during the 1970s above the pub. The hotel lies a mile west of the Windermere car-ferry beside B5285.

## WHERE TO EAT

**Queen's Head.** Main St., Hawkshead, near Ambleside, Cumbria LA22 0NS. ☎ **015394/ 36271.** Fax 015394/36722. Reservations recommended. Main courses £5–£12.75 ($8–$20.40). MC, V. Daily noon–2:30pm and 6:45–9pm. ENGLISH.

This is the most famous pub in town. It's really more an inn than a pub, as it rents 13 bedrooms, all with private bath, TV, and phone. Behind a mock black-and-white timbered facade, it's a 17th-century structure of character. The pub serves a special brew, Robinson's of Stockport, from old-fashioned wooden kegs. Try a sizzling sirloin steak, grilled rainbow trout, or perhaps pheasant in casserole. Lunches are always bar menus, where clients order their food at the counter. Dinner can also be a bar menu, or taken from a more formal menu in the dining room. The comfortably old-fashioned bedrooms rent for £45 ($72) single and £60 ($96) double. An English breakfast is included in the rates.

## 7 Keswick

22 miles NW of Windermere; 294 miles NW of London; 31 miles NW of Kendal

Keswick opens onto Derwentwater, one of the loveliest lakes in the district. It makes a good center for exploring the northern half of Lake District National Park. The small town has two landscaped parks, and above the town is a historic Stone Circle thought to be some 4,000 years old.

St. Kentigern's Church dates from 553, and a weekly market held in the center of Keswick can be traced back to a charter granted in the 13th century. It's a short walk to the classic viewing point—Friar's Crag—on Derwentwater. The walk will also take you past boat landings with launches that operate regular tours around the lake.

Around Derwentwater there are many places with literary associations that evoke memories of Wordsworth, Robert Southey (poet laureate), Coleridge, and Hugh Walpole. Several of Beatrix Potter's stories were based at Keswick. The town also has a professional repertory theater that schedules performances in the summer. There is a modern swimming pool, plus an 18-hole golf course at the foot of the mountains 4 miles away.

Close at hand are villages and lakes, including Borrowdale, Buttermere, and Bassenthwaite, whereas the open country of "John Peel" fame is to the north of the 3,053-foot Skiddaw.

## ESSENTIALS

**GETTING THERE**   Take a train to Windermere (see above) and proceed the rest of the way by bus.

Cumberland Motor Services (CMS) (☎ 01946/63222) has a regular bus service from Windermere and Grasmere (bus no. 555).

From Windermere, drive northwest on A591.

**VISITOR INFORMATION**   The **Tourist Information Centre** is at Moot Hall, Market Square (☎ 017687/72645). Open April to June, daily from 9:30am to 5:30pm, in July and August, daily from 9:30am to 7pm, from September through March, daily from 10am to 4pm. Closed Christmas and New Year's day.

## WHERE TO STAY

**Allerdale House.** 1 Eskin St., Keswick, Cumbria CA12 4DH. ☎ **017687/73891.** 6 rms. TV TEL. £46–£68 ($73.60–$108.80) double. All rates include English breakfast. No credit cards.

This large Victorian-era home close to the town center might be an ideal base near Derwentwater. Here you get real Lakeland hospitality, a warm welcome, and comfortable bedrooms, each a double. The rooms are pleasantly furnished and well maintained. Guests are accepted year-round and they can also arrange to have a home-cooked dinner in the evening for £10 ($16). This is a nonsmoking facility.

**George Hotel.** 3 St. John St., Keswick, Cumbria CA12 5AZ. ☎ **017687/72076.** Fax 017687/75968. 17 rms, none with bath. £22 ($35.20) single; £44 ($70.40) double. All rates include English breakfast. AE, DC, MC, V.

Visited from time to time by Wordsworth, Southey, and Coleridge when it was known as the George & Dragon, this hotel was conceived as a coaching inn in the 1590s. Painted an easy-to-spot black and white, it lies on the upper part of the town's main street, near the Market Square. The bedrooms are cozy, comfortable, and suitably old-fashioned, in many cases with their original ceiling beams still intact. Restaurant dinners cost £12.50 ($20) for three well-prepared courses, although residents of the hotel pay a supplement of only £8 ($12.80) per person for an equivalent meal. On site are two Old-World bars where snacks and pub grub are served daily from noon to 2pm and 7 to 9pm. Platters cost £4 to £8 ($6.40 to $12.80).

**Linnett Hill Hotel.** 4 Penrith Rd., Keswick, Cumbria CA12 4HF. ☎ **017687/73109.** 10 rms, all with shower only. TV. £22.50–£24.50 ($36–$39.20) single; £45–£49 ($72–$78.40) double. All rates include English breakfast. MC, V.

The Linnett Hill has been thoroughly modernized, yet it retains oak beams and other typical characteristics. This private town house dates from 1812. Sylvia and Richard Harland offer bedrooms with electric-shaver outlets and central heating. Smoking is not allowed. The establishment charges another £13 to £16 ($20.80 to $25.60) for an evening meal. The meals are not only large, but they're also well prepared and served. The hotel has a comfortable lounge, a small private bar, and a private parking area. It's situated in the center of Keswick opposite the River Green and Fitz Park, with open views of Skiddaw Range and Latrigg, 15 minutes' walk to the lakeshore.

## WHERE TO EAT

✪ **Dog & Gun.** 2 Lake Rd. ☎ **017687/73463.** Main courses £5.50–£6.60 ($8.80–$10.55). No credit cards. Mon–Sat 11am–3pm and 6–11pm; Sun 11am–3pm and 6–10:30pm. ENGLISH.

Talked about as the most famous pub in Keswick, this joint evokes hunting sports and has a warmth and character that fills the tavern rooms with welcome. Dating from 1690, the Dog & Gun offers an atmosphere of low beams, slate floors, brass bric-a-brac, and open fires in winter where patrons can have anything from bar snacks to full-size meals. Main courses are hearty and may include an authentic and spicy Hungarian goulash that's a favorite with local climbers, roast chicken, and baked Borrowdale trout.

**The Langstrath Inn.** Stonethwaite, near Borrowdale. ☎ **017687/77239.** Main courses £3.50–£8 ($5.60–$12.80); lunch £1.95–£4 ($3.10–$6.40). MC, V. Daily noon–2pm and 3–5pm (afternoon tea); 6:30–9pm. Bar: Mon–Sat 11:30am–11pm and Sun 11:30am–10:30pm. ENGLISH.

This bar restaurant, tucked into a cozy country inn with plenty of lively atmosphere that's buffered by dark woodwork, beams, and tables, provides a selection of healthy foods all cooked using local, fresh products. Lunchtime offerings are usually along the lines of hearty homemade soups like French onion or carrot, a fell-walkers lunch of cheeses, ham, and crusty bread; and open-face sandwiches with prawn, ham, and bacon, lettuce, and tomato. The larger dinner menu of regional specialties includes stir-fried duckling, freshly prepared steak-and-kidney pie, Scottish salmon, Cumberland sausage, and a cornucopia of vegetarian dishes.

## AN EXCURSION TO BORROWDALE & SCAFELL PIKE

One of the most scenic parts of the Lake District, Borrowdale stretches south of Derwentwater to Seathwaite in the heart of the county. The valley is walled in by fellsides, and it's an excellent center for exploring, walking, and climbing. Many use it as a center for exploring Scafell, England's highest mountain at 3,210 feet.

This resort is in the Borrowdale Valley, the southernmost settlement of which is Seatoller. The village of Seatoller at 1,176 feet is the terminus for buses to and from Keswick. It's also the center for a Lake District National Park Information Center at Dalehead Base, Seatoller Barn (☎ **017687/77294**).

After leaving Seatoller, B5289 takes you west through the Honister Pass and Buttermere Fell, one of the most dramatic drives in the Lake District. The road is lined with towering boulders. The lake village of Buttermere also merits a stopover.

You can stay the night (provided you bring your own bedding) at **Swallow Barn** (☎ **017687/72803**), part of the National Park camping barn network, for just £3 ($4.80) a night per person. Swallow Barn is located near Loweswater, 4¹/₂ miles from Buttermere.

# 8 Penrith

290 miles NW of London; 31 miles NE of Kendal

This one-time capital of Cumbria, in the old Kingdom of Scotland and Strathclyde, takes its name, some say, from the Celts who called it "Ford by the Hill." This namesake hill is marked today by a red-sandstone beacon and tower. Because of Penrith's central location right above the northern Lake District and beside the northern Pennines, this thriving market center was important to Scotland and England from its very beginning—and eventually prompted England to take it over in 1070.

The characteristically red-sandstone town has been home to many famous and legendary figures through the ages, including Richard, duke of Gloucester who was the Guardian of the West Marches and governor of Carlisle but who chose to reside in his royal fortress known as Penrith Castle; William Cookson, the grandfather of William and Dorothy Wordsworth; and, it is said, the giant Ewan Caesarius who supposedly was a slayer of monsters, men, and beasts. Caesarius's grave allegedly rests in St. Andrew's Churchyard. Today, Penrith still remains best known for its role as a lively market town.

## ESSENTIALS

**GETTING THERE**   Trains from London's Euston Station arrive in Penrith four times a day (a 4-hour trip). For train schedules and information, call ☎ **0345/ 484950.**

To take a bus from London to Penrith, hop on one of the two daily National Express buses to Carlisle and then take a Stage Coach Cumberland bus to Penrith (an 8-hour trip). The Stage Coach Cumberland buses leave every hour. For schedules and information, call National Express at ☎ **0990/808080** and Cumberland Motor Services at ☎ **01946/63222.**

By car, take the M1 out of London, then get on the M6 to Penrith (a 6-hour drive).

**VISITOR INFORMATION**   **The Tourist Information Centre,** Robinson's School, Middlegate, Penrith (☎ **01768/867466**), is open November to Easter, Monday to Saturday from 9:30am to 5pm; Easter through May and the month of October, Monday to Saturday from 9:30am to 5pm and Sunday 1pm to 5pm; June through September, Monday to Saturday from 9:30am to 6pm and Sunday 1pm to 6pm.

## SEEING THE SIGHTS

For an historical perspective of Penrith and the surrounding area, a visit to the **Penrith Museum,** Robinson's School, Middlegate (☎ **01768/212228**), is in order. Constructed in the 1500s, the museum building was turned into a poor girls' school in 1670 by native son, William Robinson, who made his fortune in London in the grocery industry. Later it was transformed into a "proper school" and continued to be in use into the 1970s. Today, the museum offers a survey of the archaeology and geology of Penrith and the Eden Valley, which was a desert millions of years ago. Open June to September, Monday to Saturday from 9:30am to 6pm and Sunday 1pm to 6pm; October to May, Monday to Saturday from 10am to 5pm. Admission is free.

Just across from the train station along Ullswater Road, you'll find a park that contains the massive ruins of **Penrith Castle** (no phone). William Strickland, the Bishop of Canterbury, started construction of the castle in 1399. For the next 70 years, the castle continued to expand in size and strength until it finally became the royal castle and oftentimes residence for Richard, duke of Gloucester, who was the Guardian of the West Marches and governor of Carlisle Castle. The park and ruins are open June through September, daily from 7:30am to 9pm; October to May, daily from 7:30am to 4:30pm. Admission is free.

For an English garden walk, see **Acorn Bank Garden,** Temple Sowerby, 6 miles east of Penrith on the A6 (☎ **017683/61893**), with its varied landscape of blooming bulbs, foliage plants, and walled spaces. Its claim to fame is its extensive herb garden, said to be the best in all of northern England. The Acorn Bank Garden is part of an estate dating from 1228 and is now owned by the National Trust. Buildings on the estate include a partially restored watermill, parts of which also date to the 13th century, and a red sandstone, primarily Tudor house, which is presently not open to the public. The garden is open Good Friday to the beginning of October, daily 10am to 5:30pm, with the last admission at 5pm. Admission is £2.10 ($3.35) for adults, £1 ($1.60) for children, and £5.50 ($8.80) for a family ticket for two adults and two children.

## SHOPPING

For a small market town of 12,500 people, you'll find a heavy concentration of shops to explore. Major shopping areas include the covered shopping precinct of Devonshire Arcade with its name-brand stores and boutiques, the pedestrian-only

Angel Lane and Little Dockray with an abundance of family-run specialty shops, as well as Angel Square just south of Angel Lane.

For handmade earthenware and stoneware from the only remaining steam-powered pottery in Britain, stop by **Wetheriggs Country Pottery,** Clifton Dykes, 2 miles south of Penrith on the A6 (☎ **01768/892733**). In the 130-year-old **Briggs & Shoe Mines,** Southend Road (☎ **01768/899001**), you'll have an extravaganza of a shopping experience. It's the largest independent shoe shop in the Lakelands.

**Eden Valley Woollen Mill,** Armathwaite, along the M6 heading toward Carlisle (☎ **016974/71457**), is where Steve Wilson and his small and talented team design and weave using restored looms dating from the early 1900s. Their wares include jackets and skirts in traditional and modern tweeds, rugs, throws, ruanas, hats, ties, and scarves. The showroom also carries individual knitwear and yarns.

# WHERE TO STAY
## DOUBLES FOR LESS THAN £45

**Barco House.** Carleton Rd., Penrith, Cumbria CA11 8LR. ☎ **01768/863176.** 3 rms, 2 with bath. TV. £25 ($40) single; £38 ($60.80) double. All rates include English breakfast. No credit cards.

A slow 10-minute walk from the center of town will lead you to this double-fronted, black-and-white sandstone Victorian B&B, built as a private residence in 1848. Slightly elevated from the road, the house has a well-kept front garden and a backyard walled garden. Inside, an effort has been made to maintain the Victorian character of the house, with its stripped pine woodwork and furnishings. A wide staircase with a large arch window ushers guests to their rather spacious rooms with soft pastel color schemes. Public rooms include a bar with seating area and a welcoming dining room that looks out onto the Lakeland Hills. Guests can have, if ordered ahead of time, a three-course evening meal for £12 ($19.20).

**Norcroft Guesthouse.** Graham St., Penrith, Cumbria CA11 9LQ. ☎ and fax **01768/862365.** 8 rms, 5 with bath. TV. £16 ($25.60) per person without bath (single or double); £19.50 ($31.20) per person with bath (single or double). All rates include English breakfast. No credit cards.

"More room than needed to swing a cat." That's how the owner describes this huge red sandstone Victorian B&B and its guest rooms. Built in 1854, this house sits in a quiet residential part of town, very near the town center. Inside, the rooms are particularly grand, awash with good pictures, dark wood, and an original English staircase that leads up to a huge first-floor landing. Located on the upper two floors, all guest rooms are individually decorated with antiques, excellent carpet, and walls dressed with English hunt and flower prints. The front rooms look out onto one of the few Victorian churchyards in England—a favorite place for guests to wander. Guests are drawn to the focal point of the house, the dining room, where they meet, socialize, and have breakfast as well as dinner, if they wish.

**Queens Head Inn.** Tirril, near Penrith, Cumbria CA10 2JF. ☎ **01768/863219.** Fax 01768/863243. 7 rms. TV. £37 ($59.20) single; £42 ($67.20) double. All rates include English breakfast. MC, V.

This white country inn, dating from 1719, sits in the very middle of the little village of Tirril, 2 miles from Penrith. In the 1830s, the inn was owned by the poet William Wordsworth and his brother. Throughout the interior, guests can see a variety of pictures of the inn during the Wordsworth era as well as words that are said to have been carved into one of the bars by William. The upstairs bedrooms are small to medium in size and have been recently renovated to expose more of the characteristic beams and to update furnishings. The ground floor, with its oak beams and low ceilings, houses the public areas of the inn and include two bars, with open stone fireplaces, and a restaurant that serves lunch and dinner.

## WHERE TO EAT

**Passepartout.** 51 Castlegate. ☎ **01768/865852.** Main courses £5.75–£13 ($9.20–$20.80). MC, V. Tues–Sat 7–11pm. FRENCH/ENGLISH.

Housed in a 400-year-old building, this cozy, candlelit dining room is set amongst painted stone walls and accent colors of greens, browns, and dusky pinks. The chef has designed an imaginative menu around fresh, local food items, and dishes may include Herdwick lamb sautéed in butter, rosemary, juniper berries, and served in a red wine sauce; grilled Scottish salmon in a creamy lime butter sauce; and Scottish venison marinated in red wine and herbs. All main courses are served with vegetables and salad. Dessert favorites range from homemade butterscotch ice cream to a hot cherry meringue with chocolate. In warmer months, patrons relax with drinks in a Spanish-style open courtyard in back of the dining room.

## PENRITH AFTER DARK

Once a retreat for William Wordsworth, the **Royal** (☎ **01768/482356**), located just west of Penrith, off the A66 in Dockray, is situated in the midst of several good local walks, making it a fine central base for a day of tramping about. The barroom is spacious and light with plushly padded seating and pink and green carpet underfoot. An adjacent area reveals the pub's flagstone floors and has basic wooden bar furniture—good for muddy or dusty hikers. The traditional pub dishes are homemade daily and will sustain you through even a vigorous hike; ales include Jennings Cumberland, Mitchells ESB, and there are several good malt whiskies from which to choose. Outside, there is not only a garden, but a field and pond as well.

Located 4 miles south of town, off the A6 in the village of Askham, the **Punch Bowl** (☎ **01931/712443**) is a sturdy, stone-walled pub with a comfortable interior and a beautiful setting on the lower village green. Join tradition and stick some coins in the cracks of the old wooden beams (management periodically takes these out and makes donations to various charities), then settle back in a Chippendale chair and savor a pint of Morlands Old Speckled Hen, Whitbreads Castle Eden, or Marstons Pedigree. There are some interesting and tasty menu items prepared with local fish, fowl, and game. In warm weather, you can sit on the front terrace and enjoy the view of the village green.

# Yorkshire & Northumbria

Yorkshire, known to readers of *Wuthering Heights* and *All Creatures Great and Small*, embraces both the moors of North Yorkshire and the dales. With the radical changing of the old county boundaries, the shire is now divided into North Yorkshire (the most interesting from the tourist's point of view), West Yorkshire, South Yorkshire, and Humberside.

A remarkable roster of peoples has crossed this vast region, including the Romans, the Anglo-Saxons, the Vikings, the monks of the Middle Ages, kings of England, lords of the manor, craftspeople, hill farmers, and wool growers, all leaving their own mark. They all left their mark, evidence of which you can still see today: Roman roads and pavements, great abbeys and castles, stately homes, open-air museums, and craft centers, along with parish churches, old villages, and cathedrals.

Some cities and towns remain scarred by the Industrial Revolution, but there's also wild and remote beauty to be found—limestone crags, caverns along the Pennines, mountainous uplands, rolling hills, chalk land wolds, heather-covered moorlands, broad vales, and tumbling streams. Yorkshire offers not only beautiful inland scenery, but also 100 miles of shoreline, with rocky headlands, cliffs, and sandy bays, rock pools, sheltered coves, fishing villages, bird sanctuaries, former smugglers' dens, and yachting havens. In summer, the moors in North York Moors National Park blossom with purple heather. You can hike along the 110-mile Cleveland Way National Trail, encircling the park.

The most visited city in Yorkshire is the walled city of York. York Minster, part of the cathedral circuit, is noted for its 100 stained-glass windows. There's also a great folk museum, York Castle Museum, and the National Railway Museum. From York, you can visit Castle Howard, Harewood House & Bird Garden, and Fountains Abbey. In West Yorkshire is the literary shrine of Haworth, the home of the Brontës.

Northumbria comprises the counties of Northumberland, Cleveland, and Durham. Tyne and Wear is one of the more recently created counties, and has Newcastle upon Tyne as its center.

# The Northeast: Yorkshire & Northumbria

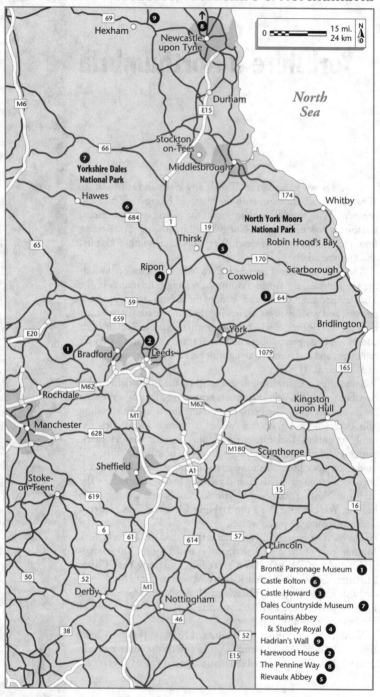

0    15 mi.
     24 km

N

**North Sea**

Hexham

Newcastle upon Tyne

M6

Durham

E15

Stockton-on-Tees

Middlesbrough

**Yorkshire Dales National Park**

Hawes

Whitby

**North York Moors National Park**

Robin Hood's Bay

Thirsk

Ripon

Coxwold

Scarborough

York

Bridlington

Bradford

Leeds

Rochdale

Kingston upon Hull

Manchester

Sheffield

Scunthorpe

Stoke-on-Trent

Derby

Nottingham

Lincoln

Brontë Parsonage Museum ❶
Castle Bolton ❻
Castle Howard ❸
Dales Countryside Museum ❼
Fountains Abbey & Studley Royal ❹
Hadrian's Wall ❾
Harewood House ❷
The Pennine Way ❽
Rievaulx Abbey ❺

696

The Saxons who came to northern England centuries ago carved out this kingdom, which at the time stretched from the Firth of Forth in Scotland to the banks of the Humber in Yorkshire. Vast tracts of that ancient kingdom remain natural and unspoiled. Again, this slice of England has more than its share of industrial towns, but you should explore the wild hills and open spaces and cross the dales of the eastern Pennines.

The whole area evokes ancient battles and bloody border raids. Unfortunately, we can't embark on a detailed discussion of this area, which is often overlooked by the rushed North American visitor. However, if you are able to come here, you should at least see Hadrian's Wall, a Roman structure that was one of the early wonders of the western world. The finest stretch of the wall lies within the Northumberland National Park, between the stony North Tyne River and the county boundary at Gilsland. And about 40 miles of the 150-mile Pennine Way meanders through the park; the Pennine Way is one of Britain's most challenging hiking paths. On your way to Hadrian's Wall, we recommend spending the night in the ancient cathedral city of Durham, a great medieval city.

# 1 York

203 miles N of London; 26 miles NE of Leeds; 88 miles N of Nottingham

Few cities in England are as rich in history as York. The northeastern city is still encircled by 13th- and 14th-century city walls—about 2¹/₂ miles long, with four gates. One of these, Micklegate, once grimly greeted visitors who made the journey north with the heads of traitors. To this day, you can walk the footpath of the medieval walls.

The crowning achievement of York is its minster, or cathedral, which makes the city an ecclesiastical center equaled only by Canterbury. In spite of this, York is one of the most overlooked cities on the international cathedral circuit. Perhaps foreign visitors think that this great city is too far north. Actually, it lies only 203 miles north of London on the Ouse River and can easily be combined with a car trip to Edinburgh. Or, after visiting Cambridge, you could make a swing through England's too-often-neglected cathedral cities: Ely, Lincoln, York, and Ripon.

Over the centuries, there was a Roman York (Hadrian came this way), a Saxon York, a Danish York, a Norman York (William the Conqueror slept here), a medieval York, a Georgian York, and a Victorian York (the center of a flourishing rail business). Today a good amount of 18th-century York remains, including Richard Boyle's restored Assembly Rooms.

At some point in your exploration, you may want to visit the Shambles; once the meat-butchering center of York, it dates from before the Norman Conquest. The messy business has given way, but the ancient street survives and teems with jewelry stores, cafes, and buildings that huddle so closely together you can practically stand in the middle of the pavement, arms outstretched, and touch the houses on both sides of the street.

Recent interest has focused on discoveries of the Viking era, from 867 to 1066, when the city was known as Jorvik, the Viking capital and a major Scandinavian trade center. Incidentally, the suffix "gate" used for streets and sites in York derives from the Scandinavian word for "street"—a historical reminder of the earlier Viking period.

Today, visitors crowd York; you'll hear a lot of American accents as you walk around this medieval maze. It's easy to explore York by foot; most attractions lie within the city's walls. "What about life today in modern York?" we asked an old-timer. He looked puzzled. "Didn't know it existed," he said. "Everybody comes here for a look at our past—not what we're up to now. In fact, most of us here earn our bread by showing off that past."

## ESSENTIALS

**GETTING THERE**    British Midland flights arrive at Leeds/Bradford Airport, a 50-minute flight from London's Heathrow Airport. Connecting buses at the airport take you east and the rest of the distance to York.

From London's King's Cross Station, York-bound trains leave every 10 minutes. The trip takes 2 hours. For schedules and information, call ☎ **0345/484950.**

Four National Express buses depart daily from London's Victoria Coach Station for the 4¹/2-hour trip to York. For schedules and information, call ☎ **0990/808080.**

If you're driving from London, head north on M1, cutting northeast below Leeds at the junction with A64, heading east to York.

**VISITOR INFORMATION**    The **Tourist Information Centre** is at De Grey Rooms, Exhibition Square (☎ **01904/621756**). Open daily from 9am to 5pm.

## ✪ YORK MINSTER

One of the great cathedrals of the world, York Minster traces its origins back to the early 7th century; the present building, however, dates from the 13th century and stands at the converging point of several streets: Deangate, Duncombe Place, Minster Yard, and Petergate.

Like the cathedral at Lincoln, York Minster is characterized by three towers built in the 15th century. The central tower is lantern-shaped in the perpendicular style and from the top of the tower on a clear day there are panoramic views of York and the Vale of York. The climb up a stone spiral staircase is steep and not recommended for very elderly or very young visitors, or anyone with a heart condition or breathing difficulties.

The most memorable and distinguishing characteristic of the cathedral is its stained glass from the Middle Ages—in glorious Angelico blues, ruby reds, forest greens, and honey-colored ambers. See especially the Great East Window, the work of a 15th-century, Coventry-based glass painter. In the north transept is an architectural gem of the mid–13th century: the Five Sisters Window with its five lancets in grisaille glass. The late–15th-century choir screen has an impressive lineup of historical figures—everybody from William the Conqueror to the overthrown Henry VI.

At a reception desk near the entrance to the minster, groups can arrange a guide, if one is available. Conducted tours are free but donations toward the upkeep of the cathedral are requested.

The Chapter house, foundations and treasury, and tower are open Monday to Saturday from 10am to 6pm, Sunday from 2 to 6pm (closing time in winter is 4:30pm). The crypt is open Monday to Friday from 10am to 4:30pm, Saturday from 10am to 3:30pm, Sunday from 1 to 3:30pm. Admission to the Chapter house is 70p ($1.10) for adults, 30p (50¢) for children; to the crypt, 60p (95¢) for adults, 30p (50¢) for children; to the foundations and treasury, £1.80 ($2.90) for adults, 70p ($1.10) for children; to the tower, £2 ($3.20) for adults, £1 ($1.60) for children. Call ahead to verify times; they are subject to change (☎ **01904/639347**).

Check out St. William's Restaurant at the front of St. William's Cottage (☎ **01904/634830**), close to the east end of the Minster. This splendid timbered building is a good place for coffee, an affordable lunch, or tea. Here you can get tasty quiches, homemade soups, and luscious desserts. Not only that, but if you can arrange for a party of 35 or more, you can have a medieval banquet staged on your

# York

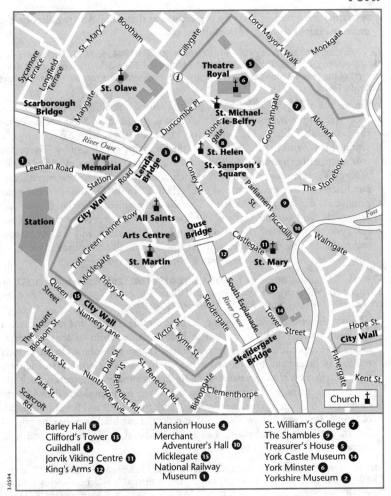

| | | |
|---|---|---|
| Barley Hall **8** | Mansion House **4** | St. William's College **7** |
| Clifford's Tower **13** | Merchant | The Shambles **9** |
| Guildhall **3** |   Adventurer's Hall **10** | Treasurer's House **5** |
| Jorvik Viking Centre **11** | Micklegate **15** | York Castle Museum **14** |
| King's Arms **12** | National Railway | York Minster **6** |
| |   Museum **1** | Yorkshire Museum **2** |

behalf, complete with minstrels, jesters, and jugglers. For more information, call ☎ **01904/634830.** One way to do this is to post a notice at your hotel and get people to sign up and invite newly made acquaintances. In one day our party swelled to nearly 50 and we were regally fed and entertained.

## MUSEUMS & MORE

**Treasurer's House.** Minster Yard. ☎ **01904/624247.** Admission £3.30 ($5.30) adults; £1.65 ($2.65) children; family ticket £8 ($12.80). Apr–Oct Sat–Thurs 10:30am–5pm (last entry 4:30pm). No bus route; less than half a mile (left) from the train station.

The Treasurer's House lies on a site where a continuous succession of buildings has stood since Roman times. The main part of the house, built in 1620, was refurbished by Yorkshire industrialist Frank Green at the turn of the century; he used this elegant town house to display his collection of 17th- and 18th-century furniture, glass, and china. An audiovisual program and exhibit explain the work of the medieval treasures and the subsequent fascinating history of the house. It has an attractive small garden in the shadow of York Minster. An appealing licensed restaurant, where Yorkshire specialties are served, is open the same hours as the house. An art gallery on the premises exhibits the work of local artists.

✪ **York Castle Museum.** Eye of York, off Tower St. ☎ **01904/653611.** Admission £4.50 ($7.20) adults; £3.20 ($5.10) children. Nov–Mar Mon–Sat 9:30am–5:30pm; Sun 10am–5:30pm; the rest of the year the museum closes at 4pm. A 15-minute walk, across the river and behind Clifford's Tower.

On the site of York's Castle, this is one of the finest folk museums in the country. Its unique feature is a re-creation of a Victorian cobbled street, Kirkgate, named for the museum's founder, Dr. John Kirk. He acquired his large collection while visiting his patients in rural Yorkshire at the beginning of this century. The period rooms range from a neoclassical Georgian dining room to an overstuffed and heavily adorned Victorian parlor to the 1953 sitting room with a brand-new television set purchased to watch the coronation of Elizabeth II. In the Debtors' Prison, former prison cells display craft workshops. There is also a superb collection of arms and armor. In the Costume Gallery, displays are changed regularly to reflect the collection's variety. Half Moon Court is an Edwardian street, with a gypsy caravan and a pub. During the summer, you can visit a watermill on the bank of the River Foss. We recommend allowing at least 2 hours for your museum visit.

✪ **National Railway Museum.** Leeman Rd. ☎ **01904/621261.** Admission £4.80 ($7.70) adults; £2.70 ($4.30) children. Daily 10am–6pm. Closed Dec 24–26. From the train station, left on Station Rd., left on Leeman Rd.; a 5-minute walk from there.

This was the first national museum to be built outside London, and it has attracted millions of visitors since it opened in 1975. Adapted from an original steam-locomotive depot, the museum gives visitors a chance to see how Queen Victoria traveled in luxury and to look under and inside steam locomotives. In addition, there's a collection of railway memorabilia, including an early–19th-century clock and penny machine for purchasing tickets on the railway platform. More than 40 locomotives are on display. One, the *Agenoria,* dates from 1829 and is a contemporary of Stephenson's well-known *Rocket.* Of several royal coaches, the most interesting is Queen Victoria's Royal Saloon; it's like a small hotel, with polished wood, silk, brocade, and silver accessories.

**Jorvik Viking Centre.** Coppergate. ☎ **01904/643211.** Admission £4.95 ($7.90) adults; £3.50 ($5.60) children; £4.60 ($7.35) seniors and students. Apr–Oct daily 9am–5:30pm; Nov–Mar daily 9am–3:30pm. Near Clifford's Tower and the Castle Museum (see above), in Coppergate Shopping Centre.

This Viking city, discovered many feet below present ground level, was reconstructed as it stood in 948. In a "time car," you travel back through the ages to 1067, when Normans sacked the city, and then you ride slowly through the street market peopled by faithfully modeled Vikings. You also go through a house where a family lived and down to the river to see the ship chandlers at work and a Norwegian cargo ship unloading. At the end of the ride, you pass through the Finds Hut, where thousands of artifacts are displayed. The time car departs at regular intervals.

## Impressions

*The external appearance of an old cathedral cannot be but displeasing to the eye of every man, who has any idea of the propriety of proportion, even though he may be ignorant of architecture as a science; and the long slender spire puts one in mind of a criminal impaled, with a sharp stake rising up through his shoulder.*

—Tobias Smollett (1721–71)

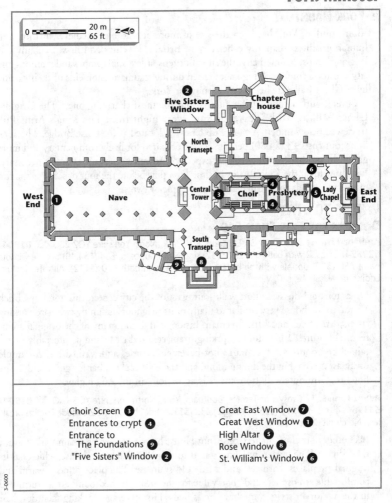

Choir Screen ❸
Entrances to crypt ❹
Entrance to
  The Foundations ❾
"Five Sisters" Window ❷

Great East Window ❼
Great West Window ❶
High Altar ❺
Rose Window ❽
St. William's Window ❻

## TEATIME

The best place for afternoon tea is **Betty's Café & Tea Rooms,** 6–8 St. Helen's Sq. (☎ **01904/659142**). We also recommend **St. William's College Restaurant,** 3 College St. (☎ **01904/634830**); and **Theater Royal Café Bar,** St. Leonard's Place (☎ **01904/632596**).

## ORGANIZED TOURS

The best way to see York is to go to Exhibition Square (opposite the Tourist Information Center), where a volunteer guide will take you on a free, 2-hour walking tour of the city. You'll learn about history and lore through numerous intriguing stories. Tours are given April through October, daily at 10:15am and 2:15pm, plus from June to August at 7pm; from November to March, a daily tour is given at 10:15am. Groups can book by prior arrangements contacting the Association of Volunteer Guides, De Grey Rooms, Exhibition Square, York YO1 2HB (☎ **01904/640780**).

## IS YORK HAUNTED?

After London, York has been the site of more beheadings, medieval torture, and human grisliness than any other city in Britain. Psychics and mystics claim it is England's most haunted city, the site of dozens of lost souls who wander among the city's historic core, resolving issues raised during traumatic moments of their earthly lives. Ghost walks are held every evening in York.

Several outfits conduct these tours, but the most charming one, "The Original Ghost Walk of York," leaves at 8pm every night from The King's Arms Pub (reviewed below under "A York Pub Crawl"), located at the Ouse Bridge. The 1 1/2-hour tour costs £3 ($4.80) per person. Be prepared for lively commentary and more ghoulishness than you might have expected. Advance reservations aren't necessary: Just show up at the King's Arms in time for a pint before the tour departs, as the fun of this tour tends to be enhanced after a tipple or two.

# WHERE TO STAY

## DOUBLES FOR LESS THAN £40

**Aberford House Hotel.** 35–36 E. Mount Rd., York, North Yorkshire YO2 2BD. ☎ **01904/622694.** 6 rms, 2 with bath. TV. £20 ($32) single without bath; £34 ($54.40) double without bath, £50 ($79) double with bath; family rm for 4 with bath £70 ($112). All rates include English breakfast. AE, MC, V.

On a quiet cul-de-sac a short walk southwest of the city center, this hotel in a brick Victorian rowhouse very similar to many of its neighbors is run by two hardworking sisters, Mrs. Snell and Mrs. Freeman. Inside, you'll find many of the original architectural features, a handful of working fireplaces, and clean and comfortably maintained bedrooms. Each contains hot-beverage facilities and washbasins. An ample breakfast is served in the dining room, and there's a cocktail bar for guests only. The hotel is a 5-minute walk from the railway station, off the A64 highway.

**Arnot House.** 17 Grosvenor Terrace, Bootham, York, North Yorkshire YO3 7AG. ☎ **01904/641966.** 4 rms. TV. £16 ($25.60) single; £32 ($51.20) double. All rates include English breakfast. No credit cards. Bus: no. 8.

Like other houses on the terrace, Arnot House has views over Bootham Park, toward the Minster. The owners welcome guests to this 1870 Victorian house, which has its original fireplaces, cornices, and a fine old staircase. The place offers a warm and comfortable atmosphere and good value for the area. The bedrooms are all furnished in the Victorian style; some have brass beds. Hot beverage–making facilities, hair dryers, and remote control TV are standard in the rooms. A four-course fixed-price dinner is served in the candlelit dining room and costs £12.50 ($20) and up. Grosvenor Terrace is a 15- to 20-minute walk from the train station, off Bootham (A19), 400 yards outside the city walls at Bootham Bar.

**The Avenue Guest House.** 6 The Avenue, Clifton, York YO3 6AS. ☎ **01904/620575.** 7 rms, none with bath, 2 with shower only. TV. £14–£18 ($22.40–$28.80) single without bath; £26–£34 ($41.60–$54.40) double without bath, £30–£40 ($48–$64) double with shower. All rates include English breakfast. No credit cards. Take A19 north of the city.

Appealing and cheerful, this brick-sided guest house was constructed around 1900 across the road from one of northern England's most venerable private schools. (St. Peters was built on land owned by the Fawkes family, and counts Guy Fawkes, leader of the Catholic insurgency during the Protestant Reformation, among its graduates.) Owned by Adèle and Clive Allen, the guest house boasts two rare laburnum trees in the front garden, turn-of-the-century charm, and a delightful interior. The bedrooms contain tea-making facilities and, in most cases, Laura Ashley–styled flowered fabrics and accessories. It's in the district of Clifton, a 10-minute walk north of York's center, a few steps from the edge of the Ouse River.

**City Guest House.** 68 Monkgate, York YO3 7PF. ☎ **01904/622483.** 7 rms, 6 with bath. TV. £14 ($22.40) single without bath, £22 ($35.20) single with bath; £32 ($51.20) double without bath, £48 ($76.80) double with bath. All rates include English, continental, or vegetarian breakfast. MC, V.

Harvey and Liz Leigh are the proprietors of this small B&B close to the heart of York. The couple offers warm, friendly service in the 1860 Victorian house. Although the rooms are fairly basic, the accommodation is a good value. The large, filling breakfast that is served will surely fill even the hungriest tourist. The Leighs are happy to help guests in choosing sights to see and restaurants or pubs in the area.

**Clifton Green Hotel.** 8 Clifton Green, York, North Yorkshire YO3 6LH. ☎ **01904/623597.** 8 rms, 3 with bath. TV. £20 ($32) single without bath; £35 ($56) double without bath, £45 ($72) double with bath. All rates include English breakfast. No credit cards. Bus: no. 9. Take the A19 rd. toward Thirsk.

About a 10-minute walk north of Bootham Bar, the north gate of old York, this immaculate, small hotel is nestled amid a row of similar red-brick turn-of-the-century houses. Since it's in front of a village green ringed with a white picket fence, it evokes one of the most rural settings in York, despite being close to the city center. The bedrooms, rented by Ben and Gloria Braithwaite, are carpeted and have central heating, hot- and cold-water basins, hot-beverage facilities, wardrobes, dressing tables, and other amenities.

The hotel also operates the **Inglewood Guest House,** next door at 7 Clifton Green (☎ **01904/653523**), which charges the same tariffs.

**Craig-Y-Don.** 3 Grosvenor Terrace, Bootham, York, North Yorkshire YO3 7AG. ☎ and fax **01904/637186.** 8 rms, 2 with bath. TV. £15.50–£17 ($24.80–$27.20) single without bath; £31–£34 ($49.60–$54.40) double without bath, £37–£39 ($59.20–$62.40) double with bath. All rates include English breakfast. MC, V. Bus: no. 9.

Mr. and Mrs. Oliver are two of the most hospitable hosts in the heart of York. They run an immaculately kept and most inviting home and serve a large Yorkshire breakfast. The bedrooms are well maintained and offer routine comfort. Children are welcome. Readers cite the exceptional kindness of Mr. and Mrs. Oliver; one California woman reported that she'd washed some clothing and hung it on the line outside. Upon her return, she found all the clothes ironed and hanging in the closet!

**Dairy Wholefood Guest House.** 3 Scarcroft Rd., York, North Yorkshire YO2 1ND. ☎ **01904/639367.** 5 rms, 2 with bath. TV. £26 ($41.60) single without bath, £34 ($54.40) single with bath; £34–£38 ($54.40–$60.80) double without bath, £42 ($67.20) double with bath. All rates include English breakfast. No credit cards.

You'll find this lovely Victorian town house decorated throughout with ideas and furnishings in the "Habitat, Sanderson, Laura Ashley" style. Architectural charm is found in such features as stained- and etched-glass windows, pitch pine doors and staircase, cast-iron fire grates, and wonderfully ornate ceiling roses and cornices. Each individually decorated bedroom has color TV, beverage-making facilities, hair dryer, and an alarm clock, along with such personal touches as toiletries, maps, books, games, and information folders. Your host, Keith Jackman, is an ex-accountant–professional drummer in Australia. He still performs, playing hand-drums, didgeridoo, and blues harmonica. His place lies only 200 yards south of the medieval city walls, within easy access of car parking. Breakfast choices range from traditional English to whole-food vegetarian.

**Feversham Lodge.** 1–3 Feversham Crescent, York, North Yorkshire YO3 7HQ. ☎ **01904/ 623882.** 10 rms, 7 with shower only. TV. £17 ($27.20) single without bath; £34 ($54.40) double without bath, £40 ($64) double with bath. All rates include English breakfast. AE, DC, MC, V. From Bootham Bar, proceed north along Gillygate; Feversham Crescent is a left turn.

This lodge is a 19th-century Methodist manse converted to receive guests in 1981. It still retains its lofty dining room, and there's a TV lounge. Bob and Jill Peacock maintain neatly kept bedrooms, all of which have central heating and tea-making equipment. Some rooms open onto views of the minster. There is space to park.

✪ **Sycamore Guest House.** 19 Sycamore Place, Bootham, York, North Yorkshire YO3 7DW. ☎ **01904/624712.** 7 rms, 3 with bath. TV. £16–£30 ($25.60–$48) single without bath; £30– £38 ($48–$60.80) double without bath, £35–£40 ($56–$64) double with bath. All rates include English breakfast. No credit cards.

Built as a private dwelling in 1902, this house has been carefully converted to maintain much of its original splendor. Now it's a family-owned and -run hotel that offers a high level of accommodation. The rooms have hot and cold running water, central heating, hair dryers, and hot-beverage facilities. The location is close to the city center off A19 to Thirsk (a 10-minute walk to the minster, a 15-minute walk to the rail station), yet it's on a quiet cul-de-sac. Guests receive keys, and parking is available.

## DOUBLES FOR LESS THAN £55

**Byron House Hotel.** The Mount, York YO2 2DD. ☎ **01904/632525.** Fax 01904/638904. 10 rms, 7 with bath. TV TEL. £25 ($40) single without bath, £28 ($44.80) single with bath; £52–£70 ($83.20–$112) double with bath. All rates include English breakfast. AE, MC, V. Take A1036 southeast of York.

Byron House is located just outside of York, about a 10-minute walk from the city walls, a railway station, and the racecourse. The proprietors provide friendly service to their guests in the early–19th-century hotel. All rooms are equipped with hot beverage-making facilities and offer pleasant views of the countryside. There is also a comfortable lounge and a room where a cooked-to-order dinner at £18.50 ($29.60) is served at 7pm.

✪ **Nunmill House.** 85 Bishopthorpe Rd., York, North Yorkshire YO2 1NX. ☎ **01904/ 634047.** Fax 01904/655879. 8 rms. TV. £21–£22 ($33.60–$35.20) single; £40–£44 ($64– $70.40) double; £60 ($96) family rm for 4. All rates include English breakfast. No credit cards. Closed Dec–Jan.

Fronted by a small garden, this brick-with-stone-trim Victorian house was built in 1887. Today it functions as a cozy and much-restored bed-and-breakfast hotel, set in a residential neighborhood about a 20-minute walk southeast of York's cathedral. The individually designed bedrooms aspire to elegance, with an occasional four-poster or half-tester bed. Each of the affordable, comfortable accommodations has beverage-making equipment and color TV. Each unit is a double. Only breakfast is served.

## A YOUTH HOSTEL

**YHA York International Youth Hostel.** Water End, Clifton, York, North Yorkshire YO3 6LT. ☎ **01904/653147.** Fax 01904/651230. 39 rms. 150 beds. Rooms: £17 ($27.20) single; £35 ($56) double; £49 ($78.40) triple; £49.50–£69.50 ($79.20–$111.20) family rm. Dorm: £13.85 ($22.15) adult; £10.30 ($16.50) children. All rates include breakfast. MC, V.

In the town center, this hostel offers standard youth hostel rooms which sleep from two to eight persons, and it also has family rooms which sleep from three to six people (a family must include at least one child under the age of 14). Also available are premium single, double, and triple rooms which have color TV and tea- and coffee-making facilities. This is really a superior grade hostel, offering good facilities such as a communal kitchen, piping hot showers, laundry room, and a TV room. Although breakfast is included with the rate, packed lunches for £2.45 ($3.90), £2.85 ($4.55), and £3.25 ($5.20) depending on the size you want, and dinner for £4.25 ($6.80) are available at the on-site restaurant. The food is cafeteria style but filling. The hostel is open year-round, and its reception is open from 6:30am to 10:30pm with 24-hour access. This is one of the few hostels where there is no curfew. The location is a mile from the heart of York. From Exhibition Square, head for three-quarters of a mile toward Bootham/Clifton, turning left at Water End. Otherwise, take the Clifton Green bus from the center which lets you off about a quarter of a mile away.

## WHERE TO EAT

For lunch, many budget travelers like to pick up the makings for a picnic. The most interesting place to shop for goodies is the **Newgate Market** between The Shambles and Market Street in the center of town. Here you can buy fruit, vegetables, cakes, pies, and prepared meats. The market is open Monday through Saturday from 8am to 5pm. Another good place to shop is **Tullivers Herbs & Wholefood,** 29 Goodramgate (☎ **01904/636437**). It bakes really good fresh bread, and you can also pick up deli items. At the tiny supermarket **Jackson's,** 25 Bootham (☎ **01904/ 623558**), you pick up a pizza. A final choice, and a good one, is **Holland & Barrett,** 39 Parliament (☎ **01904/641232**), which hawks whole food.

If you work up an appetite while exploring the National Railway Museum, stop in its licensed restaurant, **The Brief Encounter,** in the South Hall of the museum on Leeman Road (☎ **01904/621261**). The simply decorated, self-service restaurant with its many pictures of old trains serves a range of food from sandwiches to hot dishes and pastries. A selection of three main hot dishes changes daily and may include such items as beef stroganof, penne pasta with salmon and roasted red peppers, or a vegetarian dish like avocado with Mediterranean vegetables and feta cheese. They don't accept credit cards here and keep the same hours as the museum, daily from 10am to 6pm. Prices range from £1.95 ($3.10) for sandwiches to £5.25 ($8.40) for a main course.

✪ **Betty's Cafe Tea Rooms.** 6–8 St. Helen's Sq. ☎ **01904/659142.** Main courses £5.45– £6.75 ($8.70–$10.80); tea from £1.70 ($2.70); pastries from £1.90 ($3.05). MC, V. Daily 9am– 9pm. ENGLISH.

Established in 1919, and now one of the most visible tearoom chains in Yorkshire, Betty's invites you to drop in for a quick coffee and pastry or treat yourself to a full English breakfast, a Yorkshire cheese lunch, or a Yorkshire rarebit. Genteel afternoon teas with scones as well as fish-and-chips high teas are favorites, and selections of healthy salads and whole-food quiches are also available. Betty's is famous for its cream cakes. The light suppers and wide variety of cooked and cold meals make this a good place to stop in the evening, and you can order a fine Alsatian wine to complete your meal. A cafe concert (usually a pianist) entertains customers some evenings as they dine, usually between 6 and 9pm. Families with children are made especially welcome. The interior retains lots of its original paneling and its Edwardian-era stained-glass windows.

**Blake Head Vegetarian Café.** 104 Mickelgate. ☎ **01904/623767.** Main courses £5 ($8); 3-course lunch £8 ($12.80). MC, V. Sun–Fri 10am–4:30pm; Sat 9:30am–5pm. VEGETARIAN.

This inviting place is a sort of countercultural center, and is a favorite rendezvous point for the students of York. It is located in the back of a book store. The canopy roof lets in light to give a bright and cheerful atmosphere, and you can also dine on the patio in fair weather. Salads are serious business here. Lunch is served daily from noon to 3pm when their set menu is one of York's best food values. The menu for this changes daily. You can browse for a good book from the store and can enjoy one of their homemade cakes or desserts—and, of course, a good cuppa.

**Oscar's Wine Bar and Bistro.** 8 Little Stonegate, Off Stonegate. ☎ 01904/652002. Main courses £3–£5 ($4.80–$8) at lunch; £5–£7.95 ($8–$12.70) at dinner. MC, V. Daily 11am–11pm. INTERNATIONAL.

This wine bar and bistro, located in an old, historic building, offers good, affordable food—hearty fare in big portions. They serve a variety of burgers from vegetarian to Cajun to Mexican. Also dished up are lasagna, chili, Yorkshire sausage, and sizzling sirloin steaks. When the weather permits, you can dine in the courtyard. It's a lively and bustling place which often has music available. For special occasions, there may be live jazz or blues, and on the weekends a DJ spins dance music. Happy hour, which is big at this bistro, is Monday through Friday from 5 to 7pm, on Monday and Wednesday from 8 to 11pm, and on Sunday until 10:30pm.

**Rubicon.** 5 Little Stonegate, off Stonegate. ☎ 01904/676076. Fixed-price 2-course lunch £6 ($9.60); fixed-price 3-course dinner £12.50 ($20). No credit cards. Tues–Sat noon–2pm; daily 5–10pm. VEGETARIAN.

This restaurant offers vegan and gluten-free food in a very tidy, warm, relaxed, and intimate atmosphere with candlelight. You can bring your own wine at no extra charge and enjoy starters such as Stilton walnut and port pâté or baked eggplant followed by moussaka or lasagna verde, both delicious vegetarian dishes. This is a nonsmoking establishment.

**Russells Stonegate.** 34 Stonegate. ☎ 01904/641432. Reservations recommended. Snacks £2.50–£6 ($4–$9.60); fixed-price meals £6.50–£12.99 ($10.40–$20.80) at lunch, £7.99–£14.99 ($12.80–$24) at dinner. MC, V. Daily 10am–10pm (may close earlier in winter). ENGLISH.

With another branch in York at 26 Coppergate (☎ 01904/644330), Russells restaurants are, in the words of one observer, "probably the only true British restaurants in York." Although this point may be arguable, Russells does offer fresh food of a high standard. Many of its recipes are "just like mother used to make"—that is, if your mother came from northeast England. The fare includes roast beef with Yorkshire pudding, along with roast potatoes and seasonal vegetables. A good range of appetizers is also offered, and the desserts are very English and very fattening, especially bread-and-butter pudding. Wine is available by the glass or bottle, and the kitchen always has a good selection of English cheese. The place works like a carvery system, where waitresses bring appetizers, desserts, and drinks to your table, and where clients carry their plates up to the carvery for their roast joints and main courses. The restaurant sits beside York's most ancient street, a 1-minute walk from the cathedral.

**Tandoori Night.** 23 Bootham. ☎ 01904/613366. Main courses £4.10–£7.10 ($6.55–$11.35). MC, V. Mon–Fri noon–2:30pm and 6pm–midnight; Sat–Sun noon–midnight. INDIAN.

Some of the best and most affordable Indian meals in town can be found here, including chicken Malaya (cooked with fruit). You can select from a variety of chicken, lamb, or rice dishes. They also serve special Malayan dishes with fruit, rice, and coconut and a variety of Indian dishes which vary, according to your taste, from very mild to very hot. You'll feel as if you are dining in India in this exotically decorated restaurant.

## YORK AFTER DARK

Being billed as the most haunted city in Europe means that ghosts figure heavily in York's nightlife. At **Haunted Walk** (☎ 01904/628436), for an adult fee of £3 ($4.80) and a children's price of £2 ($3.20), you can join a walking tour of the city that includes a big dose of history along with the ghost stories. Tours begin at Exhibition Square every evening at 8pm. For a more dramatic account of York's ghosts, join thespian Ray Alexander as he leads you on his **Original Ghost Walk** (☎ **01759/373090**). Alexander's tales will make you laugh and give you the willies at the same time. The admission fee and starting time are the same as the Haunted Walk, but the tour begins at the Kings Arms Pub at King's Straith (see "Is York Haunted?" above for more details).

There's no phantom of the opera lurking here, but performances can be haunting when touring or amateur groups take to the stage at the **Theatre Royal,** St. Leonard's Place (☎ **01904/623568**). This building has housed a theater continuously for the last 253 years, and presently, as a repertory theater, it hosts productions of musicals, opera, comedy, and drama. The box office is open Monday through Saturday from 10am until 8pm, with tickets ranging from £5 to £15 ($8 to $24).

Hosting orchestral and chamber concerts from October through June, the **University of York Department of Music** (☎ **01904/432439**) provides entertainment from within its ranks as well as featuring an array of international performers. Tickets generally run from £3 to £11 ($4.80 to $17.60).

With two dance rooms to choose from, you can probably find something you want to groove to at **Toffs Nightclub & Restaurant,** 3–5 Toft Green (☎ **01904/ 620203**), where DJs play everything from indie to commercial dance music. The cover charge ranges from £2.50 to £6 ($4 to $9.60), but students can get in for £1.75 ($2.80) on Tuesday through Thursday. It may sound like a part of a college campus, but **York Arts Centre,** Micklegate (☎ **01904/627129**), situated in a converted medieval church, is all about club dancing, with DJs playing everything from acid jazz to trip hop on Friday and Saturday nights only. The cover charge is £5 ($8).

Live music is well represented in York, and **Fibbers,** Stonebow House, The Stonebow (☎ **01904/651250**), mixes it up as well as anyone, featuring local and touring bands playing everything from blues, folk, and jazz, to rock and Britpop, with the cover charge varying from £2 to £5 ($3.20 to $8). Entertainment is usually scheduled at the **Bonding Warehouse,** Skeldergate (☎ **01904/622527**), 2 or 3 nights a week and veers from jazz, rock, and blues to original fringe theater productions. When you need air, you can step out onto the longest balcony overlooking the River Ouse. Cover charge is £1.50 to £3.50 ($2.40 to $5.60). Don't get confused by the fact that there are four pubs with this name.

The **Punch Bowl,** 7 Stonegate (☎ **01904/622305**), is the one haunted by four ghosts—three murders and a suicide—that features blues of all variations on Monday through Thursday nights, when the music is yours for the price of a pint.

It doesn't feature live entertainment, but the place called **Roman Bath,** St. Sampson's Square (☎ **01904/620455**), draws people because it's built over a real Roman bath, one of the city's tourist attractions. Even upstairs in the pub you're reminded it's there by the legions of Roman bathers, eyes upon you, depicted in murals covering the walls. Ales on tap include Theakstons XB or Best.

## A YORK PUB CRAWL

**The Black Swan.** Peaseholme Green. ☎ **01904/625236.** Reservations not necessary. Main courses £3.95–£4.50 ($6.30–$7.20). V. Mon–Sat 11am–11pm; Sun noon–10:30pm. Food service: Mon–Sat 11:30am–2pm; Sun noon–2:30pm. ENGLISH.

One of the city's oldest inns, the Black Swan is a fine, timbered, frame house that was once the home of the lord mayor of York in 1417; the mother of Gen. James Wolfe of Quebec also lived here. You can enjoy pub meals in front of a log fire in a brick inglenook. There are sandwiches, homemade soups, and Yorkshire puddings filled with beef stew.

This is one of York's "musical pubs," featuring live jazz on Monday and folk on Tuesday, with admission charges ranging from £1.50 to £3.50 ($2.40 to $5.60). There are two double rooms with private bath, which are available for £25 ($40) per person, bed-and-breakfast.

**King's Arms Public House.** King's Staith. ☎ **01904/659435.** Reservations not accepted. Main courses £3.50–£6 ($5.60–$9.60). No credit cards. Mon–Sat 11:30am–2:30pm; Sun noon–2pm. Otherwise, pub hours. ENGLISH.

At the base of the Ouse Bridge, a few steps from the edge of the river, this 16th-century pub is boisterous and fun. A historic monument in its own right, it's filled with charm and character and has the ceiling beams, paneling, and weathered brickwork you'd expect. A board records various disastrous flood levels, the most recent of which inundated the place in 1991. In summer, rows of outdoor tables are placed beside the river. Your hosts serve a full range of draft and bottled beers, the most popular of which (Samuel Smith's) is still brewed in Tadcaster, only 10 miles away. Place your lunch food order at the counter for bar snacks, which could include burgers, homemade curries, soups, and steak-and-kidney pie. No dinner is served. The ghost walk we recommend leaves here every night at 8pm (see above).

**Ye Olde Starre Inne.** 40 Stonegate. ☎ **01904/623063.** Reservations not accepted. Main courses £3.80–£4.95 ($6.10–$7.90). AE, DC, MC, V. Mon–Sat 11:30am–11pm; Sun noon–10:30pm. ENGLISH.

On a pedestrian street in Old York, this pub dates back to 1644 and is York's oldest licensed pub. Some inn (of one kind or another) might have stood on this spot since 900. In a pub said to be haunted by an old woman, a little girl, and a cat, you enter into an atmosphere of cast-iron tables, an open fireplace, oak Victorian settles, and time-blackened beams. In addition to standard alcoholic beverages and several malt whiskies, the pub offers an array of such English staples as Yorkshire pudding, Cumberland sausage, and savory minced beef and onion. Recently, the owners have added a year-round glassed-in garden. In all types of weather, guests can enjoy the plants and the view of the minster from their tables here.

## 2 Yorkshire's Country Houses, Castles & More

Yorkshire's battle-scarred castles, Gothic abbeys, and great country manor houses (from all periods) are unrivaled anywhere in Britain. Here are some of the highlights.

## IN NORTH YORKSHIRE
### ✪ CASTLE HOWARD

In its dramatic setting of lakes, fountains, and extensive gardens, Castle Howard, at Malton (☎ **01653/648444**), the 18th-century palace designed by Sir John Vanbrugh, is undoubtedly the finest private residence in Yorkshire. The principal location for the TV miniseries *Brideshead Revisited*, this was the first major achievement of the architect who later created the lavish Blenheim Palace near Oxford. The Yorkshire palace was begun in 1699 for the third earl of Carlisle, Charles Howard.

The striking facade is topped by a painted and gilded dome, which reaches more than 80 feet into the air. The interior boasts a 192-foot-long gallery, as well as a chapel with magnificent stained-glass windows by the 19th-century artist Sir Edward Burne-Jones. Besides the collections of antique furniture, porcelain and sculpture, the castle has many important paintings, including a portrait of Henry VIII by Holbein and works by Rubens, Reynolds, and Gainsborough.

The seemingly endless grounds around the palace also offer the visitor some memorable sights, including the domed Temple of the Four Winds, by Vanbrugh, and the richly designed family mausoleum by Hawksmoor. There are two rose gardens, one with old-fashioned roses, the other featuring modern creations.

Castle Howard is 15 miles northeast of York, 3 miles off A64. It is open to the public daily from mid-March to late October: The grounds are open from 10am to 5pm; the house, from 11am to 5pm, with last admission at 4:30pm. Admission is £6.50 ($10.40) for adults, £5.50 ($8.80) for seniors and students, and £3.50 ($5.60) for children. You can enjoy sandwiches, hot dishes, and wines in the self-service cafeteria. They now have stable courtyards which include glass blowing and sales, a gift shop, a hayloft cafeteria, all operating during the same hours as the castle.

**Yorktour,** Tower Street, York (☎ **01904/645151**), provides a daily coach service to Castle Howard from June to September on Tuesday, Friday, and Sunday and to Fountains Abbey and Studley Royal on Saturday. The coaches leave in the afternoon for a half day of sightseeing.

## ✪ FOUNTAINS ABBEY & STUDLEY ROYAL

At Fountains, 4 miles southwest of Ripon off B6265, stands Fountains Abbey and Studley Royal, Fountains (☎ **01765/608888**), on the banks of the Silver Skell. The abbey was founded by Cistercian monks in 1132 and is the largest monastic ruin in Britain. In 1987 it was awarded World Heritage Site status. The ruins provide the focal point of the 18th-century landscape garden at Studley Royal, one of the few surviving examples of a Georgian green garden. It's known for its conservation work in the water gardens, ornamental temples, follies, and vistas. The garden is bounded at its northern edge by a lake and 400 acres of deer park. The Fountains Hall and Elizabethan Mansion are undergoing restoration.

It's best to visit the site by private car, although it can be reached from York by public transportation. From York, take bus no. 143 leaving from the York Hall Station to Ripon, 23 miles to the northwest (A59, A1, and B6265 lead to Ripon). From Ripon, it will be necessary to take a taxi 4 miles to the southwest, although some prefer to go on foot, as it's a scenic walk.

It is open October through March, daily from 10am to 5pm; and April through September, daily from 10am to 7pm. It is closed December 24 to 25 and on Friday in November and January. Admission is £4.20 ($6.70) for adults, £2 ($3.20) for children; a family ticket is £10 ($16).

# IN WEST YORKSHIRE
## ✪ HAREWOOD HOUSE & BIRD GARDEN

At the junction of A61 and A659, midway between Leeds and Harrogate, stands **Harewood House,** Harewood (☎ **0113/288-6331**), the home of the earl and countess of Harewood, one of England's great 18th-century houses, which has always been owned by the Lascelles family. The fine Adam interior has superb ceilings and plasterwork and furniture made especially for Harewood by Chippendale. There are also important collections of English and Italian paintings and Sèvres and Chinese porcelain.

The gardens, designed by Capability Brown, include terraces, lakeside and woodland walks, and a 4¹/₂-acre bird garden with exotic species from all over the world, including penguins, macaws, flamingos, and snowy owls. Other facilities include an art gallery, shops, a restaurant, and cafeteria. Parking is free, and there is a picnic area, plus an adventure playground for the children.

Harewood is located 7 miles south of Harrogate, 8 miles north of Leeds on the Leeds-Harrogate road (at the junction of A61/A659) at Harewood Village; 5 miles from A1 at Wetherby, and 22 miles west of York. From York, head west along B1224 toward Wetherby and follow the signs to Harewood from there.

Admission to the house, grounds, Bird Garden, and the Terrace Gallery is £6.50 ($10.40) for adults, £5.50 ($8.80) for seniors, and £4.50 ($7.20) for children. To tour the grounds only, the cost is £4 ($6.40) for adults, £3 ($4.80) for seniors, and £2 ($3.20) for children 15 and under. The house, bird garden, and adventure playground are open March to October, daily from 10am to 6pm.

## 3 North York Moors National Park

The moors, on the other side of the Vale of York, have a wild beauty all their own, quite different from that of the dales. This rather barren moorland blossoms in summer with purple heather. Bounded on the east by the North Sea, it embraces a 554-square-mile area, which England has turned into a national park.

## ESSENTIALS

**GETTING THERE** Because the park sprawls over such a large area, you can access its interior from five or six different gateways. Most visitors enter it from the side closest to York, by following either the A19 north via the hamlet of Thirsk, or by detouring to the northeast along the A64 and entering via the hamlet of Scarborough. You can also get in through the hamlet of Helmsley, where the park's administrative headquarters are located; just follow the roads from York that are signposted Helmsley. Gateways along the park's northern edges, which are less convenient to York, include the hamlets of Whitby (accessible via the A171), and Stokesley (accessible via the A19).

**VISITOR INFORMATION** For information before you go, especially accommodation and transportation data, contact **North York Moors National Park,** The Old Vicarage, Bondgate, Helmsley, York YO6 5BP (☎ **01439/770657**).

## THE GEOGRAPHY OF THE MOORS

Bounded by the Cleveland and Hambleton hills, the moors are dotted with early burial grounds and ancient stone crosses. At Kilburn a white horse can be seen hewn out of the hillside.

**Pickering** and **Northallerton,** both market towns, serve as gateways to the moors. ✪ **Cleveland Way National Trail,** stretching for 110 miles, encircles the national park; two regional routes, 35-mile ✪ **Esk Valley Walk** and 40-mile **Tabular Hills Walk,** offer the best views of the area.

The isolation and the beauty of the landscape attracted the founders of **three great abbeys:** Rievaulx near Helmsley, Byland Abbey near the village of Wass, and Ampleforth Abbey. Nearby is **Coxwold,** one of the most attractive villages in the moors. The Cistercian Rievaulx and Byland abbeys are in ruins, but the Benedictine Ampleforth still functions as a monastery and well-known Roman Catholic boys' school. Although many of its buildings date from the 19th and 20th centuries, they contain earlier artifacts.

Along the eastern boundary of the park, North Yorkshire's 45-mile coastline shelters such traditional seaside resorts as Filey, Whitby, and Scarborough, the latter claiming to be the oldest seaside spa in Britain, located supposedly on the site of a Roman signaling station. The spa was founded in 1622, when mineral springs with medicinal properties were discovered. In the 19th century its Grand Hotel, a

Victorian structure, was acclaimed the best in Europe. The Norman castle on the big cliffs overlooks the twin bays.

You can drive through the moorland while based in York, but if you'd like to be closer to the moors, there are places to stay in and around the National Park.

## TREKKING THE MOORS

In the British collective unconscious, the North York Moors are richly associated with doomed trysts between unlucky lovers and ghosts who wander vengefully across the rugged plateaus of their lonely and windswept surfaces. Although the earth is relatively fertile in the river valleys, the thin, rocky soil of the heather-clad uplands has been scorned by local farmers as wasteland, suitable only for sheep grazing and healthy—but melancholy—rambles. During the 19th century, a handful of manor houses were built on their lonely promontories by moguls of the Industrial Revolution, but not until 1953 was the 554-square-mile district designated the North York Moors National Park.

Encompassing England's largest expanse of moorland, the park is famous for the diversity of heathers, which thrive between the sandstone outcroppings of the uplands. If your visit occurs between October and February, be warned that the smoldering fires you'll see across the landscape are deliberately controlled attempts by shepherds and farmers to burn the omnipresent heather back to stubs. Repeated in age-old cycles every 15 years, the blazes encourage the heather's renewal with new growth for the uncounted thousands of sheep that thrive in the district.

Although public footpaths and bridleways take you to all corners of the moors, true aficionados usually opt for two clearly demarcated trails that are the most comprehensive moor walks in Europe. The shorter of the two is the **Lyle Wake Walk,** a 40-mile east-to-west trek that connects the hamlets of Osmotherly and Ravenscar. It traces the rugged path established by 18th-century coffin bearers. The longer trek— **the Cleveland Way**—is a 110-mile circumnavigation of the national park's perimeter. A good section of it skirts the edge of the Yorkshire coastline, other stretches take climbers up and down a series of steep fells in the park's interior.

Ghostly references permeate both walks. One of the most ghoulish involves macabre tales of the local villagers' habits. Every village contained a hangman's gibbet placed prominently at the town's highest point. For centuries, the amputated hands of the hangman's victims were prominently displayed in the doorways of Moorland cottages as a deterrent to thievery.

Don't even consider an ambitious moor trek without arming yourself with stout shoes or hiking boots, a compass, an ordinance survey map, and a guidebook specifically written for such promenades. With descriptions of geologically interesting sites, safety warnings, and listings of inns and farmhouses (haunted or otherwise) offering overnight stays, they sell for less than £4 ($6.40) each at any local tourist office.

Advice and information about the mysterious beauty of the North York Moors can be obtained at the **Sutton Bank Visitor Centre,** Sutton Bank, near Thirsk, North Yorkshire YO7 2EK (☎ **01845/597426**). Another well-inventoried information source is **The Moors Centre,** Danby Lodge, Lodge Lane, Danby, near Whitby YO21 2NB (☎ **01947/820500**).

## WHERE TO STAY & EAT IN & AROUND THIRSK

✪ **Brook House.** Ingramgate, Thirsk, North Yorkshire YO7 1DD. ☎ **01845/522240.** Fax 01845/523133. 3 rms, none with bath. TV. £16 ($25.60) per person. All rates include English breakfast. No credit cards. Discounts available for children.

This large Victorian house is set in 2 acres of land, some of which is filled with flower beds. It overlooks the open countryside, yet the Market Square is only a 3-minute walk away. Owner Margaret McLauchlan is charming and kind, and has even been known to do a batch of washing for guests at no extra cost (but we can't promise that). She serves a hearty and filling Yorkshire breakfast, plus an English afternoon tea. Tea-making facilities are also available for the guests, and a spacious and comfortable living room has a color TV. The house is centrally heated, and in the guests' drawing room is an open log fire in cool weather. There's ample parking.

Note in advance that the modern brick-sided bungalow set adjacent to Brook House's driveway also accepts overnight guests, but is not associated in any way with the McLauchlan family or its enterprises.

**St. James House.** 36 The Green, Thirsk, North Yorkshire YO7 1AQ. ☎ **01845/524120.** 4 rms, 2 with bath. TV. £26 ($41.60) single without bath; £32 ($51.20) double without bath, £40 ($64) double with bath. All rates include English breakfast. No credit cards. Closed Nov–Feb.

This three-story, 18th-century, Georgian brick house on the village green is near the former maternity home where James Herriot's children were born. The guest house, operated by Mrs. Liz Ogleby, is tastefully furnished, with some antiques. The attractive bedrooms, each a double, have such touches as good bone china to use with the hot beverage–making facilities.

✪ **Sheppard's Hotel, Restaurant & Bistro.** Front St., Sowerby, near Thirsk, North Yorkshire YO7 1JF. ☎ **01845/523655.** Fax 01845/524720. 8 rms. TV. £59–£62 ($94.40–$99.20) single; £75–£84 ($120–$134.40) double; £88 ($140.80) 4-poster room. All rates include English breakfast. MC, V. Take A19 half a mile south of Thirsk.

James Herriot treated his last horse on these premises, but now the Sheppard family has turned it into one of the finest lodging choices in the area. This family-run concern operates out of an old stable block and granary (now a restaurant and bistro, with well-furnished bedrooms overhead). A country atmosphere prevails with pine furniture, and the decor often consists of nailed horse brasses on the beams. Many guests request the "fat bedroom," so named because of its over-sized double bed. All the buildings in the complex are grouped around a cobblestone courtyard.

Many visitors come here just to dine. Since 1982 the restaurant has operated out of the old stables. In 1990 a garden-room bistro was opened in the granary and the courtyard was covered over to make an atrium. Guests eat informally by candlelight in a setting of potted plants and palms. Fresh local produce is emphasized. Main-course dishes are served with a selection of fresh vegetables, and include such dishes as "fowl and fish" (chicken breast with crayfish ravioli) or supreme of duckling lightly grilled and fanned over a kumquat glaze. Fillet of Moors lamb is oven roasted with rosemary.

The family still runs its Church Farm Bed & Breakfast, Front Street, Sowerby, North Yorkshire YO7 1JF (☎ 01845/523655), across the way. There you can be lodged less expensively. Singles cost £35 ($56) without bath, £40 ($64) with bath; doubles, £40 ($64) without bath, £50 ($80) with bath—including a full English breakfast.

## 4  Haworth: Home of the Brontës

45 miles SW of York; 21 miles W of Leeds

This village, on the high moor of the Pennines, is famous as the home of the Brontës, the most visited literary shrine in England after Stratford-upon-Avon.

# ESSENTIALS

**GETTING THERE**   To reach Haworth by rail, take the West Yorkshire Metrotrain from Leeds City Station to Keighley (it leaves approximately every 30 minutes). Change trains at Keighley and take the Keighley and Worth Valley Railway to Haworth and Oxenhope. Train services operate every weekend throughout the year, with 7 to 12 departures. From late June to the end of August, trains also run four times a day Monday through Friday. For general inquiries, call ☎ **01535/645214;** for 24-hour timetable details dial ☎ **01535/647777.**

Yorkshire Rider, a private company, offers bus service between Hebden Bridge (which has rail links to Leeds and York) and Haworth. Bus no. 500 makes the trip between Hebden Bridge and Haworth from June through September only, four trips per day Sunday through Friday and one on Saturday. For information, call ☎ **01422/365985.**

If you're driving from York, head west toward Leeds on A64 approaching the A6120 Ring Road to Shipley; then take A650 to Keighley, and finally link up with the B6142 south to Haworth.

**VISITOR INFORMATION**   The **Tourist Information Centre,** is at 2–4 West Lane in Haworth (☎ **01535/642329**). Open April through October, daily from 9:30am to 5:30pm; November through March, daily from 9:30am to 5pm (closed December 24 to 26).

## ✪ THE BRONTË PARSONAGE MUSEUM

Anne Brontë wrote two novels, *The Tenant of Wildfell Hall* and *Agnes Grey;* Charlotte wrote two masterpieces, *Jane Eyre* and *Villette,* which depicted her experiences as a teacher as well as several other novels; and Emily is the author of *Wuthering Heights,* a novel of passion and haunting melancholy. Charlotte and Emily are buried in the family vault under the Church of St. Michael, and the parsonage where they lived has been preserved as the Brontë Parsonage Museum, Church Street (☎ **01535/642323**), which houses their furniture, personal treasures, pictures, books, and manuscripts.

The stone-sided parsonage, built near the top of the village in 1777, was assigned for the course of his lifetime as the residence of the Brontë's father, Patrick, the Perpetual Curator (incumbent) of the Church of St. Michael and All Angel's Church. Regrettably, the church tended by the Brontës was demolished in 1870 because of unsanitary conditions of the crypt in the cellar; it was rebuilt in its present form the same year. The parsonage contains a walled garden very similar to the one cultivated by the Brontës, five bedrooms (whose occupants changed according to which family member was in residence at the time), and a collection of family furniture (some bought with proceeds from Charlotte's literary success), as well as personal effects, pictures and paintings, and original manuscripts. It also contains the largest archive of family correspondence in the world.

Remarkably, the town's population of approximately 6,500 is about the same as when the Brontës lived here, although the number of buildings in town has increased.

The museum is maintained by a professional staff selected by the Brontë Society, an organization established in 1893 to perpetuate the memory and legacy of Britain's most famous literary family. Contributions to the society are welcomed. The museum tends to be extremely crowded in July and August. It may be visited April to September, daily from 10am to 5pm; October to March, daily from 11am to 4:30pm. It's closed from mid-January to early February and at Christmastime. Admission is

£3.80 ($6.10) for adults and £1.20 ($1.90) for children. A family ticket, good for two adults and three children, costs £8.80 ($14.10). Children under 5 are admitted free.

## SHOPPING

While in Haworth, you'll want to visit the **Brontë Weaving Shed,** Townend Mill (☎ **01535/646217**). The shop is not far from the Brontë Parsonage, featuring the famous Brontë tweed which combines browns, greens, and oranges to evoke the look of the local (Brontë) countryside.

## WHERE TO STAY IN & AROUND HAWORTH

**Weaver's** (see "Where to Eat," below) also rents rooms.

✪ **Ferncliffe.** Hebden Rd., Haworth, Keighley, West Yorkshire BD22 8RS. ☎ **01535/643405.** 6 rms, all with shower only. TV. £19.50 ($31.20) single; £39 ($62.40) double. All rates include English breakfast. V. Closed Dec 26–30.

Ferncliffe offers one of the area's most outstanding accommodations. Modern and comfortable, the hotel and its dining room open onto views of the surrounding *Wuthering Heights* countryside. A rock garden in front contains a wide spectrum of alpine plants, which are maintained by the affable owner/managers, Elizabeth Corboy and Tom Martin. Built after World War II and converted into a hotel with enlargements in the early 1980s, the hotel offers clean and cozily decorated bedrooms, each with beverage-making facilities. The hotel serves good Yorkshire cooking as part of fixed-price dinners costing £9.75 ($15.60) for three courses and coffee. The hotel is about a mile east of Haworth, on the outskirts of the neighboring town of Keighley.

**Moorfield Guest House.** 80 West Lane, Haworth, Keighley, West Yorkshire BD22 8EN. ☎ **01535/643689.** 6 rms, 5 with bath. TV. £18–£25 ($28.80–$40) single with bath; £37 ($59.20) double without bath, £37–£38 ($59.20–$60.80) double with bath. All rates include English breakfast. MC, V. Closed Jan and Christmas.

In a rural setting overlooking the moors, Moorfield has unrestricted views of the Brontë countryside. It is located between Haworth Village and the Moors and is a 3-minute walk to the center of Haworth and the Brontë Parsonage. The owners rent well-furnished and comfortable bedrooms to guests in their nonsmoking inn.

**Ponden Hall.** Stanbury, near Keighley, West Yorkshire BD22 0HR. ☎ **01535/644154.** 3 rms, 1 with bath. £17.50 ($28) per person. Rate includes English breakfast. No credit cards.

About 3 miles from Haworth, this 1590s farmhouse, a Brontë landmark, lies a third of a mile from the main road between Ponden Reservoir and the moors. The wide, rough track that's part of the Pennine Way long-distance footpath leads to this Elizabethan farmhouse that welcomes children and pets with traditional hospitality. The hall was extended in 1801 and is reputedly the model for Thrushcross Grange, Catherine's home after her marriage to Edgar Linton in Emily Brontë's *Wuthering Heights.* Today it provides rather barebone but hospitable farmhouse accommodation. The dining hall has an open fire, a traditional flagstone floor, original oak beams, timbered ceilings, and mullioned windows. A home-cooked dinner is offered for £9.50 ($15.20), and vegetarian and special diets are catered to.

### Impressions

*Though I knew I looked a poor creature, and in many respects actually was so, nature had given me a voice that could make itself heard, if lifted in excitement or deepened by emotion.*

—Charlotte Brontë

## A YOUTH HOSTEL

**Haworth Youth Hostel.** Longlands Hall, Longlands Dr., Haworth, West Yorkshire BD22 8RT.
☎ **01535/642234.** Fax 01535/643023. 104 beds. £8.50 ($13.60) adults; £5.70 ($9.10) children under 18. MC, V.

Built by a local mill owner in 1884, this hostel retains many of the characteristics of its English country heritage—leaded painted–glass windows, lots of wood paneling, and a wide, sweeping staircase that doubles back on itself leading to a first-floor balcony. Most of the rooms, with ornate fireplaces, are original size and, as such, are quite large—sleeping anywhere from 2 to 16 people. Breakfast costs £2.85 ($4.55), lunch needs to be ordered the night before and is £2.45 ($3.90) or £3.25 ($5.20), and dinner costs £4.25 ($6.80). No smoking is allowed inside. The hostel opens from February through December. There is an 11pm curfew, and the reception is open from 7:30 to 10am and from 1 to 11pm.

## WHERE TO EAT

**The Black Bull Hotel.** 110 Main St. ☎ **01535/642249.** Main courses £4.50–£9 ($7.20–$14.40). MC, V. Mon–Sat noon–3pm and 5–8:30pm; Sun noon–8:30pm Bar: Mon–Sat 11am–11:30pm; Sun noon–10:30pm. ENGLISH.

This 350-year-old stone building has been a regular watering hole for many down through the ages—most notably Bramwell Brontë. He used to come here whenever he was having a gray day, sit in his favorite chair, and partake of some local ale to try to pick himself up. Today, his chair has become a shrine and a must-see destination for Brontë devotees. Some even say that his spirit still mopes around. The bar and restaurant both have lots of dark wood panels, tables, and doors. The same menu serves both lunch and dinner and may include sandwiches, roast beef or lamb, Yorkshire pudding, and traditional English pies—strictly standard fare.

**The Cobbled Way Tea Room.** 60 Main St. ☎ **01535/642735.** Main courses £2–£4 ($3.20–$6.40); fixed-price meal £5.95 ($9.50); tea with sandwich £2.85 ($4.55). No credit cards. Apr–Sept daily 10:30am–7pm; Oct–Mar daily 10:30am–5pm. ENGLISH.

Look up when seeking out this tearoom. It sits at the top of a steep street, in a row of similarly constructed houses, yet stands out by way of its large roof-top sign. This small cafe—with its airy, dare we say coquettish, atmosphere of fine lace and frills—serves a fixed-price menu consisting of a starter, a main course such as roast beef, pork, turkey, or lamb, and a sweet. Main dishes include vegetarian pastas and hearty lasagnas. Afternoon teas and cream teas with homemade cakes and scones are specialties.

✪ **Weaver's.** 15 West Lane. ☎ **01535/643822.** Reservations required. Main courses £8–£14 ($12.80–$22.40); fixed-price meals £10.95–£12.50 ($17.50–$20). AE, DC, MC, V. Tues–Sat 6:45–9:15pm. Closed Sun. Follow the signs for the Brontë Parsonage Museum. ENGLISH.

Once a group of cottages for weavers, this place has been turned into Haworth's best restaurant. British to the core, it not only has an inviting and informal atmosphere, but serves excellent food made with fresh ingredients. Jane and Colin Rushworth have a great talent in the kitchen; try a classic, such as Yorkshire pudding with gravy, or, if featured, a Gressingham duck, which is widely praised in Britain for the quality of the meat. For dessert, you might select a Yorkshire cheese or one of the homemade desserts. Weaver's also rents a few guest rooms. Each has a private bath, along with television, telephone, hot-beverage making facilities, and a trouser press. The rooms are decorated comfortably with antiques and have pleasant views of the village and the Brontë Parsonage. Singles are £49.50 ($79.20), and double rooms are £69.50 ($111.20).

## Hawes: A Base for Exploring Yorkshire Dales National Park

About 65 miles northwest of York, on A684, Hawes is the natural center of Yorkshire Dales National Park. On the Pennine Way, it's England's highest market town and the capital of Wensleydale, which is famous for its cheese. There are rail connections from York taking you to Garsdale, which is 5 miles from Hawes. From Garsdale, bus connections will take you into Hawes.

Hawes is a good center for exploring the **Yorkshire Dales National Park,** some 700 square miles of water-carved country. In the dales you'll find dramatic white limestone crags, roads and fields bordered by dry-stone walls, fast-running rivers, isolated sheep farms, and clusters of sandstone cottages—all hallmarks of the impressive Yorkshire Dales.

Malhamdale receives more visitors annually than any dale in Yorkshire. Two of the most interesting historic attractions are the 12th-century ruins of Bolton Priory and the 14th-century Castle Bolton, to the north in Wensleydale.

In Hawes, the **Dales Countryside Museum,** Station Yard (the old train station; (☎ **01969/667494**), traces folk life in the Dales, a story of 10,000 years of human history. Peat cutting and cheese making, among other occupations, are depicted. The museum is open April through October, daily from 10am to 5pm. Winter opening hours vary; you'll have to check locally. Admission is £2.50 ($4) for adults, £1.75 ($2.80) for children, students, and seniors.

About 1¹/₂ miles north of Hawes on the road signposted to Muker, you can stay and eat at **Simonstone Hall** (☎ 01969/667255; fax 01969/667741). Constructed in 1733, this building has been restored and converted into a comfortable family-run, country-house hotel offering 18 spacious bedrooms, each a double. It's the former home of the earls of Wharncliffe. Rooms cost £70 to £105 ($112 to $168) per person, and include half board. You can have drinks in the Tawny Owl Bar and enjoy good food in the hotel's dining room. Nonresidents can enjoy home-cooked bar meals or order a two-course or a four-course dinner. Dinner can be complemented with good wines from the extensive cellar.

If you'd like to stay in the center of Hawes, opt for **Cockett's Hotel & Restaurant,** Market Place, Hawes, North Yorkshire DL8 3RD (☎ 01969/667312; fax 01969/667162), which has eight rooms renting for £49 to £69 ($78.40 to $110.40)

## 5 The North Yorkshire Coast

If you're looking for a beach vacation where the hot sun and warm water beckon, the North Yorkshire Coast is the wrong place for you. The climate here is cool because of the brisk waters of the North Sea. Even the summer months aren't extremely warm. Many Britons do visit North Yorkshire for beach vacations, however, so you will find a beach town atmosphere along the coast. Brightly colored stalls line the sea fronts, and the people seem to be a bit more relaxed than their inland counterparts.

The beauty and history of the area are the real reasons to visit North Yorkshire. The North Yorkshire Moors National Park is perfect for lonely strolls and peaceful tours. For remnants of the area's exciting days of smugglers and brave explorers, visitors can follow the Captain Cook Heritage Trail down the coast. The fishing industry is still very much alive in the area, although the whaling ships of yesteryear have been anchored (for obvious reasons) and the fishmongers now concentrate on smaller trappings.

in a double, including an English breakfast. Charming, with reminders of its age, this building has the date of its construction (1668) carved into one of its lintels. A table d'hôte evening meal (four courses plus coffee) costs £15.95 ($25.50) per person. Lunches from £3.95 ($6.30) are served Easter through October, and substantial mid-afternoon cream teas at £2.60 ($4.15) per person. Major credit cards are accepted.

Richmond, the most frequently copied town name in the world, stands at the head of the dales and, like Hawes, is another good center for touring the surrounding countryside.

Even cheaper is the **Hawes Youth Hostel,** Lancaster Terrace, Hawes, North Yorkshire DL8 3LQ (☎ **01969/667368**). This two-story building, was built in 1972 as a youth hostel. The owners have taken care, though, to create a very homelike environment, with matching duvets and curtains, nice carpeting throughout, flowers on tables, fresh wallpaper, and even Van Gogh landscapes. There are 12 bedrooms, 10 upstairs and two downstairs, with two to eight beds in each room. Breakfast is £2.85 ($4.55); lunch, which needs to be ordered by 7pm the previous night, costs £2.45 ($3.90) and £3.25 ($5.20); and dinner is available for £4.25 ($6.80). This hostel is located right on the edge of town, a 10-minute walk from the town center. Guests are welcome from mid-February to the beginning of January. It's closed Sunday in May and June. The 11pm curfew is taken very seriously here, and the reception is open from 8:45 to 10am and from 5 to 10:30pm. It rents 58 beds, charging £8.50 ($13.60) for adults or £5.70 ($9.10) for children under 18. MasterCard and Visa are accepted.

The most reasonable place to eat in Hawes is **The Crown,** Market Place (☎ **01969/667212**). This old stone building, a pub since the early 1900s, is a local favorite. You can enjoy good ales, like Theakston's Old Peculiar and John Smith, as well as food. Main courses include roast chicken or duck served with new potatoes, hearty lasagna, and a house specialty of paella. In warmer months, patrons sit on the outdoor terrace with its spectacular views of the hills, known as the Butter Tubs. Main courses range from £4 to £9 ($6.40 to $14.40), and service is Monday through Saturday, noon to 2:30pm and 6:30 to 9:30pm; Sunday, noon to 2:30pm and 7 to 9pm.

It's a simple trip to follow the main road from Bridlington north to Scarborough and on to Robin Hood's Bay and Whitby. As you drive up the coast, you'll see small fishing ports and wide expanses of moorland.

# SCARBOROUGH

18 miles NW of Bridlington; 34 miles NE of York; 253 miles N of London

Scarborough, one of the earliest seaside resorts in Britain, has attracted visitors for more than 3 centuries. A mineral spring discovered in the early 17th century led to a spa that lured clients with promises of its water's healing benefits. In the 18th century, swimmers were attracted to the waters off the coast—sea bathing had come in vogue, and the beaches of England swarmed with tourists taking part in the craze.

The city of Scarborough is divided into two unique districts separated by a green headland that holds the remains of Scarborough Castle, which dates from Norman times. South of the headland, the town conforms to its historical molds. High cliffs and garden walks interspersed with early Victorian residences dominate the landscape.

The north side is more touristy; souvenir shops and beach eateries line the promenade—each selling a range of seaside memorabilia and English junk food. "Rock" (brightly colored hard candy that can be etched with the saying of your choice) and cotton candy ("candyfloss" to Britons) satisfy even the sugariest sweet tooth.

## ESSENTIALS

**GETTING THERE**   Trains leave London's Victoria Station approximately every hour headed for York, where you'll have to transfer to another train. The entire trip takes just under 3 hours. For more information on schedules and prices call ☎ **0345/ 484950** once you are in England.

One bus a day leaves London heading for York, another will take you from York to Scarborough. If you're taking the bus, plan on spending most of a day riding. National Express bus service can be reached at ☎ **0990/808080;** this number cannot be dialed from North America.

**VISITOR INFORMATION**   For more information about what to see and do while you're in Scarborough, call the **Tourist Information Centre,** St. Nicholas Cliff (☎ **01723/373333**). The people here will tell you about their city or send helpful brochures and hotel guides to help you plan your trip. The center is open in the summer daily from 9:30am to 6pm; the rest of the year it's open 10am to 4:30pm.

## SEEING THE SIGHTS

The ruins of **Scarborough Castle,** Castle Road (☎ **01723/372451**), stand on the promontory near a former Viking settlement. From the castle, you can look out over the North Bay, the beaches, and the gardens along the shore. Throughout the summer, there are fairs and festivals that celebrate days of yore with mock battles, pageantry, and falconry displays. The castle is open March to September, daily from 10am to 6pm; in October and November it closes at 4pm. During the winter, Scarborough Castle is open Wednesday through Sunday only from 10am to 1pm and 2 to 4pm. Admission is £1.80 ($2.90) for adults, £1.40 ($2.25) for seniors and persons with disabilities, and 90p ($1.45) for children.

Nearby is the medieval **Church of St. Mary,** Castle Road (no phone), where Anne Brontë, the youngest of the three sisters of literary fame, was buried at in 1849. She died in Scarborough after being brought from her home in Haworth in hopes that the sea air would revive her health.

**Wood End Museum,** The Crescent (☎ **01723/367326**), was once the vacation home of writers Edith, Osbert, and Sacheverell Sitwell. It now houses a library of their works as well as the collections of the **Museum of Natural History.** The house is open from May to September, Tuesday through Sunday from 10am to 5pm. The rest of the year it opens Friday through Sunday from 11am to 4pm. Admission is free.

Also located at The Crescent is **The Art Gallery** (☎ **01723/374753**). The gallery's permanent collection features pieces ranging from 17th-century portraits to 20th-century masterworks. Many of the works relate to the Scarborough area. Changing exhibitions by young artists and local craftspeople are also shown. If you're interested in learning how to create your own works of art, you may want to spend a while at the **Crescent Arts Workshop,** located in the basement of the gallery. Local artists offer courses and demonstrations in their respective media. The Art Gallery is open May to September, Tuesday to Sunday from 10am to 5pm. The rest of the year it opens Friday to Sunday from 11am to 4pm. There is no admission charge. For information about workshop offerings call ☎ **01723/351461.**

Local history collections as well as displays of important archaeological finds can be found at the **Rotunda Museum,** Vernon Road, just down the street from Wood End (☎ **01723/374839**). The museum is housed in a circular building constructed in 1829 for William Smith, the "Father of English Geology," to display his collection; it was one of the first public buildings in England to be constructed specifically for use as a museum. A schematic section of the Yorkshire coast circles the upper gallery walls. The Rotunda is open from May to September, Tuesday through Sunday from 10am to 5pm; October to April, Friday through Sunday from 11am to 4pm. There is no admission charge.

More than 70 species of sea creatures are housed at **Sea Life Centre,** Scalby Mills, North Bay (☎ **01723/376125**). An acrylic tunnel passes under the watery habitat of rays and sharks and feeding pools; hands-on displays encourage interaction with the animals. A favorite of children and adults alike is the Seal Rescue and Rehabilitation Centre, which takes in and cares for stray pups and provides a haven for resident adult gray seals. The center is open daily from 10am to 9pm in the summer and from 10am to 5pm the rest of the year. Admission is £4.50 ($7.20).

If it's a dreary day and you've already visited the Sea Life Centre, **Kinderland,** Burniston Road, North Bay (☎ **01723/354555**), is an excellent choice for entertaining the kids. The park caters to children under 14. Rides and activities, plus an array of play equipment, are sure to keep both the young and the young-at-heart occupied. Admission to the park is £3.95 ($6.30); opening times vary, so call ahead.

## WHERE TO STAY

**Lyncris Manor Hotel.** 45 Northstead Manor Dr., Scarborough, North Yorkshire YO12 6AF. ☎ **01723/361052.** 6 rms, 4 with bath. TV. £15 ($24) single without bath, £18 ($28.80) single with bath; £33 ($52.80) double without bath, £36 ($57.60) double with bath. All rates include English breakfast. No credit cards.

Situated on the North Bay overlooking Peasholm Park, Lyncris Manor is ideally suited as a base for touring the area. The proprietors have created a comfortable and friendly environment for their guests and provide helpful advice about what to see and do during your stay in Scarborough. The large dining room is attractively decorated and offers good home cooking at a reasonable price. Vegetarian choices and children's portions are served.

**The Old Mill Hotel.** Mill St., off Victoria Rd., Scarborough, Yorkshire YO11 1SZ. ☎ **01723/ 372735.** 11 rms. TV. £22.50 ($36) per person. Rate includes English breakfast. V.

This hotel is an interesting alternative to the standard accommodations in the area. The owners have converted an old corn mill and its surrounding courtyard buildings into the main building and guest rooms. The mill, which was originally driven with power from six sails, is no longer used for its original purpose; it now houses the hotel's common areas, including a homey dining room. The guest rooms are fairly large but sparsely decorated and have hot beverage–making facilities.

**The Pickwick Inn.** Huntriss Row, Scarborough, North Yorkshire YO11 2ED. ☎ **01723/ 375787.** 11 rms. TV TEL. £22.50–£27 ($36–$43.20) single; £35–£44 ($56–$70.40) double. All rates include breakfast. AE, DC, MC, V.

A stately building in the center of Scarborough, The Pickwick Inn is convenient to the beach and promenade, as well as a variety of pubs and restaurants. The bedrooms are comfortably furnished with the rooms located on the upper floors offering pleasant views of the city. All bedrooms are equipped with hot beverage–making facilities, a hair dryer, and a trouser press, and some have regal four-poster beds.

## WHERE TO EAT

**Lanterna.** 33 Queen St. ☎ **01723/363616.** Reservations recommended. Main courses £9.50–£14 ($15.20–$22.40). MC, V. Tues–Sat 7–10pm. ITALIAN.

The Arecco family has run this small Italian eatery since 1973. The place is well known for its good-tasting straightforward dishes that feature local seafood.

Small scallops called "Queenies" are sweet tasting and perfect in light marinara sauce served over homemade pasta. Many diners end their meal with one of the decadent desserts, such as zabaglione or baked Alaska.

## 6  Durham

250 miles N of London; 15 miles S of Newcastle upon Tyne

This medieval city took root in 1090 after the Normans, under William the Conqueror, took over. They began construction of Durham's world-renowned cathedral and castle on a peninsula surrounded by the River Wear. The cathedral, "Half Church of God, half Castle 'gainst the Scots," was built as a shrine to protect the remains of St. Cuthbert, while also providing a sturdy fortress against the warring Scots to the north.

It was as a result of the cathedral that Durham gained importance as both a protective border post for England and as a pilgrimage site for Christians paying tribute to St. Cuthbert—a monk on Lindisfarne, whose life of contemplation and prayer led to his consecration as bishop in 685 and sainthood after death. For centuries, Durham Castle was the seat of the Prince Bishops—kings of the wild northern territories in all but name—and today is the cornerstone of Durham University.

Today Durham is an excellent base for exploring Durham County, with its many castles and churches, a stretch of North Sea coast, and, in the west, the unspoiled rolling hills and waterfalls of the Durham Dales in the North Pennines.

## ESSENTIALS

**GETTING THERE**   Trains from London's King's Cross Station arrive hourly during the day, with the trip taking about 3 hours, and trains from York arrive every 2 hours, with travel time being about an hour. Durham lies on the main London to Edinburgh rail line. For schedules and information, call ☎ **0345/484950.** Contact the Durham County travel hotline at ☎ **0191/383-3337** for more information on public transportation in the area.

Blue line buses from London arrive twice daily, with the trip taking about 5 hours. For schedules and information, call ☎ **0990/808080.**

Motorists from London can follow the A1/A1(M) north to Durham.

**VISITOR INFORMATION**   The **Durham Tourist Office** is at Market Place (☎ **0191/384-3720**), and is open July and August, Monday through Saturday from 9:30am to 6pm, Sunday from 2 to 5pm; June and September, Monday through Saturday from 10am to 5:30pm; October through May, Monday through Friday from 10am to 5pm, and Saturday from 9:30am to 1pm.

## EXPLORING DURHAM

From the centrally located cathedral, perched on a sandstone bluff with views of the surrounding area, Durham's long history is evident all along the narrow, winding streets that lead from the university, in the bustling shopping district, and along the beautiful wooded riverbanks. From here, ancient footbridges allow you to explore both sides of the River Wear as it loops around the city's center.

You can get a better feel for the town by visiting the **Durham Heritage Centre,** St. Mary le Bow Church, North Bailey (☎ **0191/386-8719**), another medieval church, that houses exhibitions, including audiovisual shows, of Durham's history. It is open Easter week, daily 2 to 4:30pm; the week after Easter until May 25, Saturday and Sunday, 2 to 4:30pm; May 26 through June 30, daily 2 to 4:30pm.

July 1 to August 31, daily 11:30am to 4:30pm. September 1 through 20, daily 2 to 4:30pm. September 1 through 21, daily from 2 to 4:30pm. Admission is 80p ($1.10) for adults, 30p (50¢) for children.

The university adds to the diversity of the city by offering its **Oriental Museum,** Elvet Hill off South Road (☎ **0191/374-7911**), the nation's only museum devoted entirely to eastern culture and art. The museum covers all major cultures and periods of the east from ancient Egypt through India, as well as relics from Tibet, China, and Japan. The attractions are displayed in a way designed to make them understandable to the nonspecialist. Temporary exhibitions are also mounted throughout the year. The museum is open Monday through Friday from 9:30am to 1pm and 2 to 5pm, and on Saturday and Sunday from 2 to 5pm. Admission is £1.50 ($2.40) for adults and 50p (80¢) for children.

The Durham University **Botanical Garden,** Hollingside Lane off South Road (☎ **0191/374-7971**), covers 18 acres of mature woodlands, including plant life from areas as farflung as North America and the Himalayas. You can also visit the Prince Bishop Gardens, a tropical house, cactus house, visitor center, and cafe. The garden and glasshouses are open daily from 9am to 4pm, and the visitor center is open March through October, daily from 10am to 5pm (off-season hours are daily from 11:30am to 4pm). Admission is currently free (under review) but a donation is requested.

✪ **Durham Cathedral.** Palace Green. ☎ **0191/386-4266.** Cathedral: Free admission. May–Aug daily 7:15am–8pm; Sept–Apr daily 7:15am–6pm. Guided Tour: May 27–Sept 6 Mon–Fri 10:30am. Tower: Admission £2 ($3.20) adults; £1 ($1.60) children. Mon–Sat 9:30am–4pm, except during services. Treasury: Admission £1 ($1.60) adults; 20p (30¢) children. Mon–Sat 10am–4:30pm; Sun 2–4:30pm. Monk's Dormitory: Admission 80p ($1.30) adults; 20p (30¢) children. Apr–Oct Mon–Sat 10am–4pm; Sun 12:30–3:30pm and 4:30–6pm. Audiovisual Visitors' Exhibition: Admission 50p (80¢) adults; 20p (30¢) children. Mar–Oct Mon–Sat 11am–3pm.

Under construction for more than 40 years, the cathedral was completed in 1133, and today is Britain's largest, best-preserved Norman stronghold and one of its grandest surviving romanesque palaces. The structure is not only breathtaking, it is also architecturally innovative, being the first building featuring ribbed vault construction. It is also the first stone-roofed cathedral in Europe, an architectural necessity because of its role as a border fortress.

The treasury houses such relics as the original 12th-century door knocker, St. Cuthbert's coffin, ancient illuminated manuscripts, and more. You can still attend daily services in the sanctuary.

**Durham Castle.** Palace Green. ☎ **0191/374-3800.** Admission £2.50 ($4) adults; £1.50 ($2.40) children; £6 ($9.60) family ticket. Guided tours: Mar 22–Apr 27 and July–Sept Mon–Sat 10am–noon and 2–4:30pm; Sun 2–4:30pm; other times of the year, Mon, Wed, Sat 2–4:30pm. Closed Christmas break.

Adjoining the cathedral, the castle was the seat of the Prince-Bishops of Durham for more than 800 years. In 1832, it became the first building of the fledgling local college, now Durham University, and today still houses University College. During university breaks, it offers unique bed-and-breakfast accommodations to the public.

## OUTDOOR PURSUITS

Fishing is good sport all along the rivers Tees and Wear, as well as in the several reservoirs and ponds scattered throughout the county.

Boating is also available, and **Brown's Boat House,** Elvet Bridge (☎ **0191/386-3779**), rents rowboats for pulls up or down the River Wear, as well as offering short cruises from April through October, at the price of £2 ($3.20) for adults or £1 ($1.60) for children.

The 150-seat *Prince Bishop* **River Cruiser** (☎ **0191/386-9525**) departs regularly from Durham City Centre, and offers views of the riverbanks and cathedral. For land-lubbers, horseback riding is available through any of the more than a dozen stables located around the county. The tourist office (see "Visitor Information," above) will supply complete details if you're interested.

Hikers can either take the challenge provided by the 270 miles of trails (40 miles of which are in the county) along the **Pennine Way,** the **Weardale Way's** 78-mile course along the River Wear from Monkwearmouth in Sunderland to Cowshill in County Durham, or the **Teesdale Way,** running 90 miles from Middleton in Teesdale to Teesmouth in Cleveland. More centralized rambles along public foot-paths have recently been supplemented by more than 50 miles of former railway. Seven such trails make use of interlinked routes and range from the $4^1/_2$-mile **Auckland Walk,** to the $10^1/_2$-mile **Derwent Walk.** If you don't feel like going it alone, there are also more than 200 guided walks throughout the county, providing background on the history, culture, and plant and animal life of the surrounding area.

Cyclists are not neglected either, and can opt for either roadway travel along quiet country roads and converted railway routes, or trail riding in **Hamsterley Forest.** The **C2C national cycle route,** winner of the British Airways Tourism for Tomorrow Global Award, passes through the Durham Dales and North Durham, along a 140-mile signposted route. Both road and mountain-bike rentals are available at several locations; among these is **Dave Heron Cycles,** 29 Claypath St. (☎ **0191/384-0319**), open Monday through Saturday from 9am until 6pm. A bike costs £15 ($24) a day, with a £30 ($48) deposit.

For those who like their sports more competitive, the county offers 21 golf courses, a full schedule of National Hunt horse racing at the **Sedgefield Racecourse** (☎ **0174/062-1925**), and First Class County Cricket, featuring some of the best-known names in the sport, at the new **County Cricket Ground,** Chester-le-Street Riverside (☎ **0191/387-1717**). Additional information on all outdoor activities such as golf is available by contacting Marketing & Promotion, Economic Development and Research Unit, **Durham County Council,** County Hall, Durham DH1 5UF (☎ **0191/383-4117**).

## WHERE TO STAY

**Bay Horse Inn.** Brandon Village, Durham DH7 8ST. ☎ **0191/378-0498.** 10 suites, all with shower. TV TEL. £30 ($48) single; £39 ($62.40) double; £53 ($84.80) family rm. All rates in-clude breakfast. MC, V.

Three miles from the heart of Durham stand 10 stone-built chalets that offer some of the best and most affordable bedrooms in the area. Each room is comfortable and well equipped, with a shower, toilet, TV, beverage-making equipment, and phone. One room is suitable for families, and the others are either double or twins (singles can occupy one of these rooms, however, at the rates quoted). Lunch is available, but most people are out exploring. However, if you make arrangements, the owners will prepare a filling and hearty dinner for only £6.50 ($10.40).

**Bees Cottage Guest House.** Bridge St., Durham DH1 4RT. ☎ **0191/384-5775.** 4 rms. TV. £35 ($56) single; £46 ($73.60) double; £55 ($88) family rm. All rates include breakfast. No credit cards.

Located in the center of town, this old farmhouse is more than 200 years old, although no one seems to know the exact age. It is situated conveniently for walking, biking, or driving to the surrounding sights. There are fresh flowers in every room, and breakfast is a full English offering with vegetarian alternatives. This is a nonsmoking establishment.

**Castle View Guest House.** 4 Crossgate, Durham DH1 4PS. ☎ and fax **0191/386-8852.** 6 rms. £38 ($60.80) single; £48 ($76.80) double. All rates include breakfast. No credit cards.

This 250-year-old Georgian home sits near the river's edge with a great view of the cathedral and castle. Although no pace-setter, each room is comfortably furnished and well maintained. One triple is suitable for families. The English breakfast is excellent, fit fortification for the day.

**Georgian Town House.** 10 Crossgate, Durham DH1 4PS. ☎ **0191/386-8070.** 5 rms, 1 suite. TV. £37.50 ($60) single; £48 ($76.80) double; £55 ($88) suite. All rates include breakfast. No credit cards.

This is the most desirable B&B in Durham, an unusually decorated place lying on a steep, cobbled Georgian terrace street, close to everything, including the cathedral. It is a wonder of decoration, as exemplified by the reception hallway with its stenciled pillars and leaf patterns—like entering an arbor in sunny Sicily. In the bottle-green lounge, "stars" twinkle on the walls. Sofas upholstered in deep stripes are placed around the fireplace where guests meet fellow guests. Bedrooms, except for a cramped single, are tastefully decorated and light and airy, again with vibrant fabrics and stencil work. The house has a panoramic view of the cathedral and castle. Mr. and Mrs. R. M. D. Weil can also help you find your way through Durham's maze of one-way streets to the destination of your choice. Their grilled English breakfast is a hearty way to start the day without all the grease.

## WHERE TO EAT

**Bistro 21.** Aykley Heads House, Aykley Heads. ☎ **0191/384-4354.** Reservations recommended. Main courses £7.50–£12.50 ($12–$20); fixed-price 2-course lunches £11.50–£13.50 ($18.40–$21.60). AE, DC, MC, V. Tues–Sat noon–2:30pm and 6–10:30pm. INTERNATIONAL.

A big hit locally, this is the latest addition to owner Terence Laybourne's popular "21" eateries (21 Queen St., in Newcastle upon Tyne, and Cafe 21 in Ponteland). Chef Adrian Watson has moved from sous duties at Queen Street to take over the kitchen at this bright farm-theme bistro. The cuisine is precise and carefully prepared, with market-fresh ingredients that are allowed to keep their natural essence, without being overly sauced or disguised. You'd be wise to stick to the blackboard specials for some of the tastier treats. The food is full of flavor and rather forceful, borrowing from the Mediterranean, but also patriotically remaining in Britain at times, certainly in its dish of deep-fried plaice and chips. The a la carte menu includes starters such as fish soup with garlic croutons, and main courses like smoked haddock fish cakes with poached egg and hollandaise sauce or roasted chicken with sage onion polenta and crispy bacon. You can finish with one of the rich desserts, including double chocolate truffle cake or custard tart with lemon curd ice cream. But if you want to be terribly old fashioned, you'll ask for the toffee pudding with butterscotch sauce, which is prepared to perfection here.

## DURHAM AFTER DARK

Outside of the seasonal festivals, much of Durham's nightlife revolves around the university students. When school is in session, **Brewer and Firkin,** 58 Saddler St.

(☎ 0191/386-4134), is popular with the students, and hosts disco dancing Friday and Saturday nights and live alternative/punk music on Sunday nights. It's open Monday through Saturday from 11am to 11pm, and Sunday from noon until 10:30pm.

**Coach and Eight,** Bridge House, Framwellgate Bridge (☎ 0191/386-3284), has disco dancing Thursday through Sunday nights, and is open Monday through Saturday from 11am to 11pm, and Sunday from 11am to 10:30pm.

The university's student union, **Dunelm House,** New Elvet, just north of Church Street (☎ 0191/374-3316), is closed during the summer, but during the school year the bar is open from 7 to 11pm, offering a live jazz cafe on Mondays and an eclectic mix of bands on Friday nights.

Seasonal offerings include the **Durham Folk Festival,** held the last weekend in July, where you can sing, clog, or just cavort to music—with almost every event offered free. The weekend also includes free camping along the River Wear, though you'd better arrive early on Friday if you want to get a choice spot.

In mid-June, crowds swarm along the riverbank to cheer the crew racing of the **Durham Regatta,** and the first weekend of September brings the sodden celebration of the nation's second-largest **beer festival.**

## 7  Hexham, Hadrian's Wall & the Pennine Way

304 miles N of London; 37 miles E of Carlisle; 21 miles W of Newcastle upon Tyne

Above the Tyne River, this historic old market town has narrow streets, an old market square, a fine abbey church, and a moot hall. It makes a good base for exploring Hadrian's Wall and the Roman supply base of Corstopitum at Corbridge-on-Tyne, the ancient capital of Northumberland. The tourist office has lots of information on the wall for walkers, drivers, campers, and picnickers.

In Hexham, the Abbey Church of St. Wilfrid is full of ancient relics. The Saxon font, the misericord carvings on the choir stalls, Acca's Cross, and St. Wilfrid's chair are well worth seeing.

## ESSENTIALS

**GETTING THERE**   Take one of the many daily trains from London's King's Cross Station to Newcastle upon Tyne. At Newcastle, change trains and take one in the direction of Carlisle. The fifth or sixth (depending on the schedule) stop after Newcastle will be Hexham. For schedules and information, call ☎ 0345/484950. Hexham lies 14 miles southeast of Hadrian's Wall. If you are primarily interested in the wall (rather than in Hexham), get off the Carlisle-bound train at the second stop (Bardon Mill) or at the third stop (Haltwhistle), which are 4 miles and 2 1/2 miles, respectively, from the wall. At either of these hamlets, you can take a taxi to whichever part of the wall you care to visit. Taxis line up readily at the railway station in Hexham, but less often at the hamlets. If you get off at one of the above-mentioned hamlets and don't see a taxi, call ☎ 01434/344272 and a local taxi will come to get you. Many visitors ask their taxi drivers to return at a prearranged time (which they gladly do) to pick them up after their excursion on the windy ridges near the wall.

National Express coaches to Newcastle and Carlisle connect with Northumbria bus service no. 685. The trip to Hexham from Carlisle takes about 1 1/2 hours and from Newcastle about 1 hour. For schedules and information, call ☎ 0990/808080. Local bus services connect Hexham with North Tynedale and the North Pennines.

If you're driving from Newcastle upon Tyne, head west on A69 until you see the cutoff south to Hexham.

**VISITOR INFORMATION**   The **Tourist Information Centre** at Hexham is at the Manor Office, Hallgate (☎ **01434/605225**). Open Easter to mid-May, Monday through Saturday from 9am to 5pm, Sunday from 10am to 5pm; mid-May to October, Monday through Saturday from 9am to 6pm (9am to 5pm in October), Sunday from 10am to 5pm; November through March, Monday through Saturday from 9am to 5pm.

## ✪ HADRIAN'S WALL & ITS FORTRESSES

Hadrian's Wall, which extends for 73 miles across the north of England, from the North Sea to the Irish Sea, is particularly interesting for a stretch of 10 miles west of Housesteads, which lies 2³/₄ miles northeast of Bardon Mill on B6318. Only the lower courses of the wall have been preserved intact; the rest were reconstructed in the 19th century using original stones. From the wall, there are incomparable views north to the Cheviot Hills along the Scottish border and south to the Durham moors.

The wall was built in A.D.122 after the visit of the emperor Hadrian, who was inspecting far frontiers of the Roman Empire and wanted to construct a dramatic line between the empire and the barbarians. Legionnaires were ordered to build a wall across the width of the island of Britain, stretching 73¹/₂ miles, beginning at the North Sea and ending at the Irish Sea.

The wall is a major Roman attraction in Europe. The western end can be reached from Carlisle, which also has an interesting museum of Roman artifacts; the eastern end can be reached from Newcastle upon Tyne (where some remains can be seen on the city outskirts; there's also a nice museum at the university).

Along the wall are several Roman forts, the most important of which is **Housestead Fort and Museum** (☎ **01434/344363**), called *Vercovicium* by the Romans. It lies 3 miles northeast of Bardon Mill on B6318. This substantially excavated fort, on a dramatic site, contains the only visible example of a Roman hospital in Britain. Admission is £2.50 ($4) for adults, £1.90 ($3.05) for seniors and students, and £1.30 ($2.10) for children. It's open April through September, daily from 10am to 6pm; October through March, daily from 10am to 4pm. Closed December 24 to 26 and January 1.

Just west of Housesteads, **Vindolanda** (☎ **01434/344277**) is another well-preserved fort south of the wall. It is located on a minor road 1¹/₄ miles southeast of Twice Brewed off the B6318. There is also an excavated civilian settlement outside the fort with an interesting museum of artifacts of everyday Roman life. Admission is £3.50 ($5.60) for adults, £2.90 ($4.65) for seniors and students, and £2.50 ($4) for children. It's open February through October, daily from 10am to 5pm. In July and August, the site remains open until 6:30pm.

Near Vindolanda at the garrison fort at Carvoran, close to the village of Greenhead, the **Roman Army Museum** (☎ **01697/747485**) traces the growth and influence of Rome from its early beginnings to the development and expansion of the empire, with special emphasis on the role of the Roman army and the garrisons of Hadrian's Wall. A barracks room depicts basic army living conditions. Realistic life-size figures make this a strikingly visual museum experience. Admission is £2.80 ($4.50) for adults, £2.40 ($3.85) for seniors and students, and £1.90 ($3.05) for children. It's open March to September, daily from 10am to 4:30pm; in October daily from 10am to 5pm. It's located at the junction of A69 and B6318, 18 miles west of Hexham.

Within easy walking distance of the Roman Army Museum is one of the most imposing and high-standing sections of Hadrian's Wall, Walltown Crags, where the height of the wall and magnificent views to the north and south are impressive.

**Impressions**

*Over the heather the wet wind blows, I've lice in my tunic and a cold in my nose. The rain comes pattering out of the sky, I'm a Wall soldier, I don't know why.*

—W. H. Auden, Roman Wall Blues

## VISITING THE WALL

From early May to late September, the Tynedale Council and the Northumberland National Park run a bus service that visits every important site along the wall, then turns around in the village of Haltwhistle and returns to Hexham. Buses depart Saturday and bank holidays from a point near the railway station in Hexham at roughly 10am, noon, 2pm, and 4pm; and Sundays at 11am and 1:30pm. From late July to late August, the tours are given daily. Call ☎ **0191/212-3000** for more information. The cost is £4 ($6.40) for adults, £2 ($3.20) for children, and £10 ($16) for a family ticket. Many visitors take one bus out, then return on a subsequent bus 2, 4, or 6 hours later. Every Sunday a national park warden leads a 2¹/₂-hour walking tour of the wall, in connection with the bus service. The Hexham tourist office (see above) will provide further details.

## ✪ HIKING THE PENNINE WAY IN NORTHUMBERLAND NATIONAL PARK

Northumberland National Park, established in 1956, encompasses the borderlands that were a buffer zone between the warring English and Scots during the 13th and 14th centuries. Today, the park encompasses almost 400 square miles of the least-populated area in England; it is noted for its rugged landscape and associations with the northern frontier of the ancient Roman Empire.

Touching on the border with Scotland, the park covers some of the most tortured geology in England—the Cheviot Hills—whose surfaces have been wrinkled by volcanic pressures, inundated with sea water, scoured and gouged by glaciers, silted over by rivers, and thrust upward in one of the most geologically complicated series of natural events anywhere. Much of the heather-sheathed terrain here is used for sheep grazing; woolly balls of fluff adorn hillsides ravaged by high winds and frequent rain.

Northumberland includes the remains of Hadrian's Wall, one of the most impressive classical ruins of northern Europe. Footpaths run alongside it, and there are a variety of walks in the country to the north and south of the monument. One of the most challenging hiking paths in Britain, the Pennine Way, snakes up the backbone of the park. The 80 miles of the 250-mile path that are in the park are clearly marked; one of the most worthwhile (and safest) hikes is between Bellingham and the Hamlet of Riding Wood.

A map of the trails, priced at less than £1 ($1.60), can be purchased for these and other hiking trails at almost any local tourist office in the district. There are National Park Centres at Once Brewed (☎ **01434/344396**), Rothbury (☎ **01669/620887**), and Ingram (☎ **01665/578248**). The Head Office is at Eastburn, South Park, Hexham, Northumberland NE46 1BS (☎ **01434/605555**).

## WHERE TO STAY

**Beaumont Hotel.** Beaumont St., Hexham, Northumberland NE46 3LT. ☎ and fax **01434/602331.** 23 rms. TV TEL. £56 ($89.60) single; £86 ($137.60) double. All rates include English breakfast. AE, CB, DC, DISC, MC, V.

In the town center overlooking the abbey and a park, the Beaumont offers excellent facilities, including two comfortable bars and a delightful restaurant. Martin and Linda Owens have completely refurbished the bedrooms, which contain tea- and coffee-making facilities. A table d'hôte dinner costs £18.50 ($29.60).

**West Close House.** Hextol Terrace, Hexham, Northumberland NE46 2AD. ☎ **01434/603307.** 4 rms, 1 with bath. £17.50–£19.50 ($28–$31.20) per person without bath; £21.50–£23.50 ($34.40–$37.60) per person with bath. All rates include English or continental breakfast. No credit cards.

Located in a 1920s house on a private road, West Close House is owned and operated by Patricia Graham-Tomlinson, who greets guests with warmth and hospitality. The bedrooms are more spacious than many competitors' and are equipped with hot beverage–making facilities and a hair dryer. There is a sitting room where guests may watch TV.

## A YOUTH HOSTEL

**Once Brewed Youth Hostel.** Military Rd., Bardon Mill, Hexham, Northumberland NE47 7AN. ☎ **01434/344360.** Fax 01434/344045. 87 beds. £8.50 ($13.60) adults; £5.70 ($9.10) children under 18. AE, MC, V.

This is a great little hostel to stay at when touring this underpopulated part of Britain. Within a 5-minute walk, you find yourself in the midst of the Roman wall, forts, and castles. The hostel had its humble beginnings in 1934 and was completely rebuilt in 1967, with more renovations taking place in 1987. The majority of its 21 rooms house four or five travelers. Breakfast costs £2.85 ($4.55), a packed lunch is £3.35 ($5.35), and dinner is £4.25 ($6.80). Other services/amenities offered to guests include group tours of the area, a small gift shop, and free tea and coffee. Once Brewed is open from February through November, and is closed on Sunday during November, February, and March. There is an 11pm curfew, and the reception is open 7 to 10am and 1 to 11:30pm.

## WHERE TO EAT

**The Twice Brewed Inn.** Military Rd. ☎ **01434/344534.** Main courses £5–£7 ($8–$11.20). No credit cards. Mon–Sat 11am–11pm; Sun noon–3pm and 7–10:30pm. ENGLISH.

Aside from a youth hostel and tourist information office, you'll not find much else in the area especially in the way of food. So, diners and pubgoers are lucky that this is a decent place. The inn dates from 1715 and was built as a drovers inn—the midway stopping point for the sheep drive from Carlisle to Newcastle. The bar and restaurant are in two different rooms but both have the same dark-wood-and-beam atmosphere. The bar, which serves snacks, has a fireplace and pool table for distraction. The restaurant offers traditional pub meals, including beef pies, scampi, lasagna, and even vegetarian dishes.

# Index

# WHEREVER YOU TRAVEL, *H*ELP IS NEVER FAR AWAY.

From planning your trip to providing travel assistance along the way, American Express® Travel Service Offices are always there to help you do more.

---

### *London*

---

American Express Travel Service
1 Savoy Court
0171/240-1521

American Express Travel Service
78 Brompton Road
0171/584-6182

American Express Travel Service
111 Cheapside
0171/600-5522

American Express Travel Service
6 Haymarket
0171/930-4411

American Express Travel Service
89 Mount Street Mayfair
0171/499-4436

American Express Travel Service
102 Victoria Steet
0171/828-7411

**Travel**

http://www.americanexpress.com/travel

**American Express Travel Service Offices are found
in central locations throughout the United Kingdom.**